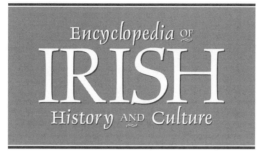

Encyclopedia OF

IRISH

History AND Culture

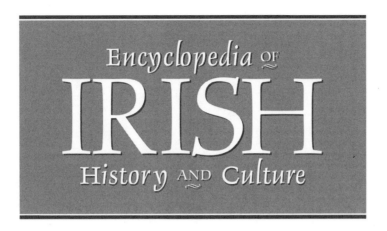

Encyclopedia of IRISH History and Culture

James S. Donnelly, Jr.

EDITOR IN CHIEF

Karl S. Bottigheimer, Mary E. Daly, James E. Doan, and David W. Miller

ASSOCIATE EDITORS

Volume

1

A–O

MACMILLAN REFERENCE USA

An imprint of Thomson Gale, a part of The Thomson Corporation

THOMSON

GALE

Detroit • New York • San Francisco • San Diego • New Haven, Conn. • Waterville, Maine • London • Munich

Encyclopedia of Irish History and Culture
James S. Donnelly, Jr., Editor in Chief

For permission to use material from this product, submit your request via the Web at http://www.gale-edit.com/permissions, or you may download our Permissions Request form and submit your request by fax or mail to:

Permissions Department
The Gale Group, Inc.
27500 Drake Road
Farmington Hills, MI 48331-3535
Permissions hotline:
248 699-8006 or 800 877-4253, ext. 8006
Fax: 248 688-8074 or 800 762-4058

LIBRARY OF CONGRESS CATALOGING-IN-PUBLICATION DATA

Encyclopedia of Irish history and culture / James S. Donnelly Jr., editor in chief.
    p. cm.
    Includes bibliographical references and index.
    ISBN 0-02-865902-3 (set hardcover : alk. paper) — ISBN 0-02-865699-7 (volume 1) — ISBN 0-02-865903-1 (volume 2) — ISBN 0-02-865989-9 (e-book)
    1. Ireland—History—Encyclopedias.
    2. Ireland—Civilization—Encyclopedias. I. Donnelly, James S.

DA912.E53 2004
941.5'003—dc22   2004005353

This title is also available as an e-book.
ISBN 0-02-865989-9
Contact your Gale sales representative for ordering information

Printed in the United States of America
10 9 8 7 6 5 4 3 2 1

Editorial Board

Editorial and Production Staff

Contents

List of Maps

Preface

The purpose of this encyclopedia is to provide a basic source of reference for the extremely wide audience of people interested in the history and culture of Ireland, from the earliest times down to the present day. Although scholars will have many reasons to consult these two volumes, the editors and the publisher have had especially in mind the educated lay public in the selection and presentation of the wealth of material that appears in these pages. We hope that the merits of this encyclopedia will strongly commend it to public libraries and university libraries in North America, and indeed in those many other parts of the world where interest in Ireland and the Irish has also taken deep root. That such an interest is remarkably widespread can hardly be denied. Among some observers the phenomenon has earned the sobriquet of "Celto-mania." In relation to this encyclopedia that phrase is at least suggestive of the outpouring in recent decades of both scholarly and popular writing on Ireland—an outpouring that the editors of this volume, and above all the contributors, have sought to distill and explore.

From the outset of this enterprise the editors and the publisher have made a serious intellectual commitment to developing a standard work of reference covering the whole spectrum of Irish history and culture. The list of articles reflects the editors' firm resolve to embrace and to give a reasonable amount of attention to all the major chronological periods (early, medieval, early modern, modern, and contemporary) and to the different varieties of history (political, social, economic, and cultural). The members of the team of editors who came together to plan and construct these volumes— James E. Doan, Karl S. Bottigheimer, David W. Miller, James S. Donnelly, Jr., and Mary E. Daly—were origi-nally chosen with a deliberate view to securing the range of expertise that would allow the project to achieve its goal of comprehensiveness. In turn, the editors enlisted a similarly broad range of experts (the contributors number 205) in the writing of the articles that comprise about 70 percent of the whole work.

The articles themselves—just over 400 altogether—were selected on the basis of a carefully considered plan that aims to provide (in articles of over 2,000 words) fairly sweeping coverage of long periods and large topics as well as in-depth analysis of important subjects and major historical figures in articles of intermediate (1,000–2,000 words) and shorter length (under 1,000 words). When designing articles treating individuals, the editors decided that we did not wish to produce a work that had the features of a biographical dictionary. The space devoted to major figures in separate articles is therefore limited deliberately. In our view it is more important in a work of this kind to address the major developments and broader trends in the long evolution of Irish history and culture, and we generally place leading personalities firmly within those contexts.

Among the special features of this encyclopedia is a copious selection of historical documents that collectively comprise almost a quarter of the entire two-volume work. These documents are intended to amplify many of the articles (articles are tied to the documents by systematic cross-references), to provide detailed substantiation for a host of important matters, and to allow readers to gain an appreciation for the rich variety of ways in which contemporary actors and observers perceived or responded to events or developments. The editors and the publisher have also expended much energy and treasure in choosing and gathering an impressive array of illustrations to enrich and enliven the encyclopedia. Drawn from many different sources or created expressly for this work, the illustrations include maps, diagrams, engravings, paintings, photographs, and even some cartoons. There is a strong visual dimension to the encyclopedia that accentuates its overall intellectual impact. At the front of the encyclopedia the editors have inserted an extensive chronology of important events and other significant dates in Irish history and culture.

In assembling a work of this scale and scope, the editors have incurred a series of debts that they freely wish to acknowledge. Jill Lectka, the commissioning editor at Macmillan Reference when we began this project, brought her great experience to bear in helping us to lay solid foundations at the outset. Dawn Cavalieri did a superb job in communicating with the contributors, in supervising the laborious editorial process, and in driving the enterprise relentlessly forward. We cannot praise too highly the dedication and professionalism that she lavished on this grand cooperative enterprise. For his support of our project at an especially critical juncture, the editors are very grateful to Frank Menchaca, publisher at Macmillan Reference. We appreciate the expert assistance rendered by Eric G. Zuelow, especially in compiling the chronology. During the production process the editors were the beneficiaries of skilled assistance from Senior Editor Sharon Mooney Malinowski and others, but above all from Alja K. Collar, whose steady hand at the tiller and unerringly wise decisions as an editor have guided this big ship safely into port. Our heaviest debt is to our contributors. We salute every one of them for their hard work and their patience with our penchant for revisions.

James S. Donnelly, Jr.

List of Articles

~

List of Contributors

Alan R. Acheson
Trinity College Dublin
CHURCH OF IRELAND: SINCE
1690

Dorothy Africa
CHURCH REFORM
SAINT PATRICK, PROBLEM OF

Ian Armit
Queen's University Belfast
CELTIC MIGRATIONS

Paul Arthur
University of Ulster
ANGLO-IRISH AGREEMENT OF
1985 (HILLSBOROUGH
AGREEMENT)
BLOODY SUNDAY
DECOMMISSIONING
HUNGER STRIKES
NORTHERN IRELAND:
CONSTITUTIONAL SETTLEMENT
FROM SUNNINGDALE TO GOOD
FRIDAY
NORTHERN IRELAND: THE
UNITED STATES IN NORTHERN
IRELAND SINCE 1970
ULSTER POLITICS UNDER
DIRECT RULE

Ronald G. Asch
University of Osnabrück
WENTWORTH, THOMAS, FIRST
EARL OF STRAFFORD

Margot Gayle Backus
University of Houston
BECKETT, SAMUEL

Jonathan Bardon
Queen's University Belfast
BELFAST
DERRY, SIEGE OF

Toby Barnard
*Hertford College, University of
Oxford*
CROMWELLIAN CONQUEST
DUBLIN PHILOSOPHICAL
SOCIETY
GREATOREX, VALENTINE
PETTY, SIR WILLIAM
PURITAN SECTARIES

Terry Barry
Trinity College Dublin
CLONTARF, BATTLE OF
DÁL CAIS AND BRIAN BORU
NORSE SETTLEMENT
O'CONNORS OF CONNACHT

Síghle Bhreathnach-Lynch
National Gallery of Ireland, Dublin
VISUAL ARTS, MODERN

Lisa M. Bitel
University of Southern California
MONASTICISM IN THE EARLY
MIDDLE AGES

Allan Blackstock
University of Ulster
MILITARY FORCES FROM 1690
TO 1800

John Bowman
RTÉ
NORTHERN IRELAND: POLICY OF
THE DUBLIN GOVERNMENT
FROM 1922 TO 1969

D. George Boyce
University of Wales Swansea
POLITICS: 1800 TO 1921—
CHALLENGES TO THE UNION

John Bradley
*Economic and Social Research
Institute, Dublin*
ECONOMIC RELATIONS BETWEEN
NORTHERN IRELAND AND
BRITAIN

Ciaran Brady
Trinity College Dublin
SIDNEY, HENRY
SPENSER, EDMUND

Joseph Brady
University College Dublin
DUBLIN

Rand Brandes
Lenoir-Rhyne College
HEANEY, SEAMUS

Dorothy Ann Bray
McGill University
HAGIOGRAPHY

Monica A. Brennan
St. Joseph's College, New York
GRANUAILE (GRACE O'MALLEY)
SURRENDER AND REGRANT

Philip Bull
La Trobe University
CONGESTED DISTRICTS BOARD
LAND QUESTIONS
PLUNKETT, SIR HORACE CURZON
UNITED IRISH LEAGUE
CAMPAIGNS

Neil Buttimer
University College Cork
LANGUAGE AND LITERACY:
DECLINE OF IRISH LANGUAGE
LITERATURE: GAELIC
LITERATURE IN THE
NINETEENTH CENTURY
RAIFTEARAÍ (RAFTERY),
ANTAINE

Mary Cahill
National Museum of Ireland
BRONZE AGE CULTURE

Jerrold I. Casway
*Howard Community College,
Columbia, Maryland*
O'NEILL, OWEN ROE

Wayne K. Chapman
Clemson University
LITERARY RENAISSANCE (CELTIC
REVIVAL)
YEATS, W. B.

Aidan Clarke
Trinity College Dublin
DARCY, PATRICK
GRACES, THE
RESTORATION IRELAND
SMITH, ERASMUS

Caitriona Clear
*National University of Ireland,
Galway*
CLARKE, KATHLEEN
CUMANN NA MBAN
GONNE, MAUD
MARKIEVICZ, COUNTESS
CONSTANCE
ROBINSON, MARY
WOMEN IN IRISH SOCIETY
SINCE 1800

John Coakley
University College Dublin
POLITICAL PARTIES IN
INDEPENDENT IRELAND
POLITICS: IMPACT OF THE
NORTHERN IRELAND CRISIS ON
SOUTHERN POLITICS
PROPORTIONAL REPRESENTATION

Marilyn Cohen
Montclair State University
FACTORY-BASED TEXTILE
MANUFACTURE
WOMEN AND CHILDREN IN THE
INDUSTRIAL WORKFORCE

R. V. Comerford
*National University of Ireland,
Maynooth*
DUFFY, JAMES
FENIAN MOVEMENT AND THE
IRISH REPUBLICAN
BROTHERHOOD
INDEPENDENT IRISH PARTY

E. Margaret Crawford
Queen's University Belfast
INDIAN CORN OR MAIZE

William H. Crawford
Queen's University Belfast
RURAL INDUSTRY
TOWN LIFE FROM 1690 TO
THE EARLY TWENTIETH
CENTURY

Maura Cronin
*Mary Immaculate College,
Limerick*
BALLADRY IN ENGLISH

Michael Cronin
Dublin City University
TOURISM

Virginia Crossman
Staffordshire University
LOCAL GOVERNMENT SINCE
1800

Bernadette Cunningham
Royal Irish Academy, Dublin
ANNALS OF THE FOUR MASTERS

Nancy J. Curtin
Fordham University
UNITED IRISH SOCIETIES FROM
1791 TO 1803

Mary E. Daly
University College Dublin
CONDITIONS OF EMPLOYMENT
ACT OF 1936
JEWISH COMMUNITY
SOCIAL CHANGE SINCE 1922
STATE ENTERPRISE

Marcus de Búrca
*County Tipperary Historical
Society, County Library, Thurles,
Co. Tipperary*
CUSACK, MICHAEL
GAELIC REVIVALISM: THE
GAELIC ATHLETIC
ASSOCIATION

Enda Delaney
Queen's University Belfast
DIASPORA: THE IRISH IN
BRITAIN
MIGRATION: EMIGRATION AND
IMMIGRATION SINCE 1950

Michael W. de Nie
Texas Christian University
DAVIS, THOMAS
MITCHEL, JOHN
O'CONNELL, DANIEL
STEPHENS, JAMES

David Dickson
Trinity College Dublin
GEORGIAN DUBLIN, ART AND
ARCHITECTURE OF

James E. Doan
Nova Southeastern University
TARA

James S. Donnelly, Jr.
University of Wisconsin–Madison
MARIANISM
ROMAN CATHOLIC CHURCH:
SINCE 1891

Martin W. Dowling
Arts Council of Northern Ireland
AGRICULTURE: 1690 TO 1845
TENANT RIGHT, OR ULSTER
CUSTOM

Patrick J. Duffy
*National University of Ireland,
Maynooth*
CLACHANS
ESTATES AND DEMESNES
LANDSCAPE AND SETTLEMENT
ORDNANCE SURVEY
RURAL SETTLEMENT AND FIELD
SYSTEMS

Seán Duffy
Trinity College Dublin
ENGLISH GOVERNMENT IN
MEDIEVAL IRELAND
MACMURROUGH, DERMOT,
AND THE ANGLO-NORMAN
INVASION
MAGNATES, GAELIC AND
ANGLO-IRISH
NORMAN CONQUEST AND
COLONIZATION
RICHARD II IN IRELAND

Lindsey Earner-Byrne
University College Dublin
DIVORCE, CONTRACEPTION,
AND ABORTION
MCQUAID, JOHN CHARLES

Owen Dudley Edwards
University of Edinburgh
GAELIC SOCIETY IN THE LATE
MIDDLE AGES
NORMAN INVASION AND
GAELIC RESURGENCE

Steven G. Ellis
*National University of Ireland,
Galway*
POLITICS: 1500 TO 1690

Sean Farrell
The College of Saint Rose
CARSON, SIR EDWARD
CONNOLLY, JAMES
LARKIN, JAMES
ORANGE ORDER: ORIGINS,
1784 TO 1800
REDMOND, JOHN

Diarmaid Ferriter
*St. Patrick's College, Dublin City
University*
POLITICS: INDEPENDENT
IRELAND SINCE 1922
PRESIDENCY
SODALITIES AND
CONFRATERNITIES

David Finnegan
University of Cambridge
JACOBITES AND THE
WILLIAMITE WARS
LAND SETTLEMENTS FROM
1500 TO 1690

Eithne Fitzgerald
Trinity College Dublin
HEALTH AND WELFARE SINCE
1950, STATE PROVISIONS FOR

David Fitzpatrick
Trinity College Dublin
DIASPORA: THE IRISH IN
AUSTRALIA
RURAL LIFE: 1850 TO 1921

Tony Flannery, C. Ss. R.
RELIGIOUS ORDERS: MEN

Alan J. Fletcher
University College Dublin
MIDDLE ENGLISH LITERATURE

Michael Foley
*School of Media, Dublin Institute
of Technology*
MEDIA SINCE 1960

Alan Ford
University of Nottingham
BEDELL, WILLIAM
CALVINIST INFLUENCES IN
EARLY MODERN IRELAND
EDWARDIAN REFORM
MARIAN RESTORATION
TRINITY COLLEGE
USSHER, JAMES

Brian Frykenberg
*Museum of Painting, North
Andover, Massachusetts*
KINGS AND KINGDOMS FROM
400 TO 800 C.E.

Daniel Gahan
University of Evansville
EMMET, ROBERT
FITZGERALD, LORD EDWARD
NEILSON, SAMUEL
TANDY, JAMES NAPPER

Finn Gallen
FDI consultant, Dublin
CELTIC TIGER
INVESTMENT AND
DEVELOPMENT AGENCY
(IDA IRELAND)
OVERSEAS INVESTMENT

Yvonne Galligan
Queen's University Belfast
WOMEN'S PARLIAMENTARY
REPRESENTATION SINCE 1922

Elizabeth Garber
SUNY Stony Brook
BOYLE, ROBERT

Frank Geary
University of Ulster
SHIPBUILDING

Laurence M. Geary
University College Cork
PLAN OF CAMPAIGN

P. M. Geoghegan
Trinity College Dublin
GOVERNMENT FROM 1690 TO
1800
TONE, THEOBALD WOLFE

Peter Gray
University of Southampton
GREAT FAMINE

Timothy W. Guinnane
Yale University
FAMILY: MARRIAGE PATTERNS
AND FAMILY LIFE FROM 1690
TO 1921

Peter Harbison
Royal Irish Academy
ARTS: EARLY AND MEDIEVAL
ARTS AND ARCHITECTURE
HIGH CROSSES
SCULPTURE, EARLY AND
MEDIEVAL

Suzanne C. Hartwick
*Hoard Historical Museum, Fort
Atkinson, Wisconsin*
IRISH TITHE ACT OF 1838
TITHE WAR (1830–1838)

Anthony Harvey
Royal Irish Academy
LATIN AND OLD IRISH LITERACY

Helen E. Hatton
University of Toronto
RELIGIOUS SOCIETY OF FRIENDS
(QUAKERS)

Charlotte J. Headrick
Oregon State University
DRAMA, MODERN

Gráinne Henry
*Presentation Secondary School,
Listowel, Co. Kerry*
WILD GEESE—THE IRISH
ABROAD FROM 1600 TO THE
FRENCH REVOLUTION

A. C. Hepburn
University of Sunderland
ANCIENT ORDER OF HIBERNIANS

Michael Herity
University College Dublin
CRUACHAIN
O'DONOVAN, JOHN
PREHISTORIC AND CELTIC
IRELAND

Jacqueline Hill
*National University of Ireland,
Maynooth*
PROTESTANT ASCENDANCY:
DECLINE, 1800 TO 1930

Myrtle Hill
Queen's University Belfast
METHODISM
PEACE MOVEMENT IN
NORTHERN IRELAND
WOMEN'S MOVEMENT IN
NORTHERN IRELAND

Barbara Hillers
Harvard University
LITERATURE: EARLY AND
MEDIEVAL LITERATURE

Edmund M. Hogan
*Archives, Society of African
Missions, Ireland*
OVERSEAS MISSIONS

Finlay Holmes
Union Theological College, Belfast
ABERNETHY, JOHN
COOKE, HENRY
PRESBYTERIANISM

Janice Holmes
University of Ulster, Coleraine
EVANGELICALISM AND REVIVALS

Patrick Honohan
Dublin
IRISH POUND

Michael A. Hopkinson
University of Stirling
ANGLO-IRISH TREATY OF 1921
STRUGGLE FOR INDEPENDENCE
FROM 1916 TO 1921

Arnold Horner
University College Dublin
WOODLANDS

Stephen Howe
Ruskin College
ENGLISH WRITING ON IRELAND
BEFORE 1800

Áine Hyland
University College Cork
EDUCATION:
NONDENOMINATIONAL
SCHOOLING

Tom Inglis
University College Dublin
SECULARIZATION

Colin A. Ireland
Arcadia University, Dublin
EARLY MEDIEVAL IRELAND AND
CHRISTIANITY

Alvin Jackson
Queen's University Belfast
NORTHERN IRELAND: HISTORY
SINCE 1920
UNIONISM FROM 1885 TO
1922

Henry A. Jefferies
Thornhill College, Derry
MONARCHY
PROTESTANT REFORMATION IN
THE EARLY SIXTEENTH
CENTURY

Walford Johnson
University of Ulster
SHIPBUILDING

David Seth Jones
Australian National University
LAND PURCHASE ACTS OF
1903 AND 1909

Donald E. Jordan, Jr.
Menlo College
HOME RULE MOVEMENT AND
THE IRISH PARLIAMENTARY
PARTY: 1870 TO 1891
LAND ACTS OF 1870 AND
1881
LAND WAR OF 1879 TO 1882

Sandra Joyce
Irish World Music Centre
CAROLAN, TURLOUGH

James Kelly
*St. Patrick's College, Dublin City
University*
ACT OF UNION
EIGHTEENTH-CENTURY
POLITICS: 1714 TO 1778—
INTEREST POLITICS
EIGHTEENTH-CENTURY
POLITICS: 1778 TO 1795—
PARLIAMENTARY AND
POPULAR POLITICS
FLOOD, HENRY
GRATTAN, HENRY
O'CONOR, CHARLES, OF
BALENAGARE
PROTESTANT ASCENDANCY:
1690 TO 1800

Joseph Kelly
College of Charleston
SWIFT, JONATHAN

Patricia Kelly
University College Dublin
TÁIN BÓ CÚAILNGE

Finola Kennedy
*Institute of Public Administration,
Dublin*
EQUAL ECONOMIC RIGHTS FOR
WOMEN IN INDEPENDENT
IRELAND
WOMEN AND WORK SINCE THE
MID-NINETEENTH CENTURY

Kieran A. Kennedy
*The Economic and Social Research
Institute, Dublin*
ECONOMIES OF IRELAND,
NORTH AND SOUTH, SINCE
1920
INDUSTRY SINCE 1920

Liam Kennedy
Queen's University Belfast
POPULATION EXPLOSION
POPULATION, ECONOMY, AND
SOCIETY FROM 1750 TO
1950

Michael Kennedy
Royal Irish Academy, Dublin
BOUNDARY COMMISSION
COMMONWEALTH
DECLARATION OF A REPUBLIC
AND THE 1949 IRELAND ACT
ECONOMIC RELATIONS BETWEEN
NORTH AND SOUTH SINCE
1922

Dáire Keogh
St. Patrick's College, Drumcondra
RICE, EDMUND
TROY, JOHN

Vera Kreilkamp
*Pine Manor College, Chestnut Hill,
Massachusetts*
COUNTRY HOUSES AND THE
ARTS

Brigid Laffan
University College Dublin
EUROPEAN UNION

Michael Laffan
University College Dublin
CIVIL WAR
HOME RULE MOVEMENT AND
THE IRISH PARLIAMENTARY
PARTY: 1891 TO 1918
SINN FÉIN MOVEMENT AND
PARTY TO 1922

Marie-Louise Legg
*Birkbeck College, London
University*
NEWSPAPERS

C. D. A. Leighton
Bilkent University, Ankara
CATHOLIC COMMITTEE FROM
1756 TO 1809
KEOGH, JOHN
PENAL LAWS
ROMAN CATHOLIC CHURCH:
1690 TO 1829

Pádraig Lenihan
University of Limerick
CONFEDERATION OF KILKENNY

Colm Lennon
*National University of Ireland,
Maynooth*
COUNCIL OF TRENT AND THE
CATHOLIC MISSION
EDUCATION: 1500 TO 1690
ENGLISH POLITICAL AND
RELIGIOUS POLICIES,
RESPONSES TO (1534–1690)
LOMBARD, PETER
OLD ENGLISH

James Livesey
Trinity College Dublin
BURKE, EDMUND

Ute Lotz-Heumann
Humboldt University
CHURCH OF IRELAND:
ELIZABETHAN ERA
PROTESTANT IMMIGRANTS
RELIGION: 1500 TO 1690

Maria Luddy
*University of Warwick, Coventry,
United Kingdom*
LADIES' LAND LEAGUE

Charles C. Ludington
Columbia University
BOYNE, BATTLE OF THE

Matthew Lynch
Kerry Group plc
POTATO AND POTATO BLIGHT
(*PHYTOPHTHORA INFESTANS*)

Patricia A. Lynch
University of Limerick
HIBERNO-ENGLISH

Mary Ann Lyons
St. Patrick's College, Drumcondra
FITZGERALD, THOMAS, TENTH
EARL OF KILDARE ("SILKEN
THOMAS")

Patricia Lysaght
University College Dublin
BLASKET ISLAND WRITERS

Dermot McAleese
Trinity College Dublin
ECONOMIC RELATIONS BETWEEN
INDEPENDENT IRELAND AND
BRITAIN

Lawrence W. McBride
Illinois State University
EDUCATION: SECONDARY
EDUCATION, MALE

Michael MacCarthy Morrogh
Shrewsbury School, England
COLONIAL THEORY FROM 1500
TO 1690
DESMOND REBELLIONS

Fearghal McGarry
Queen's University Belfast
IRISH REPUBLICAN ARMY (IRA)

Thomas McGrath
Trinity College Dublin
CULLEN, PAUL
DOYLE, JAMES WARREN
EDUCATION: PRIMARY PUBLIC
EDUCATION—NATIONAL
SCHOOLS FROM 1831
MACHALE, JOHN
MAYNOOTH
MURRAY, DANIEL

James McGuire
University College Dublin
BUTLER, JAMES, TWELFTH
EARL AND FIRST DUKE OF
ORMOND
EIGHTEENTH-CENTURY
POLITICS: 1690 TO 1714—
REVOLUTION SETTLEMENT
KING, WILLIAM
MOLYNEUX, WILLIAM
SARSFIELD, PATRICK
TOLAND, JOHN

Allan I. Macinnes
University of Aberdeen
SOLEMN LEAGUE AND
COVENANT

Gillian McIntosh
*Institute of Irish Studies, Queen's
University Belfast*
EUCHARISTIC CONGRESS

James MacKillop
Syracuse New Times
MYTH AND SAGA

Timothy G. McMahon
Marquette University
COLLINS, MICHAEL
GAELIC REVIVAL
GAELIC REVIVALISM: THE
GAELIC LEAGUE
GRIFFITH, ARTHUR
HYDE, DOUGLAS
PEARSE, PATRICK

Eoin Magennis
Queen's University Belfast
OAKBOYS AND STEELBOYS
WHITEBOYS AND WHITEBOYISM

Christopher Maginn
*National University of Ireland,
Galway*
ECONOMY AND SOCIETY FROM
1500 TO 1690
URBAN LIFE, CRAFTS, AND
INDUSTRY FROM 1500 TO
1690

Mary Peckham Magray
Madison, Wisconsin
EDUCATION: SECONDARY
EDUCATION, FEMALE
NAGLE, HONORA (NANO)
RELIGIOUS ORDERS: WOMEN

W. A. Maguire
*Institute of Irish Studies, Queen's
University Belfast*
RURAL LIFE: 1690 TO 1845
SUBDIVISION AND SUBLETTING
OF HOLDINGS

William J. Mahon
University of Wales, Aberystwyth
LITERATURE: EARLY MODERN
LITERATURE BEFORE THE
STUARTS (1500–1603)
LITERATURE: GAELIC WRITING
FROM 1607 TO 1800

Elizabeth Malcolm
University of Melbourne
TEMPERANCE MOVEMENTS

J. P. Mallory
Queen's University Belfast
EMAIN MACHA (NAVAN FORT)

Alan Matthews
Trinity College Dublin
AGRICULTURE: AFTER WORLD
WAR I
COMMON AGRICULTURAL
POLICY

Patrick Maume
Queen's University Belfast
BROOKE, BASIL STANLAKE,
FIRST VISCOUNT
BROOKEBOROUGH
COSGRAVE, W. T.
CRAIG, JAMES, FIRST
VISCOUNT CRAIGAVON
FAULKNER, BRIAN
HUME, JOHN
LABOR MOVEMENT
LOYALIST PARAMILITARIES
AFTER 1965
MURPHY, WILLIAM MARTIN
PAISLEY, IAN
ROYAL ULSTER CONSTABULARY
(INCLUDING SPECIALS)
SPECIAL POWERS ACT

Timothy J. Meagher
The Catholic University of America
DIASPORA: THE IRISH IN
NORTH AMERICA

David W. Miller
Carnegie Mellon University
DEVOTIONAL REVOLUTION
POLITICS: 1690–1800—A
PROTESTANT KINGDOM
RELIGION: SINCE 1690
RELIGIOUS GEOGRAPHY
ROMAN CATHOLIC CHURCH:
SINCE 1891

Kerby Miller
University of Missouri—Columbia
AMERICAN WAKES
MIGRATION: EMIGRATION FROM
1850 TO 1960
MIGRATION: EMIGRATION FROM
THE SEVENTEENTH CENTURY
TO 1845

Kenneth Milne
Dublin
PROTESTANT COMMUNITY IN
SOUTHERN IRELAND SINCE
1922

Colette Moloney
Waterford Institute of Technology
MUSIC: MODERN MUSIC

Hiram Morgan
University College Cork
NINE YEARS WAR
O'NEILL, HUGH, SECOND EARL
OF TYRONE

Marc Mulholland
St. Catherine's College
NORTHERN IRELAND:
DISCRIMINATION AND THE
CAMPAIGN FOR CIVIL RIGHTS
O'NEILL, TERENCE
TRIMBLE, DAVID
ULSTER UNIONIST PARTY IN
OFFICE

Eileen M. Murphy
Queen's University Belfast
EISCIR RIATA
RATHS

John A. Murphy
University College Cork
CORK

Grace Neville
University College Cork
NORMAN FRENCH LITERATURE

Kenneth Nicholls
University College Cork
AGRICULTURE: 1500 TO 1690
BRUCE INVASION
GAELIC RECOVERY

Ben Novick
University of Michigan
GREAT WAR

Sean T. O'Brien
*Keough Institute for Irish Studies,
University of Notre Dame*
LITERATURE: ANGLO-IRISH
LITERATURE IN THE
NINETEENTH CENTURY

Niall Ó Ciosáin
*National University of Ireland,
Galway*
CHAPBOOKS AND POPULAR
LITERATURE
LITERACY AND POPULAR
CULTURE

Rory O'Connell
Queens University Belfast
EQUAL RIGHTS IN NORTHERN
IRELAND

Emmet O Connor
Magee College, University of Ulster
IRISH WOMEN WORKERS'
UNION
TRADE UNIONS

Patrick J. O'Connor
University of Limerick
MARKETS AND FAIRS IN THE
EIGHTEENTH AND NINETEENTH
CENTURIES
TOWNS AND VILLAGES

Thomas O'Connor
*National University of Ireland,
Maynooth*
IRISH COLLEGES ABROAD UNTIL
THE FRENCH REVOLUTION

Donnchadh Ó Corráin
University College Cork
BREHON LAW
UÍ NÉILL HIGH KINGS

Dáibhí Ó Cróinín
*National University of Ireland,
Galway*
HIBERNO-LATIN CULTURE
RELIGION: THE COMING OF
CHRISTIANITY

Ruan O'Donnell
University of Limerick
EIGHTEENTH-CENTURY
POLITICS: 1795 TO 1800—
REPRESSION, REBELLION, AND
UNION

Anne O'Dowd
National Museum of Ireland
MIGRATION: SEASONAL
MIGRATION

Mary O'Dowd
Queen's University Belfast
FAMILY: MARRIAGE PATTERNS
AND FAMILY LIFE FROM 1500
TO 1690

Donal Ó Drisceoil
University College Cork
BREWING AND DISTILLING
GUINNESS BREWING COMPANY

Diarmuid Ó Giolláin
University College Cork
RELIGION: TRADITIONAL
POPULAR RELIGION

Gearóid Ó hAllmhuráin
University of Missouri–St. Louis
MUSIC: EARLY MODERN MUSIC

Tadhg Ó hAnnracháin
University College Dublin
O'MAHONY, CONOR, S. J.
RINUCCINI, GIOVANNI BATTISTA

Philip Ollerenshaw
*University of the West of England,
Bristol*
BANKING AND FINANCE TO
1921
INDUSTRIALIZATION

Ciarán Ó Murchadha
St. Flannan's College, Ennis
FAMINE CLEARANCES
POOR LAW AMENDMENT ACT
OF 1847 AND THE GREGORY
CLAUSE

Pádraig Ó Riagáin
Linguistics Institute of Ireland
LANGUAGE AND LITERACY:
IRISH LANGUAGE SINCE 1922

Cóilín Owens
George Mason University
ARTS: EARLY MODERN
LITERATURE AND THE ARTS
FROM 1500 TO 1800

Gary Owens
Huron University College
CATHOLIC EMANCIPATION
CAMPAIGN
REPEAL MOVEMENT
YOUNG IRELAND AND THE IRISH
CONFEDERATION

Senia Pašeta
*St. Hugh's College, University of
Oxford*
EDUCATION: UNIVERSITY
EDUCATION
EDUCATION: WOMEN'S
EDUCATION

Hans S. Pawlisch
*Office of the Chairman, The Joint
Chiefs of Staff*
LEGAL CHANGE IN THE
SIXTEENTH AND SEVENTEENTH
CENTURIES

Michael Perceval-Maxwell
McGill University
REBELLION OF 1641

Éamon Phoenix
Stranmillis University College
ADAMS, GERRY
POLITICS: NATIONALIST
POLITICS IN NORTHERN
IRELAND

Thomas P. Power
University of Toronto
CATHOLIC MERCHANTS AND
GENTRY FROM 1690 TO
1800

Aidan Punch
Central Statistics Office, Dublin
FAMILY: FERTILITY, MARRIAGE,
AND THE FAMILY SINCE 1950

Oliver P. Rafferty
John Carroll University
ROMAN CATHOLIC CHURCH:
1829 TO 1891

Susannah Riordan
CONSTITUTION
DE VALERA, EAMON
GAELIC CATHOLIC STATE,
MAKING OF
MOTHER AND CHILD CRISIS

Bill Rolston
*University of Ulster at
Jordanstown*
CÚ CHULAINN

Paul Rouse
University College Dublin
ANGLO-IRISH FREE TRADE
AGREEMENT OF 1965
ECONOMIC DEVELOPMENT, 1958
FARMING FAMILIES
FLEADH CHEOIL
GAA "BAN"
MUSIC: POPULAR MUSIC
SPORT AND LEISURE
TRANSPORT—ROAD, CANAL,
RAIL

Michael Ryan
Chester Beatty Library, Dublin
ARCHITECTURE, EARLY AND
MEDIEVAL
MANUSCRIPT WRITING AND
ILLUMINATION
METALWORK, EARLY AND
MEDIEVAL

Neil Sammells
Bath Spa University College
WILDE, OSCAR

Robert J. Savage, Jr.
*Boston College Irish Studies
Program*
LEMASS, SEÁN

David C. Sheehy
Dublin Diocesan Archives
WALSH, WILLIAM JOSEPH

Joseph M. Skelly
College of Mount Saint Vincent
KENNEDY, JOHN F., VISIT OF
NEUTRALITY
UNITED NATIONS

Geraldine Smyth
*Irish School of Ecumenics, Trinity
College Dublin*
ECUMENISM AND INTERCHURCH
RELATIONS

James Smyth
*Keough Institute for Irish Studies,
University of Notre Dame*
DEFENDERISM

Clodagh Tait
*National University of Ireland,
Maynooth*
BURIAL CUSTOMS AND
POPULAR RELIGION FROM
1500 TO 1690
PLUNKETT, OLIVER

Patrick F. Tally
University of Colorado, Boulder
BUTT, ISAAC
DAVITT, MICHAEL
PARNELL, CHARLES STEWART
SULLIVAN BROTHERS (A. M.
AND T. D.)

Spurgeon Thompson
Cyprus College
ANTIQUARIANISM

R. W. Tomlinson
Queen's University Belfast
BOGS AND DRAINAGE

Thomas M. Truxes
*Trinity College, Hartford,
Connecticut*
TRADE AND TRADE POLICY
FROM 1691 TO 1800

Michael Turner
University of Hull
AGRICULTURE: 1845 TO 1921

Maria Tymoczko
*University of Massachusetts
Amherst*
JOYCE, JAMES

Diane Urquhart
*Institute of Irish Studies,
University of Liverpool*
PARKER, DAME DEHRA
WOMEN IN NATIONALIST AND
UNIONIST MOVEMENTS IN
THE EARLY TWENTIETH
CENTURY

Bernard Wailes
University of Pennsylvania
DÚN AILINNE

Brian Walker
Queen's Univesity Belfast
ELECTORAL POLITICS FROM
1800 TO 1921
ORANGE ORDER: SINCE 1800

Eamonn Wall
University of Missouri–St. Louis
ARTS: MODERN IRISH AND
ANGLO-IRISH LITERATURE
AND THE ARTS SINCE 1800
FICTION, MODERN
POETRY, MODERN

Ann Owens Weekes
University of Arizona
LITERATURE: TWENTIETH-
CENTURY WOMEN WRITERS

Christopher J. Wheatley
The Catholic University of America
LITERATURE: ANGLO-IRISH
LITERARY TRADITION,
BEGINNINGS OF

Bernadette Whelan
University of Limerick
MARSHALL AID

Irene Whelan
Manhattanville College
EDUCATION: PRIMARY PRIVATE
EDUCATION—"HEDGE
SCHOOLS" AND OTHER
SCHOOLS
KILDARE PLACE SOCIETY
SECOND REFORMATION FROM
1822 TO 1869
VETO CONTROVERSY

Peter C. Woodman
University College Cork
STONE AGE SETTLEMENT

Padraig Yeates
The Irish Times, Dublin
LOCKOUT OF 1913
O'BRIEN, WILLIAM

Eric G. Zuelow
University of Madison–Wisconsin
CHRONOLOGY

Chronology

~

c. **3000 b.c.e.** Organized farming and food production at the Céide Fields in County Mayo.

3000 b.c.e. Megalithic period begins.

c. **2500 b.c.e.** Passage tombs at Newgrange, Knowth, and Dowth constructed.

c. **2000 b.c.e.** Bronze Age begins.

Third century b.c.e. Iron Age begins.

297–c. 450 Irish launch raids on Roman Britain.

431 Pope Celestine sends Palladius to Ireland as first bishop of Ireland.

432 Reputed date of St. Patrick's mission to Ireland.

c. **490** Earliest Irish monastery on Aran founded by St. Éndae.

493 Reputed death of St. Patrick.

520–c. 620 High point of early Irish monastic period.

546 St. Colum Cille (Columba) founds Derry.

547/48 St. Ciarán founds Clonmacnoise.

c. **550–c. 600** Earliest Irish texts written.

563 Iona founded.

c. **590** St. Columbanus undertakes Irish mission to the Continent.

c. **597** The oldest known Irish manuscript, the *Cathach*, written.

c. **650–750** Period of fine Irish metal and stonework, including construction of early high crosses. High point of the Brehon legal system.

c. **668–730** Dynastic polity gradually replaces old tribal social structure.

c. **700–c. 900** Classical Old Irish linguistic period.

c. **750–800** *St. Gall Gospels* and the *Book of Kells* illuminated at Iona.

c. **770–c. 840** Céle Dé reform movement.

795 First Viking raids.

807–813 Vikings raid west coast of Ireland.

837–876 Period of intense Viking activity in Ireland.

841 Vikings establish permanent camps at Dublin and Annagassen, Co. Louth.

876–916 Period of relative peace ("40-year peace").

900–1100 While Latin learning goes into decline, native Irish traditions are elaborated. Monastic schools are increasingly secularized. Middle Irish literature flourishes.

c. **909–c. 924** Scripture-based high crosses constructed at Monasterboice, Co. Meath, Clonmacnoise, Co. Offaly, and elsewhere.

916–937 Renewed period of Viking activity.

978 Brian Bóruma mac Cennétig (Brian Boru) becomes king of Munster after defeating Máel Muad mac Brain.

999 Máel Morda, king of Leinster, and Sitric Silkbeard are defeated by Brian Boru at Glen Máma.

1000 Dublin captured by Brian Boru.

1002 Brian Boru acknowledged as high king of Ireland.

1005 On a visit to Armagh, Brian Boru confirms primacy of see of Armagh.

1006 After claiming hostages from the north, Brian Boru becomes undisputed high king of Ireland.

23 APRIL 1014 After Brian Boru's death at the Battle of Clontarf, Máel Sechnaill II assumes high kingship.

1022–1072 High kingship dormant.

c. 1090–1120 Irish Romanesque metalwork flowers.

1101 First Synod of Cashel.

1111 Synod of Ráith Bressail—diocesan organization of Irish church planned.

1124 Round tower at Clonmacnoise finished.

1127–1226 Flourishing of Romanesque architecture and sculpture.

1132 St. Malachy made archbishop of Armagh.

1134 Consecration of Cormac's chapel at Cashel.

1142 Foundation of Mellifont Abbey, Ireland's first Cistercian house.

1152 Synod of Kells convened, later moved to Mellifont.

29 SEPTEMBER 1155 Invasion of Ireland considered and rejected at the Council of Winchester.

NOVEMBER 1155–JULY 1156 John of Salisbury visits Rome and attains papal approval for planned invasion of Ireland by Henry II.

1162 Synod of Clane reaffirms primacy of Armagh and orders that only alumni of Armagh should be recognized as lectors in Irish churches.

Control of Dublin attained by Diarmait Mac Murchada.

1166 Tigernán Ua Ruairc marches to Ferns and sacks Diarmait Mac Murchada's castle.

Mac Murchada flees to Bristol after being banished from Ireland by Ruaidrí Ua Conchobair.

1167 After returning to Ireland with a small Flemish force commanded by Richard fitz Godebert of Rhos, Mac Murchada reclaims kingdom of Uí Chennselaig.

1169 Mac Murchada captures Wexford with Norman assistance.

23 AUGUST 1170 Strongbow (Richard de Clare) lands at Wexford.

25 AUGUST 1170 Strongbow captures Wexford and marries Diarmait Mac Murchada's daughter Aoife.

21 SEPTEMBER 1170 Mac Murchada and Norman allies capture Dublin.

1 MAY 1171 After Mac Murchada's death his son-in-law Strongbow succeeds him.

17 OCTOBER 1171 Henry II of England lands near Waterford.

11 NOVEMBER 1171 The English Pale is shaped when Henry II arrives in Dublin and receives submission of kings of north Leinster, Bréifne, Áirgialla, and Ulster.

1 APRIL 1172 Henry II grants Meath to Hugh de Lacy.

20 SEPTEMBER 1172 Pope Alexander III asks Irish kings to offer fealty to Henry II.

6 OCTOBER 1175 Treaty of Windsor.

MAY 1177 John, Henry II's ten-year-old son, made "Lord of Ireland."

25 APRIL–17 DECEMBER 1185 John, lord of Ireland, visits Ireland.

c. 1200 Bardic schools standardize classical Modern Irish grammar.

1204 Center of royal administration established at Dublin Castle.

1207 Minting of first national coinage to feature the harp.

20 JUNE 1210 King John lands at Waterford.

28 JULY 1210 The de Lacys flee after Carrickfergus is captured by King John.

1216–1227 "Conspiracy of Mellifont."

12 NOVEMBER 1216 Magna Carta issued for Ireland.

1224 Dominicans establish their first foundations at Dublin and Drogheda.

c. 1224–1230 Irish Franciscans establish their first foundations at Youghal and Cork.

21 MAY 1227 Richard de Burgh is given all of Connacht as a fief.

1257 Battle of Credran, Co. Sligo; O'Donnells stop northward advance of Maurice FitzGerald, lord of Sligo.

1258 The sons of the kings of Thomond and of Connacht acknowledge Brian O'Neill as king of Ireland at Caeluisce, Co. Sligo.

16 MAY 1260 Battle of Downpatrick.

1261 Battle of Callan.

1262–1263 Haakon IV, king of Norway, is offered high kingship of Ireland in exchange for support in expelling English from Ireland.

18 JUNE 1264 Parliament of Castledermot.

1270 Battle of Áth in Chip.

1297 Widespread political representation begins at the parliament in Dublin where liberties and counties are both represented.

9 FEBRUARY 1310 Parliament of Kilkenny passes a statute banning the reception of Irishmen into Anglo-Irish religious houses.

26 MAY 1315 Edward Bruce arrives at Larne.

29 JUNE 1315 Edward Bruce inaugurated "high king" after capturing Dundalk.

1315–1317 Widespread famine in western Europe and Ireland.

c. 1 MAY 1316 Edward Bruce crowned king of Ireland.

14 OCTOBER 1318 Bruce defeated and killed by John de Bermingham at Battle of Faughart.

c. 1327–1328 "Divers men of Ireland" submit petition to Edward III asking that English law be available to Irishmen without special charter.

1331 Ordinances for conduct of Irish government decree that there should be one law for the Irish and the Anglo-Irish.

AUGUST 1348 Plague strikes at Howth and Drogheda.

19 FEBRUARY 1366 Parliament of Kilkenny: "Statute of Kilkenny" announced.

1394 First visit of Richard II to Ireland.

1399 Second visit of Richard II to Ireland.

1 APRIL 1435 Irish poets and musicians banned from Anglo-Irish areas.

1446 "Pale" used for the first time to describe area under Dublin control.

8 FEBRUARY 1460 Parliament at Drogheda.

30 DECEMBER 1460 Duke of York killed at Battle of Wakefield.

29 MARCH 1461 After Henry VI is deposed on 4 March, Edward IV, son of Richard, duke of York, replaces him as king.

1 APRIL 1463 Thomas Fitzgerald appointed lord deputy by Edward IV after succeeding his father as eighth earl of Desmond.

22 AUGUST 1485 Richard III killed at the Battle of Bosworth (England) and succeeded by Henry VII.

1 DECEMBER 1494 Poynings' Law enacted.

23 MAY 1520 Thomas Howard, earl of Surrey and lord lieutenant of Ireland, travels to Ireland with 500 troops.

SEPTEMBER 1520 Surrey ordered to subdue Irish by legal means.

30 JUNE 1521 Surrey submits program to the king for reconquest of Ireland.

1–3 MAY 1536 "Reformation parliament" meets in Dublin.

OCTOBER–DECEMBER 1537 Acts passed by parliament against authority of the pope.

1539 Beginning of dissolution of monasteries within the Pale.

AUGUST 1539 Lord Deputy Grey routes O'Neill and O'Donnell at Bellahoe.

1540–1543 Initiation of "surrender and regrant."

18 JUNE 1541 Act of Irish parliament makes Henry VIII "king of Ireland."

1542 First Jesuit mission to Ireland.

1547–1553 Edwardian Reformation in Ireland.

14 MARCH 1549 First English Act of Uniformity.

1555 Beginning of plantation of Offaly and Laois as King's and Queen's Counties.

14 APRIL 1552 Second English Act of Uniformity.

1553–1558 Marian reaction in Ireland.

JULY 1559 Shane O'Neill succeeds Conn O'Neill as The O'Neill.

11 JANUARY–12 FEBRUARY 1560 Elizabeth's first Irish parliament restores royal supremacy.

1561–1567 Shane O'Neill's rebellion.

1568–1573 First Desmond rebellion.

JUNE 1571 First Irish-language printing in Dublin.

1573–1576 Attempt by earl of Essex to establish colony in Antrim.

26 JULY 1575 Rathlin Island massacre by Essex's soldiers.

1579–1583 Second Desmond rebellion.

26 APRIL–25 MAY 1586 Hugh O'Neill takes seat in House of Lords as earl of Tyrone.

DECEMBER 1585 Scheme for plantation of Munster.

SEPTEMBER 1588 Some 25 ships from Spanish Armada wrecked off Irish coasts.

3 MARCH 1592 Incorporation of Trinity College, Dublin.

14 AUGUST 1598 Battle of Yellow Ford: Victory of Hugh O'Neill over English army led by Henry Bagenal.

1595–1603 Hugh O'Neill, earl of Tyrone, leads rebellion.

OCTOBER 1598 Earl of Desmond attacks Munster plantation.

24 DECEMBER 1601 Battle of Kinsale.

24 MARCH 1603 Accession of James I.

30 MARCH 1603 Tyrone surrenders at Mellifont and is pardoned in exchange for surrender.

JANUARY–FEBRUARY 1606 Gavelkind banned by royal judges.

4 SEPTEMBER 1607 "Flight of the Earls."

DECEMBER 1607 Departed earls declared traitors and their lands forfeit.

1608–1610 Beginning of plantation of six Ulster counties found forfeit.

APRIL–MAY 1610 British undertakers assigned lands in Ulster.

18 MAY 1613 Dublin parliament opened.

20 JANUARY 1621 Approval of plantations in parts of Leitrim, King's County, Queen's County, and Westmeath.

24 MAY 1628 Charles I grants fifty-one "Graces" in return for financial subsidy.

1632–1640 Thomas Wentworth, first earl of Strafford from 1640, becomes lord deputy and then lord lieutenant of Ireland.

AUGUST 1640 War breaks out in Scotland.

23 OCTOBER 1641 Rising in Ulster begins.

19 MARCH 1642 "Adventurers' Act" offers Irish land in return for loans.

SUMMER 1642 First Civil War begins in England.

14 OCTOBER 1642 "Confederate Catholics" convene at Kilkenny.

15 SEPTEMBER 1643 Truce between Confederates and royalists.

1646 End of First Civil War in England.

28 MARCH 1646 "Ormond Peace."

12 AUGUST 1646 Rinuccini and O'Neill condemn "Ormond Peace."

19 JUNE 1647 Dublin surrendered to parliamentary forces.

MAY–AUGUST 1648 Second English Civil War.

17 JANUARY 1649 Second Ormond Peace.

30 JANUARY 1649 Charles I executed.

15 AUGUST 1649 Oliver Cromwell arrives in Dublin.

11 SEPTEMBER 1649 Cromwell takes Drogheda.

11 OCTOBER 1649 Cromwell takes Wexford.

19 OCTOBER 1649 New Ross surrenders to Cromwell.

12 AUGUST 1652 "Act for the Settling of Ireland."

JUNE–SEPTEMBER 1653 Arrangements for "Transplantation to Connacht."

3 SEPTEMBER 1658 Death of Cromwell.

FEBRUARY 1660 Dublin parliament restored.

14 MAY 1660 Charles II made king.

13 SEPTEMBER 1660 Navigation Act; Ireland and England made one economic unit.

27 JULY 1663 "Cattle Act" protects English producers from Irish exports.

28 SEPTEMBER 1678 Popish Plot alleged.

1 JULY 1681 Oliver Plunkett executed in London.

6 FEBRUARY 1685 James II crowned.

5 NOVEMBER 1688 William of Orange arrives in England; James II flees.

18 APRIL 1689 Siege of Derry begins.

22 JUNE 1689 Temporary repeal of Cromwellian land settlement.

28 JULY 1689 Siege of Derry ends.

1 JULY 1690 Battle of the Boyne (12 July on modern calendar).

9–30 AUGUST 1690 First siege of Limerick.

26 SEPTEMBER 1690 First meeting of Presbyterian Synod of Ulster.

12 JULY 1691 Battle of Aughrim.

SEPTEMBER–OCTOBER 1691 Second siege of Limerick.

3 OCTOBER 1691 Treaty of Limerick.

1691–1703 Williamite land confiscations.

7 SEPTEMBER 1695 First "Penal Laws" enacted in Irish parliament.

25 SEPTEMBER 1697 Irish parliament banishes Catholic bishops and regular clergy, that is, those in orders.

26 JANUARY 1699 Export of Irish woolens restricted by English and Irish parliaments.

4 MARCH 1704 Sacramental test imposed for public office on both Catholics and Protestants, excluding both Catholics and Dissenters.

2 NOVEMBER 1719 Toleration Act for Protestant Dissenters (Protestants not taking communion in the Church of Ireland).

7 APRIL 1720 "Declaratory Act" passed by British parliament.

JUNE 1726 Non-subscribing Presbyterians separate from Synod of Ulster to form presbytery of Antrim.

6 MAY 1728 Catholics lose franchise.

14 JUNE 1739 Duties on imports of Irish woolen yarn into Britain removed.

1739–1741 Catastrophic famine.

DECEMBER 1753 Money Bill crisis.

20 JUNE 1758 Importation of Irish cattle into Britain legalized.

MARCH 1760 Formation of Catholic Committee.

OCTOBER–DECEMBER 1761 Whiteboy movement develops in Munster.

1763 Oakboy disturbances in Ulster.

7 JUNE 1766 Tumultuous Risings Act.

14 OCTOBER 1767 Lord Townshend begins viceroyalty.

16 FEBRUARY 1768 Octennial Act.

JULY 1769 Steelboy disturbances begin in Ulster.

2 JUNE 1772 Catholics attain right to lease bog land.

27 OCTOBER 1775 Henry Flood appointed vice-treasurer.

15 DECEMBER 1775 Henry Grattan delivers his maiden speech in House of Commons and inherits Flood's place as leader of opposition.

APRIL 1776 New anti-Whiteboy legislation.

17 MARCH 1778 Volunteer movement begins (Belfast).

14 AUGUST 1778 Catholic Relief Act grants right to lease land and inherit property.

4 NOVEMBER 1779 Volunteers march as champions of free trade.

24 FEBRUARY 1780 Free-trade legislation passes.

15 FEBRUARY 1782 Dungannon convention.

16 APRIL 1782 Grattan proposes Irish legislative independence for the third time and the motion is carried unanimously in the Irish parliament.

4 MAY 1782 Catholic Relief Act gives Catholics right to own land outside parliamentary boroughs.

4 MAY 1782 Bank of Ireland established.

21 JUNE 1782 Declaratory Act repealed.

27 JULY 1782 Yelverton's Act.

Catholic Relief Act grants Catholics education rights.

17 APRIL 1783 Renunciation Act.

8 SEPTEMBER 1783 Second Volunteer convention at Dungannon.

10 NOVEMBER–2 DECEMBER 1783 National Volunteer convention in Dublin.

19 NOVEMBER 1783 Rejection of Volunteers' parliamentary-reform bill.

14 MAY 1784 Corn Law imposes sliding scale for export subsidies based on domestic prices.

JULY 1784 Emergence of Defenders and Peep o' Day Boys in Ulster.

SEPTEMBER 1785 Renewed Whiteboy (or Rightboy) disturbances.

AUGUST 1785 Antiburgher Seceding Presbyterian Synod founded.

5 NOVEMBER 1788–10 MARCH 1789 Regency crisis.

AUGUST 1791 Publication of Theobald Wolfe Tone's *Argument on Behalf of the Catholics of Ireland.*

14 OCTOBER 1791 Foundation of the Society of United Irishmen in Belfast.

9 NOVEMBER 1791 Formation of the Dublin branch of the United Irishmen.

18 APRIL 1792 Catholic Relief Act grants Catholics the right to practice law.

25 JULY 1792 Tone made assistant secretary of the Catholic Committee.

3–8 DECEMBER 1792 Catholic Convention.

DECEMBER 1792 Deputation from Catholic Convention presents civil-rights petition to the king.

11 MARCH 1793 Suppression of the Volunteers.

9 APRIL 1793 Catholic Relief Act—Catholics receive franchise if qualified, the right to serve in the military, and other benefits.

15 FEBRUARY 1794 Publication of the United Irishmen's plans for parliamentary reform.

1 MARCH 1794 Catholics given statutory right to attend Trinity College, Dublin.

23 MAY 1794 Suppression of the Dublin branch of the United Irishmen.

4 JANUARY–23 MARCH 1795 Fitzwilliam affair.

21 SEPTEMBER 1795 Battle of the Diamond.

1 FEBRUARY 1796 Tone arrives in France.

24 MARCH 1796 Insurrection Act.

22 NOVEMBER 1796 French fleet, including Tone, sails into Bantry Bay.

7 DECEMBER 1796 French forced to leave by stormy weather.

SUMMER AND AUTUMN 1797 Severe measures taken by government to disarm the disaffected in the North.

8 MARCH 1798 Orange Order meets in Dublin and begins nationwide movement.

12 MARCH 1798 Arrest of leaders of United Irishmen.

MAY–JUNE 1798 Rising of United Irishmen in Leinster.

21 JUNE 1798 Wexford rebels finally defeated at Vinegar Hill.

8 SEPTEMBER 1798 French invasion force defeated near Ballinamuck.

19 NOVEMBER 1798 Tone dies six days after cutting his throat rather than be hanged for treason.

21 MAY 1800 Consideration of Act of Union begins in Irish parliament.

1 JANUARY 1801 Union of Great Britain and Ireland takes effect.

23 JULY 1803 Robert Emmet leads rising in Dublin.

MAY–SEPTEMBER 1808 Controversy about royal veto over Catholic episcopal appointments brings Daniel O'Connell to prominence.

AUGUST 1808 Edmund Rice founds the Christian Brothers in Waterford.

30 APRIL 1811 Grattan introduces Catholic Relief Bill at Westminster. It is narrowly defeated on 24 May.

AUGUST–OCTOBER 1816 Potato-crop failure leads to famine, made worse by outbreak of typhus.

1817 Typhus epidemic continues, claiming 50,000 lives.

1818 Wesleyan Methodist connexion formed; Primitive Wesleyan Methodists remain in communion with Church of Ireland.

10 JULY 1818 Burgher and Antiburgher Presbyterians unite to form Secession Synod.

SEPTEMBER–NOVEMBER 1821 Potato-crop failure.

12 MAY 1823 Daniel O'Connell founds Catholic Association.

24 JANUARY 1824 "Catholic rent" introduced.

19–29 JUNE 1826 General election returns pro-Catholic Members of Parliament (MPs) following extensive efforts by O'Connell to mobilize voters.

24 JUNE 1828 O'Connell wins County Clare by-election.

13 APRIL 1829 Catholic Relief Act provides Catholic emancipation.

30 JULY 1829 O'Connell returned to parliament unopposed.

25 MAY 1830 Remonstrant Synod of Ulster formed by non-subscribing Presbyterians forced out of Synod of Ulster.

3 MARCH 1831 Tithe war begins.

NOVEMBER 1831 National Education system initiated.

7 AUGUST 1832 Parliamentary Reform Act increases Irish seats from 100 to 105 and enlarges the electorate to 1.2 percent of the population.

29 AUGUST 1833 Tithe Arrears Act.

22–30 APRIL 1834 House of Commons debates Repeal following a motion by O'Connell.

17 DECEMBER 1834 First railway in Ireland opens between Dublin and Kingstown.

18 FEBRUARY 1835 First meeting leading to "Lichfield House Compact."

14 APRIL 1836 Dissolution of the Grand Orange Lodge of Ireland.

20 MAY 1836 Irish Constabulary formed.

10 APRIL 1838 Father Mathew and William Martin found total-abstinence movement.

31 JULY 1838 Poor Law extended to Ireland.

15 APRIL 1840 Daniel O'Connell forms National Association. Organization renamed Loyal National Repeal Association on 16 July.

10 JULY 1840 Synod of Ulster and Seceding Synod unite to form General Assembly of the Presbyterian Church of Ireland.

10 AUGUST 1840 Municipal Reform Act.

17 APRIL 1841 Thomas Davis joins Repeal Association.

JANUARY 1842 Having attracted three million people, Father Mathew's total-abstinence movement reaches its peak.

15 OCTOBER 1842 First issue of the *Nation* published.

15 AUGUST 1843 Huge throng attends "Monster Meeting" at the Hill of Tara.

7 OCTOBER 1843 "Monster meeting" at Clontarf prohibited. O'Connell cancels it rather than face violent confrontation with crown forces.

10 FEBRUARY 1844 Daniel O'Connell and others convicted of conspiracy and other charges. Sentence overturned on 4 September.

9 SEPTEMBER 1845 Dublin newspaper reports appearance of the potato blight.

9–10 NOVEMBER 1845 Peel orders purchase of Indian corn from America to provide famine relief.

18 NOVEMBER 1845 Government appoints relief commission.

5 MARCH 1846 Parliament authorizes county relief works to alleviate distress in Ireland.

26 JUNE 1846 Peel secures "repeal" of the corn laws.

30 JUNE 1846 Lord John Russell succeeds Peel as prime minister.

28 JULY 1846 O'Connell and Young Irelanders split over question of physical force. Young Irelanders soon form Irish Confederation.

26 FEBRUARY 1847 "Soup Kitchen Act" allows outdoor relief. More than 3 million fed at soup kitchens by July.

8 JUNE 1847 Poor Relief Act permits outdoor relief to non-able-bodied but incorporates the "Gregory Clause" facilitating mass evictions.

29 JULY 1848 William Smith O'Brien leads Confederate (Young Ireland) "rising" at Boulagh Commons near Ballingarry, Co. Tipperary.

28 SEPTEMBER–23 OCTOBER 1848 Confederate leaders tried and convicted of treason. Death sentences commuted to transportation for life on 5 June 1849.

NOVEMBER 1848 Beginning of cholera outbreak.

12 JULY 1849 Sectarian riot at Dolly's Brae in County Down.

OCTOBER 1849 Queen's Colleges of Belfast, Cork, and Galway opened.

9 AUGUST 1850 Foundation of Irish Tenant League.

22 AUGUST–10 SEPTEMBER 1850 Synod of Thurles led by Archbishop Paul Cullen initiates major reforms within Catholic Church.

19 AUGUST 1851 Formation of Catholic Defence Association.

JULY 1852 General election returns roughly 40 MPs favoring the Tenant League.

DECEMBER 1853 Queen's Island shipyard opens in Belfast.

JULY–SEPTEMBER 1857 Sectarian rioting in Belfast follows controversial street preaching.

17 MARCH 1858 James Stephens founds what is later called Irish Republican Brotherhood (IRB) in Dublin.

MARCH–NOVEMBER 1859 Religious revival occurs in Belfast.

APRIL 1859 John O'Mahony founds Fenian Brotherhood in New York.

10 NOVEMBER 1861 Funeral for Terence Bellew McManus held at Glasnevin by the IRB.

7 AUGUST 1862 Poor Relief Act abolishes "Gregory Clause."

8–25 AUGUST 1864 Sectarian rioting in Belfast precipitated by Protestant reaction against unveiling in Dublin of O'Connell monument.

22 JUNE 1866 Archbishop Cullen becomes first Irish cardinal.

5–6 MARCH 1867 Fenian rising in Munster counties and around Dublin.

20 JUNE 1867 Foundation of Clan na Gael in New York City.

17 AUGUST 1867 Colonel Thomas J. Kelly succeeds Stephens as head of the IRB.

18 SEPTEMBER 1867 IRB rescue of Kelly and Captain Timothy Deasy in Manchester.

23 NOVEMBER 1867 "Manchester Martyrs" (Allen, Larkin, and O'Brien) executed.

13 JULY 1868 Irish Parliamentary Reform Act extends borough franchise.

26 JULY 1869 Irish Church Disestablishment Act.

19 MAY 1870 Isaac Butt launches Home Rule movement Dublin.

1 AUGUST 1870 Gladstone's first Land Act.

16 JUNE 1871 "Westmeath Act."

18 JULY 1872 Ballot Act.

18–21 NOVEMBER 1873 Home Rule League founded in Dublin.

FEBRUARY 1874 General election returns 60 Home Rulers.

30 JUNE–2 JULY 1874 Butt's Home Rule motion debated and defeated at Westminster.

19 APRIL 1875 Charles Stewart Parnell returned to parliament as MP for County Meath.

31 JULY–1 AUGUST 1877 Parnell and other MPs engage in parliamentary obstruction.

28 AUGUST 1877 Parnell becomes president of the Home Rule Confederation of Great Britain at Liverpool.

1877–1879 Major agricultural depression.

27 OCTOBER 1878 American Fenian leaders announce the "New Departure."

20 APRIL 1879 Land war begins with meeting at Irishtown, Co. Mayo.

21 OCTOBER 1879 Foundation of Irish National Land League in Dublin.

MARCH–APRIL 1880 General election provides substantial victory for Parnell, Home Rule, and the Land League.

17 MAY 1880 Parnell becomes chairman of the Irish Parliamentary Party.

24 SEPTEMBER–25 NOVEMBER 1880 "Boycotting" employed by tenants after Captain Charles C. Boycott attempts to enforce payment of rents due to Lord Erne.

26 JANUARY 1881 Land League establishes Ladies' committee under Anna Parnell. Forerunner of Ladies' Land League in Ireland.

2 MARCH 1881 Protection of Person and Property Act.

21 MARCH 1881 Peace Preservation Act.

22 AUGUST 1881 Second Gladstone Land Act legalizes the "three Fs."

13 OCTOBER 1881 Arrest of Parnell and other Land League leaders.

18 OCTOBER 1881 No Rent Manifesto.

20 OCTOBER 1881 Land League declared illegal.

APRIL 1882 Parnell agrees to "Kilmainham Treaty." On 2 May the cabinet approves it.

2 MAY 1882 Release of Parnell and other Land League leaders.

6 MAY 1882 Phoenix Park murders.

12 JULY 1882 New Coercion Act.

18 AUGUST 1882 Arrears of Rent Act.

17 OCTOBER 1882 Irish National League founded to succeed banned Land League.

JUNE 1884 Fenians launch "dynamite campaign" in England.

1 NOVEMBER 1884 Gaelic Athletic Association founded.

6 DECEMBER 1884 Franchise Act triples Irish electorate.

1 MAY 1885 Foundation of Irish Loyal and Patriotic Union.

21 NOVEMBER 1885 Parnell calls on Irish in Great Britain to vote against Liberals.

23 NOVEMBER–19 DECEMBER 1885 Home Rule party wins 86 seats in general election and seems to hold balance of power at Westminster.

8 APRIL 1886 Introduction of Gladstone's Home Rule bill at Westminster.

8 JUNE 1886 Home Rule bill defeated by 30 votes.

3 JUNE–25 OCTOBER 1886 Rioting in Belfast, occasioned by Home Rule bill, causes 32 fatalities, £90,000 in property damage.

23 OCTOBER 1886 Plan of Campaign—a rent strike—announced.

APRIL–DECEMBER 1887 *The Times* publishes "Parnellism and Crime" articles.

13 NOVEMBER 1887 Over 100 injured during clash of radicals and Irish nationalists with police in London: "Bloody Sunday."

20 APRIL 1888 Rome condemns Plan of Campaign and boycotting.

13 AUGUST 1888 Special commission created to investigate charges by *The Times* against Parnell.

20–22 FEBRUARY 1889 Special commission finds that articles published in *The Times* were forged.

24 DECEMBER 1889 Captain William O'Shea files petition for divorce, citing his wife's adultery with Parnell.

13 FEBRUARY 1890 Parnell and associates exonerated of weightiest charges made in *Times* articles.

17 NOVEMBER 1890 O'Shea divorce granted.

25 NOVEMBER 1890 Parnell re-elected chairman of Irish parliamentary party.

25 NOVEMBER 1890 Publication of Gladstone-Morley letter pressuring Parnell to resign as party leader.

1–6 DECEMBER 1890 Committee Room 15 debates leading to Irish party split.

10 MARCH 1891 Irish National Federation (anti-Parnellite body) launched.

25 JUNE 1891 Parnell marries Katharine O'Shea.

5 AUGUST 1891 Arthur Balfour's Land Purchase Act.

6 OCTOBER 1891 Parnell dies in Brighton.

11 OCTOBER 1891 Parnell buried at Glasnevin after massive Dublin funeral.

DECEMBER 1891 John Redmond succeeds Parnell as leader of Irish party minority.

17 JUNE 1892 Ulster Unionist Convention in Belfast.

29 SEPTEMBER 1892 Formation of Belfast Labour Party.

13 FEBRUARY 1893 Introduction of Gladstone's second Home Rule bill.

25 FEBRUARY 1893 Report of Evicted Tenants Commission.

21–22 April 1893 Second reading of Home Rule bill leads to disturbances in Belfast.

31 July 1893 Gaelic League founded.

2 September 1893 Home Rule bill passes House of Commons by 301 to 267.

9 September 1893 House of Lords rejects Home Rule bill by 419 to 41.

27–28 April 1894 First Irish Trade Union Congress.

29 May 1896 Irish Socialist Republican Party formed.

12 August 1898 Local Government Act.

8 May 1899 Irish Literary Theatre (founded 1898) debuts in Dublin; it becomes the Abbey Theatre in 1904.

6 February 1900 Redmond elected leader of newly united Irish party.

30 September 1900 Arthur Griffith founds Cumann na nGaedheal.

11 June 1903 Independent Orange Order set up in Belfast.

14 August 1903 "Wyndham Act" passed—greatly extends land purchase.

27 December 1904 Abbey Theatre opens in Dublin.

3 March 1905 Ulster Unionist Council formed.

5 May 1906 Griffith's *Sinn Féin* first published.

21 April 1907 Sinn Féin League established.

28 August 1907 Evicted Tenants Act.

5 September 1907 National Council and Sinn Féin League combine to create new body—called Sinn Féin from September 1908.

29 December 1908 Irish Transport and General Workers' Union formed.

29 April 1909 "People's Budget" introduced by David Lloyd George.

16 August 1909 Fianna Éireann—a movement of girl scouts—formed.

January–February 1910 Irish party holds balance of power after general election.

21 February 1910 Sir Edward Carson elected chairman of Irish unionist MPs.

December 1910 Irish party once again holds balance of power after another general election.

18 August 1911 Parliament Act removes absolute veto power of House of Lords and grants suspensive veto of two years.

9 April 1912 Andrew Bonar Law promises Tory support for Ulster unionists.

28 September 1912 Ulster unionists sign Solemn League and Covenant in opposition to Home Rule— "Ulster Day" ceremony.

16 January 1913 Third Home Rule bill narrowly passes House of Commons.

30 January 1913 Third Home Rule bill defeated in House of Lords by large margin.

31 January 1913 Ulster Volunteer Force (UVF) established.

July 1913 Home Rule bill again passes Commons but fails in Lords.

30 August–1 September 1913 Labor disturbances in Dublin.

3 September 1913 "Lock-out" by Dublin employers begins against Irish Transport and General Workers' Union.

24 September 1913 Unionist leaders plan "provisional government" for Ulster.

19 November 1913 Irish Citizen Army founded.

25 November 1913 Irish Volunteers founded under Eoin MacNeill.

January–February 1914 "Lock-out" ends in heavy defeat for workers.

20 March 1914 "Curragh Incident"—a near-mutiny against Home Rule.

2 April 1914 Cumann na mBan—female branch of Irish Volunteers—founded.

24–25 April 1914 Larne gun-running—UVF now well armed.

25 May 1914 Home Rule bill passes the House of Commons for the third time.

21–24 July 1914 Buckingham Palace conference fails to solve Ulster question.

26 July 1914 Howth gun-running brings some arms to nationalists.

3–4 August 1914 First World War begins.

18 September 1914 Third Home Rule bill suspended after receiving royal assent.

20 September 1914 Redmond calls on Irish Volunteers to support British war effort.

24 September 1914 Redmond's leadership rejected by small minority (Irish Volunteers) but accepted by vast majority (National Volunteers).

20 April 1916 *Aud* captured by Royal Navy— German arms for rising lost.

24 April 1916 Easter Rising begins.

29 APRIL 1916 Pearse orders rebels to surrender. Casualties amount to about 3,000 (450 killed).

3–12 MAY 1916 Fifteen leaders of the Easter Rising shot by British military.

5 FEBRUARY 1917 Count Plunkett elected as Sinn Féin candidate for Roscommon North.

9 MAY 1917 Joseph McGuinness elected as Sinn Féin candidate for Longford South.

10 JULY 1917 Eamon de Valera elected as Sinn Féin candidate for Clare East.

23 APRIL 1918 General strike against conscription—part of furious nationalist opposition to threat of enforced enlistment.

11 NOVEMBER 1918 First World War ends.

14–28 DECEMBER 1918 General election returns large Sinn Féin majority (73 seats won).

21 JANUARY 1919 Two policemen are killed at Soloheadbeg in Tipperary—later viewed as start of war for independence.

21 JANUARY 1919 First meeting of Dáil Éireann.

20 AUGUST 1919 Dáil decides that the Volunteers must pledge allegiance to the "Irish Republic" and to the Dáil itself. The Irish Volunteers gradually become known as the Irish Republican Army (IRA).

12 SEPTEMBER 1919 Dáil Éireann proscribed by British government.

2 JANUARY 1920 First British recruits join Irish police units later called "Black and Tans."

21 JUNE–4 JULY 1920 Catholics expelled from Belfast shipyards and engineering works.

25 OCTOBER 1920 IRA commander and Cork May or Terence MacSwiney dies on hunger strike.

21 NOVEMBER 1920 "Bloody Sunday": following IRA killings of the "Cairo Gang," police "Auxiliaries" fire on a crowd at Croke Park, killing twelve.

23 DECEMBER 1920 Government of Ireland Act attempts to confer Home Rule separately on North and South.

4 FEBRUARY 1921 Sir James Craig elected leader of Ulster unionists.

24 MAY 1921 General election in Northern Ireland returns a unionist majority. Southern nationalists in effect boycott Dublin parliament.

7 JUNE 1921 James Craig elected prime minister of Northern Ireland.

11 JULY 1921 Truce between British army and IRA comes into effect.

16 AUGUST 1921 Sinn Féin MPs elected in the South meet as second Dáil Éireann.

6 DECEMBER 1921 Anglo-Irish Treaty signed in London.

7 JANUARY 1922 Dáil Éireann approves Anglo-Irish Treaty by 64 to 57. Anti-treatyites storm out.

7 APRIL 1922 Special Powers Act (Northern Ireland).

31 MAY 1922 Royal Ulster Constabulary formed.

16 JUNE 1922 General election in South returns protreaty majority to Dáil Éireann.

22 JUNE 1922 IRA assassinates Field Marshall Sir Henry Wilson in London.

28 JUNE 1922 Civil War begins with attack on IRA garrison in the Four Courts.

12 AUGUST 1922 Arthur Griffith, president of Dáil Éireann, dies.

22 AUGUST 1922 Michael Collins, commander in chief of the National (Free State) Army, killed in ambush at Béal na mBláth, Co. Cork.

9 SEPTEMBER 1922 William Cosgrave elected president of provisional government.

25 OCTOBER 1922 Constitution of Irish Free State approved by Dáil.

17 NOVEMBER 1922–2 MAY 1923 77 "Irregulars" (members of the antitreaty forces) executed by Free State government.

5 DECEMBER 1922 British government approves Free State Constitution Act.

6 DECEMBER 1922 Irish Free State formally established. T. M. Healy sworn in as first governor general of Free State.

7 DECEMBER 1922 Both houses of Northern Ireland parliament opt out of Free State.

31 MARCH 1923 Customs barriers become effective between Free State and United Kingdom (including Northern Ireland).

24 MAY 1923 Civil War ends with de Valera's order to "Irregulars."

16 JULY 1923 Censorship of Films Act becomes law in Free State.

8 AUGUST 1923 Gárda Siochána (Civic Guard, or police) founded.

27 AUGUST 1923 Cumann na nGaedheal wins plurality in Free State elections.

10 SEPTEMBER 1923 Free State joins League of Nations.

15 SEPTEMBER 1923 Belfast branch of BBC radio opened (2BE).

6 JUNE 1924 Incorporation of Irish Tourist Association.

6 NOVEMBER 1924 First meeting of the Boundary Commission.

10 DECEMBER 1923 W. B. Yeats receives Nobel Prize for Literature.

1925 George Bernard Shaw wins Nobel Prize for Literature; his prize announced in 1926.

4 JULY 1925 Authorization of the Shannon hydro-electric scheme.

3 DECEMBER 1925 Free State, United Kingdom, and Northern Ireland agree to existing borders and termination of the Boundary Commission.

1 JANUARY 1926 2RN, later RTÉ, begins radio broadcasts in Dublin.

16 MAY 1926 De Valera launches Fianna Fáil party.

10 JULY 1927 Assassination of justice minister Kevin O'Higgins.

11 AUGUST 1927 Fianna Fáil TDs take seats in Dáil Éireann.

16 APRIL 1929 Proportional representation abolished for elections to Northern Ireland parliament.

12 FEBRUARY 1930 Censorship board appointed under Censorship of Publications Act.

17 SEPTEMBER 1930 Free State joins League of Nations council.

5 SEPTEMBER 1931 De Valera's *Irish Press* begins publication.

11 DECEMBER 1931 Statute of Westminster confers broad powers on dominions.

16 FEBRUARY 1932 Fianna Fáil wins Free State general election. De Valera heads Executive Council.

30 JUNE 1932 De Valera withholds payment of land annuities owed to Britain and thus launches the "Economic War."

4–13 OCTOBER 1932 Labor unrest in Belfast.

16 NOVEMBER 1932 Parliament buildings at Stormont open near Belfast.

22 FEBRUARY 1933 Eoin O'Duffy dismissed as Gárda Siochána head.

20 JULY 1933 Army Comrades Association ("Blueshirts") adopts name "National Guard."

22 AUGUST 1933 National Guard proclaimed illegal.

2 SEPTEMBER 1933 United Ireland party (later called Fine Gael) launched on amalgamation of Cumann na nGaedheal, National Guard, and the Centre party.

21 DECEMBER 1934 Coal-Cattle Pact between Free State and Britain.

18 JUNE 1936 IRA banned in Free State.

14 AUGUST 1936 Aer Lingus established by law as national airline.

12 DECEMBER 1936 External Relations Act recognizes crown for purposes of external relations only.

14 JUNE 1937 De Valera's constitution bill approved by the Dáil.

1 JULY 1937 Voters approve new constitution in referendum.

25 APRIL 1938 Anglo-Irish agreement returns "treaty ports" to Irish control.

25 JUNE 1938 Douglas Hyde becomes first president of Ireland.

16 JANUARY 1939 Yearlong IRA bombing campaign in Britain begins.

14 JUNE 1939 Offences against the State Act becomes law.

27 JULY 1939 Irish Tourist Board established.

2 SEPTEMBER 1939 De Valera announces Irish neutrality in wartime.

3 JANUARY 1940 Oireachtas receives two emergency anti-IRA bills.

25 NOVEMBER 1940 J. M. Andrews becomes prime minister of Northern Ireland.

27 DECEMBER 1940 Consecration of John Charles McQuaid as archbishop of Dublin.

15–16 APRIL 1941 German air-raids on Belfast kill over 700 and badly wound 400.

1 MAY 1943 Sir Basil Brooke becomes prime minister of Northern Ireland.

8 DECEMBER 1943 Córas Iompair Éireann (CIE) established.

14 JANUARY 1944 National Labour party founded.

25 APRIL 1945 Fifteen trade unions form Congress of Irish Unions.

8 MAY 1945 War ends in Europe—"VE Day."

16 JUNE 1945 Seán T. O'Kelly elected president of Ireland.

1 JUNE 1946 Bord na Móna (Turf Board) established.

6 JULY 1946 Clann na Poblachta (republican party) founded.

JULY–AUGUST 1946 Ireland applies for membership in United Nations (UN).

4 FEBRUARY 1948 General election deals defeat to de Valera; John A. Costello soon becomes taoiseach (prime minister) and head of first interparty government.

Health Services Act introduces British-style National Health Service to Northern Ireland.

7 SEPTEMBER 1948 Costello announces forthcoming repeal of External Relations Act.

21 DECEMBER 1948 Republic of Ireland Act.

18 APRIL 1949 Ireland declared a republic and leaves Commonwealth.

11 APRIL 1951 Health minister Noël Browne resigns over the "Mother and Child Scheme."

13 JUNE 1951 De Valera becomes taoiseach again after Fianna Fáil wins general election on 30 May.

14 JUNE 1952 Social Welfare Act sets up social-insurance system.

25 JUNE 1952 Seán T. O'Kelly becomes president of Ireland a second time.

3 JULY 1952 Tourism Traffic Act establishes An Bord Fáilte for tourism development and Fogra Fáilte to promote Irish tourism.

13 DECEMBER 1952 Adoption legalized in Republic.

5–23 APRIL 1953 Republic of Ireland holds first An Tóstal festival.

3 MAY 1953 Gael-Linn established to promote Irish language.

2 JUNE 1954 Costello of Fine Gael again becomes taoiseach and head of second interparty government.

21 MARCH 1955 Fogra Fáilte and An Bord Fáilte combined to create Bord Fáilte Éireann.

21 JULY 1955 First regular television service in Northern Ireland launched.

14 DECEMBER 1955 Republic of Ireland admitted to UN.

5 MARCH 1957 General election returns de Valera and Fianna Fáil to power.

25 MARCH 1957 Treaty of Rome establishes European Economic Community (EEC).

20 MARCH 1958 General election in Northern Ireland returns another unionist majority. Brooke continues as prime minister.

11 NOVEMBER 1958 First *Programme for Economic Expansion* presented to the Oireachtas (both houses of the Irish parliament).

17 JUNE 1959 De Valera elected president of Ireland. Proposal to abolish proportional representation in elections defeated by referendum.

23 JUNE 1959 Seán Lemass succeeds de Valera as taoiseach and leader of Fianna Fáil.

27 JULY 1960 Republic sends first Irish troops to serve with UN forces in the Congo. Ireland is a frequent participant in future UN missions.

20 SEPTEMBER 1960 F. H. Boland elected president of UN General Assembly.

9 APRIL 1961 Census records population of Irish Republic at 2,818,341—lowest figure on record.

SUMMER 1961 Ireland announces intentions to apply for membership in the EEC in response to news of British intention to apply for membership.

4 OCTOBER 1961 General election in Republic returns Fianna Fáil to government.

31 DECEMBER 1961 Radio Éireann begins television broadcasts.

31 MAY 1962 Unionists win another general election in Northern Ireland. Brooke continues as prime minister.

6 JULY 1962 *The Late Late Show* with Gay Byrne debuts on RTÉ.

25 MARCH 1963 Captain Terence O'Neill becomes prime minister of Northern Ireland.

26–29 JUNE 1963 John F. Kennedy visits Ireland.

22 AUGUST 1963 *Second Programme for Economic Expansion* published.

14 JANUARY 1965 Historic Lemass–O'Neill meeting in Belfast concerning cross-border cooperation in tourism promotion, electricity supply, etc.

2 FEBRUARY 1965 Nationalist party accepts role as official opposition at Stormont.

9 FEBRUARY 1965 O'Neill visits Lemass in Dublin.

7 APRIL 1965 General election returns Fianna Fáil to power in the South. Seán Lemass continues as taoiseach.

25 NOVEMBER 1965 General election in Northern Ireland. O'Neill continues as prime minister.

14 DECEMBER 1965 Anglo-Irish Free Trade Agreement signed.

10 APRIL 1966 Commemoration of fiftieth anniversary of Easter Rising begins.

17 APRIL 1966 Census records population of Irish Republic at 2,884,002—first significant increase since the famine.

APRIL–MAY 1966 Ulster Volunteer Force (UVF) established.

1 JUNE 1966 De Valera re-elected president of Ireland.

28 JUNE 1966 UVF declared illegal.

26 JULY–19 OCTOBER 1966 Reverend Ian Paisley and followers imprisoned for failing to pay £30 fine for unlawful assembly.

10 SEPTEMBER 1966 Donagh O'Malley, minister for education (Republic), pledges to introduce universal free post-primary education in September 1967.

8 NOVEMBER 1966 Lemass announces his forthcoming resignation (10 November).

9 NOVEMBER 1966 Jack Lynch elected leader of Fianna Fáil party.

10 NOVEMBER 1966 Lynch succeeds Lemass as taoiseach.

19 DECEMBER 1966 Lynch meets U.K. prime minister Harold Wilson to discuss issues of common interest in relation to the EEC.

29 JANUARY 1967 Northern Ireland Civil Rights Association (NICRA) formed.

11 MAY 1967 Republic and United Kingdom reapply for EEC membership.

11 DECEMBER 1967 Lynch and O'Neill meet at Stormont.

8 JANUARY 1968 O'Neill and Lynch meet in Dublin.

24 AUGUST 1968 First of a series of civil-rights marches in Northern Ireland (Coalisland to Dungannon).

3 OCTOBER 1968 Intended civil-rights and Apprentice Boys' marches banned.

5 OCTOBER 1968 Clash between police and civil-rights marchers in Derry leads to riots.

9 OCTOBER 1968 Formation of Derry Citizens' Action Committee.

Body later called People's Democracy set up in Belfast.

16 OCTOBER 1968 Heavy defeat of referendum on abolition of proportional representation in Republic.

22 NOVEMBER 1968 Announcement of O'Neill's five-point reform program for Northern Ireland.

11 DECEMBER 1968 Craig dismissed as minister of home affairs in Northern Ireland.

4 JANUARY 1969 Ambush of People's Democracy March from Belfast to Derry by militant Protestants.

24 JANUARY 1969 Unionist party split worsens when Brian Faulkner resigns as Northern Ireland's minister of commerce.

24 FEBRUARY 1969 General election in Northern Ireland returns unionist majority yet again. O'Neill continues as prime minister.

3 MARCH 1969 Cameron Commission appointed to investigate Northern Ireland violence since October 1968.

MARCH 1969 *Third Programme: Economic and Social Development, 1969–1972*, presented to Oireachtas.

12 APRIL 1969 Riots in Derry.

23 APRIL 1969 O'Neill wins small majority for "one man, one vote" principle.

28 APRIL 1969 O'Neill resigns and is succeeded by James Chichester-Clark.

18 JUNE 1969 General election in Republic returns Fianna Fáil to government. Lynch continues as taoiseach.

12–16 JULY 1969 Further riots in Derry.

5 AUGUST 1969 Bombing of RTÉ headquarters in Dublin by UVF.

12–15 AUGUST 1969 Rioting in Derry spreads to Belfast, resulting in the deployment of British troops.

19 AUGUST 1969 "Downing Street Declaration" embraces principle of civic equality for all Northern Ireland citizens.

12 SEPTEMBER 1969 Publication of Cameron Commission report on recent violence in Northern Ireland.

10 OCTOBER 1969 Release of Hunt Committee report calling for disbandment of "B-Specials" (sectarian police reserves) in Northern Ireland.

23 OCTOBER 1969 Samuel Beckett wins Nobel Prize for Literature.

25 NOVEMBER 1969 Northern Ireland Electoral Law Act broadens local-government franchise but postpones elections until 1971.

18 DECEMBER 1969 Ulster Defence Regiment established.

11 JANUARY 1970 IRA split into "Official" and "Provisional" groups at Sinn Féin convention in Dublin.

26 MARCH 1970 Police force in Northern Ireland reshaped and partly reformed.

21 APRIL 1970 Alliance party founded in Northern Ireland.

30 APRIL 1970 Ulster Defence Regiment assumes duties of "B-Specials."

29 MAY 1970 Macrory report recommends reforms of both local government and the provision of social services in Northern Ireland.

26–29 June 1970 MP Bernadette Devlin arrested, leading to further demonstrations and the first Provisional IRA activity in Belfast.

6 May 1970 Ministers Charles Haughey and Neil Blaney dismissed from government in Republic after allegations of arms smuggling. Third minister (Kevin Boland) resigns over Northern Ireland policy of Republic.

28 May 1970 Haughey and Blaney arrested and charged with conspiracy to import arms.

25 June 1970 Catholic bishops drop old prohibition on Catholics attending Trinity College, Dublin.

21 August 1970 Social Democratic and Labour party (Northern Ireland) formed.

6 February 1971 First British soldier killed in Northern Ireland conflict since 1968.

20 March 1971 Chichester-Clark resigns and is soon succeeded by Brian Faulkner as prime minister of Northern Ireland.

9 August 1971 Internment without trial reintroduced in Northern Ireland, setting off furious nationalist reaction.

August 1971 Ulster Defence Association (UDA) appears in Belfast.

27 August–8 September 1971 Tripartite talks at Chequers between Heath, Lynch, and Faulkner.

30 January 1972 "Bloody Sunday": 13 civilians killed by British paratroopers in Derry after banning of civil-rights march.

2 February 1972 British embassy in Dublin burned.

24 March 1972 Stormont parliament is suspended and direct rule from Britain is introduced.

10 May 1972 Referendum on entry of Irish Republic into EEC approved by 83 percent of voters.

29 May 1972 Official IRA suspends operations in Northern Ireland.

26 June–9 July 1972 Truce between Provisional IRA (PIRA) and British army.

21 July 1972 "Bloody Friday" in Belfast: 22 PIRA bombs kill 11 and injure 130 in single day.

30 October 1972 Publication of *The Future of Northern Ireland* Green Paper declaring that Britain does not oppose Irish unity by consent.

7 December 1972 "Special position" of the Catholic church removed from Republic's constitution by referendum.

1972 Peak year of violence in Northern Ireland leaves 467 dead. The total number of killings since 1969 reaches 678.

1 January 1973 Irish Republic, United Kingdom, and Denmark join EEC.

20 January 1973 Car bomb in Dublin kills one and injures 17.

28 February 1973 General election results in a Fine Gael–Labour coalition headed by Liam Cosgrave.

30 May 1973 Erskine Childers elected president of Ireland.

28 June 1973 General election for Northern Ireland assembly demonstrates splintering of unionism into warring factions.

18 July 1973 Northern Ireland Constitution Act abolishes Stormont parliament and provides for appointment of new executive.

31 July 1973 Disorder concludes first meeting of Northern Ireland assembly.

22 November 1973 Agreement reached by Official Unionists, Alliance, and SDLP to form power-sharing executive under Brian Faulkner's leadership.

6 December 1973 United Ulster Unionist Council formed by militant Protestant groups to oppose "power-sharing."

6–9 December 1973 Sunningdale Agreement: Conference of British, Irish, and Northern Irish political leaders at Sunningdale in Berkshire reaches agreement on power-sharing and the "Irish dimension."

1 January 1974 Northern Ireland executive assumes office under Faulkner.

17 May 1974 Car bombs in Dublin and Monaghan town kill 29 people and injure over 100.

28 May 1974 Resignation of Faulkner and unionist members of executive after paralyzing strike by the Ulster Workers' Council.

29 May 1974 Direct rule from Westminster revived and strike canceled.

17 November 1974 Childers, president of Ireland, dies.

3 December 1974 Cearbhall Ó Dálaigh chosen as president of Ireland.

1 May 1975 General election for Northern Ireland constitutional convention returns strong anti-Sunningdale unionist majority.

8 May 1975 Northern Ireland convention meets.

7 NOVEMBER 1975 Northern Ireland convention rejects power-sharing by 42 to 31.

5 DECEMBER 1975 Internment without trial terminates in Northern Ireland.

5 MARCH 1976 Northern Ireland convention dissolved.

18 AUGUST 1976 Faulkner's intended retirement from politics announced.

23 OCTOBER 1976 President Ó Dálaigh resigns with great dignity after defense minister calls him "a thundering disgrace."

9 NOVEMBER 1976 Patrick Hillery selected as president of Ireland.

16 JUNE 1977 Fianna Fáil regains power in general election, with Lynch becoming taoiseach.

8 JANUARY 1979 Oil-tanker explosion causes disaster at Whiddy Island (Cork).

13 MARCH 1979 European Monetary System instituted.

30 MARCH 1979 End of one-for-one parity with sterling announced.

27 AUGUST 1979 Earl Mountbatten and three others assassinated by PIRA at Mullaghmore, Co. Sligo; 18 British soldiers killed in IRA ambush at Warrenpoint, Co. Down.

29 SEPTEMBER–1 OCTOBER 1979 Pope John Paul II visits Ireland and attracts 2.7 million to events.

5 DECEMBER 1979 Lynch announces intention to resign as taoiseach and is succeeded by Charles Haughey on 11 December.

21 MAY 1980 Haughey and Prime Minister Margaret Thatcher meet to discuss Northern Ireland situation.

1 MARCH 1981 Bobby Sands begins hunger strike at the Maze prison and is later joined by other republican prisoners.

9 APRIL 1981 Sands elected Sinn Féin MP for Fermanagh–South Tyrone.

5 MAY 1981 Bobby Sands dies. Between 12 May and 10 August nine other hunger-strikers die. Serious violence results. Militant nationalist recruits flock to Provisional Sinn Féin and IRA.

11 JUNE 1981 General election results in Fine Gael–Labour coalition government led by Garret FitzGerald as taoiseach.

6 NOVEMBER 1981 FitzGerald and Thatcher meet in London and agree to set up Anglo-Irish Intergovernmental Council.

18 FEBRUARY 1982 General election returns Fianna Fáil to power. Haughey again becomes taoiseach.

6 APRIL 1982 Publication of White Paper *Northern Ireland: A Framework for Devolution*.

2 MAY 1982 Irish government affirms neutrality in relation to Falklands war.

6 OCTOBER 1982 Haughey survives no-confidence vote.

20 OCTOBER 1982 General election for Northern Ireland assembly returns unionist majority.

24 NOVEMBER 1982 General election brings Garret FitzGerald and Fine Gael–Labour coalition to power in Republic.

7 SEPTEMBER 1983 Referendum to acknowledge constitutional right to life of the unborn carried by margin of 2 to 1.

7 NOVEMBER 1983 First session of Anglo-Irish Intergovernmental Council meets.

3 DECEMBER 1983 Dr. Patrick Hillery begins second term as president of Ireland.

12 OCTOBER 1984 PIRA bomb explodes at Conservative party conference in Brighton, England, killing 5 and wounding 34.

15 NOVEMBER 1985 FitzGerald and Thatcher sign Anglo-Irish Agreement giving the South a consultative role in certain affairs of the North.

21 NOVEMBER 1985 Dáil Éireann approves Anglo-Irish Agreement.

27 NOVEMBER 1985 House of Commons approves Anglo-Irish Agreement.

21 DECEMBER 1985 Party called Progressive Democrats formed in Republic.

26 JUNE 1986 Referendum in Republic continues ban on divorce.

14 FEBRUARY 1987 General election in Republic returns Fianna Fáil to government, with Charles Haughey as taoiseach.

1987–1992 Government in Republic puts its financial house in order, setting stage for "Celtic Tiger" beginning in 1993.

8 MAY 1987 British Special Air Service (SAS) soldiers kill eight Provisionals at Loughgall, Co. Armagh.

26 JULY 1987 Stephen Roche wins Tour de France cycle race after winning the Giro d'Italia in June. Later the same year, he wins the world championship.

8 NOVEMBER 1987 PIRA bomb kills 11 and wounds 63 at Enniskillen Remembrance Day ceremony.

6 MARCH 1988 SAS soldiers kill 3 Provisionals in Gibraltar. Loyalist Michael Stone attacks Gibraltar funerals at Milltown cemetery in Belfast, killing 3 mourners (16 March).

12 JULY 1989 Fianna Fáil and Progressive Democrats form coalition led by Haughey.

1 JANUARY 1990 Northern Ireland Fair Employment Act.

9 NOVEMBER 1990 Mary Robinson elected president of Ireland.

6 FEBRUARY 1992 After Haughey's resignation, Albert Reynolds becomes leader of Fianna Fáil and taoiseach.

18 JUNE 1992 Referendum approves Maastricht Treaty.

10 AUGUST 1992 UDA banned.

25 NOVEMBER 1992 General election in Republic.

12 JANUARY 1993 Reynolds elected taoiseach and heads Fianna Fáil-Labour coalition government.

15 DECEMBER 1993 Reynolds and John Major sign Downing Street Declaration—landmark in cooperation between British and Irish governments on Northern Ireland "peace process."

31 AUGUST 1994 PIRA cease-fire announced—greeted skeptically by Britain.

15 DECEMBER 1994 John Bruton becomes taoiseach following collapse of Fianna Fail–Labour coalition and heads "Rainbow Coalition" consisting of Fine Gael, Labour, and Democratic Left.

JULY–AUGUST 1995 Orange Order March es at Drumcree, Portadown, Ormeau Road (Belfast), and elsewhere lead to violence.

8 SEPTEMBER 1995 David Trimble assumes leadership of Ulster Unionist party.

8 SEPTEMBER 1995 *Irish Press* stops publication.

5 OCTOBER 1995 Seamus Heaney wins Nobel Prize for Literature.

24 NOVEMBER 1995 Divorce referendum passes by extremely narrow majority.

24 JANUARY 1996 Mitchell Commission report recommends that decommissioning and inclusive interparty talks occur in tandem.

9 FEBRUARY 1996 Canary Wharf bombing in London (2 killed, over 100 injured) ends first PIRA cease-fire.

JULY 1996 Swimmer Michelle Smith wins three Olympic gold medals. Her achievement is later tarnished by evidence of drug use.

2 JUNE 1997 Alban Maginness (SDLP) elected first nationalist lord May or of Belfast.

6 JUNE 1997 General election results in Fianna Fáil–Progressive Democrat coalition government, with Bertie Ahern as taoiseach.

20 JULY 1997 IRA cease-fire reinstated.

20 JULY 1997 Unveiling of national memorial to commemorate the Great Famine.

SEPTEMBER–OCTOBER 1997 Sinn Féin agrees to "Mitchell principles" and all-party talks begin.

7 OCTOBER 1997 Foreign minister Ray Burke resigns over bribery allegations.

31 OCTOBER 1997 Mary McAleese elected president. Mary Robinson soon becomes UN Commissioner for Human Rights.

10 APRIL 1998 Historic Good Friday or Belfast Agreement reached, transforming Northern Ireland politics and North-South relations.

22 MAY 1998 Good Friday Agreement endorsed by referendums in both North and South.

15 AUGUST 1998 Omagh bombing by dissident republicans ("Real IRA") kills 29 people and injures 220 in worst single event of the whole conflict since 1968.

10 DECEMBER 1998 David Trimble and John Hume receive Nobel Peace Prize in Oslo.

2 JANUARY 1999 Euro launched.

APRIL 1999 Republic achieves a record exchequer surplus of over £IR1 billion.

2 DECEMBER 1999 Northern Ireland devolution occurs. David Trimble becomes first minister of power-sharing executive.

19 JANUARY 2000 Legislation announced to replace Royal Ulster Constabulary with "Police Service of Northern Ireland."

27 MARCH 2000 Saville inquiry into "Bloody Sunday" (30 January 1972) opens.

26 JUNE 2000 Some IRA arms dumps opened to inspectors.

28 JULY 2000 Last of 428 prisoners released as part of Good Friday Agreement.

21 AUGUST 2000 Loyalist feud in Belfast brings British troops back onto streets.

21 SEPTEMBER 2000 "Real IRA" rocket attack on MI6 headquarters in London.

30 DECEMBER 2000 Ireland's national debt reaches record low-point.

2001 Pace of "Celtic Tiger" slows considerably.

12 FEBRUARY 2001 European Union (EU) Commission reprimands Irish government for allowing tax cuts and tolerating fiscal laxity.

23 February 2001 Outbreak of foot-and-mouth disease among livestock in United Kingdom, leading to rapid response by Irish authorities.

28 February 2001 Foot-and-mouth disease breaks out in Northern Ireland.

22 March 2001 Single case of foot-and-mouth disease occurs in County Louth.

7 June 2001 Irish voters reject Nice Treaty on expansion of the EU.

30 June 2001 Trimble announces resignation as first minister in North.

6 August 2001 IRA releases plans to put weapons "beyond use."

7 August 2001 Trimble rejects IRA plans.

10 August 2001 Northern assembly suspended for 24 hours.

13 August 2001 Three members of IRA/Sinn Féin arrested in Colombia for training FARC guerrillas.

14 August 2001 IRA withdraws decommissioning offer. But IRA and Sinn Féin are soon forced by Colombia episode and by events of 11 September in the United States to begin actual decommissioning at last.

1 January 2002 Euro adopted as official currency in Irish Republic.

6 March 2002 Referendum designed to tighten Irish Republic's laws on abortion is narrowly defeated.

17 May 2002 General election in Republic returns Fianna Fáil–Progressive Democrat coalition. Bertie Ahern remains taoiseach.

28 September 2002 Interim Flood Tribunal report on political and financial corruption published, bringing massive public response.

14 October 2002 Northern executive suspended after Trimble demands Sinn Féin's exclusion following discovery of an IRA/Sinn Féin spying operation at Stormont and elsewhere.

19 October 2002 Nice Treaty referendum passes with 62.8 percent of the vote, allowing enlargement of EU to proceed.

A

Abernethy, John

Irish Presbyterian minister John Abernethy (1680–1740), an early leader of the New Light movement, which challenged the Presbyterian Church's traditional Calvinism and obligatory subscription of the Westminster formularies by ordinands, was born on 19 October 1680, the son of the Rev. John Abernethy of Brigh, Co. Tyrone. All of Abernethy's siblings died in the violence of 1689 in Ulster, but he escaped to his mother's family in Scotland.

After studies in Glasgow and Edinburgh universities Abernethy was ordained in Antrim in 1703. He was one of the founders of the Belfast Society, whose members exchanged books and discussed theological and philosophical questions. A sermon preached by him to the society in 1719 and published in 1720, *Religious Obedience Founded on Personal Persuasion*, began a controversy between conservatives and liberals, subscribers and nonsubscribers in Irish Presbyterianism, which continued until the 1820s.

The conservative John Malcolme of Dunmurry accused Abernethy and his associates of "pretending to give New Light to the world in the room of church government," and the name "New Light" stuck; the conservatives were known as "Old Lights." New Light was often unpopular in Ulster Presbyterian congregations, and Abernethy lost some members of his Antrim congregation before moving in 1730 to Dublin to succeed the eminent Joseph Boyse in his fashionable Wood Street congregation. There Abernethy had greater freedom to preach liberty of opinion in religion. He advocated the supreme authority of the enlightened individual conscience in defiance of the authority of church or state.

Abernethy died of gout in 1740. He was twice married, and the famous London surgeon John Abernethy was his grandson. His *Discourses on the Being and Attributes of God* were much admired and frequently reprinted, but his autobiographical diary has been lost.

SEE ALSO Presbyterianism

Bibliography

Barlow, S. "The Career of John Abernethy (1680–1740), Father of Non-Subscription in Ireland." *Harvard Theological Review* 78 (1985): 399–419.

Brown, A. W. G. "John Abernethy, 1680–1790, Scholar and Ecclesiast." In *Nine Ulster Lives*, edited by G. O'Brien and P. Roebuck. 1992.

Duchal, J. *A Sermon on the Occasion of the Much Lamented Death of the Late Revd. John Abernethy.* 1741.

Holmes, Finlay. "The Reverend John Abernethy: The Challenge of New Theology to Traditional Irish Presbyterian Calvinism." In *The Religion of Irish Dissent, 1650–1800*, edited by K. Herlihy. 1996.

Malcolme, John. *Personal Persuasion No Foundation for Religious Obedience.* 1720.

Witherow, T. *Historical and Literary Memorials of Presbyterianism in Ireland.* 1879.

Finlay Holmes

Act of Union

By the Act of Union in 1800, the British and Irish parliaments created the United Kingdom of Great Britain and

Ireland, whose continued existence had become the central issue in Irish politics by the end of the nineteenth century, when Irish politics was sharply divided into unionist and nationalist camps. In return for consenting to the abolition of its venerable legislature, Ireland was empowered to send one hundred representatives to the House of Commons and twenty-eight representative peers to the House of Lords at Westminster. Significantly, because the Act of Union did not provide for the abolition of the executive, headed by a lord lieutenant and a chief secretary, and allowed for the gradual amalgamation of the financial structures of the two kingdoms over a quarter-century, the degree of integration achieved was far from complete. This fact was lost sight of in the nineteenth century, no less completely than the fact that the Act of Union was welcomed by many in Ireland. British support for a union had grown during the late eighteenth century in response to mounting problems in Ireland, while the concession to Irish Catholics of the parliamentary franchise in 1793 persuaded many Irish Protestants of the desirability of a closer connection with their British coreligionists. Given this context, it was therefore not surprising that the outbreak of rebellion in Ireland in 1798 should be the spur that prompted Prime Minister William Pitt, who had long believed that a union was the optimal solution to Anglo-Irish relations, to authorize Lord Cornwallis, the lord lieutenant of Ireland, and his chief secretary, Lord Castlereagh, to secure Irish approval for the measure in 1799. But their preparations were insufficient to overcome the opposition of a complex of commercial metropolitan, Whig, Patriot, and ascendancy interests, and the scheme could not proceed at this point. Determined to prevail, Cornwallis and Castlereagh redoubled their efforts. Through the distribution of an exceptional amount of patronage, the authorization of funds to compensate borough owners, public lobbying, and the suggestion to Catholics that Emancipation would follow the implementation of a union, they were able to present the measure to the Irish Parliament in 1800 with greater confidence of success. The coalition of opposition interests put up a robust rearguard resistance, but the deployment of secret-service funds transmitted illegally from Great Britain was indicative of official determination to ensure that the measure reached the statute book. The inability of the opposition to sustain strong public resistance, or to overcome their own internal suspicions and animosities was also important, with the result that the administration prevailed by a comfortable margin in every division that mattered. The British Parliament passed the same measure without serious dissent, and it took effect on 1 January 1801.

SEE ALSO Eighteenth-Century Politics: 1795 to 1800—Repression, Rebellion, and Union; Government from 1690 to 1800; Orange Order: Origins, 1784 to 1800; Politics: 1690 to 1800—A Protestant Kingdom; Repeal Movement; Unionism from 1885 to 1922; **Primary Documents:** Irish Act of Union (1 August 1800)

Bibliography

Bolton, Geoffrey C. *The Passing of the Irish Act of Union.* 1966.

Geoghegan, Patrick M. *The Irish Act of Union: A Study in High Politics.* 1999.

Kelly, James. "The Origins of the Act of Union: An Examination of Unionist Opinion in Britain and Ireland, 1650–1800." *Irish Historical Studies* 25, no. 99 (May 1987): 236–263.

Kelly, James. "Popular Politics in Ireland and the Act of Union." *Transactions of the Royal Historical Society* 6, ser. 10 (2000): 259–287.

James Kelly

Adams, Gerry

Born into a strongly republican family in the Falls area of West Belfast on 6 October 1948, Gerry Adams was a vice president of Sinn Féin and was instrumental in bringing about the Belfast Agreement of 1998. A scholarship boy, he was educated locally by the Irish Christian Brothers, leaving school at seventeen to become a barman. Radicalized by the 1964 "Tricolour Riots" in Belfast (when nationalists clashed with the Royal Ulster Constabulary which had removed an Irish flag), he joined Sinn Féin and, at its inception in 1967, the Northern Ireland Civil Rights Association (NICRA).

Following the split in the republican movement in 1970, Adams aligned himself with the militant Provisional wing in Belfast's Ballymurphy estate. Interned on suspicion of Irish Republican Army (IRA) involvement in March 1972, he was released dramatically in July to take part in secret but abortive talks in London between an IRA delegation and the British secretary of state, William Whitelaw. He was again imprisoned by the British authorities in 1973 and 1978 but was acquitted of IRA membership.

On his release, Adams was elected vice president of Sinn Féin (1978) and played a key policy-making role

Sinn Féin leader Gerry Adams arrives at Hillsborough Castle, Northern Ireland, for peace talks, 5 May 2000. Martin McGuinness is pictured behind Adams (left). © REUTERS/CORBIS. REPRODUCED BY PERMISSION.

during the 1981 Hunger Strike (when ten republican prisoners starved themselves to death in support of political-prisoner status), from which his party emerged as a serious political force. In 1983 he became president of Sinn Féin and abstentionist MP for West Belfast, unseating the former Social Democratic and Labour Party (SDLP) leader Gerry Fitt.

Though badly wounded by loyalist gunmen in 1984, Adams steadily pushed Sinn Féin toward greater political participation, overthrowing the southern-based "Old Guard" and paving the way for recognition of the Dáil in 1986 and the Hume-Adams dialogue between 1988 and 1994. These secret conversations between Adams and John Hume, the respected leader of the nonviolent SDLP, on the possibility of a peaceful alternative to "armed struggle" culminated in the first IRA cease-fire of August 1994 through February 1996.

Following its reinstatement in July 1997, Adams led his party into the all-party talks, which resulted in the Belfast Agreement of 1998, swinging grassroots support behind it. When Sinn Féin won a record 17.6 percent of the vote in the subsequent Northern Ireland Assembly elections, Adams steered his party into the new power-sharing executive, the devolved administration under the agreement first set up in December 1999, while declining a cabinet post himself.

In October 2001 Adams welcomed the IRA's historic decision to put some arms "beyond use," which helped to stabilize the Belfast Agreement and acknowledged unionist fears of Irish unity. In 2002 he launched his party's bid to gain a foothold in the Dáil, but he courted controversy in the United States by his refusal to testify at a congressional hearing on alleged IRA involvement in Colombia.

SEE ALSO Decommissioning; Hume, John; Irish Republican Army (IRA); Northern Ireland: Constitutional Settlement from Sunningdale to Good Friday; Northern Ireland: The United States in Northern Ireland since 1970; Trimble, David; Ulster Politics under Direct Rule; **Primary Documents:** Irish Republican Army (IRA) Cease-Fire Statement (31 August 1994); Text of the IRA Cease-Fire Statement (19 July 1997); The Belfast/Good Friday Agreement (10 April 1998)

Bibliography

Sharrock, David, and Mark Devenport. *Man of War, Man of Peace? The Unauthorized Biography of Gerry Adams.* 1997.

Éamon Phoenix

≈

Agriculture

1500 TO 1690

In agricultural practice, as in social and political structures, Ireland in 1500 fell into two distinct zones, with a large transitional area in between. In the Pale counties (Dublin, Meath, Louth, most of Kildare, and part of Westmeath) and some outlying areas of the southeast, agriculture in general followed a typical Western European pattern, with a strong emphasis on tillage. In the purely Gaelic areas of the north and west, however, there was a much greater emphasis on pastoralism, and tillage tended to be a monoculture of oats. The difference between the plow of the former colonial areas and the more primitive "short plow" of Gaelic Ireland was notable. Although both were drawn by a team of four horses, hitched abreast, and led by a driver ahead, the short plow also required the services of a "beam-holder" to hold the front of the plow in the ground, and was usually drawn by being tied to the horses' tails. There is evidence from County Louth of the occasional use of plow oxen in this period. By 1500 the old colonial areas seem to have universally adopted the three-course rotation of autumn-sown crop, spring-sown crop, and a fallow year in which the land was plowed but left unsown until the autumn. The autumn-sown crops were wheat, bere (six- or four-rowed barley) or, to a lesser extent, rye; the usual spring crop was oats, although peas, beans, and spring-sown barley are also recorded. So invariable was the three-course rotation that crops in these regions were universally reckoned in "couples," a couple being the unit of an acre of autumn-sown "hard corn" and an acre of oats. In the transitional areas, as in the Gaelic regions, the low population and

abundance of land could lead to the fallow year being extended for much longer. In the Gaelic regions it was usual to cultivate oats—the standard food crop—for two years and then to let the ground grow grass for several years. Flax was grown extensively, at least in the Gaelic regions, to supply the widespread linen trade, but as a crop grown in small patches by the poor, it was rarely noted. There is some uncertainty about the seventeenth-century spread of the potato. The surviving evidence suggests that Irish crop yields, at least in the Pale, did not differ appreciably from those in contemporary England, but there is no information on the ratio between seed sown and crops reaped. The townland was commonly treated as an agricultural unit for cultivation or grazing; boundary banks were usual between townlands, while otherwise the fields lay open and unenclosed. When it was necessary to make enclosures to protect crops, this was done with fences of posts and wattles, with an expected lifetime of two years. In the agricultural zones there existed around the coasts a belt in which abundant supplies of seaweed for fertilizer made possible an intensive agriculture in which corn crops could be raised, year after year, from the same land. The evidence suggests that in this period and in many areas, both Gaelic and Old English, there existed a class of "rural capitalists" who cultivated large areas with the help of their dependents, laborers, and share-croppers of varying status. Conversely, without the stock or dependents to adequately exploit it, land could be of little value to those who owned or worked it.

THE PASTORAL ECONOMY

In Gaelic Ireland pastoralism was more important than tillage. Its mainstay was cattle, which provided not only meat and milk products but also the hides that were Ireland's principal export. Cattle were a mobile asset that could be quickly and easily moved to a safer locality in time of war as well as in search of fresh pasture. There has perhaps been too much readiness to identify all movements of the herds with transhumance ("booleying"), the movement from winter quarters in the lowlands to upland summer grazing. Gaelic legal custom allowed the grazing of unoccupied land either by the neighbors, if they were ready to pay tribute due to the lord out of the land, or by the lords themselves. The adverse side of this mobility was the prevalence of cattle raiding or rustling, not only in time of war. The herds—the *caoruigheachta* or *creaghts*—were particularly large and mobile in Ulster. The Gaelic Irish did not make hay, and the practice was instead to leave certain lands unused during the summer to provide winter grazing for the cattle. Irish cattle of the period are described as small, a description supported by what information there is on dead weights, but there was a larger breed in eastern Ulster. Sheep and pigs played a lesser role in the economy, but there is evidence of very large flocks of sheep in Munster. The native Irish sheep seems to have resembled the present Shetland breed, with a long coarse fleece, which was plucked in summer instead of being sheared and from which the famous Irish rug mantles were made. Pigs were fed on acorns in the woods in the usual European manner. To complete the pastoral picture, lords and other important persons kept great herds of mares for breeding purposes.

THE SEVENTEENTH CENTURY

From the time of the Munster Plantation of the 1580s, English settlers (the "New English") moved into Ireland in large numbers, importing English agricultural techniques and the superior English breeds of cattle and sheep. Although interrupted by the Rising of 1641 and the subsequent wars, this immigration continued through the seventeenth century. The greater financial resources of the settlers, as well as their farming expertise, made English tenants as welcome on the lands of native Irish landlords as on those of the New English. Among the innovations that they brought were the liming of land with lime produced by burning limestone and the digging and spreading of marl, a lime-rich subsoil. The Irish before this time seem to have used only local sources of agricultural lime, such as seaside-shell sands and rare inland deposits of lime-rich sand. The coming of the settlers coincided with an expansion of the native population, leading to a more intensive utilization of the land and a shift from pastoralism to tillage. As a result of this, and of a timber trade supplied by unsustainable exploitation of Irish forests, the period saw a rapid clearance of woodland. It also saw the beginnings of the process of permanent enclosure, hastened by the increasing scarcity of wood for the traditional temporary fences. It is difficult to tell how far the imported techniques influenced the native Irish, but evidence indicates that in County Sligo haymaking was already common by 1638. That English agricultural practices were not more widely adopted by the native Irish may have been due as much to lack of the necessary capital for innovation as to innate conservatism. The Scottish settlers in Ulster and the bordering regions, unlike the English, had little to teach the Irish in the way of tillage practices but the cattle which they brought with them were, to judge by their higher value, of a better breed than the native stock.

The most striking development in seventeenth-century Irish agriculture was the introduction of the potato. Research has shown that the potato, introduced into Ireland probably by merchants from the southern ports trading into Spain some time around 1600, must have been the Chilean variety, already adapted to a temperate climate, rather than the Peruvian, which required a longer growing season than was available in the British Isles (O'Riordan 1988). By the 1640s potatoes were being widely grown across the southern half of the country. The acid soils so prevalent in Ireland suited the potato, and it became an ideal crop for land reclamation. It was eventually to transform the hitherto unproductive wastelands of Ireland.

By 1700 over most of southern and eastern Ireland a class of large progressive farmers—usually of English origin—had emerged side-by-side with a native population, who were often relegated to the poorer lands and who continued to farm by traditional methods. Much of the Scottish settler population in Ulster resembled the latter class rather than the former.

SEE ALSO Economy and Society from 1500 to 1690; Land Settlements from 1500 to 1690; Petty, Sir William; Restoration Ireland; **Primary Documents:** From *The Total Discourse of His Rare Adventures* (1632)

Bibliography

Boate, Gerard. *Ireland's Naturall History.* 1652.

Gillespie, Raymond G., ed. *Settlement and Survival on an Ulster Estate.* 1988.

National Archives of Ireland. Chancery Pleadings. c. 1560–1640.

Nicholls, Kenneth W. "Land, Law, and Society in Sixteenth-Century Ireland." O'Donnell Lecture, National University of Ireland. 1976.

Nicholls, Kenneth W. "Gaelic Society and Economy in the High Middle Ages." In *The New History of Ireland*, vol. 2, edited by Art Cosgrove. 1987.

O'Riordan, Tomás Anthony. "Potatoes, Poverty, and the Irish Peasantry: A History of the Potato in the Irish Diet, c. 1590–1900 AD." M.Phil. thesis, National University of Ireland, 1988.

Pinkerton, William. "Ploughing by the Horse's Tail." *Ulster Journal of Archaeology* 6 (1858): 212–220.

Kenneth Nicholls

1690 TO 1845

Between 1690 and 1845 a number of European regions experienced massive transformations from rural-based economies toward urban industrialization. The Irish economy, on the other hand, was still as strongly based in the countryside in 1845 as it had been a century and a half earlier. By the eve of the Great Famine the economy had changed utterly in its intensity and efficiency, supporting three or four times as many people as it had in the seventeenth century. However, it was still essentially a supplier of its own subsistence and an exporter of food to industrial Britain. Outside the textile center of the northeast, Ireland had no identifiably industrial regions.

UNSTABLE GROWTH: 1690 TO 1745

Like the rest of Europe in the 1690s, Irish agriculture was beginning a recovery from nearly a century of political and economic instability, war, depressed prices, and lackluster growth. The new colonial property system set in place during the course of the previous century, under which Scottish and English settlers owned approximately 80 percent of the land, was still taking root. The political upheaval of the previous century had left the native commercial classes in a shambles, with market and credit systems in an undeveloped state. According to William Petty, a trustworthy observer during this period, over 90 percent of profitable land was under grass in the 1680s. The production of crops was largely restricted to a region in the southeast of the country that had supplied wheat to Dublin and abroad. The mass of the rural population was still occupied in a pastoral, livestock-based economy that had not fundamentally changed for centuries.

The 1690s saw a promising resurgence of the agricultural economy, particularly in tillage, a trajectory of development that continued into the early eighteenth century. This modest growth was strongly influenced by the incentives and constraints of a framework of trade legislation that included the Cattle Acts of the 1660s, the various Navigation Acts passed in the second half of the seventeenth century, the Woollen Act of 1699, and the legislation of 1705 placing bounties on Irish linen exports. The Cattle Acts, which banned the export of livestock to England, and the Navigation Acts, which banned imports from the new world directly into Ireland, skewed Irish agricultural and industrial development. Although the livestock export trade was shut down, the Irish were allowed to supply beef for the provisioning of Atlantic trading and war vessels. Prohibited from exporting either live sheep or woolen goods, Irish graziers responded by exporting raw wool. The textile industries in Ireland were largely suppressed by this legislation, with the crucial exception of linen. The legislation of 1705 allowed linen exports not only to England but directly to the American colonies and the continent as well.

The effect of this legislative framework was to create hothouse conditions for provisions and linen goods in the Atlantic economy. Rapid commercialization and increased specialization ensued. Linen production developed rapidly, with flax producers and importers supplying a far-flung network of rural handspinners whose output in turn supplied the growing ranks of farmer-weavers in the north. The business of cattle rearing saw rapid specialization and commercialization as well. A wide variety of producers—dairymen selling young cattle, small farmers who raised young cattle but also engaged in tillage farming, spinning, and/or weaving, and larger graziers buying two- or three-year-old cattle for maturing and final fattening for market—all interacted in a mushrooming network of markets and fairs. However, until the 1740s the countryside still proved to be tragically vulnerable to the type of subsistence crises that historians associate with a primitive economy. The high level of emigration to the New World, particularly by the Protestant population of the north, is additional evidence of this economic fragility.

The Atlantic shipping trade also fuelled the relentless deforestation of the Irish countryside to meet the demand for barrels, staves, and other equipment. The process began in the early seventeenth century but greatly increased in pace in the first half of the eighteenth, so that by the early nineteenth century Ireland had been almost completely denuded of its forests.

A GREAT ACCELERATION: 1745 TO 1815

The second half of the eighteenth century saw a tremendous expansion of this commercial agrarian economy. Two interrelated factors were important. First, Ireland began to play an important role in supplying food to the rapidly urbanized and industrialized British economy. By mid-century, food prices were rising sharply across England. By the 1770s Britain had become a net importer of food, and much of those imports came from Ireland. By the end of the century Ireland was supplying over 40 percent of Britain's imports of grain, meat, and butter, and by the 1820s this figure had reached 75 percent. Secondly, the liberalization of trade legislation removed the straightjacket constraining the economy in the first half of the century. The restrictions on Irish cattle exports were lifted by legislation in 1758. The Navigation Acts were mostly removed in 1778, though exports of crucial industrial products such as wool, woolen manufactures, and cotton were still prohibited. And in 1784 the Irish Parliament passed legislation consolidating a system of export bounties on agricultural products.

Expanding pastoral production was an important component of the great acceleration of the late eighteenth century, but the real driving force was an explosion of tillage and textile production from the small-farm sector. Linen remained the leading export. Unlike wool and cotton, its production methods remained labor-intensive and suited to cottage hand production throughout the eighteenth century. Most linen producers, whether they were flax growers, spinners, weavers, or all three, also tilled the land, producing oats or wheat for distant markets and potatoes and other garden crops for local consumption. To these may be added a third key component of small-farm land use: the quasi-agricultural activity of harvesting turf. Turf cutting and saving, worth nearly £2 million a year in 1840, provided not only cheap energy but opened up new cultivable land. Successive crops of potatoes prepared former bog for grain cultivation, and potatoes then became a permanent part of the rotation of grain cultivation, simultaneously providing subsistence and renewing the soil. Together, these activities formed an interlinked microeconomy that fuelled not only a great increase in output but also demographic explosion and a massive expansion in land use. The period of the Napoleonic wars, by artificially increasing and sustaining food prices in England, fanned the flames of an already roaring productive and demographic acceleration.

PRODUCTIVITY AND DISTRIBUTION: 1785 TO 1845

Between 1785 and 1845 the fruits of the agricultural economy were unevenly distributed. From the early eighteenth century on, profits flowed overwhelmingly into the hands of landowners, middlemen, and the large graziers and stockholders. The three decades after 1785 were golden years for substantial farmers, but the benefits trickled down even to the lower reaches of society, with real wages for farm and construction labor rising. Irish rural life in this era was crowded, dirty, and short of luxuries, but the inhabitants of the countryside were relatively tall, well fed, and long-lived. Though the nature of agricultural and hand textile work was often backbreaking and monotonous, Irish workers had considerably more leisure time than their counterparts in industrial Britain.

Research published in the 1980s shows that, by comparison to the rest of the United Kingdom, Belgium, and France, Irish agriculture before the famine was reasonably productive. But the nature of its productivity was peculiar and impoverishing. Ireland lacked a number of crucial features of agricultural efficiency obtaining elsewhere: centuries of farm enclosure and rationalization, strong urban industrial development to soak up excess rural populations, strong incentives for capital accumulation and a well-developed system for its circu-

lation. Nevertheless, the Irish climate gave rural producers unique endowments, and they were generally exploited effectively. Though its soils were poor, Ireland's climate gives it a natural advantage in grass, and therefore in livestock, production. Though lacking in capital intensity, Irish agriculture made very effective use of cheap labor and capital-poor techniques (such as better weeding, more intensive spadework, and more intensive seeding) suited to rocky and wet soils.

The decades after Waterloo saw a reversal in the upward price trend in agricultural products that lasted until the Crimean War of 1853 to 1856. In addition, technical advances in the mechanical wet spinning of linen yarn in the 1820s and the beginning of a shift in demand away from linen to lighter textiles painfully undercut the rural hand-spinning and weaving trades. While the corn law of 1815 offered some protection to Irish farmers from the prevailing trend in grain prices, the mass of the peasantry lacked access to sufficient land to produce grain and livestock efficiently. This scenario caused poverty and inequality to increase dramatically in the 1830s and 1840s. Grain producers with access to land were able to capitalize on a flooded labor market and produce crops profitably. Landless laborers, on the other hand, were faced not only with declining money wages but also with rising prices of land offered by farmers in "conacre," on a short-term arrangement that allowed laborers to produce a subsistence crop of potatoes. These developments left a growing population in a position of heightened risk of impoverishment. Although Ireland was certainly not careening toward a Malthusian apocalypse in the 1840s, the structure of the economy, and the political and legislative circumstances that governed it, left the countryside completely vulnerable to the terrible shock of the potato blight in the late 1840s.

SEE ALSO Banking and Finance to 1921; Family: Marriage Patterns and Family Life from 1690 to 1921; Great Famine; Land Questions; Migration: Emigration from the Seventeenth Century to 1845; Population, Economy, and Society from 1750 to 1950; Population Explosion; Potato and Potato Blight (*Phytophthora infestans*); Protestant Ascendancy: Decline, 1800 to 1930; Rural Life: 1690 to 1845; Subdivision and Subletting of Holdings; Transport—Road, Canal, Rail; **Primary Documents:** On Irish Rural Society and Poverty (1780)

Bibliography

Crotty, Raymond. *Irish Agricultural Production: Its Volume and Structure.* 1966.

Cullen, Louis M. *The Emergence of Modern Ireland.* 1981.

Dickson, David. *New Foundations: Ireland, 1660–1800.* 2d edition, 2000.

Ó Gráda, Cormac. *Ireland before and after the Famine: Explorations in Economic History, 1800–1925.* 2d edition, 1993.

Ó Gráda, Cormac. *Ireland: A New Economic History, 1780–1939.* 1994.

O'Hearn, Denis. *The Atlantic Economy: Britain, the United States, and Ireland.* 2001.

Solar, Peter M. "Agricultural Productivity and Economic Development in Ireland and Scotland in the Early Nineteenth Century." In *Ireland and Scotland: Parallels and Contrasts in Economic and Social Development,* edited by Tom Devine and David Dickson. 1983.

Solar, Peter M., and Martine Goosens. "Belgian and Irish Agriculture in 1840–1845." In *Land, Labour, and Livestock: Historical Studies in European Agricultural Productivity,* edited by Bruce M. S. Campbell and Mark Overton. 1991.

Thomas, Brinley. "Food Supply in the United Kingdom during the Industrial Revolution." In *The Economics of the Industrial Revolution,* edited by Joel Mokyr. 1985.

Whelan, Kevin. "Settlement and Society in Eighteenth-Century Ireland." In *The Poet's Place: Ulster Literature and Society,* Essays in Honour of John Hewitt, 1907–1987, edited by Gerald Dawe and John Wilson Foster. 1991.

Martin W. Dowling

1845 TO 1921

The extraordinary decline in crop production and conversely the rise of cattle and milk production characterized Irish agriculture in the eight decades after the Great Famine. In land-use terms the country became greener. The hay and pasture acreage increased from nearly 10 million acres in 1851 to 12.4 million acres by 1911. Conversely, over the same period the cultivated acreage declined from 4.6 to 2.3 million acres. The wheat acreage alone declined dramatically from half a million acres in 1851 to 150,000 acres by 1881, and finally to 45,000 acres by 1911. There was a brief turnaround in these trends during the plough-up campaign during World War I: In 1918 the arable area recovered to 3.1 million acres, hay and pasture fell to 11.2 million acres, and wheat lands rose to 157,000 acres (this last slipping back to 43,000 acres by 1921). At its lowest level, in 1904, there were only 31,000 acres of wheat. The only significant extension of the cultivated area occurred in response to the demand for animal-fodder crops. The turnip was formerly a neglected crop, but in the second half of the nineteenth century it was grown in large quantities. The ratio of pasture to arable rose from 2:1 in 1851 to nearly 6:1 in 1921. By 1900 one-half or more of all land was under permanent grass. This move toward pasture occurred everywhere in Ireland.

Land use captures the essence of agricultural change, but one specific regional observation might be made. For every hundred acres of hay and pasture (i.e., per unit of the main animal food), it was the northern counties (Ulster) that had the greatest density of cattle in the middle to late nineteenth century. It was not until the turn of the century that the counties of the south and west came into their own as substantial cattle producers. This reflects the more mixed and highly developed farming systems in the north around mid-century, but it also suggests the potential that existed for larger change elsewhere. Mixed farming continued to characterize Ulster in the second half of the nineteenth century.

AGRICULTURAL OUTPUT AND AGRICULTURAL CHANGE

In terms of the value to Irish agricultural output, tillage represented nearly 60 percent of final output in the early 1850s, but it slumped more or less progressively thereafter to less than 20 percent by the late 1890s. Conversely, the share of livestock and livestock products rose from about 40 percent in the early 1850s to over 80 percent by 1900, and peaked at 84 percent in 1910. The cash crops of wheat, barley, and flax declined from between 8 and 5 percent of output in the early 1850s to only 1 or 2 percent each from the 1880s. Potato output fell from a fifth or a quarter of output in the early 1850s to about 10 percent or less from 1860 onwards, and to an all-time low of about 5 percent in 1897. Conversely, cattle output rose from 20 percent in 1860 to over 30 percent by the late 1870s. Milk, as revealed in butter production, also accounted for 20 percent in 1860, though it declined after 1880 to about 18 percent. Therefore, the two components of cattle output contributed close to 40 percent of final agricultural output in the 1860s, rising to nearly 50 percent by the early 1870s, with a peak of 59 percent in 1903. By 1914 even hens and ducks added more to agricultural output than wheat, oats, and potatoes combined—crops that had contributed more than half of output in about 1840.

The postfamine changes illustrated by these statistics were not induced by the famine alone. In fact, the total cultivated area rose during the first twenty years or so after the famine, but thereafter it declined. The severe decline in population from 6.55 million in 1851 to 4.39 million by 1911 helps to explain the fall in the cultivated area, but not entirely the changes within agriculture. Purely for the purposes of self-sufficiency a much smaller land area was adequate as the decades proceeded, but the population of animals actually grew in numbers. In other words, the developments in Irish agriculture were not just negative responses to the famine; they were also positive responses to other circumstances.

Livestock fairs, held in the streets of many Irish towns, were common scenes until the 1950s. On these occasions business and recreation were fused together, as this 1870 sketch of a lively pig fair at Trim in County Meath suggests. Publicans and shopkeepers quickly relieved pig-sellers of some of their gains. FROM ILLUSTRATED LONDON NEWS, 7 MAY 1870.

The increase in North American grain reaching Western Europe at lower and lower prices by the late 1870s in an atmosphere of free trade may have led to the steep decline of corn growing in England, but in Ireland the economy had already adjusted output to cash products other than wheat before the 1870s. This is an important conclusion for the history of Irish agriculture, indicating that its reconstruction was ahead of that of many European rivals. While the flight from cereal production was pronounced in Ireland, in both Denmark and Germany there was actually an increase in the land devoted to cereals, and in France and Holland the cereal acreage held up very well.

External economic stimuli were increasingly important, but in Ireland, even on the eve of the Great Famine, the export trade accounted for as much as 27 percent of all Irish agricultural output. Thereafter it grew in response to the rise in demand for meat and dairy products generally in Western Europe, especially after the 1870s and particularly in Britain. At first, the milk and butter trades were important, but this gave way to the rising tide of fat-cattle and store-cattle rear-

ing and export, especially after 1880. This was reflected in animal numbers. Milch cattle constituted about 70 percent of all cattle over two years of age in 1855, but thereafter their numbers dwindled, falling to less than 60 percent by the end of the century and only recovering slightly thereafter. The export trades to Britain were at full steam. By 1908, 58 percent of the net value of livestock production came from exports. In the 1850s between 35 and 40 percent of the cattle that "disappeared" each year from the annual enumeration were exported to Britain, increasing to 50 percent in the mid-1860s and to 70 percent by the end of the century. From 1850 to 1875 annually between 30 and 50 percent of the sheep were exported, and more than 30 percent of the pigs were exported as live animals and an untold proportion in the form of bacon.

AGRICULTURAL DEPRESSIONS AS TURNING POINTS

Apart from the short-lived period in the mid-1850s during the Crimean War, when grain prices generally

Butter-making was a mainstay of agriculture in Munster province before and after the famine. So much butter made on Munster farms went to the Cork Butter Exchange for inspection and sale that it became by far the largest such market in Ireland. In this post-1880 photograph, exchange employees are standing amid one day's supply of firkins and boxes full of butter. PHOTOGRAPH COURTESY OF JAMES S. DONNELLY, JR.

rose in Western Europe, giving some respite to the arable sector, there were two agricultural depressions in Ireland during the period. These were the depressions of 1859 to 1864 and 1879 to 1882. They have both been identified as watersheds in Irish agriculture, the first related to agricultural change, and the second very much associated with the tenant and landlord conflict known as the Land War. In the first period, for six continuous seasons, either grassland suffered from drought or the arable and fodder sector experienced either drought or too much rain. Crop yields turned down dramatically, but now the price for such crops was influenced more by the larger British or European market than by conditions in Ireland itself. Coincidentally, the cotton famine spilling over from the U.S. Civil War gave a brief encouragement to Irish flax production, and for this rea-

son alone the depression hit Ulster less severely than elsewhere. The war also gave a brief respite to wool prices. But Ireland emerged from the depression finally realigned to pastoral agriculture. Before the depression the milk and butter trade was relatively ascendant, but it was already under threat from the cattle trade. The ratio of calves to milch cows declined from 45 per hundred in 1854 to only 34 in 1861, indicating the growing sale of calves to the veal trade and a greater concentration on milk and butter. Thereafter this ratio rose dramatically until in about 1865 it was 74 per hundred, and it remained at about 70 per hundred in subsequent years. The store-cattle trade had come into its own, and it flourished as the second half of the century unfolded.

It has been suggested that for much of the third quarter of the century there was a rising tide of expectation in the agricultural sector, especially for the stability or even improvement of tenant incomes. If true, this adds weight to the interpretation of the second depression, between 1879 and 1882, as a watershed in tenant-landlord relationships. The rising tide was stopped and replaced by a disgruntled tenantry struggling to pay their fixed rents at a time when their incomes were in rapid decline. The ensuing rent arrears had consequences in terms of credit restrictions, credit-worthiness, and the reduced incomes of the large service sector of shopkeepers and other suppliers on whom agriculture depended. The general malaise of relative and sometimes absolute poverty also hit landlords whenever their tenants were in arrears with their rents. The ensuing spate of land legislation resulted in a large transfer of ownership to the tenants. In 1870 perhaps 3 percent of Irish holdings were owner-occupied, but by 1908 the corresponding figure was about 46 percent.

SEE ALSO Banking and Finance to 1921; Congested Districts Board; Family: Marriage Patterns and Family Life from 1690 to 1921; Famine Clearances; Great Famine; Indian Corn or Maize; Migration: Emigration from 1850 to 1960; Plunkett, Sir Horace Curzon; Poor Law Amendment Act of 1847 and the Gregory Clause; Population, Economy, and Society from 1750 to 1950; Potato and Potato Blight (*Phytophthora infestans*); Protestant Ascendancy: Decline, 1800 to 1930; Rural Life: 1850 to 1921; Subdivision and Subletting of Holdings; Transport—Road, Canal, Rail

Bibliography

Donnelly, James S., Jr. "The Irish Agricultural Depression of 1859–64." *Irish Economic and Social History* 3 (1976): 33–54.

Donnelly, James S., Jr. "Landlords and Tenants." In *A New History of Ireland*, vol. 5, *Ireland Under the Union, I, 1801–70*, edited by W. E. Vaughan. 1989.

Kennedy, Liam. "The Rural Economy, 1820–1914." In *An Economic History of Ulster, 1820–1939*, edited by Liam Kennedy and Philip Ollerenshaw. 1985.

Turner, Michael. *After the Famine: Irish Agriculture, 1850–1914*. 1996.

Vaughan, W. E. *Landlords and Tenants in Mid-Victorian Ireland*. 1994.

Winstanley, M. J. *Ireland and the Land Question, 1800–1922*. 1984.

Michael Turner

AFTER WORLD WAR I

At independence in 1922 the agricultural sector in the Republic accounted for about one-third of the gross domestic product, just over half of total employment, and almost three-quarters of merchandise exports (Kennedy, et al. 1988). Economic growth over the past century has reduced the relative importance of agriculture dramatically. In the year 2000 it contributed 3 percent, 7 percent, and 6 percent of national output, employment, and exports respectively. Similar trends can be observed in Northern Ireland, although the more industrialized status of the North has meant that agriculture there was always less important in the economy. It accounted for 2.6 percent of Northern output and 5 percent of employment in 2000. This shift from an agrarian economy to a predominantly urban, postindustrial one is the defining change in Irish society during this period. Although the declining importance of farming is something that Ireland shares with all developing economies, the particular pattern of adjustment that it experienced was influenced by a specific combination of historical legacy, market constraints, and policy interventions.

POST-WORLD WAR I TO 1960

The fortunes of the agricultural sector in the Republic over the past century can usefully be chronicled by distinguishing between three periods: spanning the early independence period from World War I to 1960; a brief burst of growth between 1960 and the mid-1980s; and a period of adjustment to tightening farm supports since then. In the period from the aftermath of World War I to around 1960 there was very limited growth in overall agricultural output. The policy dilemma throughout this period was that the pursuit of Ireland's comparative advantage in grass-based cattle production conflicted with the social imperative of employment creation. Cattle farming had been substituting for tillage production since the middle of the previous century, but its limited labor requirements meant that it was accompanied by a substantial decrease in the demand for rural labor. The extensive nature of cattle farming was also unsuited to the structure of predominantly small, family-owned farms inherited as a result of the land reforms at the end of the nineteenth and beginning of the twentieth centuries. The promotion of efficiency in farming conflicted with the social objective of maintaining the maximum number of farm families on the land.

Successive governments responded to this dilemma in different ways. The Cumann na nGaedheal government (1922–1932) rejected any policy of widespread support to the sector on the grounds that in a predomi-

A horse-drawn plow. Agriculture remained the most important souce of income for independent Ireland until the 1960s. COURTESY OF THE HEAD OF THE DEPARTMENT OF IRISH FOLKLORE, UNIVERSITY COLLEGE DUBLIN.

nantly rural economy the costs of farm support would fall largely on farmers themselves. Both internal and external circumstances changed in the 1930s. The onset of the Great Depression led to a general rise in protectionist barriers. Fianna Fáil came to power in 1932 on a platform of stimulating local industry, including arable agriculture, behind tariff barriers. Price supports were paid to encourage local wheat, dairy, and sugar production. The refusal to pay the land annuities led to the "Economic War" with the United Kingdom, in which Britain placed tariffs on imports of Irish cattle. The costs of this episode were largely borne by agriculture, which also saw its terms of trade fall during the period. The conflict ended with the Anglo-Irish Agreement of 1938, which relaxed access conditions for cattle to the U.K. market again.

Irish agriculture failed to capitalize on the U.K. market deficit during the Second World War, in part because input shortages limited the potential expansion in output and in part because the United Kingdom put mo-

nopoly-purchasing arrangements in place that limited the scope for price increases. The 1948 trade pact with the United Kingdom signalled a return to a more export-oriented agricultural strategy. Though agricultural output slowly increased during the 1950s, intense competition in the main export market in the United Kingdom and inadequate attention to marketing meant that prices were depressed and farm incomes remained low.

THE PRODUCTIVIST PERIOD: 1960S TO MID-1980S

An important change in the Republic was the emergence of a nascent urban-based industrial sector in the 1960s, which allowed the possibility, for the first time, of significant net transfers to the farm population. Price guarantees were strengthened for dairy products and extended to beef under the terms of the 1965 Anglo-Irish Free Trade Agreement. The next quarter-century saw a brief flowering of the "productivist" period in Irish agriculture. Deliberate efforts were made, under

Encyclopedia of Irish History and Culture

Milk being brought to the creamery by donkey and cart, 1969. This traditional image, beloved of tourists, was not in keeping with the needs of a modern dairying industry. COURTESY OF THE HEAD OF THE DEPARTMENT OF IRISH FOLKLORE, UNIVERSITY COLLEGE DUBLIN.

successive Programmes for Economic Expansion, to stimulate agricultural output through grant aid and other incentive schemes. Agricultural output responded; the output volume in 1970 was 31 percent higher than in 1960. But the growing budgetary cost of providing support would not have been sustainable without the benefits granted to the Republic by its membership in the European Union (EU) beginning in 1973.

Agricultural output per worker was marginally lower in Northern Ireland compared to the South in the 1920s, but the South subsequently lost most of its advantage. Indeed, over the period 1926 to 1962, output growth in the North of 150 percent contrasted with the growth of output in the South of just 30 percent

(Ó Gráda 1994). The U.K. policy of free trade in grains stimulated farmyard-enterprise production in the North (i.e., pigs, eggs, and poultry), and beef and dairy farmers benefited from the introduction of postwar price supports in the United Kingdom. Southern agriculture suffered from policy disincentives in the 1930s, input shortages in the 1940s, and underinvestment in the 1950s, but with the increased protection given to farmers in the Republic in the 1960s, overall agricultural performance converged.

The importance of EU membership for the Republic lay not so much in the improved terms of trade for farm produce that access to the high-price EU market brought about, for this was quite short-lived. Rather, it was the fact that for the first time since World War I, Irish agriculture had unrestricted access to its main export markets. At the same time the cost of farm support was no longer borne by the Irish exchequer but by the EU taxpayer and consumer. Agricultural output continued to grow rapidly by a further 52 percent from 1970 to 1985. New technologies, including the use of fertilizers, silage-making instead of hay-making for forage conservation, improved animal breeds, and greater use of compound feeds, led to a marked improvement in productivity. Average farm incomes narrowed the gap with nonfarm incomes and in some years exceeded them. Agriculture in the Republic also began to reverse the productivity gap that had emerged with Northern Ireland agriculture as successive governments in the South exploited the limited discretion available within the EU's agricultural policy in favor of farmers, while policy in the United Kingdom (and hence Northern Ireland) tended to keep prices lower in favor of consumers.

Not all farms shared in the growing prosperity. The modernization of farming was accompanied by the growing marginalization of the small-farm sector. A significant divide opened up between the larger farmers in the south and east of the country who were quick to adopt the new technologies and the smaller farmers in the more disadvantaged western region who fell farther behind. The self-sustaining nature of the small-farm economy began to break down as the deterioration in its relative economic position was reflected in a growing proportion of single, elderly farmers without immediate heirs. While the acceptance of off-farm employment became an increasingly important strategy for viability on smaller farms, a growing proportion of farm households disengaged from commercial agriculture and became increasingly dependent on state welfare payments to maintain their living standards.

TIGHTENING OF FARM SUPPORTS: MID-1980s TO THE PRESENT

The productivist period in Irish farming was relatively short, brought to an end in the mid-1980s by changes in EU farming policy. The costs to the EU of farm support were spiraling out of control, and increasing awareness of the environmental, animal-welfare, health, and food-safety consequences of intensive agricultural practices forced new concerns onto the policy agenda. The growth of milk output, which had expanded by 5 percent per annum over the previous two decades, was brought to a halt by the introduction of milk quotas in 1984. Grant aids for farm modernization were severely curtailed in the reform of EU structural policy in the following year. The MacSharry and Agen-

da 2000 CAP reforms substituted direct payments for market-price support, but in doing so, they introduced effective ceilings on beef, sheep, and cereal output. The growth of agricultural output slowed from 2.6 percent in the period 1970 to 1985 to 1.4 percent between 1985 and 2000 and 0.7 percent between 1990 and 2000.

Similar trends are evident in Northern Irish agriculture, although the strength of sterling in the second half of the 1990s relative to the euro and the difficulties caused for beef exports by the "mad cow" crisis have meant that farm incomes in the North have been under much greater pressure. Total income from farming at the end of the 1990s was less than half what it was at the beginning of the decade in real terms.

On the threshold of the new century agriculture faces a number of challenges. Farm incomes, though comparable to nonfarm incomes on average, remain hugely dependent on subsidies or off-farm income. EU farm-support mechanisms are under considerable challenge both externally, in the context of World Trade Organization negotiations on trade liberalization, and internally, because of the budgetary implications of extending these levels of support to farmers in the candidate countries of central and eastern Europe. Farmers also face the challenge of integrating environmental concerns into agricultural production, including stricter pollution regulations and the public's desire for environmentally benign and animal-friendly (but technically inefficient) management practices. Farmers must also respond to the calls for traceability and quality production from consumers who, in light of an increasing number of health scares, want ever-higher standards of reassurance that their food supply is safe and wholesome. The role of agriculture may have shrunk in importance over the past century, but its capacity to cause controversy and debate remains undiminished.

SEE ALSO Common Agricultural Policy; Economies of Ireland, North and South, since 1920; *Economic Development*, 1958; Economic Relations between North and South since 1922; Economic Relations between Northern Ireland and Britain; European Union; Farming Families; Marshall Aid; Transport—Road, Canal, Rail; **Primary Documents:** Speech to Ministers of the Governments of the Member States of the European Economic Community (18 January 1962)

Bibliography

Breen, Richard. "Agriculture: Policy and Politics." In *Understanding Contemporary Ireland: State, Class, and Develop-*

ment in the Republic of Ireland, edited by Richard Breen, Damian Hannan, David Rottman, and Christopher Whelan. 1990.

Crotty, Raymond. Irish Agricultural Production: Its Volume and Structure. 1966.

Kennedy, Kieran A., Thomas Giblin, and Deirdre McHugh. "Agriculture." In The Economic Development of Ireland in the Twentieth Century. 1988.

Matthews, Alan. "Agriculture, Food Safety, and Rural Development." In The Economy of Ireland: Policy and Performance of a European Region, edited by John O'Hagan. 2000.

Matthews, Alan. Farm Incomes: Myths and Reality. 2000.

Ó Gráda, Cormac. Ireland: A New Economic History, 1780–1939. 1994.

Ó Gráda, Cormac. A Rocky Road: The Irish Economy since the 1920s. 1997.

Sheehy, Seamus J. "The Common Agricultural Policy and Ireland." In Ireland and the European Community, edited by P. J. Drudy and Dermot McAleese. 1984.

Sheehy, Seamus. J., James T. O'Brien, and Seamus McClelland. Agriculture in Northern Ireland and the Republic of Ireland. 1981.

Alan Matthews

∼

American Wakes

The American wake—sometimes called the live wake, farewell supper, or bottle night—was a unique leave-taking ceremony for emigrants from rural Ireland to the United States. American wakes took place prior to the Great Famine, but most evidence survives from the late 1800s and early 1900s, when the custom prevailed among Catholics, especially in western Ireland where traditional customs remained potent. Usually held on the evening prior to an emigrant's departure, the American wake resembled its ceremonial model, the traditional wake for the dead, and its most common name signified that many Catholic country people still regarded emigration as death's equivalent—a permanent breaking of earthly ties. Usually hosted by the emigrant's parents, the American wake, like a traditional wake, was attended by kinfolk and neighbors, featured the liberal consumption of food and drink, and exhibited a seemingly incongruous mixture of grief and gaity, expressed in lamentations, prayers, games, singing, and dancing.

Although its format was archaic, the American wake was an adaptation to postfamine Ireland's social, cultural, and political exigencies. Because emigration was potentially threatening to communal loyalties and values, the leave-taking ceremony interpreted Irish emigration so as to ensure that the emigrants overseas would remain dutiful to the community left behind. The songs, ballads, and other rituals enacted during the American wakes represented a stylized dialogue between the emigrants and the parents, priests, and nationalist politicians who governed Irish Catholic society. Songs that expressed the latter's perspective often ignored the economic causes of emigration and accused the allegedly "selfish," "hard-hearted" emigrants themselves of "abandoning" their aged mothers and fathers and, by extension, "holy Ireland" itself. In response, the ballads sung from the emigrants' perspective portrayed them not as eager, ambitious, or alienated from Irish poverty or from parental and clerical repression, but as sorrowing "exiles," victims of British or landlord oppression, who would be miserably homesick overseas until they returned as promised to their parents' hearths. Such songs also excused the emigrants' departures and expiated their guilt by pledging that they would send their parents money from the United States and would remain loyal to their religion and to the cause of Irish freedom. Arguably, then, the harrowing effects of the American wake on young emigrants, at the moment they were leaving home and hence were psychologically most vulnerable, helped to ensure their unusually high levels of remittances, religious fidelity, and nationalist fervor in the New World.

SEE ALSO Great Famine; Migration: Emigration from the Seventeenth Century to 1845; Migration: Emigration from 1850 to 1960; Population, Economy, and Society from 1750 to 1950; Rural Life: 1850 to 1921; Town Life from 1690 to the Early Twentieth Century

Bibliography

Miller, Kerby A. Emigrants and Exiles: Ireland and the Irish Exodus to North America. 1985.

Schrier, Arnold. Ireland and the Irish Emigration, 1850–1900. 1958.

Kerby Miller

∼

Ancient Order of Hibernians

The Ancient Order of Hibernians (AOH) of the United States is a benevolent association founded in New York

City in 1836. There was a parent association in Ireland which probably had its origins among the secret societies of the eighteenth century, but the early history of the order in Ireland is largely unknown. The AOH itself was never a secret society, though it did have some secret procedures similar to those in Freemasonry and Orangeism. The secret Molly Maguires, who sought to improve Pennsylvania coalminers' conditions through violence during the 1870s, operated within the AOH but were soon disclaimed; the "Mollies" remained as a pejorative nickname for the order in Ireland. At their heights around 1910 the U.S. order had 100,000 members and the Irish order 60,000. The organizational unit was the division, which elected representatives to county/state and national bodies. Membership at first was restricted to Catholics of Irish parentage, then broadened to include those of Irish descent. Initially proscribed by Catholic Church authorities, the AOH later won their acceptance, although some leading Irish clergy never liked the existence of such a specifically Catholic organization under lay control.

Though linked historically, and by an agreement to accept the transfer cards of migrating members, the orders in Ireland and the United States were independent. The U.S. order was split during the years 1884 to 1898, mainly over the predominance of the New York City divisions and rivalry between the factions of leaders John Devoy and Alexander Sullivan. The Irish order was small until the moderate nationalist Joseph Devlin (1871–1934) developed it as a political machine to stiffen the declining United Irish League. His movement benefited from recognition of the AOH as an approved society by the United Kingdom's National Insurance Act of 1911. Under Devlin's influence the U.S. order favored constitutional nationalism for Ireland in the years 1902 to 1906 and 1910 to 1914; at other times it supported revolution. The main purpose of both orders was mutual support among emigrant and minority communities, underpinned by an appeal based on parades and nostalgia. It was thus stronger in divided Ulster and in Britain than in southern Ireland. After 1918 its political importance waned: In Britain it delivered Irish support to the Labour Party, whereas in Northern Ireland it acquired a "green Tory" image. By the 1980s it had about 20,000 members in the United States and a smaller number in Ireland.

SEE ALSO Orange Order: Since 1800; Roman Catholic Church: 1829 to 1891; Roman Catholic Church: Since 1891; Sodalities and Confraternities

Bibliography

Funchion, Michael F., ed. "The Ancient Order of Hibernians in America." *Dictionary of Irish-American Organizations.* 1983.

Hepburn, A. C. *A Past Apart: Studies in the History of Catholic Belfast.* 1996.

A. C. Hepburn

Anglo-Irish Agreement of 1985 (Hillsborough Agreement)

The Anglo-Irish Agreement (AIA) was signed at Hillsborough Castle (the symbolic seat of British power in Northern Ireland) on 15 November 1985 by the British and Irish premiers, Margaret Thatcher and Garret Fitz-Gerald. It was the sixth in a series of intergovernmental summits that began in May 1980. Hillsborough was qualitatively different in that the earlier summits had taken place in an atmosphere strained by the hunger strikes, the Falklands/Malvinas War, and the Brighton bomb. The communiqué accompanying the agreement recognized its historic significance. It came into effect on 29 November after it was ratified by the Dáil and the British House of Commons and was registered at the United Nations on 20 December 1985.

The agreement had a strong institutional framework. Article 2 represented one powerful axis. In part 2(a) it established an Intergovernmental Conference concerned with Northern Ireland and with relations between the two parts of Ireland to deal on a regular basis with "(i) political matters; (ii) security and related matters; (iii) legal matters, including the administration of justice; and (iv) the promotion of cross-border cooperation"; and 2(b) stated that "the United Kingdom Government accepts that the Irish Government will put forward views and proposals on matters relating to Northern Ireland within the field of activity of the Conference insofar as those matters are not the responsibility of a devolved administration in Northern Ireland." It could be said that Article 2 gave constitutional nationalism greater influence than it had ever enjoyed since partition. The countervailing axis existed in Article 1, which attempted to reassure unionists of the prevailing constitutional status of Northern Ireland, and in Articles 4(b), 5(c), and 10(b), which acted as a catalyst toward achieving devolution in place of an enhanced role for the conference. Additionally, Article 11 allowed for a review of the working of the conference within three years.

The AIA is significant for three reasons. First, both governments were now committed to working together on the historic Anglo-Irish conflict. A permanent Anglo-Irish secretariat (staffed by senior personnel from Dublin and London) was a manifestation of its rigor. The structures were built to withstand boycotts, physical threats, general strikes, or whatever. The Inter-governmental Conference, chaired by the British secretary of state and the Irish foreign minister, represented both structure and process. Second, the agreement received much international approbation. A goodwill manifest in Article 10(a) promoted cross-border social and economic development by securing international support through the International Fund for Ireland (IFI), which was established on 18 September 1986 with financial support from the United States, Canada, and New Zealand. In the next fourteen years the IFI was associated with investing 1.1 billion pounds. Third, the agreement symbolized profound attitudinal change. Article 1 represented a historic shift in Irish nationalists' attitude toward Northern Ireland. Equally, British concessions to the Irish heralded an era of intense intergovernmental cooperation. They had set in motion a process of change that was to culminate in the Belfast Agreement of April 1998.

SEE ALSO Northern Ireland: Constitutional Settlement from Sunningdale to Good Friday; Northern Ireland: The United States in Northern Ireland since 1970; Ulster Politics under Direct Rule; **Primary Documents:** Anglo-Irish Agreement (15 November 1985)

Bibliography

Arthur, Paul. "The Anglo-Irish Agreement: Events of 1985–86." *Irish Political Studies* 2 (1987): 99–107.

Aughey, Arthur. *Under Siege: Ulster Unionism and the Anglo-Irish Agreement.* 1989.

FitzGerald, Garret. *All in a Life: An Autobiography.* 1991.

Hadden, Tom, and Kevin Boyle. *The Anglo-Irish Agreement: Commentary, Text, and Official Review.* 1989.

Paul Arthur

Anglo-Irish Free Trade Agreement of 1965

The Irish attempt to gain entry into the European Economic Committee (EEC) failed in January 1963 with France's veto of its application, but the government led by Seán Lemass was determined to continue to reorganize the Irish economy in preparation for a world of freer trade. In a classic paradox of Irish trade policy, it was the desire to reduce dependence on the British market that led Ireland once again to seek closer ties with Britain. To prepare Ireland for the eventual entry to the EEC to which it aspired, while expanding its markets in Britain, Taoiseach Seán Lemass sought trade talks with the British government in March 1963. Little progress was made until Harold Wilson replaced Harold Macmillan as British prime minister in November 1964. At a summit of the two leaders in July 1965 it was agreed that a free-trade area between the countries was desirable, and the Anglo-Irish Free Trade Agreement was signed on 15 December 1965. Its preamble firmly rooted it within the context of the principles and objectives of the General Agreement on Tariffs and Trade (GATT), the harmonious expansion of world trade through the removal of barriers, and the continuing progress toward European economic cooperation. For industry it was agreed that Britain would abolish all import duties on Irish goods on 1 July 1966. On that same date Ireland would cut import duties on all British goods by 10 percent—and by another 10 percent each successive year until all industrial duties eventually disappeared in 1975. For agriculture the agreement allowed unrestricted, duty-free access to the British market for Irish store cattle, store sheep, and store lambs, while the Irish undertook to export at least 638,000 head of cattle per annum. In respect of other agricultural products it was agreed that access to the British market would be related to international commodity agreements involving all substantial producers.

Reaction to the agreement was generally positive, though far from unanimously so. There was dissent, even within the government, on the grounds that Ireland was exposing itself to a stronger economy with which it could not compete in industrial trade, and that the agricultural openings presented did not compensate for this. On balance it appears that the agreement was of greater benefit to Britain. The reduction in Irish protective tariffs enabled British manufacturers to increase sales in Ireland, but the agreement did not exempt Irish manufactured goods from the emergency import taxes that Britain imposed to protect its currency, and Irish agricultural exports had to contend with price cuts and quotas that were not foreseen when the agreement was signed. On a philosophical level, the removal of tariffs imposed since the 1930s marked the symbolic end of the dream of national self-sufficiency. The agreement lapsed on the entry of both countries to the EEC in 1973.

SEE ALSO Economic Relations between Independent Ireland and Britain; Economies of Ireland, North and South, since 1920

Bibliography

Daly, Mary E. *Social and Economic History of Ireland since 1800.* 1981.

Kennedy, Kieran A., Thomas Giblin, and Deirdre McHugh. *The Economic Development of Ireland in the Twentieth Century.* 1988.

Kennedy, Liam. *The Modern Industrialisation of Ireland, 1940–88.* 1989.

Maher, D. J. *The Tortuous Path: The Course of Ireland's Entry into the EEC, 1948–73.* 1986.

Rouse, Paul. *Ireland's Own Soil: Government and Agriculture in Ireland, 1945–65.* 2000.

Paul Rouse

Anglo-Irish Treaty of 1921

The Articles of Agreement for a treaty between Great Britain and Ireland were signed in London by representatives of the British and Dáil Éireann governments in the most melodramatic of circumstances in the early hours of 6 December 1921. The terms specified stated that a Free State should be established for the twenty-six counties of the south and west of Ireland with a large measure of independence along Canadian and Australian dominion-status lines. An imperial contribution was to be made to the British Exchequer and the so-called treaty ports were to remain under British jurisdiction in order to safeguard defense interests. An oath to the British Crown, watered down to make some allowance for republican sensibilities, had to be sworn by Irish TDs (members of the Dáil Éireann), and a governor-general was to be appointed. Clause XII made provision for a Boundary Commission to be established if Northern Ireland opted out of membership of the new state. The boundary was to be readjusted "in accordance with the wishes of the inhabitants, so far as may be compatible with economic and geographical conditions."

The treaty was quickly accepted by all in the British parliament, except for a small Tory diehard contingent, as the means by which Anglo-Irish relations could be stabilized and the Irish Question taken out of British politics. In Northern Ireland, however, the document provoked massive violence and disturbance over the next six months, while in the South political and military divisions over the treaty resulted in the Civil War from June 1922; these divisions continued to plague Irish politics and society for much of the rest of the twentieth century and into the twenty-first.

The treaty's signing ended five months of complex negotiations. Following the truce of 11 July 1921, which halted military hostilities in the Anglo-Irish War, Eamon de Valera led a small group of Dáil ministers to London. After personal meetings with the Irish leader, British prime minister Lloyd George offered a limited dominion-status settlement, which was rejected first by de Valera and then by the Dáil. There ensued a prolonged and convoluted correspondence over the following two months, which sought a form of words on the identity of the Dáil government that would allow full negotiations to begin. Eventually, it was agreed that a conference should discuss "how the association of Ireland with the community of nations known as the British Empire may best be reconciled with Irish national aspirations." The conference began on 11 October.

Much controversy, at the time and since, centered on the choice of Irish delegates. De Valera decided not to go to London, and Arthur Griffith was chosen to lead the delegation in the hope that his moderate reputation would win firm concessions from the British. The rest of the team was picked as representing distinct interests: Michael Collins, that of the army and the IRB; Robert Barton and George Gavan Duffy, together with Erskine Childers as the secretary, to provide a republican safeguard. Eamon Duggan, along with Duffy, offered legal expertise. The delegates had the status of plenipotentiaries but were honor-bound to refer any settlement to the Dáil cabinet in Dublin before signing any agreement. This ambiguity was exploited by Lloyd George at the end of the negotiations. The delegation failed to preserve unity within its ranks during the conference and had increasingly strained relations with the Dáil cabinet. The British delegation, by contrast, comprised experienced negotiators, and Lloyd George's choice of prominent Conservatives for the team, notably Lord Birkenhead and Austen Chamberlain, helped to reconcile the Tory Party to previously unpalatable concessions.

Despite preliminary sparring on defense issues, it soon became clear that the make-or-break points were the British insistence that the new state should remain part of the commonwealth and swear allegiance to the Crown, and the Irish determination to make no concessions on either sovereignty or the North. De Valera's strategy for compromise rested on his sophisticated notion of "external association," in which any recognition

David Lloyd George (far left) with Lord Birkenhead and Winston Churchill leaving No. 10 Downing St., London, and going to the House of Commons, 1922. © HULTON ARCHIVE/GETTY IMAGES. REPRODUCED BY PERMISSION.

of British authority would apply solely to foreign and not to domestic affairs. There was never any prospect that the British would agree to this. Lloyd George resorted to private meetings with Griffith, and sometimes Collins, to find some means by which Irish concessions on constitutional status could be related to assurances on "essential unity." When the Northern Irish prime minister James Craig refused to bow to Lloyd George's pressure to accept any form of control from Dublin, Lloyd George proposed to Griffith the establishment of the ill-defined Boundary Commission as a means to prevent the North from blocking a settlement. Griffith's vague acceptance of this overture was made without reference to the rest of the Irish delegation.

As in so many such negotiations, the crucial developments occurred at the very end. On the weekend before the treaty's signing, a meeting of the Dáil cabinet revealed deep divisions over the British terms. Making last minute concessions on fiscal autonomy, Lloyd George insisted that all members of the Irish delegation sign the final document there and then on the evening of 5 December or face the consequence of "immediate and terrible war"; this threat was probably the most

cynical of tactical maneuvers. After a stormy private meeting all of the Irish delegates—Barton and Duffy with extreme reluctance—signed. The Dáil cabinet, by a majority of one, accepted the treaty, but de Valera publicly rejected the terms. Three weeks of vitriolic debate ensued in the Dáil, at the end of which a motion in support of the treaty was passed by a mere seven votes. Although public bodies and the press spoke up overwhelmingly in favor of the document, around 70 percent of the IRA and a majority of active Sinn Féiners rejected it. In the following months British insistence on adherence to the application of the terms rendered futile desperate efforts for compromise within Sinn Féin and the IRA.

It was scarcely surprising that the failure to preserve either the ideals of a republic or those of Irish unity provoked opposition from committed republicans. No document could have been better calculated to reinforce the divisions within the Sinn Féin movement between pragmatists and idealists. Much of the support came from those desiring peace and normality rather than from any enthusiasm for the terms. The circumstances of the treaty's signing, moreover, exacerbated the split and infused it with personal animosities.

For all the histrionic circumstances at the time of the treaty's signing, the details of the settlement were predictable and, with the exception of Clause XII, represented the best possible compromise available at that time. A dominion-status settlement had been frequently mooted during the last year of the Anglo-Irish War and supported by powerful interests in Southern Ireland and in Britain. As Michael Collins predicted in the Dáil treaty debates, the terms did have considerable potential for movement toward a republic, but distrust of British intentions and adherence to republican nostrums were widespread. The Civil War in the South and the abject failure of the Southern leadership to focus attention on the needs of the North was to prevent the Boundary Commission from undermining the settlement. The Irish Question, somewhat fortuitously, was largely removed from British consciousness for nearly half a century. Developments in Northern Ireland since 1969 have thrown a new perspective on the document's evasions and shortcomings over Irish unity. Although Lloyd George achieved the Coalition government's short-term survival, Michael Collins was correct to say that he had signed his own death warrant.

SEE ALSO Boundary Commission; Civil War; Collins, Michael; Commonwealth; Cumann na mBan; de Valera, Eamon; Griffith, Arthur; Markievicz, Countess Constance; Political Parties in Independent Ireland; Politics: 1800 to 1921—Challenges to the Union; Protestant Ascendancy: Decline, 1800 to 1930; Struggle for Independence from 1916 to 1921; Unionism from 1885 to 1922; **Primary Documents:** The Anglo-Irish Treaty (6 December 1921); "Time Will Tell" (19 December 1921); Speech in Favor of the Anglo-Irish Treaty of December 1921 (7 January 1922); Speech at the Opening of the Free State Parliament (11 September 1922); Constitution of the Irish Free State (5 December 1922)

Bibliography

Hopkinson, Michael. *Green against Green: The Irish Civil War.* 1988.

Pakenham, Frank. *Peace by Ordeal.* 1935.

Michael A. Hopkinson

Annals of the Four Masters

The *Annals of the Kingdom of Ireland* (*Annála Ríoghachta Éireann*), as the *Annals of the Four Masters* were originally called, consist of short entries relating to significant personalities and events in Irish history, arranged in chronological order and compiled in the years 1632 to 1636. Together with other earlier annalistic compilations, the *Annals of the Four Masters* are a major source for the ecclesiastical and secular history of early and medieval Ireland. The earliest entry purports to record an event forty days before the Biblical Deluge (Anno Mundi 2242). The final entry relates to the death of Hugh O'Neill, earl of Tyrone, in 1616 C.E. The structure of the chronological framework is provided by the succession of kings, and the length of the reign of individual kings is usually documented.

Many of the entries are in the form of obituaries that record the deaths of kings and local lords, saints, bishops, abbots, and other clergy. The focus throughout the *Annals* is on the elite of society, both secular and religious. Disputes between rival kin groups are documented. Occasional reference is made to external events and to occurrences in the natural world, such as abnormal weather or the appearance of comets. Within the entry for each individual year personalities and events are mentioned in order of their importance as perceived by the compilers. The annalists left blank spaces throughout the manuscript so that further material could subsequently be inserted at the appropriate place.

The historical material that is now preserved in the *Annals of the Four Masters* is an amalgam derived from a variety of earlier texts written at various dates between the middle of the sixth century and the early seventeenth century. The precise sources for the entries relating to events that occurred before the twelfth century are unknown, but the entries would originally have been the work of Irish monastic scribes. The late medieval entries are derived from historical compilations made by secular learned Gaelic families. The long narrative entries relating to the late sixteenth and early seventeenth centuries derive from contemporary sources, including Lughaidh Ó Cléirigh's *Beatha Aodha Ruaidh Uí Dhomhnaill* (Life of Red Hugh O'Donnell). Many of the entries relating to the Franciscans were drawn from Francis O'Mahony's *Brevis synopsis provinciae Hiberniae FF Minorum*, compiled at Louvain in 1617–1618 and subsequently translated into Irish.

The *Annals of the Four Masters* differ from earlier annalistic compilations in that their focus is on the whole of Ireland. Earlier annals, such as the *Annals of*

Loch Cé or the *Annals of Connacht*, had a more local focus. However, the O'Donnell bias of some of the entries in the *Annals of the Four Masters* reflects the Donegal origins of the compilers.

The initiative that led to the production of these historical annals in the early seventeenth century came from the Irish Franciscan College of Saint Anthony at Louvain in the Spanish Netherlands. There, a number of scholarly men from Irish learned families had joined the Franciscan order and undertook a major research project on the history of Ireland and its saints. A prime objective of the Irish Franciscan scholars at Louvain was to present Ireland in a favorable light to Catholic Europe, building on the image of Ireland as an "island of saints and scholars." The need to counteract Scottish claims that the early saints from "Scotia" might have been Scottish rather than Irish was an important stimulus to research and publish the lives of Irish saints. An ambitious program of research and publication was planned in the 1620s, and much of it was implemented over the following twenty years. While the primary focus was on collecting the lives of Irish saints, special attention was also given to researching the history of early Ireland because genealogical and historical research into the families from which Irish saints emanated was deemed necessary to demonstrate their noble origins. A lay Franciscan brother from Donegal, Micheál Ó Cléirigh, was chosen to return from Louvain to Ireland to undertake research on manuscripts still in the hands of the scholarly community there. Ó Cléirigh prepared the *Martyrology of Donegal*, a new recension of *Leabhar Gabhála Éireann*, and assembled a set of genealogies of Irish saints and kings. The compilation of *Annals of the Kingdom of Ireland* was Ó Cléirigh's major achievement.

The annals were written at Bundrowes, Co. Donegal, between 22 January 1632 and 10 August 1636 from source material collected throughout Ireland. Ó Cléirigh was assisted by other scholars, including Cúchoigríche Ó Cléirigh, Fearfeasa Ó Maolchonaire, and Cúchoigríche Ó Duibhgeannáin. These four were referred to as the "Four Masters" by the Louvain Franciscan John Colgan in the preface to his *Acta Sanctorum Hiberniae* (1645) in acknowledgment of their scholarship. Conaire Ó Cléirigh, a "fifth master," was also involved. The patronage of Feargal Ó Gadhra of Coolavin, Co. Sligo, provided the necessary financial support for the research work in Ireland. Two sets of the annals were made, one for the patron (now preserved as Royal Irish Academy, MS C iii 3, and Trinity College, Dublin, MS 1301) and one for Saint Anthony's College Louvain, (now Royal Irish Academy, MS 23 P 6–7, and University College, Dublin, FLK MS A13).

After the text was completed in August 1636, approbations of the kind that prefaced printed works were obtained from bishops and hereditary historians. It was probably intended that the annals would be printed at Louvain, but this did not happen. Hugh Ward, who had commissioned the work, died in November 1635, a few months before the annals were completed. The copy of the annals that was taken to Louvain was used extensively by John Colgan in his work on Irish saints' lives. Some passages from the annals were quoted in Latin in Colgan's publications.

Given the concern of Irish Catholic writers in the early seventeenth century to demonstrate that the Catholic Church was the true church, it is no surprise to find that the *Annals of the Four Masters* presented a version of Irish history that conformed to the ideals of the Counter-Reformation. The annals were part of a major scholarly corpus that emphasized the continuity of the Catholic faith in Ireland and helped to cultivate the idea that loyalty to Catholicism was a defining characteristic of the Irish people.

The text of the *Annals of the Four Masters* was published in its entirety in 1851 in a scholarly, heavily footnoted seven-volume edition edited and translated by John O'Donovan.

SEE ALSO Education: 1500 to 1690; Irish Colleges Abroad until the French Revolution; Literature: Gaelic Writing from 1607 to 1800; O'Donovan, John; **Primary Documents:** Accounts of the Siege and Battle of Kinsale (1601)

Bibliography

Jennings, Brendan. *Michael Ó Cleirigh, Chief of the Four Masters, and His Associates.* 1936.

O'Donovan, John, ed. *Annála Ríoghachta Éireann: Annals of the Kingdom of Ireland by the Four Masters from the Earliest Period to the Year 1616.* 7 vols. 1851. Also available at http://www.ucc.ie/celt.

Ó Muraíle, Nollaig. "The Autograph Manuscripts of the Annals of the Four Masters." *Celtica* 19 (1987): 75–95.

Walsh, Paul. *The Four Masters and Their Work.* 1944.

Bernadette Cunningham

Antiquarianism

Until the late eighteenth century the word *antiquarianism* meant the study of ancient cultures and civilizations specifically, and mainly referred to those of Greece and Rome. That Ireland would have been excluded up to this point from such lofty company makes historical and political sense. Its indigenous culture did not constitute a "civilization" by the standards of most British or continental European classicists and scholars; more often it was characterized as barbarous, as in the well-circulated and repeatedly cited writings of Edmund Spenser and Giraldus Cambrensis. All of this changed, however, when a retired British general, Charles Vallancey, began his foundational work in the recovery, interpretation, and promotion of Irish antiquities. That Vallancey was completely wrong about almost every assertion he made concerning ancient Ireland, and especially the Irish language, is not nearly as important as his act of valorizing native Irish culture. Although his work, which was published in serial form (alongside the work of others) in *Collectanea de Rebus Hibernicis* (1770–1804), was full of "fantastical speculations and etymological solecisms," as Joep Leerssen writes, it was of immense political value to an emerging strand of Irish nationalism in the last decades of the eighteenth century. And so Irish antiquarianism has its roots in the enthusiasm of an amateur who could bestow upon it respectability and political significance, if not philological accuracy.

Charles Vallancey was the main force behind the establishment of a Dublin Society select committee on the study of antiquities in May 1772. One of its members, Sir Lucius O'Brien, would invite the prominent Catholic advocate Charles O'Conor to become a member in a letter that included the following formulation of its purpose: "If our Researches shall turn out of any service to the Publick or of any Honour to Ireland; If by shewing that the Inhabitants of this Islands were at all Times Respectable & often the Masters & more often the Instructors of Brittain we can Convince our Neibours that, alltho Providence has at present given them superior strength, yet ought they not to treat the Irish as a Barbarous, or a Contemptible People" (cited in Leerssen 1997, pp. 347–348). This political objective was later more fully articulated by others, including O'Conor, and it forms the basis for an apologistic nationalism which asserts that the Irish deserve better treatment because they are the inheritors of a civilization older and richer than that of Britain. Arguably, this is one of the rhetorical bases from which Daniel O'Connell made the case for Catholic Emancipation four decades later. Such

a model also paved the way for the familiar analogical linking of Ireland with Greece and Britain with Rome by the Irish Literary Revival, not to mention Matthew Arnold's related characterization in "On the Study of Celtic Literature."

Foundational as it was for so many political, social, and literary modes of thinking, antiquarianism consolidated into its most influential institutional forms in the two decades before the union. The successor to the Dublin Society select committee was the Hibernian Antiquarian Society (HAS), which sustained itself from 1779 to 1783. In 1882, just before the demise of the HAS, Vallancey cofounded the Royal Irish Academy, setting as one of its aims the recovery and study of Irish antiquities. With the establishment of the Royal Irish Academy (RIA) came a flood of interest in Irish antiquarianism from both Irish nationalist and unionist quarters. The founding of the RIA meant new respectability and prestige for studies like Vallancey's. That Vallancey—or the arguments surrounding his "strange researches," in Seamus Deane's words—remained central to these institutions was affirmed when the eminent Irish nationalist Henry Flood bequeathed a chair of Irish philology at Trinity College, Dublin, for him in the following terms: "if he shall be then living, Colonel Charles Vallancey to be the first professor thereof . . . , seeing that by his eminent and successful labours in the study and recovery of that language he well deserves to be so first appointed" (cited in Leerssen 1997, p. 362). The support and credibility that Vallancey inspired is further evidenced in letters that O'Conor, his close associate, wrote to colleagues and activists. O'Conor praised him in the highest terms, as, for example, in a letter of 1786 to Joseph Walker: "The extent of his oriental learning and skill in modern languages is vast. In my last to him I ventured to predict that his last performance will draw on him the attention of all the academics of Europe. . . ." (O'Conor 1980, p. 471). "Attention" is one way to put it—debunking, cynical attacks is more accurate. Vallancey's work sparked a fierce debate over the origins of the Irish (a debate that echoed and derived from that which took place over James Macpherson's Ossianic "translations"). Vallancey's most important contribution to Irish antiquarianism was his assertion—without any reliable evidence and without even a basic knowledge of the Irish language—that Irish was a language derivative of ancient Phoenician. This claim was attended by his assertion—again without evidence—of the ancient Carthaginian origins of the Irish people. (Carthage, of course, was located in North Africa. For a helpful map charting Vallancey's speculations, see Elizabeth Butler Cullingford's *Ireland's Others*, Part 2.) These two claims won widespread approval from a broad range of camps. Even James Joyce, lecturing to a university audience in Trieste in 1907, would cite Vallancey as a respected authority. Writing in 1907, Joyce explained the origins of the Irish language in this way: "This language is eastern in origin and has been identified by many philologists with the ancient language of the Phoenicians, the discoverers, according to historians, of commerce and navigation. . . . The language that the comic dramatist Plautus puts in the mouth of the Phoenicians in his comedy *Poenula* is virtually the same language, according to the critic Vallancey, as that which Irish peasants now speak" (Joyce 2000, p. 110). This was neither true nor even demonstrable, but as Joyce's adoption of this theory indicates, it found a broad and enduring base of support.

The persistence of Vallancey's credibility is a testament not to his academic assiduity but rather to the necessities of certain forms of cultural nationalism, such as the kind that Joyce would articulate in Trieste. Vallancey's unprovable, "speculative and mystifying" ideas (in Leerssen's words) about Irish origins would have consequences beyond enabling apologistic strands of nationalism, however. The reaction to his work, as enshrined in Edward Ledwich's *Antiquities of Ireland* (2d edition, 1804) formed the basis of nineteenth-century Irish antiquarianism and set the standard for the early-twentieth-century division of the subjects encompassed by antiquarianism into formal categories such as history, archaeology, linguistics, and physical anthropology. The *Proceedings of the Royal Irish Academy* became a forum in which to continue this reaction and the debates surrounding Vallancey's assertions. At the same time, as Seamus Deane has observed, the special section in the *Proceedings* on antiquities became a place where "amateur scholars like Charles O'Conor and Edmund Ledwige [and] politicians like Sir Lawrence Parsons all brought some offering to the new shrine of cultural nationalism, where the new gods of Language and of War presided, converting the old accusations of crudeness in speech and turbulence into symptoms of natural spontaneity and of valour" (Deane 1986, p. 62).

SEE ALSO Arts: Modern Irish and Anglo-Irish Literature and the Arts since 1800; Gaelic Revival; Literature: Anglo-Irish Literature in the Nineteenth Century; Literature: Gaelic Literature in the Nineteenth Century; O'Donovan, John

Bibliography

Cullingford, Elizabeth Butler. *Ireland's Others: Gender and Ethnicity in Irish Literature and Popular Culture.* 2001.

Deane, Seamus. *A Short History of Irish Literature.* 1986.

Joyce, James. *Occasional, Critical, and Political Writing.* Edited by Kevin Barry. 2000.

Leerssen, Joep. *Mere Irish and Fíor-Ghael: Studies in the Idea of Irish Nationality, Its Development and Literary Expression prior to the Nineteenth Century.* 1997.

O'Conor, Charles. *Letters.* 2 Vols. Edited by C. C. Ward and R. E. Ward. 1980.

Spurgeon Thompson

Architecture, Early and Medieval

The study of Irish architecture in the medieval period divides naturally into two broad phases. The earlier period began with the conversion of Ireland to Christianity in about 400 C.E. and ended in the twelfth century, when the impact of new styles from Europe and western England became commonplace. After the Anglo-Norman invasion in 1169, the pace of change accelerated largely because of English influence. The initial prosperity of the Anglo-Norman colony led to a steady increase in the building of churches, monasteries, and castles, which was only halted by the economic decline of the later thirteenth century and the calamities of the fourteenth. What emerged subsequently was a distinctive style in ecclesiastical and military architecture, modest in scale but unusual in character, which lingered until the seventeenth century in places.

THE EARLY PERIOD

No architecture survives from the missionary period of the fifth and early sixth centuries, but we can infer that dedicated places of Christian worship were constructed and that these were probably of wood. Contemporary domestic architecture favored round wooden houses, but churches were probably rectangular. The earliest extended description of an Irish church occurs in the life of Saint Brigit of Kildare, written in the late seventh century. It describes a large church catering to a double monastery of males and females, divided longitudinally, with what appears to have been a kind of chancel screen hung with images. Flanking the altar were the tombs of Saint Brigit and Bishop Conlaed, over which were suspended crowns. Some idea of the appearance of a complete timber church can be gleaned from the Temptation page of the *Book of Kells*, where the Temple of Jerusalem is shown in the manner of an Irish church with a shingled roof and gabled finials. Miniature versions of churches form the finials of high crosses and are clearly

Beehive stone huts on Skellig Michael, Co. Kerry, dating to the seventh to eighth century. These huts are round outside and square inside, some with wall cupboards (for books and vessels). © MICHAEL ST. MAUR SHEIL/CORBIS. REPRODUCED BY PERMISSION.

also the models for the portable metalwork reliquaries known as house-shaped shrines.

There are hints that some churches may have been made of stone as early as the seventh century—the place name Duleek in County Meath means "stone church." Churches of wood continued to be built into the twelfth century and probably later. Along the Atlantic seaboard, especially in areas where timber for building was scarce, churches and monastic sites were often constructed of drystone masonry. Many have survived in a remarkable state of preservation. Simple corbelled "beehive" huts, such as those found on the island monastery of Skellig Michael, Co. Kerry, were adapted from secular dwellings. Their simplicity makes them difficult to date. Simple rectangular churches with a profile like that of an upturned boat, such as Gallarus Oratory in County Kerry, have been noted on a number of sites. Rectangular in plan, with inward-curving walls, they represent an adaptation of the corbelling principle of beehive huts to a rectangular form. In structural terms this was not an entirely successful marriage, as the long sides had a tendency to sag inwards and collapse. A range of dates from about the seventh to the twelfth

centuries has been proposed for them. At Church Island, Co. Kerry, excavation showed that there a stone church had succeeded an earlier timber structure.

As far as we can tell, the building of larger churches in mortared stone began in Ireland in the later eighth century. A reference to a stone church at Armagh is the first clear indication of the new fashion. In the absence of documentation, radiocarbon dating has demonstrated the construction of a number of churches over the following four centuries. They were at first simple structures and were typically about one-third longer than they were wide. Construction was of dressed (shaped to fit by hammering) large stones, closely jointed—usually somewhat irregular in shape—and sometimes giving the impression of being exceptionally massive. Doorways (at the west end) were normally of trabeate form—that is, a single massive lintel-stone spanned the entrance. They were occasionally enriched with a simple cross motif or a low-relief carved architrave. Roofs were of slate or shingle, but gradually the classic Irish stone roof evolved. At first this was a simple gabled structure with the weight of the roof propped by trusses. Later, under Romanesque influence, the roofs were created with lofts or voids to reduce weight and were supported on barrel vaults, such as at Saint Columb's House at Kells, Co. Meath. Other distinctive features included *antae*, a term that denotes projection of the sidewalls beyond the gables. These are thought to have mimicked the corner posts of wooden structures. In some churches it seems that the antae were carried up the gable to meet at the apex. In others the antae stopped at the beginning of the roof-slope and may have been intended to support bargeboards, which met and crossed at the apex. A common feature, which survives on some churches, was a gable finial, which mimicked in carved stone the crossing of the boards.

By the tenth century Irish kings and churchmen were commissioning substantial stone churches, perhaps as part of a consolidation process, following the wars of the early Viking age. The cathedral at Clonmacnoise was one such church: It was probably constructed in the early tenth century at the behest of King Flann Sinna. The great church at Clonfert, Co. Galway, was another. At Inish Cealtra an important church was erected by Brian Boru around the year 1000 C.E.

The round tower, one of the most dramatic inventions of Irish architecture, appeared in the tenth century. These tall, tapering towers, built usually on slight foundations, often rose to a height of 100 feet or more. With their conical caps and windows more or less aligned on the cardinal points, they have been variously identified as watchtowers and refuges. They are suited to be neither. The Irish word for the tower was *cloigtech*, bell-house, and clearly they copied continental campanile. They may have had secondary uses as refuges and storehouses, but history suggests that they were death traps in times of crisis. Round towers were significant statements about the status of important churches, and with their great height they served as a dramatic advertisement of religious foundations—hardly a wise thing if refuge was their predominant purpose. Doorways are often elevated—for sound structural reasons, given the shallow foundations—and frequently of trabeate form. Later examples have arched doorways. One built around 1200 C.E. at Ardmore, Co. Waterford, was constructed of finely cut ashlar masonry. A small number of churches had a diminutive round tower incorporated as a steeple; a good example is Saint Kevin's Kitchen at Glendalough.

IRISH ROMANESQUE

Scholarship now emphasizes a twofold division in the Irish Romanesque. The first part is marked by the appearance of the barrel vault, which survives on a number of unadorned Irish churches. A good example is

Round tower in the center of the Glendalough monastery, Wicklow mountains. © MICHAEL ST. MAUR SHEIL/CORBIS. REPRODUCED BY PERMISSION.

Saint Columb's House at Kells, a structure probably built originally around the ninth or tenth century and then later substantially modified. The churches of the second phase are those which, from the twelfth century onwards, were decorated in the Romanesque style. The only really true Romanesque church in Ireland is Cormac's Chapel at Cashel, built with a porch and twin towers of finely cut ashlar: It carries a rich variety of Romanesque ornament. It is roofed in stone in the Irish manner. The chapel, consecrated in 1134, was built under the influence of western English style, symbolizing in stone the changes in church governance that the reformers of the twelfth century were promoting. Elsewhere, Romanesque decorative features were added to traditional Irish architecture; some influence from French sources has also been detected. The spread of the style has been associated with the organization of regular dioceses. Many older churches were modified by the addition of chancels, and many others were being built anew with integrated chancels. A fashion for south doors rather than the traditional western opening can also be detected at this time. These tendencies may well signal liturgical change that is otherwise undocumented.

Irish churches were often located within a circular or subcircular bank that defined the sacred enclosure. This is not unique, for enclosed monasteries were a feature of Merovingian Gaul and parts of western Britain. As late as the twelfth century larger Irish foundations tended to build clusters of smaller churches rather than single large ones. This had its roots in early traditions of church layout and contributed to the appearance of what were in a real sense spiritual cities in a largely townless landscape. A harbinger of change was the introduction of the Cistercian Order, which established its first Irish house at Mellifont in 1142 on the regular continental model.

GOTHIC ARCHITECTURE

The Anglo-Norman invasion in 1169 brought with it a new style of architecture. The magnates of the conquest supported the foundation of many Cistercian and Augustinian monasteries. Built on a unified plan in the gothic style, they were very influential. The most ambitious buildings, however, were the two cathedrals of Dublin, Christ Church and Saint Patrick's, both begun in the early thirteenth century in the early English style. With their mural galleries and ribbed vaults they were fine and substantial buildings. Other ambitious constructions (for example, Tuam Cathedral in County Galway and Athasssel Abbey in County Tipperary) were never completed. Other cathedrals were more modest—most Irish dioceses were small and perhaps unable to afford great architecture. The decline of the Anglo-Norman colony retarded the development of architecture in Ireland, and when building resumed in the fifteenth century, a simplified gothic emerged which was inward-looking and rather plain and conservative. The greatest monuments of this time were the friaries, many of them in the west and surviving largely intact if unroofed. Their distinctive slender towers rising at the junction of choir and nave are their most striking feature. Fine examples are preserved at Rosserk and Rosserily, Co. Mayo, and Muckross, Co. Kerry.

The construction of massive donjons (keeps) within curtain walls with defensive towers is characteristic of the later twelfth and early thirteenth centuries; especially fine examples are Trim and Carrickfergus castles. Royal castles placed the stamp of government on the towns of the colony. Wood and earthen motte-and-bailey castles were also constructed together in the countryside while lesser stone buildings appeared in towns. The tribulations of the early fourteenth century brought the construction of massive fortifications to an abrupt halt. From the late fourteenth century, castle architecture was dominated by the construction of more modest freestanding towers, often surrounded by a wall but less elaborate than those of earlier times. The fourteenth century saw the emergence of the tower house; about two thousand were erected in Ireland. These were usually modest rectangular towers—essentially fortified houses. Now seen usually in isolation, most were originally enclosed by *bawns* (walled courtyards). Some of these had modest towers. In Ulster both tower houses and more comfortable, but still defended houses of Scottish influence were constructed during plantation in the early seventeenth century. Although the widespread use of artillery made them obsolete, tower houses were constructed in Ireland as late as the seventeenth century; one example, at Derryhivenny, Co. Galway, was built in 1643.

SEE ALSO Arts: Early and Medieval Arts and Architecture

Bibliography

Craig, Maurice. *The Architecture of Ireland.* 1982.

Hughes, Kathleen, and Ann Hamlin. *The Modern Traveller to the Early Irish Church.* 1977.

Henry, Françoise. *Irish Art in the Early Christian Period to AD 800.* 1965.

Henry, Françoise. *Irish Art during the Viking Invasions, 800–1020 AD.* 1967.

Henry, Françoise. *Irish Art in the Romanesque Period.* 1970.

Herity, Michael. *Studies in the Layout, Building, and Art in Stone of Early Irish Monasteries.* 1995.

Leask, Harold G. *Irish Castles and Castellated Houses.* 1941.

Leask, Harold G. *Irish Churches and Monastic Buildings.* 3 vols. 1955–1960.

Manning, Conleth. *Early Irish Monasteries.* 1995.

Stalley, Roger. *The Cistercian Monasteries of Ireland.* 1987.

Stalley, Roger. *Irish Round Towers.* 2000.

Sweetman, David. *The Medieval Castles of Ireland.* 1999.

Michael Ryan

Arts

EARLY AND
MEDIEVAL ARTS
AND
ARCHITECTURE

PETER HARBISON

EARLY MODERN
LITERATURE AND
THE ARTS FROM
1500 TO 1800

CÓILÍN OWENS

MODERN IRISH AND
ANGLO-IRISH
LITERATURE AND
THE ARTS SINCE
1800

EAMONN WALL

EARLY AND MEDIEVAL ARTS AND ARCHITECTURE

The century that saw Saint Patrick's mission in Ireland is as dark from the artistic point of view as it is from the contemporary native documentation. Yet the fifth century acts as an interesting transition from the age of prehistory to the achievements of early medieval Irish artists and craftsmen. Ireland cannot have been as isolated from the dying Roman Empire as many think, and the knowledge of writing that it received from the neighboring island of Britain led not only to the use of the Ogham script on standing stones (some carved with Christian symbols), but also to a first "lost generation" of manuscripts that would have accompanied the flowering of Christianity in the country.

Iron Age Ireland had a vigorous metal industry that produced objects with La Tène decoration, and what survived of it in the fifth century got new impetus from late Roman Britain, as can be seen by the adoption of new clothing fashions that required the use of a bronze penannular brooch with pin to keep cloaks fastened. Over time, this brooch-type was to be adapted to Irish tastes, with the closure of the opening for the ring making the brooch more ornamental than functional and leading to heights of perfection such as the Tara Brooch, which, like so many of the metal objects mentioned below, is preserved in the National Museum of Ireland in Dublin. It is still unclear how far the enamel techniques used in decorating earlier brooches in the series were descended from prehistoric Irish workshop practice, or were influenced by a British metal industry at the time, or a combination of both. For all we know, decorative wood—and leather—work, too ephemeral to have survived, may have been carried on traditionally from the prehistoric period, using motifs and patterns that were to be given new life by Christian craftsmen.

A number of early manuscripts associated with Saint Columba and his monastic foundations show the influence of metalwork. The shape of a cross in one of the initial letters of the *Cathach* (c. 600) suggests Mediterranean metal prototypes, and the decoration on the figure of the Evangelist Matthew in the *Book of Durrow*

Silver chalice from Ardagh, Co. Limerick, c. 700 C.E. COPYRIGHT © NATIONAL MUSEUM OF IRELAND. REPRODUCED BY PERMISSION.

reflects designs that must have come from metal-enamellers.

The three major manuscripts with Columban affiliations—the *Cathach* in the Royal Irish Academy, and the *Book of Durrow* and the *Book of Kells* in the Library of Trinity College, Dublin, each roughly a century apart—are survivors from probably a much larger corpus. The *Cathach*, a copy of the Psalms traditionally ascribed to the hand of Saint Columba himself, has an already identifiable Irish script and betrays a combination of Celtic spiral ornament with a fish of Mediterranean origin. By the time that the *Book of Durrow* came to be illuminated, interlace was added to the treasury of Italian motifs used in Irish art, and folio 192v displays animals which can be understood as adaptations of Anglo-Saxon ornament—both of which, when combined with the revitalized La Tène spiral shapes, make up the most important compendium of motifs practiced in myriad variations in early Irish manuscripts and metalwork (though there are of course others, such as fretwork).

EARLY MEDIEVAL METALWORK

Probably sometime around the late seventh century, a spark was ignited by some unknown and ingenious craftsman that was to lead to the creation of metal masterpieces in the following century and more, which were to find few if any equals elsewhere in Europe at the time. One of these is the Ardagh Chalice used to administer wine, which has two handles reflecting models on sumptuous late Roman silver vessels. Silver, too, was the chalice's basic material, added to which were decorations in twisted gold and bosses of enamel, while the concentric circles surrounding the rock crystal at the

The Chi-Rho page from the Book of Kells *(c. 800 C.E.), Hiberno-Saxon manuscript illumination. This page, the beginning of St. Matthew's Gospel, deals with the Incarnation. The X and P represent the first two letters of Christ's name in Greek (Chi and Rho).* THE BOARD OF TRINITY COLLEGE DUBLIN. REPRODUCED BY PERMISSION.

center of the underside of the foot present copybook examples of the three major types of art motifs mentioned above—animals, spirals, and interlace.

A more unusual, yet equally high-quality liturgical vessel came to light in 1980 at Derrynaflan, Co. Tipperary, along with another (somewhat later) chalice and a (baptismal?) ladle. This is a silver paten (plate used to carry the Eucharist) on its own stand, the paten decorated with panels bearing human and animal motifs in gold wire, and interspersed with ornate silver-grille and enamel bosses, the stand using the same materials but often differing motifs and techniques, such as die-stamping.

That the Ardagh Chalice was found with four decorative brooches of varying ages raises the question as to whether the Tara Brooch was used with some liturgical garment rather than having been created for a lay client. It shares the use of enamel bosses with the chalice and packs so much ornament into both faces (which have a diameter of only 3.5 inches) that it must be adjudged the most intricate piece of eighth-century jewelry to have survived in Europe. Ecclesiastical use can, however, be ascribed with virtual certainty to a door-handle and two discs discovered at Donore, Co. Meath, which must be among the earliest surviving pieces of church furniture in Ireland. The animal-headed handle is earlier than the lion-headed examples on Charlemagne's cathedral at Aachen, and the discs are engraved with breathtakingly ingenious spiral and trumpet pattern designs which are the superb product of an artistically labyrinthine mind, every bit as complicated as that of any of the illuminators of the *Book of Kells*.

MANUSCRIPTS

The *Book of Kells*, limned perhaps around 800 on Iona or at Kells itself, is the culmination of the art of adornment that had been evolving for more than a century in both Ireland and Britain, and a continuation of the scriptorial triumph that is the *Book of Lindisfarne*. Lindisfarne's ornament is controlled and orderly, while that of Kells is characterized by a wild imagination luxuriating within the bounds of an overall design, the marvelous creation of a gifted team of artists combining successfully to adorn a gospel book for the greater glory of God. They drew on various sources of inspiration, many of them unidentified, with scholars arguing inconclusively about potential influence from great manuscripts emanating from the Court of Charlemagne, of which the *Book of Kells* is certainly a truly worthy but more riotously and richly ornamented insular equivalent. Its joy in coloring, variety in motif, complexity of design (as in the famous Chi-Rho page in-

troducing Christ's name for the first time in the Gospels), depth of meaning, subtlety in multiple interpretation, sheer inventiveness, and perfection of execution at a miniature scale make it into the most decorative codex to have survived from the insular monastic schools of illumination active in the first millennium. Other Irish manuscripts of the period, such as that numbered 51 in the library at Saint Gall in Switzerland, are comparable, if not equal, yet both delight in representing the human figure in stilted or stylized form, either individually or grouped in a narrative context.

STONE CARVINGS

The same attractive stiffness is found in the smaller pocket gospel books created for personal use in the eighth and ninth centuries, but also on stones standing free, particularly in the western half of Ireland, whose dating is contentious. These include representations of pilgrims(?) at Killadeas, Co. Fermanagh, and Ballyvourney, Co. Cork, but also Crucifixions on the County Mayo islands of Inishkea North and Duvillaun More, and a number of different carvings in County Donegal. These include the massive, pedimented slab at Fahan Mura, which finds affinities in Pictish sculpture in Scotland, and the cross at Carndonagh—both of which are seen by many as the first tentative steps in the development of the Irish High Cross in stone, because of the comparison of their interlace ornament with that of the *Book of Durrow* and the presence on the Fahan slab of a Greek inscription bearing a doxology approved by the Council of Toledo in 633. But their seventh/eighth-century dating is by no means secure, and, if they were precursors of the High Crosses, their style would not suggest that they had any direct influence on the development of High Crosses farther south.

Located in a county that had close relations with Scotland since the sixth century, they may, rather, represent the reaction of a local school of talented stone-carvers to experiments they had seen being made in the northern half of Britain. The unique figures on White Island in County Fermanagh are another local product, but without any obvious parallels anywhere.

HIGH CROSSES

These Donegal monuments in particular may be reflecting a growing appreciation of the monumentality of stone that begins to become apparent in the decades around 800, as manifested artistically in the rise of High Crosses in the midlands, east, and north of Ireland. Whereas stone crosses, plain or decorated, may well have been erected in Ireland in the eighth century (for which dating evidence is lacking) the first stirrings to-

Cormac's Chapel, Cashel, Co. Tipperary (1127–1134), Irish Romanesque, showing the influence of German and English Romanesque church-building techniques. © SEAN SEXTON COLLECTION/CORBIS. REPRODUCED BY PERMISSION.

ward free-standing stone crosses in the midlands are found around 800 in the area around Clonmacnoise, where pillars and the Bealin cross are decorated with horsemen and lions that may be paying deference to the reigning Pope Leo III (795–816). The same feeling of stylization found there is also reflected in the joyfully graphic (and probably only marginally later) carvings on the cross at Moone, Co. Kildare. Standing in strong contrast with it are the "classic" High Crosses with scriptural panels at places like Clonmacnoise and Durrow, Co. Offaly, Kells, Co. Meath, and Monasterboice, Co. Louth, where the figures—unlike much of early Irish art—are shown in a naturalistic, if somewhat squat fashion, suggesting influence coming ultimately from late antique and early medieval Rome. These Irish crosses comprise the largest corpus of biblical sculpture in Europe for the last quarter of the first millennium, and the composition of their biblical scenes is frequently comparable to those of continental frescoes, both Carolingian and earlier, suggesting that the High Crosses (which were probably painted originally, though no traces of color survive) may have served the same pious, devotional function as frescoes. Late-twentieth-century readings of fragmentary inscriptions on some crosses reveal an unexpected political dimension in that the crosses were commissioned by, or with the aid of, two high kings who were members of the Clann Cholmáin

branch of the southern Uí Néill dynasty—Maelsechnaill I (846–862) and his son Flann Sinna (879–916). Lack of similar patronage may have been a cause of the discontinuation of such crosses later in the tenth century. Although Viking looting of prototype metal crosses could conceivably have been a factor in the creation of these nonremovable High Crosses in the earlier ninth century, it is open to debate as to whether Viking raids could also have been responsible for the increasing simplification of design on metalwork and in the few surviving illuminated manuscripts as the century progressed, or whether both of these media were unable to keep up with the impossibly high standards of the previous century.

ARCHITECTURE

However, the Viking incursions may well have contributed to one important architectural development that corresponds to the idea of an increasing realization of the monumentality of stone around 800, and that is the initial stages of changing from wood to stone in the building of ecclesiastical structures to counteract Viking (and Irish!) arsonists. As with the houses of the affluent for many centuries to come, almost all churches in the first four centuries of Christianity in Ireland were built of wood. A contemporary description exists of an important and perhaps sizeable seventh-century church in Kildare, and wooden churches continued to be built up to the twelfth century. Although a few churches may have been built in stone before 800, it is only in the ninth century that references to them begin to become more common in the Irish annals. Mortar datings suggest that some of the earliest surviving church structures are oratory shrines, such as Teampull Chiaráin at Clonmacnoise or Teampull Molaise on Inishmurray, Co. Sligo, and such buildings may have come into being because earlier wooden shrines protecting the relics of the founding saint would have become too easy a prey for Viking firebrands.

THE ROMANESQUE STYLE

Simple Irish stone churches, and even the tenth-century cathedral at Clonmacnoise, probably copied their wooden forebears in style and scale with, typically, the side walls projecting out beyond the gables. But they atrophied in this state until the advent of the Romanesque in Ireland early in the twelfth century as an expression of church reform in Munster, best exemplified in Cormac's Chapel on the Rock of Cashel. So startling were its innovations that details were copied in other churches, but not its overall concept. It may have been preceded by more humble churches decorated in the Romanesque style, much influenced by England, which continued in the decoration of doorways and chancel arches of small nave-and-chancel churches up to the end of the twelfth century, and even into the early thirteenth century west of the Shannon. Similar ornament was also applied to Round Towers at Timahoe, Co. Laois, and Devenish, Co. Fermanagh, though the genre had been common on Irish monastic sites since the mid-tenth century. The awakening delight in carving decoration on stone churches in Romanesque style during the twelfth century was accompanied by a revival of interest in High Crosses, but now with a very different form, where biblical scenes retreat in favor of high relief figures of Christ and an ecclesiastic. Manuscripts, too, became bearers of a rich and colorful decoration of reds and blues using new variations of animal ornament with a Scandinavian flavor, which was also found to brilliant effect on some of the metalwork shrines of the period, such as that of Saint Lachtin's arm, or Saint Manchan's reliquary in Boher, Co. Offaly.

The twelfth century proved to be a pivotal one for Ireland. The new church reform that had started the century drained the life-blood of many of the old Irish monasteries that had been the fosterers of arts and crafts for many hundreds of years, bringing about the gradual decline of their culture that had managed for so long to set Irish art apart from that of the rest of Europe. Instead, Ireland lost much (though not all) of its artistic individuality and vigor, but it came into the mainstream of European architecture through the two major new arrivals during the twelfth century—the Cistercians and the Normans. The former, followed in the thirteenth century by other monastic orders such as the Franciscans and Dominicans, brought in a new architectural style for their churches that dwarfed and differed from the simple nave-and-chancel churches built by the Irish prior to 1200. These were larger churches, taller, with nave aisles and transepts, and standing on one side of a quadrangular cloister with monastic quarters attached—a total transplant from the Cistercian motherhouses in France, which were to set the tone for two centuries of Irish church building. Most of them respected Cistercian simplicity in ornamentation, though the Irish as opposed to the Norman houses of the order could not resist decoration, and the naturalistic plant capitals at Corcomroe, Co. Clare, of about 1200, were already anticipating developments that took place later elsewhere in Europe.

THE GOTHIC STYLE AND THE NORMANS

At first, the Cistercian Irish churches such as those at Mellifont, Co. Louth, and Baltinglass, Co. Wicklow, were Romanesque in style, but they were responsible for introducing the Gothic arch into Irish churches be-

fore the end of the twelfth century. The new style was, however, also encouraged by the new Norman arrivals in the cathedrals they completed in Dublin, Kilkenny, and elsewhere. But being more warriors than churchmen, they are best known for their castles with which they staked a fortified claim to the lands that they had conquered speedily from the Irish. None of the Irish twelfth-century castles known from historical sources survive, so that the oldest existing castles are Norman, of which the most notable are those with central keeps at Trim, Co. Meath (begun in the 1170s), and Carrickfergus, Co. Antrim, started scarcely a decade later. Some were in towns (e.g., Nenagh, Co. Tipperary, and Limerick), while others used imposing sites in the countryside (e.g., Castleroche, Co. Louth), and they display various ground plans, of which the most typically Irish is the rectangular keep with rounded turret at each corner, as exemplified in the ruined examples at Ferns, Co. Wexford, and Carlow town. By the end of the thirteenth century the Norman castles in Ireland were sometimes even ahead of their British counterparts in the development of new defensive techniques. By that stage, too, the Normans had long been ornamenting the tombs of their dead with carved effigies of knights, ladies, laymen, and ecclesiastics, which generally aped styles in England, though the Irish nobility occasionally aped themselves in turn (e.g., at Roscommon).

But all of this thriving activity came to an abrupt end with the Black Death of 1348 to 1350. It took fifty years for architecture to recover, and then it was not the Normans but the Franciscans, particularly in the western half of Ireland, who revived monastic architecture and occasionally sculpture in ways that created a new Irish contribution to the architecture of Europe, as there are few adequate parallels elsewhere to these long-halled churches with off-center towers and adjoining two-story cloisters. Carvings in Ennis friary of about 1470 show the skill of Irish stonemasons in adapting successfully to foreign models in the form of English alabasters or continental *Pietàs*. Irish woodcarvers were also able to reproduce competent religious statuary, usually adapting styles current elsewhere, and the O'Dea mitre and gold crozier of 1418 (now on display in the Hunt Museum in Limerick) are among the few late medieval masterworks to have survived the Reformation. They, along with the wooden misericords in the same city's cathedral, show what talent was available, of which so little is known.

The quality of carving in the west of Ireland was, however, also manifest in the eastern parts of the country, where the Plunkett family in Meath set up their tombs bearing armored knights and their ladies in the second half of the fifteenth century, but now supported by "weeper figures." The same family began erecting wayside crosses, thereby initiating a custom that was to last for centuries, though cities such as Dublin and Kilkenny had already long had their market crosses. The Butlers of Ormond were soon to emulate the Plunketts, and their own workshop—a rival one run by the O'Tunney family produced similar tomb-sculpture best seen in Saint Canice's Cathedral in Kilkenny. The Butlers were also responsible for the imaginative variety of figures on the cloister of the Cistercian abbey at Jerpoint in the same county, and for some of Ireland's finest fifteenth-century stonework at Holy Cross Abbey in County Tipperary.

While the Franciscans and other orders were spreading their friaries throughout the land, the Irish and gaelicized Normans built themselves tower-houses which, though having the reputation of having been sparsely furnished, may sometimes have been decorated with festive frescoes, such as those discovered at Ardamullivan, Co. Galway. These tower-houses were the landowner's status symbol of the time, a family residence unlike the earlier Norman castles that were fortified barracks. Some of the stoutest examples, such as those at Bunratty, Co. Clare, and Blarney, Co. Cork, were built by native chieftains, while the hibernicized Butlers built themselves castles like that at Cahir, Co. Tipperary. Most of the tower-houses were angular towers, but some were round, and the tower was frequently adjoined by a tall bawn wall to protect both livestock and humans. An unusual feature is the addition of a banqueting hall at Malahide Castle and at a number of locations in County Limerick.

THE LATER MIDDLE AGES

Noah's Ark in the Book of Ballymote and the Crucifixion in the Leabhar Breac, both of about 1400 and in the Royal Irish Academy, are among the rare large illustrations in later medieval Irish manuscripts. But in the realm of smaller arts and crafts, what has been handed down to us from the later Middle Ages is probably only a tiny percentage of what once existed, both Norman and Irish. From what little has survived, we can guess that much work of high quality must have perished through time or the Reformation. The visible strengths of the later medieval heritage in Ireland are the buildings—and the sculptures they contain—which are an important Irish addition to the architecture and sculpture of the time. They often remain underestimated because they stand in the shadow of the towering masterpieces of metalwork, manuscript decoration, and High Cross carving in the earlier Middle Ages, which had made Ireland into a very individualistic culture province in the corpus of European art and architecture.

SEE ALSO Architecture, Early and Medieval; Hiberno-Latin Culture; High Crosses; Literature: Early and Medieval Literature; Manuscript Writing and Illumination; Metalwork, Early and Medieval; Middle English Literature; Norman French Literature; Sculpture, Early and Medieval

Bibliography

Alexander, J. J. G. Insular Manuscripts, 6th to the 9th Century. 1978.

Bourke, Cormac, ed. From the Isles of the North: Early Medieval Art in Ireland and Britain. 1995.

Cone, Polly, ed. Treasures of Early Irish Art, 1500 B.C. to 1500 A.D. 1977.

Cosgrove, Art, ed. A New History of Ireland. Vol. 2, Medieval Ireland, 1169–1534. 1987.

Harbison, Peter. The High Crosses of Ireland: An Iconographical and Photographic Survey. 3 vols. 1992.

Harbison, Peter. The Golden Age of Irish Art: The Medieval Achievement, 600–1200. 1999.

Henry, Françoise. Irish Art. 3 vols. 1965–1970.

Henry, Françoise. Studies in Early Christian and Medieval Irish Art. 3 vols. 1983–1985.

Hourihane, Colum, ed. From Ireland Coming. 2001.

Hunt, John. Irish Medieval Figure Sculpture, 1200–1600. 2 vols. 1974.

Leask, Harold G. Irish Castles and Castellated Houses. 1941.

Leask, Harold G. Irish Churches and Monastic Buildings. 3 vols. 1955–1960.

O'Mahony, Felicity, ed. The Book of Kells. Proceedings of a Conference at Trinity College Dublin, 6–9 September 1992. 1994.

Ryan, Michael. Ireland and Insular Art, A.D. 500–1200. 1987.

Ryan, Michael, ed. Treasures of Ireland: Irish Art, 3000 B.C.–1500 A.D. 1983.

Spearman, R. Michael, and John Higgitt, eds. The Age of Migrating Ideas: Early Medieval Art in Northern Britain and Ireland. 1993.

Stalley, Roger. The Cistercian Monasteries of Ireland. 1987.

Stalley, Roger. Ireland and Europe in the Middle Ages: Selected Essays on Architecture and Sculpture. 1994.

Sweetman, David. Medieval Castles of Ireland. 1999.

Werner, Martin. Insular Art: An Annotated Bibliography. 1984.

Youngs, Susan, ed. The Work of Angels: Masterpieces of Celtic Metalwork, 6th–9th centuries A.D. 1989.

Peter Harbison

EARLY MODERN LITERATURE AND THE ARTS FROM 1500 TO 1800

The cultural history of this three-hundred-year epoch can most easily be understood as divided into two periods: between the accession of the Tudors (1485) and the conclusion of Cromwell's campaign (1650), and between the subsequent plantation and the Act of Union (1800). The first of these periods features the gradual destruction of the cultural institutions shared by the Irish and the Anglo-Normans since the thirteenth century, and the second is characterized by the coexistence of the Anglo-Irish colonial culture of Dublin and the remains of Gaelic high culture that dwindled into folk forms.

The period can be summarily described as the time of the forcible uprooting of the intertwined Celtic and Christian civilizations that had been growing for the previous millennium, and the transplanting of Anglo-Saxon and Protestant cultural colonies from England and London into the cleared spaces. The relationship between these two cultural traditions during this epoch may be further divided into three stages: the final efflorescence of Gaelic culture during the seventeenth century (as exemplified by Geoffrey Keating's history and Aogán Ó Rathaille's poetry), the burgeoning of Dublin as a center for all the arts during the eighteenth century (as exemplified by Jonathan Swift's writings and James Gandon's architecture), and toward the end of the same century, the beginnings of a rapprochement between these cultures in the rediscovery by antiquarians and folklorists of the remains of the seemingly vanquished native culture (as exemplified by Charlotte Brooke's *Reliques of Irish Poetry* and Edward Bunting's collection, *The Ancient Music of Ireland*).

ANGLO-IRISH LITERATURE

Irish writing in the English language is called Anglo-Irish literature to distinguish it from classical English literature on the one side and Gaelic literature on the other. The duality in the term *Anglo-Irish* reflects a tension in the changing political climate under which English-language writers functioned between William Molineux's *Case of Ireland . . . Stated* (1698) and Maria Edgeworth's *Castle Rackrent* (1800).

Anglo-Irish writers of this period were typically sons of English officials, educated at Irish Protestant grammar schools and Trinity College, Dublin. They usually migrated to London, the center of the literary life of the time, and soon adopted its view of the world. Thus the major Irish literary figures of the age—Jonathan Swift (1667–1745), Sir Richard Steele (1672–1729), Edmund Burke (1729–1797), and Richard Brinsley Sheridan (1751–1816)—were variously active in British politics. In his *Drapier's Letters* (1724–1725), Swift makes his dramatic contribution to the claim of the Anglo-Irish to political distinctiveness, briefly insti-

tutionalized in the Irish parliament in 1782. Although he was the voice of eighteenth-century Protestant Ireland, he had some personal links with Gaelic Ireland that appear in some of his poetry and vestigially in *Gulliver's Travels* (1726). Burke, on the other hand, while more partial to Catholic Ireland's complaints, expressed himself as a representative of England's global responsibility. Similarly, the essays of Sir Richard Steele and the fiction and poetry of Oliver Goldsmith reveal little of the social origins of these authors. Goldsmith's reputation as the most distinguished poet of Irish birth during the eighteenth century rests on his celebration of rural life in the ambiguously situated *Deserted Village* (1770).

During the sixteenth and seventeenth centuries there was little poetry of any merit in English. Luke Wadding's *Small Garland of Pious and Godly Songs* (1684) exhibits the influence of the English metaphysicals. Similarly, during the eighteenth century Anglo-Irish verse is barely distinguishable from English verse of the times. The satirical *Irish Hudibras* (1689) and Samuel Whyte's "The New Ferry" are full of Graeco-Roman references; William Dunkin's brilliant mock epic *The Murphaeid* (1728) and his "Parson's Revels" show the influence of English Augustinianism, just as James Orr's "The Irishman" demonstrates the sentimentality of many late-century English poems. Eighteenth-century fiction reveals a similar concern with cultural and political identity. Thus, William Chagineau's picaresque novel *History of Jack Connor* (1752), Thomas Amory's Rabelaisian fantasy *The Life of John Buncle* (1756, 1766), and Henry Brooke's sentimental *The Fool of Quality* (1766–1770) are various expressions of the colonial's persistent dilemma: loyal to but estranged from England, yet alien from and fearful of Gaelic Ireland. Again, as in the case of poetry, Goldsmith's genial *Vicar of Wakefield* (1766) and Laurence Sterne's wildly inventive *Tristram Shandy* (1759–1767)—neither of which engages Irish affairs—are the only novels of distinction by Irish-born writers of the eighteenth century.

DRAMA AND THEATER

The short-lived Werburgh Street Theatre (1637–1641) was succeeded by Smock Alley (1662–1786), the first Dublin playhouse to be built after the Restoration, and by Spranger Barry's rival Theatre Royal at Crow Street (1758–1820). The cultural programs of these theaters were exclusively from London: John Fletcher and Thomas Shadwell resided in Dublin for brief periods, and many of the most distinguished dramatists of the period were in fact Irish-born and got their start in the Dublin theater. One could go further and assert that the English comedy of manners from the Restoration to the rise of Romanticism was principally the creation of brilliant Irishmen—George Farquhar, William Congreve, Charles Macklin, Oliver Goldsmith, and Richard Brinsley Sheridan. Farquhar (?1677–1707), author of the blackly humorous *The Beaux' Strategem* (1707), began as a Smock Alley actor. Congreve (1670–1729), author of the Restoration masterpiece *The Way of the World* (1700), was a fellow student of Swift's at Trinity College, Dublin. Macklin (?1697–1797), who moved from Smock Alley to Drury Lane, wrote *Love à la Mode* (1759). These figures were followed by Oliver Goldsmith (1728–1774), author of the laughing comedy *She Stoops to Conquer* (1773), and Richard Brinsley Sheridan, whose many plays include the sensations of the age *The Rivals* (1775) and *The School for Scandal* (1779).

As might be inferred from these names and titles, the eighteenth-century theater was predominantly Protestant and colonial, having its focus on London with its clubs, theaters, and townhouses. The only trace of their Irish roots that these writers betray is their occasional injection of the "stage Irishman" into their dramas. This hard-drinking, sentimental figure, eloquent in his thick brogue, spendthrift but generous, pugnacious though cowardly, unmannerly and illogical, was a stereotype on the English stage for two centuries. The character enabled these dramatists to ingratiate themselves with their London audiences, though some, out of patriotic sentiment, criticized the stereotype.

Not surprisingly, this lively theatrical environment produced many distinguished figures on the eighteenth-century stage: the Shakespearean actor Spranger Barry (1719–1779), Thomas Sheridan (1719–1788), actor and father of Richard Brinsley, and the actresses Peg Woffington (?1718–1760) and her rival, Mrs. Bellamy (1727–1788).

GAELIC LITERATURE

The last phase of the early modern or classical modern period in Gaelic literature (1500–1650) is characterized by the prevalence of a standard literary language maintained by professional poets or scholars called *filidh* in Irish and frequently *bards* in English. Their verse compositions are a large part of the literature of the period, principally praise-poems to their patrons among the aristocracy, but also much religious and personal poetry. Among the more distinguished of this mainly hereditary class were Tadhg Dall Ó hUiginn (1550–1591), Eochaidh Ó hEódhasa (?1560–1612), and, one of the last in the tradition, Fear Flatha Ó Gnímh (?1540–?1630). They also adapted narrative and pious matter from French and English sources, as well as love poetry in the *amour courtois* (courtly love) genre. A major example is the *Betha Colaim Cille* (Life of Saint Colum Cille), commissioned in 1532 by Maghnus Ó Domhnaill, lord of Tyrconnell, which is a stylish compilation of legend, prose, and verse about the patron saint of Donegal.

The early modern period ends with two major syntheses of the record of Gaelic civilization: *Annála Ríoghachta Éireann* (Annals of the kingdom of Ireland), compiled under the supervision of Micheál Ó Cléirigh (?1590–1643), and Seathrún Céitinn's narrative history *Foras Feasa ar Éirinn* (The basis for a knowledge of Ireland). Seathrún Céitinn (Geoffrey Keating, ?1580–1644) was a vindicator of his nation's honor in the face of English colonial interpretation (from Giraldus Cambrensis to Richard Stanihurst) and a master Irish prose stylist. For poetry, the loss of aristocratic patronage and the need for a more popular audience led to the replacement of the classical syllable-count meters by stress-count meters called *amhrán*. The most prominent poets of the period were the Dominican priest Pádraigín Haicéad (?1600–1654), Dáibhí Ó Bruadair (?1625–1698), and perhaps the most accomplished Gaelic poet of any age, Aogán Ó Rathaille (1670–1729).

A major theme of their poetry, shared with *Foras Feasa*, is the lament for a glorious past unappreciated by the thugs around them, whether Irish or Cromwellian, who are deaf to the poetry of Ireland. Even after literary patronage had totally ceased in the eighteenth century, the traditional literary art was maintained by priests, cultured farmers, artisans, and hedge schoolmasters. These classes continued to make and circulate manuscripts, and to compose occasional and personal poems, sermons and pious material, and prose narratives. They were overshadowed in the popular imagination by more rakish and talented figures such as Cathal Buí Mac Giolla Ghunna (?1680–1756) in southeast Ulster, and in the west Munster tradition, Eoghan Rua Ó Súilleabháin (1748–1784). The most celebrated single work from the last century of this tradition is the long satirical poem by the Clare mathematics teacher Brian Merriman (?1745–1805), *Cúirt an Mheán Oíche* (The midnight court), an Augustan parody of the Gaelic *aisling* (poem of vision).

As the number of poets dwindled, they were reduced to beggary. Their works remained in the folk memory, however, and influenced the style of the popular songs that finally replaced their written compositions. The tradition of folk poetry produced the classic lament *Caoineadh Airt Uí Laoire* (Lament for Art O'Leary) by Eibhlín Dubh Ní Chonaill (?1743–?1800). The oral and manuscript traditions preserved the Fionn or Ossianic sagas from the late Middle Ages, inspiring verse and prose compositions into the eighteenth century. An outstanding example is Mícheál Ó Coimín's *Laoi Oisín ar Thír na nÓg* (Oisin's song about the land of youth, 1750), which later inspired Yeats. The Ossianic poems of James Mcpherson (1736–1796), partially drawn from the parallel oral tradition of Gaelic Scotland, stimulated an interest among the Anglo-Irish gentry in the culture of their tenantry. This interest resulted in English translations of Fenian and other poems from hitherto ignored sources, as in Joseph Walker's *Historical Memoirs of the Irish Bards* (1786) and Charlotte Brooke's *Reliques of Irish Poetry* (1789).

ARCHITECTURE

The rebellions and plantations of the seventeenth century resulted in the change of ownership of land and wealth and the destruction of much of the previously accumulated architectural capital. These uncivil circumstances required designers to accommodate the primary needs of defense. The most distinctive pattern found among the planters, especially in the North, therefore, was the tower house and bawn, a four-story stone dwelling surrounded by a fortified enclosure. Nearly three thousand of these were built by the rising gentry between 1400 and 1650. It was only after 1660 that nonfortified domestic houses were built in town and country, the finest surviving examples of which are Rothe House in Kilkenny city and the Anglo-Dutch Beaulieu in County Louth. Meanwhile, the vast majority of the Irish people lived in stone or clay cottages, a type that remained unchanged into the twentieth century.

The period of the Restoration in England and the arrival in 1662 of the Duke of Ormond as viceroy marked the beginning of one of the greatest ages in the history of Irish civilization. The last decades of the seventeenth century saw the rise of buildings in Dublin and elsewhere in the new classical style. The first such public building was the Royal Hospital, Kilmainham, in Dublin. Designed by Sir William Robinson and built between 1680 and 1684, it was a home for retired soldiers modeled on *Les Invalides* in Paris.

During the first quarter of the eighteenth century Palladian architecture, which aimed at a strict reading of classical convention, appeared in Ireland. Many of the larger country houses of the period, such as Castletown (1722–1732) and Russborough (1742), reflect the style. Its leading practitioner was Edward Lovett Pearce, whose Parliament House (1729) was one of the first large-scale Palladian buildings in Ireland. The German architect Richard Castle designed several Palladian mansions during this period: Leinster House (1745), the Rotunda Hospital (1751), and country houses at Westport, Powerscourt, and Carton.

The prosperity of Anglo-Ireland after 1750 allowed for the dramatic expansion of Dublin, provincial cities, and market towns. This prosperity enabled architects of style and vision to execute works of permanent distinction. At this point, Palladian style gave way to neoclassicism, looking directly to ancient Rome for inspiration. One of the earliest buildings in this style was Thomas Cooley's Royal Exchange (1770s). The great architect of this period was James Gandon (1742–1823). He designed some of the most beautiful public buildings in Dublin, including the Custom House and the Four Courts (1780s), each with a columned riverside facade and topped with a magnificent dome. Among Irish-born architects of the period, Thomas Ivory, Francis Johnston, and Richard Morrison were the most distinguished. Johnston designed many Irish Georgian castles, the General Post Office, and Nelson's Pillar. These works brought the classical tradition in Irish architecture to a close.

Plasterwork was practiced from at least the sixteenth century in Ireland, where new styles introduced by foreign stuccadores were adopted by native craftsmen. The Italian Francini brothers arrived in Ireland around 1735, bringing with them an international late baroque style. Much of their work is characterized by large-scale figure sculpture, fruit, and foliage, in complete departure from the preceding native style. They worked in some of the greatest houses of eighteenth-century Ireland, including the salon at Carton House, Co. Kildare. They were succeeded in the 1750s by the native plasterworker Robert West and later by Michael Stapelton, who returned to a sparer classical style.

The second half of the eighteenth century saw a new interest in town planning, particularly in the cities of Dublin, Cork, and Limerick, where wide streets and residential and market squares and diamonds were created. Elegant townhouses were erected, many decorated with fanlights over their doorways and fine plasterwork interiors. Led by local landlords, commissioners planned many smaller estate towns with visas, tree-lined walks, or village greens. The growing discontent of Catholics, increasing sectarian tensions, the1798 rebellion, and the Act of Union brought this period of prosperity to an abrupt end.

ART

John Derricke's *Image of Irelande* (1581)—a famous set of twelve woodcuts of events during the rule of Sir Henry Sidney—is one of the first visual records of Irish life and landscape. These colonial images are a dramatic indication of a seismic shift: The dissolution of the monasteries, for a millennium the principal patrons of the visual arts in Ireland, had occurred some sixty years before. Art became a Protestant preserve. At first, guilds

James Barry, Self-Portrait as Timarthes *(1803 or 1804), an Irish historical painting in the neoclassical style.* NATIONAL GALLERY OF IRELAND, CAT. NO. 971. REPRODUCED BY PERMISSION.

of urban craftworkers emerged, influenced by England and continental Europe to serve the new order and its ruling class, who sought images of itself from painters and sculptors. Thus, by the mid-seventeenth century the decorative arts of goldsmithery, plasterwork, silver, glass, and furniture flourished under the auspices of such guilds as the Goldsmiths' Company of Dublin. As easel painting replaced tapestry and wall painting, family pride rather than aesthetic interest dictated that early paintings were either portraits or maps. A "painters guild," formed in 1670, included in its number such artists as Garrett Morphey (fl. 1680–1716) and James Latham (1696–1747), whose styles derived from contemporary Dutch painters. Morphey was the first Irish painter of quality, and Latham was the best and most influential portrait painter in the first half of the eighteenth century (his most famous work depicted Bishop Berkeley). Other subsequent notable portrait painters were Charles Jervas (?1675–1739), portraitist of Swift and principal painter to the king in 1723, Nathaniel Hone (1718–1784), the fine miniaturist Horace Hone (1756–1825), and Robert Healy (fl.1765–71), whose masterpiece is the group portrait of the Connolly family at Casteltown House (1768).

The foundation of the Dublin Society (1731) for the purpose of "improving husbandry, manufacture, and the useful arts and sciences" and the foundation of its art schools in the mid-1740s mark a great advance in artistic life in Ireland: For the first time, there was professional training for portrait and landscape painters, sculptors, silversmiths, stuccodores, and so on. Consequently, the third quarter of the century was the greatest period for the visual arts since the Middle Ages. Although heavily inflected by other cultures, a distinctive Irish style, seen in the applied arts such as stucco, silver, and furniture, appeared in the 1760s and 1770s. Simultaneously, artists and intellectuals debated one of the century's most influential works on aesthetics, Edmund Burke's *A Philosophical Enquiry into the Origin of Our Ideas of the Sublime and the Beautiful* (1756). Two major figures of the period, the landscape artist George Barret (1732–1784) and historical painter James Barry (1741–1806), were both protégés of Burke. Expressing the excitement of pain or danger (the sublime) or love (the beautiful), the subject matter of painting broadened to include historical and some landscape work, often with classical or mythological allusions.

The precedents for the landscape tradition were the occasional watercolors accompanying mapmaking and some unknown primitives in the 1740s (e.g., at Stradbally and Westport House). Significant examples in this genre are the widely influential landscapes of the Dutchman William Van der Hagen (d. 1745), the illustrations of Waterford and Cork by Anthony Chearnley (fl. 1740–1785), the topographical views of Gabrielle Ricciardelli (fl. 1748–1777), the landscapes of Susannah Drury (fl. 1733–1770), "Powerscourt Waterfall" by George Barret, the brilliant and influential lakes and mountains of Thomas Roberts (1748–1778), and the cultivated scenery of William Ashford (1746–1824). A truly indigenous and rich Irish landscape style was thus developed by a group of painters who thrived on the robust commercial movement between Dublin, Cork, and London; the leading figures of this group were George Mullins (fl.1763–1775) and Nathaniel Grogan (1740–1807). Of particular historical note for his major canvasses on contemporary Irish affairs (1779–1783) is Francis Wheatley (1747–1801). His example encouraged the engravers Thomas Malton and Jonathan Fisher, the products of a school of engravers that had been established between 1730 and 1750. Thomas Malton's *Views of Dublin* (1793) are the finest ever done, and Jonathan Fisher's *Scenery of Ireland* (1796) were immensely popular.

Irish delftware was manufactured in Belfast from the seventeenth century, in Dublin from the early eighteenth century, and subsequently in Limerick and

Rostrevor, Co. Down. Thomas Frye (1710–1762) founded a Bow porcelain factory in Dublin, and the most distinguished maker in mid-century was Henry Delamain, whose designs parallel those of Chinese, Dutch, and English examples. The ancient craft of silverware was revived with the establishment of the Dublin Goldsmiths' Company in 1637, and it thrived to the end of the eighteenth century. Similarly, Irish furniture-making was closely allied in style to English fashions. For a brief period (1735–1775), however, it was distinctive: It was made of very dark mahogany and heavily carved. It was subsequently replaced by straight lines and inlaid satinwood after the Adam fashion. Lead glass-making dates from 1690; it flourished in Belfast, Cork, and Waterford until 1825, when new taxes killed it.

Music

As with the other native arts, the Flight of the Earls in 1607 meant the demise of the patronage upon which professional Gaelic musicians depended. Nevertheless, an impoverished remnant of the class of harpers and composers continued to the end of the eighteenth century. The most distinguished of these was the blind harper, composer, and poet Toirdhealbhach Ó Cearbhalláin (Turlough Carolan, 1670–1738). Patronized equally by those of native and planter stock, his songs, dance tunes, laments, and religious pieces drew on native tradition as well as the on European baroque composers Vivaldi, Corelli, and Geminiani.

Shortly after Carolan's death, collections of Irish music began to appear in print, but none had greater scope or impact on Anglo Ireland than Edward Bunting's *General Collection of the Ancient Music of Ireland* (3 vols., 1796, 1809, 1840). This collection began with Bunting's transcriptions from the Belfast Harp Festival (1792), where he heard from the surviving exponents of an ancient performance tradition, ten aged men. The massive work documented the centrality of music to Gaelic culture, its poetry, dance, and antiquities, and provided the airs for the famous *Irish Melodies* (10 volumes, 1808–1834) to which Thomas Moore matched his patriotic verses. Thousands of popular songs in Irish that were not collected remained in use by the common people, conveying into the eighteenth century some of the formal qualities of classic Gaelic poetry. But as the use of the language declined, street ballads in English replaced them. These ballads celebrated political and topical issues—such as the 1798 rebellion—and were set to traditional airs, exhibiting some of the verbal decorations of Gaelic verse. Meanwhile, the traditional dances—jigs, reels, and hornpipes—were more formally arranged after 1750.

On the other side of the cultural divide, the aristocracy of the Pale cultivated a taste for continental musical culture. Ballad operas and oratorios were especially popular, drawing on the resident choirs of Saint Patrick's and Christ Church cathedrals. This hospitable climate drew George Frideric Handel for an extended visit in 1741 and 1742, leading to the celebrated premiere of the *Messiah* on 13 April 1742 in the Fishamble Street music hall.

SEE ALSO Carolan, Turlough; Country Houses and the Arts; English Writing on Ireland before 1800; Georgian Dublin, Art and Architecture of; Hiberno-English; Literacy and Popular Culture; Literature: Anglo-Irish Literary Tradition, Beginnings of; Literature: Early Modern Literature before the Stuarts (1500–1603); Literature: Gaelic Writing from 1607 to 1800; Music: Early Modern Music; Swift, Jonathan

Bibliography

Craig, Maurice. *The Architecture of Ireland.* 1982.

Deane, Seamus, et al., eds. *The Field Day Anthology of Irish Writing.* Vol. 1. 1991.

Flood, W. H. Grattan. *A History of Irish Music.* 1905.

Kiberd, Declan. *Irish Classics.* 2000.

McHugh, Roger, and Maurice Harmon. *A Short History of Anglo-Irish Literature.* 1982.

Potterton, Homan. "The Seventeenth and Eighteenth Centuries." In *Irish Art and Architecture: From Prehistory to the Present,* edited by Peter Harbison, Homan Potterton, and Jeanne Sheehy. 1978.

Cóilín Owens

MODERN IRISH AND ANGLO-IRISH LITERATURE AND THE ARTS SINCE 1800

The nineteenth century opened with the members of the Irish parliament voting themselves out of existence by their approval of the Act of Union. Just two years before, the 1798 Rebellion ended with the bitter defeat of the insurgents and great bloodshed. The mood of the country and its distressed state did not seem conducive to the production of a lively literature. Nevertheless, notable work was produced and the seeds sown that would lead to a great flowering in the twentieth century. The first important figure to emerge was Thomas Moore, who published his *Irish Melodies* between 1807 and 1834. Although his lyrics are sentimental, they took on great power when sung to native airs, and became enormously popular in England and Ireland. For the English, Moore's *Melodies* were an introduction to Irish Celtic culture which prepared them for what would follow throughout the century. These melodies also became the most popular musical items of the century. Samuel Ferguson produced the century's most important work in translation in such works as *Lays of the Western Gael* and *Lays of the Red Branch*, which introduced readers to the rich poetic tradition in Irish poetry and mythology, and which had much to do with rebuilding a sense of identity that had been lost and diluted through the deprivations of the previous centuries. Thomas Davis was a founder of the *Nation* newspaper in 1842, the organ of the Young Ireland movement, though his greatest legacy has been the political ballad, first published in book form in 1843, and reprinted regularly throughout the century. Another contributor to the *Nation* was James Clarence Mangan, author of "Dark Rosaleen," one of the most famous of all Irish poems. Although Mangan knew little Irish, he was able, with the help of translations, to treat of ancient Irish themes and in this way continue the cultural revival and forward notions of national awareness. Many have considered Mangan to be the Irish Poe by virtue of his decadent work, his addictions, and his early death.

NINETEENTH-CENTURY LITERATURE AND THE ARTS

The first—and to some readers the best—Irish novel of the century, was Maria Edgeworth's *Castle Rackrent*, published in 1800. Here, using the voice of Thady, a simpleton narrator, we are shown how the fortunes of the estate-owning Rackrents have been dissipated through four generations of mismanagement. One of Edgeworth's main objectives in her work as a whole is to provide a blueprint for the improvement of the landlord class in Ireland. Time and time again, she urges absentee landlords to return to their estates from London and learn how to manage them properly, a message she conveyed most effectively in *Ennui* and *The Absentee*. Another well-known novelist and a contemporary of Edgeworth's was Lady Morgan, the author of such historical romances as *The O'Briens and the O'Flaherty's*. The first of the great Irish Gothic novelists of the century was Charles Robert Maturin, the author of *Melmoth the Wanderer* and other novels, and he was followed by Joseph Sheridan le Fanu, whose best-known novel is *Uncle Silas*, and by Bram Stoker, whose *Dracula* remains the most revered work in the genre. Nearly all of these Gothic novels are set in the decaying Big Houses of the Protestant Ascendancy whose decay allows for the emergence of deranged souls to fill the vacuum. Appear-

ing at the end of the century was Oscar Wilde's *The Picture of Dorian Gray*, a remarkable Gothic novel by an Irish writer using an English setting. William Carleton is the author of *Traits and Stories of the Irish Peasantry* (1830–33), in which he provides the most honest and sympathetic portrayal of rural Irish life during the early part of the century. Other notable figures are Gerald Griffin, whose most important work is *The Collegians* (a novel that was granted a second life when it was dramatized as *The Colleen Bawn* by Dion Boucicault in 1860), and John and Michael Banim, who wrote *Tales of the O'Hara Family*.

Many important developments occurred in the final years of the nineteenth century that set the literary agenda for the following century. The Gaelic League was founded in 1893, an organization whose purpose was the promotion of Irish language and culture. One of its guiding spirits was Douglas Hyde, who would eventually become the first Irish president, and it was his belief that Ireland needed to be de-anglicized in order for it to assume an identity separate from England. Hyde was also the collector and translator of the *Love Songs of Connacht*, a popular and important contribution to the literature of the time. Yeats was a prime mover in the founding of the National Literary Society in Dublin in 1892, which, in turn, led to the founding of the Irish National Theatre Society in 1902 and the Abbey Theatre in 1904. A decade that had begun with the fall and death of the Home Rule leader Charles Stewart Parnell in 1891, and the gloom and division that followed, closed with a great degree of forward movement on the cultural and literary front. At the same time as important work was being produced in Ireland, Irish writers resident in England continued to be prominent. Oscar Wilde's plays *Lady Windermere's Fan*, *A Woman of No Importance*, and *The Importance of Being Earnest* were written and performed with great success, and George Bernard Shaw, who had begun to take a central place in London' cultural and political life, published his volume *Plays Pleasant and Unpleasant*.

As a result of the mid-century potato famine, emigration, and continuing efforts to suppress it, the Irish language was not spoken as widely throughout Ireland at the end of the nineteenth century as it was at the beginning. Nevertheless, some notable writers made their marks. Brian Merriman, author of *Cúirt an Mheán Oíche* (The midnight court), the great burlesque poem, lived until 1803. Antaine Raiftearaí wrote many poems, the most famous being the short lyric, "Mise Raiftearaí" (I am Raiftearaí). The most important nineteenth-century painters are Daniel Maclise and William Mulready. Maclise is best known for his large narrative paintings, most notably *The Marriage of Aoife and Strongbow*, while

Daniel Maclise, The Marriage of Aoife and Strongbow, *shown in 1854, an example of Irish Romantic painting dealing with historical subject matter.* NATIONAL GALLERY OF IRELAND, CAT. NO. 205. REPRODUCED BY PERMISSION.

Mulready's best work is to be found in such small scale narratives as "The Last In."

TWENTIETH-CENTURY LITERATURE AND THE ARTS

In twentieth-century Irish literature certain important themes recur and are explored, defined, and refined in poetry, fiction, and drama. Irish writers have continued to focus on their relation to place, politics, history, the private world, and those points where the public and the private collide. The early agenda is set by William Butler Yeats, whose figure and achievement continues to cast a large shadow over the enterprise. The principal concerns present in Yeats's work are Irish mythology, Ireland of the revolutionary and postrevolutionary periods with its attendant heroes and villains, and the poet's preoccupations with love, mortality, and his search for immortality through mysticism and art. Although his work is compelling throughout his career, his greatest achievements as a poet are to be found in the second half of his career in such landmark poems as "Easter 1916," his poem about the Easter Rising; "The Wild Swans at Coole," a vision of rural paradise; and "Sailing to Byzan-

tium," a profound meditation on aging and the quest for immortality. Throughout his life as a writer, Yeats continued to produce drama for the Abbey Theatre, most notably *At the Hawk's Well*, *The Words upon the Window-Pane*, and *Purgatory*. He continued to take a leadership role in the Abbey Theatre and was instrumental in seeing many great Irish plays performed at the theatre in the early part of the century. Of particular importance are Lady Gregory's *Cuchulain of Muirthemne*, J. M. Synge's *The Well of the Saints* and *The Playboy of the Western World* (the latter causing some patrons to riot because they felt Synge had insulted Irish womanhood) and Sean O'Casey's *The Shadow of a Gunman* and *The Plough and the Stars*. Yeats was awarded the Nobel Prize for Literature in 1923. A contemporary of Yeats's was George Moore, whose memoir *Hail and Farewell* provides an entertaining account of Irish cultural life in the early part of the century, and who also wrote *The Untilled Field*, an important collection of short fiction.

James Joyce, in common with his younger disciple, Samuel Beckett, spent most of his adult life outside Ireland. His most important works are *Dubliners*, a collection of short fiction, and his novels: *A Portrait of the*

Artist as a Young Man, *Ulysses*, and *Finnegans Wake*. Beckett is best known for *Waiting for Godot*, his absurdist play, and for *Molloy*, *Malone Dies*, and *The Unnamable*, his trilogy of novels. Even though both Joyce and Beckett were considered major innovators internationally, they were slow to be accepted by Irish critics and readers. Another important disciple of Joyce is Flann O'Brien, the author of the comic novels *At-Swim Two Birds* and *The Third Policeman*. O'Brien wrote in both English and Irish, and his novel *An Béal Bocht* (*The Poor Mouth*) along with Máirtín Ó Cadhain's *Cré na Cille* (*Graveyard Clay*) are the two most important works of fiction written in the Irish language during the first half of the century.

The middle period of twentieth-century Irish poetry is dominated by Austin Clarke, Louis MacNeice, and Patrick Kavanagh. Clarke is best known for his long poems *Mnemosyne Lay in Dust* and *Tiresias*, and for the short, often pointed lyrics which comprise the major part of his *Selected Poems*. Louis MacNeice was born in Belfast, educated in England, and spent much of his adult life in London. He wrote many memorable Irish poems, the most famous being "Carrickfergus," an autobiographical account of his Ulster upbringing. Patrick Kavanagh, born and raised on a farm in County Monaghan, is the most important poet of this period, and his work has had an enormous influence on many of the poets who were to follow him, Seamus Heaney and Eavan Boland in particular. In his long poems, *The Great Hunger* and *Lough Derg*, Kavanagh shows that the romantic version of rural life presented by Yeats does not match reality. The rural world, in Kavanagh's view, is dominated by various hungers: social, intellectual, sexual, and economic. Toward the end of his life, Kavanagh produced his great lyric poems: "Canal Bank Walk," "Lines Written on a Seat on the Grand Canal, Dublin . . . ," and "The Hospital." Other notable poets of the period include the trio of modernists, Denis Devlin, Thomas MacGreevy, and Brian Coffey, as well as the two most prominent Irish language poets, Máirtín Ó Direáin and Seán Ó Ríordáin. Much of the best fiction during the period is in the short story, and the most prominent figures in this genre are Sean O'Faolain, author of *Midsummer Night Madness and Other Stories*; Frank O'Connor, who wrote *Guests of the Nation*; and Mary Lavin, author of *Tales from Bective Bridge*. Also important is Elizabeth Bowen, who wrote *The Last September*, one of the best of the Big House novels, and the trio of James Stephens, Mervyn Wall, and Eimar O'Duffy, all of whom wrote Irish-based fantasies.

In the 1950s a new generation of writers emerged who finally brought Irish writing out from under the shadow of Yeats, Synge, and Joyce and provided it with new energy. The poets sought to explore and define a new, more prosperous and outgoing Ireland that had begun to replace the isolation of the post-independence nation. Their work has remained thematically innovative and formally daring. In *The Rough Field*, John Montague provides the first extended poetic meditation on the role of history and place in the developing "Troubles" in the North of Ireland, while in *The Dead Kingdom*, he explores the lives of those Irish who became lost in America as part of the Irish diaspora. Thomas Kinsella, a more hermetic poet than Montague, has explored the realm of loss of language and one's place in the world. James Liddy is the most exuberant poet of this generation. His work is influenced primarily by that of the American Beat Generation, and it is through his work that the beat influence was introduced into Irish poetry. The poet Richard Murphy is primarily associated with the west of Ireland, County Galway in particular, and is notable for his exploration of the natural world and the lives of fishermen. Another notable poet of this generation is Pearse Hutchinson, whose work, written in both English and Irish, explores the lives of ordinary people, in particular the urban dispossessed.

The fiction produced by the writers who began publishing in the 1950s is similarly rich. Brian Moore's most acclaimed works are his early Belfast novels, *The Lonely Passion of Judith Hearne* and *The Emperor of Ice Cream*. A significant amount of Moore's work is set outside of Ireland, reflective of the fact that he spent most of his adult life in Canada and the United States, and of a new direction among Irish fiction writers. John McGahern is well known as both a novelist and short-story writer whose best work is *Amongst Women* and *High Ground*. William Trevor has written many novels and collections of short fiction, although his most acclaimed work remains *The Ballroom of Romance*, whose title story is an important exploration of loneliness and sexual longing in rural Ireland. Aidan Higgins has written many volumes of fiction and memoirs, the best of which is his first novel, *Langrishe, Go Down*, an exploration of the Big House on the verge of collapse. Edna O'Brien has been the most controversial writer of this generation. *The Country Girls*, her first novel, banned by the state censor and burned in her local village, became in time a trilogy of groundbreaking work that explores the inner lives and aspirations of women. In drama, the dominant figures are Brian Friel, author of many important plays, the best known of which are *Philadelphia Here I Come*, *Translations*, and *Dancing at Lughnasa*, and Tom Murphy, who wrote *The Morning After Optimism* and *Bailegangaire*. Throughout the century the Abbey has remained the dominant Irish theater, although it has often been challenged by the Gate, and by Galway's Druid Theatre.

The 1960s saw the resumption of the "Troubles" in the North of Ireland as well as the emergence of an important group of poets who have dominated Irish poetry since their inception. The best known of these poets is Seamus Heaney, recipient of the Nobel Prize for Literature in 1995. Heaney, born at Mossbawn, about thirty miles northwest of Belfast, has produced a remarkable body of varied work over the last thirty years. Although the political turmoil of Northern Ireland has an important place in his poetry, the work has not been overwhelmed by it. Heaney examines the points of intersection between the natural and human worlds. By contrast, Derek Mahon's complex, elegant, and highly structured work notes the loss of order in the contemporary world. Michael Longley's poetry is classical in tone and influence. He gazes at Belfast through the prism of classical literature and philosophy to help define the city, its people and its predicaments.

In the last two decades of the twentieth century a new second wave of poets from the North has emerged. The most prominent figures in this group are Paul Muldoon, Ciaran Carson, Medbh McGuckian, Tom Paulin, and Frank Ormsby. Muldoon's work, centered both on Ireland, where he grew up, and on the United States, where he lives now, ranges wide in themes, forms, and attitudes, and provides his readers with an ironic and postmodern view of the Irish experience. Ciaran Carson's best-known book is *Belfast Confetti*, a volume of narrative verse whose purpose is to reveal the vital essences of contemporary Belfast. Medbh McGuckian's work is sometimes considered difficult, even inscrutable by readers. In her luminous poetry, she reveals the interiors of experience. In recent times important works of fiction have also emerged from the North of Ireland, the most important of which are Robert MacLiam Wilson's *Ripley Bogle* and *Eureka Street*, and Deirdre Madden's *Remembering Light and Stone*.

An important development in Irish poetry from the 1980s to the present is the appearance of a brilliant generation of women poets. Until recently, women poets felt excluded and marginalized in the Irish literary world. To date, the most important figure, as both writer and influence, is Eavan Boland. She has articulated the struggles that she faced as a young woman, mother, and poet in her volume of memoirs, *Object Lessons: The Life of the Woman and the Poet in Her Time*, and in many of her poems. Nuala Ní Dhomhnaill has published a number of important volumes, including *The Astrakhan Cloak*, in which Irish mythology is wedded to an original feminist outlook to produce a new Irish poetic vision. Ní Dhomhnaill writes in Irish, and her success has given fresh impetus to other contemporary Irish-language poets, such as Michael Davitt, Louis de Paor,

and Cathal Ó Searcaigh, all of whom have published distinguished recent works. Mary O'Malley, in such volumes as *The Knife in the Wave* and *Asylum Road*, also introduces mythology into her work. In addition, her explorations of the west of Ireland are important and constitute the first sustained feminist interpretation of the western landscape. In Paula Meehan's work, in addition to many fine poems of love and family, ordinary Dubliners are given a voice. Other recently important women poets include Mary O'Donnell, Rita Ann Higgins, Sara Berkeley, and Moya Cannon. Besides the work produced by women, much important poetry has been published by Theo Dorgan, Tony Curtis, Greg Delanty, Sean Lysaght, Gerard Donovan, Dennis O'Driscoll, Michael Coady, and Pat Boran.

The contemporary theater continues to be dominated by Friel and Murphy, with the most important new talents being Sebastian Barry (*The Steward of Christendom*), Marina Carr (*The Mai*), and Conor McPherson (*The Weir*). Younger Irish fiction writers have found great international success. Roddy Doyle was the first Irish writer to be awarded the prestigious Booker Prize, in 1993, for *Paddy Clarke Ha Ha Ha*, and his *Barrytown Trilogy* has been widely read. Patrick McCabe has found great success, both in literature and film, with *The Butcher Boy*, a gruesome tale of rural deprivation and madness. Similarly gruesome and equally impressive is John Banville's *The Book of Evidence*. Colm Tóibín's best-known novel is *The Heather Blazing*, an exploration of how the political and personal could collide in modern Ireland. Colum McCann's novels *Songdogs* and *This Side of Brightness* are notable for their lyricism and range; McCann views the Irish experience as local, global, and multi-ethnic. Such issues are also explored by Philip Casey in *The Bann River Trilogy*.

Although Ireland is most renowned for its contribution to twentieth-century literature, many notable artists of distinction have also emerged to enrich the other arts. During the period of the Literary Revival, painting was dominated by Nathaniel Hone, Roderic O'Conor, Walter Osborne, Sir William Orpen, Sir John Lavery, and John B. Yeats, whose work was diversely focused on landscape, historical themes, and portrait painting. The most important of the modern painters, Jack B. Yeats, brother of the poet, was able to produce important figurative and landscape painting, and, later in his life, brilliant abstract work. From the 1950s to the present, the best-known visual artists have been Barrie Cooke, Louis de Brocquy, Mainie Jellett, Robert Ballagh, Norah McGuinness, Derek Hill, Camille Souter, and Kathy Prendergast. The founding of Comhaltas Ceoltóirí Éireann in 1951 to encourage the development and promotion of traditional music and arts and to train young people, provided a great boost to traditional music. In the following year the first Fleadh Cheoil festival of traditional music brought musicians together from all over the world. Since the 1950s, Irish traditional music has become popular worldwide. Ireland has also made highly important contributions to popular music, notably though the work of U2 and Van Morrison. From the 1980s to the present, Irish film directors have made many remarkable films, most notably Jim Sheridan's *The Field* and *In the Name of the Father*, and Neil Jordan's *The Crying Game* and *Michael Collins*.

SEE ALSO Antiquarianism; Arts: Early Modern Literature and the Arts from 1500 to 1800; Beckett, Samuel; Blasket Island Writers; Drama, Modern; Fiction, Modern; Gaelic Revival; Gonne, Maud; Heaney, Seamus; Joyce, James; Literary Renaissance (Celtic Revival); Literature: Anglo-Irish Literature in the Nineteenth Century; Literature: Gaelic Literature in the Nineteenth Century; Literature: Twentieth-Century Women Writers; Music: Modern Music; Poetry, Modern; Raiftearaí (Raftery), Antaine; Visual Arts, Modern; Wilde, Oscar; Yeats, W. B.; **Primary Documents:** From "The Necessity for De-Anglicising Ireland" (25 November 1892); "Easter 1916" (1916);

"The End" (1926); "Pierce's Cave" (1933); "Scattering and Sorrow" (1936); "An Irishman in Coventry" (1960); "Punishment" (1975); "Inquisitio 1584" (c. 1985); "Feis" ("Carnival") (c. 1990)

Bibliography

Arnold, Bruce, *A Concise History of Irish Art.* 1977.

Deane, Seamus. *A Short History of Irish Literature.* 1986.

Jeffares, A. Norman. *Anglo-Irish Literature.* 1982.

Kenneally, Michael, ed. *Irish Literature and Culture.* 1992.

Kiberd, Declan. *Irish Classics.* 2001.

Leerssen, Joep. *Remembrance and Imagination: Patterns in the Historical and Literary Representation of Ireland in the Nineteenth Century.* 1997.

O'Leary, Philip. *The Prose Literature of the Gaelic Revival, 1881–1921.* 1994.

Ó Tuama, Seán. *An Duanaire, 1600–1900: Poems of the Dispossessed.* Translated by Thomas Kinsella. 1981.

Rafroidi, Patrick. *Irish Literature in English: The Romantic Period, 1789–1850.* 2 vols. 1980.

Vallely, Fintan, ed. *The Companion to Traditional Irish Music.* 1999.

White, Harry. *The Keeper's Recital: Music and Cultural History in Ireland, 1770–1970.* 1998.

Eamonn Wall

B

Balladry in English

The ballads or popular songs of nineteenth-century Ireland, as elsewhere, included songs of place, love songs, comic or bawdy compositions, and narratives of shipwrecks, battles, and executions. But those most popular among both the Catholic majority and the loyal Protestant population dealt with the local community in conflict with the authorities or with another hostile community, or with other political subjects.

TYPES OF BALLAD

Political ballads in nineteenth-century Ireland were of three main types. First, there were Irish compositions, generally transmitted orally or in manuscript. The second type was the street ballad, usually an anonymous composition in English (or, infrequently, in Irish), printed on broadsheet by jobbing printers like Haly of Cork or Brereton of Dublin, and sung in public places by traveling singers. The third was the patriotic song composed in English as propaganda by groups or individuals committed to a particular political cause, and published in either newspapers or in specially produced songbooks.

The common characteristic of all ballads was thematic simplicity. Typically, a ballad was based on a single incident and underdeveloped characters, and focused on narrative rather than analysis. It made no attempt to challenge its audience's majority value system. Precisely because of this thematic simplicity, and because its main audience was among the poorer, disaffected sections of society, the ballad was a powerful expression of and shaper of contemporary popular feeling and therefore was regarded by the authorities and by respectable society as disruptive.

THE DISRUPTIVE POWER OF STREET BALLADS

The ballads' power to disturb was threefold. First, by referencing contemporary social distress, millenarian prophecies, and successive O'Connellite reform movements, they fueled popular expectations of great change. Produced within the community, they proved a potent mixture of exciting narrative, emotive words, and familiar airs. Moreover, the mode of their transmission was guaranteed to cause disturbance, sung and sold as they were wherever large crowds gathered, as at fairs, markets, and on the corners of streets.

Second, the ballads were powerful instruments of communal recall, mostly of relatively recent events such as elections, political meetings, or riots. For the Catholic majority, memories that inspired ballads included bloody tithe-war incidents like the killing of a tithe proctor and his police guard at Carrickshock in south Kilkenny in 1831. Among loyalists, ballad memories centered on Orange marches and clashes between Orangemen and their Catholic opponents; the famous incidents at Garvagh in 1813 and at Dolly's Brae in 1849 were typical. Some more long-term recollections, too, proved particularly emotive: the 1798 rebellion, still within living memory in particular areas, was guaranteed to summon phantoms on both sides of the political and religious divide.

Such recall of popular memories was inseparable from the third function of the ballads: the enforcement of communal solidarity through the incitement of popular hostility towards "the enemy." Magistrates, unpopular public representatives, and informers were typical scapegoats, but the main targets were sectarian—either "heretics" or "papists," as time, place, singer, and audience demanded. Territorial and denominational loyalties fused in a powerful sense of identity. Thus one Orange ballad warned its Catholic opponents to: "Stop counting beads and quit midnight parades, / And put on Orange shoes when you come to Kilrea," while a popular ballad from south Leinster in 1835, recalling 1798, proclaimed: "Success to Kildare and Sweet Wexford, / Their children were never afraid!" (McIlffatrick 1995, p. 19; Cronin 2001, p. 124).

Street ballads were most influential before the Great Famine purged Irish society of its most serious social and economic problems, though they still provoked popular feeling over the following half-century, especially during the Fenian scare of the 1860s and early 1870s and during the Home Rule campaign and Land War of the 1880s. Typical was the Dublin ballad of 1883 targeting James Carey, who had given evidence against those who had assassinated Lord Frederick Cavendish and Thomas Henry Burke in Phoenix Park in 1882: "May every buck flea from here to Bray / Jump through the bed he lies on, / And by some mistake may he shortly take / A flowing pint of poison" (Zimmermann 1967, p. 283).

THE EMERGENCE OF THE PATRIOTIC SONG

By the 1890s the patriotic song had taken center stage. Sharing the street ballad's one-sidedness and naiveté, and usually of little intrinsic literary merit but extremely emotive when wedded to an appropriate air, this type of song was less a spontaneous reaction to recent events than a deliberately created instrument of politicization. Its genesis can be found in the 1790s when the United Irishmen used song to transmit republican and secular ideas. Many of their compositions, such as "Freedom Triumphant" and "Plant, Plant the Tree," were published and disseminated in *Paddy's Resource*, which first appeared in Belfast in 1795 and was re-issued in Dublin in 1798. On the other side, loyal Protestants, fearful of the passions unleashed during the 1798 rebellion, responded with songs such as "Croppies Lie Down" and "The Tree of Liberty," the latter effectively turning revolutionary imagery on its head: "Around this fair trunk we like ivy will cling, / And fight for our honour, our country, and king; / In the shade of this Orange none e'er shall recline / Who with murderous Frenchmen have dared to combine" (Zimmermann 1967, p. 310). Political song writing, however, really took off in the 1840s when Thomas Davis, romantic nationalist poet and founder/editor of the *Nation* newspaper, and the Young Ireland cultural movement which he represented produced song after song proclaiming a nonsectarian nationalism modelled on the ideals of the United Irishmen of the late eighteenth century and on contemporary European romantic nationalism. Emphasizing that a common Irishness must replace the denominational animosities that inspired the street ballads, Young Ire-

land's songs turned the guns on the "the Saxon," replacing anti-Protestantism with anti-Englishness as the mainstay of popular nationalism: "We hate the Saxon and the Dane, / We hate the Norman men— / We cursed their greed for blood and gain, / We curse them now again" (O'Sullivan 1944, p. 438).

First published in the *Nation* newspaper, and then in successive editions of the *Spirit of the Nation* songbook, these songs were initially more limited in their popular impact than the street ballads. But as literacy and popular competence in the English language increased, a retail economy developed, and a more militant popular nationalism and reactive loyalism grew from 1848 onwards, the broadsheet with its single song was supplanted by the song collections of the cheap songbook sold in shops and railway stations. The titles echoed the contents: on the nationalist side, *Wearing of the Green Songbook*, *O'Donnell Abu Songbook*, *Spirit of 'Ninety-Eight Songbook* and, on the loyalist side, *The Marching of the Lodges*, *The Boyne Book of Poetry and Song*, and *The Protestant Boys' Songbook*. However, at times the distinction between the old street ballad and the published political songs was blurred. Davis's songs were sold on broadsheets as late as the 1860s; two decades later, anti-Home Rule broadsheet songs were printed by Nicholson of Belfast; and in the late 1890s old street ballads were rewritten and published to mark the upcoming centenary of the 1798 rebellion.

The centenary compositions and anti-Home Rule songs accelerated the transition from sectarianism and localism to a broader sense of identity. Anti-Home Rulers avoided abuse of "blind-led papists," stressing instead Irish loyalists' staunch and ill-recompensed stand against betrayal: "We've been true to Old England, the land of the brave, / But we'll never submit to be treated like slaves" (Zimmermann 1967, p. 319). On the other side, writers like P. J. McCall and Eithne Carbery emphasized high-minded nationalism, epitomized in the closing stanzas of McCall's "Boolavogue": "God grant you glory, brave Father Murphy, / And open heaven to all your men; / The cause that called you may call tomorrow / In another fight for the green again" (Zimmermann 1967, p. 291). The new songs, unlike the street ballads, were somewhat artificial creations, yet they were still powerful reflectors and shapers of communal memories and political attitudes. Despite the competition of other mass entertainments, they continue to be sung in the twenty-first century, particularly in areas and times of political crisis.

SEE ALSO Davis, Thomas; Duffy, James; Literacy and Popular Culture; Newspapers; Young Ireland and the

Irish Confederation; **Primary Documents:** "God Save Ireland" (1867)

Bibliography

Carolan, Nicholas. "Irish Political Balladry." In *The French Are in the Bay: The Expedition to Bantry Bay, 1796*, edited by John A. Murphy. 1998.

Cronin, Maura. "Popular Memory and Identity: Street Ballads in North Munster in the Nineteenth Century." In *Explorations: Centenary Essays, Mary Immaculate College, Limerick*, edited by Liam Irwin. 1998.

Cronin, Maura. "Memory, Story and Balladry: 1798 and Its Place in Popular Memory in Pre-Famine Ireland." In *Rebellion and Remembrance in Modern Ireland*, edited by Laurence Geary. 2001.

McIlfatrick, James H. *Sprigs Around the Pump Town: Orangeism in the Kilrea District.* 1995

Munnelly, Tom. "1798 and the Balladmakers." In *The Great Irish Rebellion of 1798*, edited by Cathal Poirtéir. 1998.

Murphy, Maura. "The Ballad Singer and the Role of the Seditious Ballad in Nineteenth-Century Ireland: Dublin Castle's View." In *Ulster Folklife* 25 (1979): 79–102.

Ó Cíosáin, Niall. *Print and Popular Culture in Ireland, 1750–1850.* 1997.

Ó Lochlainn, Colm, ed. *The Complete Irish Street Ballads.* 1984.

O'Sullivan, T. F. *The Young Irelanders.* 1944

Shields, Hugh. *Narrative Song in Ireland: Lays, Ballads, Come-All-Yes, and Other Songs.* 1993.

Zimmermann, Georges-Denis. *Songs of Irish Rebellion: Political Street Ballads and Rebel Songs, 1780–1900.* 1967.

Maura Cronin

Banking and Finance to 1921

The emergence of formal banking institutions in Ireland was preceded by development of credit facilities in internal and cross-channel trade. The shortage of banks was to some extent offset by the fact that some important areas of economic activity (linen markets, e.g.) functioned mainly on a cash basis while much of the credit for cross-channel trade was provided by London merchants. Such credit could be quite extended (as long as six or seven months), and by 1785 perhaps 1 million pounds was provided for the linen trade in this way.

The legal code governing banking in eighteenth-century Ireland was dominated by an act of 1756, passed by the Irish Parliament, that prohibited anyone who undertook "trade or traffick as merchants in goods or merchandise imported or exported" from setting themselves up as bankers. This legislation deterred the emergence of the overseas trader-banker in Ireland. Four years later another act seemed to prevent bankers from paying interest on deposits, and a third measure, in 1782, which established the Bank of Ireland (opened 1783) by royal charter, also limited all other banks to a maximum of six partners. The first of these two acts meant that banking in Ireland would develop in a way different from elsewhere in the British Isles, and the third ensured that any new banking ventures would necessarily be relatively small.

Despite its large size, the Bank of Ireland did not open any branches until 1825 and proved itself highly conservative in the provision of credit, refusing to grant overdrafts on current accounts until the 1830s. Moreover, its staff and Court of Directors were overwhelmingly Anglican. Presbyterians in the north were determined to seize the financial initiative and set up banks of their own, thus diminishing their dependence on Dublin. The formation of three new banking partnerships—the Belfast Bank (1808), the Commercial Bank (1809), and Northern Bank (1809)—indicated the extent to which religion and finance combined to produce a set of durable banking houses firmly rooted in Ulster's industrial and commercial development.

It is probably no accident that these banks were founded after some thirty years of increasingly direct export from Ulster in the linen trade, and also after the most intensive decade of investment in cotton mills in the Belfast area. Because of the uniqueness of Belfast as a manufacturing area, banks were in a relatively favorable position to provide a whole range of services to the manufacturing sector. It is also probably the case that the textile industries, although they were undoubtedly unstable, helped to protect the northern banks from the worst effects of the agricultural depression and deflation that followed the end of the Napoleonic wars in 1815, thereby helping to ensure their survival.

Within a few years of the return of peace in 1815, the banks established "agencies" in country towns and villages. The principal function of them was to increase note circulation through the discounting of bills of exchange, thereby facilitating industrial and commercial development. Bank agents usually combined their banking functions with other, usually complementary, pursuits and normally worked from home or their own business establishment. They were the forerunners of the branch managers.

Financial instability in the decade following the end of the Napoleonic wars caused bank failures, which led to legislation in the mid-1820s permitting the formation of banks with more than six partners. Especially in the years 1824 to 1827 and 1834 to 1838, some old banks converted to "joint-stock" concerns with many shareholders, and other banks were created as entirely new institutions. Joint-stock bank promotion greatly increased competition for customers. By the middle of the nineteenth century all banks, with the exception of the Dublin-based Royal Bank, operated branch networks. Only the Provincial Bank (established in 1825, with a head office in London) and the Bank of Ireland had networks with almost national coverage. Three others—the Northern Bank (a private bank converted in 1824 to become the first joint-stock bank in Ireland), the Belfast Bank (converted to joint stock from two private banks in 1827), and the Ulster Bank (a new concern in 1836)—were confined to the province of Ulster. The Tipperary Joint Stock Bank (established in 1838) had a small network in County Tipperary and the surrounding area; the National Bank (established in 1835) possessed the largest number of branches in 1850, although it had not yet penetrated the industrial northeast; and the smallest system was operated by the Dublin-based Hibernian Bank (established in 1825).

Between 1850 and 1913 the Irish banking system continued to expand, from fewer than 200 offices to around 850. The main reason for this expansion was the need to maximize deposits, a key determinant of lending capacity and of profitability. By 1913 some 320 offices were open only on specified days of the week, particularly market or fair days, to cater for local need. Most of the deposits came from rural areas, and branch networks enabled banks to utilize them to fund industrial expansion in larger towns as well as to spread their risks. The great majority of banks were both stable and profitable. Bank failure was comparatively rare in Ireland. The most notable joint-stock failures were those of the Tipperary Bank (1856) and the Cork-based Munster Bank in 1885, and in fact from the latter institution emerged the successful Munster and Leinster Bank. In order to protect their shareholders, banks adopted limited liability, especially following the Companies Act of 1879.

The various Irish banks offered a similar range of services, chief among them deposit-taking and the provision of credit facilities, such as discounting bills of exchange, overdrafts, and fixed-period loans. Many of them also issued their own notes. In most areas banking was a reflection of the type of local economic activity: farming, estate management, or professional services, as well as industry and trade. For this reason seasonal rhythms typified business, as in the linen and the provisions trades. In buoyant economic conditions banks were more likely to extend credit, but downturns in economic activity brought curtailment and demands for

repayment. Thus in Irish agriculture the Great Famine of the late 1840s and the depressions of 1859 to 1864 and 1877 to 1879 all saw the banks make determined efforts to limit exposure to bad debts by calling in loans and being cautious about new agricultural business. There is considerable evidence that banks were closely involved in the industrial expansion in nineteenth-century Ulster, meeting the diverse demands of short- and long-term credit by a range of producers, from the small firm to the largest linen companies and shipyards. Sometimes the demand for credit—such as the demand that occurred during the expansion of the linen industry that accompanied the American Civil War of 1861 to 1865, for example—could be enormous, but, as in the agriculture business, the banks exercised caution during recession and depression (e.g., in 1847–1848, 1857–1858, 1879, 1886, and 1908–1909).

The First World War from 1914 to 1918 brought great prosperity for much of Irish agriculture and led to a huge increase in deposits. This helped to provide fiscal stability for the country after partition. The banks generally kept out of the public debates on Irish politics before 1920.

SEE ALSO Agriculture: 1690 to 1845; Agriculture: 1845 to 1921; Industrialization; Irish Pound; Transport—Road, Canal, Rail

Bibliography

Barrow, Gordon Lennox. *The Emergence of the Irish Banking System, 1820–1845.* 1974.

Cullen, Louis M. *Anglo–Irish Trade, 1660–1800.* 1968.

Hall, Frank G. *The Bank of Ireland, 1783–1946.* 1949.

Ollerenshaw, Philip. *Banking in Nineteenth-Century Ireland.* 1987.

Philip Ollerenshaw

Battle of Clontarf

See Clontarf, Battle of.

Battle of the Boyne

See Boyne, Battle of the.

Beckett, Samuel

The acclaimed author of *Waiting for Godot*, Samuel Barclay Beckett (1906–1989) was born in Foxrock, Co. Dublin, on Friday, 13 April 1906. Close to his father and brother but periodically at odds with his pious Protestant mother, Beckett was at school in Dublin during the 1916 Rising, and in Eniskillen, in his second year at Portora Royal School, when Ireland was partitioned.

In 1923 Beckett went to Trinity College, where he completed an arts degree. In 1928 he became an exchange lecturer at the *École Normale Supérieure* in Paris, where he met a number of artists and writers, including James Joyce. Upon his return to Ireland in 1930, he quarreled with his mother over his writing and his unwillingness to pursue a normal career, and in 1931 he abruptly left a teaching position at Trinity College.

He started his first novel in Paris in 1932. A short story collection, *More Pricks than Kicks*, was published in 1934. He completed his novel *Murphy* in 1935. Beckett was active in the French Resistance throughout World War II, fleeing Paris to Roussillon when his cell was betrayed (Knowlson 1997), and rejoining the Resistance in Roussillon. In the years following the war Beckett produced "a torrent of work" in French (Knowlson 1997, p. 355), writing (in French) and translating (into English) the novels *Molloy*, *Malone Dies*, and *The Unnamable*.

Beckett became famous with the first performances of his plays *Waiting for Godot* (1952) and *Endgame* (1957) in 1953 and 1957, respectively. In 1959 he completed the comparatively lyrical *Krapp's Last Tape*. Thereafter, he honed his minimalism, producing short plays and prose works in which the boundaries between life and death, reality and the imagination, are annihilated. These include *Eh Joe* (1967), *Not I* (1972), *That Time* (1977), *Footfalls* (1977), *Company* (1979), *Ill Said, Ill Seen* (1981), and *Rockaby* (1982).

Beckett hated publicity—he went into hiding upon receiving the Nobel Prize for literature in 1969. Although he refused interviews, he was nonetheless willing to make political statements. He withheld the performance rights to his plays in apartheid South Africa, but endorsed a 1976 production of *Waiting For Godot* by a black cast before nonsegregated audiences (Knowlson 1997, p. 637). He also opposed censorship in the Soviet bloc countries, and he dedicated his 1979 play *Catastrophe* to fellow playwright Vaclav Havel, Czechoslovakia's foremost dissident (and later president of Czechoslovakia and the Czech Republic). Because Beckett insisted, at times irrationally, on his work's apolitical and asocial character, his recurring interest in Manichean social relations and power dynamics—as in the case of *Molloy*—in a clearly Irish context has yet to be elucidated fully.

SEE ALSO Arts: Modern Irish and Anglo-Irish Literature and the Arts since 1800; Drama, Modern; Fiction, Modern

Bibliography

Harrington, John P. *The Irish Beckett*. 1991.

Knowlson, James. *Damned to Fame: The Life of Samuel Beckett*. 1997.

McCormack, W. J. *From Burke to Beckett: Ascendancy Tradition and Betrayal in Literary History*. 1994.

Mercier, Vivian. *Modern Irish Literature: Sources and Founders*. 1994.

Margot Gayle Backus

Bedell, William

William Bedell (1571–1642) was provost of Trinity College, Dublin and bishop of Kilmore and Ardagh. Born in Black Notley, Essex, in 1570, he was educated at the Puritan seminary of Emmanuel College, Cambridge, where he obtained an M.A. in 1592, became a fellow in 1593, and was awarded a B.D. in 1599. After university Bedell returned to East Anglia, where he would have remained as a country parson had he not twice been plucked from obscurity to serve abroad. First, in 1607 he was chosen to go to Venice as chaplain to the British ambassador Sir Henry Wootton. Bedell remained there until 1610, translating the *Book of Common Prayer* into Italian in an effort to encourage the Venetians to renounce Catholicism. Then, in 1627 he reluctantly agreed to go to Ireland as provost of Trinity College, where he instituted a much-needed reform program, seeking in particular to ensure that students destined for a clerical career had the opportunity to learn Irish. In 1629 he was chosen bishop of Kilmore and Ardagh, straddling the border of the Ulster plantation (though he resigned Ardagh in 1633 because of a principled objection to pluralism). Unlike most other English Protestant bishops in Ireland, Bedell was favorably disposed to the Irish language and culture: He sought to provide a resident, Irish-speaking, preaching ministry in his parishes, and he set into motion the translation of the Old Testament into Irish in order to supplement the existing printed Irish versions of the New Testament and Prayer Book. His determined efforts at reform led him to clash with vested interests within the church, but he did win the respect, if not the religious allegiance, of the local Irish population. When in 1641 the Catholic Irish rose against the English settlers, Bedell was not immediately harmed. Eventually imprisoned, he died of natural causes and was accorded a guard of honor at his funeral by the local Irish chieftain.

Though from a Puritan background, Bedell was culturally sensitive and theologically open and enquiring, with a special interest in the vexed issue of the relationship of grace to baptism. Unique among Irish Protestant clerics, he was the subject of three seventeenth-century biographies, one by his son, another by his son-in-law, and the last by the English bishop and historian Gilbert Burnett, all of which painted him as a noble and conciliatory model of a Christian bishop.

SEE ALSO Rebellion of 1641; Trinity College; Ussher, James; Wentworth, Thomas, First Earl of Strafford

Bibliography

Clarke, Aidan. "Bishop William Bedell (1571–1642) and the Irish Reformation." In *Worsted in the Game: Losers in Irish History*, edited by C. F. Brady. 1989.

Ford, Alan. "The Reformation in Kilmore to 1641." In *Cavan: An Irish County History*, edited by Raymond Gillespie. 1995.

Shuckburgh, E. S. *Two Biographies of William Bedell*. 1902.

Alan Ford

Belfast

Flanking the River Lagan estuary, Belfast has an exceptionally attractive setting, with the Castlereagh Hills to the east and a striking escarpment of the Antrim plateau to the west. Belfast also has the unenviable reputation of being the most continuously disturbed city in western Europe since the end of World War II.

Until the twelfth century Belfast was no more than a crossing-place at the mouth of the river where mud banks were exposed at low tide—hence its name, *Béal Feirste*, which means "approach to the sand-bank crossing." A modest village that grew up around a castle built there by Normans all but disappeared when the Clandeboye O'Neills overwhelmed the earldom of Ulster in the fifteenth century.

Granted Lower Clandeboye (a Gaelic lordship encompassing south County Antrim) at the close of the Elizabethan conquest, Sir Arthur Chichester, the principal architect of the Ulster plantation, encouraged English and Scots to settle in Belfast, and he ensured that it became an incorporated town in 1613. Belfast came through the turbulence of the seventeenth century remarkably unscathed, coming under siege only once. Neglected by Chichester's descendants, the earls of Donegall, the town languished in the first half of the eighteenth century, and its recovery and development thereafter were largely due to the initiative of Presbyterian entrepreneurs. By setting up powered machinery to spin cotton, these men made the town the most dynamic industrial center in the island. Fired by news of the American and French revolutions, they also turned Belfast into the most radical town in Ireland, and it was in Crown Entry in October 1791 that the Society of United Irishmen was founded. The reality of violence in 1798, however, quickly extinguished radical fervor in the town.

More than anywhere else in Ireland, Belfast prospered under the union and was arguably the fastest-growing urban center in the United Kingdom in the nineteenth century. The town's population was a mere 19,000 in 1801; it rose to over 70,000 in 1841; and by 1901 it was the largest city in Ireland, with almost 350,000 citizens. Belfast was given official status as a city in 1888, by which time it was the third most important port in the U.K., after London and Liverpool. The sumptuous city hall, opened in 1906, was in part an expression of pride in Belfast's achievement in producing the world's largest shipyard, ropeworks, aerated-waters factory, linen mill, tea machinery and fan-making works, handkerchief factory, spiral-guided gasometer, linen-machinery works, and tobacco factory.

Though Belfast had much in common with British city ports such as Liverpool, Glasgow, and Newcastle-on-Tyne, it was an Irish city with Irish problems. The tens of thousands coming in from rural Ulster to seek employment in Belfast had recollections of dispossession, massacre, confiscation, and persecution etched into their memories. By the 1830s about a third of Belfast's citizens were Catholics, though the proportion fell to around a quarter by the beginning of the twentieth century. The unstable and invisible lines dividing Protestant and Catholic districts frequently became sectarian battlegrounds, notably in the protracted riots of 1857, 1864, 1872, and 1886. Such conflicts were intensified by the debate over Ireland's political future. Between 1912 and 1914 Belfast was the pivot of resistance to the third Home Rule bill, and as the Anglo-Irish War got under way, intercommunal hatreds gushed to the surface. Between 1920 and 1922, as Northern Ireland was brought to birth, 416 Belfast citizens lost their lives in a vicious conflict.

The deep scars left by the violence might have healed in time had Belfast enjoyed a long period of prosperity after 1922. However, the economic slump that had begun in the winter of 1920 developed into a protracted depression as the city's traditional staple industries of linen, shipbuilding, and engineering continued to contract. The German air raids of the spring of 1941 demonstrated the failure of the city government to provide the most basic air-raid protection for citizens, and the corporation was suspended and placed under the control of commissioners for more than three years. By mid-1942, however, Belfast was making a notable contribution to the Allied war effort in the production of ships, weapons, ammunition, and uniforms. In the quiet years after 1945 there was a steady increase in living standards, and when traditional industries declined again in the late 1950s, overseas firms, many of them manufacturing synthetic fibers, began to set up in Belfast's periphery.

Sectarian violence in the city led to fatalities on 14 and 15 August 1969, propelling whole districts of Belfast into chaos. For years much of Belfast resembled a war zone: Barricades blocked the entrances to working-class enclaves; hundreds of families were forced from their homes; the rising death toll was composed mainly of innocent citizens; familiar landmarks were destroyed as paramilitaries detonated bombs directed at commercial premises and installations; gun battles raged almost every night; and the city center was almost deserted after 7 P.M. and on weekends. A formidable security fence ringed the city center, and eventually twenty-six peacelines, high-security walls erected at the request of local people, separated the most troubled enclaves. Nevertheless, a significant reduction in violence beginning in the late 1970s encouraged the government to clear dilapidated dwellings, and by the early 1990s much of the city had been transformed, with the quality of planning, building design, and construction attracting well-warranted praise from housing experts around the world. The city center remained a shared space and nightlife made a rapid recovery there in the early 1980s. After decades of decline, Belfast's population rose modestly to 279,237 for the area administered by the city council, and to 475,967 for the greater Belfast area in 1991. Though mutual distrust and occasional confrontations proved impossible to eliminate, following the paramilitary ceasefires of 1994 there was a gradual realization that a new era in the city's history was arriving. Nowhere was the transformation of Belfast more apparent than by the River Lagan: There the Waterfront Hall—a concert hall and conference center without rival in Ireland—was opened in 1997; well-lit walkways were constructed along the river; and a Hilton Hotel and entertainment and commercial complexes sprang up on previously derelict sites. Confrontations in the Ardoyne district during 2001 nevertheless indicated the enduring character of Belfast's intercommunal problems.

SEE ALSO Cork; Dublin; Factory-Based Textile Manufacture; Landscape and Settlement; Shipbuilding; Towns and Villages; **Primary Documents:** On Presbyterian Communities in Ulster (1810, 1812); From *Belfast Fifty Years Ago* (1875)

Bibliography

Bardon, Jonathan. *Belfast: An Illustrated History.* 1982.

Brett, C. E. B. *Buildings of Belfast, 1700–1914.* 1985.

Maguire, W. A. *Belfast.* 1994.

Jonathan Bardon

Blasket Island Writers

The major cultural-revival association founded in 1893, the Gaelic League, conferred new significance on the Irish language, oral culture, and the traditional way of life of the *Gaeltachtaí*, or Irish-speaking areas of Ireland. Interest in the Celtic languages generated by the rise of European philology in the latter half of the nineteenth century, and the "gaelicization" policy of the new Irish state influenced by the Gaelic League, brought growing numbers of scholars and students to the Dingle peninsula of County Kerry in the southwest to study modern Irish, and especially to the Great Blasket Island lying about three miles offshore, which had a special attraction for linguists, medievalists, and folklorists owing to its remoteness.

The interest shown by scholars such as Carl Marstrander, Robin Flower, and Kenneth Jackson in the lan-

Tomás Ó Criomhthain (1856–1937), author of Allagar na hInise *(1927) and* An tOileánach *(1929). FROM* THE ISLANDMAN, *BY* TOMÁS Ó CRIOMHTHAIN (1934). COURTESY OF THE GRADUATE LIBRARY, UNIVERSITY OF MICHIGAN.

guage and folklore of the island, the influence of the Gaelic League on the islanders' perception of the importance of their language and culture, and the encouragement of language enthusiasts from the mainland developed an increasing awareness among islanders of the need to record their disappearing way of life. Tomás Ó Criomhthain (or O'Crohan) (1856–1937) was the first to do so in his journal of island life (*Allagar na hInise*, 1927), his classical autobiographical work (*An tOileánach*, 1929, translated into English as *The Islandman* by Robin Flower), and his topography of the Blasket island group (*Dinnsheanchas na mBlascaodaí*, 1935), in which he vividly and incisively depicts his natural environment, life on the island, and the mentality of the island community.

Muiris Ó Súilleabháin's celebrated depiction of a young man's view of Blasket Island life, *Fiche Blian ag Fás*, appeared in 1933. Owing much to the inspiration of the English classicist and student of modern Irish, George Thomson, it became, on translation into English, a world classic.

The gifted Blasket storyteller Peig Sayers (1873–1958) left three dictated accounts of her life (*Peig*, 1936, *Machtnamh Seana-Mhná*, 1939, and *Beatha Pheig Sayers*, 1970), providing a female perspective on island experience. *Peig* became known to generations of schoolchildren as it featured at intervals as a prescribed text on the Leaving Certificate Irish syllabus from 1943 to 1995, and it may still (2001–2003) be read for the optional course.

Among the next generation of Blasket writers, after the evacuation of the island in 1953 (due to population decline through emigration, and the lack of essential services), were Peig Sayers's son, Micheál Ó Guithín, whose elegiac autobiography (*Is Trua na Fanann an Óige*) appeared in that same year, and Tomás Ó Criomhthain's son, Séan, whose account (*Lá dár Saol*, 1969) is an epilogue to the story of the Great Blasket and to the tale of how the islanders settled on the mainland.

The Blasket Island literature, emphasizing autobiography as a literary medium and epitomizing the Gaelic League's ideal of the language and folklore of the *Gaeltacht* as the well-spring of a new literature in Irish, influenced genre, content, form, and style of the prose literature of the Gaelic revival for several decades. The Blasket writers were also important to the folklore movement through their use of oral tradition and their detailed depiction of a traditional society. An important corpus of folklore was collected from Peig Sayers by Robin Flower and Kenneth Jackson, and by her most important collector, Seosamh Ó Dálaigh, on behalf of the Irish Folklore Commission, after her return to the mainland in 1942. Flower's collection of folklore from Tomás Ó Criomhthain, *Seanchas ón Oileán Tiar*, appeared posthumously in 1949.

SEE ALSO Arts: Modern Irish and Anglo-Irish Literature and the Arts since 1800; Fiction, Modern; Gaelic Revivalism: The Gaelic League; Language and Literacy: Decline of Irish Language; Language and Literacy: Irish Language since 1922; **Primary Documents:** "The End" (1926); "Pierce's Cave" (1933); "Scattering and Sorrow" (1936)

Bibliography

Literature

Flower, Robin. *The Western Island or The Great Blasket.* 1941.

Mac Conghail, Muiris. *The Blaskets: People and Literature.* 1994, 1987.

Ní Aimhirgin, Nuala. *Muiris Ó Súileabháin.* 1983.

Nic Eoin, Máirín. *An Litríocht Réigiúnach.* 1982.

Ó Muircheartaigh, Aogán, ed. *Oidhreacht an Bhlascaoid.* 1989.

Texts

Flower, Robin, ed. "Sgéalta ón mBlascaod." *Béaloideas* 2 (1930): 97–111, 199–210.

Flower, Robin, ed. "Measgra ón Oileán Tiar." *Béaloideas* 25 (1957): 46–106.

Ó Criomhthain, Seán. *Lá dár Saol.* 1969.

Ó Criomhthain, Tomás. *Allagar na hInise*, edited by Pádraig Ó Siochfhradha (An Seabhac). 1928. New enlarged edition edited by Pádraig Ua Maoileoin, 1977.

Ó Criomhthain, Tomás. *An tOileánach.* 1929, 1967. New edition by Pádraig Ua Maoileoin, 1973. New edition by Seán Ó Coileáin, 2002.

Ó Criomhthain, Tomás. *Dinnsheanchas na mBlascaodaí.* 1935.

Ó Criomhthain, Tomás. *Island Cross-Talk: Pages from a Diary.* 1928. Translated by Tim Enright. 1986.

Ó Criomhthain, Tomás. *Seanchas ón Oileán Tiar.* Edited by Séamus Ó Duilearga. 1956.

Ó Criomhthain, Tomás (Pádraig Ua Maoileoin). *Allagar II.* 1999.

O'Crohan, Seán. *A Day in Our Life.* Translated by Tim Enright. 1992.

Ó Crohan, Tomás. *The Islandman.* Translated by Robin Flower. 1934, 1943, 1951, 1978.

Ó Gaoithín, Micheál. *Is Truagh ná Fanann an Óige.* 1953.

Ó Gaoithín, Micheál. *Beatha Pheig Sayers.* 1970.

O'Guiheen, Micheál. *A Pity Youth Does Not Last.* Translated by Tim Enright. 1982.

Ó Súileabháin, Muiris. *Fiche Blian ag Fás.* 1933, 1976, 1978.

O'Sullivan, Maurice. *Twenty Years A-Growing.* Translated by Moya Llewelyn Davies and George Thomson. 1933. Revised translation, 1953.

Sayers, Peig. *Peig.i: A Scéal Féin do Scríobh Peig Sayers.* Edited by Máire Ní Chinnéide. 1936.

Sayers, Peig. *Scéalta ón mBlascaod.* Edited by Kenneth Jackson. 1938, 1998.

Sayers, Peig. *Machtnamh Seana-Mhná.* Edited by Máire Ní Chinnéide. 1939.

Sayers, Peig. *Peig: School Editions.* Edited by Máire Ní Chinnéide. 1954?, 1970.

Sayers, Peig. *An Old Woman's Reflections.* Translated by Séamus Ennis. Introduction by W. R. Rogers. 1962.

Sayers, Peig. *Peig: The Autobiography of Peig Sayers of the Great Blasket Island.* Translated by Bryan MacMahon. 1974.

Sayers, Peig. *Machnamh Seanmhná.* New edition by Pádraig Ua Maoileoin. 1980.

Sayers, Peig. *Peig. A Scéal Féin.* New rev. edition by Máire Ní Mhainnín and Liam P. Ó Murchú. 1998.

Patricia Lysaght

~

Bloody Sunday

Bloody Sunday occurred on 30 January 1972 in Derry/Londonderry, Northern Ireland, when an illegal march of up to 20,000 civil-rights demonstrators protesting against the British policy of internment was fired on by the British army. A section of the crowd had been stoning soldiers, and the army maintained that shots had been fired at them from the republican Bogside area of the city and that petrol bombers were among the crowd of demonstrators. The consequences of the army's actions were thirteen dead and an injury that would later prove to be fatal. Republicans claimed that their personnel had stood down on that day because they believed that the army wanted to draw them into a full-scale battle. It was not until 1992 that John Major, then prime minister of Great Britain, acknowledged in a letter to the local MP, John Hume, that the victims should be regarded as innocent of any allegation that they had been shot while handling firearms or explosives. It was a tacit acceptance that the original public inquiry under Chief Justice Lord Widgery was flawed in that it was rushed and did not consider all the available evidence. New evidence, including new eyewitness accounts, medical evidence, and new interpretations of ballistics material, as well as a detailed Irish government assessment of the new material and of Lord Widgery's findings in light of all the material available, prompted another inquiry. In a parliamentary statement on 29 January 1998, Prime Minister Tony Blair announced another tribunal to investigate the events of Bloody Sunday, to be chaired by Lord Saville. The novelty of this inquiry was that the government was at least prepared to look at the uncongenial possibility that the killings were unlawful.

There is clear evidence that relations between the local Catholic community and the security forces deteriorated throughout 1971. One particular incident had been the army's killing of two local youths in a Bogside riot in July: an unofficial inquiry chaired by Lord Gifford found that both youths were unarmed. By November the semiweekly local nationalist newspaper, the *Derry Journal*, recorded incidents such as applause in court after riot charges had been dismissed; strikes and traffic disruption following a wave of protests by teachers, dockers, and factory workers after army raids in the area; the condemnation of army tactics by tenants' associations after soldiers had killed a mother of six children and 4,000 people had attended her funeral; a meeting of 500 business and professional people to support a campaign of passive resistance; and the army detention of John Hume after he had refused to be searched.

The army's own records show that following the two July killings, the Catholic community had "instantly turned from benevolent support to community alienation." The situation was compounded in August with the introduction of internment, so that "all combined to lead to a situation in which the security forces were faced by an entirely hostile Catholic community." By the end of the year the chief of the general staff was warning that whereas the Irish Republican Army (IRA) "were under pressure and becoming disorganised, in Londonderry the situation was different. The IRA could still count on the active support of the Roman Catholic population, and a major military operation here could have widespread political consequences." By early January 1972 the general officer commander admitted, "I am coming to the conclusion that the minimum force necessary to achieve a restoration of law and order is to shoot selected ringleaders among the DYH [Derry Young Hooligans], after clear warnings have been issued." On the weekend before Bloody Sunday a protest was held outside an internment camp. It led to a clash between paratroopers and protestors—a clash described by one commentator as "the brutal act of an arrogant military." It served as a mild rehearsal for Bloody Sunday.

The impact of Bloody Sunday was immense. It led to a huge resurgence in violence: In the three years before Bloody Sunday, about 250 people had been killed in the violence, whereas 470 died in the ensuing eleven months. It acted as an enormous recruiting device for the IRA. It pitted official Ireland against the British government. The Irish government recalled its ambassador in London, and the British embassy in Dublin was burned to the ground. The attendance of the Catholic primate of all Ireland, a bishop, 200 priests, five Irish government ministers, and nine mayors from the Republic at the victims' funerals made clear the sense of outrage throughout nationalist Ireland. The international pressure on the British government was such that within two months the Stormont regime was suspended and direct rule from London imposed. The unseemly haste of the Widgery report—published within eleven weeks of the day—did not prevent the coroner at the inquests from describing the deaths as "sheer, unadulterated murder" in August 1973.

The coroner's remarks encapsulated a raging sense of injustice among the nationalist community, as demonstrated by the unremitting campaign conducted by the victims' relatives and by John Hume to have the case reopened. It was "compelling new evidence" that led Tony Blair to announce a new inquiry on the twenty-sixth anniversary. It met for the first time in Derry in April 1998 and was chaired by Lord Saville of Newdi-

gate with the assistance of two other Commonwealth judges. The first phase of the tribunal ended in September 2002 after more than 500 civilian witnesses and experts had been cross-examined in Derry. The second phase moved to London for the examination of 250 soldiers and some senior British politicians before it moved back to Derry, where it completed its public fact-finding on 13 February 2004. The Saville Report was scheduled to be published in 2005. Time will tell whether the Saville tribunal will be an instrument of justice.

SEE ALSO Irish Republican Army (IRA); Northern Ireland: History since 1920

Bibliography

McClean, Raymond. *The Road to Bloody Sunday*. 1997.

McKittrick, David, et al. *Lost Lives: The Stories of the Men, Women, and Children Who Died as a Result of the Northern Ireland Troubles*. 1999.

Mullan, Don, ed. *Eyewitness Bloody Sunday*. 3d edition, 2002.

Paul Arthur

Bogs and Drainage

Peat bogs in Ireland may be divided broadly into raised and blanket bogs. Raised bogs, characteristic of central Ireland (Midlands), are so described because of their domed shape and because they hold water above the water table of their surroundings. Many are formed over basins, often in underlying glacial clays, in which water accumulated. Gradually reeds and other fenland plants colonized, and as they died, their remains did not decay fully in the waterlogged anaerobic conditions; fen peat began to form. As layers of fen peat built up, the surface gradually grew above the level of the surrounding land and of the surface runoff. Plants became reliant on rainfall for water and nutrients, and because the nutrient concentration of rainfall is low, there was a change to species tolerant of low-nutrient conditions. Fenland plants gave way to those of acid bog conditions, particularly the bog mosses (*Sphagnum* species). Continued upward growth of the bog led to the characteristic convex or domed profile.

A pristine raised bog has several distinctive parts. The central area or dome is flat or very gently sloping;

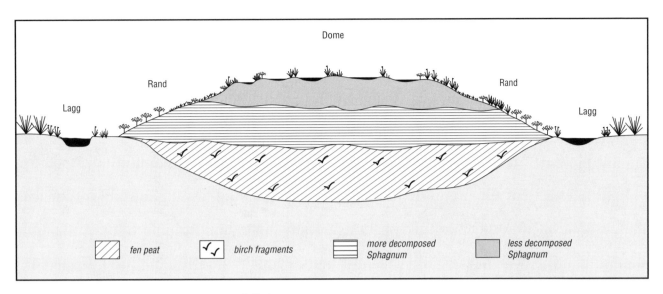

Dome

Rand

Rand

Lagg

Lagg

| ▨ fen peat | ✓✓ birch fragments | ☰ more decomposed Sphagnum | ▨ less decomposed Sphagnum |

Diagram of a raised bog showing its structure and distinct parts.

it is often extremely wet and may have a micro-topography of pools and hummocks. Pools are some-times occupied by aquatic *Sphagnum* species but may be open water. The hummocks have *Sphagnum* species re-quiring drier conditions, deer sedge (*Trichophorum cespitosum*), cotton sedge (*Eriophorum vaginatum*), and heathers (*Calluna vulgaris* and *Erica tetralix*). On the more steeply sloping bog edge (rand), the water table is slightly deeper, there is some water flow through the upper peat, and there is a better supply of nutrients; bog myrtle (*Myrica gale*) and common heather (*Calluna vulgaris*) are frequent. The bog may be surrounded by a lagg, an area of mobile water, sometimes with a small stream, and with large tussocks of purple moor grass (*Molinia caerulea*). Few raised bogs in Ireland are pris-tine; most have been subject to domestic peat cutting by spade for fuel, and because this extended inward from the bog edges, laggs and rands are rare. Climatic condi-tions varied throughout the development of raised bogs, some of which began to form 7,000 or even 9,000 years ago, and many display distinct horizons in the peat. For example, wetter, cooler conditions after 500 B.C.E. in-creased *Sphagnum* growth, and many bogs have an upper layer of poorly humified, reddish peat, whereas below, the peat is more humified and blacker.

The origin of raised bogs is generally natural, but blanket bog development, although regionally complex, came about probably through a combination of deterio-rating climate and clearance of woodland by early farmers around 3,000 to 4,000 years ago. With in-creased percolation, plant nutrients and finer soil parti-cles were washed down the soil profile, leaving acidic upper horizons. Plants adapted to these conditions colo-nized (heathers, sedges, mosses), and their remains

began to accumulate in the cool, wet environment where biological breakdown was slow. As bog mosses invaded, the organic soils became waterlogged, any re-maining trees died, and peat formed. Tree stumps and even Neolithic field systems, as at Céide fields, Co. Mayo, in the west of Ireland, may be seen beneath blanket peat—often exposed by cutting.

Hand cutting of fuel peat has little effect in any one year because the peat face extends into the bog by about one-half to one meter per year, but over centuries, espe-cially since the seventeenth century when population increase was rapid, the impact has been extensive. By the late twentieth century hand cutting had declined considerably; electricity reached almost everyone and oil was readily available. With rural to urban move-ments, the people required to dig, stack, turn, and transport turf to homesteads were no longer present. Where peat (turf) is still used for fuel, since the 1980s it has often been obtained by compact harvesters at-tached to a farm tractor; a year's supply can be cut in a few hours. Particularly after Bord na Móna was estab-lished in 1946 as a statutory body to develop Ireland's peat resources, the large raised bogs, especially those in the Midlands, became the focus for extensive peat ex-traction. Bogs were drained, surface vegetation was re-moved, and the peat was milled. Once dried, the milled peat was collected and burnt in peat-fired power sta-tions. Some peat is still used in this way, but many bogs are reaching exhaustion and public attitudes have changed; there has been increasing recognition of the in-ternational value of bogs. Ireland's bogs are examples of ecosystems relatively rare in Europe, and through their plant, pollen, and other microfossil remains they enable the vegetational history to be explored. They are also

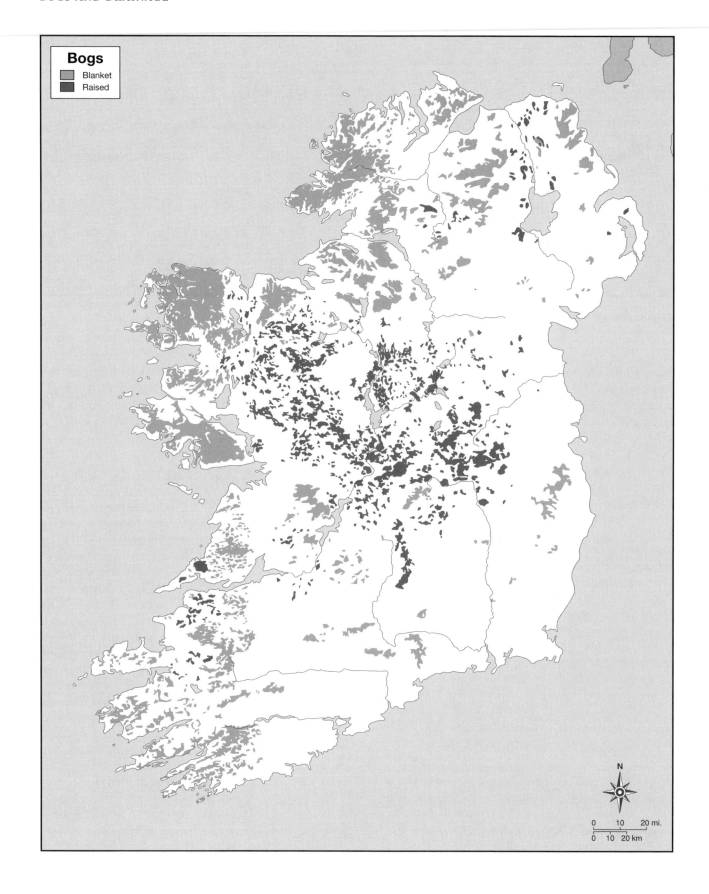

important carbon sinks. Governments in the Republic and Northern Ireland have designated conservation sites, but outside of those, human impact continues. Forestry expansion has been largely on western peatlands, and the increased sheep population, following European agricultural policies, has resulted in overgrazing and erosion.

SEE ALSO Landscape and Settlement; Rural Settlement and Field Systems; Woodlands

Bibliography

Aalen, F., K. Whelan, and M. Stout, eds. *Atlas of the Irish Rural Landscape.* 1997.

Feehan, J., and G. O'Donovan. *The Bogs of Ireland. An Introduction to the Natural, Cultural, and Industrial Heritage of Irish Peatland.* 1996.

Hammond, R. *The Peatlands of Ireland.* 1979.

R. W. Tomlinson

Boundary Commission

The Boundary Commission established in Article 12 of the 1921 Anglo-Irish Treaty was intended to redefine, "in accordance with the wishes of the inhabitants, so far as may be compatible with economic and geographic conditions, the boundaries between Northern Ireland and the rest of Ireland" (Fanning et al. 1998, p. 358).

The notion of a boundary commission had first been voiced in 1912 during the discussions surrounding the third Home Rule bill, but the form of the commission proposed in the 1921 treaty had its origins in the procedures for boundary revision in Eastern and Central Europe laid down in the treaties of the postwar Paris Peace Conference of 1919. The proposal for an Irish Boundary Commission emerged from an agreement between Minister for Foreign Affairs and Chief Delegate of the Irish delegation Arthur Griffith and British Prime Minister David Lloyd George in November 1921 during the treaty negotiations in London. The remit of the proposed commission was loosely defined, but it was accepted by the Sinn Féin delegates, who expected large territorial transfers from Northern Ireland and the collapse of the reduced territory of the Northern Ireland state, or rump, that would remain following any trans-

fers of its territory to the Irish Free State. Their acceptance enabled Lloyd George to prevent the Irish delegates from breaking off the negotiations on Ulster as they had planned, and it neatly pushed the issue of Northern Ireland beyond the immediate treaty talks.

During negotiations in early 1922, the chairman of the Irish Free State provisional government, Michael Collins, and the Northern Irish prime minister, Sir James Craig, hoped to decide the North-South boundary without recourse to the commission, but agreement proved impossible. The commission was triggered on 7 December 1922, when Northern Ireland exercised its right under Article 12 of the treaty to opt out of the Irish Free State, which had come into official existence on 6 December 1922. Civil war in the Irish Free State from June 1922 to May 1923, the ill health of Sir James Craig, and the rapid change of governments in Britain all delayed the initiation of the commission's work. So too did difficulties in interpreting the responsibility of the commission, particularly the problem of reconciling the "wishes of the inhabitants" and "economic and geographic conditions," as laid down in Article 12.

The Irish Free State appointed Minister for Education Eoin MacNeill as its Boundary Commissioner on 12 July 1923. In May 1924 the Northern Ireland government refused to appoint its Boundary Commissioner, arguing that it was not a party to the 1921 treaty. After the passage of special legislation at Westminster it was agreed that Britain could appoint the Northern Ireland commissioner. The commission, when it finally met for the first time in November 1924, was comprised of MacNeill (representing the Irish Free State), J. R. Fisher (representing Northern Ireland), and South African Supreme Court Justice Richard Feetham (for Britain), who was also the chairman.

Through late 1924 and early 1925 the commission toured the border region seeking written submissions regarding local views on possible boundary changes and on the work of the Commission and holding meetings in towns and villages to hear the views of nationalists and unionists. Though the Northern Ireland government did not recognize the commission, it did not openly hinder its work. Belfast was secure in its belief that possession of its territory was nine-tenths of the law: "not an inch" and "what we have, we hold" were the contemporary slogans in Northern Ireland. It would be very difficult to remove territory from the control of the Northern Ireland government.

The Free State government, which had established the North-Eastern Boundary Bureau in 1922 to collect material on partition and to press the Free State case for revising the boundary in its favor, doggedly believed it would be awarded large territorial transfers by the commission. However, there is evidence to suggest that W. T. Cosgrave, President of the Executive Council of the Irish Free State and Kevin O'Higgins, Minister for Home Affairs of the Irish Free State, were less sanguine about the chances of the commission finding for the Free State. One of the most striking failures in the Free State's handling of the Boundary Commission was the apparent lack of contact between Dublin and James McNeill (Eoin MacNeill's brother), who was Irish high commissioner in London. Dublin should have been able to use McNeill to get an insight into the opinions of senior British figures towards the Commission and they should have queried him about his brother, Eoin, who was Irish Free State Boundary commissioner. Another shortcoming on the part of the Free State was the weak case that the Free State counsel made to the commission when legal arguments were heard in December 1924. A certain weariness and an overall lack of realism not evident in other areas of foreign policy pervaded the Free State's Boundary Commission policy. Perhaps government ministers were lulled into a false sense of security by a dogmatic belief in their own rhetoric and propaganda.

In the summer of 1925 the commissioners retired to London to write their report in secret. A well-founded and accurate leak in the British pro-Conservative *Morning Post* newspaper on 7 November 1925 suggested that the commission would recommend only minor alterations to the existing border. More worrisome, the paper also suggested that the commission's report would recommend that the Free State cede territory to Northern Ireland (something Dublin had never envisaged) and vice versa. The first draft of the commission's report had been finalized on 5 November, two days before the leak, and J. R. Fisher, with his strong unionist views and press connections as a former editor of the unionist *Northern Whig*, was strongly suspected of leaking the document. The disclosure led to the resignation of Eoin MacNeill as Irish boundary commissioner on 20 November, and as Free State minister for education on 24 November. (Historians question why, before the leak, MacNeill remained supportive of the commission when he must have known that the proposed transfers were not going to find favor in Dublin.)

The press leak threatened a political crisis in the Free State that, it was feared, would bring down the Cosgrave government: A main plank in its policy of implementing the 1921 treaty had fallen away. Hurried meetings between the Irish, Northern Irish, and British governments were held in London and at Chequers to try to avert a catastrophe. By an agreement signed in London on 3 December 1925 by representatives of the three governments, the Boundary Commission was revoked and its report shelved. The political crisis predict-

ed for the Free State never occurred and the Cosgrave government remained in power. The border between the Irish Free State and Northern Ireland remained as it had stood since partition in 1920. Dublin received a sweetener of sorts: the December 1925 agreement forgave a considerable portion of public debts and war-pension payments owed to Britain under Article 5 of the 1921 treaty. The planned North-South Council of Ireland was also quietly shelved, to be replaced by periodic meetings of prime ministers. Even so, the first meeting between the two prime ministers in Ireland did not take place until January 1965. The 1925 report of the Irish Boundary Commission was not finally made public until January 1968.

SEE ALSO Anglo-Irish Treaty of 1921; Civil War; Collins, Michael; Griffith, Arthur; Politics: Independent Ireland since 1922

Bibliography

Fanning, Ronan, Michael Kennedy, Eunan O'Halpin, and Dermot Keogh, eds. *Documents on Irish Foreign Policy, Volume 1, 1919–1922.* 1998.

Fanning, Ronan, Michael Kennedy, Eunan O'Halpin, and Dermot Keogh, eds. *Documents on Irish Foreign Policy, Volume 2, 1923–1926.* 2000.

Kennedy, Michael. *Division and Consensus: The Politics of Cross-Border Relations in Ireland, 1922–1969.* 2000.

Lord Longford. *Peace by Ordeal.* Reprint, 1972.

Report of the Irish Boundary Commission. 1969.

Michael Kennedy

Boru, Brian

See Dál Cais and Brian Boru.

~

Boyle, Robert

Robert Boyle (1627–1691), the most eminent natural philosopher in England in the seventeenth century before Isaac Newton, was born in Lismore Castle the seventh son of the first earl of Cork by his second wife, Catherine Fenton. His academic abilities were recognized early, and he was schooled at Eton, privately, and on a Grand Tour with his brother Francis. Settling in Geneva (1638), he was introduced to the natural philosophy of Galileo. He also went through a profound religious experience that shaped his life and science.

These travels ended when rebellion broke out in Ireland in 1641 and the party returned to London. A younger son, Boyle avoided public life and immersed himself in medicine and chemistry, to which he was introduced by Samuel Hartlib, the eminent acquaintance of his sister Catherine (Lady Ranelagh). Boyle could reconcile medicine and chemistry with his religious conscience because of their imagined social utility. He moved to Oxford in 1654 and joined a politically diverse group in experimentally investigating the new philosophy. Boyle believed that experiment revealed the structure of nature and that theorizing was a separate activity. Even as he compared the numerical results of his experiments on the "spring of air" (pressure) with the predictions of theory, others deduced from them what is now known as Boyle's Law. Although he was dependent on the design and laboratory skills of men such as Robert Hooke, Boyle became a skilled chemist and an important contributor to chemical theory. He refuted Scholastic arguments against the existence of a vacuum and against the particulate nature of matter. Some of his explanations were Cartesian, yet he rejected many others because he could find no experimental evidence for them.

His scrupulosity as a Christian gentleman also marked his science and included painstaking descriptions of his methods, instrumentation, and results. He delineated for the fledgling scientific community (especially for members of the new scientific institution the Royal Society, of which he was a founding member) the proper conduct of natural philosophers and the methods of natural philosophy. The precarious position of the Royal Society in the early Restoration period was alleviated by Boyle's presence in London after 1668.

Boyle's elevated social position made him a symbol and representative of the new science and he spent much time entertaining important visitors to London for scientific activity. Boyle never married and seems to have suffered ill health for most of his life. In his will he established a series of public lectures (named after him) that were used by his contemporaries to refute atheism through use of the new science. Of all Irish-born scientists, he is the most distinguished.

SEE ALSO Dublin Philosophical Society; Petty, Sir William; Restoration Ireland

Bibliography

Harwood, John T., ed. *The Early Essays and Ethics of Robert Boyle.* 1991.

Hunter, Michael. *Robert Boyle (1627–1691): Scrupulosity in Science.* 2000.

Maddison, R. E. W. *The Life of the Honourable Robert Boyle.* 1969.

Shapin, Steven. *A Social History of Truth: Civility and Science in Seventeenth-Century England.* 1994.

Elizabeth Garber

Boyne, Battle of the

Undoubtedly the most famous military engagement in Irish history, the Battle of the Boyne occurred on 1 July 1690 (old style; 12 July, new style) along the river of the same name, roughly two miles to the west of the town of Drogheda. There, some 36,000 troops commanded by King William III defeated an army of approximately 25,000 troops led by King James II. For the entire year prior to the battle there were no major military engagements between the two cautious armies. But when William arrived in Protestant-controlled Ulster in mid-June, he moved quickly to engage his rival, whose supporters controlled the rest of Ireland. While James's French advisors suggested burning Dublin and retreating west of the river Shannon, James decided to guard the capital. He chose to make his stand along the river Boyne, the best defensible obstacle between Ulster and Dublin. Drogheda, at the mouth of the river, was well garrisoned, but the Boyne was fordable a few miles to the west near Oldbridge, and this is where James placed his army. Unfortunately for James, there was a loop in the river at Oldbridge, a geographical feature that helped to determine the outcome of the battle. Arriving on the north side of the river on 30 June, William and his advisors recognized their advantageous position and decided upon a diversionary, flanking movement further upstream. On the morning of 1 July, as mist cleared, James decided to split his troops—the French to the left flank and the Irish in the center—lest they all be encircled from behind. With over half of James's troops drawn off, the bulk of William's army easily forded the river at Oldbridge, where they outnumbered the Irish infantry and cavalry by three to one. The latter held out for three hours of fierce fighting before giving way, and news of the action at Oldbridge prompted a general Jacobite (supporters of James) retreat to Duleek, where in

The Battle of the Boyne [River], 1 July 1690 (old style), about forty miles north of Dublin, was one of the major engagements between James II and his French and Irish allies, on the one hand, and William III and his heavily Dutch forces on the other. William was victorious, and James fled the field and Ireland, though his army fought on for another year. COURTESY OF THE DIRECTOR, NATIONAL ARMY MUSEUM, LONDON. REPRODUCED BY PERMISSION.

confusion the entire army crossed the river Nanny. The Williamite army pursued them no further that day, but the victory was theirs. Within three days James was on a boat to France, never to return to Ireland or any of his three former kingdoms, and within a week William was crowned king of Ireland in Dublin.

One of the most striking aspects of the battle was the internationalism of both armies. William's best troops, the Blue Guards, came with him from Holland, while the rest of his army was comprised of French Huguenots, Germans, Danish, English, and Irish. Although the Williamite army was overwhelmingly Protestant, a number of regiments were predominantly Catholic. James's army was primarily Irish and French, but there were also large numbers of Germans, Walloons, and English. The diverse origins of the soldiers who fought at the Boyne reflect many of the key participants' feeling that the battle was not primarily about who ruled Ireland, or even who was the rightful ruler of England. Rather, the battle was part of a much larger,

pan-European conflict between William and Louis XIV of France, who supported James's claim to the crowns of England, Scotland, and Ireland. William's victory at the Boyne was seen in Europe as a defeat for the French, not for the Irish Catholics. This point is illustrated by the behavior of Pope Innocent XI—no friend of Louis XIV owing to the king's lack of support at Innocent's first papal nomination and to his subsequent extension of secular authority in France—who greeted news of the battle with joy, although not, as has sometimes been claimed, with a *Te Deum* at St. Peter's.

Despite this international dimension, within Ireland the outcome of the battle had dramatic consequences. William's victory gave his forces control of Leinster and much of Munster as well, while placing the supporters of James on the defensive and confining them to Connacht. A year later at Aughrim they were decisively smashed. Jacobites and their spiritual descendants have downplayed the military importance of the Boyne precisely because it was such a great, symbolic victory for the Williamites: two kings, one Catholic, one Protestant, fighting each other on Irish soil for the crown of Ireland, with the Protestant king victorious. Irish Protestants at the time, and indeed many more hence, came to see William's victory as a sign of divine providence and as the event that saved their lands and their lives from Irish Catholics. In Northern Ireland, the Battle of the Boyne is commemorated annually as a state holiday on 12 July, known commonly as "Orange Day."

SEE ALSO Jacobites and the Williamite Wars

Bibliography

Foster, Robert Fitzroy. *Modern Ireland, 1600–1972.* 1988.
Hayes-McCoy, Gerard Anthony. *Irish Battles.* 1969.
Murtagh, Harman. "The War in Ireland, 1689–1691." In *Kings in Conflict: The Revolutionary Ireland and Its Aftermath, 1689–1750,* edited by W. A. Maguire. 1990.

Charles C. Ludington

Brehon Law

Brehon law (sometimes called Irish law or Irish vernacular law) was the law of Ireland from the earliest historical period to the English invasion in 1169. From then until its abolition by English statute in the early seventeenth century, it was the law of the parts of Ireland controlled by Gaelic and gaelicized lords, though at that point it was heavily influenced by English law. The term *brehon* derives from Old-Irish *brithem*, meaning "judge." Though the earliest law texts belong to the seventh century (and possibly before), they are preserved in manuscripts from the twelfth to the seventeenth centuries. These contain three kinds of legal material: the ancient text in Old Irish, often written in large letters; glosses or explanations of terms, later than the original texts, written between the lines and in margins; and lengthy commentaries by later legal scholars, some being legal tracts in their own right. The earliest texts occur in different contemporary styles: nonstanzaic verse, highly ornate prose, and concise technical unornamented prose. There was an unbroken literary transmission of legal materials within a professional class of jurists for over a millennium.

PAGAN AND CHRISTIAN ELEMENTS

Irish law draws on two main sources: law inherited from the pre-Christian past, and Christian law-making of the early Middle Ages, mostly in Latin; the balance between these has been keenly debated by scholars. Irish shares important legal concepts and terminology with Brittonic (Welsh and Breton). Examples are Irish *macc*, Welsh *mach*, "surety, guarantor"; Irish *dedm*, Welsh *deddf*, "enacted law, ordinance"; Irish *athgabál*, Welsh *adauayl*, Breton *adgabael*, "distraint" (the seizure of property to discharge a debt); and Irish *enech* and Welsh *wyneb*, both meaning "face" and a person's honor in the sense of social worth. These examples show that the Irish and the Welsh share a legal culture that goes back to remote Celtic times, not later than 500 B.C.E. Irish lawyers of the Middle Ages were keenly aware of a pagan past.

By the time of the first records Irish law, however, had been profoundly influenced by Christianity. In the sixth and seventh centuries the laws were written down in the standard Old Irish developed and taught in the Christian schools. Law was not merely written: it was developed as the Christian law of a Christian people. *Cáin Fhuithirbe*, datable to 678 to 683 C.E., states explicitly: *ro dílsiged le dub in díchubus*, "that which is contrary to [Christian] conscience has been made forfeit by ink." The church took over the inherited legal culture and drew on its own laws to enrich it. For example, *Córus bésgnai*, a tract on the relationship of the church with lay society, provides a developed concept of pastoral care. A most notable achievement of the Middle Ages was the elaboration of Irish Church law in Latin. The contemporary canon law collection, the *Hibernensis*, is a compilation by Ruben (d. 725) of Dairinis (near Lismore) and Cú Chuimne (d. 747) of Iona, drawing on a rich earlier archive of canons, writings of the Fathers, councils, and synods. Some canons (for example, about heiresses) are so close to the vernacular laws that the two legal traditions seem to be merging, drawing on common sources and shared personnel. The *Hibernensis* is a remarkable undertaking—nothing less than an attempt to draw up, outside a Roman environment, a comprehensive legal framework for all aspects of Christian life. Brehon law is no less ambitious. Though some historians speak of the survival of pagan law schools and of lay legal culture, there is little evidence for either. In fact, nearly all the lawyers mentioned in the Irish annals between the early ninth and the twelfth centuries are clerics, and often church superiors, poets, or historians as well. Lay legal schools occur some time after the twelfth-century reform of the Irish Church when the church's legal and literary schools ceased to function, and Irish law was cultivated by hereditary legal families, notably, the MacEgans, O'Davorens, MacClancys, and O'Dorans.

THE LEGAL COLLECTIONS

The largest collection is *Senchas már* of the eighth century from Northern Ireland, possibly Armagh: some twenty-five tracts on private distraint, pledges, fosterage, kindred, clientship, relations of lord and dependent, marriage, personal injuries, public liability, theft, title to real estate, law of neighborhood (trespass and liability), honor-price, and the contractual obligations of clergy and laity. Other tracts deal with legal and court procedure, suretyship, contract, and much else. There are other collections, notably *Bretha nemed* from Munster Province, which contains valuable texts on the poets and the learned classes and on the relationship of clergy to society.

HISTORICAL EVIDENCE

These tracts offer a contemporary profile of society. Unlike Roman law people were not equal before the law in Ireland. It was class based in that a person's legal entitlements depended on social position, birth, and wealth, but social mobility was possible. Honor-price was the legal expression of that status. Compensations for offenses against persons were calculated as a fraction or multiple of their honor-price, and dependents had a fraction of the honor-price of those they depended on. For example, a man's wife, son, or daughter normally had half his honor-price; his concubine, a quarter. Important law tracts, such as the *Miadshlechta*, *Uraicecht becc*, and *Críth gablach*, deal with class and social structure. *Críth gablach* (c. 700) is a minute analysis of class structure, ranging from the lowest level of commoner through the nobles' grades to the highest level of kings, and is a unique piece of sociological analysis from the European Middle Ages.

The medico-legal tracts *Bretha crólige* and *Bretha Déin Chécht* deal with personal injuries and the liabilities of the injurer. Injured persons are brought to their homes and are looked after by their families for nine days. If they die within this period, the injurer must pay the full penalties for homicide. If they survive but are disabled or disfigured, the injurer must pay compensation. If they need further medical attention, they must be taken to the safe houses of third parties and nursed under strict conditions of care and quiet. The injurer must pay the physician, supply food (specified in detail) for the injured and their visitors, and provide substitutes to carry out the work of the injured. *Bretha Déin Chécht* deals expertly with the compensations for various kinds of physical injuries. The penalties vary with the person's class and the nature of the injury, and the physician's fee is half of the fine for major injuries and a third for minor ones.

Apart from unusual circumstances and councils of notables, the king had little role in framing law, and courts other than the king's lacked compulsory jurisdiction. As judge, the king sat with his royal judge. However, justice was mainly private, and law the province of a professional class of lawyers who developed a sophisticated system of sureties and guarantors that made their judgments effective. Irish law avoided capital punishment and provided a refined set of legal norms and procedures that sought to resolve conflict by arbitration. These principles include highly developed concepts in regard to evidence, witnesses, and legal proof, and take intentionality as well as act into account in arriving at judgment.

SEE ALSO Hiberno-Latin Culture; Early Medieval Ireland and Christianity; Kings and Kingdoms from 400 to 800 C.E.; Legal Change in the Sixteenth and Seventeenth Centuries; **Primary Documents:** From *A Discovery of the True Causes Why Ireland Was Never Entirely Subdued* (1612)

Bibliography

Binchy, Daniel A. "The Linguistic and Historical Value of the Irish Law Tracts." *Proceedings of the British Academy* 29 (1943): 195–227.

Binchy, Daniel A., ed. *Críth gablach.* 1941.

Binchy, Daniel A., ed. *Corpus iuris hibernici.* 6 vols. 1978.

Breatnach, Liam. "The Original Extent of the *Senchas már.*" *Ériu* 47 (1996): 1–43.

Charles-Edwards, T. M. *Early Irish and Welsh Kinship.* 1993.

Jenkins, Dafydd, ed. *Celtic Law Papers.* 1973.

Kelly, Fergus. *A Guide to Early Irish Law.* 1988.

McLeod, Neil, ed. and trans. *Early Irish Contract Law.* 1992.

Ó Corráin, Donnchadh. "Irish Vernacular Law and the Old Testament." In *Ireland and Christendom: The Bible and the Missions,* edited by Próinséas Ní Chatháin and Michael Richter, 1987.

Ó Corráin, Donnchadh, Liam Breatnach, and Aidan Breen. "The Laws of the Irish." *Peritia* 3 (1984): 382–438.

Wasserschleben, Herrmann. *Die irische Kanonensammlung.* 2d edition, 1885.

Donnchadh Ó Corráin

Brewing and Distilling

The modern Irish industries of brewing and distilling took shape in the late eighteenth and early nineteenth centuries. Prior to this period both beer-making and whiskey- (or spirit-) making were carried on at a mainly small-scale, local level. Whiskey was produced in small stills, both legal and illicit, often in one-person operations. Most beer was brewed by retail brewers—publicans who sold the beer they produced themselves. Whiskey became the most popular drink during the eighteenth century and remained so until the early nineteenth century, after which public taste shifted toward porter and stout, the stalwarts of the growing Irish brewing industry. By the end of the nineteenth century Guinness's brewery of Dublin was the world's largest, and Scotland had replaced Ireland as the world's leading whiskey producer.

Draconian excise legislation introduced in 1779 and 1780 led to the closure of many of the smaller legal distilleries, which in turn led to a huge upsurge in illicit distillation in the countryside and a concentration of the legal industry in larger distilleries in the cities and large towns. Use of illicit stills, which produced the colorless spirit *poitín* (or poteen), was widespread until the 1860s, when improved law enforcement, better-quality legal whiskey, and a shift to porter and stout consumption led to their decline; illicit distillation continued, but on a far smaller scale. In 1830 the distilling industry was revolutionized by the invention of the Coffey patent still, which allowed more economical production of increasingly popular lighter and blended whiskies. While the major distillers of Dublin and Cork clung to the old pot-still method, the Northern distilleries followed the Scottish lead by investing in patent-still production, prompting a shift in the Irish industry to the North: large-scale patent-still production, combined with superior marketing, ensured Scottish domination of international markets. By the 1920s, many of the leading Ulster distillers had been taken over by the Distillers Company Ltd. of Scotland and closed down, and Dublin (led by Jameson) and Cork (Cork Distillers Company) became the main Irish distilling centers in the twentieth century. Through amalgamation and improved technology and marketing, the Irish distilling industry regained a solid domestic foundation and international market presence.

The demand for whiskey waned throughout the nineteenth century because of increased prices, a successful temperance campaign, and the growing popularity of porter and stout. Since the mid-eighteenth century the small-scale Irish brewing industry had suffered from competition from the large British porter breweries. The decline was reversed toward the end of the century as brewing was reorganized into larger and more efficient units. Commercial brewers were growing in size and gradually displacing the formerly dominant retail operators. The larger-scale and more technically efficient Irish porter breweries, particularly Guinness of Dublin and Beamish and Crawford of Cork, rapidly overcame British competition and established brewing as a major Irish industry. Between the 1850s and the eve of the First World War output trebled; about 40 percent was exported. The extraordinary growth of Guinness's brewery was largely responsible for this. By the early twentieth century it was the largest brewery in the world, having managed to capture the expanding Irish market in the second half of the nineteenth century and to establish a crucial presence in the British market. About a dozen substantial breweries that catered to local markets managed to survive Guinness's domination in the twentieth century. The only two stouts to survive were Beamish and Murphy's, both brewed in Cork city. A key to their survival was the breweries' operation of "tied house" systems, whereby public houses in Cork city and county were owned or controlled by the breweries, providing a captive market.

Following Irish independence the number of breweries and distilleries decreased, reflecting economic hardship, new duties on alcoholic products, and restrictions on public-house licenses. Guinness remained dominant, aided by its huge export market, and brewing continued to be the country's leading industry primarily due to the Dublin brewery's success. The opening up of the Irish economy in the 1960s and shifts in consumer tastes changed the face of the industry. Guinness took over many of the last small breweries, while Murphy and Beamish were taken over by foreign multinationals. The three major Irish breweries extended their product ranges to include newly popular lagers and ales, primarily through trade agreements with foreign breweries, and the entire industry underwent extensive modernization. Stout is still the most popular beverage in Ireland, and Guinness still dominates the industry.

SEE ALSO Guinness Brewing Company; Industrialization; Industry since 1920; Rural Industry; Transport—Road, Canal, Rail

Bibliography

Bielenberg, Andy. "The Irish Brewing Industry and the Rise of Guinness, 1790–1914." In *The Dynamics of the Interna-*

tional Brewing Industry since 1800, edited by R. G. Wilson and T. R. Gourvish. 1998.

Connell, K. H. "Illicit Distillation." In *Irish Peasant Society: Four Historical Essays*. 1968.

Dennison, S. R., and Oliver MacDonagh. *Guinness, 1886–1939: From Incorporation to the Second World War*. 1998.

Magee, Malachy. *Irish Whiskey: A 1000-Year Tradition*. 1991.

Maguire, E. B. *Irish Whiskey: A History of Distilling, the Spirit Trade and Excise Controls in Ireland*. 1973.

Ó Drisceoil, Diarmuid, and Donal Ó Drisceoil. *The Murphy's Story: The History of Lady's Well Brewery, Cork*. 1996.

Donal Ó Drisceoil

Bronze Age Culture

The precise nature of the influences which resulted in Ireland in the change from a Neolithic economy predominately dependent on stone for the production of tools and weapons is not fully understood. What is known is that together with changes in burial practices and pottery types, other important technological changes also took place. These changes occurred from about 2500 B.C.E. and were responsible for the introduction not simply of objects made from copper and gold but of the complete metalworking process. The knowledge that results in the production of finished metal objects is complex, involving many different stages, including the sourcing of the raw materials, the winning or mining of the ores, the production of metal by smelting and refining the ores, and the fabrication of objects. It has been generally accepted that the people who introduced a new type of pottery called *Beaker* pottery, which occurs also in Britain and continental Europe, were instrumental in the introduction of metalworking.

THE EARLY BRONZE AGE

Ireland had rich sources of copper ores, especially in the southwest, which were identifiable by these early prospectors, and which resulted in the development of a significant copper- and later, bronze-working industry. One of the most important sites for the production of copper ore and metal was discovered at Ross Island, Killarney, Co. Kerry. Excavations here have produced thousands of stone hammers used to break up the ore-bearing rock as well as evidence of smelting ores and habitation debris, including Beaker pottery. Radiocarbon dates ranging from 2400 to 2000 B.C.E. have shown that Ross Island is the earliest dated copper mine in western Europe. It is likely that it produced the major portion of the copper requirements of Ireland in the earliest stages of the Bronze Age. An important technological improvement occurred with the development of the copper/tin alloy called bronze, which is a more durable metal. This occurred at about 2100 B.C.E. The tin mines of Cornwall, in the southwest of England, were the most likely source of the tin used in Ireland. The objects produced at this time were chiefly axeheads, daggers, and halberds, cast in one-piece or two-piece stone molds and finished by hammering. The change from copper to bronze can be observed in the gradual improvements in the functionality of the tools and weapons being made.

At the same time gold was also being used to produce a range of ornaments made from sheet gold. Although the sources of the gold used in Ireland throughout the Bronze Age have not yet been located, gold is found in different parts of the country. The products of the Early Bronze Age include the so-called basket earrings, decorated discs and plaques usually found in pairs, and collars of crescentic shape called *lunula(e)*. More than eighty lunulae have been found in Ireland. A small number were found in Britain and western Europe; some of them were exported from Ireland and others are copies of the Irish form. The finest of them show that gold-working skills were developed to a high degree, as the thinly beaten gold sheet and delicate patterns of geometric motifs demonstrate. The carefully executed patterns of incised lozenges, triangles, zigzag motifs, and groups of lines are symmetrically arranged, producing original compositions from a very limited repertoire of motifs. Similar decorative patterns are also seen on pottery and some types of bronze axehead.

Burial practices also changed; gradually, large tombs built above ground were replaced by burials placed in small stone-lined structures called *cists*. The classic Beaker burial, consisting of a single crouched inhumation accompanied by a ceramic vessel and other objects such as barbed and tanged flint arrowheads and stone wrist bracers, does not occur in Ireland. However, the same rite of burial, accompanied by a highly decorated pottery Bowl and occasionally objects of stone, bone, or bronze, was adopted. Other pottery types, including Vases and different types of urns (vase urns, encrusted urns, cordoned and collared urns) were also used. A variety of burial rites which included cremation and the placing of the cremated remains (in many cases representing more than one person) in a large urn to be buried upside down in a pit, were adopted. These burials occur in isolation, in flat cemeteries, or under or within mounds of earth and/or stone. These burial practices continued until about 1400 B.C.E., when they were replaced by the interment of cremated remains in pits or in large undecorated vessels similar to pots from domestic sites. This became the predominant burial rite for the remainder of the Bronze Age. These are found in unmarked cemeteries and other sites, such as ring barrows or ring ditches.

Settlement or habitation sites vary throughout the Bronze Age and include enclosed and unenclosed sites containing round or oval houses and other ancillary structures, some of which may have been used for storage or for housing animals. Lakeside settlements and the use of artificial islands called *crannógs* and small natural islands were a feature of Late Bronze Age society, and the building of large enclosures on hilltop sites from the end of the second millennium is thought by some to suggest a lack of stability and a need for defensive enclosures. Another view is that these sites were places of assembly for important seasonal events.

THE MIDDLE BRONZE AGE

During the period called the Middle Bronze Age (c. 1700–1200 B.C.E.) the production of bronze and gold metalwork continued, but there were changes in metallurgical techniques and in the types of objects being produced. Axeheads and daggers continued to be made while spearheads and rapiers were introduced. The hafting of tools and weapons was continuously improved as fully socketed forms were developed. Casting techniques also improved, and sophisticated two-part stone molds and eventually clay molds were used. Work in gold also continued, although the ornaments produced were very different from those of the earlier period. Probably through influences from the Mediterranean, objects of twisted bars and strips of gold became common. Some, such as the pair of torcs from Tara, Co. Meath, are extremely large and heavy, suggesting that rich sources of ore were available. Sheet gold was still used, but chiefly for armlets decorated with raised ribs and grooved bands, such as those from Derrinboy, Co. Offaly.

The occurrence of monuments such as stone circles, stone alignments (two or more stones in a row), and standing stones suggests a continuing interest in the building of structures that dominate the landscape. Some of these monuments are oriented in ways that suggest alignment on specific solar events. Others have been used for burials. The monuments known in Ireland as *fulachta fiadh*—mounds of cracked and burnt stone surrounding timber- or stone-lined pits—occur in large numbers in many parts of the country. They may have been used as cooking places, for bathing, or for another as yet unknown purpose that required large quantities of hot water.

This gold collar from Gleninsheen, Co. Clare, was found concealed in a rock fissure in 1932. The collar is formed from a single sheet of gold with two terminal discs attached to it with twisted gold wire and dates to the Late Bronze Age (c. 800–600 B.C.E.). COPYRIGHT © NATIONAL MUSEUM OF IRELAND. REPRODUCED BY PERMISSION.

The construction of hillforts from about 1200 B.C.E. and the appearance in the artifactual record of large numbers of bronze swords suggest that the later stages of the Bronze Age (1000–500 B.C.E.) were unsettled. Nevertheless, the manufacture of bronze and gold objects continued, with many new forms being introduced. Further technological advances produced cast bronze horns, while sheet-work skills were perfected in the fabrication of cauldrons and shields.

Similar techniques were used to produce a huge variety of gold ornaments, including sheet-gold collars (called *gorgets*) and ear-spools, while cast and hammered bars were used to make a great variety of bracelets and dress-fasteners. Collars and ear-spools are decorated with raised ribs and cable patterns, conical bosses, and groups of concentric circles. These were produced using a wide range of goldsmithing techniques, such as repoussé, chasing, stamping, and raising. Finely beaten gold foils were used to cover split-ring ornaments of different types, pinheads, and *bullae* (amulets) of base metals. Gold wire was used to stitch the component parts of gold collars together, to decorate as filigree, and to make the biconical ornaments called *lock-rings*.

Large and small quantities of objects, as well as single objects, were regularly abandoned both on dry land and in wet and boggy places, many in situations from which they could never be recovered. Some hoards, such as the one from a bog at Dowris, Co. Offaly, contained hundreds of bronze objects, including axeheads, spearheads, horns, crotals, and cauldrons. The hoard found at Mooghaun, Co. Clare, contained hundreds of gold bracelets and many gold collars. The custom of hoarding was common all over Europe and must have been part of the wider social and ritual lives of the people.

While metalwork, ceramics, and stone predominate during the Bronze Age in Ireland, other media such as wood, leather, bone, jet, amber, wool, and other natural materials were used to provide a range of everyday and special objects.

From about 700 B.C.E. a gradual change from a mainly bronze-working economy to one based on the use of iron as the preferred metal took place. These changes were profound and irreversible, affecting all aspects of society. Eventually, iron replaced bronze as the preferred metal for the production of tools and weapons, and bronze was restricted mostly to objects of a more decorative nature. Gold was almost completely abandoned and was never again used in Ireland to the same extent or with the same degree of unbounded plenitude.

SEE ALSO Prehistoric and Celtic Ireland; Stone Age Settlement

Bibliography

Armstrong, E. C. R. *Catalogue of Irish Gold Ornaments in the Collection of the Royal Irish Academy.* 1920. Reprint, 1933.

Cahill, Mary. "Later Bronze Age Goldwork from Ireland—Form, Function, and Formality." In *Ireland in the Bronze Age,* edited by John Waddell and E. Shee Twohig. 1995.

Cahill, Mary. "Before the Celts: Treasures in Gold in Bronze." In *Treasures of the National Museum of Ireland: Irish Antiquities,* edited by Patrick F. Wallace and Raghnall Ó Floinn. 2002.

Cooney, Gabriel, and Eoin Grogan. *Irish Prehistory: A Social Perspective.* 1994.

Eogan, George. *Hoards of the Irish Later Bronze Age.* 1983.

Eogan, George. *The Accomplished Art: Gold and Gold Working in Britain and Ireland during the Bronze Age.* 1994.

Waddell, John. *The Prehistoric Archaeology of Ireland.* 1998.

Mary Cahill

~

Brooke, Basil Stanlake, First Viscount Brookeborough

Basil Stanlake Brooke, First Viscount Brookeborough (1888–1973), unionist politician and prime minister of Northern Ireland, was born on 9 June at Colebrooke House, County Fermanagh, the family seat. The Brooke family had been Fermanagh landowners since the Ulster plantation. Brooke was educated at Pau (France) and Winchester, joining the British army at the age of 20. During home leave in 1912 to 1913 he joined the anti–Home Rule campaign, working with the Fermanagh Ulster Volunteer Force (UVF). Brooke lost his religious faith during the First World War. He left the army in 1919 and returned to Fermanagh. During the "Troubles" of 1919 to 1921 he revived the UVF as a local defense body, the nucleus of the Ulster Special Constabulary. Brooke's attitude toward Catholics and nationalists was permanently embittered by his experiences during the troubles. In 1929, Brooke became a member of the Northern Ireland Parliament for the Lisnaskea division of County Fermanagh, serving until 1965. Between 1933 and 1941 he was a competent minister for agriculture. Several speeches in 1933, calling on Protestant employers to employ only "Protestant lads and lasses," made him a particularly hated figure for Catholics and nationalists. In 1941 Brooke became minister of commerce, and was seen as the most effective member of a cabinet dominated by geriatric veterans of the Craigavon era. In 1943 he led a revolt by junior ministers that unseated J. M. Andrews and brought a new generation to power within the Unionist Party. Two of his sons died in the Second World War. Brooke's early years as premier were buoyed by the postwar economic boom, the welfare state, and British sympathy for Ulster unionism in reaction against Irish wartime neutrality. In 1952 he became Viscount Brookeborough. His term is often seen as a missed opportunity to reconcile the Catholic minority. A liberal unionist faction emerged, denounced by populist hardliners including the young Ian Paisley. Brooke was committed fully to neither liberals nor hardliners; but in the last resort, he preferred to exploit the nationalist threat, emphasized by the Republic's misconceived antipartition campaign and the Irish Republican Army's border campaign of 1956 to 1962. In the mid-1950s Northern Ireland's traditional industries resumed their decline; Brooke's amateurish governance was visibly inadequate to address the province's economic problems. The Northern Ireland Labour Party made significant progress in the 1958 and 1962 Stormont elections. When Brooke retired in 1963, he was felt to have stayed too long. His son John later became Stormont minister for home affairs. Brooke lived to see the fall of Stormont and died on 18 August 1973. He epitomized the narrowness, determination, and ultimate inadequacy of the traditional unionist elite.

SEE ALSO Declaration of a Republic and the 1949 Ireland Act; Ulster Unionist Party in Office

Bibliography

Barton, Brian. *Brookeborough: The Making of a Prime Minister.* 1988.

Hennessy, Thomas. *A History of Northern Ireland, 1920–1996.* 1997.

Patterson, Henry. *Ireland since 1939.* 2002.

Patrick Maume

Bruce Invasion

The Bruce invasion of Ireland (1315–1317) was in fact an episode in the Scottish War of Independence, arising from the attempt of Edward I of England to annex Scotland following the extinction of the direct line of native kings in 1286. A national resistance movement at once emerged, and in March 1306 Robert Bruce had himself inaugurated as king of the Scots. Forced almost at once to flee, he returned to conduct a successful guerrilla campaign against the English. In June 1314 a large invading army was destroyed by Bruce at the battle of Bannockburn, near Stirling. Nevertheless, the English refused to accept Scottish independence.

It was probably as a means of bringing pressure on England, and of depriving it of the resources that it was drawing from the Irish colony, that Robert, in May 1316, sent his brother Edward with a force to Ireland. The invasion was accompanied by an appeal to the native Irish to throw off the English yoke. After being joined by Domhnall Ó Néill, acknowledged head of the Irish of Ulster, Edward Bruce was proclaimed king of Ireland. A letter—the famous "Remonstrance"—was sent by Ó Néill to the pope, setting out the oppressions of the Anglo-Normans and asking him to transfer the sovereignty of Ireland from the English to Edward Bruce, to whom Ó Néill transferred any hereditary right he had to the kingship. Two and a half years of indeci-

sive warfare followed, ending with Edward's death in battle at Faughart, Co. Louth, on 14 October 1318. The campaign coincided with three years of exceptionally bad weather, which led to the worst European famine of the Middle Ages.

The Bruces had hoped to find widespread support in Ireland, but this failed to materialize. They may not have been aware of the depth of racial antagonism between Gael and Anglo-Norman that existed at this time in Ireland, since it did not exist in Scotland. Only some minor Anglo-Norman landowners in Ulster and Meath joined the Scots, all the major barons staying loyal to the English crown. The factional divisions of the Gaelic Irish ensured that—as happened with the O'Briens—if one faction allied themselves with the Scots, their rivals would join the English. Nevertheless, the opportunities provided by the invasion were seized upon by the Gaelic Irish, especially in the provinces of Leinster and Connacht, to attack the local colonial settlements, and after the invasion large areas passed out of the control of the Dublin administration. If the Bruce invasion failed in its aim of establishing an independent Irish kingdom allied with Scotland, it accelerated the Gaelic Recovery and the progress of gaelicization among the Anglo-Norman elites.

SEE ALSO English Government in Medieval Ireland; Gaelic Recovery; Gaelic Society in the Late Middle Ages; Norman Invasion and Gaelic Resurgence

Bibliography

Barrow, Geoffrey W. S. *Robert Bruce and the Community of the Realm of Scotland.* 3d edition, 1988. Reprint, 1992.

Duffy, Seán, ed. *Robert the Bruce's Irish Wars.* 2002.

Frame, Robin. "The Bruces in Ireland: 1315–1318." In *Irish Historical Studies* 19 (1974): 3–7. Reprinted in Robin Frame, *Ireland and Britain, 1170–1450.* 1998.

McNamee, Colm. *The Wars of the Bruces: Scotland, England, and Ireland, 1306–1328.* 1997.

Kenneth Nicholls

Burial Customs and Popular Religion from 1500 to 1690

In early modern Ireland, as in Europe, death was a public drama. The dying individual would be visited by friends, relatives, and clergy, and was expected to spend time preparing for death and putting worldly affairs in order. In certain areas bells were rung on death and again at the funeral. The body was washed and placed in a shroud that was knotted or tied at head and feet; special shroud pins might also be used. This work was the preserve of women. Corpses were usually laid out and buried with hands lying on the pelvis or at the sides. Catholics increasingly wished to die or be buried in religious habit—that of the Franciscans was particularly popular—as a means of eliciting the patronage of important saints. Most people would have been buried in the shroud alone, although archaeological evidence suggests that coffin burial became increasingly common. Parishes often hired out biers and coffins, particularly in the late seventeenth century.

THE WAKE

Prior to interment the corpse was laid out in his or her own home. Family and friends continually watched the body, with a substantial company often gathering at this wake. Drinking of alcohol, dancing, and rowdy games were a feature of wakes until the early twentieth century. The practice of keening over the corpse, both at the wake and the funeral, was frequently commented upon in the early modern period, usually negatively. For onlookers, howling and crying were the main features of the keen, though it sometimes came across as quite musical. Keeners, who were usually female, might also drink the blood of the deceased, clap their hands, and tear at their hair and clothes. The keen was more than a lament: it also served as an expression of protest (against death and other wrongs suffered by women and society), and it might occasionally be used in contexts other than funerals. Wakes and keening faced increasing opposition from the Catholic Church and the civil authorities on both national and local levels from the early seventeenth century onwards, as attempts were made to impose new forms of "civilized" and reverent behavior.

Few mentions of the *banshee* (*ban sí*, "fairy woman"), whose keen warned of or announced a death, survive from this period. However, it is clear that among the Gaelic Irish in particular, belief in death omens was widespread.

WRITTEN EVIDENCE

Private commemoration of and grief for the dead was expressed in personal documents and poetry. In Gaelic areas the deaths of important individuals often occasioned the creation of praise-poetry by the bards, though this reveals little about funerary practice or real feelings. Indeed, for Gaelic areas in particular, many aspects of the process of death and the treatment of the dead are difficult to retrieve from the patchy sources that survive from this period. Elsewhere, wills and other sources give some indications of the ways in which official proscriptions against donations to the Catholic Church could be sidestepped, and it is clear that significant resources were expended on prayers, pious works, and masses to aid the dead in purgatory. Irish Protestants tended to express strong confidence in meeting their loved ones in heaven, whereas all sides of the religious divide were quick to consign their enemies to hell.

BURIAL

Many burials were accomplished within a day of death, though two to four days was the usual interval between death and burial for the middle and upper classes in the 1630s. For the very wealthy, several weeks or months of preparation might go into the elaborate and costly funerals orchestrated by the heralds, whose office in Ireland was founded in 1552, and this delay might necessitate the embalming of the corpse. Heraldic funerals reached the height of their popularity in the early to mid-seventeenth century, especially among recently established New English settler families, for whom such display served to underline their new titles and entitlements. Their subsequent decline reflected the social disruption of the 1640s and 1650s as well as the rise of the new fashion for nocturnal funerals. Central to heraldic and other funerals was the procession in which the community gathered in hierarchical order. Military funerals might involve the participation of soldiers, while the inclusion of the poor might demonstrate the deceased's charity. (Catholics also perceived large numbers of mourners as an important source of prayer for the dead.) There was considerable communal participation in funerals in all parts of the country. Edifying sermons might occur at both Protestant and Catholic funerals.

Funerals occasionally become the site of conflict, both between and within religious denominations. Several examples of resistance to Protestant interference in Catholic funerals exist, as do accounts of rivalry between the Catholic clergy and religious orders. As church buildings gradually came under Protestant control, Catholic funeral services seem increasingly to have been held in private houses. However, burial in parish cemeteries and Protestant-controlled churches continued after the Reformation. Burial in the graveyards of old monastic sites also remained popular. Changes in the use of some of these buildings, especially in the towns, led to some adjustments in burial practice, though in many areas monasteries were protected by local Catholic landowners.

The long-established custom of burial within church buildings seems generally to have begun to decline in the late seventeenth century as overcrowding became an increasing problem. Previously, church burial was considered to be more prestigious than cemetery burial (it was also more expensive), and parts of the church, such as the east and south sides, were deemed particularly desirable. For Catholics burial near religious images and holy people was also popular. This, along with the practice of chantry-chapel creation and burial, was somewhat disturbed after the Reformation, though many Catholics long retained burial rights in family chapels, and even, through the building of new mortuary chapels, aimed to continue their association with church buildings while isolating themselves from their heretical functions. The arrival of new religious groups, such as the Quakers, led to the foundation of new burial grounds and the introduction of different burial practices (such as the south–north rather than west-east orientation of graves). Meanwhile, those considered outsiders by society—criminals, suicides, heretics, and so on—might be relegated to interment in unconsecrated ground, refused burial, or even exhumed and destroyed. In times of war and plague, bodies were frequently disposed of in mass graves. The visiting of graves seems to have been common, and the graves (and remains) of holy people, such as those perceived as martyrs for Catholicism, might become places of pilgrimage.

COMMEMORATION

Increased control over the running of churches and cemeteries during this period saw the gradual removal there from of the commercial and social activities (such as markets, taverns, and game playing) that they had formerly housed. In the later 1600s, gravestones began to appear and would eventually transform the graveyard landscape. Previously, people had largely been commemorated within churches by monuments that took on much variety in size and shape in the sixteenth and seventeenth centuries. The range of choice available made commemoration accessible to those of quite modest means. The wealthy might employ foreign craftspeople to produce large modern monuments, such as those of the first earl of Cork in Youghal and Dublin. Elsewhere local schools of craftsmen, such as the Kerins and O'Tunneys in the midlands, or individual masons competently provided for the needs of the local Catholic business and landowning classes. In their iconography and inscriptions funerary monuments reflect attitudes to death, desires to commemorate family ties and earth-

ly achievements, the ambitions of the upwardly mobile, and some of the religious concerns of Catholics and Protestants, particularly ideas about the afterlife.

SEE ALSO Calvinist Influences in Early Modern Ireland; Church of Ireland: Elizabethan Era; Family: Marriage Patterns and Family Life from 1500 to 1690; Religion: 1500 to 1690; Religion: Traditional Popular Religion; **Primary Documents:** Act of Uniformity (1560)

Bibliography

Gillespie, Raymond. "Funerals and Society in Early Seventeenth Century Ireland." *Journal of the Royal Society of Antiquaries in Ireland* 115 (1985): 86–91.

Gillespie, Raymond. "Irish Funeral Monuments and Social Change 1500–1700: Perceptions of Death." In *Ireland: Art into History*, edited by Raymond Gillespie and B. P. Kennedy, 1994.

Fry, Susan. *Burial in Medieval Ireland: 900–1500*. 1999.

Tait, Clodagh. "Colonising Memory: Manipulations of Burial and Commemoration in the Career of the 'Great' Earl of Cork." *Proceedings of the Royal Irish Academy* 101 (2001): 107–134.

Tait, Clodagh. *Death, Burial and Commemoration in Ireland, 1550–1650*. 2002.

Clodagh Tait

Burke, Edmund

The statesman and writer Edmund Burke (1729–1797) was born in Dublin on 12 January 1729 and died at Beaconsfield in England on 9 July 1797. In his writings and career Burke sought to understand and exemplify the virtues of the emerging British empire. He sought to explain how the distinctive virtues of English constitutional and social traditions were capacious enough to absorb new populations, such as that of Ireland, and to expand to new territories, especially North America. While never a systematic philosopher, he laid the basis for a distinctive brand of conservative liberalism that exists to this day.

Burke's father, Richard, was a Protestant attorney at the Court of Exchequer, while his mother, Mary Nagle, was a Catholic with connections in Munster. Burke's vision of an inclusive model of empire was therefore generated from his family background. His

Edmund Burke (1729–1797) is best known for his career as a philosopher and statesman in England. He was, however, born in Ireland and used his Irish connections to play a significant role in Anglo-Irish affairs. © BETTMAN/CORBIS. REPRODUCED BY PERMISSION.

olution in France (1790) were of more long-term importance than his political career.

SEE ALSO Eighteenth-Century Politics: 1714 to 1778—Interest Politics; Eighteenth-Century Politics: 1778 to 1795—Parliamentary and Popular Politics; Eighteenth-Century Politics: 1795 to 1800—Repression, Rebellion, and Union

Bibliography

Langford, Paul, et al., eds. *Writings and Speeches of Edmund Burke*. 7 vols. 1981–.

O'Brien, Conor Cruise. *The Great Melody: A Thematic Biography and Commented Anthology of Edmund Burke*. 1992.

James Livesey

early education was in the Quaker school at Ballitore in Kildare, and he attended Trinity College from 1743 to 1748 (B.A. 1748). There he was a founding member of the Historical Society. He left Ireland in 1750 but maintained Irish interests particularly as private secretary to Charles Watson-Wentworth, second marquis of Rockingham, leader of the parliamentary Whigs. Burke argued for Catholic Emancipation and was paymaster of the forces in the Rockingham administration that repealed Poynings' Law and granted legislative independence to Ireland in 1782. Burke spoke on Irish affairs as a British MP for Wendover from 1766 to 1794. He was a correspondent of the Catholic Committee, and his son was its agent in London until 1790. His Irish interests often hindered his English career, notably by costing him his Bristol seat.

Catholic Emancipation of Ireland was only one of his five great causes, which also included parliamentary reform, conciliation with America, reform of the Indian administration, and opposition to the French Revolution. None of these was achieved in his lifetime. His writings, notably *A Philosophical Enquiry into the Origin of Our Ideas of the Sublime and Beautiful* (1757), *A Letter to the Sheriffs of Bristol* (1777), and *Reflections on the Rev-*

Butler, James, Twelfth Earl and First Duke of Ormond

James Butler, twelfth earl and first duke of Ormond (1610–1688), lord lieutenant of Ireland, was born on 19 October 1610 at Clerkenwell, London, into the greatest of the old English families. Placed as a royal ward under the direction of the archbishop of Canterbury, he grew up a committed adherent of the Protestant Established Church. Inheriting the earldom (1633), he sat in the 1634–1635 Irish parliament. With the outbreak of the Irish rising in October 1641, he was given command of the king's army in Ireland. When the Gaelic Irish were joined by the Catholic Old English, including prominent figures related to Ormond, his loyalty to the king never wavered. He was made marquis of Ormond in August 1642, soon after the outbreak of the English civil war. Having agreed to a truce with the Catholic Confederates (September 1643), he was soon after appointed lord lieutenant of Ireland with instructions to negotiate a peace that would free up an army to support the beleaguered king in England. Ormond's task was complicated by the king's secretly authorizing the earl of Glamorgan to offer the Confederates more favorable terms on both religion and land than the Protestant Ormond would have thought prudent or proper. When the Glamorgan initiative ended in failure, Ormond reopened talks with the Confederates. The ensuing first Ormond peace (March 1646) was condemned by Archbishop Rinuccini, the papal nuncio, who excommunicated its adherents and secured its repudiation by the Catholic Confederacy (February 1647). The military failure of the king's cause in England, together with the seeming impossibility of agreement with the Confederates in Ireland, led Ormond to surrender Dublin to a parliamentary army under Colonel Michael Jones (June 1647). He left for England in late July, meeting the king and later traveling to Paris to confer with the queen. He returned to Ireland in the autumn of 1648. With news that the king was to stand trial, it was imperative for all who feared the parliamentary radicals in England to unite, and a new peace (the second Ormond peace) was agreed in January 1649. In the summer Ormond's attempt to take back Dublin ended in a rout at Rathmines. When Oliver Cromwell and a huge English army arrived in August, Ormond was in no position to take them on, though he had some modest, if short-lived, successes. Relations with the Catholic bishops again deteriorated, his position became untenable, and he left for France in December 1650.

Throughout the 1650s Ormond was one of Charles II's closest advisors at the exiled Stuart court, and so he remained immediately after the Restoration (1660). Appointed lord lieutenant of Ireland, he arrived in Dublin (July 1662) in time to give the royal assent to the Act of Settlement (1662). Faced with Catholic disappointment at the limited scope for restoration of confiscated estates, and with Protestant fears that the court of claims was conceding too much, he recognized that a second land act was necessary and was in London in 1664 to 1665 while the terms of the Act of Explanation (1665) were hammered out.

The most consistent aspect of Ormond's government was unequivocal support for the established church. He tolerated Protestant dissent only to the extent that it did not threaten the Church of Ireland, and his generally suspicious attitude toward the Catholic clergy was the result of his experience in the 1640s. The encouragement that he gave to the supporters of a Catholic remonstrance of loyalty was as much designed to provoke division among Catholic clergymen as to find a basis on which the Catholic Church might be tolerated. His inability to manage government finances was used by his enemies at Whitehall to argue for his recall, and whatever the king's reasons, Ormond was replaced as viceroy in 1669.

Reappointed for his last stint as viceroy (1677–1685), he maintained a stable order in Ireland while England was engulfed by the popish plot and exclusion crises. In James II's reign he went into retirement in England after a public life whose guiding principles were loyalty to the Crown, the established church, and the house of Ormond.

SEE ALSO Confederation of Kilkenny; Jacobites and the Williamite Wars; Puritan Sectaries; Restoration Ireland

Bibliography

Barnard, Toby, and Jane Fenlon, eds. *The Dukes of Ormonde, 1610–1745.* 2000.

Beckett, J. C. *The Cavalier Duke: A Life of James Butler, 1st duke of Ormond, 1610–1688.* 1990.

Carte, Thomas. *The Life of James, Duke of Ormond.* 6 vols. 1851.

James McGuire

Butt, Isaac

Barrister and Home Rule Party leader Isaac Butt (1813–1879) was born on 6 September in Glenfin, Co. Donegal. The only son of a Church of Ireland rector, Butt attended Trinity College, Dublin, where he helped to found the *Dublin University Magazine* in 1833. Butt was appointed professor of political economy at Trinity in 1836 and was called to the bar in 1838. He began his political career in the 1840s as a conservative opponent of Daniel O'Connell's Repeal movement. Elected MP for Youghal as a Liberal-Conservative in 1852, he moved to London and lived there until he lost his parliamentary seat in 1865. During this period Butt fathered two illegitimate children and ran up huge debts that left him in a precarious financial position for the rest of his life.

While in Parliament, Butt championed the rights of Irish tenants, and after 1865, at great financial cost to himself, he further enhanced his reputation with Irish nationalists by defending many Fenians in the trials that followed the suppression of the *Irish People* in 1865 and the failed rising of 1867. In 1868 Butt assumed the leadership of the amnesty movement, which sought the release of the imprisoned Fenians. In the following year Butt also became a leader of the Irish Tenant League, which campaigned for tenant-right legislation. After Gladstone's government failed to satisfy either of these movements, granting only a partial amnesty in 1869 and passing the limited Land Act of 1870, Butt argued that only a domestic Irish parliament could redress Irish grievances and launched the Home Government Association in 1870.

Although Butt was elected MP for Limerick in 1871, at first few other Home Rule candidates were successful. However, when the Catholic middle classes joined the new Home Rule League, and Fenians gave it their tacit support, Butt and his followers captured over half the Irish seats in the 1874 general election. Because the Home Rule Party was ill-disciplined, Butt accomplished very little. Soon some of Butt's impatient followers, led by Joseph Biggar and Charles Stewart Parnell, challenged his hesitant leadership by engaging in parliamentary obstruction. Although Butt retained control of the Home Rule League until his death on 5 May 1879, leadership of the Irish national movement had passed to Parnell in 1878. Butt won the support of Fenians, tenant-right advocates, clergy, and middle-class Catholics for a Home Rule Party, but because of his indecisive parliamentary leadership he failed to bring Home Rule any closer.

SEE ALSO Fenian Movement and the Irish Republican Brotherhood; Home Rule Movement and the Irish Parliamentary Party: 1870 to 1891; Land Acts of 1870 and 1881; Parnell, Charles Stewart; Tenant Right, or Ulster Custom; **Primary Documents:** Resolutions Adopted at the Home Rule Conference (18–21 November 1873); Speech Advocating Consideration of Home Rule by the House of Commons (30 June 1874)

Bibliography

Comerford, R. V. *The Fenians in Context.* 1996.

Thornley, David. *Isaac Butt and Home Rule.* 1964.

Patrick F. Tally

Calvinist Influences in Early Modern Ireland

John Calvin's *Institutes* (first published 1536, final edition 1559) is one of the major theological achievements of the Reformation, a systematic attempt to develop a biblical theology taking Luther's theology as its starting point, but developing it in new directions. If one defines Calvinism in relation to the model church structure that Calvin established in Geneva, with its insistence on the relative powers of church and state, its three-fold non-episcopal ministry, and its distinctive disciplinary structure, then the formal history of Calvinism in early modern Ireland, thus defined, began with the arrival of the Scottish army in Ulster in 1642 and the consequent establishment of Calvinist presbyteries in various Ulster towns. These subsequently grew into the Irish Presbyterian church(es), which after the Restoration in 1660 became the largest dissenting group in Ireland. Even within this tradition, however, the relationship to the classic English statement of Calvinist theology, the Westminster Confession of 1646, was complicated, with splits in the early eighteenth century between Old Lights (conservative Calvinists) and the more liberal New Lights, who rejected the need to subscribe to that definition of the faith.

In broader theological terms, the influence of Calvin's theology spread well beyond those churches that were formally Calvinist in their structure. The theology of the Church of England by the early seventeenth century was largely Calvinist in its approach to salvation and the Lord's Supper. By the time that the Church of Ireland began to develop a theological identity in the late sixteenth and early seventeenth centuries, it was this "informal" Calvinism that shaped both its theology and

its first seminary, Trinity College, Dublin, founded in 1592. The first full-time provost of Trinity, Walter Travers, had been a leader of the unsuccessful effort by English Puritans in the 1580s to create a Presbyterian presence within the Church of England, and Trinity in its early decades had a reputation for so-called Puritanism. Indeed, the Church of Ireland went beyond the Church of England in incorporating this theological bent into its confession of faith. Whereas the English Thirty-Nine Articles of 1563 allowed for Calvinist doctrine but did not prescribe it, the Irish Articles of 1615 were much more explicitly Reformed: For instance, they committed the church to double predestination by incorporating the Lambeth Articles of 1596 (which had been rejected by the Church of England), and they were more nuanced in their approach to episcopacy, and much more firm in their opposition to the Roman Catholic Church. The theology of James Ussher (1581–1656), Church of Ireland archbishop of Armagh (1625–1656) and the leading intellectual figure in the seventeenth-century Irish church, closely reflected the Calvinism of the Irish Articles.

As a result of this theological coloration, the Church of Ireland in the first three decades of the seventeenth century proved able to incorporate many Puritan clergy from England and Presbyterians from Scotland who had been judged too radical by the authorities across the Irish Sea. In particular, the urgent need for Protestant clergy to serve the great influx of Scottish settlers in Ulster led some Church of Ireland bishops in that province to admit to the ministry Scots Presbyterians, a feat which was made easier by the absence of any rigorous disciplinary structures to enforce conformity within the Church of Ireland.

This interesting experiment in inclusiveness ended in the mid-1630s as Ireland was sucked into the campaign by Charles I and his chief ecclesiastical adviser,

Archbishop Laud of Canterbury, to moderate the Calvinist theology of the Church of England. The arrival in Ireland in 1633 of the new Lord Deputy Thomas Wentworth and his chief ecclesiastical advisor, Bishop John Bramhall of Derry, marked the beginning of a decisive shift in theological outlook. Ussher was gently pushed to one side, and Bramhall and Wentworth used the 1634 Irish convocation to radically alter the Church of Ireland's doctrine and constitution by forcing through, in the face of considerable opposition, two key reforms: The Irish Articles of 1615 were replaced by the English Thirty-Nine Articles, and new disciplinary canons were approved. Over the next two years Bramhall forced the Presbyterian clergy in Ulster out of the Church of Ireland. The link between the Church of Ireland and Presbyterianism was not wholly broken, however, for the Westminster Confession used as one of its primary sources the Irish Articles of 1615. And in the late eighteenth and nineteenth centuries the Church of Ireland developed a distinctly evangelical outlook which can be seen as a throwback to its earlier flirtation with Calvinism.

SEE ALSO Burial Customs and Popular Religion from 1500 to 1690; Puritan Sectaries; Solemn League and Covenant; Ussher, James

Bibliography

Ford, Alan. "The Church of Ireland, 1558–1641: A Puritan Church?" In *As by Law Established: The Church of Ireland since the Reformation*, edited by Alan Ford, James McGuire, and Kenneth Milne. 1995.

Ford, Alan. *The Protestant Reformation in Ireland*. 2d edition, 1997.

Alan Ford

Carolan, Turlough

The Irish harper and composer Turlough Carolan (Toirdhealbhach Ó Cearbhalláin; 1670–1738), whose compositions make up the vast majority of surviving Old Irish harp music, was born near Nobber, Co. Meath. Carolan's family moved to County Roscommon, probably when he was about fourteen years old, and his father was employed there by the MacDermott Roe fami-

J. Rogers, Carolan: The Celebrated Irish Bard (c. 1809), a stippled engraving of the famous blind Irish harpist. NATIONAL GALLERY OF IRELAND, CAT. NO. 11343. REPRODUCED BY PERMISSION.

ly. The lady of the house took a particular interest in Carolan's education, especially when, at age eighteen, he was debilitated by smallpox, which left him blind. Mrs. MacDermott Roe arranged harp lessons for him for three years with a harper also called MacDermott Roe and then equipped him with a horse, a guide, and a gratuity to enable him to begin his career as a traveling musician.

Carolan traveled the roads of Connacht, north Leinster, north Munster, and south Ulster over a period of about forty years. His fame grew steadily in his own lifetime, no doubt helped by the fact that he was regarded as an eccentric and colorful character. However, his composing skills were apparently far superior to his performing abilities, and this is the reason that he remains an important figure in Irish traditional music today. His music was influenced on the one hand by the native, oral, art-music tradition of his Irish harping predecessors and on the other hand by the Italian baroque music popular among the gentry at that time, in particular the music of Corelli, Vivaldi, and Geminiani. The audience for Carolan's music is thought to have been divided into three groups—Gaelic, Old English, and the Protestant Ascendancy—in whose homes he was a welcome visitor. The vast majority of his surviving music is named after individuals representing each of these groups (e.g., Elizabeth MacDermott Roe, Lady Athenry, and Mervyn Pratt respectively).

Carolan's fame can be attributed at least in part to the fact that his musical life coincided with a great interest in Irish culture and identity in general as the eighteenth century progressed. However, this era was also one in which the economy and culture that had supported the medieval class of male, professional Irish harpers disappeared. Therefore Carolan was a member of one of the last generations of these harper/composers. Fortunately his musically active years also coincided with the development of the music-publishing industry in both Ireland and Britain. Carolan's compositions made up the majority of the tunes in the earliest known collection of Irish music published in Ireland, *A Collection of the Most Celebrated Irish Tunes*, published in 1724 by John and William Neal(e). His music continued to be published in Ireland and Britain in the eighteenth, nineteenth, and twentieth centuries, appearing in operas by eighteenth-century composers such as Coffey and Shield, in popular-song collections such as those by Thomas Moore, and in antiquarian-inspired collections such as those by Bunting and Petrie.

More than two hundred pieces attributed to Carolan survive, although some have been attributed erroneously. His music continues to have great importance today and is regarded as distinct from the mainstream dance-music tradition.

SEE ALSO Arts: Early Modern Literature and the Arts from 1500 to 1800; Music: Early Modern Music; Music: Modern Music

Bibliography

Moloney, Colette Mary. *The Irish Music Manuscripts of Edward Bunting (1773–1843): An Introduction.* 2000.

O'Sullivan, Donal. *Carolan: The Life, Times, and Music of an Irish Harper.* 2 vols. 1958.

Rimmer, Joan. *The Irish Harp.* 1969.

Yeats, Gráinne. *Féile na gCruitirí, Béal Feirste, 1792.* 1980.

Sandra Joyce

Carson, Sir Edward

One of the founders of Northern Ireland and a central leader of Irish unionism, Edward Carson (1854–1935) was born and raised in Dublin. Educated at Trinity College, Dublin, Carson became a very successful barrister, participating in the first Oscar Wilde trial and other landmark cases of the 1890s. Carson's spectacular legal career was confirmed by his selection as the Conservative solicitor-general, a post he held from 1900 to 1906.

But it was politics, not law, that made Carson's reputation. Named leader of the Irish Unionist Party in 1910, Carson effectively led unionist opposition to Irish Home Rule, consistently outmaneuvering John Redmond and his nationalist lieutenants throughout the ensuing decade. Carson was by no means alone; his political leadership received the critical aid of James Craig, who focused on mobilizing and organizing supporters. While privately concerned about the dangers of extremist violence, Carson publicly aligned himself with Ulster hard-liners between 1912 and 1914, signing the Ulster Covenant, helping to fund the formation of the Ulster Volunteer Force, and supporting the Larne gunrunning. The August 1914 outbreak of World War I allowed Carson to avoid facing up to the contradictions between his own social conservatism and his leadership of an increasingly militant unionist rank and file.

Carson occupied important government positions throughout the war years, becoming in July 1917 a full member of the cabinet, where he was well-positioned to articulate unionist opposition to Home Rule. While less enthusiastic than his Ulster colleagues about partition, the Dublin-born Carson accepted the idea as the best option available. The real crisis came in 1916 when, in the wake of the Easter Rising, the British government seemingly moved to implement Irish Home Rule with a temporary exclusion for Ulster. Famously rejecting this compromise as a "temporary stay of execution," Carson received private assurances that Ulster would not be coerced into a Home Rule Ireland. The issue quickly became moot when John Redmond backed away from negotiations. Although plans for all-Ireland Home Rule were raised again in 1918 (Carson resigned from the cabinet in protest), Carson and Craig were able to steer Ulster clear throughout the war years.

After Edward Carson oversaw the creation of Northern Ireland with the 1920 implementation of the Government of Ireland Act, he quickly handed over the leadership of the Ulster Unionist Party to James Craig (later Lord Craigavon). Accepting a life peerage in 1921, Carson remained active in the House of Lords until 1929; he died six years later in 1935.

SEE ALSO Craig, James, First Viscount Craigavon; Redmond, John; Unionism from 1885 to 1922; **Primary Documents:** Address on the Ulster Question in the House of Commons (11 February 1914)

Bibliography

Fitzpatrick, David. *The Two Irelands, 1912–39.* 1998.

Jackson, Alvin. *The Ulster Party: Irish Unionists in the House of Commons, 1884–1911.* 1989.

Jackson, Alvin. *Sir Edward Carson.* 1993.

Laffan, Michael. *The Partition of Ireland, 1911–23.* 1987.

Stewart, A. T. Q. *The Ulster Crisis, 1912–14: Resistance to Irish Home Rule.* 1967.

Sean Farrell

~

Catholic Committee from 1756 to 1809

The Catholic Association, the forerunner of the Catholic Committee, was established in July 1756 by Charles O'Conor of Belanagare, John Curry, and Thomas Wyse, who were Catholic gentlemen whose family fortunes had greatly suffered in the confiscations of the previous age. The establishment of this body, together with the pamphleteering activity of O'Conor and Curry, can be taken as a noteworthy signal of a major turning point in the political history of Irish Catholics. Until after the middle of the eighteenth century the Catholic community rested its hopes on a Stuart restoration and saw little point in dialogue with Ireland's Protestant community, beyond the obligation to engage in religious polemic. Now minds were turning to the problem of finding a place for the upper ranks of Catholic society under a Hanoverian regime likely to endure.

The establishment of the association was probably a little premature, if for no other reason than the outbreak of the Seven Years' War. This inevitably sharpened the anxieties of Protestants, whom Catholics feared to provoke. Clerical fears of laymen making blundering statements about Catholic principles and continuing Jacobite commitments also rendered the approaching of politicians a cause of division. However, the 1760s saw the defeat of France, banishing Jacobitism from the realm of practical politics, and the emergence of an issue suitable for Catholic agitation. This was the quarterage

dispute, occasioned by the attempt of the Protestant-controlled urban trade guilds to coerce Catholics into remaining within their structures (and thus preserve guild monopolies) without giving them access to economic or political power, that is, as mere "quarter brethren." The guilds and their champion, the "Wilkes of Ireland," Charles Lucas, were unpopular among many and failed to gain the necessary political support for this. Henceforth, though the guilds retained their constitutional power in the municipalities, their economic influence was substantially lost. Not only was there this victory, but the Catholic trading interest, a disproportionately large part of the respectability of the Catholics by virtue of the laws regulating landholding, had been politicized.

Catholic relief, when it began with the acts of 1778 and 1782, owed very little to Catholic campaigning. Indeed, the Catholic Committee had ceased to function for a few years before 1778. Then a desire to raise troops among the enthusiastically anti-American Catholics brought concessions. More came in 1782 from an attempt by the government to divide those Protestants seeking Irish legislative independence and to keep Catholics from giving them support. The attempt failed when the government's opponents united to match its display of generosity. In the following years, too, both the government and proponents of political reform sought to use the Catholics in their struggles. Most members of the committee thought an uncommitted stance the one most likely to bring what was still desired—commissions in the army, admission to the bar, and perhaps even to the franchise. However, the adoption of partisan positions by some of the most influential created division. The ideological depth of this division became manifest in the winter of 1791 to 1792, when again events outside Ireland had brought Catholic relief onto the political agenda and intensified the activity of the Catholic Committee. Viscount Kenmare led those who sought to resolve the Catholic question by the integration of Catholics and their church with the established order. When despite government pressure the committee declined to repudiate a tract that expressed hostility to any kind of confessionalism, the viscount and his followers seceded from the committee. Despite ecclesiastical support and their own status as the Catholic landed interest, those who seceded lacked substantial support among activists. In any case, they were not as submissive to the government's wishes as was imagined and were reconciled with the Catholic Committee. The Catholic Convention of 1792, which the committee organized, manifested Catholic unity as well as boldness, and contributed to the passing in 1793 of the relief act that was judged necessary for the conciliation of Catholics at the onset of the war with revolutionary France.

With Catholics now admitted to the franchise, the committee declared its work at an end. Indeed, this was true as nothing more could be achieved for a very long time. The Catholic Committee was revived at the time of the viceroyalty of the 2d Earl Fitzwilliam (1794–1795), and a Catholic Association was brought into existence when Charles James Fox and William Wyndham, Lord Grenville came to power in 1806. Such events rendered Catholic activists sanguine. However, as the fate of Fitzwilliam and the general election of 1807 showed, their hopes were unrealistic. Catholic demands were now seen to constitute a threat to Britain's essentially Protestant constitution and the Protestant control of Ireland, and traditional forms of Catholic activism were impotent in the face of firm rejection.

SEE ALSO Catholic Merchants and Gentry from 1690 to 1800; Eighteenth-Century Politics: 1714 to 1778—Interest Politics; Eighteenth-Century Politics: 1778 to 1795—Parliamentary and Popular Politics; Eighteenth-Century Politics: 1795 to 1800—Repression, Rebellion, and Union; Keogh, John; O'Conor, Charles, of Balenagare; Penal Laws; Religion: Since 1690; Roman Catholic Church: 1690 to 1829; Tone, Theobald Wolfe; **Primary Documents:** The Catholic Relief Act (1778); The Catholic Relief Act (1782); The Catholic Relief Act (1793)

Bibliography

Bartlett, Thomas. *The Fall and Rise of the Irish Nation: The Catholic Question, 1690–1830.* 1992.

Leighton, Cadoc D. A. *Catholicism in a Protestant Kingdom: A Study of the Irish* Ancien Régime. 1994.

Wall, Maureen. *Catholic Ireland in the Eighteenth Century: Collected Essays of Maureen Wall.* 1989.

C. D. A. *Leighton*

Catholic Emancipation Campaign

Legal restrictions placed upon Roman Catholics during the late seventeenth and early eighteenth centuries—the so-called Penal Laws—had been reduced considerably by the 1790s. Many statutes had been allowed to lapse; others were modified or struck down by a series of Catholic Relief Acts in 1778, 1782, and 1793. Neverthe-

less, Catholics still labored under certain disadvantages: They were prohibited from holding senior government offices; they could not serve as judges, be admitted to the inner bar, or become sheriffs of counties. Above all, the oath of supremacy that was required of all members of Parliament effectively excluded Catholics from that body because it declared their faith to be heretical. Efforts to remove these restrictions and thereby "emancipate" Catholics began in the 1790s, but despite the support of influential figures such as Prime Minister William Pitt, they foundered against the staunch opposition of King George III, the Protestant Ascendancy in Ireland, and a majority in the British parliament, particularly in the House of Lords.

EMANCIPATION: QUALIFIED OR UNQUALIFIED?

Many supporters of emancipation believed that their opponents might be won over if sufficient safeguards or securities accompanied the lifting of the remaining Catholic disabilities. They proposed, therefore, that the government retain a veto over the appointment of Catholic bishops and possibly parish priests, and that the state control the salaries of the clergy. This was the position of the aristocrats, lawyers, and merchants who dominated the Catholic Committee, a Dublin-based pressure group that had led the fight for Catholic rights since the 1760s. By the first decade of the nineteenth century others on the committee began to promote an alternative strategy: a demand for unqualified emancipation by which Catholics would receive full rights without qualifications or safeguards. The most articulate proponent of this position was a young Catholic barrister from County Kerry, Daniel O'Connell, who argued that religious liberty was a universal right, that it could admit of no limitations, and that Catholicism was fully compatible with loyalty to the Crown. Bitter wrangles over qualified versus unqualified emancipation split the Catholic movement for the better part of two decades, rendering it less effective than it might otherwise have been. Even so, it is difficult to imagine that even the most unified of campaigns could have succeeded against the implacable resistance of the king and a majority in the House of Lords.

THE CATHOLIC ASSOCIATION

By the early 1820s the prospects of achieving full rights for Catholics appeared dimmer than ever. Though a Catholic Relief Bill containing veto provisions squeaked through the House of Commons in 1821, the Lords rejected it decisively. Moreover, the new monarch, George IV (1820–1830), was even more unyielding and vocal in his opposition to emancipation than his father had been. "What is to be done now?" lamented O'Connell to a colleague following the Lords's rejection of the Catholic Relief Bill in April 1821. "We are cast down by our enemies, and we may make ourselves despicable by either a stupid acquiescence or by absurd dissension" (O'Connell, *Correspondence* II, p. 901).

It was clear that if emancipation were to succeed, its supporters would have to do more than merely petition and lobby British statesmen. A new strategy emerged in 1823 when O'Connell and a group of colleagues launched an organization called the Catholic Association. The association was originally a small body with a restricted membership, but in 1824 O'Connell proposed that it open its ranks to anyone who could pay dues of one penny per month. As a consequence, the association transformed itself into a mass-based political organization that was without precedent in Europe. Tens of thousands of ordinary Irish people flocked to join, and in so doing, they acquired a sense of participating in a mighty crusade that would bring substantial improvements to their lives. At the same time, their regular dues, known as the "Catholic rent," provided the association with the resources to conduct a vigorous campaign on behalf of emancipation. After four years the rent totaled almost 52,000 pounds.

In order to collect the monthly contributions the Catholic Association created a network of local agents and committees around the country. This network, which consisted mainly of townsmen, members of the rural middle classes, and Catholic clergymen, helped to bind the association from top to bottom as it fed the movement's campaign coffers. Sympathetic national and provincial newspapers kept members apprised of the association's activities, and through their coverage of meetings and speeches, articulated Catholic grievances on a broad range of issues from tithes to the partiality of the judicial system. The association also encouraged its members to gather frequently in public meetings. People regularly came together at the parish level in what were nothing less than local political clubs; they also gathered from time to time in county, provincial, and national meetings of the association that often featured O'Connell himself. With the possible exception of the Democratic Party in the United States, the Catholic Association was the most advanced political organization in the world at that time.

CONTESTING ELECTIONS

The emancipation campaign suffered a temporary setback in 1825 when the government outlawed the Catholic Association and all similar political bodies of longer than fourteen days' duration. Though the organization

eventually reconstituted itself as the New Catholic Association, a fresh challenge soon presented itself when the government called for a general election in the summer of 1826. In eight of the thirty-two county constituencies the association supported candidates who declared themselves in favor of emancipation. It was the first election since the Act of Union in which the electorate had an opportunity to vote on political issues rather than in line with traditional local rivalries. The most famous contest took place in County Waterford, where a young pro-emancipation candidate, Henry Villiers Stuart, challenged Lord George Beresford, who represented one of the wealthiest and most powerful landed families in Ireland. Stuart won decisively, thanks in large part to the organizational efforts of the Catholic Association. As in Waterford, voters in five other counties also defied their landlords and elected candidates favoring emancipation.

The parliamentary contests of 1826 demonstrated the effectiveness of concerted party organization and the potency of Catholic emancipation as an issue. These were put to the test two years later in what became the most dramatic parliamentary election in modern Irish history. O'Connell himself ran against William Vesey Fitzgerald, the incumbent and a newly appointed cabinet member, in a County Clare by-election in June 1828. It was the first time that a Catholic had stood for election since the seventeenth century. It was also an overt challenge to government leaders who would, if O'Connell won, be forced to choose between granting emancipation and confronting a popular upheaval in Ireland. After a vigorous campaign that saw the Catholic Association and its clerical allies mobilize enormous, well-ordered crowds on O'Connell's behalf, the Clare electorate returned a stunning verdict: 2,057 votes for O'Connell, 982 votes for Fitzgerald.

By that point Prime Minister Wellington and Home Secretary Sir Robert Peel realized that emancipation was unavoidable. Nevertheless, months of private negotiations followed, during which crowds in the tens of thousands, many in homemade uniforms, turned out in Munster to show their support for O'Connell. The demonstrations ended after a few weeks, but the situation remained volatile throughout the winter of 1828 to 1829. Finally, on 13 April 1829 Parliament passed the Catholic Emancipation Act, striking down the oaths of supremacy, allegiance, and abjuration. Catholics were henceforth allowed to sit in Parliament and hold all offices except regent, lord chancellor, and lord lieutenant. The victory, though long in coming, brought with it a new model for political action in Ireland and elsewhere.

SEE ALSO Electoral Politics from 1800 to 1921; O'Connell, Daniel; Politics: 1800 to 1921—Challenges to the Union; Protestant Ascendancy: Decline, 1800 to 1930; Veto Controversy; **Primary Documents:** Origin of the "Catholic Rent" (18 February 1824); The Catholic Relief Act (1829)

Bibliography

Hinde, Wendy. *Catholic Emancipation: A Shake to Men's Minds.* 1992.

Jenkins, Brian. *The Era of Emancipation: British Government of Ireland, 1812–1830.* 1988.

O'Connell, Maurice R., ed. *The Correspondence of Daniel O'Connell.* 8 vols. 1972–1980.

O'Ferrall, Fergus. *Catholic Emancipation: Daniel O'Connell and the Birth of Irish Democracy.* 1985.

Reynolds, James A. *The Catholic Emancipation Crisis in Ireland, 1823–1829.* 1954.

Gary Owens

Catholicism

See Religion: The Coming of Christianity; Religion: 1500 to 1690; Religion: Since 1690; Roman Catholic Church: 1690 to 1829; Roman Catholic Church: 1829 to 1891; Roman Catholic Church: Since 1891.

~

Catholic Merchants and Gentry from 1690 to 1800

Although the penal laws passed from 1695 to 1728 appear severe, the reality was that Catholic gentry and merchants enjoyed wide tolerance in the practice of their religion, their conduct of affairs and commercial activities, and their freedom of association and expression.

GENTRY

About 80 percent of the land of Ireland changed hands in the seventeenth century, so that at the outset of the eighteenth, outside of Counties Galway and Mayo and a scattering of pockets elsewhere, Catholic ownership of land was minimal, with the Province of Ulster having no Catholic landed class. Propertied Catholics survived, prospered, and from 1750 increased in number. The proportion of land in Catholic hands increased over the century if the definition of ownership is broadened to include converts and leaseholders. The oft-cited statistic of the decline of such ownership from 14 percent in 1702 to 3 percent in 1776 is misleading, for it does not include those Catholic landowners who converted to the Anglican Established Church but who, for all intents and purposes, retained an allegiance to Catholicism. Nor does it take account of the considerable Catholic leasehold interest that in some cases amounted to substantial holdings. By law Catholics were prohibited from holding leases in excess of thirty-one years or for lives, yet their holdings increased largely because they benefited from preferential treatment in lease renewals. In most cases the wealth of these substantial Catholic leaseholders (e.g., the Scullys, Keatings, and McCarthys in County Tipperary, the O'Connells in County Kerry, and the Nagles in County Cork) exceeded that of the few Catholic landowners. Their wealth was created through extensive pastoral farming, which benefited from the demand for cattle in the provision trade and in dairying.

POLITICAL ACTIVITY

Catholic exclusion from political influence has been assumed because Catholics were deprived of the vote between 1728 and 1793. Yet there was an active Catholic lobby that contested many anti-Catholic measures in the Irish Parliament. There were also attempts from the 1720s to formulate a special oath whereby Catholics could express loyalty to the state, though this did not materialize until 1774. Taking of the oath was voluntary and occurred most in those areas (Counties Cork, Kilkenny, Tipperary, and Waterford) where the Catholic interest was strongest and where there had been sectarian tension in the 1760s. From the mid-1750s onwards, Catholic merchants were active in the Catholic Committee, a conservative lobby group that supported neither the Jacobite cause nor the United Irishmen. Rather, the committee viewed their role as seeking relief from the penal laws, especially those dealing with property, trade, and the professions. Such efforts bore fruit with the Relief Acts of 1778 and 1782. Locally, the remnant of those landowners, the large leaseholders, and the converts could influence the voting patterns of Protestant tenants. This was especially the case in Galway, Mayo, and Tipperary.

CATHOLIC MERCHANTS: DOMESTIC AFFAIRS

The argument of Maureen Wall that the decline in Catholic landownership caused an exodus to the towns where former proprietors reestablished themselves as a prosperous middle class is now dated. The experience was more complex and regional in its dimensions. Certainly, from the mid-seventeenth century foreign trade was no longer mainly in the hands of Catholics in the ports of the east and southeast: that is, in Dublin, Wexford, Waterford, and Cork. In these ports and other hinterland towns in the region a Protestant dominance was probably in place by the 1690s, with the wholesale trades and guilds becoming Protestant dominated. Catholic mercantile interests from these centers either became reestablished on the Continent or experienced downward social mobility at home.

However, as early as the 1720s a Catholic majority had reestablished itself in Cork, Dublin, and Waterford owing to an influx from the rural areas of unskilled persons (as opposed to dispossessed proprietors) able to secure employment in the growing provision trade, construction, and service industries. This trend was to form the basis of a subsequent Catholic middle class of traders and merchants, as opportunities in retailing and manufacturing stimulated upward mobility. In 1780 about one-third of Dublin's merchants were Catholics, though the volume of trade in their hands was less. In Cork city there was a two-to-one Catholic majority in the 1730s, and by 1800 this figure was four-to-one, though in 1758 only 20 percent of the city's foreign traders were Catholic. Limerick and Galway retained a Catholic majority, whereas in Waterford the trend replicated that of Cork, though on a smaller scale.

In Dublin at mid-century Catholics were to the fore as bakers, distillers, brewers, carpenters, grocers, skinners, tanners, woolen drapers, and distillers. By contrast, their representation in the roles of apothecary, cooper, goldsmith, butcher, shoemaker, surgeon, and physician was moderate or low. With the exception of Galway, banking continued largely in Protestant hands until the early nineteenth century. Urban Catholic wealth was a distinct reality, but it may have remained static relative to the increase in overall wealth by the end of the century. An index of Catholic mercantile wealth is that after the relaxation of the ban on their purchase of land by the act of 1782, many Catholic merchant families in Dublin and Cork purchased large rural properties.

Legal restrictions imposed on Catholic merchants, such as those relating to the number of apprentices and to quarterage or guild membership payments, were irritants rather than real restrictions. Catholic participation in the different trades and occupations administered by the guilds was only possible as quarter brothers through payment of fees called quarterage. Catholics lobbying to have it declared illegal succeeded in 1759.

The role of the guilds in relation to the trades they regulated was on the decline after 1760, and by the 1790s was irrelevant, thus making the guilds' political function more critical. After 1793, Catholics could be freemen of the guilds but were still excluded from key administrative offices in Dublin and other cities. Catholics were effectively excluded from membership of town corporations until 1840. The ban on their purchase or leasing of urban property was the most tangible disability. Catholic merchants were also constrained by church teaching from taking interest on money loaned, though this is unlikely to have affected the larger merchants unduly.

CATHOLIC MERCHANTS: FOREIGN AFFAIRS

Overseas, an Irish Catholic diaspora of mercantile communities, established largely as a result of the property changes of the seventeenth century, continued to function and expand in the eighteenth century as outlets for family members who were unable to retain their social position in Ireland. Thus Catholic Irish commercial houses in the ports of Bordeaux, Cadiz, Nantes, Bruges, Rotterdam, and London maintained kinship links that worked to advantage in the Atlantic, European, and Caribbean trades. Former landowning families (particularly from the hinterlands of Waterford and Galway) established commercial centers or built upon existing trading links overseas in France, Spain, and Portugal, as well as developing new centers in the Atlantic trade—thus a flow of aspirants into foreign commerce continued.

Irish Catholic gentry families, especially in the hinterlands of the ports of the Province of Munster, were deeply involved in the placement of their sons in trade through overseas connections as well as in the law (through conversion), the army, and the church. By such means a complex web of career strategies evolved which, when coupled with the significant surge in Catholic proprietorship, served to buttress the Catholic interest in key areas.

SEE ALSO Catholic Committee from 1756 to 1809; Eighteenth-Century Politics: 1690 to 1714—Revolution Settlement; Eighteenth-Century Politics: 1714 to 1778—Interest Politics; Eighteenth-Century Politics: 1778 to 1795—Parliamentary and Popular Politics; Eighteenth-Century Politics: 1795 to 1800—Repression, Rebellion, and Union; **Primary Documents:** An Act to Prevent the Further Growth of Popery (1704)

Bibliography

Connolly, Seán J. *Religion, Law, and Power: The Making of Protestant Ireland, 1660–1760.* 1992.

Cullen, L. M. "Catholics under the Penal Laws." *Eighteenth-Century Ireland* 1 (1986): 23–36.

Fagan, Patrick. *Catholics in a Protestant Country: The Papist Constituency in Eighteenth Century Dublin.* 1998.

Power, Thomas P., and Kevin Whelan, eds. *Endurance and Emergence: Catholics in Ireland in the Eighteenth Century.* 1990.

Power, Thomas P. *Land, Politics and Society in Eighteenth-Century Tipperary.* 1993.

Wall, Maureen. *Catholic Ireland in the Eighteenth-Century: Collected Essays of Maureen Wall.* Edited by Gerard O'Brien. 1989.

Thomas P. Power

Celtic Migrations

Modern Ireland is habitually referred to as a Celtic country, and it is generally taken for granted that this distinctive identity derives at least in part from incursions by prehistoric Celtic people. Addressing the question of Celtic migrations into Ireland involves teasing apart the major components that contribute to our modern concept of the ancient Celts (the classical literature, language, and material culture), each of which provides an alternative definition of Celticness. In the past it has proved tempting to combine these definitions, invoking the notion of a culturally unified Celtic people in prehistory. As part of their migratory spread, these Celts were thought to have established themselves in Ireland, introducing the ancestral form of the Irish language. This idea of prehistoric Celtic colonialism was further bolstered by the accounts of successive migrations into Ireland presented in early Irish documents such as the *Lebor Gabála Érenn* (Book of invasions), a medieval amalgam of myth and pseudohistory. Although population movement undoubtedly played a part in the emergence of Ireland's Celtic identity, the full picture is likely to be rather more complex.

THE CLASSICAL CELTS

It is clear from the writings of the classical authors that the Mediterranean world was rocked to its foundations during the fourth and third centuries B.C.E. by the belligerent attentions of migratory bands known as *Keltoi* (to the Greeks) or *Celtae* (to the Romans). Sweeping south across the Alps, these tribal groups, linked in loose confederacies, enjoyed a series of remarkable successes. Rome itself was sacked in 390 B.C.E., and Celtic settlements were established in northern Italy, across much of eastern Europe, and as far east as Asia Minor. The tide eventually turned, however, and the expansion of Roman control in the second and first centuries B.C.E. led eventually to the virtual extinction of continental Celtic culture.

No classical source refers to the presence of Keltoi or Celtae in Ireland. Indeed, Caesar makes an explicit statement in his *Gallic Wars* that the Celtae were just one of three ethnic groupings in Gaul (modern France). His near-contemporary Strabo explicitly states that Ireland lies beyond "Celtica." In this rather limited sense, then, there was no prehistoric Celtic population in Ireland.

LINGUISTIC CONNECTIONS

It was the linguistic definition of a "Celtic" language family, linking living languages such as Irish and Scots Gaelic, Welsh, Cornish, and Breton to vanished tongues such as ancient Gaulish, that first saw the term *Celtic* applied to Ireland. This language family was defined in the first decade of the eighteenth century by the Welsh polymath Edward Lhuyd, building on the work of the Breton scholar Paul-Yves Pezron. Similarities of grammar and vocabulary demonstrate that Irish is a descendant of languages spoken widely across Europe during the Iron Age. This is, however, a much looser use of the term *Celtic* than that applied by Caesar and the other classical authors.

The earliest evidence for the existence of Celtic languages in Ireland is contained in a series of fragmentary and ambiguous classical texts. A lost sailing manual that may date from before 500 B.C.E. seemingly calls the Irish by the Celtic name *Hiernii*. As the relevant text survives only in a much later poem, however, the reference may be misleading. Indeed, the first secure written source is Caesar, who described the island of "Hibernia" in his mid-first-century B.C.E. *Gallic War*. By the second century C.E. the Greek geographer Ptolemy was able to list more than fifty tribal groups and places with Celtic names. Clearly, therefore, Ireland was Celtic-speaking by the period of Roman influence, and possibly many centuries earlier.

ARCHAEOLOGY AND THE CELTS

In order to identify the nature and extent of any prehistoric migrations that may have introduced Celtic languages into Ireland, we have to rely on the evidence of

Carved stone (cult monument) with La Tène curvilinear patterns, from Turoe, Co. Galway, dating to the Early Iron Age. PHOTOGRAPH COURTESY OF BERNARD S. WAILES.

archaeology. Since the middle of the nineteenth century archaeologists have identified the Celtae of classical literature with the distinctive Iron Age art style known as La Tène. This exuberant art style, dominated by abstract curvilinear patterns usually applied to aristocratic paraphernalia such as weaponry, personal adornment, and religious objects, seems to have originated in the indigenous Iron Age (Hallstatt) communities of central Europe around 450 B.C.E. The appearance of distinctive La Tène material in migration-period cemeteries in northern Italy confirmed that the bearers of La Tène art formed at least one group among the classically attested Celtae.

Over a period of some 200 years La Tène art spread both north and west, making its first appearance in Ireland some time around 300 B.C.E. (although the majority of the objects are from several centuries later). The arrival of this alien art style has been widely accepted as evidence of further Celtic incursions into areas where no literate commentators were available to record their actions. Unfortunately for proponents of the invasion hypothesis, La Tène objects in Ireland are quite distinct in

form and character from those of the continent, and actual imports are exceptionally rare. Equally problematically, La Tène material in Ireland is highly localized and concentrated in the northern half of the island, and is all but restricted to objects associated with the military or religious elite. Although the ideas embodied in La Tène art were clearly imported, their execution was overwhelmingly native in character. It is hard, therefore, to maintain that there was ever any La Tène migration into Ireland beyond a trickle of warriors and craftsmen. It seems improbable that such limited incursions could have so rapidly transformed the linguistic map of the whole island.

Some commentators, recognizing the inadequacy of the La Tène period as a point of origin for Celtic Ireland, have suggested that the migration of Celtic speakers may have occurred earlier. Continental archaeologists are agreed that the makers of La Tène art were the descendants of central European Hallstatt communities, and some distinctive Hallstatt material does occur in Ireland in the seventh century B.C.E. Hallstatt material in Ireland, however, is largely restricted to bronze swords deposited in rivers, most probably as part of ritual performance. As with the later La Tène material, these swords appear to be locally made, and their riverine deposition is similar to that of earlier bronze weaponry in Ireland. In terms of the broader linguistic picture, the seventh century B.C.E. would be a convenient "window of opportunity" for the introduction of Celtic languages to Ireland. The archaeological evidence, however, is extremely slight.

If the adoption of these exotic forms of material culture do not represent Celtic migrations, how then did Celtic languages come to be spoken in Ireland? An alternative view has been propounded recently which suggests that, rather than arriving in Ireland fully formed, Celtic languages evolved across a wide area of western Europe, including Ireland, as a by-product of the intense trading activities of the Late Bronze Age (around 1200–700 B.C.E.). Proponents of this view suggest that early forms of Celtic emerged as common trading languages to facilitate communication between people whose first languages were mutually unintelligible. Because of their association with the prestigious bronze trade, these early Celtic languages may have been adopted first by the social elite and ultimately by the lower orders through a process of social emulation. In this way, like the later language diffusions associated with Swahili and Malay, Celtic languages might have been widely disseminated without the need for actual population movement on any numerically significant scale.

It remains entirely possible, of course, that there may have been substantial movements of population that left no archaeological traces. Many periods are not characterized by archaeologically distinctive material, and it would be naïve to suppose that every event of significance in prehistory should leave an archaeological signature. Nonetheless, the wholesale migration of prehistoric Celtic peoples into Ireland seems improbable, and a more diffuse pattern of smaller-scale movements by high-status individuals, families, craftsmen, war bands, and other collectives seems a more likely mechanism for the emergence of Irish Celtic identity.

SEE ALSO Myth and Saga; Prehistoric and Celtic Ireland

Bibliography

Ian Armit

Celtic Tiger

For long the laggard of Europe, the Irish economy during the late 1990s was the most successful, not just in the European Union (EU), but in the entire Organisation for Economic Co-operation and Development (OECD). For the period between 1995 and 2000, gross domestic product (GDP) grew in volume at an average annual rate of 10 percent, far ahead of any other industrial country, including the United States and Japan. In terms of GDP per capita, Ireland passed the United Kingdom in 1997. Its GDP per head in 1999 was $25,200 in PPPs (purchasing-power parities, which allow for currency fluctuations and eliminate price differentials between countries), placing Ireland eighth among OECD economies. The value of GDP in 2000 was E103.5 billion, equivalent to E27, 322 per capita, more than 115 percent of the EU average.

GDP is the measure of a country's output; gross national product (GNP) quantifies income and is a truer reflection of the wealth retained in an economy. For most major industrial countries the two figures are broadly comparable. But in Ireland's case GNP is typically significantly lower than GDP: Capital outflows from the large foreign-owned sector are not matched by inflows of repatriated earnings from the relatively small corps of Irish subsidiaries overseas. Irish per capita GNP increased from 62 percent of the EU average in 1973 to 93 percent in 2000. The principal problems of the economy—high unemployment and mounting government debt—have disappeared. The unemployment rate dropped from 15.7 percent in 1993 to 3.6 percent in 2001; government debt shrank from over 120 percent of GDP in 1987 to 34 percent in 2001. The OECD, not given to hyperbole, has described Ireland's recent economic performance as "stunning." Growth is likely to slow to more sustainable levels of 4 to 5 percent for the period to 2010.

The defining characteristic of the modern Irish economy is its openness. Ireland relies heavily on trade and foreign investment, with the combined value of imports and exports equivalent to about 140 percent of GDP, one of the highest such ratios in the world. It was not always so. When Ireland became independent in 1922, it was essentially an agricultural country. Inevitably perhaps, the newly independent nation, seeking to be self-sufficient, adopted a policy of economic nationalism. High tariffs on imports, quotas, and a policy of import substitution were designed to protect the nascent inward-looking economy. Despite sporadic periods of economic growth, this approach failed. At the beginning of the 1950s the continuing flight from the land, high unemployment, massive emigration, economic stagnation, and a balance-of-payments crisis led to a fundamental shift in policy.

Throughout the 1950s and 1960s the process of opening up the Irish economy to international trade and foreign investment gathered momentum. The architects of the volte-face included most notably T. K. Whitaker, secretary of the Department of Finance and subsequently governor of the Central Bank, and Seán Lemass as industry minister and later prime minister (taoiseach). By 1952 the newly established Irish Trade Board was promoting exports. The Industrial and Development Authority (IDA), set up in 1949, was given the mandate to create jobs by promoting investment by indigenous and foreign firms, offering capital grants and tax breaks as incentives. In 1965 Ireland agreed to a free-trade area with Britain; in 1967 it joined the General Agreement on Tariffs and Trade (GATT); and the apotheosis of the new policy came in 1973 when Ireland joined the European Economic Community (EEC), the precursor of the European Union.

Established in the late 1980s, Dublin's International Financial Services Centre (IFSC), home to many international companies, played a key role in creating the Celtic Tiger. The IFSC has expanded to include shops, hotels, and other residential and commercial buildings in Dublin's city center. © PETER BARROW PHOTOGRAPHY. REPRODUCED BY PERMISSION.

The Celtic Tiger economy of the 1990s has been hailed as an overnight phenomenon, but modern Irish development began in the 1960s as a result of these radical policy changes, in tandem with massive investment in technological education and communications and a surge of inward investment attracted by competitive costs; an available, efficient, English-speaking workforce; investment incentives, including a low rate of corporation tax; and free access to the vast European market.

But free trade initially was a two-edged sword. While foreign direct investment (FDI) grew by an average of 27 percent a year between 1973 and 1981, domestic companies in traditional sectors—textiles, apparel, and engineering—were decimated by the exposure to competition. The oil crisis of the 1970s and mounting government debt in the 1980s further diluted the benefits of EU membership. But the economy did grow by over 3 percent a year between 1973 and 1988.

By 1987 the public finances were in crisis; government debt was equivalent to an untenable 120 percent of GDP. A newly elected government made swingeing cuts in public expenditure and negotiated the first in a series of national wage agreements with unions and employers. These agreements were in effect social contracts, with moderate wage increases linked to tax cuts and enhanced spending on agreed social and economic programs. The agreements brought stability to industrial relations, maintained Ireland's competitiveness, and bolstered investor confidence. The year 1987 set the scene for a period of unprecedented growth in the Irish economy.

THE EUROPEAN UNION

Arguably, Ireland has benefited more than any other member state from being a part of the European Union. Certainly, per capita, Ireland has received the most funding; cumulative Common Agricultural Policy

(CAP), Structural Fund, and Cohesion Fund transfers amount to more than E30 billion. These funds have greatly aided the development of industry, infrastructure, research, and education and training. Membership in the union has brought relative currency stability, and enhanced fiscal discipline, and it has helped to create a modern Irish society that is more open, more confident, and more international. For the industrial sector free access to the European market has been the sine qua non of the dramatic surge in exports and inward investment.

INDUSTRY

Ireland was not a part of the original Industrial Revolution and so was able to avoid the rust belt–smokestack blight of the more industrialized countries. The transition from an essentially pastoral society, with half the workforce in farming, to a modern high-technology economy, began in the 1960s. In the apt metaphor of Sir Donald Tsang, former financial secretary of Hong Kong, "Ireland went from potatoes to chips in a generation." Foreign direct investment has been the catalyst, the driving force behind the economic renaissance. Some critics argue that Ireland is over-reliant on inward investment, particularly from the United States, which leaves it highly vulnerable to shocks in the American economy.

Indigenous companies are strongest in the traditional industries and export mainly food and drink, clothing, fabrics, and handicrafts; there are a number of major Irish multinationals in the agriculture-based businesses. A flourishing new Irish high-technology sector, supported by Enterprise Ireland, the state agency responsible for developing native enterprises, is dominated by software companies (such as Iona Technologies) that are world leaders in their particular niche.

AGRICULTURE

Agriculture remains an important, if declining, sector of the economy, accounting for about 4 percent of GDP and 7 percent of total employment, with both figures well above the EU average. It has benefited greatly from EU Common Agricultural Policy price supports: Annual CAP transfers to Ireland were equivalent to approximately 4 percent of GDP on average during the 1990s.

SERVICES

Services continue to expand, most notably the internationally traded sector—teleservices and telecommunications, shared services, and e-business—mainly foreign owned. Dublin's new International Financial Services Centre (IFSC) has four hundred of the world's leading banks and finance houses, providing specialist financial services to international clients. The Irish Stock Exchange (ISEQ) separated from London in 1995. Tourism has been buoyant; Ireland attracts 6.5 million visitors annually.

DEMOGRAPHICS

From a low of 2.8 million in 1961 the population reached 3.84 million in April 2001, the highest level for 120 years; and net immigration, growing throughout the 1990s as labor shortages lured skilled workers to Ireland, reached an historic high of 26,300. The number at work surged from 1.088 million in 1989 to 1.710 million by the end of 2000. Ireland has a growing population, with 40 percent of people under the age of twenty-five, compared with 29 to 32 percent in that age group in the other EU countries. Irish governments have boosted investment in education, especially technological education, since the 1960s. About half of secondary school graduates progress to third level; six out of ten third-level graduates major in business studies, engineering, or science/computer science. But fewer entrants to secondary schools are now opting for the basic science subjects. At the other end of the scale the new government-sponsored Science Foundation Ireland, with a budget of E635 million, is trying to promote in Ireland world-class research in biotechnology, and in information and communications technologies (ICT).

The dynamic economy has brought challenge as well as beneficence. Dublin has attracted more than its share of new investment, particularly in services; the gap in living standards between the more affluent eastern region and the rest of the country is widening. But the capital's streets are clogged with traffic, property prices have spiraled, there is a shortage of affordable housing and there is a tight labor market.

An influx of foreign workers and asylum-seekers has presented Ireland with the challenge of adapting to a multiracial, multicultural society practically overnight. Young Irish people, of a generation who "has never known failure" in the phrase of one historian, expect to have, in their own place, a lifestyle and a standard of living to match any in the world.

SEE ALSO European Union; Investment and Development Agency (IDA Ireland); Irish Pound; Migration: Emigration and Immigration since 1950; Overseas Investment; Trade Unions; Women and Work since the Mid-Nineteenth Century

Bibliography

Gray, Alan, ed. *International Perspectives on the Irish Economy.* 1997.

Ireland: National Development Plan, 2000–2006. 1999.

Kennedy, Kieran, Thomas Giblin, and Deirdre McHugh. *The Economic Development of Ireland in the Twentieth Century.* 1988.

Mac Sharry, Ray and Padraic A. White. *The Making of the Celtic Tiger: The Inside Story of Ireland's Boom Economy.* 2000.

Ó Gráda, Cormac. *Ireland: A New Economic History.* 1994.

Sweeney, Paul. *The Celtic Tiger.* 1998.

Finn Gallen

Chapbooks and Popular Literature

The growth of literacy in Ireland during the eighteenth century created a market for printed material that was within the means of even fairly humble purchasers. This market was mainly rural, supplied by traveling peddlers who sold books along with other small consumer goods. It was already established by the early eighteenth century with some Dublin printers aiming advertising specifically at "country dealers" and peddlers. Because the rural population was predominantly Catholic, Catholic printers, who were prevented by legislation from playing a full part in the mainstream print market, tended to specialize in the country trade.

The potential buyers of chapbooks—little books of stories or songs—were not wealthy, and their purchases were infrequent. Profit margins were therefore low, the books themselves were small and poorly printed on inferior paper, and the list of titles changed slowly. In these respects, cheap print products in Ireland resembled those in other European countries, such as chapbooks in England and the booklets of the *Bibliothèque Bleue* in France. They also resembled them in content. Most of the genres found elsewhere occur in Ireland also, and indeed many Irish texts are reprints of English ones or Irish counterparts to types available in England and Europe.

The ability to read was usually acquired in school, and the most common cheap texts were schoolbooks, either reading primers or catechisms. Reading primers such as the *ABC of Reading* or *Reading Made Easy* had a constant sale. Church of Ireland catechisms were produced regularly beginning in the late seventeenth century. The Presbyterian Westminster catechism survives in editions from most decades since the 1680s. Ireland's Catholic catechisms were printed in Europe until the 1730s, then in Dublin, and editions proliferated from the 1770s onwards. In their early days in school, children used these readers and catechisms as schoolbooks. Because there were few texts specifically aimed at more advanced pupils, they tended to use chapbooks as readers.

Initially, most Irish chapbooks were reprints of the more popular texts from England and continental Europe. Because of the low profit margins of this branch of the book trade everywhere, these were not original texts but abridgements, sometimes radical, of medieval and early modern romances. Titles included *Valentine and Orson*, *The Seven Wise Masters of Rome*, *The Seven Champions of Christendom*, and *Don Belianis of Greece*, all of which were reprinted continually during the eighteenth and early nineteenth centuries. As in England, some more modern works, mostly from the early decades of the eighteenth century, were also published in severely abridged versions. Among those most frequently printed were *Gulliver's Travels* and *Robinson Crusoe*.

In contrast, texts of another popular genre, criminal biographies, were specific to Ireland. By far the most widely read was *The Lives and Actions of the Most Notorious Irish Tories, Highwaymen, and Rapparees*. First printed in the 1740s, it was a collection of short lives of outlaws and highwaymen, ranging from Redmond O'Hanlon, who was active in the 1670s, to Charles Dempsey, a horse thief who died in 1735. It was a counterpart to similar collections published in England in the 1720s and 1730s. Next to this in popularity was an autobiography, *The Life and Adventures of James Freney*, first published in 1754. Freney was a Kilkenny housebreaker who was active in the 1740s. Later, less widely distributed examples were *The Life of Jeremiah Grant* (1816) and *The Life of Michael Collier* (1849). Other specifically Irish texts included *The Battle of Aughrim*, a verse play about the decisive action of the war of 1689 to 1691, first printed in 1728. There is no record of this play having been performed professionally, but it was frequently acted in rural areas as a folk play.

Almost all this corpus of popular print was produced in English, though probably half the population spoke Irish during the eighteenth century. By 1800, an Irish-language print trade had developed. Its productions consisted almost entirely of religious texts, and Catholic catechisms in Irish survive from every decade from the 1760s to the 1840s. The predominant work in this tradition was the *Pious Miscellany* of Timothy O'Sullivan (Tadhg Gaelach Ó Súilleabháin), a collection of twenty-five religious songs composed in east Munster in the late eighteenth century. First printed in 1802, it had at least seventeen other editions between then and 1845, mostly produced in Cork and Limerick. Although the *Pious Miscellany* was an Irish production, the genre to which it belongs, the religious canticle, was a prominent feature of printing in regional languages such as Breton and Scots Gaelic.

By the late eighteenth century there was a well-established and flourishing trade in cheap books in most parts of Ireland, with specialized printers working in Belfast, Cork, and Limerick as well as in Dublin. Its rudimentary reading public was open to other forms of printed material, and the 1790s saw the beginning of a series of deliberate and large-scale interventions into the chapbook and cheap print market. The radical United Irishmen mobilized support for their program of parliamentary reform, and later for armed rebellion, through the production of propaganda material, much of which imitated genres of popular literature such as ballads, catechisms, and prophecies.

In response a series of conservative organizations produced cheap texts aimed at countering not only the radical propaganda but also the traditional chapbook literature, which they saw as contributing to political disturbance. Some of these organizations, such as the London Hibernian Society (1806), were straightforwardly evangelical, distributing Bibles and religious tracts. Others took a broader approach, aiming at political stability through education and economic improvement. They established schools and supplied them with reading primers, and published moralizing and instructive fiction. The earliest of these organizations was the Association for Discountenancing Vice (1792), which initially reprinted the tracts of Hannah More, written for a similar organization in England. The most successful was the Society for Promoting the Education of the Poor of Ireland, known as the Kildare Place Society (1811). It established a large network of schools and a major publishing operation; between 1816 and 1830 it brought out about eighty small books, nearly all of them specially written for the society. Some of these were religious, but most were books of "useful knowledge," such as natural history or practical manuals. They were made to resemble as much as possible the older chapbooks that they aimed to supplant, and to be sold likewise by peddlers. Print runs were substantial, but it is unclear whether the books achieved the circulation sought; the impact on their intended audience is unknown.

By the middle decades of the nineteenth century, a far greater range of cheap texts was available and the older chapbook titles no longer dominated the market. The O'Connellite political campaigns of the 1820s and the 1840s produced enormous quantities of cheap printed material, and the national schools were supplied with special approved readers. After the Great Famine the removal of newspaper duties made the popular press much more accessible. Some chapbooks, such as *James Freney* and the *Seven Champions of Christendom*, continued to be reprinted in the late nineteenth century, but by then they were becoming increasingly archaic.

SEE ALSO Duffy, James; Education: Primary Private Education—"Hedge Schools" and Other Schools; Education: Primary Public Education—National Schools from 1831; Kildare Place Society; Literacy and Popular Culture

Bibliography

Adams, J. R. R. *The Printed Word and the Common Man: Popular Culture in Ulster, 1700–1900.* 1987.

Ó Ciosáin, Niall. *Print and Popular Culture in Ireland, 1750–1850.* 1997.

Pollard, M. P. *Dublin's Trade in Books, 1550–1800.* 1989.

Niall Ó Ciosáin

Church of Ireland

| ELIZABETHAN ERA | UTE LOTZ-HEUMANN |
| SINCE 1690 | ALAN R. ACHESON |

ELIZABETHAN ERA

After the accession of Elizabeth I in 1558, the Irish Parliament met in 1560 and adopted the Acts of Supremacy and Uniformity. Thus the Church of Ireland was pronounced independent of Rome, and the new queen was declared "supreme governor" of this reestablished state church (similar legal situations had existed before in the reigns of Henry VIII and Edward VI). Through the Act of Uniformity, the *Book of Common Prayer* was reintroduced in Ireland, making the Church of Ireland a nominally Protestant church. However, the existing fabric and personnel of the church, which had been Catholic under Elizabeth's predecessor Mary, remained in place and the religion of the greatest part of the population of Ireland remained the Catholicism of the Middle Ages. Elizabethan reformers hoped gradually to transform the Church of Ireland into a Protestant church and to educate the people in the new faith.

In England, this plan of reform was largely realized during Elizabeth's reign. The Reformation was spread through the land, creating an overwhelmingly Protestant nation. In Ireland, however, the Reformation was not a success, but a failure, and the Church of Ireland did not succeed in spreading the Protestant faith. On the contrary, by the end of Elizabeth's reign, the state church catered only to the English (and later Scottish) colonial minority in Ireland, while the majority of the people adhered to the Roman Catholic Church. The older historiography as well as some works of the 1980s and 1990s argue that there was either an unwavering disposition toward Catholicism among the Irish or that the battle over the religious disposition of the inhabitants was quickly won by Catholicism in the first half of the sixteenth century. However, in the historiography of the 1990s, a consensus has developed that Elizabeth's reign was a true watershed. Thus, Elizabethan church formation, and the development of the Church of Ireland between 1560 and 1603, can be seen as a decisive component of the failure of the Reformation in the western island.

During the first years of Elizabeth's reign, until about 1580, the religious (as opposed to the ecclesiastical) situation in Ireland remained largely unaltered. Although the population, especially the so-called Old English (the medieval English settlers in Ireland), displayed varying degrees of conformity to the state church, they continued to exhibit medieval religiosity. This situation has been called "survivalism" or "church papistry" by historians, denoting that the population of Ireland was in a kind of limbo: The church that the people knew had officially been altered, but they could not embrace, or be embraced by, a vitally Protestant state church, such as was coming into existence in much of England and Wales.

During this period the weakness of the English government in Ireland was a major reason why the key mechanisms of church formation were not set in motion in the Church of Ireland. The government controlled only a small part of the island and was constantly threatened by uprisings. Consequently, the state was too weak to assist Protestant church formation effectively or to enforce religious conformity throughout the land. In addition, the financial resources of the established church were unequal to the task. Many of its churches were ruinous, and its benefices poor, thus making it unattractive to educated clergy. As a consequence, the Church of Ireland remained a weak church, failing to control or to convince either the clergy or the laity of the new faith.

In contrast to England, the Marian bishops in Ireland were not replaced with Protestant recruits, who might have provided leadership to the lower clergy. The latter were left to their own devices and often preserved medieval religiosity by adapting the services based on the *Book of Common Prayer* to resemble the old Latin Mass. This was made easier because use of the Latin Prayer Book remained legal in Ireland. At the beginning of her reign, Elizabeth had provided money to translate the Prayer Book into Gaelic and have it printed, but the bishops did not act and had to be reminded in 1567 to proceed with the translation or to return the money. Still, the *Book of Common Prayer* in Irish Gaelic was printed only in 1608, although the Gaelic Protestant catechism had appeared in 1571, and a Gaelic New Testament had been published in 1603. Thus, Ireland lacked a Protestant clergy to educate the people and Protestant religious texts in the language of the majority of the population.

The institutions that were meant to ensure the conformity of clergy and laity, the Commission of Faculties and the Commission of Ecclesiastical Causes, were hindered by corruption and internal squabbles, and consequently the oaths of supremacy and uniformity, which were also vital to ensure the conformity of clergy and secular officials, could not be systematically enforced. Episcopal visitations, one of the most successful aids to church formation in England and on the continent, were rarely conducted and were restricted to individual dioceses. Only in the seventeenth century were regal visitations covering the whole of Ireland carried out. Moreover, the education of the next generation, which was so important to Protestant reformers in the rest of Europe, was largely neglected. Schools were not brought under Protestant control, and there were no successful initiatives to establish a Protestant educational system in Ireland. The training of an indigenous Protestant clergy would have required a Protestant university in Ireland; only after much effort was Trinity College, Dublin, founded in 1592 for that purpose.

During the 1580s the religious situation in Ireland changed gradually, but nevertheless dramatically. The close identification of the Protestant church with the English state, its officials and its plantation projects, increasingly discredited the Reformation in the eyes of the majority of the Irish population. The Church of Ireland discovered in the last two decades of the sixteenth century that it now had a rival for the religious allegiance of the population: a resurgent Catholic Church, influenced by the Council of Trent and the Catholic reform movement on the continent and staffed by the sons of Old English and Gaelic Irish families, who had been educated on the continent. Thus, the religious vacuum of the first part of Elizabeth's reign was increasingly filled by Catholicism, which was now a clearly defined confessional alternative. The Protestant state church found its position rapidly eroding. Catholic missionaries were actively providing pastoral care. Older clergy died out and others left their benefices to work underground as Catholic priests. And recusancy, that is, the refusal to attend the services of the state church, was massively on the increase among the laity. "As the religious divide between the two churches hardened," Alan Ford observed, "the middle ground crumbled" (1997, p. 40).

As the religious limbo was eliminated in favor of a rigid division in late-sixteenth-century Ireland, the established church was forced to inaugurate a process of church formation. Although its status as an all-embracing state church existed only in theory and not in practice, it reacted to the Catholic resurgence by successfully implementing some measures of church formation. For example, as it did not manage to educate and recruit Protestant clergy in Ireland, it "imported" Protestant clergy from England and Scotland. As a corollary of this, the Church of Ireland increasingly catered to the New English (and later Scottish) settlers. Trinity College became an institution for the colonial elite, and the Church of Ireland became a privileged minority church, which is what it remained until the mid-nineteenth century.

While the reigns of James I (1603–1625) and Charles I (1625–1649) saw an intensification of Protestant church formation, this served only to integrate the small group of Protestants in Ireland. Catholics, by contrast, came to feel even more alienated from the state church when it became firmly Protestant in the early seventeenth century. The confessional divide, which had begun to open in Elizabeth's reign, was thus institutionalized for the rest of the early modern period.

SEE ALSO Burial Customs and Popular Religion from 1500 to 1690; Council of Trent and the Catholic Mission; Edwardian Reform; Marian Restoration; Old English; Protestant Reformation in the Early Sixteenth Century; Puritan Sectaries; Religion: 1500 to 1690; Trinity College; **Primary Documents:** Act of Uniformity (1560)

Bibliography

Bottigheimer, Karl S., and Brendan Bradshaw. "Debate: Revisionism and the Irish Reformation." *Journal of Ecclesiastical History* 51 (2000): 581–591.

Bottigheimer, Karl S., and Ute Lotz-Heumann. "The Irish Reformation in European Perspective." *Archiv für Reformationsgeschichte* 89 (1998): 268–309.

Clarke, Aidan. "Varieties of Uniformity: The First Century of the Church of Ireland." In *The Churches, Ireland and the Irish*, edited by W. J. Sheils and Diana Wood. 1989.

Ellis, Steven G. "Economic Problems of the Church: Why the Reformation Failed in Ireland." *Journal of Ecclesiastical History* 41 (1990): 239–265.

Ford, Alan. *The Protestant Reformation in Ireland, 1590–1641.* 1997.

Ford, Alan, James McGuire, and Kenneth Milne, eds. *As By Law Established: The Church of Ireland since the Reformation.* 1995.

Lennon, Colm. *Sixteenth-Century Ireland: The Incomplete Conquest.* 1994.

Lotz-Heumann, Ute. *Die doppelte Konfessionalisierung in Irland. Konflikt und Koexistenz im 16. und in der ersten Hälfte des 17. Jahrhunderts* [The dual confessionalization process in Ireland. Conflict and coexistence in the sixteenth and the first half of the seventeenth century]. 2000.

Ute Lotz-Heumann

SINCE 1690

As the official state church in the period 1690 to 1870, subject to parliamentary control, and as an independent, self-governing body since 1871, the Church of Ireland has preserved its polity as a Protestant Episcopal church, while conscious of its catholicity—its adherence to the ancient Catholic creeds and historic episcopate. By destroying the Jacobite threat, the Williamite military victory of 1690 to 1691 ensured the church's survival; the penal legislation of the next two decades, by defining the Protestant Ascendancy, guaranteed its security. The church's external power thus consisted of both legal privilege and property—the twenty-two Protestant prelates were substantial landed proprietors. Church life was vibrant initially. The charismatic Caroline tradition (after Carolus, or Charles) outlived the Stuarts and persisted into the Hanover era. Its vitality in the period of 1690 to 1710 especially found expression in scholarship, popular religious societies, charity schools, attempts to evangelize the native Irish, and a devotional spirit best personified in James Bonnell (1653–1699), the accountant general of Ireland. Leadership was provided by Primate Narcissus Marsh, who founded the Dublin library that bears his name, and the energetic William King, archbishop of Dublin (1703–1729), who built churches to provide for Dublin's rapidly growing population and administered his province with exemplary zeal.

THE GEORGIAN CHURCH, 1730 TO 1822

Among the heirs of the Carolines was the philosopher George Berkeley, bishop of Cloyne (1735–1753). The contrast between the saintly Berkeley and the profligate Frederick Hervey, earl of Bristol, the bishop of Derry (1768–1803), epitomized the decline of the church, which was dominated by an "English interest" and permeated by the latitudinarian spirit of the age. Faced with a largely Tory clergy and gentry, Whig governments were dependent on the votes of bishops in the Irish House of Lords and therefore nominated politically reliable and mostly English-born prelates to Irish sees. Jonathan Swift, dean of Saint Patrick's, Dublin (1713–1745), inveighed against this Erastianism (control of the church by the state in the state's own interest) and its injurious consequences. By the end of the century, the combined influences of absentee bishops, nonresident clergy, lack of material resources, and widespread lethargy endangered the established church. Ruined churches, want of ecclesiastical discipline, and pastoral negligence drove Protestants to the Roman Catholic Church in Connemara and other neglected areas.

This depressing picture was, however, modified by positive influences in church life, particularly works of private benevolence. Primate Richard Robinson (1765–1794) was an imaginative benefactor of Armagh city. Cathedral libraries were founded by bishops, and urban charities by lay persons. New churches were built, often in the auditory style, in Dublin and Cork, and in those parts of Ulster where the linen industry had brought prosperity (and where a steady influx of English settlers strengthened the church). The small but ethnically distinct communities of Huguenots and Palatines maintained the reformed faith; and the Methodists societies, fostered by John Wesley's twenty-one visits to Ireland, infused new life into the church.

The Act of Union (1800) conjoined the English and Irish church establishments, and Parliament allocated substantial resources for churches and glebehouses. The simple tower-and-hall churches of the Irish countryside date from the largesse of the early nineteenth century. Resident bishops, freed from regular parliamentary duty by the Act of Union and armed with legislation, effected reforms. The evangelical revival of the period also enhanced the church's recovery. It was strong among the landed and professional classes. They built proprietary churches, supplied resources for missionary work, provided leadership and organization, and withstood initial episcopal hostility. A revival of the High Church tradition, associated with Bishop John Jebb and the lay theologian Alexander Knox, also made a distinctive contribution to the church's effectiveness. Meanwhile, a symbiotic relationship with the newly founded Orange Order was developed, notably in County Armagh.

THE GOLDEN AGE, 1822 TO 1870

The church's response to the opportunities and crises of pulsating, pre-famine society was heroic. To satisfy its thirst for knowledge, schools were founded, and bibles and tracts were distributed. Poverty and disease were tackled by a plethora of voluntary agencies. The expanding populations of Dublin, Limerick, and Belfast were provided with district churches and chapels attached to charitable institutions. Under the leadership of Archbishop Power Trench of Tuam (1819–1839), starving people were fed during the famines of 1822 and 1831 on the western seaboard. During the Great Famine (1845–1851), more than forty Anglican clergy died in the course of their sacrificial work in famine relief. During this period, the church presented a missionary character akin to that of the early Celtic church. Irish involvement in missions in tropical Africa and India was considerable. Irish-born bishops and clergy, of both evangelical and High Church traditions, and trained in the thorough theological syllabus adopted by Trinity College, Dublin in 1833, worked in England and the United States and in the developing Anglican churches in Australia, Canada, New Zealand, and South Africa. Irish churchmen also served as colonial governors. At home the church reached out to the Irish people in those areas of the west where, before the Great Famine, the Roman Catholic Church was underresourced. As a result, the accusation of pastoral neglect was repudiated, and that of proselytism raised. But the integrity and evangelical motivation of the engagement were beyond reproach.

The church establishment underwent radical change in this period. Where government could add resources, it could also reform and, finally, remove. The Irish Church Temporalities Act (1833) abolished two provinces (Cashel and Tuam), reduced through mergers the number of sees by ten, imposed a tax on wealthy benefices, and entrusted the church's administration to ecclesiastical commissioners. Lord John George Beresford, a wise and resourceful primate (1822–1862), accommodated the church as best he could to the new order, but after 1833 the establishment lived on borrowed time. The census of 1861 disclosed that, despite all endeavors, the church still served a minority. William Gladstone, a devout Anglican and Liberal prime minister, decided on disestablishment. The Irish Church Disestablishment Act (1869) took effect on 1 January 1871. Under its terms the church took over from the state responsibility for ecclesiastical policy and government, whether in respect of doctrine and worship, finance, appointments to sees and benefices, or national, diocesan, and parochial administration.

TOWARD THE TWENTY-FIRST CENTURY

Since 1871 the church has been governed by its General Synod and its resources have been managed by the Representative Church Body established by the 1869 act. It first revised the Prayer Book in 1878 and, under the impetus of liturgical renewal, adopted an Alternative Prayer Book in 1984. In 1990, it became the first of the Anglican churches in Great Britain and Ireland to ordain women to the priesthood. Its cathedrals developed innovative ministries, so countering the partial demise of the parochial system. In the late twentieth century also, the church supported ecumenism and exerted influence in the Anglican communion: Archbishops George Simms, Henry McAdoo, and Robin Eames enjoyed international reputation for, respectively, scholarship, ecumenical leadership, and diplomatic skill. The church's unity was tested but not destroyed by the strains arising from partition and from the Orange standoff at Drumcree in Armagh in the late 1990s. Its mission was, however, crushed under its institutional weight and curbed by active prejudice toward its evangelical wing. It lacked the capacity to reform its institutions, but evangelical revival in the 1990s positioned the church to recover ground lost since 1970 both to secularism and to independent religious groupings.

SEE ALSO Evangelicalism and Revivals; Government from 1690 to 1800; King, William; Orange Order: Origins, 1784 to 1800; Orange Order: Since 1800; Overseas Missions; Protestant Ascendancy: 1690 to 1800; Protestant Ascendancy: Decline, 1800 to 1930; Protestant Community in Southern Ireland since 1922; Second Reformation from 1822 to 1869; Temperance Movements; Toland, John; Trinity College

Bibliography

Acheson, Alan R. *A History of the Church of Ireland, 1691–1996*. 1997. Second edition, 2002.

Akenson, Donald H. *The Church of Ireland: Ecclesiastical Reform and Revolution, 1800–85*. 1971.

Bolton F. R. *The Caroline Tradition of the Church of Ireland, with Particular Reference to Bishop Jeremy Taylor*. 1958.

Bowen, Desmond. *The Protestant Crusade in Ireland, 1800–70*. 1978.

Ford, Alan, James McGuire, and Kenneth Milne, eds. *As by Law Established: The Church of Ireland since the Reformation*. 1995.

Ford, Alan, and Kenneth Milne, eds. *The Church of Ireland: A Critical Bibliography, 1536–1992*. 1994.

McDowell, R. B. *The Church of Ireland, 1869–1969*. 1975.

Milne, Kenneth, ed. *Christ Church Cathedral, Dublin: A History*. 2000.

Alan R. Acheson

Church Reform

The medieval church had to adapt its institutional organization and administrative system to a new cultural environment in Ireland. The dwindling in size of population centers and the weakening civic powers of the state were already evident as Christianity was carried into the frontier regions of Gaul and Britain, but in Ireland even the vestiges of Roman culture and imperial administration in sub-Roman Britain were absent. Consequently, ecclesiastical organization in Ireland was as decentralized as its native systems of secular governance, and its centers of ecclesiastical prominence were monastic rather than metropolitan. During the sixth century, monastic communities were founded throughout Ireland. These centers followed customs of life established by their founders, but only a few monastic Rules survive from the early monastic period in Ireland between the sixth and twelfth centuries. This dearth of information makes references to reform movements somewhat misleading because there appears to have been no standard practice to reform. The term is useful, however, as a description of periodic efforts made within the Irish church to gain or recapture a larger Christian unity of practice.

THE EASTER CONTROVERSY

The earliest movements noted in the annals and other written records were both internal dissensions within Ireland, though with larger ramifications extending to England and the continent. The first dispute, which erupted in the early seventh century and was not resolved until the early eighth century, concerned the proper calculation of Easter. The problems over the calculation of Easter had their origins in continental practice. The mathematical calculations were difficult, and so the church issued standard tables, or cycles, listing when the date would fall over a period of years. These tables were subject to change or refinement, however, creating a potential rift in practice. This potential was realized in Ireland, where the most influential communities at Counties Armagh, Bangor, and Iona employed an eighty-four-year cycle established in the fifth century, but Irish communities in the south appear to have adopted a sixth-century version attributed to Victorious of Aquitaine and also favored on the Continent. Leading ecclesiastics from both north and south attempted to resolve the matter by appealing to Rome, but the papal response failed to settle the question. The conflict between the two systems was a major factor in two major political confrontations outside Ireland. One took place on the Continent between the churches of the insular mission led by Columbanus of Bangor and Frankish ecclesiastics in 610, the other in England at the Synod of Whitby in 664 between supporters of Iona and those backing Wilfrid of York. Eventually, the adherents of the older cycle were persuaded to abandon it in favor of the majority view in the early eighth century.

Céli-Dé

A second issue of potential discord arose within Ireland's monastic culture in the mid-eighth century when some influential figures and communities became advocates for the adoption of a stern ascetic regimen. By the early ninth century, adherents of these practices had become known as Céli-Dé (Culdees), or the companions of God. The term was itself probably older than this ascetic movement but became closely identified with it. The ascetic model for the movement was the communal life of the early Christian monastic communities in Egypt and the desert hermits as described by John Cassian, and other hagiographical texts such as *The Life of Anthony* by Athanasius. The attempts to emulate these holy men prompted some to seek out sites of extreme isolation. The large number of medieval Irish place-names with the element *dysert* or *disert* (desert) in them shows that the ideal of the desert hermit was popular across Ireland.

There were also groups of Céli-Dé attached to larger monastic communities or forming separate monasteries. The monastic community of Tallaght under its abbot Maél Rúain (d. 792) was an early proponent and center for the asceticism favored by the Céli-Dé. There are some texts attributed to the community, the most famous of which is the *Martyrology of Tallaght*. It is clear from their books that communal life was as important as that of the hermit to the Céli-Dé, but the focus was clearly on the spiritual purification of those committed to the religious life rather than to missionary work or pastoral care. In the eleventh century there were a few reports of groups of Céli-Dé at some large monasteries, but asceticism no longer figured as a flourishing ideal within the church.

Diocesan Organization

Even as the ideals of the Céli-Dé ossified as a monastic ideal within the Irish church, a new reform movement was on the horizon. During the eleventh century, Ireland had come into closer and more frequent communication with England and the Continent through a variety of channels. By the late eleventh century some of the Viking port communities established in Ireland, such as Dublin, Waterford, and Limerick, had subordinated themselves to English ecclesiastical centers, notably Canterbury and Winchester. There was also a series of papal legates to Ireland in the twelfth century, with both connections serving to assist indigenous Irish reformers in their efforts to renovate and reform Christian social and religious life in Ireland and to establish a diocesan system of governance. Reports of the divergence in Ireland followed in ecclesiastical customs and law from the rest of the church brought intense criticism and rebuke from the outside, heightening the concerns of native Irish churchmen. Beginning in the later eleventh century and extending into the twelfth, another reform movement arose in Ireland, this time centering its attention on ecclesiastical organization and institutional structure rather than the inner religious life.

As noted earlier, prominent abbots and other officials of monastic communities dominated the affairs of the Irish church in the early medieval period. These clerics often came from ecclesiastical families closely related to local secular dynasties. In addition, annal records name abbots and other ecclesiastical officials who inherited their positions from their fathers or were succeeded by their sons, indicating either that they remained laymen, or that the Irish church did not require them to be celibate. The Irish church was also castigated for its neglect of pastoral care and instruction to the laity, in part, perhaps, as a consequence of the ideal of the reclusive ascetic cultivated by the Irish religious. Some of the Irish reformers came from the same prominent families historically associated with powerful monasteries. This insider status gave these men the social and political access essential to effecting changes, and the discernment necessary to gauge the pace of change acceptable to contemporary society.

In 1101 there was enough internal sympathy toward the cause of reform for a synod to be convened at Cashel. The most prominent ecclesiastic at the synod was Bishop Maél Muire Ua Dunáin. Little is known of his early life and career, but he was clearly of high office and greatly revered. Ua Dunáin may have begun his ecclesiastical career at the community of Clonard, an old and prominent foundation in Meath, where he died in 1117. He was also probably acting at the synod as the papal legate of Pope Pascal II. The brief reports on the resolutions of the synod indicate that it took cautious steps toward reform. The synod moved on several fronts to limit lay control and influence over ecclesiastical property and offices. It also issued a decree against marriage among close family members.

Perhaps encouraged by the gains of the Cashel synod, another meeting convened ten years later at Rath Breasail. Ua Dunáin was in attendance, but the presiding ecclesiastic was Gille Easpuig (Gilbert), the bishop of Limerick and successor to Ua Dunáin as papal legate.

The details of Gilbert's origins and career are also largely unknown. He was probably of Norse-Irish origin and is known principally for his surviving work, *De statu ecclesiastico*, on the organization of the church. Also present was Cellach, the prominent reform-minded abbot of Armagh. The gathering at Rath Breasail adopted for Ireland a full-scale reorganization of the administrative structure of the church under two metropolitans, each with a dozen suffragan (diocesan) bishops. The two metropolitan seats were assigned to Counties Armagh and Cashel, and the dioceses assigned to each were generally named according to the old monastic and tribal centers. This allocation was immediately challenged by entrenched contemporary powers, secular and lay, resulting in substantial changes to the original plan in the immediate aftermath of the conference. Continuing the work begun earlier at Cashel, the synod also formally removed all churches in Ireland from lay control.

The period between the meeting at Rath Breasail and the Synod of Kells in 1152 was politically very turbulent, but the reform movement continued to advance under the guidance of the successor to Abbot Cellach of Armagh, Maél Maédóc Ua Morgair (Malachy). Malachy had ties to native ecclesiastical families through both his parents, but he allied himself firmly with the cause of reform. He became abbot of Armagh upon the death of Cellach in 1129, and, despite initial hostility toward him, he instituted there the observance of the canonical hours, the practice of regular confession, and other customs of the church. Malachy left the abbacy of Armagh to become first abbot of Bangor, and then a regional bishop, but he continued to work for the national cause of reform. He was instrumental in the introduction into Ireland of the Cistercian order and the spread of the order of Augustine canons. He also presided over meetings to amend the diocesan system drawn up at Rath Breasail. In 1140 Malachy made a trip to Rome, where he requested palls (church vestmants, or cloaks, worn by archbishops) for the two metropolitans from Pope Innocent II. The pope directed Malachy to convene another meeting to confirm the choice before he would grant the request. Malachy returned to his work in Ireland, but did not abandon his hopes for formal recognition of the Irish ecclesiastic centers. He presided over a synod at Inis Pádraig near Dublin in 1148, which provided the needed confirmation, but he died at Clairvaux in 1149 on his way back to Rome. The palls that Malachy had sought arrived in Ireland in 1152 and were conferred upon the metropolitan sees established by the Synod of Kells held in that year. That synod added two additional metropolitan seats at Tuam and Dublin to the original ones at Armagh and Cashel, as well as additional dioceses, but otherwise the earlier scheme was left largely intact.

The arrival of the Normans in Ireland in force after 1170 brought new leadership to the Irish church, but the organizational structure created by the reformers remained. The Normans assisted the introduction of continental orders and practices into Ireland, but they were not any more successful in curbing the Irish social practices so disturbing to the church than the earlier reformers had been. Throughout the late medieval period complaints about the marital failings of the native Irish and the crassness of the Irish clergy continued, though these reports are often suspect in light of the political and religious divisions of the period.

SEE ALSO Early Medieval Ireland and Christianity

Bibliography

Bernard of Clairvaux. *The Life and Death of Saint Malachy the Irishman.* Translated and annotated by Robert T. Meyer. 1978.

Bethell, Denis. "English Monks and Irish Reform in the Eleventh and Twelfth Centuries." *Historical Studies* 8 (1971): 111–135.

Carey, John. *King of Mysteries: Early Irish Religious Writings.* 1998.

Charles-Edwards, Thomas M. *Early Christian Ireland.* 2000.

Gwynn, Aubrey. *The Irish Church in the 11th and 12th centuries.* Edited by Gerard O'Brien. 1992.

Hughes, Kathleen. *The Church in Early Irish Society.* 1966.

Dorothy Africa

≈

Civil War

The Civil War of 1922 to 1923 was a bitterly ironic conclusion to the struggle for independence and also a savage, destructive prelude to the history of independent Ireland. It resulted from a particular circumstance—a controversial article of the 1921 Anglo-Irish Treaty—and from structural faults within both the Sinn Féin movement and the Irish Republican Army (IRA).

THE ANGLO-IRISH TREATY

A minority of Irish nationalists was passionately committed to achieving the republic that had been pro-

The cost of the Irish Civil War (1922–1923) is estimated at approximately one-quarter of the annual gross national product (GNP). It crippled the early years of the Irish Free State politically and economically. NATIONAL ARCHIVES OF IRELAND. REPRODUCED BY PERMISSION.

claimed during the Easter Rising in 1916; most, however, were satisfied with a less complete and less specific form of independence. These divisions were reinforced by civil-military tensions. During the course of the Anglo-Irish War of 1919 to 1921 many IRA units grew accustomed to acting without civilian authorization, and their members often regarded politicians with contempt. Such habits proved enduring. A final contributing factor to the split of 1921 was the growing distrust that had built up between some of the principal figures in the Irish leadership—in particular, between Eamon de Valera, who was president of Sinn Féin and the Dáil (the Irish parliament), and Michael Collins, the most significant military figure in the recent conflict. Collins and Arthur Griffith headed the Irish delegation that went to London, while de Valera remained behind in Dublin.

Before and during the negotiations the British rejected the idea of an Irish republic; their maximum concession was to accept the Irish Free State as a dominion that would have the same powers as Canada or South Africa. The Irish cabinet and the Dáil split over the treaty and in particular over the clause that laid down that members of the new Irish parliament would swear an oath of fidelity to the king. It was often wrongly described as an "oath of allegiance." Many radical nationalists could not accept this recognition of the Crown, and de Valera was among its harshest critics. The treaty's supporters argued that it represented the best terms that were then available and that it provided a basis from which further advances could be made. Opponents claimed that more concessions could have been extracted from the British, that the treaty abandoned the republic, and that the delegates had exceeded their powers by signing it. Partition did not feature prominently in the debates—only two deputies spoke about the matter at any length, one from each side—and it did not figure in the later Civil War. In 1921 and 1922 supporters and opponents of the treaty were concerned with questions of sovereignty, the republic, and the oath. They dis-

Sackville Street, now O'Connell Street, suffered major destruction during the 1916 Rising and the Civil War; most of the street was rebuilt during the 1920s. © HULTON ARCHIVE/GETTY IMAGES. REPRODUCED BY PERMISSION.

played little interest in Northern Ireland, which had already been established months before the treaty negotiations began.

The Dáil finally supported the treaty by sixty-four votes to fifty-seven, de Valera resigned as president and was defeated when he ran for reelection, and Collins became chairman of a new provisional government. He and his colleagues began taking over the administration of the future Free State from the British.

THE FIGHT FOR A REPUBLIC

The treaty was popular with the Irish public, whose main concern was with peace, but most of the IRA was hostile. Without any clear lead from the politicians, soldiers tended to follow their inclinations and their local commanders. Many of the units that had been most vigorous in the war against the British were now determined to carry on the fight for a republic—even against

an Irish government consisting of their former colleagues. In some areas, however, radical zeal was a compensation for earlier torpor.

In the course of the next six months the country slid slowly toward civil war. Rival military groups tried to seize evacuated British barracks, and conflicts broke out between them. In March an army convention met in Dublin, withdrew its allegiance from the Dáil, and established its own executive. In the following month a group of republican extremists seized the Four Courts and other buildings in Dublin and barricaded them against a counterattack. Collins played for time, and IRA representatives from both sides tried to negotiate a truce.

Elections in June revealed massive public support for the treaty; Collins now had a mandate from the people, and he no longer felt obliged to temporize. The republican IRA was unimpressed—but it had never placed much faith in public opinion. The Four Courts garrison increased its provocations, and the British cabinet pressured Collins to assert his authority. On 28 June government forces attacked republican positions in Dublin, and within days the capital was under their control. This was the decisive phase of the war, and henceforth Collins held the initiative. He displayed his usual energy as he took command of the protreaty campaign, and soon his army controlled most of the country north of a line running from Limerick to Waterford. This "Munster Republic" was attacked by land and by sea, and republican positions fell one by one. By early August every town in Ireland was under government control, although some were recaptured briefly by antitreaty forces. Most of the population in republican-controlled areas welcomed the arrival of government troops.

GUERRILLA WARFARE

This "conventional" war was followed by a long-drawn-out guerrilla campaign in which the republicans modeled themselves on the IRA's recent fight against the British. The principal victim was Collins himself, who was killed in an ambush on 22 August. The republicans tried to sap the government's will and undermine its support through violence and destruction. Their actions also served to lure the government into repressive measures, and here too the pattern of 1919 to 1921 was followed. The principal differences between the two conflicts were that the rebels lacked the popular support that the IRA had earlier enjoyed, and they faced more determined opponents.

Collins's successors showed themselves even more ruthless than their enemies, and from November 1922 onward seventy-seven republicans were executed. The most notorious case followed the murder of a protreaty Dáil deputy, when four prominent republican prisoners were shot in retaliation. The government was goaded into brutality, and in several parts of the country—particularly in Kerry—its troops carried out atrocities. But the pattern of 1916 and 1919 to 1921 was not followed during the Civil War, and Irish public opinion did not swing in favor of the republicans. Most people appear to have realized that only one side could win the war, the protreaty army, and they were prepared to turn a blind eye to harsh measures that might hasten the return of peace.

Gradually the republicans' position weakened, but Liam Lynch, their chief of staff, refused to tolerate the idea of compromise. So too did the Free State government, which was determined that the war was "not going to be a draw, with a replay in the autumn." Only with Lynch's death in April 1923 did more realistic voices predominate within the antitreaty leadership,

and a month later republicans were instructed to stop fighting. Ireland slowly began to become a normal society. De Valera had been marginalized by the military commanders, but now he reemerged as the leading figure among the opponents of the treaty.

AFTERMATH

The Civil War crippled the Irish economy, and although there is still disagreement concerning the death toll, it probably cost about 1,500 lives. It polarized the new Irish Free State and ensured that Irish public life would be dominated for decades by two rival parties whose disagreements centered on the events of 1921 to 1922. But it also confirmed—in a bloody manner—that the governments of independent Ireland would be responsible to the people rather than to the army.

SEE ALSO Anglo-Irish Treaty of 1921; Boundary Commission; Collins, Michael; Cosgrave, W. T.; de Valera, Eamon; Irish Republican Army (IRA); Political Parties in Independent Ireland; Politics: Independent Ireland since 1922; Sinn Féin Movement and Party to 1922; Struggle for Independence from 1916 to 1921; **Primary Documents:** "Time Will Tell" (19 December 1921); Provisional Government Proclamation at the Beginning of the Civil War (29 June 1922); Constitution of the Irish Free State (5 December 1922); Republican Cease-Fire Order (28 April 1923)

Bibliography

Curran, Joseph M. *The Birth of the Irish Free State, 1921–1923.* 1980.

Garvin, Tom. *1922: The Birth of Irish Democracy.* 1996.

Hopkinson, Michael. *Green against Green: The Irish Civil War.* 1988.

Litton, Helen. *The Irish Civil War: An Illustrated History.* 1995.

Prager, Jeffrey. *Building Democracy in Ireland: Political Order and Cultural Integration in a Newly Independent Nation.* 1986.

Regan, John M. *The Irish Counter-Revolution, 1921–1936.* 1999.

Michael Laffan

Clachans

The house cluster, consisting of irregular groupings of farmhouses often in association with an unenclosed and communally worked field system, was found extensively in the western regions of Ireland in the nineteenth century. This settlement form contrasted with the dispersed single farmstead, which is most characteristic of the Irish landscape in modern times. The geographer Estyn Evans christened these clusters *clachans* (a term with no known provenance in Irish linguistic tradition) on the basis of a similarity with a Scottish settlement of this name. The associated field system, referred to as *rundale*, was characterized by intermixed holdings that were frequently redistributed among different owners. In 1939 Evans suggested that such small house-clusters in Donegal represented a continuity of settlement type with early medieval antecedents, which coexisted with the raths or ringforts, the contemporary equivalent of the single dispersed farmstead.

Many historians and geographers searched for this elusive settlement cluster, but little convincing evidence has been found for any longstanding dichotomy. Most of these western clusters in fact originated quite late in the eighteenth-century agricultural and population boom, and represented cultural, economic, and ecological responses to marginal environments and material poverty—situations in which survival depended on cooperative farming systems. The earlier discourse on *clachans* attempted to demonstrate long continuities in patterns of settlement in the Irish landscape. The idea of the *clachan* is largely a construction of a particular school of thought about the history of the Irish landscape. Classical models of settlement and related patterns present in civilizations in the core of Europe were applied to Ireland to produce a stereotyped archaic Celtic civilization on the Atlantic fringes of Europe. German scholars, especially in late nineteenth century, were interested in morphological and genetic classifications of rural settlements. Much of the work of historical geographers in the 1950s and 1960s followed this approach. Much of the theorizing on *clachans* and settlement studies is based on dubious scholarship and defective readings of Irish and early medieval sources.

SEE ALSO Landscape and Settlement; Raths; Rural Settlement and Field Systems

Bibliography

Aalen, Frederick H. A., Kevin Whelan, and Mathew Stout, eds. *Atlas of the Irish Rural Landscape.* 1997.

Doherty, Charles. "Settlement in Early Ireland." In *A History of Settlement in Ireland*, edited by Terry Barry. 2000.

Patrick J. Duffy

~

Clarke, Kathleen

Kathleen Clarke (1878–1972), lifelong political activist, first woman lord mayor of Dublin, and one of the first women to be elected to any parliament worldwide, was born Kathleen Daly in Limerick city. Her mother ran a very successful dressmaking establishment; her father, a Fenian from the 1860s, died in 1890, leaving nine daughters and a son born posthumously. Kathleen, a dressmaker/shopkeeper all her life, gave up a successful business when she went to New York City in 1901 to marry Thomas Clarke. Clarke had spent fifteen years in prison for Fenian activities, and he continued to be active in Clan na Gael circles in the United States. On their return to Ireland in 1907 both Thomas and Kathleen became involved in revolutionary activity; Kathleen was not only a founding member of Cumann na mBan in 1914, but was also trusted with the Irish Republican Brotherhood plans before Easter Week of 1916. As a mother of young children (three boys under the age of fifteen), she took no active part in the Rising, but Thomas and Kathleen's brother Edward, who had commanded the garrison at the Four Courts, were executed for their involvement. In the months following the Rising she came to political prominence not only because of her bereavement but because of her management of the prisoners' dependents' fund. Arrested in 1918 for her involvement in the "German plot"—an attempt by the British government to link Irish nationalists with the Germans—she spent several months in Holloway gaol with Maud Gonne and Constance Markievicz. She was one of the "black women" (so called because they wore mourning dress) elected to the second Dáil in 1920. She was not re-elected in 1922, and like the majority of Cumann na mBan, she opposed the Anglo-Irish Treaty. A founding member of the Fianna Fáil Party, Kathleen sat in the Seánad from 1928 to 1936. Although she had never priortized the feminist struggle, she defended women's rights, speaking out against the Conditions of Employment Act (1936), which barred women from certain kinds of industry, and advocating equal pay. She also objected to the articles in Eamon de Valera's constitution (1937) that referred to women. At the end of a long career in local government, she became in 1940 the first woman lord mayor of Dublin and then retired from politics later in the 1940s.

SEE ALSO Conditions of Employment Act of 1936; Cumann na mBan; Equal Economic Rights for Women in Independent Ireland; Political Parties in Independent Ireland; Politics: Independent Ireland since 1922; Women and Work since the Mid-Nineteenth Century

Bibliography

Litton, Helen, ed. *Revolutionary Woman: Kathleen Clarke, 1878–1972: An Autobiography.* 1991.

Caitriona Clear

Bibliography

Ryan, John. "The Battle of Clontarf." *Journal of the Royal Society of Antiquaries of Ireland* 68 (1938): 1–50.

Terry Barry

~

Clontarf, Battle of

The battle of Clontarf in 1014 was the most decisive military engagement in the history of early medieval Ireland. It was fought to the north of the city of Dublin, probably somewhere in the modern suburb of Clontarf, but its exact site has never been satisfactorily identified. Two years before the battle, in 1012, Brian Boru, the high king of Ireland and leader of the Dál Cais sept of County Clare, began a violent quarrel against the men of Leinster. The king of Leinster, Máel Morda, eventually attempted to involve the northern rulers in his dispute against Brian. This dispute widened, with the Dublin Norse also supporting the men of Leinster against Brian. As a result, Brian beseiged Dublin for about three months until Christmas 1013. By the end of that year Brian and his forces left for home, but the men of Leinster and the Hiberno-Norse of Dublin sought the aid of their kinsmen from the Scottish Isles and from the Isle of Man.

By early 1014 these forces had joined up into a great Viking fleet that directly challenged the power and authority of Brian. On Good Friday of that same year Brian and his troops fought this coalition in a protracted and bloody battle in which the Norse and the men of Leinster were resoundingly defeated. But in the hour of victory Brian Boru was assassinated on the field of battle. Tracts such as the famous *Cogadh Gaedhel re Gallaibh* (War of the Irish with the foreigners) portrayed the battle as a struggle for the control of Ireland and the victory of Brian as the conclusive defeat of their Viking conquerors. But although the Vikings from Man and the Isles who had fought against Brian went home, the Ostmen of Dublin still controlled their city even after their defeat. Therefore, the battle can be seen more accurately as the last attempt by Brian Boru to force his lesser rivals to acknowledge him as high king. Although Brian's forces prevailed, his death brought about a temporary decline in the power of the Dál Cais.

SEE ALSO Dál Cais and Brian Boru; Norse Settlement

~

Collins, Michael

Revolutionary leader, signatory of the Anglo-Irish Treaty, and commander in chief of Free State forces during the Civil War, Michael Collins (1890–1922) was born on his family's farm at Woodfield, Clonakilty, Co. Cork, on 16 October. He emigrated to London in 1906, where he held several clerical jobs and participated in the Gaelic League, the Gaelic Athletic Association (GAA), and, from 1909, the Irish Republican Brotherhood (IRB).

After his internment at the Frongoch prisoner-of-war camp for his role in the Easter Rising in 1916, Collins established contacts with other internees who aided his advance in the IRB and the reorganized Sinn Féin Party. Elected MP for South Cork, he entered Dáil Éireann in January 1919. As Eamon de Valera's minister for home affairs and minister for finance, he spearheaded the successful campaign to raise loans for Dáil operations in defiance of the Crown regime. Concurrently, as director of organization and director of intelligence for the Irish Volunteers, he oversaw arms acquisitions and, critically, established an effective network of spies and a squadron of gunmen that blunted the Dublin and provincial police through intimidation and assassination. Some colleagues (notably minister for defense Cathal Brugha) distrusted the use of the IRB, of which Collins was president.

In autumn 1921, Collins and Arthur Griffith led the Irish plenipotentiaries who negotiated the Anglo-Irish Treaty. Although the treaty recognized a separate Northern Ireland state and identified the Irish Free State as a Crown dominion, Collins signed it on 6 December 1921, believing that it offered the Irish people a stepping-stone to total independence. He and Griffith carried this argument in the Dáil in January 1922 despite opposition from de Valera and others. When these opponents withdrew, Collins became chairman of the provisional government formed to implement the treaty. Attempting to avoid a rupture in Volunteer and Sinn Féin ranks, Collins cooperated with antitreaty forces in the north and agreed with de Valera to run Sinn Féin candidates as a bloc in the June 1922 general election. Under pres-

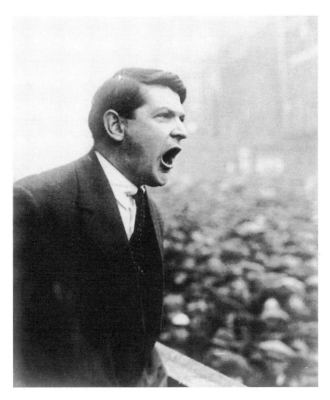

Michael Collins (1890–1922) fought in the Easter Rising and was interned with other Rising prisoners at Frongoch in Wales. His ascent after his release in December 1916 was rapid: adjutant-general of the Irish Volunteers, member of the First Dáil, minister for home affairs (1919–1922) and for finance, chief negotiator (with Arthur Griffith) of the 1921 Treaty, and chairman of the Free State Provisional Government in 1922. While acting as commander in chief of the National Army, he was killed in his native west Cork by anti-treatyites in August 1922. He is best remembered for the ruthless intelligence system he directed during the independence war of 1919–1921. He is pictured here addressing a crowd in favor of the treaty at College Green in Dublin in March 1922. AP/WIDE WORLD PHOTOS. REPRODUCED BY PERMISSION.

sure from Britain and from antitreaty forces that had seized positions in Dublin and the provinces, he belatedly abandoned this strategy. Protreaty candidates won the election, and civil war erupted. As his Free State troops advanced rapidly in the south and west, Collins was ambushed and killed at Béal-na-mBláth, Co. Cork, on 22 August 1922, while making an ill-considered inspection tour.

In his brief career Collins established a controversial dual legacy. Some decry his methods, and others emphasize his willingness to compromise as fundamental to the ultimate establishment of an Irish Republic in 1949. What is clear is that his direction and discretion were indispensable to achieving the settlement of 1921 to 1922.

SEE ALSO Anglo-Irish Treaty of 1921; Boundary Commission; Civil War; de Valera, Eamon; Griffith, Arthur; Irish Republican Army (IRA); Sinn Féin Movement and Party to 1922; Struggle for Independence from 1916 to 1921; **Primary Documents:** The Anglo-Irish Treaty (6 December 1921)

Bibliography

Béaslaí, Piaras. *Michael Collins and the Making of a New Ireland.* 1926.

Coogan, Tim Pat. *The Man Who Made Ireland: The Life and Death of Michael Collins.* 1992.

Ó Broin, Leon. *Michael Collins.* 1980.

Timothy G. McMahon

Colonial Theory from 1500 to 1690

Although Ireland had been invaded in the twelfth century and came to be dominated by the "Normans," its status as a colony largely disappeared in the later middle ages. The distinction between ruler and ruled—the essential component defining a colony—had withered. With the exception of those areas around Dublin and the other seaports, widespread integration between the newcomers and the original inhabitants occurred. During the early modern period, however, the expanding Tudor state proceeded to establish direct control over the whole of Ireland. This entailed a reconquest of the island, which was completed by 1603, and subsequent English expeditions in the 1650s and 1690s to reassert central authority. To assist the process, about 100,000 people from England and Scotland settled in Ireland over these years, forming a new breed of colonists, almost all Protestants, who occupied confiscated land. Their arrival could be regarded as the application of colonial theory.

This theory had developed out of the need to rule. Conquest had come to be seen an endless process and expense: Irish lords could be defeated, but their successors continued to resist. Moreover, the local people refused to reform and assume English customs. If the Irish declined to become English in their manners, actions, and speech, then new thinking recommended their replacement with genuine Englishmen, not merely English landowners, but tenants and artisans, with their families. In short, English society would be transplanted to Ireland.

Renaissance thinkers had little difficulty in finding precedents for such colonization—they were well acquainted with classical history and with Greek and Roman colonization. It became fashionable to appeal to the ancients when advocating colonization; the more daring Elizabethans cited Machiavelli as well. There has been much study on the most glamorous of them, Edmund Spenser (1552–1599), the poet and author of *A View of the Present State of Ireland*, but his actual impact on English immigration is hard to determine.

There was also little difficulty in justifying their actions. Any uneasiness came from the proposed treatment of the local inhabitants and their reaction. Were they to be allowed to remain to serve their new landlords (and perhaps contaminate them with Irish ways); or were they to be removed to adjacent areas; or even transplanted far away?

The first early modern colonies in Ireland, or plantations as they became known, were those of soldier-farmers in Leix and Offaly during Queen Mary's reign (1553–1558). They were on a small scale, however, and involved comparatively little settlement. More ambitious were the various schemes (projects or "plats") applied in the years after 1565 for settlements in Ulster and Munster. The inspiration for many of these "adventures" came from Queen Elizabeth's secretary of state Sir Thomas Smith. The colonies in Ulster failed to prosper, but the government did have some success with its official plantation in Munster, founded in the 1580s after the crushing of the Desmond rebellion. Various literate gentlemen involved with this plantation, produced erudite treatises on the nature of colonization, packed with classical allusions—among them not only Spenser but also William Herbert and Richard Beacon.

Other theorists are mainly associated with the American colonization experience of the 1580s. Sir Walter Raleigh, Sir Richard Grenville, and Sir Humphrey Gilbert all moved between settlements in Munster and exploration in America. For these men, all from southwest England and related to each other, there existed a connection between their Irish and American ventures, and this was the beginning of an Irish-American interchange that continued throughout the seventeenth century, principally with the southern American colonies and the Carribean.

In the early seventeenth century, colonization in Ireland accelerated with the large-scale Ulster plantation. This time not only English settlers were involved, but Scottish families, symbolizing the union of crowns under James VI and I. The lowland Scots who came were further armed with Presbyterianism, an ideal persuasion for an embattled people. The Ulster plantation entailed the confiscation of six entire counties with its settlers segregated from the Irish, who were given a lesser share of the land in distinct areas. The idea was not to repeat the Munster plantation, a piecemeal affair in which the local inhabitants were mixed with the settlers.

Although there were to be more so-called plantations in the first half of the seventeenth century, they attracted little emigration. And the massive land confiscations of the 1650s and 1690s led to relatively few British settlers crossing the Irish sea. The Cromwellian settlement of 1650 envisaged a small number of investors and a larger number of soldiers becoming the new landowners of much of Ireland, with the dispossessed inhabitants transplanted to Connacht. The land transfer did take place but its popular impact was limited, and the Irish remained among the new landlords with their regained possession in the late nineteenth century and early twentieth century.

SEE ALSO Desmond Rebellions; English Writing in Ireland before 1800; Land Settlements from 1500 to 1690; Legal Change in the Sixteenth and Seventeenth Centuries; Spenser, Edmund; Wild Geese—The Irish Abroad from 1600 to the French Revolution; **Primary Documents:** From "Notes of His Report" (1576); From *Solon His Follie* (1594); From *A View of the Present State of Ireland* (1596); From *A Direction for the Plantation of Ulster* (1610); From *A Discovery of the True Causes Why Ireland Was Never Entirely Subdued* (1612)

Bibliography

Bottigheimer, Karl. *English Money and Irish Land.* 1971.

Canny, Nicholas. *Making Ireland British, 1580–1650.* 2001.

Quinn, David Beers. *Raleigh and the British Empire.* 1947.

Quinn, David Beers. *The Elizabethans and the Irish.* 1966.

Michael MacCarthy Morrogh

Common Agricultural Policy

The Common Agricultural Policy (CAP) has been an integral part of the European Union (EU) since its foundation as the European Economic Community in 1958. All of the founding member states had national policies to support agriculture designed to promote greater food self-sufficiency and to modernize a farming sector characterized by small farms and backward technology. One of the significant achievements of the EU was to create a single, integrated market for agricultural products, with a common price level and support arrangements during the following decade, so that by 1968 agricultural products were traded freely without trade barriers between the original member states.

The CAP has two main elements. The most important component is its market-management policies intended to stabilize and raise farm prices in order to support farm incomes. The other element has been its structural policy under which payments are made to encourage the modernization of farming and the food-processing industry. The price-support element has dominated CAP expenditure for much of its existence. Recent reforms have put greater emphasis on supporting rural development, and this "second pillar" of the CAP is now attracting greater budget resources than before.

Success in establishing the CAP came at a price. In order to secure the agreement of the original member states to merge their national policies, agricultural prices within the EU were and are supported at levels much higher than world prices. The high prices, combined with the accelerated modernization of farming, encouraged the overproduction of food. This caused struggles to control the budget costs of the CAP during the 1980s, and ultimately led to reforms that reduced farm prices, compensated farmers by increased direct payments, and limited production volumes.

Irish farming benefited from access to other EU country markets and from the high support prices guaranteed by the CAP. EU agricultural subsidies contributed to the growing prosperity of rural Ireland in the period of EU membership and helped to maintain larger numbers of farmers on the land than otherwise would have been possible. But the high dependence on subsidies means that Irish agriculture is vulnerable to any changes in this policy. Farm incomes in enterprises such as cattle and sheep production are now completely dependent on the continuation of EU payments. The way in which the CAP adjusts to the challenges of absorbing the countries of central and eastern Europe and to further agricultural-trade liberalization under the auspices of the World Trade Organization will be crucial for the future of Irish farming.

SEE ALSO Agriculture: After World War I; European Union; Farming Families

Bibliography

Ackrill, Robert. *The Common Agricultural Policy.* 2000.

Fennell, Rosemary. *The Common Agricultural Policy.* 1997.

Alan Matthews

Commonwealth

The Irish Free State became a dominion in the Commonwealth under the 1921 Anglo-Irish Treaty. The Irish treaty negotiators neither desired nor were pleased with the new state's status. It was an improvement on Home Rule as enacted in the Government of Ireland Act (1920), but was hardly the independent Irish republic proclaimed in Dublin at Easter 1916. Although the Irish Free State would have the same status as the other dominions (Canada, South Africa, Australia and New Zealand), it was different because whereas they had evolved from colonies to dominion status, the Free State was the first dominion created through a treaty. It did not see itself as a colony evolving toward statehood or as a new state created by a treaty. Ireland was an historic European nation and a mother country in its own right.

The Anglo-Irish Treaty redefined the entire Commonwealth by loosening the bonds of empire on the dominions. The use of the term *treaty* in the Irish settlement of 1921 (or more correctly, "Articles of Agreement for a Treaty") was a breakthrough as it implied an agreement between two sovereign independent states. Britain contended that the Commonwealth was a single international unit and that international treaties between its members were not possible. Relations between the members of the Commonwealth (*inter se* relations) were not therefore international relations. With its very title, the Anglo-Irish Treaty set a precedent for the international independence of the dominions. So too, much to Britain's annoyance, did its registration with the League of Nations as an international treaty in July 1924.

The Irish Free State constitution of 1922 was also a defining document in the evolution of the Commonwealth. All powers of government in the Free State were derived from the people of Ireland and not from the Crown, as in, for example, Canada. The governor general, the king's representative, had fewer powers in the Free State than in Canada. The supremacy of the Irish national courts over the Privy Council in London was all but explicitly defined in the constitution.

For the Free State, the evolving nature of dominion status would vindicate Michael Collins's interpretation of the treaty as a stepping-stone to a republic. The government of W. T. Cosgrave intended to remove the restrictions imposed by dominion status and to ensure that the Free State had full and unrestricted domestic and international sovereignty. The Irish Free State sought to transform the Commonwealth into an association of independent states.

Coming straight from Ireland's admission to the League of Nations in Geneva, the Irish delegation to the 1923 imperial conference—a periodic meeting of the prime ministers and senior ministers of the various nations of the Commonwealth to discuss matters they had in common—followed a reformist agenda. The Free State had joined the League in September 1923 not as a dominion, but as Saorstát Éireann (Irish Free State), an overt expression of the Free State's international independence. The Irish were the newcomers to the imperial conference, but they were immediate participants, seeking to break down notions of imperial unity and opposing any move toward a united-empire foreign policy. Free State delegates argued against the imperial conference gaining any executive or legislative function. To them the triennial conference was purely a consultative forum.

The appointment of Timothy Smiddy as Irish minister to the United States in October 1924 marked another precedent in the international evolution of the dominions. For the first time, a dominion was represented separately from Britain in a foreign capital. The breakthrough meant that dominions could now be seen as individual international actors, and notions of imperial unity were further weakened.

For the 1926 imperial conference the Irish fielded a strong delegation, with Minister for Home Affairs Kevin O'Higgins the leading figure. The issues most important to the Irish were tackled in the meeting of the Committee on Inter-Imperial Relations. The discussion resulted in the Balfour Declaration, which laid down that dominions were "autonomous Communities within the British Empire, equal in status, in no way subordinate one to another in any aspect of their domestic or external affairs, though united by a common allegiance to the Crown, and freely associated as members of the British Commonwealth of Nations" (Harkness 1969, p. 96). This declaration ensured the international co-equality of the dominions, an issue that had been at the heart of Irish Commonwealth policy since 1923. Having achieved co-equality (for all), the Free State was the most radical and forward-looking of the dominions.

In the late 1920s Irish diplomats insisted that individual dominions had the right to control their own foreign affairs and that the Free State could not be bound by British-negotiated treaties. The Free State argued the right to appoint plenipotentiaries and to negotiate, sign, and ratify treaties in its own right. These rights were first exercised by the Free State in 1928 over the Kellogg-Briand Pact, which outlawed war as means of pursuing international relations. From that point on, the king would sign treaties negotiated by Ireland not as the British monarch, but as the king of Ireland.

At the 1930 imperial conference the Free State achieved its greatest success in the Statute of Westminster (1931), which allowed dominions to repeal acts of the British Parliament that referred to them and that they found repugnant. For the Irish, it allowed the repeal of the 1921 Treaty, but W. T. Cosgrave gave his word to the British government that this would not occur.

Nineteen-thirty-one saw another important Irish Commonwealth precedent: Britain had clung desperately to the notion of a single-empire great seal. In January 1931 the executive council advised the king to sign a treaty of commerce and navigation with Portugal and for it to be authenticated with the new great seal of the Irish Free State. This was effected in March 1931, removing another area of British interference in the affairs of the Irish Free State.

As the 1930s began, the Commonwealth policy of the Free State's ruling party, Cumann na nGaedheal, was evolving along lines later followed by Fianna Fáil. After the 1930 imperial conference the Irish contemplated removing the right of appeal to the Privy Council, and also considered introducing a separate Irish nationality act that created a distinct Irish citizenship. Cumann na nGaedheal also considered repealing the much disliked oath of allegiance to the Crown, but preliminary negotiations with the British failed. (Removal of the oath became one of the issues on which Fianna Fáil successfully campaigned for election in 1932.) By the time that Fianna Fáil came to power the Free State's most activist years in the Commonwealth were over. Ireland attended the Ottawa Economic Conference in 1932, but her concerns were more with Anglo-Irish relations. Building on the achievements of Cumann na nGaedheal, Fianna Fáil removed the right of appeal to the Privy Council, abolished the oath of allegiance, introduced a separate Irish nationality act, and abolished the office of the governor general. Fianna Fáil's most important act relating to the Commonwealth was the 1936 External Relations Act. Introduced during the abdication of Edward VIII, the act made the Free State an internal republic within the Commonwealth for domestic matters and left the state associated with the Commonwealth through the Crown for external affairs. The

British monarch would continue to sign the credentials of Irish diplomats and Ireland would remain in the Commonwealth.

By the end of the 1930s, Ireland's active participation with the Commonwealth was almost over. An Irish delegation did not attend the 1937 imperial conference. The 1921 treaty was replaced by a new constitution in 1937. A president replaced the monarch as head of state for internal matters. India, Pakistan, Burma, and Britain's former colonies in Africa closely examined Irish dominion and commonwealth policy in the 1920s and 1930s as they sought independence in the 1940s and 1950s. Ireland's final act in the Commonwealth was to leave it following the repeal of the 1936 External Relations Act in 1948 and the declaration of an Irish republic in 1949.

SEE ALSO Anglo-Irish Treaty of 1921; Constitution; Declaration of a Republic and the 1949 Ireland Act; **Primary Documents:** On the Republic of Ireland Bill (24 November 1948)

Bibliography

Fanning, Ronan, Michael Kennedy, Eunan O'Halpin, and Dermot Keogh, eds. *Documents on Irish Foreign Policy, Volume 1, 1919–1922.* 1998.

Fanning, Ronan, Michael Kennedy, Eunan O'Halpin, and Dermot Keogh, eds. *Documents on Irish Foreign Policy, Volume 2, 1923–1926.* 2000.

Harkness, David W. *The Restless Dominion.* 1969.

Kennedy, Michael. *Ireland and the League of Nations, 1923–1946.* 1996.

McMahon, Deirdre. "A Larger and Noisier Southern Ireland: Ireland and the Evolution of Dominion Status in India, Burma, and the Commonwealth, 1942–9." In *Irish Foreign Policy, 1919–1966: From Independence to Internationalism,* edited by Michael Kennedy and Joseph M. Skelly. 2000.

Michael Kennedy

Conditions of Employment Act of 1936

The 1936 Conditions of Employment Act was a landmark piece of legislation that determined the working conditions in Irish industry for many decades. The act incorporated the directives of the International Labour Organisation (ILO) into Irish law; the Irish Free State was an active member of the ILO. This legislation provided for a 48-hour week, with stringent controls on overtime, shift work, and night work, and a ban on outworking could be imposed by ministerial order. Workers were entitled to six public holidays every year, and a one-week vacation, and they were protected against wage reductions consequent on reduced working hours. Wage agreements between a representative group of employers and workers could be registered and made legally enforceable. Employment of persons under fourteen was forbidden, and a maximum 40-hour week was set for those under eighteen years; there was also provision for a ban to be imposed on the employment of young persons in a particular industry, following consultation between employers and workers. The legislation is evidence of the Fianna Fáil government's wish to placate trade union demands, provided that they did not conflict with other objectives.

When the act was introduced, criticism was expressed at the fact that workers were entitled to six public holidays, but not to the church holidays that were traditionally celebrated in rural Ireland. The most controversial clauses were those relating to women. The act enabled the minister for industry and commerce to ban women from working in a particular industry and gave him the right to set a quota for female employment. These clauses reflected criticism of women's ability to corner the majority of the new jobs that had been created in manufacturing industry. This was contrary to the idea of the male as the primary breadwinner, a view widely endorsed by government ministers, trade unions, and the Catholic Church. Women university graduates were the only group who opposed these clauses; female trade union leaders remained silent, and some even supported the measure. There is no evidence that these clauses were ever enforced; the minister for industry and commerce rejected a number of requests to implement them in specific industries. Nevertheless, they were not repealed until the mid-1970s when they were seen to conflict with European Economic Community equality directives. They signaled that the Irish state did not favor female factory employment, and this undoubtedly had an influence on the types of new industries that were established during the 1960s and 1970s.

SEE ALSO Clarke, Kathleen; Equal Economic Rights for Women in Independent Ireland; Irish Women Workers' Union; Trade Unions; Women and Work since the Mid-Nineteenth Century

Bibliography

Daly, Mary E. *Industrial Development and Irish National Identity, 1922–1939.* 1992.

Jones, Mary. *These Obstreporous Lassies: A History of the Irish Women Workers' Union.* 1988.

Mary E. Daly

~

Confederation of Kilkenny

In October 1641 Irish-Catholic insurgents attempted a bloodless coup. The insurgents were fearful of the Scottish covenanter and English parliamentary opposition's forcing Charles I into intensified anti-Catholic measures and sought to secure their position within the Stuart composite monarchy. The coup failed to secure strategically important ports and, moreover, it was quickly accompanied by a popular Catholic uprising marred by widespread atrocities against Protestant settlers. Shocked and temporarily united by exaggerated reports of a general massacre of settlers, Charles I and the English Parliament agreed to mobilize a large army of reconquest. This would be financed by loans "adventured" on the promise of postconquest repayment from a land bank of two and a half million acres of Catholic-owned Irish land. This attribution of collective guilt, also apparent from the indiscriminate brutality of the government counterattack, brought home to the insurgents that they could make no negotiated settlement in the short term.

THE CONFEDERATE CATHOLICS

In this crisis a national ecclesiastical congregation convened at Kilkenny in May 1642 and invited Catholic lay leaders to join them in setting up a new government for the two-thirds of Ireland under insurgent control to coordinate a nationwide military effort. The generally accepted name of this government, the "Confederation of Kilkenny," is retrospective; the participants described themselves as "Confederate Catholics," emphasizing that they were bound as individuals by an "oath of association." The Confederation of Kilkenny was so called because the executive or supreme council (first convened in June 1642; the last was convened in January 1649) most commonly convened in Kilkenny. The general assembly, or quasi-parliament, the other main organ of government (first convened in October 1642) met on nine occasions altogether.

NEGOTIATIONS WITH CHARLES I

The motto of the Confederation *Pro Deo, Rege, et Patria Hiberni Unanimes* (literally, We Irish united for God, king, and country) encapsulated the Irish-Catholic aspiration of reconciling religious affiliation with secular allegiance to a Protestant monarch, a utopian aspiration, perhaps, in a Europe where religious and political loyalties were inextricably linked. The cease-fire of September 1643 between the Confederation and Charles I, and the protracted search for a definitive treaty illustrate the complexity of reconciling these aspirations. Charles I refused to grant the concessions demanded by the Confederate Catholics in return for their sending an army of ten thousand soldiers to support him in fighting the English Parliament and Scots Covenanters. He would later prove more accommodating as his military position weakened, but definitive agreement nonetheless proved elusive.

To judge from the attitude of the secretary of the council, Richard Bellings, most of the supreme council would have been content with verbal assurances from the king on the key issue of religion, to the effect that he "would soon redress our grievances and tolerate the free exercise of our religion." The opportunity for a definitive agreement existed only so long as this council could continue to monopolize Confederate policy making and marginalize potential opposition from the clergy and the general assembly. The clergy, on the contrary, aspired to religious freedom rather than toleration. Given the need for a timely agreement, the king's choice of James Butler, earl of Ormonde, as his deputy and intermediary in Ireland was unfortunate. Admittedly, he had influential partisans among the Catholic leadership, including his close relatives and clients. But, regardless of family affiliations, he was a member of the Protestant community in Ireland and, as such, more reluctant than Charles I to offer concessions to Irish Catholics, preferring to subvert such peace efforts, as he did with the mission of the earl of Glamorgan in 1645, and to foment divisions within the Confederates.

THE INTERVENTION OF THE PAPAL NUNCIO

The clergy remained quiescent until the arrival of a papal nuncio, Giovanni Battista Rinuccini, late in 1645. The nuncio urged what one might call an "Ireland first" strategy: the Confederates should intensify their military effort to seize the remaining hostile enclaves and ports. Then they could send help to the king or, at worst, be in a better posture to deter invasion in the event of a parliamentary and covenanter triumph in Britain. To date their larger operations, such as the expeditions against the Covenanters in Ulster and Scotland in 1644, had been primarily intended to bolster the royalist war effort in Britain. Rinuccini's strategy and his prestige were boosted by the Irish victory over the Scots Covenanters near Benburb, Co. Tyrone, in June 1646.

To forestall a resurgent clerical interest, the supreme council concluded a definitive peace with Ormonde, who retained control of Dublin and its hinterland, on 30 July 1646. It quickly became apparent that the supreme council had misjudged the mood of the populace and, more importantly, the clergy and the Confederate Catholic armies. The manner in which the clergy administered the oath of association implied that they were the legitimate arbiters of that oath; on 12 August a specially convened ecclesiastical congregation declared unanimously that the peace violated the oath, mainly because of the lack of religious concessions. The Ulster army, fresh from Benburb, most of the Leinster army, and some units of the Munster army backed Rinuccini and forced Ormonde to return to Dublin. Rinuccini was able to oust the "Ormondist" supreme council and have it replaced with a new "clericalist" executive, soon superseded by pragmatic moderates advocating consensus, the primacy of the general assembly and a more favorable peace treaty with the royalists.

Descriptions of the power struggle in 1646 as a clash between "Gaelic" or "Old Irish," and "Old English," respectively, are simplistic. The fault lines did not open around putative ethnicity alone but involved class interests, familial allegiance, individual religious conviction, and pragmatic assessment of what objectives were reasonably achievable.

"Affliction gave the rejectors of the late [1646] peace understanding," crowed Bellings. The first "affliction" struck when a large Ulster-Leinster composite army besieging Dublin broke up in mutual recrimination in December 1646. Ormonde subsequently (July 1647) surrendered Dublin to a parliamentary army. In August 1647 Thomas Preston's Leinster Confederate army captured nearly all Dublin's satellite garrisons, but he was intercepted and his army annihilated at Dungan's Hill, Co. Meath. In November the parliamentarians of Munster, led by Murrough O'Brien, Lord Inchiquin, inflicted a heavy defeat on a Confederate army at Knocknanuss, Co. Cork.

FAILURE OF IRISH OBJECTIVES

At this critical juncture the threat of a concerted attack on Kilkenny from the Dublin and Cork enclaves receded with the creation of a new pan-archipelagic royalist coalition of moderate Covenanters or "Engagers," English

royalists, and disaffected parliamentarians. One of the latter, Inchiquin, agreed to a cease-fire with the supreme council in May 1648. A week later Rinuccini excommunicated all supporters of the cease-fire. On this occasion, in contrast to 1646, he did not enjoy the unanimous support of the clergy or, indeed, of a political nation disheartened by the military reverses of the preceding eighteen months. In follow-up negotiations the Confederate Catholics secured significant concessions compared with the 1646 agreement, and in January 1649 the Confederation was subsumed within a new royalist alliance in Ireland headed by Ormonde. A factional civil war in the summer of 1648 saw the bulk of Owen Roe O'Neill's Ulster army threatening Kilkenny from the midlands before being forced to retreat north in the autumn by converging counterattacks.

However impressive the achievements of the Confederate Catholics in mobilizing large military forces with minimal foreign aid, any assessment must be overshadowed by Oliver Cromwell's destruction of Irish-Catholic political and military power in the 1650s. The Catholic Confederates might have been able to avert this by securing an earlier definitive agreement with the king and by sending timely military aid to avert a parliamentary victory in the first English Civil War. Alternatively, they might, with the aid of foreign powers, have been able to secure control of Ireland and deter any future intervention; "by failing to decide between these viable but incompatible policies, the Confederates failed to achieve their principal objectives and thus safeguard their own survival" (Ohlmeyer 1993, p. 119).

SEE ALSO Butler, James, Twelfth Earl and First Duke of Ormond; Cromwellian Conquest; Darcy, Patrick; O'Neill, Owen Roe; O'Mahony, Conor, S. J.; Rebellion of 1641; Rinuccini, Giovanni Battista; **Primary Documents:** Confederation of Kilkenny (1642)

Bibliography

Cregan, John. "The Confederate Catholics of Ireland: The Personnel of the Confederation, 1642–1649." *Irish Historical Studies* 29, no. 116 (1995): 490–512.

Lenihan, Pádraig. *Confederate Catholics at War, 1641–1649.* 2001.

Lowe, John. "Some Aspects of the Wars in Ireland, 1641–1649." *Irish Sword* 4, no. 15 (1959): 81–87.

Lowe, John. "Charles I and the Confederation of Kilkenny, 1643–1649." *Irish Historical Studies* 14, no. 53 (1964): 1–19.

Ohlmeyer, Jane. *Civil War and Restoration in the Three Stuart Kingdoms: The Career of Randal Mac Donnell Marquis of Antrim, 1609–1683.* 1993.

Ohlmeyer, Jane. "Ireland Independent: Confederate Foreign Policy and International Relations during the Mid-Seventeenth Century." In *Ireland from Independence to Occupation*, edited by Jane Ohlmeyer. 1995.

Ó hAnnracháin, Tadhg. "Rebels and Confederates: The Stance of the Irish Clergy in the 1640s." In *Celtic Dimensions of the British Civil Wars*, edited by John Young. 1997.

Ó Siochrú, Micheál. *Confederate Ireland, 1642–1649.* 1999.

Pádraig Lenihan

≈

Congested Districts Board

The Congested Districts Board was established under the Purchase of Land Act of 1891, and its powers were extended and consolidated under the Congested Districts Board Acts of 1893, 1894, 1899, and 1901. The purpose of the board was to combine unprofitable agricultural holdings and to aid migration and emigration, agriculture, and industry in areas of Ireland where population outstripped available resources. It was a product of developments in Conservative and Unionist policy characterized as "Constructive Unionism." This approach to Irish problems was identified in particular with A. J. Balfour, chief secretary for Ireland, but also was influenced by the more interventionist ideas of Joseph Chamberlain, whose Liberal Unionists formed part of the Unionist coalition that governed the United Kingdom for most of the period 1886 to 1905.

The board sought to improve transportation, especially roads and railways, to provide better facilities for local industries, and to purchase estates from landlords for resale to the tenant occupiers. Its membership included a component representative of the Irish nationalist and Roman Catholic majority, and through this a more effective partnership was established with those with whom the board needed to work. Several of its accomplishments were initiated by the nationalist MP William O'Brien, including the establishment of a reproductive-loan fund from which new boats and equipment could be provided for the fishermen of Murrisk, Co. Mayo; the construction of a road through Dhuloch Pass in County Mayo as a stimulus to tourist traffic; and the purchase of Clare Island, in Clew Bay, Co. Mayo, and its resale in 1894 to the occupying tenants. The successful transfer of Clare Island was a model for the use of purchase and resale as a solution to the intractable conflict over land tenure, providing evidence to the government of its effectiveness in reducing agrarian conflict and reassuring tenant farmers elsewhere of its

efficacy for them. However, after passage of the Land Purchase Act of 1903 (Wyndham Act), which completed land purchase for most farmers, the board's work was increasingly complicated by the conflict between the rival claims of small-holders from the congested districts and local landless for redistributed land in non-congested areas. Under the Liberal government's Land Purchase Act of 1909 the board was reconstituted, making it even more susceptible to such popular pressures. The board was dissolved in 1923, by which time it had purchased over two million acres, to which it had made extensive improvements prior to resale.

SEE ALSO Agriculture: 1845 to 1921; Home Rule Movement and the Irish Parliamentary Party: 1891 to 1918; Land Purchase Acts of 1903 and 1909; Land Questions; Land War of 1879 to 1882; Plan of Campaign; Plunkett, Sir Horace Curzon; Rural Life: 1850 to 1921; United Irish League Campaigns

Bibliography

Curtis, L. P. *Coercion and Conciliation in Ireland, 1880–1892: A Study in Conservative Unionism.* 1963.

Micks, W. L. *An Account of the Constitution, Administration, and Dissolution of the Congested Districts Board for Ireland from 1891 to 1923.* 1925.

O'Brien, William. *An Olive Branch in Ireland and Its History.* 1910.

Philip Bull

≈

Connolly, James

Both socialist and nationalist revolutionary, James Connolly (1868–1916) was born to an Irish immigrant family in Edinburgh, Scotland. Connolly first came to Ireland in 1896 to organize the Dublin working class and founded the *Workers' Republic*, Ireland's first socialist newspaper. He left Ireland in 1903 for the United States, where he worked with the International Workers of the World for seven years. Returning in 1910, he was soon appointed Belfast organizer of the Irish Transport and General Workers' Union (ITGWU), James Larkin's fast-growing labor organization. With Larkin, he led Dublin workers during the Lockout of 1913. Following that catastrophic defeat and Larkin's departure for the United States, Connolly assumed leadership of the ITGWU.

James Connolly (1868–1916) was closely associated with James Larkin in the work of the Irish Transport and General Workers' Union between 1911 and 1914. After Larkin's departure for the United States, Connolly led Dublin labor and headed the Citizen Army alongside the Irish Volunteers in the 1916 Rising. Severely wounded during the conflict, he was executed after being propped up in a chair—one of the British blunders that turned their military victory into political defeat. © BETTMANN/CORBIS. REPRODUCED BY PERMISSION.

But it was not within the world of working-class politics that Connolly would make his name. Convinced that more extreme tactics were necessary, he revived the Irish Citizen Army, an armed militia of the Dublin left. At the same time, he began talks with Patrick Pearse and other advanced nationalist leaders who were actively planning a wartime rising. This reflected Connolly's belief that Ireland had to win its freedom before a socialist republic could effectively be created. Apparently, he believed that the socioeconomic grievances of the Irish poor would be better addressed by Irish nationalist leaders than by the British, whom Connolly hated as the creators of Dublin's tenement slums.

Connolly quickly became one of the chief figures of the revolutionary nationalist conspiracy. When the Rising occurred on Easter Monday, 1916, Connolly played a leading role, taking active military command in Dub-

lin. He was gravely wounded in the conflict, shot in the ankle while leading a sortie outside the General Post Office. But Connolly's influence was more than military; his hand can also be seen in the Proclamation of the Irish Republic, which expressed an egalitarian socioeconomic vision and an implicit commitment to women's suffrage rarely seen in Irish nationalist circles.

When the Rising ended with the arrest of the Irish insurgents, Connolly and fifteen other leaders were given capital sentences. Combined with widespread arrests, the British military's semi-secret and prolonged execution of the leaders of the Easter Rising transformed Irish public opinion, which had originally been rather ambivalent and conflicted toward the nationalist rebellion. Connolly's execution was particularly important in this shift. Too weak to stand, he was shot sitting on a chair. Connolly quickly became one of Ireland's most celebrated martyrs, a man whose vision of a more just and equitable society remains inspirational for those seeking change in Ireland and abroad.

SEE ALSO Labor Movement; Larkin, James; Lockout of 1913; Markievicz, Countess Constance; Murphy, William Martin; O'Brien, William; Struggle for Independence from 1916 to 1921; Trade Unions; **Primary Documents:** The Proclamation of the Irish Republic (24 April 1916); "What Is Our Programme?" (22 January 1916)

Bibliography

Connolly, James. Labour in Irish History. 1967.

Edwards, Ruth Dudley. James Connolly. 1981.

Greaves, C. Desmond. The Life and Times of James Connolly. 1971.

Townshend, Charles. Political Violence in Ireland. 1983.

Sean Farrell

Constitution

On 16 June 1922, the same day as the general election that was inter alia intended to ratify it, the Provisional Government published the constitution of the Irish Free State. A committee of legal and other experts, formally headed by Michael Collins, had drafted the constitution.

The document reflected a diverse range of influences, including the constraints of the 1921 Anglo-Irish Treaty, the Westminster model of government, the European and American constitutional traditions, conservative populism, and the radical contribution to the revolution.

In many respects the 1922 constitution was a conventional liberal-democratic document of its time. Despite the inclusion of the Crown (and the governor general as the Crown's representative) in the structure of government, and despite the incorporation of the treaty itself—insofar as legislation repugnant to the treaty was to be repugnant to the constitution—the constitution declared that all power derived from the people. It established a bicameral legislature, consisting of Dáil and Senate, with the government responsible to the Dáil, and the separation of powers between legislature and judiciary.

However, these structures also contained unique elements that reflected the perceived realities of Irish political life. The necessity (under the treaty) and the desire to give adequate representation to minorities led to the introduction of voting by proportional representation (single transferable vote) and of a partially nominated Senate with the power to delay legislation. The belief (ultimately inaccurate) that two-party politics would not develop and that there should be a comparatively unmediated relationship between government and the popular will led to the introduction of extern ministers and the powers of referendum and initiative. Extern ministers were not subject to collective cabinet responsibility and might not be members of the Dáil. They were appointed sporadically in the early years of the Cumann na nGaedheal administration. The powers of initiative and referendum were intended to allow a degree of popular control over legislation. In practice Cumann na nGaedheal bypassed these powers, which became obsolete.

The 1922 constitution also guaranteed a limited range of rights. The investment of the state with rights to the country's natural resources and the right of citizens to a free elementary education derived from the 1919 Democratic Programme of the Dáil. The main body of individual rights—such as the rights to freedom of expression, freedom of assembly, and habeas corpus—stemmed from the liberal-democratic tradition. Religious rights were confined to an assertion of the freedom to practice any religion.

Significantly, the government retained the power to amend the constitution without referendum beyond what had been initially intended to be a transitory period; this power was inherited by Fianna Fáil in 1932. In consequence the 1922 constitution was changed be-

yond recognition by the passage of public-safety and other legislation under various governments, and more particularly by de Valera's legislative assault on the treaty.

In April 1935 de Valera commenced drafting a new constitution. It was a personal project, carried out in consultation only with a few hand-picked civil servants, notably John Hearne of the Department of External Affairs, and with members of the Jesuit community in Dublin.

Bunreacht na hÉireann, ratified on 1 July 1937, reflected de Valera's desire to replace a dictated constitution with one that would require little adjustment if and when partition ended; this established a form of government that more closely approximated the demands of republicans and that was attuned to Irish—in reality, nationalist and Catholic—values.

With partition in effect and with a view to maintaining links with the British Commonwealth, which he saw as necessary to persuade Ulster Unionists to enter a thirty-two-county state, de Valera declined to declare a republic. Nonetheless, his constitution set out a fundamentally republican form of government, with a president replacing the monarch as internal head of state. Though the powers of the president were limited and largely ceremonial, the office was responsible for the defense of the people and the constitution against arbitrary government—an essential role from the perspective of the international environment of the 1930s.

The question of partition was dealt with directly in Article 2, which defined the national territory as the whole island of Ireland (thereby establishing a constitutional claim to jurisdiction over Northern Ireland), and in Article 3, which restricted this jurisdiction to the twenty-six-county area, "pending the re-integration of the national territory."

The forms of government and the guaranteed rights in the constitution differed little from those of its predecessor and reflected a continuity of the same traditions. The bicameral legislature was reinstated—the Senate having been abolished temporarily in 1936—although the non-nominated members of the Senate were henceforth to be elected by vocational panels rather than directly.

However, the constitution also reflected de Valera's commitment to Gaelic and Catholic values. The state was renamed "Éire," and Irish was adopted as the first national language. Article 44, on religion, referred to the "special position" of the Catholic Church, and the constitution was deeply influenced by Catholic social teaching. De Valera was motivated by the social principles set out in the encyclical *Quadragesimo Anno* promulgated by Pope Pius XI in 1931. The underlying philosophy of the encyclical was the quest for a middle road between socialism and capitalism through the reorganization of society on vocational lines and according to the principle of subsidiarity, or decision-making at the lowest possible level. These principles suggested the method of election to the Senate and informed the social provisions and directives of the constitution, the existence and nature of which mark the most significant difference between the two constitutions.

The social provisions included a reference to the family as "the fundamental unit group of society" (Article 41). Following from this, the rights of the state in educational matters were circumscribed (Article 42) and the introduction of divorce legislation was prohibited (Article 41). Article 41 also acknowledged the contribution made to the state by woman "by her life within the home," which led to a feminist protest in 1937 against the introduction of a gendered concept of citizenship.

Although the explicitly Catholic tenor of the constitution was subjected to increasing criticism from the 1960s onward, it aroused little antipathy when it was written. Article 44 represented a characteristic de Valera compromise between Catholic absolutism and pluralism and was drafted in consultation with leaders of all faiths. The social provisions were admired internationally, and they later provided a model for the constitutions of newly independent nations such as India and Pakistan.

Amendments to the constitution require a referendum and have generally reflected a changing political and social environment rather than a desire to alter the structure of government. Attempts by Fianna Fáil in 1959 and 1968 to abolish proportional representation were rejected. Among the most significant referenda have been those removing the "special position" of the Catholic Church (1972); permitting entry into the EEC (1972) and ratifying subsequent treaties; removing the ban on divorce (1995); and establishing and modifying the right to life of unborn children (1983 and 1992), thereby imposing a ban on abortion. In 1998, in the wake of the Good Friday Agreement, Articles 2 and 3 were replaced by articles emphasizing the common nationality of citizens of both parts of the island and of the Irish diaspora.

SEE ALSO Commonwealth; Declaration of a Republic and the 1949 Ireland Act; de Valera, Eamon; Gaelic Catholic State, Making of; Northern Ireland: Policy of the Dublin Government from 1922 to 1969; Politics: Independent Ireland since 1922; Presidency; Roman Catholic Church: Since 1891; **Primary Documents:** Constitution of the Irish Free State (5 December 1922); From the 1937 Constitution; The Belfast/Good Friday Agreement (10 April 1998)

Bibliography

Chubb, Basil. *The Politics of the Irish Constitution.* 1991.

Farrell, Brian, ed. *De Valera's Constitution and Ours.* 1988.

Kohn, Leo. *The Constitution of the Irish Free State.* 1932.

Litton, Frank, ed. *The Constitution of Ireland, 1937–1987.* 1987.

Murphy, Tim, and Patrick Twomey, eds. *Ireland's Evolving Constitution.* 1998.

O'Leary, Don. *Vocationalism and Social Catholicism in Twentieth-Century Ireland.* 2000.

Susannah Riordan

Cooke, Henry

Henry Cooke (1788–1868), Irish Presbyterian minister, champion of trinitarian orthodoxy and evangelicalism in religion and of conservatism and unionism in politics, was born near Maghera, Co. Londonderry, on 11 May 1788 and educated at Glasgow University. Cooke personified and led the nineteenth-century Irish Presbyterians' reaction against their eighteenth-century radicalism, which had involved them in the United Irish national and reform movements and the rebellion of 1798. The first target of his polemics was the Academical Institution, which provided higher education in rapidly growing Belfast, and whose founders had United Irish associations. Cooke denounced it as a "seminary of Arianism," endangering the faith of its Presbyterian ordinand students. Arianism rejected the full divinity of Christ and the Christian Doctrine of the Trinity. Harnessing the rising forces of Orangeism and Evangelicalism, he forced the Arian, antitrinitarian minority in the Synod of Ulster to withdraw to form a separate synod, opening the way for the Synod of Ulster to unite with the ultra-orthodox Secession Synod to form the numerically strong Presbyterian Church in Ireland.

Following his victory in the Synod of Ulster Cooke enjoyed enormous popularity and prestige, but many Presbyterians disapproved of his increasing identification with the Protestant Ascendancy in politics and his opposition to Catholic Emancipation, the tenant-right movement, and the disestablishment of the Church of

Rev. Henry Cooke (1788–1868) dominated Irish Presbyterianism from the 1820s to the 1840s. Among Presbyterian churchmen he is remembered for insisting on adherence to rigorous Calvinist doctrinal standards. Other Ulster folk remember him for his opposition to Daniel O'Connell's assertive political leadership of Irish Catholics. BY COURTESY OF THE NATIONAL PORTRAIT GALLERY, LONDON.

Ireland. Few Presbyterians shared his Toryism, but many approved of his resistance to O'Connell's campaign to repeal the Union, and he was hailed as "the Cook who dish'd Dan" when O'Connell declined his challenge to debate the repeal question in Belfast in 1841 on the grounds that he did not want to appear opposed to the Presbyterians of Ulster. In death, as in life, Cooke, whose statue stands in the center of Belfast, remains a hero to some Irish Presbyterians and a villain to others.

SEE ALSO Presbyterianism

Bibliography

Porter, J. L. *Life and Times of Henry Cooke*. 1875.
Holmes, R. F. *Henry Cooke*. 1981.

Finlay Holmes

Cork

Corcach Mór Mumhan—the great marsh of Munster—was the ancient name of the modern *Corcaigh*, anglicized as *Cork*. *The marsh*, a term still used colloquially to describe the heart of the old city, was the area where the river Lee became estuarial, threading itself through various islands. Old Cork was bounded by the two main channels (north and south) of the river, famously described by Edmund Spenser: "The spreading Lee that like an island fayre / Encloseth Cork with his divided flood." The seminal urban settlement was the seventh-century monastery and school associated with Saint Finbarr (or Bairre). It was situated on a ridge overlooking the river from the south side, not far from where the modern (Church of Ireland) Saint Fin Barre's Cathedral stands on the site of its predecessors.

The Scandinavian settlement of the "south island," the present South Main Street area, dates from the mid-ninth century. Native Irish as well as foreigners figured in this early urban development. With the arrival of the Anglo-Normans in the later twelfth century, the physical layout of the city was established in a form that lasted essentially until the late eighteenth century—one main street running from south gate to north gate with a separating strip of water midway, along what later became the filled-in Castle Street and Liberty Street.

Cork's earliest surviving charter was granted by King John in 1185. The city was primarily dependent on agricultural produce from the hinterland and therefore on commercial contacts with the Gaelic Irish who stood in uneasy relationship with the burgesses, particularly so during the native resurgence from the late fourteenth century. The sense of a city under siege is well documented at that period. Moreover, the small population (between 1,300 and 2,000) was ravaged by the Black Death in 1349. Nevertheless, the city prospered in the thirteenth and fourteenth centuries, the important port greatly facilitating its development. Trade was conducted with England (notably with Bristol), Scotland, and France; the exports included skins, hides, beef, grain, and wool, and the main imports were wine, cloth, and spices.

The great political, religious, and plantation upheavals from the mid-sixteenth century saw the Old English ruling class (loyal in politics but Catholic in religion) eventually supplanted in Cork by a New English/Protestant elite. The period from the middle of the eighteenth century to the end of the Napoleonic wars in 1815 was a golden age for Cork's economy. The population grew rapidly—to 41,000 in 1750, 57,000 in

1796, and a remarkable 80,000 by 1821. Cork remained Ireland's second city (after Dublin) until 1841; thereafter, industrial Belfast pulled ahead.

The Cork butter market handled nearly half of all Irish butter exports by 1789. Beef and pork exports were similarly impressive—provisioning British navy and army supply ships was a thriving business—and prosperous textile and tanning industries provided substantial employment and goods for export as well as the domestic market.

Cork has always identified itself with its harbor. The motto on the city's crest is *statio bene fida carinis*— "a trustworthy anchorage for ships." The harbor was important for British naval supremacy but was even more vital for commercial life. Cork was always a commercial rather than an industrial city, but a general decline in both sectors set in after the Napoleonic wars. There was a sharp decrease in agricultural prices and a falling-off in the provisioning trade, a result of the adverse impact of Anglo-Irish market integration following the Act of Union.

Meanwhile, the city was undergoing significant physical expansion beginning in the late eighteenth century. Channels were filled in and numerous bridges, including the imposing Saint Patrick's Bridge, were built, with Saint Patrick's Street becoming Cork's main thoroughfare. Throughout the nineteenth century suburban residence became the norm for the middle classes, and the areas of Sunday's Well, Tivoli, and Blackrock were variously favored by the merchant princes. Beginning in 1898 the tramline system offered citizens a reliable and economic means of enjoying residence in the suburbs while working and shopping in the city.

Queen's College (from 1908, University College) opened in 1849, making Cork a university town as well as a port and harbor city. In terms of nineteenth-century suburban growth the college was the catalyst for the development of the striking western approaches to the city. The handsome buildings and riverside grounds have given a distinctive and elegant appearance to that neighborhood over a hundred and fifty years.

Over 70 percent of all Cork families were living in slums during the second half of the nineteenth century. Leaders of the working classes were conservatives, socially speaking, concerned with preserving the aristocracy of the artisans against the unskilled workers. The lower classes were encouraged by the churches and the media to accept their "station in life" and they were diverted from socialist objectives by the lure of nationalist aspirations. Meanwhile, the professional and merchant classes were divided along sectarian lines. Catholics were envious of Protestant Ascendancy in municipal politics until something of a level playing field for the religious majority was eventually created by such measures as the Municipal Corporations Act of 1840 and the Local Government Act of 1898, and the city council gradually became more representative.

Cork nationalist politics were exciting and turbulent in the faction-ridden years after the death of Charles Stewart Parnell, MP for the city from 1880 to 1891. The most colorful and volatile figure at the turn of the century was journalist and politician William O'Brien. Later, the radical nationalist tradition in Cork found strong expression in the resurgence of Sinn Féin after 1916. The momentous highlights of this period were the murder of Lord Mayor Tomás MacCurtain in March 1920; the death from hunger strike in October of his mayoral successor, Terence MacSwiney; and the burning of the city center by Crown forces in December. Since then, the office of lord mayor has had particular prestige in Cork.

Notwithstanding urban growth and spread throughout the twentieth century, there is an immemorial charm about old Cork that was once described (doubtless with the genteel grandeur of Sunday's Well and Montenotte in mind) as "a city of tattered grace." The winding channels of the Lee and its numerous bridges make for a variety of Italianate vistas, glimpsed by the walker from midstream bridges or through narrow lanes. These views often feature Cork's symbolic and most famous landmark, the clock tower of Saint Anne's, Shandon, with its nostalgic bells "that sound so grand on / The pleasant waters of the river Lee" (O'Mahony, "The Bells of Shandon").

Industrialization in Cork in the decades after independence (1922) was dominated by such plants as Ford's and Dunlop's, which afforded steady employment for decades to great numbers of Cork workers. The Sunbeam textiles factory was also important in the Cork economy. Under native government there were great advances in public housing, and in Cork vast local-authority estates were built on the south side at Ballyphehane and on the steep slopes above the North Cathedral, siphoning the population away from the decayed "marsh" area in the city center. Meanwhile, the outer suburbs continued to proliferate.

When the staple employment industries of car assembly and textiles collapsed in the 1970s under Common Market pressure, they were replaced in time by chemical plants, electronic businesses, and high-tech industries with a new wave of inward investment from multinationals. Cork shared in the remarkable "Celtic Tiger" prosperity of the 1990s and was worried by the signs of slowdown in 2001.

In the last decades of the millennium, enlightened municipal management arrested and reversed inner-city dereliction. Mean alleys have been transformed into settings for continental-style bistros and boutiques, fine plazas have been created, and there has been much imaginative pedestrianization. A land-use and transportation study (LUTS) was gradually implemented to deal with ever-growing traffic problems.

The harbor, so crucial to the Cork economy for centuries, has continued to play a central role in greatly changed circumstances. In earlier years, grain, coal, fruit, and timber imports brought about storage and workhouse facilities in the dock areas. Various harbor activities, as well as the vital business of dredging, came under the auspices of the Harbour Commissioners, whose splendid headquarters is a notable architectural landmark in respect of both facade and interior. The political significance of the harbor was underlined in 1938 when the British handover of naval bases, in Cork harbor as elsewhere, completed the process of sovereignty transfer that had begun in 1922. Today, large cross-channel and continental ferries constitute another facet of harbor business, as do the numerous industrial and chemical sites from Little Island to the lower harbor in the Ringaskiddy area. Meanwhile, international travel in and out of the city was transformed and intensified by the development of the thriving Cork Airport (opened in 1961), which combines efficiency with a warm and distinctive local flavor. According to the latest census figures, there were 127,000 people living within the municipal limits in 1996, with a further 53,000 in the suburbs.

Finally, we may observe that traditional rivalry between north side and south side is subsumed in a general Cork personality, recognized as distinctive by natives and outsiders alike. Apart from their renowned sing-song-accented speech, Cork people tend to be perceived elsewhere in Ireland as wily, opinionated, self-confident to the point of hubris, ambitious, with a penchant for taking over the top jobs nationally, able, witty, garrulous, and ostensibly friendly and charming but clannish to a degree!

SEE ALSO Belfast; Dublin; Landscape and Settlement; Towns and Villages

Bibliography

Cork Corporation Millennium Year Book. 2000.

Journal of the Cork Historical and Archaeological Society. 1891–.

O'Flanagan, Patrick, and Cornelius G. Buttimer, eds. Cork: History and Society. 1993.

O'Mahony, Francis Sylvester (Father Prout). "The Bells of Shandon." In The Cork Anthology, edited by Seán Dunne. 1993.

John A. Murphy

Cosgrave, W. T.

W. T. [William Thomas] Cosgrave (1880–1965), Irish nationalist and head of government, was born in Dublin on 5 June. After education by the Christian Brothers he became a publican. He was active in Arthur Griffith's Sinn Féin and was a member of Dublin Corporation from 1909. Cosgrave served as second in command of the rebel garrison at the South Dublin Union during the 1916 Easter Rising and was sentenced to death. His sentence was commuted to life imprisonment, and he was released a year later. In August 1917, Cosgrave was the successful Sinn Féin candidate in a parliamentary by-election for Kilkenny city; he represented North Kilkenny in the first Dáil (1918–1920), then Carlow-Kilkenny from 1920 to 1927 and Cork city from 1927 to 1944. In 1919, Cosgrave became minister for local government in the underground Dáil administration, with Kevin O'Higgins as junior minister. In 1922, Cosgrave was a pivotal supporter of the Anglo-Irish Treaty and emerged as leader of the pro-Treatyites (later Cumann na nGaedheal) after the deaths of Arthur Griffith and Michael Collins. The harsh measures taken by the Cosgrave government during the Civil War (including reprisal executions, death sentences imposed after summary trials by military courts and semiofficial death squads) were widely criticized; Cosgrave always defended them as upholding the will of the people. As president of the executive council of the Irish Free State from 1922 to 1932 Cosgrave operated as "chairman," balancing competing cabinet factions, but was increasingly dominated by conservative technocrats associated with O'Higgins. Cosgrave himself was an effective campaigner, cultivating a "man in the street" image and emphasizing his Dublin accent. His government secured civilian control over the armed forces, restored the public finances, asserted Irish independence within the Commonwealth, and undertook prestigious projects such as the Shannon hydroelectric scheme. However, its harsh fiscal and security policies and disdain for populism led many former protreaty supporters to support Fianna Fáil after that party entered the Dáil in 1927. Cosgrave's acceptance of electoral defeat in 1932 rather than retaining power by force was perhaps his finest hour. After a second defeat in 1933, Cosgrave gave way to Eoin O'Duffy as leader of the new Fine Gael Party. Cosgrave became Fine Gael leader in 1934 after O'Duffy's resignation, holding the post until 1943 as his party declined. Cosgrave died in Dublin on 16 November 1965. His son Liam was taoiseach from 1973 to 1977. The elder Cosgrave is generally seen as a competent leader who played a significant role in consolidating the new state.

SEE ALSO Civil War; Political Parties in Independent Ireland; Politics: Independent Ireland since 1922; **Primary Documents:** Speech at the Opening of the Free State Parliament (11 September 1922); Speech on Ireland's Admission to the League of Nations (10 September 1923)

Bibliography

Collins, Stephen. *The Cosgrave Legacy.* 1996.

Regan, John M. *The Irish Counter-Revolution, 1921–36.* 1999.

Patrick Maume

Council of Trent and the Catholic Mission

The successful implementation of the doctrinal and disciplinary decrees of the Council of Trent (an assembly of Catholic bishops and priests that met from 1545 to 1563 to reform the Roman church) was premised on state cooperation with a Catholic establishment of resident bishops who were committed to regulating the devotional lives of laity and clergy. The bishops would ideally hold regular diocesan and metropolitan synods, visit Rome (the font of orthodoxy) regularly, and monitor liturgy and organizations in the parishes. Stable social and political conditions were necessary for the Tridentine vision of a renewed Catholic Church to become a reality.

The three Irish bishops who attended the closing session of the council in 1562 to 1563 returned instead to a mission field where the Catholic Church was outlawed and its structures dislocated. Although their dioceses in the north and west of Ireland were outside the reach of the Protestant state church, the decades since Ireland's breach with the papacy under Henry VIII in the 1530s had witnessed great upheaval in the organization of the Roman church in Ireland. Some areas had bishops that conformed to the royal supremacy, and other sees such as Dublin and Meath were to remain without papally appointed prelates for many years. The closure of many monasteries across the country had disrupted parish activity, since many of the benefices had been in the gift of monastic orders. As a result, church livings that had in the later Middle Ages been endowed upon the monasteries by pious benefactors were now in the possession of the new lay grantees. Despite their best efforts, the remaining Catholic bishops were operating without a proper structure of ecclesiastical command or a proper parish system.

In an effort to kick-start the drive toward reorganization, Pope Paul IV appointed a Limerick Jesuit, David Wolfe, as commissary in 1558 with the task of rebuilding the Roman episcopate in Ireland. One of his key nominees was a fellow Limerick priest, Richard Creagh, who became archbishop of Armagh in 1564. He was a zealous protagonist of Tridentine reform, but the failure of his episcopal mission makes clear the obstacles to implementing the conciliar decrees in the Ireland of the 1560s and 1570s. He never got a foothold in his archdiocese because of political turbulence and crown suspicion, so Creagh's plans for convening synods and enforcing discipline came to naught. His position on state-church relations—that the papal warrant of Catholic agents should be recognized and tolerated in return for the church's acceptance of royal sovereignty in temporal affairs—was unacceptable to the state authorities. The excommunication of Elizabeth I by Pope Pius V rendered this approach increasingly intolerable to the Crown after 1570. Creagh spent most of his twenty-two years as a bishop in prison in London or Dublin.

During the latter half of the Elizabethan period up until 1603, growing Catholic militancy in Ireland led to the involvement of both laypeople and ecclesiastics in insurrections in all of the Irish provinces. Archbishop Edmund Magauran of Armagh (who died in a skirmish in south Ulster) and Archbishop Maurice MacGibbon of Cashel went on delegations to Spain seeking military aid. Other bishops such as Dermot O'Hurley of Cashel and Patrick O'Healy of Mayo were executed by the state as traitors. In the popular mind the deceased clerics were accounted martyrs, and their example inspired a more zealous dedication to Catholic activism. In particular, lay community leaders among the gentry and merchant elites were moved to make available the considerable resources of ecclesiastical tithes and clerical appointments that they possessed to a reviving Catholic organization. They also chose to eschew the newly founded Trinity College in favor of sending their offspring to Irish continental colleges, which became seminaries for a new Catholic priesthood that returned to staff the Irish Catholic Church beginning about 1600.

With a newly confident Catholic lay elite, and in spite of sporadic bouts of government prosecution of religious dissent, a church alternative to Anglicanism began to firmly take root in Ireland in the early seventeenth century. The return of a resident episcopate, spearheaded by David Rothe of Ossory, and the re-establishment of religious orders provided an ecclesiastical leadership for the movement. New religious societies such as the Jesuits and Capuchins joined the older established ones, such as the Dominicans, Franciscans, and Carmelites, to refound religious houses in most parts of the country.

Because the older church buildings and parish structures were now possessed by the Anglican Church, the emerging Catholic organization came to be based in the homes of the gentry in the countryside and in the houses of prominent merchants in the towns. These unofficial "mass-houses" were frequented by laypeople who heard mass celebrated there by seminary-trained priests, while the parish churches of the Anglican Church of Ireland were by and large thinly attended. Aristocratic patronage of the systems of worship and pedagogy was key to the success of the Counter-Reformation church in the late seventeenth century.

Diocesan organization was slowly re-established by the 1640s, with most areas of the country served by Catholic bishops and an adequate supply of priests. Diocesan and metropolitan synods were held from 1614 onwards, legislating for the implementation of the decrees of Trent in areas such as worship, the sacraments, and discipline among clergy and laity. When the enforcement of a strict code of practice came into conflict with the social mores of the Gaelic world (with respect to marriages and funerals, for example), compromises were worked out. By the 1640s there was a strong Catholic organization that incorporated the decrees of Trent and had gained the loyalty of most of the population. One of the attractions of the Counter-Reformation church was the ease with which priests communicated with their congregations orally in the native tongue, and the deft use of Irish in published form for catechisms and works of devotion was a most useful aid to the Catholic priests. (By contrast, most of the ministers of the Protestant reformed religion were committed to the advancement of the faith through English exclusively.) The Catholic Church had successfully molded itself to the contours of the native Gaelic and Old English societies, and its leaders were anxious to be seen accepting the temporal authority of the state.

The rebellion of the 1640s and the subsequent Cromwellian regime of the 1650s dislocated the nascent church, and when the monarchy was restored in 1660, a great deal of rebuilding had to be done. Some bishops and priests were among those who had been executed for resisting the Cromwellian armies, and most others had withdrawn from the country and had to be replaced. A slow recovery took place in the 1660s and 1670s, but the fragility of the Catholic position, dependent as it was on the grace and favor of the monarch, was made clear from the prosecution and execution of Archbishop Oliver Plunkett of Armagh for his alleged part in an antiroyalist Catholic conspiracy. The brief reign of James II in the late 1680s brought about an official Catholic restoration, but the Glorious Revolution and its aftermath cast into doubt once again the position of Catholicism in Ireland. The victorious Protestant Ascendancy was determined to consolidate its political, constitutional, and social position through the parliamentary vehicle of the penal laws. Aimed primarily at suppressing Catholic social and economic ambitions, the laws did make the practice of Catholicism very difficult, but there was some flexibility through local cooperation in the areas of clerical activity such as arrangements for baptisms, marriages, burials, and schooling for Catholic youth. Although the penal laws did constrain the Catholic community socially and politically, the Irish Counter-Reformation church of the seventeenth century proved robust enough to endure and provide a relatively vibrant Catholic Church in the eighteenth century and after.

SEE ALSO Church of Ireland: Elizabethan Era; English Political and Religious Policies, Responses to (1534–1690); Irish Colleges Abroad until the French Revolution; Lombard, Peter; Plunkett, Oliver; **Primary Documents:** An Act to Prevent the Further Growth of Popery (1704)

Bibliography

Bossy, John. "The Counter-Reformation and the People of Catholic Ireland." *Historical Studies* 8 (1971): 153–170.

Bottigheimer, Karl S. "The Failure of the Reformation in Ireland: *Une Question Bien Posée.*" *Journal of Ecclesiastical History* 36 (1985): 196–207.

Bradshaw, Bradshaw. "The Reformation in the Cities: Cork, Limerick and Galway, 1534–1603." In *Settlement and Society in Medieval Ireland*, edited by John Bradley. 1988.

Corish, Patrick J. *The Catholic Community in Seventeenth and Eighteenth Centuries.* 1981.

Forrestal, Alison. *Catholic Synods in Ireland, 1600–1690.* 1998.

Jones, Frederick. "The Counter-Reformation." In *A History of Irish Catholicism*, edited by Patrick J. Corish. 1967.

Lennon, Colm. "The Counter-Reformation." In *Natives and Newcomers: Essays on the Making of Irish Colonial Society, 1534–1641*, edited by Ciaran Brady and Raymond Gillespie. 1986.

Lennon, Colm. *An Irish Prisoner of Conscience of the Tudor Era: Archbishop Richard Creagh of Armagh, 1523–1586.* 2000.

Colm Lennon

Country Houses and the Arts

By the late twentieth century, Irish country houses built by members of the Protestant Ascendancy class began to be viewed as a significant part of the nation's cultural heritage. Growing support for preservation of these buildings marked a striking change in attitude; in the decades before and after independence in 1921, these estates were perceived as alien presences in the landscape by most Irish nationalists. Burnt-out shells of such houses are stark reminders of the destruction of Ascendancy homes during the Anglo-Irish and Irish Civil Wars. Unlike England's great houses, which were incorporated into the concept of national heritage early in the nineteenth century, the Ascendancy "big house" (an ambivalently derisive term for the country house that is unique to Ireland) signaled not community but division. In a colonial and postcolonial country, such division marked not just differences of class and wealth between landlords and tenants but also divisions of political allegiance, religion, and language.

ARCHITECTURAL HISTORY

Ireland's remarkable architectural flowering occurred during the eighteenth century when members of an Anglo-Irish Protestant oligarchy eager to display their growing wealth and status began a sustained program of building unfortified country houses. A young Irishman, Edward Lovett Pearce, carried out and supplemented the plans of the Italian architect Alessandro Galilei, who designed the central block of Ireland's major Palladian home, Castletown, Co. Kildare (since 1967 the headquarters of the Irish Georgian Society). Although a few examples of Classical and Palladian building existed before Pearce, his work revolutionized the architectural taste of a newly ascendant aristocracy. After Pearce's early death his influence was carried on by the German-born Richard Castle, who built some of

Ireland's grandest houses. Pearce and Castle's architecture introduced wide-spreading Palladian elements already popular in England, particularly the center block joined to subordinate wings by straight or curved lines, a plan that was rapidly adapted to local needs in Ireland. Generally, the two architects modified and toned down the English Palladian style. In Ireland, for example, the wings were typically occupied by offices and farm buildings, instead of by additional reception rooms as in England.

Another characteristic form of eighteenth-century Irish architecture was the familiar vertical rather than horizontal Georgian block house. Three stories tall, with five to seven bays, these houses appear to be as high as they are wide. Such comparatively small eighteenth-century houses were often built in remoter parts of the countryside. Literary associations with several of them—Bowen's Court in County Cork (Elizabeth Bowen), Tyrone House in County Galway (Somerville and Ross), and Moore Hall in County Mayo (George Moore)—have brought this vertical Georgian architectural style to the attention of readers of big-house fiction.

Although Palladian architecture remained popular until the 1760s (later in the provinces), the influence of English neoclassical and Greek Revival architecture began to be felt by the second half of the century. In the 1760s, for example, the English architect James Chambers designed the exquisite neoclassical pleasure house, Marino Casino, beside the earl of Charlemont's villa at Clontarf, on the outskirts of Dublin. Later in the century and after union, architects such as James Wyatt and Francis Johnston introduced major neoclassical country houses.

Gothic Revival building arrived in Ireland as early as 1762, when under the sway of Horace Walpole's Strawberry Hill in England, the married owners of what was to be Castle Ward, in County Down, unable to agree on a single architectural style, imposed a Gothic side on a house with a Classical entrance front. In subsequent years, influenced by the Romantic movement and growing nostalgia for an antique past, many houses were pulled down and rebuilt in the newly revived Gothic style; others, retaining their classical shells, had battlements, arrow slits, and elaborate Gothic gateways added, with mock portcullises and coats of arms. The Gothic style played on the prominence of ruins in Ireland, where country estates often incorporated the remains of an old Norman tower or an abbey.

Generally, Irish country houses were smaller than their English counterparts (termed "great houses"), and changes in design and construction techniques came to Ireland twenty or thirty years after England. Architec-

Classical front, Castle Ward, Strangford, Co. Down (mid-eighteenth century). Because the Wards could not decide in which style to build their house, the entrance front was made Classical, whereas the garden front was Gothic. © CHRISTOPHER J. HALL; CORDAIY PHOTO LIBRARY LTD./ CORBIS. REPRODUCED BY PERMISSION.

tural critics celebrate not just the grandest Irish buildings, but the high quality of countless well-proportioned and elegant small houses, whose creators were, according to Maurice Craig, "imbued with the language of classicism" (Craig 1976, p. 23). Although some of these buildings were designed by distinguished architects, others were put up by local builders working with pattern books.

INTERIORS

High ceilings, well-proportioned rooms, and magnificent stairways are typical of large and small houses, but elaborate plaster-work decoration was a spectacular feature of the grander eighteenth-century buildings. Although the Italian stuccodores, the Francini brothers, Paul and Philip, and Bartholomew Cramillion are the most famous names, native artisans had worked with plaster even before the Palladian period, and the majority of neoclassical interiors were by Irish craftsmen. The Francinis introduced human figures into plaster decoration; their 1739 saloon ceiling at Carton, Co. Kildare, is a masterpiece that inspired a growing fashion. The lead-

ing Irish stuccodore, Robert West, learned and adopted the Italian designs and techniques, preferring the bird in flight to the human figure. His rococo plaster work was in turn followed by Michael Stapleton's neoclassical decoration, on occasion including painted roundels in the style of Robert Adam.

The furnishings of the grander Irish houses were generally purchased on the continent, but native Irish furniture existed and has become increasingly popular on the antiques market. In the pieces created between 1725 to 1775, before artisans adopted English Sheridan styles, exuberant carvings on dark wood often featured grimacing human, satyr, or animal faces reminiscent of the figures decorating pages of the Celtic medieval *Book of Kells*. Plain oval dining tables made with folding sides, so they could be carried outdoors, were called wake tables, as they were also used to display a coffin, surrounded by food and drink.

GARDENS

The walled demesnes, or private park lands, of Ireland's country houses formerly occupied nearly 6 percent of the country and always retained their function as farms for the landlords. The late-seventeenth- and early-eighteenth-century geometrically planned grounds were dominated by tree-lined avenues and symmetrical gardens filled with statues and topiary surrounding the new unfortified country houses. But by the mid-seventeenth century Irish landscapers reacted against symmetrical formal gardens and adopted the revolutionary new English landscape park designs that were well suited to the Irish terrain. Houses now overlooked carefully constructed "natural" parklands of expansive lawns, clumps of trees, and even newly dug lakes; sunken fences, or ha-has, obscured the demarcation between the lawns and the further demesne lands; vegetables, fruits, and flowers were banished to walled gardens isolated from the house. Elaborate gateways and ornamental lodges at the demesne entrances offered a preview of the owner's taste and wealth, and eccentric follies and mausoleums attested to the Irish gentry's love of show.

With shortages of money and labor after the Great Famine of the late 1840s, few new parklands were created. A new enthusiasm for the collecting of exotic plants and trees led to the reintroduction of formal beds around houses. After the 1880s, however, the philosophy of the great Irish horticulturist William Robinson encouraged natural woodland gardens, bog gardens, and an ecological landscaping that became increasingly popular throughout the twentieth century.

DECLINE OF THE COUNTRY HOUSE

Many houses were built in the decades following union, as some members of the nobility and gentry retreated from Dublin into the countryside. However, after the Great Famine only the richest families built or remodeled, often in the Tudor Revival or Victorian Baronial style. The process of land redistribution that began with the Land Act of 1870 encouraged tenants to buy their own land from their landlords, and as great estates lost rental income and property, landlords increasingly became unable to maintain their homes and demesnes. Ironically, the neglect that led to the ruin of some houses also protected others from Victorian "improvements"; thus relatively more surviving Irish than English country houses retain their original features. The burning of approximately two hundred houses between 1920 and 1923 during the Anglo-Irish and subsequent civil war, particularly if the owner was thought to be pro-British, underscored the political hostility elicited by these monuments of Ascendancy culture and politics. Private stewardship of Irish country houses continued to decline long after independence. Many owners, now without the resources to support their former lifestyles, sold their homes for conversion into schools, convents, and hotels, or abandoned them to slow deterioration and eventual ruin or demolition.

The Irish Georgian Society was formed in 1958 to work for preservation in the Republic. Since the 1970s the decay and disappearance of country houses have received increasing attention, as public sentiment began to support tax concessions to owners of heritage properties viewed as major tourist attractions. In Northern Ireland important estates are owned by the National Trust, and in the Republic changes in the tax structure have aided owners struggling to maintain their houses. The Office of Public Works has taken several important buildings under its wing, and some houses are maintained through partnerships between owners and local authorities. The 1988 publication of *Vanishing Country Houses of Ireland*, however, dramatically called attention to the "decay, loss and destruction" of almost 500 country houses in the Republic alone (Knight of Glin 1988, p. 6).

BIG-HOUSE LITERATURE

Literature written about declining Irish country houses reflects the preoccupations of a landlord class facing extinction. Maria Edgeworth's *Castle Rackrent* (1800) initiated a series of conventions that reappear in many subsequent novels: the improvident landlord, the decaying house and declining gentry family, and the rise of a predatory middle-class antagonist who seeks to acquire the landlord's property and position. Gothic novelists working in the tradition depict corrupt and guilt-ridden proprietors. The big-house motif appears in literature throughout the nineteenth and twentieth centuries, predominantly in Irish novels by Edgeworth, Charles Lever, William Carleton, Charles Maturin, Joseph Sheridan Le Fanu, George Moore, Somerville and Ross, Elizabeth Bowen, Jennifer Johnston, Molly Keane, William Trevor, Aidan Higgins, and John Banville. In contrast to the generally ironic indictment of an improvident gentry class emerging from most big-house fiction, the early-twentieth-century poetry of William Butler Yeats celebrates the Anglo-Irish country estate as the symbol of a beleaguered spiritual aristocracy.

SEE ALSO Arts: Early Modern Literature and the Arts from 1500 to 1800; Estates and Demesnes; Georgian Dublin, Art and Architecture of

Bibliography

Aalen, F. H. A., Kevin Whelan, and Matthew Stout. *Atlas of the Irish Rural Landscape.* 1997.

Bence-Jones, Mark. *Ireland.* Vol. 1 of *Burke's Guide to Country Houses.* 1978.

Bence-Jones, Mark. *Twilight of the Ascendancy.* 1987.

Craig, Maurice. *Classic Irish Houses of the Middle Size.* 1976.

Guinness, Desmond, and William Ryan. *Irish Houses and Castles.* 1971.

Hyams, Edward, and William Mac Quitty. *Irish Gardens.* 1967.

Knight of Glin, David J. Griffin, and Nicholas K. Robinson. *Vanishing Country Houses of Ireland.* 1988.

Kreilkamp, Vera. *The Anglo-Irish Novel and the Big House.* 1998.

Moynahan, Julian. *Anglo-Irish: Literary Imagination in a Hyphenated Culture.* 1995.

O'Reilly, Sean. *Irish House and Gardens.* 1998.

Rauchbauer, Otto, ed. *Ancestral Voice: The Big House in Anglo-Irish Literature.* 1992.

Vera Kreilkamp

Craig, James, First Viscount Craigavon

James Craig, First Viscount Craigavon (1871–1940), was the prime minister of Northern Ireland from 1920 to 1940. © Hulton-Deutsch Collection/Corbis. Reproduced by permission.

James Craig (1871–1940), Ulster unionist and prime minister of Northern Ireland, was born in Sydenham, Co. Down, on 8 January 1871. Craig worked as a stockbroker and served in the British army during the Boer War before entering politics. He represented a new generation of leaders (predominantly from the Presbyterian Belfast professional and business classes) who replaced the landed parliamentarianism of Edward Saunderson with a more populist, sectarian, and Ulster-centered unionism. In 1905, Craig cofounded the Ulster Unionist Council. He was Unionist MP at Westminster for East Down (1906–1918) and Mid Down (1918–1921). Craig organized the Ulster campaign against the third Home Rule bill as Carson's principal Ulster-based lieutenant, and helped to organize the 36th Ulster Division during the First World War. He served as a junior minister at Westminster from 1916 to 1918 and from 1919 to 1921. In 1921, Craig succeeded Carson as unionist leader and became the first prime minister of Northern Ireland. In 1926 he became first Viscount Craigavon. Craig successfully resisted British pressure during the Anglo-Irish Treaty negotiations to make concessions toward Irish unity for the sake of keeping all of Ireland within the British empire; he refused to accept the legitimacy of the Boundary Commission (replying to proposed boundary changes with the slogan "Not an inch"), and his political skills (coupled with na-

tionalist maladroitness) did much to ensure that Northern Ireland remained undiminished. A violent challenge to the new state by the Irish Republican Army was met with harsh security policies, local councils were gerrymandered to ensure unionist control, and the electoral system was altered to perpetuate the unionist-nationalist divide by making it harder for smaller parties to win seats. Even after external threats receded, Craig put unionist solidarity above intercommunal relations; attempts by the Northern nationalist leader Joseph Devlin to work within the political system in the late 1920s were spurned. Pressure from unionist hardliners, and the activities of Eamon de Valera, partly explain but cannot excuse Craig's notorious view that Northern Ireland was "a Protestant state for a Protestant people." Craig's ability to extract financial assistance from British governments partly offset his failure to address the economic devastation caused by the decline of Northern Ireland's traditional industries. His later years as prime minister were marked by declining health, long holidays, lavish official commemorations, and high-profile tours of the province during which Craig distributed "bones" (government assistance) without consulting his cabinet or the civil service. Despite increasing physical and mental decrepitude, he retained his position until his death on 24 November 1940.

SEE ALSO Carson, Sir Edward; Ulster Unionist Party in Office; Unionism from 1885 to 1922; **Primary Documents:** On "A Protestant Parliament and a Protestant State" (24 April 1934)

Bibliography

Buckland, Patrick. *The Factory of Grievances: Devolved Government in Northern Ireland, 1921–39.* 1979.

Buckland, Patrick. *James Craig.* 1980.

Jackson, Alvin. *The Ulster Party: Irish Unionists in the House of Commons, 1884–1911.* 1989.

Patrick Maume

Cromwellian Conquest

Between August 1649 and June 1652, Ireland was largely reconquered by English forces. Since October 1641 the island had seen campaigns in which locally raised contingents of Protestants and separate armies dispatched from England and Scotland struggled against the insurgent Confederate Catholics, who controlled much of the country outside Dublin and eastern Ulster. The need to reconquer Ireland acquired greater urgency following the execution of Charles I in January 1649 and the establishment in England of a Commonwealth, because it was feared that the numerous opponents of this republican regime would use Ireland as a base from which to attack it.

On 15 August 1649 an army of approximately 12,000, commanded by Oliver Cromwell, landed near Dublin. Its task was eased by the victory over the Confederates of a local Protestant force under Michael Jones a fortnight earlier at Rathmines, close to Dublin. Cromwell rapidly captured the strategic garrisons of Drogheda (11 September 1649) and Wexford (11 October 1649). With those successes he shortened the campaign and reassured his employer, the Westminster parliament, that he was spending its money well, but the savagery meted out to civilian inhabitants as well as to the garrisons was at odds with Cromwell's restraint in England. It attested to the hostility of English and Scottish Protestants toward the Irish Catholics, and in the longer term it blackened Cromwell's and England's reputations in Ireland. Although Cromwell met setbacks, as at Clonmel in May 1650, where his force suffered heavy casualties, he was confident enough that resistance had been broken to leave Ireland in the following month. His son-in-law Henry Ireton took over the command, but he died of plague while campaigning in November 1651. Besides English officers, some local Protestants, such as Roger Boyle, Baron Broghill (later earl of Orrery), and Sir Charles Coote (subsequently earl of Mountrath) joined the campaign. By April 1653, with the surrender of Cloughoughter, the entire island was again under nominal English control.

The Westminster parliament appointed parliamentary commissioners to govern Ireland, and peacetime administration was slowly restored. However, English rule could be maintained only with the help of large garrisons. These arrangements kept costs high and impoverished Ireland, wasted by warfare throughout the 1640s and more recently depopulated by plague. In the early 1650s, as much as a third of the total population may have died. Many of the defeated went into continental exile, some entering the armies of Spain, Portugal, and France.

For the Irish administration the most pressing task once military resistance had been contained was to reallocate property. It was assumed that the future security and prosperity of Ireland could best be guaranteed by confiscating the lands of the rebels and transferring them to others. In addition, it was hoped that this action would finance the military campaign. The essential measures that reserved the Irish insurgents' estates to pay for the reconquest had been taken by the English parliament in 1642. Its successors in 1652 and 1653 amplified the earlier acts. Two groups benefited: civilians, mainly in England, who had invested money in the reconquest on the security of future grants of Irish property; and soldiers serving in Ireland after 1649 who were to be paid largely in Irish lands. Furthermore, as a guarantee of future security, those implicated in the uprising of 1641 were also to be expelled from the boroughs and from coastal areas. As much as 11 million acres—55 percent of the total acreage of Ireland—was supposed to be at the disposal of the state. The work of surveying these holdings taxed the regime and provoked controversy. First, the wisdom of such a wholesale expropriation and the proposed banishment of the surviving rebels west of the river Shannon into the province of Connacht and County Clare was questioned. Next, the competence of the original surveyor, Benjamin Worsley, was impugned. Then, once Sir William Petty, Worsley's successor, had completed his Down Survey, quarrels erupted between the civilian investors and the soldiery. The redistributions eventually created 8,000 new proprietors, not all of whom settled on their new holdings. Of these, only about 500 were civilian adventurers or their heirs; the rest were soldiers, many of whom, rather than waiting to receive their portions, made over their claims to superior officers or civilian speculators. The undoubted beneficiaries from the upheavals were the members of some of the Protestant families who had settled in Ireland before 1641. Those dispossessed during the Cromwellian interregnum hoped that the Stuarts, once restored to power after 1660, would reinstate them. Lucky individuals did regain their estates, but the essential contours of the Cromwellian settlement were not altered between 1660 and 1688. The dramatic impact is clear from a simple statistic: In 1641 Catholics owned about 59 percent of the land in Ireland; by 1703 this total had dropped to 14 percent.

Some constructive measures accompanied the confiscations. As earlier, the English conquerors insisted that they only wanted to break the power of the traditional leaders of Catholic Ireland. Their prime targets were therefore the priests, heads of the *septs* (clans), lawyers, and military men. The English administration hoped to persuade the bulk of the people of the merits of its rule through a program of social and legal reforms. At the same time, efforts to convert Catholics to Protestantism were redoubled, but resources—of manpower and money—proved too meager to transform Irish society. Schemes to bring the law within the reach of more were disappointing, as were attempts to improve the provision of education and Protestant preaching. Initiatives such as the creation of a second university college in Dublin were short-lived. So, too, were schemes to map and exploit natural resources. A further difficulty was that the English regime in Ireland was no longer monarchical but republican, and this characteristic was detested by some Protestants as well as by many Catholics.

The regime tended toward introversion and quarrelling. Necessarily, it concentrated on routine affairs. Most efforts were directed toward guarding against internal subversion and foreign invaders. These threats worsened when in 1656 the Cromwellian protectorate went to war with Spain, a frequent ally of Irish Catholics and confederate of the exiled Charles Stuart. It had also to collect taxes and try to restore a measure of prosperity so that tax yields could be increased. In addition, it was hampered by unresolved differences over how best to treat the Catholic majority. As in the past, opinions varied between coercion and conciliation. Yet if this regime failed to put down deep roots among the Catholic populace, it did gradually endear itself to many with-

in the Protestant population, who saw their grip on property, office, and power tighten. Irish Catholics, despite English professions to the contrary, were subjected to a series of discriminations that depressed almost all into the condition of "hewers of wood and bearers of water," where once they had owned and governed the island. For this reason, the decade after 1649 can be seen as inaugurating in outline, if not in name, what would be known in the eighteenth century as the Irish Protestant Ascendancy.

SEE ALSO Confederation of Kilkenny; Land Settlements from 1500 to 1690; Petty, Sir William; Puritan Sectaries; Solemn League and Covenant; **Primary Documents:** On the Capture of Drogheda (17 September 1649); From *The Great Case of Transplantation Discussed* (1655); From *The Interest of England in the Irish Transplantation Stated* (1655); From *The Memoirs of Edmund Ludlow* (1698)

Bibliography

Barnard, T. C. *Cromwellian Ireland: English Government and Reform in Ireland, 1649–1660.* 1975. Reprint, 2000.

Bottigheimer, K. S. *English Money and Irish Land.* 1971.

Corish, P. J. "The Cromwellian Conquest, 1649–53," and "The Cromwellian Regime, 1650–1660." In *A New History of Ireland*, vol. 3, *Early Modern Ireland, 1534–1691*, edited by T. W. Moody, F. X. Martin, and F. J. Byrne. 1976.

Ohlmeyer, J. H., ed. *Ireland from Independence to Occupation, 1641–1660.* 1996.

Toby Barnard

Cruachain

References in early Irish literature identify *Crúachu* ("the mounded place") as an assemblage of burial mounds at which an *oenach* (assembly) was held, and as a dwelling place of the earth goddess Medb and her husband Ailill, both of them rich in cattle. Oweynagat nearby was the gateway to the otherworld in the early tale *Echtra Nerai*. The site of Carnfree (*Carn Fraich*) was the inauguration place of the O'Connor kings of Connacht, their ancestors and forerunners, from time immemorial until the fourteenth century. Both these sites are foci around which hundreds of monuments, constructed over at least four millennia, are concentrated.

Fifty mounds I certify,
Are at Oenach na Cruachna,
There are under each mound of them
Fifty truly fine warlike men.
(from a poem in *Leabhar na Uidhre* [*Book of the Dun Cow*], quoted with translation in Petrie 1845, p. 104)

The monuments of the Cruachain/Carnfree complex stand on two great ridges 400 to 500 feet above sea level, running northeast to southwest on the ancient plain of *Magh n-Aí* west of the Shannon in County Roscommon. Dominating the northwest end is the cemetery around Rathcroghan (*Ráth Cruachan*), a natural mound over 6 meters in height, scarped and built into a roughly circular form 100 meters across, with a circular bank and ditch on top which identify the mound as a ring-barrow. Around it is a ditched enclosure 370 meters in diameter. Within the cemetery complex are Stone Age megalithic tombs, two Early Bronze Age tumuli, and several late prehistoric ring-barrows, with a few tiny round cairns and standing stones. Prominent features of the complex are three parallel avenues running straight along the axis of the ridge, two of them overlain by ring-barrows. Four named wells in the area demonstrate the importance of drinking water for cattle in this prime grassland. On the more southerly ridge 6 kilometers to the southeast stands Carnfree, a burial cairn of the early Bronze Age; it lies close to a classic "bowl barrow" of the same period. A later cemetery of ring-barrows and three standing stones surround these focal tombs.

These twin cemeteries encircle spaces that reputedly were in early historic times an oenach site and an inauguration site. The sacred character of the cemeteries probably led to the creation of a zone of exclusion around each of them, outside of which several ringforts were built between 500 and 1000 C.E. In that era many tales about these sites were written down. The great spring well of Ogulla between Rathcroghan and Carnfree, the most powerful in the area, is pointed out as the meeting place of Saint Patrick and the daughters of King Laoghaire of Tara at the dawn of Christianity in the second half of the fifth century.

SEE ALSO Cú Chulainn; Dún Ailinne; Myth and Saga; Prehistoric and Celtic Ireland; Tara

Bibliography

Herity, Michael. "A Survey of the Royal Site of Cruachain in Connacht, I." *Journal of the Royal Society of Antiquaries of Ireland* 113 (1983): 121–142.

Petrie, G. *Trans. Royal Irish Acad.* xx (1845): 104.

Michael Herity

Cú Chulainn

The myth of Cú Chulainn (Cuchulainn) is told in the *Táin Bó Cúailnge* (the *Cattle Raid of Cooley*), first fully transcribed in the twelfth century C.E. (see Kinsella 1970). The epic tale tells of rivalry between Queen Medb (Maeve) of Connacht and her husband Ailill as to which of them had the richest possessions. They were evenly matched except in one respect—that Ailill had a large bull. So Medb set out with her army to the Cooley peninsula in Ulster to steal a large brown bull belonging to Dáire mac Fiachna, owner of the brown bull of Cooley, casting a spell on the defending warriors of Ulster—the Red Branch (Craobh Rua) heroes. One warrior did not succumb to the spell: Cú Chulainn was semidivine, the son of the princess Deichtine (Dectera) and the sun god Lugh. As Medb made her way back to Connacht with the stolen bull, Cú Chulainn employed guerrilla tactics to harass her army until the Red Branch heroes shook off the spell and came to his aid. A further tale tells how Cú Chulainn acquired his name. As a young boy known as Sétanta, he was making his way to the house of Culann for a feast when Culann's wolfhound attacked him. Sétanta struck a hurling ball with his stick so forcefully that he killed the wolfhound instantly. By way of reparation Sétanta promised to be Culann's guard dog, thereby changing his name to Cú Chulainn, the hound of Culann. Another tale tells of his death: Mortally wounded in battle, Cú Chulainn tied himself to a rock so that he might die upright. As he expired, a raven landed on his shoulder. This is significant because the raven would not land on the shoulder of a live person. It indicates that the hero is really dead.

The popularity of the myth of Cú Chulainn has waxed and waned through the centuries, and each revival has served a political purpose. The O'Neill clan revived the myth in the fifteenth century to justify their rule in Ulster against the usurping Elizabethans (Morgan 1993). The Gaelic revival of the late nineteenth century saw the exploits of Cú Chulainn reworked by scholars such as Standish O'Grady for an emerging nationalist consciousness. The Gaelic scholar and revolutionary Padraic Pearse in particular viewed Cú Chulainn as the embodiment of the nationalist ideal, and when Pearse was executed for his role in the doomed 1916

Easter Rising, it was perhaps inevitable that Cú Chulainn should come to symbolize not just nationalist aspirations but also republican struggle. Thus Cú Chulainn was the obvious choice when Taoiseach Eamon de Valera, himself one of the leaders of the 1916 Rising, sought an emblem to sum up the spirit of 1916. The sculptor Oliver Sheppard had already begun casting a bronze statue of the dying Cú Chulainn in 1914, and for the twentieth anniversary of the Rising, at the direction of de Valera, the completed statue was placed in the General Post Office in Dublin, the headquarters of the republican insurgents.

Ironically, in 1991 the image of the Sheppard sculpture was meticulously reproduced in a loyalist wall mural in East Belfast—one of a half-dozen murals that, for the most part, display the weaponry and activists of the Ulster Defence Association (UDA), the largest loyalist paramilitary group. This imaginative attempt to convert Cú Chulainn to the loyalist cause began with Belfast doctor—and later lord mayor—Ian Adamson, who argued that Ulster was once inhabited by Cruthin (or Picts) who were progressively forced out by the invading Celts from Europe, pushing their way up from the west and south of Ireland. In this interpretation Queen Medb is a Celt and Cú Chulainn the brave Cruthin defending Ulster. Not only does this serve to emphasize that Ulster is historically, culturally, even racially separate, but it also justifies the role of the UDA—Cú Chulainn becomes, in effect, the first UDA man.

Historians agree that Adamson's reinterpretation is fatally flawed. More significant, though, is the question of how it has been accepted by loyalists. Although the officer cadres of the UDA (and on one occasion, the Ulster Volunteer Force, the other major loyalist paramilitary group) have sponsored Cú Chulainn murals in Rathcoole (north Belfast), Highfield (west Belfast), and Derry, as well as on the walls of the UDA wings in Long Kesh prison, rank-and-file loyalists appear to be unconvinced by the revisionism. Most people interpret the Cú Chulainn image in its traditional republican light, and indeed republicans have transposed the Sheppard emblem onto the walls in their own murals in Turf Lodge and Lenadoon (west Belfast), as well as in Armagh. In this setting Cú Chulainn justifies the struggle of republican militants, prisoners, and hunger strikers.

SEE ALSO Cruachain; Emain Macha (Navan Fort); Myth and Saga; Prehistoric and Celtic Ireland; *Táin Bó Cúailnge*

Bibliography

Adamson, Ian. *The Cruthin: A History of the Ulster Land and People.* 1974.

Kinsella, Thomas, trans. *The Tain.* 1970.

Morgan, H. J. "Deceptions of Demons." *Fortnight* (September 1993): 34–36.

Rolston, Bill. *Drawing Support 2: Murals of War and Peace.* 1995.

Bill Rolston

Cullen, Paul

Paul Cullen (1803–1878), Ireland's first cardinal (1866), was born on 29 April into a strong farming family in Prospect, County Kildare. He was educated at the Quaker school at Ballitore and at Carlow College, and his outlook was marked by thirty years spent in Rome (1820–1850). There he served as rector of the Irish College beginning in 1832. He was consecrated archbishop of Armagh in 1850, in which year he was papal legate to the National Synod of Thurles. The synod condemned the third-level Queen's Colleges and called for a Catholic university to be established.

Upon the death of Archbishop Murray, Cullen transferred to Dublin as archbishop in 1852. He invited John Henry Newman to Dublin to become first rector of the Catholic University, a largely unsuccessful project. He pursued a policy of having his own candidates appointed to Irish bishoprics, favoring young and active pastors. Cullen oversaw the completion of the Tridentine model of the church in a reinvigorated post-penal and postfamine church, which was confident of its own strength for the first time since the Reformation.

In politics he was much more of a nationalist before he became archbishop than afterward. He condemned the militant nationalist Fenians, a secret oath-bound society. He pursued a policy of alliance with Liberal governments, and Irish Liberals MPs needed Cullen's goodwill to be certain of their seats. He denounced "priests in politics" who took a line contrary to his own. He had poor relations with his rival, Archbishop MacHale of Tuam.

He was suspicious of Protestants, and his pastorals condemned evangelical proselytism in Dublin. In the 1860s he argued successfully for the disestablishment of the Anglican Church in Ireland. He was influential at the First Vatican Council of 1869 and 1870. Cautious

Paul Cardinal Cullen (1803–1878). From Harper's Weekly, *30 November 1878.* COURTESY OF THE WISCONSIN HISTORICAL SOCIETY. REPRODUCED BY PERMISSION.

and secretive by nature, he took an uncompromising line for the Catholic Church in accord with the Ultramontane policy of Pope Pius IX (1846–1878). He even regarded Maynooth College with suspicion for its alleged independence from Roman thinking. In the absence of strong lay leadership between the death of Daniel O'Connell and the rise of Charles Stewart Parnell, Cullen was a dominant figure in Irish public life.

SEE ALSO Roman Catholic Church: 1829 to 1891

Bibliography

Larkin, Emmet. *The Making of the Roman Catholic Church in Ireland, 1850–1860.* 1980.

Larkin, Emmet. *The Consolidation of the Roman Catholic Church in Ireland, 1860–1870.* 1987.

Thomas McGrath

Cumann na mBan

Cumann na mBan—literally, "league of women"—was founded in Dublin in April 1914 as a women's auxiliary to the Irish Volunteers. The founders were Agnes O'Farrelly (one of the first women professors in the National University of Ireland), Agnes MacNeill, Nancy O'Rahilly, Louise Gavan Duffy, Mary Colum, and Mary McSwiney. Cumann na mBan members were to train in signals and first aid, and their role was envisaged as a noncombatant one. Although it had its own command structures, the Cumann as a whole was subordinate to the Volunteers' organization. Leading Irish suffragists of the day criticized it, claiming that these "slave-women" would become nothing more than "animated collecting boxes." Prominent Cumann member Helena Molony spoke for many members when she responded that there could be no free women in an enslaved nation. Initially the membership was drawn from the leisured middle class, but gradually, more and more lower-middle-class and working-class women came to be represented in the organization. Typical was the trained hospital midwife Elizabeth O'Farrell, who delivered the surrender at the end of the 1916 Rising.

The Volunteers split in the autumn of 1914 when the majority of its members voted to answer Britain's call to arms. In Cumann na mBan, however, the majority voted to stay with the minority of the Volunteers who served "neither King nor Kaiser, but Ireland." The Cumann played an important role in the 1916 Rising, performing vital life-maintenance work in the garrisons and carrying messages. From 1916 to 1918 it was women who were largely in charge of revolutionary nationalism, campaigning for prisoners' dependents' relief, upholding the cult of the dead 1916 leaders, sustaining the anticonscription movement, and electioneering for Sinn Féin's landslide victory in the 1918 election. The number of branches of Cumann na mBan soared from 100 in 1917 to 600 in 1918. During the War of Independence the women played vital yet hidden roles as keepers of safe houses, dispatch riders, and first-aid workers. The truce and the subsequent Anglo-Irish Treaty saw the country bitterly divided, but Cumann na mBan was the first nationalist organization to publicly reject the treaty. The Cumann were active during the Civil War, during which many of its members were imprisoned, and it continued to be the most politically radical (usually left-wing) political organization in Ireland until the revolutionary generation died out.

SEE ALSO Anglo-Irish Treaty of 1921; Clarke, Kathleen; Markievicz, Countess Constance; Sinn Féin Movement and Party to 1922; Struggle for Independence from 1916 to 1921; Women in Nationalist and Unionist Movements in the Early Twentieth Century

Bibliography

Ward, Margaret. *Unmanageable Revolutionaries: Women and Irish Nationalism.* 1983.

Caitriona Clear

Cusack, Michael

Michael Cusack (1847–1906), founder of the Gaelic Athletic Association, was born in the Burren, Co. Clare, on 20 September and qualified in 1866 as a primary-level schoolteacher. In 1877, three years after he moved to Dublin, he opened the Civil Service Academy, preparing students for the army, police, and civil service. He also ran weekly courses in the educational column of a nationalist magazine.

From boyhood Cusack had participated in the traditional athletics of rural Ireland, and in Dublin he joined in the management of amateur athletics. Convinced that Irish athletics urgently needed reforming to open them to nationalist youths, who were de facto barred from competing, and to end abuses such as betting and rigging of results, he advocated the formation of a new athletics body. However, largely because of his quarrelsome personality and his constant preaching of nationalist views to loyalist audiences, his efforts were continually thwarted. In 1882 he decided to go it alone.

In 1884 Cusack received backing from Maurice Davin, an Irish athlete of international repute, to start a new body that would revive the ancient Celtic game of hurling and reform athletics. At a meeting in the Tipperary town of Thurles on 1 November 1884, Cusack and Davin launched the Gaelic Athletic Association. Because Cusack had carefully laid the organizational foundations in provincial Ireland, the new body spread rapidly. But rifts in the association's executive led to Cusack's dismissal as chief officer in July 1886, and for the remaining twenty years of his life he remained on the fringes of the association.

By the late 1890s Cusack, dependent on private tutoring for his livelihood, had met the undergraduate James Joyce. By then having lived more than twenty years in Dublin, Cusack was a familiar figure in the city—with a bushy beard, frock coat, and broad-brimmed hat, and accompanied by his dog Garryowen. He became the model for the Citizen, the main character in the Cyclops episode of Joyce's *Ulysses*, who dominates the boisterous gathering in Kiernan's pub near Green Street courthouse. Both as the founder of the Gaelic Athletic Association and as the model for an immortal character in *Ulysses*, Michael Cusack carved out his own distinctive niche in Irish history.

SEE ALSO Gaelic Revivalism: The Gaelic Athletic Association; Literacy and Popular Culture

Bibliography

de Búrca, Marcus. *Michael Cusack and the GAA.* 1989.
Ó Caithnia, Liam P. *Micheál Cíosóg.* 1982.

Marcus de Búrca

D

Dáil Éireann

See Griffith, Arthur; Sinn Féin Movement and Party to 1922.

~

Dál Cais and Brian Boru

The origins of the Dál Cais, a dynasty of early medieval Ireland, are found in east Limerick, but around the start of the eighth century they were forced to expand into County Clare. They forged alliances with Cormac Cas, who was descended from the Eóganacht, a loose grouping of people who provided many early kings of Munster, and thus attempted to claim a major interest in the kingship of Cashel. From the tenth to the twelfth centuries, just as the fortunes of the Eóganacht declined, the Dál Cais dominated the province of Munster, initially under the leadership of Cenétig mac Lorcáin, and then under his sons Mathgamhain and Brian Boru.

Brian Boru, arguably the most famous king of this dynasty, succeeded to the kingship on the violent death of his brother Mathgamhain in 976. He spent the first part of his reign attempting to consolidate his power over Munster, but when he tried to expand the area of his control into Leinster, he came up against Maél Sechnaill II, then the high king of Ireland. They made a truce in 997, and as a result were able to join together and defeat the Dublin Hiberno-Norse at the battle of Glenn Máma in 999. Brian was the first ruler not from the Uí Néill who made a claim for the high kingship of Ireland, and he was finally acknowledged as such by Máel Sechnaill II in 1002. From the security of his base in the southern part of the country Brian Boru fought several campaigns against the leading dynasties of the northern half of the island. He was slain at the battle of Clontarf in 1014, but not before his army had routed the forces of Leinster and their Norse allies. It was his strategic skills, especially the construction of defensive fortifications and his employment of naval power, that made him such an effective military leader. His astute political sense and the appointment of many of his relations to major offices within the church of Munster ensured the close control of the church. Therefore, it is hardly surprising that, following Clontarf, he was buried in Armagh, the primatial capital, and he was also given the title *Imperator Scotorum* (emperor of the Irish) in the *Book of Armagh*, a ninth-century gospel book.

Despite the death of Brian, the Dál Cais were able to maintain their control of Munster through other strong leaders, some of whom were descendants of Brian Boru, right up until the early part of the twelfth century. But after the death of Muirchertach O'Brien in 1119, the O'Briens, as they came to be called in memory of Brian Boru, had a more limited role in the politics of Munster.

SEE ALSO Clontarf, Battle of; Norse Settlement; O'Connors of Connacht; Uí Néill High Kings

Bibliography

Byrne, Francis John. *Irish Kings and High-Kings.* 1973.

Ryan, John. "Brian Bóruma, King of Ireland." In *North Munster Studies*, edited by Étienne Rynne. 1967.

Terry Barry

Brian Boru describes himself as Imperator Scotorum *(Emperor of the Irish) in an early-eleventh-century inscription from the* Book of Armagh. THE BOARD OF TRINITY COLLEGE DUBLIN. REPRODUCED BY PERMISSION.

Darcy, Patrick

Patrick Darcy (1598–1668) was born into a leading Galway merchant family and laid the foundations of his prominent legal career at the Middle Temple, one of the four Inns of Court that controlled the education of lawyers in England, under the patronage of the earl of Clanricard, who retained his services after he qualified. He played an active role both in the Old English parliamentary opposition to Wentworth's government in 1634 to 1635 and in the resistance to the official program for the confiscation and plantation of lands in Connacht between 1635 and 1637. Though he was disbarred for leaving Ireland without license to deliver a petition to the king, his practice flourished, and his clients included influential members of the nobility and government. He was returned to Parliament in a by-election in May 1641 and at once joined the leadership of the opposition coalition of Old and New English members. When rebellion broke out in October 1641, Darcy remained aloof and cooperated in efforts to preserve neutrality in Galway, but he supported the move to establish an alternative government, was closely involved in drafting the constitution adopted by the Confederate Catholics, as the allied Irish and Old English rebels styled themselves, at Kilkenny in October 1642, and accepted appointment as lord chancellor, the chief legal officer in the rebel administration. Deeply involved in the protracted peace negotiations, Darcy's political behavior became erratic after the king's defeat in England and the failure of the first Ormond peace in the summer of 1646, and his influence declined thereafter.

Darcy lived quietly in Ireland in the 1650s and resumed his practice after Restoration. His contribution to both parliamentary opposition and Confederate ideology was embodied in "An Argument," presented at a conference of Lords and Commons on 9 June 1641, in which he reviewed the legal and constitutional objections of the Commons to developments in the practice of government under Wentworth. In a programmatic analysis of the constituents of legal authority in Ireland, which he identified as the common law of England and the parliamentary statutes and lawful customs of Ireland, he not only stripped the powers traditionally vested in the king of their discretionary character and subordinated them to the law but also excluded English parliamentary authority from Ireland. The essence of his position, that Ireland was a separate kingdom, subject to the same crown as England yet distinct from it, was not novel. However, at a time when the English parliament was taking over royal powers, including the right to rule Ireland, the clarity and force of his state-ment of the public-law relationship between the English and Irish parliaments was extremely influential. When it was delivered, Darcy's "Argument" expressed the views of Protestant colonists as well as of Catholics. During the Confederate years, when it was published (in 1643) and legislative independence was a Confederate aim, it validated the claim to be loyal to the Crown while fighting in self-defense against Parliament. In later years it became an important source in the case for Irish legislative independence, which was controversially stated by William Molyneux in 1698 and espoused by Protestant "patriots" in the eighteenth century.

SEE ALSO Confederation of Kilkenny; Rinuccini, Giovanni Battista

Bibliography

Clarke, Aidan. "Patrick Darcy and the Constitutional Relationship between Britain and Ireland." In *Political Thought in Seventeenth-Century Ireland: Kingdom or Colony*, edited by Jane H. Ohlmeyer. 2000.

Darcy, Patrick. "An Argument." In *Camden Miscellany*, vol. 31, edited by C. E. J. Caldicott. 1992.

O'Malley, Liam. "Patrick Darcy, Galway Lawyer and Politician, 1598–1668." In *Galway: Town and Gown, 1484–1984*, edited by Diarmuid Ó Cearbhaill. 1984.

Aidan Clarke

Davis, Thomas

A journalist, poet, and unofficial leader of Young Ireland, noted especially as the first to articulate the idea of cultural nationalism, Thomas Davis (1814–1845) was born at Mallow, Co. Cork, on 14 October 1814. The son of an English army surgeon and an Irish woman, Davis was educated at Trinity College and called to the Irish bar in 1838. In 1841 he joined the Repeal Association with his close friend John Blake Dillon and quickly made a name for himself in nationalist circles for both his comprehensive vision of Irishness and his stirring political ballads.

In October 1842 Davis and Dillon, along with Charles Gavan Duffy, founded the *Nation*, a newspaper that advocated Irish self-government and national pride. Within a year the *Nation* had the most paid sub-

Thomas Davis (1814–1845) was one of a trio of journalists who founded the Nation *newspaper in October 1842 and quickly turned it into the most influential weekly paper of its time. His nationalist verse and prose helped to stimulate a burst of cultural nationalism. Widely admired leader of the Young Ireland group within the Repeal Association, Davis died of scarlatina at 30 in September 1845. Pencil drawing by Sir Frederick Wilheim.* NATIONAL GALLERY OF IRELAND, CAT. NO. 2032. REPRODUCED BY PERMISSION.

scribers of any Irish newspaper and Davis had become the principal editor and contributor, using the editorial page to develop his romantic concept of Irish identity. In his view Ireland was a spiritual reality based on historic cultural tradition, and anyone who adopted Ireland as his homeland, regardless of his religion or when he arrived, was Irish. Davis's editorials, patriotic verse, and enthusiastic support for reviving the Irish language made him the most respected and admired of the Young Irelanders.

Politically, Davis and the other Young Irelanders regarded Ireland's claim to self-government as a fundamental demand that could not be compromised. Davis also believed strongly that Irish national identity should be secular and disapproved of what he saw as undue clerical influence on Daniel O'Connell and the repeal movement. Davis's dissatisfaction with O'Connell's management of the Repeal Association and his opposition to nondenominational education led to a famous verbal clash between the Young Irelanders and O'Connell on 26 May 1845. Reconciliation was achieved, but tensions remained, and a little over one

year later the Young Irelanders seceded from the repeal movement entirely, but by then Davis had died unexpectedly on 16 September 1845 after a short illness. Davis was a significant literary and political influence on his contemporaries, but his ideas had an even greater impact on subsequent generations, providing a foundation for the Gaelic revival at the turn of the twentieth century.

SEE ALSO Balladry in English; Mitchel, John; Newspapers; O'Connell, Daniel; Repeal Movement; Young Ireland and the Irish Confederation

Bibliography

Davis, Richard. *The Young Ireland Movement.* 1987.

Nowlan, Kevin B. *The Politics of Repeal: A Study in the Relations between Great Britain and Ireland, 1841–50.* 1965.

Sloan, Robert. *William Smith O'Brien and the Young Ireland Rebellion of 1848.* 2000.

Michael W. de Nie

Davitt, Michael

Fenian and Land League founder Michael Davitt (1846–1906) was born on 25 March in Straide, Co. Mayo. In 1850 his family's landlord evicted them from their small farm, and they emigrated to Haslingden, an industrial town in Lancashire, England. At age eleven, when he was working in a cotton mill, a machine crushed his right arm, and it was later amputated. Ironically this injury allowed him to resume formal schooling, and in 1861 he became a post office clerk. In 1865 Davitt, like many young Irishmen in Lancashire, joined the Irish Republican Brotherhood (IRB), or Fenians. He rose quickly through the ranks and in February 1867 helped to lead the ill-conceived raid on Chester Castle. Appointed IRB organizing secretary for England and Scotland in 1868, during the next two years Davitt traveled clandestinely around Britain organizing arms shipments to Ireland. In 1870 the authorities arrested and tried Davitt for arms trafficking. A jury found him guilty, and he was sentenced to fifteen years' penal servitude.

Davitt's mistreatment in prison became a cause célèbre, and many Irish nationalists campaigned for his

Michael Davitt (1846–1906) was the son of an evicted Mayo tenant whose family emigrated to Lancashire, where as a mill-hand at age eleven, he lost his right arm in a factory accident. Once the chief arms buyer for the Fenians, he spent over seven years in British jails under degrading treatment before his release in 1877. The real founder of the Land League in 1879, his espousal of state ownership of the land helped to marginalize him politically after 1882. Photograph c. 1879. © CORBIS. REPRODUCED BY PERMISSION.

release. Davitt thus emerged with a high public profile when he was released eight years early in 1877. He went to the United States in 1878 and with John Devoy set the nationalist movement on a new course by promising American Fenian support for both Charles Stewart Parnell's constitutional campaign for self-government and renewed land agitation. This "new departure" bore fruit when agricultural depression hit Ireland in the late 1870s. In October 1879 Davitt founded the Irish National Land League, and Parnell became its president. The league united large farmers, small farmers, laborers, constitutional nationalists, and Fenians in a great agrarian movement that received substantial financial backing from Irish Americans. The ensuing Land War forced the British government to grant the 1881 Land

Act, which gave Irish tenants the famous "three Fs"—fair rent, fixity of tenure, and free sale.

After 1882 Davitt began advocating land nationalization. This put him at odds with most Irish nationalists, who sought tenant ownership of the land. In 1890, after news surfaced of Parnell's long-standing love affair with a married woman, Davitt became a leading anti-Parnellite. He served as an anti-Parnellite MP from 1893 until 1899, when he resigned his seat to protest the Boer War. Davitt spent the rest of his life traveling, mostly as an investigative journalist. By founding the Land League, Davitt had begun the process that fundamentally transformed Irish landholding.

SEE ALSO Home Rule Movement and the Irish Parliamentary Party: 1870 to 1891; Home Rule Movement and the Irish Parliamentary Party: 1891 to 1918; Ladies' Land League; Land Acts of 1870 and 1881; Land War of 1879 to 1882; Parnell, Charles Stewart; **Primary Documents:** Establishment of the National Land League of Mayo (16 August 1879)

Bibliography

Davitt, Michael. *The Fall of Feudalism in Ireland; or, The Story of the Land League Revolution.* 1904.

Moody, T. W. *Davitt and the Irish Revolution, 1846–82.* 1982.

Patrick F. Tally

Declaration of a Republic and the 1949 Ireland Act

Under the External Relations Act of December 1936 the role of the British crown in internal Irish affairs was removed, though the Irish state remained associated with the Commonwealth for external affairs. External association with the Commonwealth had been devised by Eamon de Valera in 1921 as a compromise between dominion status and an outright republic. He hoped in vain that the 1936 act, with its remaining link with the Commonwealth, would facilitate Irish unity by allowing Ulster unionists a path into a united Ireland. The 1937 constitution complemented the External Relations Act, and through the two documents Ireland effectively became a republic within the Commonwealth, though no official declaration to this effect was ever made. A consequence was that though Ireland had a president beginning in 1937, the British monarch continued to sign the credentials of Irish diplomats, so it appeared to the international community that the British king, not the president of Ireland, was the head of the Irish state.

De Valera was careful not to formally break the link between Ireland and the Commonwealth, because such an action would allow Britain to treat Irish citizens living in Britain as aliens and it could lead to the curtailment of Irish exports to Britain. In the run-up to the 1948 general election it seemed as if de Valera was prepared to repeal the External Relations Act, declare a republic, and keep Ireland within the Commonwealth. The interparty government that came to power in February 1948 was led by Fine Gael's John A. Costello, a former Irish Free State attorney-general and veteran of Irish delegations to the imperial conferences of the 1920s. Many members of the government, including its minister for external affairs, Seán MacBride (who was the leader of Clann na Poblachta, a small radical republican party), felt that the External Relations Act was damaging to Ireland's international status. On 1 September 1948, during a speech to the Canadian Bar Association, Costello criticized the External Relations Act and hinted that it would be removed. On 5 September 1948 the Irish *Sunday Independent* reported that the External Relations Act was to be repealed and that Ireland would leave the Commonwealth. There was general surprise among the members of Costello's cabinet, and there is evidence that the story, written by Hector Legge, the newspaper's editor, was encouraged by MacBride in the hope of forcing Costello's hand. On 7 September, at a press conference in Ottawa, Costello confirmed the story that the External Relations Act was to go and that Ireland would leave the Commonwealth.

The rationale for Costello's action has been debated since 1948. Some have argued that Costello acted on impulse after being snubbed at a banquet given by the pro-unionist governor general of Canada, Lord Alexander, when a replica of "Roaring Meg," a cannon used in the siege of Derry, was placed on the table in front of Costello. Others have said that coalition partners, such as Sean MacBride, forced Costello's hand, or that Costello was countering Eamon de Valera's worldwide antipartition campaign of 1948 and 1949. Fine Gael had always been seen as a pro-Commonwealth party, and the declaration of a republic by a Fine Gael taoiseach was regarded by some as an attempt to steal Fianna Fáil's republicanism is the wake of de Valera's world tour. Another theory is that the government was trying to avoid embarrassment over questions about Ireland's international status that had been asked in the Dáil by independent

Teachta Dála (Dáil Deputy) Peadar Cowan. Costello may have felt that it was better for the government to take the initiative in repealing the External Relations Act than to be forced into repealing the act by a backbencher such as Cowan introducing a private member's bill in the Dáil. (A backbencher is a Teachta Dála who is not a member of the government or of the opposition front bench, or shadow cabinet. A certain amount of time is allotted in each Dáil sitting for private-member bills to be introduced. They are bills that are not part of the government programme and are introduced into the Dáil for consideration by individual backbench Teachta Dálas.)

Curiously, there is no mention in the 1948 cabinet minutes of a decision to declare a republic and repeal the External Relations Act. Interparty government Minister for Health Noël Browne later suggested that no such official government decision had been made. However, under the interparty government, informal ad hoc cabinet meetings took place, and its nonappearance in the written minutes does not necessarily mean that the government did not make the decision. There appears to have been a general agreement among government members that the act should be repealed. This was also the view in the Department of External Affairs, and the British representative in Ireland, Lord Rugby, had informed London before Costello's statement in Canada that the External Relations Act would be repealed before the end of 1948. London was infuriated by Costello's announcement and threatened through Lord Rugby that Ireland might lose access to valuable British markets if it left the Commonwealth. After Costello's death, Noël Browne suggested that because of this pressure from London, Costello considered resigning (though this story has little foundation). But the Irish government refused to back down, and it was supported by Commonwealth prime ministers.

The Republic of Ireland Bill was passed by the Dáil and signed into law in December 1948 by President Seán T. O'Kelly. The act came into effect on Easter Monday, 19 April 1949, the thirty-third anniversary of the 1916 Easter Rising. There was a parade to mark the occasion in Dublin, and smaller parades occurred nationwide. Costello's unorthodox declaration did at least have popular support in the new Republic.

It has been suggested, notably by Dennis Kennedy in *The Widening Gulf* (1988), that the declaration of the Republic of Ireland further increased the gulf between North and South in Ireland. Northern Irish prime minister Sir Basil Brooke (later Viscount Brookeborough) used the occasion to call a general election in which his Unionist Party was returned with an increased majority. The British Ireland Act of May 1949, which recognized the Republic of Ireland, guaranteed northern unionists that the union with Britain would not be broken without the consent of the Northern Ireland parliament. The British act came as a shock to Dublin, but ironically the years between 1950 and 1955 saw unprecedented cooperation between Dublin and Belfast over such issues as electricity generation, the running of the Dublin-to-Belfast railway, and the establishment of the cross-border Foyle Fisheries Commission.

The declaration of the Republic of Ireland enhanced Ireland's international status: Irish ambassadors now had their credentials signed by the president of Ireland, and the independence of the Republic was clearly defined. Ireland was now a fully sovereign independent state. However, some problems persisted; for example, a dispute raged from 1955 to 1964 between Ireland and Australia about whether to refer to the Irish state as "Ireland" (insisted upon by Dublin) or "Republic of Ireland" (insisted upon by the pro-unionist governor general in Australia). As a result of the dispute, Ireland had no ambassadorial representation in Canberra from 1956, when Ambassador Brian Gallagher was withdrawn in protest, until 1964.

The declaration of the Republic of Ireland ended the saga of Ireland's international and national status that began with the 1921 treaty. From 1949 onward, economic development, not the question of sovereignty, would be the key theme in Irish politics.

SEE ALSO Brooke, Basil Stanlake, First Viscount Brookeborough; Commonwealth; Constitution; de Valera, Eamon; Politics: Independent Ireland since 1922; Northern Ireland: Policy of the Dublin Government from 1922 to 1969; **Primary Documents:** On the Republic of Ireland Bill (24 November 1948); From the 1937 Constitution

Bibliography

Kennedy, Dennis. *The Widening Gulf: Northern Attitudes to the Independent Irish State, 1919–1949.* 1988.

Kennedy, Michael. *Division and Consensus: The Politics of Cross-Border Relations in Ireland, 1922–1969.* 2000.

McCabe, Ian. *A Diplomatic History of Ireland, 1948–49: The Republic, the Commonwealth, and NATO.* 1991.

McCullagh, David. *A Makeshift Majority: The First Inter-Party Government, 1948–1951.* 1998.

Michael Kennedy

Decommissioning

Decommissioning entered the lexicon of the Irish peace process obliquely. It was not mentioned specifically in the Downing Street Declaration of December 1993, which stated that only parties committed to "exclusively peaceful means" could fully engage in the political process. Nor did a clarification of the declaration the following May make any specific reference to disarmament. It made its official entrance only in March 1995 in a speech given by the Northern Ireland secretary of state in Washington, D.C. The "Washington 3" speech contained three elements: the acceptance of the principles of disarmament; the modalities by which it could be achieved; and a gesture of decommissioning as an act of good faith prior to all-party talks. Paramilitary groups balked at the third because it was interpreted as surrender. Washington 3 had followed the cessation of violence by the Irish Republican Army (IRA) in August 1994 and an Ulster Unionist Party policy paper the following January that proposed establishing an International Commission on Decommissioning (adopted by the British in June 1995). In addition, Washington 3 was launched two weeks after the Frameworks Document, which was considered to be too nationalist by unionists.

So decommissioning was wrapped in ambiguity. Republicans set it in the wider context of total demilitarization as part of a process rather than accepting it as a condition of entry into all-party talks. The Irish government worried that it was an examination that republicans could not pass. In November 1995 the two governments attempted to break the impasse with their "twin-track" process of making progress on decommissioning in parallel with all-party negotiations. An independent body chaired by former U.S. Senator George Mitchell, reporting in January 1996, made the stark point that "success in the peace process cannot be achieved simply by reference to the decommissioning of arms." It enunciated six fundamental principles of democracy and nonviolence. But it was too late: In February an IRA bomb exploded in London. The cease-fire was not reinstated until July 1997 after Labour had won a massive general election victory in May and the secretary of state had announced that decommissioning was "secondary to actually getting people into talks."

An Independent International Commission on Decommissioning (IICD) was instituted to stimulate the process. In the Belfast Agreement of April 1998 the parties affirmed their commitment to paramilitary disarmament and to using their influence to achieve decommissioning within two years. In June, Sinn Féin spoke of "a voluntary decommissioning [as a] natural development of the peace process" and appointed Martin McGuinness as its representative to the IICD in September. Many unionists countered with a "no guns, no government" policy, meaning that Sinn Féin could not be in government unless the IRA began decommissioning. It was not until June 2000 that an inspection of an IRA dump was carried out, followed by a second inspection in October and a third in May 2001. On 23 October 2001 the IRA publicly declared that it would be putting its weapons permanently and verifiably beyond use. But by the deadline of February 2002 full-scale decommissioning had not happened, and the deadline was extended for another year, with an option until 2007. The secretary of state put all of this in context when he said that decommissioning would not be finished for a generation, and that ultimately it is "culture and the mindset that has to be decommissioned."

SEE ALSO Adams, Gerry; Irish Republican Army (IRA); Northern Ireland: Constitutional Settlement from Sunningdale to Good Friday; Northern Ireland: The United States in Northern Ireland since 1970; **Primary Documents:** Irish Republican Army (IRA) Cease-Fire Statement (31 August 1994); Text of the IRA Cease-Fire Statement (19 July 1997); The Belfast/Good Friday Agreement (10 April 1998)

Bibliography

Hauswedell, Corinna, and Kris Brown. *Burying the Hatchet: The Decommissioning of Paramilitary Arms in Northern Ireland.* Bonn International Center for Conversion Brief 22. 2002.

Hennessey, Thomas. *The Northern Ireland Peace Process: Ending the Troubles?* 2000.

Mallie, Eamon, and David McKittrick. *The Fight for Peace.* 1997.

Mitchell, George J. *Making Peace.* 1999.

Paul Arthur

Defenderism

The Defender movement, which originated in County Armagh in the mid-1780s and whose participants were

once described by a historian as "rural rioters," used to be closely associated with older traditions of agrarian unrest such as Whiteboyism, and indeed the two phenomena had much in common. Both the Whiteboys, who first emerged in Tipperary in the early 1760s, and the Defenders were overwhelmingly rural, lower-class, Catholic, oath-bound secret societies; both used quasimilitary and masonic terminology ("Captains" and "brothers"); and both used violence and intimidation to police what the historian E. P. Thompson later conceptualized as the "moral economy"—fair rents, tithes, taxes, access to common lands, and so on. The Defenders in County Meath in the early 1790s were sometimes referred to as "regulators."

However, the differences between Defenderism and Whiteboyism are at least as important as the similarities. First, the local mid-Ulster context from which the Defenders arose contrasted markedly with the Whiteboy heartlands of Munster and South Leinster. Since almost all Irish landlords were Protestant, Whiteboys were sectarian by default. In Armagh, on the other hand, the Defenders confronted lower-class Protestants and in fact were born out of sectarian conflict. The precise causes of this conflict are obscure but are intimately related to the relaxation of the anti-Catholic penal laws. By the 1780s Catholics who had hitherto been barred from owning land were in a position to bid—and to outbid their Protestant neighbors—for leases. Another and more important bone of contention concerned the ownership of firearms. The right to bear arms denoted citizenship, and Catholics had been duly stripped of that right by one of the earliest penal laws. By the 1780s, however, in the new atmosphere of religious toleration promoted by some of the Volunteers, Catholics had enrolled in Volunteer companies and armed themselves. In response, the lower-class Protestant vigilante bands—known as the "Peep o' Day Boys" because they raided Catholic homes at "the peep of day" in search of illegal guns—began re-enforcing the penal laws. Defenderism constituted a response to these arms raids.

Another difference between the Defenders and the Whiteboys was the social profile of the membership. Many of the first Defenders were weavers by trade; significantly, the Peep o' Day Boys destroyed Catholic-owned looms in addition to confiscating firearms. Later on, as the movement spread, the typical Defender was as likely to be a canal worker, blacksmith, or schoolmaster as a tenant farmer, cottier, or landless laborer.

High levels of politicization represent the third major difference between Defenders and Whiteboys. In 1789 the Defender movement had scarcely spread beyond the borders of Armagh, but by 1795 Defender lodges were established across much of Leinster (especially in Meath) and Ulster, in Dublin city, and in Connacht. A faction in a local sectarian feud had been transformed into a mass revolutionary organization. There are three main reasons for this startling development: the radicalizing effect in Ireland of the French Revolution, the steep escalation in agitation surrounding the "Catholic question," and the antimilitia riots. Both reformers (such as the United Irishmen) and the newly militant Catholic Committee had mobilized mass movements behind their campaigns, and the Defenders were politicized along with the rest of a crisis-ridden society. (There is even evidence that the Catholic Committee directly enlisted the covert support of the Defenders.) The sense of alienation from the state and the Protestant Ascendancy generated by the campaign for Catholic relief was intensified by the introduction of a new militia and conscription by ballot in 1793. Widespread rioting spurred recruitment for the Defenders, and Defenders conscripted into militia regiments served as emissaries for the movement in the counties where they were stationed. The organization meanwhile evolved its own "middle-class" Ulster-based central leadership, and it was the alliance, albeit shaky, between this group and the underground United Irishmen in 1795 and 1796 that created one of the most formidable revolutionary movements in Irish history.

SEE ALSO Eighteenth-Century Politics: 1778 to 1795—Parliamentary and Popular Politics; Eighteenth-Century Politics: 1795 to 1800—Repression, Rebellion, and Union; Irish Tithe Act of 1838; Tithe War (1830–1838); Oakboys and Steelboys; Orange Order: Origins, 1784 to 1800; Whiteboys and Whiteboyism

Bibliography

Bartlett, Thomas. "Select Documents 38: Defenders and Defenderism in 1795." *Irish Historical Studies* 24, no. 95 (1985): 373–394.

Cullen, L. M. "The Political Structures of the Defenders." In *Ireland and the French Revolution*, edited by Hugh Gough and David Dickson. 1990.

Miller, David W., ed. *Peep o' Day Boys and Defenders: Selected Documents on the County Armagh Disturbances, 1784–96.* 1990.

James Smyth

Derry, Siege of

King James II, after being forced to flee England in 1688, landed in Kinsale, Co. Cork, and swiftly secured control of all of Ireland except for Enniskillen and Derry, the last walled city to be built in western Europe. Lord Antrim was ordered to replace the largely Protestant garrison in Derry, but when his troops began to cross the River Foyle from the Waterside on 18 December 1688, thirteen apprentice boys seized the keys from the main guard, raised the drawbridge at Ferryquay gate, and closed the gates. Around 30,000 Ulster Protestants loyal to William of Orange sought sanctuary in the city. Lieutenant-Colonel Robert Lundy, the military governor of the city, whose loyalty was in question, was allowed to slip away. Major Henry Baker and the Reverend George Walker were appointed joint governors in his place. The siege intensified when King James joined his army. When he advanced toward the walls and offered terms on 18 April 1689, he was greeted with cries of "No surrender!" At the end of May a train of heavy guns arrived to intensify the bombardment. The rain of shells, bombs, and cannonballs never threatened to breach the walls, but it did exact a heavy death toll on the densely packed defenders. By the beginning of July those inside the walls were starving, and as fever spread, as many as 15,000 may have died. After hesitating for weeks at the mouth of Lough Foyle, a naval relief force commanded by Major-General Percy Kirke made its way upstream on 28 July. The *Mountjoy* smashed through a Jacobite boom made of logs and chains, other vessels followed, and the siege was raised. This epic 105-day defense not only provided William with a vital breathing space in his war with Louis XIV but also gave Ulster Protestants inspiration for more than three centuries to come.

SEE ALSO Eighteenth-Century Politics: 1690 to 1714—Revolution Settlement; Jacobites and the Williamite Wars

Bibliography

Macrory, Patrick. *The Siege of Derry.* 1980.

Jonathan Bardon

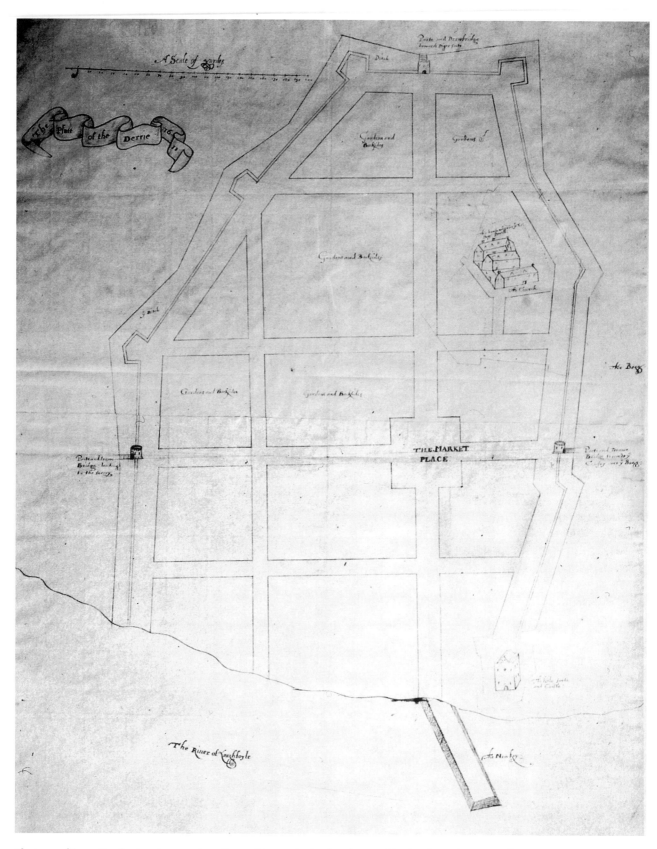

The town of Derry (Londonderry) was perhaps the most impressive landmark created in the Ulster Plantation of the early seventeenth century. As this 1625 sketch by Thomas Raven shows, the site was heavily fortified several decades before the famous siege. THE BOARD OF TRINITY COLLEGE DUBLIN. REPRODUCED BY PERMISSION.

Desmond Rebellions

Of the three great Anglo-Norman earldoms—Kildare, Ormond, and Desmond—the last was the most remote from English authority and administration in the sixteenth century. The earl's territories stretched over much of Munster in southwest Ireland. His palatinate in north Kerry gave him unusual jurisdiction over a large area, though he possessed other, more valuable land in counties Limerick, Cork, and Waterford. In the same region were further members of the numerous FitzGerald family, known collectively throughout Ireland as the Geraldines, holding their land in varying degrees of subordination to the earl. Many of the Geraldines, not least the earl himself, had adopted certain Irish ways and customs. As the Tudor government exerted itself to bring this area of Ireland under control, Desmond's autonomy and way of life was threatened. Some sort of resistance became likely.

Feud with the House of Ormond

Gerald FitzGerald, the fifteenth earl (c. 1538–1583), faced other problems besides advancing English centralization. The Desmonds were traditional enemies of the house of Ormond, whose representative was Black Tom Butler, the tenth earl (1531–1614). Ormond outshone his rival at court and in personal ability. In fact Desmond had little experience of England, having been brought up with a haphazard education in his homeland. In 1565 their private armies had met in open battle, with Desmond being defeated and carried off wounded by his opponents. (Despite his inadequacies, it is said that the earl managed some smart repartee, replying to the taunts of "Where was the great earl of Desmond now?" by retorting "On the backs of the Butlers where he belongs.") The government summoned both nobles to London, decided in favor of Ormond, fined his rival, and detained him in England until 1573.

Taking advantage of the earl's absence, his cousin, James Fitzmaurice FitzGerald, claimed to be his deputy and led much of the province into rebellion from 1569 to 1573. With him joined numerous Geraldines, including the earl's brothers, a few dissident Butlers, and some Irish lords, principally MacCarthy Mór. Their motives were: concern over the destruction of Desmond's traditional military power base; dismay at the attempts by English adventurers, colonizers, and swordsmen to confiscate and occupy lands by claiming that the local inhabitants had insufficient land titles; and, in Fitzmaurice's case particularly, a defense of the Roman Catholic religion—the first overt sign of the Counter-Reformation in Ireland.

The rebellion commenced with small numbers of English settlers being attacked and driven off their lands. Cork and other towns were then threatened; however, the insurrection lost momentum with the return of Ormond and the arrival of Sir Henry Sidney, the lord deputy. Fitzmaurice's supporters soon fell away. Pacification of the province continued under the ruthless policies of Sir Humphrey Gilbert and the first lord president of Munster, Sir John Perrot. In 1573 Fitzmaurice capitulated and soon went abroad to plot his return.

Reinforcements from Abroad

By the late 1570s Ireland was beginning to be drawn into the greater European power play. Now the pope openly (and Spain covertly) was prepared to aid insurrection in Ireland as a means of attacking English Protestantism in general. Gathering together a motley band of papal troops left over from a bizarre expedition against Muslims in Morocco, Fitzmaurice reappeared in Munster in 1579, calling for a political and religious rising against the queen and the new religion. Instantly, this charismatic rebel was joined by many Munster Geraldines, including the earl of Desmond's capable brothers. The second, and last, Desmond rebellion of 1579 to 1583 had been launched.

Desmond Lends Support to Rebellion

The earl himself was not among those first supporters of the rebellion. Despite some restless behavior since his release from sequestration in England, he had cooperated, by and large, with the authorities in Munster, particularly the sympathetic Sir William Dury, lord president of Munster in the late 1570s. It was in Desmond's own interests, moreover, to adopt certain of the new reforms pushed by the administration. Much of his wealth and power came from unwieldy and controversial feudal services merged with Gaelic custom, a prime example being coign of vantage and livery whereby a lord could billet his troops on his tenants. Such a custom was open to abuse and resistance, and from the government's point of view it resulted in large numbers of swordsmen being maintained in quarrelsome idleness. It made sense for both the earl and the government when such services were commuted to an agreed rent in 1578. Less enamored of this development, however, were the MacSheehy gallowglass and other of Desmond's professional soldiers, now threatened by unemployment, and hence willing recruits to Fitzmaurice's call.

Once the rebellion had broken out in 1579, the earl of Desmond was placed in an awkward position. To support the government unambiguously would mean losing control over many of his followers, already seduced by his cousin, who was fast becoming an open rival. Even Fitzmaurice's death in a confused inter-Irish scuffle did not lessen the pressure, for his banner was seized by Desmond's brothers, Sir John and Sir James of Desmond. On the other hand, to challenge the Crown meant the possible loss of lands and life. Such conflicting pressures explain Desmond's equivocal actions and protestations in the first few months after Fitzmaurice's landing. In addition, suspicious English officials, particularly the new lord president of Munster, Sir Nicholas Malby, put the worst possible gloss on the earl's reactions, hoping perhaps to encourage Desmond to take that last, fatal step. After the battle of Monasternenagh in October, when Malby destroyed Sir John of Desmond's army, the victor proceeded to attack the earl's castles and execute his followers. Eventually, the earl of Desmond was proclaimed a traitor in November 1579.

Over the next four years the rebellion waxed and waned. At times Desmond inflicted his will, as in the sacking of Youghal in 1579 and of Cahir in 1582. More often, he was a fugitive, with comparatively few troops, dodging Crown forces as they marched about his territories. His strategy seems to have been to stay in the field until strengthened by foreign aid or further Irish rebellion. But the Baltinglass rebellion in the Pale and the landing of papal reinforcements at Smerwick in 1580 were both dealt with effectively by Lord Deputy Grey. The latter suppression became a cause célèbre, with the entire force of some six-hundred odd men being massacred after their surrender. (It took an hour's concentrated stabbing and thrusting to kill the naked prisoners. One of the two army captains in charge of this operation was Walter Raleigh; another Renaissance luminary, Edmund Spenser, was Grey's secretary and vigorously defended his employer's actions against later criticism.) In 1581 the Jesuit Nicholas Sanders, the intellectual éminence grise behind the rebellion, died; in the next year Desmond's two brothers were killed. These disasters and defeats encouraged many in Munster to swap sides. Many of the Irish lords had not participated in this Geraldine venture in the first place, and soon the rebellion resembled a civil war within Munster. The scorched-earth policy by government troops and retaliatory depredations by the rebels caused unspeakable suffering and plentiful examples of famine throughout the province, especially in Desmond's heartlands. Yet it proved impossible to administer the final blow. It was not until the appointment of the earl of Ormond as overall commander in 1583 that at last the rebellion was extinguished. The queen allowed him to issue pardons indiscriminately, with the result that Desmond soon was left with a bare handful of followers. After stealing some cattle, revenging Moriartys surprised his men in camp and simply cut off the earl's head.

THE MUNSTER PLANTATION

After the rebellion the government recognized that this was a supreme moment to impose a new order on the province. The confiscated lands of Desmond and his associates came to about 300,000 acres, two-thirds of the value belonging to the earl. To grant this massive area to the usual favorites on the Irish establishment would effect no permanent social change. Instead the plantation of entire English families would provide a sheet anchor for security and a powerful impetus toward Anglicization. There had been minor English settlements in the Irish midlands in the middle of the century, but the scale of these Munster confiscations presented the opportunity for much more radical measures.

It was decided largely by Lord Burghley—very much the instigator and planner of the entire venture—that portions of land, ranging up to 12,000 acres, would be granted to suitable individuals in England, who then would undertake to settle or "plant" it with a stipulated number of English families. The resultant Munster plantation gradually got off the ground in the half dozen years after Desmond's death, and by 1598 the English population might have reached four thousand. In that year the plantation was destroyed by the extension of the Nine Years War from the north; however, in the early seventeenth century it was reestablished and thereafter became the nucleus of the substantial English presence in Munster. Various Geraldines survived the plantation, though most were to follow the last earl of Desmond into oblivion, owing to the Cromwellian and Williamite land confiscations of the seventeenth century.

SEE ALSO Colonial Theory from 1500 to 1690; English Political and Religious Policies, Responses to (1534–1690); Land Settlements from 1500 to 1690; Nine Years War; Sidney, Henry; Spenser, Edmund

Bibliography

Berleth, Richard. *The Twilight Lords.* 1978

Canny, Nicolas P. *The Elizabethan Conquest of Ireland.* 1976.

Ellis, Stephen. *Tudor Ireland, 1470–1603.* 1985.

Hayes-McCoy, G. A. "The Completion of the Tudor Conquest and the Advance of the Counter-Reformation, 1571–

Eamon de Valera was the most significant political figure of twentieth-century Ireland. When he died in 1975, thousands of ordinary Irish people queued to attend the lying in state. PHOTOGRAPH COURTESY OF THE IRISH TIMES.

1603." In volume 3 of *A New History of Ireland, 1534–1603*, edited by T. W. Moody, F. X. Martin, and F. J. Byrne. 1976.

MacCarthy-Morrogh, Michael. *The Munster Plantation: English Migration to Southern Ireland, 1583–1641*. 1986.

Michael MacCarthy Morrogh

~

de Valera, Eamon

President of the Executive Council of the Irish Free State, taoiseach (prime minister), and president of the Republic of Ireland, Eamon de Valera (1882–1975) was born on 14 October in New York and raised near Bruree in County Limerick. In 1908 he joined the Gaelic League, where he met his future wife, Sinéad Flanagan. He joined the Irish Volunteers in 1913 and commanded the

Boland's Mills garrison during the 1916 Rising. Although he was sentenced to death, his sentence was commuted, and he was released from prison in June 1917. De Valera was subsequently elected Sinn Féin MP for East Clare and in October, the president of the party and of the Volunteers. Interned in May 1918, de Valera escaped from Lincoln prison. He returned to Dublin briefly and was elected president of the First Dáil, the separatist parliament established by Sinn Féin MPs in January 1919, before beginning a propaganda tour of the United States, which lasted until December 1920.

Following the truce in the Anglo-Irish war in July 1921, de Valera met Lloyd George in London but did not join the Irish delegation to the treaty negotiations of October through December 1921. He subsequently rejected the treaty, leading the opposition in the Dáil debates and trying to gain support for his own scheme of "external association." When the Dáil endorsed the treaty, de Valera resigned his presidency and during the Civil War (June 1922–May 1923) he remained political leader of the antitreaty forces. Unable to wean Sinn Féin away from abstentionism, de Valera founded a new constitutional republican party, Fianna Fáil, in 1926. Fianna Fáil entered the Dáil in 1927 and came to power after the general election of 1932.

Initial fears that the Fianna Fáil commitment to republican principles and social reforms would undermine the democratic nature of the state proved unfounded. De Valera's administration was both constitutional and conservative, and during his period in office he took harsh measures to confront threats from both the right-wing Blueshirt movement and the IRA. Furthermore, although de Valera articulated strong opposition to partition throughout his career, he took few practical steps to end it.

Once in office, de Valera undertook a fundamental revision of the treaty. The office of the governor-general, the king's representative, was undermined; the contentious oath of allegiance to the Crown was abolished; and a series of constitutional changes reduced the scope of Westminster authority. In 1936, following the abdication of King Edward VIII, the remaining references to the Crown were removed from Irish law. By this time the 1922 constitution, based on the treaty settlement, had been dismantled and in 1937 de Valera introduced a new constitution.

De Valera made judicious use of foreign policy as a means of furthering Irish claims to independent nationhood, acting personally as minister for external affairs. He inherited both a temporary seat on the council of the League of Nations and the revolving presidency. His first speech to the League in September 1932, criticizing it for failing to protect weaker nations, attracted world attention and launched de Valera's career as a respected international statesman, and in 1938 he served as president of the Assembly of the League. His adherence to a "small nations" policy served to distance him from the British presence at the League, but it also reflected a sincere belief in the League ideal. This commitment led to criticism at home when he refused to adopt policies consistent with the views of the Catholic Church. He applauded League sanctions against Italy following the invasion of Abyssinia (Ethiopia) in 1935, supported the admission of the USSR to the League in 1934, and adhered to the Nonintervention Agreement during the Spanish Civil War (1936–1939).

Throughout the 1930s de Valera pursued cultural and economic as well as political self-determination. His promotion of Gaelic and Catholic values was more overt, if more pragmatic, than his predecessors' and whereas his social policies were somewhat more liberal, they were countered by the effects of promoting a self-sufficient and labor-intensive economy through the adoption of high tariffs. His policy of withholding annuities payable to the British government under the treaty led to a tariff war that furthered both his economic and political goals. The Anglo-Irish Agreement of 1938, which resolved the "economic war," also transferred control of the naval ports retained by Britain under the treaty to the Dublin government, a development that allowed de Valera to pursue a policy of neutrality during the World War II.

De Valera remained in power until 1948 and was returned to office again between 1951 and 1954 and in 1957. His chief political goals had been achieved by 1945, and future administrations were less vigorous and beset by economic crises. In 1959 he resigned as taoiseach and was elected to the presidency. Despite his age and virtual blindness, de Valera served two terms as president. He retired, in his ninety-first year, in 1973 and died on 29 August 1975.

SEE ALSO Anglo-Irish Treaty of 1921; Civil War; Collins, Michael; Constitution; Declaration of a Republic and the 1949 Ireland Act; Gaelic Catholic State, Making of; Griffith, Arthur; Lemass, Seán; Media since 1960; Neutrality; Newspapers; Political Parties in Independent Ireland; Politics: Independent Ireland since 1922; Presidency; Sinn Féin Movement and Party to 1922; Struggle for Independence from 1916 to 1921; **Primary Documents:** The Anglo-Irish Treaty (6 December 1921); "Time Will Tell" (19 December 1921); Republican Cease-Fire Order (28 April 1923); "Aims of Fianna Fáil in Office" (17 March 1932); "Failure of the League of Nations" (18 June 1936); From the 1937 Constitution; "German Attack on Neutral States" (12 May 1940); "National Thanksgiving" (16 May 1945)

Bibliography

Coogan, Tim Pat. *De Valera: Long Fellow, Long Shadow.* 1993.

Earl of Longford, and Thomas P. O'Neill. *Eamon de Valera.* 1970.

Edwards, Owen Dudley. *Eamon de Valera.* 1987.

Susannah Riordan

Devotional Revolution

In a 1972 article the historian Emmet Larkin argued that in the third quarter of the nineteenth century Irish

Respectably dressed mass attendees at a country chapel, reflecting the rising prosperity and increasingly observant religious practice of those who survived the famine. From Harper's Weekly, *9 July 1870.* COURTESY OF THE WISCONSIN HISTORICAL SOCIETY. REPRODUCED BY PERMISSION.

Catholicism underwent a "devotional revolution" that made "practicing Catholics of the Irish people." Prior to the Great Famine, he maintained, the church lacked the human and material resources to address the spiritual needs of the swollen, nominally Catholic population. Adverse ratios of clergy to laity were complicated by scandalous lapses of clerical discipline in some dioceses, and in many districts there was seriously deficient lay compliance with canonical obligations. Analysis of an 1834 religious census by David Miller corroborates this picture by demonstrating that virtually universal weekly mass attendance, which would be the norm in Ireland in 1972 when Larkin wrote, was largely confined before the famine to the relatively affluent south-eastern countryside and a few towns. Larkin attributed

the reversal of this situation to the determined efforts of Paul Cullen, archbishop of Armagh (1850–1852) and of Dublin (1852–1878); Cullen used his influence in Rome to ensure the appointment of reform-minded bishops, promote parish missions (the Catholic version of what Protestants called "revivals"), and introduce a variety of new devotional practices from the Continent. Those efforts were facilitated by the reduction of population to more manageable levels as a result of the famine, Larkin suggests, and perhaps also by direct psychological effects of the famine and by the key role of Catholicism in the formation of Irish national identity.

Critics of the devotional-revolution thesis have taken issue both with its factual claims (including those made by Miller in his analysis of the 1834 mass-attendance data) and with Larkin's interpretation of those facts. Some of the initial questions about levels of prefamine religious observance reflect simple misunderstandings of quantitative methods. There is now little doubt that prefamine levels of religious practice were remarkably low by mid-twentieth-century standards, especially in the north and west; in some areas as few as 20 percent of Catholics attended mass on a typical Sunday. Whether this situation dated to the remote past or was specifically an artifact of the population explosion that began in the late eighteenth century is unresolved.

Critics have also suggested that devotional changes may have begun earlier than 1850. Some scholars have identified prefamine devotional innovations in towns and in the relatively affluent southeastern agricultural districts. It was during the archepiscopate of Cullen, however, that such changes had their initial impact on most Irish Catholics. The changes included more frequent confessions and communions than canonically required, as well as special rites such as the forty-hours devotion and the "perpetual adoration" and benediction of the Blessed Sacrament. Devotion to the Sacred Heart became much more widespread, and Marian exercises (above all, the praying of the rosary) flourished, increasingly taking on forms that originated in continental Catholicism, such as devotion to the Immaculate Conception and to Our Lady of Lourdes. The spread of various lay confraternities introduced many Catholics to more earnest and purposeful practice of their faith.

Criticisms of Larkin's interpretation of the facts are also interesting. Sociologist Eugene Hynes (1978) offered the intriguing hypothesis that canonical religious practice was a class-specific behavior, and that the famine eliminated much of the nonpracticing underclass while leaving largely unscathed an already observant class of better-off farmers. Hynes's explanation has been taken up by another sociologist, Michael Carroll, who sees the devotional revolution as a late-eighteenth-century initiative by wealthy Catholics whose effects were obscured by the presence of the huge underclass until after the famine. Carroll calls this initiative the "second" devotional revolution and theorizes that there was an earlier "devotional revolution" in the seventeenth century. In this "first" devotional revolution, he argues, the lay elite of seventeenth-century Irish Catholicism resisted clerical efforts to implement the decrees of the Council of Trent and instead promoted folk religious practices, such as patterns (festive outdoor observances of patron saints' days) and pilgrimages to holy wells, which would later be misunderstood as survivals of pagan Celtic religion. This initiative ensured that antagonistic kin groups would not have to interrupt their feuds in order to gather peaceably together

for mass every Sunday. Both Hynes and Carroll offer important insights into devotional change in the nineteenth century, but on the issue of Carroll's thesis of a "first" devotional revolution, the jury of early modern Irish historians is still out.

The most sweeping critique of Larkin's interpretation has been offered by Thomas McGrath (1990), who argues that what Larkin calls a "devotional revolution" was actually the final stage of a "tridentine evolution." The fact that for about a century after 1875 Irish Catholics almost universally complied with canonical norms is attributed to the decision of the Council of Trent in 1563 that it should be so. Lack of compliance during much of the seventeenth and eighteenth centuries is blamed on the restrictions placed upon Catholic clergy, who longed to implement the tridentine standards but were only able to do so effectively as the penal laws were gradually relaxed. Though McGrath is right to criticize proponents of the devotional-revolution hypothesis for failing to situate the religious changes of the nineteenth century in a longer temporal perspective, his placement of the cause as far back as 300 years before the effect has found little support.

Some of the initial negative reaction to Larkin's argument was probably due to his provocative—and ahistorical—suggestion that "the Irish people" were not "practicing Catholics" before the famine. It is sometimes suggested—equally ahistorically—that at the end of the twentieth century Ireland has become a "post-Catholic society." It *is* historically accurate to say that the nearly universal religious observance whose erosion prompts the latter claim is no older than a century and a half.

SEE ALSO Marianism; Religion: Traditional Popular Religion; Religious Orders: Men; Religious Orders: Women; Roman Catholic Church: 1829 to 1891; Sodalities and Confraternities

Bibliography

Carroll, Michael P. *Irish Pilgrimage: Holy Wells and Popular Catholic Devotion*. 1999.

Corish, Patrick. *The Irish Catholic Experience: A Historical Survey*. 1985

Donnelly, James S., Jr. "The Peak of Marianism in Ireland, 1930–60." In *Piety and Power in Ireland, 1760–1960*, edited by S. J. Brown and D. W. Miller. 2000.

Hynes, Eugene. "The Great Hunger and Irish Catholicism." *Societas* 8 (spring 1978): 137–156.

Larkin, Emmet. "The Devotional Revolution in Ireland, 1850–75." *The American Historical Review* 77 (June 1972): 625–652.

McGrath, Thomas G. "The Tridentine Evolution of Modern Irish Catholicism, 1563–1962: A Re-Examination of the

'Devotional Revolution' Thesis." *Irish Church History Today: Cumann Seanchais Ard Mhacha Seminar 10 March 1990*, edited by Réamonn Ó Muirí. 1990.

Miller, David W. "Irish Catholicism and the Great Famine." *Journal of Social History* 9 (fall 1975): 81–98.

Miller, David W. "Mass Attendance in Ireland in 1834." In *Piety and Power in Ireland, 1760–1960*, edited by S. J. Brown and D. W. Miller. 2000.

Taylor, Lawrence J. *Occasions of Faith: An Anthropology of Irish Catholics.* 1995.

David W. Miller

≈

Diaspora

THE IRISH IN AUSTRALIA	DAVID FITZPATRICK
THE IRISH IN BRITAIN	ENDA DELANEY
THE IRISH IN NORTH AMERICA	TIMOTHY J. MEAGHER

THE IRISH IN AUSTRALIA

The first half-century of white settlement in Australia, beginning with the "First Fleet" of 1788, was dominated by convicts from Britain and Ireland. About 36,000 of Australia's 163,000 convict settlers were from Ireland, most of them of "peasant" background in contrast to the mainly urban laborers and artisans from Britain. Colonial indignation prevented further transportation to New South Wales and Van Diemen's Land (Tasmania) after the 1840s, and the last shipload of convicts, containing sixty-three Fenian rebels, reached Western Australia in 1868. Irishmen were also prominent among those supervising the convicts, ranging from common soldiers to officials such as Sir Richard Bourke from Thornfield, Co. Limerick, who initiated assisted immigration while governor of New South Wales from 1831 to 1837.

Between 1840 and 1914 about a third of a million Irish people emigrated to the Australian colonies. Until after the World War I the Irish were second only to the English as a component of Australia's immigrant population. In 1891, when the number of Irish immigrants peaked at almost 230,000, they accounted for nearly a quarter of foreign-born Australians, with little variation between the eastern states. No other regions of settlement apart from some of Canada's eastern provinces drew so heavily upon Irish settlers. If Australia was a minor destination for the Irish, Ireland was a major source for the Australians.

The flow from Ireland to Australia was sometimes a trickle, sometimes a minor flood. By comparison with the immense emigration elsewhere during the years of the Great Famine, there was rather little movement to Australia, where demand for immigrant labor was sluggish until the discovery of gold in 1851. The effect of economic fluctuations was blurred and indirect. Few Irish immigrants could afford the full fare of about 17 pounds at the best of times, being reliant upon assistance from governments whose readiness to invest in emigration was affected by political as well as economic calculation. More than any other stream of Irish settlers, those choosing Australia were subject to state management.

Every Australian colony offered financial encouragement for emigration, under schemes that were often cumbersome, restrictive, and liable to sudden amendment or termination. Inducements ranged from land guarantees to free passages, with many intermediate varieties of partial funding from the state, typically supplemented by contributions from those already in the colonies. A combination of British recalcitrance, Irish eagerness, and colonial demand for unskilled labor ensured that the Irish were consistently overrepresented among assisted immigrants, especially in New South Wales and Victoria. Over the entire period 1836 to 1919, subventions were provided for nearly a quarter of a million Irish immigrants, about half the number from Britain. Ireland's persistent poverty ensured that the Irish were underrepresented among those wealthy enough to pay their own way. The withdrawal of assistance was therefore a major factor in reducing the ratio of Irish to British immigrants as well as in increasing the proportion from Ulster.

State funding was supplemented by private benefactors such as landlords and colonial philanthropists. But the main sources of private funding were those already in the colonies who contributed toward further immigration under the various nomination and remittance schemes. Irish settlers, everywhere adept at forging chains of migration from their localities of origin, made far more intensive use of these facilities than did British settlers. The increasing preference of colonial governments for nomination schemes devolved most of the selection process to previous immigrants, encouraging self-replication in terms of background.

Political concern about the quality of assisted immigrants ensured that remarkably detailed statistics were compiled. Over two-thirds of Irish assisted immigrants arriving in New South Wales between 1848 and

1870 were aged between fifteen and twenty-nine years. About two-fifths traveled in family groups. In a country chronically starved of women, the Irish were unique in their response to the inducements for female immigration. The most spectacular importation of Irish girls as servants and potential wives occurred during the Great Famine, with the removal of over 4,000 female orphans from Irish workhouses. Women greatly outnumbered men among Irish assisted immigrants. With men predominating among unassisted immigrants, Irishmen and Irishwomen settled in Australia in virtually equal numbers. Every other immigrant stream was dominated by men.

The typical Irish assisted immigrant embodied "human capital" in the form of vigor rather than skill. The vast majority of men described themselves as plain laborers or agricultural laborers, and the women as domestic servants. That many Irish immigrants had worked only within the family unit did not detract from their capital value, in a primitive economy with insatiable demand for unskilled manual labor. A more serious impediment to success in Australia was illiteracy. Until the 1860s, only a minority of Irish immigrants were reportedly able to read and write. Subsequently there was a rapid improvement in basic literacy, among both immigrants and the population of origin.

The most controversial attribute of Irish immigration was the predominance of Catholics, who usually accounted for about four-fifths of the total. This slightly exceeded the Catholic component in the regions of Ireland most inclined to provide Irish Australians. The predominance of Protestants among unassisted immigrants probably explains the surprisingly large non-Catholic component (29%) of Australia's Irish-born population in 1911. The Protestant element in Australia's Irish population was less important than in New Zealand or Canada, but presumably greater than in Britain or the United States.

The prevalence of chain migration ensured that the distribution of county origins changed remarkably little between the later 1840s and the end of the century. Two regions were particularly inclined to send settlers to Australia, neither being particularly poor but both being overwhelmingly rural. Clare and Tipperary were almost invariably the two counties sending most assisted immigrants to Australia, with a secondary cluster in south Ulster. Once in Australia, the Irish dispersed throughout the settled districts with striking uniformity. In contrast to their compatriots in the United States, they were no more inclined to cluster together than were other immigrant groups. The Irish showed no ten-dency to avoid agricultural districts, and English settlers were usually more urbanized than the Irish.

While Irish immigrants penetrated every trade and profession, their aggregate occupational status remained low throughout the nineteenth century. The first comprehensive occupational census for different religious groups was conducted in New South Wales in 1901. The male occupations most heavily colonized by Irish immigrants were (in descending order) religion, "independent means" (having private sources of income), refuse disposal, and road construction. Building construction, a trade often regarded as being quintessentially Irish, attracted few Irish workers in New South Wales. By 1901, the admittedly aging population of Irish-born women was no longer overrepresented in domestic service. For most women, however, paid employment was only a secondary indicator of status, since the majority entered the workforce only as a prelude or sequel to housewifery. Marriage probably offered better chances of upward mobility than employment. By 1911 the majority of both Irish husbands and Irish wives were married to persons born outside Ireland. Even so, ethnic and especially religious networks continued to affect Irish marriage choices. The statistics indicate a marriage market that was neither fully open nor firmly closed, so permitting alternative strategies for social mobility through marriage. Such findings suggest that most Irish men and women made fairly effective use of their opportunities in Australia before World War I.

After federation in 1901 Irish immigration slowed to a trickle, causing the Irish-born population to decline from 186,000 in 1901 to 106,000 in 1921, and to its nadir of 45,000 in 1947. Though a few former servicemen and others from Northern Ireland received assistance from empire-settlement schemes, citizens of the Irish Free State were ineligible for assistance. The postwar resumption of assisted immigration caused a recovery to 70,000 by 1981, representing 0.5 percent of the population and only 2.3 percent of those born outside Australia. The Irish presence in twentieth-century Australia was dominated by those, often of mixed descent, who considered themselves Irish, an identity fostered energetically by the Catholic Church through its network of schools and social clubs. As the Catholic community was transformed by the influx from continental Europe, Irishness became increasingly a sentimental affiliation or a flag of convenience in the stormy waters of multicultural Australia.

SEE ALSO Diaspora: The Irish in Britain; Diaspora: The Irish in North America; Migration: Emigration from the Seventeenth Century to 1845; Migration: Emigration from 1850 to 1960; Migration: Emigration and Immigration since 1950

Bibliography

Fitzpatrick, David. *Oceans of Consolation: Personal Accounts of Irish Migration to Australia.* 1995.

O'Farrell, Patrick. *Letters from Irish Australia, 1825–1929.* 1984.

O'Farrell, Patrick. *The Irish in Australia.* 1986.

David Fitzpatrick

THE IRISH IN BRITAIN

Until the 1970s the Irish-born population was the largest immigrant group in British society. Historically, Ireland's nearest neighbor had been one of the most significant destinations for emigrants since medieval times. Surviving records indicate that even in the fifteenth and sixteenth centuries, poor Irish immigrants were the cause of concern on the part of municipal authorities in the growing towns and cities of Tudor England. Yet the greatest influx of Irish migrants occurred in the nineteenth and twentieth centuries. Second only to the United States, Britain was a central destination of the Irish diaspora from the early nineteenth century.

One of the consequences of the end of the Napoleonic wars in 1815 was the emergence of mass migration, as agricultural depression resulted in declining Irish standards of living, thereby strengthening the imperative for people to leave for North America and Britain. In the period before the Great Famine of the late 1840s, substantial numbers of men and women left Ireland in search of work in the expanding British industrial economy. In the 1830s and early 1840s the large numbers of Irish migrants settling in Britain were perceived as a problem because so many of them were poor, and it was assumed that they would make little positive contribution to the evolving industrial society. Social commentators such as J. P. Kay in his well-known essay on the Irish in Manchester in 1832 underlined the negative effects of large-scale Irish immigration on the living conditions of the poor in that city, especially in the infamous "Little Ireland" district. Sometime later, Friedrich Engels in 1844 described the poverty and squalor of the Irish in Manchester. Social theorists lamented that the abysmal conditions in which the Irish lived would in time lower the living standards of the British working classes. To a large extent this hostility toward the Irish in Britain was a clash of values because Irish customs,

Irish-born population of Britain, 1841–1991	
Year	Population
1841	415,725
1851	727,326
1861	805,717
1871	774,310
1881	781,119
1891	653,122
1901	631,629
1911	555,040
1921	523,767
1931	505,385
1951	716,028
1961	950,978
1971	952,760
1981	850,387
1991	836,934

SOURCE: Extracted from U.K. census, 1841–1991.

ways of living, and cultural practices were often considered alien. The stark poverty of many Irish migrants meant that they were a highly visible presence in the poorer slum districts of large British cities. Geographical proximity and the ability of the Irish labor to move freely between the two islands ensured that, notwithstanding deeply engrained anti-Irish prejudice, Britain continued to be a popular destination for Irish migrants throughout the nineteenth and early twentieth centuries.

Two distinct waves of Irish emigration to Britain can be noted, the first lasting from the 1840s until the 1860s, and the second from the 1930s until the 1960s. In the nineteenth century the most sustained inflow of Irish men and women was directly related to the famine crisis of the late 1840s. The Irish-born population in England and Wales nearly doubled between 1841 and 1861. Famine refugees arrived in huge numbers in Liverpool, Glasgow, and in other smaller ports such as Newport in South Wales, prompting a strong sense of panic about the influx of diseased and poverty-stricken migrants from Ireland. This alarm was compounded by the fact that the Irish migrant's arrival coincided with an economic recession in Britain in 1847 to 1848. Throughout the second half of the nineteenth century Britain retained its importance as a center of Irish settlement. Estimates suggest that from 1852 until the outbreak of World War I in 1914 between one-fifth and one-quarter of all emigrants from Ireland traveled to Britain. This resulted in the Irish-born population of Britain remaining relatively stable during the second half of the nineteenth century, though it declined in numbers in the early decades of the twentieth century (see table). In the mid-1930s, as a result of restrictions imposed on American immigration in the 1920s and its swift economic recovery from the Great Depression in the early 1930s, Britain became the principal destination for the hundreds of thousands of Irish who sought new lives abroad. Approximately four out of every five migrants who left independent Ireland after 1921 traveled to Britain. The 1950s saw the peak in Irish emigration, and by 1971 the Irish-born population of Britain numbered nearly one million people.

The Irish settled where employment was available. In the nineteenth century Lancashire, the west of Scotland, and London were the major regions of Irish settlement, though many Irish migrants were also found outside the large conurbations of Liverpool, Glasgow, and Manchester. From the mid-1930s on, the migrant flow was directed toward the midlands and southeastern England, principally London, reflecting the changes in employment location in twentieth-century Britain. The other obvious trend was the decline in the Irish population of Scotland. In 1841 nearly one-third of the Irish-born population in Britain lived in Scotland, but by 1991 the figure had declined to just 6 percent.

In contrast with most other migrations, men and women left nineteenth- and twentieth-century Ireland in roughly equal proportions. Until the 1860s more Irish women than men settled in Britain, but thereafter (until 1921) the position was reversed, though the overall differences were slight. From the 1920s to the early twenty-first century, Irish women have outnumbered Irish men in Britain. This is a reflection of the wide range of employment available for female migrants and the obvious shortage of similar jobs for women in Ireland.

Until 1921 Irish migrants could enter Britain without any hindrance, and visas or employment permits were not required. This remained the situation even after the end of the legislative union in 1921 and the foundation of the independent Irish state. Irish citizens, however, were required to have a visa during World War II and for a short period after the end of the war in 1945. In the context of restrictions on the entry of citizens from the "New" Commonwealth in the 1960s, that the Irish were excluded from legislation to control immigration is striking. Irish migrants could enter Britain as often as they wished and take up any form of employment. This special status was justified on the grounds of the long and close historical relationship between the two countries, though it was also perceived that because Irish migrants were white, they were unlikely to provoke racial tension.

The absence of expressions of a hyphenated identity by Irish migrants living in Britain, such as "Irish British" is in sharp contrast to the experience of Irish Americans in the United States. There is no obvious explanation for this, but the tangled and sometimes fraught political relationship between the two countries is one reason. Irish identity in Britain, however, was not monolithic, and it was shaped by religion, class, and the wider social environment. What marked Irish migrants as different from the British population, apart from their accents, cultural practices, and perhaps forms of dress, was adherence of the majority to Catholicism. The degree of attachment to some form of Irish identity varied among individual migrants. The Irish in Britain were mobilized in support of campaigns for Home Rule in the 1870s and 1880s, but they lacked the political focus that existed for Irish Americans in the late nineteenth and early twentieth centuries.

SEE ALSO Diaspora: The Irish in Australia; Diaspora: The Irish in North America; Migration: Emigration from the Seventeenth Century to 1845; Migration: Emigration from 1850 to 1960; Migration: Emigration and Immigration since 1950; **Primary Documents:** From *Narrative of a Recent Journey* (1847); "An Irishman in Coventry" (1960)

Bibliography

Delaney, Enda. *Demography, State, and Society: Irish Migration to Britain, 1921–1971.* 2000.

Devine, T. M., ed. *Irish Immigrants and Scottish Society in the Nineteenth and Twentieth Centuries.* 1991.

Fitzpatrick, David. "'A Peculiar Tramping People': The Irish in Britain, 1801–70." In *A New History of Ireland*, vol. 5, *Ireland under the Union (1801–1871)*, edited by W. E. Vaughan. 1989.

MacRaild, Donald M. *Irish Migrants in Modern Britain, 1750–1922.* 1999.

Enda Delaney

THE IRISH IN NORTH AMERICA

In 1980 over 40 million people in the United States and millions more in Canada claimed Irish ancestry. The Irish diaspora in North America was ten or more times as large as the population of Ireland itself and several times larger than the Irish diasporas in Europe, Africa, Australia, or any other continent.

EIGHTEENTH CENTURY

The huge Irish presence in North America began with only a small trickle of largely anonymous immigrants—perhaps no more than 5,000 in the seventeenth century (Fogelman 1998)—but the numbers increased considerably in the eighteenth century. Curiously, the people leaving did not come from among impoverished Irish Catholics but from the Presbyterian descendants of Scottish migrants who had settled in Ulster from the early seventeenth century. The first large group of Ulster Presbyterians left Ireland for North America in 1717 and 1718. Thereafter the emigrant tide ebbed and flowed, picking up momentum in the late 1720s and again in the 1740s and reaching a climax in the years before the American Revolution.

Historians agree more or less on the periodization of eighteenth-century Irish migration, but because of incomplete documentation, numerical estimates vary from about 100,000 (Dickson 1966, Fogelman 1998, Griffin 2001) to more than 200,000 (Miller 1985, Doyle 1989). Estimates of the proportion of Irish immigrants and their descendants in the American population by the end of the colonial era vary from about 9.5 percent to 14 percent or even more.

Why did so many people leave Ireland, or more specifically Northern Ireland, for America in the eighteenth century? Because most of these emigrants (though by no means all) were Presbyterians, older histories often stressed the religious and political discrimination that these men and women faced because they were not members of the established Church of Ireland. Although such discrimination rankled with Ulster's Presbyterians and probably loosened their commitment to Ireland, a bundle of related economic changes had a more powerful effect in pushing the migrants out of Ulster and making North America an attractive alternative. The dramatic rise in rents in Ulster over the course of the eighteenth century and severe depressions in the linen industry, especially in the 1760s and early 1770s, contributed to emigration. The linen trade had cultural and psychological as well as economic effects. It encouraged Ulster Presbyterians to break out of a traditional peasant agriculture, and because much of the linen trade was with North America, it made them aware of possibilities in the new colonies. Regular trading links between the colonies and Northern Ireland also provided the ships that were the means of escape to the New World. For these reasons and many more specific ones, such as occasional droughts or excessive cold, Ulster emptied out periodically through the eighteenth century. There was some migration from the other provinces of Ireland to North America; for example, from the Waterford area to Newfoundland. The great mass of impoverished Catholics in the South of Ireland, however, did not stir in the eighteenth century.

The first Irish migrants had gone to Boston expecting to be welcomed by their fellow Dissenters there, the descendants of the Puritans. Instead the New England Yankees spurned them, and throughout the rest of the eighteenth century most Irish immigrants entered the United States through Philadelphia and New Castle, Delaware. The reason was not simply Pennsylvania's famed tolerance but also the more practical reason that Pennsylvania was a critical source of flax for linen manufacture. Most Irish immigrants did not tarry long in their ports of entry. About 36 percent in the eighteenth century came as indentured servants, committing themselves to a contract of a few years of labor for the cost of their passage to America. Although urban artisans and shopkeepers picked up the contracts of some of these, more were sold for plantation or farm labor. Free Irish immigrants usually headed to the frontier, having been nudged or lured there by large landowners with vacant lands or by colonial officials eager to use the new immigrants as buffers between Native Americans and colonial settlements. Irish immigrants moved farther and farther west and north in Pennsylvania, then south along the Great Wagon Road through western Maryland and Virginia's Shenandoah Valley into the Carolina backcountry. Western Pennsylvania and the western Carolinas became the Ulster Irish heartland. As much as 17 percent of North Carolina's population, 25 percent of South Carolina's, and 23 percent of Pennsylvania's consisted of Irish or Scotch Irish by 1790 (Doyle 1981).

REVOLUTIONARY PERIOD AND EARLY NINETEENTH CENTURY

Irish immigrants gained a reputation for violence and hard drinking that made them quite visible and notorious to colonial officials, but they seemed to vanish into an undifferentiated American frontier mainstream within a generation. They played critical roles in the American Revolution, though these roles varied according to local political configurations. The Scotch-Irish in Pennsylvania and New Jersey were patriot zealots, but in the Carolinas they were more ambivalent about the conflict. The Revolution, however, broke down whatever barriers to success Irish Presbyterians had known before 1776 and eased their absorption into American society. The religious hothouse of eighteenth- and nineteenth-century America, with its many competing evangelical sects, also sapped the strength of Presbyterianism, the chief marker of Ulster Scots' sense of difference in the New World.

Irish immigration to America was interrupted by the Revolution but resumed in huge numbers almost immediately after: an estimated 5,000 emigrants left Ireland for America in 1783. The river of immigrants continued to run strong through the 1790s but ebbed in the early nineteenth century. After peace returned to

Europe and America in 1815, Irish migration picked up again, steadily building to 50,000 or more migrants by the late 1830s.

Between the Revolution and the Great Famine there was a change in the destination of the immigrants. By the early nineteenth century Irish migrants to the United States were choosing New York City, not Philadelphia, as their principal port of entry and settling in northern cities, not the southern countryside. A substantial number began to go to British North America (Canada), encouraged by British regulations that made trips to American ports more expensive and by grants of cheap land in Canada. This migration to Canada peaked in the 1830s but remained strong through 1847. In all, more than 450,000 Irish entered North America through Canadian ports between 1825 and 1845—50,000 more than came in through U.S. ports. Perhaps as many as two-thirds of Irish emigrants to Canada quickly re-emigrated to the United States, but the population of Canada was substantially remade by Irish migration. Already by 1841 Canada counted 122,000 Irish-born among its people.

There were changes too in the immigrants' geographic and class origins and religious backgrounds. Gradually the main sources of immigration shifted south and west into south Ulster and northern Connacht and then to the southern province of Munster. As migration drew increasingly from these largely Catholic-dominated areas, Catholics became a majority of Irish immigrants, probably surpassing Protestants by the early 1830s. Immigrants were perhaps also coming from poorer strata in the population than before, though they were probably still wealthier and better educated than the mass of the Irish at home.

All of these changes reflected new conditions in Ireland. The end of the Napoleonic wars in 1815 severely cut the demand for Irish grain and sent Ireland's economy into decline, while slowing but not halting the rise in population. Competition for land and the contraction of cottage industry undermined peasant household economies. At the same time, integration of ever-expanding areas of Ireland into the British and even international economy forced more and more Catholics in the southern provinces to learn English, the language of the market, but also made them vulnerable to the market's booms and busts.

By the 1820s and 1830s many Irishmen in America were navvies, construction workers on projects like the Erie, Chesapeake and Ohio, and Blackstone canals. For many of these men life was brutal, harsh, and insecure in the work camps, but studies of the Irish in Worcester and Lowell, Massachusetts, suggest that some settled into relative prosperity after their canal-building days.

Most urban Irish immigrants were blue-collar workers, and those outside the cities were mainly small farmers. Although not rich, they did not seem to suffer the dire poverty that would afflict masses of famine-era immigrants. In the lands of Ontario opened to settlement in the 1830s, for example, both Catholic and Protestant Irish seem to have found opportunities to build farms and carve out decent lives for themselves.

One group of Irish emigrants—refugees of the 1798 United Irish Rebellion—was small in number but had a powerful impact on the new nation. They quickly became leaders of the Jeffersonian Democratic-Republicans, editing newspapers, writing books and pamphlets, and organizing political clubs and campaigns that helped secure their political party's triumph over the Federalists. They also defined an identity that was stoutly Irish or Irish-American but republican in ideology and insistent in its nonsectarianism. In the early nineteenth century optimistic revolutionary republican ideals were still powerful, and because Irish Catholics and Protestants were both strong supporters of the Democratic-Republican Party, they shared common political interests. Such alliances between "orange" and "green" were struck in Canada in this era as well, however, even without the nourishment of republican influences.

Nevertheless, as Irish immigrant numbers and the proportion of Catholics among them increased, American Protestant suspicions rose. Nativist anti-immigrant and anti-Catholic movements fed off of the Protestant religious revival called the Second Great Awakening. The party system that pitted Democratic-Republicans against Federalists was supplanted by a new pairing of Democrats and Whigs, polarized in many places along religious lines. The possibility of a nonsectarian Irish-American community was passing; its death knell perhaps sounded in 1844 when Irish Protestant and Catholic workers clashed in deadly riots on the streets of Philadelphia.

THE GREAT FAMINE AND ITS AFTERMATH

It would be difficult to overestimate the impact of the Great Famine of the late 1840s on Irish America. About 1.5 million people left for the United States between 1845 and 1855; 340,000 traveled to Canada and about 200,000 to 300,000 settled in Britain. More people left Ireland in just eleven years than during the previous two and half centuries (Miller 1985). Trends and patterns that had emerged before the Great Famine now hardened with the flood of migrants who had left to escape catastrophe.

Ever since Archbishop John Hughes called the famine Irish immigrants "the debris of the Irish nation," the dominant assessment of their experience has been that it was a tragedy—for many immigrants a horror that seemed little more than an extension of the horrors of the famine in Ireland itself. Several historians have found that depiction too gloomy and generalized, noting significant variation in Irish experience among the regions of the United States. The Irish in Philadelphia were not nearly as forlorn as those in Boston, for example; fewer were laborers or residents of squalid, disease-ridden tenements. Substantial numbers of the Irish who settled in Detroit or San Francisco even became prosperous, and in San Francisco some moved quickly into the political or economic elite.

Nevertheless most famine Irish immigrants experienced difficult, often brutally hard conditions that improved only marginally over time. One study found that Irish famine immigrants fared much worse in the American economy than German or British immigrants, even when class was held constant. The Irish who landed in New York between 1840 and 1850 were much less likely than German immigrants to move inland to presumably richer opportunities in the Midwest. In most big cities the Irish quickly became the majority of inmates in prisons, hospitals, lunatic asylums, and poorhouses. Today's Irish Americans have focused on the deaths of immigrants' on the so-called coffin ships to America, but many more, hundreds of thousands more, enfeebled by famine, bewildered by uprooting and transit across the Atlantic, died within three or four years of their arrival in America. Irish death rates in Boston and New York were particularly catastrophic. Conditions may have been better farther west, but most Irish did not live in the West (Ferrie 1999).

Historians disagree as to whether Irish culture, or more specifically Irish Catholic culture, hindered Irish immigrant adaptation to America. Kerby Miller has argued that Irish Catholic immigrants were burdened by a culture rooted in an ancient Celtic world that privileged communalism over individualism and tradition over innovation. The most strongly essentialist notions in Miller's argument—that ancient Gaelic roots were more important than years of oppression or a stunted economy in shaping the culture that hindered Irish mobility in America—are open to question, but clearly life in rural Ireland had not prepared the vast majority of Irish newcomers for the rapidly industrializing and urbanizing United States. A further threat to Irish immigrants came from nativism, which peaked in 1854 with victories by the anti-Catholic Know-Nothing Party in city, town, and state elections across the United States.

Popular interpretations of Irish-American history often dwell on the patriotism of Irish Americans during the Civil War, as exemplified in their heroic sacrifices in such bloody battles as Antietam and Gettysburg. Sacrifices there were, but the battle casualties that seemed so glorious to later generations of Irish Americans did not seem so much heroic as horrific to Irish immigrants themselves at the time. They were also dismayed by what they perceived as a shift in the war's purpose from preserving the union to the destruction of slavery in the Emancipation Proclamation. In July 1863 Irish immigrant discontent erupted in protests against military conscription. Draft riots broke out in Boston, the Pennsylvania coal fields, and most notably in New York City, where at least 119 people died and whole sections of the city were taken over by rioters.

Communal and familial values that may have inhibited upward mobility nonetheless nurtured and protected famine-era immigrants caught in the harsh realities of poverty and squalor. Neighborhoods were often laced with ties of friendship, reinforced by gatherings at saloons or by credit received at local groceries and reflected in the clustering of people who hailed from the same counties or even the same estates in Ireland on specific blocks or streets in American cities.

Parish churches emerged as the centers of such neighborhoods, but Irish Catholic immigrants' commitment to the norms and requirements of an institutional Catholicism was not a given. In Ireland the church limped out of the penal era with a shortage of chapels, schools, and priests, and America too suffered from such shortages. Jay Dolan estimates that only about 40 percent of Irish Catholic immigrants attended mass regularly in New York City at mid-century. Yet over time the church became central to Irish-American identity. A devotional revolution much like the one that was sweeping Ireland was transforming Irish America.

Nationalism also helped to define Irish-American life in the famine era. Irish-American support for Ireland's freedom had begun with the United Irish exiles. Through the early and mid-1840s a mass base began to develop as clubs sprang up all across the country backing Daniel O'Connell's campaign to repeal the Act of Union. Yet it was the Fenians, founded in 1858 in New York and Dublin and rising to prominence just after the American Civil War, who established nationalism firmly as a central organizational nexus in the Irish-American community. The Fenians would claim up to 50,000 members in the United States, but it seems clear that their sympathizers far exceeded that number.

LATE NINETEENTH AND EARLY TWENTIETH CENTURIES

Trends that had been occurring in eastern Ireland before the famine spread across the island after it—conversion from tillage to pasturage and impartible inheritance being the most important. These changes meant that all children but male heirs and daughters with dowries confronted bleak futures in Ireland. Many left the country, contributing in turn to those who would come after or sending remittances to help sustain parents at home. Migration thus flowed more or less steadily from Ireland to North America—especially to the United States—in the late nineteenth and early twentieth centuries. Emigration fell with the hard times in America during the 1870s but rose again during Ireland's agricultural crisis later in that decade. After the 1880s it very slowly diminished, but it did not stop until the late 1920s, when increased American regulation of immigration and the onset of the Great Depression in the United States helped to reorient the flow of Irish migration to nearby Britain. An increasing proportion of postfamine migrants came from western Ireland, the province of Connacht and western parts of Munster. Rocked by disastrous harvests in the late 1870s, these areas had become increasingly vulnerable to economic and cultural change thereafter. (The much smaller migration to Canada in this era drew largely from Ulster.) More and more of the migrants were single women as it became clear that their opportunities for economic advancement or marriage were shrinking in Ireland in the late nineteenth century.

If there were changes in the character of Irish immigration, there was a disappointing consistency in the economic performance of these immigrants in America. In 1900 over half of Irish immigrant women worked as domestic servants, and about one-quarter of Irish-born men were unskilled workers, mostly day laborers. The proportion of immigrants who broke into white-collar work remained small; as before, however, the percentages varied significantly from city to city. It appeared that there were fewer Irish slums than at mid-century, but death rates among the Irish-born remained exceptionally high into early twentieth century. As late as 1915 the death rate among the Irish-born in New York was among the highest of any group in the city.

In the late nineteenth century children of the Catholic famine migrants began to find their place in American life. These second-generation Irish were very different from their Irish-born parents. They were far more likely to be white-collar or skilled blue-collar workers. They were also less likely to live in inner-city slums or neighborhoods that were exclusively Irish. Intermarriage rates among the second-generation Irish varied: one-quarter in Worcester, Massachusetts, in 1900; about one-third in New York City in the 1910s; and half or more farther west in the 1910s. Yet everywhere in the nation the second-generation Irish rates of inter-

marriage were greater than the rates among Irish immigrants. The new generation also avidly embraced the new urban American popular culture emerging at this time. Many stars of the era, including baseball players "King" Kelly, John McGraw, and Connie Mack, boxing champions John L. Sullivan and Jim Corbett, and vaudeville or theater performers Ned Harrigan, Tony Hart, Maggie Cline, and George M. Cohan, were second-generation Irish.

Yet all this did not mean the easy assimilation of Irish Americans into the mainstream, for American culture, society, and politics were still rigidly divided along religious lines. In the 1880s Catholic liberals, led by the Irish-born archbishop John Ireland and the second-generation Irish cardinal James Gibbons, sought to work out an accommodation with Protestant culture and society that might soften religious tensions and earn American Catholics some acceptance. In the same decade, Irish-American labor leaders like the second-generation Terence Powderly took another tack, trying to unite workers and their sympathizers of all ethnic backgrounds in defense of old republican ideals and workers' rights in the face of industrial change. Neither of these efforts endured. In the 1890s and 1900s Irish-American labor recoiled from the nascent radical potential of the Knights of Labor in order to embrace the antiradical business unionism of the American Federation of Labor. Catholic liberalism collapsed at the same time, caught between revivals of both American nativism and Vatican orthodoxy.

By the 1910s and 1920s the possibilities of Irish-American identity had narrowed considerably, and that definition hardened into a form that would last more or less until the 1950s. Irish-American Catholics were militant Catholics, suspicious of and hostile to the dominant Protestant and secular mainstream, but they were also fervently patriotic Americans, convinced that they were indeed the best of all Americans. Most Irish Americans were liberals in politics, at least on economic issues like labor legislation and extension of the welfare state, but they were also fiercely antisocialist and anticommunist. The people who defined this new Catholic militancy were largely second-generation Irish Americans. Cardinal William O'Connell of Boston was their most authoritative voice, and the Knights of Columbus, which grew from about 40,000 members to over 600,000 in the early twentieth century, was the organizational backbone of the new militant American Catholicism.

This new identity was not simply a compromise between the new American-born generation's ambitions and the realities of a Protestant-dominated America. It also was a strategic effort to secure Irish leadership of the rapidly growing immigrant and Catholic populations of Boston, Chicago, New York, and other cities across the Northeast and Midwest and to rally them against the dominant white Anglo-Saxon Protestants (WASPs). As patriotic Americans but Catholic outsiders, Irish Americans stood across the boundary between inside and out and brokered between people on either side.

Local differences in social structures and political cultures produced significant variations in this pattern. Irish Americans seemed already integrated into the broader societies and even the elites of western cities like San Francisco, for example, thus softening if not stilling Catholic militancy. Irish Catholic Canadians, by contrast, faced a formidable rival within their own church in a huge, entrenched French Canadian population as well as confronting a powerful and militant Protestantism suffused with "Orangeism." In the late nineteenth century an estimated one in three Canadian Protestant males belonged to the Orange Order. Irish Catholics in Canada were thus in no position to mobilize Catholic outsiders against Protestant insiders. Confronting this difficult situation, they followed quieter, more timid assimilationist strategies than the Irish south of their border.

The militant American Catholic identity dominated in the Irish-American community even as the Irish became politically powerful as members of the Democratic Party's ruling coalition in the 1930s, asserted cultural power through the church over American movies in the same decade, and began to surpass native-stock Yankees as well as other ethnics in the occupational hierarchy by the 1920s and 1930s.

IRISH NORTH AMERICA SINCE THE 1960S

A series of events and movements in the 1960s finally undercut the religious division that sustained the old militant American Catholicism: John F. Kennedy's election and death, the ecumenism of the Second Vatican Council, and the powerful impact of the civil-rights movement and subsequent ethnic and racial assertions on American conceptions of pluralism and difference. In this new environment Irish-American identifications became "optional"—no longer socially or politically constrained—in a way that they had never been before in the Irish American heartland of the Northeast.

People did not stop thinking of themselves as Irish Americans; they just found new meanings for that identity. Some Irish found their "Irishness" in a revival of republican nationalism as conflict erupted in Northern Ireland. In the 1980s, Ireland's economic troubles forced a whole new wave of immigrants to leave the island and find jobs in America. These newcomers had

definitions of Irish identity very different from those of previous immigrant generations as well as those of American-born Irish. Most Irish Americans, however, perhaps began to understand their Irishness through one or another versions of Irish culture. Traditional Irish music and dance nearly died in America in the 1950s, but, riding the American folk-music boom (or in some cases leading it) and the broader American post-1960s obsession with authenticity, Irish folk music and dance achieved an unheard-of prominence in America by the end of the twentieth century. Irish high culture also enjoyed a new popularity, as university Irish studies programs multiplied and imports of Irish drama and fiction flourished in the 1980s and 1990s.

Irish America, then, had not yet disappeared. It had merely changed, as it had so many times before in the history of Irish North America.

SEE ALSO Diaspora: The Irish in Australia; Kennedy, John F., Visit of; Migration: Emigration and Immigration since 1950

Bibliography

Diner, Hasia. *Erin's Daughters in America: Irish Immigrant Women in the Nineteenth Century.* 1983.

Dolan, Jay P. *The Immigrant Church: New York's Irish and German Catholics, 1815–1865.* 1975.

Doyle, David. *Ireland, Irishmen, and Revolutionary America, 1760–1820.* 1981.

Doyle, David. "The Irish in North America, 1776–1845." In *Ireland under the Union, 1801–70.* Vol. 5 of *A New History of Ireland,* edited by W. E. Vaughan. 1989.

Erie, Steven P. *Rainbow's End: Irish Americans and the Dilemmas of Urban Machine Politics, 1840–1985.* 1988.

Ferrie, Joseph P. *Yankeys Now: Immigrants in the Antebellum United States, 1840–1860.* 1999.

Fogelman, Aaron. "From Slaves, Convicts, and Servants to Free Passengers: The Transformation of Immigration in the Era of the American Revolution." *Journal of American History* 85 (June 1998): 43–76.

Griffin, Patrick. *The People with No Name: Ireland's Ulster Scots, America's Scots Irish, and the Creation of a British Atlantic World.* 2001.

Houston, Cecil J., and William J. Smyth. *Irish Emigration and Canadian Settlement: Patterns, Links, and Letters.* 1990.

Kenny, Kevin. *The American Irish: A History.* 2000.

McGowan, Mark G. *Waning of the Green: Catholicism, the Irish and Identity in Toronto, 1887–1922.* 1999.

Miller, Kerby A. *Emigrants and Exiles: Ireland and the Irish Exodus to North America.* 1985.

Miller, Randall. "Catholic Religion, Irish Ethnicity, and the Civil War." In *Religion and the American Civil War,* edited by Randall Miller, Harry Stout, and Charles Reagan Wilson. 1998.

Murphy, Terrence, and Gerald Stortz, eds. *Creed and Culture: The Place of English-Speaking Catholics in Canadian Society, 1750–1930.* 1993.

Wilson, Andrew J. *Irish America and the Ulster Conflict, 1968–1995.* 1995.

Wilson, David A. *United Irishmen, United States: Immigrant Radicals in the Early Republic.* 1998.

Timothy J. Meagher

Direct Rule

See Ulster Politics under Direct Rule.

Divorce, Contraception, and Abortion

In the socially conservative climate of Ireland in the 1920s and 1930s the issues of divorce, contraception, and abortion were settled with little controversy and were not to become major issues again until the late 1960s and early 1970s. Abortion was outlawed in Ireland under the Offences against the Persons Act (1861). Legal abortion was introduced in Great Britain in 1967 but was not extended to Northern Ireland owing to the united opposition of church leaders. Under the Criminal Justice (Northern Ireland) Act (1945) anyone attempting to destroy a fetus capable of being born alive was deemed to have committed an offense, but abortion was permitted to save the life of the mother. The advocacy and sale of birth control devices were outlawed in the Irish Free State under the Censorship of Publications Act (1929), and the remaining loopholes regarding the importation of contraceptives were closed under the Criminal Law Amendment Act (1935). Divorce by civil process was available in England from 1857, but extension of this process to Ireland was strongly opposed by both Catholic and Protestant clergy. In the early years of the Irish Free State the introduction of private divorce bills in Dáil Éireann caused alarm and led to the official banning of divorce in 1925. To solidify this position the 1937 Constitution of Ireland included an unequivocal ban on divorce. Northern Ireland continued to receive divorce bills after partition and legislation for divorce was introduced in 1939. Under the Matrimonial Causes (N.I.) Act (1939) divorce was permissible on the grounds of desertion, cruelty, and incurable insanity. It was not until the Matrimonial Causes (N.I.) Order (1978) that the grounds for divorce ceased to be solely offense based.

In Southern Ireland the papal encyclical *Casti connubii* (On Christian marriage), issued on 31 December 1931, was regarded as the ultimate Catholic guide to the sanctity of marriage and the immorality of birth control. In a state with an overwhelming Roman Catholic majority there was little room for dissent, and in the prevailing social climate people were generally satisfied with the legal restrictions on divorce, contraception, and abortion. Whereas the Irish state's legal position on civil divorce and abortion remained relatively uncontroversial until the early 1980s, the issue of family planning reared its head considerably earlier primarily because of concerns regarding maternal health. In 1963 the pharmaceutical companies were able to introduce the Pill as a "cycle regulator," but it was not advertised as a contraceptive. Nonetheless, it was at a grassroots level that change gradually began, involving key members of the medical profession and concerned volunteers. There was a general sense of optimism among Catholic liberals that the spirit of the Second Vatican Council would translate into some kind of a tacit acceptance of Catholics' right to limit their families by artificial means. The papal encyclical *Humane vitae* (On human life), which was issued in 1968, was therefore considered a major setback as it reiterated the Roman Catholic Church's opposition to contraception. The archbishop of Dublin, John Charles McQuaid, used the encyclical to institute a ban on contraceptive advice being issued in the Dublin hospitals under his control.

The tide of change, however, was not stemmed. Women began to give sex education talks in some Protestant schools, and the Fertility Guidance Company set up a family-planning clinic in Dublin in 1969. The group of medical volunteers behind this company issued free advice and free contraceptives, circumventing the law by not selling the contraceptives. On 22 May 1971, the Irish Women's Liberation Movement traveled to Belfast on what became known as the "contraceptive train" in order to bring back contraceptives across the border to the Irish Republic, thereby raising public awareness. Meanwhile, a young Catholic lawyer, Senator Mary Robinson (née Bourke) drafted a bill to legalize contraceptives and placed her Criminal Law Amendment Bill before the Senate in March 1971. Both of Robinson's attempts to have her bill ratified failed. In 1973 the Supreme Court's decision to reverse the High Court decision on the McGee case was considered a watershed in the contraception debate. Mrs. McGee claimed that she had attempted to import contraceptives via the post for personal use and her package had been intercepted

Solidarity's anti-divorce march in Dublin, November 1995. The second attempt to remove the constitutional ban on divorce in November 1995 was carried by a margin of only 9,000 votes. © LEWIS ALAN/CORBIS SYGMA. REPRODUCED BY PERMISSION.

by customs. She had taken a case against the attorney general, claiming that the Criminal Law Amendment Act (1935) was inconsistent with the section of the 1937 Constitution that vowed to respect the rights of citizens. The Supreme Court's ruling that Mrs. McGee's rights had been interfered with opened the way for Irish citizens to import contraceptives for their own use.

On 13 December 1978 Charles Haughey, the minister for Health in the Fianna Fáil government, introduced a Health (Family Planning) Bill, which allowed contraceptives on prescription to be available to married couples and legalized the importation of contraceptives for sale in chemist shops. This law became operative in 1980, though it remained illegal until 1985 to sell contraceptives to anyone without a medical prescription. Although the attitude to the distribution of condoms became more relaxed in the 1980s because of growing

anxiety regarding HIV and AIDS, the Irish Family Planning Association was still fined in 1990 for selling condoms in the Virgin Megastore in Dublin. Department of Health figures released in 1992 revealed that 108 Irish people had died from AIDS. It was the concern regarding sexually transmitted diseases, more than any other issue, that helped to liberalize the access to barrier methods of contraception and contraceptive information.

In Southern Ireland abortion and divorce remained contentious issues well into the 1980s and 1990s. The abortion debate began in earnest in 1981 when antiabortionists, concerned that Europe might impose an abortion law on Ireland, requested a referendum to insert an antiabortion clause in the Irish constitution. Despite an acrimonious national debate the eighth amendment to the constitution was passed by 66.9 percent, with an electoral turnout of only 54.6 percent. In 1989 the Supreme Court ruled in favor of an injunction preventing the publication of phone numbers and addresses of British abortion clinics in student-welfare clinics in Ireland. The official figure for Irish women traveling to Britain for abortion services was 4,000 in 1990, rising to an estimated 6,000 in 1999. The so-called X case brought the issue of Irish women seeking abortions abroad to a head and generated considerable national debate. In 1992 the High Court prevented a pregnant fourteen-year-old girl, the victim of an alleged rape, from traveling to England for an abortion. The Supreme Court overturned the ruling by a four-to-one margin and accepted that abortion was legal in limited cases where there was a real danger that the pregnant woman was suicidal. As a direct result of the X case a referendum was held on 25 November 1992, in which the Irish people voted on the right to abortion information and the right to travel. The voting public affirmed the right to information and travel but rejected the wording for a new amendment allowing abortion in cases of maternal ill health.

In 1997 another case, the C case, once again brought the issue of abortion to the fore. The C case involved a thirteen-year-old girl pregnant as a result of rape. The High Court ruled in this case that, by virtue of the Supreme Court judgment in the 1992 X case, a girl who was suicidal was entitled to an abortion within the Irish state. In September 1999 the Irish government published a Green Paper on abortion. An all-party Oireachtas Committee on the constitution was invited to collect written submissions regarding abortion. On 6 March 2002 the Irish people narrowly defeated a third abortion referendum. The situation remains unresolved.

The issue of civil divorce became increasingly pressing in the 1980s, with mounting statistics of marital breakdown in the Republic of Ireland and growing concerns regarding the legal injustices imposed on the children of subsequent unions. In 1986 there was a referendum to permit divorce in restricted cases, which was rejected by the voters. As a result the Judicial Separation and Family Law Reform Act (1989) was introduced to permit permanent judicial orders of separation and to formalize a custody and property-settlement process for those experiencing marital breakdown. In November 1995 the Irish electorate voted in favor of legal divorce.

SEE ALSO Family: Fertility, Marriage, and the Family since 1950; Gaelic Catholic State, Making of; Secularization; **Primary Documents:** From the Decision of the Supreme Court in *McGee v. the Attorney General*

and the Revenue Commissioners (1973); On the Family Planning Bill (20 February 1974)

Bibliography

Barrington, Ruth. *Health, Medicine, and Politics in Ireland, 1900–1970.* 1987.

Desmond, Barry. *Finally and in Conclusion.* 2000.

Jones, Greta. "Marie Stopes in Ireland: The Mothers' Clinic Belfast, 1936–1949." *Social History of Medicine* 5, no. 2 (1992): 265–267.

McAvoy, Sandra. "The Regulation of Sexuality in the Irish Free State." In *Medicine, Disease, and the State in Ireland, 1650–1940,* edited by Elizabeth Malcolm and Greta Jones. 1999.

Solomons, Michael. *Pro Life? The Irish Question.* 1992.

White, John H. *Church and State in Modern Ireland, 1923–1970.* 1971.

Lindsey Earner-Byrne

~

Doyle, James Warren

James Doyle (1786–1834), Catholic bishop of Kildare and Leighlin from 1819 to 1834, was born in New Ross, Co. Wexford. An Augustinian educated at Coimbra in Portugal, he taught at Carlow College before becoming bishop at the age of 33. Pastorally, politically, and educationally, Doyle was the outstanding church figure in Irish public life in his time.

As bishop, Doyle undertook the renewal and reform of religious life in his extensive diocese. He promoted Sunday-school catechesis, confraternities, and chapel libraries. His firm pastorate was a model of Tridentine church administration.

Politically, Doyle was a powerful supporter of the Catholic Association, though his important relationship with Daniel O'Connell was often strained. He was the author of numerous works under the monogram J. K. L.—James of Kildare and Leighlin. His most outstanding book, *Letters on the State of Ireland* (1825), is a searing attack on state policy in Ireland. A key Catholic architect of the national system of education, which was established in 1831, he favored the education of Catholic and Protestant children together, and there is an ecumenical dimension in his thought even though the spirit of the times was very inimical to ecumenism.

Doyle published extensively on religious controversy during the "Second Reformation" campaign in the

James Warren Doyle (1786–1834), Catholic bishop of Kildare and Leighlin. COURTESY OF THE GRADUATE LIBRARY, UNIVERSITY OF MICHIGAN.

1820s. He defended his church from Protestant evangelical attacks and criticized the wealth of the Established Church. In the tithe war of the early 1830s he coined the slogan, "may your hatred of tithes be as lasting as your love of justice."

Doyle's name dominated parliamentary discussion of Ireland during his episcopacy. He gave lengthy evidence before parliamentary committees in 1825, 1830, and 1832. An active theorist for an Irish poor law based on parochial assessment, he received little support from Irish politicians. He thought that Daniel O'Connell should pursue an alliance with the Whigs in 1830 rather than repeal of the union. He did not see how repeal could be achieved at that time, and he sought legislative reform instead. Doyle's brilliant career was cut short by his early death. He was one of the most talented of the modern Irish Catholic bishops.

SEE ALSO Roman Catholic Church: 1690 to 1829; Roman Catholic Church: 1829 to 1891

Bibliography

McGrath, Thomas. *Politics, Interdenominational Relations, and Education in the Public Ministry of Bishop James Doyle of Kildare and Leighlin, 1786–1834.* 1999.

McGrath, Thomas. *Religious Renewal and Reform in the Pastoral Ministry of Bishop James Doyle of Kildare and Leighlin, 1786–1834.* 1999.

Thomas McGrath

~

Drama, Modern

Modern Irish drama was initiated in 1897 at a meeting of three people: William Butler Yeats, Lady Augusta Gregory, and Edward Martyn. In 1903 they founded the Irish Literary Theatre, now called the Irish National Theatre Society, and in 1904 opened the Abbey Theatre with a double bill of Lady Gregory's *Spreading the News* and Yeats's *On Baile's Strand*. From its inception, the Abbey was dedicated to cultural nationalism and committed to staging native plays with Irish themes. Rather than simply serving as a stage for British imports (Dublin had long been a stop on the eighteenth-century circuit of London, Bath, Dublin), the Abbey was and is still today a central venue for shaping modern drama. In fact, the history of modern Irish drama is inextricably linked to the history of Irish theater.

Many of Yeats's plays were based on Irish mythology and legend, in accordance with the Abbey's celebration of Ireland and Irish traditions. Those of Lady Gregory were based on her interest in Irish folk tales and mythology. According to theater historian Oscar Brockett, Lady Gregory "virtually invented the Irish folk-history play based primarily on oral tradition" (p. 454). For example, her *Kincora* (1905) revolves around a mythic Irish king. Thematically, both Yeats's and Lady Gregory's plays were in reaction to the stereotypical "stage Irishman" character so often the object of ridicule in plays imported from England. Lady Gregory's plays were very popular with audiences but were not given the critical praise that Yeats's have received.

In 1906 Edward Martyn withdrew from the Abbey in disagreement with the policy of excluding non-Irish plays; he went on to help form the Theatre of Ireland and later started the Irish Theatre Company (1914–1920). He was replaced at the Abbey by a future star of modern Irish drama, John Millington Synge. In 1908 the talented Fay brothers (Frank and W. G.), who had been important figures in the work of the early Abbey, left to work in England and the United States.

Although Yeats had envisioned an ideal theater that would be separate from politics, the fervent Irish nationalism that led to the birth of the Irish Free State also

Scene from a production of the Charabanc Theatre Company's Lay Up Your Ends, *Belfast, 1983, with Brenda Winter, Eleanor Methven, and Marie Jones (left to right).* PHOTOGRAPH BY CHRIS HILL PHOTOGRAPHIC. © CHRIS HILL. REPRODUCED BY PERMISSION.

brought changes to the Abbey. In the early 1900s, the Abbey became a center of Irish cultural and political friction. Audience protests at the Abbey occurred due to differing artistic and political attitudes and also reflected tensions in society. The nationalists protested certain plays that they felt did not represent an accurate view of Irish life. The artistic staff of the Abbey was interested in promoting new Irish writing on a variety of themes. The public wanted plays that presented positive views that countered the stereotypes of the stage Irishman. The peasant plays of the Abbey were the "bread and butter" (Owens and Radner 1990, p. 7) of the theater. If a character was felt to portray the national character in a negative way, that character, play, and playwright were subject to protests.

The Abbey was the site of Synge's early work, including *The Playboy of the Western World*, whose initial production in 1907 provoked the infamous Playboy riots that started when some audience members object-

ed to his portrayal of the national character and his mention of the word *shifts* (female undergarments). Others objected to the play's depiction of the Irish peasantry. Despite the lasting influence of his work (his plays continue to be staged in the twenty-first century), some critics believe that Synge, in his peasant characters and invented peasant language, created unflattering stereotypes of the Irish people. Other scholars consider his *Riders to the Sea* (1904), which deals with a mother's loss of her fishermen sons, to be one of the best short plays ever written in the English language.

Between 1904 and 1930, the Abbey continued to produce new plays on Irish themes (family life, Big House stories, social issues), culminating with Sean O'Casey's trilogy of Dublin life during the Irish Civil War: *The Shadow of the Gunman* (1922), *Juno and the Paycock* (1924), and *The Plough and the Stars* (1926). This last play provoked protests by those who felt that O'Casey was mocking Irish patriotism and the Irish people. Just as Synge was criticized for his portrayal of the Irish common people, O'Casey was criticized for showing the gritty hardships of Dublin city life, particularly prostitution. Although O'Casey's Dublin trilogy is realistic, his later plays such as *The Silver Tassie* (1928) are expressionistic. His change in style led to a break with the Abbey, and O'Casey, like Shaw before him, moved to England.

In 1914 George Bernard Shaw's 1904 play about British imperialism in Ireland, *John Bull's Other Island* (1904), was finally produced. Shaw, like his fellow expatriate O'Casey, became and remains one of the major figures of world drama. Although he left Ireland and most of his plays do not have Irish settings, he took great pride in his Irish heritage. Using comedy as a tool to explore and promote social issues, his plays are full of the political ideas of the day. In *Major Barbara*, a munitions manufacturer is found to be a greater humanitarian than his daughter, a member of the Salvation Army. *Arms and the Man* questions, through the mode of comedy, romantic attitudes about love and war.

In addition to O'Casey, other playwrights of note in the early twentieth century include Theresa Deevy (*Katie Roche*, 1936), Lennox Robinson (*The Whiteheaded Boy*, 1916), Padraic Colum (*The Land*, 1905), Denis Johnston (*The Old Lady Says No!* 1929), and St. John Ervine (*Mixed Marriage*, 1911). Deevy's *The King of Spain's Daughter* (1935) deals with a young woman who escapes reality into a fantasy world, and Ervine's *Mixed Marriage* deals with the problem of mixed Roman Catholic and Protestant marriage. Thematically, these plays reflect social concerns that continue to be examined in contemporary plays.

At the same time that the Abbey was developing, several other theaters were founded in Dublin and elsewhere in Ireland. In 1928 Micheál Mac Liammóir and Hilton Edwards founded the Dublin Gate Theatre. In Galway in 1928 the Irish-language theater Taibhdhearc na Gaillimhe was founded. In the North, in Belfast, the Ulster Literary Theatre was established in 1902; it was followed by the Ulster Group Theatre in 1940 and in 1951, Mary O'Malley's Lyric Players, which acquired its home, the Lyric Theatre, in 1968.

1930–1960

According to Fintan O'Toole, after O'Casey's plays were produced in the late 1920s, the great, first era of Irish theater ended and there began a "long period of decline" (p. 48). He earmarks the "second revival" of Irish theater as starting in the 1950s and continuing into the 1980s. (The first revival spanned the period between the founding of the Abbey and the end of the 1920s.) Despite the

conservative atmosphere in Ireland from the 1930s to the 1950s, Ireland in the 1950s saw the work of two internationally important playwrights, Samuel Beckett and Brendan Behan. Behan's *The Hostage* (1958) holds a crucial place in the annals of political theater; Beckett's *Waiting for Godot* (1953) is a landmark in theater history. In 1954 the Pike Theatre presented the first Irish production of Beckett's *Waiting for Godot*, a classic work of the theatre of the absurd, a twentieth-century movement that examines humankind's growing isolation in the aftermath of World War II. In this and many other of Beckett's plays, characters are unable to control a world that seems to be disintegrating around them. Like Shaw and O'Casey, Beckett also left Ireland, moving to France and settling there permanently in 1938; he aided the French Resistance during World War II and was awarded the Nobel Prize for literature in 1970.

1960–1980

The two most vital voices of the period between 1960 and 1980, whose plays continue to shape modern theater into the twenty-first century, are Brian Friel (*Philadelphia, Here I Come*, 1967) and Tom Murphy (*A Whistle in the Dark*, 1961). Friel's influence cannot be denied, and his works command an international audience. *Philadelphia, Here I Come* and *A Whistle in the Dark* fall into the larger genre of immigration/emigration plays, which include M. J. Molloy's *The Wood of the Whispering* (1953), John Murphy's *The Country Boy* (1959), John B. Keane's *Many Young Men of Twenty* (1961), Dermot Bolger's *In High Germany* (1990), Sebastian Barry's *White Woman Street* (1992), and Charabanc's *Gold in the Streets* (1986). Along with Murphy and Friel, Hugh Leonard (*Da*, 1973), Thomas Kilroy (*Talbot's Box*, 1979), and John B. Keane (*The Field*, 1965) are also major and influential playwrights. The work of Tom MacIntyre (*The Great Hunger*, 1983; revised 1986) is also of merit, especially for its experimental aspects. Besides emigration, Christopher Murray identifies several other major themes of late-twentieth-century Irish writing: sexual identity, religious consciousness, and politics (Murray 1997, pp. 165–186). He divides the last into several subcategories: the rural-urban divide, the history play, and the political allegory. With the occupation of Northern Ireland by British troops in 1969, the atmosphere on the streets, particularly in Belfast, gave rise to the important genre of "Troubles" plays. Along with the earlier playwrights Sam Thompson (*Over the Bridge*, 1960) and John Boyd (*The Flats*, 1971), the premier dramatist was the brilliant Belfast playwright Stewart Parker. Parker's untimely death in 1988 robbed the theater of one of its most gifted talents. He is particularly known for *Spokesong* (1975) and *Pentecost* (1987).

1980 TO THE PRESENT

Since 1980, Ireland has seen exciting and innovative theater staged in the Republic and in Northern Ireland, and the establishment of numerous companies. In 1983 the Belfast-based Charabanc Theatre Company was founded by five out-of-work actresses. Known for the vitality and balance of their work, Charabanc's plays, researched and developed by the company, include *Lay Up Your Ends* (with Martin Lynch, 1983) and *Somewhere over the Balcony* (1988). Until its dissolution in 1995, the company toured all over Ireland and internationally. Field Day Theatre, established by Brian Friel and Stephen Rea in 1980, had as its first production Friel's landmark *Translations*, a play that is now widely produced and anthologized. Field Day disbanded in 1982, leaving a lasting legacy in the new work they created, but they were also widely criticized for marginalizing women in their directorship, their work, and their publications. With the publication of the three volumes of its work in 1991, supervised by its all-male board (four other male directors having been added), Field Day was reproached for the absence of women writers. A proposed fourth volume was to be devoted to the work of Irish women; however, after several years it was clear that the original board had no interest in seeing the women's volume published. A group of women scholars finally brought the long-awaited volumes to press (published by Cork University Press in 2002).

In 1990 Friel's *Dancing at Lughnasa* was a great success not only at the Abbey but also in London and New York and in other theaters around the world. Besides Friel, until the late 1990s the other most widely produced playwright was Frank McGuinness, known particularly for his *Someone to Watch Over Me* (1992) and *Observe the Sons of Ulster Marching toward the Somme* (1985). The 1980s also saw the success of playwrights Anne Devlin (*Ourselves Alone*, 1985) and Christina Reid (*Tea in a China Cup*, 1982), both from Belfast.

The second half of the 1990s saw a tremendous surge and success in Irish dramatic writing. Marina Carr (*Portia Coughlin*, 1996) was one of the few women to have her plays produced at the Abbey (the lack of women playwrights at the Abbey has been decried by feminist critics, especially during the 1990s). Sebastian Barry's plays (for example, *The Stewart of Christendom*, 1995) were noted for their autobiographical bent. Marie Jones, a founding member of Charabanc, has been internationally successful with her 1999 *Stones in His Pocket*. The Leenane Trilogy (*The Beauty Queen of Leenane*, 1996; *A Skull in Connemara*, 1997; and *The Lonesome West*, 1997) by Martin McDonagh has made him one of the most widely produced Irish playwrights of the late 1990s. Like Marina Carr, McDonagh often explores the

dark side of Irish life, but unlike Carr's plays, which can be emotionally bleak, McDonagh's dramas in their violence satirize the peasant world of J. M. Synge. In McDonagh's *The Lonesome West*, the priest Father Welsh is a man so insignificant that no one can remember the correct pronunciation of his name. Defeated by his inability to reach his parishioners, Welsh has become a drunk who eventually kills himself. Like Friel, who often sets his plays in the imaginary depressed small town of Ballybeg, Marina Carr has a favorite location for her plays, the Irish midlands, and in this setting she takes often disturbing looks at the dark underbelly of Irish life. The leading character of *The Mai* (1994) kills herself; *By the Bog of Cats* (1998) is a reworking of *Medea*, with the Medea character Hester Swane killing not only her child but also herself at the end of the play; *On Raferty's Hill* (2000) is about a cycle of incestuous abuse.

Dublin has been a dynamic center for new theater companies and new writing. Particularly outstanding is the Rough Magic Theatre Company (artistic director Lynne Parker), which has had a strong commitment to new writing. Also based in Dublin is Conor McPherson, a writer known for his monologues who has earned praise for his modern ghost story, *The Weir* (1997). Galway is the home of the celebrated Druid Theatre Company and its artistic director Garry Hynes, the first woman to win a Tony Award for direction (in 1998); Druid first produced the work of Martin McDonagh and of Vincent Woods (*At the Black Pig's Dyke*, 1992). Also based in Galway is Patricia Burke Brogan, whose *Eclipsed* (1992) helped to expose the tragedy of the Magdalene laundries. Unwed mothers and troubled young women were "committed" to these laundries that were attached to Roman Catholic orders and were more or less indentured to the church; their babies were taken from them and in many cases adopted by Catholic families. One of the newest voices in modern Irish drama is Gary Mitchell (he calls himself British rather than Irish) whose prize-winning examinations of Northern Protestant life in Belfast can be seen in his *In a Little World of Our Own* (1997) and *The Force of Change* (2000).

Modern Irish drama was born at the end of the nineteenth century; at the beginning of the twenty-first century, Irish drama (modern, postmodern and contemporary) still holds a central position in the arts and the culture of the island, capturing the imagination of audiences worldwide with its power, diversity, and vitality.

SEE ALSO Arts: Modern Irish and Anglo-Irish Literature and the Arts since 1800; Beckett, Samuel; Fiction,

Modern; Literary Renaissance (Celtic Revival); Literature: Twentieth-Century Women Writers; Poetry, Modern; Yeats, W. B.

Bibliography

Brockett, Oscar. *The History of the Theatre.* 1995.

Fairleigh, John, ed. *Far from the Land: Contemporary Irish Plays.* 1998.

Fitz-Simon, Christopher, and Sanford Sternlicht. *New Plays from the Abbey Theatre, 1993–1995.* 1996.

Griffiths, Trevor R., and Margaret Llewellyn-Jones, eds. *British and Irish Women Dramatists since 1958: A Critical Handbook.* 1993.

Harrington, John, ed. *Modern Irish Drama.* 1991.

Irish Women's Writings and Traditions. Vols. 5 and 6 of *The Field Day Anthology of Irish Writing.* 2002.

Jordan, Eamonn, ed. *Theatre Stuff: Critical Essays on Contemporary Irish Theatre.* 2000.

Leeney, Catherine, ed. *Seen and Heard: Six New Plays by Irish Women.* 2001.

McGuinness, Frank, ed. *The Dazzling Dark: New Irish Plays.* 1996.

Murray, Christopher. *Twentieth-Century Irish Drama: Mirror up to Nation.* 1997.

O'Toole, Fintan. "Irish Theatre: The State of the Art." In *Theatre Stuff*, edited by Eamonn Jordan. 2000.

Owens, Cóilín D., and Joan N. Radner, eds. *Irish Drama, 1900–1980.* 1990.

Roche, Anthony. *Contemporary Irish Drama: From Beckett to McGuinness.* 1994.

Sternlicht, Sanford. *A Reader's Guide to Modern Irish Drama.* 1998.

Trotter, Mary. *Ireland's National Theaters: Political Performance and the Origins of the Irish Dramatic Movement.* 2001.

Watt, Stephen, Eileen Morgan, and Shakir Mustafa, eds. *A Century of Irish Drama: Widening the Stage.* 2000.

Charlotte J. Headrick

Dublin

Dublin, the capital city, is located on the east coast of Ireland, on both sides of the River Liffey along a wide sweeping bay with mountains to the south that shelter it from the prevailing southwesterly winds. This situation ensures low annual precipitation (averaging 750 millimeters) but can exacerbate problems of air quality. Growth has accelerated since the mid-1990s and the population of the built-up area is approximately one million, with another half million in the hinterland. Dublin is a primate city, that is, a city which dominates the urban system, in that it has five times the population of Cork, the second largest city in the Republic. The city is low density: Over 85 percent of housing dates from the twentieth century, and most dwellings are one-family, three- or four-bedroom houses. Apartments in the central area have become popular with young professionals only since the 1990s. In 1991, 75 percent of households were homeowners and only 15 percent occupied public housing.

Dublin is the center of government administration and the location of most of the corporate headquarters in Ireland. Three out of four workers are employed in the service sector by 37,000 service companies. The most important sectors are business and financial services, information technology, and public administration. There are some 1,300 manufacturing companies with concentrations in electronics and engineering, food, drink, tobacco, and paper and printing. Companies are generally small; only forty employ more than 1,000 people and about 200 companies have 200 or more workers. There are over 800 overseas companies, including some 350 U.S. companies, mainly in software, electronics, and financial services. Over 40,000 people are now employed in tourism. The importance of this industry has grown steadily, and the city is one of the most popular city destinations in Europe, attracting 4.4 million visitors annually.

Since the mid-1980s government-supported programs of urban renewal have eliminated much inner-city blight and attracted people back to the city center. The docklands have been redeveloped into an international financial services center, and there has been significant investment in the development of the city's tourism industry. The city center is low-rise, with few buildings over ten stories. High-rise buildings will be permitted in the future in specifically designated areas. Issues of concern to the city authorities include managing traffic (particularly, reducing the use of private cars for commuting), limiting urban sprawl, and managing waste disposal.

THE HISTORY OF THE CITY

In Celtic times there was an important ford on the Liffey, and this may have supported a small settlement. There is also evidence of a monastic establishment. In the ninth century Vikings established a raiding base along the river, and by the tenth century Dublin had developed into an important Viking trading town. It passed into the hands of the Anglo-Normans in the late twelfth century and became the center of the feudal

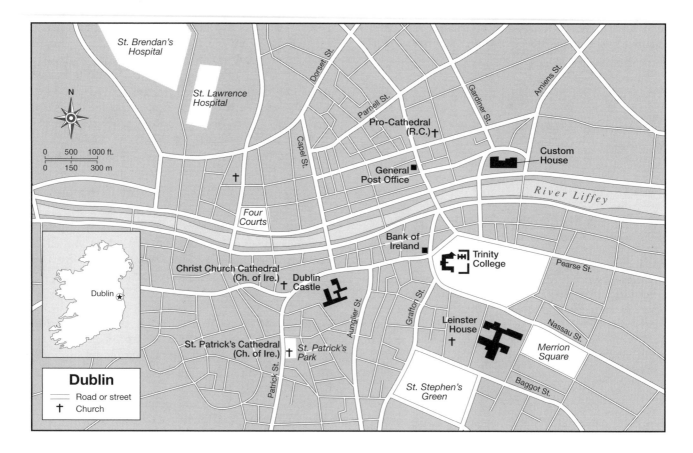

Dublin

— Road or street
† Church

lordship of Ireland. By 1610, the date of the earliest surviving map, Dublin was a small walled town (approximately 12 hectares) on the south bank of the Liffey with substantial suburbs on both sides of the river. The combined population of the town and suburbs is estimated to have been 10,000, with 3,800 within the walls. Little remains of this city today, with the exception of two cathedrals, Dublin Castle, and elements of the street plan.

Dublin flowered in the eighteenth century as both city authorities and private speculators developed the city beyond the medieval walls. A Wide Streets Commission established in 1757 oversaw development and acted as a planning authority for almost a century. The city was provided with wide, straight streets, residential squares, and impressive public buildings—the Four Courts, Custom House, and Parliament buildings—in a style greatly influenced by contemporary European ideas. By 1790 the city's elegance and charm was widely admired in Europe.

In the nineteenth century a number of circumstances combined to produce serious social problems. In the years after 1801, following the implementation of the Act of Union, the economy of the city suffered as many wealthy citizens moved to London. More importantly, the better-off moved in large numbers to legally independent townships just outside the municipal

boundary, thus reducing the tax base of the city. Two townships south of the city, Pembroke and Rathmines, became particularly important as higher-status enclaves. At the same time many people migrated from the countryside to the city, fleeing abject poverty and sometimes famine. They found themselves in a city without sufficient labor-intensive industry to absorb them productively. By 1851 the city's population had risen to 258,000 from 182,000 (in 1800), and there were problems of public health and housing of such intensity that it was well into the twentieth century before they were satisfactorily addressed. Nonetheless, Dublin continued to function as an important regional center, many infrastructural improvements were undertaken, and the better-off continued to come to the city for business and recreation. The municipal authority, Dublin Corporation, was reformed under the Municipal Corporations (Ireland) Act of 1840, and control quickly passes into the hands of the national politicians. Tension resulted between the Corporation and the British and unionist establishment, which continued until Irish independence. This manifested itself in many ways—for example, in arguments over the naming and placement of civic monuments and in the failure of the Corporation to win approval for the absorption of the Pembroke and Rathmines townships into the city.

The suburbs grew dramatically during the twentieth century. The southeastern sector, the location of the most successful nineteenth-century townships, expanded and retained its high social status. Extensive programs of social housing from the mid-1920s onward also produced large suburban developments. In the south city these were mainly to the west, creating a west/east social gradient. However, north of the Liffey, the social geography of the city did not develop such a clear-cut pattern, and areas of different social status are smaller and less spatially differentiated. Until recently, the trend in Dublin was towards suburban living, and most of the inner city experienced population decline. Industry also moved from the increasingly congested central areas to cheaper and more accessible sites in suburban industrial estates and business parks. Nonetheless most employment continues to be located in the city center, and the lack of an efficient public transport system together with increased car ownership has made commuting more time consuming. As a consequence, new housing developments in older and more central suburban and inner city areas have proved very popular since the 1990s.

For most of the twentieth century, Dublin grew without a strategic plan and with a fragmented system of local government. There was no real attempt to manage change until the 1960s when, following a state-sponsored strategic review, the Myles Wright Report, it was decided to concentrate growth into new towns on the western edge. Attempts to continue strategic planning in the 1980s and 1990s came to nothing, but the Irish government intends that urban growth in the twenty-first century will be managed in the context of a national and regional strategy.

SEE ALSO Belfast; Cork; Landscape and Settlement; Towns and Villages

Bibliography

Brady, Joseph, and Anngret Simms, eds. *Dublin through Space and Time.* 2001.

Clarke, Harold B., ed. *Medieval Dublin: The Making of a Metropolis.* 1990.

Daly, Mary E. *Dublin, the Deposed Capital: A Social and Economic History, 1850–1900.* 1984.

de Courcy, John W. *The Liffey in Dublin.* 1996.

MacLaren, Andrew. *Dublin: The Shaping of a Capital.* 1993.

Pearson, Peter. *The Heart of Dublin.* 2000.

Prunty, Jacinta. *Dublin Slums, 1800–1925: A Study in Urban Geography.* 1998.

Joseph Brady

~

Dublin Philosophical Society

Established in 1683, the Dublin Philosophical Society copied the Royal Society in London and other recently established scientific groups in Oxford and Edinburgh. It owed much to the enthusiasm of two young members of Dublin University, the brothers William (1656–1698) and Thomas Molyneux (1661–1733), and drew in others from the university, including some senior to the Molyneuxs. It attested to the spread into Ireland of interest in scientific and technological speculation, and raised hopes that its discoveries might correct apparent Irish backwardness.

Earlier efforts had been made to inquire systematically into the natural resources of Ireland, to chart improvements, and to identify how further improvements could best be achieved. These had been pursued during the Cromwellian interregnum of the 1650s, when the island looked receptive to change, but official backing was meager and more urgent matters intervened. Yet at least one pioneer of the 1650s, Sir William Petty, survived into the 1680s. Continuities between the earlier endeavors and the Dublin Society were suggested when Petty was installed as the society's president. Furthermore, much of the underlying philosophy and many of the practical schemes harked back to the earlier project. Indeed, Petty drew up rules for the infant society, stressing experiment and personal observation rather than dependence on tradition. In addition, he insisted that "the rules of number, weight, and measure" were to be strenuously applied to its inquiries. What had changed since the 1650s, enabling the society to take on a solid existence, was the presence of a larger interested group. It had also become easier to link up with similar organizations in Britain and continental Europe.

Much of the thinking behind the society derived from Francis Bacon (1561–1626), who had advocated an empirical and experimental approach to the natural world. Importance was attached to the collection of information about phenomena and resources across Ireland. To this end William Molyneux solicited informants in each county to supply accounts. Once these were collected and published, it was hoped that the problems of agricultural and commercial underdevelopment could be effectively addressed. The material sent to Molyneux varied greatly in length, detail, and quality. It was not published, so the immediate impact of these researches was negligible. In the absence of a national survey that would publicize its activities and intentions, the society contented itself with correspondence with interested parties in Ireland, Britain, and further afield.

In this way, it was hoped, useful innovations could be introduced into Ireland. The members met in Dublin, where they conducted experiments and discussed these and other scientific matters, intending through collaboration to advance knowledge with useful applications.

Membership of the society was concentrated among graduates and fellows of Trinity College in Dublin and the officials and professionals of Protestant Dublin. Its first meeting on 28 January 1684 was attended by fourteen people; of these, nine were associated with Dublin University. As with the Royal Society of London, fashion and a wish for diversion encouraged participation. Interest was often transitory, making it difficult for the directors to sustain the society. Even before enthusiasm for the meetings waned, political events conspired to halt its operations. The mounting unease among the Protestants of Dublin as the Catholic takeover under James II and Tyrconnell, lord deputy from 1687, gathered pace removed many active members. However, its meetings were merely suspended, not abandoned. After 1690, once the Protestant interest reestablished itself more securely, the society soon revived. Optimism arising from the conclusive defeat of the Catholics (in 1690 to 1691) and the desire to make good the perceived deficiencies of previous generations of Protestants in Ireland favored ventures of collective improvement such as those advocated by the society. It was, moreover, a program which, for all its practical applications and material benefits, was inseparable from religious ideologies. The proper use of the natural world, first by understanding and surveying it and then by exploiting it for the common good, was enjoined on active Christians. Indeed, a fuller comprehension of creation amounted to a form of worship, in which the power of God was at once perceived and acknowledged. In this mood clergymen of the Protestant Church of Ireland were prominent in the society, and some pursued theological exercises that paralleled their work for the society itself.

In April 1693 the revived society attracted fresh faces. Its base was still in Trinity College, but it was joined by important civil administrators such as Sir Cyril Wyche and Sir Richard Cox. Once more, efforts were directed toward a comprehensive description of the surface and history of the island. Despite its enlarged membership, the Philosophical Society depended—dangerously as it proved—on the direction of the Molyneuxs. With William Molyneux preoccupied with public affairs (he was both a barrister and an MP), the society declined. His premature death in 1698 seemed to signal an end to the organization. However, his son Samuel Molyneux, while an undergraduate at Trinity College, reanimated the society in 1707. He was helped by a new generation interested in this type of collective activity and by the patronage of the current viceroy, Lord Pembroke. But this phase lasted only a year. Even more than its two predecessors, this incarnation of the society relied on the energies of a Molyneux, and Samuel Molyneux's were soon diverted into making a career for himself.

If concrete achievements were few, the Dublin Philosophical Society represented an important stage between the more diffuse work of Petty and his associates in the 1650s and the sustained activity of the Dublin Society, set up in 1731 and incorporated by royal charter in 1733. There were continuities between these groups in their agenda, especially in the eagerness to collect and disseminate information. All subscribed to an optimistic view that Ireland's potential was great, but would be realized only when it had been properly mapped and its resources identified and quantified. All accepted a duty to use the materials at hand for the benefit of the entire population, which thereby might be delivered from famine, idleness, ignorance, and poverty, though sometimes members were naïve in assuming that methods of cultivation and manufacture successfully adopted elsewhere could be introduced profitably into Ireland. Almost a quarter of the recorded discussions of the Dublin Philosophical Society centered on medical inquiries. These had local and practical applications, and may have improved the training of physicians in the capital. Much of the time, though, the society functioned essentially as a club for a circle of privileged Protestants, and amusement as much as betterment—ethical or material—resulted. Also, if the remit of the group did not tie it to any particular confession, it nevertheless failed to become a place where Protestants and Catholic virtuosi mingled. Only one Catholic, Mark Baggot, was admitted to the circle, and he took little part in the proceedings. Essentially a Protestant monopoly from the start, it also tended to celebrate the achievements of the Protestant interest in Ireland, crediting it alone with most of the cultural and material advances of the seventeenth century. In this it looked forward to its successors, the Dublin Society and the Physico-Historical Society of the 1740s. Nevertheless, the Philosophical Society did encourage closer and more systematic study of the natural and civil histories of Ireland. It also helped to popularize such endeavors among the propertied and professionals of Protestant Ireland. Moreover, through its questionnaires and inquiries it connected provincials with what was happening in the capital, and (more generally) linked Ireland with the wider world of educated speculation and experiment.

SEE ALSO Boyle, Robert; Molyneux, William; Petty, Sir
William; Trinity College

Bibliography

Barnard, T. C. "The Hartlib Circle and the Origins of the Dublin Philosophical Society." *Irish Historical Studies* 19, no.
73 (1974): 56–71.

Hoppen, K. Theodore. *The Common Scientist in the Seventeenth
Century: A Study of the Dublin Philosophical Society.* 1970.

Simms, John Gerald. *William Molyneux of Dublin.* 1982.

Toby Barnard

Duffy, James

An enterprising publisher of patriotic and religious
works for a mass market, James Duffy (c. 1809–1871)
was a native of County Monaghan, but the exact date
of his birth and the circumstances of his background are
unknown. He is believed to have received a hedge-school
education before going to Dublin to start in business as
a bookseller. Reputedly, he made an early fortune by
buying cheap Bibles bestowed on unappreciative Catholics by Protestant missionaries and reselling them in Liverpool, where they commanded a considerable profit. As
a beginner in publishing, Duffy issued editions of established lowbrow favorites such as *The Life of Freney the
Robber*, but it was as the publisher of respectable literature in inexpensive but tasteful formats that he made
his mark. By the 1840s the growth of literacy and the
flourishing of Irish Catholicism created a thriving market for works of piety and devotion. Duffy tapped that
market and extended it to the Catholic Church throughout the British empire, winning business around the
globe. Eager to find a medium for the propagation of an
elevated nationalism, Thomas Davis and Charles Gavan
Duffy of the *Nation* turned to Duffy to publish their
multivolume series of low-priced works of literature,
history, and reference, the Library of Ireland. Twenty-
two volumes appeared between 1845 and 1847. Several
of them, such as Gavan Duffy's anthology *The Ballad
Poetry of Ireland* and Davis's *Literary and Historical Essays*, were enormously successful. Diversifying his
trade, Duffy ventured in 1847 into the thriving but volatile periodical sector with *Duffy's Irish Catholic Magazine* (although there was no commitment on the publisher's part to the more comprehensive ideals of the

Young Irelanders). He experimented with successive titles, ending with *Duffy's Hibernian Sixpenny Magazine* in
1864. By then Duffy had assembled a book list that encapsulated a large segment of the emerging canon of
popular patriotic literature. His entrepreneurial ethic allegedly denied holidays both to himself and to his employees, and there is little hint of warmth in the tributes
paid to him after his death on 4 July 1871. There is no
known cache of personal or business papers, and this
major Irish pioneer of print capitalism has not yet attracted a full-length study.

SEE ALSO Balladry in English; Chapbooks and Popular
Literature; Education: Secondary Education, Female;
Education: Secondary Education, Male; Literacy and
Popular Culture

Bibliography

Hayley, Barbara, and Enda McKay, eds. *Three Hundred Years
of Irish Periodicals.* 1987.

MacManus, M. J., ed. *Thomas Davis and Young Ireland.* 1945.

R. V. Comerford

Dún Ailinne

Dún Ailinne, located in Knockaulin Townland, near Kil-
cullen, County Kildare, was one of the preeminent royal
sites of pre-Christian Ireland—the Leinster equivalent to
Emhain Macha in Ulster, Cruachain in Connacht, and
Tara in Mide. Reputedly, it was constructed by the earliest Leinster king (Art Mess Telmann or Setna Sithbacc).
Although these sites were deserted by the medieval period, they retained great symbolic significance (see Grabowski 1990).

Dún Ailinne is an oval hilltop site of about 15 hectares, enclosed by a bank and ditch with an entrance on
the eastern side. It was excavated between 1968 and
1975. The main excavation area was on the top of the
hill, near the center of the site. Here, pottery, flaked flint,
and ground stone artifacts show Neolithic and (very
slight) Bronze Age activity (see Johnston 1990). The nature of this activity is quite unclear, however, because
of extensive disturbance by the construction of three
successive circular timber structures in the Iron Age.

These were large: The diameter of the first was 28 meters, the second 38 meters, and the last 42 meters. The entrance of each faced roughly east-north-east. Each in turn was dismantled and, after the last had been taken down, accumulations of burnt stone, ash, charcoal, and animal bone indicate periodic feasting. Radiocarbon dates for these Iron Age activities lie between the fifth century B.C.E. and the third century C.E., while bronze, iron, and glass artifacts are mostly of the first century B.C.E. and first century C.E.

Survey and excavation of the site entrance revealed a roadway eight meters wide running through the entrance into the interior. Its alignment is directly toward the entrances of the circular timber structures on the top of the hill. All available evidence indicates that Dún Ailinne in the Iron Age was a ritual and ceremonial site, which later fell into disuse (see Wailes 1990). The ENE orientation of the timber circles and the roadway suggests that they may have been aligned with sunrise on or about the festival of Beltane (1 May), the traditional beginning of summer. Pam Crabtree's 1990 analyses of the animal and plant remains suggest that Iron Age activities at the site were mainly around that time, and in the fall.

SEE ALSO Cruachain; Emain Macha (Navan Fort); Prehistoric and Celtic Ireland; Tara

Bibliography

Crabtree, Pam. "Subsistence and Ritual: The Faunal Remains from Dún Ailinne, Co. Kildare, Ireland." *Emania* 7 (1990): 22–25.

Grabowski, Kathryn. "The Historical Overview of Dún Ailinne." *Emania* 7 (1990): 32–36.

Johnston, Susan A. "The Neolithic and Bronze Age activity at Dún Ailinne, Co. Kildare." *Emania* 7 (1990): 26–31.

Wailes, Bernard. "The Irish 'Royal Sites' in History and Archaeology." *Cambridge Medieval Celtic Studies* 3 (1982): 1–29.

Wailes, Bernard. "Dún Ailinne: A Summary Excavation Report." *Emania* 7 (1990): 10–21.

Bernard Wailes

Early Medieval Ireland and Christianity

The history of early medieval Ireland can be understood only against the background of the conversion to Christianity that introduced ideas that changed the culture and society of pagan Ireland forever. Christian doctrine and theology shaped social behavior and altered cultural practice, yet much was kept that did not contravene Christian conscience as affirmed by some early Irish law tracts. Christianity, as the "religion of the book," required literacy so that believers could read the Bible and perform the Latin liturgy. With literacy in Latin came literacy in the vernacular, that is, in Irish (Gaelic). The early Irish took readily to these intellectual pursuits, and Ireland produced the earliest, and arguably the richest, vernacular literature in medieval Western Europe.

The richness and variety of literary texts in the early Irish language has encouraged many to see this literature as a repository of pre-Christian lore and belief. But most Celticists accept that it is impossible to recreate accurately the pagan beliefs and practices of pre-Christian Ireland based on archaeology and the surviving literature. Most medieval texts that purport to represent pre-Christian Irish characters and events were compiled several centuries after the introduction of Christianity, and vast cultural and societal changes separate them from the times they pretend to portray. Many texts reveal direct influence from identifiable Christian authors and their writings. Critics now accept that a tenth-century Irish saga from the Ulster Cycle, for example, tells us as much about Ireland in the time of its tenth-century redactor as it does about the pre-Christian Irish characters depicted in the saga.

THE EARLY SAINTS

The first firm date in Irish history does not come from Irish sources but rather from the south of France in a chronicle written by Prosper of Aquitaine (c. 390–463). Prosper's *Chronicle* states that in 431 a certain Palladius was ordained bishop by Pope Celestine and sent "to the Irish believing in Christ." Prosper made it clear that Saint Patrick was not the first Christian missionary to Ireland. In addition to Palladius, there are traditions of Christian saints and their communities in Ireland, particularly in the south and east, before Patrick's arrival. These pre-Patrician Christians may have developed the earliest Irish writing system, known as *ogham*.

Saint Patrick may have flourished any time during the period around 432, when Irish chronicles say that he arrived in Ireland, to around 492, when they claim that he died. These dates represent a period that critics accept as being too long to accurately reflect Patrick's career in Ireland. Most scholars state simply that Patrick flourished sometime in the mid to late fifth century. Although we do not have firm dates for Saint Patrick, we are fortunate that writings by him do survive—his *Confession* and the *Letter to (the soldiers of) Coroticus*. Both reveal much about the character and personality of the man even if they tell us little about Ireland in his time.

By the late seventh century the richness of early Irish literature becomes evident in several saints' lives written in Latin. Irish hagiography (from the Greek words meaning "writings about holy persons") includes early texts about the saints Patrick, Brigit, and Columba. Besides their emphasis on religious topics, we see their propaganda value as they attempt to promote certain regions and dynastic families who supported an individual saint's cult.

Two surviving seventh-century lives of Saint Patrick reveal much about how Irish clerics of that period

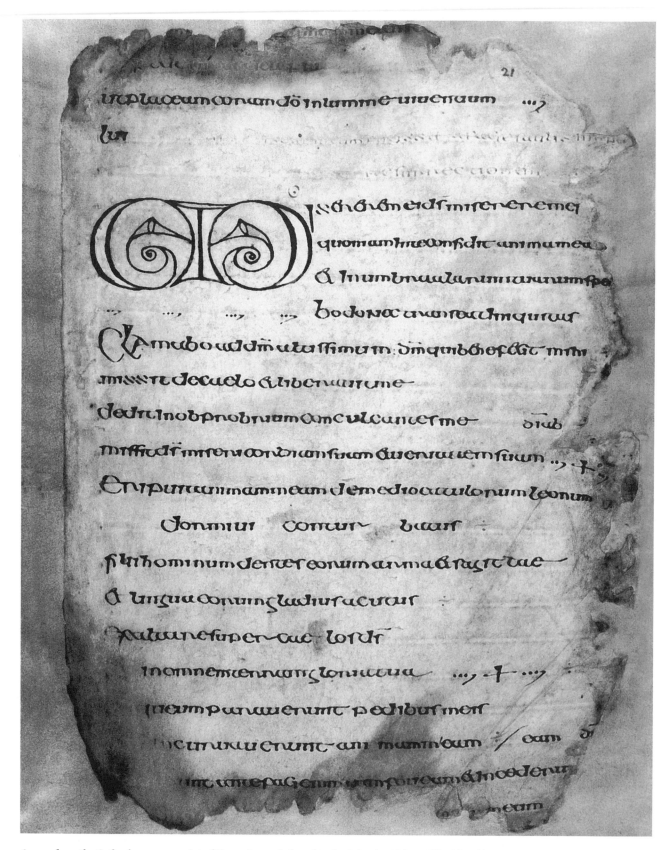

A page from the Cathach, a manuscript of the psalms, attributed to St. Columba (Colum Cille) himself (c. 600 C.E.). COURTESY OF THE ROYAL IRISH ACADEMY. PHOTOGRAPH BY DECLAN CORRIGAN PHOTOGRAPHY. REPRODUCED BY PERMISSION.

viewed Patrick, but they do not add much reliable information about Patrick himself or about Ireland in his lifetime. Tírechán of Armagh compiled around 670 a collection of anecdotes about Saint Patrick (*Collectanea de Sancto Patricio*). A near contemporary of Tírechán, Muirchú maccu Machthéni, wrote a life of Saint Patrick around 690 (*Vita Sancti Patricii*) that is a more finished work of hagiography than Tírechán's. Muirchú's work relates, among other episodes, the conversion of King Lóeguire at Tara and Patrick's contests with Lóeguire's druids. Both of these seventh-century hagiographical works reveal a northern bias in their acceptance of the primacy of the see of Armagh and Patrick as patron saint of all Ireland, and both stress the role of the Uí Néill (O'Neill) dynastic family.

While the hagiography about Patrick tended to emphasize sites and families in central and northern Ireland, Leinster in the east also had its special saint. Cogitosus wrote around 680 a life of the female saint Brigit (*Vita Sanctae Brigitae*). Brigit's cult is centered in Kildare, a monastic city that became famous for its *scriptorium* and a center from which many Irish scholars departed for the continental schools in the Carolingian age. There is no firm historical evidence for Brigit, and she may be the one case of an early pagan Celtic goddess being transformed into an Irish saint. The struggle between the Uí Néill dynasts of the north and the ruling families of Leinster are reflected in the competition between Armagh and Kildare, with Armagh eventually gaining supremacy throughout Ireland but allowing Kildare and its saint Brigit to maintain their importance within Leinster.

The first firmly historical Irish saint was Saint Columba (Columba the Elder, c. 521–597; *Colum Cille* in Irish). Adomnán (+704), abbot of Iona, wrote a life of Columba (*Vita Sancti Columbae*) sometime in the last decade of the seventh century. The life of Columba follows typical hagiographical motifs rather than offering historical details and describes prophetic revelations and miracles. Columba, like Patrick, was a missionary. As the first Irish pilgrim (*peregrinus*) saint, Columba left Ireland sometime around 563 and founded the monastery of Iona on a small island off the coast of Scotland. Tradition relates that Columba went into exile as a penance for his part in the dynastic wars of his Uí Néill relatives.

Columba's self-imposed exile from Ireland reveals much about the monastic ideals of his period. It was considered a penance to leave one's homeland to reside among foreign people. But to do so for the love of God, or for Christ's sake, was a powerful act of piety. We see this ideal in Patrick's writings and actions. Patrick, who was originally from Britain, was captured by Irish raiders and taken in his teens as a slave to live in Ireland. When he escaped after years of servitude, his religious faith drove him to return to Ireland to convert to Christianity those who had enslaved him rather than return to his home in Britain. *Deorad Dé* ("exile of God") was the Irish term for a person willing to undergo self-imposed pilgrimage (*peregrinatio*) or exile as an act of piety.

Many examples of Irish pilgrim exiles exist. One of the most famous is Columbanus (Columba the Younger, c. 543–615)—not to be confused with Columba the Elder—who spent roughly twenty-five years on the continent as a pilgrim and founded several monasteries in France and one in Italy. Columbanus was educated at the monastery of Bangor, Co. Down, in Northern Ireland. He composed Latin texts that include sermons, a penitential, a monastic rule, and letters, some of which were addressed to popes. His writings reveal the depth of the education that he received at the monastic school in Ireland. He left Bangor sometime around 590, at about the age of fifty, and traveled with twelve companions on the continent, particularly in what is now France, where he founded monasteries at Annegray, Luxeuil, and Fontaines. But Columbanus was eager to move on and visit Rome. Although he never fulfilled his wish, he succeeded in founding the most important of his monasteries at Bobbio in Italy. Columbanus died around 615.

This pattern of pilgrim saints founding monasteries on the continent was repeated frequently in subsequent centuries. One of Columbanus's Irish disciples, a monk named Gall, was too ill to travel to Italy with Columbanus and stayed back, eventually founding a monastery at Saint Gallen in Switzerland. Gall died around 630. Another Irish missionary, Kilian, departed Ireland more than a century later with a group of companions and founded a monastery at Würzburg in Germany. Kilian is one of the few Irish pilgrim saints to have been martyred. He was assassinated, along with two companions, as a result of political intrigue after a trip to Rome around 687/9.

MONASTERIES

The ideals of Irish monastic life can be seen in the missionary work and training activities of Irish monasteries. During the early decades of the seventh century many Anglo-Saxon nobles were educated at Irish monasteries in northern Britain, specifically at Iona. When these Irish-educated English nobles returned to England, they invited Irish missionaries into their pagan kingdoms to evangelize. The Anglo-Saxon king Oswald invited the Irish bishop Aidan from Iona into his kingdom, and Aidan founded the monastery at Lindisfarne on the coast of Northumberland around 635. The English historian Bede (+735) shows that Irish missionary activity in northern England was more successful at converting the pagan English than that started by Rome in 597 from Canterbury in the south of England.

Monastic schools in Ireland became centers of excellence for peoples from all over Europe, as can be seen by tracing the English who came to study and train as missionaries in them. The historian Bede and an earlier English contemporary Aldhelm (+709) report that sizeable contingents of English students trained as missionaries in Ireland, specifically at Rath Melsigi, Co. Carlow, in Leinster. These English monks trained in Ireland in order to convert their pagan Germanic relatives on the continent. Several of them had successful ecclesiastical careers after their Irish training.

Bede and Aldhelm, as clerics, emphasized religious training, but both confirm that secular subjects were also taught at Irish monastic schools. Study of the scriptures was paramount, but they both make it clear that students often traveled from site to site seeking out teachers who had specialized knowledge in secular subjects as well. Bede said that the Irish willingly welcomed the English students, gave them food, and provided them with books and instruction, without seeking any payment (Book iii, chapter 27).

Much early Irish literature is associated with monasteries, which shows that many of the learned persons of Ireland, whether secular or religious, received their educations at monastic schools. This means as well that the literature associated with these monasteries is preserved in both Latin and Irish.

The monastery of Iona, founded by Columba, encouraged literary production in both languages. For example, one of its more famous abbots, Adomnán (679–704), mentioned already as the author of the Latin "Life of Columba," wrote a description in Latin of the significant sites in the Holy Land called "On the Holy Places" (*De Locis Sanctis*). Abbot Adomnán also wrote and promulgated a law (*Cáin Adomnáin*, 697), written in Irish, which was intended to protect women, children, and clerics from the ravages of warfare.

Columba himself, the founder of Iona, has a Latin hymn, "Exalted Creator" (*Altus Prosator*), attributed to him, although not all critics accept the attribution. Three poems in praise of Columba rank among the oldest complete poems in the Irish language. One of them, the "Eulogy for Columba" (*Amra Choluim Chille*), has been dated on linguistic grounds to around 600, which coincides well with Columba's death date of 597. According to tradition, Dallán Forgaill, a professional poet, composed it in order to eulogize Columba on his death.

This poem is important for several reasons besides its great age. It reflects an ancient tradition of praising secular rulers, but it is unusual for praising instead a religious leader. It demonstrates how the learning of the monasteries blended native customs with Christian teachings. For example, it complies with the norms of secular eulogy by noting Columba's aristocratic background and by providing genealogical information that can be corroborated in other sources. Columba is called a great champion, but rather than battling against his enemies and sharing largesse among his subjects, Columba excels in self-denial and Christian learning. His praiseworthy qualities are not those of a secular ruler, but of an ascetic, scholarly cleric.

The monastery at Bangor also produced learned religious texts in Latin beside a vibrant vernacular literature of Irish tales. We have already noted that Columbanus, the Bangor-educated missionary to the continent, corresponded with popes and wrote sermons, a penitential, and a monastic rule in Latin. In the late seventh century a collection of beautiful religious poems and hymns in Latin, the "Antiphonary of Bangor," was compiled there.

Important vernacular literature also came from Bangor. "The Voyage of Bran" (*Immram Brain*), perhaps the earliest example of the Irish "otherworld voyage," was written at Bangor. It tells of Bran's voyage across the Western Ocean and recounts the wonders that he encountered in a sinless otherworld. It employs a motif whereby characters in a pre-Patrician context prophesy the coming of Christianity and the salvation of the Irish. Tales in Irish about the early cultural hero Mongán mac Fiachnai also originated at Bangor. The tales about Mongán portray the Irish Sea as a highway between Ireland and Britain and relate episodes that involve battles against English kingdoms.

The mixture of Latin and Irish writings, like the texts produced at monasteries, is well illustrated by early Irish law tracts. Most, but not all, law texts produced for the church tend to be written in Latin. The "Irish Collection of Canons" (*Collectio canonum hibernensis*) of about 725, the primary example of Irish church law, is based on biblical and patristic sources. Penitentials and monastic rules represent the Irish tendency, evident in the vernacular law tracts, to codify and schematize social organization and behavior. A group of ecclesiastical laws in the vernacular is represented by *cána* (sg. *cáin*), of which *Cáin Adomnáin* (Adomnán's Law, 697) has already been cited. Other examples include *Cáin Phátraic* (Patrick's Law, 737) and *Cáin Domnaig* (Law of Sunday).

The majority of secular law tracts, written in Irish, were redacted between around 650 and around 750. A collection of vernacular law tracts called the *Senchas Már* (the "Great Tradition") appears to have been compiled in the northern midlands. A separate group of "poetico-legal" texts called the "*Nemed* school" probably originated in Munster. These law tracts reveal a great deal about the hierarchical nature of early Irish society and social custom. They discuss social rank and status, kinship structure, distribution of inheritance, rights to property, making and enforcing of contracts, the grading of professions, and so on. It is significant that the law tracts tended to be compiled during the same period that saw the spread of ecclesiastical literature.

KINGSHIP

The study of early Irish politics is made difficult by the proliferation of names of petty kings, none of whom ever clearly rose to prominence. The genealogies and regional king-lists preserved from early Irish sources are particularly rich when compared to other parts of medieval Western Europe. Part of the problem can be understood by recognizing that the Irish word translated as "king" (*rí*) does not designate a centralized, powerful monarch, as we might encounter on the continent, for example. Instead, it is used to describe the leader of any small local group based on blood kinship (*tuath*). These groups existed in varying hierarchical relationships to one another so that a local "king" might be a vassal to a stronger "king" in the next valley, and that neighboring "king" would in turn be subject to a regional "king" who might control, at least nominally, an entire province.

The politico-geographical divisions of Ireland have a long history, whether the divide is between north (*Leth Cuinn*) and south (*Leth Moga*) or into the provinces that exist to this day: Ulster, Connacht, Munster, and Leinster. The notion that one king could rule all of Ireland—usually called the "High King of Tara"—had developed by our period, although it remained an ideal rather than a reality. Nevertheless, this ideal implies the incipient concept of an Irish nation encompassing the entire island.

The idealized concept of kingship was circumscribed by certain inherited proscriptions. For example, a king must not be physically blemished, as this implied an imperfection in his reign. The sacral character of kingship is shown by the idea that a just, righteous king would have a peaceful, prosperous reign; his "king's truth" (*fír flathemon*) guaranteed the land's fertility. Sovereignty, as an abstract concept, was portrayed as a female so that a king, when he assumed the kingship, symbolically married his kingdom.

Kingship was not based on a strict father to son (or closest male relative) succession, but rather eligibility for kingship was based on blood kinship extending over several generations. This meant that grandsons and great-grandsons might be eligible to contend for the kingship if they could muster support from relatives and political allies. This system appears on the surface to provide a democratic method of selecting the most qualified and popular candidate, but it often led to social strife and political division.

In the northern half of Ireland the Uí Néill dynasts dominated the political scene, but the Uí Néill must be understood as interrelated families who exerted the greatest political control. The Uí Néill themselves divided into northern and southern divisions, and each of these subdivided again into various branches. Each branch of the Uí Néill claimed descent from Niall of the Nine Hostages (*Niall Noígiallach*), a quasi-historical fifth-century character. The various branches of the Uí Néill, north and south, alternated as they supplied the high king of Tara, without any branch ever clearly predominating. Other dynastic families from other parts of Ireland frequently occupied the high kingship during this time as well.

The hierarchical nature of early Irish society is well illustrated in this concept of descent through prominent families. It can be seen functioning in Irish monasteries as well. For example, nearly all of the abbots at Iona from Columba (+597) to Adomnán (+709) were descended from Columba's own family, the Cenél Conaill branch of the northern Uí Néill.

In Munster a high kingship was centered on the ecclesiastical site at Cashel, Co. Tipperary. The ruling dynastic families in Munster were known as the Éoganachta, descended from Corc of Cashel, a contemporary of Niall of the Nine Hostages. The Éoganachta of Munster, like the Uí Néill, divided into two major divisions, this time between east and west, and these two major branches had their own subdivisions. Connacht takes its name from the Connachta, a tribal group descended from Conn the Hundred-Battler (*Conn Cétchathach*), who is also an ancestor of Niall of the Nine Hostages. The Uí Briúin produced the major dynastic families of Connacht. In Leinster by the early historical period the Uí Cheinnselaig and Uí Dúnlainge were the families that dominated the region, but the major Leinster dynastic families had already passed their peak of influence.

THE VIKING PERIODS

In 795 the first recorded Norse raid took place on Ireland's north coast. This Irish raid came soon after the first attacks in England. Iona was also attacked in 795 and again in 802. In 806 sixty-eight persons were killed at Iona by raiders. In 807 a new monastic community was begun at Kells, Co. Meath, and was completed by 814, by which time much of the administration had been moved from Iona to Kells. It was during this period or immediately before it that the magnificent illuminated manuscript, the *Book of Kells*, was completed.

There are two great periods of Norse activity in Ireland. The first centers on the first four decades of the ninth century. During this period the incursion consisted primarily of hit-and-run raids conducted by fast-moving, seagoing Vikings. In the second half of the ninth century the Norse began establishing permanent settlements that eventually became important commercial and trade centers. These include modern port cities such as Dublin, Wicklow, Wexford, Waterford, Cork, and Limerick. Permanent Norse settlements were more prominent in the southern half of Ireland, in part because of the success of the northern Uí Néill at resisting their incursions.

These Norse cities came to represent small kingdoms within Ireland that traded with, fought against, and in turn allied themselves with Irish kingdoms. By the early decades of the tenth century Irish kingdoms were often as not successful in their struggles against the Norse kingdoms. The Norse kingdoms tended to remain independent of each other and never presented a unified force against the Irish. The Norse in Ireland never controlled large areas the way they did in England, where vast territories came under the Danelaw. In France the entire province of Normandy memorializes the Norse kingdom that was established there and which eventually came to exert power over much of western Europe, including Ireland.

The Battle of Clontarf (1014) has often been presented as the defeat of the Viking invaders by the Irish king Brian Boru. But, in fact, the battle represents the successful dynastic wars of the Uí Briain/O'Brien descendants of Brian Boru of Munster in their rise to supremacy and reveals Norse and Irish kingdoms allied with and against each other. The Uí Briain were allied with the Norse of Limerick against the Norse of Dublin and their Irish allies from Leinster. While Brian Boru's victory (he was killed in the battle) may have marked the gradual demise of the Norse kingdom in Dublin, its real significance was the rise of the Uí Briain dynasts of Munster. With the decline of the Norse kingdoms we can recognize the outlines of modern Ireland emerging as the trading cities founded by the Norse continued to thrive.

SEE ALSO Brehon Law; Church Reform; Hagiography; Hiberno-Latin Culture; Kings and Kingdoms from 400 to 800 C.E.; Latin and Old Irish Literacy; Monasticism in the Early Middle Ages; Norse Settlement; Religion: The Coming of Christianity; **Primary Documents:** "To Mary and Her Son" (c. 750); "The Vikings" (Early Ninth Century); "Writing out of Doors" (Early Ninth Century)

Bibliography

Anderson, Alan Orr, and Marjorie Ogilvie Anderson, eds. and trans. *Adomnán's Life of Columba.* 1961. Revised, 1991.

Bieler, Ludwig, ed. *The Patrician Texts in the Book of Armagh.* 1979.

Byrne, Francis John. *Irish Kings and High-Kings.* 1973. Revised, 2001.

Charles-Edwards, T. M. *Early Christian Ireland.* 2000.

Clancy, Thomas Owen, and Gilbert Márkus, OP. *Iona: The Earliest Poetry of a Celtic Monastery.* 1995.

Colgrave, Bertram, and R. A. B. Mynors, eds. *Bede's Ecclesiastical History of the English People.* 1969.

De Paor, Liam. *Saint Patrick's World: The Christian Culture of Ireland's Apostolic Age.* 1993. Reprint, 1996.

Edwards, Nancy. *Archaeology of Early Medieval Ireland.* 1990.

Flower, Robin. *The Irish Tradition.* 1947. Reprint, 1994.

Hughes, Kathleen. *The Church in Early Irish Society.* 1966.

Hughes, Kathleen. *Early Christian Ireland: Introduction to the Sources.* 1972.

Kelly, Fergus. *A Guide to Early Irish Law.* 1988.

Kenney, James F. *The Sources for the Early History of Ireland: Ecclesiastical, An Introduction and Guide.* 1929. Reprinted, 1993.

Lapidge, Michael, and Richard Sharpe. *A Bibliography of Celtic-Latin Literature, 400–1200.* 1985.

Ó Cróinín, Dáibhí. *Early Medieval Ireland, 400–1200.* 1995.

O'Loughlin, Thomas. *Celtic Theology: Humanity, World, and God in Early Irish Writing.* 2000.

Richter, Michael. *Medieval Ireland: The Enduring Tradition.* 1988.

Ryan, John. *Irish Monasticism: Origins and Early Development.* 1931. 2d edition, 1972. Reprint, 1992.

Sharpe, Richard, trans. *Life of St. Columba.* 1995.

Sherley-Price, Leo, trans. *Ecclesiastical History of the English People.* 1955. Revised, 1990.

Smyth, Alfred P. *Scandinavian York and Dublin: The History and Archaeology of Two Related Viking Kingdoms.* 1975–1979.

Walker, G. S. M., ed. *Sancti Columbani Opera.* 1957. Reprinted, 1970.

Williams, J. E. Caerwyn, and Patrick K. Ford. *The Irish Literary Tradition.* 1992.

Colin A. Ireland

Economic Development, 1958

Completed in May 1958, *Economic Development* was a 250-page study of the Irish economy initiated and supervised by T. K. Whitaker, who had been appointed secretary of the Department of Finance in May 1956. The work was framed by the social and economic crises of the mid-1950s, which saw emigration from the country exceed 45,000 per annum—75 percent of the birth rate. Ireland had remained removed from the economic boom enjoyed across Western Europe and the United States, as total employment in the country fell by 12 percent between 1950 and 1958 and the volume of GNP increased by just 6.5 percent. As a further backdrop to Ireland's economic stagnation, increased acceptance of the potential of economic planning among the country's political elite, as well as the moves toward freer trade between countries evidenced by the development of the Common Market, challenged the traditional assumptions on which the Irish economy was operated. In light of these internal and external pressures, and an emerging consensus that economic change was necessary, in the early months of 1957 Whitaker assembled a team that worked in small groups finalizing sections of the study under the coordination of Charlie Murray, an official from the Taoiseach's Department. Following the release of the May 1958 draft, *Economic Development* was amended to reflect departmental and governmental contributions in the intervening months, then formed the core of the white paper titled *Programme for Economic Expansion* published in November 1958.

Intended as a blueprint for the economy from 1958 to 1963, the *Programme* again stressed that agriculture should drive the economy, mostly through increased export of cattle and beef. Although considerable insight was offered into existing policies, no formal planning methodology was applied in constructing new ones. The only policy instrument specified for agriculture was the provision of fertilizer subsidies, and the *Programme* largely avoided the recommendation in *Economic Development* that agricultural grants be redirected away from relief of rates toward increased production. Furthermore, agriculture was to receive only 14 million of the £53.4 million investment promised in the *Programme*. Ultimately, agricultural growth was exceptionally slow, and the net-output index increased by merely 1.6 percent between 1957 and 1963, despite the fact that 1957 was an extremely depressed year. Crucially, industry easily exceeded the modest goals set for it. Better access to loans and the courting of foreign investment, as well as improved grants to new industries and tax relief for manufactured exports, facilitated major advances in the industrial sector, which were largely responsible for overall economic growth of 23 percent through the duration of the *Programme*. By 1965, 80 percent of all investment came from foreign capital, and through the 1960s, 350 new foreign companies were established in Ireland. While *Economic Development* was not quite the revolutionary document that its most enthusiastic supporters claimed, it nonetheless played a significant role in redirecting the Irish economy toward a more industrial path.

SEE ALSO Agriculture: After World War I; Economies of Ireland, North and South, since 1920; Investment and Development Agency (IDA Ireland); **Primary Documents:** From *Economic Development* (1958)

Bibliography

Daly, Mary E. *Social and Economic History of Ireland since 1800.* 1981.

Fanning, Ronan. *The Irish Department of Finance.* 1978.

Kennedy, Kieran A., Thomas Giblin, and Deirdre McHugh. *The Economic Development of Ireland in the Twentieth Century.* 1988.

Kennedy, Liam. *The Modern Industrialisation of Ireland, 1940–88.* 1989.

Lee, J. J. *Ireland, 1912–85: Politics and Society.* 1989.

McCarthy, John F., ed. *Planning Ireland's Future: The Legacy of T. K. Whitaker.* 1990.

Rouse, Paul. *Ireland's Own Soil: Government and Agriculture in Ireland, 1945–65.* 2000.

Paul Rouse

Economic Relations between Independent Ireland and Britain

Ireland won its independence armed with the strong conviction that its poverty relative to Britain and its failure to develop were largely the fault of its colonial master. The common belief was that free trade with a powerful Britain meant that any emerging Irish-owned industry would be swiftly overwhelmed by the superior firepower of British industry, while integration in the U.K. fiscal system meant that Ireland paid a disproportionate share of tax relative to its meager resources. In any conflict of interest between Ireland and Britain, precedence would always be given to Britain. Some pushed the argument even further: a British government had no particular wish to see Ireland develop and compete with its own industry—a poor Ireland, supplying cheap food and plentiful labor to the cities of England, suited England just fine. Against this background it was not surprising that the new Irish government had support for proactive programs to assist domestic industry against U.K. competitors and also to build up a physical infrastructure (such as an electricity network) to complement it. The restraining factor was that Irish exports remained heavily dependent on the U.K. market: 83 percent went to Britain and 14 percent to Northern Ireland.

PROTECTION AND THE ANGLO-IRISH ECONOMIC WAR

By closing off the possibilities of emigration to the United States and the United Kingdom, the Great Depression of the late 1920s and 1930s accentuated the pressure on the Irish government to find ways of employing people at home. Export markets were becoming increasingly difficult to access, so attention focused on the domestic market. Economic policy changed toward the espousal of full-blooded protection. High, often prohibitive, import barriers were imposed across a wide range of industrial goods, accompanied by measures to restrict foreign investment so that the new import-competing industries would be the breeding ground for a new cadre of Irish entrepreneurs. Given the importance of the Irish market to Britain, the change in policy orientation had unfavorable repercussions for many British exporters. Around this time the Irish government decided to withhold payment of the land annuities due to the British government for landholdings purchased prior to independence. This action was met with retaliation in the form of duties on Irish food exports to the United Kingdom. Ireland retaliated in turn with restrictions on coal, steel, cement, and other imports from Britain. There followed a round of tit-for-tat measures that led to a severe depression in Irish agricultural prices, a fall in British exports to Ireland, and a general severe deterioration in Anglo-Irish relations.

The "Economic War" came to an end in 1938 with the signing of a trade agreement that involved considerable generosity on the part of Britain. After that, more normal economic relations were restored insofar as one can think of anything being normal during the Second World War. Reviewing this episode in Irish economic history, scholars have come to the rather surprising conclusion that the Anglo-Irish trade war might not have been such a bad thing for the economy. To be sure, some sectors of the economy suffered severe losses, but the overall economy benefited from a gain in the terms of trade (that is, import prices fell more than Irish export prices) and from an expansion in employment.

POSTWAR DOLDRUMS

Ireland's immediate postwar economic performance was extremely poor, and this was reflected in high emigration, unemployment, and depressed living standards. The British economy also experienced difficulties, especially in comparison with its continental neighbors. Given Ireland's heavy export dependence on the U.K. market, there was an inevitable negative spillover effect, and a slow-growing British industry was unable to generate much investment abroad even if it had been made welcome. Britain's determination to keep food prices down, a logical policy for a net food importer, was also bad news for a net exporter like Ireland. Thus, to some extent, Ireland's poor growth could be attributed to its more powerful neighbor's different priorities and different economic performance. It was tempting to revert to the old culture of blaming slow-growing Britain for Ireland's economic woes. But Britain was only partly to blame, as a landmark report, *Economic Development* by T. K. Whitaker, then secretary of the Department of Finance, demonstrated in 1958. Ireland's inward-looking approach to economic development, with its emphasis on isolating the domestic market from foreign competition, worked well at first but rapidly encountered diminishing returns. There was a limit to how much growth could be achieved through focusing on the domestic market. Also, as the Whitaker report implied and as subsequent experience would demonstrate, a small country can buck the trend set by even the largest economic neighbor. These considerations led to a root-and-branch reappraisal of Irish economic policy that culminated in a shift from inward-looking to outward-looking policies, the dismantling of protection, and the reversal of policy from restrictions to incentives to inward foreign investment.

THE EUROPEAN COMMUNITY—AN ALTERNATIVE PARTNER

Membership in the European Economic Community (EEC) pointed to an eagerly grasped resolution to Ireland's dilemma. Unlike the United Kingdom, the European Community favored agriculture with higher than world prices, and any new member could participate in the new regime. Its economy was also dynamic; German industry in particular was strong and was ready to invest in Ireland given the right conditions. The promise of guaranteed access to the European market would also, it was hoped, prove attractive to U.S. investors. Britain's simultaneous application made the decision to apply for membership all that much easier. There were some dissenting voices, fearful of job losses in protected industries, and many believed that the Irish government's willingness to join even without Britain was overly ambitious. Perhaps fortunately for Ireland, both countries were turned down in 1963 following objections from France's president, Charles de Gaulle.

In order to maintain the momentum of trade liberalization the Irish government reduced protection unilaterally in two 10-percentage-point steps in the early 1960s and then capped this with a comprehensive trade agreement with Britain that came into effect in 1966. The Anglo-Irish Free Trade Area Agreement (AIFTA) had features similar to those of numerous agreements that fill the trade-negotiation landscape today. Trade barriers were abolished on most industrial goods over a ten-year transition period. There were exceptions for sensitive industries, and liberalization of trade in agricultural produce was tentative and took the form of individual product arrangements, most often subject to quotas. In a study of the economics of the 1966 agreement McAleese and Martin (1971) concluded that the balance of advantage was fairly evenly spread. Irish industry, the study predicted, would lose some jobs, but more would be generated in export industries, and there would be gains for the farm sector. Clearly, however, the AIFTA was a staging post on the way to a renewed application for membership in the EEC, which eventually was accepted in 1973. This was the big prize, long sought and gratefully received by the Irish voters: 83 percent of the electorate voted "yes" to membership in the national referendum in 1972.

ANGLO-IRISH RELATIONS AT PRESENT

At the time of independence more than 90 percent of Ireland's trade was with Britain. By the end of the 1980s it had fallen considerably, to 37 percent, and at the turn of this century the U.K. market accounted for only 22 percent of Irish exports and 32 percent of imports. Measured by trade flows, there has been a remarkable and sustained de-linking of the two economies. Equally striking is the diminished role of U.K. investors in the Irish economy. The United States is by far the dominant investor in the manufacturing sector, and there has been a substantial influx of investment from the Continent. The link with sterling was broken in 1979, much to the relief of the Irish authorities, since sterling's role as an anchor of price stability had been undermined by high U.K. inflation rates during the 1970s (the rate reached 24 percent in 1974). The break with sterling was further sealed when the Irish government adopted the Euro, notwithstanding the United Kingdom's abstention.

However, the United Kingdom remains an important influence on Ireland's economy. U.K. subsidiaries are still highly visible in the retail sector. London continues to act as a powerful magnet and a congenial host for many Irish people in search of employment, higher education, or simply new horizons. Ireland continues to import economic-policy ideas from England. Prime Minister Margaret Thatcher's regime, though not warmly admired in Ireland, nonetheless had a powerful impact on the conduct of industrial relations and on attitudes to government spending. One could go further and suggest that the adoption of these policies played a large role in creating the 1990's Celtic Tiger economy.

Although Ireland joined the Euro area without Britain, it is clear that the new currency will not deliver all its potential benefits to the Irish economy as long as a trade partner of Britain's importance stays aloof. Paradoxically, after being the sick man of Europe for much of the postwar period, Britain has now become something of an economic star relative to slow-growing economies of continental Europe. Northern Ireland may also experience a resurgence as peace becomes more firmly entrenched. The long, steady trend toward greater de-linking of the two economies may be coming to an end and some reversal might even be in store.

At the turn of the twenty-first century Ireland's living standards are equal to Britain's, something few ever imagined possible, and mass emigration to British cities has come to an end. Ireland's export markets are becoming more and more diversified, and economic dependence on the United Kingdom is a thing of the past. Together and in friendship the peoples of Britain and Ireland seek to maintain economic prosperity in the context of a vastly more globalized world, where nothing is certain to last and where both of their economies seem very small indeed.

SEE ALSO Anglo-Irish Agreement of 1985 (Hillsborough Agreement); Economic Relations between North and South since 1922; Economic Relations between Northern Ireland and Britain; Irish Pound; Economies of Ireland, North and South, since 1920; Industry since 1920; Lemass, Seán; **Primary Documents:** From *Economic Development* (1958); Speech to Ministers of the Governments of the Member States of the European Economic Community (18 January 1962)

Bibliography

Drudy, P. J. "Migration between Ireland and Britain since Independence." In *Ireland and Britain since 1922*, edited by P. J. Drudy. 1986.

McAleese, Dermot, and John Martin. *Irish Manufactured Imports from the UK in the Sixties: The Effects of AIFTA.* 1973.

McAleese, Dermot. "Political Independence and Economic Performance: Ireland Outside the U.K." In *The Economics of Devolution: Proceedings of Section F of the British Association for the Advancement of Science*, edited by Edward Nevin. 1977.

McAleese, Dermot. "Anglo Irish Interdependence: Effects of Post-1979 Changes in the British Economy on Ireland." *Irish Banking Review* (spring 1986): 3–16.

McAleese, Dermot. "Anglo Irish Interdependence: From Excessive Intimacy to a Wider Embrace." In *Ireland and Britain since 1922*, edited by P. J. Drudy. 1986.

McAleese, Dermot, and Michael Gallagher. "Developments in Irish Trade in the 1980s." *Irish Banking Review* (autumn 1991): 3–18.

Neary, J. P., and C. Ó Gráda. "Protection, Economic War, and Structural Change: The 1930s in Ireland." *Irish Historical Studies* 27 (May 1991): 250–266.

Dermot McAleese

Economic Relations between North and South since 1922

The political partition of Ireland, effected by the Government of Ireland Act of 1920, had a grave impact on economic life across the island of Ireland, particularly in border areas. A cold war began in 1920 between the Dublin and Belfast governments that ensured that cross-border trade was slow to develop. Partition was never meant to be economic, but it led to towns such as Derry, Enniskillen, Sligo, Clones, Dundalk, and Newry losing important sections of their economic hinterlands. Dublin's policy of a "Belfast Boycott" between 1920 and 1922 did little to help this situation, and economic partition became a reality on 1 April 1923 when the Irish Free State government imposed a customs barrier around Northern Ireland. Though the economic protectionism of successive southern governments enhanced economic partition, limited cross-border trade continued. The balance of trade between North and South remained in the South's favor from 1924, except between 1944 and 1946, when southern exports dried up during the Second World War.

While trade relations between North and South remained poor in the postwar years, economic contact in other areas developed. During and immediately after the Second World War North and South cooperated to construct a hydroelectric power station on the River Erne, though the supply went solely to the South. In the early 1950s Dublin and Belfast combined forces to prop up the ailing Great Northern Railway, which linked Dublin with Belfast and Derry. Though the joint operation agreement ended in 1958, close cooperation between transport companies on both sides of the border continued over the Dublin-to-Belfast railway. The most successful form of cross-border economic cooperation came with the 1952 establishment of the Foyle Fisheries Commission, which, following protracted legal wrangling over fishing rights in the lough situated between Derry and Donegal, put fish stocks and their development in the Lough Foyle catchment area under the control of an independent cross-border body.

In the late 1950s calls were made for North-South economic cooperation through the relaxation of cross-border tariffs. From 1954 to 1958 northern imports from the South had increased from £16.3 million to £20.4 million, and northern exports to the South increased from £2.9 million to £8.4 million (Kennedy 1997). Northern manufacturers, finding southern imports eroding their home markets, were interested in improving their exports across the border. They did not receive support from the Stormont government, which felt that supporting cross-border free trade would have dangerous political consequences. By the time that Seán Lemass became taoiseach of the Republic in June 1959, northern manufacturers had begun to lobby Dublin to develop cross-border trade. Lemass sought to remove duties on northern exports to the Republic in order to create a level playing field for exporters on both sides of the border. He had two agendas: in the shorter term he hoped that the removal of tariffs would prepare the way for the Republic's entry into the European Economic Community (EEC); in the longer term he hoped that an improvement in cross-border trade could lead to Irish unity. Dublin began to remove the tariffs on selected imports from Northern Ireland in September 1962. The Northern Ireland government refused to take part in the process, though the British government welcomed the move. Further concessions followed in 1962 and 1963. Northern Irish manufacturers traveled to Dublin in increasing numbers to seek further concessions; secretly, the Northern Ireland government supported them.

Following France's veto of Britain and Ireland's application for EEC membership in January 1963, Dublin and London began talks that would lead to an Anglo-Irish free-trade area. Northern Irish ministers were worried that these developments would swamp northern agricultural exports to Britain with southern Irish produce. Belfast followed the Anglo-Irish trade negotiations in London, always seeking to protect Northern Ireland's agricultural base, but had little influence over British negotiators.

North-South economic contact gained real meaning after the meetings in January and February 1965 between Sean Lemass and Northern Ireland Prime Minister Terence O'Neill. Further ministerial-level meetings set the agenda for a fruitful period of North-South cooperation from 1965 to the outbreak of the Troubles in 1969. In January 1966 the northern and southern Irish tourist boards joined forces to promote Ireland to Britain and North America. Following an agreement signed in 1967, a cross-border electricity interconnector came into operation in 1969, but it never lived up to its full potential in the energy-starved 1970s and was destroyed in a terrorist attack in 1975.

After the Lemass-O'Neill meetings, the trading relationship between North and South became enmeshed in the Anglo-Irish free-trade area talks. Northern Ireland was covered in a side-document to the Anglo-Irish Trade Agreement of December 1965, which allowed accelerated tariff reduction in favor of Northern Ireland goods exported to the Republic. Commentaries on the agreement predicted the gradual re-opening of markets closed in the 1920s, and it was expected that this agreement would benefit mainly Northern Ireland industries. In a remarkable turnaround by the Northern Ireland government, Brian Faulkner, the Northern Ireland minister of commerce, welcomed the agreement. By the late 1960s the volume of trade across the border had increased significantly, though it was still a small percentage of the overall international trade of both Northern Ireland and the Republic of Ireland. In 1960 the Irish Republic's imports from Northern Ireland were valued at £7.4 million, and exports were valued at £20.3 million. By 1970 the respective figures were £29.9 million and £57.2 million (Kennedy 1997). The Troubles ended much of the direct intergovernmental cooperation between North and South, but civil-service-level contacts continued. North-South tourism also declined because of the Troubles, a sign that many of the spinoff contacts arising from intergovernmental cooperation had ended.

Cross-border trade continued to develop as part of the overall increase in international trade of North and South. In 1983 annual exports from the South to the North were reaching £500 million, and imports from the North £312 million. By 1995 the relevant figures were £789 million and £645 million respectively as cross-border trade edged towards parity, but by the late 1990s they were again turning in favor of the South (Kennedy 1997). The terrorist cease-fires of the mid-1990s and the Good Friday Agreement of 1998 led to greater North-South economic contact, though fluctuations between the British sterling pound and the Irish punt were a restraining force.

The Good Friday Agreement contains cross-border implementation bodies that have a direct impact on North-South economic relations. They cover inland waterways, food safety, trade and business, special European Union programs, language promotion (Ulster Scots and Irish), and mariculture and aquaculture in a body known as the Foyle, Carlingford, and Irish Lights Commission, which includes the work of the Foyle Fisheries Commission. All-Ireland tourism is also promoted. Electricity interconnection has existed since the 1990s, and in the autumn of 2001, agreement was reached on a cross-border gas link. The climate created by the "peace process" and the Good Friday Agreement has significantly improved North-South economic relations; at the very least, they have contributed to a situation where the populations on both sides of the border come into greater contact in everyday life.

SEE ALSO Agriculture: After World War I; Economic Relations between Independent Ireland and Britain; Economic Relations between Northern Ireland and Britain; Economies of Ireland, North and South, since 1920; Faulkner, Brian; Industry since 1920; Irish Pound; Lemass, Seán; Northern Ireland: Constitutional Settlement from Sunningdale to Good Friday; Northern Ireland: History since 1920; O'Neill, Terence; **Primary Documents:** The Belfast/Good Friday Agreement (10 April 1998)

Bibliography

Kennedy, Dennis. *The Widening Gulf.* 1988.

Kennedy, Michael. "Towards Co-operation: Seán Lemass and North-South Economic Relations, 1956–1965." *Irish Economic and Social History* 24 (1997): 42–61.

Kennedy, Michael. *Division and Consensus: The Politics of Cross-Border Relations in Ireland, 1925 to 1969.* 2000.

O'Halloran, Clare. *Partition and the Limits of Irish Nationalism.* 1987.

Michael Kennedy

Economic Relations between Northern Ireland and Britain

Before partition in 1922 the Irish economy had been fully integrated into the U.K. fiscal and monetary system since the Act of Union in 1801. After partition, under the Government of Ireland Act of 1920, Northern Ireland was governed by a local parliament at Stormont. However, policy continued effectively to be fully integrated within U.K. structures. The main change was that economic and financial legislation enacted at Westminster usually needed to be transmitted to Northern Ireland through enabling acts of its local parliament. A wide range of trade, fiscal, and monetary policies were "excepted" or "reserved" and were framed by Westminster. In all matters concerning public expenditure there was close supervision and control by the U.K. treasury (Birrell and Murie 1980).

Given the industrial strength of the Northern Ireland economy in the immediate aftermath of the First World War, it had never been envisaged that the newly devolved region would become dependent on outside subvention. Indeed, there had been an expectation that Northern Ireland would make a net financial contribution toward the cost of imperial services (Wilson 1989). That this did not occur was due mainly to the collapse of the Northern Ireland industrial sector during the 1920s and 1930s. The quality of public services in the North was initially inferior to that in Britain, and the gap was difficult to close because the North was required to be generally self-sufficient at a time when its main industrial bases—shipbuilding and linen—suffered serious decline. It was not until 1946 that there was a commitment to parity of services and taxation between Great Britain and Northern Ireland.

The major pressure on public expenditure in Northern Ireland came from the growth of the U.K. welfare state. In a context where tax rates, social-insurance contributions, and social-welfare benefits were equalized within the United Kingdom, expenditure in excess of local tax revenue in Northern Ireland was driven by greater local needs. However, it was not until the mid-1960s that public expenditure per head in Northern Ireland equalled that in England, and only in the early 1980s (after the abolition of the Stormont parliament) did it exceed the level in Scotland and Wales (Wilson 1989).

The decline of Northern manufacturing from a historically high level mirrored the more general U.K. process of deindustrialization, but was exacerbated by the outbreak of civil unrest in the late 1960s and the abolition of Stormont in 1972. The imposition of direct rule led to efforts to improve social and economic conditions in the North, and the expansion of the public sector offset the decline of private-sector activity. By the mid-1990s the external subvention had reached nearly one-third of GDP (Bradley 1998).

Today there are structural weaknesses in the economy of Northern Ireland, and these problems are moving toward center stage in the aftermath of the restoration of devolved government under the Belfast Agreement of 1998 (Heath et al. 1999). There is a continued dependence on traditional sectors such as textiles, clothing, and shipbuilding, which are particularly vulnerable to low-cost competition. Insufficient education exacerbates low productivity and high structural unemployment. A dependence on public assistance has emerged as a consequence of an inability to attract foreign direct investment in sufficient quantity to offset the decline in traditional domestic industry. The problems are aggravated by the disruption of civil unrest, together with collateral problems of labor-market segmentation and discrimination.

Difficulties experienced by policymakers as they tackle these problems can be traced to the very limited degree of policy autonomy within Northern Ireland, which effectively prevents appropriate region-specific policy variations from national U.K. norms. Within the new devolved administration in Belfast, social and economic policies are still set mainly according to U.K. standards, but a discretionary pattern of public expenditure can be set within the overall block grant received from London, and this has been used in the design of generous subsidy-based industrial incentives. Nevertheless, the fact remains that policy norms in the North are designed with the wider United Kingdom in mind. While the subvention assistance can be used to design and operate beneficial policies to address Northern Ireland's structural problems, some of these problems may originate in the first place from the application of U.K.-wide policies to Northern Ireland (Dunford and Hudson 1996; NIEC 1996; Bradley 1998).

The United Kingdom is a highly centralized state and has devolved only limited powers of economic governance to its regions. The recent devolution for Northern Ireland has relaxed the degree of centralization only to a modest extent. Economic success depends increasingly on the ability to mobilize regional resources and policymaking powers to improve competitive performance. Without such devolved powers Northern Ireland is at a severe disadvantage relative to regions that have extensive devolved or federal policymaking structures and are prepared to use them creatively.

SEE ALSO Agriculture: After World War I; Economic Relations between Independent Ireland and Britain; Economic Relations between North and South since 1922; Economies of Ireland, North and South, since 1920; Industry since 1920; Northern Ireland: History since 1920; **Primary Documents:** "Ulster at the Crossroads" (9 December 1968); The Belfast/Good Friday Agreement (10 April 1998)

Bibliography

Birrell, Derek, and Alan Murie. *Policy and Government in Northern Ireland: Lessons of Devolution.* 1980.

Bradley, John, ed. *Regional Economic and Policy Impacts of EMU: The Case of Northern Ireland.* Research Monograph 6. 1998.

Dunford, Michael, and Ray Hudson. *Successful European Regions: Northern Ireland Learning from Others.* 1996.

Heath, Anthony F., Richard Breen, and Christopher T. Whelan, eds. *Ireland North and South: Perspectives from Social Science.* 1999.

Northern Ireland Economic Council (NIEC). *Decentralised Government and Economic Performance in Northern Ireland.* Occasional Paper 7. 1996.

Wilson, Tom. *Ulster: Conflict and Consent.* 1989.

John Bradley

Economies of Ireland, North and South, since 1920

When Ireland was partitioned in 1921, the combined population of the two parts was 4,354,000, of which 3,096,000 were located in the South. With a total land area of 32,000 square miles, the population density was comparatively low—137 persons per square mile compared with almost 500 in Great Britain. The North was the more heavily populated part with nearly 30 percent of the island's population but only one-fifth of its land area. The most striking fact about the Irish population in 1921, however, was that it was little more than half the level of eighty years earlier. The decline in population dated from the Great Famine of 1845, during which more than one million people died. In the course of the famine and its immediate aftermath, about two million persons emigrated, and four million more left the country in the seventy years from 1852 to 1921. The average standard of living in Ireland in the early 1920s was much lower than in Britain—approximately three-fifths of the British level—and it was about 10 percent higher in the North than in the South.

THE PERIOD 1920–1960

Prior to independence there were great hopes that political autonomy would facilitate economic development,

leading to an end to emigration. As it happened, progress in the South proved to be slow and difficult until the 1960s. In the absence of sufficient job opportunities at home, substantial emigration continued and the population of the South went on declining until 1961. Neither was there any progress in this period in closing the gap in living standards compared with the United Kingdom.

This poor rate of progress may seem surprising given that the new Irish state began with inherited advantages not possessed in the same degree at the time by many of the European countries that later outpaced it. The country was no longer overpopulated; it had no national debt and possessed substantial external capital reserves; there was an extensive rail network; the banking system was widely spread; communications were satisfactory by contemporary standards; and education levels were not inferior to those generally prevailing elsewhere.

Yet the South also suffered from certain limitations that made development difficult in the world economic climate between the two World Wars and during the Second World War. The severe fall in world agricultural prices after World War I and the subsequent long-term downward trend was bound to adversely affect the South, where agriculture employed over half the labor force and accounted for almost 90 percent of goods exports. The widespread resort to agricultural protectionism in the 1930s restricted market access almost exclusively to the United Kingdom, where the indigenous farmers were subsidized in a way that kept prices low. The South made matters worse for its own agriculture in the 1930s on the U.K. market by engaging in a trade war commonly known as the "Economic War" and based on a dispute between the two governments about land-annuity payments. Even apart from this, conditions were never for long conducive to a strong agricultural performance prior to accession to the European Community in 1973.

As regards industry, the partition of Ireland deprived the new independent state of the only region with substantial industrial development. Manufacturing in the South accounted for only 10 percent of the labor force, and of this, two-thirds were engaged in processing of food and drink. A big drive to develop industry might have been expected, especially given that the need for industrialization featured strongly in the nationalist philosophy leading up to independence. In the first decade of independence, however, the new government took the view that the overall prosperity of the economy depended on agriculture, and economic policy concentrated primarily on raising the efficiency of that sector. The use of protectionism to develop new manufacturing activities was limited because of the adverse impact on agricultural costs.

The change of government in 1932 brought a switch from the long-established position of free trade to a radical experiment in protectionism and economic nationalism. Indeed, pressure for change had mounted even before Eamon de Valera took office. By 1931 the worldwide Great Depression, which had begun two years earlier, had taken its toll on Irish agricultural exports. The tightening of U.S. immigration laws and reduced job opportunities abroad had led to a fall in emigration, so the need to create jobs at home was even more urgent. The government had been forced to yield to these pressures in 1931 by restricting the dumping of cheap imports on the Irish market.

The new government in 1932 made widespread use of tariffs, quotas, import licenses, and other such devices to shelter the domestic market from foreign competition, and it also extended state-sponsored bodies in industry and commerce. The high levels of protection persisted until the 1960s. This approach led to sizeable increases in manufacturing output and employment in the 1930s, but had little further momentum after the Second World War once the immediate postwar recovery ended. Although manufacturing employment had doubled by then, the initial base was so low that this increase was quite insufficient for Ireland's employment needs, and there was little further progress during the 1950s. The chief benefit of protection was that it led to the establishment of many firms that would not have existed without it. Indeed, in the troubled world economic conditions of the 1930s it is doubtful if any other approach would have achieved as much. Nevertheless, the hasty and indiscriminate application of the strategy resulted in an industrial base that was weak and vulnerable.

During the Second World War the shortage of imported supplies dispelled all notions of economic development and the paramount need was to secure basic necessities. Even as late as 1950 the degree of trade dependence on the United Kingdom had not been reduced, and nearly 90 percent of exports went to that market. Neither had the composition of exports been much altered—live animals and food still comprised more than three-quarters of the total. The 1930s and 1940s were not auspicious times for increasing the scale or diversifying the destination and composition of trade, even if Irish policy had been directed more effectively toward that goal. The growth rate of real GDP in Western Europe from 1913 to 1950 was only 1.2 percent per annum, and the total volume of merchandise exports in 1950 was less than in 1913.

In the 1950s, when the Western world moved toward restoring free trade, the limits of the protectionist strategy were gradually recognized in Ireland. A new outward-oriented strategy began to emerge, but at a pace too slow to make any impact in providing jobs for the large numbers leaving agriculture, so the 1950s became a decade of high emigration and great economic gloom about the future of the country. The slow progress in moving to an export-oriented strategy is apparent in the fact that the volume of merchandise exports did not regain the prewar peak until 1960—long after most West European countries had recovered from an even greater decline in trade during the Second World War.

Northern Ireland did not fare well either in the interval between the First and Second World Wars. The North was the only part of Ireland to have experienced an industrial revolution in the nineteenth century. When the country was partitioned, there were more manufacturing workers in the North, even though its population was less than half that of the South. Manufactured goods accounted for two-thirds of the North's exports. The major manufacturing industries of Northern Ireland—linen and shipbuilding—depended almost entirely on sales outside the area, however, and were highly exposed and vulnerable to fluctuations. Linen was also adversely affected by long-term changes in consumer tastes and habits. Its critical U.S. market was severely damaged by the Great Depression, and the industry never recovered fully again in Northern Ireland.

Shipbuilding was also badly affected by the Great Depression, which led to worldwide overcapacity in shipping, intense competition, and weak markets for new ships. A stay of execution was granted to the Belfast shipyards by the Second World War, which brought booming demand for new ships and repair work—a demand that was well maintained in the early postwar years. In fact, unlike its impact on the South, the war's effect on the economy of the North was highly beneficial. Subsequently, however, shipbuilding in Northern Ireland shared in the long-term decline of the industry in the United Kingdom. Competition from low-cost countries and unstable demand were at the root of the decline, but these forces were aided and abetted by poor management.

Agriculture in Northern Ireland enjoyed more favorable access to the British market in the 1930s when trade barriers developed, and this advantage continued until the 1960s, when the South negotiated improved access to the British market. But agriculture was much less significant to the overall economy in the North than in the South. In both areas the economy as a whole fell behind Britain in the period from 1920 up to the Second

World War—in terms of the growth of total output and output per head of population. Wartime demand in Britain for ships and other manufactured goods led to boom conditions in Northern Ireland, which gained substantially during the Second World War relative to the South and to Britain. In the postwar period up to 1960 the growth of income per capita in both areas of Ireland kept pace with that in Britain, but in the South only because of massive emigration and significant population decline. Population in the North had largely ceased to decline in the twenty years before partition, and thereafter it followed an upward trend.

THE PERIOD 1960–1990

The new outward-looking strategy developed gradually in the South during the 1950s and was most fully articulated in 1958 by the then secretary of the Department of Finance, T. K. Whitaker, in the report *Economic Development*. The strategy had three main elements. First, capital grants and tax concessions were provided to encourage export-oriented manufacturing. Second, the Industrial Development Authority was given the task of attracting foreign firms to Ireland, again aimed at exports. And third, protection was gradually dismantled in return for greater access to markets abroad, culminating in an Anglo-Irish Free Trade Area Agreement in 1965 and accession to the European Community in 1973. Great efforts were also made to improve the physical infrastructure—electricity, telephones, roads, and other transport facilities. Perhaps most important of all, even though the benefit took a long time to show up, was the emphasis placed on education in the seminal report *Investment in Education*, completed in 1965 under the chairmanship of Professor Patrick Lynch, which foreshadowed the major expansion in education.

The outward-looking strategy worked well in the buoyant world economic conditions of the 1960s. The strategy began to be questioned, however, following the first oil crisis in 1973. Although a vast increase in manufactured exports had been achieved, most of the increase had come from new foreign-owned enterprises that exported the bulk of their output. Concerns about the high and rising dependence on foreign industry were exacerbated in the 1980s when the flow of foreign investment fell and nearly 10,000 jobs were lost in foreign firms. This highlighted once more the need for indigenous industry, but the situation of the indigenous firms was even worse, owing to the combined effect of import penetration after the elimination of trade barriers and the disturbed economic conditions following the oil crises.

The 1980s were also made difficult by poor macroeconomic-policy decisions and excessive public borrowing in the 1970s, especially by the new 1977 government. The first half of the 1980s would have been difficult anyway because of the repercussions of the second oil crisis, but the South's problems were greatly exacerbated by the struggle to restore order to the public finances—a task that was tackled with the necessary determination only by the government elected in 1987.

In every quinquennium of the period 1960 to 1990 (apart from the first half of the 1980s) the South experienced an average annual GNP growth rate of about 4 percent, but this proved insufficient to make any significant impact on the central problems of surplus labor and relatively low living standards. Population decline had been arrested in 1961, and over the years 1961 to 1986 a significant increase had been achieved, amounting to 25 percent during this period. With the depressed conditions in the 1980s, however, and a renewed surge in emigration in the second half of that decade, population began to fall once again. In 1993 total employment was only just back to the 1980 level after the large fall in the first half of the 1980s, and the 1993 level was still 7 percent below that of the 1920s—an altogether unique experience in contemporary Europe. In terms of living standards, the South had begun to narrow the gap vis-à-vis the United Kingdom, but the record of the United Kingdom was a poor one in comparison with continental West European countries. Accordingly, with the average level of GNP per capita in the South remaining throughout the period 1960 to 1990 in the range of 60 to 65 percent of the average for the European Union, there was no convergence toward European living standards.

In Northern Ireland the government was accorded increased powers to develop industry in the postwar period and took advantage of them to attract external investment in particular. These efforts enjoyed some success until the outbreak of conflict in 1969 hampered efforts to attract investment. On top of the unstable political situation came a series of adverse shocks—the two oil crises, the weakening of U.K. regional policy, and the strengthening of sterling following the exploitation of North Sea oil. Northern Ireland suffered a catastrophic fall in manufacturing employment up to the mid-1980s, followed by an essentially static level. The North is a classic example of an area specialized in a narrow range of activities vulnerable to world market forces. In such a setting industrial survival depends on adapting to higher-value products based on new technologies. Northern Ireland essentially failed to adapt, so it has suffered massive deindustrialization. Its overall growth in GDP per capita in the postwar period up to 1990 just about kept pace with that of the United King-

The giant Intel plant at Leixlip, Co. Kildare. Ireland's success in attracting high-tech firms, such as Intel, has been the key to its recent economic success. COURTESY OF INTEL IRELAND LTD.

dom, so the South, which had been catching up on it since 1960, surpassed the Northern level by the early 1990s. There was never significant economic interdependence between the two parts of Ireland, and a further impediment was introduced in 1979 when the South broke the long-standing link with sterling and joined the European Monetary System.

THE CELTIC TIGER

The extraordinary transformation in the economy of the South in the 1990s has been commonly designated as the "Celtic Tiger." In this phase the South experienced a wholly novel phenomenon of rapid and sustained growth in employment. The rate of employment growth from 1993 to 2000—averaging 4.75 percent per annum—was without precedent in Irish history. As a result, the unemployment rate fell from 16 percent to below 4 percent—close to full employment and less than half the average rate of the European Union nations. Significant net immigration also developed, comprising both returning Irish and inflows of refugees and other foreign immigrants attracted by the buoyant

labor market. The focus of attention in labor-market policy swung from labor surplus to labor scarcity.

The remarkable growth in employment was made possible by a substantial acceleration in the growth rate of the total volume of output to an average of almost 9 percent per annum. The employment boom led to a big increase in the ratio of employment to population, with important consequences for the standard of living. Hitherto, a low employment rate had been a major factor in depressing Irish living standards in comparison with other European countries. That low employment rate stemmed from three historically unfavorable factors: a relatively high proportion of the population in the dependent age groups, a low rate of participation in the labor force (especially by married women), and a high rate of unemployment. Now all three factors moved in a favorable direction. As a result, whereas in 1993 every ten workers had to support, on average, twenty-one dependents (all those not in gainful employment), by 2000 the average number of dependents had been reduced to fourteen for every ten workers.

The acceleration in the growth of output and employment in the Celtic Tiger economy was fueled by an enormous growth in exports. The volume of Irish goods exports rose at the phenomenal rate of 17 percent per annum from 1993 to 2000—a rate that would lead to a doubling of exports every four and one-half years, and more than twice the average rate achieved in the preceding thirty years. Tourist earnings also rose rapidly. By 2000 the South had reached the remarkable situation where its exports of goods and services were nearly as large as its total GDP.

Ireland's success in attracting an increasing and disproportionately large share of U.S. manufacturing investment in Europe, particularly in the area of electronics, was a major factor in boosting exports and output. As a member of the European Union, Ireland had free access to the markets of other member countries following the initiation of the Single European Market in 1992. This, combined with the generous tax incentives available to foreign investors, the sound macroeconomic policies pursued by the government since 1987, and the plentiful supply of well-educated English-speaking labor, made the South an exceptionally attractive and profitable location for U.S. multinationals. The foresight of the Industrial Development Authority in the 1980s in targeting the new high-tech enterprises and its dynamism in marketing Ireland's competitive advantages proved to be important elements. Profitability was enhanced by the social-partnership agreements entered into approximately every three years since 1987 by the government, trade unions, and employer organizations, which helped to secure pay restraint in return for income-tax cuts and to maintain industrial peace.

It would be wrong to think that foreign investment was the only motor driving the Celtic Tiger. Indigenous enterprise also flourished. Indeed, the most striking indicator of the globalization of the South's economy has been the emergence of substantial Irish multinational enterprises. By the end of the 1990s Irish multinationals employed nearly 65,000 persons in the United States. While this figure falls well short of the 100,000 employed in Ireland by U.S. firms, it nevertheless represents a remarkable growth from a negligible level in the mid-1980s.

No Celtic Tiger appeared in Northern Ireland in the 1990s. Nevertheless, the economy performed reasonably satisfactorily. Basically, it kept pace with the U.K. economy, which was doing well at this time relative to mainland European countries. There was a significant increase in employment, and the unemployment rate fell from nearly 14 percent in 1993 to less than 7 percent in 2000. There was no convergence with the United Kingdom in terms of living standards, however—the level of GDP per capita in Northern Ireland remained at about four-fifths of the British level. The South had already converged with the U.K. level of GDP per capita by 1997 and was about 15 percent above it in 2000. It is important to note, however, that GDP per capita overstates average living standards in the South, chiefly because of the large and increasing outflow of profits in multinational enterprises, which do not add to domestic living standards. A better measure is GNP per capita, which excludes net international capital flows, and on this measure the South was at about the same level as the United Kingdom in 2000, which would put it about 25 percent above the corresponding level in the North. A further qualification must be made in comparing living standards of the North with those of the South. Northern Ireland, as a poorer part of a larger and richer country, benefits from net fiscal transfers from the U.K. exchequer. Because incomes are lower, the North pays relatively lower taxes, while it still enjoys much the same level of social benefits as the United Kingdom generally. Using a measure that takes account of the impact of net fiscal transfers, disposable household income per capita, the North is less than 15 percent below the corresponding U.K. level. This still leaves Northern living standards in 2000 a little behind those in the South, though not as far below as the more commonly used figures for GDP/GNP per capita suggest.

While the South has gained on the North in the long run, the North scored better than the South in one significant respect: In 1995 its population had finally regained the immediate prefamine level, whereas the population in the South is still little more than half that of 1841.

SEE ALSO Agriculture: After World War I; Anglo-Irish Free Trade Agreement of 1965; Celtic Tiger; *Economic Development*, 1958; Economic Relations between Independent Ireland and Britain; Economic Relations between North and South since 1922; Economic Relations between Northern Ireland and Britain; Industry since 1920; Irish Pound; Marshall Aid; Overseas Investment; Tourism; Trade Unions; **Primary Documents:** From *Economic Development* (1958)

Bibliography

Barry, Frank, ed. *Understanding Ireland's Economic Growth.* 1999.

Goldthorpe, John H., and Christopher T. Whelan, eds. *The Development of Industrial Society in Ireland.* 1992.

Harris, Richard I. D., Clifford W. Jefferson, and John E. Spencer, eds. *The Northern Ireland Economy: A Comparative Study in the Economic Development of a Peripheral Region.* 1990.

Johnson, David. *The Interwar Economy in Ireland.* 1985.

Kennedy, Kieran A., Thomas Giblin, and Deirdre McHugh. *The Economic Development of Ireland in the Twentieth Century.* 1988.

Kennedy, Liam. *The Modern Industrialisation of Ireland, 1940–1988.* 1989.

Kennedy, Liam, and Philip Ollerenshaw, eds. *An Economic History of Ulster, 1820–1939.* 1985.

Lee, Joseph J. *Ireland, 1912–1985: Politics and Society.* 1989.

MacSharry, Ray, and Padraic White. *The Making of the Celtic Tiger: The Inside Story of Ireland's Boom Economy.* 2000.

Meenan, James F. *The Irish Economy since 1922.* 1970.

Northern Ireland Statistics and Research Agency, and Central Statistics Office. *Ireland North and South: A Statistical Profile.* 2000.

Ó Gráda, Cormac. *Ireland: A New Economic History, 1780–1939.* 1994.

O'Malley, Eoin. *Industry and Economic Development: The Challenge for the Latecomer.* 1989.

Sweeney, Paul. *The Celtic Tiger: Ireland's Economic Miracle Explained.* 1998.

Kieran A. Kennedy

~

Economy and Society from 1500 to 1690

At the beginning of the sixteenth century there existed in Ireland separate Gaelic and English political and cultural communities that, taken together, formed something approaching the modern notion of a collective economy and society in Ireland. Though the latter community claimed lordship over the entire island, its political power by 1500 was concentrated in the fertile eastern region between Dublin and Dundalk (known as the English Pale), east Munster, some fifty scattered port and market towns and their hinterlands, and several isolated outposts in Connacht and Ulster. The remainder of Ireland was dominated by scores of thinly populated independent Gaelic lordships unified by a common language, legal system, and social structures, but devoid of any political or administrative cohesion capable of surmounting traditional regional differences. The largest and most powerful of these lordships were those furthest removed from English areas, such as the O'Neill or O'Brien lordships in Ulster and west Munster respectively. The native Gaelic elite looked upon the English community as *Gaill*, or foreigners, with varying degrees of hostility, while English administrators contemptuously referred to the Gaelic clans living outside the "civility" of the Tudor state as "wild Irish" or the Crown's "Irish enemies." The sixteenth century witnessed the struggle between these two societies for dominance in Ireland.

SEPARATE BUT DEPENDENT ECONOMIES IN SIXTEENTH-CENTURY IRELAND

Markedly different forms of economic organization reinforced Ireland's inherent political and cultural divisions. The Gaelic economy was primarily pastoral in nature, with milk-related products, such as butter and sour curds, forming the staple diet of the population; pigs and especially sheep were raised for additional food. Cultivation of oats and wheat existed in most lordships as a dietary supplement, and corn was regularly harvested in several lordships, but the extent of these practices varied greatly and was dictated by the quality and location of the land. The pattern of earlier English settlement in Ireland meant that Gaelic lordships tended to be located in terrain unconducive to widespread cultivation. Gaelic wealth was more often manifested in cattle (moveable property) than fields, and chiefs amassed vast numbers of four-footed chattel. Cattle, usually small and black, were well-suited to this environment, and the migration of communities from winter grazing lands to summer pasture, referred to as "booleying," was common in the purely Gaelic areas of Connacht and Ulster. This, coupled with a natural aversion to nucleated settlement, lent an impermanence or transience to Gaelic society that was often mistaken for nomadism by outside observers. Commercial activity was limited by the absence of a widely circulated native coinage, and with few Gaelic urban centers or sizeable port towns available to export surpluses, trade remained generally localized. Gaelic society, moreover, did not produce an identifiable merchant class, and the responsibility for trade was left to chiefs who rarely built their own ships and relied instead on the English infrastructure to carry their goods over long distances.

By contrast, the English economy at the same time was founded on a system of extensive tillage in which the town was the principal economic outlet for agrarian surpluses, mainly wheat and barley, produced in its hinterland. English areas of Ireland normally employed a three-crop rotation system: two fields in use in the growing season and the third left fallow. All towns held annual fairs with the purpose of selling their goods and attracting commerce, but it was the older quasi-autonomous, walled port towns, of which Dublin and Waterford were the largest, that fostered regular trading links abroad. Although Dublin was Ireland's most prosperous trading town, earning mainly through its trade with England about £80,000 annually, commercial traffic was distributed among over a half-dozen of these port towns. The southern and western ports—Waterford, Cork, and Galway—exported fish, beef, tallow, and animal hides to the Iberian peninsula and France, where wine, iron, salt, and other luxury goods were purchased to be sold in Bristol. Commerce, both internal and external, was further facilitated by the ready availability of specie: a mint in Dublin produced native coins in the king's name until its closure in about 1506; afterward, the English community imported its coinage from England. Barter was not uncommon, especially in areas removed from urban centers. Taken together, the independent economies of the counties and towns underpinned English society and government in Ireland. But the settled conditions implicit in this decentralized economic organization also forced English areas to adopt a defensive posture against neighboring Gaelic clans, whose tendency to prey upon the wealth of English settlements was long established. Thus the different forms of economic organization contributed to the development of a siege mentality among the English, who regularly erected physical barriers—castles, towers, and ditches—in an effort to protect their property from their Gaelic neighbors.

Yet these ostensibly separate economies were in fact linked. Neither Gaelic resentment of the upstart *Gaill*, nor repeated English legal measures prohibiting Englishmen from interacting with the Gaelic population, entirely succeeded in keeping these neighboring societies apart. Economic forces in sixteenth-century Ireland made commercial as well as cultural interaction unavoidable and led to a symbiotic relationship. The declining English population during the fifteenth century created a labor shortage on farmlands, and a greater proportion of Gaelic peasants were thus attracted to English areas to replace English tenants. This inroad into the lower levels of English agrarian society strengthened Gaelic customs and language in areas hitherto dominated by English culture, while concurrently introducing English agricultural methods to the Gaelic population. Overseas demand for animal products (such as skins, hides, and wool) and the lucrative taxes they yielded, united the English government, the port towns, and the Gaelic hinterland in a common economic interest. Similarly, demand for timber and other raw materials in English areas formed an important internal export from Gaelic areas. To meet this demand Gaelic chiefs traded in English coinage (they became quite adept at discerning the precious metal content of various coins following the Tudor debasement after 1534), and they routinely chartered English ships to carry their goods through English port towns. In areas where the Gaelic economy was inherently weak—urban and maritime trade or the production of coinage, for instance—the Gaelic population appropriated English economic channels in order to rise above traditional restrictions.

But Gaelic reliance on the English infrastructure adversely affected the development of independent growth within the Gaelic economy. There was no internal redistribution of these profits, and for many Gaelic lordships adjacent English settlements represented an irresistible and limitless source of goods and money from which they might exact tribute (known colloquially as "black rents") through the threat of depredation. More often, however, Gaelic clans would simply take by raiding what they did not produce. The Tudor administration, together with the local English gentry, responded by launching sporadic punitive expeditions into what they believed to be predatory or recalcitrant Gaelic lordships. This destructive aspect of Gaelic-English interaction bred unsettled conditions that limited the potential of the English economy in Ireland, while stunting economic growth in most Gaelic areas. The English population looked to the Crown to intercede on its behalf and repeatedly pointed to the economic benefits that would flow to England if the Crown's "Irish enemies" were fully subjugated.

THE TUDOR CONQUEST: THE CATALYST FOR ECONOMIC AND SOCIAL CHANGE

By the mid-sixteenth century conciliatory efforts to integrate the Gaelic polity, both politically and economically, into the Tudor state had met with only limited success. The resort to coercive methods committed the Tudors to an unprecedented level of military expenditure, reducing the opportunities for capital investment or commercial development. Instead, the Tudors grudgingly financed an increasingly large standing army and a number of expensive military garrisons to protect and further English interests. Subventions from the English exchequer to support the army in Ireland had risen from negligible amounts prior to the Kildare rebellion in 1534 to £196,000 per annum by 1599. Gaelic lordships responded in kind and organized their economies to sustain a state of perpetual war. In the 1560s it was reported that Shane O'Neill had broken with Gaelic convention and armed the peasantry within his lordship. O'Neill's repeated confrontations with the Crown reveal also the strong economic and social links between Gaelic Scotland and Ulster, and the proclivity of chiefs in the latter to import large numbers of Scots mercenaries. In these unsettled conditions normal economic development was almost everywhere eclipsed by military necessity. The Tudor administration in Dublin recognized this and at the 1569–1571 Irish parliament enacted legislation encouraging the manufacture of processed commercial goods for export. Henry Sidney, as lord deputy, even attracted a group of Flemish tanners to relocate to Swords in north County Dublin in the 1570s. In the main, however, English attempts to diversify the economy at the local level were hampered by the predominance of soldiers and soldier-settlers over skilled craftsmen and artisans. In a society subject to bouts of political instability this was perhaps unavoidable; yet seen in a wider context, the Irish economy was displaying signs of improvement in the later sixteenth century.

Imports from England grew steadily, indicating greater domestic wealth and demand in Ireland, and the government's tax receipts also reveal an increase in profits from exports. This can be attributed to the fact that the walled port towns—the engines of the English economy in Ireland—were insulated from much of the political instability that plagued inland areas. And as inflation soared in England, Irish prices remained comparatively low, thus allowing Ireland a competitive advantage over its principal trading partner. For the Gaelic polity the increasingly militarized political environment, coupled with deteriorating relations with the Tudor state, brought about closer contact with continental powers and continental economies. Importation of supplies and ultimately arms and munitions from abroad, however, at once bolstered the economic strength of the English port towns and contributed to Irish resistance.

The suppression of broad-based Gaelic opposition in 1603, and the resulting extension of royal authority throughout Ireland in subsequent years, enabled the new Stuart monarchy to begin a gradual process of demilitarizing Irish society. Tudor observers had long agreed that the destruction of what they believed to be the tyrannical Gaelic noble class would liberate the allegedly tractable and hard-working Gaelic "churl," or peasant, allowing him to assimilate more fully to English culture. But the arrival of a mainly Protestant New English settler class, originally intended to serve as a model for its Gaelic neighbors, proved provocative instead. By 1600 significant amounts of land formerly held of Gaelic lordships had been transferred or mortgaged to English settlers, and as the threat of Gaelic rebellion seemed to recede, this trend accelerated.

The Ulster plantation, begun in 1607, followed the example of earlier, less extensive Tudor plantations in the midlands and in Munster, but reflected English dominance in this once purely Gaelic district. The aim of plantation was to effect swift economic and social change in Gaelic areas. The extension of a standardized English system of landholding and property rights ran concurrently with the transfer of land, and English cultural norms like primogeniture replaced the Gaelic custom of partible inheritance. In some respects the trans-

fer of land from native to newcomer was more apparent than real, for many Gaelic lords in the late sixteenth century had voluntarily adopted the English system of landholding and stayed on as landowners. In other cases, English landowners were absentees, and the native population continued to live and work on their traditional lands without interruption. As Irish society was demilitarized after 1603, the English economy became dominant, destroying the remnants of an independent Gaelic economy and many of its social foundations.

THE UNIFICATION AND GROWTH OF THE IRISH ECONOMY IN THE SEVENTEENTH CENTURY

The early seventeenth century was characterized by steady population growth and substantial economic expansion. The population of Dublin alone grew from less than 10,000 people in the late sixteenth century to nearly 50,000 in 1690. The southern and western port towns underwent similar, though less dramatic, expansion. A large labor supply allowed exports of hides, yarn, and particularly unfinished wool to increase significantly. In the late 1580s Ireland exported between 1,400 and 2,800 pounds of wool a year; in 1639, more than 93,000 pounds of wool were exported. Local merchants established commercial fishing centers in Munster to begin harnessing this lucrative natural resource that had long been dominated by foreign interests. Increasingly, large numbers of trees were felled for export in Ireland in dwindling forested areas in Wicklow, south Derry, and parts of Munster. It was, however, the export of cattle and other livestock that became the dominant feature of the Irish economy in the early seventeenth century. More than 15,000 animals were being exported annually to Chester alone by the 1630s. Compared with the negligible amount of livestock exported in the sixteenth century, and taken together with marked increases in population and exports, the Irish economy appears to have undergone a substantial transformation. But the economy was not so much transformed as unfettered from the political instability and economic divisions that had limited its potential in the previous century. The extension of royal authority and the integration of the Gaelic economy had allowed for more efficient exploitation of Ireland's existing resources, while the continued absence of an Irish mint ensured that trade outstripped the production of money. This created a deflationary and, in effect, competitive economy.

The outbreak of war in 1641, however, revealed that the ethnic and religious differences thought to have been permanently resolved by military conquest in 1603 were still capable of causing serious political unrest and vast economic damage. The rebellion, originally conceived in Ulster as an armed protest over property rights and religious freedom, resulted in the sectarian massacre of several thousand settlers there before spreading slowly throughout Ireland. In the half-century following the destruction of the Gaelic hierarchy, with its emphasis on armed personal followings and communal landed possessions, individual ownership of land within the English legal system had become the primary measure and source of wealth. Rumors of a future confiscation of lands by the increasingly anti-Catholic English parliament pushed the predominantly Catholic Gaelic and Old English populations toward making common cause with royalist supporters in the English civil war. The following decade (1641–1655) brought war-induced plague, famine, and depopulation; trade was brought to a near-standstill, and the Irish economy was devastated. Such political and economic instability provoked the subsequent Commonwealth government to undertake an even more extensive land redistribution scheme in 1652–1655 than any witnessed hitherto. It has been estimated that in 1641, 61 percent of profitable land was in the hands of Catholic landowners, but that by 1688 the figure had fallen to a mere 27 percent. A major turnover in population, however, did not occur, for it was difficult to attract large numbers of English settlers to a war-torn and dangerous Ireland. Many Gaelic inhabitants either remained on their lands or drifted back to them after a few years. Yet the significance of the transfer of land from Catholic landowners to mostly English Protestants should not be underestimated. The land settlement utterly transformed landownership and laid the foundation for the estate system that survived intact until the late nineteenth century. On another level the concentration of Ireland's landed interests in a class closely affiliated with the Protestant administration in England caused Ireland to become more fully integrated into the English economy after 1653, allowing for a speedy economic recovery in the decades that followed.

The dependence of the Irish economy on the English market in the 1650s and 1660s was clearly reflected in exports: in 1665, 75 percent of Irish exports were directed toward England. Cattle remained the principal export, but English cattle-breeders, disadvantaged by the favorable trade conditions extended to Irish imports, successfully lobbied Parliament to place restrictions on the number of cattle and sheep imported from Ireland. The resulting Cattle Acts, passed in 1663 and 1667, hastened a trend already underway toward the development of more diversified exports such as barrelled beef, wool, and butter. The English parliament's willingness to support these restrictions, however, highlights the subordination of the Irish economy to the English poli-ty. Irish merchants and landlords, many of whom were English-born Protestants, had little choice but to practice economic diversification in the face of restrictions on livestock. The diversification of Irish exports, and the regional specialization that was required to furnish the market with more labor-intensive products such as butter or wool, prompted a reorganization of the economy as merchants relied more heavily on inland market towns to direct their goods for export from expanding urban centers like Dublin, Cork, and Belfast. Diversification was also evident in the destination of Irish exports after 1667. A flourishing trans-Atlantic trade developed to the West Indies and the American colonies. Ireland exported barrelled beef and livestock and imported large quantities of tobacco. In 1665 Ireland imported 1,818,000 pounds of tobacco; and by the mid-1680s an average of 2,850,000 pounds were arriving annually. The continental market was also developed, and France in particular imported large amounts of Irish butter. By 1683 only 30 percent of Irish exports were directed toward England. Thus by the 1680s the Irish economy had sufficiently reorganized itself both internally and externally to meet a changed economic relationship with England and was showing signs of unprecedented prosperity. Though the outbreak of the Williamite wars in 1689 served as a reminder of Ireland's continued political subordination to England, physical destruction and depopulation were not extensive, and the Irish economy emerged largely unscathed.

In the two centuries after 1500 the economy and society of Ireland underwent an important transformation. The Tudor conquest ended centuries of political uncertainty and paved the way for the integration of the Gaelic economy and society into a developing British state that stretched to the New World. The Irish economy responded positively to the more settled political conditions ushered in by the extension of English rule. Merchants, both Gaelic and English, could now draw upon Ireland's once separate economies and channel their resources toward a single commercial goal. After 1641, however, it was clear that the conquered Gaelic society, and to a lesser extent the Catholic Old English community, had become marginalized in an increasingly commercialized Irish economy that revolved around the possession of land dominated by British Protestants. As Aidan Clarke has noted, the economic gains of the seventeenth century "accrued to individuals, while the social cost was borne by the conquered community" (p. 186). This calls into question the extent to which economic and social change penetrated Irish society. In the 1680s the Irish economy continued to be almost exclusively pastoral in nature, with 80 percent of outgoing trade emanating from livestock. Where once an Irish farmer sold his cattle to be fattened on English pasture, now he simply slaughtered them to sell as barrelled beef at home. Similarly, dairy products and wool were wholly dependent on livestock. In 1683, a good harvest year, grain and other crops contributed less than 4 percent to Ireland's total export trade. Sharp differences between English and Gaelic society also continued to be apparent into the 1680s. It was more likely for people of British descent to occupy the more fertile districts, to participate in local government, and to own land. The native Irish, moreover, were still dismissed by British society as a barbarous people lacking civility. Thus in some respects the Irish economy and society in 1690 bore a striking resemblance to conditions in the early sixteenth century. This qualification, however, should not overshadow the profound changes that had occurred during this crucial period when Ireland became fully integrated into a developing British state.

SEE ALSO Agriculture: 1500 to 1690; Protestant Immigrants; Urban Life, Crafts, and Industry from 1500 to 1690

Bibliography

Andrews, John H. "Land and People, c.1685." In *A New History of Ireland, III: Early Modern Ireland, 1534–1691*, edited by T. W. Moody, F. X. Martin, and F. J. Byrne. 1976.

Canny, Nicholas. *From Reformation to Restoration: Ireland, 1534–1660.* 1987.

Clarke, Aidan. "The Irish Economy, 1600–60." In *A New History of Ireland, III: Early Modern Ireland, 1534–1691*, edited by T. W. Moody, F. X. Martin, and F. J. Byrne. 1976.

Cullen, Louis M. "Economic Trends, 1600–90." In *A New History of Ireland, III: Early Modern Ireland, 1534–1691*, edited by T. W. Moody, F. X. Martin, and F. J. Byrne. 1976.

Ellis, Steven G. *Ireland in the Age of the Tudors, 1447–1603: English Expansion and the End of Gaelic Rule.* 1998.

Gillespie, Raymond. *The Tranformation of the Irish Economy, 1550–1700.* 1991.

Lennon, Colm. *Sixteenth-Century Ireland: The Incomplete Conquest.* 1994.

Longfield, Ada K. *Anglo-Irish Trade in the Sixteenth Century.* 1929.

Nicholls, Kenneth W. *Gaelic and Gaelicised Ireland in the Later Middle Ages.* 1972.

O'Brien, George. *The Economic History of Ireland in the Seventeenth Century.* 1919.

O'Dowd, Mary. "Gaelic Economy and Society." In *Natives and Newcomers: Essays on the Making of Irish Colonial Society*, edited by Ciarán Brady and Raymond Gillespie. 1986.

Quinn, David B. "'Irish' England and 'English' Ireland." In *A New History of Ireland, II: Medieval Ireland, 1169–1534.* 1987.

Christopher Maginn

Ecumenism and Interchurch Relations

Religious division and political conflict have played a formative role in Irish society. The reality that Protestantism and Catholicism often serve as badges of ethnopolitical identity continues to impede interchurch relations both in the Republic of Ireland with its 91.7 percent Catholic majority, and in Northern Ireland where the 53 percent Protestant-unionist majority often views itself as under siege. Stormont Castle in Belfast, described by one former unionist leader Lord Craigavon as "a Protestant parliament for a Protestant people," provided (in the words of another unionist leader, David Trimble) "a cold house for Catholics." Following the historic Good Friday Agreement (1998), a power-sharing legislative assembly was established in Belfast, but relationships within it have been embattled and its capacity to survive has been under constant threat.

Throughout much of the past century, sociopolitical division was intensified by religious separation: segregated schools, an effective Catholic-Church ban (until 1970) on Catholics attending Trinity College, discrimination against Catholics in jobs and housing allocation (especially in the North), and bitter memories of church-supported proselytizing and even boycotts. In such conditions ecumenism could not flourish. The Catholic Church, under its *Ne Temere* decree regulating "mixed marriages" between Catholics and Protestants (1911, somewhat modified in 1970), had stringently exacted that both partners in a marriage raise their children as Catholics. Until the Second Vatican Council (1962–1965), ecumenism for Roman Catholicism implied a "return to the fold." Protestant churches kept themselves aloof as the best protection against absorption and cultivated inter-Protestant solidarity. Encouraged by international ecumenical involvement, Protestant churches addressed themselves sporadically to the possibilities of "Protestant reunion" alongside bipartite and later tripartite conversations (Presbyterian-Methodist-Anglican). Although interest in reunion faded, the century's end saw a de facto mutual recognition of clerical ministries, nudged forward by interconnecting agreements with various European churches. Anglican-Methodist conversations resumed in 1989, culminating in the signing of a Covenant (2002) "to share a common life and mission" and "to grow together so that unity may be visibly realized." For Irish Catholicism, interchurch relationships were problematic not only because of Protestant alignment with unionism but also theologically. Independently sponsored ecumenical encounters in the 1940s and 1950s inspired neither Protestant confidence nor the approval of Rome, but certain Dominican, Jesuit, and Maynooth theologians steadfastly continued to pave the way.

THE TURN TO ECUMENISM AND THE START OF THE TROUBLES

Vatican II was the needed catalyst. Its movement of renewal enlivened a static Catholic ecclesiology, retrieving such concepts as the "pilgrim people of God" and modifying the offensive claim that the Roman Catholic Church is the one true church by avowing instead that the church of Christ "subsists in" the Catholic Church. The bishops supplied ecumenical directives for Catholic involvement (updated in 1976 and 1983). Kevin Mac-Namara—later archbishop of Dublin—envisioned the Catholic Church's future as "profoundly linked to the progress of ecumenism [and as] a test of its fidelity to the will of Christ" (1966, p. 152).

Seasoned and fledgling ecumenists rallied. In 1970 the Irish Council of Churches (ICC), an all-Protestant council of churches and religious communities (e.g., the Quakers and the Salvation Army, which were not strictly churches) formed with the Catholic Church a "Joint Group on Social Problems" to advise the Catholic hierarchy and ICC on social issues such as poverty, unemployment, and alcohol abuse. There was initial reluctance to tackle concerns such as civil rights or the causes of political conflict. That the ecumenical thrust coincided with the outbreak of the "Troubles" in Northern Ireland was painfully ironic. Violence and terror lent desperate urgency to ecumenical relations, but politicized religion crippled their effectiveness. By ministering restrictedly to their respective communities, churches, although they condemned violence, urged restraint, or acted as mediators, were accused of being "chaplains to their tribes" and were themselves vulnerable to sectarianism.

SUCCESSES AND SHORTCOMINGS OF INTERCHURCH RELATIONS: BALLYMASCANLON AND BEYOND

Nevertheless, formal ecumenical associations were crafted, most decisively the Irish Inter-Church Meeting (1973). Ballymascanlon, close to the border between North and South, was chosen as a neutral venue, and the "Ballymascanlon conferences" that took place there became a mainstay of official relationships, facilitating debate (not always progressive enough for some) on the ecumenical demands of unity-in-diversity. Papers were prepared on neuralgic areas (e.g., human rights), and a

standing committee wrestled with the pastoral challenge of "mixed marriages." Through virtually annual meetings, sustained and sustaining relationships took root among participants, engendering trust, forthrightness, and tact in the face of differing cultural identities, political reservations, and theological traditions. Initiatives on youth ministry and peace education emerged, but no bold venture on interchurch education. Two commissioned reports are noteworthy: the incisive *Violence in Ireland* (1976), which was received more enthusiastically in political groups than in church circles, and *Sectarianism: A Discussion Document* (1993), which examined churches' collusion in sectarianism.

For the most part, churches support the peace process. Though they have been powerless to prevent nearly 4,000 deaths, the churches' foremost ecumenical challenge now is to give witness to the gospel pattern of boundary-crossing and healing. An inclusive ecumenical structure is one necessary factor in this. The fact that the ICC (minus Catholic representation) and the more inclusive Irish Inter-Church Meeting (Ballymascanlon) operate in parallel has militated against concerted action, but protracted discussions have failed to achieve an integrating structure. In addition, the Catholic Church remains outside ICC; its joining would present untenable difficulties for the Presbyterian Church, which alone of the main Protestant denominations stands outside the World Council of Churches (having resigned in 1980 over funding of resistance groups in Africa). Most Irish churches are variously associated with the "Churches Together in Britain and Ireland" body, but there is unmistakable discomfort with any movement toward full union.

It is often asserted that the churches have lacked a prophetic stature, failing to make needed gestures of "institutional self-sacrifice," proffering "a palliative rather than a cure." Their contribution to the reconciliation of histories—with undoubted exceptions—has been lackluster. The vision of interchurch unity has not found strong resonance in the congregational mainstream. Yet, incontrovertibly, a network of relationships once unimaginable now exists: shared worship, pulpit exchange, joint hospital and university chaplaincies, and local interchurch forums, along with meetings, appearances, and appeals of "the four church leaders," are now routine. Ecumenism is alive on the ground too, with projects abounding. The Corrrymeela Community, founded by the Presbyterian minister Ray Davey (1967), promotes peace between communities. The Irish School of Ecumenics, founded by Michael Hurley, S. J. (1970), remains a powerhouse of research and learning, collaborating with churches and community groups across civil society. Innumerable independent bodies contribute to this ecumenical world through partnerships or through groups dedicated to study, writing, and action for reconciliation. By opening spaces for ecumenical worship and hospitality to interested Christians, conferences like those at Greenhills or Glenstal Abbey are, since the 1960s, annual highlights, together with events focusing on the Week of Prayer for Christian Unity and the Women's World Day of Prayer.

Whether official or informal, interchurch relationships have sustained perseverance, ensuring that neither internal conflicts nor embarrassing actions lead to rupture, but rather compel the rebuilding of trust. Recent challenges to reconciliation include Catholic unease with the association of Protestant churches with the Drumcree "right to march"; the new "obstacle" for official Catholic ecumenism as Protestant churches break with ancient tradition by ordaining women; the irritation of Catholics when perceived as not "Christian"; the consternation of Protestants at the Vatican's "downgrading" of Anglican and Reformed Churches in its *Dominus Iesus* declaration and accompanying "Note" (2000), which, when taken with the episcopal document *One Bread, One Body* (1998), appears to run counter to Vatican II and to Pope John Paul II's encyclical letter on commitment to ecumenism (1995). Although doctrine remains important, since the search for truth is inherent in the quest for unity, it is often historical prejudice and other nondoctrinal factors that constitute the stumbling blocks. Some expostulations following President Mary McAleese's partaking in Anglican holy communion (1997) exposed a lamentable ignorance of changing historic patterns in eucharistic theology, and of the degree of Anglican–Roman Catholic agreement already achieved.

Mícheál Mac Gréil's now classic 1977 survey *Prejudice and Tolerance in Ireland* revealed a majority perception that the churches contributed to divisions and that Christian unity was desirable. Yet, a 1998 inquiry intimated that Irish churches were still "imprisoned within structures." In a globalized world churches are called to overcome violence and to make peace. On an increasingly pluralist island where Christians may turn out to be Eastern Orthodox as well as Catholic or Protestant, and where people of many faiths now seek a home, churches are charged "to widen the space of their tent."

SEE ALSO McQuaid, John Charles; Protestant Community in Southern Ireland since 1922; Religion: Since 1690; Roman Catholic Church: Since 1891

Bibliography

Clegg, Cecelia, and Joseph Liechty. *Moving beyond Sectarianism: Religion, Conflict, and Reconciliation in Northern Ireland.* 2001.

Ellis, Ian. *Vision and Reality: A Survey of Twentieth-Century Irish Inter-Church Relations.* 1992.

Hurley, Michael, S. J. *Christian Unity: An Ecumenical Second Spring?* 1998.

Mac Gréil, Mícheál. *Prejudice and Tolerance in Ireland.* 1977.

MacNamara, Kevin. "Ecumenism in the Light of Vatican II." *Irish Ecclesiastical Record* 105 (1966): 152.

Smyth, Geraldine. "Churches in Ireland: Journeys in Identity and Communion." *Ecumenical Review* 53, no. 2 (April 2001).

Geraldine Smyth

Education

1500 TO 1600	COLM LENNON
PRIMARY PRIVATE EDUCATION— "HEDGE SCHOOLS" AND OTHER SCHOOLS	IRENE WHELAN
PRIMARY PUBLIC EDUCATION— NATIONAL SCHOOLS FROM 1831	THOMAS MCGRATH
NONDENOMINATIONAL SCHOOLING	ÁINE HYLAND
SECONDARY EDUCATION, FEMALE	MARY PECKHAM MAGRAY
SECONDARY EDUCATION, MALE	LAWRENCE W. MCBRIDE
UNIVERSITY EDUCATION	SENIA PAŠETA
WOMEN'S EDUCATION	SENIA PAŠETA

1500 TO 1690

The official policy of the colonial government in late medieval Ireland dictated that there should be strict segregation of the Gaelic and English educational systems, but in practice there were points of overlap. In Gaelic Ireland the caste of literati, including judges, medics, and poets, operated a system of apprenticeship through the "bardic schools" which ensured the hereditary nature of traditional learning. In some of the towns, particularly in the south and the west, the populations that were mainly of English origin appear to have had access to these schools. As elsewhere, the church (which was also divided into English and Gaelic zones) exerted a powerful influence over education through monastic and parish schools. Cathedral schools functioned in, for example, the Dublin foundations of Christ Church and Saint Patrick's.

A salient feature of pre-Reformation education was the expanding role of lay institutions and individuals in the provision of schooling. Through their power of appointment of chantry chaplains (priests employed to sing or say mass in endowed chapels) supernumerary to the diocesan clergy, lay people ensured the availability of priests who could be expected to teach as well as to celebrate mass for deceased benefactors. Besides endowing large religious guilds with many chantry priests, wealthy families established colleges, which, while not formal academies of learning, nevertheless supported a number of chaplains to instruct youths, even if only in singing and choral techniques. Aristocratic and gentry patronage of these and other forms of schooling was evident in the late medieval period, while in the boroughs such as Dublin, the civic corporations began to establish municipal schools. In the towns there also was training through the apprenticeship system, which was organized by the trade and craft guilds.

As part of a burgeoning humanistic movement for social and cultural reform, an act for "the English order, habit and language" was passed in the Dublin parliament in 1537, the first state measure for education in Ireland. In the context of King Henry VIII's assertion of royal sovereignty in church and state, its purpose was to foster English civility throughout as much of the country as could be made responsive to governmental authority. The key educational provision was for the setting up of primary schools in every parish for the teaching of English language and culture, and also "Christ's religion" (which meant the pristine religious practice of the early Christian church, or, more simply, real Christianity). Although there was little or no success in implementing the legislation in Gaelic Ireland, the response was positive in some areas of the Englishry, but lack of resources and the impropriation (or lay possession) of many parishes mitigated the effects. Because the act coincided with the coming of the ecclesiastical Reformation to Ireland under Henry, the impulse toward educational reform that underpinned it tended to be confused with the campaign for religious change. A small minority of leaders in church and state who were charged with implementing Protestantism beginning in about 1549 were enthusiastic about a pedagogical initiative through the medium of the Irish language, possibly with the aid of the printing press. The strong majority view in the Church of Ireland, however, was that the principles of the reformed religion should be inculcated as part of a program of anglicization. Thus the 1537 act came to be invoked in the succeeding decades to justify the teaching and preaching of the gospel exclusively in English.

INITIATIVES IN SECOND- AND THIRD-LEVEL EDUCATION

The failure of the Protestant Reformation to embrace the world of Gaelic learning alienated the older Irish population, but reformers with Old English backgrounds pinned their hopes for social and religious advancement on a proper system of state-sponsored second- and third-level education. The impetus for the act for the erection of diocesan grammar schools in 1570 came mainly from this sector of society, since its members were influenced by the Erasmianism or moderate Christian humanism of the mid-sixteenth century. Already the extralegal activity of Catholic schoolteachers in some of the southwestern boroughs (including members of the Society of Jesus, who also aspired to the foundation of a Catholic university) was eliciting a popular response. The challenge to the state authorities was to devise an educational structure and curriculum that would counteract the agents of the Roman church while retaining the loyalty of the Old English. The measure that emerged from Parliament was for secondary schools jointly regulated by church and state to be founded in each Irish diocese. The measure's supporters argued that the new schools would eventually provide a student body for a university in Ireland that would in turn be a seminary for a Protestant ministry.

This scheme proved to be problematic for a number of reasons. Few diocesan schools emerged as a result of the legislation before the seventeenth century. The bishops, in whose interest it was to promote academic reform as well as evangelization, were reluctant to pledge their scarce revenues to the establishment of schools. The conservative Old English elites in town and country became alienated from the Anglican Church by the 1570s and 1580s, identifying it with the newly arrived English agents of radical constitutional and social change. This lay leadership that might have been expected to be supportive of state educational initiatives possessed extensive ecclesiastical revenues and property rights, and began to channel these resources into an alternative Catholic system of religious practice and schooling. Nor could agreement be reached on the site and nature of a university for Ireland that might have canalized all the reforming impulses, social, cultural, and religious. By the time that internal Protestant divisions were resolved to allow for the foundation of Trinity College in 1592, there was already a vibrant system of second-level Catholic schools and an emergent network of seminaries on the continent.

PROTESTANT AND CATHOLIC EDUCATIONAL SYSTEMS

By the late seventeenth century there were two educational systems operating in Ireland, reflecting the polarized nature of politico-religious ideology. On one side was the official Anglican educational sphere, radiating out from Trinity College and incorporating municipal schools, diocesan schools, and the newly established royal schools in the plantation settlements in Ulster. On the other was the unofficial but ubiquitous Catholic nexus, transcending diocesan and county boundaries, and molding itself to the contours of urban and county society. This system of schooling was for much of the century not clandestine—teachers and their patrons made arrangements quite openly for the tuition of pupils. There was even a short-lived Jesuit-run Catholic university in Back Lane in Dublin in the 1620s that was closed by agents of the state government in 1629. Some mixing of the religious groups did occur within the educational sphere, however. For example, the Dublin municipal school was under Protestant control in the early seventeenth century, but of its 122 pupils in 1622, 43 did not attend Church of Ireland services. Since 1610, 100 of its graduates had gone to Trinity College, but 160 went overseas, several returning as Catholic priests. And in the 1610s the graduates of Isaac Lally's school in the diocese of Tuam were going on to both the Protestant Trinity College and to the Catholic Irish college at Salamanca.

Salamanca and other continental colleges provided pedagogues who returned to Ireland to supplement the catechesis of the burgeoning Counter-Reformation. Though technically outside the law, this unofficial schooling played a powerful part in securing the majority of the population for the Catholic cause, in part at least because it enshrined the use of the Irish language in its secular and religious curricula. The dominance of the Catholic educational system thus restricted the influence of the Protestant one to a mostly New English minority community during the Stuart period.

SEE ALSO *Annals of the Four Masters*; Irish Colleges Abroad until the French Revolution; Smith, Erasmus; Trinity College

Bibliography

Corcoran, Timothy, ed. *State Papers in Irish Education*. 1916.

Ford, Alan. *The Protestant Reformation in Ireland, 1590–1641*. 1997.

Giltrap, Risteárd. *An Ghaeilge in Eaglais na hÉireann*. 1990.

Hammerstein, Helga. "Aspects of the Continental Education of Irish Students in the Reign of Elizabeth I." *Historical Studies* 8 (1971): 137–154.

Lennon, Colm. *Richard Stanihurst the Dubliner*. 1981.

Lennon, Colm. "Education and Religious Identity in Early Modern Ireland." *Pedagogica Historica: International Journal of the History of Education, Supplementary Series* 5 (1999): 57–75.

Lennon, Colm. *An Irish Prisoner of Conscience of the Tudor Era: Archbishop Richard Creagh of Armagh, 1523–1586*. 2000.

Colm Lennon

PRIMARY PRIVATE EDUCATION— "HEDGE SCHOOLS" AND OTHER SCHOOLS

Until the late eighteenth century the availability of primary education reflected the realities of political and religious life in Ireland. Ever since the Reformation, Protestant schools (known variously as "parish," "diocesan," and "royal" schools) had received state support. These schools were English in orientation and catered for the children of the nobility and the middle classes. They complemented concurrent efforts to suppress the native culture and the Catholic religion. As a result of penal laws Catholics were forbidden to establish or endow schools for much of the eighteenth century. Such education as Catholics received was necessarily clandestine, though from the middle of the eighteenth century Catholic teaching orders in the larger towns were openly running schools for the children of those who could afford to pay. In the countryside the clandestine system provided the foundation for the celebrated "hedge schools," an informal system in which itinerant schoolmasters supported by the community taught basic numeracy and literacy. Following the relaxation of the penal laws affecting education in 1782, both the hedge-school system and the schools of the religious teaching orders spread with remarkable speed. This development prompted the foundation of new teaching orders (such as the Christian Brothers) and drew the attention of the political establishment to the dangers posed by the hedge-school system and to the need for state involvement in the education of Catholics.

The only attempt at state involvement in the education of Catholics in the eighteenth century was the establishment of the Charter Schools beginning in 1733.

Influenced by Enlightenment rationalism, the founders of the Charter Schools hoped that the schools would serve as a means through which poor Catholic children would be trained to earn their living in trade and industry. The system was never a success and developed a scandalous reputation because of its abuse of resources and the neglect and exploitation of the children in Charter Schools.

The educational initiatives the early nineteenth century were an immediate result of the fears inspired by the events of the 1790s. The spread of revolutionary republicanism was seen as intimately linked to the growth of mass literacy, and it was clear that hedge-school masters had played a key role in disseminating widely the radical ideas that had led to the rebellion. The first two decades of the nineteenth century were therefore a period of great debate on popular education, which increasingly came to be seen as fundamental for future political and social stability and for economic progress. The early nineteenth century was also an age of experimentation in both the public and private spheres. The reformers who were inspired by the ideals of the evangelical revival hoped that education would be the vehicle through which the rising generation of Irish children would be converted to the Protestant faith—a happy outcome, as they saw it, that would ensure loyalty, industrious behavior, and obedience to the law. A variety of voluntary agencies, such as the London Hibernian Society and the Association for Discountenancing Vice, appealed with great success to landlords to support the agencies' educational initiatives. Schools funded by these agencies (often employing the newest educational methodology developed by theorists, such as Heinrich Pestalozzi in Switzerland and Bell and Lancaster in Britain) soon began to appear on the estates of improving landlords concerned with disseminating a Bible-based morality.

Simultaneously, a government commission was established (it sat from 1806 to 1812) and reported on the condition of education at the national level. In its last and most influential report it recommended that government funds be made available to launch a national, nondenominational educational venture. The organization that came closest to meeting these conditions was the Kildare Place Society—the product of a Quaker initiative committed to the provision of nondenominational education for the poor. Formally established in 1811, the Kildare Place schools had spread across the country by the early 1820s and were educating Catholic children in large numbers. A powerful evangelical lobby on the Kildare Place board of trustees, however, led Catholics to suspect that the society was working in tandem with other, more overtly proselytizing bodies like the London Hibernian Society. Strident criticism from the Rev. John MacHale and Daniel O'Connell led to a general attack on the system, and the wholesale withdrawal of Catholic children from Kildare Place schools after 1824 effectively destroyed the society.

The attack on the Kildare Place Society precipitated yet another government commission that sat from 1824 to 1827 and issued as many as nine reports. In the most detailed and exhaustive of these reports, which appeared in 1825, it was revealed that the majority of Catholic children (between 300,000 and 400,000) were continuing to be educated in the hedge-school system. Catholic representatives interviewed by the commissioners also made clear that Catholic clergymen were unlikely ever to agree to the attendance of Catholic children at schools in which the Protestant Bible was used for educational purposes. The immediate outcome of the commission was the recommendation by Chief Secretary Edward Stanley that a National Board of Education be set up to oversee a national system of primary education in which the religious-education requirements of the different denominations would be accommodated.

The National Board, which was duly established in 1831, was to be run by a body of commissioners who would entrust particular schools to a patron; this patron would then appoint a manager who would be responsible for hiring the teaching staff. Although the term *undenominational* was applied to the system as envisaged by Stanley, in the decades following the setup of the board the denominational interests who participated in the system modified the rules such that religious education was provided in accordance with the wishes of the patron and manager. As the system evolved, the patron was generally the bishop of the diocese and the manager was normally the local priest or clergyman. This meant that national schools in Catholic areas were exclusively Catholic and taught religious doctrine accordingly. The same held true in the Presbyterian areas of the north where the national system was also embraced. Because the rules of the National Board did not satisfy the demands of the Church of Ireland, a separate Church Education Society was founded in 1839 to cater to the more stringently religious demands of Irish Anglican leaders.

The schools of the National Board quickly became institutionalized at all levels of Irish society. By the 1840s they had replaced not only the hedge schools but also the schools of the Kildare Place Society and the evangelical agencies. In many instances these older schools were formally incorporated into the national system and their management and curricula were adjusted accordingly. By 1849 almost half a million children were receiving an education in the schools of the National Board, and provisions were in place for an inspectorate, a system of teacher training, and a curriculum whose materials were so advanced that they were used as models in Britain.

The success of the national system meant that the children of the poor were receiving the education they craved. It also endowed Ireland with a progressive and sophisticated system of primary education at least a generation before most countries in Europe, including Britain. On the debit side, the manner in which the religious and administrative issues were settled meant that the clergy of the different denominations managed and controlled the schools—a result that was the complete antithesis of the original promoters' vision. What evolved was a system rigidly denominational in character and practically akin to a form of religious apartheid among children of school-going age. The foundation was also established for a society in which the clergy, through their role as school managers, would come to wield an extraordinary degree of control in Irish society. On the credit side, the national schools laid the basis for mass literacy in English, which was undoubtedly a major advantage—in terms of skill, confidence, and general awareness—for the millions of Irish who emigrated to find work in English-speaking countries.

SEE ALSO Chapbooks and Popular Literature; Education: Nondenominational Schooling; Education: Primary Public Education—National Schools from 1831; Kildare Place Society; Literacy and Popular Culture; Religion: Since 1690; Rice, Edmund; Roman Catholic Church: 1829 to 1891

Bibliography

Akenson, D. H. *The Irish Education Experiment: The National System of Education in the Nineteenth Century.* 1970.

Whelan, Kevin. *The Tree of Liberty: Radicalism, Catholicism, and the Construction of Irish Identity, 1760–1830.* 1996.

Irene Whelan

PRIMARY PUBLIC EDUCATION— NATIONAL SCHOOLS FROM 1831

The national system of education established by the state in 1831 was the outstanding educational innovation in nineteenth-century Ireland. In the 1820s education at the elementary level was a major battleground between Protestant evangelicals and the Catholic Church. The foundation of the national school system came about because of Catholic opposition, led by Bishop James Doyle of Kildare and Leighlin, to the voluntary (though state-funded) Kildare Place Society, which operated on Protestant principles, as well as to other educational societies which had proselytizing aims.

Educational modernizers and the government hoped that the new national schools would replace the widespread "hedge schools" which were deemed to be unsatisfactory because of their primitive physical conditions, the poor quality of their teachers, and the antiquated curriculum that they taught. The new, well-built schools were to demonstrate best practice in education. Lancasterian methods were implemented, a system of inspection was established, and a teacher-training college was set up.

The new national education board, which administered the system, comprised seven members: three Anglicans, two Presbyterians, and two Catholics. Remarkably, the Catholic and Protestant archbishops of Dublin sat on the board. However, the representative composition of the board, inconsistent as it was with respect to the country's religious demography, would later become an issue.

The guiding principle of the system was outlined in 1831 by Chief Secretary Edward Stanley in his letter to the president of the new board, the duke of Leinster. It was to be "a system of education from which should be banished even the suspicion of proselytism, and which, admitting children of all religious persuasions, should not interfere with the peculiar tenets of any."

Combined literary and moral instruction was to be given on four or five days of the week. It could not be doctrinal or dogmatic. Separate religious instruction was to be given on the other days of the week or before or after the school day.

A sum of 30,000 pounds in public funds was withdrawn from the Kildare Place Society and put at the disposal of the Irish lord lieutenant for the board. Two-thirds of the money required to build new national schools was available from the board, provided that one-third was raised locally. The board sought joint applications for aid to build schools from Catholic and Protestant ministers or from any combination of Catholics and Protestants.

The hope that clergy of all denominations would cooperate in managing local national schools was thwarted. Out of a total of 4,795 schools in 1852, only 175 were under joint management. The Anglican Church generally opposed the new system as an interference with its traditional prerogatives in elementary

The system of national schools established in 1831 was a major agent in the process of anglicization, even though the decline of the Irish language had begun decades earlier. These primary schools were also responsible for striking improvements in literacy levels over the next two generations. In this pre-1914 photograph girls and boys play outside a country school in County Monaghan. © SEAN SEXTON COLLECTION/ CORBIS. REPRODUCED BY PERMISSION.

education. It was opposed to the rule that the Bible could not be used in national schools at any time during any day. Anglican opposition led to the formation of the Church Education Society in 1839.

Presbyterian opposition was based on similar grounds but was, if anything, more deeply felt, and resulted in attacks on and the destruction of some new national schools in Ulster in the mid-1830s. By 1840, however, the Presbyterian Synod of Ulster had secured modifications acceptable to it and had entered the system.

Changes made to suit Presbyterian objections led the Catholic archbishop of Tuam, John MacHale, to attack the system as no better than the proselytizing educational societies of the 1820s, even though his fellow archbishop, Daniel Murray of Dublin, sat on the board. A majority of bishops supported Murray. This dispute ended in 1841 when Rome decreed that each bishop in his own diocese should decide on the merits of the system.

Usually, where schools were mixed in the religious allegiance of students, the denominational numbers were very lopsided. In 1862, the first year for which this information is available, 53.6 percent of all national schools were mixed. This statistic hides the reality that normally there was an overwhelming majority of Catholics and only a few Protestants in mixed schools.

In the second half of the nineteenth century the Catholic Church sought to make what was already a de facto denominational education denominational in theory as well; this was achieved by 1900. Under the leadership of Archbishop Paul Cullen of Dublin, the Catholic Church in 1863 boycotted the twenty-six regional "model schools" that had been established for teacher-training purposes. Catholic children and student-teachers were ordered out of the model schools. One result of this was that the percentage of untrained teachers in Ireland was very high. The total number of trained teachers in 1874 was 3,842; the number untrained was 6,118. Sixty-six percent of teachers had not received formal training; only 27 percent of Catholics were trained, compared with 52 percent of Protestants. As a result of church pressure, denominational teacher-training colleges were sanctioned in 1883.

While there had been fears that the hedge schools had been academies of sedition, no such criticism was made of the national schools, where inculcation of loyalty to the established order and respect for authority were taught. Irish cultural identity was not on the agenda of the national schools. Irish language, history, heritage, and games did not find a place in the curriculum. The culture of the schools was more British than Irish. The textbooks produced by the national board were so successful that they were the best-selling books to elementary schools in England.

The number of schools and pupils went up from 789 with 107,000 children in 1833 to 4,321 schools with 481,000 children in 1849. By 1870 the number of schools had increased to 6,806 with 998,999 pupils. In 1871 there were still 2,661 schools with 125,000 children outside the national-school system. More than 1,100 of these were Church Education Society schools, though that body was in rapid decline because of financial pressure.

A majority of children remained in school only until they had attained functional literacy. To learn to read was the fundamental objective of schooling; writing was a secondary concern. Voluntary attendance had long been poor. In 1871 it averaged only 37 percent. In 1892, for the first time, education was made compulsory for children between ages six and fourteen, but the legislation was full of loopholes. Daily attendance was only 62 percent in 1900.

The Royal Commission of Inquiry into Primary Education, or Powis Commission, reported in 1870 and followed English and Scottish commissions in recommending payment by results in order to improve standards in the national schools. The payment-by-results policy was introduced in 1872, but it was heavily criticized and abolished in 1899, also following the English and Scottish pattern.

The Commission on Manual and Practical Instruction, or Belmore Commission, reported in 1898. It was appointed to bring Ireland into line with educational thinking on the European continent. It concentrated on practical and child-centered education rather than the mere rote learning of the three Rs. Resident Commissioner William Starkie implemented the recommendations in the revised program for national schools in 1900.

The removal of illiteracy in English was a major achievement of the national-school system in the nineteenth century. In 1851, 47 percent of people 5 years old and older could neither read nor write in English; in 1871 the corresponding figure was 33 percent, and in 1901 it was 14 percent. From 1879 it became possible to teach Irish in national schools, though only outside school hours. Irish was not taught in national schools during school hours until 1900. In 1904, Irish, for the first time, became the main medium of instruction in national schools in Irish-speaking areas. Many within the Gaelic League (founded in 1893) believed that Irish had been lost because of an anglicizing policy in nineteenth-century national schools, and that it could be revived through a gaelicization policy in twentieth-century national schools. In the Irish Free State the argument that Irish had been lost in the national schools was used to attempt the restoration of the Irish language by placing the burden of learning it on primary-school pupils. Arguably, greater damage had been done to Irish in the hedge schools, which were primarily concerned with learning to read in English, in the century before 1831.

SEE ALSO Chapbooks and Popular Literature; Education: Primary Private Education—"Hedge Schools" and Other Schools; Education: Secondary Education, Female; Education: Secondary Education, Male; Language and Literacy: Decline of Irish Language; Kildare Place Society; Literacy and Popular Culture; Presbyterianism; Religion: Since 1690; Rice, Edmund; Roman Catholic Church: 1829 to 1891; Roman Catholic Church: Since 1891

Bibliography

Akenson, D. H. *The Irish Education Experiment: The National System of Education in the Nineteenth Century.* 1970.

McGrath, Thomas. *Politics, Interdenominational Relations, and Education in the Public Ministry of Bishop James Doyle of Kildare and Leighlin, 1786–1834.* 1999.

Thomas McGrath

NONDENOMINATIONAL SCHOOLING

The system of education in Ireland, north and south, developed during the nineteenth and early twentieth centuries as a denominational system under the control and management of the main Christian churches. This occurred despite the fact that when the national (elementary) school system was set up in Ireland in 1831, its main objective "was to unite in one system children of different creeds." While some of the schools that were funded by the Commissioners of National Education in the early years were jointly managed, the main Christian churches put pressure on the government to allow aid to be given to schools under the management of individual churches. This pressure was so effective that by the mid-nineteenth century, 96 percent of schools funded by the government were under the control of one or other of the main Christian churches and remained so. In this respect, the Irish system of education is fundamentally different from systems of education in other parts of the Western world. In most western countries "parallel" systems have evolved; that is, denominational schools exist side by side with publicly controlled schools.

After independence was granted to the twenty-six counties of the Irish Free State in 1921 to 1922, very little change occurred in the control and management of the school system in the south. Three-quarters of a century were to pass before comprehensive legislation in the form of the 1998 Education Act became law. In the north, the education system was immediately restructured after partition to bring it into line with the system in England and Wales, and the 1923 Education Act set up democratic local authority structures to run primary education in the north. However, because the Roman Catholic Church insisted on maintaining the autonomy and separateness of its schools, the education systems in both the north and south remained religiously divided. On both sides of the border virtually all schools, primary and secondary, catered separately to either Catholic or Protestant pupils.

It was not until the 1960s that the system of control and management of schooling began to be questioned. During the 1960s and 1970s there was a growing interest in education in Ireland. Vatican II had encouraged involvement of the Roman Catholic laity in what had traditionally been a clerically dominated church. Some Roman Catholics argued that a strong case could be made from the reading of the documents of Vatican II for the introduction of integrated schools. The troubles in Northern Ireland had erupted afresh, and after 1969 many Irish people were anxious to break down barriers between Protestant and Catholic on the island of Ireland. They felt that the introduction of multidenominational or integrated education could contribute to breaking down these barriers.

In the south the Dalkey School Project (DSP) was set up in 1975 with the aim of opening a school that would be multidenominational, co-educational, and under a democratic management structure, and which would have a child-centered approach to education. The task confronting the project was formidable. The national school system had been undisturbed for over 100 years. There was an established equilibrium between the Department of Education, the churches, and the Irish National Teachers' Organisation, the only teacher union representing primary teachers in the Republic of Ireland. There was a price for the churches' control of education: They provided sites for schools and they paid the local contribution toward the capital and running costs of their schools. The state paid the teachers' salaries, the larger share of the capital costs (averaging 85 percent), and an annual capitation grant towards maintenance costs. The DSP realized that the entry fee for any new partner into the network would be high and that it would have to raise funds on a very large scale if it was to succeed in setting up a school.

Four years of lobbying, fund-raising, and preparation were to pass before the first multidenominational primary school—the DSP National School, with about eighty pupils on its roll—was recognized by the southern government in 1978. Politicians of all political parties supported the concept, but there were also powerful antagonists, within and outside government, opposed to such a development. Some bureaucrats at both local and central levels had difficulty in accepting that a multidenominational school could be a valid part of the Irish education system. The DSP National School functioned in temporary premises for six years, and in 1984, when the school moved to a purpose-built school, it had over 300 pupils on the rolls and employed ten teachers.

In 1984 Educate Together was set up as a national coordinating body for schools and groups interested in setting up multidenominational schools. Since then, the number of schools has grown to twenty-eight, catering to more than 4,000 pupils (about 1 percent of all primary school pupils) and employing 200 teachers. These schools aim to meet a growing need in Irish society for schools that recognize the developing diversity of Irish life and the modern need for democratic management structures. Educate Together guarantees children and parents of all faiths and none equal respect in the operation and governing of education. It is facing unprecedented demand for places in its schools and for increased services to schools, and it is under pressure to open new schools in new areas. It is also being urged to promote its philosophy in the wider context of secondary education and pre-school provision. This growing demand can be attributed to various factors in modern Irish life such as the rapid diversification of society, economic growth, increasing population, globalization of the economy, and improved communications. It can also be attributed to the increasing demand of Irish parents to participate as partners in the educational process and to see their children grow up at ease with social, religious, and cultural difference.

In the mid-1970s, when the Dalkey School Project was struggling to obtain state sanction, some parents in Northern Ireland were also actively engaged in trying to convince the Northern Ireland government to provide support for what they referred to as an "integrated" school. Integrated education is described as the bringing together in one school of pupils, staff, and governors in roughly equal numbers from both Protestant and Catholic traditions. It is about cultivating the individual's self-respect and therefore respect for other people and other cultures. Integrated education means bringing children up to live as adults in a pluralist society, recognizing what they hold in common as well as what separates them, and accepting both.

The first integrated school, Lagan College, was established in Belfast in 1981 by the campaigning parent group All Children Together (ACT). In 1985 three more integrated schools opened in Belfast, offering parents in the city an alternative choice to the existing segregated schools. In 2003 there were forty-six integrated schools in Northern Ireland, comprising seventeen integrated second level colleges and twenty-nine integrated primary schools. In addition there were thirteen integrated nursery schools, most of which were linked to primary schools. Like Educate Together schools in the south, integrated schools in Northern Ireland were oversubscribed: in the academic year 2000 to 2001 some 1,140 applicants for places in integrated education had to be turned away due to lack of places. (The coordinating body for integrated education in Northern Ireland is NICIE—the Northern Ireland Council for Integrated Education.)

Over the years multidenominational education in the south and integrated education in the north have at-

tracted both supporters and detractors, and the growth of the sector has not come without opposition. Opinion polls, however, continue to show widespread support for the concept of multidenominational and integrated education.

SEE ALSO Education: Primary Private Education—"Hedge Schools" and Other Schools; Education: Primary Public Education—National Schools from 1831

Bibliography

Cooke, Jim. *Marley Grange: Multi-Denominational School Challenge.* 1997.

Survey of Attitudes and Preferences towards Multi-Denominational and Co-Education. 1976.

Áine Hyland

SECONDARY EDUCATION, FEMALE

The last quarter of the nineteenth century witnessed what has been called a revolution in the education of Irish women. Though Irish girls were beneficiaries of the comprehensive, publicly funded, national elementary school system established earlier in the century (with the passage of Stanley's Education Act in 1831), their access to secondary and university education was a much later development, and its accomplishment was fraught with controversy.

EARLY DEVELOPMENT

Whereas female secondary education was not unheard of before the last quarter of the nineteenth century, the availability of advanced instruction was rare, the quality of that instruction variable, and the distinction between elementary and secondary or higher education unclear. Census returns from 1871 show four national schools providing secondary education to Protestant and Catholic girls (though they numbered a mere twenty-four pupils). There were also some Catholic convent boarding schools (run by the Ursuline, Dominican, Loreto, Brigidine, and Saint Louis Sisters) that offered what was called "superior" education, distinguished by a curriculum that included foreign languages. For girls from families lacking the resources to pay the £40 annual fee required at such institutions, the Mercy and Presentation sisters (founded originally to work with the poor) developed the pension day school during the middle decades of the nineteenth century. Located in the larger towns throughout the country, the schools offered both elementary and more advanced education to Catholic girls for one-tenth of the cost of a boarding school.

Despite the existence of schools offering what might be called secondary instruction to a limited number of Irish girls, both lack of access as well as the inferior quality of educational content drew criticism during the middle decades of the nineteenth century. Protestant educational reformers objected to curricula that emphasized the teaching of so-called accomplishments (singing, drawing, music, and needlework) at the expense of academic or technical subjects (languages and literature, higher mathematics, and physical sciences) that would better prepare women for employment or afford them the opportunity to know intellectual achievement.

In demanding female access to technical, classical, and professional education on the same terms as males, these women were players in larger social and cultural dramas. As elsewhere in the industrializing world, growing numbers of middle-class women in Ireland needed paid employment but could not secure it. Educational reformers like the Quaker Anne Jellicoe lobbied for female access to improved secondary and university education as a way for women to gain better, life-sustaining employment. Some proponents of expanded educational access, like the feminist Isabella Tod (again, part of a larger feminist movement that was organizing throughout the nineteenth-century industrializing world), called for expanded female educational access not only as a necessity but also, quite simply, as a right.

Consequently, in the late 1850s Protestant women began opening a series of new educational institutions for young women, providing both secondary and higher education. Margaret Byers (Ladies' Collegiate School, later Victoria College, 1859, Belfast), Anne Jellicoe (Queen's Institute, 1861; Alexandra College, 1866; and Alexandra School, 1873, all in Dublin), and Isabella Tod (Ladies' Institute, 1867, Belfast) were among the most prominent founders of more than seventy Protestant female secondary schools begun by the end of the nineteenth century. Run by a Protestant committee of both lay and clerical leaders (usually male), these schools prepared young women between the ages of fourteen and eighteen for jobs as governesses and teachers and eventually for university degrees and civil-service positions.

Although liberal Protestant reformers may have been critical of the traditional forms of female education, Catholic educational leaders, both men and women, were not. Their wealth, prominence, and nationalist aspirations flourishing at this time, Irish Catholics clung to their Catholicism and its traditions for reasons of both religious loyalty and political and cultural resistance. Liberal Protestant social critiques, in this case of female education, did not resonate with them. In their eyes female education was as it should be, training up religiously and morally upright women whose societal role was, and ought to be, centered on family life.

This is exactly what convent superior boarding schools did their best to accomplish. Curricula included not only English, French, Italian, history, geography, writing, and arithmetic, but also needlework, drawing, deportment, and conduct. End-of-term competitions meant prizes and marks for those girls deemed to be most refined in the art of politeness. Employment needs or aspirations, let alone intellectual pursuits, were believed to be not only frivolous but dangerous as well. Domestic accomplishments—be they those required by the wealthy, the middle ranks, or the lower classes—were the proper courses of study for Irish girls and women. Yet regardless of whether convent superiors approved of the new demands for female educational reform, change was on its way.

STATE SUPPORT OF SECONDARY EDUCATION

After a decade of lobbying efforts by several reform movements aimed at winning publicly funded secondary education, the British government passed the Intermediate Education Act in 1878. The law provided limited state support for schools offering education beyond the primary level, and it included female secondary institutions. This act was followed by the creation of the Royal University of Ireland in 1879, which opened university exams to women (though they were still barred from attending classes or taking degrees at the country's universities). Taken together, these two pieces of legislation accelerated the reform of female education and helped to lay the groundwork for eventual access to full educational rights in the early twentieth century.

Beginning in the summer of 1879, schools throughout Ireland were invited to present advanced students for public examinations. Topics for the exams were set by a national examining board (consisting of both Protestants and Catholics), and students deemed by the examiners to have passed or excelled in the various subjects tested were given monetary awards and honors. In addition, schools received results fees that were determined by the success of their students. The system of public exams and prizes that was used to distribute state money—customary practice in Irish schools—was believed to be an effective means of raising educational standards. The major subject areas stressed were Latin, Greek, and English language, history, and literature; higher mathematics (algebra, geometry, trigonometry); Irish (though Irish history was included later than was the Irish language) and French; and to a lesser extent, the sciences (botany and zoology). Schools did not have to present students in all subject areas but could compete in fields of their choosing. Convent schools, for example, competed regularly in English and French, but were slower than Protestant schools to begin teaching girls Latin.

Exams were held in forty cities and towns throughout the country at the end of the summer term and lasted for nearly two weeks. Though the system was criticized for encouraging a rigid educational curriculum (undermining intellectual pursuit and excellence in areas outside those tested) and also for leading to a "cramming" culture within the schools, those Protestant women who had led the push for expanded female education believed that the intermediate act had produced nothing short of a revolution in education for women in Ireland.

Catholic educators were not so impressed. Though some among the Catholic elite did desire a more academically challenging educational experience for their daughters, mother superiors were slow to back the secondary education system. They complained of the travel and long stays away from school necessitated by the examination system. They worried about their pupils being exposed to a range of influences not to their liking and outside their control. They questioned the long-term effects of an education that seemed to be of no great purpose and to devalue women's central domestic role.

Yet they faced a dilemma on several levels. Though they did not like the system of examinations or the curriculum being developed, still, they did not like turning away state money that could be put to good use. Also, convents possessed a competitive spirit—especially when the competition was with the Protestant community. It is no surprise, then, that convent superiors were loath to see Protestant girls' schools take top prizes year after year. Finally, growing numbers of young Catholic women themselves wanted secondary and university educations; the best among them began to attend the Protestant-managed Alexandra School and College in Dublin, which admitted students of all denominations. It was not until 1893, after Archbishop William Walsh of Dublin approved the foundation of Saint Mary's University College in response to this very issue that convents throughout the country felt free to take up the challenge. In 1892 twenty convent schools competed for prizes and results fees. In 1893 twenty-nine did so; and by 1898, forty-five convent schools (60 percent of Catholic girl's secondary schools) were among those on the results list. In 1899 the Saint Louis convent in Monaghan was the first Catholic school to place second in the country, and in 1901, the Eccles Street Dominican School in Dublin placed first. With the support of the Catholic hierarchy and their initial reservations now behind them, mother superiors never looked back. In the twentieth century they won accolades (from both the British and Irish governments and the church hierarchy) for their able, effective, and successful administration of female secondary education.

SEE ALSO Duffy, James; Education: Primary Public Education—National Schools from 1831; Education: Secondary Education, Male; Education: Women's Education; Literacy and Popular Culture; Religion: Since 1690; Roman Catholic Church: 1829 to 1891; Roman Catholic Church: Since 1891

Bibliography

Breathnach, Eibhlín. "Charting New Waters: Women's Experience in Higher Education, 1879–1908." In *Girls Don't Do Honours: Irish Women in Education in the 19th and 20th Centuries*, edited by Mary Cullen. 1987.

Luddy, Maria. "Isabella M. S. Tod." In *Women, Power and Consciousness in 19th Century Ireland*, edited by Mary Cullen and Maria Luddy. 1995.

Magray, Mary Peckham. *The Transforming Power of the Nuns: Women, Religion, and Cultural Change in Ireland, 1750–1900.* 1998.

McElligott, T. J. *Secondary Education in Ireland, 1870–1921.* 1981.

O'Connor, Anne V. "The Revolution in Girls' Secondary Education in Ireland, 1860–1910." In *Girls Don't Do Honours: Irish Women in Education in the 19th and 20th Centuries*, edited by Mary Cullen. 1987.

O'Connor, Anne V. "Anne Jellicoe." In *Women, Power and Consciousness in 19th Century Ireland*, edited by Mary Cullen and Maria Luddy. 1995.

Mary Peckham Magray

SECONDARY EDUCATION, MALE

Defining the state's role in education and establishing an appropriate curriculum for middle-class Irish adolescents complicated the question of how best to provide a system of secondary education during the late nineteenth and early twentieth centuries. Attempts to address these issues were affected by the Catholic bishops' determination to manage their local schools and thereby shield their students from proselytization, and by debates over the value of including subjects with Irish cultural and historical content in the curriculum.

After 1831 the national schools provided primary education to an expanding number of children, but in 1870 less than 5 percent of the pupils, or some 25,000 students, advanced to the secondary level. Secondary schools were managed either privately, or by dioceses, or by Catholic religious teaching orders. They varied widely in endowment, enrollment, quality of facilities, and skill of the teaching staff. There were few religiously mixed schools, and boys and girls attended separate schools. Only forty-seven secondary schools were under Catholic management, and the hierarchy, among others with an interest in education, looked for a way to provide further education for middle-class youths with scholastic ability.

Proponents of educational reform collaborated in 1878 with the Conservative government to secure passage of the Intermediate Education Act (Ireland). The act maintained the principle that Ireland would have publicly funded and locally managed denominational education—the defining characteristic of the Irish national schools. The legislation established the Intermediate Board of Education; additional parliamentary activity in 1900, 1913, and 1914, several official inquiries, and annual reports provided information for subsequent administrative adjustments. Prominent Irishmen were selected to represent Catholic or Protestant interests on the seven-member board, which was responsible for a system that encompassed, on the eve of partition, 356 schools and 27,250 students, 16,093 male and 11,157 female, aged fourteen to eighteen. The annual interest on a grant of one million pounds, made available from the disestablishment of the Church of Ireland, was designated for intermediate education; later, a percentage of customs and excise taxes supplemented the budget. No provision was made for building, equipping, or maintaining new schools, and no provision was made for the training of secondary teachers. The Irish Christian Brothers operated the only training college for secondary teachers. Lay teachers, who were outnumbered by teaching members of religious orders, were chronically underpaid and enjoyed no security of tenure. The salaries of women teachers (forty-eight pounds in 1905) was about half the amount earned by male teachers; both earned less than the better-trained national-school teachers. For good or ill, secondary teachers, unlike their national-school counterparts, were not subjected to the periodic visits from school inspectors until 1908, when officials were appointed for the principal subjects.

The curriculum for preparatory, junior, middle, and senior grades was conceived along classical lines: A liberal education was considered by policymakers to be the best preparation, particularly for males who hoped to enter the professions. Subjects included Latin and Greek (important to Catholic leaders, who saw intermediate schools as fruitful recruiting grounds for the priesthood), English, German, Italian, French (favored by girls), drawing and music, history and historical geography, the natural sciences, algebra and arithmetic, and bookkeeping.

A dominant feature of secondary pedagogy was the payment-by-results policy. At the beginning of the academic year the board issued a program of study that effectively determined the amount of instructional time that teachers devoted to various subjects. At the end of the year students presented themselves for public examinations in which their demonstrated ability was recognized by prizes, exhibitions, medals, and certificates. The board awarded teachers extra fees according to their pupils' achievements. This policy prompted teachers to encourage students to cram into their heads as much detail as possible in order to roll up points on a given examination. In the early 1880s, about four times as many boys as girls presented themselves for examination, but that gap was closing by 1920. Boys, however, generally maintained a slightly higher overall pass rate: 52 percent to 48 percent was a typical margin.

The payment-by-results policy seems stultifying, but contemporaries believed that preparation of the memory was appropriate for postsecondary students, who would encounter similar examinations for the civil service, for clerkships in businesses, and for admission to universities. Catholic schools found the policy especially lucrative. They quickly surpassed Protestant schools in the production of prizewinning students; by the end of the century Catholic students were regularly sweeping up over three-fourths of the exhibitions. Catholic secondary schools also competed with their rivals—one teaching order versus another—to boast of the highest number of awards. The negative effect of the emphasis on testing was the psychological toll on those students, about half, who were deemed insufficiently prepared to take the examinations, and on those who failed the examinations, thereby hurting their schools' financial and competitive positions.

In time the Christian Brothers' secondary schools in Dublin and Cork, which attracted male students largely from the lower socioeconomic strata, were winning nearly 50 percent of the fees payable after the annual examinations. Renowned for their teaching ability at the primary level, the Brothers' success at the secondary level was remarkable because their schools enrolled only about 3,000 students, less than 10 percent of the total receiving a secondary education. Moreover, their curriculum did not coincide with the standard intermediate program, as the Brothers placed heavy emphasis on

Irish subjects and did not offer much Latin or Greek, subjects that the Intermediate Board favored with some 25 percent of prizes awarded. The Brothers' success strained their relationship with both the elite Catholic boarding schools and the Intermediate Board: The former complained that the Brothers had overstepped their bounds by presenting lower-class boys for examination; the latter would not heed the Brothers' requests to implement curricular reforms in Irish history and the Irish language that would further increase their students' opportunities on the examinations.

The Brothers were not alone in criticizing the curriculum. Various advocates complained that the classical curriculum was inappropriate for Irish needs and that it ought to be revised to prepare students for specific careers, including agriculture. The most persistent critics, however, were cultural nationalists who demanded curricular reform to promote the development of the students' knowledge and understanding of their nationality and heritage. Cultural nationalists, sparked by the ideas of Young Ireland writers of the 1840s and following the lead of the Gaelic Athletic Association and Gaelic League in the 1880s and 1890s, fostered widespread interest in Irish history and culture, particularly the language and its literature. Cultural-revival enthusiasts protested rightly that courses in these subjects were relegated to minor positions in the curriculum, and pointed out that the thousands of students who studied them were discriminated against in the awarding of points on the annual examinations. The board would not bow to this pressure and was consequently branded an antinational institution that aimed to transform Irish youths into anglicized West Britons. This criticism became a crucial part of the revolutionary rhetoric that advanced nationalists in the Sinn Féin movement levelled against Dublin Castle rule. Many significant Sinn Féin leaders and supporters of the movement for Irish independence were Christian Brothers' boys.

The administration of the intermediate system was divided when the country was partitioned in 1921. The new government in Northern Ireland did not disrupt local control of Catholic secondary schools, and the existing curriculum remained largely in place. The Provisional Government in Dublin, however, abolished the Intermediate Board in 1922 and instituted a dramatically revised curriculum designed along cultural nationalist lines.

SEE ALSO Duffy, James; Education: Primary Public Education—National Schools from 1831; Education: Secondary Education, Female; Literacy and Popular Culture; Religion: Since 1690; Religious Orders: Men; Rice, Edmund; Roman Catholic Church: 1829 to 1891; Roman Catholic Church: Since 1891

Bibliography

Coldrey, Brian M. *Faith and Fatherland: The Christian Brothers and the Development of Irish Nationalism, 1838–1921.* 1988.

McElligott, T. J. *Secondary Education in Ireland, 1870–1921.* 1981.

Titley, E. Brian. *Church, State, and the Control of Schooling in Ireland, 1900–1914.* 1983.

Lawrence W. McBride

UNIVERSITY EDUCATION

Commonly known as "the university question," the attempt to establish a university system that offered accessible and good quality education without offending the religious sensibilities of Irish Roman Catholics, Anglicans, and Presbyterians was one of the most difficult tasks faced by all late-nineteenth- and early-twentieth-century British governments. Before 1845 only Trinity College provided laymen with third-level education in Ireland. A lay college at Maynooth functioned only from 1795 until 1817, when the institution turned exclusively to training priests. Trinity College was perceived to be the university of the Protestant Ascendancy, and Catholics were encouraged by their bishops to shun the college. Both the expansion of a Catholic professional and mercantile middle class and a perception that Catholics were discriminated against in the realm of university education encouraged demands for the establishment of a university that was suitable for Catholics.

In 1845 Sir Robert Peel's government created the Queen's Colleges. Established at Belfast, Cork, and Galway and linked to form the Queen's University in 1850, the colleges offered low fees, good scholarships, and a vocational ethos. They were secular institutions, but provision was made for the pastoral care and religious instruction of students of various denominations. The colleges were an expensive attempt both to undermine the demand for repeal and to provide institutions in which Irish students of different religious backgrounds could be educated together. This attempt to institute "mixed education" met with fierce resistance from many quarters, but was welcomed by such political progressives as Young Ireland.

The Catholic hierarchy condemned the colleges, which were denounced as "godless." By 1850 ecclesiastics were forbidden to have any dealings with the new

Before 1960 university education in Ireland was reserved for the privileged few. Of the meager total of 3,200 university students in 1901, about 1,000 attended Trinity College (pictured here in 1918). Trinity's connections with Anglicanism were still very strong, though non-Anglicans had been admitted to fellowships and scholarships in 1873. Irish Catholics generally went elsewhere in Ireland when they attended university at all. © HULTON ARCHIVES/GETTY IMAGES. REPRODUCED BY PERMISSION.

colleges, priests were barred from accepting college offices, and the laity were instructed to shun them at all costs. Some Catholics did attend them, but the Cork and Galway colleges attracted fewer students than the Belfast college, which drew a steady flow of Presbyterian students. In response to this initiative, in 1854 the Catholic bishops founded the Catholic University under the rectorship of the famed English convert John Henry Newman. This institution labored under almost constant financial difficulty. Its medical school in Cecilia Street earned a good reputation, but as the institution received neither a charter nor an endowment, it failed to live up to the expectations of its clerical founders. W. E. Gladstone's proposal in 1873 for a single Irish university consisting of the Belfast and Cork colleges, Trinity, the Presbyterian Magee College, and the Catholic University led to the fall of his government and was met with almost universal rejection in Ireland.

One of the most important nineteenth-century initiatives in the realm of higher education was the introduction in 1879 of the University Education (Ireland) Act, which made way for the dissolution of the Queen's University and the establishment of the Royal University of Ireland. The Royal University was an examining body only. It had the power to grant degrees to anybody who passed its examinations; where or by whom students were educated made no difference, except in the case of medical students, who were required to attend approved medical schools. In 1882 the Catholic University was restructured to consist of a number of affiliated Catholic educational institutions whose students could register at the Royal University. The old Catholic University became one of these and was renamed University College, Dublin; the Jesuit fathers undertook the running of the college in 1883. The teaching of medicine continued at Cecilia Street under the title of the Catholic

University Medical School. The Board of the Royal University distributed thirty-two university fellowships to approved colleges throughout Ireland; the main recipients were the old Queen's Colleges, which continued to exist but had no special role or privileges in the new university, and University College, Dublin, which was regularly awarded half of the Royal University's fellowships. In this way indirect funding was given for denominational education.

In some respects the Royal University was remarkably progressive. University prizes and scholarships were open to male and female students of all denominations, and the numbers of students presenting themselves for examinations grew rapidly. But the Royal University was largely viewed as merely temporary. The system encouraged intense rivalry and competition as results were published and widely dissected, while students in unendowed private colleges were under heavy pressure to win cash prizes. But the main objection was the lack of a collegiate life that could compare with Trinity's. In the absence of an acceptable Catholic teaching university or university college, various secondary schools and newly established colleges became de facto university colleges that were deemed unsatisfactory by lay and clerical Catholics. By 1901 the majority of students sitting Royal University examinations were educated privately or at miscellaneous schools. Calls for the abolition or major reorganization of the Royal University continued.

In the early twentieth century numerous schemes were suggested, including the establishment of a second college, Catholic in atmosphere and administration, alongside Trinity in the University of Dublin. This proposal met with fierce rejection from the Trinity authorities, as did another plan to incorporate Trinity, the old Queen's Colleges, and a new Dublin college into a federal structure. Royal Commissions on University Education in 1902 to 1903 and on Trinity College in 1906 to 1907 failed to reach agreement on the issue, which continued to provoke debate in Ireland and in Britain. Despite a number of near settlements, commissions, and debates, it was only when the Catholic hierarchy finally conceded that a Catholic University would not be endowed by governments hostile to denominational education, and that Trinity would not be interfered with, that a settlement seemed likely. Augustine Birrell's National University scheme of 1908 finally placated most interested parties, but it was hardly greeted with enthusiasm. The Irish Universities Bill of 1908 allowed for the establishment of two new universities: the National University of Ireland, a federal institution that encompassed the old Queen's Colleges in Galway and Cork, and a transformed and endowed University College, Dublin, and

Queen's College, Belfast, which became the Queen's University. Trinity College was left untouched.

The colleges were formally nondenominational, but the university senates and governing bodies of each of the institutions were to reflect the religious affiliation of most college members; the Belfast institution would cater mainly to Presbyterians, while University College, Dublin—which retained many of its professors—catered primarily to Catholics. The Catholic Medical School was merged with the new National University, and Maynooth became a recognized college in 1913. The Gaelic League demanded that Irish be included as a compulsory matriculation subject in the new university. This provoked fierce debate, but the requirement was formalized for all native-born Irish candidates in 1913.

SEE ALSO Education: Women's Education; Maynooth; Presbyterianism; Roman Catholic Church: 1829 to 1891; Roman Catholic Church: Since 1891; Trinity College

Bibliography

Akenson, D. H. *The Irish Education Experiment: The National System of Education in the Nineteenth Century.* 1970.

Atkinson, N. *Irish Education: A History of Educational Institutions.* 1969.

Coolahan, John. *Irish Education: History and Structure.* 1983.

Dowling, P. J. *A History of Irish Education: A Study of Conflicting Loyalties.* 1971.

McElligott, T. J. *Education in Ireland.* 1966.

McElligott, T. J. *Secondary Education in Ireland, 1870–1921.* 1981.

Ó Buachalla, Séamas. *Education Policy in Twentieth Century Ireland.* 1990.

Senia Pašeta

WOMEN'S EDUCATION

Before 1878 the secondary education of female students was largely undertaken by private tutors or in fee-paying schools that usually reflected the religious and class backgrounds of students. Provision of postprimary education for working-class girls was virtually nonexistent. The first attempts to improve women's higher education were made by bourgeois Protestant campaigners who established a number of women's colleges, including the Ladies' Collegiate School (later Victoria College) in 1859, the Queen's Institute in 1861, and Alexandra College in 1866. In 1882 they founded the Central Association of Schoolmistresses and Other Ladies Interested in Education to lobby for the extension of women's access to higher education. Middle-class Catholic women were mostly taught by nuns, especially the Ursuline and Loreto orders which brought a strong French tradition to Irish Catholic schools—particularly boarding schools—by emphasizing literary subjects, refinement, order, and discipline.

Women's access to higher education was revolutionized by the introduction of intermediate education in 1878. This system of secondary education was open to all Irish students, male and female, and was administered by the Intermediate Education Board, which examined students annually and paid fees to the schools that produced the highest-scoring students in junior, middle, and senior grade examinations. A number of girls' secondary colleges entered their students for these examinations, and although fewer women than men presented themselves for examinations, by the turn of the twentieth century women were outperforming men in almost all subjects.

The establishment of several women's colleges in the 1880s and 1890s that aimed to prepare women for intermediate examinations raised the standard of women's education enormously. Many of these colleges were adapted to prepare women for entrance to the Royal University, which was established in 1879. Based on the University of London, this university was an examining body only, whose annual examinations, prizes, and scholarships were available to male and female students. It allocated a number of fellowships to teachers at approved institutions, but the preparation of students was left almost entirely to individual schools and private tutors. Since women's colleges received none of the Royal University's fellowships, inadequate teaching in classical languages and mathematics made the task of penetrating such traditionally male subjects as medicine and philosophy nearly impossible. Despite this, Protestant schools once again took the lead with several colleges, including Alexandra College, establishing departments that prepared women for Royal University examinations. Fearful that ambitious Catholic women would go to Protestant schools, Catholic schools followed suit by similarly introducing university classes for women. This began in 1883 with the Dominican convent school in Eccles Street, Dublin. Its women's university classes were taken over in 1893 by Saint Mary's University College, Dublin, which was soon joined by Loreto College, Saint Stephen's Green, and Saint Angela's in Cork. In addition, the old Queen's Colleges began gradually to admit women to classes that prepared them for Royal University examinations: Belfast in 1882, Cork in 1886, and Galway in 1888 (de-spite fierce opposition from the local Catholic bishop). The Cecilia Street Medical School—a remnant of the old Catholic University—admitted women in 1896. In total, fourteen educational institutions opened their doors to female students of the Royal University between 1879 and 1889.

Despite these improvements, teaching provisions at most women's colleges were so poor that many women were forced to resort to expensive private tuition in order to pass their examinations. Very fortunate women's colleges occasionally managed to engage a Royal University fellow for an hour or two, but the vast majority of female students had no contact with fellows, which were the only teaching provisions offered by the Royal University. The absolute refusal by University College, Dublin, to allow women to attend the lectures given by university fellows—of which University College, Dublin, was usually awarded half—placed women at a severe disadvantage.

By 1902 Catholic and Protestant women together formed the Irish Association of Women Graduates and Candidate Graduates, which presented evidence about the position of women in higher education to the Royal Commission on University Education in Ireland in 1902. The majority of the association's members were graduates of the Royal University, but others had studied at medical schools and other tertiary institutions. University College, Dublin, became the focus of a prolonged feminist campaign. Women were determined to gain admission to it as it was the only institution in Dublin that boasted any sort of collegiate life. Some sympathetic Royal University senators took up the women's cause and offered the use of university rooms to University College fellows who agreed to repeat their lectures to women. This unsatisfactory arrangement lasted only a few years because many fellows refused to repeat lectures, and others charged fees well beyond the means of women students. Finally in 1901, under enormous pressure, college authorities were forced to admit women to lectures in University College. Only second- and third-year arts students, mainly drawn from Catholic colleges, were allowed into lecture halls. First-year students were excluded and women were still barred from becoming full members of the college community. All these restrictions were lifted in 1908 with the establishment of the National University of Ireland. University College, Dublin, and the Queen's Colleges in Cork and Galway became constituent colleges of the new university, while the Belfast Queen's College became Queen's University. Women were awarded full equality in these institutions in the areas of teaching, degrees, and staff appointments.

Every university in the United Kingdom with the exception of Durham had admitted women (without giving them degrees) by 1892, and even Oxford and Cambridge had allowed women to attend lectures and to be placed on examination lists. Female activists reminded the authorities that the Irish universities and university colleges lagged behind the rest of the United Kingdom. Beginning in the 1880s, Trinity College was inundated by petitions and memorials from advocates of women's education. Although some university fellows supported women's demands, the university board made only meager concessions, such as the decision in 1896 to allow women only very limited access to certain examinations, but not to teaching facilities. Under considerable pressure from campaigners, Trinity College finally admitted women in 1904.

Although the degrees of all Irish universities were open to women by 1908, objections to mixed-sex education remained. Alexandra College supported the admission of women to the degrees of Trinity College but argued that their education should be arranged separately from men's. Alexandra's college department sought affiliation with Trinity College, but its bid was unsuccessful. The first women who attended Trinity College did so under highly restrictive conditions, but the provision of a lady registrar, a women's hostel, and the growth of social activities for women ensured that their active involvement in university life increased year by year. Victoria College made a similar application for affiliation to the Queen's University in Belfast, but that too was turned down and women were integrated into the new university alongside men. The education of nuns presented another problem, as the Catholic authorities were reluctant to allow them to mix freely with male students in the colleges of the National University. Several Catholic women's colleges applied for affiliation with the National University, but their bids were unsuccessful, and nuns began to attend college lectures on a regular basis beginning in the mid-1920s. Although fewer women than men completed secondary school and entered university for much of the first half of the twentieth century, this pattern was largely reversed by the 1980s. Female participation and performance statistics in secondary education are now equal to or better than male rates, and women make up just over half of all undergraduate and postgraduate students in Irish universities. In addition, women's participation in the traditionally male fields of medicine, law, and accountancy have now reached or exceeded 50 percent.

SEE ALSO Education: Secondary Education, Female; Education: University Education; Religious Orders: Women; Trinity College; Women and Work since the Mid-Nineteenth Century; **Primary Documents:** From the *Report of the Commission on the Status of Women* (1972)

Bibliography

Connolly, Brid, and Ann Bridget Ryan, eds. *Women and Education in Ireland.* 2 vols. 1999.

Coolahan, John. *Irish Education: History and Structure.* 1983.

Cullen, Mary, ed. *Girls Don't Do Honours: Irish Women in Education in the Nineteenth and Twentieth Centuries.* 1987.

McElligott, T. J. *Secondary Education in Ireland, 1870–1921.* 1981.

Senia Pašeta

Edwardian Reform

The death of Henry VIII and the accession of his sickly nine-year-old son as Edward VI in 1547 led to a dramatic change in religious policy in England. The new king and his advisors were firmly Protestant and ensured that the break from Rome became closely linked to a commitment to the reformed religion. The archbishop of Canterbury, Thomas Cranmer, led the way with two new prayer books in 1549 and 1552, the latter containing a clearly Protestant communion service, and he was working on a new confession of faith, the Forty-Three Articles, in 1553 when religious reform was brought to a sudden halt by the death of Edward and the succession of his Roman Catholic half-sister Mary in 1553.

The rapid progress of the Edwardian Reformation was a reflection not just of the power of the centralized English state, but also of the commitment of Cranmer and many others to the new religious ideas. But the speed of change aroused opposition among conservative clergy and much of the population. In Ireland, where Protestants were much fewer and the power of the government far weaker than in England, religious resistance was more formidable. Such limited success as had been achieved in the reign of Henry VIII was focused upon securing compliance with the jurisdictional change from the pope to the new "supreme head," the monarch. But Edwardian Protestantism led to important changes in personnel, theology, and liturgy, and marked a dramatic new departure in Irish religious policy.

Lord Deputy Bellingham, with the reluctant cooperation of Archbishop Brown of Dublin, issued injunctions against Catholic practices and imposed the new Protestant communion service. In 1551 the first English *Book of Common Prayer* was introduced to Ireland and used in many churches there. Bishop Staples of Meath set out to preach Protestant doctrine, scandalizing his more conservative clergy and laity by attacking prayer to the saints and the sacrifice of the mass. The archbishop of Armagh, George Dowdall, resolutely refused to countenance such innovations, and in 1551 he fled Ireland rather than conform to the new faith. In his place the new lord deputy, Sir James Croft, in 1552 secured the service of two English Protestants: John Bale, who was appointed bishop of Ossory, and Hugh Goodacre, who succeeded Dowdall at Armagh but died soon after. This marked an important shift in English religious policy away from slow reform relying upon local clergy toward a much more rapid process necessarily relying upon clergy imported from England.

Bishop Bale's uncompromisingly Protestant religious principles came as something of a shock for the Church of Ireland. At his consecration in Dublin on 2 February 1553 he refused to let Archbishop Browne use the old ordinal, insisting on the new English one. As bishop in Ossory, he preached on Protestant doctrine regularly to the congregation in Kilkenny Cathedral, attacked Catholic idolatry, and used the new 1552 prayer book. Bale, however, was unusual in the vigor of his commitment to the new religion. More typical was Archbishop Browne, who went along with the reforms, but without much commitment. Not surprisingly, after the death of Edward in July 1553, Ireland swiftly returned to the papal fold.

SEE ALSO Church of Ireland: Elizabethan Era; Marian Restoration; Protestant Reformation in the Early Sixteenth Century; Religion: 1500 to 1690

Bibliography

Bradshaw, B. I. "The Edwardian Reformation in Ireland." *Archivium Hibernicum* 34 (1977): 83–99.

Hayes-McCoy, G. A. "Conciliation, Coercion, and the Protestant Reformation, 1547–71." In *A New History of Ireland*, Vol. 3, *Early Modern Ireland, 1534–1691*, edited by T. W. Moody, F. X. Martin, and F. J. Byrne. 1976.

Alan Ford

Eighteenth-Century Politics

1690 TO 1714—REVOLUTION SETTLEMENT	JAMES MCGUIRE
1714 TO 1778—INTEREST POLITICS	JAMES KELLY
1778 TO 1795—PARLIAMENTARY AND POPULAR POLITICS	JAMES KELLY
1795 TO 1800—REPRESSION, REBELLION, AND UNION	RUAN O'DONNELL

1690 TO 1714—REVOLUTION SETTLEMENT

To many Protestants the Articles of Limerick (3 October 1691) conceded too much and left open the possibility of future Catholic, indeed Jacobite, resurgence. The initial determination of William III's government to honor what had been agreed at Limerick saw Protestant anxiety turn into political resentment. The all-Protestant parliament that met in Dublin in October 1692 was implacable, assertive and short-lived. Although the government did not seek parliamentary ratification of the Articles of Limerick, it met opposition at every turn, most significantly on the key issue of financial supply. When the commons claimed a "sole right" to determine how taxes could be raised and to initiate the heads of money bills, the lord lieutenant (Viscount Sydney) somewhat disingenuously chose to regard these claims as a breach of Poynings' Law and brought the session to an end in early November. This parliament never met again.

The breakdown in relations between the political nation and the administration posed the questions: How was Ireland to be governed? Could another parliament be summoned? The solution came from Sir Henry Capel, a lord justice from 1693 and later lord deputy (1695–1696), who advised that a parliament might safely meet if a *modus vivendi* were established with the Protestant political nation. The strategy he devised involved compromise on money bills (the sole right was not accepted in principle, though the House of Commons' control of draft money bills was largely conceded), a legislative program designed to meet the perceived insecurities of the Protestant elite (including penal or "popery" laws, as contemporaries called them), and a

View of the Battle of the Boyne, 1 July 1690 (old style), etching by Romeyn de Hooghe. The critical battle in which the forces of James II were defeated by those of William of Orange, enabling him to occupy Dublin. NATIONAL GALLERY OF IRELAND, CAT. NO. 11655. REPRODUCED BY PERMISSION.

skillful use of patronage that allowed for parliamentary management (significantly lacking under Sydney in 1692). Capel's handiwork in 1695 became the template for government-parliament relations into the later decades of the eighteenth century, occasionally breaking down but never irretrievably.

The 1695 parliament outlasted Capel, who died in office in 1696. By the time of its dissolution in 1699 it had enacted a substantial number of statutes, including four penal laws, restraining foreign education (1695), disarming papists (1695), banishing Catholic bishops and members of religious orders (1697), and preventing Catholics from being solicitors (1699). An act ratifying the Articles of Limerick also passed (1697), but its terms were restrictive and honored the letter rather than the spirit of what had been agreed in 1691. Further penal measures were passed in subsequent Irish parliaments, especially in the 1703 to 1711 parliament during Queen Anne's reign. The most far-reaching was the "act to prevent the further growth of popery" (1704), which denied Catholics the right either to buy land or to lease property for more than thirty-one years and altered the law of succession (primogeniture replaced by gavelkind) so that on the death of a landowner the property could not be willed to the eldest son but must be divided among all sons, unless the eldest son conformed to the Protestant Established Church. The penal laws of the 1690s and early 1700s were never intended as a coherent code. It is clear nonetheless that they were meant, in different ways and by attacking differing targets, to buttress Protestant security and to ensure that the former Catholic political and social elite would never again

challenge, as they had in the later 1680s, the Protestant hegemony that had been established in the mid-seventeenth century.

Protestants who refused to conform to the established church were also the subject of legislative discrimination. Hopes of a limited toleration for Protestant dissent, along the lines of the English Toleration Act of 1689, were not realized until 1719. Indeed, the 1703 popery act had included a sacramental-test clause that effectively excluded Protestant Dissenters from civil office and borough politics. Dissenters, especially Ulster Presbyterians, had few supporters in the Irish parliament, and they faced implacable opposition from senior Church of Ireland clergy, who strongly objected to legal toleration. The contrast in the treatment of Protestant dissent in England and Ireland can be explained by the proportionately greater threat that Dissenters posed to the established church in Ireland, seen in the concentration in parts of Ulster of a Presbyterian population overwhelmingly Scots in character and sympathy. Occasionally, government in Dublin Castle and Whitehall might seek toleration for Dissent, and the *regium donum*, a modest stipend for Presbyterian ministers, was paid by Whig and Tory administrations, but the Protestant elite remained obdurately opposed to concession.

The *modus vivendi* achieved in the government-parliament relationship in the mid-1690s did not remove the potential for resentment at the unequal constitutional relationship with England. Such resentment usually arose when the English (British from 1707) parliament legislated on matters touching Irish trade or land. This occurred twice in William III's reign, first with the passing in 1699 at Westminster of an act to prohibit the export of Irish woollens to overseas markets, and again in 1700 with the act of resumption that nullified William III's grants of forfeited Jacobite estates. Since the latter had either been sold or leased to Protestant proprietors, their resumption by the English parliament was deeply destabilizing for a landed elite which had so recently come out of the Jacobite crisis. Even for those with no economic interest in the woollen trade or the forfeited estates, this sort of legislation suggested that Ireland's status as a kingdom was purely nominal, and that its relationship with England was more that of a colony to the imperial power. William Molyneux had seen the implications of such legislation in 1698, when a draft woollen bill was being considered at Westminster, and the terms in which his *Case of Ireland's Being Bound by Acts of Parliament in England Stated* had been condemned in the English House of Commons served to underline the subordinate status of King William's loyal Protestant subjects in Ireland even before the offending acts had reached the statute book. Under the circumstances it was hardly surprising that in the first parliamentary session of Queen Anne's reign the Irish House of Commons should petition the queen for union. Even Molyneux had referred to union as a "happiness we can hardly hope for" (Simms 1982, p. 106). The advantage of union was that it would remove the possibilities for legislative discrimination and provide instead the benefits of representation and consent. But pleas from Ireland for union evoked neither interest nor sympathy at Whitehall or Westminster, where the wider English interest was seen as better served by Ireland remaining both separate and subordinate. There was also an inconsistency, even selectivity, in the expression of Protestant Ireland's resentment at English legislative supremacy. It was after all an act passed at Westminster in 1691 which prevented Roman Catholics from sitting in any future Irish parliament, and Protestant Ireland was happy to accept the English Act of Settlement (1701), which paved the way for the Hanoverian succession.

SEE ALSO Catholic Merchants and Gentry from 1690 to 1800; Derry, Siege of; Eighteenth-Century Politics: 1714 to 1778—Interest Politics; Eighteenth-Century Politics: 1778 to 1795—Parliamentary and Popular Politics; Eighteenth-Century Politics: 1795 to 1800—Repression, Rebellion, and Union; Government from 1690 to 1800; Jacobites and the Williamite Wars; Military Forces from 1690 to 1800; Molyneux, William; Penal Laws; Politics: 1690 to 1800—A Protestant Kingdom; Protestant Ascendancy: 1690 to 1800; Trade and Trade Policy from 1691 to 1800; **Primary**

Documents: An Act to Prevent the Further Growth of Popery (1704)

Bibliography

Connolly, S. J. *Religion, Law, and Power: The Making of Protestant Ireland, 1660–1760.* 1992.

McGrath, Charles Ivar. *The Making of the Eighteenth-Century Irish Constitution: Government, Parliament, and the Revenue, 1692–1714.* 2000.

McGuire, James. "The Irish Parliament of 1692." In *Penal Era and Golden Age: Essays in Irish History, 1690–1800*, edited by Thomas Bartlett and D. W. Hayton. 1979.

Simms, John G. *William Molyneux of Dublin, 1656–1698.* Edited by P. H. Kelly. 1982.

James McGuire

1714 TO 1778—INTEREST POLITICS

The inauguration of the Hanoverian succession with the coming of George I to the throne in 1714 put a sudden and immediate end to the politics of party in Ireland. Deprived of their primary rationale, Tories across the kingdom either stepped hastily into the political wilderness or embarked on a campaign of political reinvention, whereas the now dominant Whigs availed of the opportunity to consolidate their command over the levers of power. Locally, this usually resulted in the exclusion of Tory activists from boroughs and corporations, as a result in some instances of specific acts of the Irish parliament. At the national level the imputation of disloyalty was sufficient to ensure that Toryism dissolved as a political force.

New and familiar cleavages based on court and country, personality, and simple ambition soon moved to take the place of party allegiances. The decline in the likelihood of a French invasion facilitated greater tolerance, though the introduction of a formal prohibition in 1727 on voting by Catholics reflected a commitment to uphold the penal laws. Meanwhile, successive lords lieutenant, unwilling to reside permanently in Ireland, were dependent on the guidance that they received from the leaders of the major (Protestant) political interests in their management of the Irish parliament. This in effect obliged them to decide during George I's reign (1714–1727) between the skillful and influential William Conolly and the ambitious and less predictable Alan Brodrick. Most opted for Conolly, though even he might dissent from such unpopular policies as the controversial attempt between 1724 and 1725 to introduce low-denomination copper coin—Wood's halfpence. This and other constitutional and fiscal crises energized a "patriot" sensibility in the kingdom. Perceiving that British politicians regarded Ireland as a dependent kingdom—an impression underlined by the Declaratory Act (1720), by which the Westminster legislature assumed the power to make law for Ireland—Irish Protestants welcomed the vigorous restatement of their legislative rights provided by Jonathan Swift's *Drapier's Letters* (1725). Swift's commentaries on the famine conditions that gripped the kingdom in the late 1720s also served as an important stimulus to economic patriotism.

In the wake of the dispute about Wood's halfpence, lords lieutenant expanded the role of selected Irish politicians ("undertakers") who "undertook" to manage the government's legislative program. The undertaker system was at its most effective under the direction and guidance of Henry Boyle, who performed that role for over twenty years from 1733. By ensuring that the key financial legislation was enacted at every biennial session, and by neutralizing such threats to political stability as emerged from the Dublin radical Charles Lucas, Boyle ensured that Irish politics remained on an even keel. By the early 1750s, however, a coalition of Irish politicians eager to assume his influence and officials resentful of his power sought to diminish his authority. The resulting crisis—the Money Bill dispute (1753–1756)—did not put an end to the undertaker system, but it did serve to introduce a degree of instability into the political process and controversy into public discourse. Stimulated to promote a political program that blended traditional Whig principles with civic virtue, a loose connection of Patriot politicians had emerged as a force to be reckoned with in the House of Commons by the late 1760s. Officials and ministers in London concluded that something needed to be done to affirm the authority of the crown in Ireland. A number of options were canvassed, but the one that found most favor was that of requiring lord lieutenants to reside in Ireland for the duration of their appointment. Because they did not much like the undertaker system, the Patriots might have been expected to support George, Lord Townshend (lord lieutenant, 1767–1772), when he challenged that system by residing in Ireland. But their conviction that his real object was to promote an aristocratic reaction, such as they perceived was also being promoted in England and America, prompted them to take the opposite course. Nevertheless, Townshend put an end to undertaking, thus prompting popular hopes for a more principled era. Increasingly vigorous demonstrations of support for parliamentary reform in the early 1770s had little impact on the House of Commons until the outbreak of hostilities between the Crown and the American colonies changed the context utterly.

SEE ALSO Burke, Edmund; Catholic Committee from 1756 to 1809; Catholic Merchants and Gentry from 1690 to 1800; Eighteenth-Century Politics: 1690 to 1714—Revolution Settlement; Eighteenth-Century Politics: 1778 to 1795—Parliamentary and Popular Politics; Eighteenth-Century Politics: 1795 to 1800—Repression, Rebellion, and Union; Flood, Henry; Government from 1690 to 1800; Grattan, Henry; Military Forces from 1690 to 1800; O'Conor, Charles, of Balenagare; Penal Laws; Politics: 1690 to 1800—A Protestant Kingdom; Protestant Ascendancy: 1690 to 1800; Trade and Trade Policy from 1691 to 1800

Bibliography

Bartlett, Thomas, and David W. Hayton, eds. *Penal Era and Golden Age.* 1979.

Burns, Robert E. *Irish Parliamentary Politics in the Eighteenth Century, 1714–60.* 2 vols. 1989–1990.

McNally, Patrick. *Parties, Patriots, and Undertakers: Parliamentary Politics in Early Hanoverian Ireland.* 1997.

Magennis, Eoin. *The Irish Political System, 1740–1765: The Golden Age of the Undertakers.* 2000.

James Kelly

1778 TO 1795—PARLIAMENTARY AND POPULAR POLITICS

Although the allocation of four thousand Irish troops to fight against the Americans in their war for independence and the imposition of an embargo on trade were the subject of heated debate in the Irish parliament, the full implications of the war on Irish domestic politics were not manifest until 1778. The entry of the French into the war on the side of the Americans generated alarm that the French might attempt to use Ireland as a back door to attack Britain, reinforced fears about the loyalties of the Catholic population, and prompted thousands of Protestants to band together in civilian Volunteer corps in order to supplement the depleted military. To encourage Catholic goodwill while the war was in progress, the Irish parliament was persuaded to ratify a bill that removed a number of burdensome restrictions on the rights of Catholics to lease land. Meanwhile, the Westminster legislature refused to implement a proposal in the summer of 1778 to allow Irish merchants to trade on the same terms as their British counterparts. A number of radical activists, with James Napper Tandy to the fore, responded with a campaign for nonimportation and nonconsumption of British goods in 1778 to 1779. Animated by Volunteer support, Henry Grattan and other Patriot leaders brought sufficient pressure upon ministers of the Crown that agreement was reached to concede Ireland free trade in the winter of 1779 to 1780.

The successful achievement of free trade inevitably prompted demands for constitutional reform, though there was less unanimity within the Patriot coalition on this issue. Some, such as the duke of Leinster objected in principle to the involvement of a paramilitary body like the Volunteers. Others were not convinced that the repeal of the Declaratory Act (1720) and the modification of Poynings' Law in a manner that deprived the British and Irish privy councils of the right to initiate, amend, and lay aside Irish legislation was in the best interest of a secure Anglo-Irish nexus. When the Irish parliament reconvened in the autumn of 1781, the Patriots made little headway until the Ulster Volunteers took up the cause. Their public pronouncement in support of legislative independence at a delegate meeting at Dungannon in February 1782 galvanized the faltering campaign and provided the Patriot leadership of Henry Grattan and Lord Charlemont with the authority, following a change of government in England, to secure the desired concessions at Westminster and College Green in the summer of 1782.

The ratification of legislative independence, which brought about what is conventionally but misleadingly known as "Grattan's parliament," increased the powers of the Irish parliament to make law. But it did not address the relationship of the Irish parliament to the Irish executive based at the Dublin Castle. The ratification, also in 1782, of a further measure of Catholic relief seemed to mark a new dawn politically, but the Patriots were increasingly weakened by internal differences. Grattan and Henry Flood disagreed over the advisability of requiring the British parliament formally to renounce its right to make law for Ireland. Flood enjoyed the support of most rank-and-file Volunteers, and when the Ulster Volunteers took up the issue of parliamentary reform in 1783, his readiness to support a plan that did not include the enfranchisement of Catholics was received with little enthusiasm by many erstwhile advocates of free trade and legislative independence. Encouraged by evidence of the fragmentation of the once powerful Patriot coalition, Prime Minister William Pitt boldly proposed a commercial union between Britain and Ireland. Irish suspicion of the proposal as a surreptitious attack on legislative independence prevented it from reaching the statute book—an outcome that left the Anglo-Irish connection dangerously unregulated in British eyes.

The political mood changed in the late 1780s, and the initiative in domestic Irish affairs shifted from the Patriots, with whom it had largely rested since 1779.

Indeed, the emergence of a more ideologically conservative viewpoint, encouraged by the fears generated by the agrarian movement, the Rightboys, acted as a disincentive to reform for a number of years. The Anglo-Irish relationship briefly returned to the political agenda in the winter of 1788 to 1789 with the incapacitation of George III, but of greater consequence was the formation (from the ranks of the Irish opposition) of the Whig Club and the radicalizing effects of the French Revolution. The failure of the parliamentary opposition to achieve significant further reform disillusioned radicals, who were attracted to the newly formed United Irish Society from the early winter of 1791. In practice, the radical strategy, which was to recreate the conditions that had wrought reform in the early 1780s, wanted for originality, and in the absence of overwhelming public support it never seemed likely to prevail. Catholic enfranchisement was approved in 1793, but it was in response to the independent activity of the Catholic Committee. Indeed, though some steps were taken to respond to the Whigs' eagerness to curb the pensions list, the formal replacement of the Volunteers with a state-controlled militia, the proscription of representative conventions, and the rejection of bills for parliamentary reform in 1793 and 1794 signaled that the political initiative remained firmly with the administration and its largely conservative supporters in the Irish parliament. This was underlined by the arrest and prosecution of the leadership of the Dublin United Irish Society, which caused several key figures in the movement either to withdraw from radical politics or to go into exile. The unexpected appointment of the liberal Whig, 2d Earl Fitzwilliam, as lord lieutenant in 1794 provided the proponents of reform with one more opportunity to reverse the tide. Guided by Grattan and his Whig colleagues, Fitzwilliam seemed intent on governing in accord with moderate reform principles. But by his sweeping changes of personnel and his promotion of Catholic emancipation, he exceeded his instructions. His recall not only destroyed the prospects of reform but also facilitated the adoption of a revolutionary strategy by those who had lost confidence in parliamentary government.

SEE ALSO Burke, Edmund; Catholic Committee from 1756 to 1809; Catholic Merchants and Gentry from 1690 to 1800; Defenderism; Eighteenth-Century Politics: 1690 to 1714—Revolution Settlement; Eighteenth-Century Politics: 1714 to 1778—Interest Politics; Eighteenth-Century Politics: 1795 to 1800—Repression, Rebellion, and Union; Fitzgerald, Lord Edward; Flood, Henry; Government from 1690 to 1800; Grattan, Henry; Keogh, John; Military Forces from 1690 to 1800; Neilson, Samuel; Orange Order: Origins, 1784 to 1800; Penal Laws; Politics: 1690 to 1800—A Protestant Kingdom; Protestant Ascendancy: 1690 to 1800; Tandy, James Napper; Tone, Theobald Wolfe; Trade and Trade Policy from 1691 to 1800; United Irish Societies from 1791 to 1803; **Primary Documents:** The Catholic Relief Act (1778); The Catholic Relief Act (1782); The Catholic Relief Act (1793)

Bibliography

Curtin, Nancy. *The United Irishmen: Popular Politics in Dublin and Ulster, 1791–1798.* 1994.

Dickson, David, et al., eds. *The United Irishmen.* 1993.

Elliott, Marianne. *Wolfe Tone: Prophet of Irish Independence.* 1989.

Kelly, James. *Prelude to Union: Anglo-Irish Politics in the 1780s.* 1982.

Kelly, James. "The Genesis of 'Protestant Ascendancy': The Rightboy Disturbances of the 1780s and Their Impact upon Protestant Opinion." In *Parliament, Politics, and People*, edited by Gerard O'Brien. 1988.

Kelly, James. "Conservative Protestant Political Thought in Late Eighteenth-Century Ireland." In *Political Ideas in Eighteenth-Century Ireland*, edited by S. J. Connolly. 2000.

McDowell, Robert B. *Ireland in the Age of Imperialism and Revolution, 1760–1801.* 1979.

James Kelly

1795 TO 1800—REPRESSION, REBELLION, AND UNION

The basic strategy of the United Irish leadership remained unchanged between 1795 and 1803. The vigilance of the Irish administration following the declaration of war on France in 1793 and security contingencies adopted to combat the Catholic insurgents known as the Defenders ensured that the republican organization could hope to triumph only with the assistance of foreign allies. The raising of the Irish militia in 1793 and the civilian yeomanry in late 1796 represented major accretions of the state's garrison strength. The recall of the liberal Viceroy Lord Fitzwilliam in 1795 at the behest of Irish ultraconservatives had closed with finality the option of peaceful reform of Parliament and set the stage for armed conflict on Irish soil. Lord Camden, Fitzwilliam's hard-line successor, actively fostered Protestant sectarianism and loyalist supremacy by permitting state agents to assist the newly formed Orange Order. Orangemen frustrated United Irish efforts to infiltrate the yeomanry and militia, and the gradual spread of their lodges exacerbated popular fears of loyalist atrocities.

The French government was expected to provide the men and material necessary to render the United Irishmen effective auxiliaries who, from 10 May 1795, re-coalesced as an oath-bound revolutionary body. New dynamism was injected by Theobald Wolfe Tone's successful negotiation of the French fleet, which moored in Bantry Bay, Cork, under General Lazare Hoche in late December 1796. The French forces were prevented from disembarking by severe weather conditions, but the scare strengthened the hand of republican militants. This reprieve spurred Camden into a sustained crackdown on the Ulster United Irishmen in the spring of 1797. The "dragooning of Ulster," characterized by house burning, mass deportation of suspects, and murderous rampages, was followed by the extension of martial law into midland and southeastern counties. The key issue between March 1797 and May 1798 was whether the United Irishmen could retain sufficient cohesion to offer support to the French. Executions, such as that of Antrim's William Orr, proved counterproductive, but the shooting of militia infiltrators probably reduced the prospect of mass defections. Camden's cultivation of the ultraconservatives introduced the unpredictable element of loyalist extremism into Irish politics, while the concurrent isolation of liberal magistrates exacerbated grievances in counties in which martial law was either threatened or enforced.

REBELLION OF 1798

The United Irish leadership, contrary to popular belief, was never penetrated by agents of Dublin Castle, although an intelligence breakthrough led to the arrest of senior activists in Leinster on 12 March 1798 and left the organization in the hands of a coterie headed by Lord Edward Fitzgerald and Samuel Neilson. Capturing Dublin was the primary focus of the Fitzgerald/Neilson faction, which with great reluctance decided to rise without the French, whom, it was assumed, would quickly rally to the United Irishmen. The dispatch of Napoleon's army to Egypt in mid-May 1798 greatly lessened this prospect. United Irishmen reasoned that a surprise revolt in the capital, aided by rebels from adjacent counties, would disrupt military communications long enough for their members to overcome local garrisons. Disaster struck when Fitzgerald was detained on 19 May, a blow seconded by the loss of Neilson on 23 May, the day set for the rebellion. While the turnout of city rebels that night was much more significant than once believed, a last-minute warning enabled Dublin Castle to occupy the chosen mobilization sites with government forces. Skirmishes ensued in the northern and western suburbs of Dublin, and by daylight much of Kildare was in rebel hands.

The manner in which the rebellion commenced ensured that the effort was a disjointed series of minor actions rather than a massive blow to government interests. The first news available from the censored press was of numerous rebel defeats attended by heavy casualties. The situation was actually more fluid, with a degree of rebel ascendancy achieved in parts of Kildare, Wicklow, and Meath on 23–24 May, but the military gradually contained the situation once reinforcements from north Munster and east Ulster arrived. The inactivity of United Irishmen in the provinces therefore facilitated critical government victories in Leinster by 31 May. A massacre of surrendering rebels in Kildare, however, steeled their comrades into greater militancy and tied down troops urgently needed to stabilize the situation in north Wexford and south Wicklow. Successes at Oulart Hill and Enniscorthy on 27–28 May yielded the Wexfordians the ability to win battles of more strategic consequence. They were slow to press their advantage prior to 1 June, by which time the government had massed on their borders. While the Castle counterattack met with failure at Tubberneering on 4 June, heavy rebel reverses at Newtownbarry, New Ross, and Arklow between 1 and 9 June cost thousands of lives and the tactical initiative.

The rebellion spread belatedly after 6 June to Ulster, where a split in the provincial leadership hindered the turnout in Antrim and Down. Success at Antrim town, Saintfield, and elsewhere promised greater achievement, but the struggle for Ballynahinch on 12–13 June ended in failure for Henry Joy McCracken and Henry Munro and presaged the collapse of the Ulster effort. The landing of over 10,000 reinforcements from Scotland, England, and Wales decisively tipped the balance against the United Irishmen. On 21 June the rebels were driven from their central camp at Vinegar Hill (Enniscorthy) and divided into two major bodies. Father John Murphy's column pressed into Kilkenny and Queen's County in search of support that was not available and was largely dispersed on the long march home. The second body, under Edward Fitzgerald of Newpark and Garret Byrne of Ballymanus, had greater success in mountainous districts of Wicklow and north Wexford until early July, when it too began to disintegrate. A desperate foray from Wicklow into Kildare, Meath, and north County Dublin proved a costly failure and emphasized the futility of further resistance. All but the hard core spurned the generous amnesty offered by the new administration of Lord Cornwallis and waged a destructive guerrilla war in the Wicklow mountains under Joseph Holt into November.

The appearance of 1,100 French veterans near Killala, Co. Mayo, on 22 August 1798 had raised United

A United Irishman captured by crown forces at Ballynahinch, Co. Down, on 13 June 1798, the decisive battle in the northern phase of the rebellion. Detail of Thomas Robinson, Battle of Ballynahinch (1798). REPRODUCED BY PERMISSION OF THE OFFICE OF PUBLIC WORKS, DUBLIN. PAINTING IN THE COLLECTION OF ÁRAS AN UACHTARÁIN. PHOTO COURTESY OF THE NATIONAL GALLERY OF IRELAND.

Irish spirits and spurred offensives in Sligo, Longford, Westmeath, and Leitrim. Franco-Irish forces under General Jean-Joseph Humbert won a signal victory at Castlebar on 27 August but were diverted from their path into Ulster on 5 September at Collooney. When confronted by an overwhelmingly superior army at Ballinamuck, Co. Longford, on 8 September, the invasion quickly faltered. Efforts to disembark Tone and French soldiers on the northwest coast of Ulster on 12 October, moreover, were prevented by the Royal Navy. It seemed that in the absence of effective French intervention the military was equal to the challenge posed by ill-coordinated insurgent campaigns.

PASSAGE OF THE ACT OF UNION

Ireland remained highly disturbed into 1799, and the United Irishmen continued to petition the French. Robert Emmet and Malachy Delaney went to the Continent to negotiate with Napoleon and Tallyrand in mid-1800 and argued that the imposition of the Act of Union had not lessened popular determination to found an independent Irish Republic. The bill had a difficult passage through the Irish Commons during 1799 and 1800, and, after its initial rejection, officials relied in the final analysis on considerable bribery to secure its implementation on 1 January 1801. An important part of the union agenda was to provide for effective security of the islands of Britain and Ireland, which the United Irishmen had shown to be weak during time of war. The operation of the union made virtually no difference to the vast majority of Irish people owing to the nondemocratic nature of both pre- and post-union parliaments and the failure of London to grant the mooted concession of Catholic emancipation. Emmet's machinations, however, created a major security crisis in Dublin and London in July 1803, which obliged Westminster to garrison Ireland as it would a vulnerable colony.

SEE ALSO Act of Union; Burke, Edmund; Catholic Committee from 1756 to 1809; Catholic Merchants and Gentry from 1690 to 1800; Defenderism; Eighteenth-Century Politics: 1690 to 1714—Revolution Settlement; Eighteenth-Century Politics: 1714 to 1778—Interest Politics; Eighteenth-Century Politics: 1778 to 1795—Parliamentary and Popular Politics; Fitzgerald, Lord Edward; Flood, Henry; Government from 1690 to 1800; Grattan, Henry; Keogh, John; Military Forces from 1690 to 1800; Neilson, Samuel; Orange Order: Origins, 1784 to 1800; Penal Laws; Politics: 1690 to 1800—A Protestant Kingdom; Protestant Ascendancy: 1690 to 1800; Tandy, James Napper; Tone, Theobald Wolfe; Trade and Trade Policy from 1691 to 1800; United Irish Societies from 1791 to 1803; **Primary Documents:** United Irish Parliamentary Reform Plan (March 1794); Grievances of the United Irishmen of Ballynahinch, Co. Down (1795); Speech Delivered at a United Irish Meeting in Ballyclare, Co. Antrim (1795); The Insurrection Act (1796); The United Irish Organization (1797); Statement of Three Imprisoned United Irish Leaders (4 August 1798); Account of the Wexford Rising (1832)

Bibliography

Curtin, Nancy J. *The United Irishmen: Popular Politics in Ulster and Dublin, 1791–1798.* 1994.

O'Donnell, Ruan. *The 1798 Diary.* 1998.

Smyth, Jim. *The Men of No Property: Irish Radicals and Popular Politics in the Late Eighteenth Century.* 1992.

Whelan, Kevin. *The Tree of Liberty: Radicalism, Catholicism, and the Construction of Irish Identity.* 1996.

Ruan O'Donnell

Eiscir Riata

The Eiscir Riata is a system of eskers (glacial ridges) that runs across the midlands of Ireland from east to west, dividing the island into two parts of roughly equal size. The esker system formed at the end of the Midlandian glaciation during the dissolution of its ice sheets at around 15,000 B.C.E. Meltwater from the glacier, often transporting massive quantities of sediment during deglaciation, formed tunnels beneath the ice. Changes in the amount of flowing water could lead to an increase in the deposition of sediment, choking a section of tunnel. When the ice melted, a ridge of sand and gravel from the tunnel would emerge as an esker, which can run across the countryside over several kilometers.

In protohistory the Eiscir Riata was used to divide the island between the kings Conn Céadchathach and Mógh Nuadhat in the wake of the battle of Magh Léna, an event attributed to the early second century C.E. Conn ruled the northern territory (Leath Cuinn), and Mógh was given the southern lands (Leath Mógha). Apart from this possible use as a territorial division, the well-drained glacial ridge was also employed as a routeway for travelers across the boggy land of central Ireland. Starting in the east near Dublin and extending to Clarinbridge in County Galway, the Slighe Mhór (the Great Road) ran along the Eiscir Riata as one of ancient Ireland's five great roadways.

The importance of the Eiscir Riata to travellers is further emphasized by the establishment of a number of early Christian ecclesiastical sites along its length, including Durrow and Clonmacnoise, both in County Offaly. These monasteries needed easy access to good communication networks; Clonmacnoise, for example, was particularly well sited because it was located at a point where the river Shannon cut through the Eiscir Riata. The monastery thus stood at a major crossroads in the middle of Ireland.

SEE ALSO Landscape and Settlement

Bibliography

Hogan, Edmund. *Onomasticon Goedelicum Locorum et Tribuum Hiberniae et Scotiae: An Index, with Identifications, to the Gaelic Names of Places and Tribes.* 1910.

King, A. Heather, ed. *Clonmacnoise Studies.* Vol. 1, *Seminar Papers 1994.* 1998.

Ó Lochlainn, Colm. "Roadways in Ancient Ireland." In *Essays and Studies Presented to Professor Eoin MacNeill on the Occasion of His Seventieth Birthday,* edited by John Ryan. 1940.

Eileen M. Murphy

Electoral Politics from 1800 to 1921

During the period of the union the character of Irish elections changed considerably, not only in the types of constituencies and the number of electors but also in the political and social backgrounds of the MPs. Normally, Irish electoral politics were very local in nature, and it was only at times of unusual political agitation that national issues became dominant.

Under the Act of Union Ireland returned 100 MPs to the U.K. parliament at Westminster. The number increased to 105 in 1832, fell to 103 after two boroughs were disfranchised in 1870, and rose again to 105 in 1918. From 1800 to 1885 each of the thirty-two counties of Ireland returned two MPs, thirty-three towns or cities returned either one or two MPs, and Dublin University returned two MPs. From 1885 onwards seats were allocated on a roughly equal population basis, which resulted in eighty-five single-seat county constituencies, fourteen single-seat borough constituencies (with one double-seater), and two university seats. Redistribution in 1918 led to the creation of eighty single-seat county constituencies, twenty-one single-seat borough constituencies, and three university constituencies (returning four MPs).

For most of the period from 1800 to 1921 the right to vote was connected to some form of property ownership. It was restricted to males until 1918. At the beginning of this period the franchise was based mainly on the 40-shilling freeholder, but in 1829 (following Catholic Emancipation) it was limited to the 10-pound free-holder, a change that dramatically reduced the size of the Irish electorate. In 1832 the vote was extended to 10-pound householders in the boroughs, in parallel with the new urban franchise introduced in England and Wales by the Great Reform Bill of that year. In 1850 the vote was further broadened to include occupiers of property valued at 12 pounds or more for county electors and 8 pounds or more for borough electors; the borough qualification was reduced to 4 pounds in 1868. Far more important than these modest extensions, however, was the legislation of 1884 that tripled the size of the Irish electorate by granting the vote to all adult male householders. In 1918 the vote was granted to all adult males and to all females over thirty years old.

In the political system created by the Act of Union there was no religious bar to voting, but only after Catholic Emancipation in 1829 were Catholics allowed to become MPs. Until the 1880s the majority of MPs were drawn from the leading landowning families, and they were mainly members of the Church of Ireland. Beginning with the arrival of Daniel O'Connell in Parliament in 1829 there was a rise in the number of Catholic MPs, but it was not until 1874 that Catholics constituted a majority of Irish MPs. for the first time. The social status of members of the Irish contingent at Westminster was also changing as the Home Rule movement gathered momentum in the 1870s and 1880s. From the general election of 1880 onwards most Irish MPs were no longer from a landowning family.

In the early decades of the nineteenth century relatively few elections proceeded to a poll, though even without a contest an Irish election could still provoke considerable political excitement. The MPs returned to Parliament were usually identified by whether they supported or opposed the government of the day. With the rise in importance of the question of Catholic Emancipation and with the formation of the Irish Parliamentary Party led by Daniel O'Connell, national political issues became more salient and party labels started to emerge. In 1832 O'Connell's party, which sought to repeal the Act of Union, won thirty-nine seats while the Conservatives took thirty and the Whigs and Liberals captured thirty-six in total. The Conservatives wanted to protect the Anglican Church and to preserve the Protestant Ascendancy in Ireland in general, whereas the Whigs and Liberals were ready to reduce Anglican privileges and to weaken the Protestant Ascendancy in various ways. From 1835 to 1841, while the Whigs were in office, the O'Connellites in Parliament supported them in return for concessions in the matters of political appointments, tithes, and municipal government. But the alliance with the Whigs hurt the O'Connellites' elec-

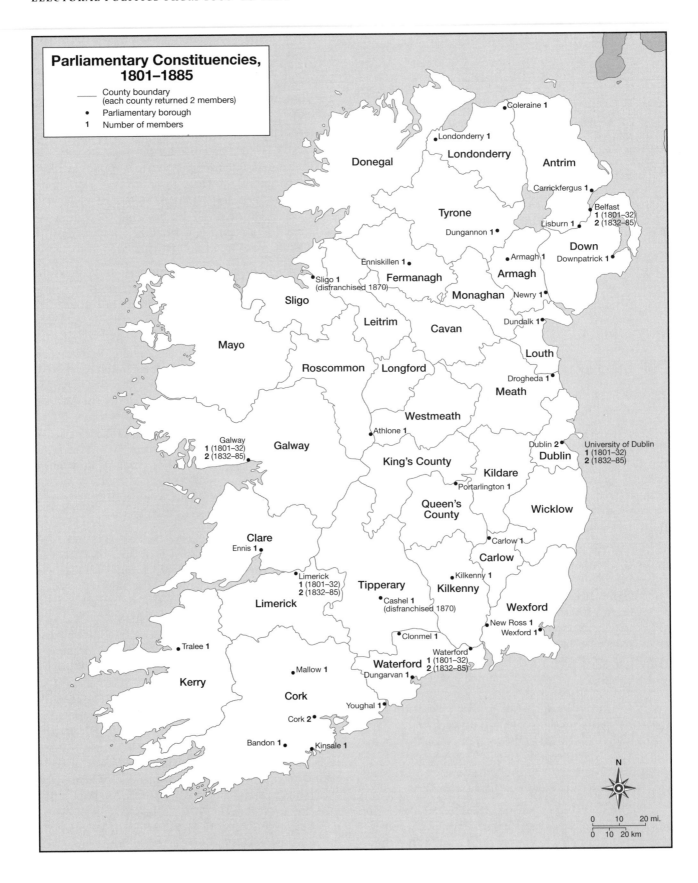

Parliamentary Constituencies, 1801–1885

— County boundary
  (each county returned 2 members)
• Parliamentary borough
1 Number of members

Coleraine 1

Londonderry 1

Londonderry

Donegal

Antrim

Carrickfergus 1

Belfast
1 (1801–32)
2 (1832–85)

Tyrone

Dungannon 1

Lisburn 1

Down

Enniskillen 1

Armagh 1

Downpatrick 1

Fermanagh

Armagh

Sligo 1
(disfranchised 1870)

Monaghan

Newry 1

Sligo

Leitrim

Cavan

Dundalk 1

Mayo

Roscommon

Longford

Louth

Drogheda 1

Meath

Westmeath

Athlone 1

Galway
1 (1801–32)
2 (1832–85)

Galway

King's County

Dublin 2

University of Dublin
1 (1801–32)
2 (1832–85)

Dublin

Kildare

Portarlington 1

Queen's
County

Wicklow

Clare

Ennis 1

Carlow 1

Carlow

Limerick
1 (1801–32)
2 (1832–85)

Tipperary

Kilkenny 1

Kilkenny

Limerick

Cashel 1
(disfranchised 1870)

Wexford

Clonmel 1

New Ross 1

Wexford 1

Tralee 1

Waterford
1 (1801–32)
2 (1832–85)

Mallow 1

Waterford

Dungarvan 1

Kerry

Cork

Youghal 1

Cork 2

Bandon 1

Kinsale 1

N

0   10   20 mi.

0   10   20 km

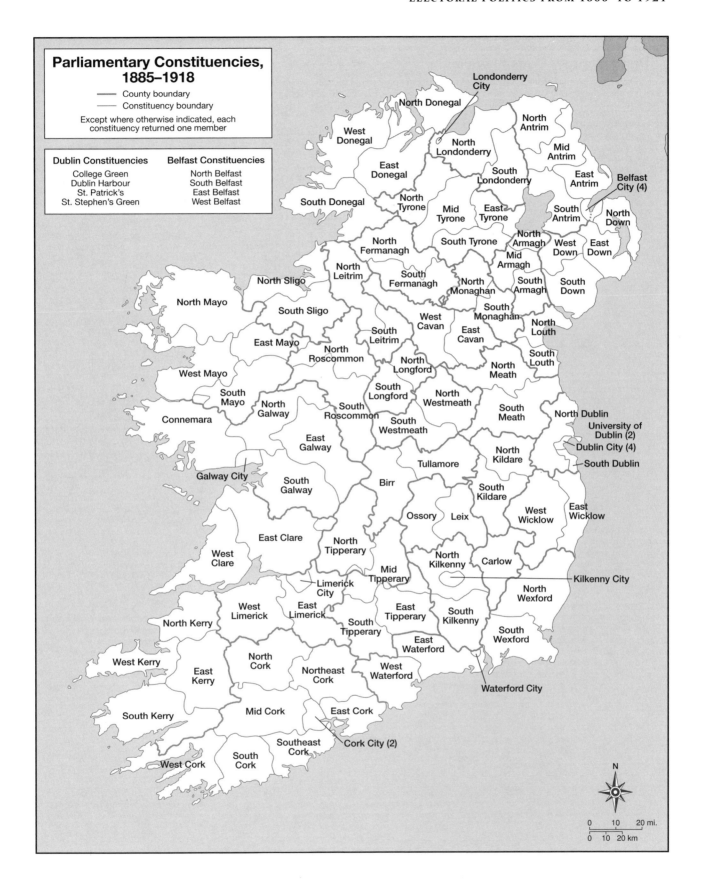

Parliamentary Constituencies, 1885–1918

——— County boundary

- - - - - Constituency boundary

Except where otherwise indicated, each
constituency returned one member

Dublin Constituencies

College Green
Dublin Harbour
St. Patrick's
St. Stephen's Green

Belfast Constituencies

North Belfast
South Belfast
East Belfast
West Belfast

Londonderry City

North Donegal

West Donegal

North Antrim

Mid Antrim

East Donegal

North Londonderry

South Londonderry

East Antrim

South Donegal

North Tyrone

Mid Tyrone

East Tyrone

South Antrim

North Down

Belfast City (4)

South Tyrone

North Armagh

West Down

East Down

North Fermanagh

Mid Armagh

South Armagh

North Sligo

North Leitrim

South Fermanagh

North Monaghan

South Down

North Mayo

South Sligo

West Cavan

East Cavan

South Monaghan

North Louth

East Mayo

South Leitrim

North Roscommon

North Longford

North Meath

South Louth

West Mayo

South Longford

North Westmeath

Connemara

South Mayo

North Galway

South Roscommon

South Westmeath

South Meath

North Dublin

University of Dublin (2)

Galway City

East Galway

Tullamore

North Kildare

Dublin City (4)

South Dublin

South Galway

Birr

South Meath

North Kildare

South Kildare

East Wicklow

East Clare

Ossory

Leix

West Wicklow

West Clare

North Tipperary

Mid Tipperary

North Kilkenny

Carlow

North Wexford

Kilkenny City

Limerick City

West Limerick

East Limerick

South Tipperary

East Tipperary

South Kilkenny

South Kilkenny

South Wexford

North Kerry

North Cork

East Waterford

Waterford City

West Kerry

East Kerry

Northeast Cork

West Waterford

South Kerry

Mid Cork

East Cork

West Cork

South Cork

Southeast Cork

Cork City (2)

N

0   10   20 mi.

0   10   20 km

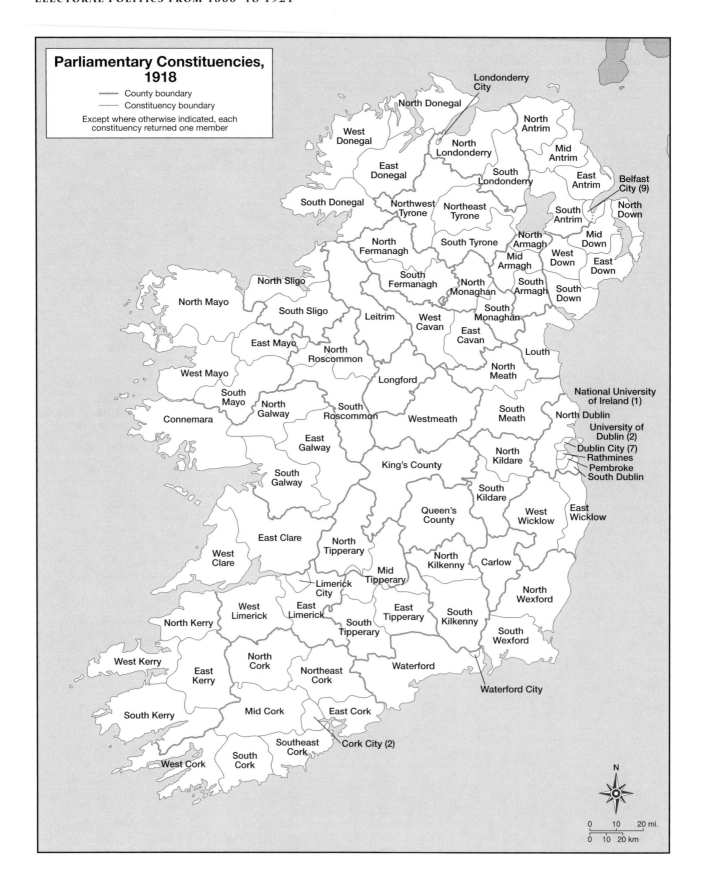

Parliamentary Constituencies, 1918

—— County boundary
—— Constituency boundary

Except where otherwise indicated, each
constituency returned one member

Londonderry City

North Donegal

West Donegal

North Antrim

North Londonderry

Mid Antrim

East Donegal

South Londonderry

East Antrim

Belfast City (9)

South Donegal

Northwest Tyrone

Northeast Tyrone

South Antrim

North Down

North Fermanagh

South Tyrone

North Armagh

Mid Down

South Armagh

West Down

East Down

North Sligo

South Fermanagh

North Monaghan

Mid Armagh

South Down

North Mayo

South Sligo

Leitrim

West Cavan

South Monaghan

East Cavan

Louth

East Mayo

North Roscommon

Longford

North Meath

West Mayo

South Mayo

North Galway

South Roscommon

Westmeath

South Meath

National University of Ireland (1)

Connemara

East Galway

King's County

North Kildare

North Dublin

University of Dublin (2)

Dublin City (7)
Rathmines
Pembroke
South Dublin

South Galway

South Kildare

West Wicklow

East Wicklow

East Clare

North Tipperary

Queen's County

North Kilkenny

Carlow

West Clare

Mid Tipperary

Limerick City

North Wexford

West Limerick

East Limerick

East Tipperary

South Kilkenny

North Kerry

South Tipperary

East Cork

South Wexford

West Kerry

East Kerry

North Cork

Northeast Cork

Waterford

Waterford City

South Kerry

Mid Cork

East Cork

West Cork

South Cork

Southeast Cork

Cork City (2)

N

0   10   20 mi.

0   10   20 km

toral popularity in Ireland, and after the Tories returned to office in 1841, O'Connell briefly restored the political standing of his party by leading an immense but unsuccessful popular movement for Repeal.

From O'Connell's death in 1847 until 1874 electoral politics were mostly dominated by the Liberals and Conservatives. The majority of elections went uncontested and politicians were concerned primarily with local issues. Beginning in the early 1870s, however, national issues came back into prominence. In 1874 Isaac Butt's Home Rule Party captured sixty seats, and Home Rule became the main issue at elections. Under Butt the loosely organized and not particularly zealous Home Rule MPs made little impression at Westminster, but after Charles Stewart Parnell took over the leadership of the party in 1880, he and his colleagues brought Home Rule to the center of the political stage in Britain. In the election of 1885 the nationalists under Parnell won eighty-five seats (plus one more in Liverpool), and the Conservatives and unionists (based largely in the north of Ireland) captured only eighteen seats. The Liberal leader William Gladstone embraced Home Rule early in 1886, and thus there commenced an alliance between the Liberals and Irish nationalists that was to last for three decades.

The general elections of 1885 and 1886 marked a number of important changes in the nature of Irish elections. The vast extension of the electorate in 1884, embracing many small farmers and agricultural laborers, was an enormous electoral boon to the nationalists, and their new constituency structures, based on local branches of the National League and the active support of the Catholic clergy, introduced a level of dynamic, centralized party organization that had not been seen previously at Westminster elections. The unionists also created strong local electoral organizations, in their case with close links to the Orange Order. At previous elections there had always been a certain amount of voting across denominational boundaries (for example, in support of Liberal candidates in the previous two decades), but by 1886 voters were polarized along religious lines, with Protestants supporting unionist candidates and Catholics backing nationalist ones—overwhelmingly in both cases.

Over the next three and a half decades until 1921 there was little alteration in the comparative strength of unionists and nationalists at elections, which were often uncontested, with local issues again assuming special importance. On a number of occasions, however, considerable political activity was generated at election time within the major parties. Parnell's overthrow as party leader in 1890 led to bitter rivalry among nationalist factions at the general elections of 1892 and 1895. Early in the new century the unionists witnessed heated intraparty quarrels at elections over land and labor issues.

Although the nationalist party was reunited in 1900, the failure of the Liberals in Britain to deliver Home Rule either before or during World War I helped to undermine the nationalist party, and its electoral chances were further weakened by the political blunders of the British government over the Easter Rising of 1916 and the threat of military conscription at a late stage of the war. In the general election of December 1918 the Home Rule nationalists were virtually eliminated (the number of seats they held plummeted from sixty-eight to only six). A relatively new party, Sinn Féin, which stood for independence from Britain and for abstention from Westminster, swept to victory, capturing seventy-three seats that they did not take up. Instead, Sinn Féin's successful candidates (or at least those who were not imprisoned by the British) established a revolutionary Irish parliament in Dublin (Dáil Éireann) in January 1919. Between then and the end of the union in 1921, the unionists, who had won twenty-six seats in the 1918 election, were the only representatives from Ireland sitting in the Westminster parliament, aside from the tiny remnant of Home Rule MPs who carried on for a few years after their debacle in December 1918.

SEE ALSO Catholic Emancipation Campaign; Fenian Movement and the Irish Republican Brotherhood; Great War; Griffith, Arthur; Home Rule Movement and the Irish Parliamentary Party: 1870 to 1891; Home Rule Movement and the Irish Parliamentary Party: 1891 to 1918; Independent Irish Party; Local Government since 1800; Politics: 1800 to 1921—Challenges to the Union; Protestant Ascendancy: Decline, 1800 to 1930; Redmond, John; Repeal Movement; Sinn Féin Movement and Party to 1922; Young Ireland and the Irish Confederation; **Primary Documents:** The Irish Parliamentary Party Pledge (30 June 1892)

Bibliography

Hoppen, K. Theo. *Elections, Politics, and Society in Ireland, 1832–1885*. 1984.

Walker, Brian M., ed. *Parliamentary Election Results in Ireland, 1801–1922*. 1978.

Brian Walker

Elizabethan Conquest

See Nine Years War; Land Settlements from 1500 to 1690; Sidney, Henry; Desmond Rebellions.

~

Emain Macha (Navan Fort)

Emain Macha, the traditional seat of the kings of Ulster and the capital of the Ulstermen (*Ulaid*) depicted in the Ulster Cycle of tales, has been identified as the present Navan Fort, an enclosure approximately two miles west of the city of Armagh. This monument, measuring 236 meters across, is situated on a small hill and is surrounded by several other prehistoric sites, most notably Loughnashade, a natural lake that has yielded evidence of Iron Age depositions; Haughey's Fort, a late Bronze Age hillfort; and the King's Stables, an artificial pond created circa 1000 B.C.E. Navan was excavated between 1961 and 1971.

Emain has been variously identified with two sites in Ptolemy's second-century C.E. geographic dictionary of Ireland: *Isamnium*, whose linguistically reconstructed form (**Isamonis* or **Isamnis*) might be the antecedent of **Emnae Emain*; or the northern *Regia* ("royal site"). In early Irish tradition the name of the site was fancifully derived either from the *eo-muin* (neck-brooch) that Queen Macha, the eponymous founder of Emain Macha and euhemerized Celtic deity, employed to draw out the shape of the enclosure, or from the *emain* (twin[s]) that the semidivine Macha Sanreth gave birth to at the site after defeating the royal chariot team in a race. Early Irish pseudohistorical or traditional genealogies and king-lists indicate that Emain served as the capital of the Ulstermen from the seventh (or fourth) century B.C.E. until the last Ulaid king at Emain was killed in 324 or 332 C.E., when "rulership of the Ulaid departed from Emain" (O'Brien 1962, p. 325).

The site was initially occupied in the Neolithic period, circa 3500 B.C.E., and then again during the Bronze Age, circa 1000 B.C.E. At this time the occupants constructed on top of the hill a small enclosure formed by a wide but shallow ditch and an internal row of timber uprights—perhaps a ritual precinct. The interior of the enclosure was subsequently occupied by a figure-eight structure that was renewed on a number of occasions; the skull of a Barbary ape, imported from North Africa, was found in one of the wall-slots. A larger figure-eight enclosure (with rings 30 meters and 20 meters across) was then erected nearly adjacent to the first set of rings;

this structure appears to have been burnt. By 95 B.C.E. the initial area of building had been cleared, and a circular forty-meter structure was erected, with a massive central post and five concentric rings of 280 oak posts. This building (there is debate as to whether it was roofed or not) was then filled with limestone cobbles, timber around the perimeter was fired, and the entire edifice was covered with sods to produce an earthen mound. At about the same time the hill was enclosed by an earthen bank and an inner ditch.

Emain Macha has been traditionally interpreted as a royal site along with Tara, Knockaulin, and Rathcroghan, the first two having figure-eight ritual structures similar to Emain's. The medieval literature that describes royal activities on these sites may be anachronistic reconstructions, but the archaeological evidence suggests that all of these sites were major ritual centers during the Iron Age.

SEE ALSO Dún Ailinne; Cú Chulainn; Myth and Saga; Prehistoric and Celtic Ireland; *Táin Bó Cúailnge*; Tara

Bibliography

O'Brien, M. *Corpus Genealogiarum Hiberniae.* 1962

Waterman, D. M. *Excavations at Navan Fort, 1961–71.* Completed and edited by C. J. Lynn. 1997.

J. P. Mallory

~

Emmet, Robert

A United Irishman and the leader of a failed rebellion in 1803, Robert Emmet (1778–1803) was the younger brother of Thomas Addis Emmet, a prominent United Irishman of 1798. Robert joined the United Irishmen in December 1796 and led the society at Trinity College, Dublin, but fled the country in April 1798 and was in France during the rebellion of that summer. In the autumn of 1798 he became involved in a movement to revive the United Irishmen and initiate a second rebellion. He was back in Ireland by the spring of 1799 and worked actively toward this goal. He left Ireland again in August 1800 and traveled around much of Europe over the next two years, arranging for support from United Irish exiles and foreign governments. Emmet returned to Ireland for the final time in October 1802 and, in cooperation with James Hope, William Putnam McCabe, and Thomas Russell, created a formidable revolutionary network embracing as many as nineteen counties. His immediate strategy was based on the idea of a quick seizure of Dublin, followed by rebellion in outlying counties, all coinciding with a French landing. An accidental explosion in one of several arms depots he had established in Dublin, in addition to the work of spies, led both to the government's discovery of Emmet's plot and to his hurried decision to initiate the rebellion on 23 July 1803 rather than in August (when he mistakenly expected a French landing). After a brief struggle in Dublin the rebel mobilization disintegrated and Emmet and more than two dozen other leaders fled, but they were rounded up within a few weeks. Emmet was tried and found guilty. Before his execution in October, he made one of the most famous of all Irish patriotic speeches from the dock. For this reason as well as because he was among the first to conceive of the Irish separatist struggle as one that must be based primarily on Irish efforts rather than foreign assistance (despite his own intense efforts to secure such assistance), he occupies an important place in the story of Irish nationalism.

SEE ALSO United Irish Societies from 1791 to 1803; **Primary Documents:** Speech from the Dock (19 September 1803)

Bibliography

Elliott, Marianne. *Partners in Revolution: The United Irishmen and France.*1988.

Madden, R. R. *The Life and Times of Robert Emmet.* 1847.

Daniel Gahan

~

English Government in Medieval Ireland

The Anglo–Norman intervention in Ireland from 1167 onwards had little official involvement until King Henry II decided to intervene in person in October 1171. From then on, Ireland was an English colony and had to be governed as its new lord, the king of England, thought appropriate. Henry stayed less than a year and can have made little headway in instituting a system of government in a territory that was still a volatile frontier. At an organizational level his biggest achievement was to assemble a church synod at Cashel, which issued decrees for ecclesiastical reform, specifying that the Irish church should henceforth be modeled on that of England. As it was vital that the invasion be a stimulus to commerce, Henry also, having taken the towns into his own hands (Dublin implicitly being made the capital), issued charters of privileges allowing them access to a de facto free-trade zone within his territories in Britain and France. He legalized the status of invaders who claimed territory in Ireland by granting charters specifying the extent of their lands and the terms under which they held them. Finally, he appointed as his deputy the new lord of Meath, Hugh de Lacy, whose role as chief governor was similar to that of the justiciar of England in the king's absence.

From the start, and expressly by order of King John (1199–1216), the law of the new colony was the common law of England, Irish Brehon law being regarded as barbaric. The native Irish had no direct access to the law, and although a few exceptions were made and an individual grant of access could be bought, by and large they remained the enemy in the eyes of the law, and without legal remedy throughout the Middle Ages. Legislation passed in England tended to apply also in Ireland, a copy of Magna Carta, for instance, being sent to Ireland in 1217. It was only in the fifteenth century that the Anglo-Irish began to question the mandatory application to Ireland of legislation enacted in England, and the subject was one of great controversy thereafter.

Although Irish cases were sometimes heard in the courts of England, by the reign of Henry III (1216–1272) a system of itinerant justices was in place in Ireland, holding courts in various towns throughout the colony. Dublin was also home to a resident court of common pleas dealing with civil cases. But as his name suggests, the justiciar governing in the king's name had his own court, over which he presided in dispensing justice as he traveled about. He was also head of the civil administration and chief military officer; he had his own armed retinue and summoned the king's tenants to perform military service; for example, campaigning against Irish rebels. The justiciar (later known as the lieutenant) was advised by a council of ministers and by the great magnates of the land, an informal body that gradually gained a fixed structure during the thirteenth century. Parliament was an extended version of this council and existed in Ireland by at least the 1260s, but it was closer to the end of the century before it had matured into a formal judicial and legislative assembly

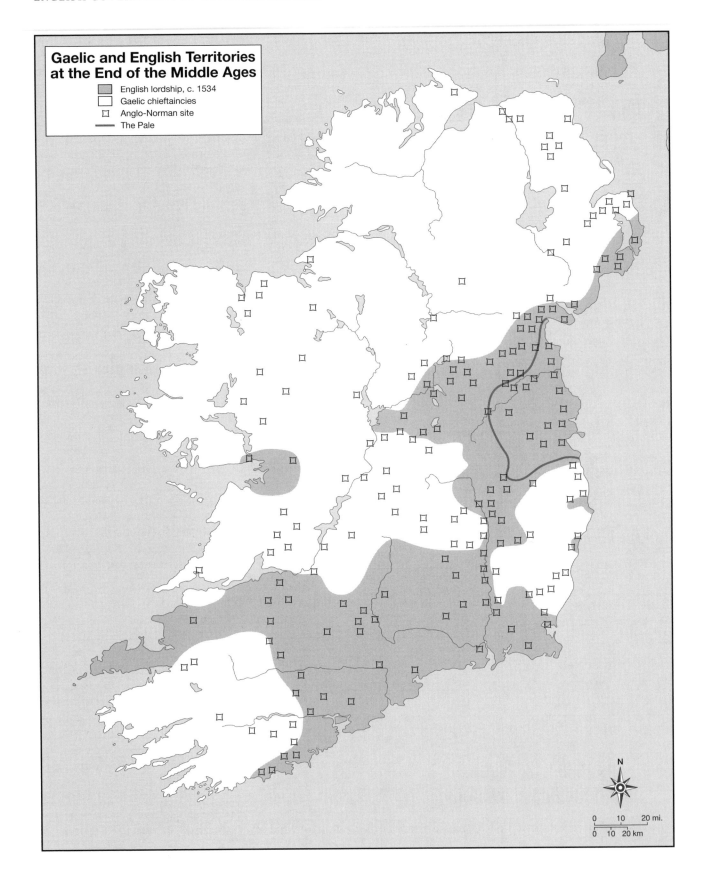

Gaelic and English Territories at the End of the Middle Ages

- English lordship, c. 1534
- Gaelic chieftaincies
- Anglo-Norman site
- The Pale

N

0   10   20 mi.

0   10   20 km

Albrecht Dürer, Irish Warriors and Peasants Armed for War, *engraving from 1521. This image depicts heavily armed Scottish gallowglasses with claymores and lighter-armed Irish kerns. Note the characteristic Irish glibs (forelocks) as well as the large Irish mantle.* © BILDARCHIV PREUSSISCHER KULTURBESITZ/ART RESOURCE, NY. REPRODUCED BY PERMISSION.

composed of both individuals and representatives of communities.

Since the courts levied fines and the king was entitled to rents and (with Parliament's approval) taxes, the oldest department of state was the exchequer where these were accounted for. It was based in Dublin and had the treasurer as its chief clerk. The latter, second in importance to the justiciar in the early years, was subsequently superseded by the chancellor, who ran the chancery, the letter-writing office of government. Because the chancellor had possession of the great seal that authenticated government documents, he traveled around the colony with the justiciar. They dealt with the local agent of government, the sheriff, who collected revenues and debts due to the Crown from the localities (for which he accounted at the exchequer), had the task of arraigning persons charged to appear before the justiciar's court, had custody of prisoners, and also adminis-

tered the county court. The county or shire was the system of local government inherited from England, Dublin being the first to make an appearance, followed gradually by Cork, Waterford, Limerick, Tipperary, Louth, Kerry, Connacht (or rather part thereof), Roscommon, Kildare, Carlow, and part of Meath. Some of these subsequently became liberties, like Ulster (the only earldom in the colony until 1316), Wexford, and the rest of Meath. Although not entirely exempt from central control, liberties were free on a day-to-day basis from government interference and had similar, if smaller, structures as the central government. At any one time about half of the colony was held as liberties, and the division of the country into counties was never completed in the Middle Ages.

The ecclesiastical equivalent of the shire was the diocese, the system established before the invasion remaining largely intact thereafter, although diocesan sees were sometimes relocated to more heavily colonized centers, and a rather half-hearted attempt to give primacy to Dublin over Armagh was solved by awarding the archbishop of the former the title "primate of Ireland" and the latter "primate of all Ireland." Senior clerics, particularly the archbishop of Dublin, were frequently royal nominees, and as such they were government ministers and instruments of English royal policy in Ireland: it was useful to be certain of their loyalty. Armagh, on the other hand, was in hostile Irish territory, so that its incumbent rarely visited the primatial see itself and resided in safety in one of his manors in County Louth.

Louth was one of the most heavily anglicized areas where the government's writ ran efficiently except in troubled times, but the Irish revival that began in the late thirteenth century eroded the authority of government in regions where it had previously functioned well. The consequence was that local settler communities were less subject to government control and all the safeguards that it brought in terms of protection of life and limb and access to legal redress. The corollary was that they could literally get away with murder, and we find that the lords of the great liberties, especially after the creation of the three new earldoms of Kildare, Desmond, and Ormond in the early fourteenth century, were not amenable to external authority and ruled their lordships with impunity, having their own private armies, meting out their own justice, and adopting from Gaelic society the onerous exactions claimed by lords in terms of the abuse of hospitality and the billeting of troops on local communities.

Central government abandoned its responsibilities in outlying areas out of sheer financial exigency. Annual revenue that amounted to about £6,000 at the start of Edward I's reign in 1272 had dropped, because of constant warfare and agricultural decline, to less than a third of that a century later under his grandson, Edward III, after which point an annual subsidy was habitually provided by the English exchequer. Government had to concentrate its limited resources on the area where they could be most effectively employed, the four "obedient" counties at its core—Dublin, Louth, Meath, and Kildare—and by the mid-fifteenth century these were known as the Pale, and were literally protected from beyond by a ditch that ran intermittently from the vicinity of Dundalk to Dalkey. Of this area alone, by the end of the Middle Ages, one could say that English government in Ireland operated effectively.

SEE ALSO Bruce Invasion; Legal Change in the Sixteenth and Seventeenth Centuries; Magnates, Gaelic and Anglo-Irish; Monarchy; Norman Conquest and Colonization; Norman Invasion and Gaelic Resurgence; Richard II in Ireland; **Primary Documents:** The Treaty of Windsor (1175); Grant of Prince John to Theobold Walter of Lands in Ireland (1185); Grant of Civic Liberties to Dublin by Prince John (1192); Magna Carta Hiberniæ (The Great Charter of Ireland) (12 November 1216); The Statutes of Kilkenny (1366); King Richard II in Ireland (1395); Declaration of Independence of the Irish Parliament (1460); Poynings' Law (1494)

Bibliography

Cosgrove, Art, ed. *A New History of Ireland.* Vol. 2, *Medieval Ireland, 1169–1534.* 1987. Reprint, 1993.

Hand, Geoffrey Joseph. *English Law in Ireland, 1290–1324.* 1967.

Orpen, Goddard Henry. *Ireland under the Normans.* 4 vols. 1911–1920.

Otway-Ruthven, Jocelyn Annette. *A History of Medieval Ireland.* 1969.

Richardson, Henry Gerald, and George Osborne Sayles. *The Irish Parliament in the Middle Ages.* 1952.

Richardson, Henry Gerald, and George Osborne Sayles. *The Administration of Ireland, 1172–1377.* 1963.

Watt, John Anthony. *The Church and the Two Nations in Medieval Ireland.* 1970.

Seán Duffy

English Political and Religious Policies, Responses to (1534–1690)

The political and religious reforms implemented in Ireland after the defeat of the Kildare rebellion of 1534 and 1535 reflected Henry VIII's anxiety over imposing a unitary sovereignty in church and state. Under the aegis of the policy, managed by Thomas Cromwell, a new English coterie was established in a Dublin administration more directly answerable to London. No major initiative with respect to Gaelic Ireland was envisaged. With the fall of Cromwell in 1540 and the arrival of Sir Anthony Saint Leger as chief governor in 1541, however, a radical new constitutional framework was put in place, within which the island's older English and Gaelic communities would share on a basis of equality of citizenship and privilege. Within the overarching design of a newly declared kingdom of Ireland, a series of agreements was to be concluded by peaceful means with the hitherto alienated Gaelic and gaelicized lordships to bring them into full communion with the monarchy. The English objectives were to introduce political and social stability by extirpating systematic taking and billeting such as coign and livery, to promote succession of the eldest son, and also to foster English economic and cultural norms through agrarian changes and religious and educational reform.

The indigenous populations responded positively to the early phase of reform. The session of Parliament that proclaimed Henry's kingship of Ireland in 1541 necessitated the unprecedented translation of the proceedings into the Irish language. The Old English anticipated that they would have a central role to play in the implementation of the reforms through civil and judicial administration in the provinces; they were further conciliated by Saint Leger by land grants of dissolved monastic property in Leinster and Munster. For the dozens of Gaelic lords who were likewise assimilated within Saint Leger's system and rewarded with monastic grants, the compacts were acceptable—their lands were assured in return for their recognition of the king's sovereignty. This was the policy of "surrender and regret" whereby the principal Gaelic and gaelicized lords surrendered their lands and titles to the Crown and received new grants of those lands and titles to be held directly from the Crown. Leading chiefs were given such titles as earl of Thomond (O'Brien), earl of Tyrone (O'Neill), and baron of Upper Ossory (Macgillapatrick). Little real social, political, or cultural change was required of them, though all were agreeable to the royal supremacy in ecclesiastical matters. Under Saint Leger's governorship, political relations were generally harmonious, and the painful effects of the religious reformation were significantly mitigated.

During the reigns of King Edward VI (1547–1553) and Queen Mary (1553–1558) there were many ominous signs that the consensus built in the early to mid-1540s was unlikely to persist. Radical religious doctrinal changes under Edward were introduced without the sanction of an Irish parliament or consultation with the Old English political leadership. The innovations proved to be unpopular in the dioceses and parishes where they were implemented. Although as yet unaffected by this Protestant Reformation, Gaelic Ireland was not to be treated as a special case in linguistic and cultural terms, for the emphasis was to be heavily on evangelization through the English language. Under Queen Mary there was an overwhelmingly popular response in the towns and countryside of the Englishry to the restoration of Roman Catholicism. During the mid-Tudor period a

succession of viceroys with differing priorities came and went. The Old English community felt the weight of increased military expenditure as Sir Edward Bellingham and Sir James Croft campaigned vigorously in the Gaelic midlands and elsewhere, mainly targeting the O'Connor and O'More clans, who were regarded as having breached their "surrender and regrant" agreements. The ensuing rebellions in the region, as well as continuing succession disputes elsewhere, gave rise to questions about the efficacy of the compacts made in the 1540s. When a plantation scheme was undertaken for the newly shired King's County (Offaly) and Queen's County (Leix) in the mid-1550s, discontinuity in government policy was more manifest than ever: Although some of the compliant Gaelic clans retained land in the planted zone, as did a few selected Old English, the bulk of the new settlers were military personnel from England who were expected to do double duty as soldiers and farmers.

The advent of the earl of Sussex to the governorship in 1556 initiated a new, systematic approach to reform of the Tudor realm of Ireland. Carefully costed, preselected objectives were to be met within an agreed time frame. This programmatic style of governance drew a variety of responses from the more established communities, ranging from full acceptance to outright rejection. In the first phase, until about 1571, the continuing emphasis on assimilation and persuasion of target populations elicited native support. In respect to the religious changes introduced in the Reformation parliament in 1560, for example, a policy of leniency ensured that matters of conscience were not publicly contentious. The Old English, among whom the reformed religion was expected to take root first, remained aloof from the Anglican Church of Ireland, but their dissent was not an issue at this stage. What did rile their political leadership in the early Elizabethan period was the mounting burden of the cess (a range of government impositions, including levies on goods and services) and a burgeoning campaign of constitutional opposition in Parliament and at court began to take shape. The regimes of Sussex (1556–1563) and Sir Henry Sidney (1565–1571) persevered with the policy of surrender and regrant, and were able to win over some Gaelic lords in Leinster, Munster, and Connacht. The inclusion of some of the compliant Leinster chiefs such as O'Dempsey and Macgillapatrick in the plantation of Leix and Offaly proved the government's intent to proceed with moderation in the process of social and political engineering. Major problems arose, however, because the government failed to engage all levels of the Gaelic political system, so although sitting chieftains and their immediate families were content with the changes, those who might reasonably have expected to succeed to the chieftaincy through the Gaelic mode of election were to be disappointed. Also, if the attempted demilitarization of the Gaelic lordships were to succeed, the class of armed retainers would be left without a raison d'être.

Perhaps the most serious case of the failure of surrender and regrant occurred in Ulster, where Shane O'Neill, the successor by clan election to Conn, first earl of Tyrone, was not accommodated in the original agreement. O'Neill's bellicosity in central Ulster disturbed the arrangements already made with the lesser lords such as O'Reilly and O'Rourke. For a number of years until his untimely death in 1567, O'Neill rampaged in much of the north of Ireland, rejecting the legitimacy of his half-brother's succession and demanding royal acknowledgment of his claims to rule in Ulster. While Sussex's regime foundered because of the failure to contain O'Neill, Sidney claimed credit for Shane's killing by the MacDonalds, but into the vacuum entered another formidable O'Neill, Turlough Luinech, who dominated the region for more than two decades.

The arrival of new settlers in the territories of Old English and Gaelic families led to revolts in Leinster and Munster in the later 1560s. Besides the ongoing attacks by the O'Mores and O'Connors on the plantation of Leix and Offaly, an armed rebellion was staged in 1569 by leading members of the Butler family against the claim of an Englishman, Sir Peter Carew, to some of their land in Carlow. In the southern province a more serious outbreak was sparked by James Fitzmaurice, a leading member of the Fitzgeralds of Desmond, in response to the presence of newcomers in his territory in County Cork. His campaign was also affected by his Catholic militancy, for which he sought aid from Spain and Rome. The revolts of the Butlers and Fitzmaurice (both members of old Norman houses) were supported by disgruntled Gaelic leaders, and though both were put down by rigorous state military actions, the implications of these alliances for the whole reform program were extremely worrying.

The pace of governmental reform speeded up in the mid-Elizabethan period until 1585, with extreme reactions from the native communities. None of the viceroys—Sir William Fitzwilliam (1571–1575), Sidney again (1575–1578), Lord Grey (1580–1582) or Sir John Perrot (1584–1588)—set out to make the religious reforms central to their programs of government, but the issue became highly charged during the major rebellions of the 1570s and 1580s. Most of the Old English preferred a quietist type of recusancy that was, for the most part, tolerated in private. Their main concern at this point was the agitation against the cess, which took on the dimensions of a constitutional struggle for the preservation of traditional customary rights (including liberty of conscience) in the face of the assertion of royal prerogative. At the parliament of 1585 to 1586, the Old English leadership successfully forged a coherent opposition to government designs. On the positive side, in conjunction with the establishment of a presidency system in Munster and Connacht, a more refined type of surrender and regrant was devised under Sidney that provided for the commuting of dues and levies payable by all levels of political leadership into annual rental payments to the president. This system, known as composition, barely worked in the southern province, but it provided the foundation for an elaborate and successful framework of agreements in Connacht. There, many of the leading magnates agreed to drop all demands on lesser lords in return for the protection of the presidency, which would in turn be funded by the contributions of all. In the south of the province the earls of Clanricard and Thomond, of Norman and Gaelic backgrounds respectively, became fully assimilated in Connacht.

Elsewhere the program of monarchical expansion into the provinces provoked violent reactions. In Leinster grievances caused by the overbearing actions of local English seneschals (mayors), the burden of supporting growing numbers of troops, and the curtailment of religious freedom all combined to bring together a coalition of insurgency in 1580 headed by the Old English gentleman, James Eustace, Viscount Baltinglass, and the Gaelic leader Feagh MacHugh O'Byrne. The spirit of the Counter-Reformation animated Baltinglass, and after his defeat and flight in 1581, the execution of many of his supporters helped to crystallize a growing sense of Catholic identity among Old English people.

These events were mirrored in the renewal of the revolt of James Fitzmaurice in Munster in 1579 in the form of a Catholic crusade with continental backing that drew the earl of Desmond into military opposition to the regime. The attempts to win Desmond and his cohorts to the new presidency system had broken down irrevocably, but upon his defeat and death in 1583, the vast Desmond estates in Munster were forfeited to the Crown. A highly centralized scheme of plantation was then organized under which English undertakers took over large estates with the duty of establishing socioeconomic institutions drawn from their homeland. Many of the existing occupiers claimed to be blameless in the recent uprising and made strenuous efforts to establish their rights through the courts. Meanwhile, two private colonial enterprises in Ulster—by the earl of Essex in Antrim and Sir Thomas Smith in the Ards—failed disastrously, but not before the region was badly affected by instability and agitation by the leaders of the threatened lordships and their neighbors. As elsewhere, the massacre of civilians, in this case on Rathlin Island, left a legacy of bitterness and mistrust.

The unrest spilled over in the climactic period before the death of Queen Elizabeth in 1603. The government pushed ahead with its policies of shiring territory in Connacht and Ulster and of reorganizing Gaelic lordships with redistributions of land and power, sparking a major conflict known as the Nine Years War (1593–1603) that eventually affected most of Ireland. For the Old English, events of the era provoked a tension between their ingrained loyalty to the monarchy and their allegiance to the Roman church, the official restoration of which came to be championed by Hugh O'Neill, earl of Tyrone. Although many of their offspring had migrated to Catholic continental centers for university training, the Old English for the most part eschewed the politico-religious cause espoused by the Spanish monarchy. Thus, while their commitment to Catholicism deepened during the 1590s, they argued the tenability of their dual loyalty in church and state, and many became active in the government's campaign against the northern Irish confederates. Apart from preventing the Old English from siding with the insurgents, the government had few policy successes through the later 1590s. The earldoms of Thomond and Clanricard in Connacht remained bastions of loyalty right throughout the Nine Years War, providing a bulwark in the west between Ulster and Munster. And the containment of the struggle in the north until the later 1590s provided breathing space for the hard-pressed military planners in Dublin Castle. But eventually discontents in all provinces confronted the state with the very real prospect of the complete overthrow of English authority in Ireland.

The shipwrecking of Spanish sailors and troops from the ill-fated Armada on the north and west coasts of Ireland in 1588 unsettled many of the lordships there. While some of the local rulers were unsympathetic to the stranded Spaniards, others such as Brian O'Rourke provided hospitality (a deed for which he was executed in 1591). The ruthless methods of the president of Connacht, Sir Richard Bingham, compounded the disaffection of the leaders of the northern part of the province who were susceptible to the influence of Hugh O'Donnell of Tir Conaill (Donegal). In the southern Ulster lordships, including west Breifne (Leitrim) and Fermanagh, there was resistance to government plans to reorganize the lands and redistribute power within an English county framework, along the lines of the Monaghan settlement of 1590. In Monaghan the MacMahon lordship was broken up and individual freehold-

ing landlords were established. The campaign of O'Donnell, Hugh Maguire, and Brian Oge O'Rourke gathered momentum and acquired a religious dimension when Catholic bishops supported the cause for Spanish intervention. Hugh O'Neill, earl of Tyrone, was faced with the dilemma of continuing to cooperate with the Dublin government and losing face with the Gaelic of Ulster, or throwing in his lot with the militant chieftains and risking the loss of all his lands and authority, as had happened to the earl of Desmond. Eventually, in 1595, he took the field on the side of the insurgents and initiated a highly successful military strategy in Ulster, culminating in his victory over the English army at the Yellow Ford in 1598. The triumphant O'Neill took the war to other parts of Ireland including Munster, and in Leinster and Connacht there were sympathetic uprisings. His most decisive move, however, was to internationalize the conflict by appealing for Spanish aid in the name of the Catholic cause. By the time of the arrival of a fleet from Spain at Kinsale in 1601, Sir George Carew was already subduing Munster, and O'Neill was under severe pressure from Lord Deputy Mountjoy. The battle at Kinsale saw the routing of the confederate forces, and O'Neill was forced to surrender just over a year later. Although the terms granted at Mellifont in 1603 were better than what he might have reasonably expected, O'Neill lost his autonomous Ulster sovereignty and was threatened with being fully circumscribed by English power.

The conquest of Ireland was more or less complete when James I began his reign in 1603, and the flight of the northern chiefs, including O'Neill in 1607, left Ulster leaderless. The consequent plantation of Ulster introduced a large number of Scottish and English settlers to the province. Yet the identities forged in the smithy of the crisis of the 1590s buoyed the older communities in their struggle to preserve their endangered heritages. For the Old English, the survival of their political, economic, and religious liberties was threatened by the absolutist-tending government of the Stuarts. The clearest manifestation of this threat came in the parliament of 1613 to 1615, when a series of constitutional and political clashes revolved around the question of representation of the recusant Old English majority. In the towns their fellows battled to preserve their guild and corporate rights in the face of government centralization and New English infiltration. These campaigns brought into sharper focus their long-established heritage of civic and religious freedom. For the Old Irish, whose senior figures had been sidelined or fled into exile, the absence of a constitutional focus in the form of a legislative forum or even a viable political leadership was damaging. The resilience of some of the Gaelic lords in adapting to the new political and social order contrasted with the failure of many more to come to terms with the market conditions brought about by colonization and the innovative estate-management techniques introduced by the newcomers. For both of the indigenous communities, the early decades of the seventeenth century were fraught with difficulty.

The prospect of an improvement over the position of de facto toleration of the Old English beckoned in the 1620s when Charles entered into negotiations with community leaders over the question of money and aid in return for a more robust form of recognition of their religious and political rights. Although the bargain was not concluded, the raising of the key issues seemed to promise the possibility of a solution. Contemporaneously, the political thought of Irish Catholic churchmen of English and Gaelic backgrounds appeared to diverge. The Old English Catholics were quite prepared to accept the legitimacy of the Stuart monarchy in return for limited toleration of their beliefs. Some exiled Gaelic priests and scholars, on the other hand, argued that the Stuarts were illegitimate because of their adherence to heresy, and they formulated a brand of Catholic nationalism that melded patriotism and religious zeal, branded "faith and fatherland" by later commentators. Meanwhile, on the ground in town and country, the Catholic Church, spearheaded by continentally trained priests, grew stronger despite the periodic bouts of repression in 1604 to 1605, 1611 to 1612, and 1629. The 1630s witnessed regression on all fronts as the absolutism of Thomas Wentworth (lord deputy, 1633–1640) alienated all groups in Ireland. Threats of a plantation in Connacht were raised, potentially affecting Old English and Gaelic Irish landowners and compounding the already existing resentments of the displaced landowners of Ulster after the resettlement in the north.

In the 1640s the Old English and Old Irish were drawn together into a major uprising that resonated throughout the British kingdoms. At stake were the constitutional, religious, and property issues that had loomed large in the previous decades, but now the monarchy, in jeopardy itself, was prepared to enter into talks with the communities in Ireland. Beginning in July 1642, the Old English, through the representative confederation of Kilkenny, sued for religious toleration and a guarantee of their political standing within the kingdom. The Old Irish, also in the assembly but with their own, separate military organization, pushed for full re-establishment of Catholicism and restoration of their lands within the kingdom of Ireland. Divisions that opened up among confederates were not exactly along ethnic lines, but the arrival in 1645 of Archbishop Rinuccini, the papal legate, complicated the matter of whether the terms offered by Ormond, the king's representative, should be accepted or not. Rinuccini, who championed the full reestablishment of the Catholic Church, lost the argument and withdrew, but the divided confederates soon had to face the English army of Oliver Cromwell, which swept all before it in 1649 and 1650.

Out of the upheavals of the 1640s and 1650s there emerged a restored monarchy by 1660, but the position of the older indigenous Irish communities had been irreparably eroded. The Old English lost their socially ascendant role in the counties, and their urban counterparts were excluded from political and economic power. The Catholic Church had suffered severe dislocation in the mid-century decades and faced a painful process of recovery. The arbitrary nature of the toleration of dissent was graphically shown in the fate of Oliver Plunkett, the archbishop of Armagh, who was executed on charges of treason in 1681. The Old Irish presence as a political grouping was further diluted by the Cromwellian and Stuart settlements: The real spiritual home of the community lay outside Ireland among the exiled literati and churchmen who fanned the flames of Catholic nationalism. Key to this resurgence was the use of the Gaelic language in print in the Tridentine catechism. The reign of James II offered a brief period of hope to the older Catholic communities that their positions could be restored, but the defeats at the Boyne (1690) and Aughrim (1691) dashed these hopes. Thereafter, the Old English and the Old Irish ceased to exist as coherent politico-religious groupings, and the process of unification of the Catholics of Ireland, designated "Irish papists" indiscriminately by Cromwell, continued on into the eighteenth century. The era of the penal laws shaped a different kind of Catholic community.

SEE ALSO Council of Trent and the Catholic Mission; Desmond Rebellions; Lombard, Peter; Monarchy; Nine Years War; O'Neill, Hugh, Second Earl of Tyrone; Plunkett, Oliver; Rebellion of 1641; Rinuccini, Giovanni Battista; Sidney, Henry; **Primary Documents:** From *Solon His Follie* (1594); From *A Direction for the Plantation of Ulster* (1610)

Bibliography

Bradshaw, Brendan. *The Irish Constitutional Revolution of the Sixteenth Century.* 1979.

Brady, Ciaran. *The Chief Governors: The Rise and Reform of Reform Government in Tudor Ireland, 1536–1588.* 1994.

Brady, Ciaran, and Raymond Gillespie, eds. *Natives and Newcomers: Essays on the Making of Irish Colonial Society, 1534–1641.* 1986.

Caball, Marc. *Poets and Politics: Reaction and Continuity in Irish Poetry, 1558–1625.* 1998.

Canny, Nicholas. *Making Ireland British, 1580–1650.* 2001.

Clarke, Aidan. *The Old English in Ireland, 1625–1642.* 1966.

Crawford, Jon. *Anglicizing the Government of Ireland.* 1994.

Cunningham, Bernadette. *The World of Geoffrey Keating.* 2000.

Ellis, Steven G. *Reform and Revival: English Government in Ireland, 1470–1534.* 1986.

Ellis, Steven G. *Ireland in the Age of the Tudors, 1447–1603.* 1998.

Ford, Alan. *The Protestant Reformation in Ireland, 1590–1641.* 1997.

Lennon, Colm. *The Lords of Dublin in the Age of Reformation.* 1989.

Lennon, Colm. *Sixteenth Century Ireland: The Incomplete Conquest.* 1994.

Morgan, Hiram. *Tyrone's Rebellion.* 1993.

Morgan, Hiram, ed. *Political Ideology in Ireland, 1541–1641.* 1999.

Ó Siochrú, Micheál. *Confederate Ireland, 1642–9: A Constitutional and Political Analysis.* 1999.

Simms, J. G. *Jacobite Ireland, 1685–91.* 1969.

Simms, J. G. "The Restoration, 1660–85." In *Early Modern Ireland, 1534–1691.* Vol. 3 of *A New History of Ireland*, edited by T. W. Moody, F. X. Martin, and F. J. Byrne. 1976. Reprint, 1991.

Colm Lennon

English Writing on Ireland before 1800

The boundaries of this subject are more than a little blurred, and more than a trifle contentious. For medieval writing, the very categories "English" and "Irish" may be anachronisms: historians argue vigorously over how far back in time such national labels can aptly be applied. In more recent periods particular individuals and groups evidently had changeable or hybrid identities—the same person might be viewed either as English or as Irish, as both or indeed neither, from different perspectives or at different times. "Old English" and later "Anglo-Irish" identities in early modern Ireland are the most obvious cases in point. But there would also be scope for dispute over the categorization, for instance, of a figure such as Jonathan Swift (1667–1745), who was Dublin-born but of English parentage, and divided his adult life between the two countries, adopting different literary personae according to circumstances and polemical intent.

Among the earliest surviving "English" texts dealing with Ireland are medieval Anglo-Irish annals of Irish historical events; that is, ones apparently set down by monks of English origin, though resident in Ireland. They differ from their counterparts kept in Gaelic Irish monasteries mainly in that the latter confine themselves largely to happenings within Ireland, whereas the Anglo-Irish chronicles detail English and Welsh events as well. A little later, Giraldus (Gerald) Cambrensis depicted Ireland more extensively in his *Topography of Ireland* (1188) and *Expugnatio Hibernica* (c. 1189). As his name suggests, Gerald was of Welsh birth, but his writings clearly reflect the viewpoints of Ireland's and Wales's Norman invaders. Indeed, Gerald is often seen as the effective founder of a long English literary tradition of viewing the Irish as primitive, barbaric, semi-heathen, and fit only to be dominated, if not destroyed, by England.

A great deal of the early English writing about Ireland came from clergymen and was religious in character. After the Protestant Reformation, a major theme was naturally anti-Catholic polemic, often coupled with lamentation at the alleged theological ignorance, immorality, and backsliding of the Irish clergy and people. Suffolk-born John Bale (1495–1563), for instance, was bishop of Ossory from 1552 to 1553. His tenure was brief because his attempts to enforce Protestant worship in the diocese met a violently hostile reaction from local people. Bale's account of this fiasco is among the most important records of early responses to the Reformation in Ireland. Among the later English ecclesiastics who resided in and wrote about Ireland, perhaps the most prolific and influential was Anglican bishop Jeremy Taylor (1613–1667).

English-born writers contributed to Counter-Reformation polemic too. The English Jesuit Edmund Campion (?–1581) stayed in Dublin in 1570 and 1571 and wrote his *Histories of Ireland* (published only in 1633, well after Campion's execution for treason) to acclaim the record of the Catholic Old English there. His manuscripts were heavily drawn on by Richard Stanihurst (1547–1618), who wrote most of the Irish sections of Raphael Holinshed's *Chronicles.* The latter was the most widely read historical work in Elizabethan England. As is well known, it formed in its turn the main source for Shakespeare's history plays. But although Shakespeare's *Henry V* features a famous cameo appearance by a belligerent Irish soldier, Macmorris, there are no major Irish themes or settings in his oeuvre. England's greatest seventeenth-century poet, John Milton, similarly made only fragmentary (and unflattering) allusions to Ireland in his works. Indeed, very few—perhaps surprisingly few—of England's major

Depiction of the flight of the Irish. English horsemen are pursuing the Irish cavalry. In the background the Irish foot soldiers are flying, annoyed by the English arquebusses. The piper has been thrown down, with his bagpipe beside him. FROM JOHN DERRICKE'S *THE IMAGE OF IRELANDE* (1581).

early playwrights, poets, or novelists seem to have given much attention to Ireland before the eighteenth century. The most prominent exception was Edmund Spenser (c. 1552–1599), whose *View of the Present State of Ireland* (which remained unpublished until 1633) advocated a harsh policy of repression or even extermination. Historians have differed over how representative or influential such extreme proposals may have been, and also on how far Spenser's epic *Faerie Queene* (1590–1596) should be read as presenting a similar view in allegorical form.

Nonfiction accounts—histories, geographical surveys, and religious and political arguments—were more numerous and extensive. Many came from the pens of English soldiers or administrators in Ireland. Sir John Davies (1569–1626) in his *Discovery of the True Causes Why Ireland Was Never Entirely Subdued* (1612) celebrated the extension of English law across Ireland and the sweeping away of indigenous and Old English institutions. William Camden (1551–1623) espoused fiercely anti-Catholic sentiments, while his *Britannia* (1586) also included references to the Irish as lazy, filthy in their habits, bellicose, and promiscuous. Other major contributions to this literature included John Dymmok's *Treatise of Ireland* (c. 1600), Robert Payne's *Brief Description of Ireland* (1589), Luke Gernon's *Discourse of*

Ireland (1620), and various works by Fynes Moryson (1566–1630). Others became more famous for their images than their words—above all, John Derricke's 1581 *Image of Irelande.*

The relative weights of anti-Catholicism and of anti-Irishness in much of this writing have been lastingly contentious, but claims that the supposedly deplorable character of the Irish people was caused above all by their religion seem to have gained strength in the early seventeenth century. Still, not all were uniformly hostile. Payne, for instance, found much that was positive to say about Irish honesty, hospitality, and (perhaps surprisingly at that time) their obedience to the law, and the Elizabethan courtier Sir John Harrington (1561–1612) was positively effusive about the people's good qualities. Yet these, it is often pointed out, were exceptions, while new political conflicts gave impetus to antagonistic imagery. Thus the "depositions" of Protestant settlers who had suffered in the 1641 rebellion were heavily drawn upon in Sir John Temple's *History of the Irish Rebellion* (1646). Temple's claims about the number of settlers massacred in the rising were greatly exaggerated but had a lasting effect on Protestant historical consciousness.

Several of those who came with Oliver Cromwell in and after 1649 left important accounts. Some, like *Ire-*

Triumphant return of the English soldiers. Henry Sidney, the lord deputy, is escorted by a guard of English troops, preceded by trumpeters and standard bearers. FROM JOHN DERRICKE'S *THE IMAGE OF IRELANDE* (1581).

land's *Natural History* (1652), the posthumously published survey by Gerard Boate (1604–1650), who was actually Dutch-born, or the later *Interest of Ireland in Its Trade and Wealth* (1682) by the former Cromwellian colonel Richard Lawrence (?–c. 1684) were explicitly designed to encourage colonization and commercial development. The most influential of them, however, was Cromwell's physician-general, William Petty (1623–1687), whose economic and demographic surveys of Ireland included *The Political Anatomy of Ireland* (1691) and *Hiberniae Delineatio* (1685).

After the end of the Williamite wars a seemingly more tranquil Ireland attracted numerous English travel writers. The most famous—and in many later critics' eyes, the most accurately informative—was the 1780 *Tour in Ireland* by agrarian reformer Arthur Young (1741–1820). But the genre became so popular that even an Irish-authored account—Thomas Campbell's *Philosophical Survey of the South of Ireland* (1776)—was presented as if written by an English tourist. English-born members of the Ascendancy, such as Mary Delany (1700–1788) and Emily Fitzgerald, duchess of Leinster (1731–1814), also left significant portrayals, which are among the first widely known women's views of Ireland. Some began to be infused with the emerging and novel Romantic enthusiasm for wild countryside, mountains, and lakes, for "unspoilt" peasant communities and their folklore. Thus it became possible and in-

creasingly popular to see the west of Ireland no longer as its most barbaric part, but as the most picturesque and interesting—indeed, as more "truly Irish" than other regions. This structure of feeling had, of course, a lasting influence not only on outsiders' depictions of the country but on Irish literary self-images too.

Literary depictions of the Irish—especially on the London stage—also became more numerous, more varied, and at least in some cases, less scornful during the eighteenth century. The stock figure of the comic, usually foolish "Stage Irishman" was already well established, but now a wider range of stereotypical characters began to emerge in the writings of Henry Fielding, Tobias Smollett, and other popular English writers: the impudent fortune hunter, the sham squire, but also the gallant army officer and the naturally eloquent peasant. An image of the Irish as sentimental, poetic, musical, and courageous took shape. It was often a condescending representation at best, but it was no longer a ferociously hostile one. Nonetheless, such affectionate stereotypes did not entirely replace those of the Irish as congenitally idle, drunken, violent, and treacherous. The latter, indeed, were to re-emerge with renewed force in the era of Daniel O'Connell's Repeal campaigns and the Great Famine of the late 1840s.

So diverse a body of writing, extending across several centuries, cannot easily be subject to general judgment. Yet dispute over the dominant character of English works and views on Ireland has nonetheless been vigorous, not least since the 1990s. Some commentators would emphasize a general tendency of English writing about Ireland and the Irish to stereotype, denigrate, and scorn its subjects. They see a great deal of it as directly linked to and supporting England's attempts at conquest, domination, and exploitation. Other critics, by contrast, would stress that many English literary views of Ireland were by no means uninformed, unfriendly, or unsympathetic.

SEE ALSO Arts: Early Modern Literature and the Arts from 1500 to 1800; Colonial Theory from 1500 to 1690; Literature: Anglo-Irish Literary Tradition, Beginnings of; **Primary Documents:** From *The Topography of Ireland* (1188); From *Expugnatio Hibernica* (1189); From *Vocation of John Bale to the Bishopery of Ossorie* (1553); From *Two Bokes of the Histories of Ireland* (1571); From "Notes of His Report" (1576); Letter to Elizabeth (12 November 1580); From *The Image of Irelande* (1581); From "The Sons of Clanricard" (1586); From *A View of the Present State of Ireland* (1596); From *A New Description of Ireland* (1610); From *A Discovery of the True Causes Why Ireland Was Never Entirely Subdued* (1612); From *An Itinerary* (1617); From *Discourse of Ireland* (1620); From *The Total Discourse of His Rare Adventures* (1632); From *Travels* (1634–1635); From *A Philosophical Survey of the South of Ireland* (1777); On Irish Rural Society and Poverty (1780); From *A Description of the . . . Peasantry of Ireland* (1804); From *Narrative of a Residence in Ireland* (1817)

Bibliography

Canny, Nicholas. *Making Ireland British.* 2001.

Duggan, G. C. *The Stage Irishman: A History of the Irish Play and Stage Characters from the Earliest Times.* 1937.

Eagleton, Terry. *Crazy John and the Bishop and Other Essays on Irish Culture.* 1998.

Hadfield, Andrew, and John McVeagh, eds. *Strangers to That Land: British Perceptions of Ireland from the Reformation to the Famine.* 1994.

Leerssen, Joep. *Mere Irish and Fíor-Ghael: Studies in the Idea of Irish Nationality, Its Development and Literary Expression prior to the Nineteenth Century.* 1986. Rev. edition, 1996.

Stephen Howe

Equal Economic Rights for Women in Independent Ireland

Until the closing decades of the twentieth century the social model around which rights to property, employment, and social-welfare payments revolved in Ireland was the male breadwinner. The model was supported by a firm legal framework: The property of a married woman was vested in her husband; priority in employment and pay went to men; and married women were barred from work in the public service and from a range of other jobs, including teaching, nursing, and banking. In relation to certain social-welfare payments, including unemployment assistance, married women did not have an entitlement of their own; instead, their husbands were entitled to a payment for a dependent wife. Children's allowances were paid to fathers.

Until the late nineteenth century a wife did not have a legal right to hold property in her own name separately from her husband. Husband and wife were regarded as one person in law, and the husband held all the property. By an enactment in 1882, when Ireland was still part of the United Kingdom, a wife was allowed to hold property and could enter a contract separately from her husband. The Married Women's Status Act of 1957 represented an important development regarding the property rights of married women. The act permits one spouse to sue the other in court, and a section of the act has been used to determine proprietary rights to the family home. Prior to the Succession Act of 1965 it was possible for one spouse to exclude the other from benefiting from his or her estate. As the bulk of property was held by men, this left wives in a parlous state. The Succession Act guarantees a minimum of one-third of the deceased spouse's estate to a surviving spouse. When introduced by the then minister for justice, Charles Haughey, the Succession Bill aroused terrific hostility, partly owing to the possibility of property passing out of a family of origin following a childless marriage.

In achieving equal rights for women in employment and social welfare, an important catalyst was the *Report of the Commission on the Status of Women,* published in 1972. In November 1969 the taoiseach announced the establishment of a Commission on the Status of Women which would operate under the minister for finance. Dr. Thekla Beere was appointed chairperson. (Beere, a legal and political science graduate of Trinity College, made history when she was appointed secretary of the Department of Transport and Power, the first woman to hold the post of secretary of a government department in Ireland.) Shortly after it was established, the commission was asked by the minister for finance to prepare an interim report on the question of equal pay with particular reference to the public sector. In the event, and reflecting the position at the time, almost the entire Final Report dealt with equal pay and other issues related to the employment of women, as well as aspects of politics and public life, taxation and social welfare.

A recommendation of the commission for a payment to women working full-time in the home as careers sprang from the concern of the commission that "the introduction of equal pay will not accentuate further the present undervaluation of the role of mother and housewife." Alone among the recommendations of the commission, this recommendation for a payment for women in the home was not implemented. However, another recommendation, that the entitlement to children's allowances should be paid to mothers was given effect in the Social Welfare Act of 1974. This proposal had been made by Deputy Liam Cosgrave, TD, thirty years earlier in 1943, when the bill to introduce children's allowances was being debated in the Dáil. An important innovation in the social-welfare code that was introduced following a recommendation by the Commission of the Status of Women was a payment for a single mother who rears her child herself. The payment was revolutionary at the time that it was introduced. Subsequently, it was extended to include fathers who rear children on their own.

Two pieces of legislation enacted in the 1970s contributed to strengthening the economic rights of women. These were the Family Law (Maintenance of Spouses and Children) Act of 1976 and the Family Home Protection Act of 1976. The former contains a code relating to the maintenance of spouses and children and provides for enforcement of maintenance orders through attachment of earnings, while the latter prevents either spouse from disposing of the family home without the written consent of the other, although it does not give any right to ownership.

Beginning in the 1930s, the era of the Great Depression and the Economic War with Britain, restrictions were gradually introduced to limit the sphere of women's work. In 1936 the Conditions of Employment Act was passed. It provided ministerial authority to prohibit the employment of women in certain forms of industrial work, to fix the proportion of female workers who could be hired by an employer, and to outlaw the employment of women in industry between 10 P.M. and 8 A.M. These restrictions applied to all women; certain further restrictions were imposed on married women. For example, a marriage bar against the employment of married women primary teachers was introduced in

1933. The growth in employment of married women has been facilitated by the removal of such discriminatory regulations against them. One of the most significant changes in the regulations governing the employment of married women was the removal in 1958 of the ban on married women primary teachers introduced twenty-five years earlier.

A series of significant changes in regulations followed Irish entry into the European Economic Community (EEC) in 1973. On 31 July 1973 the marriage bar in the civil service was ended. The Anti-Discrimination (Pay) Act of 1974 came into operation in December 1975, establishing the right of men and women employed at like work by the same employer to equal pay. The Employment Equality Act came into operation on 1 July 1977, prohibiting discrimination on grounds of sex or marital status in recruitment, training, or provision of opportunities for promotion.

Other important laws were the Unfair Dismissals Act of 1977 and the Maternity (Protection of Employees) Act of 1981. The Unfair Dismissals Act protects employees, including pregnant employees, from unfair dismissal by laying down criteria by which dismissals are to be judged unfair and by providing an adjudication system and redress for an employee who has been dismissed unfairly. The Maternity Act of 1981 was particularly important in ensuring the right of a woman to return to work following the birth of a child. The act provides maternity protection for pregnant employees by granting an entitlement to maternity leave and the right to return to work.

The basis for equality in the social-welfare system derives from the Equality Directive of the European Community (Directive 79/7/EEC). This directive on the progressive implementation of equal treatment for men and women came into force in Ireland in 1984. At the time, a number of elements of discrimination existed in the social-welfare code. One discriminatory practice that operated against married women was the lack of direct access to unemployment assistance; instead, their husbands received an allowance for a "dependent spouse." The legislation providing for equality of treatment for men and women in the social-welfare code (Social Welfare Amendment No. 2, Act of 1985) allows either member of a married couple to claim the main payment, and a spouse can apply to obtain the dependent payment part directly. Subsequent delays in making payments led to litigation all the way to the European Court. The matter was finally resolved in 1992.

As the twentieth century drew to a close, there was general awareness of the extent to which the agenda seeking equal rights for women had been achieved, and attention refocused on possible areas of discrimination against men and on the difficulties for men and women of sharing domestic and labor-market tasks, especially in relation to the care of children and other dependents, including elderly and disabled relatives.

SEE ALSO Clarke, Kathleen; Conditions of Employment Act of 1936; Family: Fertility, Marriage, and the Family since 1950; Health and Welfare since 1950, State Provisions for; Robinson, Mary; Women and Work since the Mid-Nineteenth Century; Women in Irish Society since 1800; **Primary Documents:** From the *Report of the Commission on the Status of Women* (1972)

Bibliography

Commission on the Status of Women. *Report to the Minister for Finance.* 1972.

Kennedy, Finola. *Cottage to Crèche: Family Change in Ireland.* 2001. Reprint, 2002.

Second Commission on the Status of Women. *Report to Government.* 1993.

Shatter, Alan. *Family Law in the Republic of Ireland.* 1997. 4th edition, 1998, 2000.

Finola Kennedy

Equal Rights in Northern Ireland

The period of devolved government in Northern Ireland (1921–1972) saw an entrenched unionist and Protestant majority discriminating systematically against a large nationalist and Catholic minority. Despite a constitutional ban on discrimination, Catholics were discriminated against in local elections, housing, and public and private employment. Alienation, segregation, and disadvantage were serious problems. The police and security services were almost exclusively Protestant. In education, single-denominational schools were the norm; educational underachievement among Catholics compounded their disadvantage.

REFORMS SINCE THE 1960S

The unionist and London governments introduced some belated reforms in the 1960s: The more crass discriminatory practices in housing and elections were removed; complaint mechanisms and community-relations bodies were introduced; and the exclusively Protestant police reserve was replaced with a new force. The 1973 Northern Ireland Constitution Act reinforced the prohibition on explicit discrimination by public bodies on grounds of religion or political opinion, and it also established the Standing Advisory Commission on Human Rights (SACHR) to advise on human-rights matters.

In 1976 the government introduced measures to combat discrimination in the private sphere. The British ban on sex discrimination in employment and in the supply of services was extended to the Irish province (but not the prohibition on race discrimination, since the government did not believe that the province had a problem of racial discrimination). The 1976 Fair Employment Act (FEA), which was limited to Northern Ireland, banned discrimination on grounds of religion or political opinion in employment. The statutes on sex discrimination and fair employment established independent bodies to promote equality. The FEA applied only to employment. More seriously, it prohibited only direct, explicit discrimination and not indirect discrimination, which includes cases where, for example, an employer hires someone on the basis of educational achievement; this indirectly works to the disadvantage of some groups. The 1976 act did not undo the situation of persistent disadvantage. Pressure groups in the United States urged corporations and legislators investing in Northern Ireland to respect the "MacBride principles," a code of conduct for U.S. firms that encourages nondiscrimination and equality of opportunity in Northern Ireland. In 1987 SACHR reported that the Catholic male unemployment rate was two and one-half times higher than the Protestant male unemployment rate and had not changed since 1976. SACHR recommended a new law to promote equality of opportunity.

The 1989 Fair Employment Act implemented some of SACHR's recommendations. Indirect discrimination was outlawed, and many (though not all) employers were put under a duty to monitor the religious composition of their workforces. The act permitted limited forms of affirmative action, including training programs that would be accessible to the underrepresented Catholics and would encourage them to apply for jobs. Reverse discrimination—explicit preferences for Catholics—remained illegal. The 1989 act prompted definite improvements, but Catholic disadvantage, single-religion places of employment, and occupational segregation persisted. SACHR, the equality bodies, the Committee on the Administration of Justice (CAJ—a civil-rights group established in 1981), and others promoted a new policy of "mainstreaming" equality, which would emphasize working proactively to achieve equality rather than simply avoiding discrimination. They also advocated more robust affirmative-action and enforcement measures.

There were important developments apart from the fair-employment laws. The United Kingdom's accession to the European Community prompted many changes. A 1986 European Court of Justice (ECJ) decision limited the scope for national-security defenses in sex-discrimination cases. In 2000 the European Community adopted new measures barring discrimination based on race, religion, disability, age, or sexual orientation. Rulings of the European Court of Human Rights (ECHR) resulted in the decriminalization of gay sexual practices (1981) and in limits being placed on the national-security defense to claims of religious discrimination (1997). Both ECJ and ECHR cases provided greater protection for people who had undergone gender-reassignment surgery. Discrimination against people with disabilities was banned in 1995, and so too was racial discrimination in 1997. Independent bodies were established to enforce these laws. The 1997 Labour government's constitutional reforms included the 1998 Human Rights Act, which requires public authorities to respect the 1950 European Convention on Human Rights. The convention prohibits discrimination in the enjoyment of such rights. Its extensive and open-ended list of prohibited grounds (e.g., age, sexual orientation, lifestyle, etc.) captures some types of official discrimination that would not otherwise be illegal. Women's rights also began to receive attention. In 1996 a new party with a focus on equality—the Women's Coalition—entered the male world of Northern Irish politics.

THE BELFAST OR GOOD FRIDAY AGREEMENT

The Belfast or Good Friday Agreement promises wide-ranging equality and human-rights reforms. The Women's Coalition played a role in ensuring this. Under the 1998 Northern Ireland Act the assembly and executive may not violate the European Convention on Human Rights. The act creates two bodies to promote human rights and equality: the Northern Ireland Human Rights Commission (replacing SACHR) and the Equality Commission (replacing four earlier bodies). The Human Rights Commission is working on a bill of rights for Northern Ireland. The act adopts the policy of "mainstreaming" equality. All public authorities must devise equality schemes to explain how they promote equality of opportunity between people, irrespective of religion, political opinion, race, age, marital status, or sexual orientation, and between people with or without a disability and with or without dependents. This duty extends to all the functions of a public authority. Public authorities must also consider how to promote good relations between persons of different religions, political opinions, and races. This new duty is expected to encourage a more proactive approach and more transparent and participatory decision making.

The London government's Fair Employment and Treatment Order (FETO) of 1998 replaced the earlier fair-employment legislation. FETO extended the prohibition of religious discrimination to nonemployment fields. Affirmative action was extended somewhat—for instance, employers may actively recruit from the ranks of the long-term unemployed. (Previously, this would have been unlawful indirect discrimination against Protestants.) Since 1998 the Office of the First and Deputy First Minister is responsible for equality law; its charge is to unify the diverse equality laws. The peace process also required a major review of the police, a force that was still unrepresentative of Northern Ireland's diverse population. To remedy this, the 2000 Police Act requires that 50 percent of new recruits be Catholics.

Much has been achieved in Northern Ireland. Catholic disadvantage in employment and education has diminished; for example, in 2001, except in security occupations, Catholic participation in public employment equalled Catholic representation in the private workforce. The new measures undertaken since 1998, although they stop short of the SACHR recommendations, are impressive, but they also indicate how bad things had become in Northern Ireland. A quota for the police was necessary because less than 10 percent of the force was Catholic. The FETO had to make an exception for affirmative action targeted at the long-term unemployed because two-thirds of the long-term unemployed are Catholic. In many areas of life separation and mistrust remain: Sectarian violence continues, residential segregation is prevalent, many private associations are restricted to a single community, most schools are single-denominational, and the main political parties attract support from only one community. Furthermore, the equality measures are controversial, with some members of the unionist community regarding them (especially the quota for the police) as rank reverse discrimination.

Other forms of inequality are also significant. Serious socioeconomic deprivation affects members of both communities. Homelessness is a bigger problem than in the rest of the United Kingdom. The Women's Coalition has exposed crude sexism in political life. According to a 2002 Northern Ireland assembly research paper, women are significantly more likely than men to experience poverty. In 2002 the Equality Commission felt the need to issue a "wake-up call" on the dangers of race discrimination. If the new equality measures are striking initiatives, that is only because Northern Ireland still needs to tackle serious problems of inequality, segregation, and disadvantage.

SEE ALSO Equal Economic Rights for Women in Independent Ireland; Women in Irish Society since 1800; **Primary Documents:** The Belfast/Good Friday Agreement (10 April 1998)

Bibliography

Boyle, Kevin, and Tom Hadden. *Northern Ireland: The Choice.* 1994.

Equality Commission for Northern Ireland. Web site available at http://www.equalityni.org.

Farrell, M. *Northern Ireland: The Orange State.* 1976.

Fearon, Kate, and Monica McWilliams. "Swimming against the Mainstream: The Northern Ireland Women's Coalition." In *Gender, Democracy, and Inclusion in Northern Ireland,* edited by C. Davies and Carmel Roulston. 2000.

McCrudden, Christopher. "Mainstreaming Equality in the Governance of Northern Ireland." In *Human Rights, Equality, and Democratic Renewal in Northern Ireland,* edited by Colin Harvey. 2001.

Northern Irish Assembly. Web site available at http://www.ni-assembly.gov.uk.

Sheehan, M., and M. Tomlinson. *The Unequal Unemployed: Discrimination, Unemployment, and State Policy in Northern Ireland.* 1999.

University of Ulster. The Northern Ireland Conflict (1968 to the Present). Conflict Archive on the Internet. Available at http://cain.ulst.ac.uk.

Whyte, J. "How Much Discrimination Was There under the Unionist Regime, 1921–68?" In *Contemporary Irish Studies,* edited by Tom Gallagher and James O'Connell. 1983.

Wilson, Tom. *Ulster: Conflict and Consent.* 1989.

Rory O'Connell

Estates and Demesnes

Visually significant components in the modern Irish landscape, estates and demesnes are particular Irish expressions of a system of landownership and social control that was characteristic of much of western Europe and had its origins in the feudal manorial system of the Middle Ages. They have been mainly associated with the Protestant Ascendancy class in Ireland, though some estates were owned by Catholic families and others who were not part of the ascendancy. It might be more accurate to characterize them as being held by a heterogeneous group of landowners who belonged to the "gentry."

ORIGINS

The estate system grew out of an amalgam of Anglo-Norman medieval manors, lands which were confiscated by the Crown and granted to or purchased by new British planters and settlers in the sixteenth and seventeenth centuries, in such projects as the Munster (1586) and Ulster (1610) plantations and the Cromwellian settlement in the 1650s, as well as some Gaelic sept lands which survived confiscation. Plantations introduced many representatives of the new mercantilist British state, like Richard Boyle (later earl of Cork) or Moses Hill (later the marquis of Downshire) in County Down, who were intent on the vigorous economic development of their new lands. Some landowners in the eighteenth century owned estates in both England and Ireland.

STRUCTURE

Estates varied greatly in size and economic capacity, reflecting the impact of initial plantation settlements, subsequent speculative land purchases, incremental additions to the original holding, marriage endowments, and random sales. As a result of defective land surveys, the initial plantation schemes in Munster and Ulster sometimes allotted estate properties that were too large and beyond the investment potential of the Undertakers or Adventurers (who "undertook" to plant the land with settlers or who "adventured" their capital in the enterprise). The Downshire and Kildare estates comprised 120,000 and 67,000 acres respectively, but most were properties of less than 10,000 acres. Economic viability, however, was determined more by land quality: the Lansdowne estate in Kerry (95,000 acres) consisted mostly of mountain and bogland.

The plantation of a landed elite in Ireland had the economic objective of stabilizing regional economic and political conditions. Estates were leased in farms to tenants for specified periods at agreed rents. Tenants were bound by their contracts to develop the landholding, build a house, pay the rent, and so on. Leases reflected contemporary economic conditions. During the seventeenth-century wars and economic recession, leases were long and cheap in order to attract tenants. Many obtained long leases on large portions of estates, which they subsequently subleased in smaller sections at higher rents, and shorter leases. These leaseholds produced what became known as the middleman system,

The great house of the Butlers, earls (and later dukes) of Ormond, erected around 1570 at Carrick-on-Suir, Co. Tipperary. The remains of the medieval castle are visible in the background. COURTESY OF FAILTE IRELAND. REPRODUCED BY PERMISSION.

which in places allowed fragmentation of landholdings and the growth of unsustainable population densities. By the time of the Napoleonic wars and the wartime boom in agriculture, rents rose significantly and leases were shortened by landlords (in many cases smaller farms were let on annual tenancies). Population rose rapidly as farms were subdivided on many estates in the decades prior to the Great Famine. In general, subdivision among tenant families, and subletting to landless laborers or cottiers occurred most often on poorly managed estates, especially in more marginal western districts that had little economic potential beyond rental farming. In regions of commercial agriculture, estates were more carefully managed by their owners, with tenant leases and laborer numbers controlled.

Larger properties usually had an array of estate officials to help with management, such as land agents, stewards and bailiffs, as well as an office holding records of the tenancies and the estate's business—of vital importance to modern historians. Management practice often varied between resident and nonresident (or absentee) owners. Smaller, more fragmented properties,

often on poorer lands that may have had a history of speculative ownership, may have had a less alert management. There were, for example, many estates where the tenants were largely unknown to the owners in the 1840s.

These differences were reflected in landscape and settlement patterns that echo down to the present. The texture of farms and fields, hedges and trees, road networks, and housing density reflected varied management strategies. For example, estates in south Monaghan, which contained many house clusters in the 1770s, were characterized by dispersed farmsteads by the 1830s as a result of land-reform policies pursued by Lord Bath, an influential landlord from Wiltshire in England.

In the eighteenth century the more innovative landlords and land agents were preoccupied with improving their estates, introducing enclosure, rearranging settlement, planting trees, setting up model farms, and offering prizes to encourage better husbandry. Improvement extended to the local economy, with landowners getting involved in the development of towns and villages as focal points for markets and industry on their estates. By the mid-eighteenth century, the linen industry was developing and colonies of weavers were established in villages like Collon, Co. Louth, and Monivea, Co. Galway. Estate towns like Strokestown, Co. Roscommon, Hillsborough, Co. Down, and Kenmare, Co. Kerry, as well as encouraging the local economy, were important marks of status for the landowner.

In an age of paternalism some landlords considered that they had responsibilities as social improvers too, and appointed moral agents to look after the welfare of their tenants, especially to stem over-indulgence in whiskey drinking. Most ideas on improvement were encountered in England or on the Grand Tour in Europe. Landlords were also patrons of the arts and many Big Houses contained paintings and sculptures bought on the Continent. By the 1840s ideas on improvement encompassed schemes of assisted emigration in order to relieve many overpopulated estates of surplus tenantry.

DEMESNES

Demesne is a medieval term for lands set aside for the lord of the manor, especially deer parks, which continued in some instances into modern demesnes. By the 1650s the demesne was essentially the home farm of the landlord, and by the late seventeenth century its design began to incorporate fashionable gardens laid out in the classicalism of Le Nôtre. But by the time of the mid-eighteenth-century romantic movement, pastoral designs from nature became popular and most demesne landscapes are legacies of this period. Irish demesnes are distinguished by high enclosing walls to keep out poachers and the populace from what were called the pleasure grounds of the landlord. Rising estate incomes in the eighteenth century led to increased investment in demesnes involving a range of elements, which were as much a mark of contemporary fashion as a necessary function. Grand Tours of the Continent and seasonal visiting by the landed class led to the diffusion of fashionable gardening and architectural ideas. Vistas; winding avenues; serpentine lakes; ponds and canals, kitchen, walled, and exotic gardens; fanciful gate lodges; boathouses; Swiss cottages; shell houses; glasshouses for soft fruit; icehouses for summer drinks; and extravagant follies appeared in the most prestigious properties to match imposing mansion houses and modern farm buildings. Many examples remain as important resources of cultural tourism today—Carton, Castletown, Florence Court, Powerscourt, Kilruddery. There are also many derelict demesne landscapes and Big Houses, which reflect the demise of the estate system following the Land Acts and the burning of many houses by the IRA during the War of Independence.

SEE ALSO Country Houses and the Arts; Landscape and Settlement; Rural Settlement and Field Systems; Woodlands

Bibliography

Crawford, William H. "The Significance of Landed Estates in Ulster, 1600–1820." *Irish Economic and Social History* (1990): 44–61.

Dooley, Terence. *The Decline of the Big House in Ireland.* 2001.

Proudfoot, Lindsay J. "Spatial Transformation and Social Agency: Property, Society, and Improvement, c. 1700 to 1900." In *An Historical Geography of Ireland,* edited by Brian J. Graham and Lindsay J Proudfoot. 1993.

Reeves-Smyth, Terence. "Demesnes." In *Atlas of the Irish Rural Landscape,* edited by Frederick H. A. Aalen, Kevin Whelan, and Mathew Stout. 1997.

Somerville-Large, Peter. *The Irish Country House.* 1995.

Patrick J. Duffy

Eucharistic Congress

The Eucharistic Congress is a mass meeting of Catholics organized on an international basis and aimed at celebrating the mystery of the Eucharist through lectures, seminars, discussions, and the adoration of the Blessed Sacrament. The thirty-first congress, which was held in Dublin in June 1932, demonstrated not only the links and bonds within Irish society, North and South, but also the inherent tensions and strains (particularly in the North: for instance, trains carrying Catholics back through Northern Ireland after the event were stoned, prompting complaints from the Catholic hierarchy to the Stormont government).

Interestingly, the Northern Irish government was invited to attend the celebrations but chose to ignore the invitation, though the Northern Irish press gave detailed and balanced coverage of the event. Conversely, Eamon de Valera's government chose to use the congress as an opportunity to snub the governor-general (the representative of the British crown in Ireland), James McNeill. The congress was a coup for de Valera, who gained in world profile and prestige from association with the congress and the visit of the cardinal legate, Lorenzo Lauri. This was ironic given that de Valera's predecessor, W. T. Cosgrave, and the previous Cumann na nGaedheal government had helped to organize the event before de Valera and Fianna Fáil won their first election in February 1932.

The congress organizers presented a distinctive and selective version of life in the Free State, portraying an image of civic and religious unity. The scars of the Civil War lived on in the Free State in the 1930s, and arguably for much longer. Indeed, up to 1927 de Valera and his party had rejected the legitimacy of the state. However, in the face of such a high-profile event, and with the Catholic world watching, the organizers were keen to represent the state as now unified. In form and style, although on a much greater scale, the 1932 Eucharistic Congress owed much to the 1929 centenary celebration of Catholic Emancipation. In its similarities it reminded the audience and participants of the previous drama of the centenary, and by association, it promoted a Catholic and nationalist interpretation of Ireland's past. Carefully organized and choreographed, both observances were preceded by a week of events, including high masses and a special children's mass, building to the climax of a mass held in Phoenix Park. In both the 1929 and 1932 celebrations, the high masses were followed by processions to the center of the capital, where benedictions were held on Watling Street Bridge in the first instance and on O'Connell Bridge in the second. Although both events were meticulously planned, neither the centenary or the Eucharistic Congress were prepared for or performed cynically: They were, above all, genuine expressions of a Catholic state that tentatively was coming into its own. With these two events the relationship between church and state in the Free State was formally acknowledged and affirmed in the modern age. In an almost literal way it was (or was presented as) an act of "national communion."

SEE ALSO Gaelic Catholic State, Making of; Politics: Independent Ireland since 1922; Protestant Community in Southern Ireland since 1922

Bibliography

Harris, Mary. *The Catholic Church and the Foundation of the Northern Irish State.* 1993.

McIntosh, Gillian. "Acts of National Communion"? The Centenary of Catholic Emancipation and the Eucharistic Congress." In *Ireland in the 1930s*, edited by Joost Augusteijn. 1999.

Gillian McIntosh

European Union

In January 1972 the Taoiseach Jack Lynch and his foreign minister Dr. Patrick Hillery left Dublin airport for Luxembourg to sign Ireland's Treaty of Accession to the European Communities. Just over fifty years after the signing of the Anglo-Irish Treaty, which gave the people of twenty-six of the thirty-two counties of Ireland the right to establish a state (the Irish Free State) separate from the United Kingdom, an Irish government negotiated membership of a community that had altered the nature of statehood in Europe. Ireland as a relatively young state was preparing to pool and share its sovereignty with the other member states of the Union in a dynamic political experiment. The Irish government made its first application for European Union (EU) membership on 31 July 1961. It took twelve years to bring this key foreign-policy goal to fruition, largely because of events beyond the control of any Irish government. Throughout the 1960s successive governments remained wedded to Ireland's eventual membership of the Union. In 1972, 83 percent of those who voted in the referendum voted in favor of membership.

THE NICE NO

Ireland's engagement with the EU system was relatively smooth until the shock of the defeat of the Nice referendum in June 2001. Ireland was the only member state that had to submit the Nice Treaty to a popular referendum for constitutional reasons. In Ireland this was the fifth referendum on the EU since 1972. All of the others had been passed by a comfortable, albeit declining, majority. On 7 June 2001 the Irish electorate voted no to the Nice Treaty by 54 to 46 percent in an extremely low voter turnout of just 35 percent. The outcome of the referendum was a major reversal for the government that had negotiated the treaty, for the main opposition parties that had advocated a yes vote, and for the peak groups in civil society, notably the main business associations, farming organizations, and the Trade Union Congress. Although a second referendum in October 2002 reversed this decision by a decisive 62 to 38 percent, Irish attitudes toward the EU have since entered a more complex and a more ambivalent phase.

IRELAND'S POLICY INTERESTS

There is remarkable consistency in the policies that are accorded a high priority by Ireland in the EU. Preferences were molded by Ireland's low level of development relative to the continental European economies, by sus-

The first European Economic Community (EEC) summit in which Ireland participated, Dublin, March 1975. EEC membership brought major economic benefits to Ireland and an increased profile in international affairs. PHOTOGRAPH COURTESY OF THE *IRISH TIMES.*

tained high levels of unemployment, and by Ireland's dependence on mobile foreign investment. The aim was to try to ensure that Ireland could accommodate developments in social and economic policy at the EU level. From an Irish perspective, the key policy areas were as follows:

- The EU's Common Agricultural Policy (CAP) enabled Irish agriculture to escape from the traditional cheap-food policies of the United Kingdom. The emphasis in relation to the CAP is to maintain or improve farm incomes. Ireland and France remain the key supporters of CAP.

- Cohesion policies at the EU level assist Europe's peripheral areas in catching up. Successive Irish governments deployed considerable diplomatic effort to ensure that the EU would develop a cohesion policy and that Ireland would benefit from financial transfers from the EU budget. Following reform of the structural funds in 1988, Ireland experienced a significant increase in financial transfers from the EU budget. Given Ireland's high level of economic growth in the 1990s, the volume of transfers will be reduced progressively until 2006.

- Successive Irish governments attempted to protect the domestic space by carefully vetting policies and EU regulations that were likely to have an impact on Ireland's competitive position and on regulatory frameworks at the national level. The internal-market program was thus accorded a high priority because of the weight of EC legislation and the need to prepare Irish industry and the service sector for the competitive shock of the 1992 program. Irish administrations have been adamantly opposed to any harmonization of taxation policy in Europe and have fought a hard campaign to maintain low levels of corporation tax.

- The 1992 Maastricht Treaty on European Union (TEU) marked further integration, with provisions on a single currency, the common foreign and security policy, and cooperation among EU members on justice and home affairs. Rather than dislodging the high-ranking policies of the past, the TEU simply added priorities and concerns. Irish governments in the 1990s showed considerable commitment to the public debt philosophy and targets set out in the Maastricht Treaty and supported the full observance of the Maastricht criteria across Europe. In practice the Irish political and policy system was converted to the sound-money/tight-budget philosophy of the German Bundesbank.

Successive Irish governments have endorsed EU social and environmental regulation, provided that regulations do not impose an undue burden on Irish industry or the exchequer. The goal of maintaining Ireland's attractiveness to foreign mobile investment, particularly American capital, runs deeply through Irish policy. In promoting domestic preferences and protecting national space, Irish politicians and administrators have had to engage in coalition-building with like-minded states. Unlike other small states, such as the Nordic or the Benelux countries, Ireland does not have a natural grouping of like-minded states and thus must seek allies on a case-by-case basis: with the French on agriculture, the United Kingdom on taxation, and the other "cohesion countries" on regional funds.

Domestic adaptation to the challenge of competition and Ireland's vulnerability as a small open economy caused difficulties. Irish adjustment in the 1970s, notwithstanding the oil crises, was relatively smooth. However, by the end of the 1970s Ireland had entered a vicious circle of economic policy. Ireland had the worst economic performance in Europe during most of the

1980s as a result of international recession, which was reinforced by dramatic domestic efforts to reduce public-finance and balance-of-payments deficits and to lower inflation. By the mid-1980s Ireland's economic and social strategy was in ruins and its hope of prospering in the EU was in considerable doubt. There was a widespread sense of Ireland's failure, not unlike the prevailing mood in the 1950s. The state and its society found itself at another critical juncture. Ireland had to find the institutional and cultural capacity to overcome the failure of the 1980s. Without this, the opportunities offered by the internal European market and the deepening of integration would have been lost. Tight management of the domestic budget and a new system of social partnership meant that Ireland could take advantage of the larger market. The conditions for the remarkable boom of the 1990s were in place.

REPOSITIONING IRELAND IN THE EU

Just over thirty years of membership of the Union and over forty years since the Irish state altered its strategy of economic development, Ireland finds itself as a small, prosperous Western European state with per capita incomes that have converged with those of other wealthy EU states. The claim that Ireland is a "nation caught on the hop between the traditional and the modern, between the Bishop of Rome and the Treaty of Rome" no longer holds (Eagleton 1999, p. 177). The economic modernization represented by the Treaty of Rome has prevailed. Within the EU, Ireland will find itself as one of over twenty five small states in the decades ahead. It is no longer regarded as a deserving, small, poor state. Policy preferences are likely to change when Ireland becomes a net contributor to the EU budget Irish officials will be expected to contribute more actively to EU debates rather than concentrate on the key issues of interest to Ireland. How Ireland repositions itself in the EU system depends on the outcome of several proposed developments. The draft EU constitution, agreed by the Convention on the Future of Europe, is the subject of negotiations among the member states and represents an important development in the dynamic of European integration. The purpose of the draft constitution is to simplify the EU's constitutional and institutional framework and to add to its legitimacy by inserting a charter on rights. Major changes are foreseen in the institutional architecture and decision-making processes. In a Union of twenty-five, it will be more difficult for Ireland to have its voice heard. Managing its relations with the EU will demand greater prioritization and care from Irish governments and policy-makers. While it is highly improbable that a common European defense policy will emerge in the near future, any moves in that direction would present major difficulties for a neutral Ireland.

SEE ALSO Agriculture: After World War I; Celtic Tiger; Common Agricultural Policy; Health and Welfare since 1950, State Provisions for; Industry since 1920; Neutrality; Overseas Investment; Politics: Independent Ireland since 1922; United Nations; **Primary Documents:** Speech to Ministers of the Governments of the Member States of the European Economic Community (18 January 1962)

Bibliography

Dooge, Jim, and Ruth Barrington, eds. *A Vital National Interest: Ireland in Europe, 1973–1998.* 1999.

Eagleton, Terry. *The Truth about the Irish.* 1999.

Laffan, Brigid, R. O'Donnell, and M. Smith. *Europe's Experimental Union: Re-thinking Integration.* 1999.

Maher, Denis. *The Tortuous Path: The Course of Ireland's Entry into the EEC, 1947–73.* 1986.

Brigid Laffan

Evangelicalism and Revivals

Evangelicalism is a term used to describe a movement of religious ideas that swept the transatlantic world in the eighteenth and nineteenth centuries. Its distinctive features include the central importance of a personal conversion experience and assurance of sins forgiven. It also lays great emphasis on the doctrine of atonement and claims that the Bible is the only source of religious authority. Its adherents are known for their pragmatism, their disregard for denominational traditions, and their active efforts at evangelization and charitable work.

The origins of evangelicalism are a complicated mixture of local trends and international influences. In the late seventeenth century persecuted Protestant minorities in Central Europe developed a deeply personal and emotional form of religious worship. They stressed the need for a "new birth," which they promoted via private devotions and Bible reading, house meetings, and field preaching, which often turned into full-scale revivals. This new approach to Protestant belief spread very quickly throughout Europe and beyond.

In Ireland, Protestantism in the early eighteenth century was dominated by the Church of Ireland and the Presbyterians, both of whom were concentrated in the northern part of the island. Small groups of Protestants who had immigrated in the seventeenth century, such as the Moravians, Palatines, Huguenots, and Baptists, were based in the southwest or in urban centers such as Dublin. It was among these Protestant minorities that evangelical ideas initially began to develop. Several of the Dublin-based groups started to form religious societies in the 1730s. These stirrings were enlivened by the visits of itinerant evangelists such as John Cennick, George Whitefield, and John Wesley, the founder of Methodism. Between 1747 and 1789 Wesley made twenty-one visits to Ireland, and by 1760 there were an estimated 2,000 members of Methodist societies located mainly in southern port and market towns or near military garrisons.

The spread of evangelicalism in eighteenth-century Ireland was complicated by the Catholicism of the majority of the population, the hostility of the Church of Ireland to religious enthusiasm, and the theological preoccupations of the Presbyterians. Even Methodism, despite its initial success, made little sustained headway. It was not until the 1790s, when Ireland was wracked with agrarian unrest and rebellion, that Methodism began to grow dramatically and shift its focus northward. Between 1770 and 1820 a series of local revivals took place; between 1799 and 1802 Methodist membership more than doubled.

It was around this time that evangelicalism began to make substantial inroads into mainstream Protestantism. By the late 1780s Trinity College, Dublin, had become the focal point for evangelicals within the Church of Ireland, and by the 1850s a majority of the Anglican clergy espoused evangelical doctrines. In the early nineteenth century it was the orthodox, or Old Light, camp within Irish Presbyterianism which, under the influence of evangelical ideas, sought to expel the more liberal New Lights from the Synod of Ulster. After their success in 1829, the Presbyterian Church began to adopt an overwhelmingly evangelical tone.

The growth of evangelicalism was demonstrated most dramatically in an unprecedented outburst of religious fervor that swept the Protestant communities of the north during the summer of 1859. Characterized by frequent and lengthy church services, ecstatic manifestations of spiritual feeling, and lay leadership, the Ulster revival of 1859 served to solidify evangelical practice among Irish Protestants and to foster a wider sense of Protestant unity.

Evangelicalism has contributed significantly to the development of a distinctly Irish Protestantism, and its theological rigidity has exacerbated sectarian tensions. In the 1820s evangelicals embarked on the so-called Second Reformation, a sustained effort to convert Irish Catholics that, despite some early successes, ultimately failed to do more than antagonize the Catholic hierarchy. Throughout the nineteenth century, open-air preaching and other efforts to target the "unsaved" routinely provoked clashes with Catholic protestors. More positively, evangelicalism has prompted an active concern for wider social welfare. In the nineteenth century, Sunday schools, Bible classes, and young men's associations aimed to instruct the young. A plethora of charitable and missionary societies were established to meet the social needs of the poor in Ireland and to marshal the growing interest in overseas missions. In the twentieth century, community involvement continues to be an important focus.

Evangelicalism's theological preoccupations have had a significant impact on the political culture of Northern Ireland. Its disregard for tradition has contributed to the emergence of new charismatic religious movements both north and south of the border. Although evangelicalism has often caused tension and division, its flexibility and pragmatism have sustained its influence as a powerful element within the contemporary Irish Protestant identity.

SEE ALSO Church of Ireland: Since 1690; Methodism; Overseas Missions; Presbyterianism; Second Reformation from 1822 to 1869; Temperance Movements

Bibliography

Hempton, David, and Myrtle Hill. *Evangelical Protestantism in Ulster Society, 1740–1890.* 1992.

Hill, Myrtle. "Ulster Awakened: The '59 Revival Reconsidered." *Journal of Ecclesiastical History* 41 (1990): 443–62.

Holmes, Janice. *Religious Revivals in Britain and Ireland, 1859–1905.* 2001.

Janice Holmes

F

Factory-Based Textile Manufacture

By 1725 linen bleaching was too risky and time-consuming to be performed by household women. Capitalists—assisted by the 72 members of the Trustees of the Linen and Hempen Manufacturers of Ireland, which enforced existing laws and made efforts to extend and improve the industry—made significant timesaving innovations, including harnessing water power and introducing washmills, rubbing boards (1730s), beetling engines (1727), and vitriol (1756). By mid-century, linen bleachers were centralizing and reorganizing linen production along capitalist lines. However, in the nineteenth and twentieth centuries innovation slowed, and production processes in these small family-owned firms changed little. Although working conditions in bleachgreens were relatively healthy, skill, strength, and long hours were required of the predominantly male labor force.

The Linen Board similarly encouraged the use of water-driven machinery in scutch mills, which multiplied in number and importance in the eighteenth century. By 1800 most northeastern parishes had a scutch mill. Scutch mills were simple, cheap, and efficient, with a breastshot waterwheel driving a horizontal shaft along which scutching stocks for flax and targing stocks for tow or shorter fibers were arranged. In seasonal scutch mills wages were low and working conditions were dusty and dangerous.

By the 1770s political and economic factors favored the mechanization of linen's rival fabric—cotton. The semiautonomous Irish parliament acted to encourage and protect cotton manufacture. Thereafter, the cotton industry, with its dependence on waterpower, coal-driven steam power, machinery, imported raw materi-

als, and cheap labor, ushered industrial capitalism into Ulster's Lagan Valley. Cotton-yarn spinning required changes in the organization of production and considerable fixed capital investment. Muslin weavers earned higher wages than linen weavers, encouraging many to change jobs.

The cotton industry in Ireland was not the same as in England, due to Ireland's colonial status. In Ireland, cotton spinning did not revolutionize weaving, but instead intensified the decentralized system of putting-out mill-spun yarn by manufacturers to handloom weavers. (The putting-out system, a transitional stage in the development of capitalism, was characterized by manufacturers' supplying raw materials and marketing finished products. Producers, who owned the means of production, controlled the work process.) Irish muslin weavers earned lower wages than their English counterparts, inhibiting technological innovation, and young female workers in the dusty Belfast mills earned lower wages than workers in Lancashire. Finally, when the expanding Irish cotton industry posed a competitive threat, the English state periodically dumped cheaper English yarn and cloth in Ireland.

By the 1820s and 1830s Belfast cotton spinners could not compete, so they turned to spinning flax. Competition and innovation in the cotton industry forced similar technological changes in the linen industry. Flax, however, was far more difficult to process than cotton wool. Flax-spinning machinery capable of spinning coarse yarn had been patented in England in 1789. The coarse-linen trade was thereby captured by England and Scotland, leaving Ireland to concentrate on fine linen yarn. Then in 1825, the Englishman James Kay invented the wet-spinning process, enabling fine counts of yarn to be spun more cheaply. This threatened the future of Ireland's fine-yarn specialization. When the regulation affecting the importation of British and foreign yarn was abolished, the number of yarn-spinning mills in Ireland multiplied. The labor force in flax-spinning mills was predominantly young and female. Persistently unhealthy working conditions—dust in the preparing processes and intense heat in wet-spinning rooms—damaged the health of workers.

Although the mechanization of spinning fundamentally changed the organization of linen production, the centralization of linen weaving was an uneven century-long process. By the 1840s some handloom weavers were reluctantly working for manufacturers in shops or factories where they lost their independence and earned low piece wages. The powerloom was more slowly adopted in Ireland than in Britain because of Ireland's lower labor costs and technological problems in weaving fine-linen cloth. Before the Great Famine the low cost associated with the putting-out system inhibited innovation. After the famine the rising costs of labor and yarn and competition from powerloom weavers in Britain generated the incentive for innovation. Investment in powerlooms increased dramatically during the linen boom years of the 1860s and 1870s when the "cotton famine" induced by the U.S. Civil War stimulated demand for alternative fabrics. New flax-spinning mills and weaving factories multiplied rapidly. The labor in powerloom factories was predominantly female, and working conditions were persistently poor because of dust, moist heat, and intense noise. A new division of labor between hand- and powerloom production of linen emerged by the 1880s, with fine-linen cloth being produced on handlooms into the twentieth century.

The making-up end of textile production consisted of producing and decorating linen and cotton household articles, handkerchiefs, and apparel, and decorating these by embroidery and sewing. Making-up work entailed an intricate division of labor between tasks performed in factories and those carried out in homes. Only three processes—punch hemstitching, Swiss embroidery, and machine spoking—were always performed in factories. Swiss-embroidery machines operated by one skilled man with three female assistants dominated the higher end of the hemstitching trade by the 1860s. Most other processes, including hemming, and sewing shirts, collars, and ladies undergarments, were performed both inside and outside factories, at the discretion of the employer. Although female workers in sewing factories earned piece rates similar to those of other textile workers, cleaner and quieter working conditions resulted in their higher status.

Until World War I the north of Ireland was the world's largest producer of linen. Thereafter, the industry faced myriad problems, including a shortage of sources of flax, the dominance of private family ownership, internecine disputes among the sectors, protection in overseas markets, rival fabrics, lower labor costs elsewhere, and inadequate marketing and research. The need for modernization was particularly acute. Although flax spinning and weaving were classified as dangerous trades in 1905, by 1948 no new flax mills had been built for more than forty years, and in many plants the average age of machinery was forty or fifty years. The Re-Equipment of Industry Act (1951) subsidized the modernization of machinery and buildings. Still, the decline of the linen industry continued, with only twenty firms remaining by 1980. The few firms that survive today have done so by adopting new strategies of production and marketing, by cooperation among manufacturers, and through government investment in research and development. New spinning machinery was developed, computerized damask looms currently produce cloth cleanly and efficiently, and fashion designers creatively use Irish linen.

Between 1939 and 1951 the shortage of flax and decreased demand for linen forced northern Irish manufacturers to invest in rayon staple fabrics. The transition to rayon after 1945 was encouraged by government assistance, since rayon staple required the installation of new equipment and at times new factories. Existing wet-spinning frames and powerlooms in linen plants were unsuitable for rayon production, which required dry processing and greater regularity in weaving. Despite the early success of the rayon industry, it was vulnerable, controlled from firms outside Northern Ireland, and ultimately short-lived, collapsing in the1980s.

SEE ALSO Belfast; Industrialization; Industry since 1920; Rural Industry; Women and Children in the Industrial Workforce

Bibliography

Cohen, Marilyn, ed. *The Warp of Ulster's Past: Interdisciplinary Perspectives on the Irish Linen Industry, 1700–1920.* 1997.

Collins, Brenda. "Sewing and Social Structure: The Flowerers of Scotland and Ireland." In *Economy and Society in Scotland and Ireland, 1500–1939,* edited by Rosalind Mitchison and Peter Roebuck. 1988.

Crawford, W. H. *The Handloom Weavers and the Ulster Linen Industry.* 1972.

Gill, Conrad. *The Rise of the Irish Linen Industry.* 1925.

Green, E. R. R. *The Lagan Valley, 1800–1850.* 1949.

Kennedy, Liam, and Philip Ollerenshaw, eds. *An Economic History of Ulster, 1820–1939.* 1985.

O'Hearn, Denis. "Innovation and the World-System Hierarchy: British Subjugation of the Irish Cotton Industry, 1780–1830." *American Journal of Sociology* 100 (November 1994): 587–621.

Ollerenshaw, Philip. "Textiles and Regional Economic Decline: Northern Ireland, 1914–1979." In *Economy and Society: European Industrialization and Its Social Consequences*, edited by Colin Holmes and Alan Booth. 1991.

Marilyn Cohen

Family

MARRIAGE PATTERNS AND FAMILY LIFE FROM 1500 TO 1690	MARY O'DOWD
MARRIAGE PATTERNS AND FAMILY LIFE FROM 1690 TO 1921	TIMOTHY W. GUINNANE
FERTILITY, MARRIAGE, AND THE FAMILY SINCE 1950	AIDAN PUNCH

MARRIAGE PATTERNS AND FAMILY LIFE FROM 1500 TO 1690

In 1500 Irish customs in marriage and family life can be distinguished by ethnicity, law, and economic status. Practices in Gaelic Ireland differed from those in areas where English law was observed; and within both regions, wealthy families viewed marriage differently from poorer families.

The legal differences in marriage practices in Gaelic and Anglo-Irish Ireland should not, however, be exaggerated. In the two societies canon law formed the basis for the recognition of a valid marriage. Under church law a marriage was created when both partners freely expressed their consent to the union. Neither public ceremony nor consummation was necessary, although throughout the medieval period, the church tried, with only limited success, to promote the public solemnization of nuptials. The church also asserted the permanent nature of the marriage bond and prohibited unions between persons who were related to one another up to the degree of third cousin.

In Gaelic Ireland canon law on marriage was observed selectively. At the upper levels of society marriage was exploited as a valuable political asset. Marriages often coincided with political alliances and lasted only as long as it was politically convenient for the families of both partners. As networks and connections between families shifted and changed, so too new marriage partners were selected and old ones abandoned. Most aristocratic men and women in Gaelic Ireland married several times and usually in the lifetime of former spouses. Shane O'Neill, lord of Tyrone, for example, married four times and clearly changed his marriage partners to suit his political circumstances.

The political pressure to select a marriage partner from within the small pool of Gaelic aristocratic families meant that marriage of kinsfolk within the prohibited third degree was common. The regular petitions for papal dispensations from such unions suggest some concern to keep within the confines of canon law. The fact that dispensations were sought years after the marriage had been consummated also indicates, however, that papal church approval was not considered a matter of great urgency.

We have far less information about the duration of marriages among families outside the aristocratic elite, but the surviving records of the Armagh ecclesiastical court document women from less well-off Gaelic backgrounds complaining of their abandonment by husbands who had taken new wives. Clandestine marriages also continued to be consummated into the seventeenth century, although by that time they were mainly to be found within the landless section of society.

In Anglo-Irish society marriage was normally only dissolved on death, but given the prevalence of war in sixteenth-century Ireland and generally high mortality rates, most people married more than once. A study of marriage patterns among the landed families of the Pale in the late sixteenth and early seventeenth centuries revealed that many women in that community married three or four times. Few, however, matched the record of Genet Sarsfield from County Meath, who had six husbands.

By 1500 the payment of a dowry to the groom was customary in both Gaelic and Anglo-Irish families. Among wealthy Gaelic families dowries were usually calculated in cattle, but in the 1560s and 1570s, Scottish women also brought attractive dowries of mercenary soldiers and weaponry to their new chieftain husbands in Ulster. In the more anglicized parts of Ireland, a woman's marriage portion usually consisted of cash, animal stock, and household goods. In the towns a merchant could also offer a prospective son-in-law admission as a freeman of the city or membership of a trade guild—both passageways into the closed commercial world of sixteenth- and seventeenth-century Irish towns. At the lowest levels of rural society the bride made a valuable economic contribution to the establishment of the home of the new couple. She provided the animal stock for the land and the household utensils, such as a brass pan and a griddle iron that she would use for cooking and brewing beer.

Old English and Gaelic society also cemented social and political alliances through the fostering of children. The bond between foster parents and the foster child was strong and was often said to be stronger than that between the child and his or her natural parents. Dame Janet Eustace, who was foster mother to Thomas Fitzgerald, tenth earl of Kildare, was alleged to have had a strong influence over him, particularly at the time of his rebellion in 1534.

Gaelic society traditionally made no distinction between legitimate and illegitimate children, and the determination of the paternity of a child lay with the mother. The most famous example of this phenomenon was that of Alison Kelly who claimed in the 1530s that her son, Mathew, by then a young teenager, had been conceived following a night spent with Conn O'Neill, first Earl of Tyrone. Conn liked the boy and not only accepted him as his son, but also nominated him as his heir in the agreement that he made with the English administration in 1542, much to the dismay of his legitimate sons—particularly Shane, who refused to recognize Matthew as his father's heir.

In Old English society, only children conceived within marriage were entitled to inherit their father's property and title. Primogeniture was also universally observed by Old English families, although daughters could inherit the family property if a man had no sons. Under Gaelic law daughters were prohibited from inheriting land. In practice, however, the difference between the two systems was less stark. Many Old English families entailed their estates to male heirs only, thus effectively excluding women from landownership.

Changes in the religious and legal structure of sixteenth- and seventeenth-century Ireland had an impact on marriage customs and family life in a number of ways. First, the Protestant Reformation and the Catholic response strengthened the necessity for a formally solemnized marriage ceremony in a church. In addition, the Council of Trent asserted Catholic doctrine on the sacramental nature of marriage. The marriage of partners from different religious denominations resulted in a public discourse in the seventeenth century on what constituted a valid marriage. This was a debate that was to become increasingly bitter in the 1690s, when the Penal Laws imposed severe penalties on Protestant landowners who married Catholic or Dissenting spouses.

The triumph of English law over Gaelic custom meant the eradication of Gaelic-style divorce and the dominance of primogeniture. The replacement of Old English and Gaelic landed families by new English estate owners brought other changes. There was, for example, a noticeable increase in the number of female heiresses in seventeenth-century Ireland; and espousal to an heiress was an important means by which the large landed estates of the "Protestant Ascendancy" were created and consolidated in the late seventeenth century. Within the craft families of the new British tenancies in Munster towns, male heads of household also demonstrated a willingness to divide their goods equitably among surviving widows and children.

The legal documentation which accompanied marriage ceremonies became increasingly complex in the course of the seventeenth century, particularly among the landed elite. Marriage settlements, deeds, and wills were drawn up, often before the marriage took place, in order to ensure jointures for widows, marriage dowries for daughters, and livelihoods for younger sons. Jointures, by which land was held jointly for the use of husband and wife, replaced dowries as a means of providing for widows; and increasingly the jointure was in the form of a cash annuity rather than, as in the dowry, a specified portion of the family estate. There was also a steady increase in the amount required for marriage dowries, with cash amounts of £2,000 to £3,000 replacing the cattle and household goods of earlier times among the wealthier families. The growing tendency of Irish peerage families to look for spouses from English peerage families also exerted inflationary pressure on the cost of marriage.

SEE ALSO Burial Customs and Popular Religion from 1500 to 1690; **Primary Documents:** Act of Uniformity (1560)

Bibliography

Bourke, Angela, et al., eds. *Field Day Anthology of Irish Writing.* Vols. 4–5. 2002.

Canny, Nicholas. *The Upstart Earl: A Study of the Social and Mental World of Richard Boyle, First Earl of Cork, 1555–1643.* 1982.

Cosgrove, Art, ed. *Marriage in Ireland.* 1985.

Cosgrove, Art, ed. *Medieval Ireland, 1169–1534.* Vol. 2 of *A New History of Ireland.* 1993.

Jackson, Donald. *Intermarriage in Ireland, 1550–1650.* 1970.

Lennon, Colm. *The Lords of Dublin in the Age of Reformation.* 1989.

MacCurtain, Margaret, and Mary O'Dowd, eds. *Women in Early Modern Ireland.* 1991.

Nicholls, Kenneth W. *Gaelic and Gaelicised Ireland in the Middle Ages.* 1972.

Mary O'Dowd

MARRIAGE PATTERNS AND FAMILY LIFE FROM 1690 TO 1921

By the early twentieth century about one-quarter of adult men and women in Ireland had never married. While not unique to Ireland at the time, these patterns were unusual and have long been taken as evidence of an exceptional pattern of marriage and family life. As early as the 1840s the proportion of adults in Ireland who had never married was much lower, at about 10 percent, and was completely unremarkable by European standards. The huge increase over the second half of the nineteenth century raises the question of the role of the Great Famine in these family patterns. The reasons behind this dramatic change are not well understood, unfortunately, but the broad outlines are known and scholarship since the 1980s has at least succeeded in dispelling some old thinking.

FROM 1690 TO THE GREAT FAMINE OF 1846 TO 1850

Most western European couples between 1690 and 1850 lived in small households consisting of a married couple and their children. This couple did not marry until they were able to move out of their own parents' household and provide for themselves and their offspring. This western European marriage pattern produced what was by world standards a relatively late age at marriage. Women did not marry until their early or mid-twenties, and men married a few years later. Many adults never married at all. Depending on the time and place, some 10 percent to 20 percent of adults remained single (or celibate, to use the demographer's term) all their lives. There is strong evidence that in bad economic times adults married later, and more of them never married, reflecting the difficulty of setting up their own households.

This picture is clear for England, France, Sweden, and some other western European societies for which there are excellent historical records on marriage and households. For Ireland, with its very poor demographic records prior to the 1841 population census, the picture is much less clear. Most of what is known about marriage patterns in Ireland until the early nineteenth century comes from sources that are either inadequate to the questions at hand or that pertain to small minority groups such as Quakers.

The striking account of prefamine marriage patterns offered by Kenneth H. Connell in his classic work *The Population of Ireland, 1750 to 1845* implies that Ireland was some sort of demographic oddity. The prefamine Irish, he claimed, married at much younger ages than did their European counterparts, and virtually all of them married. Connell argued that agricultural prosperity brought about by the Anglo-French wars of the late eighteenth and early nineteenth centuries had made it easier for poor Irish people to obtain land and so to marry and raise a family. He stresses the miserable living standards to which the Irish were accustomed, which made them willing to marry an income that other Europeans would have considered insufficient to support a family. He also noted the spread of a system of land tenure that let very small strips of land in conacre, an in-kind form of rent, to the poorest families.

Research since the 1980s suggests that Connell's account was flawed in important features. A number of reliable sources, including the 1841 census (which is considered very reliable), show no trace of his teenage brides, and the proportions who never married in Ireland at that time were nearly identical to those in England and other western European societies. On the other hand, some studies (such as O'Neill's account of the parish of Killashandra, Co. Cavan), have found lower female ages at marriage, reflecting economic opportunities presented by household linen production in some regions of Ireland.

THE FAMINE AND AFTER

During the decades following the famine the proportions of Irish people who never married climbed dramatically, although not constantly. The basic patterns of this change are better documented than are household patterns before the famine. Increases in permanent celibacy were at first largely restricted to eastern and northern Ireland in the 1860s and 1870s, but then spread rapidly to western and southern Ireland. Many accounts claim that age at marriage rose dramatically, and indeed there were numerous bridegrooms in their late thirties and even older. But the increase in the age at marriage was slight when compared to the increases in the proportion of those who did not marry at all.

Some scholars have argued that this change in marriage patterns was a simple result of the famine. Early and universal marriage was restricted to the poor, the argument goes, and the famine swept away these poor, leaving only the social classes whose marriage patterns had been more "European" all along. This view contains a kernel of truth. But it cannot explain the time patterns of change; there was no dramatic rupture at the time of the famine, and marriage patterns continued to change well into the twentieth century, long after any direct impact from the famine would be expected. Kevin O'Rourke has noted that the famine made Ireland's poor more willing to emigrate and less likely to tolerate poverty in Ireland, which would imply a more drawn-out influence of the famine on marriage patterns. Connell stressed the postfamine spread of a form of marriage that he called the "match." In his account Irish farming families, who dominated the countryside after the death of many of the poor during the famine, became less and less willing to marry without larger and more prosperous farms. As these farms became more difficult to acquire, young Irish adults became more willing to postpone marriage or even avoid it altogether.

Guinnane's 1997 study of postfamine demographic patterns stresses some correctives to earlier accounts. Most accounts of marriage in postfamine Ireland claim that Irish marriage patterns were unique, but this is simply not true. Similar marriage patterns can be observed in several other regions of western Europe, all of which shared a common history of rural poverty, lack of industrialization, and heavy emigration. An explanation unique to Ireland cannot account for similar patterns in Portugal. Much of the discussion of postfamine marriage patterns also ignores the impact of emigration on every facet of Irish life. Some Irish birth-cohorts lost half of their members to emigration; those who remained were those who had in a real sense chosen Irish life and all that it meant. For many, remaining in Ireland meant giving up a chance to marry and to have a family, and this must have played a large role in many emigrants' decisions.

Less is known about the other famous feature of Irish family life—large numbers of children. During the second half of the nineteenth century most European couples began to have much smaller families, in a development historical demographers call the fertility transition. The Irish were only half-hearted participants in this development. As late as 1911 the average Irish couple had a family about 50 percent larger than the average English couple. The reasons for this high Irish fertility are not yet understood. It is true that the Roman Catholic Church, of which a large majority of Irish people were adherents, forbade contraception. But this was also true of many Protestant groups in Ireland, and the evidence on Catholic/Protestant fertility differences in Ireland is very mixed. Historians have proposed other reasons for high fertility in Ireland. One is that Irish parents did not have to bear much expense to establish their children as adults, because an inexpensive ship ticket purchased life in the United States. Another reason often noted is that there was little employment opportunity for Irish women outside the home, which made it relatively easy for Irish women to care for large broods.

SEE ALSO Agriculture: 1690 to 1845; Agriculture: 1845 to 1921; Great Famine; Indian Corn or Maize; Migration: Emigration from the Seventeenth Century to 1845; Migration: Emigration from 1850 to 1960; Population, Economy, and Society from 1750 to 1950; Population Explosion; Potato and Potato Blight (*Phytophthora infestans*); Rural Life: 1690 to 1845; Rural Life: 1850 to 1921; Subdivision and Subletting of Holdings; Town Life from 1690 to the Early Twentieth Century; **Primary Documents:** On Irish Rural Society and Poverty (1780); On Rural Society on the Eve of the Great Famine (1844–1845); From the *Report of the Commission on Emigration and Other Population Problems, 1948–1954* (1955)

Bibliography

Connell, Kenneth H. *The Population of Ireland, 1750–1845*. 1950.

Fitzpatrick, David. "Irish Farming Families before the First World War." *Comparative Studies in Society and History* 25 (summer 1984): 338–374.

Guinnane, Timothy W. *The Vanishing Irish: Households, Migration, and the Rural Economy in Ireland, 1850–1914*. 1997.

Ó Gráda, Cormac. *Ireland: A New Economic History, 1750–1939*. 1994.

O'Neill, Kevin. *Family and Farm in Pre-Famine Ireland: The Parish of Killashandra*. 1984.

O'Rourke, Kevin H. "Did the Great Irish Famine Matter?" *Journal of Economic History* 51 (spring 1991): 1–22.

Walsh, Brendan M. "Marriage in Ireland in the Twentieth Century." In *Marriage in Ireland*, edited by Art Cosgrove. 1985.

Timothy W. Guinnane

FERTILITY, MARRIAGE, AND THE FAMILY SINCE 1950

During the second half of the twentieth century the annual number of births in Ireland reached a peak of 74,000 in 1980 and subsequently decreased by over a third, to reach a low point of 48,200 in 1994. The period since 1980 has seen births decline and then pick up again, attaining a level of 57,900 in 2001. During the 1950s and 1960s births exceeded 60,000 annually—apart from 1958 (58,510) and 1961 (59,825). Having risen to 64,000 in 1964 and declined to 61,000 in 1968, births began their upward movement to reach the 1980 maximum figure—the only decline being a temporary one during the mid-1970s.

FERTILITY IN DECLINE SINCE THE 1960s

To gain a greater insight into fertility trends it is necessary to look at the number of women of childbearing age (those aged 15 to 49 years) and at the fertility levels of these women. Between 1961 and 1981 the number of women aged 15 to 49 years increased by over 30 percent. More significant was the increase of nearly 50 percent in the number of women in the prime childbearing age group (20 to 39 years). Therefore, the 20 percent increase in births observed during this period actually masked a significant decline in the underlying fertility rates of these women.

The total fertility rate (i.e., the average number of children born to each woman), which was slightly over 4 during the mid-1960s, fell to 2.08 in 1989. That was the first year in which Irish fertility fell below the replacement level of 2.1—the level at which each generation replaces itself. Having fallen further to 1.85 in 1994 and 1995, the fertility rate has recovered slightly and stood at 1.98 in 2001.

A striking change that occurred during the second half of the twentieth century was the increase in the proportion of births outside marriage. In 1950 the relevant proportion was fairly minor at 2.6 percent; by 2001 nearly one in three births were outside marriage. The proportion of nonmarital births has increased every year since 1971, with the most significant increases taking place from the mid-1980s onward. It is important to bear in mind that nonmarital births include those to single mothers as well as those to couples who choose to cohabit rather than marry. While the popular perception of a birth outside marriage may be of an unplanned pregnancy for a young girl, no fewer than 40 percent of births outside marriage in the year 2000 were to women who had previous children.

Another change was the decline in the number of home births. In the mid-1950s the proportion of home births stood at one in three. The figure had fallen below 1 percent by 1974 and has been less than 0.5 percent since 1977.

The average age of women who bore children in 1960 was 31.5 years. This fell to 29.6 years by the mid-1970s, reflecting an increase in the fertility rates of younger women—especially those in their twenties—over this period. The average age of women at childbearing has since increased and stood at 30.7 in 2001. Looking at firstborn children only, the average age of the mother increased from 25.5 in 1975 to 28.0 in 2001, indicating a tendency for women to postpone childbirth, thereby curtailing family size.

The number of births to teenage girls increased from around 1,100 a year in the mid-1950s to just over

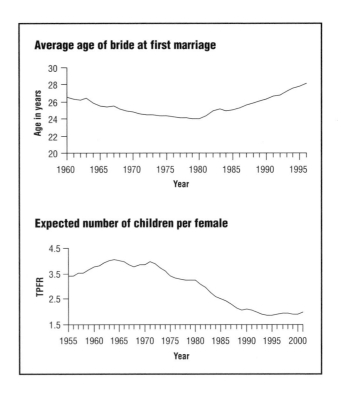

3,000 by the late 1990s. While only one in four of these births were to unmarried teenagers in the earlier part of the half-century under review, by 1980 the proportion had grown to 40 percent, and it has exceeded 90 percent since 1993. This reflects both a departure from the situation in which a pregnant teenager might hastily marry and also an actual fall in the number of marriages in which the bride was a teenager.

MARRIAGE GOING OUT OF FASHION?

The popular perception is that marriage as an institution is going out of fashion, but this overstates the actual situation. A comparison of the number of marriages in 1950 (16,000) with the 2001 total (19,200) indicates an increase of 20 percent. However, when account is taken of the growth of one-third in the underlying population, a fall in the crude marriage rate (the number of marriages per 1,000 population) is the outcome. In fact, the marriage rate, which stood at 5.4 in 1950, exceeded 7.0 for the first five years of the 1970s and then fell to 5.0 by 2001.

Although the crude marriage rate does take account of the underlying population, a more refined measure is the total female first-marriage rate, which is based on age-specific marriage rates. By this measure the probability of a female marrying has fallen by over a third in the years 1960 to 2000. During the same period the average age of the bride at first marriage declined from 26.9 years in 1960 to 24.6 in 1980 and increased to

27.9 by the late 1990s. The general picture is therefore that proportionately fewer females marry, and in the case of those who do, the average age is higher than before.

The number of private households increased from just over 660,000 in 1946 to 1.1 million fifty years later (an increase of 68.3%). Average household size fell from 4.2 to 3.1 persons during the same period, with most of the decrease occurring since 1960 as a direct result of decreasing fertility and increasing household formation.

The number of childless couples (whether married or not) increased by over a third between 1981 and 1996, while families with one or two children also grew appreciably over the same period (by 25.9% and 34.3%, respectively). Larger families have become less common, with the result that the average number of children per family fell from 2.2 to 1.8 between 1981 and 1996.

Cohabiting couples accounted for 3.9 percent of all family units in 1996, and of these, about 60 percent comprised couples without children. Given the age profile of the partners involved, there is strong evidence that cohabitation is not just a precursor to marriage but a permanent form of union.

The number of separated persons more than doubled in the ten years from 1986 to 1996. In 1986 there were 37,200 separated persons. This grew to over 55,000 by 1991, and the 1996 census recorded close to 88,000 separated persons, corresponding to 5.4 percent of ever-married persons.

FEMALE EMPLOYMENT

In 1961, when the population of Ireland was at a historically low level of 2.8 million persons, the number of persons in employment was 1,053,000. Females accounted for 26.4 percent of these. By 1996 the number of women at work had increased by 226,000, representing an increase of 81.5 percent, while male employment increased by only 28,100. The period 1996 to 2001 was one of unprecedented employment growth (greater than 29.2%). At the end of this period women accounted for 40.9 percent of total employment. Furthermore, about 45 percent of these working women were married. The corresponding figure in 1971 was only 14 percent. The labor-force participation of Irish women has now reached the European norm. In 2001 the figure for Ireland was 47.5 percent compared with an overall European Union figure of 47 percent.

IRELAND'S DEMOGRAPHY IN A EUROPEAN CONTEXT

Ireland's demography is markedly different from that of most of its Western European neighbors. Major demographic changes have tended to occur much later and at a slower pace in Ireland than elsewhere in Europe. In particular, fertility rates have been, and continue to be, higher in Ireland than in other western countries. Consequently, Ireland has a younger population profile and has yet to experience the aging of population evident in mainland Europe, with its attendant pressures on healthcare and the pension system.

Since the 1990s Ireland's population has been growing at a faster rate than those of other European Union countries. This growth has been fueled by both natural increase (the excess of births over deaths) and net immigration. Because of the young age-profile of its population, Ireland can expect a continuing, though slowing, natural increase in population; in other European countries population growth is already close to zero or even negative.

SEE ALSO Divorce, Contraception, and Abortion; Equal Economic Rights for Women in Independent Ireland; Farming Families; Migration: Emigration and Immigration since 1950; Social Change since 1922; **Primary Documents:** From the Decision of the Supreme Court in *McGee v. the Attorney General and the Revenue Commissioners* (1973); On the Family Planning Bill (20 February 1974)

Bibliography

Central Statistics Office. *Census of Population Reports.* Various.

Central Statistics Office. *Census 96: Principal Demographic Results.* 1997.

Central Statistics Office. "Women in the Workforce." 1997.

Central Statistics Office. *Census 96: Principal Socio-Economic Results.* 1998.

Central Statistics Office. *Population and Labour Force Projections, 2001–2031.* 1999.

Council of Europe. *Recent Demographic Developments in Europe.* 2001.

Aidan Punch

EJECTMENT OF IRISH TENANTRY.

The scale of the mass evictions that occurred during the famine and in the early 1850s was enormous, with 250,000 persons formally dispossessed between 1849 and 1854 alone. In this 1848 sketch a tenant and his family plead vainly to be spared. Some bailiffs are unroofing the tenant's house while others are seizing his goods. Soldiers stand ready to overawe would-be resisters. FROM ILLUSTRATED LONDON NEWS, 16 DECEMBER 1848.

Famine Clearances

During the Great Famine and in its immediate aftermath, Irish landlords engaged in a campaign of mass evictions that was unprecedented in its extent and severity. These mass evictions are known as the famine clearances. One relatively moderate estimate puts the numbers permanently expelled from their homes at about half a million persons. This estimate refers to legally sanctioned evictions and does not take account of the countless informal ejections and so-called voluntary surrenders of land during the period.

Although few parts of rural Ireland escaped clearances altogether, as a rule they occurred most frequently in the more remote, poorer regions of the country, where subdivision of holdings had been carried on to its most extreme degree. Regions of the west and south of Ireland were therefore most affected by the clearances, with residents of counties such as Clare, Tipperary, and Mayo suffering more than others. The level of evictions in Tipperary was some twenty times that of Fermanagh, the county with the lowest incidence of clearance, and in Clare it has been calculated that one in every ten persons was permanently expelled from house and holding in the years between 1849 and 1854.

Before the famine evictions had been one of the great ills of the prevailing system of landholding in Ireland, prompted by many different circumstances, ranging from nonpayment of rent to the whim of the landlord. Mass clearance-evictions were rather infrequent, and occurred mainly where landlords sought to improve and modernize their properties by ridding them of the inefficiency of large numbers of smallholding occupiers. A clearance might occur in one great consolidation, with the ejection of very large numbers at once, or it might take place piecemeal wherever the surrender of middleman leases provided the opportunity of ejecting subtenants, with the landlord either taking the land into his own hands or redistributing it among a smaller number of occupiers. Famine-era clearances followed

No other poor-law union in the whole country suffered more from clearances than Kilrush, Co. Clare: 14,000 persons (from 2,700 families) were evicted between November 1847 and mid-1850 alone. Entire villages, like Moveen in this 1849 sketch, were cleared of their occupants. Special legal procedures made mass removals relatively easy. FROM ILLUSTRATED LONDON NEWS, 22 DECEMBER 1849.

this basic pattern, but on a gigantic scale. Emerging with remarkable suddenness toward the end of 1847, the number of these clearances escalated over the next two years, peaking in 1850, after which the rate of eviction fell rapidly. By 1854 the clearances had come to an end in most parts of Ireland.

The sudden onset and exceptional severity of the famine clearances were the consequence of new government relief policies that added greatly to the economic troubles of landlords. A massive loss of rental income from successive years of crop failure and extreme deprivation, including actual starvation, together with encumbrances inherited from prefamine times, had already brought many landlords to the brink of insolvency. To these difficulties was added a hugely increased tax liability under the Poor Law Amendment Act of June 1847, which transferred the major responsibility for poor relief to Irish property owners. Most of them acted in the belief that the only way to avoid potentially ruinous liability was to eliminate their tax-bearing smallholdings altogether by the wholesale expulsion of the occupiers and the destruction of their dwellings. For the owners of large estates who were not in difficulties, the new pressures furnished a reason to finally resolve the problems of overcrowded properties and unprofitable holdings; for them the dislocation of the period presented a convenient opportunity to complete the estate consolidation begun before 1845.

Although many landlords carried out evictions directly, there was an increased demand for the services of land agents with specialized knowledge of cost-cutting legal procedures and the innumerable practical difficulties encountered at eviction sites. As well as ensuring that a professional job was done, the employment of an agent also enabled the landlord to distance himself from distressing aspects of the eviction process.

Clearances were greatly facilitated by the Gregory clause of the Poor Law Amendment Act, which landlords used to force tenants to part with their entire holding, and once begun, rapidly degenerated into a panicked scramble to clear properties before the new and higher tax rates began to bite. Behind the rush also lay the fear that the eviction option might soon be closed off forever in the event of the introduction of a tenant-right measure by government. Because of the frenzied manner of so many clearances, estates were voided of occupiers to an extent that went beyond what the landlords had originally intended, or what was economically wise for the owners. On many properties the number of tenants left behind after a series of evictions was insufficient for the redistribution of the land. Many cleared estates returned to untended wilderness and remained economically unproductive for several years. Rental income fell during this period, and land values dropped accordingly.

Resistance to evictions was a rare phenomenon in the famine clearances. By the time they began, the enormous wave of social protest and retaliatory crime that had characterized earlier phases of the Great Famine had faded away completely, and many participants and organizers were either in jail or dead of starvation or disease. Verging on disintegration after years of famine, rural communities were now leaderless, and few of those still surviving retained the physical or psychological strength to resist the so-called crowbar brigades, the demolition gangs deployed by landlords and agents at eviction sites. Indeed, the work of evictors was much eased by the fact that tenants destined for eviction were for the most part demoralized to the point of complete docility. In innumerable cases evictors took cynical advantage of this docility by inducing occupiers to destroy their own cabins in exchange for a small monetary consideration. The destruction of dwellings, either in this manner or by paid demolition gangs, was considered essential by evictors to prevent reoccupation by the former tenants. Where ejected families erected huts within or adjoining the ruins of their homes, pains were taken to level these also. Rather than face the horrors of the overcrowded workhouses, the majority of evicted families remained in the vicinity of their former dwellings. Some built crude shelters of branches and turf-sods called "scalpeens" on waste or boggy land nearby. Enormous numbers died of disease, exposure to the cold, or hunger in these hovels, and often it was only in the last stages of starvation or disease that evicted persons could bring themselves to approach the workhouses.

Not surprisingly, the famine clearances left behind many bitter memories in Irish rural communities. The cruelty of particular evicting landlords and agents was remembered sharply for generations, and general culpability was assigned to the British government for the Poor Law Amendment Act and its notorious Gregory clause. More than any other aspect of the Great Famine tragedy, the evictions provided ammunition for the nationalist belief that a genocidal intent lay behind British government famine policies. Transmitted memories of the clearances supplied much of the enraged energy behind the nationalist movements of the later nineteenth century, from physical-force separatism to constitutional demands for self-rule for Ireland and agitation for agrarian reform. There is little doubt, too, that in the long term, by engaging in clearances during the Great Famine, Irish landlords helped seal their own doom. At the end of the nineteenth century, a series of land-purchase acts, inspired by determined campaigning on the part of agrarian and constitutional nationalists, initiated the legal processes by which Irish landlordism would disappear within a generation.

SEE ALSO Agriculture: 1845 to 1921; Great Famine; Indian Corn or Maize; Land Questions; Poor Law Amendment Act of 1847 and the Gregory Clause; Potato and Potato Blight (*Phytophthora infestans*); Protestant Ascendancy: Decline, 1800 to 1930; Subdivision and Subletting of Holdings

Bibliography

Donnelly, James S., Jr. "Mass Eviction and the Great Famine." In *The Great Irish Famine*, edited by Cathal Portéir. 1995.

Donnelly, James S., Jr. *The Great Irish Potato Famine*. 2001.

Kinealy, Christine. *This Great Calamity: The Irish Famine, 1845–1852*. 1994.

Ó Gráda, Cormac. *Black '47 and Beyond: The Great Irish Famine in History, Economy, and Memory*. 1999.

O'Neill, Thomas P. "The Organisation and Administration of Relief, 1845–1852." In *The Great Irish Famine: Studies in Irish History, 1845–52*, edited by R. Dudley Edwards and T. Desmond Williams. 1956. Reprint, 1994.

O'Neill, Timothy P. "Famine Evictions." In *Famine, Land, and Culture in Ireland*, edited by Carla King. 2000.

Vaughan, W. E. *Landlords and Tenants in Mid-Victorian Ireland*. 1994.

Ciarán Ó Murchadha

Farming Families

By the 1960s Irish agricultural policy involved the existence of an ever-greater number of schemes to support the occupants of farms. Survival, not prosperous expansion, remained the goal of the majority of Irish farmers, most of whom resided on small farms that had been created or sanctioned by the state. These farming families were profoundly affected by ideological and economic division on the role of agriculture within Irish society. The struggle to reconcile the demands of modern society with the emotions and traditions of the past acutely influenced the country's agriculture. The ideal of Gaelic, industrious, prosperous (though not materialistic) farmsteads filling the countryside with an ancient and dignified way of life was fundamentally at odds with the forces governing the realities of rural life. Repeated insistence that agriculture would provide the engine of economic expansion, bringing prosperity to all the citizens of the state, ignored global trading patterns. Yet, political demands, as well as genuine fidelity to an inherited dream, severely restricted moves to restructure the Irish agricultural economy; for example, the policy of land division was continued long after it became apparent that such a policy was economically unsound.

In terms of price and accessibility, only the export of cattle to Britain offered a substantial and viable trade with a profit margin worthy of the name. The production of cattle for export, however, necessitated an extensive-farming pattern inimical to the prospects of constructing a vibrant small-farming community. Irish agriculture lived in the shadow of this conflict between economic and social needs. In essence, the expectation that agriculture could both drive the economy through export earnings and simultaneously preserve a way of life that was progressively less profitable was ill-conceived. Like all other countries, Ireland wrestled with the dilemma of viewing agriculture as either a business or a way of life, and the Irish unequivocally regarded it as both. Ultimately, agricultural policy made no attempt to distinguish between farmers seeking assistance to improve the competitiveness of Irish produce on the international market and farmers to whom assistance was socially motivated.

Where other countries freed workers from agriculture to provide labor for industrial development, the Irish constitutional, legislative, and ideological commitment to retain on the land as many families as possible was complemented by the lack of an industrial sector of any note. Farming families suffered grievously from the failure of Irish industry to contribute to the economy on anything approaching the scale achieved in Western Europe and the United States. Irish farms traditionally absorbed far more labor than they could justifiably employ, and the extended retention of family members restricted any moves toward rationalization of the agrarian structure. Throughout the 1950s huge numbers of these previously hidden, underemployed family members left the land and emigrated. As Irish industry developed through the 1960s, more of those born on farms found work in Irish cities, but the percentage was again far below the European average. Furthermore, foreign currency earned by agricultural exports was used to subsidize industrial development, while farmers also supported the inefficient chemical and fertilizer industries by paying prices above the world market. Most crucially, Ireland was unable to offer its farmers price supports funded from industrial earnings, as Britain and the United States did.

By the late 1960s a succession of *Programmes for Economic Expansion* had shifted the position of agriculture within Irish society. Agriculture had modernized, but far too slowly to satisfy the evolving materialist needs of Irish society, and it was displaced by industry as the fulcrum of the Irish economy. Inevitably, the sheer scale of agriculture in the 1960s ensured that it retained a formidable position in Irish society, and it has continued to do so in the decades since then. The influence of the farming community has waned considerably, however, and the significance of farming within the Irish economy has declined, too. Various independent farmers' bodies sought to oppose this diminution. The Irish Farmers' Association and the Irish Creamery Milk Suppliers' Association continuously campaigned for the economic advancement of farmers, and such organizations as Macra na Feirme and the Irish Countrywomen's Association offered a social outlet to young and female farmers, who often were isolated in rural areas. This voluntary sector was vital in improving the morale of farmers, but it was a constant struggle.

It was as much the experience of what happened outside farming as what happened inside it that influenced farming life. Farmers' incomes rose throughout the 1960s and in every decade after that, but, significantly, the gap between those in agricultural and in nonagricultural employment widened considerably as industrial workers continuously increased their purchasing power. The Irish state now sought to support farmers and to contain the growing disparity of income between families living in rural and in urban areas. Central to those attempts at containment was entry into the EEC. Farming organizations had campaigned in favor of Irish membership since the 1950s, and following Ireland's accession in 1973, farmers benefited from the range of measures comprised in the EEC's Common Agricultural Policy (CAP). Of all the nations in the EEC, Ireland has received the most money for its farmers, through a plethora of schemes including market-price supports and headage and premia payments (broadly comprising payments related to the number of animals owned by a farmer). Funds from Europe were complemented by payments from the Irish exchequer, and by 1998 direct payments made up 56 percent of aggregate farm income in Ireland. Even attempts to reform the CAP have not unduly affected Irish agriculture, and in 1997 money from Europe amounted to 1.7 billion pounds, or 4 percent of GNP. Essentially, entry into the EEC allowed Ireland to fund its public-policy aim of transferring income to the farming community, which in 1973 still constituted 22 percent of the workforce. There remains considerable criticism that income-support policies—particularly through price supports—have not been successfully targeted, since 60 percent of total support goes to the top-earning 20 percent of farms.

Between the 1960s and the 1980s the number whose principal occupation was farming declined by almost 2 percent per annum, although many have held onto the land, and there has not been enormous consolidation of farms. With more than a quarter of Irish farms considered incapable of generating a viable income from farming alone, the importance of part-time farming has increased considerably since the 1960s and is crucial to the survival of many farming units. By the mid-1990s 27 percent of farmers had jobs away from the farm; the number reached 41 percent on small farms. Furthermore, 16 percent of women married to farmers also held off-farm employment. The involvement of either spouse in off-farm employment alters the traditional gender roles prevalent on Irish farms. The great majority of women become involved in farming either through marriage or through the exceptional circumstance of inheriting a farm in the absence of a male heir. Women marrying into a farm usually encounter long-established structures, and are expected to preserve them by creating, in turn, their own farm families. A wife's involvement in off-farm employment significantly alters the traditional pattern. Similarly, when her husband is involved in off-farm employment, the woman assumes a more central role in day-to-day farm management, becoming the de facto farm manager. It was only in 1991 that the Central Statistics Office included the labor of farm wives in the agricultural census, and this demonstrated that women contributed a minimum of 20 percent of all labor on family farms. Significantly, farm women are credited with the exceptional performance of farm children in third-level education (where they are overrepresented), enabling them to avail themselves of professional or skilled jobs rather than in agriculture. As a result, fewer offspring from farm families are dependent on the land for income, substantiating the unmistakable reality that Ireland continues to shed its agricultural past in pursuit of an industrial and technological future. Farm households fell from 22 percent of total population in 1973 to less than 5 percent in 1997, and continue to fall sharply. Global trends and the sands of time have proved impossible to stem, let alone reverse, and agrarian Ireland seems set to suffer a long fade in its importance.

SEE ALSO Agriculture: After World War I; Common Agricultural Policy; Equal Economic Rights for Women in Independent Ireland; Family: Fertility, Marriage, and the Family since 1950; Health and Welfare since 1950, State Provisions for; Women and Work since the Mid-Nineteenth Century; Women in Irish Society since 1800

Bibliography

Crotty, Ray. *Irish Agricultural Production.* 1966.

Goldthorpe, John, ed. *The Development of Industrial Society in Ireland.* 1992.

Kennedy, Kieran A., Thomas Giblin, and Deirdre McHugh. *The Economic Development of Ireland in the Twentieth Century.* 1988.

Kennedy, Liam. *The Modern Industrialisation of Ireland, 1940–88.* 1989.

Lee, J. J. *Ireland, 1912–85: Politics and Society.* 1989.

Matthews, Alan. *Farm Incomes: Myth and Reality.* 2000.

O'Hara, Patricia. *Partners in Production? Women, Farm, and Family in Ireland.* 1998.

Rouse, Paul. *Ireland's Own Soil: Government and Agriculture in Ireland, 1945–65.* 2000.

Paul Rouse

Faulkner, Brian

Brian Faulkner (1921–1977), Ulster unionist and prime minister of Northern Ireland, was born in Helen's Bay, County Down on 18 February and educated at Saint Columba's College, Dublin. Faulkner managed the family's shirt factory during the Second World War rather than joining the British armed forces, which was often criticized in later unionist internal disputes. In 1949 he became Stormont MP for East Down. Faulkner was appointed chief whip in 1956 and minister for home affairs in 1959; he acquired a hardline reputation by supporting provocative Orange marches and was seen as a possible successor to Lord Brookeborough. From 1963 Faulkner was an outstandingly able minister for commerce under Prime Minister Terence O'Neill; he intrigued with hardliners while avoiding open confrontation. In January 1969 Faulkner resigned from the cabinet over the appointment of the Cameron Commission on civil disturbances. On O'Neill's resignation in April 1969, Faulkner contested the leadership, losing to James Chichester-Clark by one vote; instead, he became minister for development. In March 1971, Faulkner became leader of the Unionist Party and prime minister of Northern Ireland after Chichester-Clark's resignation. He attempted to combine concessions to nationalists with a harsh security policy; these approaches undermined each other, and violence continued to escalate. Faulkner persuaded the British government to introduce internment in August 1971, believing that it would end the Irish Republican Army's campaign; instead, it further alienated nationalist opinion and intensified violence. In March 1972 Faulkner and his cabinet resigned after the British government withdrew the Northern Ireland government's authority over security policy; the Stormont parliament was suspended, and Westminster resumed direct control over Northern Ireland. In May 1973, Faulkner led the Unionist Party into assembly elections intended to provide a mandate for negotiations. Negotiations between Northern Ireland politicians and the British government in October and November 1973 led to the Sunningdale Agreement, which created a power-sharing executive drawn from the Ulster Unionist Party, the Social Democratic and Labour Party, and the Alliance Party. This was unacceptable to most unionists, but Faulkner retained the support of most of his Assembly members; he resigned as party leader in January 1974. In February anti-agreement unionists won eleven of twelve seats and an absolute majority of Northern Ireland votes in the Westminster general election. The executive collapsed on 27 May after a loyalist strike paralyzed the province. Faulkner subsequently led a dwindling splinter group, the Unionist Party of Northern Ireland. In 1976 he retired from politics, accepting a life peerage as Lord Faulkner of Downpatrick. He died in a riding accident on 3 March 1977.

SEE ALSO Economic Relations between North and South since 1922; Northern Ireland: Discrimination and the Campaign for Civil Rights; Ulster Unionist Party in Office; Ulster Politics under Direct Rule

Bibliography

Faulkner, Brian. *Memoirs of a Statesman.* 1978.

Hennessy, Thomas. *A History of Northern Ireland, 1920–1996.* 1997.

Purdie, Bob. *Politics in the Streets: The Origins of the Civil Rights Movement in Ulster.* 1990.

Patrick Maume

Fenian Movement and the Irish Republican Brotherhood

Between the Great Famine (1845–1851) and the Land War (1879–1882), Ireland was apparently settling into an accommodation, internally and externally, as a subordinate part of the British empire. Several of the countercurrents to this trend found expression in the Fenian movement that began in Ireland with the foundation in Dublin on 17 March 1858 of the Irish Republican Brotherhood (IRB). Its founder was James Stephens. Others who, like him, had been radicalized under Young Ireland influence, such as Thomas Clarke Luby, John O'Leary, Jeremiah O'Donovan Rossa, and Charles J. Kickham, became stalwarts of the movement in Ireland. In 1859 a U.S. counterpart, the Fenian Brotherhood, was formed, the name referring to the warrior Fianna of Gaelic folklore and reflecting the scholarly interests of the brotherhood's leader John O'Mahony. From 1863 onward Fenianism was to become a synonym for revolutionary Irish nationalism.

Both wings gathered widespread support in the early 1860s, with the Fenian Brotherhood becoming a prominent vehicle of Irish-American self-expression. In Ireland the socioeconomic changes of the 1850s had fostered a category of apprentices and literate wage earners, especially in retail trade; Stephens attracted them to the IRB by appropriating various nationalist initiatives, most notably the funeral of the Young Irelander Terence Bellew MacManus, which was organized by the National Brotherhood of Saint Patrick and culminated in a grand procession through Dublin on 14 November 1861. By 1863, in the towns of Leinster and Munster and to a lesser extent in the other provinces, young men were organized into a national network leading back to Stephens. Young men of their social background found their recreational outlets restricted by agents of social control who were busily transforming postfamine Irish society into an exemplar of respectability—priests, policemen, and magistrates. The new organization emboldened members to engage in autonomous socialization in public houses, at sporting events, and at their supposedly secret drilling exercises. The appeal and impact of Fenianism in the mid–1860s cannot be understood without reference to this social dimension.

Thus the original intention of conducting an entirely secret society had been overtaken by the realities of Irish life, and it was further undermined when Stephens in 1863 launched his own weekly, the *Irish People*, and brought key individuals from the provinces to work at its office in Dublin. Over its lifetime of twenty-two months the *Irish People*, while not openly admitting that it was the organ of the Fenians, hinted broadly at their existence and advocated Irish independence and military action as the means to that end. Every other form of nationalist movement was denounced in intolerant fashion. Frequent cannonades against "priests in politics" were intended to strengthen the nerves of Fenians facing

Following the failed Fenian rising of March 1867, the police in Manchester luckily captured two rebel leaders—Colonel Thomas Kelly and Captain Timothy Deasy. But as depicted in this sketch, the prisoners were rescued on 18 September from a police van by a body of armed Fenians. Police sergeant Charles Brett was killed in the raid, leading to a famous trial. FROM *ILLUSTRATED LONDON NEWS*, 28 SEPTEMBER 1867.

pressure from clergy who feared a revolution. The paper helped to consolidate the organization in Ireland and to spread it among the Irish in Britain.

The IRB had been launched without a program or manifesto, as an immediate response to a critical situation. In the wake of the Crimean War (1854–1856) relations between Britain and France had become fraught, and the prospect of an Anglo–French war—the classic opportunity for Irish revolution—seemed very credible. Stephens, O'Mahony, and other Fenian strategists were determined to have a force in place ready to take advantage of this longed-for eventuality. As it happened, France did go to war in 1859, not with Britain but with Austrian power in northern Italy. Faced with the disappearance of the original raison d'être of their organizations, Stephens and O'Mahony decided to continue on the new basis of working toward a revolution in Ireland (supported by Irish Americans), even without any international crisis affecting Britain.

The U.S. Civil War introduced new and encouraging factors. Participation in the warring armies meant that tens of thousands of Irishmen in the United States were obtaining military experience and might be persuaded to put it to use in a war of Irish liberation, if one could be instigated. And the U.S. conflict caused serious tensions between London and Washington, raising the prospect of an Anglo-American war. When the Civil War ended in 1865, Stephens promised that there would be action in Ireland before the year was out. It was only the prospect of imminent rebellion that enabled Stephens to maintain his position as dictatorial controller of the IRB. In the summer of 1865 he may have had up to 50,000 at his call, but they were very poorly armed, and he hesitated to launch a rebellion with no hope of success. In September the authorities struck, seizing the *Irish People* and arresting leading figures. Stephens escaped and in May 1866 reached New York City, where he found the movement in confusion, a so-called Senate group having emerged in opposition to O'Mahony. In April and May each of the factions had in turn fomented a brief raid on Canada. Stephens took control of the O'Mahony wing and boosted his authority by reinstating the objective of a rebellion in Ireland

Five Irishmen faced trial in a Manchester courthouse (depicted here) in November 1867 for the murder of Sergeant Brett. The three who were executed on 23 November—William Allen, Michael Larkin, and Michael O'Brien—became known in Ireland as the "Manchester Martyrs." Irish republicans worshipped their memory, as did most nationalists for decades thereafter. FROM ILLUSTRATED LONDON NEWS, 9 NOVEMBER 1867.

itself by the end of 1866. Thousands of Irish-American Civil War veterans prepared to cross the Atlantic. When Stephens in mid-December announced another postponement, he was deposed and a core group of military men left for England, where they laid plans for what proved to be a desultory attempt at rebellion in Ireland, the main action occurring on 5 and 6 March 1867.

In November 1867 the execution of William O'Meara Allen, Michael Larkin, and William O'Brien for killing a policeman during an attempted rescue of prisoners in Manchester provided the Fenians with martyrs. For a few years the movement attracted vibrant support, boosted by the general exuberance associated with Gladstone's concessions to Irish popular opinion before and after the general election of 1868. The mistaken idea that these concessions had in fact been won by the Fenian threat gained ground and was given some credence by Gladstone for his own purposes. A campaign for the release of Fenian prisoners drew widespread support. The IRB was put on a new footing in 1868 when the for-

mer autocracy was replaced by a supreme council with representatives from around Ireland and Britain. Membership began changing in 1871, as a loss of interest among the urban population was partially offset by inroads on the ranks of the Ribbon societies. By 1877 the numerical strength of the IRB was concentrated among the small farmers of south Ulster and north Connacht. Meanwhile, activists had become accustomed to participation in electoral politics in alliance with the Home Rule Party, and a few prominent Fenians had even been elected to Parliament as Home Rulers.

After 1867 a number of organizations contended for the leadership of militant Irish America, and of those, Clan na Gael came to dominate thanks to the dynamic leadership of John Devoy, exemplified by his masterminding of the escape of Fenian prisoners from Western Australia on board the *Catalpa* in 1876. Devoy forged a compact with the IRB that was intended to secure Clan na Gael influence on both sides of the Atlantic. With Devoy's backing the advocates of involvement in

Home Rule politics were expelled from the supreme council in 1877. Clan na Gael was never without competitors for the support of Irish Americans: O'Donovan Rossa collected a large sum of dollars for a skirmishing fund that he launched in 1876 with the support of Patrick Ford's New York–based *Irish World*; and John O'Mahony maintained an independent, if exiguous, existence for himself and the Fenian Brotherhood until his death in 1877.

SEE ALSO Butt, Isaac; Electoral Politics from 1800 to 1921; Newspapers; Politics: 1800 to 1921—Challenges to the Union; Stephens, James; Sullivan Brothers (A. M. and T. D.); **Primary Documents:** Two Fenian Oaths (1858, 1859); "God Save Ireland" (1867); O'Donovan Rossa Graveside Panegyric (1 August 1915)

Bibliography

Comerford, R. V. *The Fenians in Context: Irish Politics and Society, 1848–82.* 1985. Rev. edition, 1998.

D'Arcy, William. *The Fenian Movement in the United States, 1858–86.* 1947.

Moody, T. W., ed. *The Fenian Movement.* 1968.

Ó Broin, Leon. *Fenian Fever: An Anglo-American Dilemma.* 1971.

Ó Broin, Leon. *Revolutionary Underground: The Story of the Irish Republican Brotherhood, 1858–1924.* 1976.

R. V. Comerford

Fianna Fáil

See Political Parties in Independent Ireland; Politics: Independent Ireland since 1922.

~

Fiction, Modern

Many of the most important works of fiction that emerged from Ireland in the early part of the twentieth century are linked by the themes obsessively explored by their authors: the simultaneous ambivalence and attraction to home place and the pain felt at separation from it; and the strong ties to family and community made complicated by equally strong desires for freedom both from family and from such institutions as the Catholic Church, which traditionally have sustained the family. The first great work of the century, and one which explores all of these themes, is George Moore's *The Untilled Field*, which first appeared in Irish in 1902, and subsequently in English the following year. Moore, who was a Catholic landlord from County Mayo, had spent time as a young man in France and learned from Gustave Flaubert and Émile Zola. In addition to the short stories that comprise *The Untilled Field*, Moore is the author of many important novels dealing with both rural and city life in Ireland, most notably *A Drama in Muslin*, *Esther Waters*, and *The Lake*.

James Joyce was a contemporary of Moore's and, like him, looked toward Europe for his literary models, to Flaubert and Henrik Ibsen in particular. In *Dubliners*, *A Portrait of the Artist as a Young Man*, *Ulysses*, and *Finnegans Wake*, Joyce produced some the landmark fiction of the century. Joyce's work, however, did not find ready approval in his home country, and was considered difficult, obscure, and even obscene by some commentators. Like many Irish writers of this period, Joyce spent much of his adult life outside of Ireland, living in Italy, Switzerland, and France. Samuel Beckett was a disciple of Joyce's who provided aid while the master sought to complete *Finnegans Wake*. Although Beckett is best known as the author of *Waiting for Godot*, a defining work in the theatre of the absurd, he also wrote many important works of fiction, the most important being his trilogy *Molloy*, *Malone Dies*, and *The Unnamable*. After 1945 Beckett abandoned English and wrote in French, the language of his adopted country. Another great modernist and disciple of Joyce is Flann O'Brien, who achieved fame as an *Irish Times* journalist, using the pseudonym Myles na gCopaleen, and who is the author of the great comic novels *At-Swim Two Birds* and *The Third Policeman*. Máirtín Ó Cadhain's *Cré na Cille* (Graveyard clay) is arguably the greatest novel written in Irish during the twentieth century and one that is similar to the work of Beckett in many respects.

Many fiction writers emerged under the umbrella of the Irish Literary Revival, which set out to examine Irish life after the Yeats model and to keep modernism at a safe distance, but also to put some distance between themselves and revival. For the most part, much of the best work done by writers from this generation was in the short story. The most notable writers in the genre are Sean O'Faolain, author of *Midsummer Night Madness and Other Stories* and *A Purse of Coppers*; Frank O'Connor, author of *Bones of Contention and Other*

Stories and *Guests of the Nation*, the title story of which is a classic antiwar narrative; and Mary Lavin, author of *Tales from Bective Bridge*. During this same period, Máirtín Ó Cadhain wrote many of his best short stories, which were later translated from the Irish in the collection *The Road to Brightcity*. However, some important novels, such as Patrick MacGill's *The Rat Pit* and Peadar O'Donnell's *Storm*, dealt, with great compassion, with the poor and downtrodden. Liam O'Flaherty wrote many novels, the most popular being *The Informer*—though *Famine*, his exploration of the famine on Aran, is probably his best. Some writers continued in the fantasy vein made popular by Yeats and Lady Gregory and produced some notable work: James Stephens's *The Crock of Gold*, Mervyn Wall's *The Unfortunate Fursey*, and Eimar O'Duffy's *King Goshawk and the Birds*.

Although the Big House novel is often most closely associated with the nineteenth century, it has also flourished in the twentieth. Edith Somerville and Violet Martin's *The Big House of Inver* and Elizabeth Bowen's *The Last September* are remarkable examples of the novel at its best. To this day, the Big House novel exerts a fascination for Irish writers, and two excellent, more recent examples are Aidan Higgins's *Langrishe, Go Down* and Molly Keane's *Good Behaviour*. Higgins is one of an important group of writers who emerged in the 1950s and 1960s and struck out in new directions, borrowing from both the Irish modernists and revivalists.

Brian Moore grew up in Belfast, but left the city after completing school and eventually settled in California. His best known works are *The Lonely Passion of Judith Hearne*, concerned with a middle-aged woman's fruitless search for love, and *The Emperor of Ice-Cream*, a coming-of-age novel, both of which are set in Belfast. John McGahern is well known both as a novelist and short-story writer whose work examines the lives of rural folk in the west of Ireland. His most acclaimed books are the novel *Amongst Women* and the story collection, *High Ground*. William Trevor has written many novels and collections of short stories, set in both Ireland and England. *The Ballroom of Romance*, which deals with the loneliness of rural life, is his most acclaimed. Edna O'Brien has been the most controversial writer of this generation. Her first novel, *The Country Girls*, was banned by the censors for obscenity and burned in her local village in County Clare. In time *The Country Girls* became a trilogy and was seen as a groundbreaking work which explored the inner lives and aspirations of women. Although *The Country Girls Trilogy* remains her best-known work, O'Brien has written many novels and *Lantern Slides*, an important collection of short fiction.

A NEW GENERATION OF WRITERS

Recently, another strong wave of Irish writers has arrived, many of whom have enjoyed wide international success. Roddy Doyle's *The Barrytown Trilogy* is a hilarious and deeply sympathetic portrayal of working-class life on Dublin's Northside, and each part has benefited from being made into a popular film. Doyle was also the first Irish fiction writer to win the Booker Prize for *Paddy Clarke Ha Ha Ha*. Philip Casey is the author of the highly regarded *Bann River Trilogy*, a work which details the ever shifting nature of love and the often ghostly links between the past and present. Patrick McCabe has found great success, both as novel and film, with *The Butcher Boy*, an impressive exploration of rural deprivation and madness. Similarly gruesome and impressive is John Banville's *The Book of Evidence*. Both Colm Tóibín and Colum McCann are writers whose work is frequently set outside of Ireland. In *The Heather Blazing*, Tóibín shows how both the political and the personal worlds become tangled in post-treaty Ireland, while *The Story of the Night* shows how the political and the sexual become entangled in contemporary Argentina. In Colum McCann's fiction, because his characters are restless and mobile, the location may shift suddenly, as is the case in *Songdogs*, a novel that takes place in Mexico, Ireland, and the United States. In *Ripley Bogle* and *Eureka Street*, Robert MacLiam Wilson has provided two moving and hilarious accounts of life in contemporary Belfast. As has been the case in poetry, women have contributed important and technically daring fiction. Anne Enright's volume of short stories, *The Portable Virgin*, is an original and hilarious take on the contemporary scene, while Deirdre Madden's *Remembering Light and Stone* is an Irishwoman's reflection of her life in Italy among expatriates. Emma Donoghue frequently focuses on the lives of lesbians though her most successful novel to date is *Slammerkin*, a historical novel about a servant girl who murdered her mistress in 1763.

SEE ALSO Arts: Modern Irish and Anglo-Irish Literature and the Arts since 1800; Beckett, Samuel; Blasket Island Writers; Drama, Modern; Joyce, James; Literature: Twentieth-Century Women Writers; Poetry, Modern

Bibliography

Brown, Terence. *Ireland, A Social and Cultural History, 1922–79.* 1981.

Deane, Seamus. *Celtic Revivals: Essays in Modern Irish Literature, 1880–1980.* 1985.

Forkner, Ben, ed. *Modern Irish Short Stories.* 1980.

Joyce, James. *Ulysses.* 1922.

Kiberd, Declan. *Irish Classics.* 2001.

McHugh, Roger and Maurice Harmon. *Short History of Anglo-Irish Literature from its Origins to the Present Day.* 1982.

Mahony, Christina Hunt. *Contemporary Irish Literature: Transforming Tradition.* 1998.

Martin, Augustine. *The Genius of Irish Prose.* 1984.

Eamonn Wall

Fitzgerald, Lord Edward

Most famous as the intended commander in chief of the Irish rebels in 1798, Lord Edward Fitzgerald (1763–1798) was arrested before the rebellion broke out and was mortally wounded by his captors; he became a legendary figure in Irish history in subsequent generations. Lord Edward was the younger son of the duke of Leinster, the premier Irish peer, and was the nephew (through his mother) of the earl of Richmond and the first cousin of Charles James Fox. The Fitzgeralds, like their English relatives, were prominent Whigs, and when he entered the Irish parliament in 1790, Lord Edward was firmly on the side of the reformist opposition. By that time he had served in several regiments of the army and had traveled extensively in Europe and North America. In the early 1790s he expressed support for the French Revolution (he had been educated in the principles of philosopher Jean-Jacques Rousseau), and he was expelled from the army in 1793 for having attended a revolutionary banquet while on a visit to Paris in 1792. In 1796 he joined the United Irishmen, which by that time had become a secret revolutionary and republican organization. He was briefly involved in their negotiations with France for an invasion of Ireland. Following the failure of the French expedition to Bantry Bay at the end of 1796, Lord Edward remained active in the movement, and in 1797 and early 1798 he was a prominent member of the Dublin leadership. In the late spring of 1798 he was among those who planned the details of the rebellion that eventually broke out on 23 May. He was frequently in contact with the spy Thomas Reynolds, and it was through information garnered from their network of spies that Dublin Castle arrested several United Irishmen leaders, Lord Edward included, shortly before the appointed date of the rebellion. He was captured on 19 May and died on 4 June from the wound he received on that occasion.

SEE ALSO Eighteenth-Century Politics: 1778 to 1795—Parliamentary and Popular Politics; Eighteenth-Century Politics: 1795 to 1800—Repression, Rebellion, and Union; United Irish Societies from 1791 to 1803

Bibliography

Moore, Thomas. *The Life and Death of Lord Edward Fitzgerald, 1763–1798.* 2 vols. 1831.

Tillyard, Stella. *Citizen Lord: The Life of Edward Fitzgerald, Irish Revolutionary.* 1997.

Daniel Gahan

Fitzgerald, Thomas, Tenth Earl of Kildare ("Silken Thomas")

Thomas Fitzgerald, Lord Offaly, tenth earl of Kildare (1513–1537), leader of the Kildare rebellion (1534–1535), was born in London and spent much of his youth in England. In February 1534, before his father, Lord Deputy Gerald Fitzgerald (ninth earl of Kildare), answered a summons to the Henrician court, he appointed Thomas as vice-deputy during his absence. By May the futility of Gerald's negotiations to preserve the Kildare dynasty's control over Ireland within the newly reformed Tudor polity was manifest. Rumors of Gerald's death and of attempts to lure Thomas to the court were rife. (Meanwhile, Thomas was in Munster soliciting support for the Geraldine cause from Conor O'Brien of Thomond.) Fearful that Thomas might be persuaded by the Irish council to go to court, his father warned him not to trust those councillors lest he should be captured. In early June, Thomas was summoned to appear before the Irish council. Guided by his father's advisors and backed by a guard of 140 horsemen, he dramatically resigned his position as vice-deputy and repudiated his allegiance to Henry VIII at a council meeting in Saint Mary's Abbey, Dublin, on 11 June. A Gaelic bard, de Nelan, invested him with the sobriquet "Silken Thomas" as his horsemen's quilted leather coats were elaborately embroidered with silk. Thomas proclaimed a Catholic crusade and initiated direct contacts with Charles V, Pope Paul III, and James V of Scotland.

The Kildare rebellion has sometimes been interpreted as a show of his dynasty's resistance to the Tudor policy of increased government centralization. Alternatively, it has been viewed as an error of judgment by the Fitzgeralds, occurring at a time when Henry VIII was especially vulnerable as he wrestled with the divorce issue and the introduction of the Reformation.

Henry's reaction was to imprison Gerald in the Tower of London on 29 June. Late in July, Thomas's forces assassinated Archbishop John Alen of Dublin and thereafter wasted the rival Butler earldom and besieged Dublin until 4 October, by which time Thomas's father had died in prison (probably from natural causes) and Thomas succeeded as tenth earl. Henry's resolve to suppress the rebellion was evidenced by the arrival of a 2,300-strong army at Dublin in late October. Thomas was publicly proclaimed a traitor and was attainted by the English parliament on about 18 December. During the winter of 1534 to 1535 he engaged in sporadic ravaging excursions through the Pale and remained hopeful that a 10,000-strong army promised by Charles V would soon arrive in Ireland. Instead, losses and defections weakened his forces, morale was waning, and support dwindled. His campaign was dealt a fatal blow when his principal fortress, Maynooth Castle, surrendered to Lord Deputy Skeffington following a siege (18–23 March). Thomas sought refuge in Munster, where he held out for several months in vain hope of military aid from Charles V. On 24 August he surrendered to his uncle-in-law, Lord Deputy Leonard Grey, on the condition that he would be allowed to live, and was conveyed to London in September and imprisoned in the Tower. The attainder of Thomas and his uncles and their execution at Tyburn on 3 February 1537 precipitated the confiscation of the Kildare estates and left the Kildare Geraldines without a leader. Thomas's revolt removed the Kildares from their position of political dominance in Ireland and facilitated reform of the Dublin government, which was thereafter in the charge of an English-born governor backed by a garrison.

SEE ALSO Monarchy

Bibliography

Bradshaw, Brendan. "Cromwellian Reform and the Origins of the Kildare Rebellion, 1533–4." *Transactions of the Royal Historical Society* 5th ser., 27 (1977): 69–93.

Ellis, Steven G. "The Kildare Rebellion and the Early Henrician Reformation." *Historical Journal* 19 (1976): 807–830.

Lyons, Mary Ann. *Gearóid Óg Fitzgerald*. 1998.

McCorristine, Laurence. *The Revolt of Silken Thomas: A Challenge to Henry VIII*. 1987.

Ó Siochrú, M. "Foreign Involvement in the Revolt of Silken Thomas, 1534–5." *Proceedings of the Royal Irish Academy*, 96C (1996): 49–66.

Mary Ann Lyons

Fleadh Cheoil

The Fleadh Cheoil (feast of music) was originally conceived in 1951 by the organization Comhaltas Ceoltóirí Éireann (CCÉ; known as Cumann Ceoltóirí Éireann at its inception in 1951 until it revised its name in 1952) as a yearly exhibition of traditional music. Although the event held in Mullingar on Whit weekend 1951 was not actually termed a fleadh, it established the model of a music festival, with competitions of music, song, and dance where medals, trophies, and other awards are given. The term *fleadh cheoil* was first used for the following year's competition in Monaghan town, and the 1951 attendance of 1,500 grew rapidly during the decade. For traditional musicians the Fleadh represented a means of bringing their music before the public, as well as an opportunity to exchange tunes. Spontaneous sessions in public houses and on the streets quickly became a singular feature of the Fleadh, drawing a progressively younger audience.

The very popularity of the endeavor provoked dissent within the traditional music community. Its proponents noted that the competition engendered by the Fleadh drew new musicians, greatly improved playing standards, and ultimately encouraged the popularization of traditional music, which previously had been the preserve of the few rather than of the many. Some lamented that the founding aims of CCÉ—the promotion of Irish traditional music in all its forms and cooperation with all bodies working for the restoration of Irish culture—were being lost and were ignored by many who attended the Fleadh. They further opposed the association of the Fleadh with music that was not indigenous, notably criticizing the balladeers singing songs far removed from the seannós (traditional Irish) style.

Yet it was the combination of the purist and the popular that produced the unique atmosphere of the festival as it moved annually across the country. By the 1960s it was a focal point of nascent youth culture in Ireland, drawing as readily from urban as from rural areas, seeking an Irish counterpart to music festivals held around the world. Drunkenness brought occasional public-order problems during the 1960s and 1970s, but this involved a tiny minority. The event has also flirted with political involvement, and the 1971 Fleadh was cancelled in protest over the introduction of internment in the North. The attendance at the All-Ireland Fleadh Cheoil regularly draws more than 100,000 people. Now held on the August bank holiday weekend, its unique atmosphere remains a compelling draw for its competing musicians, music lovers, and tourists. The establishment of branches of CCÉ across the country—by 2000 there were 400 branches—brought about the introduction of county and provincial Fleadhanna Cheoil, which reproduce the All-Ireland format on a smaller scale and are attractions in their own right. Fleadhanna form an integral part of the cultural life of Irish communities across the world: Competitors from Britain, the United States, and Australia compete annually—and successfully—in the All-Ireland Fleadh Cheoil.

SEE ALSO Music: Popular Music

Bibliography

Ceol. A Journal of Irish Music. Vols. 1–3.

Vallely, Fintan. *The Companion to Irish Traditional Music.* 1999.

Paul Rouse

Flood, Henry

Politician, and the leading Patriot spokesman of his generation, Henry Flood (1732–1791) entered the Irish House of Commons as MP for County Kilkenny in 1759, and subsequently sat for a number of borough constituencies. The most notable was Callan, Co. Kilkenny, which involved him in a tense, costly, and sometimes violent struggle for control with James Agar of Ringwood, resulting in a duel in 1769 in which Agar was killed. Meanwhile Flood achieved a considerable measure of fame as one of the most talented parliamentarians of his generation. His reputation was grounded on his exceptional skills as an orator, debater, and propagandist, but it was his advocacy of a Patriot program, embracing limited parliaments, a Protestant militia, and the curtailment of patronage, that gave it substance.

His decision to accept the position of vice treasurer in 1775 both alienated many of his Patriot colleagues in parliament and enmeshed him in an unhappy relationship with the Irish administration that cast him into the political wilderness for six years. His dismissal in 1781 freed him to press for legislative independence as the Irish parliament neared its crucial final phase, though his more radical position on the issue set him at loggerheads with Henry Grattan. Flood's successful agitation between 1782 and 1783 of a demand that the British parliament should renounce its right to make law for Ireland enabled him to supersede Grattan as the most popular Patriot politician in Ireland at this point. But his desire to prove himself on the imperial stage at Westminster meant that he devoted increasingly less attention to Irish politics thereafter. He made an exception for the issue of parliamentary reform, to which he made a strong commitment in Ireland between 1783 and 1785 and in Britain in 1790. Even this was insufficient to sustain his career, however, for though he made a number of impressive interventions, electoral difficulties and health problems ensured that he had become a figure of increasingly marginal political consequence for some years before his death in December 1791.

SEE ALSO Eighteenth-Century Politics: 1714 to 1778—Interest Politics; Eighteenth-Century Politics: 1778 to 1795—Parliamentary and Popular Politics; Eighteenth-Century Politics: 1795 to 1800—Repression, Rebellion, and Union; Grattan, Henry

Bibliography

Dickson, David. "Henry Flood and the Eighteenth-Century Irish Patriots." In *"Worsted in the Game": Losers in Irish History*, edited by Ciaran Brady. 1989.

Kelly, James. *Henry Flood: Patriots and Politics in Eighteenth-Century Ireland.* 1998.

Flood, Warden. *Memoirs of the Life and Correspondence of Henry Flood.* 1838.

James Kelly

Foreign Investment

See Overseas Investment.

G

GAA "Ban"

The GAA ban rules, which varied in force and substance, ultimately decreed that anyone who played, promoted, or attended "foreign games" (cricket, hockey, rugby, and soccer), or who was a member of the British security forces, was prohibited from membership in the Gaelic Athletic Association (GAA). Further, no GAA club was allowed to organize any entertainment at which "foreign dances" (essentially all dancing unrelated to Irish traditional, folk, or country music) were permitted, and any GAA member who attended dances run either by the British security forces or by foreign games clubs was liable to be suspended for two years. Although it was in the five decades after independence that these rules were strongest, the very first ban rules were introduced in January 1885, within two months of the founding of the GAA; they banned athletes who competed in athletics meetings run by other organizations from competing at GAA meetings. A similar ban relating to clubs involved in field games was introduced in March 1886. Essentially, both rules were intended to increase the administrative and organizational power of the GAA in its struggle to gain control of sport in Ireland. Land agitation and political turmoil in 1887 brought the GAA to ban members of the police, though not the army, from joining the GAA. When political division almost obliterated the organization in the early 1890s, it moved to remove the police ban in 1893, and then its foreign games ban in 1896, in an attempt to draw new members. By the early 1900s membership had improved as interest in organized sport increased. Nationalist sentiment in the country also grew, and this brought the return of the ban rules—involving for the first time the exclusion of army, navy, and prison officers, and all who watched foreign games—this time with the stated intention of drawing a divide between Irish Ireland and those portrayed as "West British."

The rules did not enjoy unanimous support within the association in the preindependence era, and there were almost annual attempts to have them weakened or removed—several of which failed only narrowly. After 1921 support for the ban hardened, and vigilance committees were established to police the rules, which were broadened to include a ban on "foreign music" between 1929 and 1932. Anecdotal evidence suggests that there was widespread evasion of the rules, and by the 1960s a serious campaign emerged calling for their elimination. The relative opening of Irish society in the 1960s, coupled with the televising of games from all sports, brought a reassessment of policy, and in 1971 the GAA voted to remove its ban on members playing foreign games and attending foreign dances. The ban on members of the British security forces was retained, and despite infrequent attempts at deletion, it remained until November 2001. The ban on the playing of foreign games on GAA pitches remained in place even after that date.

SEE ALSO Gaelic Revivalism: The Gaelic Athletic Association; Sport and Leisure

Bibliography

de Búrca, Marcus. *The GAA: A History.* 1999.

MacLua, Brendan. *The Steadfast Rule: A History of the G.A.A. Ban.* 1967.

Mandle, W. F. *The Gaelic Athletic Association and Irish Nationalist Politics, 1884–1925.* 1987.

Rouse, Paul. "The Politics of Culture and Sport in Ireland: A History of the GAA Ban on Foreign Games, 1884–1971.

Part One: 1884–1921." *International Journal of the History of Sport* 10, no. 3 (December 1993): 333–360.

Paul Rouse

Gaelic Athletic Association

See GAA "Ban"; Gaelic Revivalism: The Gaelic Athletic Association.

◿

Gaelic Catholic State, Making of

Independence was followed by few institutional or social innovations—the main exception was the increased prominence given to traditional Irish or "Gaelic" culture and to the Catholic religion in public life. Given the extent to which the independence movement was inspired by ideas of cultural and religious identity, this was understandable, but the result was apparent state adherence to an exclusive interpretation of "Irishness" that embraced only the majority community.

Gaelic symbolism was extensively used in the formal and ceremonial aspects of government and traditional forms of art and entertainment were encouraged, but the greatest effort was devoted to the cause of reviving the Irish language. Language enthusiasts believed that the best hope for this endeavor lay with the primary (or "national") schools. Beginning in 1922 the government implemented a policy of requiring all instruction of infant (elementary) classes to be in Irish. In the higher grades, as much instruction as possible was to be in Irish, and every incentive was offered to increase the total amount of Irish taught. Fianna Fáil Minister for Education Tomás Derrig was dissatisfied with the rate of progress in the national schools, and beginning in 1934 he reduced the time allocated to other subjects. Secondary schools were not subjected to the same requirements, but Irish was given significant prominence. In 1925 it became necessary to achieve a passing grade in Irish in order to pass the Intermediate Certificate, an examination usually taken at age 16. In 1934 the same regulation was applied to the final school examination, the Leaving Certificate. Secondary schools were also assessed for state grants according to the amount of instruction in Irish.

By the 1940s, teachers' organizations had become critical of the fact that there was little educational development other than that motivated by language revival, but the public and their representatives rarely discussed dissatisfaction. This may have been due to a commitment to the cause of language revival, or more negatively, a reluctance to be seen to be antinational. It may also have been because many jobs in the public service were reserved for Irish speakers. The one significant source of discontent was the Church of Ireland, whose members often felt culturally alienated and practically disadvantaged by the language policy. It was not easy for Church of Ireland schools to find teachers competent in Irish, and the general decline of educational standards made it more difficult for students to gain admission to universities or to secure jobs outside Ireland.

The state's commitment to the Irish language was largely confined to the schools, but the influence of Catholicism was more pervasive, if in some ways more subtle. Cumann na nGaedheal, the party in government from 1922 to 1932, had a close relationship with the Catholic hierarchy, which had contributed to establishing the government's legitimacy during the Civil War. Despite this, or perhaps because of it, Fianna Fáil was no less anxious to display its Catholic credentials. Notwithstanding the formal separation of church and state, state occasions were imbued with Catholic ritual, and Catholic moral and social ethics had a profound effect on social policy. The state had inherited a denominational education system and all political parties accepted that they should not interfere with this arrangement. Catholic social teaching of the period was deeply suspicious of the power of the state, particularly in areas of education, health, and family welfare. Successive Irish governments were content to minimize their involvement and to permit the development of a concept of social services that was heavily dependent on voluntary organizations. This arrangement led to a destabilizing conflict of interests when these services were reorganized in the postwar period.

Perhaps the most obvious and controversial influence of Catholicism was in the area of public morality. In 1925, after consultation with the Catholic archbishop of Dublin, the government took steps to circumvent the power to grant divorces that had devolved on the Irish parliament from Westminster. Given that courts were not empowered to grant divorces, either, this meant an effective ban on divorce in the Free State. Though some Protestant clergymen and lay people supported the measure, others argued that because divorce was permitted by their churches, the measure represented the removal of an existing civil right. The matter provided the occasion for a speech in the senate by the poet W. B. Yeats in which he famously set out the achievements of the Anglo-Irish community, claiming

Pilgrims to Croagh Patrick, 1948. The pilgrimage, honoring St. Patrick on the last Sunday of July, is a Christian continuation of the ancient pagan festival of Lughnasa. It continues to attract thousands of people. COURTESY OF THE HEAD OF THE DEPARTMENT OF IRISH FOLKLORE, UNIVERSITY COLLEGE DUBLIN.

that "we against whom you have done this thing are no petty people" (Brown 1985, p. 131).

Yeats and many of his fellow writers were also in the vanguard of opposition to the Censorship of Publications Act of 1929. This act was not draconian in its inception—it was intended mainly to prevent the free circulation of publications relating to contraception, an international concern at the time. However, the zeal of the Censorship of Publications Board established under the act led to the prohibition of many of the greatest works of modern Irish and world literature. These included Aldous Huxley's *Brave New World*, John Steinbeck's *The Grapes of Wrath*, Ernest Hemingway's *A Farewell to Arms*, Samuel Beckett's *More Pricks than Kicks*, and James Joyce's *Stephen Hero*. Until its liberalization in the 1960s the severity of Irish literary censorship was internationally notorious.

Cumann na nGaedheal failed to address two of the greatest sources of anxiety to the Catholic hierarchy:

the widespread growth of unregulated dance halls and the question of contraception. In 1935 Fianna Fáil responded to these concerns with a regulatory Public Dance Halls Act and a Criminal Law Amendment Act that absolutely prohibited the importation and sale of contraceptives. It was a measure that was widely applauded, but one that also drew criticism from those who believed the power of the state should not be used to enforce Catholic values in matters of public health and private conscience.

The creation of a Gaelic and Catholic state reached its apogee in Eamon de Valera's 1937 constitution, which established Irish as the first official language of the state and recognized the "special position" of the Catholic Church "as the guardian of the Faith professed by the great majority of the citizens." The Catholic ethos of the constitution was not purely symbolic: The text was deeply imbued with Catholic social theory and traditional values. The family was recognized as the fundamental unit of society, entitled as such to protection from the state. The family was also recognized as the primary educator of the child, and the state was relegated to a secondary role. In the context of family values the constitution recognized the support given by woman "by her life within the home" and stipulated that no law permitting divorce would be enacted.

In the 1920s and 1930s opposition to the increasing identification of the state with Gaelic and Catholic culture was muted, sporadic, and unorganized. It is inaccurate to regard these measures as motivated solely by a desire to establish an exclusive national identity; nonetheless, that was one of the results. Perhaps the most overt example of the confusion of nationality and majority culture is found in the preamble to the constitution, which acknowledges "all our obligations to our Divine Lord, Jesus Christ, Who sustained our fathers through centuries of trial." This was not simply a statement of Christian piety, but an understanding of the nature of the state in the context of a specific historic tradition.

SEE ALSO Constitution; de Valera, Eamon; Divorce, Contraception, and Abortion; Eucharistic Congress; Language and Literacy: Irish Language since 1922; Jewish Community; McQuaid, John Charles; Mother and Child Crisis; Politics: Independent Ireland since 1922; Protestant Community in Southern Ireland since 1922; Roman Catholic Church: Since 1891; Secularization; **Primary Documents:** Letter on the Commission on the Gaeltacht (4 March 1925); From the 1937 Constitution; Letter to John A. Costello, the Taoiseach (5 April 1951)

Bibliography

Akenson, Donald Harmon. *A Mirror to Kathleen's Face: Education in Independent Ireland, 1922–60.* 1973.

Brown, Terence. *Ireland: A Social and Cultural History, 1922–1985.* 1985.

Coolahan, John. *Irish Education: Its History and Structure.* 1981.

Farrell, Brian, ed. *De Valera's Constitution and Ours.* 1988.

Kelly, Adrian. *Compulsory Irish: Language and Education in Ireland, 1870s–1970s.* 2000.

Keogh, Dermot. *The Vatican, the Bishops, and Irish Politics, 1919–1939.* 1986.

Whyte, John H. *Church and State in Modern Ireland, 1923–1979.* 1980.

Susannah Riordan

Gaelic League

See Gaelic Revivalism: Gaelic League.

~

Gaelic Recovery

Gaelic Recovery refers here to three linked developments that occurred in Ireland between about 1250 and 1400: (1) the military and territorial revival of Gaelic Irish dynasties after a period in which the Anglo-Norman settlers had everywhere triumphed; (2) the revival of Gaelic literature and scholarship that took place after about 1330 and provided an ideological justification for the new Gaelic powers; and (3) the gaelicization over most of the country of the Anglo-Norman elites, with their assimilation in language and culture to their Gaelic neighbors. None of these processes has so far attracted a major study in depth.

REVIVAL OF GAELIC IRISH DYNASTIES

By 1250 Anglo-Norman settlement had spread over most of the level and open country suitable for agricultural settlement, except the northwest of Ireland, into which there had been only tentative advances. A more superficial occupation, with isolated castles and borough settlements, extended over forest regions such as the wooded mountains of the south, the wooded bogs of the midland plain, and the lowland forest of northern Wexford. After 1250, although colonial expansion continued along the north Ulster coast as far as Derry and the Inishowen peninsula, the drive into inland Ulster petered out, and almost everywhere else a new and militarily more efficient Gaelic opposition brought about the rapid collapse of colonial settlement and control in the forested regions, even those of eastern Leinster, which would appear to have been completely integrated into the colony. By 1260 the MacCarthy kings of Desmond had effectively ousted the colonists from the southwestern corner of Munster, and although their expansion seems to have then halted for a half century, with the coastal strip of west Cork remaining under Anglo-Norman control, it was to resume in the early fourteenth century. The settlements among the wooded bogs of the midlands also seem to have been destroyed in the 1260s, with the area reverting to effective Gaelic control. By the 1290s the O'Reillys (in the present County Cavan) and the O'Farrells (in County Longford) were slowly but steadily pushing back the colonial frontier in those regions, while the outlying castles built during the first impetus of colonization had long since been abandoned.

The increasing legal discrimination (technically referred to as "the exception of Irishry") against those of Gaelic stock may have played a part in alienating those Irish who had been prepared to be integrated into colonial society, but the major factor was certainly the improved weaponry and military techniques adopted by the Irish, with their efficient development of guerrilla techniques. After about 1280 the Irish in Ulster and Connacht also begin to employ heavily armed Scottish mercenaries from the western Highlands and Islands, the gallowglass (*galloglaigh*). The Bruce invasion dealt a shattering blow to the colony, while the deteriorating climatic conditions, which set in after 1315, weakened the tillage agriculture that was its economic base. The colonial frontier rapidly retreated everywhere. The Black Death of 1349, the first of a series of plagues, was a further blow to the urban and village communities. From the time of the Bruce invasion the O'Conor (Ó Conchobair) kingship of Connacht reemerged as a powerful political force, only to be destroyed by internal divisions at the end of the century, while the MacMurrough (Mac Murchadha) kingship of Leinster revived as a center of resistance in the forest country of Counties Wexford and Carlow, although its conversion into a solid territorial power was the work of Art MacMurrough (1376–1416). From about 1330 the Dublin administration began to formally recognize the occupation of lands by Gaelic lords in return for some sort of tribute, and some of the latter, such as the MacCarthy (MacCarthaigh) kings of Desmond, entered into much closer relations with the Dublin administration, receiving a large grant of lands in 1353 and actually entailing their lands in English legal form in 1365. Not all the new Gaelic rulers were the representatives of preinvasion dynasties: the Mageoghegans (Meic Eochagáin) of Westmeath were bandit chiefs who erected a lordship on the ruins of frontier manors, while one Gaelic dynasty, the O'Flynns of Uí Tuirtre in east Ulster, having thrown in their lot with the colonists, found themselves ousted along with the latter by the expanding O'Neills. By 1400 a new stability of frontiers had been largely established, and the network of autonomous lordships that had come into existence was to survive largely unchanged until the Tudor reconquest.

GAELICIZATION OF THE ANGLO-NORMANS

The Gaelic Recovery could perhaps be seen as involving as much the gaelicization of the Anglo-Norman elites as a revival by the Gaelic ones. It seems to have begun in Connacht, where the settlers were a thin aristocratic layer over a largely Gaelic population, and it is perhaps significant that elsewhere it seems to have come soonest in those areas where education, as it was, remained largely Gaelic. Its extension into the political sphere can be seen as a reaction to the centralizing policies of the English royal government—only briefly reversed during the Mortimer ascendancy of 1326 to 1331—which was hostile to baronial jurisdictions. Denied by English law the devolved powers that were necessary for their survival, the Anglo-Norman lords seized them for themselves. Their new situation also involved the necessity of entering into alliances, by marriage or fostering arrangements as well as militarily, with the surrounding Gaelic powers, to whom they became in varying degrees assimilated. Gerald, third earl of Desmond (d. 1398), although in 1367 to 1369 the official English governor of Ireland, wrote poetry in Irish, and his children seem to have been brought up in a Gaelic milieu. By 1400 the Dillons and Daltons on the Westmeath frontier had become completely gaelicized and passed outside royal control. Just as some of the Gaelic rulers, such as the Mageoghegans or the Fermanagh Maguires (Meig Uidhir), were "new men," so the Dillons and Daltons were knightly families who had imposed their rule on their neighbors and former equals. The fourth (the "White") earl of Ormond (d. 1452), although through much of his career the official representative of the English Crown and an important figure in England as well as Ireland, patronized Gaelic men of letters. He governed his own lordship in Kilkenny and Tipperary autonomously without reference to English norms, and he employed Gaelic lawyers (brehons) in doing so. Thus living in two worlds, he was a forerunner of the Kildares (1477–1534).

LITERARY REVIVAL

The third aspect of the Gaelic Recovery was the revival of the Gaelic learned and literary tradition. After a long period during which Gaelic literary activity had been largely confined to the writing of bardic praise-poems, the fourteenth century saw an upsurge of literary and antiquarian studies in which the greatest name was Seán Mór Ó Dubhagáin (d. 1372). Although much of the work of these scholars was politically motivated, in finding (or manufacturing) genealogies for the new Gaelic rulers and historical justifications for their territorial acquisitions or ambitions, there was also a genuine wish to recover and preserve the records of Gaelic Ireland and its culture before its disruption by the invasion. It was in this period that the great learned families of the succeeding period, such as the Mac Firbises (Mac Firbisigh), O'Mulconrys (Ó Maolconaire), O'Duigenans (Ó Duibhgeanáin), and Magraths (MacCraith), emerged into prominence and that many of the great surviving codices were written.

SEE ALSO Bruce Invasion; Gaelic Society in the Late Middle Ages; Magnates, Gaelic and Anglo-Irish; Norman Invasion and Gaelic Resurgence; Richard II in Ireland

Bibliography

Barry, T. B., Robin Frame, and Katharine Simms, eds. *Colony and Frontier in Medieval Ireland.* 1995.

Frame, Robin. "War and Peace in the Medieval Lordship of Ireland." In *The English in Medieval Ireland*, edited by James Lydon. 1984.

Nicholls, Kenneth W. "Anglo-French Ireland and After." *Peritia* 1 (1982): 370–403.

Nicholls, Kenneth W. "Worlds Apart? The Ellis Two-Nation Theory on Late Medieval Ireland." *History Ireland* 7, no. 2 (summer 1999): 22–26.

Simms, Katharine. "The O'Reillys and the Kingdom of East Breifne." *Breifne* 6 (1976–1978): 305–317.

Simms, Katharine. *From Kings to Warlords: The Changing Political Structure of Gaelic Ireland in the Later Middle Ages.* 1987. Reprint, 1998.

Simms, Katharine. "Bards and Barons: The Anglo-Irish Aristocracy and the Native Culture." In *Medieval Frontier Societies*, edited by Robert Bartlett and Angus McKay. 1989.

Kenneth Nicholls

Gaelic Revival

The Gaelic Revival, which aimed to extend the use of Irish Gaelic as a spoken language and a literary medium, was at the height of its popular influence in the first decade of the twentieth century and reached its artistic peak during the 1920s and 1930s. The revival drew together older men and women whose first language was Gaelic, and younger intellectuals, primarily from urban Ireland and from communities in Britain and the United States, who hoped to learn Gaelic because of a romantic notion of their linguistic heritage. Among this latter group were many who became leaders in the campaigns for independence from the United Kingdom between 1916 and 1922, and the cultural programs they instituted in the Irish Free State reflected one significant line of thought that emerged out of the revival. Moreover, the creative and philosophical tensions between Gaelic enthusiasts and Irish artists who wrote in English had infused Gaelic and Anglo-Irish literature with vigor, sparking debates about the proper role of art in society and revealing the insular vision of some leading revivalists.

Throughout the nineteenth century, Gaelic had continued the decline that had begun before the Great Famine. Few postfamine writers or poets produced new literature in Irish, though recent research suggests that Gaelic literature was not as moribund as contemporaries believed. Until the last decades of the nineteenth century, however, publishers printed little Gaelic matter aside from the proceedings of antiquarian bodies and the translations of Gaelic works into English by scholars such as Eugene O'Curry and John O'Donovan. By the 1891 census fewer than 700,000 people out of a population of 4.7 million even claimed a knowledge of Gaelic, and only about 38,000 of them were monolingual Irish-speakers.

Three events prefigured the nascent revival. The first, in 1877, was the foundation of the Society for the Preservation of the Irish Language (SPIL). In the following year the SPIL enlisted support from members of Parliament to make Gaelic a voluntary subject for intermediate-school students, though few availed of the opportunity for two decades. Second, between 1878 and 1880, Standish James O'Grady published his multivolume adaptation of ancient Gaelic epics, *The History of Ireland: The Heroic Period*, a work that attracted readers and later writers to an array of indigenous sources. Finally, another important fillip came in October 1881 in Brooklyn, New York, when the Galway native Michael Logan (Ó Lócháin) founded *An Gaodhal*, the first periodical published substantially in Gaelic.

THE GAELIC UNION AND GAELIC LEAGUE

What sparked the revival was a split in the ranks of the SPIL when some active members formed a new group, the Gaelic Union. In 1882 the Union founded what was until 1909 the most important bilingual publication devoted to Irish literature, *Irishleabhar na Gaedhilge* (the *Gaelic Journal*). Edited by a succession of enthusiastic scholars including David Comyn, John Fleming, Father Eugene O'Growney, Eoin MacNéill, Joseph Lloyd, and Tadhg Ó Donnchadha, the *Journal* published original works, manuscript material, folklore, and news about Gaelic and Celtic movements in Ireland and abroad. Significantly, in 1894 it became the property of the most important organization associated with the revival, the Gaelic League.

Eoin MacNéill founded the League in July 1893, eight months after Douglas Hyde's impassioned speech

"The Necessity for De-Anglicising Ireland" had inspired Eoin MacNéill to establish a popular linguistic movement. The organization gained footholds in urban centers such as Dublin, Belfast, and Cork, as well as in towns and villages in the western and southern Gaeltachts, districts that had native Irish-speaking majorities. At its peak between 1906 and 1908 the League included more than 670 Irish branches and several hundred more in émigré communities, and it claimed nearly 50,000 individual members at any given time. Although sympathy for Gaelic became widespread, the ability to speak and write Irish remained the possession of a relative few.

LITERATURE OF THE REVIVAL

The League did, however, play a critical role in encouraging new literature and Gaelic drama. Its publications committee produced the monthly *Gaelic Journal*, the weekly bilingual newspaper, *An Claidheamh Soluis* (The sword of light), and hundreds of pamphlets, books, and one-act plays. Individual branches, meanwhile, published ephemeral journals such as *Loch Léin* in Killarney and *An Craobh Ruadh* (The red branch) in Belfast. Annual competitions, particularly those at the national literary festival, the *Oireachtas* (founded in 1897), elicited folklore collections, historical essays, translations, and original poems, short stories, and plays. Much of the original work lacked merit, but older folk poets (such as Colm Wallace and Robert Weldon) and noteworthy emerging writers enjoyed success in Oireachtas competitions.

Revival writers faced complex issues as they established a modern literature after nearly a century with little innovation. Among the most important questions were: What relationship should they have with Irish writers using English? What use should be made of translations? Should authors subsume their artistic freedom to approach subjects from a specific political viewpoint? How should they overcome the dearth of indigenous models of novels and dramas? And which, if any, existing genres should they emphasize? Most revivalists were students of the language and drew on familiar English literary tropes or deferred to self-proclaimed native authorities. At times, such as when theater patrons rioted over John Millington Synge's dramatization of peasant life in *The Playboy of the Western World* in 1907, Gaelic enthusiasts displayed an overweening provincialism, but revivalist writers tended to be open-minded toward their Anglo-Irish counterparts.

Broadly speaking, two philosophical camps developed. Some, such as Father Patrick Dinneen and Father Peadar Ó Laoghaire, adopted a "nativist" viewpoint—looking almost exclusively to indigenous models and approaching subjects from generally conservative, Catholic, and nationalist perspectives. Others, such as Pádraic Ó Conaire, were open to a more "progressive" outlook—searching for themes and models that might challenge conventional perspectives. Within these categorizations further divisions emerged. Thus Dinneen's advocacy of seventeenth- and eighteenth-century forms resonated with poets like Tadhg Ó Donnchadha ("Tórna") and Osborn Bergin, and Ó Laoghaire infused his prose with the peasant idiom of his youth (the so-called "caint na ndaoine," or speech of the people).

Ó Laoghaire's ubiquitous presence as an essayist, translator, playwright, and novelist virtually ensured that most prose writers copied his style. Publication of his Faustian peasant tale *Séadna* (Words, 1904), the first Gaelic novel, should be viewed in this light as a landmark. Less influential but equally important for its incorporation of gritty realism into the novel was Ó Conaire's *Deoraidheacht* (Exile, 1910). With its urban setting and vivid attention to detail, it stood as a largely solitary achievement until well after independence. It was Patrick Pearse (an admirer of Ó Laoghaire while editor of *An Claidheamh Soluis* and later the leader of the 1916 Easter rebellion) who anticipated the form in which experimental prose proved most successful in short stories, in his *Íosogán* (1905).

After 1922 leaders of the Irish Free State, including MacNéill, then minister for education, fostered the language through sometimes misdirected initiatives. The government imposed compulsory Gaelic instruction in schools, set up the publication office An Gúm, and endowed theatrical enterprises such as the Taibhdhearc na Gaillimhe. Much of what appeared in print or on stage, however, was derivative. Some original novels were published, such as Edward MacLysaght's *Cúrsaí Thomáis* (The story of Tomás, 1927) and Séamas Mac Grianna's *Caisleáin Óir* (Golden castles, 1924), but An Gúm also delayed potentially controversial works, such as Seosamh Mac Grianna's *An Druma Mór* (The big drum, written in the 1930s, but not published until 1972). Meanwhile, Ó Conaire, Liam O'Flaherty, and Máirtín Ó Cadhain, among others, explored the short-story form, and playwrights such as Micheál Mac Liammóir infused the theater with creative energy, albeit drawing heavily upon translations. Perhaps the most lively literature of the 1920s and 1930s appeared in Gaeltacht autobiographies inspired by those revivalists who had sought out "authentic" representatives of the Gaelic tradition. Among the best known were those written or dictated by residents of the Blasket Islands—Muiris Ó Súilleabháin's *Fiche Blian ag Fás* (Twenty Years A-Growing, 1933), Peig Sayers's *Peig* (Peig, 1936), and Tomás Ó Criomhthain's *An tOileánach* (The Islandman, 1929).

Assessing the impact of the Gaelic Revival is a matter of perspective. If the yardstick applied was whether Irish became the universal language of the people in Ireland, then it must be judged a failure. If, however, one also considers the symbolic importance of Gaelic to people in southern Ireland (and to a minority in Northern Ireland) and recognizes as significant the creation of a modern literature with a limited readership, then the revival was a defining period in modern Irish cultural history.

SEE ALSO Antiquarianism; Arts: Modern Irish and Anglo-Irish Literature and the Arts since 1800; Gaelic Revivalism: The Gaelic League; Hyde, Douglas; Language and Literacy: Decline of Irish Language; Literature: Anglo-Irish Literature in the Nineteenth Century; Literature: Gaelic Literature in the Nineteenth Century; **Primary Documents:** From "The Necessity for De-Anglicising Ireland" (25 November 1892); Letter on the Commission on the Gaeltacht (4 March 1925); "The End" (1926); "Pierce's Cave" (1933); "Scattering and Sorrow" (1936)

Bibliography

Caerwyn Williams, J. E., and Patrick K. Ford. *The Irish Literary Tradition.* 1992.

Kiberd, Declan. *Inventing Ireland.* 1995.

McMahon, Timothy G. "The Social Bases of the Gaelic Revival, 1893–1910." Ph.D. diss., University of Wisconsin–Madison, 2001.

O'Leary, Philip. *The Prose Literature of the Gaelic Revival, 1881–1921: Ideology and Innovation.* 1994.

Ó Súilleabháin, Donncha. *Scéal an Oireachtais, 1897–1924.* 1984.

Ó Tuama, Seán. *Repossessions: Selected Essays on the Irish Literary Heritage.* 1995.

Ó Tuama, Seán, ed. *The Gaelic League Idea.* 1972, 1993.

Timothy G. McMahon

~

Gaelic Revivalism

The Gaelic Athletic Association	Marcus de Búrca
The Gaelic League	Timothy G. McMahon

THE GAELIC ATHLETIC ASSOCIATION

The Gaelic Athletic Association (GAA), which was responsible for reviving the ancient Irish field game of hurling and for codifying and popularizing Gaelic football, the modern version of the traditional Irish form of football, was founded in Thurles, Co. Tipperary, on 1 November 1884. The association was the earliest expression of the late-nineteenth-century Irish cultural movement that triggered the political revival that led, in turn, to the Easter Rising of 1916 and the establishment in 1921 of the modern Irish state now known as the Republic of Ireland.

The GAA was the brainchild of Michael Cusack, a Clare schoolteacher who campaigned for ten years beginning in 1874 for the reform of Irish athletics to enable all social classes to participate and for the revival of hurling, which was almost extinct mainly as a result of the famines of the late 1840s. Because Cusack had laid the organizational foundations in provincial Ireland, the new association was an instant success, spreading to most parts of Ireland in its first year. In its early years it concentrated on field and track athletics rather than on hurling or Gaelic football.

Despite its initial success, the GAA in its first fifteen years struggled to stay alive. Internally, it came under attack from two rival nationalist factions, the Irish Parliamentary Party (IPP) and the Fenian Irish Republican Brotherhood (IRB), with both attempting to gain control of it. Externally, it had to fend off a new unionist-dominated body, the Irish Amateur Athletics Association. At a stormy convention in Thurles in November 1887 the IRB gained control of the GAA, and the other delegates set up a rival body. The split was quickly healed through mediation by the GAA's charismatic patron, Archbishop Thomas Croke of Cashel, but Fenian influence on the GAA continued until 1901.

The decline in the GAA's fortunes during the 1890s was due to several factors. Feuding between the IRB faction and IPP supporters continued long after Croke's mediation and led to the resignation of the GAA president, Maurice Davin. The association's support for Charles Stewart Parnell after his involvement in a divorce case caused mass withdrawal of Roman Catholic clergy, hitherto an influential element. Continued domination of key posts by the IRB led to a steady fall in membership, which was aggravated by the GAA's failure to exploit its leading role in 1898 in the 1798 Rebellion centenary celebrations.

At the 1900 convention a group of mostly younger officials ensured the election of Alderman James Nowlan of Kilkenny as GAA president and of Luke O'Toole of Dublin as secretary. Displaced was Frank Dineen of

Limerick, who had served as either president or secretary since 1895, and who with Michael Deering of Cork had controlled the central council until Deering's sudden death before the convention. Nowlan retained the presidency for twenty years, and O'Toole the secretarial post for almost thirty. Unlike Dineen and Deering, neither was an IRB member; both belonged to a younger nationalist generation disillusioned by the Parnell split. Their elections marked a new, more competent GAA, determined to avoid the bitterness of the post-Parnell decade.

When in the early 1900s the Gaelic League's membership exploded, it brought into the GAA a new influx of members, too, and after the foundation in 1907 of Sinn Féin by Arthur Griffith, the GAA benefited from a growth in militant republicanism. Almost 300 of the participants in the Easter Rising of 1916 were GAA members. During the subsequent War of Independence (1919–1921) the association provided the backbone of what became the Irish Republican Army; many GAA officials, such as Michael Collins and Harry Boland, played leading roles in the rival underground government.

Peace returned in 1924 after five years of hostilities, and the GAA became part of the establishment of the new Irish Free State. With the appointment in 1929 of a dynamic new general secretary, Pádraig Ó Caoimh, the association began to prosper for the first time since the 1890s. Ireland's isolationism in World War II was turned to advantage by the GAA, and the 1930s saw record attendances at Gaelic games. Attendances fell steeply on the arrival of Irish television in 1961, but the ending in 1971 of the prohibition on GAA members playing or attending non-Gaelic games reflected a new mood of optimism in the association. Moreover, a radical streamlining of its administration followed a searching self-analysis by a commission, composed partly of nonmembers, which met from 1969 to 1971.

The 1984 celebrations of the GAA's centenary lasted for most of the year, beginning and ending in Ennis, the capital of Cusack's native Clare. The all-Ireland hurling final was switched from Dublin to Thurles, regarded as the cradle of the association. The importance of the GAA in the social life of modern Ireland was emphasized by some of the centenary events, which included a government reception, a history symposium at University College, Cork, and issuance of a set of commemorative postage stamps. The publication in 1980 of a history of the GAA was the first of many local histories.

In the years since 1984 the GAA has faced some major new challenges. Chief among them have been the growth of an urban society where Gaelic games have often been undervalued, the constant threat to GAA rev-

The Gaelic Athletic Association (GAA) proved highly successful in promoting Gaelic football and hurling after it was launched in Thurles in November 1884. Its lusty expansion was part of a general revival of cultural nationalism after 1880. More than a century later, GAA sporting fixtures remain extremely popular, as indicated by the vast crowd that turned out to watch the 1995 All-Ireland Hurling Final at Dublin's Croke Park. © MICHAEL ST. MAUR SHEIL/ CORBIS. REPRODUCED BY PERMISSION.

enue caused by soccer football beamed into Irish homes by television, and the implementation of a costly program to provide comfortable accommodation for family and corporate groups in the major stadia. In addition, the spread of commercial sponsorship to a basically amateur body built on voluntary effort has not been easy. Since the commercialization of the two football codes in Britain, it is difficult to see how erosion of the GAA's amateur codes can be postponed indefinitely.

Predictably, in a country where almost every activity has political undertones, the association has had its share of criticism from the start. The overlapping of politics and sport has concerned many who point to the GAA's inability to alleviate tension in Northern Ireland, where to be involved in the GAA is to be identified as a nationalist. Nevertheless, the association's contribution to modern Irish society has been impressive. In the vanguard of the cultural renaissance in the late 1800s it brought color and sporting rivalry to a drab countryside traumatized by the Great Famine. In the early 1900s the GAA played a prominent part in the shift from cultural to political nationalism. In the political and military struggle from 1919 to 1921 it supplied many of the foot soldiers of the revolution as well as some of its finest officers. In a country always in danger of being swamped by foreign sporting cultures, the GAA has held its own.

To appreciate what the GAA has achieved, one needs only to contemplate what would have happened in its absence. Field and track athletics would be run from London, and Irish athletes would compete in the Olympics in the colors of other nations. The 2,000-year-old game of hurling would almost certainly be extinct. In place of Gaelic football, now Ireland's most popular outdoor game, soccer football would reign supreme. Thanks largely to the GAA, the mass exodus from the Irish countryside, now well-nigh unstoppable, was at least slowed for the greater part of a century.

SEE ALSO Cusack, Michael; GAA "Ban"; Gaelic Revivalism: The Gaelic League; Literacy and Popular Culture; Politics: 1800 to 1921—Challenges to the Union; Sport and Leisure

Bibliography

de Búrca, Marcus. *The GAA: A History.* 1999.

Irish Independent GAA Golden Jubilee Supplement. 1934.

Irish Press GAA Golden Jubilee Supplement. 1934.

Mandle, W. F. "The IRB and the Beginnings of the Gaelic Athletic Association." *Irish Historical Studies* 20, no. 80 (1977): 418–438.

Mandle, W. F. "Sport as Politics: The Gaelic Athletic Association, 1884–1916." In *Sport in History: The Making of Modern Sporting History*, edited by Richard Cashman and Michael McKernan. 1979.

Mandle, W. F. *The Gaelic Athletic Association and Irish Nationalist Politics, 1884–1924.* 1987.

O'Sullivan, T. F. *The Story of the GAA.* 1916.

Tierney, Mark. *Croke of Cashel.* 1976.

Marcus de Búrca

THE GAELIC LEAGUE

Founded in July 1893 by Eoin MacNéill to preserve and extend the use of Irish as a spoken language, the Gaelic League was the most important organization associated with the Gaelic revival of the late nineteenth and early twentieth centuries. Although the League failed to convince a significant percentage of the population to use Irish as their everyday medium of social intercourse, it raised public consciousness of Gaelic culture, engaged in campaigns to include Irish in school curricula, inspired a modern literature in Gaelic, and energized the nationalist movement in the years before 1916.

MacNéill's emphasis on spoken Irish appealed to many younger members of existing antiquarian societies, who felt that organizations such as the Society for the Preservation of the Irish Language and the Gaelic Union lacked the dynamism necessary to safeguard Gaelic as a living language. Among these earliest adherents were the poet and folklorist Douglas Hyde, who had made a similar plea for spoken Irish during the previous year in a seminal speech to the National Literary Society in Dublin ("The Necessity for De-Anglicising Ireland"), and Father Eugene O'Growney, the professor of Irish at Saint Patrick's College, Maynooth. From 1893 until 1915, Hyde would serve as president and leading spokesman for the League, while O'Growney's five-part series of primers, the *Simple Lessons in Irish*, became important teaching tools in Gaelic League classes.

GROWTH AND ACTIVITIES

From its Dublin base the organization expanded quickly to other large cities and towns. By 1898, however, it could claim just eighty branches, and only a few of these were in the western and southern communities where Irish remained the primary language of home life. Thereafter, several factors combined to encourage more rapid expansion at the turn of the century, including growing anti-English sentiment fueled by the centenary celebrations of the 1798 rebellion and the outbreak of the Boer War; the hiring of paid *timirí* (organizers) to promote the language cause, and the advocacy of journalists such as Alice Milligan, Arthur Griffith, and D.P. Moran.

By 1906 enthusiasts had established more than 600 *craobhacha* (branches) within Ireland and several hundred more abroad. The League maintained at least one branch in every Irish county, but the highest concentrations of domestic branches were in counties with significant native-speaking populations and in the larger cities and towns, such as Dublin, Belfast, Cork, and Galway. Ironically, in those counties with high concentrations of native-speakers the League relied primarily on English-speaking town elites to lead their cause, and the organization only sporadically established lasting outposts in which native-speakers comprised the bulk of members. Similarly, outside of the Gaelic-speaking districts the vast majority of people joining *craobhacha* were English-speakers with an interest in learning some Irish and otherwise participating in what they called the "Irish-Ireland" movement.

Precise estimates of total membership are difficult to calculate, but based on average branch size, it is likely that the highest annual total was about 47,000. Because most members participated actively for only a year or two before being replaced by new recruits, it is nevertheless likely that the overall membership was significantly higher—perhaps more than a quarter of a million—in the years prior to 1910.

Within their branches members engaged in a wide variety of social and intellectual activities. Typically, they held general meetings on Sunday afternoons, at which they discussed historical or contemporary topics, and on weekday evenings interested members also attended classes in language instruction, history, dancing, or singing. Leaguers engaged in numerous public campaigns to press educational authorities to incorporate Irish classes in the national and intermediate schools; and between 1908 and 1910 they coordinated a successful island-wide effort to force the senate of the new National University of Ireland to adopt a strict standard requiring all matriculating students to have some familiarity with the Gaelic language. At other times members also promoted causes that were apparently unrelated to their linguistic mission, including temperance crusades and efforts to "buy Irish" products crafted by native hands or in factories at home.

Craobhacha regularly sponsored an array of amateur entertainment, such as concerts, *ceilidhs*, and plays, in which members took leading parts. The largest such gatherings were regional *feiseanna* (festivals) and the *Oireachtas* (national literary festival), which included competitions in storytelling, oratory, poetry, prose, singing, and dancing. Festival prizewinners often attained local or even national celebrity as instructors and entertainers at branch functions. Some Irish-Ireland purists such as Moran lamented that many of these events mirrored the entertainment provided by music halls and popular theater, but they provided townspeople with amusement during an era when town life was otherwise quite drab.

The League, moreover, was instrumental in encouraging the publication of literature, news, folklore, and drama in the Irish language. At the time of Mac-Néill's overture in 1893, O'Growney was editor of the most important Gaelic-related publication in Ireland, *Irisleabhar na Gaedhilge* (*Gaelic Journal*), which he put at the League's disposal. Until it ceased publication in 1910, this monthly offered Gaelic poets and authors an outlet for their productions. Beginning in 1898 with

Fáinne an Lae (Dawn of day) and continuing with *An Claidheamh Soluis* (The sword of light), the League published weekly bilingual newspapers, which provided another platform to propagate the language cause. In addition, the League's publications committee produced numerous original works, albeit of mixed quality, ranging from school histories and conversation guides to essay collections and novels. Thus many writers associated with the revival of Gaelic literature in the twentieth century, such as Father Peadar Ó Laoghaire and Pádraic Ó Conaire, published their early works under League auspices or received their first public recognition at League festivals.

ALL CREEDS AND ALL CLASSES?

Early League leaders hoped that their cultural program would bring together the fractious elements of Irish society, and they determined to keep their organization nonpolitical and nonsectarian in order to overcome the political and social divisions of the Home Rule era. But this aim seems in retrospect to have been merely a pious hope. Scholars believed traditionally that the organization consisted initially of upper-middle-class romantics, including both Catholics and Protestants, but that as the League grew, its increasingly politicized lower-middle-class Catholic membership discouraged Protestants from joining League ranks. Some have even concluded that the organization should be remembered primarily as a "school" for the nationalist revolutionaries who engaged in the Irish war of independence. Indeed, many revolutionaries were active in the League, including Patrick Pearse, who served as editor of *An Claidheamh Soluis* from 1903 until 1909. Also, members of the Irish Republican Brotherhood did engineer a takeover of the League in 1915, prompting Hyde's resignation from the presidency and ensuring that the League would be an important component of republican efforts in the push for independence after 1916.

Recent research, however, has qualified this portrayal. For example, McMahon has determined that the membership of the League was more broadly based across class lines from its foundation than had previously been thought, and a committed minority of Protestants continued to participate in Gaelic activities until the mid-1910s. Furthermore, although nearly all members professed loyalty to some form of political nationalism, and although ardent revolutionaries were inspired by their association with the language cause, one should not overstate the politicization of the organization until after the takeover by the Irish Republican Brotherhood (IRB) in 1915. Prior to that point efforts by politicians to use Gaelic platforms were usually rebuffed by League leaders and regular members alike.

When the IRB did capture the organization, the League had long been in decline, though it experienced a brief resurgence during and immediately after the war of independence. By the mid-1920s, however, the League had lost much of its earlier energy, and membership again tapered off as officials in Northern Ireland were intent on stamping that new state with a British identity, and as their counterparts in the Free State believed that the language should receive official sanction.

Although the League has kept a watchful eye on state policy toward the language since then and has continually encouraged Gaelic literature and arts through the annual *Oireachtas*, its major achievement belonged to the preindependence decades, when it secured a place of symbolic importance for the Gaelic language and Gaelic culture in modern Ireland.

SEE ALSO Blasket Island Writers; Gaelic Revival; Gaelic Revivalism: The Gaelic Athletic Association; Hyde, Douglas; Language and Literacy: Decline of Irish Language; Language and Literacy: Irish Language since 1922; Literacy and Popular Culture; Pearse, Patrick; Politics: 1800 to 1921—Challenges to the Union; Raiftearaí (Raftery), Antaine; **Primary Documents:** From "The Necessity for De-Anglicising Ireland" (25 November 1892); Letter on the Commission on the Gaeltacht (4 March 1925)

Bibliography

Garvin, Tom. *Nationalist Revolutionaries in Ireland, 1858–1928.* 1987.

Mac Aonghusa, Proinsias. *Ar Son na Gaeilge: Conradh na Gaeilge, 1893–1993, Stair Sheanchais.* 1993.

McMahon, Timothy G. "The Social Bases of the Gaelic Revival, 1893–1910." Ph.D. diss., University of Wisconsin–Madison, 2001.

Ó Tuama, Seán. *The Gaelic League Idea.* 1972, 1993.

Timothy G. McMahon

Gaelic Society in the Late Middle Ages

In the last hundred years before Henry VIII asserted Tudor control (c. 1430–1534), Ireland was English only from Dublin to Dundalk—thirty miles south to north, twenty east to west—and even there, in "the Pale," Gaelic speech and dress were conspicuous. "Beyond the Pale" were the increasingly gaelicized magnates: FitzGerald (Kildare, Cork, north Kerry); Butler (Kilkenny, Tipperary); Burke, also known as Mac Liaim Íochtar (Mayo); and Mac Liaim Uachtar (Galway). Various families of O'Neill held central Ulster, O'Donnell western Ulster, and with MacCarthy (southwest Cork, south Kerry) and O'Brien (Clare, west Limerick), they were the greatest of the Gaelic magnates.

Norman impact from earlier centuries survived fitfully, the north and west having remained heavily forested and most vigorously Gaelic, the south and southeast mixing and varying between English and Irish land, inheritance, and legal systems. Control of church appointments was divided similarly but was more polarized. In Ulster the English controlled the east coast dioceses and lands, whereas the rest was firmly in Gaelic hands. The O'Neills largely determined whether revenue would be collected, episcopal visitation would take place, and ecclesiastical punishment would be enforced west of the river Bann. Parish development dated only from the twelfth century, and Gaelic Ireland left the parish coterminous with family lands. Family control of dioceses and religious houses had dwindled from such reform efforts as followed the Norman invasions, but re-gaelicization meant its revival. English government rule sought to prevent "anyone of Irish blood, name, or nation" from holding major ecclesiastical office, but when William O'Reilly was chosen as minister-provincial of the Franciscan friars in 1445—the first native appointment to the two-hundred-year-old office—Henry VI (1421–1471) was persuaded to veto him, despite O'Reilly's Oxford doctorate in theology. Pope Eugenius IV (1383–1447) then overruled the king, and O'Reilly proved to be a much-needed reformer. In the church hierarchy Gaelic dynasties increased, as did widespread indifference to clerical celibacy. The bishopric and archdeaconate of Clogher went from father to son time and again in the fifteenth century, shared between the intermarrying families of MacCawell (or Campbell) and Maguire. As to monasteries, the great Gaelic families widely treated them as personal property. Lay hereditary control of bishoprics and parishes continued as in pre-Norman times. The papal anger at this situation in the twelfth century was past; Gaelic abuses were in line with the spirit of the Borgia and comparable popes of the late fifteenth century. Yet some piety remained, as in the delicate fervent poetry of Pilib Bocht Ó hUiginn.

Gaelic landholding was nonfeudal. The overlord held "mensal" land—needed to maintain food, heat,

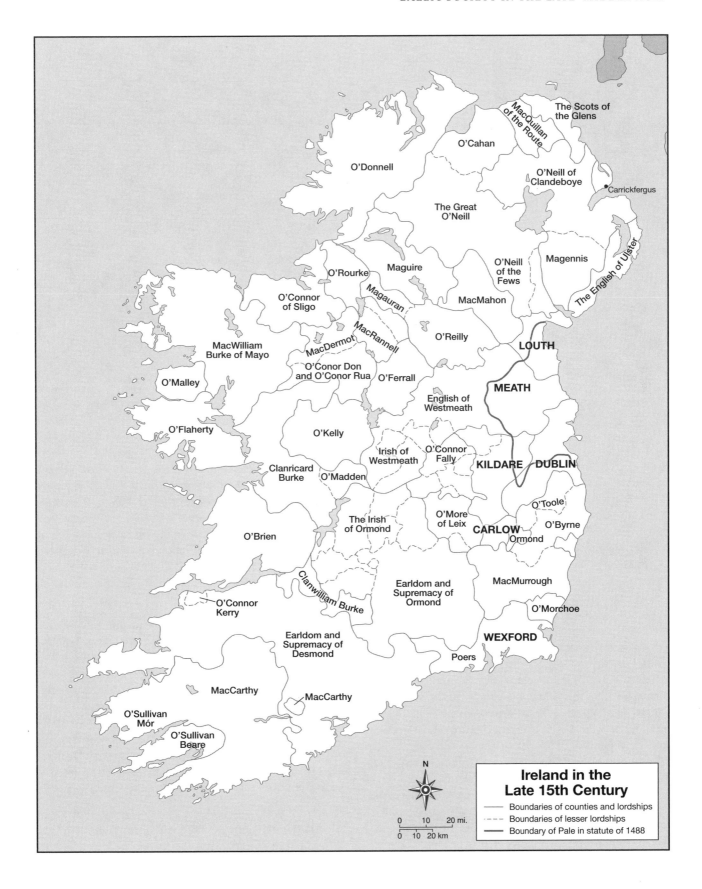

The Scots of the Glens

MacQuillan of the Route

O'Cahan

O'Donnell

O'Neill of Clandeboye

Carrickfergus

The Great O'Neill

O'Neill of the Fews

Magennis

The English of Ulster

Maguire

O'Rourke

Magauran

MacMahon

O'Connor of Sligo

MacDermot

MacRannell

O'Reilly

MacWilliam Burke of Mayo

O'Conor Don and O'Conor Rua

O'Ferrall

LOUTH

O'Malley

MEATH

O'Flaherty

O'Kelly

English of Westmeath

Irish of Westmeath

O'Connor Fally

KILDARE

DUBLIN

Clanricard Burke

O'Madden

O'Toole

O'Byrne

O'Brien

The Irish of Ormond

O'More of Leix

CARLOW

Ormond

Clanwilliam Burke

Earldom and Supremacy of Ormond

MacMurrough

O'Connor Kerry

O'Morchoe

Earldom and Supremacy of Desmond

Poers

WEXFORD

MacCarthy

MacCarthy

O'Sullivan Mór

O'Sullivan Beare

N

Ireland in the Late 15th Century

0   10   20 mi.

0   10   20 km

——— Boundaries of counties and lordships

- - - - Boundaries of lesser lordships

——— Boundary of Pale in statute of 1488

A sixteenth-century Irish chieftain's feast, depicting the MacSweenys of Donegal accompanied by their bard, harpist, and other entertainers. Derricke may have misinterpreted some of the activities at the feast, which he describes as "hoggishe." FROM JOHN DERRICKE'S THE IMAGE OF IRELANDE (1581).

style, and hunting–grounds for himself, servants, and dependants—while he lived. Another such area went to the ruling family from whom he was elected in the system called tanistry: the *tánaiste*, or heir apparent, would be chosen from the family, but the one elected was not by any means necessarily the eldest or even any son, legitimate or otherwise, of the existing king or chieftain. (The modern parliamentary term for deputy prime minister is *tánaiste*, which has definitely lost its connotation of right of succession.) The remaining land went to other branches of the family, excluded, where possible, from the succession. By the fifteenth century the results varied. In Munster, for example, MacCarthy of Muskerry held half of the available land himself, as mensal, while the ruling O'Neills of Ulster were challenged by their cousins descended from Aodh Buidhe (Yellow or Fair-Haired Hugh), who kept their lands almost independent of the rulers (the Clandeboy O'Neills). Neighboring chieftains and even Dublin viceroys entered into such disputes between kinsmen to win over what protégés and weaken what aspirants they could. The tenantry on the mensal land was of its nature short-term; a new chieftain might want new tenants. Freeholders beyond the limits of mensal land paid cows or a penny per acre to the overlord. Cow ownership was the symbol of wealth. Chargeable lands were about half the total area, and while rentable, they might also be used to billet mercenaries during the fighting season. The mass of the population had little land, constantly subdivided under a principle of gavelkind, providing for all sons. Hopes for economic success depended on livestock ownership. A churl occupying insignificant land and owning no cattle had poorer economic prospects than a landless tenant from a landless family under the immediate protection of a landowning chieftain as his follower.

The norm of secular marriage meant a succession of spouses with easy divorce. The preference was for marriage to kinsfolk, often in defiance of church law forbidding marriage to third or closer cousins, or to relations acquired by a former marriage. Clerics were frequent products or partners in such cases, to the obvious detriment of church reform. The fosterage system, by which children were reared in another household, made fathers less hostile to rape or intercourse with their little-known adult daughters. Fosterage often resulted in closer political alliances outside family limits.

Local poets and historians were deeply attached to chieftains, with fine poetic results, sometimes perhaps prompted by homosexual sentiment (as James Carney and others suggest for Eochaidh Ó hEódhasa's ode to the Maguire [i.e., Hugh Maguire]). Harpers and musicians were court pets, readily adopted by Normans in the process of gaelicization. Poets were greatly feared for their cursing powers, usually mistranslated as "satires" and doubtless of social consequence in their ridicule, but many instances were given of curses causing death within a short time. The brevity of normal life spans no doubt exacerbated the number of coincidences, but some are likely to have had serious psychological and even physical results.

SEE ALSO Bruce Invasion; Gaelic Recovery; Magnates, Gaelic and Anglo-Irish; Richard II in Ireland; **Primary Documents:** The Statutes of Kilkenny (1366)

Bibliography

Carney, James. *The Irish Bardic Poet.* 1967.

Cosgrove, Art, ed. *Medieval Ireland, 1169–1534.* Vol. 2 of *A New History of Ireland.* 1993.

Duffy, Sean. *Ireland in the Middle Ages.* 1997.

Edwards, R. Dudley. *A New History of Ireland.* 1972.

Frame, Robin. *Colonial Ireland, 1169–1369.* 1981.

Lyndon, James. *The Making of Ireland.* 1998.

Nicholls, Kenneth. *Gaelic and Gaelicised Ireland in the Middle Ages.* 1972.

Watt, John A. *The Church in Medieval Ireland.* 1972.

Owen Dudley Edwards

~

Georgian Dublin, Art and Architecture of

The term Georgian Dublin is used to describe the physical attributes of the capital city during the reign of the four Georges (1714–1830), a golden age in the architectural history of Dublin. The city's population more than tripled in these years, and the urban area expanded even more dramatically, a process linked to the beginnings of outer suburbs and the social decline of the medieval core. But Georgian Dublin's claim to fame rests on the quality and quantity of urban building, both public and private, that occurred in this period. Thanks to the city's later stagnation, most of the building stock survived intact, if dilapidated, into the twentieth century. However, a very large part of it had been swept away by the 1970s, when its historical significance began to be appreciated.

The architectural distinction of Georgian Dublin rests on four elements: a small number of architectural-ly sophisticated public buildings, a rather larger number of private palazzi, a series of speculative terrace (or row-house) developments of high architectural quality, and the strategic decisions of a precocious planning agency.

The first of the great public buildings was the new Parliament house in College Green, erected circa 1730. It was designed by a young Irish architect who had trained in London, Edward Lovett Pearce (d. 1733). The other keynote public buildings—the Lying-in Hospital, the Royal Exchange, the Public Theatre and Provost's House in Trinity College, the new Custom House, the new Four Courts, the House of Lords, and the King's Inns—were all designed by English- or German-born architects. But the rules of architecture were presumed to be universal, informed by the wisdom of "the ancients." Designing a major building did not require local knowledge, and Sir William Chambers, perhaps the greatest architect associated with eighteenth-century Dublin, never visited the city. His protégé James Gandon (d. 1823), however, came and stayed. Gandon was responsible, among much else, for the riverside icons, the Custom House (completed c. 1790), and the Four Courts (completed c. 1800).

The gentleman-architects mixed public and private commissions. Richard Castle (d. 1751), designer of the Lying-in Hospital, is more famous for Leinster House, the largest of the several dozen aristocratic houses that were constructed in the eastern half of the city. Their cut-stone and sometimes austere exteriors belied the sumptuous plasterwork and marble-work of the interiors; the staircases and public rooms in these houses were designed for entertainment and conspicuous display. Fitting and furnishing these houses required the services of dozens of crafts and sustained an army of craftsmen.

The era of constructing massive detached houses was drawing to a close by the 1770s, by which time speculative brick-faced terrace-building for an upper-class and professional clientele had become far more important. Most, but not all, of the speculative building occurred on green-field sites to the northeast and southeast of the commercial city, on the Gardiner and Fitzwilliam estates. The former property had been assembled by Luke Gardiner I (d. 1755), a highly successful functionary and banker who, despite a low public profile, became one of the most powerful figures in Irish politics. Two northside aristocratic streets were his creation, Henrietta and Sackville (later O'Connell), and his method of urban development—tight proprietorial control over the appearance and social character of the principal houses—set the precedent for activity elsewhere, most obviously on the Fitzwilliam (later Pembroke) estate, which began with the laying out of Merrion Square in

Designed by architect James Gandon, the Custom House, Dublin, late eighteenth century, is an example of neoclassical Irish architecture. © ROYALTY-FREE/CORBIS. REPRODUCED BY PERMISSION.

the 1760s and culminated in the boulevards of Ballsbridge half a century later.

The Wide Streets Commission was established as a parliamentary committee in 1757 and remained in existence for almost a century. Its initial remit was to gouge out a new street north of Dublin Castle; it evolved to become a citywide planning agency. Its principal achievements were the widening and reconstruction of Dame and Sackville Streets, the development of new streets to the south of the new Carlisle (later O'Connell) Bridge, and the completion of quays along the Liffey. Its moment of greatest activity—the 1780s and early 1790s—coincided with the preeminence of John Beresford (d. 1805), the driving force behind the Custom House project and much else. As important to the creation of Georgian Dublin as the marquis of Pombal had been in the reconstruction of eighteenth-century Lisbon, Beresford combined cultural enlightenment with political reaction. He was the epitome of the landed gentry whose burgeoning rent rolls and parliamentary ambitions had funded the architectural splendor of the city.

The gentry's fashion for wintering in Dublin faded away after the union, and the demand for high-quality housing changed markedly. However, the rise of the professions and the expansion of the middle classes insured that the classical idioms, the terrace houses and brick facades, the fanlights and the marble chimneypieces, were replicated on a more modest scale in the nineteenth-century city.

SEE ALSO Arts: Early Modern Literature and the Arts from 1500 to 1800; Country Houses and the Arts

Bibliography

Craig, M. J. *Dublin, 1660–1860: A Social and Architectural History.* 1952. New edition, 1992.

Dickson, David, ed. *The Gorgeous Mask: Dublin, 1700–1860.* 1987.

McParland, Edward. *James Gandon: Vitruvius Hibernicus.* 1985.

McParland, Edward. *Public Architecture in Ireland, 1680–1760.* 2001.

O'Brien, Jennifer, and Desmond Guinness. *Dublin: A Grand Tour.* 1994.

David Dickson

~

Gonne, Maud

Maud Gonne (1866–1953), lifelong nationalist activist, was born in England. Her father was an army officer and her mother died when she was five. The family then moved to Ireland, a country that Gonne adopted as her own. Educated privately at home, Gonne was given an unusual amount of freedom at an early age. In 1887 she went to France, where she published *L'Irlande Libre* (Free Ireland) and took part in the extreme nationalist Boulangist movement along with her lover, Lucien Millevoye, with whom she had two children, Georges (1890–1891) and Iseult (1894–1954). Back in Ireland in the 1890s, Gonne took part in the ongoing land campaign, focusing media attention on hunger and poverty in Donegal. In 1900 she founded Inghínidhe na hÉireann (Daughters of Ireland), a nationalist organization that concentrated on the teaching of the Irish language, support for Irish manufactures, and antirecruitment activities. In 1903 she married John MacBride, who had fought with the Boers against the British. Their only child, Seán, was born in 1904, and a year later, they were acrimoniously divorced. Thereafter, Gonne divided her time between her house in Normandy, where Seán was mainly reared, and Ireland, where she continued to campaign politically, presiding over the foundation of Inghinidhe na hEireann's newspaper, *Bean na hÉireann* (Woman of Ireland) in 1908. She was closely associated with James Connolly and Arthur Griffith. The outbreak of the First World War found Gonne working for the Red Cross in France. The execution of John MacBride after the 1916 Rising elevated her nationalist status as a 1916 widow and enabled her to return to Ireland with Seán. In 1918 she spent time in Holloway gaol with Constance Markievicz and Kathleen Clarke; she was also imprisoned during the Civil War of 1922 to 1923, in which she took the republican (antitreaty) side. Gonne was a lifelong republican and a tireless campaigner for prisoners' rights. Her autobiography, provocatively entitled *A Servant of the Queen*, was published in London in 1937. Many people know of Gonne only as the inspiration for some of W. B. Yeats's finest love poems, but though she was fond of "poor Willie," as she called him, she played a much greater part in his life than he did in hers.

SEE ALSO Arts: Modern Irish and Anglo-Irish Literature and the Arts since 1800; Literary Renaissance (Celtic Revival); Sinn Féin Movement and Party to 1922; Struggle for Independence from 1916 to 1921; Women in Nationalist and Unionist Movements in the Early Twentieth Century; Yeats, W. B.

Bibliography

Gonne, Maud. *A Servant of the Queen.* 1937.

Ward, Margaret. *Maud Gonne: Ireland's Joan of Arc.* 1990.

Caitriona Clear

~

Government from 1690 to 1800

Throughout the long eighteenth century (1690–1800) Ireland was governed by an executive in Dublin Castle answerable to the king's government in London and a legislature answerable to the Irish Protestant landed class, which came to be known as "the Ascendancy." This division of power was reflected in the judicial system, whose judges served at the Crown's pleasure but whose grand juries (responsible also for important aspects of local governance) were composed of leading members of the Ascendancy in each county. The government enjoyed military support from a garrison composed of British regiments paid for from Irish revenue and spiritual support from an established church, many of whose bishops were Englishmen.

The relationship between the executive and the legislature as marked by three distinct phases during this period. The first (1690–1769) followed the victory of King William III at the Battle of the Boyne and the reemergence of a more assertive Protestant nationalism.

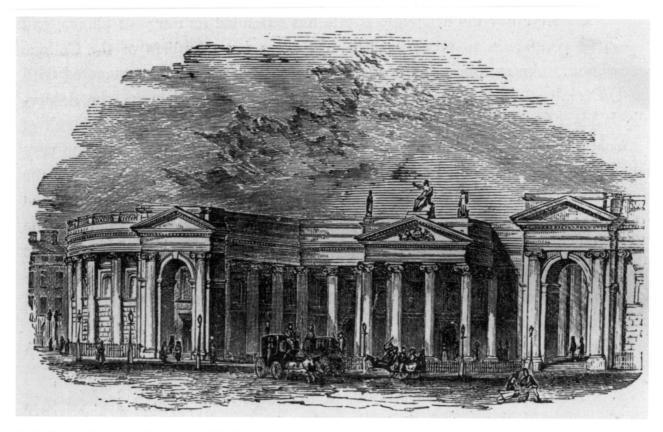

The Parliament House on College Green, Dublin, designed by Sir Edward Lovett Pearce in 1728 and completed in 1739. After the Act of Union the building was purchased by the Bank of Ireland. FROM MR. AND MRS. SAMUEL CARTER HALL, IRELAND: ITS SCENERY, CHARACTER, ETC. (1841–1843).

The executive consisted of a lord lieutenant (or "viceroy") and his staff (including a chief secretary) based at Dublin Castle, and the legislature consisted of the two houses of parliament—the House of Commons and House of Lords. The Irish parliament met regularly at roughly two-year intervals, having not met previously since the 1660s. The legislature, however, was severely constrained by the terms of Poynings' Law (1494), which allowed the king and his ministers to amend or reject bills proposed from Ireland. The Declaratory Act of 1720 further weakened the position of Parliament. This act asserted the right of the British parliament to pass legislation binding on Ireland, and it provided the terms of reference for political debate in the country for the next sixty years. The executive in this period was notoriously weak, as the lord lieutenant did not reside in the country. Instead he only visited for the parliamentary session, and thus control of patronage and much of the power devolved to others. These power brokers came to be known as the "undertakers," men who undertook to manage the business of government in return for being consulted about policy; they also had a large share of the government's patronage at their disposal. Thus, for long periods the success of an adminis-

tration often depended on the whims of the most powerful political families, and the ability of the Crown to secure results depended on its ability to cajole as much as to negotiate.

This all changed in 1767 with the appointment of Lord Townshend as viceroy. Townshend decided to reside permanently in Ireland, creating a precedent that all future lord lieutenants followed. His decision resulted in the overthrow of the undertaker system, and control over patronage and policy returned to the executive. Helped by an efficient chief secretary, George Macartney, Townshend established a new system of management which involved supporting a "Castle party" in Parliament that could be relied upon to be loyal to the Crown. The cost, however, was high: Townshend was forced to resort to a system of parliamentary corruption and was eventually recalled in 1772. Dublin Castle became increasingly important in this second phase in the government of Ireland (1767–1782), and the holder of the office of chief secretary, the key administrative assistant to the viceroy who controlled most of the business, was central to its success.

Demands for a change in the constitutional relationship between Great Britain and Ireland grew increasingly loud in the 1770s. A new spirit of patriot nationalism emerged, with its advocates unhappy about the subservient position of the Irish parliament. These demands reached their peak in 1782 with the granting of legislative independence, which was conceded reluctantly by the British government after it was forced through in the Irish parliament. The Declaratory Act was repealed, but there was no substantive change in the running of the government. The key political figure in the country remained the lord lieutenant, who dealt directly with the British cabinet on all questions of policy. Irish acts could still be vetoed by the English privy council, but this only occurred four times in the period from 1782 to 1800. The Catholic relief acts of the period (1778, 1782, and 1793) were all introduced at the instigation of the British cabinet and passed in Ireland despite much unwillingness in Parliament.

The ambiguous nature of the government of Ireland in this third phase (1782–1800) led to fears in London that Ireland would break away like the American colonies. This prompted the British prime minister William Pitt in 1784 to put forward his commercial propositions to link the countries economically so that they would be to all intents and purposes united. However, this was rejected by the Irish House of Commons, which viewed the proposals as an attack on their recently won independence. The Regency Crisis (1788–1789) only exacerbated these tensions. At a time of major constitutional turmoil created by the madness of the king, it seemed that the Irish parliament could not be relied upon to remain loyal. The French Revolution increased these fears and prompted Pitt and his ministers to consider introducing a legislative union with a view to ruling Ireland directly from London. War with France in 1793 made any attempts to alter the government of Ireland unpalatable, but the increasing political radicalism of the 1790s made change inevitable. The 1798 rebellion forced the British government to act. A new lord lieutenant, Charles Cornwallis, was sent to Ireland to quell the rebellion and introduce a legislative union. This was rejected in the Irish House of Commons in 1799, but every resource of the Crown was applied—including the use of bribery—and the union passed in 1800. It came into effect on 1 January 1801, creating the United Kingdom of Great Britain and Ireland. The Irish parliament was abolished, and 100 Irish MPs took their seats at Westminster as the government of Ireland entered a radically different phase at the start of the nineteenth century.

SEE ALSO Act of Union; Church of Ireland: Since 1690; Eighteenth-Century Politics: 1690 to 1714—Revolution Settlement; Eighteenth-Century Politics: 1714 to 1778—Interest Politics; Eighteenth-Century Politics: 1778 to 1795—Parliamentary and Popular Politics; Eighteenth-Century Politics: 1795 to 1800—Repression, Rebellion, and Union; Grattan, Henry; Military Forces from 1690 to 1800; Penal Laws; Politics: 1690 to 1800—A Protestant Kingdom; Protestant Ascendancy: 1690 to 1800; Trade and Trade Policy from 1691 to 1800; **Primary Documents:** Yelverton's Act (1782)

Bibliography

Dickson, David. *New foundations: Ireland, 1660–1800.* 2d edition, 2002.

Johnston, E. M. *Great Britain and Ireland, 1760–1800.* 1963.

Moody, T. W., and W. E. Vaughan, eds. *A New History of Ireland.* Vol. 4, *Eighteenth-Century Ireland, 1691–1800.* 1986.

P. M. Geoghegan

Graces, The

The Graces comprised fifty-one concessions promised by Charles I on 14 May 1628 after protracted negotiations, primarily with representatives of the Old English (Catholic) community. In the bitter disputes that followed, however, the term tended to be used as a convenient way of referring to the substance of the two articles that dealt with the central question of land titles. The Old English, who felt threatened and alienated by official policies of land confiscation and religious discrimination in the previous reign, had for some time looked for assurances that their origins and proven loyalty entitled them to be treated on the same footing as their fellow English colonists rather than in the same way as their Irish fellow Catholics. They were also critical of the failure of the post-conquest administration to bring Irish administrative and judicial procedures into conformity with those of England and to guarantee due legal process.

Their opportunity to take positive action came some months after Charles's accession in March 1625, when the English government began preparations to wage war on Spain and confronted the problem of defending Ireland against counterattack. An offer by the Old English to raise forces to defend Ireland at their own expense was brokered by the courtier Sir John Bath of

Drumcondra, who argued forcefully that a demonstration of official goodwill was essential to the retention of Old English allegiance. The offer was rejected on the advice of the Dublin administration, which was reluctant to "put arms into their hands of whose hearts we rest not well assured" (Clarke 1968, p. 8). Fresh negotiations were aimed at securing Old English support for an enlarged standing army financed by voluntary taxation in return for concessions; they resulted in a royal offer to suspend the collection of recusancy fines and to do away with religious requirements for inheritance, appointment to public office, and legal practice. These proposals were presented to a representative assembly in Dublin in April 1627. They met with opposition from the Protestant episcopacy, who declared that to offer to suspend the collection of fines for nonattendance at divine service (recusancy) was "to set religion to sale" (Clarke 1968, p. 13). Less predictably, the offers were received coldly by the Old English, for whom the change of emphasis, from a policy founded upon trust to one redolent of distrust, confirmed their original suspicions that the government doubted their loyalty and inclined them in turn to distrust the sincerity of the king's overtures. They reiterated their willingness to defend Ireland themselves.

The negotiations were transferred back to England, where eleven provincial representatives, eight Old English and three New English, concluded an agreement in May 1628. The demands made in this final phase reflected the experience of the previous three years of negotiations. The Old English agents no longer sought to persuade the administration to trust them, but rather to guard against the most likely consequence of its evident distrust, which was that the Crown would exploit the widespread deficiencies in titles to Irish land to expropriate them. Their chief demands, therefore, were for an act of limitation of royal title, by which the Crown would renounce all claims older than sixty years, and a supplementary act to secure titles in Connacht and Clare, where sixty years would not provide sufficient protection. The New English agents capitalized upon Protestant resistance to the original proposals to secure the withdrawal of Charles's offers to suspend recusancy fines and to allow Catholics to qualify for governmental office by taking an oath of secular allegiance rather than the statutory oath of supremacy, which involved recognizing the king as supreme governor of the church and renouncing all foreign jurisdictions. They also took the opportunity to secure the indemnification of planters from the consequences of their widespread failure to introduce the stipulated number of settlers, make adequate arrangements for defense, and observe the prohibition against taking Irish tenants.

The fifty-one articles of the final agreement included many beneficial reforms of administrative practice and legal process that went well beyond what the king had offered previously, but it was Articles 24 and 25, which contained new royal pledges to guarantee the existing distribution of land ownership by statute, that were of outstanding value to the Old English. The agreed price was a national contribution of 160,000 Irish pounds toward the support of an army of 5,000 men, to be paid over three years. Fatally, responding to the impatience of an administration that was now at war with both France and Spain, the representatives agreed that the money could be collected before the meeting of the Irish parliament which was to enact the promised bills. That Parliament was summoned so hastily that the mandatory procedures were not followed and the writs had to be recalled. This accidental delay proved decisive because time revealed that the government's position was stronger than it seemed. The contribution continued to be paid. This was paid, partly because the alternative was the billeting of the enlarged army in private houses, but mostly because most of the other Graces did not require legislation and their benefits were significant. As the international situation improved and the danger of invasion receded, the army was reduced, the bargaining power of the Old English declined, and the administration was able to renege on the king's promises.

THE DENIAL OF THE GRACES

When Viscount Wentworth came to Ireland as lord deputy in 1633 his objective was to maximize royal revenues, his intention was to convene a parliament and his difficulty was the outstanding Graces. If these were enacted, the most promising source of enhanced income, the king's title to Irish land, could not be realized. Wentworth resolved the problem without scruple. He assured the Old English that the king's promises would be honored, convened Parliament, secured assent to the revenue measures he needed, and, in November 1634, abruptly announced that "their two darling articles" would not be enacted. In the following years the consequences rapidly unfolded. Arrangements to plant Connacht and Clare were forced through, with no distinction made between Old English and native Irish proprietors. Defective titles were exploited to revise the conditions upon which land was held. Moreover, legal challenges to borough charters changed the future balance of parliamentary representation decisively to Protestant advantage. Within very few years, in short, not only were the property rights of the Old English seriously impaired, but the possibility of mounting political resistance was sharply reduced.

Nonetheless, when a new parliament was summoned in 1640 to assist the king in dealing with his rebellious Scottish subjects, circumstances conspired to favor the Old English. Wentworth's authoritarianism had also offended the New English, Charles's absolutist tendencies had aroused opposition in England, and a complex network of alliances took shape. The two colonial communities in Ireland entered into a parliamentary coalition, sealed by an agreement not to proceed with a bill for the confirmation of the plantation arrangements in Connacht and Clare. Having done so, they formed links with the English opposition, which in turn developed covert connections with the king's Scottish enemies. The immediate collective aim was to secure the impeachment of Wentworth, but the dominant Old English concern was to secure the enactment of the Graces. In April 1641, at a critical moment in Wentworth's trial, when impeachment was replaced by a bill of attainder, the king yielded to the demands of the Old English members of an Irish parliamentary delegation and ordered the Irish government to prepare a statute of limitations and a bill to revoke the plantation proceedings in Connacht and Clare. The government complied, while urging that this legislation be balanced by measures to compensate for the loss of revenue. Early in August, when it became known that the draft bills had received royal approval and were about to be returned for enactment without this condition being fulfilled, the Irish administration suspended Parliament until November. Before it met again, the Irish in Ulster had risen in rebellion. A minority opinion held that the way to prevent the outbreak from spreading to the Old English was to affirm the government's intention of having the Graces enacted, but it did not prevail.

SEE ALSO Old English; Rebellion of 1641; Wentworth, Thomas, First Earl of Strafford

Bibliography

Clarke, Aidan. *The Old English in Ireland, 1625–1642.* 1966. Reprint, 2000.

Clarke, Aidan. *The Graces, 1628–1641.* 1968.

Kearney, Hugh F. *Strafford in Ireland, 1633–1641: A Study in Absolutism.* 1959. Rev. edition, 1989.

Moody, T. W., F. X. Martin, and F. J. Byrne, eds. *Early Modern Ireland, 1534–1691.* Vol. 3 of *A New History of Ireland.* 1976. Reprint, 1991.

Treadwell, Victor. *Buckingham and Ireland, 1616–1628.* 1998.

Aidan Clarke

Granuaile (Grace O'Malley)

Chieftainess, pirate, and Gaelic heroine, Granuaile or Grace O'Malley (c. 1530–1603) was born in County Mayo on the west coast of Ireland. Her father, Owen Dubhdara O'Malley, was chieftain of the barony of Murrisk. The O'Malleys, like their neighbors the O'Flahertys, traded with Spain, Portugal, and Scotland and were famous both as pirates and fishermen. As a teenager, Granuaile was married to Donal-an-Choghaidh (of the Battles) O'Flaherty, the heir or *tanist* of the O'Flaherty of Ballinahinch. The alliance gave the two families control of the western seas and all of Connemara. Granuaile bore Donal three children before he was murdered at the hands of rival clansmen, the Joyces. Denied the one-third of her husband's property accorded by Brehon (traditional Gaelic) law, Granuaile returned to O'Malley territory with 200 followers. From Clare Island, Granuaile began to make her own fortune by raiding ships en route to the English-controlled port of Galway, charging for navigational information, and extorting money for safe passage. In 1566 she married Richard-an-Iarainn (Iron Dick) Burke, chief of the Burkes of Carra and Burrishoole, heir to the title of MacWilliam, and governor of Rockfleet Castle. The marriage brought her control of all Clare Island and Clew Bay. Brehon law permitted divorce after one year of marriage, and Richard was accordingly dismissed. Granuaile retained possession of Rockfleet, the base of her enterprises. In 1574 an English fleet under Captain William Martin was sent to capture her fortress and to put an end to her forays. This expedition failed, but the Crown continued its efforts to subdue Connacht. Most Irish chieftains had already surrendered to the Crown, exchanging their Irish titles for English ones. The O'Malleys did so in 1576. Faced with growing English opposition and uncertain of their own power base, Granuaile and Richard Burke submitted to Sir Henry Sidney in the following year. It was a ruse for time; Irish attacks on English ships soon resumed. An unsuccessful raid on the earl of Desmond ended with Granuaile's imprisonment, though she was again released on the promise of good behavior. The pledge was also broken; in 1586 she was captured and her possessions were confiscated by Sir Richard Bingham, governor of Connacht. In 1593 an impoverished Granuaile petitioned the queen for the restoration of her property, claiming that the lawlessness and discord that reigned in western Connacht had forced her and her family "to take arms and by force to maintain [my]self and [my] people by sea and land the space of forty years past" (Calendar of State Papers, Ireland. 63/170 No. 0204, quoted in

Chambers 1983). Summoned to defend herself in England, Granuaile met with Queen Elizabeth at Greenwich Palace. Particulars of the meeting are not known, but the queen was sufficiently impressed by the elderly Irishwoman to give her a pardon on condition that in the future she direct her "activities" against enemies of the Crown. Little is known of Granuaile's later life, but a 1601 entry in the Calendar of State Papers reports that her galleys, presumably illegally engaged, were attacked by English patrol ships. It is believed that Granuaile died at Rockfleet Castle in 1603; her burial site is not known.

Bibliography

Calendar of State Papers, Ireland. 1574–1601.
Chambers, Anne. *Granuaile.* 1983.

Monica A. Brennan

∼

Grattan, Henry

Politician, and the leading orator in the late-eighteenth-century Irish parliament, Henry Grattan (1746–1820) was brought into the House of Commons in 1775 by Lord Charlemont to reinforce the then somewhat depleted ranks of opposition MPs known as Patriots. Choosing at the outset to focus on financial issues, Grattan quickly demonstrated that he was possessed of exceptional oratorical skills. His penchant for "violent" language elicited disapproving comments from those who were the target of his criticism, but it earned him bouquets from his parliamentary colleagues and an increasingly politicized public. Grattan was a leading member of the Patriot interest that obliged the British government to remove long-standing mercantilist restrictions on Irish trade in the winter of 1779 to 1780. In April 1780, Grattan called on the Irish Commons to approve "a declaration of the rights of Ireland," but two years elapsed before he was able to gain approval for such a declaration by taking advantage of a change in government at Westminster and the strong support of the Volunteers, a paramilitary body of Protestant citizens formed to aid in the defence of the kingdom. It was the greatest moment in Grattan's career and ensured that the ensuing constitutional changes securing to the Irish legislature the right to make law for the kingdom of Ireland ("legislative independence") would long be identified with him ("Grattan's parliament").

Unfortunately from Grattan's perspective, a disagreement with Henry Flood as to whether the British parliament had renounced the right to make law for Ireland soured the public mood and generated a measure of bitterness between the two men that nearly culminated in a duel in 1783. Having lost the esteem of the public, Grattan sought to forge a working relationship with Dublin Castle, but he did not possess an eye for legal or administrative detail and soon gravitated toward opposition in the House of Commons. The Regency Crisis of 1788 through 1789, which provided the stimulus for the foundation of the Whig Club, more organized opposition, and the general invigoration of political discourse following the outbreak of revolution in France, created the environment in which Grattan could flourish once more. Now MP for Dublin city, his embrace of the cause of Catholic enfranchisement ensured him a leading place among the country's moderate reformers. His advocacy of Catholic emancipation at the time of Earl Fitzwilliam's controversial viceroyalty between 1794 and 1795 reinforced this image, but his inability to overcome the conservative vested interests, who were committed to upholding the values of "Protestant Ascendancy," caused him to withdraw from Parliament in 1797. Wrongly suspected of complicity with the United Irishmen in the late 1790s, he was persuaded to make a political comeback in 1800 only by the threat of an Anglo-Irish union. His fruitless opposition to the Act of Union helped greatly to reinforce his identification with legislative independence among later generations, though he served in the united Parliament from 1805 until his death in 1820. A sincere and influential presence in the Whig Party, he worked unsuccessfully to promote Catholic emancipation conditional on the Crown retaining the power to veto appointments to the Catholic hierarchy. The emergence of a demand for the repeal of the Act of Union following his death ensured that it was as the progenitor of "Grattan's parliament" that he achieved a measure of popular immortality.

SEE ALSO Eighteenth-Century Politics: 1714 to 1778—Interest Politics; Eighteenth-Century Politics: 1778 to 1795—Parliamentary and Popular Politics; Eighteenth-Century Politics: 1795 to 1800—Repression, Rebellion, and Union; Flood, Henry; Government from 1690 to 1800; Military Forces from 1690 to 1800

Bibliography

Grattan, Henry, Jr. *Memoirs of the Life and Times of the Rt. Hon. Henry Grattan.* 5 vols. 1839–1846.
Kelly, James. *Henry Grattan.* 1993.

Kelly, James. *Henry Flood: Patriots and Politics in Eighteenth-Century Ireland.* 1998.

McDowell, Robert B. *Henry Grattan.* 2001.

James Kelly

≈

Great Famine

The Great Famine of 1845 to 1850 was the most serious peacetime catastrophe to afflict any part of nineteenth-century Europe. The 1851 Irish census revealed that the population had fallen from the 8.2 million recorded in 1841 to 6.6 million; when estimates of natural growth in the early 1840s are taken into account, the "missing" amounted to some 2.4 million people, more than a quarter of the island's population. Separating the number of emigrants from the dead is difficult, but research from the 1980s suggests that the total killed by famine and its associated diseases was around 1.1 million people.

The Great Famine was the consequence of a combination of structural and triggering causes. Although there was nothing inevitable about the onset of famine, by the mid-1840s Irish society was acutely vulnerable. The rural population had grown rapidly from the mid-eighteenth century as increasing British demand for imported foodstuffs had promoted a massive growth in Irish tillage production. From around 1815, however, this agricultural boom collapsed, leading to sharper landlord-tenant conflict, increasing evictions, and the ever-worsening impoverishment of the landless and land-poor peasant families who made up a substantial part of the rural population. The following decades also witnessed a sharp contraction of the cottage-based linen-spinning industry, which had spread rapidly in the west and center of Ireland. Many families now saw their earnings collapse and were thrown into greater dependence on the one subsistence crop that they could grow in sufficient quantities in their cottage gardens, or "conacre" land plots rented from larger farmers. While these adverse economic conditions led to a reduction in the rate of population growth and promoted a modest rise in emigration, the population of Ireland had by the early 1840s reached a density on cultivated land of around 700 individuals per square mile, among the highest in Europe. Over 1.5 million of the landless laboring poor had no other significant source of food than the potato; three million more from the cottier peasant class of families renting small plots of land were also very largely dependent on this subsistence food.

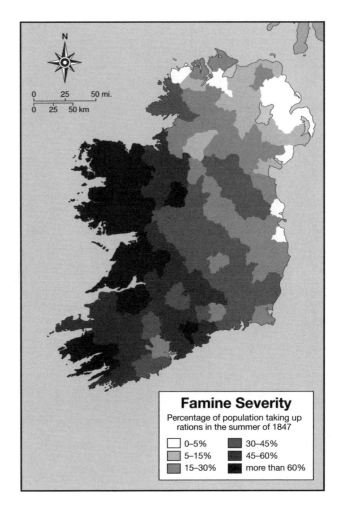

Famine Severity
Percentage of population taking up rations in the summer of 1847

- ☐ 0–5%
- ☐ 5–15%
- ☐ 15–30%
- ☐ 30–45%
- ☐ 45–60%
- ■ more than 60%

The fungal infestation of the potato blight reached Ireland from North America via the low countries and Britain in the fall of 1845. The disease was unknown and misunderstood, and no effective remedy was available to farmers until decades later. Accidental in its timing, the blight would produce an ecological catastrophe almost unparalleled in modern history. Up to a third of the Irish potato crop was lost in 1845. Mild and damp conditions favorable to the blight promoted its earlier appearance in 1846, when more than three-quarters of the crop was ravaged, leaving millions without their subsistence food or the seed vital to plant again in 1847. After a brief lapse the disease returned in 1848 and 1849, prolonging the famine crisis in many parts of Ireland. The blight faded in the early 1850s, but the potato never returned to the extraordinary levels of productivity witnessed before 1845. Further outbreaks in the early 1860s and in 1879 again threatened parts of Ireland with famine.

Much controversy surrounds the question of whether the failure of the potato crop alone was sufficient to produce famine in Ireland. Despite its economic

The poor-law system used to relieve destitution during the famine was woefully inadequate, and nowhere more so than in such western counties as Clare, where evictions raged. In this 1849 illustration the daughter of the poor-law official Captain Arthur Kennedy is distributing clothing to famished children in Kilrush. Kennedy himself publicly denounced evicting landlords; few other poor-law officials did so. FROM ILLUSTRATED LONDON NEWS, 22 DECEMBER 1849.

malaise, prefamine Ireland was continuing to export large quantities of grain and animal products to Great Britain, for the profit of landowners and larger farmers. Export of these higher-valued foodstuffs continued throughout the Great Famine period, to the outrage of many commentators who were convinced that Ireland was "starving in the midst of plenty." However, the amounts of grain exported from Ireland in 1846 and 1847 amounted in food value only to around one-tenth of the loss occasioned by the potato blight. Even if exports had been prohibited, Ireland lacked sufficient food resources to stave off famine in this year. Furthermore, food imports to Ireland in 1846 to 1847, principally cheaper grains like maize and rice, were twice the volume of exports, and this proportion increased in the following years.

These aggregate figures mask an important truth. Food imports from the United States began to arrive in bulk only in the spring of 1847, after a "starvation gap" in the preceding winter when retention of the exported Irish grain would probably have kept many thousands alive. Moreover, even when imports did begin to arrive

in bulk, driving down the price of food in Ireland from by the summer of 1847 to half the levels of six months earlier, destitution had rendered thousands incapable of purchasing what was available on the market. In its later years (1848–1850) the Great Famine changed its character from a total food deficit crisis to a "crisis of entitlement," in which mass unemployment, evictions, and physical vulnerability were more significant than aggregate food availability. As with all famines, human agency was central in determining the character and impact of the Great Famine.

The response of the British state to the Great Famine has been widely criticized. Sir Robert Peel's Conservative government did react reasonably promptly, initiating public-works schemes and establishing local relief committees and a central Relief Commission in early 1846. Peel also ordered the secret purchase of 100,000 pounds worth of American maize in order to regulate Irish grain prices and to introduce a taste in Ireland for the foodstuff that he hoped would permanently replace the potato. However, like his successors, Peel also hoped that the free market would ultimately solve the Irish problem in the wake of his repeal of the corn laws (which imposed tariffs on imported grains) in 1846. Peel was replaced in June 1846 by Lord John Russell's Whig administration, which immediately gave greater control over famine policy to the ideologue Charles Trevelyan, the senior administrator at the British Treasury. Under pressure from the merchant lobby the new government withdrew from all interference in the food trade and Trevelyan reorganized the public works to eradicate what he perceived as widespread abuses of the system by the laboring poor and self-interested landowners. The consequence in the winter of 1846 to 1847 was spiraling food prices and an overstretched public-works system, which neither produced improvements to Ireland's infrastructure nor provided the destitute with sufficient earnings to feed themselves. Outbreaks of typhus and relapsing fever, promoted by the harsh conditions of this bad winter, killed many thousands of the malnourished on the public works or in their cabins. Belatedly acknowledging the scale of human suffering, the government decided to abandon public works for direct feeding of the destitute at local soup kitchens in the late spring of 1847. These soup kitchens provided only the bare minimum of subsistence, but more than three million rations were being issued daily at their peak and undoubtedly they kept many alive.

By the late summer of 1847 the government considered the famine to be over and replaced the soup kitchens with relief through the mechanism of the Irish poor law. This decision proved catastrophic, especially in the south and west. Many devastated localities were unable to raise the heavy local taxation required to support the masses of destitute, and landowners engaged on campaigns of wholesale eviction to reduce their tax burdens and clear land for livestock farming. The overcrowded workhouses rapidly became breeding centers for diseases that continued to ravage the uprooted poor. Despite appeals from philanthropists and relief officials for government aid, virtually no state assistance was granted in the latter years of the famine. This was not the result of a deliberate policy of genocide, as nationalists later claimed, but of a dogmatic belief that relieving the famine was the responsibility of landowners and that a measure of suffering was required to break Irish so-called dependency on welfarism and state aid.

From late 1846 emigration from Ireland took on a new and extraordinary character. Over one million fled Ireland during the Great Famine years, some with savings and hopes of a better life, but the majority as economic refugees. Most first took the short and cheap crossing to Britain, frequently bringing typhus with them into the slums of port cities, and often onto the converted cargo ships that carried thousands to Canada

Mass evictions were mostly confined to the western counties during the Great Famine, but there they created misery on an appalling scale. Clare was among the counties hit hardest by evictions, and in this 1849 illustration, Bridget O'Donnell and her children have just been thrown out on the roadside with barely enough clothing to cover them. FROM ILLUSTRATED LONDON NEWS, 22 DECEMBER 1849.

in 1847. This was by far the worst route, with up to one in five emigrants dying on these "coffin ships" or shortly after arrival. Direct passage to America became more common from 1848, and while conditions were better, they were still harsh and mortality was high. Irish Catholic immigrants frequently faced hostility and exploitation on arrival in Britain, Canada, and the United States; most tended to congregate in urban areas seeking laboring work wherever available.

The Great Famine was a national catastrophe, although mortality was most acute in the southern and western counties of Ireland. The indifference to mass suffering of most of the landlord class and the government (each of which blamed the other) unquestionably worsened the situation and resulted in large numbers of unnecessary deaths. Unsurprisingly, it left a bitter memory within both Ireland and the extended Irish diaspora, which continues to this day.

SEE ALSO Agriculture: 1690 to 1845; Agriculture: 1845 to 1921; American Wakes; Family: Marriage Patterns and Family Life from 1690 to 1921; Famine Clearances; Indian Corn or Maize; Migration: Emigration from the Seventeenth Century to 1845; Migration: Emigration from 1850 to 1960; Mitchel, John; Poor Law Amendment Act of 1847 and the Gregory Clause; Population, Economy, and Society from 1750 to 1950; Population Explosion; Potato and Potato Blight (*Phytophthora infestans*); Protestant Ascendancy: Decline, 1800 to 1930; Religious Society of Friends (Quakers); Rural Life: 1690 to 1845; Rural Life: 1850 to 1921; Subdivision and Subletting of Holdings; Town Life from 1690 to the Early Twentieth Century; Young Ireland and the Irish Confederation; **Primary Documents:** On Rural Society on the Eve of the Great Famine (1844–1845)

Bibliography

Donnelly, James S., Jr. *The Great Irish Potato Famine*. 2001.

Gray, Peter. *Famine, Land, and Politics: British Government and Irish Society, 1843–1850*. 1999.

Ó Gráda, Cormac. *The Great Irish Famine*. 1989.

Ó Gráda, Cormac. *Black '47 and Beyond: The Great Irish Famine in History, Economy, and Memory*. 1999.

Póirtéir, Cathal, ed. *The Great Irish Famine*. 1995.

Woodham-Smith, Cecil. *The Great Hunger: Ireland, 1845–1849*. 1962.

Peter Gray

Greatorex, Valentine

Valentine Greatorex (1629–1683), faith healer, was born into a Protestant family in the southern Irish province of Munster. He was educated locally, but first the death of his father and then the uprising of 1641 disrupted plans for his further education. He moved to England, where he came under the influence of German mysticism. The prospect of Protestants recovering what they had lost in 1641 to the Catholic insurgents in Munster persuaded him to return to Ireland. Distressed by the cruelty and devastation of the Irish wars, he fell into deep depression, but his spirits seem to have revived with the fortunes of the local Protestants. For six years he soldiered in a local force, until about 1656, when he returned to civilian life.

The patronage of the Boyles, his landlords, and specifically of Roger Boyle, baron of Broghill, his former commander, earned Greatorex appointments as a justice of the peace, clerk of the peace in County Cork, and registrar for transplanting the Irish to Connacht. In these official capacities, he reputedly behaved with more moderation than other officials toward the Catholics. After Charles II's restoration he discovered and applied healing powers. At first, these were directed toward those in the neighborhood afflicted by scurvy, known as "the king's evil," but news of his powers quickly spread, and he was in demand to heal both notables and the humble. He attended a former comrade in the army, Robert Phaire, notorious for his religious and political radicalism, and also Broghill, now advanced to earl of Orrery and ruling Munster as lord president. Through Orrery he was introduced to other Anglo-Irish grandees and was invited to England in 1666. In London his doings were observed by theologians and scientists, including Robert Boyle, in an effort to decide the efficacy and significance of his cures. These activities, reported in pamphlets, added to his fame.

The ensuing controversy over his gifts exhumed Greatorex's past. Hostile parties suggested that he was psychologically disturbed, and that his behavior was in keeping with his unorthodox political and religious beliefs—the now discredited republican and sectarian views of the 1650s. His popularity threatened public order as patients flocked to his house, some having sailed from England. Even more ominous to ardent royalists was Greatorex's claim to the thaumaturgical role hitherto reserved for the monarch: that of therapeutically touching the afflicted. Others defended him as "a very sober, discreet, civil gentleman" (Beecher 1665, p. 5). Yet, at a time of political instability his activities were feared for their unsettling effects. His apparently magical powers were too reminiscent of the claims of the Catholic clergy, and questioned the rationalists' approach to miracles. His activities also coincided with a year of apocalyptic expectancy. In 1666 it was alleged that he had caused more conflict between laity and clergy "than anyone these 1000 years" (Duffy 1981, pp. 268–269). Aware of these controversies, he became more reticent about practicing his cures outside his immediate neighborhood, to which he retired in 1668. Thereafter nothing is known of his career.

Bibliography

[Beecher, Lionel]. *Wonders if not Miracles or, a Relation of the Wonderful Performances of Valentine Gertrux.* 1665.

A Brief Account of Mr. Valentine Greatraks, and Divers of the Strange Cures by Him Lately Performed. 1666.

Duffy, Eamon. "Valentine Greatrix, the Irish Stroker." In *Religion and Humanism*, edited by Keith Robbins. 1981.

Godfrey, Edmund, and others. Letters to V. Greatorex. MS 4728. National Library of Ireland.

Stubbe, Henry. *The Miraculous Conformist or, An Account of Severall Marvailous Cures Performed by the Stroaking of the Hands of Mr. Valentine Greatarick.* 1666.

Toby Barnard

~

Great War

War came to the United Kingdom on 3 August 1914. The leader of the Irish Parliamentary Party, John Redmond, heard the cheers in the House of Commons that greeted the announcement of war, and responded by pledging the Irish Volunteers to defend Ireland. This, he hoped, would allow the British to remove their troops from the island. But from the start Redmond wanted more for his Irish Volunteers than an active part in home defense. On 11 September, when the British minister of war, Lord Kitchener, authorized the creation of an Irish division for his second New Army, Redmond saw his chance. He wanted to get War Office approval for turning the Sixteenth Division into an "Irish Brigade," a nostalgic misnomer that confused British officialdom. This was to be an Irish Catholic fighting unit officered by veterans of Redmond's Volunteers—in effect, it was to be led by supporters of the Irish Parliamentary Party. On 20 September at Woodenbridge, Co. Wexford, Redmond committed the Volunteers to service abroad. In the ranks of the Volunteers reaction was swift. On 24 September 1914 advanced nationalists, who wished for more independence than Home Rule offered, met in Dublin under the leadership of Eoin MacNeill and broke with Redmond, splitting the Volunteers. The vast majority of the 180,000 Irish Volunteers stayed with John Redmond and reorganized under the name the "National Volunteers." For MacNeill and his ilk, the idea of fighting offensively for the British oppressor was too much to bear. The 6,000 or so Irish Volunteers who left with MacNeill, however, were men of considerable influence within the movement. In Dublin alone 2,000 joined MacNeill, including virtually all of the leaders of the 1916 Easter Rising.

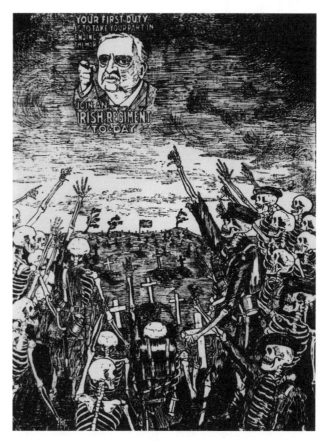

By November 1916 some 150,000 Irishmen had donned a British uniform. But military casualties were catastrophic, and the British attempt to extend conscription to Ireland in 1918 set off a furious campaign of opposition joined by both the moderate Home Rule and the more militant Sinn Féin parties. But this poster pillories Home Rule leader John Redmond, whose words, "Join an Irish regiment today," prompt the war dead to rise in condemnation. COPYRIGHT © NATIONAL MUSEUM OF IRELAND. REPRODUCED BY PERMISSION.

RECRUITING

The creation of the Sixteenth (Irish) Division completed the triumvirate of volunteer divisions that recruited in Ireland during the First World War. The other two divisions were the Tenth and the Thirty-sixth. The Tenth was part of Kitchener's first New Army created in August 1914, and it consisted of reorganized regular army divisions. The Thirty-sixth (Ulster) Division was created for the Ulster Volunteer Force (UVF) in September 1914 and was manned almost exclusively by members of the UVF until July 1916.

Recruiting in Ireland matched patterns seen in the rest of the United Kingdom. An initial rush sent more than 44,000 Irishmen into the armed forces by December 1914. After this first period, recruiting declined dramatically. Exceptions to this decline were in April and May 1915, when recruiting rose, probably in response to the allied landings at Gallipoli; and then in October 1915, when the viceroy, Lord Wimborne, led a campaign to send "personal" recruiting letters to all eligible Irishmen. After April 1916 recruiting was virtually moribund in Ireland, although historians disagree on whether or not the Easter Rising was directly responsible for this phenomenon; indeed, recruiting rose in the month following the Rising.

Recruiters enjoyed the advantages of large publicity budgets and produced massive runs of colorful posters that exhorted people to take up arms for the allied cause. The major propaganda arguments for joining the British army focused (for southern Catholics) on defending the Catholic nation of Belgium and on Britain's pledge of Home Rule following the war. In the North the argument was a simpler one that revolved around the idea of loyalty to the British empire and the Crown. No single argument seems to have made much difference to people enlisting—men joined the army for nebulous reasons of patriotism, loyalty to friends (units were often organized around local sports teams or neighborhood associations), or in order to have an adventure. The traditional recruiting hotbeds of urban poverty continued to provide a disproportionate number of recruits throughout the war. Statistically, unskilled laborers were the most likely men to volunteer, and skilled clerks and farmers' sons were the least likely. There was no great variance in recruiting patterns around Ireland, though, predictably, the more urban provinces, such as Ulster, sent more men than the rural ones, such as Connacht.

ON THE FRONT LINES

The Irish divisions to which Irish recruits went—the Tenth, Sixteenth, and Thirty-sixth—all kept their distinctively "Irish" character until they were decimated in action. The Tenth was the first to be destroyed, at Gallipoli in the summer of 1915. The Thirty-sixth was the next to go: embarking for France with a more coherent unit identity than most other divisions, it faced its destiny at the Somme on 1 July 1916. Elements of the Thirty-sixth Division were among the only British army troops to reach their original objectives on that morning; however, unsupported by their fellow soldiers, regiments of the Thirty-sixth lost close to 80 percent of their strength. That the Somme battle coincided with the anniversary of the Battle of the Boyne in 1690 was not lost on Protestant propagandists in Ulster. For the first time, the Orange marches in July 1916 memorialized the men of the Thirty-sixth Division, and even today, Orange Lodges carry banners with pictures of the Somme on them during their July marches.

The Sixteenth Irish Division, set up as the nationalist and Catholic counterpart to the Thirty-sixth, embarked for France in the February of 1916. During the war Tom Kettle, ex–Home Rule MP and professor of economics at University College Dublin, and Willie Redmond (younger brother of John) both served as officers in the Sixteenth, and both lost their lives wearing the khaki of the British army. Kettle, who had volunteered for active service after the Easter Rising, died on the Somme in September 1916. The Sixteenth Division retained its "Irish" character the longest; despite suffering intensive casualties both at the Somme and in the Third Battle of Ypres, it remained a predominantly Irish division until it was destroyed during the German offensive of March and April 1918.

AT HOME

Although the 1916 Easter Rising marked a turning point in Irish domestic politics, the enduring focus of wartime worry between 1914 and 1918 was the possibility of conscription. Conscription had been applied in the rest of the United Kingdom in January 1916, and the vast majority of the Irish, opposed to its imposition in Ireland, were fearful that they too would soon be forced to join up. And indeed, after the German army successfully drove within 30 miles of Paris in March 1918, the British government decided to bring the military draft to Ireland. This was resisted by nearly all of the Irish nationalist organizations. Because Sinn Féin had maintained a consistent antiwar stance since August 1914, its leaders, especially Eamon de Valera and Arthur Griffith, gained significant national support when conscription was successfully resisted; in contrast, the Irish Parliamentary Party, a newcomer to the cause, was shown to be a band of hypocrites.

While urban civilians formed a large percentage of the recruits for the army, the war also brought increased prosperity to those city dwellers who stayed behind. The urban poor found work in munitions factories, frequently abroad, and as in the rest of the world, many women worked in factories for the first time during the war. In the countryside farmers benefited from higher prices owing to wartime shortages. Sinn Féin combatted the appeal of these economic advantages of war by pointing out the moral dangers of young people leaving Ireland for Britain's factories, and by raising the specter of famine as food controls hit people's larders in 1917 and 1918.

CONCLUSION

The Great War marked a watershed in Irish life. In 1914 the Irish Parliamentary Party dominated the political landscape. In December 1918, one month after the war ended, Sinn Féin took power in the south in a democratic general election. One of the keys to Sinn Féin's electoral success was its propagandists' harnessing of antiwar sentiment in Ireland. Even as many Irish supported the war, there was growing frustration as Irish casualty rates grew, and a cleverly managed publicity campaign by Sinn Féin tarred the Irish Parliamentary Party as a group of murderers who were happy to see Irish men killed for a British cause. Although Sinn Féin's victory can be seen as a revolution, in fact, the election of a nationalist antiwar party following the devastation of the First World War was more of a natural evolution in Irish public opinion.

SEE ALSO Electoral Politics from 1800 to 1921; Griffith, Arthur; Home Rule Movement and the Irish Parliamentary Party: 1891 to 1918; Protestant Ascendancy: Decline, 1800 to 1930; Redmond, John; Sinn Féin Movement and Party to 1922; Struggle for Independence from 1916 to 1921

Bibiliography

Bartlett, Thomas, and Jeffery Keith, eds. *Military History of Ireland.* 1996.

Denman, Terence. *Ireland's Unknown Soldiers: The 16th (Irish) Division in the Great War, 1914–1918.* 1992.

Dooley, Thomas. *Irishmen or English Soldiers?* 1995.

Fitzpatrick, David. *Politics and Irish Life, 1913–1921: Provincial Experience of War and Revolution.* 1977.

Fitzpatrick, David, ed. *Ireland and the First World War.* 1988.

Gregory, Adrian, and Senia Paseta, eds. *Ireland during the First World War.* 2002.

Jeffery, Keith. *Ireland and the Great War.* 2001.

Novick, Ben. *Conceiving Revolution: Irish Nationalist Propaganda during the First World War.* 2001.

Ben Novick

∽

Griffith, Arthur

Founder of the Sinn Féin Party, signatory of the Anglo-Irish Treaty, and president of Dáil Éireann, Arthur Griffith (1871–1922) was born on 31 March in Dublin. Educated by the Christian Brothers and trained as a compositor, he pursued a career in journalism. With William Rooney, he founded the *United Irishman* in 1899 and pressed for a compromise between revolutionary republicanism and the constitutionalism of the Irish Parliamentary Party. His series of essays, collected and published in 1904 as *The Resurrection of Hungary*, outlined the abstentionist policy of Sinn Féin ("Ourselves"); however, the party set up in 1906 to pursue Griffith's ideas foundered for a decade until the government and the public misidentified the rebels of the Easter Rising as "Sinn Féiners."

Griffith then became increasingly involved in the struggle for independence, though he stood aside while Eamon de Valera assumed the leadership of the reformed party in 1917. In the first Dáil Éireann, Griffith served as minister for home affairs and, for eighteen months, as acting president, only reluctantly acquiescing in the campaign against the police undertaken by the Irish Volunteers.

Arrested in November 1920 and interned for seven months in Mountjoy jail, Griffith advised his colleagues from a distance, but his signal contribution came after his release. In the autumn of 1921, along with Michael Collins, he played a central role in the negotiations that led to the Anglo-Irish Treaty signed on 6 December. Although the treaty granted the twenty-six-county Free State control of its armed forces and police and fiscal autonomy, Griffith received criticism for also recognizing a separate Northern Ireland state and accepting the status of a Crown dominion. (Griffith believed that a boundary commission would rework the border and make the northern state untenable.) In December 1921 and January 1922, he, Collins, and their supporters argued that the treaty provided an opportunity for the Irish people to create their own future along "native" lines, putting the Sinn Féin ideal into practice. They carried the vote in the Dáil, prompting de Valera and the antitreaty deputies to withdraw. The remaining deputies elected Griffith president of the Dáil, and in that capacity he helped Collins to establish the provisional government of the Free State in 1922. Exhaustion overtook him as the Free State descended into civil war, and Griffith died of a cerebral hemorrhage on 12 August 1922.

SEE ALSO Anglo-Irish Treaty of 1921; Boundary Commission; Collins, Michael; de Valera, Eamon; Electoral Politics from 1800 to 1921; Great War; Home Rule Movement and the Irish Parliamentary Party: 1891 to 1918; Sinn Féin Movement and Party to 1922; Struggle for Independence from 1916 to 1921; **Primary Documents:** Resolutions Passed at the Public Meeting which Followed the First Annual Convention of the National Council of Sinn Féin (28 November

1905); Address at the First Annual Convention of the National Council of Sinn Féin (28 November 1905); Resolutions Adopted at the Public Meeting Following the First Annual Convention of the National Council of Sinn Féin (28 November 1905); The Anglo-Irish Treaty (6 December 1921); Speech in Favor of the Anglo-Irish Treaty of December 1921 (7 January 1922)

Bibliography

Colum, Padraic. *Arthur Griffith*. 1959.

Davis, Richard. *Arthur Griffith and Non-Violent Sinn Fein*. 1974.

Maye, Brian. *Arthur Griffith*. 1997.

O'Hegarty, P. S. *The Victory of Sinn Féin: How It Won It and How It Used It*. 1924, 1998.

Younger, Carlton. *Arthur Griffith*. 1981.

Timothy G. McMahon

Guinness Brewing Company

In 1759 Arthur Guinness established a brewery at Saint James's Gate in Dublin and Ireland's greatest business success story began. In 1778 Guinness began to specialize in porter and its stronger cousin, stout; by 1833 it was the largest brewery in Ireland and had begun to establish a crucial presence in the British market; by the 1880s it was the leading brewery in the United Kingdom; and by 1914 it was the largest in the world.

Technical excellence, concentration on manufacturing and product quality, and superb management skills combined to keep Guinness in a pre-eminent position. In the 1930s it began advertising for the first time in response to a declining market in Britain. The timeless slogan "Guinness is good for you" was developed, promoting the health properties of stout. Witty and attractive cartoon posters established a brand awareness that was strengthened in subsequent decades by other innovative campaigns that made Guinness a globally recognized product. Because of its continuing dominance of the Irish market, the company did not advertise locally until the late 1950s, when a diversifying market and competition from British breweries in the newly opened Irish economy forced its hand. Beginning in the 1960s, Guinness was one of Ireland's leading advertisers, utilizing RTÉ, the new Irish television channel, the print media, and outdoor posters to great effect.

In the late 1950s and early 1960s the company expanded its product portfolio in response to changing consumer tastes, through the takeover of smaller breweries and trade agreements with other international brewers. Its innovative marketing strategy was epitomized by the success of the *Guinness Book of World Records*. In 1986 the chairmanship of the company passed from family hands for the first time, and in 1997 Guinness merged with GrandMet to form Diageo, a huge global corporation.

SEE ALSO Brewing and Distilling; Industry since 1920

Bibliography

Bielenberg, Andy. "The Irish Brewing Industry and the Rise of Guinness, 1790–1914." In *The Dynamics of the International Brewing Industry since 1800*, edited by R. G. Wilson and T. R. Gourvish. 1998.

Lynch, P., and J. Vaizey. *Guinness's Brewery in the Irish Economy, 1759–1876*. 1960.

Sibley, Brian. *The Book of Guinness Advertising*. 1985.

Donal Ó Drisceoil

Hagiography

The composition of hagiography (saints' lives) in Ireland begins with three major works that date from the mid- to the late seventh century, when the three major monastic foundations of Kildare, Armagh, and Iona had firmly established themselves and were expanding their territories and influence. The first is the *Vita Sanctae Brigidae* (Life of Saint Brigit of Kildare) by a monk whose name is given as Cogitosus. Cogitosus's life of Brigit dates from about 650 C.E. and has long been considered the earliest hagiographical work in Hiberno–Latin. Another life of Brigit, the anonymous *Vita Prima Sanctae Brigidae* (First life of Saint Brigit, so called because it is the first of Brigit's biographies recorded in the *Acta Sanctorum Bollandiana*—the major collection of saints' lives first compiled by the Société des Bollandistes in Belgium in the seventeenth century), also has a claim for early composition, and there is a continuing debate over which of these two is the earlier. The relationship between these two lives has yet to be resolved, and while both seem to draw upon similar sources, their composition is different. Cogitosus's biography offers only a very brief summary of Brigit's birth, parentage, and early career in a conventional hagiographical manner and concentrates instead on a series of miracle stories (including the well-known story of how the saint hung her wet cloak on a sunbeam), leading to a lengthy description of Brigit's church and monastery. Cogitosus's aim seems to be the promotion of the monastic community as much as that of its founder and patron; the miracle stories underline Brigit's sanctity and divine power while the great size, wealth, and political and religious importance of her community are emphasized. The *Vita Prima*, on the other hand, offers a more lengthy series of miracle stories and anecdotes, including the famous birth tale in which Brigit is the daughter of a nobleman and a slavewoman, whom he sells at his wife's insistence. The woman is bought first by a poet, then by a druid; the child is born on the threshold of the dairy at dawn and washed in new milk. Both versions mix biblical references and scripturally based miracles with folkloric material.

The work of Cogitosus was followed shortly by that of Muirchú, a monk of Armagh, who composed a life of Saint Patrick around 680 C.E. In his preface he refers to the hagiographical work of his "father" Cogitosus (no doubt meaning his spiritual father) and aims in his composition to do as Cogitosus did for his patron and founder. Muirchú's work contains more biographical material than does Cogitosus's and details Patrick's early life and mission to Ireland; however, much of it is based on legend rather than history, although he clearly used some historical sources, including Patrick's own *Confessio* (Confession). Nevertheless, Muirchú's life of Patrick became the basis for subsequent lives of Patrick. A contemporary document by a bishop, Tírechán, provides further hagiographical material but is a collection of memoranda concerning Patrick and a list of his foundations rather than any kind of biography.

The third great hagiographical work of the seventh century is the life of Columba (Colum Cille) by Adomnán, ninth abbot of Iona, written between 685 and 689 C.E. Adomnán's life of Columba represents Irish hagiographical writing at its finest; his work shows not only biblical influence but the influence of major continental writers, such as Sulpicius Severus and Gregory the Great, in both his hagiographical form and Latin style. While Adomnán incorporated both written sources and the oral tradition of Saint Columba in his life, much of the work also documents the history and constitution of the Irish church in its early days. The life is divided into three parts: The first part tells of Columba's life and career, the second of his miracles and prophecies, and the third of angelic visions. Despite the legendary and folkloric material, Columba emerges in this life less as a magical figure and more as an historical personage. Like Muirchú's life of Saint Patrick, Adomnán's life of Columba became the basis for subsequent biographies of the saint in both Latin and Irish, culminating in the massive *Betha Colaim Chille* (Life of Colum Cille) compiled under the direction of the Donegal chieftain Manus O'Donnell in 1532. The works of Cogitosus, Muirchú, and Adomnán also reflect their respective communities' concerns with promoting the cults of their founders and establishing their territorial rights, thereby increasing their influence and income. Armagh and Kildare, both episcopal sees, rivaled one other for preeminence in the Irish church; Armagh and its founder saint, Patrick, eventually gained ascendance.

The Irish church witnessed an expansion of monastic communities in the seventh and eighth centuries that led to an increase in hagiographical composition. This was aided in part by a renewal of asceticism and a spiritual reform led by a new order who called themselves *céli Dé* (culdees) or "companions of God," centered at the monastery of Tallaght. The lives of saints from this period emphasize the saints' ascetic practices and virtues of self-denial, individual prayer, and meditation; the life of the anchorite, alone in his cell with only God's creation for company, is valorized, as is the saint's spiritual guidance. Irish hagiographers often ascribed to their subjects a strong empathy with the natural world and its creatures; the saints of the sixth and seventh centuries had shown this affinity with nature and wild animals, and this characteristic continued in the hagiography of the reform period, finding also new expression in the religious poetry of the time. Devotion to the saints was also an important ideal in this movement, and two major martyrologies, the *Martyrology of Tallaght* and the *Martyrology of Oengus*, are associated with the *céli Dé*.

During the eighth and ninth centuries more hagiographical texts began to appear in the vernacular, including the Old Irish life of Brigit (*Bethu Brigte*), which dates from the late eighth to early ninth centuries, and the Tripartite Life of Saint Patrick (*Vita Tripartita*) of the late ninth century, which represents the last major Patrician text of the Irish church. The Tripartite Life marks another change in the characteristics of Irish hagiography—it exhibits a strong concern with the rights and property of Patrick's church rather than with spiritual teaching. The lives of the saints from this period onward follow suit in showing such interest in their saints' churches, and the miracle stories become more fantastic and flamboyant to demonstrate the power of the saint, who appears much the same as a saga hero.

The majority of the lives written in the vernacular are in Middle Irish; many are direct translations from Latin originals and date from around and after the twelfth century. But dating is notoriously difficult, since the manuscript versions of the lives of the saints, in both Latin and Irish, cannot be dated with confidence before the late twelfth century. This is partly owing to the incursions of the Vikings in the late eighth to tenth centuries, but also to the ravages of later eras. From the sixth century Irish monks had traveled to Europe as pilgrims and missionaries, and a few, such as Saint Columbanus in the late sixth to early seventh centuries, founded several monasteries in France, Germany, and Switzerland. Many Irish monks fled to these continental Irish monasteries in the wake of the Vikings, taking their manuscripts with them. Irish hagiographical writing continued, however, both in Ireland and in Europe—the *Navigatio Sancti Brendani* (Voyage of Saint Brendan), one of the most widely read works of the Middle Ages, was composed on the continent around the tenth century, probably by an Irish monk in exile, and was later translated into several vernacular languages.

In the eleventh and twelfth centuries the Irish church moved closer to conformity with the continental church and participated in the reform movement that was associated with the Benedictine abbey at Cluny. This paved the way for new orders, such as the Cistercians, to enter Ireland. One of the main leaders of this movement in Ireland was Máel-Máedóc Úa Morgair, or Saint Malachy; an account of his life was composed after his death in 1148 by his friend, Saint Bernard of Clairvaux. Although the great heyday of Irish saints and Irish hagiography had passed, the lives of the saints remained an important part of Irish history and identity. As the Normans became increasingly absorbed into Irish society and culture, Irish literature and learning rebounded. In the thirteenth and fourteenth centuries the major collections of saints' lives—the *Codex Insulensis*, the *Codex Salmanticensis*, and the *Codex Kilkenniensis*—were compiled. The *Book of Lismore*, a private collection made for Finghín MacCarthaigh *Riabhach* (MacCarthy Reagh) and his wife Catherine, containing lives in Irish, was compiled in the late fifteenth century.

The English conquest in the sixteenth century, however, halted further hagiographical production. The traditional historians of Ireland tried to continue the task of preserving and copying existing manuscripts, while Irishmen hoping to join the priesthood had to journey to Europe for their training. In the early seventeenth century the Irish ecclesiastics on the continent, alarmed that their national history was threatened with extinction, began to collect and publish Irish manuscripts; the main proponents were Henry FitzSimon (c. 1566–c. 1645), Luke Wadding (1588–1657), Peter Lombard (c. 1555–1625), and Stephen White (1574–1646). At the College of Saint Anthony in Louvain, a group under the leadership of Hugh Ward (1590–1635), encouraged by Luke Wadding and assisted by Stephen White, undertook a major plan for a *Thesaurus Antiquitatem Hibernicarum* (Thesaurus of Irish antiquities). The first object was to collect at Louvain as many Irish historical sources as possible, including hagiographical sources, both from Europe and from Ireland. This task was discharged by John Colgan (1592–1658), Patrick Fleming (1599–1631), and Michael O'Clery (d. 1645). The mission of collecting and copying in Ireland all the manuscripts in Irish pertaining to religious history fell to O'Clery, who between 1626 and 1642 assembled and transcribed a prodigious number of manuscripts, many of which contained hagiographical material. The third volume of the whole design, published at Louvain in 1645, contains the lives of Irish saints whose festivals fall within January, February, and March; the second volume, published in 1647, contains documents pertaining to Saints Patrick, Brigit, and Columba. Both were edited by Colgan. Another collection of lives in Irish was copied by Domnall Ó Dineen in 1627, possibly for the Irish scholars at Louvain, though it remained in Ireland.

From the collections of Irish material made by these scholars and from the great Latin collections, most of the modern editions of Irish hagiography were made. The O'Clery collections now reside in the Bibliothèque royale in Brussels. Several manuscripts that remained in Ireland found their way into the collections of antiquarians, such as Sir James Ware (1594–1666) and Sir Robert Cotton (1570–1631), and from thence went eventually to the British Library and the Bodleian Library at the University of Oxford (including the great codices under the Rawlinson collection). Other manuscript sources reside in the libraries of Trinity College, Dublin and the Royal Irish Academy. The study of Irish hagiography has gained added impetus not only from modern editions but from advances in the study of the language and history of early Ireland; a large body of scholarship has appeared in recent years, making these texts accessible to the modern reader and returning them to their rightful place in Irish literary and religious history.

SEE ALSO Early Medieval Ireland and Christianity; Hiberno-Latin Culture; Monasticism in the Early Middle Ages; Religion: The Coming of Christianity; Saint Patrick, Problem of; **Primary Documents:** From Muirchú's *Life of St. Patrick* (c. 680)

Bibliography

Anderson, A. O., and M. O. Anderson, eds. and trans. *Adomnán's Life of Columba.* 1961. Reprint, 1991.

Bray, Dorothy Ann. *A List of Motifs in the Lives of the Early Irish Saints.* 1992.

Connolly, Seán. "Vita Prima Sanctae Brigidae." *Journal of the Royal Society of Antiquaries of Ireland* 119 (1989): 5–49.

Connolly, Seán, and Jean-Michel Picard. "Cogitosus: Life of St. Brigit." *Journal of the Royal Society of Antiquaries of Ireland* 117 (1987): 5–27.

Heist, W. W. *Vitae Sanctorum Hiberniae.* 1965.

Herbert, Máire. *Iona, Kells, and Derry: The History and Hagiography of the Monastic Familia of Columba.* 1988.

Howlett, D. R., ed. and trans. *The Book of Letters of Saint Patrick the Bishop.* 1994.

Hughes, Kathleen. *The Church in Early Irish Society.* 1966.

Hughes, Kathleen. *Early Christian Ireland: An Introduction to the Sources.* 1972.

Kenney, J. F. *The Sources for the Early History of Ireland: Ecclesiastical.* 1929. Reprint, 1979.

Ó hAodha, Donncha, ed. and trans. *Bethu Brigte.* 1978.

Plummer, Charles, ed. and trans. *Bethada Náem nÉrenn: Lives of Irish Saints.* 2 vols. 1922. Reprint, 1968.

Plummer, Charles, ed. *Vitae Sanctorum Hiberniae.* 2 vols. 1910. Reprint, 1968.

Sharpe, Richard. *Medieval Irish Saints' Lives.* 1991.

Sharpe, Richard, trans. *Adomnán of Iona: Life of St. Columba.* 1995.

Dorothy Ann Bray

Health and Welfare since 1950, State Provisions for

Ireland evolved from an economically backward, insular, and largely agricultural country to one of the richest nations in the world by the close of the twentieth century. Over the final quarter of the century the welfare state, which began to develop after the World War II, slowly matured from a residual system catering largely for the poor and the working class to a comprehensive one. Elsewhere in Europe, politically strong labor movements gave momentum to the development of welfare states during postwar reconstruction.

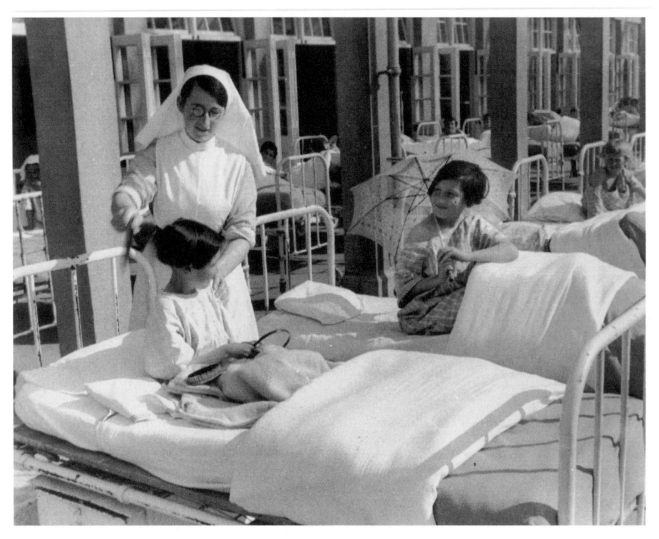

Noël Browne, minister for health from 1948 to 1951, waged a crusade against the widespread scourge of tuberculosis. He and members of his department presided over the construction of numerous specialist sanatoria that, together with the arrival of BCG vaccine, aided greatly in the eradication of the disease during the 1950s. As this photograph indicates, "fresh air" was prized in these sanatoria. © FR. BROWNE S.B. COLLECTION/IRISH PICTURE LIBRARY. REPRODUCED BY PERMISSION.

However, the Ireland of 1950 was still predominantly a rural society, with the urban working class making up less than a quarter of the workforce. The Catholic Church's social teaching, which favored a minimal welfare state, was heavily influential in the formation of policy. Initial government plans in the late 1940s proposed comprehensive social insurance and an outline national health service, both closely modeled on the recommendations of the United Kingdom's Beveridge Report (1942). However, far more timid proposals were actually implemented, in contrast to the Beveridge-style welfare state developed in Northern Ireland.

The setting up of new Departments of Health and of Social Welfare in 1947 marked a shift from local to central government as the driving force in social provision. (*Social welfare* is the term customarily used to de-

scribe both social security [social-insurance] and parallel means-tested welfare payments.) The Department of Health's ambitious hospital-building program of the 1940s and 1950s put in place a modern hospital infrastructure. The new social-insurance system (1953) rationalized previously fragmented social-security provisions into a single national scheme, but the middle class, the public service, and farmers remained outside its scope. Social-insurance pensions were not introduced until 1961. The social-insurance system closely followed the U.K. model, with flat-rate payments rather than the earnings-related benefits of continental Europe.

The Catholic Church backed the medical profession in strongly opposing a proposal for free medical care for mothers and children, in a clash that led to the fall of the government in 1951. This victory by church and medical interests helped to fix a model of mixed public and private medical care that continues in the early twenty-first century. However, in spite of initial church misgivings that such a scheme would "lower the sense of personal responsibility and seriously weaken the moral fiber of the people" (Barrington, 1987: 235), free hospital care for the low- and middle-income groups was introduced from 1956. Public-sector medical consultants retained a right to private practice. The state-run Voluntary Health Insurance Board set up in 1957 helped to underpin private hospital care. In 1991 the entire population was made eligible for free hospital care as public patients. Encouraged by speedier access to treatment for private patients, however, almost half the population were insured for private hospital care in 2000. A segregated system of free family-doctor care for the poor through dispensary doctors was abolished in 1972. Public patients now have a choice of family doctor and are treated in general practice alongside private patients.

As the more prosperous Ireland of the 1960s modernized, urbanized, and opened up to the outside world, the philosophy of a minimalist welfare state was replaced by a new emphasis on developing and expanding social services. Catholic Church influence began to wane, ironically as the post-Vatican II church now favored an active approach of expanding welfare provision and tackling poverty.

The 1970s was a decade of expansion for social welfare. Among the new payments introduced were retirement pensions at sixty-five, invalidity pensions, and death grants. The old-age-pension age was reduced from seventy to sixty-six. A uniform safety net called supplementary welfare replaced discretionary assistance dating back to the poor law. Social-insurance cover was extended to the middle class. The changing family was reflected in new schemes of unmarried mother's allowance, deserted wife's benefit, and deserted wife's allowance, modeled on payments to widows. In the 1990s these became the gender-neutral "one-parent family payment."

Since joining the European Union (EU) in 1973, Ireland has become more exposed to social-policy influences from outside the U.K. European Union laws, in particular those prescribing equal treatment for men and women, and EU-funded social programs have been important in shaping policy. Up to the 1980s Irish women's workforce participation was very low. Indeed, before 1973, women public servants lost their jobs on marriage. Ireland's social-welfare system, as in the United Kingdom, was designed around a male breadwinner. Payments to men included additions for a dependent wife and children. Up to 1986 married women's benefits were severely curtailed until the European Directive (79/7/EEC) on Equal Treatment for Men and Women in Social Security ended formal discrimination against women in the welfare code.

As women's workforce participation increased dramatically during the economic boom of the 1990s, a vigorous debate raged about state assistance toward childcare costs. Although tax relief for childcare costs was the favored option of the trade unions, the government was wary of ignoring low-income parents and of alienating full-time parents. So the chosen form of childcare subsidy, implemented from 2001, was to grant substantial increases in the social-welfare child benefits paid to all families.

Across the Western world the recession of the 1980s and changes in the dominant ideology led to moves to contain costs and to curb the welfare state. In Ireland the recession of the 1980s was particularly deep and was exacerbated by a crisis in the public finances. Health spending was restricted, and the number of hospital beds was reduced. The policy shift toward community-based care and away from large institutions brought even sharper reductions in the number of psychiatric beds.

In spite of cutbacks elsewhere, during the 1980s social-welfare benefits improved in real terms alongside a steep growth in spending as unemployment soared. The Commission on Social Welfare (1986), which conducted the first systematic review since the late 1940s, argued for benefit levels that would be adequate relative to incomes elsewhere in society. It also recommended simplified and rationalized payments to the different categories of recipients, along with comprehensive social insurance. Subsequently, social-insurance cover was extended to the self-employed, to part-time workers, and to newly recruited public servants.

The lowest rates of welfare payments were increased significantly, bringing them closer to incomes from work. To encourage movement from welfare to work, rather than cutting or limiting existing benefits, complex new benefits for the reemployed were introduced. Continued improvement in welfare provision in Ireland took place at the same time as the welfare restrictions of the Thatcher years in the United Kingdom. This brought Irish social welfare payments ahead of those in Northern Ireland for the first time.

Traditionally, services for people with disabilities depended heavily on state-aided voluntary-sector initiatives. From the 1980s however, EU training funds helped to expand day places for people with disabilities, such as in sheltered workshops. The 1990s saw the first systematic assessment of needs in relation to people with mental handicaps, along with significant funding to expand services.

The difficult economic conditions of the 1980s gave birth to a new form of social partnership. From 1987 on, a series of detailed economic and social programs were negotiated between government and the social partners, initially embracing employers, trade unions, and farmers. From 1996 on, social partnership expanded to include organizations of the unemployed and other community interests. A trade-off between modest pay rises and tax cuts has been at the heart of these national agreements. This has tilted the balance more toward tax reductions than improved public services. Social-service spending has grown but has not matched the exceptional rise in GNP experienced in the 1990s. But specific improvements in services (for example, free hospital care for all) were negotiated as part of these agreements. Influential working groups on specific topics set up under the social partnership have helped to shape the details of social policy.

From small and slow beginnings after 1945, Ireland had developed a modern welfare state by the close of the twentieth century. Flat-rate social-insurance benefits and a substantial private health-care sector have yielded an Irish welfare model closer to U.S. and U.K. systems than to those of northern Europe.

SEE ALSO Equal Economic Rights for Women in Independent Ireland; European Union; Farming Families; Mother and Child Crisis; Social Change since 1922; **Primary Documents:** Letter to John A. Costello, the Taoiseach (5 April 1951)

Bibliography

Barrington, Ruth. *Health Welfare and Politics.* 1987.

Burke, Helen. "Foundation Stones of Irish Social Policy: 1831–1951." In *Irish Social Policy in Context*, edited by Gabriel Kiely, Anne O'Donnell, Patricia Kennedy, and Suzanne Quin. 1999.

Conroy, Pauline. "From the Fifties to the Nineties: Social Policy Comes Out of the Shadows." In *Irish Social Policy in Context*, edited by Gabriel Kiely, Anne O'Donnell, Patricia Kennedy, and Suzanne Quin. 1999.

Cousins, Mel. *The Irish Social Welfare System, Law, and Social Policy.* 1995.

O'Connell, Philip, and David Rottman. "The Irish Welfare State in Comparative Perspective." In *The Development of Industrial Society in Ireland*, edited by John H. Goldthorpe and Christopher T. Whelan. 1992.

Eithne Fitzgerald

Heaney, Seamus

Born on 13 April 1939, Irish poet, playwright, critic, and translator Seamus Justin Heaney (1939–), received the Nobel Prize for literature in 1995 for the lyrical beauty and integrity of his work. The eldest of nine children, Seamus Heaney was born thirty-five miles northwest of Belfast on the small farm of "Mossbawn" near Castledawson, Co. Derry, Northern Ireland, where his father raised cattle. A gifted student, in 1957 Heaney entered Queens University, Belfast, where he was influenced by the poetry of Ted Hughes and Gerard Manley Hopkins and by Anglo-Saxon literature. Heaney married Marie Devlin in 1965 and published his first volume of poems, *The Death of a Naturalist*, in 1966. Childhood memories, disappointments, fears, and losses that are buried in the land and language and must be "dug up" by the poet are central to *Death of a Naturalist* as well as to his subsequent books, *Door into the Dark* (1969) and *Wintering Out* (1972). During the late 1960s, while teaching at Queens University, Heaney—a constitutional nationalist—became involved in the civil-rights movement for Catholic equality in Northern Ireland. He later moved his family from Belfast to Glanmore Cottage in County Wicklow in 1972. While in Wicklow, Heaney worked as a freelance journalist and published his most highly regarded book, *North*, in 1975. *North* was Heaney's most profound historical and mythological exploration of the violence in Northern Ireland. The Heaneys relocated in 1976 to Dublin, where they still reside. During the 1980s Heaney began teaching at Harvard University and helped to launch the Derry-based multicultural art alliance Field Day Theatre Company. Ancient Irish poetry as well as writers as diverse as Wordsworth and Dante and James Joyce and Patrick Kavanagh informed Heaney's *Field Work* (1979), *Sweeney Astray* (1983), and *Station Island* (1984). *The Haw Lantern* (1989) revealed the influence of contemporary eastern European writers and the increasing internationalization of Heaney's work. The pastoral gave way to the political and the transcendent, and the earthy language of his early work became more abstract and translucent in *Seeing Things* (1991), *The Spirit Level* (1996), and *Electric Light* (2001). These global shifts are recorded in Heaney's prose collections *Preoccupations* (1980), *The Government of the Tongue* (1988), and *The Redress of Poetry* (1995). However, it was the Derry dialect of his youth that inspired Heaney's highly acclaimed translation of *Beowulf* (1999) and reconfirmed his position in the pantheon of Irish poets.

SEE ALSO Arts: Modern Irish and Anglo-Irish Literature and the Arts since 1800; Poetry, Modern; **Primary Documents:** "Punishment" (1975)

Bibliography

Durkan, Michael, and Rand Brandes. *Seamus Heaney: A Reference Guide.* 1996.

Heaney, Seamus. *Opened Ground: Selected Poems, 1966–1996.* 1998.

Heaney, Seamus. *Finders Keepers: Selected Prose, 1971–2001.* 2002.

Rand Brandes

Hiberno-English

Hiberno-English, or Irish-English as it is sometimes called, is a variety of English strongly influenced by the Gaelic that was spoken by most of the Irish population until well into the nineteenth century. Other formative influences were the Englishes of the Planters who came to Ireland in the sixteenth and seventeenth centuries, from the southwest of England, and from Scotland in the case of the north of Ireland.

Formal study of the dialect has had a relatively late start. In the nineteenth century and into the twentieth, Hiberno-English was associated with what is called the "stage Irishman" in the theatre and periodical cartoons of the times, which depicted the Irish as subhuman figures of fun. The Irish accent, called a "brogue" even in the time of Jonathan Swift, was something which educational systems tried to eradicate in the children of the Irish, whether in Ireland or abroad. In the early years of Irish independence the new state tried to focus on the restoration of Gaelic, and paid little attention to Irish use of English. With the advent of postmodernism and postcolonialism, attitudes to Hiberno-English and other World Englishes have changed radically across the globe. From the late decades of the twentieth century especially, scholars through books, surveys, and dictionaries have recognised its distinctiveness, and tried to describe Hiberno-English.

Hiberno-English has a distinctive phonology; for example, a dental pronunciation of *t* and *d*, which leads to pronunciation sometimes transcribed as 'throuble' (trouble), vocabulary (e.g., words derived from the Gaelic such as *boreen* [little road]), grammar and syntax, (e.g., "I'm after washing the dishes" to indicate the recent past), and is particularly noted for its witty and expressive use of images and tropes ("He'd mind mice at a crosssroads" [O'Farrell 1980, p. 28]). It is not surprising that writers, especially dramatists, were the first to recognize the potential of Hiberno-English, beginning with Shakespeare's colorful portrayal of McMorris (*Henry the Fifth*). Nobel prize winners W. B. Yeats, Samuel Beckett, and Seamus Heaney, and other famous writers such as James Joyce, J. M. Synge, Sean O'Casey, and Brian Friel, have used it to great effect in their works. New Irish poets and fiction writers as well as playwrights, continue to use this vibrant dialect today.

In spite of Ireland's new confidence, Hiberno-English is declining. The Gaelic past is further removed in time; education and Ireland's new cosmopolitanism have also been responsible. What remains, especially in informal situations, is the pronunciation, recurrent words, and grammatical expressions, and continuing invention of new idioms and images.

SEE ALSO Arts: Early Modern Literature and the Arts from 1500 to 1800; Language and Literacy: Decline of Irish Language; Language and Literacy: Irish Language since 1922; Middle English Literature

Bibliography

Christensen, Lis. *A First Glossary of Hiberno-English.* 1996.

Dolan, T. P. *A Dictionary of Hiberno-English.* 1999.

Fippula, Markku. *The Grammar of Irish English: Language in Hibernian Style.* 1999.

Kallen, Jeffrey L., ed. *Focus on Ireland.* Varieties of English around the World. 1997.

Kiberd, Declan. *Inventing Ireland: The Literature of the Modern Nation.* 1995.

Kirk, John M., and Dónall Ó Baoill. *Language Links: The Languages of Scotland and Ireland.* Vol. 2 of Belfast Studies in Language, Culture and Politics. 2001.

O'Farrell, Padraic. *How the Irish Speak English.* 1980.

Ó Muirithe, Diarmaid. *A Dictionary of Anglo-Irish.* 2000.

Share, Bernard. *Slanguage—A Dictionary of Slang and Colloquial English in Ireland.* 1997.

Todd, Loreto. *The Language of Irish Literature.* 1989.

Patricia A. Lynch

~

Hiberno-Latin Culture

The coming of Christianity to Ireland in the fifth century brought about many changes in Irish society, one of the most profound being the introduction of the Latin language. Ireland had never been a part of the Roman Empire and therefore had never acquired the apparatus of Roman government, which included Latin as the everyday lingua franca not only of administrators but also of the population at large. The Rome that Irishmen revered was, in the words of the great Irish missionary Saint Columbanus, not the Rome of the Caesars but the Rome of the Saints Peter and Paul. Within a century of receiving formal Christianity, however, Irish scholars had acquired a remarkable mastery of Latin, but it was the Latin of the Bible and the church fathers rather than of Virgil. The image of Ireland as a haven of classical Latin literature (and even of Greek) in the decades following the fall of the Roman Empire has been greatly exaggerated, but the reality, while more modest, is no less impressive in its own way. Whether the initial impetus owed anything to the activities of the first continental missionaries, led by Bishop Palladius, is impossible to say; that Gallican mission has left no traces, either in surviving manuscripts or in any texts associated with Palladius and his followers. The only fifth-century writings to survive, Patrick's *Confessio* and letter, left no mark on later Irish writings in Latin, except insofar as Patrick's works display a mastery of what has been called biblical style by its discoverer, David Howlett, and that biblical style was to become a distinguishing feature of later Hiberno-Latin prose compositions. It is reasonable to suppose that there was continuity of Latin literacy from the fifth century on, but the hymn in praise of Patrick traditionally attributed to his disciple Secundinus (*Audite omnes amantes*) is now believed to be late sixth-century in date, and the work of Colmán Alo (of Lynally, Co. Meath, d. 610) rather than the fifth-century Secundinus. It already attests to a respectable grasp of Latin language and metrics. A possible rival in terms of dating is the remarkable poem *Altus prosator* (Ancient creator), a sort of "Paradise Lost" ascribed to Columba (Colum Cille), founder of the monastery of Iona (d. 597). However, that work is believed by modern scholars to be of seventh-century date.

It is only with the figure of Columbanus, originally of Bangor, Co. Down, later founder of monasteries in Gaul and Italy (d. 615), that the first real evidence emerges of substantial writings in Latin by Irishmen. Six of his letters survive, along with a number of poems, sermons, and two monastic rules. He mentions two mentors by name, the British writers Finnian (Uennianus) and Gildas; the latter's *De excidio Britanniae* has left definite traces on Columbanus's prose style. The evidence of surviving manuscripts makes clear the debt to British teachers in the formative stages of the Irish Church, but Columbanus's complete mastery of Latin, in a variety of different prose styles, as well as his command of both quantitative and stressed meters, demonstrates for the first time the full range of native Hiberno-Latin skills. This range finds expression in prose and verse compositions throughout the seventh century: saints' lives and instructional literature, biblical commentaries and Latin grammars, canon law and handbooks of penance, besides a rich variety of poems devoted to biblical learning and computistics (the mathematics required to calculate the date of Easter), devotional hymns, and hagiography. One of the earliest of these compositions in date, Cummian's letter on the Paschal question (632/633), is remarkable for its rich patristic sources (i.e., the writings of the church fathers—some of them unique) and for the collection of ten different Easter tables (the mathematical tables used to calculate the date of Easter) on which its author was able to draw. Sometime in the mid-seventh century the arrival in Ireland of Isidore of Seville's writings spurred a massive production of Hiberno-Latin writing on every imaginable subject, and across the full spectrum of the monastic curriculum. Newly acquired grammatical texts from late antiquity led to a surge of renewed interest in that field also, and Irish writers perfected a new type of instructional handbook, the elementary grammar, for use with beginners in Latin, which led in turn to more advanced study using exegetical grammars. By combining the methods of biblical exegetes and Latin grammarians in one text, Irish teachers perfected an instructional technique that was clearly very successful. Nowhere is this more clearly seen than in the remarkably uniform language of these different authors. Though scholars have happily used the term *Hiberno-Latin* to describe the language of Irish texts from this period; in fact, Irish Latin was indistinguishable in grammar and syntax from its continental counterpart—a testament to the efficacy of teaching in Irish schools.

Alongside the ordinary expressions of Latin culture in Ireland, however, there was also the extraordinary: the so-called *Hisperica famina* (Western sayings) make their appearance in the mid-seventh century. A "culture fungus of decay" (as one scholar, Eoin Mac Neill, described them), these bizarre colloquies are a pastiche of the pedantic hypercorrectness of some of the grammarians, and they mock the high-falutin' language and vocabulary of the schools. They are probably not to be taken too seriously (and may not be Irish at all in origin). Another exotic flowering of Irish Latin culture, however, definitely is a native concoction: The bizarre writings of Virgilius Maro "the Grammarian" are an extraordinary rodomontade (bluster) of mock learning that pokes glorious fun at the pomposities of the self-same schoolmen. The fun was probably well intended, but Virgilius Maro's more exuberant pronouncements made their way into the works of seriously minded computists and biblical commentators, with the result that continental men of learning, when they came face to face with such oddities in the eighth century, tended to look askance at Irish learning.

What most impresses, however, is the sheer quantity of Hiberno-Latin writings in the seventh and eighth centuries and the range of their subject-matter. Hiberno-Latin authors drew on a huge variety of Late Latin, biblical, and patristic sources, in addition to unorthodox writings like the commentaries of the heresiarch Pelagius, and a remarkable number of biblical apocrypha nowhere else available. They also began to gloss their Latin texts in the vernacular, very quickly passing to full texts in Old Irish. The most remarkable example of this phenomenon is the Cambrai Homily (probably mid-seventh century), a bilingual Latin-Irish text combining excerpts from the gospels, Pauline Epistles, and Gregory the Great's gospel homilies, with a parallel text in Old Irish whose language is extraordinarily archaic. The oldest known manuscript with bilingual Latin-Irish glosses dates to about 700, but the most famous is the Würzburg codex of about 800 containing Pauline epistles with a huge number of glosses in both Latin and Old Irish. This probably belonged to Clemens Scottus, master of the palace school at Aachen in Charlemagne's time, who ended his days at the shrine of the Irish saint Kilian in Würzburg.

Hiberno-Latin scholars enjoyed a very good reputation when they traveled across Europe, following in the steps of Columbanus. The eighth century saw the appearance on the continent of men like Dicuil (author of a remarkable cosmographical work, *Liber de mensura orbis terrae* [Book on the measurement of the earth], as well as computistical and grammatical texts), Dungal of Pavia, Muredach Scottus "most learned of all men" (in his own estimation, at any rate), and Joseph Scottus, friend of Alcuin. Even more remarkable, however, was the generation of scholars that followed them in the ninth century, especially Sedulius Scottus of Liège and his circle of friends, and the most famous of them all, Iohannes Eriugena ("Irish-born"). These men were the superiors of their continental contemporaries not only in terms of Latin learning but also in their knowledge of Greek. Eriugena in particular was by common consent the finest intellect of his generation. In their Latin poetry (and Greek poetry too in Eriugena's case) Sedulius and Eriugena demonstrated a complete mastery of the language. Sedulius too, with his "Handbook for Princes" (*De rectoribus Christianis*), also established a genre that was to have lasting influence in the area of political philosophy. In Eriugena's case his philosophical works (especially the *Periphyseon: On the Division of Nature*) reveal a mind that had no equal in Europe in his time, and a unique grasp of Greek philosophy.

SEE ALSO Arts: Early and Medieval Arts and Architecture; Brehon Law; Early Medieval Ireland and Christianity; Hagiography; Manuscript Writing and Illumination; Monasticism in the Early Middle Ages; Saint Patrick, Problem of; **Primary Documents:** "Columbanus to His Monks" (c. 600)

Bibliography

Bieler, Ludwig. Ireland, *Harbinger of the Middle Ages*. 1963.

Kenney, James F. *Ecclesiastical*. Vol. 1 of *The Sources for the Early History of Ireland*. 1929.

Ó Cróinín, Dáibhí. *Early Medieval Ireland, 400–1200*. 1995.

Dáibhí Ó Cróinín

High Crosses

First named as such in *The Annals of the Four Masters* in the year 957, these stone crosses reach a height of up to 20 feet. More than two hundred survive, many bearing panels illustrating biblical scenes, and they were sculpted from sandstone, granite, or limestone by master craftsmen who occasionally inscribed their names but never their status (e.g., monk or layman). The crosses were probably copied from (smaller) examples in other media, including wood and metal, and may originally have been painted.

They were erected at two different periods—the ninth/tenth century and the twelfth. A few examples may be earlier, but the normally accepted eighth-century dating for the Ahenny group of crosses in counties Tipperary and Kilkenny is now being challenged in favor of the ninth. The earlier group is characterized by a ring ("Celtic cross") which probably combined a structural function (preventing the arms from snapping off) with a cosmic symbolism, making Christ's Crucifixion at the center of the circle the crucial event in the history of the universe.

Cross of the Scriptures at Clonmacnoise (early tenth century), an example of early Christian sculpture. © GERAY SWEENEY/CORBIS. REPRODUCED BY PERMISSION.

The ring first developed in the Mediterranean area, and it was probably Rome that provided the ultimate inspiration for the biblical carvings and the unusual idea of applying them to the surface of a cross. While the interpretation of some of the figured panels is controversial, the identifiable scenes—like similar continental frescoes—portray stories from the Old and New Testaments and the lives of the desert fathers Paul and Anthony. Though the subjects selected for illustration differ from cross to cross, they generally concentrate on showing how God helps the faithful in time of danger, and illustrate the life, passion, death, and resurrection of Christ. The crosses are also decorated with sophisticated geometrical patterns of bosses, interlace, and so forth, whose symbolic meanings remain enigmatic.

Crosses of the earlier group are located on eastern and northern monastic sites, as well as in the midlands where inscriptions deciphered in the 1970s and 1980s reveal patronage from successive Uí Néill high kings in the erection of the crosses. Similar patronage from the O'Connor high kings of Connacht was involved in creating crosses of the later group at Tuam, Co. Galway, and the O'Brien dynasty and others were instrumental in raising further examples of this later group in north Munster, where they were probably associated with the religious reform movement of the twelfth century. These later crosses frequently bear high-relief figures of Christ and an ecclesiastic.

SEE ALSO Arts: Early and Medieval Arts and Architecture; Sculpture, Early and Medieval

Bibliography

Harbison, Peter. *The High Crosses of Ireland.* 3 vols. 1992.

Peter Harbison

Hillsborough Agreement

See Anglo-Irish Agreement of 1985 (Hillsborough Agreement).

~

Home Rule Movement and the Irish Parliamentary Party

1870 TO 1891   **DONALD E. JORDAN, JR.**

1891 TO 1918   **MICHAEL LAFFAN**

1870 TO 1891

The Home Rule movement that animated Irish political life for over forty years began with the formation of the Home Government Association in May 1870. It was an inauspicious beginning, a meeting of forty-nine mostly Conservative Protestants in Dublin, but it came at a propitious time for Irish nationalism. The Fenian rising of 1867, although a failure in its immediate goal of winning Irish freedom from British rule, had focused the attention of the Irish and British public on Irish grievances and compelled both British political parties to address those grievances, if for no other reason than to satisfy moderate nationalist aspirations while discrediting the radical ones of the Fenians and their supporters. In this environment Isaac Butt, the driving force behind the formation of the Home Government Association, was well situated to attempt to bring the disparate elements of Irish nationalism together.

A former Tory, an opponent of Daniel O'Connell, and a man committed to the propriety of parliamentary politics and to a continued constitutional link with Britain, Butt had distinguished himself by defending Fenian prisoners following the 1867 rising. At the time of the setting up of the Home Government Association he was president of the Amnesty Association, which he had founded in the previous year to advocate amnesty for Fenian prisoners, and was leader of the Irish Tenant League, also established in 1869. Within the Home Government Association he was able to bring together, albeit briefly, Conservatives who had become disillusioned with the union with Britain because of the disestablishment of Church of Ireland, Liberals, constitutional nationalists, and Fenians around a loosely defined platform of federalism within the United Kingdom. The Conservative Protestants and landlords were the first to bolt, realizing quickly that any form of Home Rule for Ireland would threaten their ascendancy over politics and the land. Butt's hope for a comprehensive and inclusive nationalist organization was never realized because Catholic nationalists soon dominated the association, bringing with them commitments to land reform and denominational education, along with the sanction of the Catholic hierarchy.

Throughout its three years of existence the Home Government Association remained little more than a Dublin-based organization whose primary role was to coordinate the activities of local Home Rule bodies. It had no central executive and refused to endorse candidates for election or advocate causes other than Home Rule, although Butt understood that Home Rule and land reform were inseparable. Nonetheless, a series of by-election victories for candidates professing allegiance to Home Rule demonstrated the growing strength of the movement and the ability of cadres of Fenian-inspired local nationalists, often in tenuous collusion with sympathetic priests, to turn out the vote. In November 1873 more than 800 delegates met in Dublin for a conference during which the Home Rule League was founded to replace the Home Government Association. Like its predecessor, the new league was a single-issue, inclusive organization with few resources and a desire to preserve a fragile unity under the banner of Home Rule.

THE FORMATION OF THE HOME RULE PARTY

Two months later, the growing strength of the Home Rule movement was demonstrated when fifty-nine candidates professing Home Rule sympathies were elected to seats in the House of Commons. At least half of these MPs were former Liberals who had responded to the changing political climate, but whose allegiance to Home Rule was not always firm. Soon after the election, forty-six of the Home Rule MPs established the first formal Irish political party, the Home Rule party, agreeing to work together to promote Irish reform legislation in Parliament. As its chairman, Butt had no authority to enforce discipline, and with the Tories controlling a secure majority in the House of Commons, there was little incentive to do so. Furthermore, ever-respectful of parliamentary decorum and willing to give the Tories a chance to propose reform for Ireland, Butt urged patience at a time when the countryside and a radical cadre of MPs were not inclined to do so. To Butt's dismay, Joseph Biggar, MP for Cavan, Frank Hugh O'Donnell, MP for Dungarvan, and John O'Connor Power, MP for Mayo, initiated a practice of using parliamentary procedures and interminably long speeches to obstruct legislation as a means of bringing attention to Irish grievances. They were soon joined by Charles Stewart Parnell, who in 1875 had been elected MP for Meath.

During the 1877 session of parliament Biggar and Parnell took obstructionism to new levels, and in so doing, gained attention and support in Ireland and within the Irish community in Britain while further distancing themselves from Butt and the moderate majority within the Home Rule party. The obstructionists' case that Ireland's voice must be heard in the House of Commons was strengthened by the disinterest of the Tory government in reform legislation for Ireland and the consequent failure of Butt's strategy of giving the government a chance. In August 1877 the Home Rule Confederation of Great Britain, a more radical and working-class organization than its Irish counterpart, replaced Butt with Parnell as its president, signaling a shift in public opinion that would soon sweep Ireland as well. Although Butt remained in control of the Home Rule party until his death in May 1879, Parnell demonstrated a command of parliamentary procedures and the ability to gauge and exploit popular opinion that would lead him quickly to the leadership of the party and the nation.

PARNELL AND THE LAND WAR

Parnell's obstructionism and growing popularity attracted the attention of influential Fenians, who had broken formally with Butt in August 1876 but were facing the reality that their dream of an armed insurrection against Britain was on hold, if not dead. Foremost among them were Michael Davitt, recently released from Dartmoor prison after serving seven years for arms running, and John Devoy, who had also been imprisoned for Fenian activity before emigrating to New York City, where he was a journalist and an active member of Clan na Gael, the U.S. wing of the Fenian movement. Together they worked out the details of an alliance between Parnell and the Fenians, dubbed the "New Departure." It called for an aggressive but constitutional campaign for land reform leading to peasant proprietorship through compulsory purchase, and for Irish self-government. Although a limited version of an alliance between Fenians and constitutional nationalists had been operating in the west of Ireland since 1873, the alliance proposed in 1878 brought with it the dynamic leadership of Parnell and Davitt at a time when a deteriorating economy was radicalizing the Irish countryside. Moreover, it carried with it the potential of linking effectively for the first time the land and national movements in a united campaign.

Between 1879 and 1881 the campaign for Home Rule was on hold while the immediate needs of tenant farmers for relief and the campaign for a permanent solution to the land question dominated the political agenda. The passage of the Land Act in 1881, the subsequent arrest of Irish National Land League leaders, including Parnell, and the suppression of the league in October 1881 brought an end to the first phase of the land movement. This end was formalized in May 1882 with the "Kilmainham Treaty," by which the league leadership was released from prison after Parnell agreed to curtail the land agitation in return for assurances that tenants in arrears with their rent, who had been excluded from the Land Act, would become eligible to take advantage of its provisions. Although the first phase of the Land War had not moved the campaign for Home Rule forward appreciably, it had demonstrated the potential of a mobilized rural Ireland to force concessions from a Liberal administration.

Accordingly, when in October 1882 Parnell replaced the Irish National Land League with the Irish National League, Home Rule was fixed at the head of its program. The Land League goal of peasant proprietary was included, but rather than being brought about through compulsory purchase, it was now to be accomplished through amendments to the purchase clauses of the Land Act of 1881. In keeping with this focus on parliamentary activity, Parnell sought and received assurances that the new league would be controlled by the parliamentary party and would serve its agenda. To a considerable degree, between 1882 and 1885 the National League was an organization waiting for an opportune time to mobilize the Irish countryside again. That opportunity came with the general election of 1885.

Anticipating a general election, the parliamentary and local leadership moved quickly to form league branches, with the number growing from 242 in January 1884 to 592 a year later. By the time of the general election in November–December the league had more than 1,200 branches, many of them formed solely to act as electoral agents for the Irish Parliamentary Party. In this role they functioned splendidly, mobilizing an electorate that had more than tripled as a result of franchise reform enacted in 1884. The local branches sent delegates to carefully orchestrated county conventions where they chose preselected candidates, assured that the newly enfranchised voters completed the required forms and paid their poor rates in order to be enrolled on the voters' register, and transported voters to the polling places. Parnell insisted that the general election in Ireland be fought on the single issue of Home Rule. When the polling ended, Home Rulers had secured eighty-six seats—eighty-five in Ireland and one in Britain. They had taken all but eighteen constituencies in Ireland, sixteen of those in Ulster, with the remaining two being those allotted to Trinity College, Dublin. Parnell's eighty-six supporters matched exactly the total that separated the victorious Liberals from the defeated Conservatives, thus ensuring that a Home Rule bill would be presented in the upcoming session.

THE FIRST HOME RULE BILL
AND ITS AFTERMATH

Although Liberal Prime Minister W. E. Gladstone did not consult with the Irish members as he prepared his Home Rule bill, the measure that he presented to the House of Commons on 8 April 1886 went a long way toward satisfying the aspirations of Parnell and his party. The Government of Ireland Bill of 1886 proposed to create an Irish parliament and executive with responsibility for the domestic affairs of Ireland, although the government could neither support nor discriminate against any particular religion. In addition, it would have limited control over revenue and trade, while the Royal Irish Constabulary would remain controlled from Westminster, along with defense, foreign and colonial affairs, and the powers and prerogatives of the Crown. No special provisions were made for Ulster, although the antidiscrimination provisions were clearly designed to ease Protestant concerns that Home Rule would mean "Rome Rule." Nonetheless, concerns for the religious and economic position of Protestants and for the allegedly special circumstances of Ulster featured prominently in the parliamentary debate, as did the question of whether Ireland warranted or could be entrusted with self-rule. On 8 June the bill was defeated on its second reading, forcing the resignation of the government and the dissolution of Parliament. In the subsequent general election the Conservatives were returned to office.

The Home Rule debate had solidified the alliance between the Irish Parliamentary Party and the Liberal Party. It had also demonstrated that there was a political consensus that reform was needed in the governance of Ireland. The new Conservative government was committed to reform, seeing it as an alternative to Home Rule and as a means of undermining Parnellism in Ireland. Conservative policy toward Ireland over the next six years has been characterized by L. Perry Curtis as one of "coercion and conciliation." Its primary architect was J. Arthur Balfour, Irish chief secretary from 1887 to 1891. His tenure of office began amid falling agricultural prices in Ireland which, along with a renewed militancy unleashed by the failure of the Home Rule bill, brought unrest and a restoration of the land movement that Parnell had succeeded in keeping under wraps during the previous four years. The government responded with the Criminal Law and Procedure Act of 1887 that gave the authorities emergency powers to deal with unrest, and especially with the proponents of the Plan of Campaign that had been declared in October 1886 by prominent Parnellites, although not endorsed by Parnell himself. The government also introduced the Land Act of 1887, which allowed leaseholders to take advantage of the provisions of the 1881 Land Act and for the first time enabled tenants in arrears with their rents to have them judicially reviewed and reduced, even if those rents had been fixed by the land courts established in 1881, something previously not possible. This was soon followed by the Land Purchase Act of 1888, which increased the funds available for tenants to purchase their holdings. As Virginia Crossman has pointed out in *Politics, Law, and Order in Nineteenth-Century Ireland*, Balfour's intention was to criminalize the land movement and the National League while bestowing some of its objectives from a supposedly benevolent government.

This process of criminalization of the land movement ran parallel with a judicial commission established by the government in 1888 to look into allegations made by *The Times* that Parnell and his associates in the Land and National Leagues were connected with, if not responsible for, agrarian and political crime in Ireland. Although the initial claims by *The Times* were proved to be based on forged letters, the commission heard extensive testimony and reviewed numerous documents that demonstrated the degree to which criminal acts were associated with the land and national movements. However, it was not able to establish direct connections between crime and the leaders of the movements. Although historians are not of one mind as to the degree of damage that the commission's proceedings did to Parnell, in the short term he seemed vindicated in the eyes of the Liberals, who renewed their overtures to him to pursue the alliance and to plan for a new Home Rule bill.

THE FALL OF PARNELL

To all appearances, Parnell seemed again to be in full control of the party and the Home Rule movement. The agrarian agitation associated with the Plan of Campaign was on the decline, thanks in large part to Balfour's coercion efforts as well as to the popularity of his land-reform measures. This enabled Parnell to reestablish Home Rule at the top of the agenda and to do so in the context of a revival of the alliance with the Liberals, who understood their dependence on the Parnellites if they were going to be restored to government at the next general election. In mid-December 1889, just weeks after the commission had issued its final report, Parnell and Gladstone met at Hawarden, Gladstone's estate, to plan a new campaign for Home Rule. Five days later, Captain W. H. O'Shea filed for divorce from his wife Katharine, naming Parnell as the corespondent. The full impact of this action was not apparent for nearly a year, during which time Parnell continued to command loyalty within the party and within Ireland. However, when he failed to offer a defense after the divorce petition went to trial in November 1890, Parnell's position and the Liberal alliance, on which his hopes for Home Rule rested, quickly deteriorated.

Immediately, Gladstone, pressed by British Nonconformists who formed the core of Liberal support, withdrew his support from Parnell and made it clear that both the alliance and quite possibly his own leadership of the Liberal Party would collapse if Parnell did not stand down from the leadership of the Irish party. Confronted with the prospect that the very foundation of the Home Rule campaign would be destroyed, forty-five Irish MPs split from Parnell in December 1890, leaving him with twenty-eight loyalists. This bitter split, which was to remain in effect until 1900, quickly spilled over into the Irish countryside, where in a series of by-elections in 1891 Parnell's defenders were defeated. Parnell campaigned vigorously, increasingly appealing to the more radical elements in the land and national movements from whom he had distanced himself over most of the previous decade, while at the same time condemning Gladstone and the Liberals with whom he had formulated political strategy since 1882. This campaign, during which Parnell vilified the very policy and strategies that he had been responsible for, undermined much of his authority in Ireland and weakened his already fragile health. He died on 6 October 1891 at the age of forty-five. With Parnell gone, the Liberal connection was salvaged, resulting in subsequent Home Rule bills in 1893 and 1912.

SEE ALSO Butt, Isaac; Davitt, Michael; Electoral Politics from 1800 to 1921; Ladies' Land League; Land Acts of 1870 and 1881; Land War of 1879 to 1882; Local Government since 1800; Parnell, Charles Stewart; Plan of Campaign; Politics: 1800 to 1921—Challenges to the Union; Protestant Ascendancy: Decline, 1800 to 1930; Sullivan Brothers (A. M. and T. D.); **Primary Documents:** Resolutions Adopted at the Home Rule Conference (18–21 November 1873); Speech Advocating Consideration of Home Rule by the House of Commons (30 June 1874); On Home Rule and the Land Question at Cork (21 January 1885); On Home Rule at Wicklow (5 October 1885); On the Home Rule Bill of 1886 (8 April 1886); The Irish Parliamentary Party Pledge (30 June 1892)

Bibliography

Bew, Paul. *C. S. Parnell.* 1980.

Boyce, D. George. *Nationalism in Ireland.* 1982. 3d edition, 1995.

Callanan, Frank. *The Parnell Split.* 1992.

Callanan, Frank. *T. M. Healy.* 1996.

Comerford, R. V. "Isaac Butt and the Home Rule Party, 1870–77." In *A New History of Ireland,* vol. 6, *Ireland under the Union II, 1870–1921,* edited by W. E. Vaughan. 1996.

Comerford, R. V. "The Parnell Era, 1883–91." In *A New History of Ireland,* vol. 6, *Ireland under the Union II, 1870–1921,* edited by W. E. Vaughan. 1996.

Crossman, Virginia. *Politics, Law, and Order in Nineteenth-Century Ireland.* 1996.

Curtis, L. Perry, Jr. *Coercion and Conciliation in Ireland, 1880–1892: A Study in Conservative Unionism.* 1963.

Lyons, F. S. L. *Charles Stewart Parnell.* 1977.

Lyons, F. S. L. *The Fall of Parnell, 1890–91.* 1960.

O'Brien, Conor Cruise. *Parnell and His Party, 1880–90.* 1957. Reprint, 1964.

O'Callaghan, Margaret. *British High Politics and a Nationalist Ireland: Criminality, Land, and the Law under Forster and Balfour.* 1994.

O'Day, Alan. *Parnell and the First Home Rule Episode.* 1986.

O'Day, Alan. *Irish Home Rule, 1867–1921.* 1998.

Thornley, David. *Isaac Butt and Home Rule.* 1964.

Donald E. Jordan, Jr.

1891 TO 1918

Between 1890 and 1891, a large majority of Charles Stewart Parnell's colleagues (forty-five out of seventy-three) sacrificed their leader in an effort to preserve his policy of an alliance with Gladstone's Liberal Party, a move known as the Parnell split. The result shattered the Irish Parliamentary Party. The willingness of the Irish MPs to do so has been seen as base ingratitude and as subservience to the demands of British politicians. It has also been seen as a backhanded compliment to the party's maturity and as proof that it had transcended its earlier role of a support group for one dominant individual. Under Parnell's leadership the Irish party had been characterized by unity and discipline, but for the next quarter century it would be marked by feuds and factionalism.

In three bitter by-elections that followed the split, almost two-thirds of the electors voted against Parnell's candidates. The dispute was not ended by his early death in October 1891, and rival nationalists contested the following general election with an exceptional degree of bitterness. Nine Parnellites and seventy-one anti-Parnellites were elected. Despite the disarray among his Irish allies, Gladstone introduced a new Home Rule bill in 1893. This measure passed the House of Commons, but its rejection by the Lords effectively ended prospects of Home Rule for the foreseeable future.

The party remained divided for nearly ten years, and the dominant anti-Parnellite faction was in turn weakened by disagreements over policies and personali-

Despite the defeat of the first Home Rule bill in 1886 and the disastrous split in the Irish Parliamentary Party in 1890, Home Rule long remained the goal of most Irish nationalists. The Home Rule banner of 1892 shown here signaled Gladstone's second attempt to win a parliament for Ireland (in 1893), but the House of Lords threw out the bill by a crushing majority. © PUBLIC RECORD OFFICE/TOPHAM-HIP/THE IMAGE WORKS. REPRODUCED BY PERMISSION.

ties. In particular, John Dillon adhered to the Liberal alliance and urged centralized control of the movement, while Tim Healy believed in independent opposition and a policy of decentralization.

In 1900 the party was reunited under the chairmanship of John Redmond, the leader of the minority Parnellite group, but new divisions soon emerged. Two of the leading Home Rulers soon quarreled with the leadership of Redmond and Dillon, his long-serving deputy; Healy and his followers were expelled in 1900, and William O'Brien resigned three years later. They would later join forces with other, more radical critics of the party.

A ONE-PARTY NATION

Yet until after the outbreak of the World War I the squabbling elements of the Home Rule movement encountered no serious opposition in nationalist Ireland. New ideas flourished and new movements gained widespread support, among them the Gaelic Athletic Association, the Gaelic League, and the Transport Workers' Union. Such groups displayed the vigor and inspired the commitment that had been associated with Parnellism in its prime. But in political terms nationalist Ireland remained a one-party nation, and most parliamentary candidates were returned unopposed. On rare occasions Home Rulers fought battles with unionists, above all in marginal Ulster constituencies, but the relations between the two parties more often took the form of a cold war in which each side recognized the other's sphere of

influence. From time to time dissident nationalists challenged the party's official leadership, but with the exception of O'Brien's following in County Cork they posed no serious threat.

This enduring ascendancy was made possible by the party's strengths, in particular by one basic fact: in many respects it reflected accurately the dominant elements and interests in nationalist Ireland. Its MPs tended to come from a lower social class than their British counterparts, the party paid close attention to local needs and demands, it was intimately involved in agrarian matters, and it displayed a formidable ability to infiltrate—and sometimes absorb—other bodies that might have endangered its position. This pattern was displayed with particular clarity after O'Brien formed the United Irish League in 1898. The menace that was posed by this new grouping provided a stimulus to the reunification of the Home Rule movement in 1900, and within a few years the party had taken over the league.

Redmond was forced to modify his personal taste for a policy of conciliation with British governments and Irish unionists, and Dillon's views proved to be more influential. He feared that Home Rule might be killed by kindness, as Conservative politicians hoped, and he believed that the party should distrust measures that could distract attention from the ultimate objective of a Dublin parliament. Home Rulers tended to be wary of reforms by Conservative governments, such as the Local Government Act of 1898 and the Wyndham Land Act of 1903. Even Liberal measures, such as old age pensions, could breed a dangerous degree of contentment as well as risk posing financial problems for a future Home Rule administration.

A change of government made relatively little difference to the party's general strategy; in the 1906 general election the Liberals won a massive overall majority and consequently were independent of Irish support. Many Liberals saw Irish Home Rule as a liability, associating it with the failures of Gladstone's last governments, and preferred to concentrate on other problems. An Irish council bill was proposed as a halfway house to Home Rule, but the measure was rejected by a convention of the United Irish League. Gradually nationalists became disillusioned with the party's failure to achieve Home Rule, and the alliance with the Liberals seemed to have brought a Dublin parliament no nearer. Two MPs resigned their seats, and one of them ran unsuccessfully for reelection in 1908 as a Sinn Féin candidate.

The party's fortunes were transformed by the political crisis of 1909 to 1911. The radical "People's Budget" was deeply unpopular in Ireland, but it opened new opportunities by provoking a conflict between the House of Commons and the Lords. Two general elections were held in 1910, and both of them resulted in deadlock between the main British political parties. Redmond made the most of his strong position, first assisting Asquith's government to break the power of the House of Lords and then prevailing on it to introduce a third Home Rule bill—which would not be subject to a veto by the Lords. There was widespread dissatisfaction at the inadequacy of the powers that would be devolved to Dublin under this scheme, but at least most Irish nationalists were confident that Home Rule was now unstoppable and that it would become law in a few years' time. The Parliamentary Party regained, briefly, its lost support.

RIVAL FACTIONS

Deprived of their protection from the House of Lords, the Ulster unionists felt desperate and resorted to radical measures; if necessary they would abandon political and parliamentary methods and fight to avert the threat of Home Rule. Ultimately they formed a paramilitary force, the Ulster Volunteers, and threatened rebellion if Home Rule were to be implemented. They were supported and incited by the Conservative Party, whose frustration in opposition was reinforced by outrage at what it regarded as a corrupt deal between Liberals and Home Rulers.

With victory in sight Redmond's main task was to prevent his allies from diluting their Home Rule proposals even further. Most nationalists were dismayed by

the unionists' recourse to military measures, fearing that decades of Irish constitutional activity would be undone and that the scorn that radicals felt for "Home Rule tactics" might be vindicated. Such views formed the background to the formation of the Irish Volunteers, a paramilitary force that was modeled on the unionists' rival private army. Nominally under the leadership of Eoin MacNeill, this body was from the outset influenced by the revolutionary Irish Republican Brotherhood.

As both British parties inched their way toward a compromise settlement in 1913 and 1914, Redmond yielded to government insistence that he should agree to some form of partition. This would grant Home Rule to "nationalist Ireland" but would exclude the largely unionist areas in northeast Ulster for a fixed number of years. However, no agreement was reached on the area to be excluded (what was "Ulster"?) or on how long such exclusion should last. Negotiations in Buckingham Palace between the party leaders failed to break the deadlock, and only with the outbreak of the First World War did British and Irish politicians escape an impasse that might have resulted in rebellion or civil war.

THE END OF THE HOME RULE MOVEMENT

Redmond pledged his support to the British war effort, but he also continued his efforts to ensure that Home Rule would become law. This was achieved in September 1914, although with the crucial qualifications that the act would come into effect only when the war ended and when amending legislation had been passed to deal with Ulster.

Nationalist Ireland celebrated its historic victory, but the events of August through September 1914 marked the beginning of the end of the Home Rule movement. Redmond soon went beyond his assurance that Irish forces could defend the island against German attack, and he urged members of the Irish Volunteers to join the British army and fight abroad. This action provoked a split with the original founders of the force, and the strength of his position was revealed when over 90 percent of the Volunteers followed the party leadership rather than side with its radical critics.

But the war became unpopular as the stalemate continued, month after month, year after year, and as the death toll rose steadily. Fears grew that conscription would be imposed on Ireland, particularly after January 1916 when it came into effect in Britain. One result of a ban on emigration was that large numbers of unemployed or underemployed young people were obliged to remain in the country, and many of them became restive. The unionist leader Edward Carson joined a coalition government in London while Redmond, perhaps unwisely, chose not to do so. And as Home Rule seemed to be no nearer, despite the famous victory of September 1914, fears of deception and betrayal became more widespread.

The Easter Rising of 1916, although aimed at the British, was also a devastating blow to the Irish Parliamentary Party; Redmond's claim to represent Irish nationalists now seemed less plausible. Republicans had seized the initiative, and despite the failure of their rebellion, their courage commanded the respect of enemies such as John Dillon. The insurrection was followed rapidly by new Home Rule negotiations—a halfhearted attempt to achieve a wartime settlement. Redmond felt obliged to make a new concession: the surrender of two counties with nationalist majorities, Fermanagh and Tyrone, to enlarge the excluded area of four unionist counties. This provoked much heart-searching among Home Rulers and precipitated revolt and defections by some of the party's followers in Ulster. A convention of northern nationalists supported Redmond's proposals, but he was soon faced with yet further demands and the collapse of the negotiations. It seemed to many people as if republican rebels had provided moderate politicians with one last chance to achieve Home Rule and that this opportunity had been squandered. The party's morale never recovered from the failure of the 1916 negotiations.

In the course of the following year the Redmondites began to encounter serious opposition from more radical nationalists. A motley coalition of Volunteers, Sinn Féiners, and others contested a by-election in North Roscommon and won a decisive victory. This triggered the emergence of a relatively united mass republican party, Sinn Féin, which defeated Home Rulers in a series of by-elections, spread rapidly throughout most of the country, and totally outclassed the battered Parliamentary Party. The Redmondites had been unchallenged for decades throughout much of the country, and their party machinery had fallen into disuse; they proved to be an easy target when at last they encountered a formidable opponent.

SINN FÉIN

Except for its leaders, the new party was comprised overwhelmingly of converts from the Home Rule cause, and one natural consequence was that many of the political skills it revealed were acquired from its opponents. Despite its republican program, Sinn Féin embodied some of the qualities of the old Parnellite movement—in particular an ability to associate with violent men while engaging in political measures. This

had been a feature of Parnell's early career and also of the last year of his life, but it was a pattern that the party had abandoned in recent decades.

Redmond's death in March 1918 seemed to symbolize the collapse of the movement that he had served and led for so long. The party succeeded in winning three by-elections in the early months of the year, but it was once more caught off balance when a new crisis erupted. The British government's decision to impose conscription on Ireland provoked immediate and widespread indignation among all Irish nationalists, together with a willingness to resist this threat by force. Sinn Féin and the Irish Volunteers seized the opportunity that had been presented to them, claiming that only they could provide the radical response that was needed. The Parliamentary Party was reduced to implementing Sinn Féin tactics and withdrawing its members from Westminster as a protest against the conscription act. Republican leaders were arrested shortly afterward, whereas their Home Rule allies in the fight against conscription were left unscathed. This appeared to vindicate its opponents' taunt that the party was superfluous; its members were no longer sufficiently menacing to be worth putting in jail.

When a general election was held in December 1918, at the end of the war, the party was disorganized and defeatist. Its demand for Home Rule no longer satisfied a newly radicalized nationalist electorate, yet the British government made it clear that, in the circumstances of the time, there could be no question of implementing devolved government as laid down by the 1914 act. The party had nothing to show for the nominal achievement of Home Rule and had little or nothing left to fight for. It could do no more than look back to its past achievements and warn that its opponents' policies would lead to disaster.

In the election campaign the Home Rulers were outclassed by Sinn Féin supporters' displays of discipline, enthusiasm, personation, and intimidation—all qualities the Parliamentary Party had revealed frequently in the past. Its disarray was revealed by the abandonment of twenty-five safe nationalist constituencies, which Sinn Féin won without a contest. Only in Ulster did Home Rulers perform respectably—because only there had they faced serious, sustained opposition, and only there had they needed to be efficient in amassing votes. The overall result was that Sinn Féin won seventy-three seats, the unionists twenty-six, and the recently dominant Home Rule party a mere six. Four of these were secured as the result of an antiunionist voting pact with Sinn Féin.

NATIONALIST PARTY

Under the new name the Nationalist Party, the Irish Parliamentary Party of Parnell and Redmond survived in Northern Ireland for another fifty years. In the rest of the country it died in December 1918 and—except by historians—was soon virtually forgotten. Such neglect is unfair. Over decades the party displayed skill, patience, and resilience; it built on the politicization of Irish nationalist society, which Daniel O'Connell had begun in the 1820s; and it helped to secure fundamental changes in landholding, housing, education, and other areas. It also helped to consolidate democratic values and habits, transmitting them to a new generation of politicians who simultaneously repudiated and emulated many qualities of their defeated opponent.

SEE ALSO Congested Districts Board; Davitt, Michael; Electoral Politics from 1800 to 1921; Great War; Griffith, Arthur; Parnell, Charles Stewart; Pearse, Patrick; Plunkett, Sir Horace Curzon; Politics: 1800 to 1921—Challenges to the Union; Protestant Ascendancy: Decline, 1800 to 1930; Redmond, John; Sinn Féin Movement and Party to 1922; Struggle for Independence from 1916 to 1921; United Irish League Campaigns

Bibliography

Bew, Paul. *Conflict and Conciliation in Ireland, 1890–1910.* 1987.

Bew, Paul. *John Redmond.* 1996.

Callanan, Frank. *The Parnell Split, 1890–1891.* 1992.

Callanan, Frank. *T. M. Healy.* 1996.

Collins, Peter, ed. *Nationalism and Unionism: Conflict in Ireland, 1885–1921.* 1994.

Dangerfield, George. *The Damnable Question: A Study in Anglo-Irish Relations.* 1977.

Lyons, F. S. L. *John Dillon.* 1968.

Lyons, F. S. L. *Culture and Anarchy in Ireland, 1890–1939.* 1979.

Mansergh, Nicholas. *The Unresolved Question: The Anglo-Irish Settlement and Its Undoing, 1912–1972.* 1991.

Maume, Patrick. *The Long Gestation: Irish Nationalist Life, 1891–1918.* 1999.

Pašeta, Senia. *Before the Revolution: Nationalism, Social Change, and the Irish Catholic Elite, 1879–1922.* 1999.

Michael Laffan

Hume, John

John Hume (1937–), civil-rights activist and nationalist leader, was born in Derry city on 18 January. He was educated at Saint Columb's College, Derry, and at Maynooth. Returning to Derry, he became a schoolteacher and a leading credit-union organizer, and he was prominent in the Northern Ireland Civil Rights Association. In 1969 his displacement of the Nationalist Party leader Eddie McAteer as Stormont MP for Foyle marked the emergence of a more articulate and professional nationalist politics. In 1970 Hume cofounded the Social Democratic and Labour Party (SDLP), which combined civil-rights activists, Belfast laborists, and elements of the crumbling Nationalist Party; Hume became deputy leader under west Belfast MP Gerry Fitt. In 1974 Hume was minister for commerce in the power-sharing executive established under the Sunningdale Agreement. The Ulster Workers' Council strike convinced Hume that an internal Northern Ireland settlement was impossible; the Irish Republic must act as guarantor. In 1979 Hume became SDLP leader and was elected to the European parliament; he emphasized the role of European integration in resolving territorial disputes. In 1983 he became Westminster MP for Foyle. During the 1980s Hume was immensely popular in the Irish Republic, where he was nicknamed "Saint John." His calls for peace and reconciliation were inspiring if repetitive (wags mocked his "single transferable speech"). Hume proved extremely effective at rallying external support for the SDLP through extensive contacts in Europe and the United States. Helped by the desire of the British and Irish governments to contain Sinn Féin after the 1981 hunger strike, Hume played a decisive role in securing the 1985 Anglo-Irish Agreement. Beginning in 1988 Hume entered intermittent negotiations with the Sinn Féin leadership. He was widely criticized for lending respectability to Sinn Féin, but these contacts proved crucial in developing the Northern Ireland peace process of the 1990s. Hume led the SDLP in the negotiations that produced the 1998 Belfast Agreement, and he received the 1998 Nobel Peace Prize (jointly with David Trimble). Thereafter Hume became less prominent; he stayed out of the new executive and resigned his Northern Ireland Assembly seat in 2000. Sinn Féin increasingly overtook the SDLP in popularity among Northern nationalists; Hume's leadership, always autocratic, grew increasingly tired. He resigned as SDLP leader after party setbacks in the 2001 Westminster election. Despite occasional accusations of egoism and insensitivity toward unionists, he was a figure of great political and moral stature and the most effective twentieth-century Northern nationalist leader.

SEE ALSO Adams, Gerry; Northern Ireland: Constitutional Settlement from Sunningdale to Good Friday; Northern Ireland: The United States in Northern Ireland since 1970; Trimble, David; Ulster Politics under Direct Rule

Bibliography

Drower, George. *John Hume: Peacemaker.* 1995.

Murray, Gerard. *John Hume and the SDLP.* 1998.

Routledge, Paul. *John Hume: A Biography.* 1997.

White, Barry. *John Hume: Statesman of the Troubles.* 1984.

Patrick Maume

Hunger Strikes

Hunger striking was not purely a phenomenon of the early 1980s in Northern Ireland. After a visit to fasting republican prisoners in 1978, the primate of all-Ireland, Cardinal Ó Fiaich, commented that "they prefer to face death rather than submit to be classed as criminals. . . . Anyone with the least knowledge of Irish history knows how deeply rooted this attitude is in our country's past." The cardinal recognized the two essential elements of hunger strikes: historical resonance and contemporaneous grievances. A sense of continuity and symbolism was important to republicans. Already, twelve republicans had starved to death for their beliefs in the twentieth century, most recently Michael Gaughan (1974) and Frank Stagg (1976). Gaughan's coffin was draped with the same tricolor flag that had been placed on the coffin of the legendary hunger striker Terence MacSwiney in 1920. Hunger striking, a practice that flourished in pre-Christian times in Ireland, derives from the ancient Brehon (Gaelic Irish) laws that recognized and strove to regulate the rite of "fasting against a person of exalted state in order to enforce a claim against him." The debtor had three options: to concede the claim, to mount a counterfast, or to let the hunger striker starve himself to death. None of these are congenial, as events in 1980 and 1981 were to demonstrate.

THE STRIKERS' CAMPAIGN

The contemporaneous grievance centered on prison status. Republicans believed that their struggle was political, not criminal. In an effort to bring them into the political process the British authorities granted them special-category status in 1972. This enabled them to run their own regime and strengthen their organization inside the prison to such an extent that there were fears that the prisons were being used as extensions of the militant republican campaign. Concerned that political violence was not being contained and that political concessions had not weaned republicanism away from violence, the British secretary of state, Merlyn Rees, reverted to a policy of "criminalization" in March 1976. Essentially it meant that there was no distinction between those imprisoned for "normal" crime and those fighting for a nonexistent republic. When they lost their special-category status, the prisoners embarked on a blanket and no-wash protest in which they refused to wear prison clothing or to clean out their cells. Only when these tactics failed did they resort to the ultimate protest—the hunger strike.

Criminalization was a serious political error for three reasons. In the first place, it denied republicans the respectability they felt they had earned in a legitimate and heroic struggle for Irish freedom. They had been practicing a form of social republicanism inside the ghettos whereby they had appropriated the role of the guardians of the law. In those circumstances, they asked rhetorically, how could they be criminals?

Secondly, the prisoners distinguished the sacrificial ideology of their campaign from the revolutionary ideology of the military campaign, linking themselves to the 1916 rebels who had risen not to win but to die. And their campaign was steeped in martyrology and religious symbolism, demonstrated in the grafitto in west Belfast of a dying hunger striker comforted by the Virgin Mary that bore the caption "Blessed are those who hunger for justice." The hunger strikers were portrayed in crucified postures, with the barbed wire of the prisons transformed into Jesus's crown of thorns, and the H-Block blanket (their only piece of "clothing") into a burial shroud. These religious motifs tied them into the heart of the Catholic psyche and broadened the dimensions of the campaign.

Thirdly, the campaign both diluted and strengthened the republican leadership. The decision to hunger strike had been made by the prisoners alone, against the advice of the outside leadership, who felt that it was distracting attention from the "war." But it brought onboard another layer of support. Some of the prisoners' relatives had formed a Relatives' Action Committee (RAC). Over the next few years the RACs, distributed across Northern Ireland and often independent of Sinn Féin, developed a mass movement that offered an alternative to a seemingly pointless military campaign. The strength of that movement is illustrated by comparing the numbers who protested when the first hunger striker, Bobby Sands, began his fast (about 4,000) and those who attended his funeral march (approximately 70,000). It could be seen too in the results of Northern Ireland's local government elections of May 1981 (following Sands's death). If all candidates identifying with the hunger strikes had joined together in one group, they could have become the fifth-largest party. There was a constituency to be nurtured, a fact acknowledged in an editorial in the newspaper *Republican News* in September 1982: "While not everyone can plant a bomb, everyone can plant a vote."

The first hunger strikes began on 27 October 1980 in protest against prison conditions and status. The second group began on 1 March 1981. In both instances seven volunteers were selected initially. The timing and the numbers were significant: The first strike was to culminate at Christmas (though it was called off on 18 December because the prisoners believed, wrongly, that they had extracted the necessary concessions), and the second at Easter. The seven strikers corresponded to the number of signatories to the 1916 proclamation. They believed themselves to be the revolutionary vanguard and sacred keepers of the nation's history. Bobby Sands, the Irish Republican Army (IRA) leader imprisoned in the Maze, was the first to die on 5 May 1981. By 20 August another nine republican prisoners were dead, and the rest ended their protest on 3 October. The whole business polarized the community as never before. It threatened to make constitutional nationalism redundant inside Northern Ireland; it deprived Fianna Fáil of victory in the Republic's 1981 general election when two hunger strikers were elected to the Dáil; it caused tremendous tension between the British and Irish governments; and it aroused an inordinate amount of international attention, much of it embarrassing to the British government.

INTERNATIONAL REACTION

The hunger strikes above all gave republicans what they wanted by making politics a straightforward confrontation between them and the British government in which every other party was rendered irrelevant or powerless. There is no doubt that the strikes discommoded the political and religious establishment. A survey of sixty-four newspapers in twenty-five countries conducted by the *Sunday Times* (31 May 1981) concluded that world opinion had begun to shift away from the British government and in favor of the IRA. In the United States, the home of so many descendents of the Great Famine Irish, the Irish Northern Aid Committee (NORAID), a U.S. support organization for the republican cause, raised $250,000 in the first half of 1981 (compared with an average of $110,000 every half-year for the previous seven years). In short, the hunger strikes contributed to a fundamental reevaluation of the conflict: Republicans moved into political mode while retaining the armed struggle, and the British and Irish governments, with the active support of the Reagan administration, embarked on much closer political and security cooperation that culminated in the Anglo-Irish Agreement in November 1985.

SEE ALSO Irish Republican Army (IRA); Loyalist Paramilitaries after 1965; Politics: Impact of the Northern Ireland Crisis on Southern Politics; Ulster Politics under Direct Rule

Bibliography

Arthur, Paul. "'Reading' Violence: Ireland." In *The Legitimization of Violence*, edited by David E. Apter. 1997.

Clarke, Liam. *Broadening the Battlefield: The H-Blocks and the Rise of Sinn Fein.* 1987.

O'Malley, Padraig. *Biting at the Grave: The Irish Hunger Strikes and the Politics of Despair.* 1990.

Paul Arthur

Hyde, Douglas

Poet, scholar, and politician, Douglas Hyde (1860–1949) was born on 17 January at Castlerea, Co. Roscommon, and became a leader of the Gaelic revival and, from 1938 until 1945, president of Ireland. Hyde earned a law degree from Trinity College, Dublin, and collaborated with Anglo-Irish writers such as W. B. Yeats and Lady Augusta Gregory, but his greatest achievement was his contribution to the preservation of the Irish language and literature.

He attained wide fame as president of the Gaelic League, the cultural nationalist body founded by Eoin MacNéill in 1893 in answer to Hyde's seminal speech "The Necessity for De-Anglicising Ireland." Good-natured and witty, he was equally at home testifying before government commissions and appearing at

League festivals and meetings. In 1905 and 1906 he made an extensive tour of the United States, raising more than 10,000 pounds for the organization. Under his leadership, language enthusiasts successfully pressed the educational authorities to include Gaelic as a voluntary subject in the primary and intermediate school curricula and to make a knowledge of Irish a matriculation requirement at the National University of Ireland after 1913.

Hyde continually contended with factionalism in League ranks and, after 1910, with an increasingly vocal cadre of nationalists. When they associated the organization with calls for independence in 1915, Hyde resigned and applied himself to his post as professor of modern Irish at University College, Dublin.

Hyde's scholarship, though marked by a lack of philological training, testified to his skill as a folklorist and synthesizer of the first rank. He published several groundbreaking works, including the folklore volumes *Leabhar Sgéulaigheachta* (1889) and *Beside the Fire* (1890); the *Love Songs of Connacht* (1893), which inspired subsequent writers, including Yeats, Gregory, and J. M. Synge; the monumental *A Literary History of Ireland* (1899); and, with Gregory, the *Songs Ascribed to [Anthony] Raftery* (1903). In the 1920s he helped to inaugurate the Irish Folklore Society and established an Irish studies journal, *Lia Fáil*.

Hyde received numerous public accolades, including cooption into the Free State Senate in 1925 and appointment to the Irish Academy of Letters in 1931. His highest honor, however, came in 1938 when he was elected to the largely ceremonial position of president of Ireland. He died on 12 July 1949, having invigorated indigenous interest in Gaelic literature and established the Irish language as a symbol of national identity, if not as a practical medium of everyday discourse.

SEE ALSO Gaelic Revival; Gaelic Revivalism: The Gaelic League; Literacy and Popular Culture; Literature: Gaelic Literature in the Nineteenth Century; Pearse, Patrick; Protestant Ascendancy: Decline, 1800 to 1930; Raiftearaí (Raftery), Antaine; **Primary Documents:** From "The Necessity for De-Anglicising Ireland" (25 November 1892)

Bibliography

Daly, Dominic. *The Young Douglas Hyde: The Dawn of the Irish Revolution and Renaissance, 1874–1893.* 1974.

Dunleavy, Janet Egleson, and Gareth W. Dunleavy. *Douglas Hyde: A Maker of Modern Ireland.* 1991.

Hyde, Douglas. *A Literary History of Ireland from Earliest Times to the Present Day.* 1899, 1967.

Hyde, Douglas. *Mise agus an Conradh (go dtí 1905).* 1937.

Timothy G. McMahon

Independent Irish Party

The Independent Irish Party of the 1850s, also known as Independent Opposition, marks an intermediate stage in the evolution of Irish party politics. Daniel O'Connell had utilized his fellow repeal MPs to constitute one of the interest groups on the Whig side of the House of Commons, and from 1835 to 1840 this had won him influence over government policies and patronage. The thirty-five repealers returned in 1847 after O'Connell's death but had no effective leader and did little to disturb Lord John Russell's Liberal government during the worst years of the Great Famine. That catastrophe brought to the forefront the clash of interests between landlords and tenant farmers. By 1850 campaigns for tenant right were afoot in Ulster and in the southeast, led by Presbyterian and Roman Catholic clergy respectively. Charles Gavan Duffy, running the *Nation* in greatly changed circumstances, saw in the tenant movement a substitute for the more heady nationalism of preceding years and gave it the oxygen of newspaper support. He was joined in this by several other newspaper proprietors. Duffy led the way in the organization of a conference in Dublin in early August 1850 at which representatives from all over the country formed the Irish Tenant League and adopted the program of the three Fs—fair rent, free sale, and fixity of tenure. The intention was to return to Parliament at the next election with a group of MPs pledged to make satisfactory legislation on the landlord-tenant relationship a condition for supporting any government on any issue. Two considerations gave credibility to this strategy: The party system at Westminster was in such flux that any solid block could exercise some bargaining power; and Parliament was in the process of enacting new franchise legislation for Ireland that would give the vote to many farmers.

Matters were greatly complicated a few months later when the restoration of the Roman Catholic hierarchy in England and Wales provoked a popular reaction that induced the government to introduce the Ecclesiastical Titles Bill. This proposed restriction on religious freedom was viewed by Catholics in Ireland as a reversion to the penal laws and up to twenty Irish Catholic MPs were outspokenly opposed to the measure. As they fought against the progress of the bill, a sympathetic journalist dubbed them "the Irish brigade," and many of them—including George Henry Moore, John Sadleir, and William Keogh—gained wide prominence. Their tactics included voting against the government on issues other than the offending legislation; this was a remarkable departure for a group drawn from the repeal and Whig/Liberal ranks, since it involved voting with the Tories. The opposition of the Irish brigade made a large contribution to the destabilization of the ministry, leading to its resignation in February 1852 and the accession of a caretaker Tory government under the earl of Derby.

At a conference in Dublin in late August 1851, a few weeks after the enactment of the ecclesiastical titles legislation, the Catholic Defence Association of Great Britain and Ireland had been formed. The brigadiers were prepared to take their cause to the country and seek support for their stance. At this juncture the radical MP for Rochdale, William Sharman Crawford, brokered an agreement between the tenant-right and Catholic campaigners whereby the latter agreed to support a diluted version of the Tenant League's demands in return for cooperation at the next election. It was not a happy union, but rivalry at the hustings would have been disastrous for both. At the fiercely fought general election of 1852 most constituencies were offered a candidate or

The year 1850 saw a flurry of tenant-right meetings in both the north and the south, such as the great one at Kilkenny shown here. Largely a reaction to continuing mass evictions, the movement endorsed the "three Fs"—fair rents, fixity of tenure, and "free sale" of the tenant's interest in his holding. The Independent Irish Party of the 1850s benefited from the popularity of tenant right. FROM ILLUSTRATED LONDON NEWS, 5 OCTOBER 1850.

candidates advocating both tenant right and Catholic rights, and many of the new voters risked the wrath of their landlords to support this compelling combination. At a conference organized by the Tenant League in September 1852, forty of the newly elected MPs, including all the brigadiers, pledged to hold themselves "perfectly independent of and in opposition to" any government not adopting tenant-right policy. Subsequently, about half of the group took a similar pledge with regard to Catholic rights.

The pledged members united to vote with the majority that ousted the Tory government on 17 December. The next administration was a Peelite-Liberal arrangement with Lord Aberdeen as prime minister. He had opposed the Ecclesiastical Titles Act and had no need to give concessions on policy in order to make himself attractive to Catholic interests. His accession marked the end of the titles conflict and vindicated the opponents of the legislation. This meant that for those pledged MPs who were tactical refugees from the Whig-Liberal camp, the new government was very much to their liking, and about twenty of them at once became reliable supporters. This they did without any government undertakings on tenant-right policy and so in contravention of their pledges. Two of them went further and accepted office in the new administration: These were John Sadleir and William Keogh, who were denounced as renegades and subsequently became two of the most reviled figures in nationalist demonology.

Duffy fought to maintain the coherence of the much reduced Independent Party and was supported by Moore, Archbishop John MacHale of Tuam, several newspaper proprietors, and the Tenant League. The pro-government MPs were supported by another faction of the Catholic leadership elite, most notably Archbishop Paul Cullen of Dublin. He was intent on doing business with the administration, and he used his contacts with Liberal-Catholic MPs most effectively to influence government policies affecting the church. The policy of independent opposition would in Cullen's eyes leave Irish Catholic interests unprotected. He used ecclesiastical authority in what opponents saw as an oppressive fashion to undermine clerical activism on the other side, and the resulting grievance helped exacerbate the conflict to the point that in 1854 Frederick Lucas of the *Tablet* appealed to Rome against Cullen, inevitably in vain. Support for the party gradually ebbed away, and in 1855 Duffy sold his interest in the *Nation* and left to start a new career in Australia. Agricultural prosperity had blunted the enthusiasm of farmers for agitation. The 1857 general election was a tame affair. The Independent Oppositionists entered it with about a dozen MPs and came out with the same number, and mostly the same personnel. Cooperation between Tories and Independent Oppositionists was noticeable at the 1857 elections. In office in 1858 and 1859, the Tories made various overtures to Catholic interests and seemed to be less inimical to the secular power of the papacy than were the Liberals. In a vote of confidence in the government on 31 March 1859 the identifiable Independent Oppositionists split seven against six. This marked the end of any pretense to coherence, but the Independent Oppositionists lost no ground in the general election of 1859, and as a faction in Irish politics they endured until 1874. The aspiration to the status of a party had been much less enduring. The punishment of the Liberals for the Ecclesiastical Titles Act had been the main success of the party, and once that had been secured with the accession of Aberdeen, there no longer existed the extraordinary provocation that had induced instinctive Liberals to break the conventions of parliamentary conduct. The remnant that tried to function after 1852 had an extraparliamentary organization in the shape of the Tenant League—that last met in 1858—but little else by way of party structure and no commanding leader. Even the most devoted of the Oppositionists adhered to conventional assumptions about the independence of the individual MP. The party machine was more than a generation away.

SEE ALSO Electoral Politics from 1800 to 1921; Politics: 1800 to 1921—Challenges to the Union

Bibliography

Comerford, R. V. "Churchmen, Tenants, and Independent Opposition, 1850–56." In *A New History of Ireland*, vol. 5, *1801–70*, edited by W. E. Vaughan. 1989.

Knowlton, S. R. *Popular Politics and the Irish Catholic Church: The Rise and Fall of the Independent Irish Party, 1850–59.* 1991.

White, J. H. *The Independent Irish Party, 1850–59.* 1958.

R. V. Comerford

Indian Corn or Maize

Indian corn and meal were imported into Ireland as relief food for the poor during periods of shortages in the first half of the nineteenth century. Indian corn is derived from maize; Indian meal is the ground product. Maize is grown in warm climates such as Mediterranean countries and the southern states of North America. It is resistant to drought, gives a high yield per acre, and matures quickly. Maize has acquired the reputation of being the poor man's cereal; however, in societies where maize is the subsistence crop, the poor are vulnerable to the vitamin-deficiency disease pellagra.

Pellagra is caused by a deficiency of niacin (nicotinic acid), one of the B vitamins. Maize meal is a poor source of niacin, and what is present is in an unavailable form. Niacin can be synthesized in the body from a protein called tryptophan, but the principal protein in maize (zein) contains little tryptophan. Thus a diet composed essentially of maize is deficient in available niacin and is incapable of synthesizing the missing vitamin. The consequence is pellagra, a disease characterized by diarrhea, dementia, and dermatitis.

Maize first plugged food shortages in Ireland during the subsistence crisis of 1799 to 1801, when potato and grain yields were poor. Maize was imported again in the distressed year of 1827. When the potato harvest failed in 1845, Sir Robert Peel, the British prime minister, engaged Baring Brothers and Company to purchase the first consignment of Indian meal, worth 100,000 pounds, from the United States. Large imports followed: 7,000 tons in 1845, rising to a peak of 632,000 tons in 1847.

Initially, the population hated Indian meal. Early consignments were stale and improperly ground, and cooking was inadequate. The hard corn required steel grinders, and such equipment was not at first available

The enormous food deficit during the Great Famine would have been greater still if Indian corn or maize, ground into meal, had not been imported in large quantities. In later periods of distress, such as 1879–1880, Indian corn was used again, as shown in this 1880 sketch of women carrying home sacks of meal from a relief committee in County Galway. FROM ILLUSTRATED LONDON NEWS, 20 NOVEMBER 1880.

in Ireland. The consequence was painful intestinal disorders among a populace unused to Indian meal; the irritation to the digestive system and its yellow color earned Indian meal the name "Peel's brimstone." When milling techniques improved and hunger intensified, Indian meal was more readily accepted, and many families subsisted solely upon it for prolonged periods. There is no direct evidence that pellagra was widespread during the Great Famine, but conditions suggest that it is likely, though its symptoms were masked by the many other diseases rife at the time. After the famine Indian meal gained a place in the more varied diet of the laboring classes until the end of the nineteenth century.

SEE ALSO Agriculture: 1845 to 1921; Family: Marriage Patterns and Family Life from 1690 to 1921; Famine Clearances; Great Famine; Poor Law Amendment Act of 1847 and the Gregory Clause; Population, Economy, and Society from 1750 to 1950; Pota-to and Potato Blight (*Phytophthora infestans*); Rural Life: 1850 to 1921; Town Life from 1690 to the Early Twentieth Century

Bibliography

Bourke, Austin. "The Irish Grain Trade, 1839–48." *Irish Historical Studies* 20 (September 1976): 156–169.

Crawford, E. Margaret. "Indian Meal and Pellagra in Nineteenth-Century Ireland." In *Irish Population, Economy and Society: Essays in Honour of the Late K. H. Connell*, edited by J. M. Goldstrom and L. A. Clarkson. 1981.

Donnelly, James S., Jr. "The Administration of Relief, 1846–7." In *Ireland under the Union I, 1801–70*. Vol. 5 of *A New History of Ireland*, edited by W. E. Vaughan. 1989.

Donnelly, James S., Jr. "Famine and Government Response, 1845–6." In *Ireland under the Union I, 1801–70*. Vol. 5 of *A New History of Ireland*, edited by W. E. Vaughan. 1989.

E. Margaret Crawford

Industrialization

In the eighteenth and early nineteenth centuries, industrial activity in Ireland was substantial and geographically widespread. The 1821 census of Ireland indicates that more than 40 percent of men and women who stated their occupation were "chiefly employed in trades, manufactures, or handicraft." Of the provinces, Ulster, predictably, had the highest percentage (55%), followed by Connacht (43%), Leinster (33%), and Munster (24%). Six counties outside Ulster had a greater proportion of their population in trade, manufacture, or handicrafts than in agriculture. Within all the provinces there were further great disparities and in some east Ulster baronies the percentage of workers engaged mainly in trade, manufacture, or handicraft might exceed 70 percent, but even in the west of the province, some baronies had about a half of their populations so concentrated.

From the 1820s to the end of the nineteenth century, however, the process of industrialization in east Ulster accelerated, and this led by the 1850s to a much clearer industrial demarcation of this area from the rest of Ireland. Indeed, until the 1830s Dublin and Cork led Belfast in a range of industries, most notably in brewing, distilling, flour milling, and shipbuilding, but also in others such as engineering and foundries, tanning, woolen manufacture, glass-making, and paper-making.

Cork was and remained much more a commercial than an industrial city, as reflected in the significant presence of merchants on the city council. Nevertheless, the optimistic view expressed in the 1790s that the commercial significance of the city would soon rival that of Liverpool could not have been more ill founded. In fact, the nineteenth century was one of widespread stagnation, and the 1901 population figure of 76,000 was some 5 percent less than that of 1821. Even if nineteenth-century Cork lost its dynamism, it remains the case that at least 20 percent of its male and female population was engaged in manufacturing. Census data show that on the eve of the famine 8,000 men worked in manufacturing; this had fallen by a quarter in 1851, and the figure declined still further to 4,000 in 1901. The number of women in manufacturing remained much more stable in the long term: 3,500 in 1841 and around 3,000 in 1901. There was a sharp, if short-lived, increase (to over 5,000) recorded in the 1851 census, which reflected a postfamine revival movement in cottage-based manufacturing in, for example, lace-making, net-making, and knitting.

Before the development of large-scale brewing and distilling in the later eighteenth century, sugar refining was Dublin's most significant capital-intensive industry, in which the firms catered to a countrywide market. In general terms the industrial development of eighteenth-century Dublin evolved from commercial activity, where goods were manufactured for the home market from raw materials drawn either from within Ireland itself (e.g., woolens) or were imported (as with silk or iron). During the eighteenth century, Dublin was the predominant economic and social center for the whole of Ireland, and to a considerable extent this derived from the dependence of Ulster's rapidly growing linen industry on Dublin as a financial center, marketplace, and port. Toward the end of the eighteenth century, however, this dominance began to look less secure.

In Dublin, traditional industries like cabinetmaking and carriage manufacture declined, as did clothing, the last apparently a victim of a determination to retain outdated techniques. Few manufacturing industries developed to provide substantial employment to the "deposed capital" in the nineteenth century. There was some growth in engineering, especially relating to the railways, as well as in food and drink. A small number of large firms stand out. Among these are the Quaker biscuit manufacturer W. and R. Jacob, formerly of Waterford, which opened a factory in Dublin in 1851. The firm demonstrated an early commitment to mass-production methods and became a public company in 1883; by the beginning of the twentieth century it employed more than 2,000 workers. Dominating the manufacturing sector in Dublin was Guinness, established in 1759, but its output still lagged behind Beamish and Crawford of Cork in the early nineteenth century. The trend in Irish brewing was to install much larger units in a smaller number of urban centers. Guinness rose to prominence not only because of its distinctive product but also through its high-quality management, technical innovation, and successful marketing. The firm exploited the British market, and as the transport system improved the market within Ireland increased. In both markets consumers increasingly favored high-quality stout. Decades of expansion led to the conversion of Guinness into a public company in 1886. Between that date and 1914, dividends on ordinary shares rose from 15.4 to 35.7 percent. Some members of the Guinness family entered the peerage. Firms like Jacob and Guinness, however, were very much the exception to the rule; indeed, apart from food and drink, much of the south and west of Ireland had very little industry by the early twentieth century.

LINEN IN THE PROCESS OF INDUSTRIALIZATION

Leading the industrialization process in the north of Ireland was the linen industry. Within Ireland, linen production developed from a thoroughly rural and widespread activity into a much more localized but strikingly successful example of factory-based industry centered on the Belfast area. However, factory techniques did not become widespread in spinning until the 1830s and in weaving until the late 1850s and 1860s.

The influence of Huguenot immigrants who arrived in 1698 has been shown to have been exaggerated. In fact, the industry had been growing for several decades before that. In the 1640s and 1650s substantial surpluses of linen yarn were sent from Ulster to England to be woven. A combination of cheap land, the chance to take refuge from religious persecution, and the opportunity to take advantage of the evident yarn surpluses all combined to attract migrants from the north of England and Scotland in the later seventeenth century. The earliest known reference to a significant linen industry in Ulster comes from the 1680s; from this period through the eighteenth century access to the English market was the main stimulus to Irish linen industry, especially following the abolition in 1696 of duties on flax, yarn, and cloth imported into England from Ireland. Further encouragement for Irish linen came with the formation in 1711 of the Trustees of the Hempen and Flaxen Manufactures of Ireland known as the Linen Board. The main tasks of the board were to oversee and operate the regulations governing linen duties, to promote quality control in production, and to make determined efforts through financial incentives to spread the industry more widely outside Ulster. The board continued to function until 1828, but it lacked the expertise to ensure that its grants were used in the most cost-effective way. Even so, the most balanced assessments of the board's activities have judged it to be mildly positive, and linen dominated the manufacturing sector in both Ireland and Scotland by the later eighteenth century. During the course of that century a number of significant and related developments can be identified, each of which contributed to the subsequent transition to factory production. These included the following: (1) changes in bleaching and finishing technology and the emergence of the large-scale bleachers and drapers; (2) the move away from Dublin as the main entrepôt in the Anglo-Irish trade, and the associated switch to direct exports from Ulster; and (3) the impact of the short-lived factory-based cotton industry, whose appearance coincided with the final phase of domestic spinning in the linen industry.

Taken together, these developments were crucial in the acquisition of skill, the accumulation of capital, the refinement of credit and banking networks, and the introduction of factory techniques. Ultimately, they contributed enormously to the emergence of northeast Ulster as the premier linen-producing area in the world and also to the rise of Belfast as an example of spectacular urban growth and very much a symbol of successful industrialization. Most of the flax produced for the Irish linen industry before the 1860s was grown on farms in the north of Ireland. Having been prepared, the flax was spun and wound onto bobbins by women and children, then woven into cloth by the farmer-weavers and perhaps their older children, who would then take it to market. Although the farmer-weaver predominated, by the late eighteenth century the journeyman weaver working for a variety of middlemen was increasingly in evidence and was typically provided with board and lodging and paid a wage, or, if married, he was more likely to work in his own home. One important consequence of the growth of the linen industry, often under landlord patronage, was that it stimulated competition for land, drove up rent levels, encouraged subdivision of holdings, and increased population pressure. In 1841, for example, County Armagh was the most densely settled county in Ireland.

The techniques for flax spinning and weaving remained fundamentally unaltered before the 1820s, and the same is true for the marketing arrangements for selling the webs. The brown (unbleached) linen webs were sold through a large network of brown linen markets. At the markets, some held weekly, others monthly, jobbers could supply weavers with yarn, and drapers and bleachers purchased weavers' webs. If the drapers

played a key role in organizing and marketing the cloth, the bleachers were responsible for initiating profound long-term changes in the industry. Sometime during the eighteenth century, mechanical power was applied to bleaching, thus making it the first process in the industry to experience mechanization. From the late 1780s, following Bertollet's discovery of the bleaching properties of chlorine gas, it became possible for bleaching to be carried on throughout the year. Bleachers and their agents made more frequent appearances at brown linen markets in order to buy webs for their bleach-greens (on which linen was laid on the grass to be bleached). At the same time it is clear that bleachers might supply yarn to weavers and also play an important role in the export of linen across the Irish Sea and beyond. These changes in the scale and function of bleachers had fundamental long-term significance because bleachers turned into drapers and linen merchants provided some of the earliest machine spinning and weaving.

The linen trade contributed much to the development of an embryonic credit structure based on bills of exchange. In the absence of formal banking facilities credit networks evolved directly between northern bleachers and Dublin, and between English merchants and bankers. As direct shipments from Ulster to Britain increased, the intermediate role of Dublin declined: in 1710, 88 percent of Irish linen exports to Britain had been shipped through Dublin, but by 1780 that proportion had fallen by half. A reflection of the growing importance of the industry and the reorientation of trading links was the construction in 1785 of the White Linen Hall in Belfast. This in turn led to a further decline in the proportion of linen sent to Dublin, even from such major markets as County Armagh, which traditionally had strong links with the capital. Research in the 1980s into the late eighteenth-century business community has shown that although the construction of the Linen Hall was originally advocated by drapers, other merchants quickly came forward and used the hall's management committee in order to organize shipping arrangements and the discounting of bills of exchange. This same group of merchants has also been identified as the driving force behind the formation of the Belfast Chamber of Commerce in 1783 and of the Belfast Harbour Board two years later. These developments contributed considerably to the emergence of Belfast as a leading commercial center.

COTTON AND THE TRANSITION TO FACTORY-BASED PRODUCTION

The role of Belfast as a center of textile production was transformed in the late eighteenth and early nineteenth centuries by the cotton industry, and its origins as a factory town may be said to date from this period. The need to import raw cotton, coal, and machinery meant that the Ulster cotton industry tended to be concentrated in coastal towns such as Belfast, Bangor, Larne, and Carrickfergus, although it also spread inland. In origin the region's cotton manufacturers were from a range of backgrounds, including haberdashery and, significantly, linen bleaching and drapery. The industry was stimulated by the wars with France and by the Linen Board, which provided, inter alia, some thirteen grants for cotton-spinning machinery in 1782. In 1797 the board was authorized to grant up to £350 to firms wishing to purchase steam engines. The principal type of cotton produced in Belfast was muslin, a finer and lighter product than calico, though the latter was also made. The area's experience with the manufacture of fine linens ensured a ready supply of skilled labor that could easily move into muslin production.

Another factor that contributed to the switch to manufacturing muslin rather than linen was the ease with which muslin could be bleached, making it an attractive business for the small enterprise. The rise of the large bleaching businesses forced many smaller concerns out of business, but some of them were able to turn to muslin bleaching. The Ulster cotton industry was heavily reliant on imported technology, which often proved extremely troublesome to install and maintain. Belfast did not really begin to acquire a textile machine–making industry until the 1830s and 1840s, and this was in response to the growth of flax spinning. Although the cotton industry failed to lead to the development of textile machine making, it certainly helped to stimulate credit networks and banking facilities.

Banks began to develop partly in response to demands of the cotton industry, but it was the linen industry that was of much greater significance for the region and its banks in the long run. The main reason for this lies in the contraction of the cotton industry in the late 1820s and 1830s and the introduction of factory-based wet spinning of flax at the same time. However, the ascendancy of Belfast within the Irish linen trade has been shown to predate the coming of joint-stock banking and the inauguration of regular steamship services (both in the mid-1820s). For the triennium of 1820 to 1822, six ports accounted for 98 percent of Irish linen exports, and the share of Belfast (43%) was double that of Dublin. Particularly striking were the links between Belfast and Liverpool: the latter had taken a mere 8 percent of Irish linen exports, but fifty years later the proportion was 61 percent.

The advent of the wet-spinning process provided cotton spinners with an attractive alternative in the years after 1825, when trade was depressed. Those with a great deal of fixed capital already committed in Ireland thus had an opportunity and a strong incentive to move into power spinning. For these reasons, then, it is no surprise that two of the first entrants into power flax spinning were a bleacher and a cotton manufacturer, and this in turn helps us to appreciate the technological and organizational developments in Ulster textile industries that had taken place since the late eighteenth century. Bleachers like the Murlands of Castlewellan in County Down integrated backwards into spinning, building their first mill in 1828 and their second in 1836. This set a pattern for several other bleachers such as the Richardsons at Bessbrook in County Armagh and the Adairs at Cookstown in County Tyrone. The Murlands' enterprise was an early example of factory flax spinning in the countryside using a mixture of water and steam power. The Mulhollands, by contrast, were the first to open an entirely steam-driven mill in Belfast, and their move was the first of several made by former cotton spinners who now converted to flax. By 1834 twelve mills had been built or converted and a further nine were in the process of construction. Such a rate of expansion had never been achieved by the Ulster cotton industry. Provincial production of linen was responsible for the growth of industrial villages in many parts of Ulster, especially in the period 1830 through 1870. Although most of these were in the east, some—like Sion Mills in County Tyrone, developed by the Herdman family from 1835—were in the west.

The major factor underpinning the expansion of factory spinning (and, later, factory weaving) was the growth of export markets, especially the United States. Over 40 percent of Ulster's linen exports went to the United States by the late 1850s. Textile machine making emerged soon after the advent of power spinning and by the mid-1830s was beginning to make a noticeable impact on the local economy, lessening dependence on imported technology. Mill construction continued apace, with only brief interruptions in commercial crises such as that of between 1847 and 1848, so that by 1850 there were sixty-nine spinning mills in Ireland, the vast majority of them in Ulster. One consequence was a massive increase, perhaps a doubling, in the demand for flax during the 1840s.

The advent of mill-spun yarn had an adverse effect on those households involved in hand spinning. Here both demand and wages declined drastically, and this had an adverse effect on the viability of households, especially in peripheral areas of northwest and southwest Ulster. Before the Great Famine the decline of the linen industry in these areas led to deindustrialization and emigration. To a limited extent the impact of decline was offset by the growth of embroidery and sewing trades, which, though present from the late eighteenth century, grew rapidly from about 1830 to the 1850s. Organized largely by Scottish firms, working through agents resident in Ulster, this work perhaps served as a brake on depopulation as well as a more genteel alternative to mill work for young girls of "decent" family.

Commentators on the eve of the Great Famine were well aware of the pace of growth of Belfast, and that such growth was unprecedented. Within the Chamber of Commerce by the 1820s, although textile interests (cotton, linen, and wool) were dominant, there were also representatives from shipbuilding and engineering, tanning, distilling, printing, and, among many from the service sector, members drawn from accountancy, banking, and insurance. No group lobbied more energetically on behalf of Ulster business from the later eighteenth century and the chamber continued to grow in membership, and in the range of businesses in which members were involved, during the nineteenth and early twentieth centuries. Acutely aware of the significance of Britain as a source of raw materials and intermediate goods, especially the coal and iron that underpinned industrialization, and as a market for manufactured goods, the chamber lobbied hard for more regular and cheaper cross-channel transport and postal services and for lower port dues.

From the 1820s the chamber lent its support to the promotion of railways in Britain and Ireland as well as to improvements in mail services between Belfast and the west of Ireland. It attached great importance to free trade across the Irish Sea and declared in 1834 that "it is now generally admitted that had a free intercourse existed between this country and England since the Union such as now exists that our manufactures would be at present further advanced than they are." This comment points to an increasingly important characteristic of the industrialization process in Ulster: it was perceived to be underpinned by the Act of Union of 1800. Many businessmen, especially in the larger export-oriented firms, were Protestant and the view that industry and trade were dependent on the British connection resulted in a strong and militant unionism in the business community. Indeed, Ulster unionism could scarcely have become the force it did from the 1880s to partition without the financial support and leadership from industrialists and merchants. The chamber also intervened in many other areas of public policy. Thus in December 1846, in the face of the "great national calamity" of the famine, it called for the "suspension of the use of grain in Breweries and Distilleries whereby the food of more than five millions of people is daily consumed in the United Kingdom."

The mechanization of flax spinning was of fundamental importance in extending the industrialization process in northeast Ulster. The low wages of handloom weavers, together with the technical deficiencies in the power weaving of the fine linens in which Ulster specialized meant a considerable delay in the widespread adoption of power looms. However, the labor supply was dramatically curtailed through death and emigration in the late 1840s, and as a consequence wages rose by some 20 percent to 30 percent between 1848 and 1852. This particular problem was compounded as late as the early 1850s because weavers' were to some extent locked into seasonal agricultural work. Under these circumstances the pressure to refine power loom technology intensified during the 1850s, and necessary improvements were made just in time for Ulster to reap huge benefits from the unprecedented demand for linen occasioned by the "cotton famine" during the American Civil War of 1861 to 1865.

In many ways the American Civil War period was a crucial one for the Ulster linen industry, with much new investment. A number of spinning and bleaching firms integrated weaving into their operations, but there were now more opportunities for specialist, single-process, weaving enterprises to develop. In fact, the number of looms in both types of enterprise was almost exactly equal by 1875, though there was a marked tendency for the specialist firms to increase their share of weaving capacity during the late nineteenth and early twentieth centuries. At the same time a relatively small number of large, fully integrated firms developed and became the giants of the industry between the 1860s and 1914. This process was accelerated by the decision, first taken by the York Street Flax Spinning Company in 1864, and soon by many others, to adopt a joint-stock form with limited liability. It was also aided by an immense expansion of bank credit, by the availability of flax increasingly imported from Europe, and by the development of a textile-engineering sector, which by mid-century also competed successfully in American and European markets.

The transition to factory production in the linen industry was the most significant feature of industrialization in nineteenth-century Ireland and led to a much greater role for Belfast in both manufacturing and services. Linen was also an industry subject to economic fluctuations, with frequent downturns in business leading to short-time working and unemployment in, for example, 1879, 1886, 1893, 1904, 1908 through 1909, and 1912. The majority of workers in the linen industry as a whole were women, but the diversification of the economic base in Belfast meant that men increasingly found work, and relatively high wages, in engineering and shipbuilding. The two shipyards Harland and Wolff, established in the late 1850s, and Workman Clark, set up in 1879, though subject to considerable short-term fluctuations in output, grew over the long term. From the 1880s to the First World War they came to epitomize the success and self-confidence of industrial Belfast. Good business connections, bank assistance, design flair, highly skilled labor, and a massive expansion in world seaborne trade and travel, all combined to underwrite growth. On the eve of the First World War employment at Harland and Wolff had reached 14,000. Other industries such as rope making and various branches of engineering developed as spin-offs and helped to sustain expansion when the rate of expansion of the linen industry slowed. By 1911 these sectors, together with textiles, accounted for some 40 percent of total employment in the city. While three-quarters of the working population of Belfast was described as industrial, much of it in factory production and employed by medium-sized and large firms, the proportion in Dublin was just over half, and much of this was in craft industries or in unskilled occupations. For example, less than 20 percent of the work force of Guinness, Dublin's largest employer, was skilled. The population of Belfast grew from 19,000 in 1801 to 387,000 in 1911, and increasingly the city depended on a labor force born outside its boundaries: Less than 40 percent of the population had been born inside the city in 1901. Belfast was also exceptional in Ulster terms. Derry, the province's second city, had no comparably dynamic industrial base; rather, it developed a specialization in shirt making, collar making, and embroidery, mostly using female labor.

The industrialization process in Ireland conformed to a pattern of regional growth and decline often observed in Europe since the eighteenth century. Dependence on overseas trade led to an increasing concentration of industry in the northeast in general and Belfast in particular. The economic problems following the 1914 through 1918 war inflicted permanent damage on the staple industries and helped to ensure that Northern Ireland after 1920 would never have the economic self-confidence of pre-1914 Ulster and would, moreover, always have a substantial unemployment problem.

SEE ALSO Banking and Finance to 1921; Brewing and Distilling; Factory-Based Textile Manufacture; Industry since 1920; Rural Industry; Shipbuilding; Transport—Road, Canal, Rail; Women and Children in the Industrial Workforce

Bibliography

Bielenburg, Andy. *Cork's Industrial Revolution, 1780–1880: Development or Decline?* 1991.

Bielenburg, Andy. "The Irish Brewing Industry and the Rise of Guinness, 1790–1914." In *The Dynamics of the International Brewing Industry since 1800.* 1998.

Cohen, Marilyn. *Linen, Family, and Community in Tullylish, County Down, 1690–1914.* 1997.

Cohen, Marilyn, ed. *The Warp of Ulster's Past: Interdisciplinary Perspectives on the Irish Linen Industry, 1700–1920.* 1997.

Collins, Brenda. "Protoindustrialization and Prefamine Emigration." *Social History* 7 (May 1982): 127–146.

Crawford, William H. "The Evolution of the Linen Trade in Ulster before Industrialization." *Irish Economic and Social History* 15 (1988): 32–53.

Daly, Mary E. *Dublin: The Deposed Capital: A Social and Economic History, 1860–1914.* 1984.

Dickson, David. "The Place of Dublin in the Eighteenth Century Irish Economy." In *Ireland and Scotland, 1600–1850,* edited by Thomas M. Devine and David Dickson. 1983.

Geary, Frank. "Deindustrialization in Ireland to 1851: Some Evidence from the Census." *Economic History Review* 51 (August 1998): 512–541.

Hepburn, Anthony C. *A Past Apart: Studies in the History of Catholic Belfast.* 1996.

Macneice, Denis S. "Industrial Villages of Ulster, 1800-1900." In *Plantation to Partition,* edited by Peter Roebuck. 1981.

Murphy, Maura. "The Economic and Social Structure of Nineteenth-Century Cork." In *The Town in Ireland,* edited by David Harkness and Mary O'Dowd. 1981.

Ó Gráda, Cormac. *Ireland: A New Economic History, 1780–1939.* 1994.

Ollerenshaw, Philip. "Industry, 1820–1914." In *An Economic History of Ulster: 1820–1939,* edited by Liam Kennedy and Philip Ollerenshaw. 1985.

Ollerenshaw, Philip. "Businessmen and the Development of Ulster Unionism, 1886–1921." *Journal of Imperial and Commonwealth History* 28 (January 2000): 35–64.

Solar, Peter. "The Irish Linen Trade, 1820–52." *Textile History* 21 (spring 1990): 57–85.

Takei, Akiro. "The First Irish Linen Mills, 1800-1824." *Irish Economic and Social History* 21 (1994): 28–38.

Philip Ollerenshaw

Industry since 1920

Because conditions in the nineteenth century favored free trade, manufacturing in southern Ireland became concentrated in food and drink, using raw materials from the dominant agricultural sector. Food and drink formed the bulk of exports, and Britain was the prime export market. As independence approached, the only part of Ireland that had experienced anything akin to an industrial revolution was the northeastern corner, where Belfast was the chief linen manufacturing region of the world and its shipyards were among the largest in the world—and both industries depended almost exclusively on foreign demand.

PROTECTIONISM

The nationalist perspective of Irish economic history had stressed the need for manufacturing industry and the use of tariffs to achieve that aim. Yet, the new Irish government avoided any radical departures in policy, concluding that prosperity depended on agriculture. While some farsighted steps were taken to develop the infrastructure for industry, such as the Shannon Electricity Scheme, the Cumann na nGaedheal government was reluctant to burden agriculture with higher prices—a likely outcome of industrial protection.

This changed radically with the election of Eamon de Valera's government in 1932. Fianna Fáil was happy to use the adverse impact of the worldwide Great Depression on Irish agricultural exports to launch its avowedly protectionist policy of industrial development. The objective was partly nationalistic—to keep Irish production in Irish hands—but also to provide employment and reduce emigration. Extensive use was made of tariffs, quotas, import licenses, and other protectionist instruments. There was also a wide extension of state-sponsored bodies producing industrial goods and commercial services.

Strong protectionist policies were maintained until the 1960s. Sizeable increases in manufacturing output and employment were achieved in the 1930s, but there was little further progress during and after the Second World War. The speed and scale of protectionism had evoked a plethora of undersized firms that often were engaged only in the assembly of imported parts of products for sale on the small home market. Most of these firms had neither the competence nor the resources to attain an efficient scale of operation by exploiting export markets. Foreign enterprise was frowned on, but because of the scarcity of Irish firms with the ability to run large enterprises, many foreign suppliers were allowed to establish plants to preserve their Irish sales. Such foreign subsidiaries, however, were generally prevented by their parent firms from competing in overseas markets.

THE OUTWARD-LOOKING STRATEGY

The limits of protectionism became widely recognized during the 1950s. A new outward-looking strategy evolved, though it took some time to reach its full flowering. The main ingredients were the provision of capital grants and tax concessions to encourage export-oriented manufacturing; the establishment of a new state-sponsored body, the Industrial Development Authority, to attract foreign, export-oriented firms to Ireland; and the dismantling of protectionism in return for greater access to foreign markets.

While the outward-looking strategy worked well in the 1960s when world economic conditions were favorable, it ran into problems following the first global oil crisis in 1973. Most of the output growth had come from new foreign enterprises. In the case of indigenous manufacturing, once the dismantling of protectionist policy began in earnest after 1966, there was no further rise in employment until the end of the 1970s, and between 1980 and 1988 indigenous industry shed more than one-quarter of its workforce. Neither was there much improvement in the share of output exported. The adverse situation of industry was exacerbated in the 1980s, when the flow of foreign enterprise fell and nearly 10,000 jobs were lost in such firms.

The Telesis report of 1982, commissioned by the government, documented the fragility of indigenous industry and the excessive dependence on foreign enterprise. It recommended a modification of the outward-looking strategy to give priority to building up a select number of large Irish companies to serve world markets. These new directions of policy scarcely had time to take effect before a further review was initiated, culminating in the Culliton report published in January 1992. The central message of the Culliton report was that industrial-development strategy goes well beyond industrial policy as traditionally conceived. The report called for reform of the tax system, further improvement in the physical infrastructure, and the adaptation of education and training to meet the needs of industry.

The period since the late 1980s has seen a dramatic improvement in industrial performance, with the volume of manufacturing gross output in the South rising nearly fourfold from 1986 to 2000; by 2000 it was seventy times greater than when the state was founded. Employment was slower to recover, but between 1993 and 2000 total manufacturing employment rose by more than one-quarter—a remarkable achievement at a time when it was falling in most other European countries. A big revival in new foreign enterprise has spearheaded the recovery. At the end of the 1990s foreign firms accounted for three-quarters of manufacturing gross output and for nearly half the employment. Their presence is particularly noticeable in electronics and computing, where all of the world's household names in these industries, including Microsoft, IBM, Hewlett Packard, and Intel, have major production facilities in Ireland.

While foreign enterprises have led the way, there has also been a distinct improvement in the performance of native industry. Particularly encouraging has been the emergence and growth of indigenous electronics firms specializing in sophisticated niche areas of the market. By 1999 native firms were exporting an average of one-third of their output. As recently as the mid-1980s the bulk of their exports went to only one market, the United Kingdom, but at the end of the 1990s three-fifths went further afield. It is too soon to say that indigenous industry is firmly established on a new long-term growth path; nevertheless, the success of the 1990s gives solid ground for hope.

Northern Ireland

The recent industrial progress in the South contrasts sharply with the economic picture in Northern Ireland. From the 1920s onward, manufacturing employment fell substantially in Northern Ireland owing to the secular decline in the two major industries, linen and shipbuilding, in which the North's initially strong manufacturing base was concentrated. Both industries were adversely affected by the Great Depression. Linen was also subject to long-term negative changes in consumer tastes and habits, so the industry never recovered fully following the Great Depression. The Second World War brought about a revival of activity in the shipyards, but this was not sustained beyond the early postwar years. As with the shipbuilding industry in the United Kingdom generally, competition from low-cost countries and unstable demand led to long-term decline, but the impact of these forces was exacerbated by weak management, shown particularly by an inability to adapt to changing market conditions and changing techniques of production.

Attempts to provide replacement industries in Northern Ireland enjoyed some success in the 1960s, but sufficed only to stabilize the level of employment. Following the outbreak of domestic conflict in 1969, the volatile security situation and political instability deterred foreign investment. Manufacturing employment in the North fell by nearly two-fifths until the mid-1980s, and since then the level has been static.

In his celebrated statement of the case for industrialization written in 1904, the nationalist leader Arthur Griffith argued that a country, like a person, needed two arms—industry as well as agriculture. Grafting on Griffith's second arm in the new Irish state has been a long and difficult operation, but at last it is now in place, but as the experience of Northern Ireland shows, even the strongest industrial base can be eroded unless it is constantly renewed.

SEE ALSO Brewing and Distilling; Economic Relations between Independent Ireland and Britain; Economic Relations between North and South since 1922; Economic Relations between Northern Ireland and Britain; Economies of Ireland, North and South, since 1920; Factory-Based Textile Manufacture; Guinness Brewing Company; Industrialization; Investment and Development Agency (IDA Ireland); Lemass, Seán; Marshall Aid; Overseas Investment; Shipbuilding; Social Change since 1922; Tourism; Transport—Road, Canal, Rail

Bibliography

Bielenberg, Andy. "Industrial Development in Ireland, 1780–1907." Ph.D. diss., London School of Economics, 1994.

Bradley, James F., and Brendan Dowling. Industrial Development in Northern Ireland and in the Republic of Ireland. 1983.

Girvin, Brian. Between Two Worlds: Politics and Economy in Independent Ireland. 1989.

Hewitt-Dundas, Nola, Bernadette Andreosso-O'Callaghan, Mike Crone, John Murray, and Stephen Roper. Learning from the Best: Knowledge Transfers from Multinational Plants in Ireland: A North-South Comparison. 2002.

Industrial Policy Review Group. A Time for Change: Industrial Policy for the 1990s. 1992. Commonly called the "Culliton Report" after the chairman of the group, Jim Culliton.

Isles, Keith S., and Norman Cuthbert. An Economic Survey of Northern Ireland. 1957.

Kennedy, Kieran A. Productivity and Industrial Growth: The Irish Experience. 1971.

Kennedy, Liam. The Modern Industrialisation of Ireland, 1940–1988. 1989.

McAleese, Dermot, and Tony Foley, eds. Overseas Industry in Ireland. 1991.

O'Malley, Eoin. Industry and Economic Development: The Challenge for the Latecomer. 1989.

Telesis Consultancy Group. A Review of Industrial Policy. 1982.

Kieran A. Kennedy

Employment in IDA supported companies

	1992	1993	1994	1995	1996	1997	1998	1999	2000	2001
New jobs filled	7,074	8,227	9,938	11,955	13,197	14,768	16,154	17,949	23,158	13,514
Number of companies	860	879	914	968	1,047	1,113	1,174	1,290	1,287	1,237
Full-time employment	78,583	81,264	85,761	92,585	99,690	109,423	118,351	126,972	142,030	138,009
Net change in full-time employment	1,200	2,681	4,497	6,824	7,105	9,733	8,928	8,621	15,058	−4,021
% Net change	+1.6	+3.4	+5.5	+8.0	+7.7	+9.8	+8.2	+7.3	+11.9	−2.8
Job losses	−5,874	−5,546	−5,441	−5,131	−6,092	−5,035	−7,226	−9,328	−8,100	−17,535
Job losses as % of total jobs	7.5	6.8	6.3	5.5	6.1	4.6	6.1	7.4	5.7	12.7
Temporary employment	4,273	5,331	9,028	11,573	9,462	13,475	15,094	15,587	14,793	11,632

SOURCE: *Forfás Employment Survey.*

Investment and Development Agency (IDA Ireland)

The Investment and Development Agency of Ireland (IDA Ireland) is the autonomous state-sponsored agency responsible for attracting inward investment. Funded mainly by government grant under the National Development Plan, it has an annual budget of about E250 million, of which 5 percent is supported by European Union programs. The agency reports to the minister for enterprise, trade, and employment, who appoints the chief executive and the board, which is comprised of representatives from the private and public sectors.

IDA operates under the terms of the Industrial Development Acts 1986 to 1998, but the original Industrial Development Authority dates back to 1949. Through the 1950s and 1960s it had a relatively minor promotional role as Ireland opened up to inward investment. In 1970 it was combined with a sister agency that paid grants to industry, and the new IDA became a full-service national development agency, one of the first in the world: It planned, promoted, and negotiated new investment; it could acquire land and buildings; it administered a growing range of financial incentives for investors; and it had the task of developing native industry as well as attracting companies from abroad.

Following a restructuring of the development agencies in 1994, three organisations share responsibility for industrial development. Forfás deals with overall policy advice and coordination; Enterprise Ireland develops indigenous industry; and IDA became the Industrial and Development Agency, with the mission of bringing in new overseas investors and helping to expand and secure their operations in Ireland. In September 2001, IDA changed its name again (retaining the acronym) to *Investment* and Development Agency, since only 40 percent of investment now fits the traditional industrial classification.

IDA administers a range of investment incentives: capital grants, employment grants, and grants for training and for research and development; and it provides sites and buildings, often in partnership with private developers. The most important financial incentive is the low corporation tax rate: zero on export profits (1956–1980); 10 percent (1980–2003); 12.5 percent (2003–). The agency markets abroad Ireland's advantages as a location for investment: a stable economy and society; skilled, productive young workers; access to the European Union market; and competitive production costs.

IDA is now trying to achieve a better balance of development across the more remote regions and is moving some sectoral divisions away from its Dublin head office. For the future it will focus more on innovation- and research-driven investment and will take a wider role in ensuring that the appropriate skills and facilities are available in Ireland. IDA has a staff of three hundred of whom about sixty are marketing executives based in the agency's sixteen overseas offices (six in the United States).

SEE ALSO Celtic Tiger; *Economic Development*, 1958; Industry since 1920; Overseas Investment; State Enterprise

Bibliography

Forfás. *Enterprise 2010.* 2000.

IDA Ireland Annual Report 2000. 2001.

Industrial Policy Review Committee. *A Time for Change: Industrial Policy in the 1990s.* 1992.

Finn Gallen

Irish Colleges Abroad until the French Revolution

Between the 1570s and the French Revolution about thirty colleges were established in Spain, the Spanish Netherlands, France, central Europe, Portugal, and Italy to provide the Irish Catholic Church with priests, to educate the lay Catholic elite, and to maintain the influence of European Catholic powers in Ireland. Their primary function was to train Catholic clergy.

In the medieval period Irish clerical students were educated informally, usually by parish clergy. Because medieval attempts to establish universities in Ireland failed, a small number of talented or ambitious students traditionally traveled to English, Scottish, and continental European universities to pursue further studies. These practices changed dramatically in the sixteenth century. The Council of Trent (1545–1563) laid down strict rules regarding the education of priests, the most important of which was the duty imposed on bishops to establish diocesan seminaries. The primary object of seminaries was to encourage the moral and spiritual growth of obedient and disciplined clergy in order to reform the church and combat heresy. Due to the extension of Tudor and Stuart power in Ireland, the associated introduction of the Protestant Reformation, government prohibition of Catholic schools and sheer lack of resources and organization, Irish bishops were unable to comply with the new tridentine regulations. In the sixteenth and early seventeenth centuries Irish Catholics were gradually excluded from political and civil life. For Old English Catholics, concentrated especially in Munster and Leinster, uncertainty regarding land tenure grew. For Gaelic Irish Catholics, particularly in Ulster, confiscation and plantation were stark realities. For both Catholic communities in Ireland, religious persecution became a sporadic but constantly threatening reality. In these circumstances the possibility of establishing secondary schools, seminaries, and universities in Ireland was remote.

From the late 1540s Irish students began to turn up in continental Europe, where they were accommodated in already established seminaries or in the fledgling English and Scots recusant (Catholic) colleges. In about 1578 in Paris six clerics came together under the Waterford-born priest John Lee and found lodgings in the Collège de Montaigu and later in the Collège de Navarre. As the numbers of Irish students abroad increased, the small, informal Irish communities developed into proper seminaries with church recognition and usually insecure financial patronage. About twelve colleges were set up by religious orders to train their own clerical students, and about seventeen were established for the training of secular or diocesan clergy and laymen. These secular colleges were often run by religious orders, usually Jesuits. Most of the earliest foundations were in Spain or the Spanish Netherlands because the Spanish Habsburgs had strategic interests in Ireland and were traditional champions of Catholicism, and because these territories had long-established commercial relations with Ireland and thriving universities. The Irish also established a number of colleges in France, where there was relative religious peace following the edict of Nantes (1598), in central Europe and in Rome.

The most important of the early colleges were in Spanish territories. The first successful attempt to found a college was in 1592, when the Jesuit Thomas White (1556–1622) of Clonmel secured the patronage of Philip II (1527–1598) for an institution in Salamanca. During its first fifty years it educated nearly four hundred Irish seminarians. In 1594, the Meath-born Christopher Cusack founded the Irish college of Saint Patrick at Douai in the Spanish Netherlands; from it a number of small colleges were launched in Antwerp (1600), Lille (1610), and Tournai (1616). The arrival of large numbers of Irish emigrants after the battle of Kinsale (1601–1602) led to another spate of foundations; in 1605, for instance, Eugene McCarthy established a private college at Santiago to provide for the education of the family and retinue of the Gaelic lord, Donal Cam O'Sullivan Beare. Its rather informal discipline aroused the concern of King Philip III (1578–1621), who placed the college under the care of the Jesuits in 1611.

Jesuit influence in the college network was strong but not overwhelming and was balanced by that of the Irish Franciscans, Dominicans, and others. From the late sixteenth century, pressure from the Dublin government forced the Irish Franciscans to set up a network of colleges, friaries, and student residences in continental Europe. The first Irish Franciscan college, Saint Anthony's, was founded by Florence Conry (1560–1629) in Louvain, Spanish Netherlands in 1607, with a faculty educated at the university of Salamanca. Saint Anthony's became a center for the formation of clergy for the Irish mission, especially in the Gaelic-speaking parts of both Ireland and Scotland, and consequently developed a speciality in Irish language and hagiography. Saint Isidore's in Rome, set up in 1625 by Luke Wadding (1588–1657), achieved recognition as a center for international Franciscan studies, especially in history, hagiography, and the theology of Duns Scotus (1266–1308). Pressure of numbers in Louvain and Rome obliged the Irish Franciscans to found a college at Prague in 1631. Members of its theological staff, at the invitation of the local archbishop, joined the theology faculty of the local seminary. A Franciscan friary was founded at Vielun in Poland in 1645, but owing to the opposition of local Franciscans, it closed in 1653. The friary set up in Capranica in Italy in 1656 became an important summer residence for the Irish Franciscans in Rome. The last Franciscan college was founded in 1700 at Boulay, near Metz, France under the patronage of Leopold, duke of Lorraine.

The Irish Dominicans suffered from the same pressures in Ireland as their Franciscan confreres and were obliged to establish colleges abroad, at Louvain, Lisbon, and Rome. Their Louvain college was founded in 1626, and in 1767 it boasted a community of about fifty. The remarkable Dominican Daniel O'Daly (1595–1662), who served as an outstanding diplomat for the house of Braganza, the royal house of Portugal, founded the Lisbon college in 1629. It suffered badly in the earthquake of 1755, when it had a community of more than twenty-five, all of them Irish. Associated with it was an Irish Dominican convent for female religious, also founded by O'Daly. The Dominican priory of San Clemente in Rome was established in 1677. The Augustinians set up a college in Rome in 1656, and the Capuchins had an institution in Charleville (1620). The Irish Carmelites were established in La Rochelle in 1665 and in Aix-la-Chapelle in 1677. In French territory diocesan colleges were founded in Bordeaux (1603), Rouen (1612), Toulouse (1645?), and Nantes (1689?). The college in Nantes quickly grew in importance and by 1765 housed over sixty students.

The colleges were small in the early days, rarely housing more than a dozen students at a time. They encountered great difficulty in supporting themselves financially, and many had to be closed, usually temporarily, when patronage dried up. The Irish College in Paris had a sporadic existence until the 1610s when it secured the patronage of Jean L'Escalopier, the president of the *parlement* of Paris (died 1619), and was awarded letters patent from Louis XIII (1601–1643) in 1623. The Irish pastoral college in Louvain enjoyed a relatively large number of scholarships, many of which were established between 1692 and 1783. However, these scholarships had various conditions attached to their allocation, and it was frequently difficult to find suitably qualified candidates. In other colleges priests supported themselves through Mass stipends or chaplaincies. They helped in neighboring parishes, acted as chaplains in hospitals, and gave religious instruction to the children of the local Irish community.

The places available in the colleges were not always filled, and many students split their time between two or more colleges. Students came from a great variety of backgrounds, but most had already received some informal secondary tuition in Ireland, mostly in the classics, and generally had access to at least some limited resources; for instance, Nicolas Marob, a native of Kilkenny, possessed an extensive wardrobe and a copy of Suárez's *Rhetoric* when he arrived in Salamanca in 1595. Because of the difficulties in securing education in Ireland, many of the students who traveled to Spain were already mature men in their twenties or thirties, and some were ordained priests. All students were required to take oaths of obedience, promising to observe college rules and to return to the Irish mission on completion of their studies. The students were subjected to a strict discipline, the Paris seminarians in the 1620s rising at 4:30 A.M. and following an exhausting schedule until they retired at 9:00 P.M. Students in the Irish foundations pursued their studies in the college itself or attended lectures at a neighboring university or at a local Jesuit house of studies. Those who were not already ordained priests entered the colleges at about sixteen or seventeen years old and spent about nine years in study before returning to Ireland. Those already ordained usually spent about five or six years abroad. In the eighteenth century there was a tendency to prolong the period of study. In 1742, for instance, the course of studies in the Franciscan and Dominican colleges was extended by two years.

The philosophical and theological education of the students reflected the preferences of the local universities and the college authorities. The Irish Franciscans favored the philosophy and theology of Duns Scotus, so their houses in Louvain, Rome and Prague became important centers of Scotist scholarship. Between 1630 and 1769 about 257 theological theses were defended at Saint Anthony's, and of these, the overwhelming majority (231) dealt with Scotist theology. The Franciscan colleges provided teaching staff for seminaries all over Europe, notably in central Europe, and were instrumental in propagating renewed Scotist theology in the Habsburg sphere. Some of the Irish Franciscans in the low countries and Rome, such as Florence Conry, Hugh de Burgo, and Luke Wadding, contributed to the theological and moral tendencies that later became associated with Jansenism, but in general, the Irish of the colleges, both staff and students, were careful to observe the theological disciplines favored by the local ordinaries. The Irish Franciscans in particular fostered the study of Irish history, language, and hagiography. Hugh Ward (d. 1635), Patrick Fleming (1599–1631), John Colgan (1592–1658), and Thomas O'Sheerin (d. 1673) were pioneers in these fields. The extraordinary, if wayward, Peter Walsh (1614–1688) was also educated in Louvain, and his literary output made him one of the most widely read Irish Catholic writers in England and Ireland in the 1660s and 1670s. The Irish college in Paris also produced scholars of repute, including the Meath-born third rector and hagiographer Thomas Messingham (about 1580–1638?), and David Rothe (1568?–1651), who became bishop of Ossory. In the eighteenth century the Paris college produced a number of theologians, catechists, and Gaelic scholars including the Dubliner Cornelius Nary (1660–1730), and from Roscommon, Anthony Dunlevy (1694–1746), the author of the Irish-language catechism *An Teagasc Críosduidhe* (1742). Another student was Michael Moore (about 1639–1726), who left his library to the Irish college in Paris and was a distinguished, much-published late Aristotelian and critic of Descartes. Among the products of the Irish colleges in Rome Luke Wadding was a giant, but there were many others, including the theologian Francis Molloy (d. 1660).

On the completion of their training the young priests were supposed to return to Ireland, but getting trained clergy back to Ireland was not easy. In Spain, on the completion of their courses, Irish priests could apply to the Spanish king for the royal contribution, or *viaticum*, granted under certain conditions to help pay for the journey back to Ireland. Between 1619 and 1659 at least 280 Irish priests, mostly Dominicans and Franciscans, applied for the viaticum, but from the frequent references to Irish clergy active in Spanish and French dioceses, it appears that a substantial number never returned to Ireland. Some served as chaplains in the Irish regiments, others remained to staff the colleges, and a number entered pastoral ministry in their host countries.

The fledgling institutions suffered from internal divisions, often caused by disputes concerning the selection of superiors. In the diocesan colleges they were sometimes appointed by the local bishops, but in many cases they were elected by the students, usually according to a provincial quota system that was supposed to ensure representation of all parts of Ireland. Failures of the system were a constant cause of disharmony. Provincial differences ran deep, chiefly because the Irish migrants brought to the continent the traditional provincial rivalries that divided them at home. The main disagreement was between students from Munster and Leinster, which were largely Old English, and Ulster and Connacht, where the Gaelic Irish predominated. Because the Irish Jesuits recruited chiefly in Munster and Leinster and were also anxious to gain control of the colleges, there were frequent clashes between them and representatives of the Gaelic Irish. In 1602, for example, the Connacht-born Franciscan Florence Conry, with the support of the Ulster nobleman Aodh Ruadh Ó Domhnaill (1572–1602), petitioned Philip III to remove the Jesuits from the Salamanca college, accusing them of mismanaging funds, favoring Old English seminarians, and encouraging loyalty to Elizabeth I (1533–1603). Such disagreements were all too common. In Iberia, the Jesuits tended to prevail and eventually won control of all the Irish colleges there, with the exception of Alcalá. Thus the Society of Jesus exercised a decisive influence on the training of the Irish Counter-Reformation clergy, especially in Spain.

The fate of many Irish colleges was linked with the fate of the Jesuits in Europe: Suppression of the Jesuits in Portugal in 1759 and in Spain in 1767 led to the closures of the Irish colleges they ran. Salamanca was the only Spanish college re-established after the French revolutionary wars, and while the diocesan college in Lisbon remained open throughout the wars, it closed definitively in 1834. In Prague the Franciscan college, beset by internal feuding, was dissolved by Emperor Joseph II (1741–1790) in 1786 as part of his sweeping ecclesiastical reforms. The colleges in France fared better, and in the eighteenth century, the college in Paris was the largest, with a total of 200 student places, about a third of the total number of seminary places available on the continent of Europe for Irish clerical students. Before the French Revolution, fifteen Irish bishops were Paris-trained, and Paris-educated clergy were exposed to the latest trends in theology thanks to the lectures of Dublin-born Luke Joseph Hooke (1714–1796) and others. In addition, the Irish college in Paris was an important center for the wider Irish migrant community, providing financial and legal aid as well as spiritual services to the Irish soldiers, students, and merchants resident in or passing through Paris.

The French Revolution sealed the fate of the French colleges. The passing of the Civil Consitution of the Clergy in 1791 disrupted church life and led to the seizure of the Irish college in Paris in 1793. The French invasion of the Austrian Netherlands in 1793 spelled the end of Saint Anthony's and the other colleges in the low countries. In the end it was the combined effect of the suppression of the Jesuits, the amalgamation of the smaller Spanish colleges with Salamanca, the reforms of Emperor Joseph II, the French invasion of Rome in 1798, and the confiscation of church property all over French-occupied Europe that dealt the fatal blow to most of the Irish colleges. By 1799 only three were functioning effectively. In 1795 an act of the Irish parliament (passed with a lot of arm-twisting by William Pitt [1759–1806]) effected the foundation of the Royal Catholic College of Maynooth. Henceforth the Irish church could produce its clergy at home, and consequently, the importance of the continental colleges diminished.

During their two centuries of activity, however, the Irish continental colleges were vital to the maintenance of Catholicism in Ireland, and practically every Irish ecclesiastic in the period was associated with them. The colleges provided an educated clergy; they helped to maintain the network of contacts that held together the Irish migrant communities in western Europe; they sustained the political influence of the Catholic powers in Ireland; and they were powerfully active intellectual centers, playing a pivotal role in the modernization of Irish Catholic culture in the early modern period. Their disappearance deprived the nineteenth-century Irish church of an enriching continental influence.

SEE ALSO *Annals of the Four Masters*; Council of Trent and the Catholic Mission; Education: 1500 to 1690; Wild Geese—The Irish Abroad from 1600 to the French Revolution

Bibliography

Brockliss, L. W. B., and P. Ferté. "Irish Clerics in France in the Seventeenth and Eighteenth Centuries: A Statistical Study." *Proceedings of the Royal Irish Academy*, Section C,. 87(9): 527–572.

Giblin, Cathaldus. "Irish Exiles in Catholic Europe." In *A History of Irish Catholicism*, vol. 3, edited by P. J. Corish. 1971.

O'Connor, Thomas, ed. *The Irish in Europe, 1580–1815.* 2001.

Silke, John J. "The Irish Abroad 1534–1691." In *Early Modern Ireland, 1534–1691.* Vol. 3 of *A New History of Ireland*, edited by T. W. Moody, F. X. Martin and W. E. Vaughan. 1976.

Walsh, T. J. *The Irish Continental College Movement: The Colleges at Bordeaux, Toulouse, and Lille.* 1973.

Thomas O'Connor

Irish Language

See Language and Literacy: Decline of Irish Language; Language and Literacy: Irish Language since 1922.

Irish Pound

In January 2002 the Irish pound was replaced by the euro as the legal tender and currency of the Republic, and its notes and coin are now only collectors' items. Three years earlier, management of monetary affairs passed to the European Central Bank, and legally speaking the Irish pound was already a denomination of the euro, the currency of the European Monetary Union (EMU).

Using the currency of others is not a new experience for the Irish. Indeed, for most of the past two centuries, the Irish pound has had a shadowy existence, sheltering behind the pound sterling. Just twice did the currency emerge as a truly autonomous entity—first during the Napoleonic wars and more recently for the last two decades of the twentieth century, when it fluctuated as a member of the European Monetary System (EMS). Both periods of fluctuation were uneasy ones.

EARLY YEARS

All through the eighteenth century the value of the Irish pound had been fixed at thirteen Irish to twelve sterling. There was an Irish copper coinage, but before the establishment under statute of the Bank of Ireland in 1783, larger payments were mainly made in foreign silver and gold coin and in the banknotes of the small and often short-lived private banks. At first, the Bank of Ireland's notes were convertible into gold or Bank of England notes at the fixed rate, but when convertibility of both banks' notes was suspended in 1797, the Irish notes began to depreciate more quickly, puzzling many contemporaries and prompting the establishment of a parliamentary select committee. The committee's 1804 report broke new intellectual ground in pinpointing the excessive issue of bank notes in Ireland as the source of the problem. By 1821, with the dust of the wars settled, convertibility was restored at the old fixed rate; five years later, the Irish pound was effectively merged with sterling. Irish banks continued to issue sterling banknotes (a privilege which they retain to the present day in respect of their operations in Northern Ireland).

THE STERLING LINK

The foundation of the new state a century later called for the creation of a new currency. First on the agenda was the preparation of a national coinage, admirably accomplished with the beautiful 1926 design showing Brian Boru's harp (still to be found on the euro coins) on the obverse. The reverse shows animal representations—a woodcock on the farthing, a horse on the halfcrown, and a hare, wolfhound, bull, sow, and hen on other denominations.

The financial conservatism of the early administrations of the Irish Free State is clearly exemplified by the

This £50 note, designed by Robert Ballagh, featured a piper and the crest of the Gaelic League, overlaid on a sixteenth-century manuscript from the Royal Irish Academy. The front featured a portrait of Douglas Hyde, Gaelic League founder and first president of Ireland. This note was in use from 1995 until 2002. © ROYALTY-FREE/CORBIS. REPRODUCED BY PERMISSION.

decision to establish a currency commission, on the long-established model of British colonies, rather than a full-fledged central bank. From 1928 the commission issued Irish banknotes in exchange for sterling notes. It undertook to buy back these notes on a one-for-one basis and held a full and liquid reserve of sterling and other foreign assets. The Irish banks were also allowed to continue issuing notes, but on a consolidated basis, jointly guaranteed by the banks and the commission, rather than bank by bank (these consolidated notes began to be phased out in 1943). Bank of England notes also circulated freely, as did British coin. By 1942, attracted by the international vogue for central banking, a more activist administration had established the Central Bank of Ireland with extensive powers. However, these were at first little used, and the one-for-one sterling parity of the Irish pound never came under threat. Indeed, such calls that were made for a revision in the parity were generally for an appreciation—for example, at the time of the 1949 sterling devaluation and again when inflation was being imported as a result of sterling weakness in the mid-1970s.

It has been suggested that the one-for-one link may have served as a blinker to Irish exporters, inhibiting firms from breaking into more dynamic markets in Europe and elsewhere. By 1978 the United Kingdom still accounted for 47 percent of Irish exports, though this was less than half the share recorded in 1926. But the sterling link also provided a worthwhile discipline to government policy. Only twice did governments attempt to break away from this discipline. The first was in 1955, when an attempt to hold Irish interest rates down when London rates were rising was followed by a payments crisis that precipitated a deep recession and a surge of emigration. The second was in the late 1970s, when expansionary loan-financed government fiscal policy overheated the economy. This episode could ultimately have threatened the parity, but as it happened, it was suddenly abandoned for essentially political reasons.

INTO EUROPE

It was only in 1978, when beckoned to join the EMS, a Franco-German project for a new zone of monetary

People in line outside the Central Bank in Dublin to exchange their Irish pounds for Euros on 1 January 2002. AP/WIDE WORLD PHOTOS. REPRODUCED BY PERMISSION.

stability in Europe, that the Irish government decided to make the change. At first there was some hope that it would prove possible to hold the Irish pound's value at one pound sterling while still respecting the fluctuation limits in the EMS, despite the fact that Britain had not joined the new exchange-rate mechanism. But the strength of sterling in the early months of the EMS, buoyed up as it was by North Sea oil revenues and by the tight monetary policy of the Thatcher administration, put paid to that hope. It is arguable that a continuation of the sterling link into the early 1980s would have proved politically unsupportable, considering the loss of competitiveness that it might have entailed at a time of rapidly growing unemployment associated with the fiscal adjustment of those years.

During the twenty years of the EMS the Irish pound fluctuated widely against sterling, going below 74 pence (February 1981) and as high as 110 pence (November 1992). Nor was it stable against EMS partner currencies. Realignments in the EMS were fairly frequent, averaging about one a year in the 1980s, and the Irish pound depreciated steadily against the Deutsche

Mark (DM), anchor of the system, reaching a cumulative depreciation of 34 percent at its low point in 1993. These depreciations both reflected wider weaknesses in the Irish economy in those years and served to prevent a loss of competitiveness from compounding those weaknesses. Thus, contrary to the fears of many observers, linking the currency with the DM did not impose an unsupportable discipline, largely because the option of depreciation was readily availed of. By the same token EMS membership did not help to stamp out Irish inflation; though inflation did come down in the 1980s, the reduction lagged behind that of Britain.

Overall, Ireland's experience with an independent currency in the years of the EMS was not a very happy one. Interest rates were high, giving depositors a return of about 2.5 percent per annum more than would have been available in DM-denominated assets. Implicit in the interest differentials were exaggerated fears of devaluation, especially at times of sterling weakness. High Irish interest rates in the 1980s hampered fiscal adjustment and slowed economic growth.

Perhaps reflecting the checkered experiences of currency independence in Ireland, a sizable 69 percent majority voted in favor of the euro in a constitutional referendum in 1992, though many voters surely had their eyes mainly on the other tangible benefits which economic integration into Europe had brought the country. Specialists were more narrowly divided on the issue: Though a majority favored joining the EMU, few thought that the net advantages of abandoning the national currency and adopting the euro would be substantial.

SEE ALSO Banking and Finance to 1921; Celtic Tiger; Economic Relations between Independent Ireland and Britain; Economic Relations between North and South since 1922; Economies of Ireland, North and South, since 1920

Bibliography

Hall, F. G. *The Bank of Ireland, 1783–1946.* 1949.

Honohan, Patrick. *An Examination of Irish Currency Policy.* 1993.

Honohan, Patrick. "Currency Board or Central Bank? Lessons from the Irish Pound's Link with Sterling, 1928–79." *Banca Nazionale del Lavoro Quarterly Review* 50 (1997): 39–67.

McGowan, Padraig. *Money and Banking in Ireland.* 1990.

Moynihan, Maurice. *Currency and Central Banking in Ireland, 1922–1960.* 1975.

Patrick Honohan

~

Irish Republican Army (IRA)

The Irish Republican Army (IRA) originated from the Irish Volunteers, a nationalist militia established in 1913. Following Sinn Féin's establishment of a national parliament, Dáil Éireann, in 1919 and its declaration of an Irish republic, the Volunteers became known as the Irish Republican Army. Under the resourceful leadership of Michael Collins, from 1919 to 1921 the IRA fought an effective guerrilla-warfare campaign against British rule in Ireland. In July 1921, when both sides had fought to a stalemate, a truce was agreed to allow Sinn Féin and the British government to negotiate a settlement.

The Anglo-Irish Treaty, which was signed in December 1921 and narrowly accepted by the Dáil in January 1922, split the republican movement. The treaty offered a significant degree of autonomy for southern Ireland but entailed dominion rather than republican status and required the swearing of a loyalty oath to the British crown. The partition of the unionist-dominated six northeastern counties (constituted as Northern Ireland in 1920) was not a central issue. Despite broad public support for the treaty, many Volunteers who had sworn an oath to the Republic viewed the compromise as a betrayal. Led by Michael Collins, much of the IRA's leadership supported the treaty, but many republicans, particularly those from the areas most active in the preceding war, opposed it in the Irish Civil War (1922–1923). The antitreaty IRA also drew support from rural areas with a tradition of land agitation and opposition to authority. After a short but bitter conflict the IRA dumped its arms and suspended its violent campaign.

Despite defeat, Irish republicans rejected the Irish Free State and professed loyalty to the republican Dáil, which was composed of antitreaty Sinn Féin deputies. The relationship between the military and political wings of the republican movement remained strained as many IRA figures blamed politicians for the events preceding the Civil War. Even Eamon de Valera, the leading antitreaty figure, was regarded with suspicion because of his earlier support for a settlement that fell short of establishing an independent republic. At the 1925 IRA convention, amid rumors that de Valera might enter the Free State Dáil, the IRA withdrew its allegiance to the republican Dáil and vested authority in its own executive. It restructured itself as a secret army under the command of a seven-member army council whose principal enemy was the Irish Free State rather than Britain or Northern Ireland. Abstention from parliament, suspicion of politics, and commitment to physical force became the characteristics of militant republicanism in independent Ireland.

Although too weak to militarily threaten the Free State, the IRA engaged in periodic acts of violence, notably the assassination of the deputy head of government, Kevin O'Higgins, in 1927. The ensuing spiral of IRA violence and government coercion destabilized the state, while the IRA's increasingly socialist rhetoric also provoked concern. The IRA's political initiative, Saor Éire (1931), the first of several opportunistic attempts to harness social and economic grievances to republican objectives, aroused clerical and public disapproval and the subsequent "red scare" was used by the protreaty government to suppress the IRA.

The election of Fianna Fáil (a constitutional republican party which maintained links with the IRA despite entering the Dáil) in 1932 proved a greater threat to the

The outbreak of violence in Northern Ireland in 1969 led to the revival of the Irish Republican Army. The IRA was responsible for the deaths of 1,778 of the 3,665 men and women killed in the "Troubles" between 1966 and 2001. © TOPHAM/THE IMAGE WORKS. REPRODUCED BY PERMISSION.

IRA, as the party which comprised much of the Civil War antitreaty leadership demonstrated the possibility of achieving republican objectives through peaceful means. De Valera's reforms, such as scrapping the loyalty oath and the 1922 constitution, reconciled all but the most militant republicans to the southern state government and increased dissension within the IRA. In 1934 the IRA's left-wing minority, led by Peadar O'Donnell, split to form the Republican Congress, a short-lived socialist organization. In 1936, following several murders, de Valera banned the IRA. A disastrous bombing campaign in England, begun in 1939, soon petered out. The outbreak of World War II offered the IRA an opportunity to ally with Germany, but despite some IRA-German contact, the main consequence of the emergency (as World War II was known in Ireland) was de Valera's ruthless suppression of the IRA with much public support. Draconian legislation, including the introduction of internment and the death penalty, crushed the IRA in southern Ireland. Subsequent IRA activism would focus on the North.

THE PROVISIONAL IRA

The IRA's border campaign (1956–1962) appeared to confirm the ineffectiveness of physical force and led to a process of politicization as figures such as IRA Chief of Staff Cathal Goulding urged republican participation in the Catholic civil-rights movement. However, the resurgence of sectarian violence in the summer of 1969 revived tensions between the left-wing Dublin leadership led by Goulding and northern republicans who emphasized the IRA's role as armed defenders of the Catholic community. The leadership's decision to support a left-wing united front and end abstention from the Dáil led to a split in December 1969. The dissidents, led by Seán MacStiofáin, established a rival "provisional" IRA and a rival Sinn Féin (under Ruairí Ó Bradaigh) to continue the armed struggle. The "provisional" and "official" movements coexisted uneasily, but the original IRA's Marxism and ambiguity toward physical force resulted in further splits (including one that resulted in the formation of the extremist Irish National Liberation Army in 1975) and eventual terminal decline.

The early 1970s saw the escalation of the IRA's armed campaign which, despite ruthless tactics, won support in republican areas, partly due to the Unionist government's failed security policy that resulted in mass searches, curfews, internment, and "Bloody Sunday" (when the British army killed thirteen unarmed Catholic civilians). Bloody Sunday prompted direct rule from London in 1972 and several years of intense violence. A brief cease-fire in 1975 produced no results, the IRA leadership offering a politically unrealistic "Brits out" ultimatum, and a greatly weakened IRA resumed the armed campaign. Military setback was again followed by internal debate and calls for politicization. The subsequent "long war" strategy, developed by the rising northern IRA leadership, advocated the development of a broad political base but, crucially, not at the expense of armed struggle. The IRA turned to a cell system of organization that rendered British penetration more difficult by limiting the amount of information which volunteers who were turned by security forces could provide. The 1981 hunger strikes, the culmination of a lengthy struggle between republican prisoners and the British prison authorities, appeared to end in defeat after the deaths of ten prisoners, but the public sympathy it generated provided the first evidence of a potentially strong political base for Sinn Féin, which won seats in the British parliament and the Irish Dáil.

The "armalite and ballot box" strategy produced some gains in the 1980s, but the IRA faced increasing pressure from the penetration of informers, "supergrass" trials (the mass conviction of IRA volunteers based on the evidence of a former member), and the effective deployment of Britain's Special Air Service (SAS). The strategy also produced dissension as the younger northern leadership (led by Gerry Adams, who became Sinn Féin president in 1983) began dumping Sinn Féin's historical baggage. In 1986 Ó Brádaigh resigned from the party to protest the ending of abstention from the Dáil and founded the splinter Republican Sinn Féin, which would later be associated with the dissident Continuity IRA, who oppose the "peace process."

Talks that began in 1988 between the Social Democratic and Labour Party leader, John Hume, and Gerry Adams (along with secret British-IRA contacts) raised hopes for peace. Over the next six years, republicans modified their demands and formed a closer understanding with northern nationalists, the southern government, and Bill Clinton's White House. The 1993 Anglo-Irish Downing Street Declaration, setting out the principles underpinning any settlement (most importantly, the validity of the aspiration to national self-determination and the necessity for unionist consent), was followed by an IRA cease-fire in 1994. Following the British government's reluctance to initiate further talks, the IRA returned to violence seventeen months later. A second cease-fire in 1997 was followed by all-party negotiations that produced the Good Friday Agreement in April 1998. Since then, the resulting power-sharing executive and associated institutions have functioned fitfully, constrained by the IRA's failure to fully decommission and cease all operations, disagreements over policing, dissident republican violence, and substantial unionist hostility to the agreement itself. The IRA's cease-fire has, with some transgressions, held, and Sinn Féin continues to expand, for the first time out-polling the Social Democratic and Labour Party as the largest nationalist party in the June 2001 British general election.

SEE ALSO Adams, Gerry; Civil War; Collins, Michael; Decommissioning; Hunger Strikes; Loyalist Paramilitaries after 1965; Political Parties in Independent Ireland; Politics: Nationalist Politics in Northern Ireland; Special Powers Act; Ulster Politics under Direct Rule; **Primary Documents:** Proclamation Issued by IRA Leaders at the Beginning of the Civil War (29 June 1922); Republican Cease-Fire Order (28 April 1923); On Community Relations in Northern Ireland (28 April 1967); Irish Republican Army (IRA) Cease-Fire Statement (31 August 1994); Text of the IRA Cease-Fire Statement (19 July 1997)

Bibliography

CAIN: Conflict Archive on the Internet. Available at http://cain.ulst.ac.uk.

Coogan, Tim Pat. *The IRA.* 1995 edition.

English, Richard. *Radicals and the Republic: Socialist Republicanism in the Irish Free State, 1925–37.* 1994.

O'Brien, Brendan. *The Long War: The IRA and Sinn Féin.* 1999 edition.

Patterson, Henry. *The Politics of Illusion: A Political History of the IRA.* 1989.

Taylor, Peter. *Provos: The IRA and Sinn Fein.* 1998 edition.

Fearghal McGarry

Irish Republican Brotherhood

See Fenian Movement and the Irish Republican Brotherhood.

Irish Tithe Act of 1838

The Irish Tithe Act of 1838 effectively ended the tithe war of the 1830s. Earlier legislation in 1823 and 1832 had converted the contentious and fluctuating tithe charge into a fixed, standard payment based on the quality and quantity of land that each tithe payer held. Left unresolved, however, was the basic problem that Anglican clergymen still had to collect tiny sums from thousands of Catholic parishioners, all of whom fiercely resented being forced to support the Protestant Established Church. The 1838 act addressed this problem by transferring the burden of paying tithes from the numerous occupiers of the land, who were overwhelmingly Catholic, to the relatively fewer owners of land, who were usually Anglican.

By the terms of the 1838 act, tithe was converted into a charge on the landowner at three-quarters of the original amount due to the tithe owner. A tithe owner who previously had tried to collect a total of £100 from the many occupants of a parish would now receive £75 directly from the owner of the estate. In theory, the landowner could then add up to the full amount of the original tithe to his tenants' rent, thus receiving a bonus of up to 25 percent for his trouble. The liability traveled down through the layers of subtenants, stopping just above those who held land at will or from year to year. Tenants in this latter category, comprising the vast majority of Catholic landholders, were now completely exempt from tithe. In addition, all the uncollected tithe of the 1830s was effectively written off, as was the money already advanced to Anglican clergymen in 1833 by parliamentary act. Additional money left over from that 1833 legislation was now made available to tithe owners in order to help cover their losses.

Despite eight years of fierce resistance to paying tithes, the new rent charge met with surprisingly little opposition. By removing the burden of tithe from the majority of Catholic landholders and by abandoning all efforts to collect arrears, the new measure insured that the countryside would remain undisturbed. Furthermore, nonpayment of what was now rent carried a greater risk, as a landlord could evict or refuse to renew a lease.

The 1838 act finally put an end to the hostile transaction between Anglican parsons and the rural Catholic population, while maintaining tithe as a species of property for the support of the Protestant Established Church. It provided much needed financial stability to the Church in the years before its disestablishment in 1869.

SEE ALSO Defenderism; Land Questions; Oakboys and Steelboys; Protestant Ascendancy: Decline, 1800 to 1930; Tithe War (1830–1838); Whiteboys and Whiteboyism

Bibliography

Macintyre, Angus. *The Liberator: Daniel O'Connell and the Irish Party, 1830–1847.* 1965.

Suzanne C. Hartwick

Irish Women Workers' Union

After a summer of labor unrest, the Irish Women Workers' Union (IWWU) was launched in Dublin on 5 September 1911, with James Larkin as president and his sister Delia as general secretary. James Larkin had decided that membership in the Irish Transport and General Workers' Union (ITGWU) was reserved to men; the IWWU was formed on the principle that women workers needed their own union, and it was supported by suffragists. The union claimed 1,000 members in 1912. Subsidized by the ITGWU, it suffered financially from the 1913 lockout, and Delia Larkin left her position to work in London in 1915. She was refused readmission to the union on her return in 1918.

Following the 1916 Rising, the ITGWU president Thomas Foran invited Louie Bennett (1870–1956), a socialist and suffragist from a prosperous Dublin Protestant merchant family, to reorganize the IWWU. The union expanded to represent members in nursing and some twenty other industries, chiefly traditionally feminine industries such as printing, papermaking, and laundering. It also issued a newspaper, *An Bhean Oibre* (The woman worker), from 1926 to 1928. Dublin-based, with a few provincial branches, IWWU membership varied from 5,300 in 1918 to 3,300 in 1932, peaking at 6,782 in 1949.

Bennett served as general secretary of the IWWU from 1917 to 1955 and was also prominent in the Labour Party and Irish Trade Union Congress. While committed to equal rights and equal pay for women and critical of the Conditions of Employment Act (1936) and the role prescribed for women in Bunreacht na hÉireann for providing a legal basis for the belief that a woman's place was in the home, she accepted the prevailing trade-union view that employment of women endangered family life and the wage rates of male workers. As a pacifist, she disliked conflict, though the IWWU led strikes, notably an action by laundry workers in 1945, and its moderate industrial policy was partly dictated by the weak bargaining power of its members.

Despite internal modernization, the IWWU failed to cope with industrial transformation from the late 1950s. Its new, more strident feminist rhetoric merely reflected changing social values, and the union became less distinctive. Membership declined steadily to 2,654 in 1980. In 1984, concluding that they no longer had the resources to be proactive in the fight for wage equal-ity, IWWU members voted 1,086 to 182 in favor of merging with the Federated Workers' Union of Ireland.

SEE ALSO Conditions of Employment Act of 1936; Larkin, James; Trade Unions; Women and Work since the Mid-Nineteenth Century

Bibliography

Cullen Owens, Rosemary. *Louie Bennett.* 2001.

Jones, Mary. *These Obstreperous Lassies: A History of the Irish Women Workers' Union.* 1988.

Emmet O Connor

Jacobites and the Williamite Wars

The accession of James II, the first Catholic monarch for over a century, in February 1685 presented Irish Catholics with an opportunity to overturn the Cromwellian and Restoration settlements that had deprived them of their lands. A devout Catholic who wished to improve the lot of his coreligionists, James presented a major threat to the Irish Protestants, whose monopoly of power and privilege depended entirely on English support. Within a year he had created his favorite, Richard Talbot, earl of Tyrconnell, and in February 1687 he appointed him Irish viceroy. Thereafter Tyrconnell embarked upon the Catholicization of Ireland, and he secured James's agreement not just to the creation of an almost wholly Catholic army and government, but also to preparations to revise the crucial Restoration land settlement.

While this prompted something of a major Protestant exodus from Ireland, English Protestants were prepared to tolerate him because he would be succeeded by his Protestant daughter Mary. The birth of a Catholic son to James, by his second wife Mary of Modena in June 1688, transformed the situation and confronted English Protestants with the specter of a Catholic dynasty. At the behest of leading English notables Mary's husband, William of Orange, governor-general of the Netherlands, arrived in England to challenge the actions of his father-in-law in late 1688. James fled to France, and the English parliament recognized William and Mary, jointly, as his successor. These events brought Ireland into a European orbit, for William was a key figure in the anti-French front opposing the aggressive designs of Louis XIV. Perceiving Ireland as an inexpensive means of distracting William, Louis sent a reluctant James to Ireland with French money, arms, and officers to give Tyrconnell's raw Catholic army a backbone. Despite William's accession, Tyrconnell's supporters maintained control over most of Ireland. In March 1689 Justin McCarthy had suppressed Protestant resistance in Munster, while in eastern Ulster the Williamite Mountalexander was defeated at Dromore (14 March). Only in western Ulster, where Gustavus Hamilton rallied the Protestant settlers and fortified Enniskillen and Londonderry, did William enjoy real support.

On 12 March 1689 James landed at Kinsale, where he was greeted "as if he were an angel from heaven," and made a triumphal progress to Dublin (Gilbert 1971, p. 46). He had already begun to anticipate crossing into Scotland, but first had to secure Ulster. It seemed unlikely that the key bastion of Protestant resistance, Londonderry—crammed with refugees, low on supplies, and with relief a distant prospect—could hold out for long and, believing his presence would induce Londonderry to surrender, James addressed his "Protestant subjects" on 18 April and pleaded with them to acknowledge him. The inhabitants signalled their defiance by firing on him and thereafter the most famous siege in Irish history took place. In the Protestant version of the event Londonderry's defenders, inspired by true religion and pride of race, held out against overwhelming odds. The Jacobites, hampered by inadequate siege equipment and poor leadership, had little choice but to try to starve Londonderry into submission.

By late July the starving defenders were on the verge of surrender when Major-General Kirk's small flotilla of merchantmen broke the besiegers' boom across the Foyle estuary and delivered desperately needed supplies. The Jacobites were forced to raise the 105-day siege, and the arrival of an expeditionary force

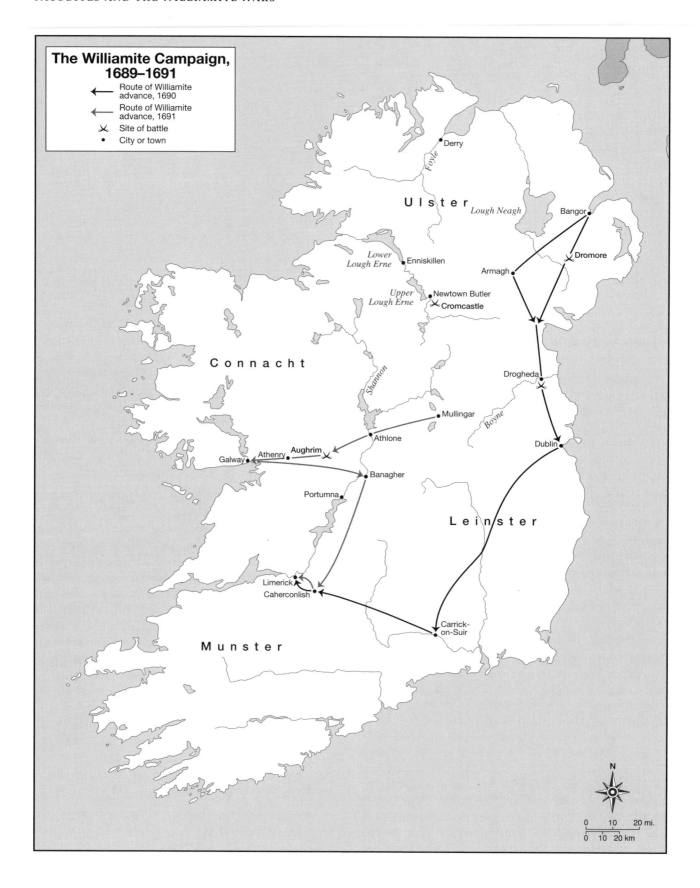

The Williamite Campaign, 1689–1691

← Route of Williamite advance, 1690
← Route of Williamite advance, 1691
✕ Site of battle
• City or town

Derry

U l s t e r Lough Neagh Bangor

Dromore

Lower Lough Erne Enniskillen Armagh

Upper Lough Erne Newtown Butler Cromcastle

C o n n a c h t *Shannon*

Drogheda

Mullingar *Boyne*

Athlone Dublin

Galway Athenry Aughrim

Banagher

Portumna **L e i n s t e r**

Limerick Caherconlish

Carrick-on-Suir

M u n s t e r

N

0   10   20 mi.
0   10   20 km

under Schomberg in the following month ensured Ulster was William's.

Both sides attempted little over the following ten months. This convinced William that only his presence would break the stalemate, and in June 1690 William landed near Belfast, took charge of an army of 37,000 men and immediately began marching south. On 1 July at the river Boyne he encountered James's force, which, although augmented by 7,000 recently arrived French troops, numbered less than 26,000 men. William's larger and better-equipped force carried the day. A diversionary flanking movement led by William himself proved decisive. As most of James's forces moved upstream to meet William's cavalry, the Williamite foot soldiers forced a passage across the river. Tyrconnell's Irish foot soldiers broke ranks and fled, but the Williamite cavalry, slowed by the river, failed to press their advantage, and the French troops covered a largely successful, albeit chaotic, retreat. James's conduct was less heroic than William's, and his flight from Ireland three days after the battle, in conjunction with his stubborn refusal to free the Irish parliament from its subordination to the English Crown, fatally damaged his reputation among his Catholic Irish supporters.

Whereas victory at the Boyne handed William control of Dublin and Leinster, as well as the military initiative, the Jacobites, though temporarily scattered, had lost fewer than a thousand men and still controlled Munster and Connacht. In these terms French dismissals of the battle as a "skirmish" are admissible. But continuing Protestant celebration of William's memory and the annual commemoration of the battle as the decisive blow for the Protestant cause reflect the powerful tradition that came into being. In the struggle for the British Crowns the Battle of the Boyne decided the issue in Williams' favor. In a European context, it represented a victory for Protestantism, yet it was also hailed by *Te deums* in Catholic Austria and Spain because it weakened the position of Louis XIV.

James's flight from Ireland and the disorganized retreat to the Shannon dealt grievous blows to Jacobite morale. Nonetheless, having regrouped at Limerick and Athlone, the Jacobites determined to use the natural line of the Shannon as a defensive boundary. While William sought to end the war that season, his failure to take either Athlone (17–24 July) or Limerick (10–30 August)—where Patrick Sarsfield's *rapparees* behind enemy lines had seriously impeded the besiegers—meant that the conflict entered a third year. Believing he had broken the back of the Jacobite opposition, William left for England after appointing General Godard van Reede Ginkel as his successor.

Patrick Sarsfield (c. 1655–1693), earl of Lucan, was the leading Catholic commander of the Williamite war (1689–1691). After an apprenticeship in the French army in the 1670s, he advanced in the army of the Catholic king, James II (r. 1685–1688), and persisted in the defense of Catholic Ireland after James left Ireland in 1690. A year later he was forced to negotiate the Treaty of Limerick in 1691, after which he left the country. THE ART ARCHIVE/JARROLD PUBLISHING. REPRODUCED BY PERMISSION.

In May 1691 Jacobite hopes were raised by the presence of the marquis de Saint Ruth, who arrived with French reinforcements. Nonetheless, Ginkel took Athlone in the following month and crossed the Shannon. Determined to regain the initiative, Saint Ruth opposed Ginkel's advance at Aughrim on 12 July. Both armies numbered about 20,000 men but Saint Ruth had chosen his ground well and, having repulsed the Williamite advance, he pursued the enemy across the field before leading his cavalry against the Williamite batteries. With Jacobite victory in sight a dramatic reversal of fortune occurred: a cannonball decapitated Saint Ruth and the Jacobites fled in disarray, ruthlessly pursued by Ginkel's regrouped cavalry. Although Sarsfield attempted to cover the retreat, some seven thousand Jacobites were slain. Shortly afterwards Galway surrendered and the surviving Jacobites limped into Limerick where they were soon besieged. Aughrim's "dread disaster" was thus the decisive engagement of the war, for thereafter the Jacobites had little prospect of successful resistance.

Irish Catholic thoughts now turned to what manner of surrender they could negotiate with Ginkel. Eager to rejoin the European war, Ginkel was persuaded to grant generous conditions, and on 3 October 1691 the Treaty of Limerick was concluded. Under its terms 14,000 Jacobite troops led by Patrick Sarsfield set sail for France on 22 December. For those who chose to stay behind, the civil terms were lenient. They would retain their lands, practice their professions, and enjoy the same rights of religious worship as they had under Charles II. These terms were not to be honored because after three major rebellions in less than a century Protestants had decided that the Catholics were totally untrustworthy. Tyrconnell's rapid Catholicization of the administration, army, and the Irish parliament convinced Protestants of the need to secure ascendancy in all walks of life. In 1691 a parliamentary act preventing Catholics from becoming MPs was passed: thereafter the Irish parliament was used by the Protestant Ascendancy to dismantle the Treaty of Limerick and introduce legislation to encumber the position of Irish Catholics.

The accession of James, which had initially given hope to Irish Catholics, in the end, greatly worsened their situation. James had provided ineffective leadership whereas his rival, in no small part owing to his own courage, won the crucial victory at the Boyne. Moreover, because of England's superior military resources the Jacobite cause was dependent on French aid, and yet Louis XIV provided wholly inadequate military assistance. Buttressing a Jacobite regime was a far less pressing objective for the French king, than securing Ireland was for William. The "War of the Two Kings" represented the climax of a century of bloody conflict in Ireland over land and religion, and the demoralizing sequence of defeats at Derry, the Boyne, and Aughrim crushed the spirit of Irish Catholics for over a century, as well as securing the Protestant Ascendancy for the next two centuries.

SEE ALSO Boyne, Battle of the; Butler, James, Twelfth Earl and First Duke of Ormond; Derry, Siege of; Eighteenth-Century Politics: 1690 to 1714—Revolution Settlement; Sarsfield, Patrick; **Primary Documents:** Treaty of Limerick (1691)

Bibliography

Bagwell, Richard. *Ireland under the Stuarts and during the Interregnum.* 1910–1916.

Baxter, S. B. *William III.* 1966.

Dickson, David. *New Foundations: Ireland, 1660–1800.* 2000.

Gilbert, J. T., ed. *A Jacobite Narrative of the War in Ireland, 1688–1691.* 1892. Reprint with introduction by J. G. Simms, 1971.

Hayton, D. W., Gerard O'Brien, and J. G. Simms, eds. *War and Politics in Ireland, 1649–1730.* 1986.

Miller, John. *James II: A Study in Kingship.* 1978.

Simms, J. G. "The War of the Two Kings, 1685–1691." In *The New History of Ireland,* vol. 3, *Early Modern Ireland, 1534–1691,* edited by T. W. Moody, F. X. Martin, and F. J. Byrne. 1976.

Simms, J. G. *Jacobite Ireland.* Reprint, 2000.

William of Orange. *The State of the Protestants of Ireland under the Late King James's Government.* 1691.

David Finnegan

Jewish Community

The first evidence of Jewish settlement in Ireland dates from 1079, when the Annals of Innisfallen record the arrival of five Jews with gifts for the king of Munster, Turlough O'Brien. King Edward II expelled the Jews from Britain and Ireland in 1290, but there has probably been a continuous Jewish presence in Dublin from the 1650s, when Oliver Cromwell invited a community of Sephardic Jews to the city. In 1818 there were reported to be only 9 Jews in Dublin, but by 1861 their numbers had increased to 324; the majority were craftsmen—jewelers, goldsmiths, and watchmakers.

The 1911 census records a Jewish population of 5,148. The exodus of Jews from eastern Europe in the closing decades of the nineteenth century saw the emergence of Jewish communities in Belfast, Cork, and Limerick and a substantial increase in Dublin's Jewish population. The new settlers were poorer than the established Jewish families: They made their living as traveling dealers, as small shopkeepers, and allegedly as moneylenders; their arrival triggered attacks on Jewish property, anti-Semitic poster campaigns, charges that they were engaged in sweated labor, and organized boycotts of Jewish businesses. The most serious incident happened in 1904 when a series of anti-Semitic sermons by a Limerick priest resulted in a boycott of Jewish businesses, and the departure of city's Jewish community, which had numbered 171 in 1901. The Limerick "pogrom" reflects one aspect of the Jewish experience in Ireland, but it is not the entire story.

The Jewish community played an active part in the campaign for Irish independence, and subsequently in Irish political life. In the early 1990s there were three

Jewish deputies in Dáil Eireann, one in each of the three major parties, an impressive record for a community of less than 1,600 people. Article 44 of the 1937 Constitution gave formal recognition to the Jewish congregation, but the Irish government was reluctant to admit Jewish immigrants who were fleeing central Europe. Irish society was introspective and somewhat xenophobic, and there was widespread resentment toward any foreigner who appeared to be taking jobs from Irish people, but the hostility and suspicion toward Jewish immigrants was exacerbated by a vein of anti-Semitism in Irish Catholicism, which was exploited by some unscrupulous politicians. After World War II a limited number of Jewish families and approximately one hundred children were admitted as refugees. The Irish Jewish population peaked in 1946 at a figure of 5,381. Since that time the population has fallen to between 1,000 and 2,000. The decline is consistent with what has happened elsewhere in Europe, especially in cities with a small Jewish population, where a combination of emigration, out-marriage, and an extremely low birthrate threatens the survival of communities that have existed for centuries.

SEE ALSO Gaelic Catholic State, Making of; Politics: Independent Ireland since 1922; Protestant Community in Southern Ireland since 1922

Bibliography

Hyman, Louis. *The Jews in Ireland from Earliest Times to the Year 1910.* 1972.

Keogh, Dermot. *Jews in Twentieth-Century Ireland.* 1998.

Shillman, Bernard. *A Short History of the Jews in Ireland.* 1945.

Mary E. Daly

Joyce, James

Arguably the most important English-language writer of the twentieth century, James Joyce (1882–1941) was born into a family of some wealth that spiraled down into economic misery during his youth. Raised in various locations in Dublin and its environs, Joyce was educated principally by the Jesuits at Clongowes Wood College and Belvedere College. He earned his university degree from University College, Dublin, in 1902, after studying modern languages, particularly French and Italian. Joyce left Ireland permanently in 1904—returning only for visits thereafter—with Nora Barnacle, whom he married in 1931 and with whom he had two children, Giorgio and Lucia. He lived on the Continent, writing primarily in Trieste, Rome, Zurich, and Paris. He was helped by patronage from and association with such writers as W. B. Yeats, T. S. Eliot, and Ezra Pound; he was lionized by the avant-garde literary circles of Paris and supported economically by his long-term benefactor Harriet Shaw Weaver. Other patrons included Mrs. Harold McCormick and Sylvia Beach, who arranged the publication of *Ulysses.*

Written in a style described in his letters as "scrupulous meanness," Joyce's first major work was *Dubliners* (published in 1914). Using covert Irish-language symbolism, *Dubliners* is a collection of fifteen short stories purporting to be "a chapter of the moral history of [his] country" and to show Dublin as "the centre of paralysis" in Ireland. *A Portrait of the Artist as a Young Man* (1916), a semiautobiographical symbolist narrative, is a landmark of varied perspective. Joyce welds together form, style, and content even as he demonstrates that the Irish artist has a dual heritage and identity, comprised of both Gaelic and English elements. *Ulysses* (1922) is Joyce's masterpiece, one of the central modernist narratives of the twentieth century, enormously influential on all of Western literature because of its stream-of-consciousness technique as well as its experiments with style and its merging of symbolist and realist aspects. Following the experiences of three principal characters in Dublin on a single day (16 June 1904), *Ulysses* challenges the canonical form of the novel, in part through the deployment of narrative techniques drawn from early Irish literature. Although Joyce had experimented with mythic substructure and Irish symbolism in his earlier narratives, in *Ulysses* his mythic technique became a major focus, intertwining principally Greek and Irish sources, and using the myth armature itself to convey political and ideological stances.

Drawing on Giambattista Vico's theory of history, *Finnegans Wake* (1939), a sui generis encyclopedic work, meshes history, myth, popular culture, and Dublin placelore, to name just a few strands. Here Joyce's syncretism extends to language itself, with the text a stream of puns, portmanteau words, and other types of wordplay, all drawing on dozens of languages, among which Irish ranks highly. Structured around the collective and personal dreamwork of a household near Dublin during a single night, *Finnegans Wake* was begun in 1922, during the Irish Civil War, and published on the eve of World War II. A thread of conflict, from the local to the global, lends a somber *basso continuo* to the text, emphasized by the circular structure whereby the first line of the book completes the last line.

Joyce's other works include two volumes of poetry, *Chamber Music* (1907) and *Pomes Penyeach* (1927); a play, *Exiles* (1918); *Stephen Hero*, a preliminary form of *A Portrait of the Artist*, which was published after Joyce's death; and numerous critical essays, lectures, and reviews.

Hailed as both modernist and postmodernist, Joyce created a new narrative type with each of his major works. He was a postcolonial writer before such a critical category existed, writing his nation's history, culture, language, and literature into all of his texts. Though in his youth he criticized the Irish Literary Revival, in many ways his works are a fulfillment of the revival's literary project. His influence is patent on writers ranging from Flann O'Brien and Samuel Beckett to William Faulkner, Gabriel García Márquez, and Toni Morrison.

SEE ALSO Arts: Modern Irish and Anglo-Irish Literature and the Arts since 1800; Fiction, Modern

Bibliography

Adams, Robert Martin. *Surface and Symbol: The Consistency of James Joyce's "Ulysses."* 1962.

Campbell, Joseph, and Henry Morton Robinson. *A Skeleton Key to "Finnegans Wake."* 1944. 2d edition, 1961.

Ellmann, Richard. *James Joyce.* 2d edition, 1982.

Gilbert, Stuart. *James Joyce's "Ulysses."* 1930. 2d edition, 1955.

Kenner, Hugh. *Joyce's Voices.* 1978.

Lawrence, Karen. *The Odyssey of Style in "Ulysses."* 1981.

Manganiello, Dominic. *Joyce's Politics.* 1980.

Tymoczko, Maria. *The Irish "Ulysses."* 1994.

Maria Tymoczko

K

Kennedy, John F., Visit of

In June 1963, as part of a wider European tour and just after his famous address at the Berlin Wall, John F. Kennedy made a memorable visit to Ireland, the first of any U.S. president during his term of office. Kennedy, also the first Irish-American Catholic elected to the Oval Office, received a tumultuous welcome during stops in Galway, Co. Limerick, Cork, and Dublin as well as in Wexford, the home of his Irish forebears. The Irish people embraced Kennedy, the great-grandson of Irish emigrants, as one of their own, and saw the success of the Harvard-educated, fourth-generation Bostonian as a vindication of their own Irish identity and proof, as one Irish newspaper noted, that they too were made of the "right stuff." Dermot Keogh recalls Kennedy's sojourn across Ireland as "days of national celebration." Alvin Jackson accurately describes the trip as "an emotionally intense occasion for both guest and hosts," and Kennedy himself, in a letter to the president of Ireland, Eamon de Valera, poignantly remembered it as "one of the moving experiences of my life."

In Ireland, President Kennedy's visit provided a boost to the opening up of Irish society, a process that had been underway since the 1950s and was then being spearheaded by the taoiseach (prime minister), Seán Lemass, who was especially committed to international trade and economic development. Speaking before the Dáil, Kennedy congratulated the Irish people, saying "[you have] modernized your economy, harnessed your rivers, diversified your industry, liberalized your trade, electrified your farms, accelerated your rate of growth, and improved the living standards of your people."

Kennedy received numerous accolades during his stay. After being awarded honorary degrees from Trinity College, Dublin, (primarily Protestant at the time) and the National University of Ireland (traditionally Catholic), he quipped, "I now feel equally part of both, and if they ever have a game of Gaelic football or hurling, I shall cheer for Trinity and pray for National." Just before returning to the United States, Kennedy promised his audience in Limerick that "I certainly will come back in the springtime"—a rendezvous that never materialized.

SEE ALSO Diaspora: The Irish in North America; Politics: Independent Ireland since 1922

Bibliography

Jackson, Alvin. *Ireland, 1798–1998.* 1999.

Keogh, Dermot. *Twentieth-Century Ireland.* 1994.

McCaffrey, Lawrence. *The Irish Diaspora in America.* 1984.

Mitchell, Arthur. *JFK and His Irish Heritage.* 1993.

O'Donnell, Kenneth, and David Powers. *"Johnny, We Hardly Knew Ye."* 1970.

Joseph M. Skelly

Keogh, John

The family origins and early life of John Keogh (1740–1817), who was among the more important figures in

John F. Kennedy's visit to Ireland in June 1963, the first visit by a U.S. president, was a major cause of national celebration. It also brought Ireland to the attention of U.S. and international media. AP/WIDE WORLD PHOTOS. REPRODUCED BY PERMISSION.

the Catholic politics of his day, are obscure. By the time he began to make his name as a member of the Catholic Committee in the 1780s, he had accumulated a considerable fortune in trade and land. In the last two decades of the eighteenth century some sought to integrate the Catholic community into the established order, while others sought to use the Catholic question as an instrument to induce fundamental political change. Keogh's adherence to the latter position quickly became clear when he joined in agitation for the admission of Catholics to political power. In the early 1790s, as a member of the United Irishmen, Keogh played an important part in displacing the conservative leadership of the Catholic

body, which now adopted a more aggressive stance. A substantial Catholic relief measure followed in 1793, but this owed its enactment chiefly to the desirability of conciliating Catholics as the war with republican France began. After a brief adherence to Wolfe Tone's revolutionary conspiracy, Keogh withdrew from political life and his attempt to reenter it in 1805 was ineffectual.

Keogh was treated with deference by his fellow political activists: they no doubt found it useful to accommodate his vain self-image as the undisputed and triumphant champion of Irish Catholics. In reality, he showed an aptitude for quick retreat from the extreme positions he had adopted, when subjected to persuasion or pressure by those in power. Such was his conduct as a Catholic negotiator in 1793 and again as a republican conspirator in 1797. Whatever gratitude the Catholic body owed to Keogh for its political advances, it owed just as much to other leaders and far more to the circumstances of the times.

SEE ALSO Catholic Committee from 1756 to 1809; Eighteenth-Century Politics: 1778 to 1795—Parliamentary and Popular Politics; Eighteenth-Century Politics: 1795 to 1800—Repression, Rebellion, and Union; United Irish Societies from 1791 to 1803

Bibliography

Bartlett, Thomas, *The Fall and Rise of the Irish Nation: The Catholic Question, 1690–1830.* 1992.

Wall, Maureen. "John Keogh and the Catholic Committee." In *Catholic Ireland in the Eighteenth Century: Collected Essays of Maureen Wall.* 1989.

C. D. A. Leighton

~

Kildare Place Society

The Kildare Place Society, known officially as the Society for the Promotion of the Education of the Poor of Ireland, was the most successful of all the voluntary educational agencies founded in the years before the establishment of the National Board of Education in 1831. Set up in 1811 explicitly to cater to the demand for education among the Catholic poor, it aimed to provide a Bible-based but nondenominational education that would be acceptable to Catholics. In 1816 the society petitioned Parliament and was awarded 10,000 pounds, an amount that was greatly increased over the following decade; this money allowed it to spread across the country and to establish the rudiments of a national system of primary education. The society aimed to modernize the teaching profession with a training college and an inspectorate, decent schoolhouses, and regular salaries for teachers. It also produced reading material aimed at a popular audience, which competed very favorably with the much-derided chapbooks that were the staple of popular reading material at the time.

Despite the commitment of the founders (many of whom were members of the Society of Friends) to re-spect denominational differences, and despite the allocation of seats for Catholics on the board of trustees, during the second decade of the century the society was increasingly drawn into quarrels over the use of the Protestant Bible for educational purposes. Particularly significant was the influence of the evangelical members of the board, especially Chief Justice Thomas Lefroy, who insisted on the compulsory use of the Bible "without note or comment" in the Kildare Place schools. This measure was openly and stridently criticized by the Reverend John MacHale in the famous *Hierophilus Letters* of 1820 and was the immediate cause of the resignations of Daniel O'Connell and Lord Cloncurry from the society's board in 1821. This gesture was followed in short order by directives to Catholic parents to withdraw their children from the schools. The substance of O'Connell's and MacHale's attacks on the Kildare Place Society was that its policies were in line with the more overtly proselytizing societies associated with the "Second Reformation" and were therefore unsuitable for Catholic children. The society did not survive the challenge. As a result of the ideological conflict over education, the government inaugurated a series of inquiries to determine what kind of educational system would be acceptable to the different denominations in Ireland, and the outcome was the setting up of the National Board of Education in 1831. Although the Kildare Place Society continued its work into the 1830s, its school system suffered an inevitable decline with the spread of the new national system.

SEE ALSO Chapbooks and Popular Literature; Education: Primary Private Education—"Hedge Schools" and Other Schools; Education: Primary Public Education—National Schools from 1831; Literacy and Popular Culture

Bibliography

Kingsmill-Moore, H. *An Unwritten Chapter in the History of Education, Being the History of the Society for the Education of the Poor of Ireland, Generally Known as the Kildare Place Society, 1811–1831.* 1904.

McGrath, Thomas. *Politics, Interdenominational Relations, and Education in the Public Ministry of Bishop James Doyle of Kildare and Leighlin, 1786–1834.* 1999.

Irene Whelan

King, William

William King (1650–1729), bishop and parliamentarian, was born on 1 May 1650 in Antrim town into a Scots Presbyterian family. Educated at Dungannon Royal School, he became an undergraduate at Trinity College, Dublin, where, rejecting his Presbyterian upbringing, he embraced with enthusiasm Church of Ireland Anglicanism. Within five years of his ordination in 1674 he was chancellor of Saint Patrick's Cathedral, Dublin, of which he became dean in 1688. The most senior clergyman left in Dublin in 1689, he was rightly suspected of Williamite sympathies by the Jacobite authorities and imprisoned on two occasions. With Williamite victory assured, King set himself to write *The State of the Protestants of Ireland under the Late King James's Government* (1691), which, whatever its author's intentions, became a hugely influential account of Protestant suffering under James II, running into several editions. Appointed bishop of Derry (1691), he became in effect the leader of the reform party in the established church, seeking to restore church finances and buildings, and he remained the leading advocate of church rights after his promotion to the archbishopric of Dublin in 1703. Inevitably, he came into conflict with Presbyterians and continued to be a strong opponent of legal toleration for Dissent. Though his attitude to Catholicism was implacably hostile, he did not support the draconian penal laws.

In 1697 he was embroiled in a legal dispute involving the diocese of Derry and the Irish Society of Londonderry. When the latter appealed to the English House of Lords over the heads of the Irish parliament, King became a staunch defender of the Irish parliament's jurisdiction. Over succeeding decades he championed "patriot" issues, including opposition to both a bank of Ireland in 1721 and Thomas Woods's patent to mint halfpence in 1722. Despite his trenchant criticisms of government policy, he was appointed a lord justice of Ireland during the absence of the viceroy on three occasions in George I's reign, though he was twice passed over (1713 and 1724) for promotion to the see of Armagh in favor of English clerics, whose appointment he deplored for both personal and "patriot" reasons.

William King, who never married, died on 8 May 1729. Had he never had a public career, he would be best remembered for his tract on the problem of evil in the world, *De Origine Mali* (1702), which the German philosopher Gottfried Wilhelm Leibniz took sufficiently seriously to write a refutation.

SEE ALSO Church of Ireland: Since 1690

Bibliography

King, C. S. *A Great Archbishop of Dublin: William King, D.D., 1650–1729. Autobiography and Selected Correspondence.* 1906.

O'Regan, Philip. *Archbishop William King of Dublin (1650–1729) and the Constitution in Church and State.* 2000.

James McGuire

Kings and Kingdoms from 400 to 800 C.E.

The institution of early Irish kingship stands rooted in a "tribal, rural, hierarchical, and familiar" society. Each basic tribal, territorial unit (*tuath*) had its king (*rí*) whose sacral, unitary functions had long since devolved upon the expert in law or brehon (*brithem*), the poet (*file*), and the historian (*senchaide*). These offices and the kingship were shared closely within kin-groups. Stemming from Indo-European antiquity, the rituals and poetic vision serving this institution endured until the Flight of the Earls in 1607 and the collapse of the old social order.

SACRAL KINGSHIP

The king was ritually wedded to the land. Early texts refer to the *feis* ("sleeping with") or wedding feast initiating a king's reign. In legend, sovereignty, personified as a woman, might become beautiful for the just king or unkempt and deadly for the unjust. Like Medb ("She who Intoxicates") of the Ulster Cycle, this figure dispensed rulership as ale (*laith*) to the ruler (*flaith*). Other preludes to kingship included donning of a royal cloak and standing upon or touching a potent stone. A king was to be free of any bodily blemish rendering him unfit to rule. Thus early sources show him accompanied by a battle-smiter, a substitute churl for legal actions against him, and other surrogates. His death, even wounding, in battle, spelled defeat. Beyond this were auspicious or inauspicious actions (*buada, gessa*) he was to perform or avoid. His good rule was the fulfillment of *fír flatha* (prince's truth); his ill rule or prince's falsehood (*gáu flatha*) was linked to economic failure and was a harbinger of his death.

Pre-Viking Ireland: Political Divisions

N

0   10   20 mi.
0   10   20 km

Dál
Riata

Cenél
nEogain

Dál
Riata

Cenél
Conaill

Ciannachta

ULAID

Cenél
nEogain

AIRGIALLA

Dál
nAraide

Dál
Fiatach

Irrus
Domnainn

Crecraige

Uí Ailello

Uí Briúin
Bréifne

Uí
Fiachrach
Muaide

Gailenga
Luigne
Conaille

Luigne

Uí Briúin Aí

Calraige

Gailenga

CONNACHTA

Ciarraige
Aí

Clann
Cholmáin

Brega

Conmaicne
Mara

Uí Briúin
Seola

Delbna

Cenél
Cairpre

Cenél
Loegaire

Síl nAedo
Sláine

Fir Thulge

Delbna

Uí Fiachrach
Aidne

MIDE

Déis Temro

Cenél
Fiachach

Cenél
nArdgaile

Uí Maine

Delbna

Uí Fáilge

Corco
Modruad

Loíges

Uí Dúnlainge

Uí Briúin
Chualann

Éle

Ailtraige

Múscraige

LAIGIN

Fortuatha

Corco
Baiscind

Múscraige

Déis
Becc

Corco Óche

Eóganacht
Áirthir
Cliach

Eóganacht
Caisil

Osraige

Uí Chennselaig

Ciarraige
Luachra

Uí Fidgeinte

Eóganacht
Áine

Fothairt

Uí Bairrche

Corco Duibne

MUMU

Déisi Muman

Eóganacht
Locha Léin

Eóganacht
Glendamnach

Corco
Duibne

Uí Liatháin

Eóganacht
Raithlenn

Corco
Loígde

INAUGURATION

Inauguration occurred at a central, sacred place (a summit or sacred tree) in an assembly. A thirteenth-century text depicts the Ó Conchobhair king standing on the mound of Carn Fraoich attended by the principal lords and ecclesiastics of Connacht, while the chief poet (*ollam*) Ó Maolchonaire gave him a rod and sang his praises and genealogy. Advice to the king for just rulership—"princes' instructions" (*tecosca ríg*)—would be uttered, followed by a proclamation affirming both the truths of kingship and the king embodying them. Later, bardic poetry mentions the king's gift of a horse to the poet, and a twelfth-century Irish *Life* of St. Maedóg notes the king's bestowal of his royal cloak upon a witness adopting the poet's role as royal bride. Annalistic texts describe the foray to neighboring territories that might follow such a ceremony, ensuring subordination by gift (*tuarastal*).

DYNASTIC SUCCESSION

All males within the *derbfine* ("certain kin"), or descendants of a common great-grandfather, were eligible for election to kingship as the "one looked-forward-to" or *tánaise*. The *tánaise* was well positioned to assume his new role before the demise of his predecessor, so that social necessities and maintenance of a robust, limited pool of aspirants counterbalanced an institution that otherwise led to segmentation of populations. The other term for heir-apparent, *rígdomna* ("makings of a king"), was used more loosely, and applied to a wider group of eligible persons.

KINGSHIP AND LAW

Every person had an honor-price ("face-value," *lóg n-enech*). For the king of a *tuath* this was seven *cumals* (female slaves) or twenty-one milchcows; for a comfortable farmer (*bó-aire*), five milchcows. Clients and dependents paid rent in food, stock, land, or goods in return for a grant of fief (*rath*). A king's free clients (*soer-chéli*) constituted his retinue (*dám*). The candidate for king had to be a prince's son of good legal standing, preferably born from his father's principal wife. His house was considered to be a sanctuary from violent pursuit of legal claims. The king presided at the fair or *oenach* ("union"), a festal gathering of the *tuath* where he and the free nobles (*gráid Féne / soer-nemed*) might enact the occasional change in legal arrangements (*rechtge fénechais*).

HIGH KINGSHIP

Closely associated with the relationship of king (*rí*) to mesne king (*ruire*) and overking (*rí ruirech*) was the con-cept of a high king (*ard-rí*) of all Ireland (the island seen as a goddess *Ériu*, "Fat, Fertile [Land]") whose incumbent would celebrate the inaugural Feast of Tara (*Feis Temro*). There were indeed high kings in Ireland, many of whom were recognized by surrounding peoples or are so described in the sources—though never one that completely dominated the island. Besides being imposed on the annals during the eighth century by the Uí Néill interloper, Clann Cholmáin Móir, in a way favorable to themselves, the myth began its progress toward reality at the end of the eighth century with consolidation of territorial lordships that grew quickly during the Viking Age.

THE PENTARCHY: THE NORTH AND THE SOUTH

Two other potent ideas influencing early Irish history were Ireland's division into *Coíceda*, "Fifths," and the concept of two halves, north and south. Thus the Doirse earthwork, sectioning off Ulster from Connacht, Leinster, Munster, and Meath, was a human construct supplementing topographical, economic, and strategic barriers between these areas. Likewise, the Escir Riata, running from Clonmacnoise to Clonard, was in Uí Néill ideology said to have been built, by agreement of ancient progenitors of the dominant northern and southern peoples, to divide "Conn's Half" from "Mug's Half," the "Head's Half" from the "Slave's Half."

EARLY POPULATION GROUPS

The social structure, like the office of kingship, was fragile yet enduring, locally based upon the aggregation and dissolution of small units. The system excluded lineage segments falling outside of the kin-group by limiting the dynastic pool. Thus, between 400 C.E. and 800 C.E. new kingdoms grew or old ones became established more firmly. Early tribal nomenclature reveals the importance of ritual and religious (even totemic) associations, for example: *dál* ("share of"); *-raige* ("-people"); *corco* ("offspring of"); and the ethnographic suffix *–ne*. Thus: *Dál mBuinne* ("Buinne's Share"); *Osraige* ("Deer People"); *Corco Duibne* ("Offspring of Duibne"); and *Luigne* ("Lug's People"). Such names, and the formula MAQI MUCOI ("Son of the Seed of"), date from the fourth and fifth centuries as inscriptions on memorial stones for kings of southern Irish populations and for their expatriate relations in West Britain. These usages were waning swiftly in the fifth century. At the same time a linguistic, ethnographic shift took place that emphasized the blood ties unifying even larger social groups: *clann* ("progeny of"); *cenél* ("kindred of"); *uí* ("descendants of"). In the earliest sources such new relationships are a fact; the earlier tribal groups are already, or nearly, subordinated, or migrating to border, coastal, or mountain regions. Tribal histories, sagas, and annals rationalized such changes by retrospective and propagandistic genealogical fictions. Thus the Déisi were expelled, the Aithechtuatha ("Vassal Peoples") revolted and were subjugated, and the "Additional Peoples" (*Fortuatha*) of Leinster relocated to borderlands. The Gailenga, Delbna, and Luigne spread out in pockets across the island. The Érainn inhabited Munster, and the Airgialla ("Eastern Hostages") encircled Ulster, according to legend by agreement with the dominant Uí Néill, though perhaps driven there or simply emerging. Of all of these earlier populations, only the Osraige (Ossory), Airgialla (Oriel) and Déis Becc of Thomond were to be future political players—a branch of Dál Riata having migrated early in the sixth century to form a new kingdom in Scotland.

DEVELOPMENT OF KINGDOMS

The strongest early populations of Leinster (Laigin) were Dál Messin Corb of Naas in Kildare, Uí Garrchon bordering Meath, Dál Cormaic by Kileen Cormac to the south, and Uí Gabla of Leix. The Uí Néill drove the northern Laigin out of the midlands early in the sixth century. Against this, archaic regal genealogies and praise-poems attest the rise of Uí Dúnlainge in north Leinster (Laigin Tuathgabair) and of Uí Chennselaig in the south (Laigin Desgabair) during the later fifth century. Within this overlordship the Uí Fáilgi inhabited Offaly and west Kildare, Uí Briúin of Cualu the northeast coast, and Uí Máil the Wicklow highlands. The Loíges held sway between Slieve Bloom and the Barrow. Amongst other peoples were the Wexford Fothairt Chairn and Uí Bairrche of the Blackstairs range and Bargy. The Osraige in Kilkenny and Carlow played off allegiances between Leinster and Munster. Powerful Uí Dúnlainge kings, such as Faelán mac Colmáin in the early seventh century, dominated Leinster until the eleventh, when Uí Chennselaig revived. In 738 the Uí Néill routed the Leinster kings at Ballyshannon, and peace ensued later in the 700s.

The Eóganachta of Munster (Mumu) held together various allied or subordinate populations: Éle and Múscraige of Tipperary and Cork, Uí Liatháin in the southeast, Corco Loígde of the Laune and Maine watersheds, Ciarraige in Kerry, Corco Óche of Limerick, Corco Baiscind, Alltraige, and Corco Modruad in Clare, Déis Becc in Thomond, Déisi of Waterford, and the Uí Fidgente northwards. The Eóganacht of Caisil commanded the Plain of Femin and routes to the north. Origin legends, and mutual, formalized relationships between the Eóganacht Caisil and their neighbors, emphasize the peaceful acquisition of Cashel as both regal seat and bishopric. Munster was an early center for literacy and for traffic with the Mediterranean and West Britain. The Eóganacht of Áine and of Airthir Cliach, in Limerick and Tipperary, neighbored the Cashel branch, challenging it during the eighth century. The southeastern Eóganacht Glendamnach (Glanworth) were ascendant in the seventh century, submerging the Fir Maige—their powerful king Cathal mac Finguine (742) a claimant to the high kingship. The southern Eóganacht of Raithliú were excluded from kingship by 590, and the kings of Loch Léin in the seventh century. By 800 the Eóganacht Caisil ruled the overkings of Munster.

In County Down, the Ulaid continued as the Dál Fiatach; they were predominant in Ulster in 600 and were variously aligned with or hostile to the Dál Riata of Antrim and the Dál nAraide between Belfast Lough and the Mournes. In 563 Dál nAraide and Dál Riata were defeated by the Uí Néill at Móin Dairi Lóthair. The Uí Néill again routed Dál nAraide at Dún Ceithirnn in 629. Together with their expatriate Argyll branch, Dál Riata, who had allied with the Uí Néill in 575 at Druimm Cett, joined themselves with Dál nAraide to strike at the Uí Néill and were routed at Mag Rath, Co. Down, in 637 by the "King of Ireland," Domnall mac Aedo mic Ainmire. Dál Riata and Dál nAraide contracted, and Dál Fiatach moved west of the Bann. By the eighth century, Ulster was no longer a major political force.

In Connacht were the minor population groups: Irrus Domnainn of County Mayo; Conmaicne and Delbna of Lough Mask and Connemara; Luigni, Gailenga, Grecraige of Lough Gara; Ciarraige of Roscommon; and Calraige of Drumlease. The Uí Maine inhabited an area along Lough Derg in East Galway. Connacht's foremost peoples were the Uí Ailello; the Uí Fiachrach—Muaide (in Mayo) and Aidne (southeast of Galway); and the Uí Briúin—Aí of central Connacht, Seola, south near Carnfree, and Bréifne. The latter expanded later during the 700s due to pressure from Uí Briúin Aí, by 734 they drove a wedge between the Northern and Southern Uí Néill. The Uí Briúin Seola dominated the homeland, consolidating their power between 700 and 723 and ousting the Uí Ailello in 764. By 766 Uí Briúin Bréifne had defeated Uí Briúin Seola. The Uí Fiachrach entered the Uí Néill ancestry in the high kings Nath Í and Ailill Molt.

The rise and hegemony of the Uí Néill in the north and midlands attended Ulaid's demise in the mid-fifth century and reached its apogee by the mid-ninth century. Pushed out of Connacht, the Uí Néill spread—eastwards from Mag nítha, southwards to defeat the Laigin between the mid-fifth and sixth centuries, and northwards to Glen Gaimin. The Cenél Conaill settled

Tirconnell, and Cenél nEogain expanded southwards to Meath and, after the Battle of Cloitech in 789, moved into Derry, Tyrone, and Fermanagh to exclude Cenél Conaill from overlordship permanently. The southern Uí Néill split between Aed Sláine, Colmáin Mór, and smaller branches during the mid-sixth century—the first at Skreen east and south of the Boyne; the second settled around Lochs Owel and Ennell in Westmeath by the seventh century. Two lordships of Brega, north of the Boyne at Knowth, and south at Lagore, worked to Clann Cholmáin Móir's advantage, and when, after 724 and into the mid-tenth century, the northern branch monopolized the Brega lordship, Clann Cholmáin Móir dominated the midlands—by 770–797 suppressing Síl nAedo Sláine. Cenél Cairpre inhabited Tethba by Granard south of Lough Sheelin and north of the Inny. Cenél Fiachach settled by the sacred center of Uisnech, Cenél Loegaire west of Tara, and Cenél nArdgaile southwards, bordering the Uí Ḟaílge of Leinster. Several sub-peoples (*fo-thuatha*) lay within Uí Néill territories: the Déis of Tara; west of these, the Fir Thulae; southwest, the Cenél Fiachach; Conaille in Muirthemne between Airthir and the sea; Gailenga; Luigne; and Ciannachta.

SEE ALSO Brehon Law; Early Medieval Ireland and Christianity

Bibliography

Binchy, Daniel A. *Celtic and Anglo-Saxon Kingship*. O'Donnell Lectures, 1967–68. 1970.

Byrne, Francis John. *Irish Kings and High-Kings*. 1973. Reprint, 1987.

Mac Niocaill, Gearóid. *Ireland before the Vikings*. Gill History of Ireland 1. 1972. Reprint, 1980.

Ó Corráin, Donncha. *Ireland before the Normans*. Gill History of Ireland 2. 1972. Reprint, 1980.

Ó Cróinín, Dáibhí. *Early Medieval Ireland, 400–1200*. Longman History of Ireland 1. 1995.

Brian Frykenberg

Labor Movement

Trade unions emerged in Ireland in the early nineteenth century, combining features of the obsolescent guilds and agrarian secret societies. Their legal status was not fully regularized until the 1860s. The sheer numbers and poverty of Irish unskilled workers made them difficult to organize, and not until the end of the nineteenth century were sustained efforts made to do so.

Before 1900 organized labor was dominated by skilled craft workers who emphasized their differential status (by restricting skills and controlling admissions). Craft unions acted as friendly societies, providing medical and other benefits for members. They operated within cross-class nationalist movements (the Dublin trades were a mainstay of nationalist processions); their emphasis on self-reliance drew many urban artisans into radical nationalist movements such as Fenianism and Parnellism. They believed that workers' interests lay in cooperation with employers to develop Irish industries, though such cooperation often proved one-sided.

Craft unions established trade councils in urban centers (Cork in 1880, Belfast in 1881, Dublin in 1886). Attempts to create U.K.-wide labor federations in the nineteenth century foundered because of organizational and communications difficulties and nationalist sentiments; an Irish Trade Union Congress (ITUC) was founded in 1894. The 1890s also saw many local Irish societies merge with larger British unions; the role of British unions in Ireland intermittently divided the Irish labor movement until the 1950s.

Small socialist groups appeared in Irish urban centers beginning in the 1870s; these were usually short-lived because of clerical and political opposition. The Dublin-centered Irish Republican Socialist Party (1894–1903) deserves particular attention as the first political venture of James Connolly (1868–1916), the Scottish-born Marxist theorist and future leader of the 1916 Rising. The first independent Labour parliamentary candidates stood for election in Belfast in 1885 and 1886. The Home Rule Party sometimes spoke of itself as a "labor party"; some members were labor activists in Britain, and the party sought British support by comparing land agitation to trade unionism. From 1892 several Home Rule MPs identified themselves as "labor nationalists" (similar to contemporary "Lib-Lab" MPs within the British Liberal Party). The "Lib-Nat" MPs voiced labor concerns but were primarily loyal to the Home Rule Party, whose relations with the British labor movement were complicated by its alliance with the Liberals and its own increasingly bourgeois character. The extension of the local-government franchise in 1899 created independent labor groups on several urban councils, but these proved divisive and ineffective.

The ITUC was hampered by divisions between pro-union northern workers and (predominantly nationalist) southern unions. The industrialization of northeast Ulster gave it disproportionate strength within the movement, but northern unions mirrored the sectarian divide. Skilled workers' unions maintained sectarian as well as craft divisions, and unskilled workers followed populist Orange or Green (Protestant or Catholic) leaders who incorporated "laborist" elements in their messages. Cross-sectarian cooperation occurred from time to time, but it was always vulnerable to constitutional and religious tensions.

The Belfast trade unionist William Walker (1871–1918) established an Independent Labour Party presence in Belfast in 1893. Walker's "gas and water socialism" included support for the union on economic grounds. His endorsement of sectarian Protestant legislation alienated Catholic support, which contributed to the defeat of his parliamentary candidacies in 1905 to 1907; he is best remembered for debating the relationship between socialism and nationalism with Connolly in 1911.

Beginning in 1873 attempts were made to organize agricultural laborers through groups such as the Irish Agricultural Labourers' Union (1873–1879), the Knights of the Plough (1890s), and the Irish Land and Labour Association (1894–1918). These faced formidable organizational difficulties; their association with the Irish Parliamentary Party encouraged factionalization and complicated relations with urban unions. They were absorbed by the Irish Transport and General Workers' Union during the First World War.

British "new unionism," which tried to organize unskilled workers in mass-membership unions, led briefly to labor unrest in Ireland when it emerged in the late 1880s. Its principal impact on Ireland began in 1907 when James Larkin (1876–1947) arrived in Belfast as an organizer for the Liverpool-based National Union of Dock Labourers (NUDL, founded in Liverpool by Irish immigrants). Belfast was already experiencing an upsurge of trade-union militancy. Larkin, an inspiring orator, organized large numbers of unskilled workers, to some extent uniting Catholic and Protestant. Employers reacted with lockouts; between April and November 1907 Belfast saw disputes involving dockers, carters, and tobacco workers. Organized strike-breaking and street unrest led to police mutiny and military intervention in which two laborers were killed and many were wounded by troops.

The NUDL leadership disliked Larkin's confrontational style and expansive recruitment. Faced with heavy demands for strike pay, it sidelined Larkin and settled on disadvantageous terms. Larkin moved to Dublin and Cork, becoming embroiled in further strikes. After his suspension by the NUDL in December 1908, Larkin founded the Irish Transport and General Workers' Union (ITGWU). The new union faced determined opposition from employers and the NUDL. In the summer of 1909, ITGWU strikers in Cork were crushed by a concerted lockout; Larkin was briefly jailed in 1910 because of a dispute over NUDL funds.

Instead of the conciliatory tactics of the older unions, the ITGWU operated in a confrontational style, enlisting the impoverished masses of unskilled urban labor and trying with some success to bring a general rise in wages through sympathetic strikes, the "closed shop," and aggressive tactics against strike-breaking. Larkin held the syndicalist belief in the general strike as a weapon of social transformation. He expressed the anger and hopes of the poor, linking their struggle to Fe-

nianism and Parnellism, which had also faced middle-class and clerical opposition. His reckless leadership was balanced by skilled (and occasionally exasperated) organizers such as William O'Brien and James Fearon.

The ITGWU joined the ITUC in 1909, moving it toward explicit socialism. Older craft unions acquiesced or were sidelined. Pro-Larkin labor councillors became the principal opposition to Dublin Corporation; Connolly returned from the United States as a political organizer and produced some of his best-known attempts to adapt Marxism to Irish conditions. In 1912 the ITUC established the present-day Irish Labour Party.

The year 1911 saw further labor conflict, with prolonged strikes in Wexford and Dundalk and a Dublin rail and timber strike in September. The weekly *Irish Worker*, written mostly by Larkin, first appeared on 27 May 1911; it denounced the employers and their allies in uncompromising terms. Meanwhile, the Dublin employers, led by William Martin Murphy, prepared concerted counteraction. The Irish Parliamentary Party, frightened by Larkin's radicalism and divided between laborist and probusiness elements, proved ineffective and was bitterly denounced by Larkin. (In some provincial centers, notably Sligo, which experienced a major dispute in 1912, local Home Rule leaders did come to terms with Larkinism.)

The great Dublin lockout of 1913 to 1914 was the climax of two years of preparations by employers and Larkinites. The dismissal of *Independent* employees who joined the ITGWU led to sympathy action by ITGWU members in other firms and to a walkout by ITGWU tramwaymen on 19 August 1913. The employers retaliated with a mass lockout aimed at destroying the union by starving out its members. The strikers received financial assistance from British unions (which, however, turned down Larkin's calls for sympathy strikes in Britain). The end of the dispute in January 1914 marked a short-term defeat for the ITGWU, but it survived. The terrible poverty of Edwardian Dublin, the determined endurance of the strikers, and the vindictive words and behavior of the employers provided the founding images for the modern Irish labor movement. The formation of the Irish Citizen Army in self-defense against widespread police brutality symbolizes the strike's radicalizing effect.

Shortly after the outbreak of the First World War, Larkin left for the United States on a fundraising tour. He returned in 1923 to a labor movement strengthened by wartime upheavals but less receptive to his form of radicalism.

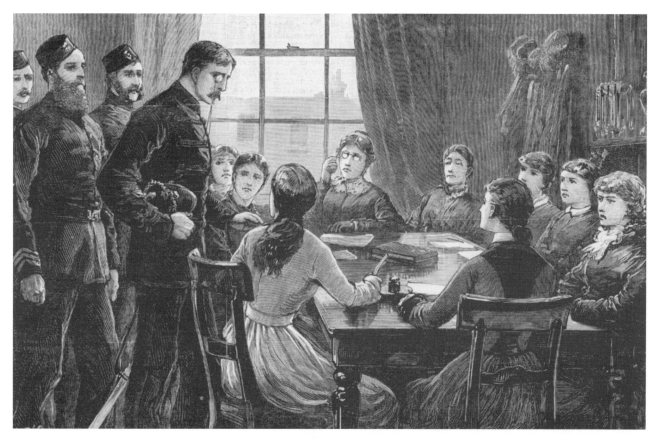

Launched publicly in Ireland by C. S. Parnell's sister Anna in January 1881, the Central Land League of the Ladies of Ireland maintained offices at 39 Upper O'Connell Street in Dublin (depicted here). Its activists were especially prominent in assisting embattled tenants after the male leaders of the land war were imprisoned in October 1881. Catholic churchmen denounced this novel women's organization. Disputes over policy between male and female activists led to its demise in August 1882. MARY EVANS PICTURE LIBRARY. REPRODUCED BY PERMISSION.

SEE ALSO Connolly, James; Larkin, James; Lockout of 1913; Markievicz, Countess Constance; Murphy, William Martin; O'Brien, William; Trade Unions

Bibliography

Boyle, John W. *The Irish Labor Movement in the Nineteenth Century.* 1988.

Cunningham, John. *Labour in the West of Ireland: Working Life and Struggle, 1890–1914.* 1995.

Gray John. *City in Revolt: James Larkin and the Belfast Dock Strike of 1907.* 1985.

O'Connor, Emmet. *A Labour History of Ireland, 1824–1960.* 1992.

Yeates, Padraig. *Lockout: Dublin 1913.* 2000.

Patrick Maume

Ladies' Land League

Realizing that the leaders of the Land League in Ireland were likely to be arrested, Michael Davitt proposed the establishment of a Ladies' Land League modeled on the Ladies' Irish National Land League that had been organized as a fund-raising body in New York in March 1880. His proposal was "vehemently opposed" by a number of his colleagues in the Land League, with many fearing public ridicule if the organization was seen to place women in a political role. However, the imprisonment of the Land League leaders led to the hasty establishment of the Ladies' Irish National Land League in Dublin on 31 January 1881.

The president of the new organization was Anne Deane, but its effective leader from the beginning was Charles Stewart Parnell's sister, Anna. During the first few months of its existence the Ladies' Land League took over the administration of the Land League, including the processing of applications for relief and the providing of grants to evicted tenants. By July 1881 there were 420 branches throughout the country. Anna Parnell traveled extensively in Ireland, England, and Scotland to explain the aims of the Land League. In October, with the Land League leaders jailed, the organization proclaimed, and a considerable level of agrarian militancy evident throughout the country, the Ladies' Land League effectively took responsibility for carrying on the land war.

From the beginning Anna Parnell viewed the Ladies' Land League as a political rather than a charitable organization and had a more radical expectation of the policies of the Land League than its leaders. With the release of the Land League leaders from prison in May 1882 Anna Parnell was anxious to dissolve the Ladies' Land League, deeming it impossible to work with the hostility displayed toward them by the Land League. The dissolution of the Ladies' Land League was finally achieved with much bitterness between Anna and her brother in August. Throughout the period of its existence the Ladies' Land League attracted considerable publicity. The press and the clergy displayed their unease with the presence of women in the land movement. The women were ridiculed as the "screaming sisterhood." Archbishop Edward McCabe of Dublin castigated the women for forgetting the "modesty of their sex and the high dignity of their womanhood." Much of the hostility toward the Ladies' Land League revolved around the public participation of women in political life. The Ladies' Land League proved to be a significant force in maintaining pressure during the land war. It also proved to be an important vehicle for women's political involvement in the late nineteenth century; many of its supporters were to remain active in nationalist politics well into the twentieth century.

SEE ALSO Davitt, Michael; Home Rule Movement and the Irish Parliamentary Party: 1870 to 1891; Land Acts of 1870 and 1881; Land War of 1879 to 1882; Parnell, Charles Stewart; Women in Nationalist and Unionist Movements in the Early Twentieth Century

Bibliography

McL. Cote, Jane. *Fanny and Anna Parnell: Ireland's Patriot Sisters.* 1991.

Parnell, Anna. *The Tale of a Great Sham.* Edited by Dana Hearne. 1986.

Maria Luddy

~

Land Acts of 1870 and 1881

The Landlord and Tenant (Ireland) Act of 1870 and the Land Law (Ireland) Act of 1881 were both products of the Liberal governments of Prime Minister William Ewart Gladstone. The first act, largely ineffectual, came in the second year of Gladstone's first government, the product of his famous statement that his "mission" as prime minister was "to pacify Ireland." The second act, more mature and substantial, came in the wake of two years of intense agrarian and parliamentary protest that shaped the bill and the debate over it.

Gladstone's hope for the 1870 bill was to give the force of law to the "Ulster Custom." This ambitious plan would have given tenants an interest in their holdings that was recognized in law, and would have legalized state intervention in the rights of landowners. The compromise that was passed did legalize the Ulster Custom where it was already in place, primarily in northern Ireland, and recognized similar customs elsewhere in the country. However, the majority of Irish tenant farmers received little more than the right to claim compensation from their landlord if they were evicted from their holdings for any cause other than nonpayment of rent, and landlords were allowed to deduct back rents from any compensation ordered. In addition, tenants who quit their holdings could claim compensation for any permanent improvements that they had made to the land. Lastly, the treasury was authorized to advance two-thirds of the purchase price of a holding to those wishing to buy their holdings, to be paid back over thirty-five years at a rate of 5 percent for each 100 pounds loaned. At this rate few tenants took advantage of the purchase provisions of the act, which overall had little impact on landlord-tenant relations during the 1870s. Although the 1870 act fell short of Gladstone's initial goals, it did establish the precedent for both government-assisted purchase and state intervention into landlord-tenant relations in Ireland that would produce more far-ranging legislation during the 1880s.

The most momentous of these laws came in 1881. Central to the new legislation was the granting of the "Three Fs" and the establishment of a Land Commission with the power to enforce its provisions, most notably the determination of what constituted a fair rent. This legislation recognized the notion of "dual ownership" of the land between landlord and tenant and firmly placed the government in the position of regulator of tenanted land in Ireland. The government was now empowered to prohibit landlords from factoring in tenant-made improvements when determining rent levels. The act also

TAKING THE (IRISH) BULL BY THE HORNS.

Solving the Irish land question proved difficult politically for the Liberal prime minister William Gladstone, shown here in a Punch cartoon of 1870 wrestling with the horns of a bull—one a tenant, the other a landlord. His 1870 Land Act made landlords pay compensation for "disturbance" and for tenant improvements—not enough to satisfy tenants, who wanted the "three Fs" (fair rents, fixity of tenure, and free sale) later granted by Gladstone's 1881 Land Act. FROM PUNCH, 26 FEBRUARY 1870.

included a land-purchase scheme similar to that in the previous bill, and a provision that empowered the government to loan money to farmers to build cabins for their agricultural laborers.

The initial response of the Irish National Land League was to view the bill with skepticism and to caution its members not to rush into the Land Commission courts. The League leadership argued that the bill fell far short of the goal of expropriating landlords and establishing peasant proprietorship in Ireland, and that by excluding tenants in arrears and leaseholders, the bill exempted a significant proportion of Irish tenant farmers from its provisions. In addition, the League was aware of Gladstone's wish that such a far-reaching bill would lessen the power of the League. To the degree that farmers ignored League cautions and rushed into the courts, where their petitions for rent reductions were most often successful, Gladstone's gamble succeeded. And it was not long before all observers realized that despite its limitations, the act set into motion the slow, but irreversible end to landlordism in rural Ireland.

SEE ALSO Butt, Isaac; Davitt, Michael; Home Rule Movement and the Irish Parliamentary Party: 1870 to 1891; Ladies' Land League; Land Questions; Land War of 1879 to 1882; Parnell, Charles Stewart; Protestant Ascendancy: Decline, 1800 to 1930; Tenant Right, or Ulster Custom; **Primary Documents:** Establishment of the National Land League of Mayo (16 August 1879); Land Law (Ireland) Act (22 August 1881)

Bibliography

Kolbert, C. F., and T. O'Brien. *Land Reform in Ireland: A Legal History of the Irish Land Problem and Its Settlement.* 1975.

Solow, Barbara L. *The Land Question and the Irish Economy, 1870–1903.* 1971.

Steele, E. D. *Irish Land and British Politics: Tenant-Right and Nationality, 1865–1870.* 1974.

Vaughan, W. E. *Landlords and Tenants in Mid-Victorian Ireland.* 1994.

Donald E. Jordan, Jr.

The 1903 Land Act broke a political impasse between landlord and tenant partisans. The law speeded up land purchase by lowering the annual payments of tenants; landlords received a bonus for selling. This 1903 Punch cartoon shows the Irish chief secretary George Wyndham putting the finishing touches on his masterpiece "The Contented Irishman"—the result that framers of this law vainly hoped for. FROM PUNCH, 25 MARCH 1903.

Land Purchase Acts of 1903 and 1909

The 1903 and 1909 Land Purchase Acts, also known as the Wyndham and Birrell Acts respectively (after successive chief secretaries for Ireland), provided the means by which most Irish tenant farmers became owner-occupiers of their land. This legislation radically extended the existing limited provision for tenant purchase, and for the first time created procedures and incentives to ensure the sale of estates as a whole to the occupying tenants.

Under the 1903 land act, tenants received from the government an advance to purchase the land, which was to be repaid through annuities (yearly installments) over a period of 68.5 years. The rate of interest was 3.75 percent. The landlords were compensated in cash that was raised by government issue of guaranteed land stock yielding a dividend of 2.75 percent. The purchase price of the land was calculated in terms of rent years (the previous rent multiplied by a specified number of years). The number of years varied: For first-term judicial rents (rents already reduced once under the fair-rent provisions of the 1881 land act), the price agreed could range only from 18.5 to 24.5 years; for second-term rents (rents that had been twice reduced), the range was 21.5 to 27.5 years. Within these ranges it was left to the landlords and tenants to agree upon a price. In the case of nonjudicial rents (rent that had not been previously reduced), the price agreed had to be approved by the Estates Commissioners, a body set up under the 1903 act to implement its provisions. Under these arrangements the average price received by the landlords was 22 years' purchase and the annuities paid by the tenants were significantly less than their previous rents. The landlords were further compensated by a 12 percent bonus if they were willing to sell their entire tenanted estates.

Unfortunately, the depreciation of land stock after 1903 meant that not enough money was raised to finance land purchase. The 1909 land act was designed to rectify this by compensating landlords in the future not with cash but with guaranteed 3 percent land stock. The average price for holdings was reduced to 19 years' purchase and the repayment period was changed to 66 years, with the rate of interest increased to 3.5 percent.

Under the 1903 and 1909 land acts, Estates Commissioners and the Congested Districts Board were for the first time given power to acquire land for the purpose of relieving congestion by enlarging and rearranging small and impoverished farms, especially in the west. To a limited extent, such powers for the first time could be exercised on a compulsory basis under the 1909 act. In cases of compulsory acquisition the landlords were entitled to compensation in cash rather than in land stock. Under these two acts, just under 11 million acres in the 32 counties of Ireland were sold, involving over 320,000 holdings (60% of the total number of holdings). In achieving a transfer of land on this scale, these acts were major steps in addressing the widespread land agitation in the Irish countryside during the last twenty years of the nineteenth century. In so doing, they also contributed to the erosion of the social and economic status of the landlord class in Ireland.

SEE ALSO Congested Districts Board; Land Questions; Protestant Ascendancy: Decline, 1800 to 1930; United Irish League Campaigns

Bibliography

Bull, Philip. *Land, Politics, and Nationalism: A Study of the Irish Land Question.* 1996.

Hooker, Elizabeth R. *Readjustments of Agricultural Tenure in Ireland.* 1938.

Jones, David Seth. *Graziers, Land Reform, and Political Conflict in Ireland.* 1995.

Kolbert, Colin Francis, and T. O'Brien. *Land Reform in Ireland: A Legal History of the Irish Land Problem and its Settlement.* 1975.

David Seth Jones

Land Questions

Conquest and dispossession are the keys to understanding the land-tenure disputes in Ireland from the late eighteenth to the twentieth centuries. While the intent of the series of conquests and plantations by which Ireland was colonized over several hundred years was to establish the principles of the Norman-derived English system of land tenure, this was done so imperfectly that traditional indigenous land-tenure practices persisted within the imported system. Thus, the traditional occupiers of the land—while they paid rent to the landed proprietors—continued to consider themselves owners of the land in ways incompatible with the theoretical basis of the landlord's own property rights. As in other premodern societies, there were mechanisms within the population by which traditional rights were defended and protected, and in Ireland such secretive bodies as the Whiteboys and Ribbonmen demonstrated the determination of the lower orders of society to protect what they saw as their rights, particularly in relation to control and use of land. The first in a long series of land questions was this contest between conflicting percep-

tions of rights, something not unique to Ireland. What distinguished this conflict in Ireland, however, was a combination of two factors: the memory of dispossession still present in the consciousness of the occupiers of the land; and the consolidation of a religious divide between landlords and tenants, due in part to the penal laws against Catholics that followed the vanquishing of the former Catholic landholding elites after the 1688 revolution. Notwithstanding these factors—or in part because of them—conflict was muted by the assumption of landlords that paternalism and protection were part of their function, as well as by a degree of ambivalence in asserting an authority that derived from an awareness of their colonizing origins. The aspiration, often unrealized in Ireland, for natural social bonds tempered landlord behavior and secured, to a limited extent at least, a sense of reciprocity in their tenants.

THE LATE EIGHTEENTH CENTURY TO THE 1840s

While these historical legacies continued to influence the course of land-tenure relations in Ireland, new elements emerging from the later eighteenth century through to the 1840s gave a sharper intensity to agrarian conflict. To a great extent these pressures grew out of the transformation occurring in British politics and society at that time. At the heart of the modernization of the British state was a series of new principles and attitudes deriving from, or in other ways closely related to, the newly fashionable ideology of laissez-faire and the economic and political imperatives associated with the consolidation of empire. Three factors in particular began to work against reciprocal relationships in the Irish countryside. In the first place, the new pressure on Irish landlords to manage their estates according to the new philosophies meant that—particularly where new owners were involved—a tendency to assert more strongly the rights of property (especially to evict, to increase rents, and to restructure farm boundaries) resulted in greater conflict. Secondly, there was a new morality about appropriate modes of behavior and management that were more distinctively English, and this increased the cultural tensions between the landlord class on the one hand and the more indigenous, largely Catholic classes of rural society on the other. Thirdly, while the transformation of the English rural economy was facilitated by a massive population exodus to the new industrial centers, in Ireland the opposite was occurring. There was a vast increase in the number of people dependent on land for survival, without alternative sources of employment through industrialization. Overarching and influencing all these factors was a growing triumphalist British imperial pride and determination to which unreformed Ireland represented a serious blot.

While changes in ideology and political outlook were causing landlords to intrude more assertively into the lives of the occupiers of the land, the occupiers themselves were becoming better equipped to use new methods to defend their own interests. The inability of the British state to address the grievances of the majority of the population, both as Catholics and as tenant farmers, encouraged the agitation that eventually transformed premodern forms of protest into modern political mobilizations. The failure of the British parliament to concede Catholic emancipation, despite a recognition of its political wisdom, led to an unprecedented popular agitation in which the techniques of political organization and tactics were introduced to vast masses of the rural populace. The equally potent grievance for Catholic farmers (and for all other farmers as well)—tithes for the support of the Protestant Established Church—provided yet another basis for a major political agitation, in which the cleavage between the landlord class and the rest of the population was again redefined. In these great movements, which culminated in O'Connell's Repeal movement, political habits were formed that would set precedents for the future pursuit of land reform.

DEFINING THE LAND QUESTION

Whatever the continuities of political culture and ancient division, the actual defining of what constituted the land question in Ireland was subject to flux and change. As the conflict heightened between more assertive landlords and a more politically organized tenantry in the 1830s and early 1840s, there emerged different definitions of what it was that the tenantry wanted. One point of view, which acknowledged the legacies of dispossession and the tenantry's sense of its proprietorship in the land, was identified initially with the landlord William Conner. It was encapsulated in his slogan "a valuation and a perpetuity." Conner believed that peace could be secured only by recognizing in law the customary assumptions of the tenantry about their right to the land. He argued for a determination of rents based on a system of valuation and then, subject to the payment of such rents, a right to perpetual occupancy. This was the proposition that would be implemented in the 1880s under the term *dual ownership.* In the 1840s it received only limited support; Thomas Davis, James Fintan Lalor, and later John Stuart Mill were among those who argued for this approach, often under the label of "peasant proprietorship." Daniel O'Connell and his Repeal movement, eager to channel potential unrest on the land and enlist tenant support, equivocated on

the issue, sometimes using the language of "fixity of tenure" but fundamentally committed to the currently acceptable principles of political economy and property rights. More carefully constructed was the defense of tenant right associated with the Ulster politician William Sharman Crawford, also a landlord. From 1835 onwards Sharman Crawford introduced bills in the House of Commons that were intended to legalize the practice of tenant right, best known to him in the form of "Ulster custom." Genuinely committed to securing a fixity of tenure, he sought, ultimately unsuccessfully, to draw Members of Parliament and the British public to an understanding of what that custom was and to convince them of its legitimacy. In his attempts, he contributed to its reinterpretation as "compensation for improvements," a notion more easily justifiable to British legislators. Political pragmatism rather than accuracy underlay this definition of tenant right.

This approach did not prove efficacious, either in achieving legislation or in adequately articulating the aspirations of the tenants. What tenant right actually was had already been defined, but in a form more accessible to historians than to contemporaries. The escalating attention given to the Irish land issue led the Peel government in 1843 to appoint a royal commission "to inquire into the state of the law and practice with respect to the occupation of land in Ireland." Although little came of the recommendations of the Devon Commission, it provided indisputable evidence of the nature and scale of the practice known as *tenant right.* Not only was it shown that this practice existed extensively outside Ulster, but the evidence disclosed that it was often practiced without the landlord's consent, and in many cases without his knowledge. It involved a payment by an incoming to a vacating tenant, determined by a formula and without any reference to the cost of improvements that the tenant may or may not have undertaken. The practice most closely correlated to the sale of an interest or of goodwill, but it can be better explained in the Irish context as a claim by the tenant to a proprietorship in the land, based upon tradition and custom. In many cases the practice was enforced by very powerful communal sanctions. Thus the evidence collected by this extensive government inquiry powerfully endorsed the understanding of Irish land-tenure usage on which the remedies proposed by William Conner, James Fintan Lalor, and other advocates of "peasant proprietorship" were based.

THE LAND ACTS OF 1870 AND 1881

It was the exigencies of politics, and especially the need to reconcile solutions to the prevailing principles of political economy, that ensured that in the contemporary political debate "Ulster custom" or tenant right was reduced to the minimal concept of "compensation for improvements." In the final days of the Great Famine, stimulated by the tenant clearances undertaken by many landlords, the demand for legal recognition of tenant right became the focal point of a new land agitation and the basis of the Independent Irish Party. Sharman Crawford's proposed legislation became for this movement the touchstone of what constituted the land question. This largely remained so after the demise of this party, during a period in which there was little formal political structure at the national level through which the land-tenure grievance could be expressed. In part at least, the growth and relative popularity of the Fenian movement must be understood in the context of the political frustrations of the rural population over this issue. It was only with the application of the energies of William Ewart Gladstone, driven partly by Fenian disturbance and outrage, that new insights into the nature of the Irish land question began to influence policy. In a process that included sending the former Indian official George Campbell to Ireland to report to him, eliciting views from informed Irish opinion, and reading extensively himself, Gladstone concluded that central to a resolution of the land question in Ireland was recognition of the "idea of restitution." By this he meant that the tenant's demand was based on an historical and customary understanding that his interest in the land was a proprietorial one, that conquest had failed to obliterate this belief, and that this had to be taken into account in any attempted resolution of the issue. Gladstone sought to shape his land legislation accordingly, but the Land Act of 1870 failed to incorporate that dimension, largely because of opposition from his cabinet colleagues. One of those colleagues displayed a possibly unintentional insight by disparaging as "tribal tenure" Gladstone's desired outcome. Instead, the legislation was a somewhat unsatisfactory compromise between recognition of customary tenant-right practice and compensation for improvements. The tenant movement had been hoist on the petard of "compensation for improvements," which in the British political discourse of the day was interpreted in a more literal sense than its Irish proponents had ever intended.

But there had been for one rare moment a convergence of understanding between the tenant farmers and the British, albeit principally in the person of the prime minister. The importance of that development was consolidated by the influence of George Campbell's views, the essence of which was "that in Ireland a landlord is not a landlord, and a tenant is not a tenant—in the English sense" and that "the whole difficulty arises from our applying English laws to a country where they are opposed to facts" (Campbell 1869, pp. 5–6). The modified definition of the land question that emerged during the consideration of the 1870 legislation, together with the failure of that measure, clarified for the English the deeper dimensions of the Irish land issue, and it consolidated for the Irish—from emerging leaders such as Isaac Butt down to the ordinary farmer—a clearer sense of the question that had to be asked in order to secure an appropriate response. The "three Fs"—fair rents, fixity of tenure, and freedom to sell—became the accepted expression of what Irish tenant farmers took to be their rights in relation to their farms. This representation locked in all the aspects of Conner's "valuation and a perpetuity" in ways that the last of the three principles, diluted to compensation for improvements, had not. While no progress was possible during the life of a Conservative government, the combination of the mobilization of land agitation through the Land League beginning in 1879 and Gladstone's return to office in 1880 meant that this new formulation became the basis of a new act in 1881. Some of its provisions were deficient (again, partly due to opposition within Gladstone's cabinet), leaving a basis still for land agitation, but this act validated the central contention of the tenant demand. The system established by this measure quickly became identified as "dual ownership."

LAND-PURCHASE LEGISLATION

For landlords, the tenant success had come not as it might have earlier on the basis of accommodation, but through increasing acrimony and conflict, and the outcome epitomized the extent to which the landlord class had become marginalized in the agrarian economy and society. But an alternative path to resolving the land issue had emerged, opening up for landlords a line of escape from a situation that was economically and socially uncomfortable, if not intolerable. Both the act of 1869 to disestablish the Church of Ireland and the Land Act of 1870 had included provisions to facilitate purchase by tenants of their farms. These provisions were extended by the 1881 act. Although land purchase was for Liberals secondary to protecting the rights of tenants, it became extremely attractive to both Conservative politicians and landlords because it offered means for removing "dual ownership," an anomalous and for them undesirable form of tenure. In 1885 the Conservative government's Land Purchase Act (the Ashbourne Act) put purchase at the center of government policy on Irish land, and through a series of mainly Conservative land acts in the 1880s and 1890s, culminating in the comprehensive and highly effective Wyndham Act of 1903, the bulk of agricultural land in Ireland was transferred into the sole ownership of the occupying tenants.

THE LEGACY OF THE LAND QUESTION

The long struggle to establish the claims of the tenant farmers to proprietorship of their land, with changing definitions of how that demand was to be met, had become so intimately associated with the question of nationalism that by the 1880s it was difficult to separate the two issues, either ideologically or organizationally. Indeed, the one issue had effectively become a metaphor for the other. In this context the settlement of the central issue of proprietorship was bound to be of great significance, not only to the future direction of the nationalist movement but also to the way in which the legacy of the question of land affected social issues and class relationships thereafter. In the half-century after the Great Famine there had been major changes in the class structure of rural Ireland, and in particular a significant shift from tillage agriculture to grazing ranches. This had produced new contests for land between the graziers and the farmers that had been subsumed to a great degree by their common commitment to the struggle against landlordism, pursued as part of a wider nationalist mobilization. Likewise, that campaign had enlisted, and often very heavily depended on, the agitations of the poorest classes of peasant farmers, especially in the western areas of Connacht. The major beneficiaries of land purchase were the prosperous and substantial farmers; neither graziers nor poor farmers gained tangible advantage from these reforms. For those with little or no land there was now a demand that the grazing ranches be broken up and the lands redistributed. The consequence was a "ranch war" against the prosperous graziers, who by then had become the backbone of both the Irish rural economy and the nationalist movement. In this struggle the farmers who had acquired the ownership of their holdings took little interest in the plight of those on small, unviable farms, supporting land redistribution only to the extent that it might provide more land for themselves or their sons. This situation was extremely divisive, and the constitutional nationalist leaders equivocated over the principles involved, leaving it to the revolutionary Dáil Éireann to issue in 1920 an unambiguous condemnation of the demand for land redistribution.

What originally had been a negotiable problem of coexistence between an indigenous agrarian society and a colonizing ruling class had been turned by ideological ardor into a struggle for absolute control of the land. In the course of that combat the increasingly dominant economic ideology of the time came to be identified in Ireland as directed more toward serving the interests of the British state and English cultural dominance than toward economic progress. Ironically, the very objective to which laissez-faire was supposedly directed, the ef-fective capitalization of Irish agriculture, was undermined by this struggle. From the time that William Conner articulated what he saw as the proper tenurial relationship between landlord and tenant in Ireland, it was clear that clarity in property rights was more important than conformity to a particular model of property law. Whether expressed as "valuation and a perpetuity," "Ulster custom," "tenant right," the "three Fs," "dual ownership," or "peasant proprietorship," these all represented a way forward toward a constructive relationship between the rural classes and a clear line of demarcation between the roles of landlord and tenant. Recognition of these rights, especially after the Great Famine, might well have provided the incentives for a more capitalist outlook among Irish farmers. John Stuart Mill identified this issue in the aftermath of the Great Famine, arguing that resistance to customary beliefs undermined economic confidence. Or as William Crawford later stressed, imposing one particular form of tenure—that favored by British opinion—was in this case to oppose the facts of what actually happened on the land in Ireland. In the long term, the attempt to negate Irish custom and practice so embittered the relationship of landlord and tenant that coexistence was impossible. The refusal of landlords to embrace accommodation ultimately led to the end of landlordism as an institution.

The question of land tenure in Ireland assumed such importance and so shaped political life over the better part of a century that it had lasting legacies. Although in economic terms the conflict was one between two classes, as the divide deepened it became also to a degree a synonym for religious and communal division. There had been those, Charles Stewart Parnell included, who believed that to concede to tenant farmers the rights they demanded was to pave the way for a reconciliation between the ruling elite and the majority of the people, thus strengthening national cohesion and nationalist aspirations. In reality, the dependency of nationalist politics on the land issue had become so entrenched that, despite the conciliation efforts of both some landlords and some nationalists after 1903, the cleavage set by the landlord-tenant conflict persisted into twentieth-century Irish life. Economically too, the obsession with land and its control tended to elevate the status of the small-tillage farmer to a point where the structure of Irish agriculture was arrested in the form that emerged after 1903. This outcome was less than constructive in terms of the competitiveness of Irish farming in the changing international climate of the twentieth century.

Between 1848 and 1935 there were approximately forty acts of the U.K. parliament that attempted either to clarify or to change the nature of agricultural-land occupation, with those after 1925 designed to finalize the process of land purchase in Northern Ireland. More than twenty more land acts, mainly concerned with the furthering of land purchase and consolidation of the principle of owner-occupation, were passed by the Irish Oireachtas between 1923 and 1992. Perhaps no other statistics better demonstrate both the intractability of the Irish land question through the nineteenth century and the long shadow that it cast over Ireland in the twentieth century. Originally it was a problem amenable to settlement by accommodation and conciliation and by recognition of the legacies of conquest. Indeed, in its essence the question was not fundamentally different from many of those addressed much later in other parts of the world where reconciliation between indigenous and colonizing peoples has become a testing issue. That was not, however, the way in which British opinion conceptualized the Irish land question in the nineteenth century, and Irish representations of the problem were insufficiently direct and forceful to avert what ultimately became an unnecessarily intractable conflict.

SEE ALSO Agriculture: 1690 to 1845; Congested Districts Board; Famine Clearances; Irish Tithe Act of 1838; Land Acts of 1870 and 1881; Land Purchase Acts of 1903 and 1909; Land War of 1879 to 1882; Oakboys and Steelboys; Plan of Campaign; Plunkett, Sir Horace Curzon; Poor Law Amendment Act of 1847 and the Gregory Clause; Population Explosion; Protestant Ascendancy: Decline, 1800 to 1930; Rural Life: 1690 to 1845; Tenant Right, or Ulster Custom; Tithe War (1830–1838); United Irish League Campaigns; Whiteboys and Whiteboyism; **Primary Documents:** On the Whiteboys (1769); Resolutions Adopted at the Tenant-Right Conference (6–9 August 1850); Resolution Adopted at the Tenant League Conference (8 September 1852)

Bibliography

Bull, Philip. *Land, Politics and Nationalism: A Study of the Irish Land Question.* 1996.

Campbell, George. *The Irish Land.* 1869.

Clark, Samuel. *Social Origins of the Irish Land War.* 1979.

Donnelly, James S., Jr. "The Land Question in Nationalist Politics." In *Perspectives on Irish Nationalism,* edited by Thomas E. Hachey and Lawrence J. McCaffrey. 1989.

Gray, Peter. *Famine, Land and Politics: British Government and Irish Society, 1843–1850.* 1999.

Jones, David S. *Graziers, Land Reform, and Political Conflict in Ireland.* 1995.

Philip Bull

Landscape and Settlement

Ireland's landscape diversity is a product of glacial processes operating on the geological base of carboniferous limestone in the central lowlands and on ancient folded mountain ridges to the north and south. Glaciations more than 12,000 years ago eroded material from the uplands and deposited it as gravels and clays (in eskers, drumlins and moraines) on the midlands. These thin out in the western counties, where the underlying rock appears on the surface, most notably in the karst landscapes of Clare and Galway and the granites of Connemara. Eskers are ridges of gravel that were formed by streams and rivers underneath the ice sheets, and were important routeways historically through the midland bogs of the island.

BOGLANDS

Seventeen percent of the surface of Ireland is composed of peat bogs. Raised bogs are found in the lowlands, while blanket bogs are more characteristic of the uplands and western regions. The lowland bogs comprise great domes of undecayed matter, mostly sphagnum mosses, which accumulated in hollows and waterlogged basins in postglacial times up to 8,000 years ago. Esker and morainic deposits of gravel obstructed the natural drainage, accelerating the growth of peat up to seven or eight meters in depth. Blanket bogs developed in the much wetter conditions of the western parts of the country, where the peat lands have spread over the hills and with their distinctive moor grasses and sedges add color and texture to the mountain landscapes. Deteriorating climatic conditions about 6,000 years ago and localized forest removal encouraged the spread of blanket peat over many prehistoric settled landscapes. The most dramatic recent discovery (in the 1970s) has been the uncovering of Céide Fields underneath the blanket peat in north Mayo, where an extensive field system with accompanying house and tomb sites dates from 3,700 to 3,200 B.C.E. Further ancient landscapes may still await discovery underneath the peatlands of Ireland.

Much of the midlands is honeycombed with fertile land as islands in the extensive wet boglands. During the early Middle Ages, this labyrinthine pattern of eskers and boglands sheltered a largely tribal localized culture familiar with the intricacies of passes through the bogs. Tyrellspass in County Westmeath commemorates one such pass through the bogs. One of the largest of these eskers was called the *Eiscir Riata*, which was an important pass in prehistory between the northern and

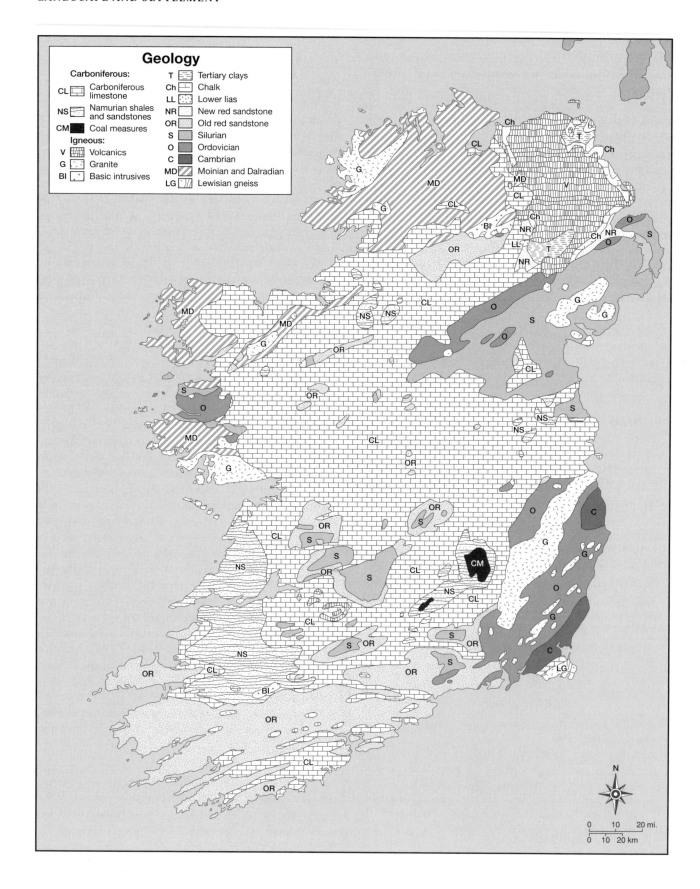

Geology

Carboniferous:

CL — Carboniferous limestone
NS — Namurian shales and sandstones
CM — Coal measures

Igneous:

V — Volcanics
G — Granite
BI — Basic intrusives

T — Tertiary clays
Ch — Chalk
LL — Lower lias
NR — New red sandstone
OR — Old red sandstone
S — Silurian
O — Ordovician
C — Cambrian
MD — Moinian and Dalradian
LG — Lewisian gneiss

southern parts of Ireland. The significance of these medieval routeways is today marked by the remains of monastic sites like Clonmacnoise, Clonfert, Terryglass, Durrow, Tihilly, Seirkieran, Kinitty, Rahugh, and Clonard.

In modern Ireland, as elsewhere in Europe, the great bogs were seen negatively as obstacles to development and refuges for rebels and other persons evading the laws of the Anglo-Norman and Tudor state. Canal construction in the late eighteenth and early nineteenth centuries had the double advantage of providing an opportunity to drain these wetlands at the same time as bringing trade and commerce to the midland regions. Historically peat harvesting was a traditional local activity—"cutting turf" with spades in local communities was a centuries-long tradition throughout Ireland. Turbary rights, which went with farm leases from the seventeenth century, were important local assets and landlord interference with these rights often led to local disturbances. Many small bogs were extinct by the twentieth century, with cutover and cutaway bog forming important landscapes in parts of south Ulster and on the margins of the midland bogs. By the twentieth century the more extensive bogs were seen as opportunities for industrial harvesting and local economic development. A state peat authority (Bord na Móna) was established in 1946 to excavate the peat mechanically for electricity generation, for domestic fuel as peat briquettes, and as a horticultural product in form of peat moss. In the last quarter of the twentieth century popular interest in the conservation of these bog landscapes increased, and tourism and local interests have realized the botanical and environmental value of these extensive landscapes.

THE PEOPLING OF IRELAND

The Irish environment has formed a stage for human settlement for thousands of years. The interaction between the environmental endowment and humanity on this small island has resulted in a tremendous topographical variety at the regional and local level, and this in turn has been one of the main driving forces for cultural tourism. Situated on the Atlantic fringes of Europe, much of Ireland's landscape and cultural experience is a product of peoples and processes diffusing out of the European mainland.

The earliest Mesolithic hunter and gatherer communities arrived in Ireland about 9,000 years ago after the end of the Ice Age. These small groups lived along riverbanks and estuaries, lake shores, and coastal districts, exploiting fish, plant, and animal resources. Neolithic settlement (from 5,000 years ago) using Stone Age technology, constituted the first farming communities—a civilization marked by the appearance of important megalithic tombs. Court, portal, passage, and wedge tombs (referring to the arrangements of spaces, particularly of the entrance to the tomb, within them) have been located in different regions, suggesting a variety of population groups settling in the landscape. The enormous passage tombs at Newgrange in County Meath and at Carrowmore in County Sligo were built about 3,500 to 3,000 B.C.E. and are part of an array of similar tombs in Brittany and western Iberia, a phenomenon that emphasizes the importance of the seaways along the Atlantic fringes in early migration flows.

The Bronze Age (c. 2,500–600 B.C.E.) was marked by copper-mining people who produced personal ornaments and jewellery of great beauty, as well as constructing large hilltop enclosures like Navan Fort near Armagh and great ceremonial circles and henges, such as those in the Boyne valley. From about 600 B.C.E. an ironworking culture spread to Ireland from continental Europe and made a significant contribution to the island's landscape and culture. Much of the linguistic and genetic heritage of the Irish people can be traced to this Iron Age Celtic culture. Most of the great fables and mythic figures, such as the Táin Bó Cuailnge, Cuchulainn, and Fionn Mac Cumhal, originated with these peoples.

The Celts made a lasting cultural impact on the Irish landscape in terms of its territorial and political order and its place-names. The historic provinces of Connacht, Leinster, Munster, and Ulster are simplified legacies of more complex divisions of the island among early Celtic population septs (lineage or kin groups). In broad terms they coincide with major environmental regions. The names of Ulster, Leinster, and Munster are ninth-century Norse constructions of earlier Irish names: Ulaidh or Cúige Ulaidh (literally the "fifth of the men of Ulaidh"), Laighin or Cúige Laighin, and Mumhan or Cúige Mumhan; the "fifth" is evidence of the probable existence of Mide as another provincial territory. Tír, the Irish word for territory, was added by the Norse to make Laighins-tír and so on. A more detailed lattice of territorial divisions emerged within the provinces, as population groups expanded and formed tribal entities. Approximately 150 tribal units known as Tuatha emerged, many of which formed a template for the medieval territorial lordships and baronies of the Gaelic and Anglo-Norman settlements. Tuatha were grouped into kingdoms, whose geographies have survived in dioceses established by the church in the twelfth century. By the Middle Ages, many of the tiny local territorial units known as townlands (of which there are more than 60,000 today) had taken shape as Gaelic landholding units, and many of their names continue in use.

Large fortified stone forts like Grianán Aileach in Donegal or Staigue in Kerry and other earthworks like Tara and Knockaulin (Dún Ailinne) were constructed during the Iron Age. Linear earthworks such as the Black Pig's Dyke (500–100 B.C.E.), which runs across the south Ulster landscape, and upwards of two hundred promontory forts in coastal locations represent attempts in this period to provide a form of regional security.

The early Christian period contributed some of the more familiar components of the Irish landscape. The ubiquitous ringforts (more properly called *rath* and *dún*) represented a pattern of dispersed farmsteads throughout the island, which are assigned to the second half of the first millennium. Raths refer mainly to sites built of earth; dún refer to larger, more prestigious examples. Ringforts in more rocky terrain were built of stone (called *caiseal* or *caher*), some of which contain the remains of houses within the enclosure. More than 50,000 of these circular enclosures (with single or multiple banks and ditches) were built in this period. They have been preserved down through the centuries as a result of superstitious associations with "fairy forts." Modern agricultural development, however, has destroyed great numbers of them. Crannogs or lake dwellings were settlements built for security in the period from 500 to 1000 C.E. on artificially constructed islands in lakeland regions especially in the northern half of the island.

The early Christian monastic church in Ireland established sites that came closest, in function if not in form, to urban centers in early Ireland. A large number of significant centers developed, such as Clonard, Clonfert, Clonmacnoise, Durrow, Devenish, Derry, and Armagh. They became the centers of federations of settlements, often located on sites with pre-Christian significance, populated not only by monks but by secular communities working at a variety of crafts. Located along important routeways through the midlands and associated with the settlement pattern of ringforts, it is likely that these monastic centers probably played a key role in contemporary rural economies. Becoming extensive owners of land, they were at the forefront in clearing woodlands, cultivating cereals, and managing livestock. As points of early wealth accumulation, they were repeatedly plundered by Viking raiders in the ninth century. Monastic sites mirrored ringfort morphology, though their circular enclosures were more extensive. The street morphologies of many small towns that originated on these sites still show the curve of ancient monastic boundaries. Throughout the Irish countryside today there are also the remains of small early medieval church sites, usually located at walking

distances in the landscape and frequently marked by circular-shaped cemeteries. These small rural parishes from the early medieval period sometimes have holy wells associated with their founder, at which pattern (patron)-day pilgrimages still occur.

Later, more lavish ecclesiastical buildings followed attempts to reform the old church in Ireland, with impressive new structures like those at the Rock of Cashel being built in the twelfth century. Abbeys such as Boyle in County Roscommon, Mellifont in County Louth, and Holy Cross in Tipperary are the work of continental orders (Cistercians and Benedictines) who came to Ireland in the early twelfth century and who pioneered a new phase in agricultural activity. Most of the medieval ecclesiastical structures in Ireland are in ruins today following the dissolution of the monasteries in 1536 at the time of the Protestant Reformation. The Established Church of Ireland inherited the ecclesiastical buildings, but never obtained the allegiance of the majority population in Ireland, so that maintenance of the structures was difficult.

A number of significant immigrations from the ninth century contributed to the modern Irish landscape. The Vikings (or Norsemen) first arrived on raiding missions from Scandinavia in the late eighth century, and although there is evidence of their having settled in parts of the countryside as farmers, they have been credited mainly with introducing the first urban overseas trading settlements around the coast in the ninth and tenth centuries, and these have endured to the present. Dublin grew into a major Norse settlement presiding over a kingdom that embraced the lower Liffey valley. Port towns were also established at Waterford, Wexford, Cork, Youghal, and Limerick, all place-names incorporating linguistic elements of Norse.

The Anglo-Norman colonization that occurred in the eighty years after 1169 represents the beginnings of Ireland's centuries-long political and cultural engagement with the neighboring island kingdom of England. The invaders who came from the western regions of England and Wales were part of the expanding Angevin empire that had engulfed Anglo-Saxon England a century earlier. The Anglo-Normans were responsible for the introduction of a fully fledged feudalism into Ireland, expressed on the ground in a manorial system of land organization, an open-field tillage economy, incastellation of the countryside, and establishment of an embryonic market system. However, it was an incomplete colonization, with large parts of the island remaining under Gaelic control. The English Pale emerged through the Middle Ages as the principal region of English control in Ireland, containing a king's representative in Dublin and a parliament that was subservient to

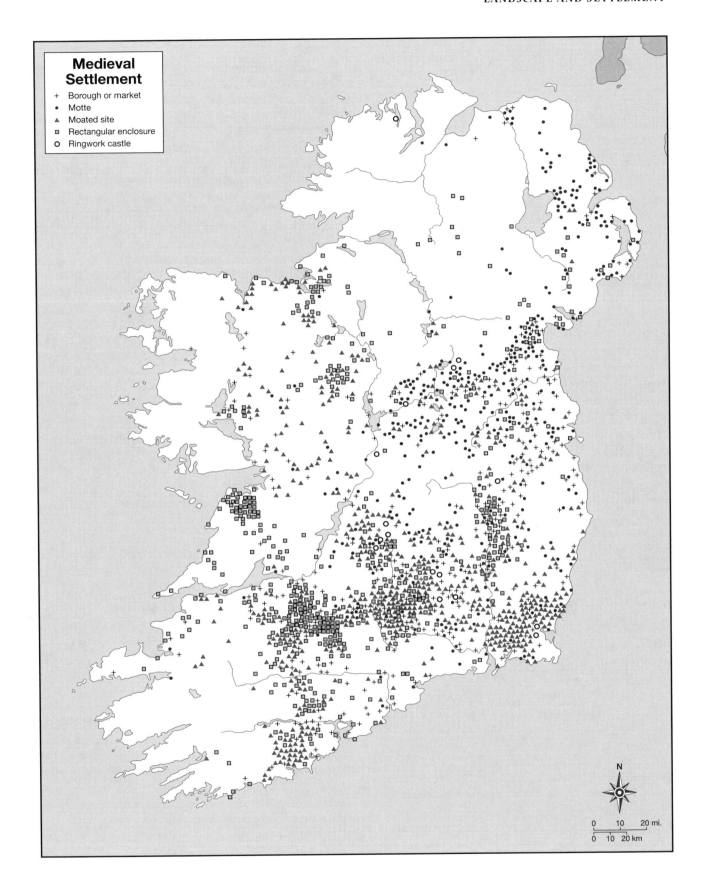

Medieval Settlement

- + Borough or market
- • Motte
- ▲ Moated site
- ▫ Rectangular enclosure
- ○ Ringwork castle

England. Outlying feudal lordships and liberties in Munster and Connacht had a weakened connection with the English crown, and pressure from Gaelic lordships on the borders of the colony from the fourteenth century resulted in contraction and gaelicization of the colony. Most of the counties of Leinster and Munster were created by the Anglo-Normans by the thirteenth century as part of the administration of the colony.

By the mid-sixteenth century the expanding English state began a process of subjugation of Ireland that involved the elimination of regional lordships and the incorporation of the island as a unitary economic and political entity. This policy was carried out through a sometimes brutal series of land confiscations and plantation schemes that encouraged planters and settlers to come from Britain. This process of settlement continued into the middle of the seventeenth century, leading to an effective modernization of the Irish landscape with the introduction of a commercial landed-estates system and the consolidation of a market economy over the entire island. Where possible, British (Protestant and Presbyterian) settler tenants were brought in to introduce new farming methods, especially in Ulster. The native (mainly Catholic) population was largely dispossessed of landownership and relegated to tenant status. New plantation towns were added to the medieval urban network and were important agents of economic development in Ulster especially. The remaining counties of Ireland were created during these sixteenth- and seventeenth-century plantations as jurisdictions of local administration.

THE WOODLANDS

Although there was continuous forest clearance in Ireland from ancient times, most of the native forests were destroyed during the seventeenth century in response to the demands of an expanding mercantile economy and a rush to exploit the country's natural resources by new British settler communities. By the middle of the eighteenth century the Dublin parliament and the owners of Irish landed estates were concerned at the denuded state of the Irish woodland resources. Reflecting a European-wide age of improvement, the Royal Dublin Society, for instance, offered incentives to landowners and tenants to plant estates with hardwoods. Much of the legacy of beech, oak, and lime trees today can be traced to this period of planting and continues to be an important feature in Ireland east of the Shannon, especially in the demesne lands of former estates. In the more windswept west of the country the landscape is largely treeless.

FIELDS

The most common features in the landscape today are the hundreds of thousands of individually enclosed fields, separated by hedges, banks, and ditches. In the rockier western regions fields are enclosed by an intricate mesh of stone walls. Most of this enclosure occurred in the largely open-field landscapes that prevailed before the eighteenth century and is part of a revolution in agriculture that diffused throughout the British Isles, reaching the west of Ireland latest after the famine in the 1840s. Unlike England, where parliamentary enclosure reorganized most of the older medieval open fields, in Ireland the land was enclosed mainly by landlord and tenant initiative. The more commercially minded landowners in Leinster and Munster were at the forefront in having their lands enclosed in the eighteenth century as part of a drive for more efficient agriculture. Usually, the outbounds of the tenant farms were enclosed initially, with the tenants being left to hedge and ditch their own fields. In the 1820s and 1830s landlords in south Ulster were giving their tenants thousands of quick sets (whitethorn hedge plants) on the November "gale days" (rent days) to plant on their farms. As population soared in the decades before the Great Famine, farms and fields were subdivided and new boundaries installed. The story of the hedging of the countryside in its characteristic patchwork-quilt pattern represents a critical formative phase in the making of the landscape and the sense of place today. Because of the intimate connection between farmer and field over generations of manual labor, field-naming was a common practice in many regions, adding another layer to place-names in the landscapes.

ESTATES

Most of the material features in the modern settlement landscape developed within the parameters of the landed estate. In common with much of Europe from feudal times, the land of the island was owned by a privileged minority. This estate system was firmly established in Ireland following its final incorporation in the expanding modern British state. Some estates traced their origins to powerful Anglo-Norman families, but most emerged from plantation schemes or purchase in the sixteenth and seventeenth centuries. Landowners, who might generally be characterized as ascendancy and gentry, leased their land to tenant farmers for rent. Tenants were expected to make the land productive, through drainage and good husbandry. It was the large and small tenant, under the managing eye of the owner or his agent, who made the landscape, and who molded and imprinted on it the marks of his community and culture. Landless laborers were employed either by the landlord or the tenant, their numbers reflecting the nature of the local agricultural economy. The busy tillage lands of Louth and Wexford had large settlements of laborer cottages near the farms.

In the cattle-grazing midlands these were fewer. As population grew and employment shrunk in prefamine decades, it was the poorly managed estates that experienced the brunt of subdivision of the landscape. Landless populations squatted on marginal lands on the edges of the bogs, high up on mountainsides, or along new roads built to open up remote areas in Munster or Connacht. Landless sons added cabins to swelling house clusters in coastal regions and mountain valleys in the west, from which bands migrated seasonally to work in eastern counties, Scotland, or England. More carefully managed properties controlled their tenant populations, or encouraged some to leave under assisted-emigration schemes in mid-nineteenth century. On these properties, mostly located in the east and south, landlords invested in large mansions and lavish walled demesnes with ornamental gardens and model farms. Many landlords were also involved in attempts to induce economic development in planned estate villages, with markets to encourage trade and frequently with colonies of textile workers. However, following the ravages of the Great Famine, the landlord system was largely discredited, and commencing with the disestablishment of the Anglican Church in 1869 and land legislation transferring ownership from landlord to tenant at the turn of the nineteenth century, the estates and the social system that they represented were dismantled. The truncated demesnes and big houses, intact or derelict, are all that remain as landscape markers of the estate system.

BUILDINGS

The Irish heritage in buildings is modest by European standards. Before the seventeenth century, Ireland was a comparatively underdeveloped and politically fragmented entity, thus preventing the articulation of a significant island-wide economy. Unlike the rest of Europe, where significant remnants of the medieval-built environment survive, military and economic instability meant that most Irish medieval structures have been in ruins for more than three hundred years. The majority of inherited structures still in use today originated largely in the eighteenth and nineteenth centuries. The more significant buildings are the mansion houses of the wealthy landed elite—referred to as the "Big Houses" of the gentry, or as "stately homes" by heritage tourism—which accompany estates. Great houses like Carton, Castletown, Powerscourt, or Florencecourt, with

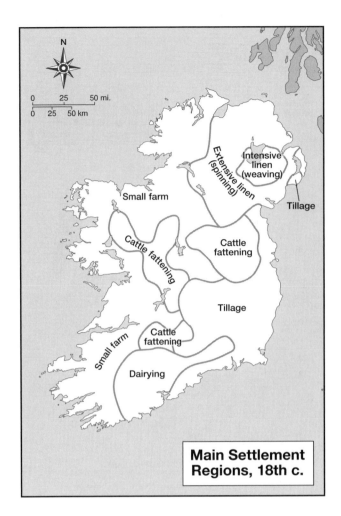

Main Settlement Regions, 18th c.

their demesne landscapes largely intact, are important components in the modern landscape.

The houses of bigger tenant farmers aped the pretensions of their masters by embellishing their houses with a second story or a porch. Smaller tenant-farmer houses were more traditional in form, consisting of two or more connected rooms. Originally thatched, some survive, though most have been slated. The poorest category of house belonging to the landless laborer was replaced in the late nineteenth and early twentieth centuries by local authority or state-sponsored cottages. Today, however, most of the traditional buildings in the countryside have been superseded by modern bungalow type dwellings, which are universal throughout the Irish landscape.

The most important distinction in buildings is between the houses of the wealthy from the seventeenth to the nineteenth centuries, which engaged with a wider world of architecture, taste, and building materials, and those of the local tenantry. Many of the eighteenth-century mansions reflect the impact of palladianism (derived from the ideas of the sixteenth-century Italian,

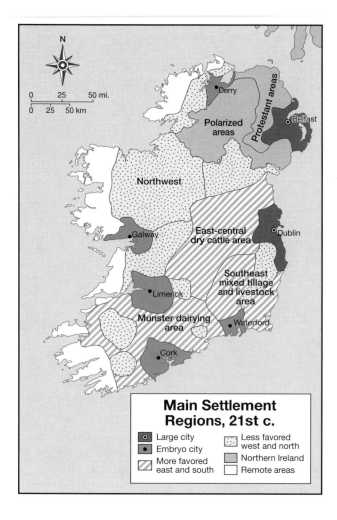

Main Settlement Regions, 21st c.

- ⊙ Large city
- ■ Embryo city
- ▨ More favored east and south
- ⠿ Less favored west and north
- ▒ Northern Ireland
- □ Remote areas

Andrea Palladio), ornamented by fashionably popular Irish architects such as Richard Castle and craftsmen from Dublin or England. Frequently, building materials were imported, like the exotic plants for landlord demesnes.

In contrast, the houses of the majority of the population were embedded in the local landscapes literally and metaphorically. Built by local craftsmen, they reflected the constraints of traditional practice and local materials in plan and construction. Consequently, as in the rest of Europe, the domestic buildings of local communities blended into the countryside, snuggling into landscapes from which stone, straw, or reeds were obtained.

CHURCHES

Church buildings in Ireland reflect diverging allegiances in the population: the majority native population which adhered to Rome after the Reformation and whose churches were impoverished and often illegal through most of the eighteenth century, and the Protestant mi-

norities whose smaller but better-built churches reflected their social and political privilege. The Established Church of Ireland, which was state endowed up until disestablishment in 1869, inherited many of the old medieval cathedrals and built many small, attractive country churches, which, because of dwindling congregations, have been abandoned throughout the south of Ireland in the twentieth century. Northern Ireland with its much bigger Anglican and Presbyterian congregations has a more extensive heritage of churches. The Catholic Church embarked on a building program from the early nineteenth century following Catholic Emancipation in 1829, though in places some older vernacular barn chapels have survived from the eighteenth century. Its churches are larger and reflect elements of a neo-gothic triumphalism in the nineteenth century.

URBANIZATION

Ireland's regional pattern of urbanization is a combination of a legacy of colonial settlement superimposed on a more ambiguous Gaelic pattern. South of a line from Dundalk to Galway lay a region of comparatively intensive urban settlements from the Anglo-Norman feudal economy. To the north the Gaelic landscape was more rural and town-less. It has been suggested that the monastic settlements of the early medieval period presented protourban settlements in which the economic activities of an "urban" class occurred. However, the fragmented nature of Gaelic political authority and the localized and disarticulated nature of economic life prevented the development of anything resembling a market economy. Small Norse trading centers were established by the tenth century, but the Anglo-Norman colonization brought the first market towns in the European mold, with streets and market spaces, protected by walls, lords, and charters. Boroughs and market centers associated with manors were at the forefront of the Anglo-Norman colonial project to attract settlers and establish economic stability, as at port towns like Kinsale, Youghal, Dundalk, and Drogheda, or inland markets like Kells, Trim, Kilkenny, Carlow, and Clonmel. Many of these medieval towns were developed on earlier monastic sites. By the thirteenth and fourteenth centuries a network of towns with market functions had been established in the Pale and the larger lordships of the colony. However, the failure of the colony to incorporate the entire island meant that periodic instability, especially in the borderlands, inhibited the development of the urban network. Towns also became the lynchpins of later British settlement plans: the Laois-Offaly plantation (1556) and the Munster plantation (1586) were based on the implementation of town plans, resulting in the modern towns of Portlaoise (originally Maryborough), Daingean (originally Philipstown), Bandon, and Clonakility; the Ulster plantation program from 1610 succeeded in creating in excess of one hundred towns in the last Gaelic and rural province of Ireland by the 1650s. In the eighteenth century some new market and industrial towns were built with the encouragement of landlords and capitalists to encourage local economic growth, but it was East Ulster in the later nineteenth century that experienced heavy urbanization that resembled that of Great Britain. Apart from a few Bord na Móna villages, urbanization stagnated in the Republic of Ireland in the long emigration phase up to the 1960s. Since then there has been a steady increase in the country's urban population, with growing state investment in the industrialization of the economy.

SEE ALSO Belfast; Bogs and Drainage; Clachans; Cork; Dublin; Eiscir Riata; Estates and Demesnes; Ordnance Survey; Raths; Religious Geography; Rural Settlement and Field Systems; Towns and Villages; Woodlands

Bibliography

Aalen, Frederick H. A., Kevin Whelan, and Mathew Stout, eds. *Atlas of the Irish Rural Landscape*. 1997.

Barry, Terry B., ed. *A History of Settlement in Ireland*. 2000.

Casey, Christine, and Alistair Rowan. *The Buildings of Ireland: North Leinster*. 1993.

Duffy, Patrick J., David Edwards, and Elizabeth Fitzpatrick, eds. *Gaelic Ireland: Land, Lordship and Settlement, c. 1250–c. 1650*. 2001.

Graham, Brian J., and Lindsay J. Proudfoot, eds. *An Historical Geography of Ireland*. 1993.

Mitchell, Frank, and Michael Ryan. *Reading the Irish Landscape*. 1986. Revised, 1990.

Moody, T. W., and F. X. Martin, eds. *The Course of Irish History*. 1984.

Royal Irish Academy. *Irish Historic Towns Atlas*. Vol. 1. 1996.

Shaffrey, Patrick, and Maura Shaffrey. *Irish Countryside Buildings*. 1985.

Simms, Anngret, and John H. Andrews, eds. *Irish Country Towns*. 1994.

Simms, Anngret, and John H. Andrews, eds. *More Irish Country Towns*. 1995.

Smyth, Alfred P. *Celtic Leinster: Towards an Historical Geography of Early Irish Civilisation, A.D. 500–1600*. 1982.

Smyth, William J., and Kevin Whelan, eds. *Common Ground: Essays on the Historical Geography of Ireland*. 1988.

Patrick J. Duffy

~

Land Settlements from 1500 to 1690

As a consequence of the Gaelic revival of the fourteenth and fifteenth centuries, only the area of the Pale (Louth, Meath, Dublin, and Wicklow) remained under direct English rule by 1500. Other anglicized enclaves throughout the country were controlled by relatively independent Anglo-Irish nobles. Throughout the later Middle Ages English monarchs had attempted to regain control, but it was only with the end of the Wars of the Roses and the reemergence of strong monarchy under the Tudor dynasty (after 1485) that this became a viable prospect. The support in Ireland for the Simnel and Warbeck conspiracies against Henry VII illustrated how England's enemies could use Ireland to launch an invasion of Britain. As an outright conquest of Ireland was initially deemed too expensive, a conciliatory strategy was adopted. The eventual aim was the total reformation of Gaelic society, and in particular an end to the chronic instability and violence associated with *tanistry* (the English name for the Gaelic inheritance system), the stimulation of economic activity, and the extension of the reformed religion. This program might well have settled the Irish Question, but it lapsed with Henry VIII's death in 1547 and with the rise of ambitious young nobles in Ireland like Shane O'Neill.

By 1550 the government concluded that certain of the "wild" Irish were incapable of reform. As conquest remained impractical, a new type of colonial expansion or "plantation" was posited. Its central tenet was the reformation of the indigenous population through exposure to small-scale colonies of civilized people from the metropolis. This was based on two suppositions: that Gaelic society was less advanced than English, but that it was sufficiently progressive to accept this fact and follow examples of English civility.

The first areas targeted were the Offaly lordship of the O'Connors and the O'More lordship of Leix. A scheme of 1556 called for two-thirds of the natives' lands to be expropriated and allocated to "Englishmen born in England or Ireland." Even with the expulsion of the natives and a substantial influx of settlers, the plantation was only a limited success: sustained resistance from the O'Connors and O'Mores continued throughout the sixteenth century. Despite Lord Deputy Sir Henry Sidney's complaint in 1575 that the "revenue of both the countries [Leix-Offaly] countervails not the twentieth part of the charge, so that the purchase of that plot is, and hath been, very dear" (Moody 1976, p. 79), and despite the Crown's reluctance to support fur-

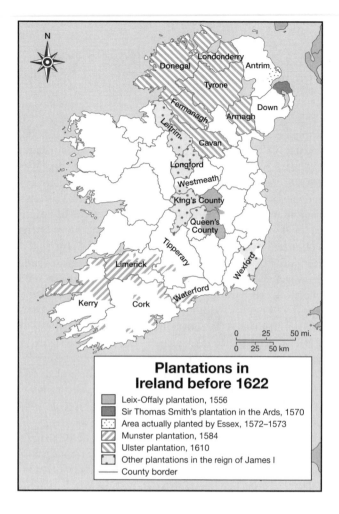

Plantations in Ireland before 1622

Leix-Offaly plantation, 1556
Sir Thomas Smith's plantation in the Ards, 1570
Area actually planted by Essex, 1572–1573
Munster plantation, 1584
Ulster plantation, 1610
Other plantations in the reign of James I
County border

ther schemes, private entrepreneurs attempted plantations elsewhere in the middle years of Elizabeth's reign. The ultimately unsuccessful ventures of Sir Thomas Smith and the first earl of Essex in eastern Ulster between 1571 and 1575 further estranged the Gaelic Irish from the government, and Sir Peter Carew's attempted plantation in Idrone in eastern Munster drove the Old English—and hitherto loyalist—Butlers into rebellion.

This extension of plantation to the Old English was a new development, and with the suppression of the Desmond and Baltinglass rebellions between 1579 and 1583, the New English argument that Irish-born magnates could not be relied upon to establish civil society was increasingly heeded in London. Thereafter, plantation was as likely to be employed against the Old English as against the Gaelic Irish, and the confiscation of the recent rebels' lands in Munster furnished an immediate opportunity to impose a large-scale plantation there. Increased state involvement sought to ensure that there was no repetition of the disastrous private plantations of the previous decade. The English officials most closely involved in the development of the project were

determined that the plantation be organized along scientific principles, and a detailed survey was conducted to plot out the Munster plantation on paper.

This survey was only partially complete by the time that the scheme had been carried out in early 1587. Almost 250,000 acres were allocated to thirty-five "undertakers" over twenty-five seignories of between 4,000 and 12,000 acres each. Most undertakers were from the English West Country because of its proximity to, and long-established trade connections with, the Munster ports. The undertakers were to construct defensible buildings, encourage English modes of agriculture, erect model villages, and equip the settlers to defend the colony against the natives. Within seven years the undertakers were to settle ninety-one families on each 12,000-acre seignory, "to be entirely maintained of mere English persons without any intermixture of the mere Irish" (Canny 2001, p. 130).

That the confiscated lands of the earl of Desmond were a mosaic rather than a unified block of property greatly complicated the process of settlement. By the time the first undertakers arrived late in 1586, many of the former proprietors were involved in litigation to reclaim their lands, and no undertaker whose grant was being contested could succeed in attracting tenants. Consequently, the transplantation of English settlers proceeded slowly, and by 1598, when the first Munster plantation was destroyed and many settlers were killed in Tyrone's rebellion, there were fewer than 4,000 settlers in Munster, less than a third of the number anticipated. Nonetheless, they had substantially altered Munster's socioeconomic structures: trade in wool, tallow, and hides exported to England (mainly through the port of Bristol) increased substantially, and the settlers yielded the Crown rents in excess of £2,000 per annum. The settlers were developing arable farming; using English breeds to improve husbandry; and putting Munster's natural resources—particularly its dense forests—to profitable use.

According to Edmund Spenser, this was the plantation's major weakness, for "only the present profit [was] looked unto, and the safe continuance thereof [was] ever hereafter neglected" (Renwick edition, p. 126). He deplored the fact that the settlers had not implemented the defensive conditions demanded by the government. Spenser insisted that settlements in isolation could not endure in Ireland, and he recommended the wholesale plantation of the country and an increased role for the army therein. This line of reasoning was consonant with that of the Dublin government and its spokesperson Sir John Davies (solicitor general, 1603–1606, and attorney general, 1606–1619). In his *Discovery of the True Causes Why Ireland Was Never En-*

tirely Subdued (1612), Davies argued that notwithstanding the Munster debacle, plantation, with some modification, remained the panacea for Ireland's ills and so following the Flight of the Earls in 1607 a modified plantation was implemented in Ulster on the lands escheated to the Crown.

To avoid the litigation that had plagued the Munster settlement, all land in Counties Armagh, Cavan, Donegal, Derry, Fermanagh, and Tyrone was confiscated. Most of this huge territory was set aside for settlement by English and lowland Scottish gentlemen of means who undertook to transfer tenants of their countries to Ulster (including laborers and craftsmen), to establish new towns, and to build defensible strongholds and arm their tenants. Undertaker estates were limited to 3,000 acres to ensure that private individuals could better afford to meet the defensive conditions demanded. The undertakers were to pay the Crown a rent of £5 6s. 8d. for each 1,000 acres. As in earlier plantations, the undertaker estates were to provide an instructive model for the native Irish, and undertakers were to settle ten British families on each 1,000 acres and were expressly forbidden to maintain Irish tenants. To ensure that these terms were met, regular surveys were to be conducted.

If nurturing civil society was the purpose behind the undertaker estates, the intent behind the involvement of servitors (men who had served the Crown in Ireland) was to maintain in good order the native Irish inhabitants of Ulster, many of whom had participated in Tyrone's rebellion. These servitors were either former army captains or current Ulster garrison commanders and were to "be seated in the places of most danger and best advantage for His Majesty's service and defense of the rest of the undertakers." These men would provide leadership in the event of a crisis, but as they lacked financial resources, they were allowed estates of no more than 2,000 acres. They could maintain Irish tenants in exchange for a rent of £8 per 1,000 acres. Coleraine was granted to the London merchant guilds, which formed a joint-stock company for the purpose of planting the area (thereafter designated County Londonderry). Although bound by the same terms of tenure as the undertakers, they were granted special privileges, as it was hoped they would both introduce skilled tradesmen throughout the settlement and develop the ports of Coleraine and Derry.

One-quarter of the plantation was reserved for the "deserving Irish" (loyal supporters of the Crown). They were settled on estates removed from the lands occupied by their kinsmen in order to undermine Gaelic kin affiliation. They could maintain Irish tenants, but they had to introduce English methods of farming and landholding. The generous endowments of church livings within Ulster, along with other measures, indicated the government's aim to promote Protestantism as well as English civility. The lenient treatment of the lesser septs aimed to "outweigh the displeasure and dissatisfaction of the smaller number of better blood." This policy did not work because few of the "deserving Irish" received what they felt they deserved. Moreover, as surveys conducted in 1611, 1614, 1619, 1622, and 1628 revealed, many of the undertakers neither implemented the defensive conditions nor cleared their estates of natives, having discovered that it was far more lucrative to maintain Irish tenants—whom they could charge extortionate rents—than to settle British tenants. This meant that there existed throughout the entire plantation a substantial, disaffected native population living in close proximity to the settlers.

Hard-line English observers justified such expropriation and its attendant violence as the inevitable and necessary march of civilization at the expense of a people who were "not thrifty, and civil and human creatures, but heathen or rather savage and brute beasts," and there was almost universal approval of the planting of "civil men brought up in the laws of England." Validating this view were a host of anti-Gaelic Irish and Old English diatribes like John Derricke's *Image of Irelande* (1581), Richard Beacon's *Solon His Follie* (1594), and Edmund Spenser's *View of the Present State of Ireland* (1596).

The personal interest taken by James VI and Charles I in the Ulster plantation encouraged the Dublin administration to develop further schemes, and there were further small-scale plantations in counties Leitrim, Longford, Offaly, and Westmeath during the latter years of his reign. As the grantees appointed in these areas were not compelled to establish British tenants on their lands, it is evident that the government was now using plantation as a tool to dismember rather than to reform Gaelic lordships by forcing the lords to divide their lands into freeholds and tenancies. By Charles I's accession in 1625 the government was actively seeking to extend these schemes throughout the country, and in particular to the province of Connacht and the Ormond lordship in south Leinster and northeast Munster.

These areas were distinctly Old English, and the landowners used their court connections to frustrate government progress. Throughout the rest of the country, however, settlers flooded in. By 1635 there were some 18,000 settlers in the re-established Munster plantation, while in Ulster there were almost 35,000. Anglicization by example was successful in some cases, and certain native proprietors established nucleated settlements of foreign tenants on their estates. By 1640 there were probably some 90,000 mainly British settlers in Ireland, the majority having been introduced via plantation.

The resentment engendered among those dispossessed by plantation exploded in the 1641 Rising, which resulted in the deaths of about 12,000 settlers, almost all Protestant. This bloodshed was used to justify the Cromwellian plantation of the 1650s, which followed the long-delayed suppression of the rebellion, but the real imperative was the need for Irish land to reimburse the state's creditors and over 33,000 unpaid Roundhead soldiers who had participated in the British campaigns. The Act of Settlement (1652) declared all land east of the Shannon to be confiscated to the Crown. Most Catholic landowners forfeited their lands and were forcibly relocated west of the Shannon, although some avoided this fate. In September 1653 the English parliament set aside four counties for the government (Carlow, Cork, Dublin, and Kildare) and ten for distribution among the state's creditors (Antrim, Armagh, Down, Laois, Limerick, Meath, Offaly, Tipperary, Waterford, and Westmeath). A tripartite survey of Ireland—by jury inquisition, gross estimation, and William Petty's historic Down Survey—was conducted to facilitate implementation of the scheme. Once established on their lands the new proprietors were to draw the natives into a civil condition. It had been hoped that the soldiers would remain in Ireland to form a strong yeoman class, but fewer than 12,000 took physical possession of their lands. Most sold their debentures to their officers, who in turn sold to the Protestant settlers resident in Ireland before 1641. Expected immigration from Britain failed to materialize and the settlement proved a crushing disappointment to those who had hoped that it would achieve the reformation of the country. Indeed, more soldiers sold their holdings thereafter, for the Restoration settlement confirmed only 7,500 soldiers in their new lands.

Overall, William Petty estimated that 11 million acres had changed hands. While the settlement substantially increased the number of Protestants in Ireland, even more importantly, it greatly increased their wealth and power. They enjoyed a complete ascendancy throughout the country, and their control over Irish political and economic life was thereafter almost absolute. The Cromwellian settlement represented the greatest early modern transformation in Irish landownership and created the estate system that lasted until the late nineteenth century. The Act of Settlement (1662), while restoring individual Catholic favorites of Charles II, did little to redress the imbalance between Catholic and Protestant landownership and left just over one-fifth of Irish land in Catholic possession.

Plantation in Ireland failed to achieve its original objective to secure the country, and the government was forced to maintain substantial forces to guard against invasion. While the upper class was anglicized, or more accurately "briticized," this was achieved through expropriation, not reformation. Such expropriation led to several centuries of ethno-religious conflict. If elite Gaelic power structures were successfully dismantled, the lower levels of Gaelic society remained largely unchanged. As successive plantations failed, the process underwent many modifications, but by the end of the 1650s plantation was less about reformation than expropriation. The scale of the Cromwellian plantation, which spectacularly manifested this change, would have astounded the original proponents of colonization. The emphasis of plantation had changed as early as the 1610s, as the Irish Protestant Reformation faltered, and the transfer of power from the Old to the New English reflected this fact. Religion became the new badges of civility, and segregation rather than integration became the hallmark of plantation. Crucially, the suffering engendered by plantation and resistance to it eventually helped to mould the Gaelic Irish and Old English into one proto-nation.

SEE ALSO Agriculture: 1500 to 1690; Colonial Theory from 1500 to 1690; Cromwellian Conquest; Desmond Rebellions; Legal Change in the Sixteenth and Seventeenth Centuries; Politics: 1500 to 1690; Sidney, Henry; Wild Geese—The Irish Abroad from 1600 to the French Revolution; **Primary Documents:** From *Solon His Follie* (1594); From *A Direction for the Plantation of Ulster* (1610); Conditions of the Plantation of Ulster (1610); From *The Great Case of Transplantation Discussed* (1655); From *The Interest of England in the Irish Transplantation Stated* (1655); From *The Memoirs of Edmund Ludlow* (1698)

Bibliography

Brady, Ciaran, and Raymond Gillespie, eds. *Natives and Newcomers: Essays on the Making of Irish Colonial Society, 1534–1641*. 1986.

Bottigheimer, Karl. *English Money and Irish Land: The Adventurers in the Cromwellian Settlement of Ireland*. 1971.

Bottigheimer, Karl. "The Restoration Land Settlement in Ireland: A Structural View." In *Irish Historical Studies* 18, no. 69 (1972): 1–21.

Canny, Nicholas. "The Ideology of English Colonization: From Ireland to America." In *William and Mary Quarterly* series 3, xxx (1973): 575–98.

Canny, Nicholas. *The Elizabethan Conquest of Ireland: A Pattern Established, 1565–76*. 1976.

Canny, Nicholas. *Making Ireland British, 1580–1650*. 2001.

Dunlop, Robert. "The Plantation of Leix and Offaly, 1556–1622." In *English Historical Review* 6 (1891): 61–96.

Ellis, Steven G. *Ireland in the Age of the Tudors, 1447–1603: English Expansion and the End of Gaelic Rule.* 1998.

MacCarthy-Morrogh, Michael. *The Munster Plantation: English Migration to Southern Ireland, 1583–1641.* 1986.

Moody, T. W., F. X. Martin, and F. J. Byrne, eds. *A New History of Ireland.* Vol. 3. 1976.

Robinson, Philip. *The Plantation of Ulster: British Settlement in an Irish Landscape, 1600–1670.* 1984.

Spenser, Edmund. *A View of the Present State of Ireland*, edited by W. L. Renwick. 1970.

David Finnegan

Land War of 1879 to 1882

The Land War of 1879 to 1882 began in the wake of three years of economic downturn that arrested the postfamine economic progress of many Irish farmers and heightened the anxiety of vulnerable small tenants, especially those along the western seaboard where postfamine prosperity had been most limited. It was given focus and leadership by a coalition of radical and constitutional nationalists. This coalition added potency to the mobilized Irish tenant farmers in a movement that forced the passage of legislation that began the dismantling of landlordism in Ireland.

The public meeting that launched the Land War occurred on 20 April 1879 at Irishtown in County Mayo. It came following two years of cold and wet weather, meager harvests, low livestock prices, and a decline in the demand for seasonal laborers in England and Scotland that left many western farmers with few sources of cash with which to pay rent, satisfy creditors, or purchase food. During the previous three years local activists in counties Mayo and Galway—most importantly James Daly, proprietor of the *Connaught Telegraph*, Matt Harris, a member of the Supreme Council of the Irish Republican Brotherhood, and John O'Connor Power, MP and a former Fenian—had promoted the formation of tenant-defense associations and had sought to forge an alliance with local Fenians, who had a long-standing aversion to public campaigns for land reform. These efforts were greatly aided with the release from prison in December 1877 of Mayo native Michael Davitt, who, in association with New York-based Irish activist John Devoy, crafted the "New Departure" that made possible the alliance between Fenians, land reformers, and advanced parliamentarians.

Following the Irishtown meeting, County Mayo was alive with meetings characterized by fiery speeches and militant resolutions, and the festive mobilization of rural Ireland that swept away the initial hesitation of the clergy to join a movement that was beyond their control. These activities resulted in the establishment of the National Land League of Mayo by Davitt in August and the spread of the movement beyond the west of Ireland. This expansion of the movement was formalized in October with the founding of the Irish National Land League, with Charles Stewart Parnell, leader of the advanced wing of the Irish Parliamentary Party, at its head. The formation of the Land League institutionalized the agitation and brought it under the direction of a central leadership that was committed to channeling the energy and rhetoric of the previous six months into a workable plan of action that Parnell hoped could be advocated in the House of Commons. The plan that emerged from the founding conference was a radical departure from the "three Fs" and from the principle of "dual ownership" advocated by earlier tenant-right organizations and Irish parliamentarians. The League plan called for an immediate and permanent reduction of rents, an end to evictions for nonpayment of rents, and legislation that would "enable every tenant to become the owner of his holding."

This strategy was bolstered in the spring of 1880 by a general election that returned to office the Liberal leader W. E. Gladstone, an advocate of land reform in Ireland, and that brought about the return of a sufficient number of MPs supporting Parnell to enable him to become leader of the Irish Parliamentary Party. In April the Land League executive convened a national conference to draft proposals for land-reform legislation consistent with the League's program. The conference was given further significance by the presence of a substantial number of large farmers and cattle graziers, who were making their initial intervention in League matters. Their attempt to ensure that the League advocated land reform that would benefit large as well as small farmers was not welcomed by western radicals, who viewed large farmers as avaricious grabbers of land who furthered the impoverishment of vulnerable small tillers. Although tension between large and small farmers over tactics and goals plagued the Land League until its dissolution, and ultimately weakened the attachment of small western farmers to it, the conference marked the transformation of the League into an organization that agitated for legislative reform that would benefit all tenant farmers. Moreover, it was doing so in alliance with a radical group of parliamentarians with whom it shared a leader.

Over the next year hundreds of local branches were formed, public demonstrations were held nearly every weekend, and the country was teeming with a campaign to topple the traditional land system. That campaign involved organized efforts to withhold rents, to resist evictions, to support tenants evicted or threatened with eviction, to intimidate landlords, their agents, process servers, and police, often through violence or the threat of it, and to use public demonstrations and branch meetings to press for land reform. The most far-reaching tactic was social and economic ostracism, dubbed "boycotting" in reference to the case of Captain Charles Boycott, the agent of the Earl Erne's Lough Mask estate in County Mayo, who was driven from his property in November 1880 following two months of a highly publicized refusal by his tenants to pay rent, his laborers to work, and local traders to provide him with any provisions.

Boycotting, and indeed the entire range of Land War tactics, were validated by a belief widely held in rural Ireland that the land belonged to the people who worked it, irrespective of the legal claims of landlords, who were seen as the descendants of English invaders who had stolen the land from its God-given owners. This belief, advanced on many League platforms, was the foundation for a code of behavior, dubbed the "lawless law" by Davitt, which called for not paying rent deemed excessive and not taking land from which the previous tenant had been evicted or compelled to leave owing to inability or unwillingness to pay excessive rents. This code was designed to protect access to land for impoverished tenant farmers as well as to render untenable the economic position of landlords. Along with the religious divide between most tenant farmers and their landlords, the tenants' confidence in the moral legitimacy of their cause produced a powerful degree of unity of purpose and action in rural Ireland.

In April 1881 Gladstone introduced a land-reform bill (which became law in August) that fell far short of what had been demanded by the League, but one that he conceded would not have come about without the sustained agitation of the previous two years. Realizing that this legislation would satisfy many tenant farmers and might undermine support for the land movement, the League called on its supporters to refrain from rushing into the newly established rent-arbitration courts to seek reductions, and instead to wait until a few carefully selected test cases could be decided. Convinced that the League executive was attempting to thwart implementation of the bill, the government arrested Parnell and much of the League's leadership in October 1881. From prison they issued a "No Rent Manifesto" that was ignored throughout Ireland but that did succeed in getting the League proclaimed an illegal organization. During the next six months the Ladies' Land League, established

in the previous January, kept the agitation going, but with the principal leaders of the Land War in prison, League branches in disarray, and eligible tenant farmers rushing into the land courts, this initial phase of the Irish Land War soon came to a conclusion.

SEE ALSO Congested Districts Board; Davitt, Michael; Home Rule Movement and the Irish Parliamentary Party: 1870 to 1891; Ladies' Land League; Land Acts of 1870 and 1881; Land Questions; Parnell, Charles Stewart; Plan of Campaign; Protestant Ascendancy: Decline, 1800 to 1930; United Irish League Campaigns; **Primary Documents:** Establishment of the National Land League of Mayo (16 August 1879); Call at Ennis for Agrarian Militancy (19 September 1880); Land Law (Ireland) Act (22 August 1881)

Bibliography

Bew, Paul. *Land and the National Question in Ireland, 1858–82.* 1978.

Bull, Philip. *Land, Politics, and Nationalism: A Study of the Irish Land Question.* 1996.

Clark, Samuel. *Social Origins of the Irish Land War.* 1979.

Comerford, R. V. "The Land War and the Politics of Distress." In *A New History of Ireland*, vol. 6, *Ireland Under the Union II, 1870–1921*, edited by W. E. Vaughan. 1996.

Donnelly, James S., Jr. *The Land and the People of Nineteenth Century Cork.* 1975.

Jordan, Donald E., Jr. *Land and Popular Politics in Ireland: County Mayo from the Plantation to the Land War.* 1994.

Moody, T. W. *Davitt and Irish Revolution, 1846–82.* 1981.

Warwick-Haller, Sally. *William O'Brien and the Irish Land War.* 1990.

Donald E. Jordan, Jr.

Language and Literacy

| DECLINE OF IRISH LANGUAGE | NEIL BUTTIMER |
| IRISH LANGUAGE SINCE 1922 | PÁDRAIG Ó RIAGÁIN |

DECLINE OF IRISH LANGUAGE

The Irish language has been in decline since the seventeenth century. Its reversal was a complex phenomenon, and it not easy to describe or analyze the processes involved. For the seventeenth and eighteenth centuries, only indirect measures of its downturn are available, but these measures at least help to identify the context of the decline in the nineteenth century. The rate of occurrence of indigenous Gaelic surnames has been used to determine the status of Irish in late seventeenth-century Dublin city and county: There was 26 percent usage in the metropolitan urban area at that stage, and more than 90 percent usage in some rural baronies around the capital. Estimates by researchers writing in the nineteenth century suggest that in the 1730s two-thirds of the country's population might have been Irish-speaking. Signs of reduction are evident from the mid-eighteenth century onwards. One indication of this downward trend was the decrease in the number of scholarships with a Gaelic component offered to and accepted by young Irishmen studying for the Catholic priesthood in French seminaries. France was the principal training ground for the Catholic clergy prior to the French Revolution in 1789. Earlier in the eighteenth century, Irish would have been the vernacular of many of the communities that priests returned to serve, but this clearly became less so over time.

The nineteenth century witnessed a continuation of the foregoing trends and their dramatic acceleration after 1850. What principally distinguishes the nineteenth century from previous periods is the growth in data specifically focused on language matters, thus facilitating the measurement of change. Statistical surveys of counties conducted by the Royal Dublin Society and other bodies are one such source. Although only some twenty counties were studied, and although the treatment of Irish differs from report to report (reflecting changes in the kinds of information elicited from informants), these organizations' publications are valuable for their data on Irish-language usage in different regions of Ireland and among different social classes. A substantial reversal in the use of Gaelic in Leinster and Ulster is apparent for the years in question (roughly 1800–1830). There were also systematic inquiries conducted by proselytizing Protestant groups seeking to convert speakers of Irish by means of their own language beginning in the late 1810s. The responses to the surveys confirm that although Irish was still strong in the south and the west, it was diminishing there too.

The Great Famine was the key turning point, not only in the fortunes of the language but also in the modes of reporting its retreat. It was evident from 1845 onwards that mortality was greatest in regions where Irish remained the principal community language. Public officials and others aware of the change were successful in having a question on the use of the language in-cluded in the population census of 1851. This was the first time that such an inquiry had been conducted, although censuses had been taken in Ireland since 1821. Questions about the Irish language were posed in all of the decennial censuses from 1851 to 1911; no census was carried out in 1921 in the turbulent conditions of the war of independence. The seven censuses conducted between the two aforementioned dates are a foundation for the analysis of the story of the language both before and after 1850.

The first systematic investigation of the census returns, and still the best overview of the position of Irish in the period on the national level, was by Brian Ó Cuív (1950 and 1969). He determined the percentages of Irish speakers for each county from the censuses of 1851 and 1891, tabulating the story for all baronies in eighteen counties. Maps were drawn up on his instructions for the two time horizons. They show a dramatic shrinkage in the intervening years (from 25 percent of the population in 1851 to less than half this total in 1891), with the speaking of Irish effectively confined by 1891 to coastal and some inland regions of the north, west, and south (counties Donegal, Mayo, Galway, Clare, Kerry, Cork, and Waterford). These districts came later to be called the *Gaeltacht*, although this term was probably borrowed from the similar designation of Gaelic-speaking areas of Scotland. Subsequent scholarship has built on and refined Ó Cuív's work. FitzGerald (1984) sought to determine from postfamine census data precisely when in the late eighteenth century significant patterns of decline might have commenced. Later studies have investigated usage or decline at more discreet levels of local administration (Nic Craith 1993).

Census questions elicit a relatively restricted range of information, and as a result, they allow only large-scale alterations over space and time to be charted. The decline of Irish involves issues pertaining to the use of the language proper. Some work has been done on characterizing the parameters of usage—for instance, categorizing speakers into monoglots, fully bilingual in either Irish or English, or partially bilingual (exhibiting greater command of either Irish or English), and examining whether such bilingualism was active or passive. There has been only limited analysis of the distribution of these capabilities across the population during the nineteenth century. Investigating the issue further will require that researchers go beyond census reports to other sources.

Greater levels of Irish-only competence are to be expected for the early nineteenth century. Contemporary manuscript materials are the most immediately relevant basis for assessing the language attainments of such speakers. More bilingualism and diminishing amounts of monoglottism were evident as the century progressed. The Irish of speakers born after 1850 survives in documentation from the early twentieth century—for instance, in oral traditions written down in the 1930s and later. Many of these records reveal the speech patterns of communities where Irish was disappearing as an everyday vernacular. Some breakdown in distinctive Gaelic linguistic characteristics such as initial mutation (sounds changing at the beginning of a word when the word's grammatical context alters) is evident from the seafaring and other traditions described by the fisherman Seán Ó hAodha (1861–1946), a native of Glandore, Co. Cork. These developments possibly reflect the decreasing use of Irish by Ó hAodha and his neighbors, rather than necessarily mirroring any predictable evolution within the structures and sounds of the language itself.

While Ó hAodha's Irish shows signs of contraction in usage, the language of his near-contemporaries from adjacent regions exhibits a continued vibrancy. This is the case for the renowned Blasket Islander Tomás Ó Criomhthain (1856–1937), whose autobiography *An tOileánach* (first published in 1929 and translated in 1937 as *The Islandman*) is an epic testimonial to his maritime people. The same is true for other male and female tradition-bearers, such as the masterful west Cork storyteller, Amhlaoibh Ó Luínse (1872–1947), and the Beara peninsula exponent of oral narrative, Máiréad Ní Mhionacháin (1860–1957). Accordingly, the concept of language decline cannot be equated automatically with morbidity (Crystal 2000) or with intrinsic weakening in the expressiveness of Irish itself. The Irish of the late nineteenth century still clearly benefited from the linguistic vitality of the prefamine period (three million people probably spoke Irish in the early 1840s). The Gaelic Revival that began in the late nineteenth century capitalized on such residual strengths. This factor and the state support that it received throughout the twentieth century have meant that Irish may not now be as close to extinction as many of the world's other less-used or minority languages (McCloskey 2001).

The causes of the decline of Irish have attracted scholarly notice, but further work on the issue remains to be undertaken. Seán de Fréine's classic account (1965) sketches the main reasons as well as their impact. They include the age-old hostility of the English authorities to the language, growing indifference toward it on the part of Irish ecclesiastical and political leaders in the nineteenth century, and the community's own willingness to jettison its use. Whether arising from enforced or voluntary circumstances, the loss of Gaelic, according to de Fréine, was reflected in the population's diminished self-confidence and self-awareness. The main

planks of de Fréine's arguments are still largely tenable, but they must be refined in light of more recent scholarship. Efforts on behalf of Irish by agencies directly or loosely associated with the government, particularly in the domains of religion, culture, and education, suggest that not all branches of the establishment were unremittingly hostile to Gaelic in the nineteenth century. And recent studies on the social and educational background of Catholic priests and bishops have given a clearer impression of how the clergy might have been predisposed to acquiesce in language change.

Much more study of important aspects of the language is needed. Though there has been significant recent work on the transformative effects of literacy and on school curricula in the critical first half of the nineteenth century, this scholarship does not investigate these issues through contemporary Gaelic manuscript sources themselves, which are replete with relevant data. Nor has there been a full investigation of the effects on Gaelic-speaking communities of industrialization and the development of modern communications networks. Perhaps the most serious omission is the failure to study the decline of Irish in comparative terms. In this connection the forces that impelled language shift in Aboriginal Australian populations in such a short space of time might be considered (Schmidt 1985). This will inevitably bring into focus the considerable literature on language and colonization. These considerations further demonstrate how complicated a topic language change is in its own right, and they reinforce the need to approach it in a broad and sophisticated manner. In Ireland's case the decline of Irish is one of the more profound transformations in the country's history, affecting a range of issues beyond language use and encompassing psychology and identity as well.

SEE ALSO Blasket Island Writers; Education: Primary Public Education—National Schools from 1831; Gaelic Revival; Gaelic Revivalism: The Gaelic League; Hiberno-English; Language and Literacy: Irish Language since 1922; Literacy and Popular Culture; Raiftearaí (Raftery), Antaine

Bibliography

Crystal, David. *Language Death*. 2000.

De Fréine, Seán. *The Great Silence*. 1965.

FitzGerald, Garret. "Estimates for Baronies of Minimum Level of Irish-Speaking amongst Successive Decennial Cohorts." *Proceedings of the Royal Irish Academy* 84 C (1984): 117–155.

McCloskey, James. *Voices Silenced: Has Irish a Future?* 2001.

Nic Craith, Máiréad. *Malartú teanga: Meath na Gaeilge i gCorcaigh san Naoú hAois Déag.* 1993.

Ó Cuív, Brian. *Irish Dialects and Irish-Speaking Districts.* 1951.

Ó Cuív, Brian, ed. *A View of the Irish Language.* 1969.

Schimdt, Annette. *Young People's Dyirbal: An Example of Language Death from Australia.* 1985.

Neil Buttimer

IRISH LANGUAGE SINCE 1922

By the end of the nineteenth century the assimilation of the Irish language community into the English-speaking world appeared to have entered its final phase. In the census of 1926, only 18 percent of the population were returned as Irish-speakers, of whom nearly half of were concentrated in scattered bilingual or monolingual areas along the western and southern coasts (collectively referred to as the Gaeltacht). The remaining Irish-speakers, most of whom had learned the language at school, were scattered throughout largely English-speaking communities. Despite the well-established dynamic of language assimilation, the small demographic base, and rural character of Irish language communities, the new native government in 1922 adopted a broad strategy to enhance the social and legal status of Irish, to maintain its use in areas where it was still spoken, and to promote and revive its use elsewhere.

Although the population of the Gaeltacht has declined in both absolute and relative terms, there has been a gradual but continual revival in the ratios of Irish-speakers in other regions. In the 1996 census, 1,430,205 were returned as Irish-speakers. This represents 43.5 percent of the national population and compares with 18 percent in 1926. About 50 percent of Irish-speakers now reside in Leinster Province (including Dublin), compared with about 5 percent in 1926. The proportion of Irish-speakers in all regions has moved toward the national average, whereas the average itself is rising.

However, the largest proportion of Irish-speakers is found in the ten- to twenty-year-old age groups (i.e., school-age populations), after which it consistently becomes smaller. Furthermore, national language surveys conducted between 1973 and 1993 suggest that most of those returned as Irish-speakers were speakers of quite limited competence; only 10 percent claimed to be fluent or nearly fluent in Irish. The available evidence on the social use of Irish indicates that fewer than 5 percent of the national population use Irish as their first or main language, while a further 10 percent use Irish regularly but less intensively. Use of the language appears to be most intensive during school years, after which it is discontinued in the case of many individuals. Bilingualism in Ireland is based on a thin distribution of family and social networks, which have a degree of underpinning from a variety of state policies in educational, work place, and media institutions. But these networks are dispersed and weakly established and are very vulnerable to the loss of members over time, as they are not sufficiently large or vibrant enough to easily attract and retain replacements.

PUBLIC ATTITUDES

Support for the Irish language is higher in many respects than the objective position of the Irish language in society would appear to justify. The relationship between the Irish language and ethnic identity on the one hand, and perceptions of its limited value as economic or cultural capital on the other, form two opposing attitudinal predispositions that determine public attitudes toward policy. A majority perceives the Irish language to have an important role in defining and maintaining national cultural distinctiveness. Thus the general population is willing to accept a considerable commitment of state resources to ensure its continuance and even to support a considerable imposition of legal requirements to know or use Irish on certain groups within the society, such as teachers and civil servants. However, where such requirements directly affect respondents' own material opportunities, or those of their children, they are less readily supported. Although a majority of the Irish public would appear to espouse some form of bilingual objective, the evidence would suggest that many of this majority seek at best simply to maintain the low levels of social bilingualism now pertaining. When taken in conjunction with the increase over the last quarter of the twentieth century of those favouring an "English only" objective, it would appear that the proportion holding the revival position as traditionally understood has slipped and may no longer represent the majority viewpoint.

THE GAELTACHT

In strictly economic terms, state-sponsored socioeconomic development in the Gaeltacht has had an appreciable measure of success since 1970. After a long period of decline population levels have increased again and nonagricultural employment has grown. However, the progressive shift to English continues. It would appear that only about half of Gaeltacht children learn Irish in the home, and a decline in the proportion of Irish-speakers in other age groups is also occurring. This is in part related to the high level of in-migration and

return migration that has accompanied economic restructuring since about 1970. While community use of Irish remains very much higher than the national average, the Gaeltacht now accounts for less than 2 percent of the national population, the communities are very fragmented, and a large minority of the residents in these areas do not use Irish at all.

EDUCATION

The maintenance of more or less stable rates of bilingualism over the past forty years is due more to the capacity of the schools to produce competent bilinguals rather than to the capacity of the bilingual community to reproduce itself. Most Irish children learn Irish in both primary and post-primary school as a subject, but despite some thirteen years of experience in the case of the average child, these programs do not generally produce highly competent active users of Irish. When they do, they are usually among those who stay in the system the longest and take the academically most demanding syllabus, or else among the small minority who attend all-Irish schools. Paradoxically, in a period when Irish language policy in the schools generally is experiencing considerable difficulties, the number of Irish-immersion primary schools in English-speaking areas continues to grow. In 1981 there were 28 such schools. In 1991 this figure had risen to 66, and it is now over 100. As a consequence, the proportion of children receiving this type of education has increased from 5 percent to 8 percent. The position in mainstream schools is not so healthy. In these schools Irish is taught as a subject only. Following the decision in 1973 to discontinue the policy of requiring students to pass state examinations in Irish in order to graduate with a certificate, a small but growing minority of students did not take the Irish paper in public examinations, and a consistently upward trend was apparent in the percentages who failed Irish.

MEDIA AND CULTURAL LIFE

An Irish-language radio station was established in 1972, and an Irish-language television service commenced broadcasting in 1996. There are two weekly newspapers in Irish, and some national and regional newspapers regularly carry Irish-language material. There is a lively literary scene in Irish, and about one hundred books are published annually. There are occasional theatrical productions in Irish in the main cities. Core audiences and readerships reflect the low levels of social use of Irish, but sizeable minorities (about 20 percent) take an infrequent but consistent interest.

Although the effort to reestablish Irish as a national language has not been successful, neither can the impact of Irish-language policy be described as negligible. Irish has not been successfully maintained in the Irish-speaking areas, although there are still residual districts where Irish is habitually used. Elsewhere, only a small minority use Irish in daily social intercourse, but this widely dispersed minority does not command any domain of language use; nor is it in itself a very efficient source of bilingual reproduction. Since 1922 there has indeed been some measure of revival, and the pattern of bilingualism has consequently shifted, but the long-term future of the Irish language is not any more secure now than it was then.

SEE ALSO Arts: Early Modern Literature and the Arts from 1500 to 1800; Gaelic Catholic State, Making of; Hiberno-English; Newspapers; **Primary Documents:** Letter to John A. Costello, the Taoiseach (5 April 1951)

Bibliography

Bord na Gaeilge. *The Irish Language in a Changing Society: Shaping the Future.* 1988.

Ó Murchú, Máirtín. *The Irish Language.* 1985.

Ó Riagáin, Pádraig. *Language Policy and Social Reproduction: Ireland, 1893–1993.* 1997

Ó Riagáin, Pádraig, ed. "Language Planning in Ireland." *International Journal of the Sociology of Language,* no. 70. 1988.

Pádraig Ó Riagáin

Larkin, James

Born in the Irish slums of Victorian Liverpool, James Larkin (1876–1947) grew to become an influential labor leader in early twentieth-century Britain, Ireland and the United States. Larkin was a firm believer in syndicalism—the notion that trade-union involvement in direct industrial action was the best vehicle to bring about the socialist revolution. A fiery speaker and charismatic leader, Larkin excelled at mobilizing and organizing workers, inspiring fervent loyalty in his followers and equally emotive hatred in his opponents.

Larkin did important work in organizing for the National Union of Dock Labourers in Britain, but it was

Socialist James Larkin (1876–1947) headed the Irish Transport and General Workers' Union during the notorious lockout of 1913. The union-busting lockout was engineered by the Employers' Federation under the lead of the wealthy businessman and newspaper proprietor William Martin Murphy. Some 20,000 Dublin workers took sympathetic action in opposition to the lockout. Early in 1914 the conflict ended in defeat for the union. A discouraged Larkin spent the next nine years in the United States. © HULTON-DEUTSCH COLLECTION/CORBIS. REPRINTED BY PERMISSION.

his Irish career that gave Larkin an international reputation. He first arrived in Ireland in 1907, determined to organize labor at Irish ports. Starting his work in Belfast, he briefly brought Catholic and Protestant workers together before his short-lived union was shattered by traditional sectarian animosities.

Undaunted by his failure in Belfast, Larkin moved on to Dublin to organize dockworkers there. It was here that Larkin achieved his greatest success, founding the Irish Transport and General Workers' Union (ITGWU) in 1908. Aided by James Connolly, Larkin oversaw the rapid growth of the ITGWU from a fledging union to a force with 14,000 members by 1913. Determined to make their mark, Larkin and Connolly took on the business empire of William Martin Murphy, one of Dublin's leading entrepreneurs. Equally determined to face down and break Larkin's union, Murphy organized the Employers' Federation, which agreed to take on the ITGWU in 1913. The showdown that ensued—the great Lockout of 1913—resulted in a bitter defeat for the union.

Larkin left Ireland for the United States in the following year.

Although he had not planned on staying so long, Larkin remained in the United States for nine years, speaking out against the war effort and participating in the foundation of the American Communist Party. When he returned to Ireland in 1923, he found conditions much changed. Faced with the aggressively conservative Catholic atmosphere of the newly formed Irish Free State, Larkin's influence was much reduced. "Big Jim" Larkin, that towering figure of Irish labor, lived out his days in relative quiet, dying in his sleep in January 1947.

SEE ALSO Connolly, James; Irish Women Worker's Union; Labor Movement; Lockout of 1913; Markievicz, Countess Constance; Murphy, William Martin; O'Brien, William; Trade Unions

Bibliography

Daly, Mary E. *Dublin, the Deposed Capital: A Social and Economic History, 1860–1914.* 1985.

Gray, John. *City in Revolt: James Larkin and the Belfast Dock Strike of 1907.* 1985.

Larkin, Emmet. *James Larkin: Irish Labour Leader, 1876–1947.* 1965.

Sean Farrell

Latin and Old Irish Literacy

The oldest physically surviving examples of Irish-language literacy are a few hundred inscriptions written in the Morse code–like alphabet called *ogham.* Almost all of these simply record names of people. They are found carved on large stones across southern Ireland (particularly Cork and Kerry) and in Irish-influenced parts of western Britain, and they date from about the fourth century C.E. to the seventh. For the invention of the ogham alphabet itself, a dating only a little earlier than that of the first extant inscriptions has been proposed, but it is certain that only a fraction of the earliest evidence has survived, so the script may have originated as soon as the influences inspiring it began to be felt in Gaeldom. The main such influence is believed to have been the Roman alphabet. This was used primarily for writing Latin (some of the stones in Britain give a Roman-letter "translation" into Latin of the Irish name that appears in ogham). By the second century C.E. at the latest, the Roman invasion of Britain had brought Latin, as a potentially culture-affecting force, to the shores of the Irish Sea (and probably across it; there is known to have been Roman trade with Ireland and arguably some transient settlement). Although Ireland was and remained outside the Roman empire, it may therefore have been as early as this that educated but hitherto illiterate Irish-speaking circles first gained the fairly minimal access to Latinity that they needed for the ogham script to be devised.

Whether or not some knowledge of Latin reached Ireland before the Christian gospel did, the language was necessarily involved in the establishment of the religion there: Irish churches could not have been part of Catholic Christendom, as they were, without using some Latin right from their foundation. Of Latin works known to have been written in early Ireland, the oldest that survive in terms of composition (not in physical terms; they are probably copies of copies) are two letters authored by the Briton Saint Patrick, probably in the fifth century. As Christianity was believed until recently to have been first introduced to Ireland by Patrick, he and his epistles have conventionally been seen as marking the necessary introduction of Latin literacy to the island as well. But not only does the ogham phenomenon precede his traditional dates, Irish Christianity is now recognized to do so too. So unless Patrick was actually active before the fifth century, Latin reached Ireland first.

Weak as Latin culture still was in Ireland in Patrick's day, his sixth-century successors established it firmly. The Latin of the writing tradition that they set up is known to have been pronounced in a markedly British fashion; thus they too were from Britain. These evangelists were doubtless inspired in many cases by the zeal that appears to have swept the larger island after the publication there of *De excidio Britanniae* (The ruin of Britain), a prophetic call for reformation in church and state by their compatriot Gildas. His ability to compose this erudite work a century or more after the fall of Rome shows that Latin learning was still strong in Britain at that time, and the prestige the work conferred probably played a major part in invigorating the stylish and productive British-Latin tradition that continued down to Norman times. Elements of that tradition surviving from the seventh century fall into a penitential genre, which spread to Ireland: We have Hiberno-Latin examples from the same century. By the year 700, Ireland had produced a significant body of Latin in other genres, too, that has come down to us, albeit preserved in later manuscripts. Accomplished authors responsible include Cummian (computistics), "Augustinus" Hibernicus (theology), Virgilius Maro Grammaticus (idiosyncratic philological discourse), and Cogitosus and Muirchú (hagiography), as well as anonymous writers of poetry and legal and historical works. Indeed, the debt of Hiberno-Latin culture to the outside world was being actively repaid during that period: Seventh-century English scholars frequently traveled to Ireland for further study, while influential Irishmen such as Saint Columbanus (d. 615) had begun to spearhead a continent-wide monastic movement that did much to keep Latin learning alive on a wider stage in troubled times.

As soon as Celtic scribes began to write Latin texts on vellum, they probably included Latinized versions of Celtic names (Patrick and Gildas both did this). But the first extant manuscript material to constitute real Celtic-medium writing consists of explanatory glosses added in Irish to Latin texts penned from the early seventh century onwards. Given their ancillary nature, these physically earliest examples have been seen as reaching us from a stage not long after the actual beginning of the (manuscript) writing of Irish. However, Irish glosses in a famous Würzburg manuscript, though themselves of the eighth century, show traces of a spelling system whose invention must predate the introduction of British-Latin pronunciation by Saint Patrick's successors. Indeed, this system shows links with ogham orthography. Can it have originated in the same period? Ogham on stone was formerly felt to have been a pagan phenomenon that gave way to the Christian practice of writing manuscripts in Roman letters on vellum. But some ogham stones also display Christian crosses. Since ogham's straight strokes are ideally suited to carving, the choice of alphabet may actually have been determined more by the medium than by the culture. So the same people who carved inscriptions using ogham may also have written on vellum using the Roman alphabet. The ogham was Irish-language; any contemporary Roman-letter material will have been primarily Latin-medium, but may it have included Celtic as well? It is true that some of the stones survive while no physically contemporary manuscript texts do; but then, only ten manuscripts (in either language) went on to survive on Irish soil from even as late as 1000 C.E., and hundreds are known to have existed by then.

At all events, once Irish-medium manuscript literacy was established in a form that comes down to us, it can be seen blossoming in a variety of genres, including theological tracts, saints' lives, legal material, poetry, and ultimately the great prose tales. Early Irish literacy also displays an astonishing assurance. By the year 700 fully bilingual material was being written, showing that (uniquely for a vernacular) Irish-medium literacy was esteemed equally with Latin. It cannot be coincidence that, during the mainstream Old Irish period that followed, this literacy went on to constitute the earliest and, for its day, by far the largest body of nonclassical vernacular written material in Europe (a distinction often, but erroneously, claimed for Old English).

SEE ALSO Early Medieval Ireland and Christianity; Literature: Early and Medieval Literature; Religion: The Coming of Christianity; Saint Patrick, Problem of

Bibliography

Harvey, Anthony. "Latin, Literacy, and the Celtic Vernaculars around the Year AD 500." In *Celtic Languages and Celtic Peoples*, edited by Cyril J. Byrne, Margaret Harry, and Pádraig Ó Siadhail. 1992.

Harvey, Anthony. "Problems in Dating the Origin of the Ogham Script." In *Roman, Runes, and Ogham*, edited by John Higgitt, Katherine Forsyth, and David N. Parsons. 2001.

Howlett, D. R. *The Celtic Latin Tradition of Biblical Style.* 1995.

Jackson, Kenneth. *Language and History in Early Britain.* 1953. Reprint, 1994.

Lapidge, Michael, and Richard Sharpe. *A Bibliography of Celtic-Latin Literature, 400–1200.* 1985.

McManus, Damian. *A Guide to Ogam.* 1991.

Stevenson, Jane. "The Beginnings of Literacy in Ireland." *Proceedings of the Royal Irish Academy* 89 C (1989): 127–165.

Anthony Harvey

Legal Change in the Sixteenth and Seventeenth Centuries

Law reform in early seventeenth century Ireland arose from the English victory over Hugh O'Neill, the Earl of Tyrone, who led the last great Gaelic uprising during the Nine Years War (1593–1603). This military victory represented a necessary and primary phase in English domination over Ireland, but a second stage of political consolidation by judicial means was equally essential. Of the Crown lawyers laboring to reform Irish administration at the beginning of the seventeenth century, the most important was Sir John Davies, an Oxford-educated Middle-Temple lawyer who also studied briefly with the Dutch civilian Paul Merula at Leyden in the Netherlands.

Davies' Jacobean Irish career as solicitor-general (1603–1606) and attorney-general (1606–1619) left a permanent mark on Irish law, administration, and jurisprudence. This legacy is best evidenced by his Irish *Law Reports*, which reveal two distinct patterns in cases argued before the central Irish courts. The first is the application of continental jurisprudence, particularly the impact of military conquest, on the laws and customs governing real property in Ireland. The second is the number of cases decided by judicial resolution or collective decision arising from either the Irish or, on at least two occasions, the English judiciaries acting in conclave.

As propounded by Davies, the right of conquest vested England with a public-law title to Ireland. He argued that conquest-right justified eradication of domestic Irish or *brehon* law since it amounted to little more than a "barbarous and lewd custom" whose only goal was to eliminate all competing foreign or Gaelic claims to Irish dominion. Davies' main objective and most difficult problem was to reconstruct land property rights, especially those held by customary Gaelic tenures derived from political authority other than the Crown.

In what has been described as a lineage or clan-based society, *brehon* law vested property rights in the corporation of the extended kin group. In practice this meant that individual holdings of land in Gaelic districts were temporary and subject to periodic redistribution, either by what contemporaries referred to as the custom of gavelkind, or by a scheme of succession known as the custom of tanistry. By the term gavelkind, Davies was referring to the distinctive custom of inheritance in Kent, by which lands descended to all legitimate male heirs in equal portions instead of by primogeniture, as was the case in the rest of England. In Ireland and Wales, however, the custom deviated from Kentish practice by excluding women from inheritance and allowing bastard males a share alongside legitimate heirs.

In addition to such temporary rights in land, there also existed in Ireland the custom of tanistry, a scheme of succession whereby the replacement of a chief or king was nominated during the lifetime of the man to be succeeded. The office of tanist usually included lands and other privileges. But Davies and other English jurists employed their own concepts of property to define tanistry as a kind of life trust in land for which there existed no ultimate proprietorship. To assimilate native forms of property and landholding, the Irish judiciary simply invalidated both gavelkind and tanistry by resolution of all the Irish justices. In practice abolition of native custom by judicial fiat meant that prior possession might be respected, but unless accepted as lawful by the sovereign or the judiciary, Irish tenures had no validity against a superior common-law title. In other words, legal sanction by the conquering power was necessary to validate or create rights over real property in Ireland. It was this perception of Gaelic law and society that influenced plantation schemes and laid the foundation for native policy in Ireland during the first decade of the seventeenth century.

That judicial resolutions became a prominent instrument for Irish law reform may surprise some who view the doctrine of precedent as a singularly modern concept. But this orthodox position neglects to take into account a development of great importance in early modern English legal history—the emergence, in England, of the Exchequer Chamber for debate. The Court of Exchequer of course had its own statutory jurisdictions, but as early as the fifteenth century and increasingly during the sixteenth and seventeenth centuries, it appears that difficult matters of law might be referred to the Exchequer Chamber for discussion by all the justices of the King's Bench and Common Pleas, together with the Barons of the Exchequer. When the assembled judiciary had reached agreement, the decision was recorded in a certificate, referred back to the original tribunal, and read before the court. This practice placed the judges in the unique position of reviewing case law to articulate authoritative principles in a manner consistent with a modern doctrine of precedent.

Davies's Irish *Law Reports* reveal that a similar practice existed in Jacobean Ireland. The reasons are complex, but most likely the absence of a malleable parliament (whose members were still mainly catholic) elevated judge-made law over statute law as the preferred instrument to consolidate the Tudor conquest of the island. The Irish judiciary proscribed the customary Gaelic forms of land tenure and succession by judicial resolution. Soon afterward, the judges applied the same resolutions to invalidate native Irish titles that stood in the way of the Ulster plantation. Other judicial resolutions sought to erode the once privileged position of the Old English and, for the most part, Catholic descendants of those who settled in Ireland before the Reformation. As in the cases voiding the customary forms of Gaelic landholding and descent, the government initiated three judicial resolutions to (1) enforce religious conformity by validating a proclamation extending to Ireland the English penal laws passed by late Elizabethan parliaments; (2) eliminate extensive corporate liberties, including appropriations of customs revenue; and (3) reform the national coinage in ways that eroded Irish trade and commerce. Taken collectively, the effect of these judicial resolutions on cases argued before the courts by Sir John Davies amounted to a wholesale redefinition of the nature of English sovereignty in Ireland.

In trials argued by Davies before the central Irish courts, the cases of gavelkind and tanistry proved the most enduring. During the eighteenth and nineteenth centuries, Davies' Irish legacy occasionally appeared in litigation arising from English claims to distant lands. As early as 1694, William Salkeld, an English sergeant-at-law, reported the case of Blankard *vs.* Galdy, referred from Jamaica to the King's Bench, in which the justices cited Davies' case of tanistry to define the status of conquered kingdoms. This doctrine provided continuity for both a colonial jurisprudence and a strategy of imperial control over conquered territories. The doctrine was to appear again in an anonymous Chancery case reported by Peer Williams in 1722. According to Williams, conquest-right allowed the English state to impose or modify whatever laws it deemed necessary to govern the conquered territory. Writing later in the century, Sir William Blackstone incorporated the principles set forward by the anonymous case of 1722 in his discussion of overseas plantations and colonies, expanding the doctrine to cover territories acquired by session as well as conquest.

The formula was later corroborated by Sir Frederick Pollock's comments on the "external conquests of the common law," in which English law was seen to regulate the legal systems of India, the Sudan, and other territories within the empire. Indeed, research done on behalf of the United Nations Educational, Scientific, and Cultural Organization (UNESCO) in 1966 strongly suggests that Davies's formula became the basis for defining the status of native law and landholding throughout British overseas possessions. His formula for Ireland—"to give laws to a conquered people is the principal mark of a perfect conquest"—helped establish a paradigm for British expansion elsewhere.

SEE ALSO Brehon Law; Colonial Theory from 1500 to 1690; English Government in Medieval Ireland; Land Settlements from 1500 to 1690; Politics: 1500 to 1690; **Primary Documents:** From *A Discovery of the True Causes Why Ireland Was Never Entirely Subdued* (1612)

Bibliography

Davies, Sir John. *Le Primer report des cases & matters en ley resolves & adiudges en les Courts del Roy en Ireland.* 1615. Translated as *A Report of Cases and Matters in Law Resolved and Adjudged in the King's Courts in Ireland.* 1762.

A Discovery of the True Causes Why Ireland Was Never Subdued Nor Brought under Obedience of the Crown of England. 1612.

McCavitt, J. "'Good Planets in Their Several Spheares': The Establishment of the Assize Courts in Early Seventeenth-Century Ireland." *Irish Jurist* (1994): 248–278.

Pawlisch, Hans S. *Sir John Davies and the Conquest of Ireland: A Study in Legal Imperialism.* 1985.

Hans S. Pawlisch

≈

Lemass, Seán

Seán Lemass (1899–1971) was born on 15 July in Ballybrack, Co. Dublin. He participated in the 1916 Easter Rising and was later involved in the War of Independence and the Civil War. Research suggests that Lemass was one of the notorious "twelve apostles," a ruthless covert unit organized by the leader of the Irish Republican Brotherhood (IRB), Michael Collins. These men destroyed the British intelligence network in Ireland on Bloody Sunday, 21 November 1920, killing eleven members of the Cairo Gang, a crack unit of British intelligence agents handpicked by Winston Churchill to destroy Collins and the IRB. During the Irish Civil War, Lemass stood with those who opposed the 1921 Anglo-Irish Treaty as a betrayal of the revolution.

Lemass was a founding member of the political party Fianna Fáil, which was established in October 1926. As one of Eamon de Valera's most trusted lieutenants, Lemass played an important role in building the impressive political machine that has dominated Irish political life. When Fianna Fáil came to power in 1932, Lemass held a number of critical cabinet posts. Initially, he was minister for industry and commerce; during the "Emergency"(World War II, when Ireland was neutral) he became minister for supplies; and in 1945 he was named tánaiste. During this period Lemass earned a well-deserved reputation for being an effective administrator. Throughout his career he promoted efficiency in all spheres of Irish life. In 1959, at the age of sixty, Seán Lemass stepped out of de Valera's shadow to become taoiseach.

He was taoiseach during a period that many observers define as a watershed in the history of modern Ireland. Along with the secretary of the Department of Finance, T. K. Whitaker, Lemass developed a critical economic initiative that helped to reinvigorate a stagnant Irish economy. In fact, he is closely associated with the remarkable transformation of Ireland's economy in the early1960s. Lemass also made a concerted effort to improve relations between Dublin and Belfast, making an

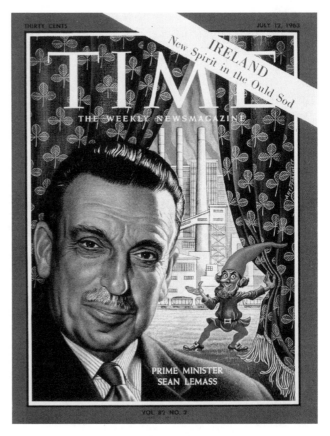

Time *magazine's cover story of 12 July 1963 presented Ireland as a country that was becoming a modern industrial economy, thanks to the leadership of Prime Minister (Taoiseach) Seán Lemass.* © TIME LIFE PICTURES/GETTY IMAGES. REPRODUCED BY PERMISSION.

historic trip to Belfast in 1965 to meet Terence O'Neill, the prime minister of Northern Ireland.

Lemass is remembered as an activist and a leader who was not afraid of taking chances to achieve results. His efforts to reinvigorate the Irish economy and to develop a dialogue with Northern Ireland were bold initiatives aimed at improving the lives of Irish citizens. His economic initiatives proved successful, but his attempt to improve relations with Northern Ireland ultimately failed.

SEE ALSO de Valera, Eamon; Economic Relations between Independent Ireland and Britain; Economic Relations between North and South since 1922; Industry since 1920; O'Neill, Terence; Overseas Investment; Political Parties in Independent Ireland; Politics: Independent Ireland since 1922; State Enterprise; United Nations; **Primary Documents:** Speech to Ministers of the Governments of the Member States of the European Economic Community (18 January

1962); On Community Relations in Northern Ireland (28 April 1967)

Bibliography

Bew, Paul, and Henry Patterson. *Seán Lemass and the Making of Modern Ireland, 1945–66.* 1982.

Horgan, John. *Seán Lemass: The Enigmatic Patriot.* 1997.

Savage, Robert J. *Seán Lemass.* 1999.

Robert J. Savage, Jr.

~

Literacy and Popular Culture

Beginning in the middle of the eighteenth century, the culture of the majority of the population in Ireland was increasingly influenced by the written word, particularly the printed word in English. The context within which this happened was an economic expansion, involving the growing commercialization of agriculture in the south of Ireland and the development of large-scale rural industry in northern areas. These processes led to greater frequency and regularity of market transactions and use of written documents, which increased the value of reading and writing not just for commercial farmers and tradesmen but also for small farmers and weavers. Moreover, a shortage of precious metals during the French wars of 1793 to 1815 led to a new reliance on paper money for even small transactions. Alongside this increased market activity, the population had greater contact with state agents and institutions: Irish recruitment to the British army was substantial between the 1760s and the 1820s, and in the early nineteenth century saw the establishment of a court system which was accessible to most of the population. These interactions raised the value and prestige of literacy.

The mechanism through which literacy was achieved for most people in Ireland was the small informal school, sometimes known as the "hedge school." These were private institutions where irregularly attending pupils received rudimentary instruction, consisting initially of reading, writing for those who persevered, and perhaps arithmetic. The autonomous nature of these schools stood in contrast to the western European norm, where elementary schooling was principally carried out by the state church. In Ireland most schools were independent not only of the state church but also of the other churches, including the Catholic

Church, to which the majority of the population belonged. This did not mean, however, that there was no religious component to education and literacy, as clergy of different denominations frequently examined the pupils in catechism.

By the middle of the eighteenth century the independence of schools was preoccupying secular and religious authorities. Their anxiety was heightened in the aftermath of the rebellion of 1798, which was concentrated in the most literate regions of Ireland, and many conservative commentators pointed to the involvement of schoolmasters in the rebellion. This led on the one hand to a series of state investigations into elementary education beginning in 1806, and on the other to the establishment of educational societies, mainly religious in inspiration, dedicated to providing alternative schooling. These had made a significant impact by the 1820s.

The earliest systematic enumeration of schools was carried out in state reports of the mid-1820s. They showed that almost 600,000 pupils, about 40 percent of the relevant age group, attended schools. More than 70 percent of these attended independent private schools, 20 percent attended the schools of the educational societies, 6 percent attended Catholic Church schools, and the rest went to Anglican Church schools. This confirmed the prevalence of "hedge schools," while the religious nature of the schools of the educational societies, coupled with the renewed prominence of the Catholic question in the politics of the 1820s, meant that education became a denominational as well as a political battleground. The state eventually favored the creation of a nondenominational national system of education, which was established in 1831. This involved less the setting up of new schools than the subsidization of existing schools, provided that certain organizational and curricular conditions were met. Over the following decades the vast majority of primary schools entered this system.

While a great deal is known about schools in the early nineteenth century as a result of state investigations, less is known about the levels of literacy they produced. The standard measurement of writing ability in early modern Europe is the ability to sign a contract or a marriage register, but few such sources survive in Ireland. The first comprehensive record is to be found in the population census of 1841. This census, and the decennial censuses that followed, measured self-assessed (rather than tested) levels of reading and writing. It also measured literacy in English only.

The 1841 census reported that 25 percent of the population over 5 years old claimed to be able to read and write, and a further 22 percent to read only. Of those able to read, levels varied between men and

In this painting of c. 1850 by Henry McManus, a well-dressed gentleman reads the Nation *newspaper to people whose dress marks them as middle class. Many sources indicate, however, that before the famine the educated often provided the unlettered with the news by reading papers aloud in public. As literacy steadily improved after 1850, newspaper sales soared.* NATIONAL GALLERY OF IRELAND, CAT. NO. 1917. REPRODUCED BY PERMISSION.

women (54 percent and 44 percent) and between town and country (64 percent and 45 percent). Geographical variation was more marked, from 85 percent or more in parts of Ulster to 15 percent or less in parts of Connacht. This is due partly to differing levels of market participation and contact with state institutions, and partly to a greater prominence of a religiously based literacy among the Protestant population of the northeast. This region had very high numbers of women who were able to read only; this was the result of a highly catechized culture that emphasized the reading of religious texts by both sexes equally.

Analysis of the 1841 population by age reveals that reading ability was present, to varying degrees, in most parts of Ireland by the late eighteenth century. It was rudimentary and infrequently practiced, however, and the culture remained mostly oral. In consequence, there was an oral element to many of the early manifestations of literacy. In this partially literate society, in which the printed word was still relatively expensive, texts would usually be read aloud in "group readings."

Over the longer term this new, mainly lower-class, reading public constituted a market for cheap printed material, and by the middle of the eighteenth century a specialized sector within the printing trade had emerged to supply it. Its products were sold principally by hawkers and peddlers in town and city streets and at fairs. They were also commonly used in schools as reading matter for pupils who had progressed beyond elementary readers, since other texts were not available. These texts were short and cheap, printed on inferior paper, and were suitable for reading or singing aloud. An example, common in Ireland as well as in Britain during the eighteenth century, was the gallows speech of a condemned criminal, printed on a single sheet and sold at the execution.

The most widespread and cheapest form of printed material was the single-sheet ballad. These usually cost a halfpenny and were sold by traveling singers. They represented the clearest combination of oral and literate, since they were purchased, read, memorized, and then absorbed into oral culture independently of their printed form. These ballads covered a wide range of subjects. Some of them, such as love songs or songs of emigration, were permanently available and constituted a corpus that remained stable for many decades. Others, related to a topical item such as a sensational murder or trial, would be sold only for a short time. The ballad trade was highly responsive to current affairs. Contested parliamentary elections prompted many ballads, usually written and paid for by the candidates or their supporters. They were also an integral part of wider political mobilization, and huge amounts were produced by the United Irish organization in the 1790s and by the O'Connellite movements of the 1820s and 1840s. Ballad production continued in the second half of the nineteenth century, but with a marked shift toward a more "respectable" content. Political ballads in particular were less violent, probably reflecting the higher social basis of political participation: ballads from the tithe war of the 1830s, for example, frequently featured graphic description of violent incidents, whereas nationalist ballads after 1850 used a more generalized rhetoric. This trend is also noticeable in Protestant or Orange ballads of the same period.

Longer texts were sold in the form of small books of 12, 24, or 48 pages, although some were as long as 144 pages. Given the relative lack of affluence of the readers and the infrequency of their purchases, the cheap-print market was slow, and there was remarkably little change in the titles available from the middle of the eighteenth century until the late nineteenth. Catechisms and yearly almanacs were probably the most commonly possessed items and demonstrate, respectively, the penetration of a uniform religious culture and the recognition of a more abstract sense of time. The favored genres of western European popular print were also obtainable—episodes from medieval and early modern chivalric romances, the lives and adventures of highwaymen and other criminals, and abridgements of more recent elite prose works such as *Robinson Crusoe.*

Like the ballads, these mainly episodic prose narratives were suited to oral performance. They were read aloud partly because not everyone could read and partly because of the relative expense for a lower-class audience of even the cheapest printed works. In this way print culture did not so much supplant oral culture as interact productively with it.

To the body of popular printed texts were added two new elements in the 1820s and 1830s. The first of these was produced by the educational societies that had been established in the early nineteenth century. Although their principal concern was with schooling and teaching basic literacy, some of them went further and became publishers of short books intended initially for use in their schools and later for wider distribution. The most active society on this front was the Society for Promoting the Education of the Poor of Ireland, known as the Kildare Place Society, which published almost eighty titles between 1817 and 1825 and distributed them widely. Like the society's schools, its texts aimed at moral and social reform of the population; their content consisted of practical advice as well as moral exhortation and argument. By the early 1820s the Kildare Place Society had come to be perceived as a proselytizing agency by Catholics, a group of whom set up in response a cheap-book company of their own, the Catholic Book Society, in 1827. This society was active for twenty years or so, publishing devotional and moral texts.

The second element was also associated with an educational innovation—the national schools. The new education system of 1831 aimed at a nationally uniform curriculum, and so commissioned its own set of graded readers whose use was a condition of affiliation with the system (and therefore of funding). There were six textbooks in all, the most advanced of which contained complex texts on science and economics; in practice, most pupils read the first two books, at most. Like the texts of the educational societies, on which indeed they were modeled, the content of these readers was predominantly moral and religious (though nondenominational). They were in use throughout the nineteenth century. Overall, with a single centrally controlled curriculum, the national schools were one of the most powerful agents of a uniform state culture in the nineteenth century and later.

Beginning in the middle of the eighteenth century, the demand for affordable printed material that accompanied the rise of popular literacy was served by a solid cheap-print and small-book trade. This vastly increased the amount of information and variety of ideas circulating in Ireland. The cheap-print business was steady rather than spectacular. It was not affected by the Act of Union of 1800, which extended copyright law to Ireland and was detrimental to elite publishing, and in fact it was boosted by periods of increased political activity and by the activities of educationalists.

More fundamentally, popular literacy was an instrument of a broader process of language shift, as English replaced Irish as the predominant spoken language in Ireland. English was the legal language, and the market functioned with documents and money (contracts and banknotes) written in English. Consequently, literacy and schooling in English was desirable. The print trade was concentrated in anglophone larger towns, particularly in Dublin, and the circulating printed texts were also overwhelmingly in English. This did not mean, however, that literary production in Irish did not exist: A tradition of manuscript production in Irish, continuous with an older Gaelic cultural order, flourished until the mid-nineteenth century, particularly in Munster and south Leinster. Until the 1840s, scribes, often schoolmasters by profession, continued to copy old poetry and prose, as well as to compose new works in Irish. More commercial print production in Irish also existed, particularly in the first half of the nineteenth century, again most markedly in Munster, with publishing centers in Limerick, Cork, and Clonmel. It was principally religious and was dominated by Catholic catechisms and short devotional works. Because these books were purchased and read by an audience that had become literate in English, and were produced by a print trade that functioned in English (there is no known printer who produced works in Irish only), their form was heavily influenced by English-language literacy. Their typefaces were roman as opposed to gaelic, their orthography was simplified, and their title pages were often in English. Even more striking is the hybrid nature of the main secular texts printed in Irish—broadsheet ballads. These used a phonetic script that was read as if it were English but sounded in Irish. Some of them mixed the two languages, with alternating verses in English and Irish demonstrating the complexity of usage in a diglossic society.

It might be expected that the Great Famine, which had a catastrophic effect on the very poor and therefore the illiterate, would be a watershed in the development of a literate popular culture in Ireland. In purely statistical terms this was not so. National levels of literacy, as reported in the population censuses, continued a steady increase from 1841 to the end of the nineteenth century. At the same time, those able to read did so with far greater ease and frequency in the second half of the nineteenth century. This was due to changes in schooling and in the availability of printed matter. Primary-school pupils spent much more time in school—five or

six years instead of one or two prefamine—with fewer seasonal interruptions, and they were taught reading and writing simultaneously. The proportion of those who could read but not write was in continuous decline and had almost disappeared by 1900. In addition, very high levels of attendance meant that the gender distribution of literacy skills, and of writing in particular, was becoming more equal. This was almost all achieved within the primary-school system (that is, in the national schools) because very few pupils proceeded to a secondary education. In 1871 almost one million children were attending primary schools and only about 25,000 secondary, a ratio of only 40 to 1.

The second development that shaped popular literate culture after 1850 was the increasing ownership of printed matter and the ease of access to it. This is particularly evident in the case of newspapers. A rise in average incomes after the Great Famine coincided with the lowering of the price of newspapers as a result of the ending of stamp tax in 1855 and of paper tax in 1861. A single issue of a newspaper in the 1860s cost a quarter of what it had in the 1840s. In addition, there was an increase in the number of newspapers from 73 in 1849 to 122 in 1879. This increase was concentrated at the cheaper end of the market (where a copy cost one penny), among dailies as opposed to weeklies, and within the nationalist press as opposed to the conservative unionist papers, which had dominated before 1850. Geographically, what stood out was the increase in the proportion of papers published outside Dublin, so that by the late nineteenth century almost all towns with a population of 3,500 or more had a newspaper; this development was facilitated by the introduction of the electric telegraph at mid-century, which dispelled the time advantage previously enjoyed by Dublin and London papers in reporting news from Britain. The press also penetrated rural areas, with a weekly paper being bought on Sundays.

All of these papers reported local news, but they were also important to the integration of Ireland into the international economy because they carried reports of market prices, as well as information and advertisements relating to emigration, which was a universal feature of Irish life after the Great Famine. The implications of these changes can be seen in the far greater role of newspapers in political agitations such as the Land War of 1879 to 1881. The organization of meetings in the early stages of the tenant campaign was carried out through local newspapers, and a prominent role was played by editors such as James Daly of the *Connaught Telegraph* in Mayo and Tim Harrington of the *Kerry Sentinel* in Tralee.

The cheap-book trade, by contrast, became more centralized after 1850, owing to changes in print technology (which increased the capital intensity of the industry) and to the greater ease of distribution on railways. Ballad and book publishing, which in the early nineteenth century had been well established in cities such as Limerick and Cork and also in towns as small as Monaghan and Strabane, was increasingly concentrated in larger firms in Dublin and Belfast. These firms marketed newer forms of popular literature in branded series. The earliest was the Parlour Library of the Belfast publishers Simms and McIntyre, begun in 1847. James Duffy of Dublin, the largest publisher of Catholic and nationalist works, had ten different series in print in the 1860s. The same processes of cost efficiency and distribution meant that the cheap-book market in Ireland could be served from outside the island. Duffy's competitors for the Catholic nationalist market, for example, included Cameron and Ferguson of Glasgow and John Denvir of Liverpool.

The centralization of the trade had dire implications for printing in Irish, for the Dublin and Belfast publishers were almost entirely anglophone. In any case, the number of Irish-speakers declined rapidly beginning in the middle of the nineteenth century, and popular literate culture in Irish declined at the same time. The production of cheap printed matter in Irish in the decades after 1850 was a fraction of what it had been. The same was true of manuscripts, and those that were produced show a marked turn toward English-language print norms, with those in Connacht often using a phonetic script. At the beginning of the twentieth century there was a striking increase in the amount of publishing in Irish, particularly in Dublin. But this was less a revival than the creation of a new literate culture in Irish among urban English-speakers. The majority of the texts sold were language primers, and there was an accompanying debate over the forms of language, orthography, and typeface to be used. Simple forms of the language were usually chosen, but so was a gaelic typeface rather than the roman to which readers were accustomed. By the middle decades of the twentieth century the revival had inspired a small but vibrant literary and literate subculture in rural Irish-speaking districts as well as in urban centers.

The vast majority of the population remained English-speaking, of course, and widespread literacy in English was achieved by the early years of the twentieth century. There was one school for every 150 children, 95 percent of pupils attended national schools, attendance was compulsory, and tuition fees had been abolished. The reading public was served by a long-standing and vigorous trade in popular printing, and for over a century there had been a print element in popular culture, not so much supplanting oral culture as coexisting with it, borrowing from it and enriching it at the same time.

SEE ALSO Arts: Early Modern Literature and the Arts from 1500 to 1800; Balladry in English; Chapbooks and Popular Literature; Cusack, Michael; Duffy, James; Education: Primary Private Education—"Hedge Schools" and Other Schools; Education: Primary Public Education—National Schools from 1831; Education: Secondary Education, Female; Education: Secondary Education, Male; Gaelic Revivalism: The Gaelic Athletic Association; Gaelic Revivalism: The Gaelic League; Hyde, Douglas; Kildare Place Society; Language and Literacy: Decline of Irish Language; Literature: Gaelic Writing from 1607 to 1800; Murphy, William Martin; Newspapers; Raifteara (Raftery), Antaine; Sullivan Brothers (A. M. and T. D.); **Primary Documents:** On Irish Society before the Famine (1841–1843)

Bibliography

Cullen, L. M. *The Emergence of Modern Ireland, 1600–1900.* 1981.

Legg, Marie-Louise. *Newspapers and Nationalism: The Irish Provincial Press, 1850–1892.* 1999.

Logan, John. "Schooling and the promotion of Literacy in Nineteenth-Century Ireland." Ph.D diss., University College Cork, 1992.

Ó Ciosáin, Niall. *Print and Popular Culture in Ireland, 1750–1850.* 1997.

Niall Ó Ciosáin

Literary Renaissance (Celtic Revival)

By the mid–1880s in Ireland the stirrings of a revival of literature had begun that was part of the cultural, artistic, and political awakening that contributed to the creation of a nation in the 1920s. Writers central to this revival tended to commit themselves consciously to the project of recovering as well as creating a national literature. As claimed by W. B. Yeats (1865–1939), the westward-moving Renaissance had been stalled for three hundred years of repressive British rule. The failure of the Parnellites to bring Home Rule to Ireland roughly coincided with the return from exile of the Fenian John O'Leary (1830–1907), around whom rallied young disciples such as Yeats, Maud Gonne (1866–1953), and T. W. Rolleston (1857–1920). Rolleston became editor of the *Dublin University Review* in 1885 and, with Yeats, a founding member of the Rhymers' Club in London and the Irish Literary Society. The Society developed a proposal for a New Irish Library, a series of books to honor Irish culture, with Rolleston and Douglas Hyde (1860–1949) as editors. Yeats' work in the press was particularly notable for defining the "best Irish books" for a public whose appetite for reading was stimulated by the mannerisms of his own richly symbolic, incantatory early poems. The lists featured the translations and scholarship of Hyde, Standish O'Grady (1846–1928), and Sir Samuel Ferguson (1810–1886), as well as poetry by close friends such as Katharine Tynan Hinkson (1861–1931) and George Russell, or "AE" (1867–1935).

The Irish Literary Renaissance had two geographic centers in Dublin and in London. A traveler between the two, Yeats acted as a synthesizing agent. As a member of the Rhymers' Club, he propounded and adapted himself to the tenets of the primarily British Decadent poets of the *fin de siècle*, including Anglo-Irish playwright Oscar Wilde (1854–1900), Ernest Dowson (1867–1900), Lionel Johnson (1867–1902), Arthur Symons (1865–1945) and others whom he dubbed "the tragic generation" (pp. 219–266). He quarreled with fellow members of the Irish National Alliance on the politics and poetry of Thomas Davis (1814–1845), particularly with friend-turned-enemy Frank Hugh O'Donnell (1848–1916), and enlisted Lionel Johnson in the defense, later publishing a collection of Johnson's poetry and the book *Poetry and Ireland* (1908), with essays by Yeats and Johnson. In Ireland, Yeats's interest in magic brought him into conflict with O'Leary, a Young Ireland Society member and the influential author of *Recollections of Fenians and Fenianism* (1896), though Yeats's interests agreed with those of his former art schoolmate, the visionary poet and editor, AE. The amalgamation of competing interests led for a time to an idealized, nationalist-oriented poetry of rarified senses and vague or fantastic symbolism named after the title of one of Yeats's books, *The Celtic Twilight* (1893) and its culminating poem, "Into the Twilight." The attempt to collect and define as a phenomenon the poetry of the Celtic Revival helped to promote the work of like-minded individuals and define a "book of the people." *A Book of Irish Verse* (1895), edited by Yeats and dedicated "To the Members of the National Literary Society of Dublin and the Irish Literary Society of London," featured poetry by Rolleston, Hyde, Tynan (Hinkson), Johnson, AE, several other friends, and notes and an introduction by himself. The effort as publicist for a cause was one with Yeats's prolific journalism and career as a self-made folklorist and editor of Irish fairy tales at this time.

By the 1890s, Lady Isabella Augusta Gregory (1852–1932), inspired by *The Celtic Twilight*, had begun collecting folktales of her own that would fill the five volumes of "Kiltartin" stories that she published between 1906 and 1910 and the two-volume *Visions and Beliefs in the West of Ireland* (1920), written in collaboration with Yeats. Though she did not make his acquaintance until 1896 when he was visiting at the country estate of Edward Martyn (1859–1923), she soon became an indispensible partner in projects undertaken for the stage. Martyn's *The Heather Field* and Yeats's verseplay *The Countess Cathleen* were performed in 1899 to celebrate the creation of the Irish Literary Theatre, which they started with Lady Gregory. When public disturbances occurred at the opening of Yeats's play, partly agitated by political opponents such as O'Donnell in the press, the young James Joyce (1882–1941) was there to take note, and in 1916 he would recreate the scene in *A Portrait of the Artist as a Young Man*, parodying the "Celtic Twilight" style, which Yeats himself tired of as he rewrote the play. Less talented imitators such as Thomas MacDonagh (1878–1916), the author of *Literature in Ireland* (1916), as well as disagreeable collaborators such as George Moore (1852–1933), drove Yeats in another direction, aided by Lady Gregory. Consequently in 1902 the first of a series of plays were performed in the name of the Irish National Theatre: AE's poetic *Deirdre* and Yeats's patriotic *Cathleen ni Houlihan* (written with Gregory). A restrictive crown patent was issued solely for production of "plays in Irish and English languages, written by Irish writers on Irish subjects" (Holloway 1967, p. 42); and thus the Abbey Theatre came into being on 27 December 1904, with the curtain rising on Yeats's heroic drama *On Baile's Strand* and Lady Gregory's comedy *Spreading the News*. Yeats, Gregory, and John Millington Synge (1871–1909) were the theater's co-directors and featured playwrights.

Saved from obscurity by following Yeats's advice to "go to the Aran Islands and find a life that had never been expressed in literature" (p. 262), Synge became the pivotal Abbey dramatist. From his notebooks he completed a book of observations called *The Aran Islands* in 1901 with illustrations by Jack B. Yeats (1871–1957), but delayed publication until just after the riotous first production of *The Playboy of the Western World* in January 1907. Among his half dozen plays, two were produced posthumously under Yeats's supervision as executor: *Deirdre of the Sorrows* and *The Tinker's Wedding*. Somewhere between the antirealism of Yeats's poetic drama and the local color of the one-act peasant plays Lady Gregory wrote in dialect (in a few instances with Yeats), Synge's work anticipated the lively and satirical tragicomedies of Gregory's protégé, Sean O'Casey (1880–1964). The grim beauty of Synge's west gave place to the squalid working-class settings of O'Casey's "Dublin Trilogy," *The Shadow of a Gunman* (1923), *Juno and the Paycock* (1924), and *The Plough and the Stars* (1926), plays that dealt critically with the realities of culture and class in time of insurrection and civil war between 1916 and 1923. Certainly, by then, the objective of reviving the literary capacity of the Irish people had been achieved. In 1923, the Nobel Prize for Literature was awarded to Yeats, and in 1926 to Ireland's great successor to Wilde in London, George Bernard Shaw.

The literary renaissance in Ireland still continues if the Celtic Revival is only its formative stage, precisely correspondent with the transitional, proto-modernist phase of international literature in English. What is Irish literature? The question was answered in 1904 by Justin McCarthy (1830–1912), editor in chief of a five-volume anthology entitled, simply, *Irish Literature*. Like the combined advisory board and contributing editors of the more recent *Field Day Anthology of Irish Writing* (1991), McCarthy and associates—Gregory, O'Grady, Hyde, Russell (AE), Rolleston, Yeats, and many others—answered the question with selections that exemplify thought at the time. Consensus is negotiated. Since then, thought has shifted from the nationalist agenda of the Celtic Revival to the global view of Ireland's place in literature as a whole. Lately, the east-to-west migration of the renaissance in Europe seems to have shifted north in Ireland.

SEE ALSO Arts: Modern Irish and Anglo-Irish Literature and the Arts since 1800; Drama, Modern; Gonne, Maud; Yeats, W. B.

Bibliography

Boyd, E. A. *Ireland's Literary Renaissance.* 1968.

Deane, Seamus, ed. *The Field Day Anthology of Irish Writing.* 3 vols. 1991.

Fallis, Richard. *The Irish Renaissance.* 1977.

Finneran, Richard J., ed. *Anglo-Irish Literature: A Review of Research.* 1976.

Holloway, Joseph. *Joseph Holloway's Abbey Theatre: A Selection from His Unpublished Journal "Impressions of a Dublin Playgoer."* Edited by Robert Hogan and Michael J. O'Neill. 1967.

Hyde, Douglas. *A Literary History of Ireland, from Earliest Times to the Present Day.* 1899.

Jeffares, A. Norman. *Anglo-Irish Literature.* 1982.

MacDonagh, Thomas. *Literature in Ireland: Studies Irish and Anglo-Irish.* 1916.

Marcus, Phillip L. *Yeats and the Beginning of the Irish Renaissance.* 2d edition, 1987.

Yeats, W. B. *The Collected Works of W. B. Yeats.* Vol. 3, *Autobiographies.* Edited by William H. O'Donnell and Douglas N. Archibald. 1999.

Wayne K. Chapman

≈

Literature

ANGLO-IRISH LITERARY TRADITION, BEGINNINGS OF

When Anglo-Irish literature begins is problematic. Some critics deny the existence of an Anglo-Irish literature distinct from British literature before 1800 and Maria Edgeworth's (1768–1849) novel *Castle Rackrent*

(1800). Indeed, at least through the first two decades of the eighteenth century, many of the English settlers and their descendants would have insisted that they were "the English of Ireland." And stylistically, even an Irish Catholic writing in English, such as playwright John O'Keeffe (1747–1833), has been described as "West British." O'Keeffe wrote at least seventy-seven plays, counting revised versions, and several of them, including *The Poor Soldier* (1783) and *The Wicklow Mountains* (1795), are set in Ireland. O'Keeffe dedicated his *Recollections of the Life of John O'Keeffe* (1826) to "George my Belov'd King, and Ireland my Honour'd Country," illustrating the difficulty of simple definitions of literary nationalism.

The Catholic Old English, descendants of the immigrants who arrived from England before the large Elizabethan plantations of the late sixteenth century, were denounced in Rome in 1659 as largely responsible for the loss of Ireland to the Protestants, thus lumping the Old and New English together as equally Anglo-Irish. The Old English long wished to insist on a difference between themselves and the native Irish, a distinction that English commentators tended to deny with the Latin tag *Hibernis ipsis* Hiberniores (more Irish than the Irish). Henry Burnell (fl. 1639–1642) in his play *Landgartha* (17 March 1639) pleaded allegorically for Charles I to remain true to the Catholic Old English rather than the Protestant New English; the native Irish, represented by the character Marfisa, while loyal to the true faith, are clearly untutored bumpkins. After the defeat of Jacobite forces at the Boyne (1690) and Aughrim (1691), and the Treaty of Limerick in the same year, the distinction between Old English and Irish dissolved, replaced by an apparently simple bifurcation between Catholics and Protestants. Even here, conversion blurs the line; for example, the actor and playwright Charles Macklin (c. 1699–1797) was born Catholic and Irish-speaking in Donegal but converted to the Church of England and moved in Protestant circles easily in the second half of his life, while continuing to write plays that challenged pejorative stereotypes of the stage Irishman.

Movement between Ireland and England was relatively easy for ambitious writers and tended to draw literary talent to the imperial center. Most of the significant comic playwrights of the London stage in the eighteenth century were from Ireland. William Congreve (1670–1729)—born in Yorkshire but educated in Kilkenny and at Trinity College, Dublin—George Farquhar (1677–1707), Sir Richard Steele (1672–1729), Oliver Goldsmith (1728–1774), and Sir Richard Brinsley Sheridan (1751–1816) are perhaps the most famous, but Arthur Murphy (1727–1805) and Hugh Kelly (1739–1777) were also very successful. Their plays im-

ported from the London stage also provided much of the repertory for Dublin's theaters. Nevertheless, it is difficult to discern a particularly "Irish" element in their works. While these playwrights were more likely than English playwrights to present positive Irish characters, a playwright whom most would regard as English, Richard Cumberland (1732–1811), whose father was bishop of Clonfert and Kilmore and who was himself Ulster secretary under Lord Halifax in 1761 and 1762, also depicted admirable Irish characters in the second half of the eighteenth century (for example, Major O'Flaherty in *The West Indian* [1771]). Cumberland's sister Mary Alcock (1742–1798) also published two volumes of poetry, and she is included in the major anthology of Irish verse in English in the eighteenth century, *Verse in English from Eighteenth-Century Ireland* (1998). It was not unheard of for English writers to move to Ireland. Charles Shadwell, already a successful English playwright, was the equivalent of playwright-in-residence at Smock Alley Theatre from 1715 to 1720; his plays reveal a firm identification with the Whig principles of the revolutionary settlement of William III, while indicating a growing sympathy toward Anglo-Irish complaints of mistreatment. Shadwell's conflicted allegiance is symptomatic. Robert Ashton's (fl. 1725–1728) *The Battle of Aughrim* (1728) presents both the English and the Irish as heroic, and the hero is a doomed English soldier who fights for both sides.

If, however, there is a characteristic that Anglo-Irish authors share, it is a sense of grievance. In the aftermath of 1691 the Anglo-Irish regarded their sacrifice in the victory over the Jacobites as insufficiently appreciated, and they increasingly protested against the English parliament's disadvantageous legislation limiting the Irish economy and usurping the ancient rights of the Irish parliament. In the late seventeenth and early eighteenth centuries the towering literary figure was Jonathan Swift (1667–1745). Swift's relationship with Ireland was profoundly ambivalent: He was frequently contemptuous of both the native Irish and the Anglo-Irish gentry, but the poor of Ireland never had a more impassioned defender than Swift, and the gentry had no more determined a supporter of Irish independence. Swift's circle included Thomas Sheridan the Elder (1687–1736), Thomas Parnell (1679–1718), Patrick Delany (c. 1685–1768) and his wife Mary Delany (1700–1788), and Matthew (1701–1774) and Laetitia Pilkington (c. 1708–1750). Together, their poems, essays, and letters provide a valuable portrait of Georgian Ireland.

In the latter half of the eighteenth century Protestant writers increasingly regarded themselves as Irish patriots, although this disaffection to English authority did not necessarily entail any allegiance to Catholic Emancipation. Novelist, playwright, and poet Henry Brooke (c. 1703–1783) wrote in support of the Dublin alderman Charles Lucas (1713–1771), whose advocacy of municipal electoral reform forced him to flee Ireland; nevertheless, he produced anti-Catholic propaganda as virulent as anything written at the time. Some cultural syncretism was present nonetheless. Brooke's daughter Charlotte (c. 1740–1793) was fluent in Irish and produced the important translations of Irish verse in *Reliques of Irish Poetry* (1789). Poets and playwrights from either side of the political spectrum in the second half of the eighteenth century wrapped themselves in Irish history, as evidenced by the radical Francis Dobbs's *The Patriot King; or Irish Chief* (1774) and the conservative Gorges Edmond Howard's *The Siege of Tamor* (1774). Moreover, individual political allegiances varied depending on the issue. During the Regency Crisis the poet and playwright Mary O'Brien (fl. 1785–1790) sided with the group surrounding Charles James Fox and Richard Brinsley Sheridan in her collection of poems *The Political Monitor; or Regent's Friend* (1790), but her play *The Fallen Patriot* (1790) is a plea for Irish economic independence (which Fox opposed) and for an Irish parliament unbribed by Dublin Castle. William Drennan (1754–1820) wrote poetry and satire in support of the agenda of the United Irishmen; his works reveal the influence of Thomas Paine and the French philosophes. As such, his politics are antithetical to those of Edmund Burke (1729–1797), whose *Reflections on the Revolution in France* (1790) is one of the masterpieces of English prose, but Burke too campaigned often for Irish rights.

Anglo-Irish literature in this period should not be thought of only in political terms or even just in terms of the relationship between Ireland and England. Lawrence Sterne's (1713–1768) birth in Ireland probably did not affect his own sense of himself as English, but James Joyce and Flann O'Brien are the aesthetic heirs of Sterne's novel *Tristram Shandy* (1759–1767). Frances Sheridan's (1724–1766) novel of suffering virtue *Memoirs of Miss Sidney Biddulph* (1761) was popular not just in Britain but also on the continent. Poets such as Lawrence Whyte (1683–1753), author of bucolics and panegyrics, Matthew Concanen (1701–1749), who celebrated Irish sport in his mock-epic *A Match at Football* (1720), and William Dunkin (1709–1765), the gleeful chronicler of Irish country life and the Hiberno-English dialect in poems such as *The Parson's Revels*, all represent a self-conscious identification with and a delight in Irish life that establishes an Anglo-Irish literary identity long before the romantic age.

SEE ALSO Arts: Early Modern Literature and the Arts from 1500 to 1800; English Writing on Ireland before 1800; Literature: Gaelic Writing from 1607 to 1800; Swift, Jonathan

Bibliography

Beckett, J. C. "Literature in English, 1691–1800." In *A New History of Ireland*, vol. 4, *Eighteenth-Century Ireland*, edited by T. W. Moody and W. E. Vaughan. 1986.

Carpenter, Andrew, ed. *Verse in English from Eighteenth-Century Ireland*. 1998.

Deane, Seamus. *A Short History of Irish Literature*. 1986.

Deane, Seamus, ed. *The Field Day Anthology of Irish Writing*. Vol. 1. 1991.

Leersen, Joep. *Mere Irish and Fíor Ghael: Studies in the Idea of Irish Nationality, Its Development and Literary Expression Prior to the Nineteenth Century*. 1986.

Leersen, Joep. *Remembrance and Imagination: Patterns in the Historical and Literary Representation of Ireland in the Nineteenth Century*. 1997.

McHugh, Roger, and Maurice Harmon. *A Short History of Anglo-Irish Literature from Its Origins to the Present Day*. 1982.

Mercier, Vivian. *Modern Irish Literature: Sources and Founders*. Edited by Eilís Dillon. 1994.

Thuente, Mary Helen. *The Harp Re-strung: The United Irishmen and the Rise of Irish Literary Nationalism*. 1994.

Vance, Norman. *Irish Literature: A Social History*. 1990.

Wheatley, Christopher J. *Beneath Iërne's Banners: Irish Protestant Drama of the Restoration and Eighteenth Century*. 1999.

Christopher J. Wheatley

ANGLO-IRISH LITERATURE IN THE NINETEENTH CENTURY

There are many possible definitions for the term *Anglo-Irish literature*. The designation can categorize works based on something as simple as the language of the work or more complicated notions such as the racial, religious, or class background of the author. The focus here is Irish writing in the nineteenth century that was composed in English by Protestant authors representing the interests of the landowning class primarily for audiences in England. Understanding Anglo-Irish writers and their work along these lines is intended to guide an initial inquiry, not to exclude anomalies, questions, and contradictions. Although the literature incorporates a wide range of themes, the tradition centrally comes to terms with the dynamic role of the landowning Protestant minority in a largely poor and Catholic country. Anglo-Irish literary works are intimately involved with three key periods of political tension and change in the century: the Act of Union of 1800, the Great Famine of 1845–1851, and the land question of 1870–1903.

Maria Edgeworth (1767–1849) was among the first authors to examine the cultural effects of the Act of Union. Beginning with the novel *Castle Rackrent* (1800), she described the anxiety of the Anglo-Irish in the United Kingdom. Since they were no longer solely the unchallenged ruling ascendancy of the island, Edgeworth was concerned with establishing an identity separate from the cultural and political challenges of the English and managing the threat of Catholic Emancipation. In her later novels *Ennui* (1809), *The Absentee* (1812), and *Ormond* (1817), she laid further groundwork for two dominant elements of this struggle for identity within Anglo-Irish literature: family secrets and the Big House.

Sidney Owenson, Lady Morgan (1776?–1859), offers a romantic sensibility in her work that contrasts with Edgeworth's reform-minded anxieties about the Irish ruling class under the union. In novels such as *The Wild Irish Girl* (1806) she reconciles the uncertainty of the union by uniting Protestant and Catholic characters in both national and social matrimony. Her work also recognizes the challenge of representing Ireland fairly both to Irish readers and to a larger, less-informed, and more metropolitan English readership.

Standing out as a kind of irregularity among Anglo-Irish writers, William Carleton (1794–1869) grew up among Catholic farmers in County Tyrone and converted to Protestantism after an abortive attempt to join the priesthood. The literary successes of his fiction, notably "Wildgoose Lodge" in *Traits and Stories of the Irish Peasantry* (1830) and *Valentine M'Clutchy* (1845), depend in part on his ability to critique the extremes of both his native Catholic and adopted Protestant cultures. His novels such as *The Black Prophet* (1847), *Emigrants of Ahadarra* (1848), and *The Tithe Proctor* (1849) portray the tragedy of famine among the Catholic peasantry for Anglo-Irish and English readers.

As both a political and human catastrophe, the Great Famine of 1845 to 1849 splits Anglo-Irish literature in two directions. One strain confronts the failure of the English government to deal with widespread starvation and emigration by moving toward cultural nationalism, while another remains entrenched in preserving the waning political capital of the ruling class. Many Anglo-Irish nationalists wrote for the *Nation*, a newspaper committed to Irish self-determination and run by both Catholics and Protestants. Important *Nation* contributors include Thomas Davis (1814–1845), the paper's founder and author of the poem "A Nation Once Again"; John Mitchel (1815–1875), whose radical

critique of the British empire led to his conviction and transportation to Van Diemen's Land, detailed in his *Jail Journal, or Five Years in British Prisons* (1854); and "Speranza" (1826–1896), the pen name of Jane Elgee, later known as Lady Wilde and the mother of Oscar, who inveighed against starvation and poverty in poems such as "To Ireland," "The Voice of the Poor," and "The Famine Year" and was among the nationalist women poets and critics writing for the *Nation*.

Although it existed well before the Great Famine, the Anglo-Irish Gothic is the representative genre of the class whose members did not become invested in one form or another of nationalism. Anglo-Irish Gothic works match Edgeworth's focus on Big Houses, locked rooms, and family secrets with a mounting anxiety about the decline of Protestant Ascendancy rule and the expanding power of the Catholic majority. Charles Maturin (1780–1824) explored the power of the fantastic to uncover the darkest secrets of the ruling class in the novel *Melmoth the Wanderer* (1820). J. Sheridan Le Fanu (1814–1873) approached this anxiety psychologically, describing different states of consciousness during intense emotional situations in novels such as *Uncle Silas* (1864) and in short stories like "Carmilla" and "Green Tea," collected in *In a Glass Darkly* (1872). At the end of the century Bram Stoker (1847–1911) blended Irish and eastern European folklore with Anglo-Irish Gothic disquiet in *Dracula* (1897), in which the aristocratic title character is both connected to and divorced from his home soil in a manner that suggests the land question.

Although Charles Lever (1806–1872) was extremely popular in England throughout his career (rivaling even Charles Dickens in the 1840s), his novels focus almost exclusively on representing Ireland and the Irish to England. His works failed, however, to engage fully with the political anxieties of the Anglo-Irish, and he often cast the Irish peasantry in an unflattering, comic light in novels such as *Harry Lorrequer* (1839). Outraged nationalist criticism for his stereotypes and accusations of plagiarism were almost certainly contributing factors in his decision to live abroad in Europe after 1845.

Edith Somerville (1858–1949) and Martin Ross (the pseudonym of Violet Martin, 1862–1915) began their careers with cheerful yarns about hunting and country life such as *Some Experiences of an Irish RM* (1899). These stories employ stereotypical "stage Irish" representations of the peasantry reminiscent of Lever's novels. However, they describe the twilight of Anglo-Irish rule as a consequence of both its own excesses and increasing Catholic political power in their more serious novels *The Real Charlotte* (1894) and *The Big House at Inver* (1925). The destruction of the Big House in the latter novel provides a grim punctuation mark for the anxieties of

Edgeworth, the hopes of Owenson, and the fears and secrets of the Gothic writers.

The collapse of the Big House did not mark the end of Anglo-Irish literature, however. By incorporating European ideas of aesthetics and bohemian society into their work, writers such as George Moore (1852–1933), Oscar Wilde (1854–1900), and W. B. Yeats (1865–1939) were able to transform the anxieties of Anglo-Irish literature into a confident cultural nationalism. Moore explored a variety of unconventional social and aesthetic innovations in his feminist novels *A Drama in Muslin* (1886) and *Esther Waters* (1894). Oscar Wilde trained his critical eye on the audience itself in plays such as *An Ideal Husband* (1895) and *The Importance of Being Earnest* (1895), thus reversing the traditional relationship between the Irish writer and the English reader. Yeats searched for a new form of literary expression by combining rereadings of heroic legends and mythology with a close examination of Irish folk culture and oral traditions in *Fairy and Folk Tales of the Irish Peasantry* (1888). Yeats's blending of Anglo-Irish literary sensibilities with folk culture, mythology, and French aesthetics took shape in his play *The Countess Cathleen* (1892) and continued in the works of numerous writers during the Irish Literary Renaissance.

SEE ALSO Antiquarianism; Gaelic Revival; Literature: Gaelic Literature in the Nineteenth Century; Wilde, Oscar; Yeats, W. B.

Bibliography

Backus, Margot. *The Gothic Family Romance: Heterosexuality, Child Sacrifice, and the Anglo-Irish Colonial Order.* 1999.

Bourke, Angela, et al., eds. *The Field Day Anthology of Irish Writing.* Vols. 5–6. 2002.

Deane, Seamus, ed. *The Field Day Anthology of Irish Writing.* Vols. 1–3. 1991.

Eagleton, Terry. *Heathcliff and the Great Hunger.* 1995.

McCormack, W. J. *From Burke to Beckett: Ascendancy, Tradition, and Betrayal in Literary History.* 1994.

Moynahan, Julian. *Anglo-Irish: The Literary Imagination in a Hyphenated Culture.* 1995.

Sean T. O'Brien

EARLY AND MEDIEVAL LITERATURE

Early Irish literature stands out for its richness and excellence, encompassing not only a wide range of religious and secular poetry but also—uniquely in early medieval Europe—a flourishing prose literature. Its range and breadth reveals a vibrant vernacular culture, unafraid of either its native roots or of the Latin Christian culture of the Continent.

Pre-modern literature in Irish is divided into periods on the basis of linguistic criteria: Old Irish (600–900), Middle Irish (900–1200), and Early Modern (or "Classical") Irish (1200–1650). The transition from the Old Irish to the Middle Irish period, generally associated with the upheavals in the aftermath of the Viking incursions, was, in literary terms, less abrupt than the transition from Middle Irish to Early Modern Irish in the wake of the Anglo-Norman invasion.

THE EARLY CENTURIES

Literacy came to Ireland through contact with the Romano-Christian world. The practice of Christianity brought with it a knowledge of Latin; however, Irish played a significant role as a literary language in the church from an early date. The monks glossing Priscian's Latin grammar in Irish used a technical vocabulary suited to describe both Latin and Irish grammar, and the same literate bilingualism informs the Old Irish primer *Auraicept na n-Éces*. Along with the clergy's adoption of the vernacular went other aspects of traditional culture. While it is impossible to reconstruct the real nature of the encounter between missionary Christianity and native pagan culture, it is significant that in later tradition it is often portrayed as a conciliatory compromise. According to the preface of the native law code *Senchas Már*, Saint Patrick endorses the native laws, as long as they did not conflict with church law. Such anecdotes express the need that medieval scholars felt to legitimize elements of native culture, to baptize, as it were, their pre-Christian gods and heroes. Modern critics have been particularly fascinated by the native culture with its roots in a pre-Christian Celtic past. However, the traditional view of the "secular" parts of Irish literature—especially saga and law—as representing pagan survivals has largely been replaced by a new scholarly consensus that regards the entire literary production as emanating directly or indirectly from the monasteries.

PROSE

Ireland has the earliest developed prose tradition in medieval Europe. The preference for prose as a vehicle for narrative was such that when the verse epics of Virgil, Lucan, and Statius were translated into Irish, they were rendered into prose rather than verse. Early Irish prose covers a number of genres, including hagiography and homily, history, and translated literature, as well as he-

The story of the conversion and death of King Lóeguire from the Book of the Dun Cow *(c. 1100), one of the major collections of Irish saga literature.* COURTESY OF THE ROYAL IRISH ACADEMY. PHOTOGRAPH BY DECLAN CORRIGAN PHOTOGRAPHY. REPRODUCED BY PERMISSION.

roic epic and myth. The narrative prose is characterized by a distinctive style particularly associated with heroic saga but found equally in saints' lives and historical tales. Quick-paced action is offset by colorful, if impressionistic description and punctuated by memorable, often laconic dialogue. The themes, motifs, and narrative style of the sagas are traditional and may hark back to preliterate storytelling. The sagas are without exception anonymous. Their authors clearly did not think that they were inventing; they were retelling traditional subject matter in a traditional manner. They thought of themselves as historians and of their subject as history, albeit history told with the flair and gusto of heroic epic.

POETRY

Although the modern reader may find the prose literature more accessible, poetry had a higher prestige. Poems were regarded as individually authored. While prose texts are anonymous, poems were often attributed, and scores of Early Irish poets are known to us by name. Irish metrics are of dazzling complexity and variety. Much of the earliest poetry is stressed and alliterative. This poetry, referred to as *rosc* or *retoiric*, is generally regarded as the original poetic mode. Stressed verse was eclipsed by syllabic verse, which soon became the dominant mode for poetry, although stressed poetry continued to be composed for several centuries, particularly in contexts that invited an archaizing treatment (Breatnach 1996). From 1200 on, the bardic schools maintained a standard literary language and a sophisticated system of metrics; the contemporary metrical tracts distinguish scores of individual meters. Syllabic poetry employs a variety of ornamentation, including alliteration, assonance, and rhyme. The definition of rhyme differs from other European traditions: Phonemes do not have to be identical in order to rhyme, but must belong to the same group of "rhyming" letters.

Modern scholarship has focused on the origins and development of Irish metrics. The lyric is well represented in anthologies (see, for example, Murphy 1956) and has received critical attention, especially the so-called "hermit" or "nature" poetry of monastic provenance; longer narrative and didactic verse fares less well. After 1200 the bulk of poetry is encomiastic.

THE EARLY MODERN PERIOD

Two events made the twelfth century a watershed in Irish literary history: the introduction of the continental monastic orders, heralded by the foundation of the Cistercian abbey of Mellifont in 1142, and the Anglo-Norman invasion of 1169. The two events combined to shift the locus of native literary production from the

monasteries to the bardic schools maintained by the dozen or so families of hereditary poets that formed the Irish intelligentsia. The bardic schools oversaw a linguistic reform that created a new literary standard after the profound linguistic changes of the Middle Irish period. This new standard language, referred to as "Classical" or "Early Modern" Irish, was used by literati from Gaelic Scotland to the south of Ireland and remained essentially unchanged until the collapse of Gaelic rule in the seventeenth century.

The foreigners introduced new literary fashions; entertainment plays a larger part in the composition of prose. Anglo-Norman tastes are reflected by the Irish adaptations of Guy of Warwick and Bevis of Hampton, of the Travels of John Mandeville and the Grail Quest. Poetry, on the other hand, remained essentially unassimilated and maintained its distinctive metrics. But even in poetry, foreign fashions had an impact; the *dánta grádha* (courtly love poetry) are informed by European love poetry and often have direct models in contemporary English poems. The first amateur practitioner of syllabic verse, the Anglo-Norman Gerald Fitzgerald, earl of Kildare, is an example of the much-invoked tendency for Ireland's invaders to "go native," becoming *Hibernis ipsis Hiberniores* ("more Irish than the Irish"). While relations between the two cultures were by no means always amicable, a cultural regrouping beginning in the thirteenth century resulted in many Anglo-Norman lords patronizing native poets. One poet, Gofraidh Fionn Ó Dálaigh, explains in a poem how he flattered native and foreign nobility alike. The poets, themselves of the aristocracy, looked at their profession as an independent institution that endowed them with the right to counsel and censure as well as praise their lords. Nevertheless, in economic terms they were largely dependent on the bounty of their patrons, whose careers they celebrated and whose deaths they lamented. Such official eulogies were preserved in a *duanaire* (poem book). A good many poem books survive, and the contents of a number of these have been published, as have the repertoires of individual poets, such as the exemplary edition of the oeuvre of Tadhg Dall Ó hUiginn (Knott 1922 and 1926).

Throughout its long history, Irish literature weathered major political upheavals and successfully accommodated foreign influence, be it Latin, Norse, or Norman. It was only when the Anglo expansion in the sixteenth and seventeenth centuries led to the disestablishment of Gaelic rule that Irish ceased, for a couple of centuries, to be a literary language.

SEE ALSO Arts: Early and Medieval Arts and Architecture; Latin and Old Irish Literacy; Middle English Literature; Myth and Saga; Norman French Literature; *Táin Bó Cúailnge*; **Primary Documents:** "The Vikings" (Early Ninth Century); "Writing out of Doors" (Early Ninth Century)

Bibliography

Breatnach, Liam. "Poets and Poetry." In *Progress in Medieval Irish Studies*, edited by Kim McCone and Katharine Simms. 1996.

Flower, Robin. *The Irish Tradition.* 1947.

Knott, Eleanor. *Irish Classical Poetry.* 1957.

Knott, Eleanor, ed. and trans. *The Bardic Poems of Tadhg Dall Ó hUiginn.* 2 vols. 1922 and 1926.

McCone, Kim, and Katharine Simms, eds. *Progress in Medieval Irish Studies.* 1996.

Murphy, Gerard. *Early Irish Lyrics.* 1956.

Williams, J. E. C., and Patrick Ford. *The Irish Literary Tradition.* 1992.

Barbara Hillers

EARLY MODERN LITERATURE BEFORE THE STUARTS (1500–1603)

Despite the unprecedented political and social destabilization brought on by the Tudors' consolidation of their colony, Irish literature in the sixteenth century exhibited a remarkable degree of formal and thematic continuity with that of earlier ages. The work of hereditary scholars continued apace, as older historical, genealogical, legal, and medical texts were assembled, revised, and copied in important manuscripts such as the *Book of Fenagh* (Rawlinson B502) and the second portion of *Yellow Book of Lecan.* The annalistic tradition continued, most notably with the *Annals of Ulster* (until 1541), the *Annals of Connacht* (to 1544), and the *Annals of Loch Cé* (to 1590). Bardic poetry was preserved in family poembooks (*duanaireadha*) such as the *Book of the O'Sweeneys* (commenced in 1513), the *Book of the O'Haras* (1597–1612), and the *Book of the O'Byrnes* (1550–1630).

This continuity is deceptive, however, for the traditional elements in prose and poetry came to be manipulated in new and subtle ways which reveal a gradual process of engagement with political and social change. It is not surprising that the poetry of the professional bards offers the clearest demonstration of this interplay between tradition and innovation. From the 1530s onwards, a series of ordinances was issued that specifically aimed at eliminating these professional classes ("Yryshe mynstrels, rymours, shannaghes, ne bardes"). Threatened with the loss of status and personal security under the colonial dispensation, a new corporate consciousness and political acuteness emerged among the poets, and a sensitive reading of their work reveals that their hypertraditionalism is partly ironic and constitutes a strategic response to external threat.

Of the score or so of poets whose work survives, the most prominent belong to the second half of the century. One of the most highly regarded and paradigmatic poets of the period is Tadhg Dall Ó hUiginn (1550–1591), a native of Sligo whose patrons included the O'Connors, Burkes, O'Rourkes, and O'Haras. In a praise poem from the 1570s, "'Fearann cloidhimh críoch Bhanbha" (The land of Ireland is sword land), there is a striking example of the poet's political use of traditional material. Ó hUiginn cites precedents from the medieval *Lebor Gabála Érenn* (Book of invasions) and urges the Lower MacWilliam Burkes to take action against the English, arguing that the gaelicized descendents of the Anglo-Norman invaders—no less than the Gaels themselves—are entitled to their land by right of conquest. In a manner anticipating Geoffrey Keating's historical project half a century later, Ó hUiginn imagines an inclusive Irish ethnicity based on shared linguistic and cultural traits.

Ó hUiginn's corpus includes two early examples of the *aisling* (vision) poem, in which the sleeping poet is visited by a mysterious woman, presumably from the otherworld. In the course of the seventeenth and eighteenth centuries this genre would be developed as the primary mode of political discourse in Irish poetry. In Ó hUiginn's *aisling* poems the motif is quasi-political insofar as it serves to reinforce the mythical underpinnings of the poet's social role.

Ó hUiginn is also credited with the earliest dateable poem in *amhrán* meter, the popular accentual form which eventually supplanted the syllabic bardic meters entirely. This poem, "Searc mná Ír dhuit, Aoidh, ná léig a bhfaill" (Do not spurn, Hugh, the love Íor's wife has for you), is addressed to Hugh O'Byrne of Wicklow (d. 1579), praising him for the authority that he asserts over the native inhabitants of the Pale. A statute of 1549 prohibiting the composition of "aurane" to anyone but the king indicates that this meter had already been adopted by the professional poets for some time before Ó hUiginn's poem was written.

Other notable poets of the period include Eochaidh Ó hEódhasa (?1560–1612), whose work offers insights into the personal relations between poet and patron; Fearghal Óg Mac an Bhaird (c. 1550–1620), who used traditional themes and motifs to question the status quo of contemporary Irish leadership; Eóghan Ruadh Mac an Bhaird (?1570–?1630), whose post-Kinsale "Rob soruidh t'eachtra, a Aoidh Ruadh" (Fare thee well on your journey, Hugh Roe) envisions the sovereignty of Ireland and all her hopes departing for Spain along with Hugh Roe O'Donnell in 1602; and Aonghus Fionn Ó Dálaigh (?1545–?), who produced an impressive body of religious verse. New themes which emerged in the bardic poetry of this period also include the degeneration of the Irish as a result of English goods and fashions, the role of divine providence in the misfortunes of the native Irish, the need for unity under a single leader, English duplicity, and the equation of Protestantism with foreign intrusion.

Narrative poetry in the sixteenth century consisted almost entirely of Fenian ballads, which were gradually collected, concorded, and arranged in manuscripts to produce an overarching "history" of Fionn mac Cumhaill and the Fianna. The *Book of the Dean of Lismore*, compiled in Scotland by Sir James MacGregor in the first quarter of the century, contains a particularly fine and representative selection of this verse. In prose, the same matter provided the background for tales such as *Eachtra an ghiolla dheacair* (The adventure of the difficult lad), *An Bruidhean Chaorthainn* (The Rowan hostel), and *Feis tighe Chonáin* (A night at Conán's), in which the device of a frame tale is used effectively to combine several such stories in a single compilation. Comic elements frequently feature in the later Fenian tales as well as in independent tales such as *Eachtra an cheithearnaigh chaoil riabhaigh* (The adventure of the slender, swarthy kern) which are rooted in the oral story-telling tradition. Other story cycles were still productive, and during this period *Oidheadh Chloinne Lir* (Tragic fate of the children of Lir, c. 1500), was reworked and grouped with *Oidheadh chloinne Tuireann* and *Oidheadh choinne Uisnigh* as the "Three Sorrows of Story-telling." Romantic tales based on continental models also continued to enjoy great popularity in this period, and Arthurian elements are featured in stories such as *Eachtra mhacaoimh an iolair* (The adventure of the eagle youth) and *Eachtra ridire na leómhan* (The adventure of the knight of the lions).

The influence of Renaissance aesthetics is notable in the life and work of Manus O'Donnell (?1490–1563), lord of Tirconnell, whose *Betha Colaim Chille* (Life of Colum Cille, 1532) was based on a variety of historical sources and written in an accessible form of the vernacular. O'Donnell also composed a number of *dánta grádha* (love poems), a courtly genre which was particularly popular with the nonprofessional poets and largely inspired by continental and English models.

After the accession of Elizabeth I, the colonial administration felt that the native language could be used to promote the Reformation in Ireland. The first book printed in Irish (in this case, in the "classical" form of the language) was John Carswell's *Foirm na nUrrnuidheadh* (Edinburgh, 1567), a translation of the Presbyterian *Book of Common Order*. Four years later, in 1571, Seán Ó Cearnaigh's Anglican catechism, *Aibidil Gaoidheilge agus Caiticiosma*, was printed in Dublin. A translation of the New Testament had been commissioned by the Crown in the 1560s, but none appeared until William Daniel's *An tiomna nuadh* (the New Testament, 1602–1603) at the beginning of the seventeenth century. Daniel based his translation on the original Greek and had the assistance of two professional poets, Maoilín Óg Ó Bruaideadha and Domhnall Óg Ó hUiginn, in formulating the Irish text.

A Catholic response to the Protestant printing venture was late in coming. During the 1590s, however, Irish recusant clerics established a number of centers in Spain and in the lowlands, and at this time Counter-Reformation elements began to appear in poetry. A notable example is "Léig dod chomhmhórtas dúinn" (Give up your vying with us) by the Franciscan Eoghan Ó Dubhthaigh (d. 1590), in which he bitterly attacks prominent clerics who had gone over to the established religion.

SEE ALSO Arts: Early Modern Literature and the Arts from 1500 to 1800; Literature: Gaelic Writing from 1607 to 1800

Bibliography

Caball, Marc. *Poets and Politics: Reaction and Continuity in Irish Poetry, 1558–1625.* 1998.

Craith, Mac. "Gaelic Ireland and the Renaissance." In *The Celts and the Renaissance: Tradition and Innovation*, edited by Glanmor Williams and Robert Owen Jones. 1990.

Ó Cuív, Brian. "The Irish Language in the Early Modern Period." In *A New History of Ireland*, vol. 3, *Early Modern Ireland, 1534–1691*, edited by T. W. Moody, F. X. Martin, and F. J. Byrne. 1976.

O Riordan, Michelle. *The Gaelic Mind and the Collapse of the Gaelic World.* 1990.

William J. Mahon

GAELIC WRITING FROM 1607 TO 1800

Seventeenth-century Gaelic literature registers the response of the traditional learned classes to the English colonial enterprise. The insecurity of the professional poets, for example, is evident in an increasing tendency to address poems to one another rather than to patrons.

In the decade following the Flight of the Earls (1607), their political differences provide the subtext for the "Contention of the Bards" (*Iomarbháigh na bhFileadh*), a poetic debate on the respective historical claims of the two halves of Ireland. Originating in a vituperative exchange between the Clare poet Tadhg mac Dáire Mac Bruaideadha (c. 1570–c. 1652), a supporter of the English interest, and Lughaidh Ó Cléirigh (c. 1580–c. 1640) of Donegal, it drew many prominent contemporaries into the fray.

The social reorientation of poetic activity was also reflected in the abandonment of the old syllabic meters and the gradual adoption of *amhrán*, a popular metrical form based on repeated patterns of stressed vowel sounds.

In this period, poets began to address the political situation faced by Ireland as a whole. Notable among these are two Tipperary-born clerics: Seathrún Céitinn (c. 1580–c. 1644), whose *Óm sceol ar ardmhagh Fáil ní chodlaim oídhche* (With this news of Ireland's pain I cannot sleep) lamented the disappearance of the old nobility who might have defended Ireland from "the litter of every foreign sow," and Pádraigín Haicéad (c. 1600–1654), whose impassioned verse reflected his hopes and disappointments as an active supporter of the Gaelic Party during the Confederate War. The disastrous events of the period between 1640 and 1660 were also detailed in six lengthy political poems, the most well known being the anonymous *An Síogaí Rómhánach* (The Roman fairy, c. 1650).

Keating and his contemporaries were the first to develop the *aisling*, or dream-vision motif, as an elegiac mode with political undertones. In an *aisling* the poet meets an otherworldly female—a personification of the locality or the nation—who laments the loss of her spouse, the deceased. Insofar as the conceit of this genre is that of a supernatural confrontation, it may be seen as a popularizing strategy whereby the poets exploit grass-roots cultural symbols connected with the traditional death ritual.

In the last quarter of the seventeenth century the personal plight of the traditional poet and the sociopolitical "shipwreck" (*longbhriseadh*) of Ireland after the Treaty of Limerick (1691) were powerfully expressed in the acerbic verse of Dáibhí Ó Bruadair (c. 1625–1698).

SEVENTEENTH-CENTURY PROSE

By the beginning of the seventeenth century many younger members of the learned classes had chosen ecclesiastical over secular patronage and entered holy orders. Established in 1606, the Franciscan College of St. Anthony of Padua in Louvain soon became a major center of Irish recusant scholarship and publishing. As part of a general Counter-Reformation strategy, the devotional works produced there were written in a simple, natural Irish and designed for popular appeal. Among the most notable first-generation Louvain scholars were Flaithrí Ó Maolchonaire (1560–1620), whose *Desiderius* (Louvain, 1616) is an expanded translation of a Catalan devotional work; Bonaventura Ó Heodhasa (d. 1614), whose catechism in prose and verse *An Teagasg Criosdaidhe* (Antwerp, 1611), was the first Catholic work to be printed in Irish; and Aodh Mac Aingil (1571–1626), author of *Sgáthán Shacramuinte na hAithridhe* (Mirror of the sacrament of repentance, Louvain, 1618), a devotional work with strong political undertones.

A project in Irish historical research was established at Louvain, and it was there that Brother Micheál Ó Cléirigh (c. 1590–1643) organized a team of scholars who returned to Ireland and produced between 1632 and 1636 *Annála Ríoghachta Éireann*, a massive compendium of Irish chronicles popularly known as the *Annals of the Four Masters*.

The most influential historical work of the period, however, was Seathrún Céitinn's *Foras Feasa ar Éirinn* (The basis for a knowledge of Ireland), an elegantly written narrative that promoted the concept of a Catholic Irish nation and established the framework in which the Irish viewed their own history for the next 250 years. Céitinn also produced important devotional works, the most important being *Trí Biorghaoithe an Bháis* (The three shafts of death), a lengthy treatise on sin, death, and judgment.

Protestant scholars were also active throughout the century. William Daniel's Irish translation of the *Book of Common Prayer* was published 1609. In 1634 William Bedell (1571–1642), the bishop of Kilmore, assembled a team of scholars to translate the Old Testament into Irish. The work was finally published in 1685, and in 1690 it was printed along with Daniel's translation of the New Testament (1603) as *An Bíobla Naomhtha*.

Popular prose at this time consisted mostly of short heroic romances and the reworking of traditional tales. Nevertheless, there were some very good works in a comical or satirical vein, the most notable being the anonymous *Parliament Chloinne Tomáis* (The parliament of Thomas's clan), a burlesque satire on the upstart peasantry, which once again registered the insecurity of the learned class.

A shift toward parody and mock-heroism had already been evident in the late Fionn-cycle literature, and it was used to full comic effect toward the end of the century in the anonymous *Siabhradh Mhic na Míchomhairle* (The hallucination of the Son of Ill-Counsel), a skillful reworking of traditional material narrated in the first person.

EIGHTEENTH-CENTURY POETRY AND PROSE

In the south of Ireland the strange mix of collegiality and factionalism that had manifested itself in the "Contention of the Bards" reemerged in the poetry of the *cúirteanna éigse,* or "courts of poetry," local poetical associations that upheld formal standards, encouraged the composition and dissemination of new verse, and saw to the preservation and copying of manuscripts. Typical of this milieu were extended displays of repartee in which poets respond in verse to one another's compositions, as for example in the work of Seán Ó Tuama (c. 1708–1775) and Aindrias Mac Craith (c. 1708–1795). Typical also was the satirical *barántas,* or "warrant poem," a parody of a legal document in which "bailiffs" were called upon to apprehend and punish someone who had offended the court by some misdeed or minor theft.

The *aisling,* however, is the poetic genre most associated with eighteenth-century Ireland. From its roots in the elegiac verse of the previous century, it was developed as a mode of presenting political allegory. The most successful examples were probably those composed by Aogán Ó Rathaille (c. 1670–1729) at the end of the first decade of the century, when there existed a genuine hope for a Jacobite invasion of Ireland. The *aisling* eventually became the conventional genre for the expression of political aspiration and was indelibly associated with the Stuart cause. Many of the later *aislings,* like those of Eoghan Rua Ó Súilleabháin (1748–1784), are admired more for their musicality and technical perfection than for their emotive power or sincerity.

The extemporaneous composition of a lament, or *caoineadh* (the English keen) was an essential feature of the funeral ritual in eighteenth-century Ireland. A particularly fine example that was preserved in oral tradition is *Caoineadh Airt Uí Laoire* ("The Lament for Art O'Leary"), composed by Eibhlín Dubh Ní Chonaill in 1773 after the occasion of her husband's murder.

The most original and brilliant example of narrative verse from this period is undoubtedly Brian Merriman's *Cúirt an Mheán Oíche* ("The Midnight Court," written in 1780), a poem of over one thousand lines in which the dreaming author, representing the men of Ireland, is forcibly brought before the fairy-queen of Thomond and put on trial for neglecting women and failing to marry. This work is an extraordinary blend of genres, successfully combining elements of the *aisling* with those of the *barántas,* and sparkling with technical virtuosity.

Prose composition did not fare so well in this century, and the most exciting experimentation occurred early on with the work of Seán Ó Neachtain (c. 1648–1729). A native of Roscommon, he eventually settled in Dublin where he and his son Tadhg were the central figures in an extremely productive circle of Irish scholars, scribes, and poets. Although he was a capable poet himself, Ó Neachtain's best work was his prose, and he is primarily admired for *Stair Éamainn Uí Chléire* (*The History of Éamonn Ó Clery,* c. 1710), a comical and picaresque moral allegory on the dangers of alcohol.

SEE ALSO *Annals of the Four Masters;* Arts: Early Modern Literature and the Arts from 1500 to 1800; Literacy and Popular Culture; Literature: Anglo-Irish Literary Tradition, Beginnings of; Literature: Early Modern Literature before the Stuarts (1500–1603)

Bibliography

Cunningham, Bernadette. *The World of Geoffrey Keating.* 2000.

Leersen, Joseph Th. *Mere Irish and Fíor-Ghael: Studies in the Idea of Irish Nationality, its Development, and Literary Expression Prior to the Nineteenth Century.* 1996.

Ó Tuama, Seán, and Thomas Kinsella. *An Duanaire, 1600–1900: Poems of the Dispossessed.* 1981.

William J. Mahon

GAELIC LITERATURE IN THE NINETEENTH CENTURY

Nineteenth-century Gaelic literature falls into two distinct and complex phases: The first extends from the revolutionary era of the 1790s to the Great Famine, and the second from the famine to the end of the century. In the first period written materials were principally transmitted via a robust manuscript tradition, as had been the case in the previous millennium. Some 2,000 documents from the period have survived, but much cataloging and editorial work has yet to be completed on these codices (de Brún 1987 and 1988). The scribal culture that persisted in Irish-speaking Ireland is reminiscent of those of other societies marginalized on geographic, ideological, or sociopolitical grounds. Ireland's output in the early nineteenth century merits comparison with the handwritten production of medieval writings in contemporary Iceland, the manuscript circulation of clandestine philosophical compositions in early eighteenth-century France, and the surviving documentation of central European Judaica.

Gaelic copyists were active throughout much of Ireland. Manuscript writing was strong in the south in counties such as Cork, Limerick, and Waterford. Parts of Leinster, notably Kilkenny, were also productive. There is also evidence of the tradition in the north midlands, the northeast (especially Belfast), and distinctively, though less vigorously, the west. It was an urban as well as a rural phenomenon. We know of writers operating in or near towns and villages in County Clare, for example, including Conchúr Ó Maoilriain and Donnchadh Ulf from Sixmilebridge, Micheál Ó hAllúráin from Kilrush, and Micheál Ó Raghallaigh from Ennistymon.

The manuscripts include business accounts, legal agreements, personal biographical details, and other records of their compilers' everyday lives, as well as literary compositions. There are two types of prefamine creative writings. The first are texts from medieval times and from the innovative seventeenth century that were recopied in the early nineteenth century, including sagas and bardic poetry as well as historical and devotional matter. The transmission of pre-1700 writings was not simply a passive, repetitive exercise. Nineteenth-century annotation of compositions such as the Deirdre story (Mac Giolla Léith 1993) reveals their compilers' thoughts about character or motivation in this and other legends. Material from the past continued to furnish literary allusions in works from the early nineteenth century. Medieval writings, especially those of the seventeenth-century chronicler and Catholic polemicist Geoffrey Keating, set standards of language and style. This holds true especially for scribes trained in reading and reproducing Gaelic script and spelling.

Original prefamine writings constitute the second strand of materials. Both verse and prose works have survived. Topics in the lives of the composers themselves feature in the compositions. The north Kerry poet Seán Ó Braonáin (de Brún 1972) was occupied with sectarian issues, millenarian hopes of delivery from English rule, the career of Daniel O'Connell, poverty, relations with his fellow scribes such as the Cork-based 1798 insurgent Micheál Óg Ó Longáin (1766–1837), and a range of other subjects. His output has particular value as the unmediated voice of the community for which he wrote; in this regard it resembles the work of other composers such as Antaine Raiftearaí (Anthony Raftery), whose texts are more obviously molded by oral culture. The compositions of Ó Braonáin and his counterparts are traditionalist in other ways. The meter of the poetry is accentual, reflecting ordinary speech patterns, but highly wrought. His verse demonstrates a continuation of poetic practices that came to fruition in the seventeenth century and were in full force

throughout the eighteenth century. Prose works that are rooted in the past, though less common than poetry, are also found in this period. The prolific County Cork writer Dáibhí de Barra (d. 1851) recast the story of his neighbors' defeat of officials levying Anglican tithes in the 1830s to make it read like a heroic saga (Ó Cuív 1960).

Other intriguing innovations in early nineteenth-century verse and prose writing deserve closer attention than they have received. One of these is the absorption into Irish poetry of the themes, style, and diction of near-contemporary literature in English, particularly various manifestations of romanticism. The works of County Louth-based Nioclás Ó Cearnaigh are a case in point. He translated pieces by Robert Burns such as "Sweet Afton" and "Highland Mary" into Irish (Ó Dufaigh and Ó Doibhlin 1989), and the process resulted in his Gaelic text having a convoluted syntax and a sentimental tone. These features resurface in the contorted language and phraseology of his own original Irish versification on topics such as love and politics. The scribe Amhlaoibh Ó Súilleabháin is best known for his diary of everyday life in Callan, Co. Kilkenny, in the years 1827 to 1835. He also completed in manuscript form a tale entitled *Tóruigheacht Chalmair* (The pursuit of Calmar) (McGrath 1937). It is in effect a short Gothic novel about economic distress. Ó Súilleabháin and Ó Cearnaigh's works typify the writings of other, mostly urban-based bilingual writers who had access to printed sources. Although awkward in style, their material has relevance in cultural terms. Irish politics were edging toward an accommodation with British authority, particularly through the parliamentary tradition; similarly, new experimental Gaelic literature appears to have consciously established a rapprochement with a linguistic medium set to dominate not only in Ireland but also internationally as the nineteenth century advanced.

How far this modernizing tendency might have developed organically after the 1840s is uncertain; its development was interrupted by the devastating events of the decade, which ushered in the second phase of Irish-language writing in the nineteenth century. The Great Famine had as damaging an impact on Gaelic literature as on other aspects of Irish life. As it swept away speakers of the language, it also undermined scribal culture, which completely died out in certain regions and was attenuated in other locations. There were some critically important survivors, however, including Kilkenny-born John O'Donovan (1809–1861), who had worked with the Ordnance Survey (the branch of the British administration charged with producing up-to-date maps of Ireland on a county basis between 1825 and 1841) in the 1830s and translated some of the works of the philosopher John Locke into Irish, and his colleague Eugene O'Curry (1796–1862), who had trained as a traditional copyist in his native Clare. In 1848 to 1851, O'Donovan issued his monumental edition and translation of the *Annals of the Four Masters*, one of the first authoritative large-scale works offering insights into life in Ireland before 1600. O'Curry became a professor of Irish history and archaeology at Newman's Catholic University in 1854. His teaching formed the basis for his *Lectures on the Manuscript Materials of Ancient Irish History* (1861). In another example of the persistence of the scribal tradition, younger members of the Ó Longáin scribal family recopied some of the codices of the Royal Irish Academy in the 1860s and 1870s, establishing bridges between the prefamine past and subsequent generations who would draw on the earlier works in creating new forms of Irish writing in the late nineteenth century. This mutually reinforcing symbiosis between scholarship and literature has existed throughout the history of Irish civilization.

In the last quarter of the nineteenth century Irish-language enthusiasts adopted an organizational approach to the promotion of Gaelic culture. The Society for the Preservation of the Irish Language was established in 1876 to arrest the decline of Irish. A recent study (Ó Murchú 2001) has shown that its program of teaching Irish in schools and supplying textbooks was very successful in encouraging writing at a basic level. An offshoot body, the Gaelic Union, set up in 1880, produced the first successful printed periodical devoted to the modern Irish language in Ireland, the *Gaelic Journal/ Irisleabhar na Gaedhilge* (1882). It became a vehicle for the creation of new verse and prose (O'Leary 1994). By far the most influential organization, however, was the Gaelic League, established in 1893 (Ó Ríordáin 2000). The League set up elaborate branch networks and sponsored cultural events featuring evenings of song, storytelling, and dance. It developed competitions in music and literature at both local (*feis*) and national (*Oireachtas*) levels. These contests produced many writings, from essays to short stories and novels, some of which were conservative (for instance, those based on folk narrative), and others that were more adventurous, particularly when translations from European literature were used as exemplars. Infrequent publishing of key periodicals had an adverse effect on the strength of the material (Nic Pháidín 1998). Another, no less important result of the competitions was the formation of a readership for the new works. The principal achievement of the revivalists was the establishment of a platform on which a fully fledged modern Gaelic literature would be built, a process due to bear fruit throughout the twentieth century.

SEE ALSO Antiquarianism; Arts: Modern Irish and Anglo-Irish Literature and the Arts since 1800; Gaelic Revival; Hyde, Douglas; Literature: Anglo-Irish Literature in the Nineteenth Century; O'Donovan, John

Bibliography

de Brún, Pádraig. *Filíocht Sheáin Uí Bhraonáin.* 1972.

de Brún, Pádraig. "The Cataloguing of Irish Manuscripts," *Newsletter of the School of Celtic Studies* 1 (1987): 33–34.

de Brún, Pádraig. *Lámhscríbhinní Gaeilge: Treoirliosta.* 1988.

Mac Giolla Léith, Caoimhín. *Oidheadh Chloinne hUisneach: The Violent Death of the Children of Uisneach.* 1993.

McGrath, Micheal, ed. *Cinnlae Amhlaoibh Uí Shúileabháin.* Vols. 1–4. 1936–1937.

Nic Pháidín, Caoilfhionn. *Fáinne an Lae agus an Athbheochan (1898–1900).* 1998.

Ó Cuív, Brian. "A Contemporary Account in Irish of a Nineteenth-Century Tithe Affray." *Proceedings of the Royal Irish Academy* 61 C (1960): 1–21.

Ó Dufaigh, Seán, and Diarmaid Ó Doibhlin. *Nioclás Ó Cearnaigh: beatha agus saothar.* 1989.

O'Leary, Philip T. *The Prose Literature of the Gaelic Revival, 1881–1921: Ideology and Innovation.* 1994.

Ó Murchú, Máirtín. *Cumann Buan-Choimeádta na Gaeilge: Tús an Athréimnithe.* 2001.

Ó Ríordáin, Traolach. *Conradh na Gaeilge i gCorcaigh, 1894–1910.* 2000.

Neil Buttimer

TWENTIETH-CENTURY WOMEN WRITERS

The overriding twentieth-century question for both the newly independent Irish state and the six counties that remained united with Britain was that of national identity. While politicians charted public perspectives, writers presented varied possibilities, some mirroring the dominant models, others projecting liberating roles. Although excluded from many public arenas, Irish women were present in nationalist, suffragist, and literary circles. Their early twentieth-century literature reflects women's responses to national questions but also expresses their neglected concerns, revealing that women's identities transcended definition by a male-dominated state or by male writers. The educational and social advances that followed the economic reforms of the 1960s liberated women as well as men to imagine and create new possibilities and opportunities, which in turn resulted in a dramatic increase in the number of writers.

Lady Isabella Augusta Gregory, née Persse (1852–1932), Irish playwright and founder of the Abbey Theatre. © HULTON ARCHIVE/ GETTY IMAGES. REPRODUCED BY PERMISSION.

WOMEN'S POSITION IN THE NEW NATION

Lady Gregory's position as codirector and founder of the important national literary endeavor the Abbey Theatre (1904) evidences her interest in national identity. A student of Irish legend and history as well as the Irish language, she, like her contemporaries in the Irish Renaissance, aimed to replace the picture of Ireland current on the British stage with that of the Irish people speaking for themselves, reflecting both historic and contemporary concerns. *Cuchulain of Muirthemne* (1902), her first major work of folklore, reintroduces and interprets this legendary character as a dignified and idealistic hero. Lady Gregory wrote more than forty plays, most with nationalist themes. One of them, *Cathleen Ni Houlihan* (1902), cowritten with William Butler Yeats, celebrates Ireland as an old woman rejuvenated by the blood of young men who fight and die for her. Controversial and influential, this concept of Ireland has been criticized by feminist scholars as concealing the concerns of actual women. The 1912 play *Grania* suggests more concern with female identity, as Gregory remains true to the myth but underscores approvingly Grania's ability to take control of her own life.

Variations on Lady Gregory's nationalistic concerns were presented by women involved in the national struggle such as Alice Milligan and Maud Gonne, but increasingly, women's issues took center stage. The plays of Teresa Deevy and Maura Laverty focus on the conflicts that faced women particularly. Deevy's plays, produced between the 1930s and 1950s, critique the institution of marriage even as the Irish Constitution of 1937 foresaw no other identity for women. *The King of Spain's Daughter* and *Katie Roche*, produced by the Abbey in 1935 and 1936 respectively, underscore the gulf between male and female marital expectations: Katie Roche's husband finds marriage a threat to his autonomy, and Katie discovers therein neither the opportunity of emotional communion nor independence. In a brief career Katherine Cecil Thurston examined many aspects of Irish and English life, notably exposing, in *The Fly on the Wheel* (1908), the fragility of Irish Catholic middle-class identity. First-generation middle-class characters, male and female, dare not deviate in their choices of job and spouse from the narrow confines tacitly approved by their class—confines that neither religion nor love can breach.

Over the course of a long career Kate O'Brien dissected and analyzed the middle class, revealing its consolidation at the expense of women's independence and happiness. In *Without My Cloak* (1931), an Irish Catholic myth of origin, the principal male characters refuse to help their sister to escape a loveless but socially approved marriage, prompting the omniscient narrator to remark that it would never occur to them to set their sister's happiness above their own surname, thus underscoring their perception of the fragility and threatened nature of their position. In this novel the heroine dies giving birth to a son needed to continue the dynasty; a generation later, the son's lover, a beautiful daughter of unmarried parents, is ruthlessly dispatched to America, her "illegitimate" status still a threat to the family's social position. Women often sacrifice other women to male interests (which often parallel class interests) in O'Brien's novels: In her dying moments, a mother arranges her irresponsible son's marriage to her competent nurse in *The Anteroom* (1934); college education is seen as a waste for women in *Mary Lavelle* (1936); a young woman's education would be sacrificed for her brother's in *The Land of Spices* (1941). Women in O'Brien's novels are denied autonomy both before and after marriage, and marriage fails to provide emotional fulfilment; but O'Brien also depicts enlightened figures, such as an Irish bishop and an English nun in *The Land of Spices*, who see the benefits of an educated, responsible female populace.

Women's position in upper-class Anglo-Irish society is addressed by Elizabeth Bowen and Molly Keane.

In *The Last September* (1929) and *A World of Love* (1955), Bowen charts the coming-of-age of young women in disintegrating Anglo-Irish society. Bowen's women look to the past as Edenic but also burdensome; in *The Last September*, set during the Irish Civil War, characters are caught between their sympathy for a rebel family, whose circle is both dangerous and exciting, and their ties to their own class, which are depicted as passionless and enervated. The "Big Houses" of the Anglo-Irish families are themselves characters in Bowen's novels, reflecting the glorious and scarred histories of their inhabitants. Molly Keane's first novels are affectionate views of the disintegrating Anglo-Irish society that focus on plucky, unconventional girls who participate compulsively in what are depicted as the almost interchangeable, exciting, beautiful sports of fox- or man-hunting; servants and non-Anglo-Irish characters are practically ignored. *Conversation Piece* (1932) introduces the first of a series of awful Keane mothers—vicious elderly women who prey on, or dominate, the young. Janet McNeill sets her work in bourgeois Belfast; her *Tea at Four O'Clock* (1956) dissects the ceremonies of gracious living to reveal onerous demands on the youngest daughter. McNeill's characters lack the viciousness of Keane's, but her women, too, are implicated in preserving the patriarchal order at the expense of their daughters.

Religious bigotry and its consequences play a role in the work of Margaret Barrington, Anne Crone, and Nora Hoult. Crone's *Bridie Steen* (1948), her most complex novel, addresses the mystery of how children learn and play together, then become Protestant and Catholic adults denied any social interaction. Barrington's *My Cousin Justin* (1939) sees religious fears as rooted in centuries of repression of the Catholic Irish and, more importantly, twentieth-century repression of the working class.

EXORCIZING MYTH, INTRODUCING MOTHER

Despite the recurrence of the "Troubles" in the 1960s, women writers turned confidently to their own neglected concerns, introducing mother-daughter relationships into a national literature that had ignored them. Mary Lavin's short stories focus sympathetically but unsentimentally on the minutiae of women's lives, the beautiful prose awakening the reader to the human drama inherent in the mundane. Her final stories concentrate on the complex relationships of grandmothers, mothers, and daughters. In her Irish-language poetry Máire Mhac an tSaoi, like Lavin, turns to the drama of the urban housewife. Edna O'Brien's *The Country Girls* (1960) introduces the author's series of abused, dispirited, and often manipulative mothers—these characters

become more complex in her later work, including *Time and Tide* (1992), which reveals a daughter's inheritance of the very manipulative traits she resents in her mother. Mother-daughter relationships have been explored at length by many other authors, too, often in works that expose the daughters' exploitation, including Caroline Blackwood's *The Stepdaughter* (1976), Helen Lucy Burke's *A Season for Mothers* (1980), Jennifer Johnston's *The Christmas Tree* (1981), Clare Boylan's *Holy Pictures* (1983), and Mary Rose Callaghan's *The Awkward Girl* (1990). Eavan Boland's poetry often speaks of the loss of the mother's story; on the other hand, the poetry of Mary Dorcey and Paula Meehan deals with the mystery of filial inheritance, the continuing presence of the mother in the psyche and personality of the daughter. Deirdre Madden's *Birds of the Innocent Wood* (1988), Johnston's *The Railway Station Man* (1984) and *The Illusionist* (1995), Boylan's *Last Resorts* (1984), Maeve Kelly's "Orange Horses" (1990), and Catherine Dunne's *The Walled Garden* (2000) all depict the mother's pain that results from the child's rejection or lack of communication. Mary Morrissy's *Mother of Pearl* (1996) investigates maternal desire; Marina Carr's play *The Mai* (1995) examines sororal and maternal relationships.

Embracing and reinterpreting traditionally negative female images, the poetry of Eiléan Ní Chuilleanáin, Rita Ann Higgins, and Nuala Ní Dhomhnaill presents female consciousness actively revising and overturning conventional formulations of women to expose the reality concealed by the myth. Eavan Boland exorcizes traditional mythic images, which she blames for concealing the experiences of real women. The most minute aspect of nature is cause for wonder in the poetry of Biddy Jenkinson; another close observer, Moya Cannon, finds maternal comfort both in the neglected but resonant Irish language and in nature. The Irish-language poetry of Ní Dhomhnaill and Caitlin Maude has been translated and is very popular, but Jenkinson has refused English translation.

SEXUALITY

Irish women were not encouraged to explore their sexuality even in literature, but unhappiness owing to repressed sexuality was apparent in the works of even early writers. Molly Keane's second series of novels, beginning with *Good Behaviour* (1981), satirically contrasts the desires of undesirable girls with their fates in a dying society. The title of an Eithne Strong volume of poetry, *Flesh—The Greatest Sin* (1980), captures the repressive atmosphere. Remembering the child who died alone birthing a baby by a statue of Mary, Paula Meehan reveals the consequences of the ignorance that accompanies repression. Positive depictions of female sexuality appear in the 1980s work of Julia O'Faolain, and the poetry of Medbh McGuckian celebrates female sexuality. *The Dancers Dancing* (1999), an experimental novel by Éilís Ní Dhuibhne, charts female coming-of-age, joyfully, in a Donegal Gaeltacht. The possibility of a lesbian relationship, which might offer more than traditional (heterosexual) arrangements, is hinted at in Bowen's *The Last September*, whereas Molly Keane caricatures such relationships. Kate O'Brien presents the first extended lesbian portrait in *Mary Lavelle* (1936), albeit a negative one. In her last novel, *As Music and Splendour* (1958), O'Brien parallels the joys and difficulties in both heterosexual and lesbian relationships; the sense of joy and emotional closeness in the latter suggests that it is a richer relationship. In 1989 Mary Dorcey's collection of short stories, *A Noise from the Woodshed*, marked a new maturity in Irish fiction. In stories that focus on aging or class struggles, lesbian characters love and fight, their relationships now an authorial given that requires neither explanation nor defense, although the characters are frequently forced to address their identities in response to the ignorance or prejudices of other characters. Dorcey's *Biography of Desire* (1997) explores the many faces of love, chiefly between women, as does her volume of poetry *The River That Carries Me* (1995). Emma Donoghue's *Stir-fry* (1994) is a lesbian bildungsroman, and her *Hood* (1995) portrays the pain of a young woman who cannot reveal that her dead friend was her lover.

SOCIAL PROBLEMS

Irish women writers investigate many social problems; several reflect actual 1980s court cases that revealed that incest was more widespread than many believed possible. Leland Bardwell's "Dove of Peace" (1987), Dorothy Nelson's *In Night's City* (1982), Jennifer Johnston's *The Invisible Worm* (1991), and Edna O'Brien's *Down by the River* (1996) focus on the pain and shame of young girls molested by their fathers; Nelson's novel also reveals the mother's anger and confusion, as she, like the father in the O'Brien novel, blames her daughter for the ensuing pregnancy. This crime crosses social boundaries—those affected include: a distinguished Catholic politician married to a Protestant descendant of the ascendancy in Johnston's text, and a Traveller, a member of a distinctive and neglected nomadic culture, in Maeve Kelly's "Orange Horses."

The indignities that face working-class women are frequent subjects in the poetry of Rita Ann Higgins, Mary Dorcey, and Paula Meehan, and in the fiction of Frances Molloy. Evelyn Conlon captures both the drabness and the humor of middle-class women who are often confined to the company of children. Maeve Kelly

moves to the twice-disprivileged world of women Travellers. Discrimination against, and the fears of, the elderly are featured in Clare Boylan's *Beloved Stranger* (1999) and Mary Lavin's "Senility" and "A Family Likeness." Patricia Brogan explores the lot of "Magdalen women," pregnant and unmarried women, practically imprisoned in laundries run by nuns in her play *Eclipsed* (1994); Emma Donoghue's novel *Slammerkin* (2000) moves from a house of prostitution to a Magdalen home. Marie Jones's *Lay Up Your Ends* (1983) depicts the hardships of Belfast mill workers. Ronit Lentin uncovers the racism in late twentieth-century Ireland in *Songs on the Death of Children* (1996), as does Clare Boylan in her humorous *Black Baby* (1988). The separation and subsequent problems of the characters in Anne Enright's highly experimental novel, *What Are You Like?* (2000), spring from Irish social conditions and contribute to Irish-immigrant identity concerns in the high-tech worlds of New York and London.

THE "TROUBLES": A SECONDARY SUBJECT

Writers in the Republic initially responded to the "Troubles" by setting them in an historic context. Arguably, Johnston's *How Many Miles to Babylon?* (1974) and *The Old Jest* (1979), set during World War I and the Irish Civil War respectively, may be seen as attempts to contextualize the conflict. Later Johnston novels set during the "Troubles" focus on personal rather than national relationships, as do other works. Julia O'Faolain's 1980 novel *No Country for Young Men* bridges two periods of "Troubles" through the unreliable consciousness of an elderly nun whose memory of the troubles of the 1920s is stirred by contemporary TV footage; Mary Leland's works *The Killeen* (1985) and *Approaching Priests* (1991) condemn a nationalism based on violence; Edna O'Brien's *The House of Splendid Isolation* (1994) looks at the reception in the 1990s of the North and Northeners in the South. Northern writers make distinctive contributions: Frances Molloy's *No Mate for the Magpie* (1985) presents the Northern Irish situation as an insult to common sense. Class and gender, Molloy's plucky heroine comes to see, are as restrictive as politics. Mary Beckett's *A Belfast Woman* (1980) and *Give Them Stones* (1987) depict the difficulty of raising a family in the midst of violence and prejudice. The heroine in Deirdre Madden's *Hidden Symptoms* (1986) imagines the violence as the acts of a madman tearing his flesh. The dramatist Anne Devlin exposes the abuse of women within paramilitary groups in *Ourselves Alone* (1986), and presents a more optimistic view of women's possibilities in *After Easter* (1994); Devlin's short stories, particularly "Naming the Names" in *The Way-Paver* (1986), are unforgettable accounts of the horrors of urban violence. Christina Reid focuses on a group of Catholic un-employed teenagers in the topical play *Joyriders* (1987); her *Belle of Belfast City* (1989) explores the divisions in Unionist families. Members of the experimental Chara-banc Theatre Company cowrote many plays between 1983 and 1990; writer-in-residence Marie Jones pro-duced *A Night in November* (first published in 1995) in 1994, focusing on sectarian hatred. The experimental poetry of Medbh McGuckian often comments obliquely on the conflict, while Eavan Boland overtly exposes po-litical violence in the North and South, past and present.

Texts by twentieth-century Irish women writers have not only represented women characters, women's concerns, and women's perspectives absent in earlier works by male writers; many of these authors have moved beyond mimesis, envisioning alternative fu-tures. In so doing, they have altered the way in which Ireland itself can be read.

SEE ALSO Arts: Modern Irish and Anglo-Irish Litera-ture and the Arts since 1800; Drama, Modern; Fic-tion, Modern; Poetry, Modern; **Primary Docu-ments:** "Scattering and Sorrow" (1936); "Inquisitio 1584" (c. 1985); "Feis" ("Carnival") (c. 1990)

Bibliography

Contemporary Irish Drama. Special Issue. *Colby Quarterly* 27 (December 1991).

Grant, David, ed. *The Crack in the Emerald: New Irish Plays.* 1994.

Haberstroh, Patricia Boyle. *Women Creating Women: Contem-porary Irish Women Poets.* 1996.

Quinn, Kathleen. "Silent Voices." *Theatre Ireland* 30 (winter 1993): 9–11.

Saint Peter, Christine. *Changing Ireland: Strategies in Contem-porary Women's Fiction.* 2000.

Somerville-Arjat, Gillean, and Rebecca E. Wilson. *Sleeping with Monsters: Conversations with Scottish and Irish Women Poets.* 1990.

Teresa Deevy and Irish Women Playwrights. Special Issue. *Irish University Journal* 25 (spring–summer 1995).

Weekes, Ann Owens. *Irish Women Writers: An Uncharted Tra-dition.* 1990.

Weekes, Ann Owens. *Unveiling Treasures: The Attic Guide to the Published Work of Irish Women Literary Writers.* 1993.

Ann Owens Weekes

Local Government since 1800

The nineteenth century saw a dramatic expansion in the scope and authority of local government together with its gradual democratization. This process was reversed in the twentieth century, with power moving back to the center.

In the early nineteenth century responsibility for urban government was shared by municipal corpora-tions (where they existed), parish vestries, and manor courts. These bodies paid little attention to the provision of local services, and in 1828 urban property holders were empowered by act of Parliament to elect commis-sioners to provide such basic services as street lighting and the construction of sewers. The powers and respon-sibilities of town commissioners were gradually in-creased over the course of the century. The vast majori-ty of Irish municipal corporations were abolished in 1840, having developed into exclusive, self-perpetuating oligarchies. Only ten (with the later addi-tion of Wexford) survived to become elected councils.

The primary organ of local administration in rural areas was the grand jury, which was empowered to raise money by means of local taxation to provide for the upkeep of roads, bridges, and public buildings such as jails and courthouses. Many of the grand jury's tax-ing powers, such as those relating to the provision of county infirmaries, were discretionary and rarely uti-lized. Growing concerns about poverty, ill health, and disorder in Ireland led to the imposition of statutory re-sponsibilities on grand juries. For example, beginning in 1817 they could be required to build and maintain dis-trict lunatic asylums that were managed by centrally appointed boards of governors. The county constabu-lary established in 1822 was similarly funded by but not administered by grand juries. As the century pro-ceeded, the grand jury thus became increasingly impor-tant as a taxing rather than an administrative authori-ty. As expenditure levels rose, criticism of the grand-jury system increased: Not only were grand juries unrepresentative of the local community, but they were also alleged to be corrupt and inefficient. Grand jurors were nominated by the high sheriff from the leading property owners of the county, excluding nobles, and were widely believed to abuse the system for their own personal gains. Government ministers shared the popu-lar dissatisfaction with the way in which grand-jury af-fairs were conducted, but they were reluctant to con-template any major reform, believing that Ireland was not ready for local democracy in rural areas. Legislation passed in 1818, 1833, and 1836 did reduce the opportunities for abuse by introducing stricter accounting procedures and by giving ratepayers a limited role in authorizing expenditures. More significantly, however, the administrative power of the grand jury was increasingly eclipsed by the poor-law board, which was composed partly of guardians elected by the ratepayers and partly of local magistrates sitting ex officio.

First introduced in 1838, poor-law boards were entrusted with a wide range of responsibilities in addition to their primary tasks of managing workhouses and distributing relief to the poor. Administration of local dispensaries was transferred from grand juries to poor-law boards in the 1850s, and the boards became the administering authorities of the health and safety legislation of the 1860s and 1870s. Changes in local expenditures illustrate the increasing importance of the poor-law system: while the level of county taxation, which had risen steeply in the first half of the nineteenth century, remained fairly static in the second half of the century, poor-law expenditure doubled. In the early decades of the poor-law system, landowners or their agents dominated most boards of guardians, but this changed in the 1880s following the radicalization of rural politics that took place during the years of the Land War. Poor-law elections were increasingly contested as part of the national campaign for self-government, and elected guardians began to replace ex-officios as board officers. The shift in power on many poor-law boards produced a far more politicized and polarized system. In addition to serving as training grounds for nationalist politicians, poor-law boards gave women, who became eligible to serve as guardians in 1896, their first experiences in holding local government office.

The Local Government Act of 1898 established a comprehensive system of democratic local government in Ireland. Based on the English measure of 1888, the act introduced a two-tier system of county and district councils. The administrative responsibilities of grand juries were transferred to elected county councils. Rural district councils took on the functions of poor-law boards and also became the sanitary authorities for their areas. (In urban areas municipal corporations and town commissioners operated largely unchanged and separate boards of guardians were retained.) The local government board was given the task of supervising the activities of the new councils, and its approval was required for many of their acts, including appointments and dismissals. All councillors and poor-law guardians were elected by a householder franchise that, unlike the parliamentary franchise, included women and peers. Following vigorous lobbying by women's organizations, women obtained the right to run for election as district councillors, though not, until 1911, as county councillors. The most significant changes produced by the Local Government Act were not to the structure of local administration, but in the composition of its constituent bodies: In contrast to unionist-dominated grand juries, county councils were, in most cases, nationalist-dominated.

As the campaign for national self-government gathered momentum in the early decades of the twentieth century, relations between central and local governments deteriorated. After the establishment of the Dáil government in 1919 many local councils refused to recognize British authority and declared their allegiance to Dáil Éireann. Irish republicans regarded both the local-government system and its practitioners with suspicion, seeing the former as extravagant and expensive and the latter as inefficient and corrupt. While the basic structures remained in place in both parts of Ireland following independence, local government in the Free State lost many of its functions, including health and welfare administration, either to central government or to national or regional administrative boards. (Poor-law boards were abolished in 1923 and rural-district councils in 1925.) The establishment in the 1930s of the city- and county-manager system, whereby council services are administered not by committees of elected councillors but under the direction of an appointed manager, and the replacement of local property taxation with block grants from central government, further weakened the power and authority of local representatives. Since 1935 a universal adult franchise has operated in local elections.

In Northern Ireland, local government became the focus of allegations of gerrymandering and discrimination, primarily against Catholics. Proportional representation in local elections, intended to ensure minority representation, was abolished in 1922, and the retention of property and businessmen's votes, long after these had been abandoned in Britain and independent Ireland, gave unionists a significant electoral advantage. Universal adult suffrage was introduced for local elections in 1969. In the following year the Stormont government accepted the report of a review body chaired by Sir Patrick Macrory recommending the reorganization of local government. This led to the establishment in 1973 of twenty-six district councils responsible for services such as refuse disposal and environmental health, and area boards, whose members were nominated by government, to control health, education, and library services. Macrory had intended that this system would work in tandem with the Northern Ireland Assembly; the absence of this top tier of local government, often referred to as the "Macrory gap," resulted in a significant democratic deficit at the local level.

SEE ALSO Electoral Politics from 1800 to 1921; Home Rule Movement and the Irish Parliamentary Party: 1870 to 1891; Protestant Ascendancy: Decline, 1800 to 1930; **Primary Documents:** Letter Advocating Federalism as an Alternative to Repeal (November 1844)

Bibliography

Aughey, Arthur, and Duncan Morrow, eds. *Northern Ireland Politics.* 1996.

Chubb, Basil. *The Government and Politics of Ireland.* 3d edition, 1992.

Crossman, Virginia. *Local Government in Nineteenth-Century Ireland.* 1994.

Feingold, W. L. *The Revolt of the Tenantry: The Transformation of Local Government in Ireland, 1872–86.* 1984.

Virginia Crossman

Lockout of 1913

The great Dublin Lockout was a seminal event in modern Irish history that marked the coming of age of the trade union movement in Ireland. Before the arrival of the lockout's charismatic leader James Larkin, efforts to organize unskilled Irish workers had been relatively unsuccessful. Larkin's great achievement was to convince workers to adopt his syndicalist tactics and use mass solidarity action, including widespread use of the sympathetic strike, to win major concessions from employers.

In the first six months of 1913 a series of strikes by the newly formed Irish Transport and General Workers' Union (ITGWU), which Larkin founded as a breakaway from the more conservative British based National Union of Dock Labourers, secured pay increases of up to 25 percent for members. In July employers agreed to a conciliation board to curb industrial unrest, despite opposition from the city's most powerful business leader, William Martin Murphy. When Larkin tried to organize workers in the Dublin United Tramways Company (DUTC), of which Murphy was chairman, Murphy began systematically purging ITGWU members. On 26 August Larkin called a strike and urged workers to "black," or boycott, DUTC trams. Murphy, who was president of the Dublin Chamber of Commerce, persuaded 400 of the city's main employers to lock out ITGWU members. Other workers who refused to sign declarations denouncing the ITGWU were sacked. Within a month 100,000 people, a third of the city's population, was suffering hardship as a result of the dispute. The general mortality rate in Dublin rose by 17 percent during the lockout and the rate for young children by almost 100 percent (Dublin Corporation Reports 1913–1914). These figures would have been much higher but for aid worth more than £93,000 sent by the British Trades Council.

Inevitably, the dispute degenerated into naked class warfare. Murphy's antipathy toward Larkin and the ITGWU was ideological as well as economic. Like many conservative nationalists, he feared syndicalism as a vehicle for anglicization, socialism, and secularization. These fears were reinforced by the "Dublin Kiddies' Scheme," which provided foster homes for strikers' children in Britain. In opposing the scheme, employers were able to mobilize support from the main churches, the middle classes, and constitutional nationalists against the strikers. Radical nationalists such as Patrick Pearse and feminists such as Countess Markievicz and Hannah Sheehy Skeffington supported the strikers.

The ITGWU and many other unions supporting its actions such as the Bricklayers, Builders' Labourers, Carpenters and Jointers, Carpet Planners and Women Workers' Union, would have collapsed without the help of the British Trades Union Congress (TUC). However, Larkin's syndicalism and his verbal abuse of leading British trade union leaders alienated the TUC as much as Dublin employers. By February 1914 most strikers had returned to work on the employers' terms. Nevertheless, the lockout marked the beginning of a decade of upheaval. Workers formed the Irish Citizen Army in November 1913 to defend themselves against the police, new alliances between socialists and radical nationalists were forged, and the lockout convinced many trade unionists that they must embrace political action to achieve their objectives.

SEE ALSO Connolly, James; Labor Movement; Larkin, James; Markievicz, Countess Constance; Murphy, William Martin; O'Brien, William; Trade Unions

Bibliography

Clarkson, J. Dunsmore. *Labour and Nationalism in Ireland.* 1970.

Greaves, C. D. *The Irish Transport and General Workers Union: The Formative Years, 1909–1923.* 1982.

Keogh, Dermot. The *Rise of the Irish Working Class.* 1982.

Larkin, E. James. *Larkin, 1876–1947: Irish Labour Leader.* 1965.

Nevin, Donald. *James Larkin: Lion of the Fold.* 1999.

Wright, Arnold. *Disturbed Dublin: The Story of the Great Strike.* 1914.

Yeates, Padraig. *Lockout: Dublin 1913.* 2000.

Padraig Yeates

Lombard, Peter

Peter Lombard (c. 1555–1625), theologian and historian, archbishop of Armagh, was born in Waterford the son of a city merchant. He attended the grammar school of Peter White at Kilkenny and studied with the historian William Camden in London. He moved then to Louvain, where he studied theology and graduated in 1575 as "primus universitatis," the leading scholar of his year. Having attained a doctorate in 1594 and taught with distinction at Louvain, Lombard went to Rome in 1598 to represent the interests of his university at the papal court. He was to spend the rest of his life there.

In his early years at Rome he became deeply involved as the agent of Hugh O'Neill, earl of Tyrone, who was championing the defense of Roman Catholicism in Ireland. To further O'Neill's campaign he wrote *De insulae Hiberniae commentarius* (Commentary on the island of Ireland) in 1600 (unpublished until 1632) to contextualize for Pope Clement VIII O'Neill's rebellion and to argue the case for the excommunication of those who refused to help him. Unlike the majority of his fellow Old Englishmen, he urged strenuously the transfer of the sovereignty of Ireland from Queen Elizabeth to a Catholic monarch, ideally a Spanish Habsburg. In constructing his case, Lombard presented a most persuasive vision of Ireland as a potentially rich and viable Catholic nation. It was due to his closeness to O'Neill that Lombard was appointed archbishop of Armagh in 1601, a post he held until his death in 1625, though he never resided in his diocese.

Thereafter, Lombard's interests centered on theological issues and the advocacy of Tridentine renewal in Ireland. As a leading Vatican theologian, he adjudicated on matters concerning grace, the heliocentric theories of Galileo, the Roman church and churches of the eastern rite, and the question of church-state relations. In respect to the last, his position had changed since 1600: in 1616 he was prepared to countenance a heretic as monarch as long as tolerance of Catholicism was assured. This was particularly relevant to Ireland as he became reconciled to the monarchy of James I. Lombard played a crucial role in promoting the Counter-Reformation in Ireland. He advised the Curia on the appointment of Irish bishops, arguing strongly for a resident episcopacy. His foresight is demonstrated by his concern for the establishment of an Irish College at Rome, though this was not fully accomplished until after his death.

SEE ALSO Council of Trent and the Catholic Mission; English Political and Religious Policies, Responses to (1534–1690)

Bibliography

O'Connor, Thomas. "Peter Lombard's *Commentarius* (1600): Ireland as a European Catholic State." In *Irish Migrants in Europe after Kinsale, 1602–1820*, edited by Thomas O'Connor and Marian Lyons. 2002.

Silke, J. J. "Later Relations between Primate Peter Lombard and Hugh O'Neill." *Irish Theological Quarterly* 22 (1955): 15–30.

Silke, J. J. "Primate Lombard and James I." *Irish Theological Quarterly* 22 (1955): 124–150.

Colm Lennon

Loyalist Paramilitaries after 1965

Hard-line unionist opposition to the modernizing policies of Terence O'Neill inspired quasi-military organizations modeled after the Ulster Volunteer Force of the Third Home Rule Bill period; these organizations also drew on near-continuous traditions of paramilitary action (especially in Belfast). Two of the most prominent were Tara (whose leader William McGrath was subsequently jailed for sexually abusing inmates of the Kincora Boys' Home) and the Ulster Protestant Volunteers (UPV), who marched in support of Ian Paisley.

The present-day Ulster Volunteer Force (UVF) was founded in 1965 by working-class loyalists on Belfast's Shankill Road. They were linked to UPV, Tara, and similar organizations; they may have had tacit support from some middle-class Ulster Unionist Party activists. The UVF was banned on 28 June 1966 after members committed three murders. O'Neill denied any connection between this "sordid conspiracy of criminals" and the Carson-era UVF. UVF leader Gusty Spence was imprisoned for the murder of a Catholic barman but the organization survived, growing rapidly in response to the upheavals of the early 1970s. The Red Hand Commandos, founded in the early 1970s by John McKeague, has usually been a satellite of the UVF.

The other principal loyalist paramilitary group, the Ulster Defence Association (UDA), was founded in 1972 as a coalition of local vigilante groups formed during sectarian rioting from 1969 onwards. After internal feuding between East and West Belfast leaders, Andy Tyrie emerged as "Supreme Commander." Both the UVF and UDA engaged in extensive sectarian murder campaigns epitomized by Lenny Murphy (d. 1982), whose UVF "Shankill Butchers" became notorious in 1975–1976 for torturing random victims to death and mutilating their bodies. UDA violence was often claimed by the "Ulster Freedom Fighters," a codename intended to preserve the UDA's legality. Some particularly sectarian or repulsive UVF crimes were attributed to the equally nonexistent "Protestant Action Force." Both groups developed youth wings and prisoner support organizations: Ulster Young Militants and Loyalist Prisoners' Aid for the UDA, Young Citizen Volunteers and Loyalist Prisoners of War for the UVF.

The upheavals of the early 1970s caused large numbers of unionists to dabble in paramilitarism either through "home-guard" organizations (which saw themselves as a reserve army to be unleashed in a doomsday situation) or the militaristic symbolism of the Vanguard organization. Thousands of working-class Protestants marched in loyalist rallies. The high point of loyalist paramilitary influence occurred in 1974: In that year loyalist paramilitaries provided the muscle for the Ulster Workers' Council strike, which brought down the power-sharing executive established under the Sunningdale Agreement. However, the paramilitaries were unable to establish a coherent political program and were further discredited by infighting, criminal activity, and extreme violence; these have persistently undermined their self-projected image as "defenders of the community." Tougher state security policies reduced fears of a doomsday situation, and mainstream unionist politicians reasserted their leadership.

In response to these setbacks, some loyalists attempted to develop a distinct political agenda; Spence tried to influence younger loyalists associated with the nascent Progressive Unionist Party (PUP) toward an explicitly socialist and secular loyalism, while in the late 1970s onwards Tyrie's deputy John McMichael advocated an independent Northern Ireland. McMichael founded the Ulster Loyalist Democratic Party (later called the Ulster Democratic Party) but received little

electoral support; at the same time he reorganized the UDA's military structure and orchestrated further sectarian murders.

Loyalist paramilitarism revived in response to the Anglo-Irish Agreement and a massive leadership upheaval in the UDA, involving the IRA's assassination of John McMichael, the resignation of Tyrie after an attempt on his life, and the removal of other leading figures by arrest or exposure as informers. (Tyrie was replaced by a collective leadership—the six-member "Inner Council" that unleashed young, more violent activists.) Individuals such as Billy Wright ("King Rat"), Portadown-based Mid-Ulster UVF "Brigadier," and Johnny Adair ("Mad Dog"), UDA commander in the Shankill area of Belfast became feared celebrity gangsters who combined extensive racketeering with sectarian murder.

The PUP (which developed a small core of experienced activists led by Hugh Smyth, David Ervine, and Billy Hutchinson) and the UDP (nominally led by McMichael's son Gary) persuaded the loyalist paramilitaries to call a cease-fire in October 1994 (after the IRA cease-fire in August). The loyalists played a significant role in the Belfast Agreement of 1998; their record allowed them to undercut DUP accusations of "a sell-out." The PUP had initial success as a working-class rival to the DUP but failed to expand outside its core support in parts of Belfast. The UDP, whose leadership was less experienced and cohesive, had little electoral success and eventually disintegrated. (It was replaced by the Ulster Political Research Group.) The loyalist ceasefires were underpinned by prisoner releases and racketeering opportunities. However, the organizations continued to engage in vigilantism and to intimidate isolated Catholic minorities. The increasing political profile of republicans and the restlessness of activists whose status derived from the gun increased internal tensions. In 1996 Wright, his profile raised by the 1995 and 1996 Drumcree protests, sought the overall leadership of loyalism; he seceded from the UVF and established the Loyalist Volunteer Force (LVF), combining anticompromise rhetoric with criminality. Wright was assassinated in prison by republicans in December 1997. Sectarian attacks were perpetrated by splinter groups calling themselves the Red Hand Defenders (generally regarded as a codename used by elements of the UDA and LVF) or the Orange Volunteers. Adair (jailed in 1994 for directing terrorism but released after the Belfast Agreement) became increasingly disruptive; in 1999 his alignment with the LVF led to a bloody UDA-UVF feud and his imprisonment. After his release in 2002, Adair attempted to displace the UDA leadership; another bloody feud again led to his arrest, while Adair supporters were driven from their Shankill power base after the assassination of an anti-Adair "Brigadier," John Gregg. Despite a renewed cease-fire loyalist organizations remained wracked by personal rivalries, criminality, and low-level violence. Loyalist paramilitary groups are generally less disciplined and politically aware than the IRA and contain a larger criminal element. (They have also been more prone to internal feuding than the IRA, though the Irish National Liberation Army [INLA] has experienced similar patterns of division and criminality.) Because of their traditional identification with the state, the loyalist working class does not have a history of creating a coherent oppositional subculture on the same scale as nationalists; the political opinions of the loyalist working class are largely reactive and their principal "oppositional" institutions—trade unions and independent churches—have been undermined by socioeconomic change. Protestant upper and middle-class elites have historically been more distant from their poorer co-religionists than their Catholic counterparts, who still tend to see themselves as part of a historically oppressed minority. The community's pro-state orientation means that potential middle-class and skilled working-class recruits tend to join the security forces, leaving paramilitaries with a relatively restricted and low-quality support base among the unskilled working class. (This forms a notable contrast to the paramilitaries' principal role model, the elite-led 1912–1914 UVF.) While shared origins have led some security force personnel to collaborate with loyalists, they also make it easier for security forces to detect, infiltrate, and capture or manipulate paramilitaries. The republican view of loyalist paramilitaries as simply state puppets is an exaggeration, but there has unquestionably been information-passing and cooperation among loyalist paramilitaries and some locally recruited security-force elements. In recent years there have also been revelations (most prominently involving the activities of Brian Nelson, a high-level infiltrator within the UDA) about the willingness of some military and police agencies to tolerate crimes by loyalist informants or even to assist loyalists in targeting particular republicans.

Loyalist paramilitaries maintain a certain constituency, but their role has been primarily reactive and destructive. It is unlikely that this will change in the future.

SEE ALSO Hunger Strikes; Irish Republican Army (IRA); Paisley, Ian; Ulster Politics under Direct Rule

Bibliography

Bruce, Steve. *The Red Hand: Protestant Paramilitaries in Northern Ireland.* 1992.

Cusack, Jim, and Henry McDonald. *UVF.* 1997. Expanded, 2000.

Dillon, Martin. *The Shankill Butchers: A Case Study of Mass Murder.* 1989.

Taylor, Peter. *Loyalists.* 1999.

Patrick Maume

M

MacHale, John

John MacHale (1791–1881), Catholic archbishop of Tuam (1834–1881), was born in Tyrawley, County Mayo, on 6 March. He was educated for the priesthood at Maynooth, and he taught there from 1820 until he became a bishop in 1825. While on the Maynooth staff, he wrote the "Hierophilos" letters criticizing the activities of Bible societies and the tithe system. The British government tried unsuccessfully to prevent him from becoming archbishop of Tuam in 1834.

MacHale condemned the national school system in 1838 against the wishes of both his fellow archbishop, Daniel Murray, who sat on the National Board of Education, and a majority of the hierarchy. In the 1840s he strongly supported Daniel O'Connell's campaign for repeal of the union of Great Britain and Ireland. MacHale was caustic in his criticisms of British government policy during the Great Famine, but he did not have any influence on that policy. MacHale opposed the third-level Queen's Colleges, which Murray favored, and he went to Rome to secure papal condemnation of the colleges.

Even though he supported the appointment of Paul Cullen as archbishop of Armagh in 1850, MacHale subsequently had a very poor relationship with Cullen, who controlled the Irish church in line with Roman policy. MacHale voted against papal infallibility at the First Vatican Council.

MacHale was interested in the Irish language and heritage; he translated classics into Irish and he preached in Irish. He is not, however, known as a great pastoral bishop. Toward the end of his lengthy episcopacy his diocese was neglected, and his relatives held the best clerical appointments. When a coadjutor was appointed to the 88-year-old MacHale, he refused to recognize him. A forceful and persistent critic of government policy in Ireland, he is regarded in Irish historiography as a powerful nationalist bishop and recalled as the "Lion of the West."

SEE ALSO Roman Catholic Church: 1690 to 1829; Roman Catholic Church: 1829 to 1891

Bibliography

O'Reilly, Bernard. *John MacHale, Archbishop of Tuam: His Life, Times, and Correspondence.* 1890.

Thomas McGrath

MacMurrough, Dermot, and the Anglo-Norman Invasion

The origins of the Anglo-Norman invasion lie in the conquest of England in 1066. William the Conqueror and his sons, who ruled England until 1135, held no fear of frontiers, manmade or natural, and within years of the Conquest were thrusting into Wales where, at least figuratively, the shores of Ireland beckoned. The closeness of Irish-Welsh contacts led to occasional friction, and it was probably only the English civil war after 1135 that prevented the Normans from taking earlier action regarding Ireland. Things changed with the accession to the English throne in 1154 of Henry II, who within a year held a royal council at Winchester to discuss the conquest of Ireland. The plan had the backing of the archbishop of Canterbury, still reeling from the decision of the papacy in 1152 to acknowledge the independence of the Irish church, ending Canterbury's dubious claim to primacy. The archbishop's secretary, John of Salisbury, was sent off to Rome, where an English abbot had been installed as Pope Adrian IV, and he obtained a letter, *Laudabiliter*, authorising Henry to invade Ireland to reform its church. This gave Henry his pretext and Canterbury its opportunity.

Unfortunately for Canterbury, Henry's influential mother advised against it, and in the following years King Henry was fully occupied in trying to keep intact an empire that stretched from Hadrian's Wall to the Pyrenees. Ireland would have to wait, and a full decade passed before there is evidence of contact. In 1165 the king was campaigning in Wales and, having spent his youth in Bristol, would have known the reputation of Ireland's Viking towns as suppliers of warships and warriors. Therefore, ships and troops were recruited from Dublin and probably Waterford and Wexford, but not in sufficient numbers to help force the Welsh into submission, so that Henry had to abandon his campaign. The overlord of these towns was the king of Leinster, Diarmait Mac Murchada (Dermot MacMurrough). As his vassals, it is unlikely that they were free to campaign without his assent, and he presumably lent his support to Henry's Welsh expedition. Perhaps he knew Henry, since Bristol was a port with trading links with Ireland's east-coast towns. In any case, it seems that after 1165 Henry owed Diarmait a favor, a return on which was soon sought.

Diarmait Mac Murchada was an ambitious ruler who had enjoyed since 1132 a successful reign in Leinster, lording it over the province's lesser rulers, although his power rarely extended further afield. He would have liked to breach Leinster's northern border, formed by the Liffey, and to conquer lands in Meath belonging to the declining southern Uí Néill dynasty, which had ruled for centuries as kings of Tara but were now gravely weakened. His problem was that the O'Connors were seeking to do the same from across the Shannon, while Tigernán Ó Ruairc, the relatively minor king of Bréifne, had similar aspirations. Conflict between them was inevitable, ongoing, and made more bitter by Mac Murchada's abduction of Ó Ruairc's wife Derbforgaill (Dervorgilla) in 1152, a slight to his honor that demanded retribution. There was little prospect of revenge while the high kingship was occupied by Muirchertach Mac Lochlainn of the northern Uí Néill dynasty, with whom Diarmait was allied; but his overthrow and death in 1166 left the high kingship in the hands of

Ruaidrí Ó Conchobair of Connacht, no friend of Mac Murchada's. It would not be long before Mac Murchada felt the brunt of his enemies' assault, especially since his own vassal kings within Leinster now rose against him.

Diarmait was fifty-nine years of age, and a lesser man might have had thoughts of retirement. Instead, when Ó Conchobair, Ó Ruairc, and the rebel Leinster kings rounded on him, Mac Murchada gathered his immediate family and on 1 August 1166 set sail for Bristol. The city fathers made him welcome and, undeterred by news that Henry II was off in Aquitaine, Mac Murchada headed for his court. Once there, he did fealty to the king, becoming his feudal vassal, holding Leinster as a fief. The potential of that act for Irish history was enormous, but first Diarmait had to recover his kingdom. He got little practical assistance from Henry—merely letters of introduction to vassals elsewhere, authorizing them to go to Mac Murchada's assistance. The latter would have known the Normans who had been in south Wales since the 1090s, and the Flemings whom Henry I had settled in Pembrokeshire a decade later, and of their thirst for adventure and skill at arms, and so headed directly for the area. Together with a small force of Flemings, led by Richard fitz Godebert (ancestor of the Roche family in Ireland), he returned to Ireland a year after his exile and recovered a foothold in his ancestral lands in Uí Chennselaig in southeast Leinster. That winter his old enemies came after him. Ó Ruairc received substantial financial compensation for the earlier insult to his honor, and Diarmait was allowed to retain possession of Uí Chennselaig, his enemies doubtless believing him suitably humbled.

It was a grave error as, in May of 1169, two fleets put ashore at Bannow Bay, Co. Wexford, the first led by the Norman-Welsh Robert fitz Stephen, as well as Maurice FitzGerald (ancestor of the Geraldines) and Robert de Barri (founder of the Barry family), the second by the Fleming Maurice de Prendergast, altogether consisting of about one hundred cavalry and at least three hundred infantry and archers. Together they conquered Wexford town and the surrounding area, which Mac Murchada bestowed on his new vassals, before proceeding to the task of recovering all Leinster. The high king, Ruaidrí Ó Conchobair, acquiesced in this, following Mac Murchada's promise to send the foreigners packing as soon as his position was secure. But the latter had no such intention, as was made plain in May 1170 when fresh Norman troops under Raymond le Gros (ancestor of the Carews) landed at Baginbun, Co. Wexford, and in August when there landed the most prominent figure yet, Richard "Strongbow" de Clare, lord of Pembroke and Chepstow. In return for his promised aid in securing all of Ireland for Mac Murchada, Strongbow was given Diarmait's daughter Aífe in marriage and the right of succession to the kingdom of Leinster. Shortly afterwards, in September 1170, the combined Norman and Leinster army marched on Dublin, by then effectively the capital of Ireland, which in spite of Ó Conchobair's best efforts they managed to storm and conquer. Their successes were so rapid and so far-reaching that few contemporaries can now have been in any doubt but that the Normans were in Ireland to stay.

SEE ALSO Norman Conquest and Colonization; Norman Invasion and Gaelic Resurgence

Bibliography

Duffy, Seán. *Ireland in the Middle Ages.* 1997.

Flanagan, Marie Therese. *Irish Society, Anglo-Norman Settlers, Angevin Kingship.* 1989.

Orpen, Goddard Henry. *Ireland under the Normans.* 4 vols. 1911–1920.

Orpen, Goddard Henry, ed. *The Song of Dermot and the Earl.* 1892.

Scott, Alexander Brian, and Francis Xavier Martin, eds. *Expugnatio Hibernica. The Conquest of Ireland by Giraldus Cambrensis.* 1978.

Seán Duffy

~

McQuaid, John Charles

Archbishop of Dublin John Charles McQuaid (1895–1973) was born in Cootehill, Co. Cavan, on 28 July 1895. Ordained a Roman Catholic priest on 29 June 1924, he served as a member of the staff at Blackrock College, a Catholic boys' school on the south side of Dublin, between 1925 and 1939. He became president of the college in 1931, a post he retained until 1939, and was ordained archbishop of Dublin on 27 December 1940.

McQuaid was opposed to interdenominational cooperation, fearing proselytism by Protestants and the moral weakness of his own flock. In 1942 he successfully objected to the proposed Anti-Tuberculosis League because of its nondenominational makeup and declared the enrollment of Catholics at Protestant Trinity College to be a mortal sin. McQuaid's anxiety to protect Catholic interests also led to proactive initiatives like the Cath-

olic Social Service Conference, a federation of previously disparate charities to aid the Catholic poor of Dublin. Within the Irish context his Catholic Social Welfare Bureau was a pioneering venture that offered protection to Irish emigrants and trained Catholic social workers.

McQuaid believed in cooperating with the Irish government to secure the predominance of Catholic principles in social policy and legislation. He played an important role in drawing up the Irish Constitution of 1937 and in shaping other pieces of legislation concerning censorship, contraception, liquor licensing, adoption, education, and health. He is best remembered for his role in the "Mother and Child Controversy" of 1951 when he objected to a new and free health scheme for mothers. His objection led to the resignation of the minister for health, Noël Browne. The controversy, heralded as the most significant church-state clash in the history of the state, revealed the latent power of the Catholic hierarchy in Ireland and exposed the raw nerves of social change. McQuaid was seen to have defeated Browne's scheme; however, he received public criticism for his interference and failed to wield as much influence when Eamon de Valera's government introduced a modified version of the same scheme in 1953. Although reassured by the papal encyclical *Humanae vitae* (On human life) issued in July 1968, which reiterated the church's stance on the immorality of contraception, McQuaid was unable to accept the new ecumenical era introduced by the Second Vatican Council beginning in 1962. He retired on 29 December 1971 and died on 7 April 1973.

SEE ALSO Ecumenism and Interchurch Relations; Gaelic Catholic State, Making of; Mother and Child Crisis; Politics: Independent Ireland since 1922; Roman Catholic Church: Since 1891; Secularization; **Primary Documents:** Letter to John A. Costello, the Taoiseach (5 April 1951)

Bibliography

Cooney, John. *John Charles McQuaid: A Ruler of Catholic Ireland.* 2000.

Feeney, John. *John Charles McQuaid: The Man and the Mask.* 1974.

Kelly, Peter. *John Charles McQuaid: What the Papers Say.* Esras Films, Radio Teilfís Éireann, 1998.

Lindsey Earner-Byrne

Magnates, Gaelic and Anglo-Irish

The Anglo-Norman invasion, by reducing the arena of warfare that was left in the hands of native Irish lords to less than half of the island, meant that the days had ended when great royal circuits of Ireland were made by provincial kings to assert their claim to the elusive high-kingship. Instead, those who retained their territories intact, primarily in the north and west of the island, raided their neighbors in petty pursuit of cattle-prey, while those who lost lands in the colonial settlement compensated by expanding into their neighbors' territory. As the colony expanded, two strategies were variously employed: one, never very effective for long, was to unite with their fellow Irish against a common threat; the other was the temptation to align with the all-conquering invader against a neighbor who had, after all, been an enemy for generations.

As for the Anglo-Normans, antagonisms fueled by land-hunger had been in evidence from the beginning, and for them too an alliance with the Irish "enemy" (frequently sealed by marriage, fosterage, or the bond of *gossipred* [sponsorship at baptism]) could prove useful if it undermined the ambitions of a rival Anglo-Norman. Thus, although there was undoubtedly an ongoing war in medieval Ireland between native lords and newcomers, the paramount powers on both sides had much in common, and as time wore on, the differences became fewer. On the Irish side, by and large, the dynasties most prominent at the time of the invasion remained so after its initial shockwave, an exception being the MacDunleavys of Ulaidh (east Ulster), while the Mac Lochlainns of Cineál Eoghain were supplanted by their O'Neill cousins in the early thirteenth century. Some thrived, but at the expense of other Irish dynasties: when the Mac Carthys lost Cork, they compensated in Kerry; when the O'Briens lost Limerick, they fell back on their Clare birthright.

It would have been harder to predict at the start of the invasion which of the invaders would stand the test of time. This was because of the feudal law of inheritance, which stipulated that an estate without a direct male heir passed to another family or families through heiresses, as in the case of Strongbow's lordship of Leinster and de Lacy's lordship of Meath. Predictability came only with the creation in the early fourteenth century of three new earldoms entailed in the male line, so that the estates were never subdivided among heiresses but were inherited by the nearest male family member. Henceforth, therefore, the paramount Anglo-Irish magnates were the Geraldine earls of Kildare and Desmond,

Tomb effigy of Thomas de Cantwell (d. 1320), Kilfane Church, Co. Kilkenny (early fourteenth century), an example of Gothic sculpture. © MICHAEL CARTER; CORDAIY PHOTO LIBRARY LTD./CORBIS. REPRODUCED BY PERMISSION.

and the Butler earls of Ormond. Unfortunately for the vast de Burgh (Burke) estate of Connacht and Ulster, it was not so entailed, and the earl's murder in 1333 saw the inheritance go to an absentee heiress, a situation having two main consequences: cadet branches of the family in Connacht filled the vacuum and flourished while the absence of a resident Anglo-Norman magnate in Ulster was an enormous stroke of luck for the O'Neill family.

These were the dominant players on the Irish political scene in the fifteenth century, troubled only by the turbulence of the contemporary English scene: the Butlers had Lancastrian affiliations and strong English landed interests, the Geraldines were Yorkist sympathizers, largely free of English interests and much more immersed in native Irish politics. Control by the various families over government waxed and waned with developments in England, the Kildares emerging preeminent, despite supporting Yorkist pretenders in the early Tudor years. Their downfall came only with their failed rebellion in 1534, a key factor in the collapse of the superstructure of power in medieval Ireland.

SEE ALSO English Government in Medieval Ireland; Gaelic Recovery; Gaelic Society in the Late Middle Ages; Norman Invasion and Gaelic Resurgence

Bibliography

Bryan, Donough. *Gerald FitzGerald, the Great Earl of Kildare (1456–1513)*. 1933.

Cosgrove, Art, ed. *Medieval Ireland, 1169–1534*. Vol. 2 of *A New History of Ireland*. 1987. Reprint, 1993.

Curtis, Edmund. *A History of Mediaeval Ireland from 1086 to 1513*. 1938.

Duffy, Seán. *Ireland in the Middle Ages*. 1997.

Ellis, Steven. *Ireland in the Age of the Tudors, 1447–1603*. 1998.

Frame, Robin. *English Lordship in Ireland, 1318–1361*. 1981.

Simms, Katharine. *From Kings to Warlords: The Changing Political Structure of Gaelic Ireland in the Later Middle Ages*. 1987.

Seán Duffy

Symbols of the Four Evangelists from the Book of Kells *(c. 800 C.E.). Clockwise from top: Man (St. Matthew), Eagle (St. John), Ox (St. Luke), and Lion (St. Mark).* © STAPLETON COLLECTION/CORBIS. REPRODUCED BY PERMISSION.

Manuscript Writing and Illumination

The promotion of Latin literacy was a high priority for the young Irish church, and later tradition frequently describes Saint Patrick leaving the necessary books in churches that he had founded. Saint Columba (Colmcille; died at Iona in 597 C.E.) was said to have been involved in a dispute in his youth about copying a new version of the psalter, and to have been copying a manuscript on his last day on earth. In later times some books were regarded as precious relics and enshrined in metal reliquaries—a practice that may have originated in an Irish reflex of the Roman tradition of keeping the book for papal masses in a sealed casket.

Scholars have disputed the locations where important Irish manuscripts of the early medieval period were written. In some cases it is impossible to establish the provenance of a manuscript, so the term *insular* is often used in preference to more precise geographical ascriptions. The earliest extended text to survive from Ireland is the bundle of wax tablets from Springmount Bog, Co.

Antrim, on which a student practiced the psalms in a script that owes much to late Roman cursive writing but is already distinctively Irish. The first almost complete manuscript that has come down to us is the *Cathach* of Saint Columba, a psalter, or book of the psalms, written on vellum in an Irish half-uncial script around the year 600 C.E. It was preserved until modern times by the O'Donnells (the saint's kin). The *Cathach* already shows the principal stylistic traits of later Irish manuscripts. Psalms begin with an enlarged capital, often embellished, followed by letters of smaller size that diminish in height until they merge with the body of the text—the effect is called *diminuendo*. The ornament is very simple: Letters are enriched by spiral scrolls and simple trumpet devices in the La Tène tradition, and Christian symbols (a dolphin or fish and the cross) appear. (The La Tène style is an abstract art form based on stylized vegetal motifs, spirals, and curvilinear scrolls associated with the Iron Age Celtic peoples of mainland Europe, Ireland, and Britain.) A fragmentary gospel book of about the same date in Trinity College Library, *Codex Usserianus Primus*, has a singe leaf devoted entirely to a painted cross of eastern style with an abbreviated Chi-Rho (monogram of Christ) and alpha and omega.

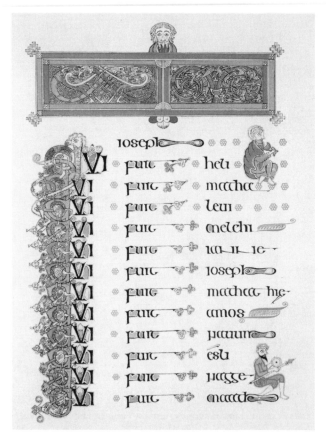

Genealogy of Christ from the Book of Kells, *a Hiberno-Saxon manuscript illumination.* © STAPLETON COLLECTION/CORBIS. REPRODUCED BY PERMISSION.

Nothing further is known of Irish manuscript production until the later seventh century, by which time Irish missions in north Britain and on the continent had created an entirely new climate. Influences from Anglo-Saxon England, Gaul, and probably Italy gave rise to a new eclectic ornamental style in monastic scriptoria.

The first manifestation of the mature insular style is the *Book of Durrow*, a luxury codex of the New Testament with prefatory matter and canon tables, which was preserved at Durrow, Co. Offaly, until it was given to Trinity College in the seventeenth century. With its remarkable carpet pages devoted entirely to ornament and to the cross and its highly original depiction of the symbols of the evangelists (Matthew, Mark, Luke, and John, the authors of the Gospels), it is a splendid hybrid. The spiral and trumpet scrolls of the La Tène tradition dominate its decoration—one carpet page is a remarkable evocation of the spirit of the bronzesmith and enameller. The initial letters and diminuendo of the *Cathach* have been recreated here with great virtuosity and magnificence. Interlace, varied in rhythm and color, makes its appearance for the first time in insular art. A page devoted to animal art of Germanic inspiration has

led some to attribute the manuscript to Northumbria or Iona. The careful observer will see even on pages that are ostensibly wholly "Celtic" stylized animal heads, but expressed in the idiom of spirals and trumpets. Gospels are prefaced by whole-page representations of the evangelists' symbols, and the genealogy of Christ in Matthew's gospel is introduced by a finely decorated Chi-Rho.

The Anglo-Saxon –style beasts have been compared to metalwork from the Sutton Hoo ship burial, suggesting an early seventh-century date for Durrow, but a late seventh-century date is more plausible. The art-historical arguments can tell us nothing about provenance, for the style could well have been present in the Irish midlands in the seventh century. The *Book of Durrow* is associated with Columba, and it is clearly related to the tradition of the later *Book of Kells*. The style could conceivably have been practiced in Durrow, itself a Columban monastery. Probably, though, it was produced in Iona and belonged to a tradition that was intimately connected, as the evangelists' symbols show, with the emergence of very similar beast symbols on Pictish carved stones, and in contact with both the Irish and Anglo-Saxon worlds.

Two manuscripts now in Durham and probably originally in the monastery of Lindisfarne (founded by Aidan of Iona in the 630s) belong to the mixed traditions of Northumbrian Christianity, which owed much to Irish ecclesiastics. One of these shows the development of a more fluid animal style that would be greatly elaborated in the eighth century; the other has the imprint of a now lost crucifixion scene in which Christ's body is enveloped in a tightly wound garment. This is the earliest evidence that painted scenes were part of the insular repertoire.

The Lindisfarne Gospels, associated with the cult of Saint Cuthbert, are remarkable. The book may have been created for the translation of Cuthbert's relics in 698 C.E. to Lindisfarne. It is the greatest and most elaborate of the earliest insular gospel books. Art-historically, a date of about 700 C.E. for the manuscript is plausible. Its animal ornament with tightly wound, fabulous, but entirely believable interlaced beasts, its elegantly caricatured birds, a remarkable cross-carpet page, stunning zoomorphized spiral scrollwork, and beautiful script make the book a tour de force. Symbolism of beasts and birds is prominent, but its evangelist portraits, bearing the unmistakable impress of the Mediterranean culture of the monasteries of Monkwearmouth and Jarrow, place this manuscript at the heart of the Northumbrian Renaissance. Nevertheless, the style of ornament is uncannily close to that of the Tara Brooch and Donore Hoard—both from eastern Ireland—and of the Hunterston Brooch from Ayrshire in Scotland (almost certainly of Irish manufacture). These seem to locate the origin of its decoration partly in the art of the metalworkers patronized by Irish potentates. The legacy of Lindisfarne is apparent in the greatly inferior Lichfield Gospels and in the persistence of elements of the La Tène style in later Anglo-Saxon manuscripts.

Irish and Anglo-Saxon manuscript styles diverged during the eighth century. The sample of Irish survivors is very small, and only a few "pocket" gospel books are known. These have a smaller, often cursive script, simplified decoration of capitals, and charming if rather naïve evangelist portraits and symbols. Good examples are the *Book of Mulling* and the *Book of Dimma* in Trinity College and part of the Stowe Missal in the Royal Irish Academy—the latter almost certainly dates from after 800 C.E.

Opinion is sharply divided on the date and origin of the famous *Book of Kells.* The current consensus is that it was created on the island of Iona toward the end of the eighth century. The book was probably brought to Kells, Co. Meath, a refuge of Columban monks from the Viking onslaught, in the tenth century C.E. It was at Kells in 1007 C.E. when it was stolen from the church and later found with the ornaments torn off the cover. The *Annals of Ulster,* recording both the theft and the recovery in that year, call it "the chief relic of the western world." It was given to Trinity College in the seventeenth century. Though 340 folios survive, the book is incomplete. Kells has highly decorated canon tables, carpet pages, evangelist portraits and symbols, and figured scenes (the Temptation, the Virgin and Child, the Arrest of Christ)—all the work of a number of artists who employed with élan interlace, animal interlace, and beast ornament, especially of felines (lions?), birds, and serpents. There are vignettes in minor initials and interlinear paintings—an eagle seizing a fish, a warrior, chickens, and butterflies—some of which reflect on the adjacent text. Christological symbolism is everywhere. A particularly important page is devoted to the Chi-Rho that introduces the genealogy of Christ. This is a remarkable composition based on La Tène spirals and trumpets, combined with tiny illustrations of cats, mice, and butterflies, and other extraordinary displays of fine, almost microscopic decoration. A fragmentary manuscript in Turin may have approached Kells in ambition, and another in the Library of Sankt Gallen shared the Kells scriptorium's interest in figured scenes, but neither approaches Kells in virtuosity and ornamental skill.

In the ninth century a gospel book decorated with animal ornament, evangelist portraits, and fine geometric ornament was written by MacRegol, abbot of Birr (d.

822). It is preserved in the Bodleian Library. A much more elegant product is the *Book of Armagh,* created by the scribe Ferdomnach for the Abbot Torbach early in the ninth century. It contains the four gospels, documents relating to Saint Patrick, and a life of Saint Martin of Tours. Its elegant script and evangelist symbols are in black ink.

The high style of manuscript production was dealt a fatal blow by the Viking wars of the ninth and tenth centuries, and later books do not approach in quality and ambition the work of the early period.

SEE ALSO Arts: Early and Medieval Arts and Architecture; Hiberno-Latin Culture

Bibliography

Alexander, J. J. G. *Insular Illuminated Manuscripts, 6th to 9th Century.* 1978.

Fox, P., ed. *The Book of Kells Ms 58 Trinity College Library Dublin.* 1990.

Henry, F. *Irish Art in the Early Christian Period to AD 800.* 1965.

Henry, F. *Irish Art during the Viking Invasions, 800–1020 AD.* 1967.

Meehan, B. *The Book of Kells.* 1994.

Meehan, B. *The Book of Durrow, a Medieval Masterpiece at Trinity College, Dublin.* 1996.

O'Mahoney, F., ed. *The Book of Kells: Proceedings of a Conference at Trinity College, Dublin, 6–9 September, 1992.* 1994.

Michael Ryan

Marianism

The antiquity of devotion to the Virgin Mary among the educated and the literate in Ireland in the Christian era before 1800 is not in doubt, but the emergence of an intense Marian piety taking organized forms among the mass of the Catholic population was mostly a development of the late nineteenth and twentieth centuries. Evidence of Marian devotion prior to 1800 survives in Bardic poetry, in traditional prayers, and in the use of the rosary among some Irish Catholics. But before the Great Famine the orientation of so much of popular religion toward sacred spaces in the natural environment (holy wells, sacred trees and stones, the reputed graves of saintly men and women, revered monastic ruins, and other ancient pilgrimage sites) meant that Catholic piety was not yet focused on the Virgin Mary.

The rapid spread of the Marian cult after 1850 can be traced to a combination of external and internal factors. During the long reign of Pope Pius IX (1846–1878) the papacy itself and the Vatican bureaucracy were squarely behind the propagation of devotion to the Blessed Mother throughout the Western world. In numerous instances this campaign impinged directly on Ireland. Rome was a vigorous proponent of parish missions as a means of religious revival and evangelization, and parish missions were perhaps the single most important agency in the extension of the Devotional Revolution in Ireland after 1850. The male religious orders that conducted parish missions usually placed a heavy emphasis on the cult of Mary by erecting statues and altars to her in the churches they visited, by establishing Marian sodalities and confraternities, and by encouraging the praying of the rosary through their preaching and example.

The swiftly multiplying female religious orders were also of great importance in the spread of the Marian cult. In their schools the nuns promoted devotion to the Blessed Mother especially by setting up sodalities, the most widespread of which were those connected with the Children of Mary. In the general extension of this sodality the apparitions at Lourdes in 1858 exercised a major impetus. The Lourdes phenomenon, which deeply influenced Catholic popular piety all over Western Europe, had an extraordinary impact in Ireland. It greatly multiplied the number of Children of Mary sodalities in Irish convent schools over the course of the following decade. More broadly, it led to a remarkable intensification of the Marian cult throughout most of Catholic Ireland. One dramatic sign of this development was the famous series of apparitions of the Virgin Mary (and other visions) beginning in August 1879 at Knock in County Mayo. That small western village became for a few years the site of great religious fervor (including claims of hundreds of cures) and the focus of large pilgrimages from other parts of Ireland.

Although Knock had steeply declined as a pilgrimage center by the late 1880s, the broader Marian wave gathered even more force and crested in the years 1930 to 1960. In those decades signs of the cult of Mary were everywhere in Ireland. There was a proliferation of books, pamphlets, periodicals, films, and plays linked to the cult. A pilgrimage to Lourdes became an annual exercise for many thousands of Irish Catholics, and many more thousands who remained at home supported the pilgrims with money, prayers, and benevolent actions. So strong was the Marian zeal gripping Irish Catholicism that Knock shrine itself experienced an extraordinary revival. According to shrine authorities, pilgrim traffic to Knock roughly tripled in the late 1930s, rising from about 80,000 in 1937 to nearly 250,000 in 1940. By the time of the "Marian Year" in 1954 the shrine authorities were boasting of a million pilgrims at Knock, though this figure appears to be a serious exaggeration.

Three explanations have been offered for the steep upward curve in Irish Marian enthusiasm over the period 1930 to 1960. First, the fierce anticlerical violence and desecration associated with the Spanish Civil War of 1936 to 1939 produced an intensified Marianism by way of reaction. A second factor was anticommunism, which flourished especially during the Cold War and took Our Lady of Fatima as its central icon. The cult of Fatima, with its central anticommunist message, eclipsed the cult of Lourdes in Ireland after 1945, and Irish Catholics embraced the praying of the rosary with unprecedented fervor. And third, there was a strong social and cultural dimension to Marianism in this period, when swiftly changing sexual mores outside of Ireland seemed to threaten the severe sexual restraint associated with the Irish demographic characteristics of late marriages and high rates of bachelorhood and spinsterhood. As the epitome of sexual purity, the Virgin Mary was perceived as the most essential bulwark of the traditional moral order.

Then, rather suddenly in the 1960s and 1970s, the Marian wave swiftly receded, and Irish Catholicism as a whole entered a troubled new era which has not yet ended. Already by the late 1960s traditionalists were bemoaning the near-collapse of the praying of the family rosary, for which they mostly blamed the impact of television on patterns of family life. Also clearly on the wane before 1970 were other Marian devotions such as May processions, the erection of household altars in the month of May, and the wearing of Miraculous Medals and Brown Scapulars. The flagship institutions of Irish Marianism—the Legion of Mary and Our Lady's Sodality—went into steep decline as well. The notorious episode of the "moving statues" in the summer of 1985, when thousands flocked to Marian shrines, was one of the last gasps of the old order. Among the leading reasons for this marginalization of Marianism in Ireland (and elsewhere) were the dramatic weakening (and eventual reversal) of the Cold War, the revolution in sexual attitudes, and the impact of the Second Vatican Council (1962–1965) in certain critical areas, especially liturgical reform (emphasizing Christ much more than Mary) and the sidelining of devotional practices linked to popular belief in miracles. These factors operated in a fundamentally new context hostile to Marian enthusiasm: From the 1960s Irish society was increasingly characterized by materialist values and cultural openness to the outside world.

SEE ALSO Devotional Revolution; Religion: Since 1690; Roman Catholic Church: 1829 to 1891; Roman Catholic Church: Since 1891; Secularization; Sodalities and Confraternities

Bibliography

Donnelly, James S., Jr. "The Marian Shrine of Knock: The First Decade." *Éire-Ireland* 28, no. 2 (summer 1993): 55–99.

Donnelly, James S., Jr. "The Peak of Marianism in Ireland, 1930–60." In *Piety and Power in Ireland, 1760–1960: Essays in Honour of Emmet Larkin*, edited by Stewart J. Brown and David W. Miller. 2000.

Larkin, Emmet. *The Historical Dimensions of Irish Catholicism.* 1976.

Larkin, Emmet. "The Parish Mission Movement, 1850–1880." In *Christianity in Ireland: Revisiting the Story*, edited by Brendan Bradshaw and Dáire Keogh. 2002.

Magray, Mary Peckham. *The Transforming Power of the Nuns: Women, Religion, and Cultural Change in Ireland, 1750–1900.* 1998.

James S. Donnelly, Jr.

~

Marian Restoration

The death of Edward VI and the succession of Mary in July 1553 marked a significant shift in religious policy in both Ireland and England, as a committed Protestant monarch was replaced by a firmly Catholic one. Mary, with the help of her cousin, the papal legate Cardinal Pole, restored England to papal obedience and the English church to Roman Catholic practice and belief. In England this was accompanied by the execution of several hundred Protestant heretics; in Ireland, however, where the Reformation's roots were far shallower, the return to Catholicism was less traumatic. Thus, rather than going to the stake for his beliefs, the Protestant archbishop of Dublin, George Browne, abandoned his wife, conformed to the new regime, and was allowed to remain as a prebendary of the re-Catholicized Saint Patrick's Cathedral. The only hint of violence was in Kilkenny, where the aggressively Protestant Bishop Bale was forced to flee the city by an angry Catholic populace.

The leading figure in the restoration of Catholicism in Ireland was George Dowdall, who returned from exile and was reinstated at his former see of Armagh in March 1553. As a good lawyer, Dowdall saw the revival of canon law as the essential vehicle for restoring Catholicism and reasserting the preeminence and standing of the church. He began by calling a provincial council of his clergy and issued seventeen canons. He may also have been influential in securing a papal bull that erected Ireland into a kingdom, thus restoring the link between Ireland, the English Crown, and the papacy that had been established by the 1155 papal bull *Laudabiliter*. Dowdall was certainly instrumental in securing the restoration of Saint Patrick's as a cathedral in 1554 to 1555 (despite the opposition of Lord Deputy Saint Leger). In 1554 a royal commission was appointed, which weeded out married bishops such as Browne, Staples in Meath, and Lancaster in Kildare and replaced them by conforming Catholics. Thus Browne was replaced in June 1555 by an English canon lawyer, Hugh Curwin, who set about restoring the Mass and the Roman Catholic liturgy to the Dublin cathedrals. The restoration of Catholicism was completed in 1557 when the Irish parliament repealed the Henrician Reformation legislation, and when a further royal commission was issued to identify and return the church plate and valuables that had been lost and distrained during the Reformation. After the death of Mary in 1558 it became apparent, from the grave difficulties which her half-sister Elizabeth I encountered in her attempts to reimpose Protestantism, just how effective the Marian re-Catholicization of Ireland had been.

SEE ALSO Church of Ireland: Elizabethan Era; Edwardian Reform; Protestant Reformation in the Early Sixteenth Century; Religion: 1500 to 1690

Bibliography

Edwards, R. D. *Church and State in Tudor Ireland.* 1935.

Hayes-McCoy, G. A. "Conciliation, Coercion, and the Protestant Reformation, 1547–71." In *A New History of Ireland*, Vol. 3, *Early Modern Ireland, 1534–1691*, edited by T. W. Moody, F. X. Martin, and F. J. Byrne. 1976.

Murray, James. "The Tudor Diocese of Dublin." Ph.D. diss., University of Dublin, 1997.

Alan Ford

Handloom weavers offering their bolts of cloth for sale to bleachers at the brown-linen market of Banbridge, Co. Down. Engraving by William Hincks, c. 1783. PHOTOGRAPH COURTESY OF DAVID W. MILLER.

~

Markets and Fairs in the Eighteenth and Nineteenth Centuries

Markets and fairs have ancient origins in Ireland, reaching back to the *aonach* (fair) in the native Irish tradition and to *margadh* (market), a loan word from the Viking world. Over the course of history, markets and fairs underwent mutations, yet their days remain fixed in the Irish psyche. *Lá aonaigh* (fair day) and *lá margaidh* (market day) engage the range of the senses and carry a raft of cultural meaning.

For the eighteenth and nineteenth centuries the most complete inventory of markets and fairs is to be found in a parliamentary report of 1853. This report records the name of each market and fair by location and county. It specifies the date of the patent or license, the name of the licensee, and the days on which the market or fair was held. The majority of the patents were allocated to individuals, usually landowners. Their provi-

sion ushered in modernizing influences. This much is clear from an analysis of some of the original licenses and from an examination of the associated tolls. Taken together, these demonstrate that the intended function of markets and fairs was to facilitate the sale of local agricultural produce for cash and thereby promote the commercialization of agriculture.

Once or twice a week the market served as an exchange center for a surrounding rural area. Most of the produce on offer, including butter, oats, wheat, flax, cattle, and horses, derived from local farms, whereas the market also afforded to landowners and their tenants opportunities for purchasing goods ranging from salt to domestic utensils and agricultural implements. The market as a mechanism of trade fitted routinely into the life of small towns and villages, of which there were 349 dispersed throughout the island in 1853.

The location of fairs was far less discriminating. According to the report of 1853, fairs were held at 1,297 different places in Ireland. However, towns and villages were the site of greatest frequency, with many of their fairs graduating to monthly occurrences by the mid-nineteenth century. This is well seen in County Limer-

Fair at Donnybrook (now a Dublin suburb) around 1840. Despite the quiet appearance in this illustration, the reputation of this fair for riotous disorder is reflected in the usage of "donnybrook" for an acrimonious quarrel. FROM MR. AND MRS. SAMUEL CARTER HALL, IRELAND: ITS SCENERY, CHARACTER, ETC. (1841–1843).

ick. By the second half of the eighteenth century this mid-Munster county had formed part of the most extensive of the fair hearths of Ireland, and the aggregate of its fairs in urban locations increased from 102 in 1787 to 175 in 1850.

Fair day spawned a whole range of transactional activity, including the buying and selling of cattle, sheep, pigs, pedlery (items and commodities offered for sale by peddlers or itinerant traders), sometimes horses, agricultural implements, and linen and woolen cloth; and it brought a much-needed injection of capital into the life of small urban settlements. About 1900, the Limerick town of Newcastle West, for instance, acted as a veritable catchall on a fair day. Here knotted gatherings assembled and broke, money changed hands, bills got paid, and publicans and shopkeepers waxed rich for the day. Even in the case of small villages the significance of fair day should not be underestimated. At Kilteely, County Limerick, for example, fairs in the 1840s drew large numbers of victuallers from County Cork and from the various towns of County Limerick, and sufficient transactional activity was generated for proceedings to last two days at a time.

Markets and fairs tended to sometimes occupy dual locations. On the one hand, the market came to be cen-

trally located in the market square or main street; on the other, the fair was consigned to a marginal venue. Such duality is well seen in estate villages like Dunlavin in County Wicklow or Milltown Malbay in County Clare, where the centrally located market house contrasts with the peripheral fair green. The first may be taken to represent the world of the landlord; the second, that of his tenants, and the symbolic interplay between the two was often expressed in terms of conflict.

Conflict and violence were common features of fair days; market days were in general more muted. At the heart of much of the violence of a fair day were: a lashing out at the makers of painful historical change by the various agrarian collectivities from the 1760s onward; an inveterate love of feuding and a commitment to clan and territory as epitomized by faction fighting; and a hardening of ethnic or religious cleavage, as exemplified by sectarian conflict. Faction fighters in particular targeted towns and villages whenever great assemblies were in session. Of these, fairs constituted the great majority, and most of the recorded encounters pertain to fair days. In the period 1806 through 1811, for example, frequent fights occurred at fairs in south Tipperary, Kilkenny, and Waterford. The contending factions were known as the Caravats (Carabhait) and Shanavests

(Sean-Bheisteanna). Hundreds of men usually took part, sometimes thousands. Once, at the fair of Kilgobnet in County Waterford, an Armageddon between the two sides failed to materialize, owing to prior disclosure to the military. But many encounters did occur at a time when the traditional faction stick was replaced by the ash plant weighted with lead. These weapons were supplemented by homemade swords and spears, and by whatever firearms could be mustered. Not surprisingly, many fights ended in fatalities. No fewer than twenty people were killed at the May fair of Golden, County Tipperary, in 1807. Altogether, hundreds must have died.

As well as notoriety, fairs also attracted celebrity. The Ould Lammas Fair at Ballycastle in County Antrim and Spancel Hill Fair in east Clare are celebrated in song. The Puck Fair of Killorglin, County Kerry, takes its name from the eponymous male goat that was "sometimes ornamented and paraded about the fair." It was the midsummer horse fair which first drew the Travellers (or Tinkers, then known as horse dealers) to Rathkeale around 1840, and a fair on the Cork-Kerry borderland brought "long-tailed" (an expression often used to denote a strong sense of identity and extensive itinerant connections) clans to converge "on a green fit / for a fabled stud of horses: / the hearth of Knocknagree." Ultimately, after 1900 nearly all the fairs and many of the markets failed to withstand the ruthless thrust of modernity.

SEE ALSO Migration: Seasonal Migration; Rural Industry; Towns and Villages

Bibliography

Clark, Samuel, and James S. Donnelly, Jr., eds. *Irish Peasants: Violence and Political Unrest, 1780–1914.* 1983.

Crawford, William H. "Markets and Fairs in County Cavan." *Breifne* 2, no. 3 (1984): 55–65.

Cronin, Denis A., et al., eds. *Irish Fairs and Markets: Studies in Local History.* 2001.

Harris, Tom. "Fairs and Markets in the Environment of County Meath." *Ríocht na Mídhe* 9, no. 4 (1998): 149–169.

Logan, Patrick. *Fair Day: The Story of Irish Fairs and Markets.* 1986.

O'Connor, Patrick J. *All Ireland Is in and about Rathkeale.* 1996.

O'Connor, Patrick J. *People, Power, Place.* 2001.

O'Flanagan, Patrick. "Markets and Fairs in Ireland, 1600–1800: Index of Economic Development and Regional Growth." *Journal of Historical Geography* 11, no. 4 (1985): 364–378.

Patrick J. O'Connor

Markievicz, Countess Constance

Constance Markievicz (1868–1927), the first Irish woman cabinet minister and the first woman to be elected to the House of Commons, was born Constance Gore-Booth to a landed Sligo family. She became a countess on her marriage to Casimir Markievicz, from whom she separated amicably in the 1890s; they had one daughter, Maeve. Her first political involvement was with Maud Gonne's Inghinidhe na hEireann; in 1909 she founded the Fianna, a nationalist equivalent to the Boy Scouts. Her association with James Connolly and her involvement in the Dublin Lockout of 1913 led her to become a member of Connolly's Irish Citizen Army, in which women and men were equal combatants. Although she was not first and foremost a feminist, she commented in 1913 that there were three great struggles in Ireland: the national question, labor, and suffrage. As an Irish Citizen Army commandant, Markievicz was second in command to Michael Mallin at the Royal College of Surgeons during the 1916 Rising. Her death sentence was commuted to life imprisonment, from which she was released in the general amnesty of 1917. Rearrested in 1918 because of the "German plot" (an attempt by the British government to prove that nationalists were conspiring with the Germans), she was elected a member of Parliament while in Holloway gaol in December of that year. As a member of the absentionist Sinn Féin, upon her release in 1919 she was appointed minister for labour in the first Dáil. She told Kathleen Clarke that she had to "bully" her male colleagues for this position, arguing that women deserved this recognition for their essential work during the Rising and after it. Markievicz was a very active minister for labour during the War for Independence of 1919 to 1921, when industrial and agricultural disputes were legion, and the Dáil was busily implementing an alternative administration. Like many other prominent nationalist women, she opposed the Anglo-Irish Treaty of 1921, and although she initially abstained from taking her Dáil seat, she eventually joined Eamon de Valera's Fianna Fáil when it was founded in 1926. A year later, having been reelected to the Dáil, she died in a public ward of Sir Patrick Dun's hospital in Dublin. The people of Dublin thronged the streets for her state funeral in testament to their affection for her. Like Maud Gonne, Markievicz was romanticized by W. B. Yeats, who played an even more marginal role in Markievicz's life than he had in Gonne's.

SEE ALSO Anglo-Irish Treaty of 1921; Connolly, James; Cumann na mBan; Labor Movement; Larkin,

James; Lockout of 1913; O'Brien, William; Sinn Féin Movement and Party to 1922; Struggle for Independence from 1916 to 1921; Women's Parliamentary Representation since 1922

Bibliography

McNamara, Maedhbh, and Paschal Mooney. *Women in Parliament: Ireland, 1918–2000.* 2000.

Caitriona Clear

Marshall Aid

On 5 June 1947, George C. Marshall, the U.S. secretary of state, painting a grim picture of the conditions prevailing in post–World War II Europe, offered financial aid, technical assistance, and economic advice to European countries. Nations that accepted the offer would have to produce a joint plan of their needs; in this way, Europe would cooperate and recover along democratic, capitalist lines. Ireland was one of the sixteen countries that accepted the invitation to participate in the European Recovery Programme (ERP), also known as the Marshall Plan.

Ireland's inclusion in the ERP was surprising because its wartime policy of neutrality still rankled in the U.S. State Department, the White House, and Congress. On the other hand, the United States could not afford to omit Ireland, because of its strategic importance to U.S. and British security and its role as an exporter of food to Britain. More importantly, excluding Ireland would have been contrary to the U.S. aim of uniting Europe. The United States did illustrate its disapprobation, though, by awarding Ireland only $128.2 million in loans and $18 million in grants between 1948 and 1952, representing the second-smallest grant awarded to any of the ERP countries.

The job of using the dollars began in September 1948 when officials from the Economic Cooperation Administration (ECA), the U.S. body that supervised the Marshall Plan, arrived in Ireland. The ECA's economic plans for Ireland initially focused on encouraging farmers and officials in the Irish Department of Agriculture to develop the sector along more modern, efficient lines. But beginning in 1949, when it became clear that dollar shortages would continue past 1952 when ERP funding

was to end, the ECA prioritized the development of the industrial sector—which could export to dollar markets—and the tourism industry. Along with spreading the messages of growth, productivity, and modernization, ECA officials oversaw the utilization of ERP-funded raw materials and goods, the establishment of the technical-assistance program, and distribution of grant funds for research, development, and educational projects that benefited the economy.

In the short term the ERP did not result in economic prosperity in Ireland. But it funded essential imports and capital projects, encouraged economic planning in the government administration, and exposed industry officials, workers, and business managers and owners to modernizing forces that could not be ignored in the long term.

SEE ALSO Agriculture: After World War I; Economies of Ireland, North and South, since 1920; Industry since 1920

Bibliography

Whelan, Bernadette. *Ireland and the Marshall Plan, 1947–57.* 2000.

Bernadette Whelan

Maynooth

There are two separate universities on the Maynooth campus in County Kildare, eighteen kilometers from Dublin: Saint Patrick's College, Maynooth, the national seminary for the training of priests, is a Pontifical University; the National University of Ireland, Maynooth, was established by an act of the Irish parliament in 1997.

The Royal College of Saint Patrick at Maynooth was founded by an act of Parliament in 1795 during a brief period when the interests of a liberal Dublin Castle administration and the Irish Catholic bishops coincided. In the 1790s both the government and the Catholic bishops feared that seminarians traveling to the Continent to be educated would be infected by democratic principles. In the nineteenth century, state funding of Maynooth was regularly attacked in Parliament by Protestant evangelicals as a "national sin." When the prime minister, Sir Robert Peel, raised the Maynooth grant in 1845, it almost split his own party. The grant was removed when the Established Church was disestablished in 1869.

Maynooth has functioned as a national seminary since its foundation, and more than 11,000 priests have been ordained there, mainly for Irish dioceses, though also for overseas missions. Pontifical-university status was not granted to Maynooth until 1896. In 1910 the College became a recognized college of the new National University of Ireland. In 1966 its doors were opened to lay students, including women, for the first time.

Since then the number of seminarians has dramatically declined while the number of lay students has equally dramatically increased. In 1997 the secular faculties were legally separated from Saint Patrick's College under a new university arrangement. The seminary suffered in the general decline in the standing of the Catholic Church in Ireland at the turn of the twenty-first century. In the popular mind Maynooth has long been considered the corporate headquarters of the Irish Catholic Church.

SEE ALSO Trinity College

Bibliography

Corish, Patrick J. *Maynooth College, 1795–1995*. 1995.
Healy, John. *Maynooth College: Its Centenary History*. 1895.

Thomas McGrath

Media since 1960

At the launch of Irish television on New Years Eve 1961, the Irish president, Eamon de Valera, knew that he was ushering in change. After suggesting that the new medium could impart knowledge, he came to what he really thought: Television, he said, "can lead through demoralisation to decadence and disillusion. Sometimes one hears that one must give the people what they want. And the competition unfortunately is in the wrong direction, so standards become lower and lower" (Hall, p. 69).

De Valera himself had been responsible for a previous seismic shift in the Irish media when he founded the *Irish Press* in 1931. The *Irish Press* was the only newspaper established since independence that overtly supported one political party, Fianna Fáil. In 1949 the *Sunday Press* was launched, and a further paper was added to the press group when the *Evening Press* was founded in 1954. By 1961 the Irish Press Group, now consisting of three newspapers, still supported the political party founded by de Valera, Fianna Fáil; the Independent Group, which also included three titles, was conservative, middle-class, and Catholic, broadly supporting the Fine Gael Party. The *Irish Times* was bought mainly by the small Protestant population but also provided a space for dissenting voices in an otherwise conformist Ireland. Around the country in every small town there were family-owned weekly provincial newspapers that reported on the local courts, the cattle marts, and other local events, much as they had done since the nineteenth century. Irish radio consisted of one station, Radio Éireann, which later became part of RTÉ (Radio Telefís Éireann), the state radio and television company, funded by license fees and advertising.

The 1960s was a period of rapid change in Ireland as elsewhere. Television, through current-affairs coverage and chat shows, was a modernizing force. The "Late Late Show," presented by Gay Byrne until the late 1990s, became a forum for discussion and debate about issues relating to the church, the family, and politics, of a kind which had never existed before. The *Irish Times*, which was in decline along with its Protestant readership, took advantage of the opportunities offered by social developments. Under its editor Douglas Gageby and news editor Donal Foley, it tapped into a middle class emerging in urban centers that worked in new industries and the public services. The newspaper became the voice for this new liberal constituency. Instead of being concerned with the traditional loyalties of newspaper buying in Ireland, where one bought the newspaper closest to one's family's political allegiance, the *Irish Times* introduced new writers, often women, and began to use specialist correspondents and more foreign news. Change at the *Independent* was slower but speeded up with the purchase of a major stake in the newspaper by an international businessman, Tony O'Reilly, in 1973. Under O'Reilly the press group Independent Newspapers became more middle-market in its audience, led by human-interest stories. It gradually shook off its Catholic conservatism, and the *Sunday Independent* especially became a platform for controversial and sometimes outrageous columnists and celebrity and fashion news. The Irish Press group, which had offered an alternative to the unionist *Irish Times* and the conservative *Irish Independent*, failed to respond to the change. By the 1980s the influence on the newspaper group of the de Valera family had ceased to be dynamic. For advertisers, the

Irish Press's readership profile compared badly with its competitors': It consisted mainly of older men living in rural Ireland with little disposable income. The company's financial problems were exacerbated by management problems, and the three Irish Press titles folded in 1995.

In addition to Irish newspapers, a number of British newspapers are sold widely in Ireland, where they are read avidly. This is not a new phenomenon, but has been growing since at least the foundation of the Free State in 1922. The enduring presence in Ireland of the British media is a colonial legacy that has never been completely explained: Nowhere else in the world does the population of one country read in such great numbers the newspapers of another. One-third of all Sunday newspaper sales in Ireland and a quarter of all daily sales are of newspapers, mainly tabloids, published in Britain. In the mid-1990s British newspapers, especially Rupert Murdoch's News International titles, began to produce so-called Irish editions, with Irish news on the front page and some sports on the back, wrapped around an essentially British product. Traditionally, Irish newspapers have seen their role as essentially serious; this has left a gap for entertainment-led media, which has been filled by British newspapers, especially the tabloids. Irish publishers have also moved to fill that market gap with newspapers that are similar in style to their British counterparts, such as Ireland's daily tabloid, *Star*, and the *Sunday World*.

While huge changes were taking place within the existing Irish media, the Broadcasting Act of 1988 was the most significant institutional change. The act allowed for the establishment of commercial radio and television, and soon there were several local radio stations. They quickly won audience approval. In time a new national radio service, Today FM, came on air and then in 1998, TV3, a national commercial television station, was launched.

Foreign ownership of the Irish media became an issue when the *Irish Press* closed in 1995. A number of overseas companies had indicated interest in buying the group's three titles, but various factors, including a purchase of 24 percent of the company by Independent Newspapers, made it a less attractive proposition. (In fact, an American newspaper owner, Ralph Ingersoll, had already invested in the *Irish Press* in 1989.) TV3 was 45 percent owned, and fully managed, by the Canadian company CanWest. Later, a British television company also bought into TV3, thereby ensuring its access to a number of popular television programs, to the detriment of RTÉ. RTÉ's public-service role is now constantly challenged by those who believe that RTÉ's license-fee income gives it an unfair advantage and distorts the market. In 2001 the commercial broadcasting regulator, the Broadcasting Commission of Ireland, changed its rules, making it easier for bigger media players to buy into Ireland's radio and television industry. The British company Scottish Radio Holdings immediately bought the national commercial radio station Today FM. Early in 2003 the government announced an increase in the license fee, which will be linked to inflation, increasing automatically rather than as the each current government sees fit. This move guaranteed the RTÉ's future.

Ireland's economic performance since the mid-1990s has attracted overseas interest, but at the same time, Ireland's largest media company, Independent News and Media, the owner of the Independent group, now dominates Irish media to an alarming extent. It has three Independent titles, including the best-selling *Irish Independent*, *Sunday Independent*, and *Evening Herald*, as well as the *Sunday World*. It also has interests in the *Sunday Tribune*, the *Star*, and a string of weekly local newspapers in the Republic of Ireland and in Northern Ireland, as well as interests in a cable-television franchise and telecommunications companies. Independent News and Media also owns the *London Independent* as well as newspaper groups in South Africa, New Zealand, and Australia.

Back in 1961 de Valera saw a small, Irish-owned, conservative media that was still coming to terms with its place in an independent Ireland. Television was the force that pushed the media to look outwards, to engage in debate about Ireland's role in the world, modernization, and social and political development. With the advent of television, the forces de Valera represented lost control of the political and cultural agenda. Today the Irish media is one of the most competitive in Europe, with four daily national newspaper titles and five Sunday national newspaper titles serving a population of around four million. Its television competes for viewers and advertising revenue with British channels, which can be accessed by over 70 percent of Irish homes. Within the Irish media, assumptions about public service, quality, ownership, and diversity are constantly challenged.

SEE ALSO de Valera, Eamon; Newspapers; Social Change since 1922

Bibliography

Farrell, Brian, ed. *Communications and Community in Ireland.* 1984.

Hall, Eamonn G. *The Electronic Age: Telecommunications in Ireland.* 1993.

Horgan, J. *Irish Media: A Critical History since 1922.* 2001.

Kiberd, D., ed. *The Media in Ireland: The Search for Diversity.* 1997.

McLoone, Martin, and John MacMahon, eds. *Television and Irish Society: 21 Years of Irish Television.* 1984.

O'Brien, Mark. *De Valera, Fianna Fáil, and the Irish Press.* 2001.

Savage, Robert J. *Irish Television: The Political and Social Origins.* 1996.

Michael Foley

St. Patrick's Bell, c. fifth century C.E.*, found in the reputed tomb of St. Patrick.* COPYRIGHT © NATIONAL MUSEUM OF IRELAND. REPRODUCED BY PERMISSION.

Metalwork, Early and Medieval

The study of metalwork in Ireland in the period from c. 450 C.E. to c. 1600 C.E. reveals much more than changing fashions in art styles. One can observe changes in the supply of raw materials, the adoption of new techniques, alternations to patterns of patronage and craft organization, and the appearance of new military tactics. Careful reading of the evidence brings to light periods of rapid development under exotic influences as well as those of conservatism and relative isolation.

EARLY MEDIEVAL PERIOD, C. 450 TO C. 800 C.E.

Archaeological evidence shows that almost every farmstead in early medieval Ireland was a site of subsistence-related ironworking for the repair of tools and farm implements. High-quality iron objects (for example, the collar and chain from Lagore, Co. Meath) were also fabricated. Sword blades were at first relatively small and made of fairly soft iron, but by the Viking period, imported blades provided models for better weapons. Decorative work in gold, bronze, and enamel was manufactured on important secular sites (for example, Lagore and Moynagh Lough crannogs, Co. Meath; Garranes, Co. Cork; and Clogher, Co. Tyrone) and on church sites such as Armagh and Clonmacnoise.

During the fifth and sixth centuries fine metalwork was predominantly in bronze, with engraved ornament of spirals, trumpets, and peltae, occasionally enamelled in red. Most bronze pieces were personal ornaments—pins, penannular (gapped-ring) brooches, and latchets (disc-shaped cloak fasteners with sinuous tails) were the principal types. Most derive from late and early post-Roman Britain, where there was a resurgence of Iron

Age La Tène style, modified by provincial Roman military taste. Debate in Ireland has centered on how much the ornament of spiral scrollwork owes to the native Irish Iron Age tradition and how much was imported. The repertoire of smiths in southern Britain before the Anglo-Saxon conquest and in Pictland was wider than that of Irish craftsmen, but the variety and sophistication of Irish work has been underestimated. By about the year 600 experiments in silver had occurred, and new embellishments in millefiore glass and new colors of enamel were adopted. Sophisticated products include the tinned bronze brooch from Ballinderry Crannog, Co. Westmeath, the decoration of which is close to that of the great enamelled hanging bowl from the Sutton Hoo burial around 630 C.E.

Irish missions in northern Britain and mainland Europe provide the context for the flowering of Irish art in the late seventh century. Sophisticated casting in silver, fire gilding, polychrome glasswork used as a substitute for gemstones, and consummate gold filigree work appeared. The range of motifs was enriched by the addition of animal ornament of Germanic (especially Anglo-Saxon) and late Roman origin. Interlace from the

The Tara Brooch, discovered in Berrystown, Co. Meath, is made of cast silver gilt covered by gold foil and precious stones, eighth century C.E. © ERICH LESSING/ART RESOURCE, NY. REPRODUCED BY PERMISSION.

Mediterranean world and a number of geometric patterns were added to the surviving traditions of spiral scrollwork. This new art was almost certainly first synthesized in monastic scriptoria and royal workshops. From simple beginnings such as the engraved curvilinear decoration of seventh-century shrines in Bobbio (Italy) and Clonmore, Co. Armagh, by 700 C.E. craftsmen were producing distinctive, yet cosmopolitan objects. The Tara Brooch—which has, like many lavish brooches of eighth- and ninth-century date, a closed ring—bears ornament similar to that of the Lindisfarne Gospels and the Donore door-furniture that harks back to classical prototypes. By the end of the eighth century surviving pieces like the Ardagh Chalice and Derrynaflan Paten had taken the symbolic filigree motifs and polychrome glasswork to the highest standards of elegance. These remarkable altar vessels copied the communion services of the great churches of Christianity. Reliquaries (containers in which sacred relics were kept)

shaped like little churches were common. The practice of enshrining books developed, and other reliquaries (for example, the Moylough belt-shrine, a major work of about 800 C.E. designed to preserve the belt of an unknown saint) show how the church challenged craftsmen to extend their range.

THE VIKING PERIOD, C. 795–1020 C.E.

The Viking raids on Ireland began in the 790s and increased in ferocity in the following century. Nevertheless, fine metalworking continued; the Derrynaflan Chalice, with its numerous gold filigree and amber ornaments, seems to have been commissioned during the ninth century. Splendid brooches were also produced, though they were less colorful and more dependent on silver for effect. By the late ninth century the increased supply of silver through Viking trade gave rise to a new series of penannular brooches, international in style but

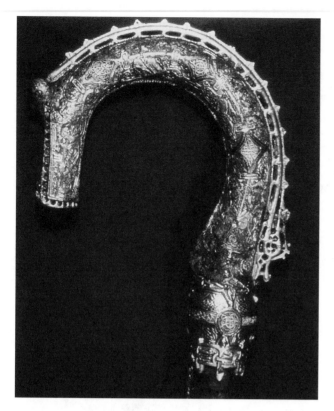

Head of crozier of the abbots of the monastery at Clonmacnoise, late eleventh century. COPYRIGHT © NATIONAL MUSEUM OF IRELAND. REPRODUCED BY PERMISSION.

of strong Irish influence, made entirely of solid silver—the "bossed" and "thistle" brooches. These are found widely in Britain and Ireland. A few brooches with long pins and hinged heads ("kite-brooches") emerged in Ireland under Viking influence; they remained in vogue into the eleventh century. A few examples are decorated with gold filigree ornament (e.g., a brooch from Waterford).

THE RENAISSANCE OF THE ELEVENTH AND TWELFTH CENTURIES

During the eleventh century large personal ornaments went out of style and effort turned to repairing some of the losses of the Viking age. Some ancient shrines were restored—for example, a silver cross embracing evangelists' symbols was applied to the restored front of the bookshrine known as the Soiscél Molaise in County Fermanagh. The later eleventh century saw the enshrinement of the *Cathach* of Saint Columba at Kells in County Meath. It carries on its sides animal ornament of Scandinavian inspiration. The badly preserved Inishfallen Crosier, decorated with fine panels of gold filigree of later Viking style, was also made at this time.

The final flowering of native metalworking took place in the first third of the twelfth century with the creation of the magnificent crosiers of Clonmacnoise and Lismore, the shrines of Saint Patrick's Bell and Saint Lachtin's Arm, and Saint Manchan's shrine in Boher, Co. Offaly. The summa of the style is the Cross of Cong (about 1120 C.E.), which was made to enshrine a relic of the True Cross. Inscriptions on most of these great pieces link prominent kings with leading churchmen in their commissioning and name the craftsmen who made them. Although all show the strong, if anachronistic, Scandinavian influence, especially in the animal ornament in the so-called Urnes style, they combine this with unmistakable efforts to revive ancient glories and elements of Romanesque influence.

Changes in church governance and dynastic warfare began to change the pattern of patronage that supported the native craftsmen in the twelfth century. Ecclesiastical metalwork from continental workshops (e.g., the crosier from Cashel, Co. Tipperary, made at Limoges) undercut native production. and the traditional workshops seem to have died out with astonishing speed.

LATER MEDIEVAL METALWORK

With the Anglo-Norman invasion came organized guilds of metalworkers based in towns. We know very little of their production because of the confiscations of the sixteenth century following the dissolution of the monasteries and the transfer of major churches from the Catholic to the Reformed Church. A few personal ornaments, such as a gold ring-brooch from Waterford in a continental style, have come to light. Some repairs to ancient shrines were made. The Domhnach Airgid (ninth century) was remodelled about 1350, adding a crucifixion scene and other religious and heraldic devices. Intact original pieces are rare. A silver-gilt crosier in gothic taste was made by a native craftsman for the bishop of Limerick in 1418 C.E. A processional cross, found at Lislaghtin, Co. Kerry, was made for John O'Connor, lord of Kerry, in 1479. International in style, its workmanship is markedly provincial. To a large extent the history of Irish fine metalworking in the High Middle Ages is mirrored in what we know of weapons and armor in the period. As late as the sixteenth century Irish warriors were appearing on the battlefield in mail shirts and fluted helmets—armor that had changed little since the fourteenth century.

SEE ALSO Arts: Early and Medieval Arts and Architecture; Sculpture, Early and Medieval

Bibliography

Harbison, Peter. *The Golden Age of Irish Art.* 1999.

Henry, Françoise. *Irish Art in the Early Christian Period, to 800 AD.* 1965.

Henry, Françoise. *Irish Art during the Viking Invasions, 800–1020 AD.* 1967.

Henry, Françoise. *Irish Art in the Romanesque Period.* 1970.

Ryan, Michael. *Metal Craftsmanship in Early Ireland.* 1993.

Ryan, Michael. *Early Irish Communion Vessels.* 2000.

Youngs, Susan, ed. *The Work of Angels.* 1989.

Michael Ryan

Methodism

Originating in mid-eighteenth-century England under the leadership of John Wesley, Methodism began as part of a wider evangelical revival within the Church of England. Wesley, an ordained Anglican minister, felt that the church had lost its sense of missionary zeal and was failing particularly to appeal to the poor in society. Heavily influenced by the pietism of the Moravians, he set out to reform and revive religious life.

ORIGIN

Ignoring the confines of ecclesiastical boundaries, Wesley journeyed extensively throughout Britain, preaching outdoors, forming local societies, and using lay preachers to spread his message of Christian perfection and justification by faith (that the individual, alienated from God by sin, is reconciled not by his merits or good works but through faith in Christ). He particularly emphasized the importance of personal salvation and conversion, and Methodism, with its emotional class meetings, spiritual discipline, and practical support, reached out to many of those neglected by the more established religions. The importance attached to thrift and temperance perhaps appealed particularly to women, while the early use of women preachers introduced a dimension of novelty into popular religious life. But although Wesley's zeal and organizational talents ensured rapid growth, both his methods and his criticism of established religious authorities led to clashes with more conventional clerics. The first annual conference took place in 1744, and with Wesley ordaining his own preachers from 1784, Methodism emerged as a distinct religious body, which broke with the Church of England after his death in 1791.

John Wesley (1703–1791), founder of Methodism who made several preaching tours of Ireland. © BETTMANN/CORBIS. REPRODUCED BY PERMISSION.

METHODISM IN IRELAND

Wesley considered Ireland to be an important mission field and visited the country on a total of twenty-one occasions, beginning in August 1747. Although Methodist preachers were often denounced as "black caps," "swaddlers" or "cavalry preachers," growth was rapid in these early years, with outdoor meetings at markets, fairs, and wakes generating intense religious emotion and excitement. Following the United Irish rebellion in 1798, a mission was established, engaging Irish-speaking preachers in an attempt to win over the Catholic peasantry. Demographic data, however, indicate that although early Methodism was strong in southern cities and market towns from the 1780s onwards, the province of Ulster was the most successful recruiting ground. Indeed, it has been suggested that Methodism was both a beneficiary of and a contributor to sectarian tensions in south Ulster during the last two decades of the eighteenth century, with its vehement anti-Catholicism helping to reinforce and revitalize northern Protestantism. Wesley's links with ascendancy figures in Ireland, and Methodist input into the so-called Second Reformation of the 1820s, also reflect the perceived link between social unrest and religious allegiance. The sect was particularly strong within traditional Anglican areas and in the "linen triangle" of south Ulster, and, by 1815, 68 percent of Irish Methodists lived north of a line drawn from Sligo to Dundalk.

Many divisions followed Wesley's death. In Ireland the Wesleyan Methodists became an autonomous Church, while the Primitive Methodists retained their Anglican links. These groups were united in 1878 following the disestablishment of the Church of Ireland. Membership numbers reached their peak in 1844. Thereafter, with increased financial and administrative responsibilities, Methodism became progressively institutionalized, moving away from outside preaching and its more spontaneous activities.

Rather than its numerical strength, however, Methodism's most important contribution to Irish society was the stimulus that it gave to a much wider evangelicalism. Many Methodist characteristics, particularly itinerant preaching, and the establishment of voluntary religious societies were taken up by individuals, missionary organizations, and eventually the main churches themselves. The 1859 revival, known as the Great Awakening, provides the best evidence of the extent to which evangelicalism had infiltrated mainstream religions by the middle of the nineteenth century.

METHODISM IN THE EARLY TWENTY-FIRST CENTURY

Today's Methodist ministers undergo a period of probation: five years for university graduates, six for others, and spend a maximum of eight years on one circuit (group of local societies of churches). Early female preaching had been brought to an end in 1804, but in line with developments elsewhere, the first Methodist woman to be ordained entered the ministry in 1977. There are currently seventy-six circuits in Irish Methodism, administered by quarterly meetings of ministers and officials. Circuits are grouped into districts, which hold a synod twice yearly. The annual conference remains the governing body and is made up of both ministerial and lay representatives who have equal voting rights. Ministerial sessions deal with the admission, probation, discipline, appointment, expulsion, and retirement of ministers, as well as with appeals and ministerial and pastoral concerns. The representative session deals with matters of government and management. The president of the Methodist Church in Ireland is elected annually from among the Irish ministers.

Concerned to spread the gospel message, the Methodist church has long been involved with overseas missions and continues to send both lay and clerical mis-

sionaries to all parts of the world. In contrast to the situation in late-eighteenth-century Ireland, it also enjoys harmonious relationships with other religious denominations, and participates in joint prayer and study groups with the Catholic Church.

SEE ALSO Evangelicalism and Revivals; Religion: Since 1690; Second Reformation from 1822 to 1869; Temperance Movements

Bibliography

Cole, Richard Lee. *A History of Methodism in Ireland, 1860–1960*. 1960.

Cooney, Dudley. *The Methodist in Ireland: A Short History*. 2001.

Crookshank, Charles Henry. *History of Methodism in Ireland*. 3 vols. 1885–1888.

Hempton, David. *Methodism and Politics in British Society, 1750–1850*. 1984.

Hempton, David, and Myrtle Hill. *Evangelical Protestantism in Ulster Society, 1740–1890*. 1992.

Myrtle Hill

Middle English Literature

Since the year 1169 and the Anglo-Norman "conquest," literature in Middle English started being written in Ireland. Its surviving quantity is comparatively small, but some is of premier historical and literary importance. It also exhibits an idiosyncratic combination of word spellings that permits us to identify it as medieval Hiberno-English, a distinctive written dialect of late Middle English.

One reason for the relative lack of surviving texts is the fact that from the late twelfth century to the fifteenth, English in Ireland was always a minority language, even if that of the powerful minority congregating in and around the colonial centers and the walled towns. (The other principal vernacular introduced after 1169, Anglo-Norman French, seems by the late fourteenth century to have been in substantial decline.)

The poetry of some major Middle English authors was imported, including William Langland's *Piers Plowman* and Geoffrey Chaucer's *Troilus and Criaseyde* (the latter appears in a 1526 catalogue of the library of the earl of Kildare). Some ambitious Middle English prose translations were also undertaken by Irishmen, including in 1422 one done by James Yonge of Dublin of the French *Secreta Secretorum*. At about this time an anonymous translator also rendered into English the late twelfth-century Latin *Expugnatio Hibernica* of Giraldus Cambrensis.

However, the most important Middle English literary collection to have survived is contained in London, Harley MS 913, an anthology mainly of verse on religious and satirical topics, compiled probably by a Franciscan friar in Waterford circa 1331. Some of his items were imported, but many are indigenous, one of the most striking being *The Land of Cokaygne*, a surreal account of monastic hedonism in which abbeys are built of food, and geese fly ready-cooked into the open mouth. (Compare this edible architecture with the motif of the land of food appearing in the late twelfth-century Gaelic story *Aisling Meic Con Glinne*.) Outside the Harley anthology, Middle English poetry from Ireland is not otherwise extensive. Middle English lyrics are known from Kilkenny and from Armagh, for example, but their quantity is small.

Absence of evidence is not evidence of absence, however. The field of drama is similar, where the chance survival of part of the text of *The Pride of Life*, the earliest known morality play in English, suggests that a dramatic tradition formerly existed that was far broader and sturdier than this solitary, sophisticated play might otherwise lead us to suspect.

SEE ALSO Arts: Early and Medieval Arts and Architecture; Hiberno-English; Literature: Early and Medieval Literature; Norman French Literature

Bibliography

Bliss, Alan and Joseph Long. "Literature in Norman-French and English." In *A New History of Ireland II: Medieval Ireland, 1169–1534*. Edited by Art Cosgrave. 1987.

Dolan, Terrence. "Writing in Ireland." In *The Cambridge History of Medieval English Literature*. Edited by David Wallace. 1999.

Fletcher, Alan J. *Drama, Performance, and Polity in Pre-Cromwellian Ireland*. 2000.

Alan J. Fletcher

Migration

EMIGRATION FROM THE SEVENTEENTH CENTURY TO 1845

The number of Irish who emigrated prior to the Great Famine (1845–1852) is uncertain and disputed. Recent scholarship (e.g., by Cullen and Wokeck) has revised steeply downward older estimates (e.g., by Dickson) of eighteenth-century migration to North America. The higher numbers remain credible, however, and other historians (e.g., Bríc and Kirkham) suggest that even these may be too low.

During the 1600s migration *to* Ireland exceeded emigration *from* Ireland. Perhaps 250,000 English, Welsh, and Scottish Protestants settled in Ireland (Canny, Smout), whereas about 50,000 Catholic soldiers and others left the island, primarily for Europe (Cullen), and perhaps as many again emigrated to the Americas. Most of that last group were Catholics—primarily indentured servants, rebels, or "vagabonds"—transported to the British West Indies. Smaller numbers of Catholic servants and convicts disembarked in the Chesapeake region, and a few seasonal migrants from east Munster—servants and laborers on the Grand Banks fisheries—settled permanently in Newfoundland. Also, the 1680s and 1690s witnessed the start of Irish Protestant migration to North America, as Ulster Presbyterians migrated to the Chesapeake, while Irish Quakers and Baptists sailed to Pennsylvania and New Jersey. The frequent wars, famines, and economic crises of the seventeenth century were the principal causes of these migrations.

Between 1700 and the American Revolution, movement *from* Ireland greatly exceeded migration *to* Ireland, and North America prevailed among overseas destinations. In the period 1700 to 1775 perhaps 25,000 Britons settled in Ireland (Canny, Landsman). By contrast,

From 1815 to 1845 alone, between 800,000 and 1,000,000 emigrants left Ireland for North America—a figure about double that of the previous two centuries. Among emigrants after 1815 the proportion of Protestant farmers and artisans from Ulster was falling and the proportion of poorer Catholic farmers and laborers from the other three provinces was rising. Traffic between Liverpool and New York City was already heavy before 1845. This illustration shows an emigrant ship leaving Liverpool in 1850. FROM ILLUSTRATED LONDON NEWS, 6 JULY 1850.

some 88,000 military and nonmilitary migrants left Ireland for Europe or Britain or to work for the British East India Company (Cullen). Moreover, at least 150,000 Irish migrated to North America, although some historians (Cullen, Wokeck) suggest that they numbered merely 60,000. Of the migrants to the New World, about three-fourths left from Ulster, and the remainder from commercialized and anglicized areas in southern Ireland. Perhaps 60 percent of the total were Ulster Presbyterians (or Scots-Irish); a fifth to a fourth were Catholics from both Ulster and southern Ireland, and (despite continued Quaker migration) most of the remainder were Anglicans, members of the legally established Church of Ireland.

Between 1700 and 1775 Catholic settlement in Newfoundland increased and migration to the West Indies diminished. However, Catholics and Anglicans were relatively reluctant to migrate to America—the former because legal discrimination in Britain's colonies reinforced archaic Catholic notions that emigration (at least to Protestant countries) was tantamount to exile or

banishment, the latter because of their privileged position in Ireland and the empire. Although indentured servitude enabled Ireland's poor to obtain free transatlantic passages, the great majority of Irish Catholics—still monolingual Irish-speakers—were insulated from America's attractions as promoted by newspapers and shipping agents. Most Catholics and Anglicans who did cross the Atlantic were subsumed in the Scots-Irish migration, and the dearth of priests and chapels in the colonies promoted the absorption of Catholic emigrants into Presbyterian sociocultural networks. Thus nineteenth-century America's "Scotch-Irish" community would include many Protestants whose ancestors had been Catholics or Anglicans.

R. J. Dickson identified four major phases of Ulster Presbyterian migration to prerevolutionary America: 1717 to 1720, when several clergymen led entire congregations to New England; 1725 to 1729, when some 8,000 Scots-Irish disembarked at or near Philadelphia and, in lesser numbers, at Charleston; 1730 to 1769, when perhaps 70,000 Presbyterians left Ulster, primarily for the Delaware River; and 1770 to 1775, when Ulster emigration, mostly to Philadelphia and to the Deep South, peaked at 40,000 or more. Voyages from Ulster typically lasted eight to ten weeks, and the costs of passage and provisions ranged between 9 pounds and 3 pounds 5 shillings. Many Presbyterian farmers could afford to transport entire families, but most Protestant artisans and laborers—and nearly all Catholic migrants—emigrated as indentured servants, bound to labor in America for three to five years in return for their passages. (Yet another 25,000 Irish migrants, mostly Catholics, were convicts sent to the southern colonies.) Most of the Scots-Irish and others initially settled in the middle colonies. However, from the 1730s through the early 1770s many of them, with their American-born offspring, moved south down the Great Path into the Virginia, Carolina, and Georgia backcountries, where they met others who had disembarked at Charleston or Savannah. By 1790 the Irish-born and their descendants comprised a fourth of the whites in Pennsylvania, more than a fourth of those in South Carolina and Georgia, and perhaps a third of those in Kentucky and Tennessee (Doyle).

In the years 1700 to 1775 Scots-Irish departures often were responses to specific crises—for example, to sharp rent increases, famines, and depressions in Ulster's linen industry. However, Quaker and Scots-Irish emigration quickly became routine and self-perpetuating, spurred by letters from America. There was also a religious and political dimension to early Scots-Irish emigration, as their spokesmen often claimed that they were fleeing Anglican "oppression." Most emigrants were motivated chiefly by America's cheap land and high wages; Presbyterians' resentments were real, coloring a communal exodus from what their clergy called "Egyptian bondage."

After the American Revolution, in the period 1783 to 1815, at least 150,000 migrants sailed to the United States, a large but unknown number settled in Britain, and 25,000 or more left home to serve in the British army and navy. Also, in 1791 British vessels began shipping Irish convicts to New South Wales, and even Irish migration to the United States was not entirely voluntary, as it included about 2,500 Protestants and Catholics who fled the suppression of the United Irish rebellion in 1798. Most transatlantic migrants were still Ulster Presbyterians, although scholars (e.g., Bríc) discern a rise in Catholic departures from southern Ireland. The 1783 to 1815 emigration may be seen as a continuation of the migration of the early 1770s or as a harbinger of the larger exodus of 1815 to 1845; evidence exists to support either perspective. Evidence on the social character of the emigrants is equally mixed: after 1783

the rapid decline of indentured servitude curtailed pauper emigration, yet while some observers reported an increase of skilled and propertied migrants, others complained that they represented "a very inferior class." Likewise, although most new arrivals followed their predecessors to the U.S. frontier, there is evidence of early Irish-American urbanization and political organization in cities such as Philadelphia (still the major debarkation port) and New York City. Finally, although most of the migration between 1783 and 1815 was crisis-driven—by economic depression in 1783 to 1785, by near-famine in 1799 to 1801, and by political upheavals and high wartime taxes from 1793 on—many emigrants followed paths blazed by kinsmen who had departed prior to 1776. Surely, overseas migration would have been even greater had not the French revolutionary and Napoleonic wars precluded many departures after 1793, and had not the 1803 British Passenger Act impeded lower-class emigration by raising passage costs.

In the prefamine era of 1815 to 1845 most of the "modern" or "classic" patterns of Irish emigration, especially to North America, were established. In the three decades prior to the Great Famine, between 800,000 and one million Irish moved to North America, and perhaps at least another half-million, unable to afford transatlantic fares, went to Great Britain. At least 35,000 more, mostly convicts, disembarked in Australia; others went to serve the British empire; and a few settled in Argentina and elsewhere. Altogether, the 1815 to 1845 emigrants were roughly twice as numerous as those who left Ireland in the two preceding centuries.

Despite a surge in departures between 1815 and 1816 and the dampening effects of the U.S. financial panics of 1819 and 1837, overall Irish migration to the New World increased steadily (from 20,000 in 1826 to 65,000 in 1832, and to a record 92,000 in 1842). Before the 1830s a majority of emigrants were Protestants—mostly Presbyterians from Ulster, although many Anglicans left southern Ireland. However, Catholic departures from both Ulster and the southern provinces steadily increased, and from the mid-1830s Catholics—primarily from the most commercialized and anglicized areas in south Ulster, Leinster, east Munster, and east Connacht—comprised a growing majority. The social complexion of the migration changed accordingly: Numbers of poor and unskilled emigrants rose steadily, outnumbering farmers and artisans by the prefamine decade. Alongside agricultural laborers were many non-inheriting sons and daughters of middling and poor tenant farmers who recently had adopted impartible inheritance—a custom whereby only one son inherited land and only one daughter received a dowry. This custom became universal after the famine. Male emigrants remained a slight majority, but departures by young, single women steadily increased. Most prefamine emigrants traveled alone or with siblings, not as members of multigenerational families. Growing numbers (a majority among Catholics) financed their passages with remittances or prepaid passage tickets sent by kinfolk in the United States. Of those who sailed directly to the United States, in voyages lasting six to eight weeks, most now sailed from Liverpool, not from Irish ports as formerly, and most disembarked at New York City rather than Philadelphia.

However, most prefamine migrants landed in British North America rather than the United States. In the 1820s British passenger laws and a growing timber trade between Canada and Britain reduced passage costs to the Maritimes or Quebec to merely 1 or 2 pounds, compared with fares to New York of 4 to 10 pounds. Fares equalized in the 1830s, however, and between 1838 and 1844 Irish migrants to the United States outnumbered those to Canada by 202,000 to 150,000. Moreover, despite British and Canadian inducements, many emigrants who landed in British America, particularly poor Catholics, quickly migrated to the United States for greater opportunities. Most prefamine emigrants to the United States (and the great majority of those who remained in Canada) pursued farming, primarily in the states/territories as far east as Ohio as well as states/territories farther west, such as Illinois and Wisconsin (rather than in the South, as formerly). However, growing numbers engaged in semiskilled and unskilled occupations on public works (such as the Erie Canal) and in construction, dock laboring, and (for women) domestic service—work located primarily in northern seaports and industrial towns. Likewise, Irish migrants to Britain concentrated overwhelmingly in urban industrial centers and on public-works sites.

The magnitude of prefamine emigration reflected the contrast between U.S. economic attractions and Irish poverty and population pressure. Between 1790 and 1844 Ireland's population grew from about four million to perhaps eight and one-half million, and from 1815 the island suffered severe economic depression and dislocation. Economic crises following the Napoleonic wars brought rapid deindustrialization in most of Ulster and southern Ireland, as rural and (outside Belfast) urban spinning, weaving, and other crafts contracted or collapsed, unable to compete with British manufactures. Consequently, most Irish country people became totally dependent on agriculture in a period when prices for farm products and wages for agricultural laborers declined steeply, when hard-pressed landlords and commercial farmers strove to rationalize their holdings by evicting "superfluous" tenants, subtenants, and laborers, and when fierce competition for land kept rent levels (especially for subtenants and laborers) exceptionally high. By the eve of the Great Famine 70 percent of Ireland's rural families lived in or barely above poverty, largely or entirely dependent for subsistence on their annual potato crops. Another consequence was increased social, religious, and political strife, which only spurred more emigration, as Catholics and Protestants competed violently for economic advantage. The rural poor joined secret agrarian societies to defend traditional economic "rights" against the agents of capitalism; and Daniel O'Connell mobilized Catholic peasants' grievances in a series of political crusades against Ireland's Protestant Ascendancy. Even had the Great Famine not occurred, emigration would have continued to rise in a country whose people were, after the Act of Union in 1800, powerless to shape economic or social policies to Irish advantage. Despite Irish-speaking Catholics' traditional reluctance to emigrate (already dissipating as a result of anglicization as well as desperation), increasing numbers of Irish people now focused their hopes for economic improvement or survival overseas.

SEE ALSO American Wakes; Diaspora: The Irish in Australia; Diaspora: The Irish in Britain; Diaspora: The Irish in North America; Family: Marriage Patterns and Family Life from 1690 to 1921; Great Famine; Migration: Seasonal Migration; Population, Economy, and Society from 1750 to 1950; Population Explosion; Potato and Potato Blight (*Phytophthora infestans*); Rural Life: 1690 to 1845; Subdivision and Subletting of Holdings; Town Life from 1690 to the Early Twentieth Century

Bibliography

Adams, William Forbes. *Ireland and Irish Emigration to the New World from 1815 to the Famine.* 1932.

Akenson, Donald Harman. *The Irish Diaspora: A Primer.* 1993.

Blethen, H. Tyler, and Curtis W. Wood, Jr., eds. *Ulster and North America: Transatlantic Perspectives on the Scotch Irish.* 1997.

Bric, Maurice J. "Patterns of Irish Emigration to America, 1783–1800." *Éire-Ireland* 36 (spring/summer 2001): 10–28.

Canny, Nicholas. "English Migration into and across the Atlantic during the Seventeenth and Eighteenth Centuries." In *Europeans on the Move: Studies on European Migration, 1500–1800,* edited by Nicholas Canny. 1994.

Dickson, R. J. *Ulster Emigration to Colonial America, 1718–76.* 1966, 1988.

Doyle, David N. *Ireland, Irishmen and Revolutionary America, 1780–1920.* 1981.

Doyle, David N. "The Irish in North America, 1776–1845." In *A New History of Ireland: Ireland Under the Union, I, 1801–1870*, vol. 5, edited by W. E. Vaughan. 1989.

Fitzpatrick, David. "Emigration, 1801–1870." In *A New History of Ireland: Ireland Under the Union, I, 1801–1870*, vol. 5, edited by W. E. Vaughan. 1989.

Fitzpatrick, David. "'A Peculiar Tramping People': The Irish in Britain, 1801–1870." In *A New History of Ireland: Ireland Under the Union, I, 1801–1870*, vol. 5, edited by W. E. Vaughan. 1989.

Houston, Cecil J., and William J. Smyth. *Irish Emigration and Canadian Settlement: Patterns, Links, and Letters.* 1990.

Jones, Maldwyn A. "Ulster Emigration, 1783–1815." In *Essays in Scotch-Irish History*, edited by E. R. R. Green. 1969.

Lockhart, Audrey. *Some Aspects of Emigration from Ireland to the North American Colonies between 1680 and 1775.* 1976.

Kirkham, Graeme. "Ulster Emigration to North America, 1680–1720." In *Ulster and North America: Transatlantic Perspectives on the Scotch-Irish*, edited by H. Tyler Blethen and Curtis W. Wood, Jr. 1997.

Miller, Kerby A. *Emigrants and Exiles: Ireland and the Irish Exodus to North America.* 1985.

Miller, Kerby A., et al. *Irish Immigrants in the Land of Canaan: Letters and Memoirs from Colonial and Revolutionary America, 1675–1815.* 2003.

Myers, Albert Cook. *Immigration of the Irish Quakers into Pennsylvania, 1682–1750.* 1902.

O'Farrell, Patrick J. *The Irish in Australia.* 1987; 2001.

O'Farrell, Patrick J. "The Irish in Australia and New Zealand, 1791–1870." In *A New History of Ireland: Ireland Under the Union, I, 1801–1870*, vol. 5, edited by W. E. Vaughan. 1989.

Truxes, Thomas M. *Irish-American Trade, 1660–1783.* 1983.

Wokeck, Marianne S. *Trade in Strangers: The Beginnings of Mass Migration to North America.* 1999.

Kerby Miller

EMIGRATION FROM 1850 TO 1960

Irish emigration between 1850 and 1960 is best divided into three periods: 1850 to 1854, when most migrants still responded to the Great Famine's immediate effects; 1855 to 1929, when (as in 1850 to 1854) the great majority of Irish migrants went to the United States; and 1930 to 1960, when Irish emigration flowed primarily to Great Britain.

In the years 1850 to 1854, between 900,000 and one million Irish emigrated overseas (i.e., to destinations other than Britain), an average of 180,000 to 200,000 per year; not until 1855 did overseas migration decline to prefamine levels. Of these, some 80 percent emigrated to the United States, another 10 to 12 percent to British North America (Canada), and most of the remainder to Australia. In addition, an unknown number settled in England, Wales, or Scotland, and by 1861 Britain contained more than 800,000 Irish-born residents (up from 416,000 in 1841 and 727,000 in 1851). About two-fifths of the overseas migrants left Munster, with another 13 percent from Connacht, and 23 percent each from Leinster and Ulster. In terms of its 1851 population Munster was overrepresented among the overseas emigrants, and Ulster was underrepresented, but the northern province probably contributed a disproportionate share of the migrants to Scotland and the north of England. Catholics likely constituted an overwhelming majority of the 1850 to 1854 migrants, as during the famine itself. Much of the migration between 1850 and 1854 reflected the famine's aftershocks—the effects of high poor-rates imposed on Irish farmers generally and of continued distress and evictions in western Ireland. However, large numbers (probably the great majority) responded to remittances and prepaid passage tickets sent by Famine emigrants who strove to reunite their families abroad. Thus, although most of the migrants of 1850 to 1854 were single men and women in their twenties and early thirties, family reunions help explain why about 40 percent were under age nineteen and 13 to 14 percent were over age thirty-five.

Between 1855 and 1929, the classic period of postfamine emigration, nearly five million Irish men and women emigrated to overseas destinations. The great majority, about 85 percent, settled in the United States; about 7 percent migrated to Canada, another 8 percent to Australia and New Zealand, and the remaining 1 to 2 percent to South Africa, Argentina, and other countries. In addition, scholars (for example, Cormac Ó Gráda) estimate that between 500,000 and one million unrecorded emigrants settled permanently in Great Britain. In all, more than two and one-half times the number of Irish people left their native land between 1855 and 1929 than had emigrated in all preceding periods combined. As a result, Ireland's population fell from 6.55 million in 1851 to merely 4.23 million in 1926. Although other European countries also experienced mass emigration in this period, only Ireland suffered what amounted to demographic catastrophe.

Except during World War I, annual Irish migration overseas in the period 1855 to 1929 never fell below 23,300 and was rarely less than 35,000. However, emigration fluctuated in response to economic conditions at home and abroad. Most notably, there was a surge in departures in the late 1870s and early 1880s; this was associated with poor harvests, evictions, agrarian turmoil (the Land War), and, most important, the steep price declines for Irish farm products that followed a period of relative prosperity in rural Ireland. Another fluctuation resulted from the U.S. economic depression of 1873 to 1877. Overseas migration normalized after 1883, but in the 1890s more than 427,000 Irish jour-

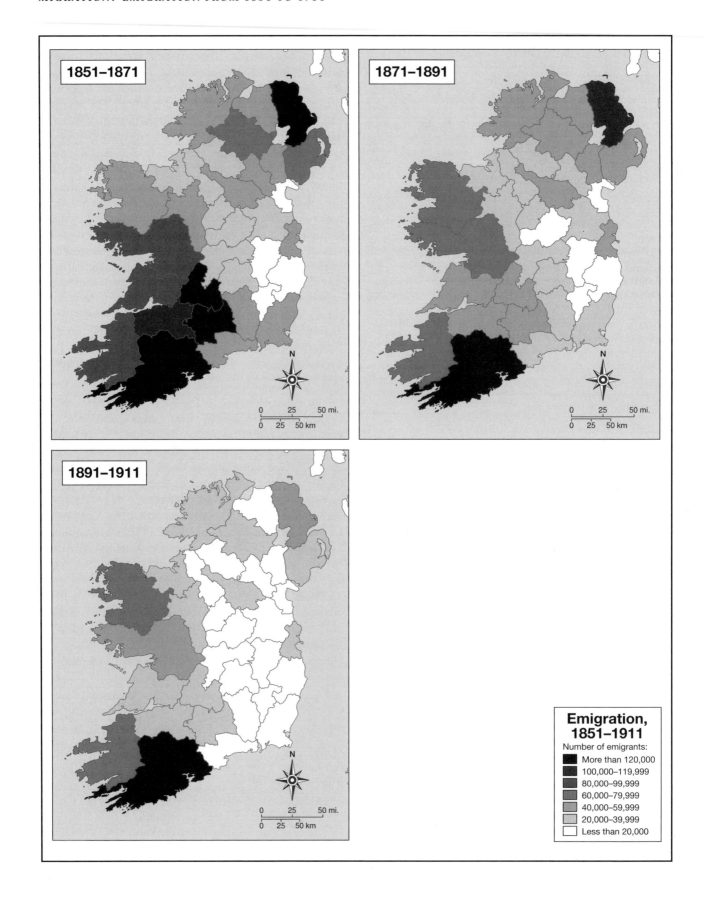

1851–1871

1871–1891

1891–1911

Emigration, 1851–1911

Number of emigrants:

- More than 120,000
- 100,000–119,999
- 80,000–99,999
- 60,000–79,999
- 40,000–59,999
- 20,000–39,999
- Less than 20,000

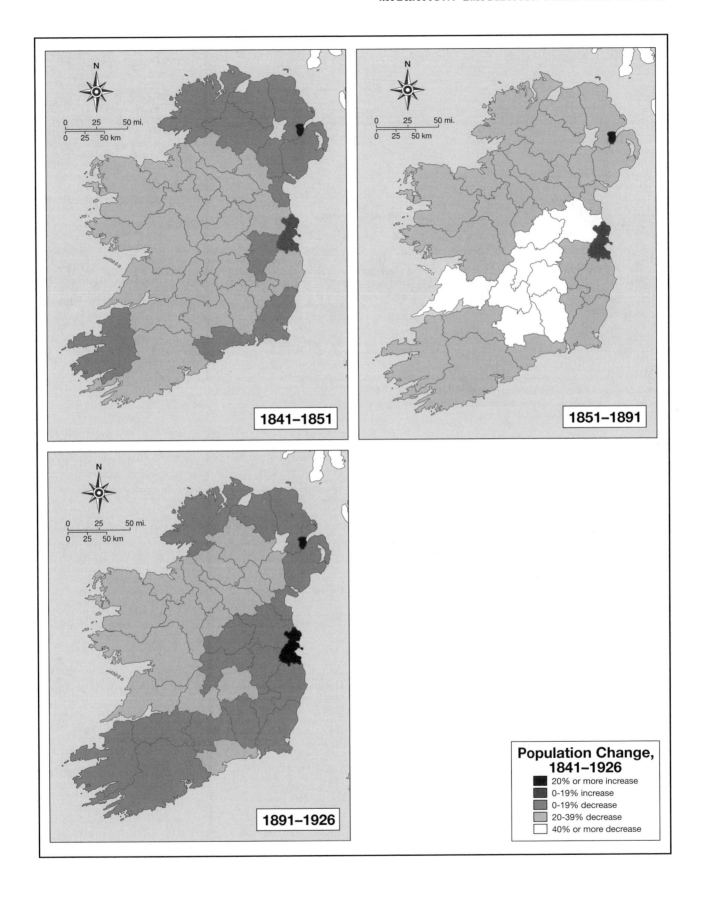

1841–1851

1851–1891

1891–1926

Population Change, 1841–1926

■ 20% or more increase
■ 0-19% increase
■ 0-19% decrease
▨ 20-39% decrease
□ 40% or more decrease

By 1900 emigration had removed nearly four million people from Ireland since 1846. The famine emigrants had a hard lot in the United States for at least a generation after their arrival. In this painting of c. 1855 by Samuel Waugh, Irish emigrants disembarking at the Battery in New York City appear to be in better circumstances than those of the great majority of Irish New Yorkers in the 1850s. © MUSEUM OF THE CITY OF NEW YORK/CORBIS. REPRODUCED BY PERMISSION.

neyed to the United States alone, and annual departures averaged about 43,000 from 1900 to 1913, and about 25,000 between the end of World War I and the Great Depression. In general, the origins of postfamine migration shifted steadily to the south and west of Ireland. Whereas most prefamine emigrants had left Ulster and Leinster, slightly more than half the overseas migrants from 1855 to 1929, perhaps 60 percent from 1880 to 1929, came from Munster and Connacht. A disproportionate share, especially from the late 1870s on, left the most impoverished and socially and culturally archaic "congested districts" in western Ireland and almost equally poor counties such as Cavan, Longford, and Tyrone. At least four-fifths of those who migrated to the United States between 1855 and 1929 were listed on shipping manifests as laborers and servants; the great majority were single men and women in their late teens and early twenties. Unusually among contemporary emigrants, women comprised about half the Irish migrants—slightly more than half after 1880. The overwhelming majority were Catholics, and given their regional origins, a large minority were Irish-speakers. In contrast to those general patterns, however, Ulster migration rose sharply in the 1870s and early 1900s, when it is probable that Protestant emigration also increased. In addition, it appears that relatively affluent, skilled and/or educated Protestants (and Catholics) from Ulster and Leinster were disproportionately repre-

sented among migrants to Canada, Australia, New Zealand, and South Africa, whereas poorer Ulster men and women probably comprised a majority of migrants to Britain.

Postfamine emigration was encouraged by cheap, improved transportation: Transatlantic steamships called regularly at Queenstown (now Cobh, Co. Cork) and at Moville (Co. Donegal), crossed the ocean in merely 10 to 15 days, and charged fares as low as 1 or 2 pounds. Most overseas migrants paid their passages with remittances or prepaid tickets sent by relatives abroad; between the Great Famine and 1900 the value of these from the United States alone exceeded 52 million pounds (260 million dollars). This in turn reflected the growth, stability, and relative prosperity of an Irish-American society, concentrated in northern centers, able to offer the newcomers shelter and employment. Also, the peculiar evolution of postfamine Irish society virtually mandated massive out-migration, even during the U.S. Civil War and the U.S. depression of 1893 to 1897. Continued deindustrialization provided no alternative to underemployed or unemployed rural and urban dwellers, only a minority of whom could be absorbed in northeast Ulster's industrialized but highly selective and sectarian job market. Most important, the increasing commercialization of Irish agriculture exposed Ireland's tenant farmers to international price fluctuations. It persuaded them (even in the west of Ireland after 1880) to adopt impartible inheritance and late-marriage patterns, which consigned most of their sons and daughters to emigration. It also dictated a pronounced shift from tillage to pasture farming, which in turn sharply reduced both employment and opportunities to rent land among agricultural laborers and noninheriting farmers' children. More broadly, the commercialization and concomitant anglicization of rural Irish society eroded the emigrants' familial, social, and cultural bonds to their homeland. These converging trends made emigration more a fundamental imperative—rooted in the inequities and processes of Irish society—than a matter of personal choice. Irish nationalists wrongly believed that winning self-government alone could bring prosperity and full employment; continued migration in the 1920s, after the creation of the Irish Free State, demonstrated that its causes were structural.

Irish migration to the United States dropped sharply after 1929 and never recovered its former levels. In the decade from 1931 to 1940, according to U.S. data, Irish emigrants to the United States numbered merely 13,000 (versus 23,000 to Australia and New Zealand), rising only to 27,500 in 1941 to 1950, and to 40,000 in 1951 to 1961. However, the Irish economy stagnated from the 1930s to the 1950s, and Britain's relatively early recovery from the depression and its enormous need for labor (and wartime nurses) during the war and in postwar reconstruction persuaded at least 634,000 Irish men and women to settle in the United Kingdom. Between 1931 and 1961 Britain's Irish-born residents increased from 505,000 to 951,000. In 1948 the Dublin government created a commission to propose policies to stem emigration, but not until the 1960s would Irish economic growth check a floodtide that had been flowing since the Great Famine.

SEE ALSO Agriculture: 1845 to 1921; American Wakes; Diaspora: The Irish in Australia; Diaspora: The Irish in Britain; Diaspora: The Irish in North America; Family: Marriage Patterns and Family Life from 1690 to 1921; Great Famine; Migration: Seasonal Migration; Population, Economy, and Society from 1750 to 1950; Potato and Potato Blight (*Phytophthora infestans*); Rural Life: 1850 to 1921; Town Life from 1690 to the Early Twentieth Century; **Primary Documents:** From the *Report of the Commission on Emigration and Other Population Problems, 1948–1954* (1955)

Bibliography

Akenson, Donald Harman. *The Irish Diaspora: A Primer.* 1993.

Delaney, Enda. *Demography, State, and Society: Irish Migration to Britain, 1921–1971.* 2000.

Doyle, David Noel. "The Remaking of Irish-America, 1845–1880." In *A New History of Ireland: Ireland Under the Union II, 1870–1921,* vol. 6, edited by W. E. Vaughan. 1996.

Drudy, P. J., ed. *The Irish in America: Emigration, Assimilation, and Impact.* 1985.

Fitzpatrick, David. "'A Peculiar Tramping People': The Irish in Britain, 1801–1870." In *A New History of Ireland: Ireland Under the Union, I, 1801–1870,* vol. 5, edited by W. E. Vaughan. 1989.

Fitzpatrick, David. "Emigration, 1801–1870." In *A New History of Ireland: Ireland Under the Union, I, 1801–1870,* vol. 5, edited by W. E. Vaughan. 1989.

Fitzpatrick, David. "Emigration, 1871–1921." In *A New History of Ireland: Ireland Under the Union, II, 1870–1921,* vol. 6, edited by W. E. Vaughan. 1996.

Fitzpatrick, David. "The Irish in Britain, 1871–1921." In *A New History of Ireland: Ireland Under the Union, II, 1870–1921,* vol. 6, edited by W. E. Vaughan. 1996.

Guinnane, Timothy. *The Vanishing Irish: Households, Migration, and Rural Economy in Ireland, 1850–1914.* 1997.

Houston, Cecil J., and William J. Smyth. *Irish Emigration and Canadian Settlement: Patterns, Links, and Letters.* 1990.

Kennedy, Robert E. *The Irish: Emigration, Marriage, and Fertility.* 1973.

Miller, Kerby A. *Emigrants and Exiles: Ireland and the Irish Exodus to North America.* 1985.

O'Farrell, Patrick J. *The Irish in Australia.* 1987; 2001.

O'Farrell, Patrick J. "The Irish in Australia and New Zealand, 1791–1870." In *A New History of Ireland: Ireland Under the Union, I, 1801–1870,* vol. 5, edited by W. E. Vaughan. 1989.

O'Farrell, Patrick J. "The Irish in Australia and New Zealand, 1870–1990." In *A New History of Ireland: Ireland Under the Union, II, 1870–1921,* vol. 6, edited by W. E. Vaughan. 1996.

Ó Gráda, Cormac. *Ireland: A New Economic History, 1780–1939.* 1994.

O'Sullivan, Patrick, ed. *The Irish Worldwide.* 6 vols. 1992–1997.

Schrier, Arnold. *Ireland and the American Emigration, 1850–1900.* 1958.

Vaughn, W. E., and A. J. Fitzpatrick. *Irish Historical Statistics: Population, 1821–1971.* 1978.

Kerby Miller

EMIGRATION AND IMMIGRATION SINCE 1950

The evolution of Irish society since 1950, north and south, was shaped fundamentally by the continued experience of emigration. Immigration was always less significant in both societies, though by the end of the twentieth century independent Ireland was an immigrant country. In the early 1950s, as they watched thousands of young people leaving Ireland for new lives

This photograph appeared in Ireland Is Building, *a government brochure that urged Irish emigrants in Britain to return to Ireland. Almost 500,000 men and women left Ireland during the 1950s to seek better opportunities abroad.* COURTESY OF THE NATIONAL ARCHIVES OF IRELAND, DEPARTMENT OF THE TAOISEACH, S14670. FROM *IRELAND IS BUILDING*, PROMOTIONAL BROCHURE PRODUCED BY THE DEPARTMENTS OF LOCAL GOVERNMENT AND SOCIAL WELFARE, 1949.

elsewhere, few contemporaries could have foreseen this development. Irish population history since the mid-twentieth century vividly illustrates how the wider economic environment determines the levels of either emigration or immigration.

The years following the end of the Second World War witnessed the large-scale movement of Irish emigrants to Britain. The late 1940s and the 1950s constituted a remarkable era of mass emigration. Over 500,000 people left independent Ireland between 1945 and 1960—stark evidence of the poor state of the Irish economy at this time. The following decade saw reduced emigration, a significant decrease that, together with substantial return migration in the 1960s, contributed to a rise in the population of independent Ireland by 1971—reversing the downward trend since the late 1840s. In the 1970s the numbers immigrating remained, for a sustained period, higher than the numbers leaving. This inflow was due mainly to the return home of emigrants who had left in the 1940s and 1950s. The 1980s and 1990s were a watershed in Irish population history. Emigration again became a major feature of life in the 1980s—the so-called new wave of Irish emigra-

tion. By the mid-1990s, however, as a consequence of the rapid economic growth associated with the Celtic Tiger, the inflow again exceeded the exodus. For instance, in 2001–2002 the population rose by 58,100 people, and the net inflow of 28,800 accounted for roughly half of this increase.

Similarly, Northern Ireland experienced large-scale emigration in the 1950s, although the northern exodus remained at less than half the rate of the southern state. In the 1960s the level of emigration decreased, mirroring the trend in independent Ireland. In the 1970s the numbers leaving Northern Ireland rose, and this trend continued into the 1980s, leading to a slight decrease in the total population by 1991. Throughout the 1990s the gross outflow averaged roughly 17,000 people, although this was offset by a slightly larger inflow of migrants.

Where did Irish emigrants travel in the second half of the twentieth century? From the 1940s on, roughly three out of every four Irish emigrants were destined for Britain, and one out of eight for the United States, with Canada, Australia, and New Zealand accounting for most of the remainder. It was only in the 1980s that the United States regained its popularity as a destination for Irish emigrants, with many of them entering the country illegally. In the 1980s about one in seven leaving independent Ireland traveled to the United States. The redirection of emigration across the Atlantic was a reflection of the employment opportunities available there, and the severity of the economic recession in Ireland and Britain. One significant feature of the "new wave" of Irish emigration of the 1980s and early 1990s was the greater variety of destinations. Mainland Europe received small but significant numbers of young Irish people in the 1980s and 1990s.

It was only with the establishment of the Assisted Passage Scheme (1947–1971) that Australia again became an attractive option. Under this scheme, which aimed to attract white settlers to Australia, emigrants were provided with assistance toward the cost of the fare, hostel accommodation on arrival, access to public housing, and voting rights within six months. Citizens of Northern Ireland, as British subjects, paid only £10 to migrate to Australia, with all their other expenses being defrayed. An agreement reached with the Irish state in November 1948 limited assistance to £30 for each adult fare for Irish citizens. The numbers leaving both parts of Ireland for Australia peaked in the 1960s and early 1970s, and by 1981 the Irish-born population amounted to almost 68,000 people.

Most other European migrant flows were dominated by single males, but Ireland, north and south, differed in this key respect, following a pattern established in the nineteenth century. In Northern Ireland the gender differential was more marked in the 1950s and 1960s, with a greater number of males emigrating than females, though by the 1980s this gap had narrowed. Throughout the 1990s roughly equal numbers of males and females emigrated from Northern Ireland. An overriding characteristic of the emigrant profile was their relative youth. Young people made up the great bulk of the outflow, as in the nineteenth and early twentieth centuries. Detailed information on the socioeconomic profile of Irish emigrants after 1950 is not available, although it appears that the majority came from poorer backgrounds, especially in parts of western and northwestern Ireland. Throughout this period the emigration of highly skilled workers was also significant, especially in the 1980s and 1990s, reflecting the huge expansion in secondary and university education in the 1970s and 1980s.

In Northern Ireland the failure of the traditionally higher birth rate among Catholics to produce a substantial rise in the Catholic share of total population is generally explained by the higher level of Catholic emigration up to the 1960s. But patterns shifted over time. In the 1950s almost two-thirds of emigrants were Catholic. In the following decade the differences narrowed somewhat, and throughout the 1970s and 1980s Protestants emigrated from Northern Ireland at a higher rate than Catholics, a trend that continued into the 1990s and reflected the demand in Britain for skilled labor and the preference of young Protestants for education at English and Scottish universities.

Inflows into independent Ireland from the 1960s onward were mostly composed of emigrants returning from Britain or the United States. In the 1970s a net inflow of over 100,000 people was recorded. From the late 1980s until the mid-1990s immigration averaged 30,000 persons per annum. Between 1997 and 2002 the average annual inflow rose to 45,000 persons. Returned Irish emigrants were the largest immigrant group throughout the 1990s, although the proportion of non–European Union (EU) nationals increased steadily from 1999 onward. The attractions of rapid economic growth together with higher living standards ensured that immigration from other parts of Europe and non-EU countries gradually increased. While the immigration of large numbers of skilled workers received little attention, the arrival of relatively small numbers of migrants, refugees, and asylum-seekers from eastern Europe, Africa, and elsewhere has generated much public controversy. For Northern Ireland the annual gross inflow between 1975 and 1990 fluctuated between 6,000 and 10,000 persons. In the 1990s immigration into Northern Ireland increased and averaged 19,000 persons per annum, many of whom were migrants returning after spending time living and working in Britain.

Emigration was a defining feature of Irish life after 1950. For most of this period it ensured that a significant proportion of each generation born in Ireland would in time leave for other countries, and only in the 1970s and 1990s did substantial immigration reverse this well-established historical pattern. From the mid-1990s the immigrant flow has included an increasing number of economic migrants from other countries—a remarkable discontinuity within the past two hundred years. For a country accustomed to bidding farewell to so many of its young citizens, welcoming immigrants, especially from non-EU countries, proves to be an extremely difficult process and remains one of the central ironies of contemporary Irish society: a nation of emigrants now displays a remarkable reluctance to embrace non-European nationals and to accept that immigration is an inevitable outcome of economic success.

SEE ALSO Celtic Tiger; Diaspora: The Irish in Australia; Diaspora: The Irish in Britain; Diaspora: The Irish in North America; Family: Fertility, Marriage, and the Family since 1950; Social Change since 1922; **Primary Documents:** From the *Report of the Commission on Emigration and Other Population Problems, 1948–1954* (1955)

Bibliography

Delaney, Enda. *Demography, State and Society: Irish Migration to Britain, 1921–1971.* 2000.

Delaney, Enda. *Irish Emigration since 1921.* 2002.

Enda Delaney

SEASONAL MIGRATION

Irish emigration has long been a subject of study, though the short-term seasonal and temporary movement of workers has not received the same attention. This is surprising considering the great number of agricultural workers involved during the heyday of seasonal migration in the nineteenth century and the interchange of ideas, values, and customs that occurred.

Although there is some evidence that Irish farm laborers were already traveling to Britain in the fourteenth and fifteenth centuries, their numbers increased only with population pressures in Ireland during the second half of the eighteenth century. With the establishment of the first regular passenger steamship service between Britain and Ireland in 1815, the one serious obstacle to reaching places where work was available—the expense of the journey—was removed. Already by the 1830s, by conservative estimate there were 35,000–40,000 Irish people working on a temporary basis in Britain, and numbers continued to increase to more than double this figure by the 1860s. In many areas of Ireland, especially in Counties Mayo and Donegal, people were dependent on earnings from seasonal work well into the opening decades of the twentieth century. The introduction of "new" agricultural crops to Britain in the late nineteenth century fostered a mutual dependence: Britain needed seasonal laborers to plant and lift potatoes, hoe turnips, pick fruit and hops, and ready crops for transport to the local market. In Scotland the extension of the railway resulted in the rapid growth of the potato industry after the 1860s, providing plenty of seasonal employment for Irish migrants. The Irish had worked as reapers of corn in the Scottish lowlands dur-

ing the Napoleonic war years and had become general agricultural laborers, working from seed-time to crop gathering, by the last quarter of the nineteenth century. They were still working as "tattie hokers" in the Scottish potato fields in the 1940s and 1950s.

Equally significant were the travels of seasonal migrants within Ireland, predominantly from western areas to counties in the east. Seventeenth- and eighteenth-century poets mention these *spailpíní*, as the workers were generally known. Their numbers were greatest during the difficult years of the 1820s and 1830s. On the whole, the seasonal workers were people who had close ties to the land: small farmers, cottiers, agricultural laborers, and generally poor people with family responsibilities and no means of earning cash at home. Women began to participate as workers to an important degree only in the middle of the nineteenth century, in the Scottish potato fields. Although there were few women migrant workers before this time, women were nevertheless an essential part of the movement in other ways: they provided support for the men by traveling with them; they begged for food and money to keep themselves and their children alive until the men returned home, and they undertook and organized essential farm work back in Ireland, thereby maintaining the small holding of land as the family home.

SEE ALSO Markets and Fairs in the Eighteenth and Nineteenth Centuries; Migration: Emigration from the Seventeenth Century to 1845; Migration: Emigration from 1850 to 1960; Population, Economy, and Society from 1750 to 1950; Rural Life: 1690 to 1845; Rural Life: 1850 to 1921

Bibliography

Collins, E. J. T. "Migrant Labor in British Agriculture in the Nineteenth Century." *Economic History Review* 14, no. 1 (1976): 38–59.

Harris, R. A. M. *The Nearest Place that Wasn't Ireland: Early Nineteenth-Century Irish Labor Migration.* 1994.

O'Dowd, Anne. *Spalpeens and Tattie Hokers: History and Folklore of the Irish Migratory Agricultural Worker in Britain and Ireland.* 1991.

Ó Fiaich, Tomás. "Filíocht Uladh mar Fhoinse don Stair Shóisialta san 18ú Aois." *Studia Hibernica* 11 (1971): 80–129.

Ó Gráda, Cormac. "Seasonal Migration and Post-Famine Adjustment in the West of Ireland." *Studia Hibernica* 13 (1973): 48–76.

Anne O'Dowd

Military Forces from 1690 to 1800

After the Battle of the Boyne, King William's army comprised about 30,000 men, composed of English, Dutch, and French Huguenots, plus locally raised Protestant regiments. The English parliament's Disbanding Act of 1699 limited the regular army in Ireland to 12,000 men in peacetime. Though in effect part of the English army, this force was paid for by the Irish parliament. It was seen as a strategic reserve that could be increased during wartime, when Irish regiments fought in Britain's overseas wars. The limit of 12,000 was maintained until 1769, when it was raised to 15,000 with the stipulation that the former total was retained for home defense. Legislation of 1701 required that no Catholics serve in this force, nor Protestant Irishmen in the ranks. The increasing demands of eighteenth-century warfare saw the removal of the bar on Protestants in 1745 and, from the 1760s, a slackening on Catholic exclusion. During the American Revolution Catholics were recruited for overseas service. During the French Revolution Ireland's military establishment expanded considerably, due to its vulnerability to French invasion and domestic insurrection. On the eve of the 1798 rebellion the total stood at over 42,000, and during the "bloody summer" of the insurrection reinforcements were rushed over from Britain, bringing the total to nearly 70,000 men. The force that defeated the United Irishmen was comprised of regular soldiers, fencible regiments enlisted for wartime service within the British Isles, Irish yeomanry, and British and Irish militia.

MILITIA

Militia were civilians who engaged to serve in an emergency. William's forces in 1690 were supplemented by a locally raised militia of 15,000 men. This hastily raised force had no statutory existence. The first militia legislation came during the Jacobite scare in 1715. In compliance with the prevailing Penal Laws, only Protestants could serve. Though there were several mobilizations during invasion scares in the 1740s and 1750s, the militia remained largely moribund, with its weapons stored away. The militia legislation lapsed after 1776 and was not renewed, because of the unavailability of finance, when the American Revolution began. With the regular troops depleted by war, the Irish Volunteers took over the militia's home-defense role. In 1793, at the outbreak of war with France, a new militia was raised. This radically different force included Catholics as privates and required full-time service. Initially, these men were levied by parish lottery, but this practice was deeply resented and rioting often resulted. The regulations were soon changed. The militia was organized in county regiments that were rotated to avoid soldiers' serving in their home districts and becoming embroiled in local unrest. The southern regiments were predominantly Catholic, and with sectarian and revolutionary tensions rising, fears were expressed about their reliability. Some did join the United Irishmen, but several well-publicized and harrowing executions discouraged defections. Despite earlier reservations, the militia fought well in 1798, when it totalled 30,000 men.

VOLUNTEERS AND YEOMANRY

The Irish Volunteers were raised in 1778 after France and Spain had joined the American colonists in their war against Britain. They were composed of Protestant civilians organized into small corps, raised by local initiative, and provided with their own arms and equipment. Volunteer officers held no commissions from the government and in many cases were elected from the ranks. They proudly saw this independence as signifying their patriotism and citizenship. The Volunteers willingly undertook law-and-order duties and were prepared to defend Ireland against invasion from France or Spain, but many sympathized with the plight of the American colonists. No invasion of Ireland came, and the Volunteer movement, which had grown from 12,000 in 1779 to over 60,000 in 1782, began functioning as an extra-parliamentary political-pressure group. A relationship was formed with the "Patriot" opposition in the Irish parliament to secure more equal treatment from the Westminster parliament, which could veto Irish legislation. Astutely realizing the British government's difficulty in fighting the unpopular war with the Americans, the Volunteers pressed for rectification of a range of their own grievances. Typically, they combined political protest with military reviews. On one occasion a cannon was paraded in front of the Irish parliament, draped with placards demanding concessions. In 1782 a Volunteer convention in Dungannon, Co. Tyrone, published political resolutions that were adopted throughout Ireland. With this public support and a change of government in London the Patriot leader Henry Grattan obtained the legislative independence of the Irish parliament.

This has been seen as the high point in Volunteering; afterward, some of the more radical Volunteers began recruiting Catholics and wanted to press on for franchise reform and full political rights for Catholics. The majority, however, were satisfied with their achievements and stood down. The radical Volunteers languished until the French Revolution of 1789 encour-

Demonstration by the Dublin Volunteers, 4 November 1779, in favor of "free trade," that is, the right of Ireland to the full benefits of membership in the British mercantile system. Painting by Francis Wheatley. NATIONAL GALLERY OF IRELAND, CAT. NO. 125. REPRODUCED BY PERMISSION.

aged them to resurrect their demands. In 1792 radical Volunteers in Dublin and in Ulster reorganized and rearmed as National Volunteers, emulating the French Gardes Nationale. With war against France beginning, the government suppressed them in 1793 when the new Irish militia was raised. Many National Volunteers were concurrently United Irishmen, and others of the original Volunteers later joined the government's new home-defense force—the Irish yeomanry. The revolutionary climate thus simplified the Volunteers' equivocal relationship with the government into polarities of loyalty and disloyalty.

In 1796, with a United Irish rebellion and a French invasion expected, the government raised a force modelled on the English yeomanry. In many respects the yeomanry was like the original Volunteers. It was part-time and was constituted in small, locally based corps of cavalry and infantry. The crucial difference was that the yeomanry was completely under government control. Its officers held commissions and its men were paid and equipped by the government. The initial levy was for 20,000 men, but the growing crisis saw that total rise to 50,000 by May 1798. Mostly Protestant in composition, the yeomanry became increasingly associated with Orangeism. Initially intended for law-and-order duties, yeomen were increasingly used in a military capacity and were heavily involved in the fighting in 1798, when, depending on one's perspective, they developed a reputation for brutality or bravery.

SEE ALSO Eighteenth-Century Politics: 1690 to 1714—Revolution Settlement; Eighteenth-Century Politics: 1714 to 1778—Interest Politics; Eighteenth-Century Politics: 1778 to 1795—Parliamentary and Popular Politics; Government from 1690 to 1800; Grattan, Henry; **Primary Documents:** The Ulster Volunteer Resolutions (1782)

Bibliography

Bartlett, Thomas, and Keith Jeffrey, eds. *A Military History of Ireland.* 1996.

Blackstock, Allan. *An Ascendancy Army: The Irish Yeomanry, 1796–1834.* 1998.

Allan Blackstock

Mitchel, John

A journalist and Irish nationalist best known for his critical analysis of British relief policy during the Great Famine, John Mitchel (1815–1875) was born at Camnish, Co. Londonderry, on 3 November 1815. The son of a Presbyterian minister, Mitchel attended Trinity College and practiced as a solicitor in Banbridge, Co. Down, for several years.

In 1843 he enrolled in the Repeal Association and two years later joined the editorial staff of the nationalist newspaper, the *Nation*. Although he was a leading figure among the Young Irelanders and the Irish Confederation, Mitchel left the *Nation* after failing to convince moderates in the Confederation to support Fintan Lalor's radical schemes for land reform. In February 1848 Mitchel established another newspaper, the *United Irishman*, in which he openly preached armed revolution. Arrested in March 1848 and charged with treason-felony for his writings, Mitchel was convicted by a jury packed by the government to ensure a conviction and sentenced to fourteen years' banishment to a penal colony in Tasmania. In 1853 Mitchel escaped to the United States, where he quickly rekindled his career as a controversial journalist. Mitchel also published several books that formed the basis of the nationalist genocide interpretation of the Great Famine, including *Jail Journal* (1854), *The Last Conquest of Ireland (Perhaps)* (1858), *An Apology for the British Government in Ireland* (1860), and his *History of Ireland* (1868).

With an acid pen Mitchel depicted the famine and resulting mass mortality and emigration as a deliberate policy pursued by officials of the British government to clear poor Irish farmers off the land. A central, although incorrect, element of Mitchel's argument was his contention that imports of maize and other grain into Famine Ireland by relief officials were far outstripped by exports of Irish foodstuffs to British markets. Mitchel also railed against the British government for its inadequate financial contributions and denounced the inequity of forcing a region of the United Kingdom to provide for its own relief. Mitchel's interpretation of the famine is best summarized by his famous maxim, "The Almighty indeed sent the potato blight, but the English created the famine" (Mitchel 1858, p. 219).

Mitchel returned to Ireland in 1875 after he was elected an MP for Tipperary, but Parliament voided the election on the grounds that he was a convicted felon. The voters re-elected Mitchel but he died shortly afterward on 20 March 1875. Mitchel is regarded as one of the founding fathers of Irish revolutionary republican-

Son of a northern Presbyterian minister, the journalist John Mitchel (1815-1875) at first took over from Thomas Davis (d. 1845) at the Nation. *Mitchel became a revolutionary after breaking with O'Connell's Repeal Association in 1846 and with Smith O'Brien's Irish Confederation in 1848. Sentenced to fourteen years' transportation for treason-felony (May 1848), he remained in Tasmania until 1853, when he escaped to the United States. A bitter antagonist of Britain and Victorian values, Mitchel did more than any other nationalist to propagate the genocide interpretation of the Great Famine.* NATIONAL GALLERY OF IRELAND, CAT. NO. 10 119. REPRODUCED BY PERMISSION.

ism and provided the most enduring nationalist interpretation of the famine.

SEE ALSO Davis, Thomas; Great Famine; Newspapers; O'Connell, Daniel; Repeal Movement; Young Ireland and the Irish Confederation

Bibliography

Donnelly, James S., Jr. "The Great Famine, Its Interpreters, Old and New." *History Ireland* 1, no. 3 (autumn 1993): 27–33.

Mitchel, John. *The Last Conquest of Ireland (Perhaps)*. 1858.

Nowlan, Kevin B. *The Politics of Repeal: A Study in the Relations between Great Britain and Ireland, 1841–50*. 1965.

Sloan, Robert. *William Smith O'Brien and the Young Ireland Rebellion of 1848*. 2000.

Michael W. de Nie

Molyneux, William

William Molyneux (1656–1698), pamphleteer and scientist, was born in Dublin on 17 April into a long-established Protestant family. Educated at Saint Patrick's Cathedral School and Trinity College, Dublin (1671–1674), he graduated with a B.A. in 1674 and was admitted to the Middle Temple (1675–1678). On his return to Dublin he threw himself into scholarly activity, which led to his prominent role in the foundation in 1683 of the Dublin Philosophical Society on the model of London's Royal Society. From 1684 to 1687 he served as chief engineer and surveyor-general in Ireland, but in 1688, like many other Dublin Protestants, he and his wife took refuge in Chester, England. After William III's victory at the Boyne they returned to Dublin, where Molyneux was reappointed as chief engineer and surveyor-general and given other official responsibilities. As MP for Dublin University in 1692 and again from 1695 to 1698, he played an active role in the House of Commons but was not associated with the vociferous opposition. In 1695 he was appointed a master in chancery.

It was in the last year of his life that Molyneux published *The Case of Ireland's Being Bound by Acts of Parliament in England Stated* (1698). He wrote it at a time when the English House of Commons was considering a bill to prohibit the export of Irish woollens overseas and the English House of Lords was asserting an appellate jurisdiction for Ireland. In effect, Molyneux argued that Ireland was a kingdom, with a parliament of medieval origin, and that subjects of William III in Ireland possessed the same right to the principles of representation and consent as subjects in England. To make his case he drew heavily not only on history and legal precedent but also on arguments based on John Locke's natural-rights theory. He readily admitted that a parliamentary union would equally guarantee to Ireland the principles of representation and consent, but that was "an happiness we can hardly hope for." The *Case* might well have faded into obscurity, as with other similar tracts based on precedent, had not the English House of Commons roundly condemned it, gaining for tract and author an enduring place in the eighteenth-century patriot canon.

Molyneux and Locke had corresponded throughout the 1690s, and though Locke was deeply unhappy at being mentioned in the *Case*, he received Molyneux with great civility when he visited England in August 1698, and was greatly saddened when he learned that Molyneux had died on 11 October, within a month of his return to Ireland.

SEE ALSO Dublin Philosophical Society; Eighteenth-Century Politics: 1690 to 1714—Revolution Settlement

Bibliography

Hoppen, K. T. *The Common Scientist in the Seventeenth Century.* 1970.

Simms, J. G. *William Molyneux of Dublin.* 1982.

James McGuire

Monarchy

On 18 June 1541 the Irish parliament declared Ireland to be a kingdom. It was a decisive change in Ireland's constitutional status that was to endure until the Act of Union created the United Kingdom of Great Britain and Ireland in 1801. Yet Ireland was no ordinary kingdom. Only in legal theory did its king exist as an individual distinct from the English monarch. The Irish kingdom remained de facto a dependency of the English Crown, but the vision of a sovereign Irish kingdom was to inspire separatist sentiments over many subsequent years.

CONSTITUTIONAL REVOLUTION?

Since Pope Adrian IV granted the bull *Laudabiliter* to Henry II, king of England, in 1155, Ireland was considered to be a papal fief held by the kings of England. With Henry VIII's breach with the papacy in 1534 the sovereignty of Ireland was disputed. The preamble of the Irish act of 1541 justified the adoption of the royal title as a means of clarifying Ireland's constitutional status, but the act was part of a broader, constitutional strategy to confederate Ireland with England and Wales.

This constitutional "revolution" was the brainchild of Sir Thomas Cusack, a local official in the Dublin administration. Cusack had been influenced by humanist thought during his legal studies at the Inner Temple in London, and he returned to Ireland with a sense of mission. He wanted to see the government of Ireland reformed so that the native Irish and the English colonial community in Ireland could live harmoniously together within a common political framework. Following recent developments in Wales, in particular the so-called Act of Union of 1536, he believed that the two communities in Ireland (Gaelic and "Old English") could be reconciled and reformed through constitutional means. Cusack won support from Sir Anthony Saint Leger, whom Henry VIII appointed as his lord deputy in Ireland in July 1540. Saint Leger was more an administrator than a soldier, and he boldly grasped the opportunity to try to pacify Ireland through constitutional means.

The 1541 "act for the kingly title" was the centerpiece of the Cusack–Saint Leger initiative. Ostensibly, the act was to encourage the Irish to accept Henry VIII as their true sovereign, but Cusack explained to the English Privy Council that it had far deeper implications. It required the abolition of the de facto constitutional and juridical division of Ireland into the English colony on the one hand and the independent Irish lordships on the other. It made all of the people of Ireland into subjects of Henry VIII, with the same rights and privileges as the king's English subjects. Henry became now honor-bound to dispense justice and good government throughout his new kingdom. A public holiday was declared in Ireland to mark the passing of the act, and it was promulgated in Dublin with a high mass, cannonades, bonfires, and free wine.

The Irish parliament that adopted the act for the kingly title was historic for another reason: an Irish layman sat as a member for the first time. He was Barnaby MacGilpatrick, made baron of Upper Ossory only two days before the parliament had convened. Other Irish lords attended as observers, ahead of their elevation to the peerage. The presence of these Irish nobles in this parliament was a revolutionary innovation. It signified that in the future the Irish parliament would become the representative assembly of all the people in Ireland—Gaelic Irish and Old English colonists alike. By involving the two communities in the government in this way, Saint Leger and Cusack hoped to unite the peoples of Ireland as the Welsh and English people in Wales had been brought together.

Surrender and Regrant

With the constitutional framework in place, Saint Leger introduced the policy known as "surrender and regrant." This involved the Irish lords surrendering their territories to the Crown in return for letters patent by which the king regranted them their lands with a title valid under English law. This formula was designed to regularize the relationship between the Crown and the greatest Irish lords. It also began the process by which the independent Irish lordships were to be transformed, more or less as they stood, into feudal lordships held of the Crown of Ireland. As part of this process each Irish

lord had to abandon his Gaelic title and accept instead an English title of nobility, such as earl or baron. He agreed to assist and obey the king's officers, to do military service for the Crown, and to pay taxes. Furthermore, the lord was obliged to learn to speak English, and to adopt English clothes and customs, and to reject the pope's authority.

Saint Leger realized that the assimilation of all of Ireland into the Tudor dominions could not be achieved overnight. He worked to bring about change gradually and relatively peacefully. He appreciated that some compulsion would be necessary on occasion to enforce the desired degree of constitutional change and social engineering. Already, the first breakthrough had come in January 1541 when James FitzGerald, fourteenth earl of Desmond, was formally reconciled to the English Crown. As Cusack observed, "the winning of the earl of Desmond was the winning of the rest of Munster at small charge." Progress with the Gaelic Irish lords was necessarily more difficult and slow. Yet, in September 1542 Conn O'Neill, lord of Tyrone and descendent of the ancient kings of Ireland, traveled to the English court to become the first earl of Tyrone. On 1 July 1543, Murrough O'Brien, prince of Thomond, traveled to court to become the first earl of Thomond. With him went Ulick MacWilliam Burke, a magnate from southern Connacht, who became the first earl of Clanrickard.

Reformation

In religion too Saint Leger made progress, winning widespread acquiescence for a moderated version of the Henrician reformation, a schismatic, if essentially Catholic religious settlement in which the pope's authority was renounced by Ireland's political and ecclesiastical elites—Irish as well as colonial—while traditional religious practices were permitted. The first Jesuit mission to Ireland, in 1542 was quickly aborted when the missioners concluded that the Irish were irredeemably lost to Rome.

Suspension

The Cusack-Saint Leger initiative was making remarkable progress toward a peaceful settlement of the political divisions in Ireland when it was suddenly suspended. In July 1543 Henry embarked on a war with France and Scotland. Many Irishmen fought with the English army against the French and the Scots; however, the constitutional revolution never recovered from its suspension. The protracted negotiations to reform the internal structures of the Irish lordships were interrupted and left incomplete, a major deficiency which undermined the prospects of future success. Saint Leger might have been able to inject new momentum into the would-be revolution once the war with France and Scotland had ended, but the death of Henry VIII in January 1547 also spelled the end of the Cusack–Saint Leger initiative. The government of Henry VIII's son and successor Edward VI, adopted militarist strategies to subjugate the Irish and rejected Saint Leger's achievement of religious consensus in favor of more full-blooded Protestantism.

CONCLUSIONS

The Irish monarchy established in 1541 failed to reconcile the people of Ireland to English, and later British, governance. In fact, the monarchy was a legal fiction that did little to diminish Ireland's constitutional subordination to the English Crown and government. Irish people were not granted political and legal rights equal to those of English subjects under Henry VIII or his son, and in Elizabeth I's reign conformity to the Anglican Church began to be used as a test of who was a true subject and who was not. Nevertheless, after the repeated failure of rebellions against Elizabeth, the idea of an Irish monarchy came to be accepted, and Irish and Old English scholars supplied the monarchy with an ancient Irish pedigree. The ideal of Ireland as a kingdom separate from England, though sharing the same monarch, was promoted at different times over the centuries by groups as diverse as the Kilkenny Confederates of the 1640s, the late-eighteenth-century Patriots, and even by the nascent Sinn Féin.

SEE ALSO English Government in Medieval Ireland; English Political and Religious Policies, Responses to (1534–1690); Fitzgerald, Thomas, Tenth Earl of Kildare ("Silken Thomas"); Old English; Politics: 1500 to 1690; Protestant Reformation in the Early Sixteenth Century; Surrender and Regrant; Wentworth, Thomas, First Earl of Strafford

Bibliography

Bradshaw, Brendan. *The Irish Constitutional Revolution of the Sixteenth Century.* 1979.

Brady, Ciarán. *The Chief Governors: The Rise and Fall of Reform Government in Tudor Ireland, 1536–1588.* 1994.

Ellis, Steven G. *Ireland in the Age of the Tudors, 1447–1603: English Expansion and the End of Gaelic Rule.* 1998.

Henry A. Jefferies

~

Monasticism in the Early Middle Ages

Irish Christians embraced monasticism as enthusiastically as they had accepted the Christian religion itself. As with the doctrines and rituals of Christianity, the Irish created a form of institutionalized ascetic life dependent upon continental originals but unique to the society and culture of Ireland. What is more, by the end of the seventh century Irish monks had thoroughly organized churches and parishes throughout the island according to monastic models, and had even begun to send missionaries abroad to bring Christianity to formerly Roman territories. They also built schools and scriptoria (copying rooms) where they began producing the artistic and scholarly works that made them famous throughout Christendom.

Both bishops and monastic men and women helped to create Irish Christianity. Saint Patrick (d. 461? or 493?), the legendary missionary to Ireland and its primary patron saint, was a bishop, not a monk, but his two fellow patron saints, Saint Brigit of Kildare (d. 524?) and Saint Columba (Colum Cille) of Iona (d. 5??), were both heads of monasteries. Around 450, Saint Patrick himself made the first possible references to people pursuing ascetic vocations in his descriptions of "virgins in Christ" and "religious women," including noblewomen who endured harassment from their parents, Irish and British slaves, and widows (*Confessio*, sec. 41, 49, trans. De Paor 1998, pp. 250–253). No communities of nuns or monks appeared in Ireland for another thirty or forty years. Patrick's female comrades in religion were probably following the advice of theologians such as Saint Jerome, who explained to Roman women exactly how to organize and educate themselves for an ascetic life in their own homes.

The first monastic community in Ireland may have been created by women at Kildare under the leadership of Brigit. Cogitosus, a monk of Kildare around 670, wrote the earliest Irish saint's life about Brigit. He suggested that she had established a church and a community of women, along with a bishop, at or near an old pagan center in the province of Leinster around 500. Kildare was patronized and staffed by the local nobility and royalty of the province. Abbesses and bishops usually came from leading families of the dynasty that controlled the kingship of Leinster or were the children of local chiefs. The monastery owned properties near its main church, and had tenants who provided income. The abbess of Kildare also demanded allegiance and revenues from other monasteries and churches scattered around Ireland dedicated to Saint Brigit, as well as from other local Leinster churches. Already a major pilgrimage site in the seventh century, Kildare had become by 650 a place of legal refuge, treasury of kings, and cultural center, where crowds flocked, as Cogitosus wrote, "for the abundance of festivals" and "to watch the crowds go by" (*Vita Sanctae Brigidae*, in Migne, *PL 72*, col. 789).

By the time that Kildare had acquired a major church and island-wide fame, it had competition as the most flourishing site of Irish monastic practice. Around the time of Brigit, many founders of ascetic communities built their settlements and established their own reputations as saintly monks and nuns. In particular, a community dedicated to Saint Patrick at Armagh in Ulster had become his primary church and acquired dependent foundations of its own. In the late seventh century, via two lives of Patrick and a collection of jurisdictional statements called the *Liber Angeli* (Book of the angel), Armagh's leaders claimed the governance of a *paruchia* (network of churches and monasteries) that spread throughout Ireland, inferior in authority and size to none. The *Liber Angeli*, supposedly handed to Patrick by an angel, declared that the bishop at Armagh had the right to adjudicate all rivalries and disputes among Irish monasteries and churches. Other *paruchiae*, especially those of Brigit and Columba (based on the Irish island monastery of Iona off the coast of Scotland) contested Armagh's claims to authority, territory, and dues in the seventh century, but Armagh eventually won the battle for dominance. As a consequence, each monastery or convent in Ireland had its own patron among the hundreds of Irish saints, but supposedly all were obedient to the abbot of Armagh.

Life in most Irish monasteries was challenging physically, intellectually, or both. No one built the stone cloisters typical of continental monasteries in Ireland until the Cistercians arrived in the twelfth century, and even then the Irish preferred their wattle and daub huts to the masonry angles of the European reformers. In the sixth and seventh centuries monasteries included everything from a single round hut built of sticks and mud to a collection of circular and rectangular buildings jostling together inside an encircling wall. Typically, though, every monastic settlement had three features: a church, a patron saint's shrine in or near the church, and a circular enclosure of walls, ditches, or both. Monks combined and augmented these elements in myriad ways. At Reask in County Kerry a rounded stone wall enclosed pairs of connected, beehive-shaped huts of stone in one half of the enclosure; separated by a stone wall through the middle, the other half contained rectangular church buildings. Elsewhere, the en-

Symbol of St. Matthew from the Book of Durrow *(seventh century), a gospel book. The flat body is covered by a checkered pattern of millefiori-type ornament. The hairstyle is similar to the Irish tonsure known from other representations of Celtic saints.* © ARCHIVO ICONOGRAFICO, S.A./CORBIS. REPRODUCED BY PERMISSION.

tirely earthen enclosure and wooden buildings have disappeared, leaving only cross-inscribed slabs to mark especially sacred spots within the now-lost enclosures—the church doorway, the shrine, a well, or a cemetery. The seventh-century *Hisperica Famina* (Western sayings), a maniacally ornate Latin poem, described life in a prosperous community of monks. One passage compared a comfortable monastic building with its poorer cousin: "This hollow hall surrounds a clean chamber / which is continually swept with switches of birch, / nor does any kindling pile up there. / Here there is a foul-smelling room / that contains hardened grains of dirt, / nor do the leafy brooms sweep the aforesaid chamber" (Herren 1974, pp. 82–83). Some wealthier settlements, such as Armagh, included special housing for nuns, students, guests, kings and queens, and domestic animals. Beyond the gates of such major monasteries lay their farms, pastures for cattle and sheep, their forests, and perhaps a mill.

Neither stone nor wood-and-earth huts would have afforded much comfort to brothers and sisters, who made do with pleasures of mind and soul. Wherever they lived, Irish monks and nuns, who had never known the Romans as rulers, took up Latin as part of their religious training. Monastic communities organized the study of this entirely foreign language, its grammar, and its major religious texts. They also formed their own idiosyncratic ways of making letters and manuscripts, thus initiating a distinguished tradition of book-learning and production. In addition to Bibles, psalters, and grammar books, Irish monks in the seventh and following centuries produced biblical commentary, prayers, letters, astronomical works, laws, penitentials, and many other texts in both Latin and Europe's earliest written vernacular, Irish. They commemorated the lives of their monastic founders in biographies of saints, beginning with Cogitosus's life of Brigit. They also wrote and rewrote the poetry and stories of their ancestors, the kings of ancient Ireland, and the myths of the pre-Christian era. Only the most prosperous communities could muster the supplies and labor to create a great library, or the gorgeously illuminated manuscripts for which Ireland became known (such as the seventh-century *Book of Durrow*, the earliest known decorated Irish manuscript); others had to borrow and copy what they could.

The historian known as the Venerable Bede (672?–735), writing in the early eighth century, spread the reputation of Irish scholars, who were already taking in foreign students by then: "The Irish welcomed them all gladly, gave them their daily food, and also provided them with books to read and with instruction without asking for any payment" (*Historica Ecclesiastica*, III.27, trans. King 1930, p. 485). From large monasteries such as Bangor, where Saint Comgall first ruled, scholars such as Columbanus (543–615) went to continental Europe and Britain to gather and offer Christian learning. (Only men went into exile; religious women were expected to stay home and, at most, teach rudimentary letters to young boys and girls.) Columbanus left a rule and penitentials for the monasteries that he founded in southern France and northern Italy, along with poems and letters to Pope Gregory the Great, among others. His writings reveal not only an elegant style and the passion of a dedicated missionary but also the training in grammar and exegesis that he gained at home early in his career. Columbanus annoyed Gregory with arguments about the date of Easter and so angered local royalty that he found himself on a boat bound for Ireland, composing a mournful poem about his forced depar-

ture. But he ended his days as a saintly abbot in Bobbio, south of the Alps. Columbanus was among the first of what would be so many Irish missionary monks that eventually the Latin word for Irishmen, *Scotti*, came to represent wandering monks of any nationality.

SEE ALSO Early Medieval Ireland and Christianity; Hagiography; Hiberno-Latin Culture

Bibliography

Bede. *Historica Ecclesiastica*. Edited and translated by J. E. King. 1930.

Bieler, Ludwig, ed. and trans. *Patrician Texts in the Book of Armagh.* 1979.

Bitel, Lisa. *Isle of the Saints: Monastic Settlement and Christian Community in Early Ireland.* 1990.

Cogitosus. *Vita Sanctae Brigidae*. PL 72, cols. 775–790.

De Paor, Liam. *Saint Patrick's World.* 1996.

Gwynn, Aubrey, and R. Neville Hadcock. *Medieval Religious Houses: Ireland.* Reprint, 1988.

Herren, Michael, ed. and trans. *The Hisperica Famina*. 2 vols. 1974, 1987.

Hughes, Kathleen. *The Church in Early Irish Society.* 1966.

Ó Cróinín, Dáibhí. *Early Medieval Ireland, 400–1200.* 1995.

Ryan, John. *Irish Monasticism: Origins and Early Development.* Reprint, 1986.

Sharpe, Richard. "Some Problems Concerning the Organization of the Church in Early Medieval Ireland." *Peritia* 3 (1984): 230–270.

Walker, G. S. M., ed. *Sancti Columbani opera.* 1957.

Lisa M. Bitel

Mother and Child Crisis

The Mother and Child Scheme was a government program to provide free maternity and child care as part of the restructuring of postwar health services approved by Fianna Fáil in 1947. Implementation of the scheme was delayed until after the first interparty government came into office in February 1948 and became the responsibility of the new minister for health, Dr. Noël Browne of Clann na Poblachta. Browne had quickly come to prominence because of his highly successful campaign to eradicate tuberculosis, but when his name came to be linked with the Mother and Child Scheme, he became one of Ireland's most controversial political figures.

Criticism of the scheme had been voiced from the outset, by Fine Gael (which had been in 1947 an opposition party, but by 1948, the senior partner in the interparty government charged with the scheme's implementation); by the Catholic hierarchy; and by representatives of the medical profession. All had expressed the belief that free treatment, regardless of means, represented state intrusion into the lives of families and was contrary to Catholic social ethics. Additionally, the bishops feared that women would learn about contraception and abortion, and family practitioners feared a loss of independence and income.

On 11 October 1950, Browne met the Catholic archbishop of Dublin, Dr. John Charles McQuaid, and other bishops to discuss their concerns. Believing wrongly that he had reassured them, he publicized his plan to put the scheme into effect, gambling that the popular response would undermine the doctors' opposition. This act precipitated a crisis when McQuaid reiterated his objections to the scheme. Pressured by the taoiseach, John A. Costello of Fine Gael, and his colleagues to come to an accommodation, Browne met McQuaid in March 1951. He asked that the bishops state definitively whether the scheme was contrary to Catholic morals and implied that the outcome might result in his leaving office. The bishops were uniformly hostile and the cabinet refused to proceed with the scheme. Browne's resignation was urged by the Clann na Poblachta party leader Seán MacBride and gladly accepted by Costello on 11 April 1951. Shortly afterwards, the interparty government, which was already disintegrating, fell from office. The affair became the subject of passionate public debate. Opinion was divided, but for the first time the Catholic bishops were widely accused of improper and harmful interference in the affairs of the state.

The Mother and Child crisis was not simply a conflict between church and state; it also arose from the ambiguous relationship between the state and interest groups such as the medical profession, and from ideological and personal differences within the interparty government and Clann na Poblachta. However, the public backlash against the bishops' influence on government policy marked the beginning of the end of the close relationship between church and state.

SEE ALSO Gaelic Catholic State, Making of; Health and Welfare since 1950, State Provisions for; McQuaid, John Charles; Political Parties in Independent Ireland; Politics: Independent Ireland since 1922; Roman Catholic Church: Since 1891; Secularization; **Primary Documents:** Letter to John A. Costello, the Taoiseach (5 April 1951)

Bibliography

Browne, Noël. *Against the Tide.* 1986.

Cooney, John. *John Charles McQuaid: Ruler of Catholic Ireland.* 1999.

Horgan, John. *Noël Browne: Passionate Outsider.* 2000.

Whyte, John. *Church and State in Modern Ireland, 1923–1979.* 1980.

Susannah Riordan

Murphy, William Martin

William Martin Murphy (1844–1919), businessman, was born near Castletownbere, Co. Cork, on 29 December. Murphy inherited the family building firm after his father's death in 1863, made a fortune through railway-construction contracts, and sat on several railway boards. In 1875 he moved to Dublin, where he dominated the Dublin United Tramways Company (created in 1880 by his father-in-law James F. Lombard) and oversaw the expansion and electrification of the city's tram system. (His company later constructed tramways in Britain and Argentina.) Murphy also managed Clery's Department Store and owned the Imperial Hotel (both in O'Connell Street). Cold, austere, and dominating, proud of his entrepreneurial skills, Murphy saw himself as a paternalist who created employment in return for complete obedience, and he remained fiercely conscious that he was a Catholic arriviste in a Protestant-dominated business community.

Murphy was a Home Rule MP from 1885 to 1892. He opposed Charles Stewart Parnell in 1890 to 1892, and in the party feuds of the 1890s he financed the political and journalistic enterprises of T. M. Healy's "Bantry Band." His political experiences gave Murphy an abiding contempt for the Irish Parliamentary Party leadership as incompetent and irresponsible opportunists. In 1905 Murphy relaunched the *Irish Independent* (initially acquired in 1900) as a halfpenny daily, employing journalistic techniques pioneered by the Northcliffe Press. The *Independent* rapidly displaced the *Freeman's Journal* as the best-selling Irish nationalist daily newspaper; by 1914 it was selling more than 100,000 copies daily. Its criticisms of the Irish Parliamentary Party allegedly assisted the rise of Sinn Féin; however, it was criticized by Irish Irelanders for sensationalism and West Britonism. In 1907 Murphy organized the Dublin International Exhibition, with King Edward VII as patron; it was denounced by nationalists for promoting imports and "flunkeyism," but it cemented Murphy's leading role in the Dublin business community. As president of the Dublin Chamber of Commerce, Murphy led the Dublin employers' resistance to James Larkin's Irish Transport and General Workers' Union, culminating in the Dublin lockout of 1913 to 1914. Murphy thought the third Home Rule bill insufficient; from 1914 he openly denounced the Irish Parliamentary Party's willingness to accept partition and advocated all-Ireland dominion status.

Murphy died on 26 June 1919; his business empire was frittered away over the next half-century by less competent descendants. Murphy's historical reputation is dominated by his ruthless treatment of the 1913 strikers, by W. B. Yeats's poetic denunciations of Murphy as the archetypal Catholic bourgeois philistine, and by the *Independent*'s calls for the execution of James Connolly after the 1916 Rising.

SEE ALSO Connolly, James; Labor Movement; Larkin, James; Literacy and Popular Culture; Lockout of 1913; Newspapers; O'Brien, William; Trade Unions

Bibliography

Callanan, Frank. *T. M. Healy.* 1996.
Morrissey, Thomas. *William Martin Murphy.* 1997.

Patrick Maume

Murray, Daniel

Daniel Murray (1768–1852), Catholic archbishop of Dublin from 1823 to 1852, was born on 18 April in Arklow, County Wicklow. He studied for the priesthood at the Irish College in Salamanca, Spain, and was ordained a priest of the Dublin diocese. He was named coadjutor archbishop of Dublin in 1809. He succeeded Archbishop Troy in the see in 1823.

As the church in Dublin emerged from the penal era, it underwent a transformation with the building of a new physical fabric. Murray oversaw a remarkable expansion of Catholic activities in Dublin, including the emergence of new orders such as the Sisters of Mercy, founded by Catherine McAuley, and the Sisters of Charity, founded by Mary Aikenhead.

Murray opposed "the veto" in the 1810s as the price of Catholic Emancipation. This would have granted the

British government an influence in Catholic episcopal appointments. A gentle personality, he relied on Bishop James Doyle in the 1820s for much of his response to the Catholic Association's campaign for Catholic Emancipation. Murray was named a member of the National Board of Education in 1831, the first Catholic bishop to be appointed to a state board in the modern period. He served in administering the system alongside the Anglican archbishop of Dublin, Richard Whately, in an unusual example of good ecumenical relations.

In 1838, Murray was attacked by a fellow archbishop, John MacHale of Tuam, for not holding firmly to a Catholic position on the National Board. Murray, however, had the support of a majority of the bishops. Throughout the 1840s Murray and MacHale disagreed on almost every issue and split the hierarchy. Murray did not approve of Daniel O'Connell's campaign for repeal of the union. He favored the third-level Queen's Colleges but was opposed by a majority of the hierarchy and by Archbishop Cullen at the Synod of Thurles in 1850. A political moderate, he was regarded by Cullen and others as being too trusting of British government intentions.

SEE ALSO Roman Catholic Church: 1690 to 1829; Roman Catholic Church: 1829 to 1891

Bibliography

Kerr, Donal A. *Peel, Priests, and Politics: Sir Robert Peel's Administration and the Roman Catholic Church in Ireland, 1841–1846.* 1982.
Kerr, Donal A. *"A Nation of Beggars"? Priests, People, and Politics in Famine Ireland, 1846–1852.* 1994.

Thomas McGrath

Music

EARLY MODERN MUSIC	GEARÓID Ó hALLMHURÁIN
MODERN MUSIC	COLETTE MOLONEY
POPULAR MUSIC	PAUL ROUSE

EARLY MODERN MUSIC

An eclectic cadre of native and foreign sources chronicles the music, song, and dance from 1500 to 1800. The most striking feature of its musical landscape is the genesis of what is known today as Irish traditional music and the decline of the harp music of the Gaelic court, a dilemma induced by the perplexities of Tudor and Stuart politics. Both Henry VIII and Elizabeth I passed decrees prohibiting music. The *píobaire* (piper), bard, and *aois ealaíon* (artistic class) were frequently outlawed. In contrast to royal skepticism, Tudor scribes Edmund Spenser and Fynes Moryson left vivid accounts of Irish music from sword dancing in the court of the lord deputy, to the Gaelic *kerne* (professional soldiers) of Fiach MacAodha Ó Broin being led into battle by pipers. Native musicians also registered their impressions of the Tudor conquest, from the Desmond rebellions (1569 and 1579) to the Nine Years War (1594–1603). A poignant eulogy to the period is the Munster air "Caoineadh Uí Dhomhnaill," which recalls O'Donnell's defeat at Kinsale (1601). The subsequent Flight of the Earls (1607) marked a watershed in Irish musical culture. Apart from a minority of performers who accompanied their chiefs into exile, those who remained behind were deprived of aristocratic patronage. Henceforth, the archaic trinity of *file* (poet), *reacaire* (reciter), and *cruitire* (harper) crumbled. Despite its displacement of native performers, the settlement of English and Scottish colonists in the northeast corner of Ireland during the Plantation of Ulster (beginning in 1609) brought a new injection of musicians, among them Gaelic-speaking Presbyterians from Galloway and Argyle.

Just as music reflected the Tudor conquest, so too did it mirror the bellicose politics of the seventeenth century, from the Ulster Rebellion (1641) to the Williamite Wars (1689–1691). Among the musical records of the period are: the "Lament for Eoghan Rua O'Neill" (composed by Carolan in memory of the Confederate leader); "Alasdruim's March" (eulogizing Alasdair MacColla, killed at Cnoc na nDos in 1647); "Seán Ó Duibhir A'Ghleanna" (lauding the exploits of John O'Dwyer during the Cromwellian Wars); "Gol na mBan san Ár" (a piping dirge simulating the march to Aughrim in 1691 and the crying of the women after the slaughter); "Marbhna Luimní" (cognate of the Scottish "Lochaber No More," lamenting the exile of Sarsfield and the Wild Geese after the fall of Limerick); "Clare's Dragoons" (extolling Wild Geese valor in the French army at Fontenoy in 1745); and "Éamonn A'Chnuic" (praising raparee, or political dissident, Éamonn Ryan, forced to become an outlaw after a fracas with a Williamite tax collector).

Although love songs like "Dónal Óg" and "Úna Bhán" composed by anonymous poets dominated the *amhráin* (vernacular songs) by the late 1600s, older airs survived in "Laoithe Fiannaíochta" (evoking the exploits of Fionn MacCumhail). *Caoineadh* (laments) also en-

"Brian Boru's Harp," the oldest surviving Irish harp, dates to the fourteenth to fifteenth centuries. THE BOARD OF TRINITY COLLEGE DUBLIN. REPRODUCED BY PERMISSION.

dured, from *amhrán bheannaithe* ("sacred songs" derived from medieval apocrypha) and keening songs, like "Caoineadh Airt Uí Laoire" (Lament for Arthur O'Leary, penned by his wife Eibhlín Dubh Ní Chonaill in 1773), to formal and semilearned *marbhna* (bardic elegies). The latter were composed by poets like Aogán Ó Rathaille (1670–1728) and Dáibhí Ó Bruadair (1625–1698). The *aisling* ("vision poem/song," in which the poet meets an enchanted lady, symbolically Ireland) evolved during the eighteenth century. "Úr Chill an Chreagáin" by the Ulster poet Art Mac Cumhaigh (1715–1774) is among the best known.

THE EIGHTEENTH CENTURY

The Williamite wars left 90 percent of Irish land in Protestant hands. By 1700 a series of harsh anti-Catholic penal laws had been passed that excluded Catholics from Parliament, the army, the legal professions, and government services. Access to land, education and religious worship was also restricted. Songs like "An Raibh Tú ar an gCarraig?" (Were you at the Rock?), "Caoineadh an tSagairt" (Priest's Lament), "Pill, Pill, Rúin Ó" (lament for the Donegal priest, Dominick O'Donnell, who converted to Protestantism under duress) and "An

Joseph Patrick Haverty, The Blind Piper *(early nineteenth century). This work, filled with nostalgia for a long-lost Ireland, was hung in engraved form throughout the country.* NATIONAL GALLERY OF IRELAND, CAT. NO. 166. REPRODUCED BY PERMISSION.

Spailpín Fánach" (recalling the demeaning hiring fairs that marked the life of the migrant laborer) all mirror the toils of the penal era.

By 1730 folk poets and musicians accepted their reduced status as clerics, farmers, peddlers, and hedge schoolmasters. Although in Munster they continued to hold courts of poetry, their folk compositions were now more community oriented and dealt with a range of religious, legal, and economic issues. Their work also acted as a form of political journalism, as in Whiteboy songs like "Príosún Chluain Meala," Riocard Bairéad's "Eoghan Cóir," and the rich corpus of Jacobite songs that emerged in the 1700s. The latter reflected a common Gaelic culture that linked Ireland with Scotland. In the wake of the Jacobite risings (1715 and 1745) poets and musicians like Seán Clárach MacDomhnaill, Piaras MacGearailt, Seán Ó Tuama, and Eoghan Rua Ó Súilleabháin lauded the Stuarts in songs like "Mo Ghile Mear" and "Rosc Catha na Mumhan," and in piping airs like "Loch na gCaor." After the Battle of Culloden (1746), the Young Pretender was immortalized in Ire-

land by musical code names like "The Blackbird," which still survives as a set dance today.

DANCING

Throughout the eighteenth century, traffic in and out of Ireland had a direct impact on music, song, and dance. Gaelic-speaking "wintermen" (fishery workers) headed to Newfoundland, dissenting Scots-Irish transplanted whole communities to Appalachia, while dissident "croppies" (United Irishment influenced by Jacobin ideas, who cropped their hair in the new French style of the 1790s) found new vocations after serving prison sentences in Australia. All these exiles helped to disperse Irish music overseas. In-bound traffic facilitated the adoption of the modern violin (*fidil* in Irish) and imported a bevy of dancing masters who sold their steps to all classes of society. These were particularly popular in Munster, where they worked with hedge schoolmasters. Sources for the early history of dancing are nebulous. By the 1600s, English accounts refer to the "hay," "fading," "trenchmore," and *rince fada* (long dance) as popular forms. The latter was danced when bonfires were lit on May Eve. Until the late 1700s, when it was ousted by new French dances, it was performed at the close of public balls. In 1780, the English geographer Arthur Young noted that "dancing is general among the poor people, almost universal in every cabin. Dancing masters of their own rank travel through the country from cabin to cabin, with a piper or blind fiddler; and the pay is sixpence a quarter. It is an absolute system of education." Young, who traveled in Ireland from 1776 to 1779, cited jigs, minuets, and cotillions as the most common dances. Reels and hornpipes did not gain prominence until the 1790s. By then, the printed collections of Golden Age masters Neil Gow and Nathaniel Gow, William Marshal, and other Scottish composers were gaining new audiences in Ireland. Hence, the presence of Scottish reels like "Miss MacLeod," "Lord MacDonald," "Lord Gordon," and "Lucy Campbell" in Irish repertories.

BARDS

Although composers like Rory Dall Ó Catháin (c. 1550–1640) had enjoyed considerable status a century earlier, by now the remnants of the bardic order were reduced to a few itinerant harpers. Patronized by ascendancy landlords and a scattering of Gaelic families, their music acquired the features of continental composers. The most prominent was Turlough Carolan (1670–1738) whose work was published during his own lifetime. Astutely aware of his working milieu, he offered music that was an eclectic mix of Irish and non-Irish tunes, composed in a variety of dialects from baroque to vernacular dance music. When it became clear that the oral art of the harper was facing extinction, efforts were made to preserve it. In 1730 a contention of the bards met in Limerick. In 1780 James Duggan, an Irishman living in Denmark, sponsored harp festivals in Longford in order to provide support for harpers and create awareness for their plight. These eleventh-hour efforts peaked at the Belfast Harpers' Festival in 1792. Fueled by republicanism and antiquarianism, this venture brought together ten exponents (nine men and a woman) to have their music transcribed by nineteen-year-old Edward Bunting. The oldest attendee was nonogenarian Denis Hempson (1697–1807), who contributed "An Chuilfhionn." Bunting's *General Collection of the Ancient Music of Ireland* (1796) contained music collected at this caucus. Adding to existing collections (Neale, Lee, and Walker), this seminal work set the tone for other collectors and composers in the nineteenth century; among them Thomas Moore, who reinvented the atrophied harp music of Gaelic Ireland for the new pianofortés and drawing rooms of Regency society.

The End of the Early Modern Era

Whereas songwriters like Antaine Raiftearaí and Tomás Rua Ó Súilleabháin were coming to prominence by the late 1790s, their work would be marginalized by *macaronic* songs (incorporating bilingual lyrics) and English language ballads. Despite their cultural distinctions, songs in both traditions continued to address familiar topics like love, work, recreation, death, and the supernatural. Political songs mirrored the events of the time (United Irishmen risings in Counties Antrim, Down, and Wexford, and the French landing in Mayo). Dance music reflected circumstances in America and France that influenced Irish politics. Just as the Industrial Revolution and the synergy of the Romantic period led to the invention of new instruments in Europe; in Ireland pipe makers perfected the unique multireed *uilleann* pipes, which reached their present state of development (combining drones, chanter, and regulators) in the 1790s. Sheet music and tutors soon followed, among them O'Farrell's *Collection of National Irish Music for the Union Pipes*, published in London in 1800.

At the end of the early modern era, Dublin's predilection for western art music, which reached an epitome in 1742 with the première of Handel's *Messiah*, would decline with the drift of colonial society to London after the Act of Union. By now, however, Irish traditional music had spread worldwide. Sustained by an expanding population, especially in the rural *clacháns* of the west of Ireland, where music making followed the cyclical calendar of the agricultural year, dance music and set dancing experienced dynamic growth in the late 1700s, only to be devastated by famine and diaspora a half century afterward.

SEE ALSO Arts: Early Modern Literature and the Arts from 1500 to 1800; Carolan, Turlough; Music: Modern Music; Raiftearaí (Raftery), Antaine

Bibliography

Breathnach, Breandán. *Folk Music and Dances of Ireland.* 1971.

Breathnach, Breandán. *Dancing in Ireland.* 1983.

Flood, W. H. Grattan. *A History of Irish Music.* 1905.

Gillen, Gerard, and Harry White, eds. *Music and Irish Cultural History.* 1995.

Ó Canainn, Tomás. *Traditional Music in Ireland.* 1978.

Ó hAllmhuráin, Gearóid. *A Pocket History of Irish Traditional Music.* 1998.

Ó Tuama, Seán. *An Grá in Amhráin na nDaoine.* 1960.

Shields, Hugh, ed. *Popular Music in Eighteenth-Century Dublin.* 1985.

Vallely Fintan, ed. *The Companion to Irish Traditional Music.* 1999.

Young, Arthur. *A Tour in Ireland.* 1780, 1892.

Discography

Clancy, Willie. *The Pipering of Willie Clancy.* Vol. 2. 1983.

Ennis, Séamus. *The Best of Irish Piping.* 1978.

Harte, Frank. *My Name is Napoleon Bonaparte.* 2001.

Kelly, James. *Traditional Irish Music.* 1996.

Ní Chathasaigh, Máire. *The New-Strung Harp.* 1985.

Ó hÉanaí, Seosamh. *Ó Mo Dhúchas/From My Tradition.* 1976.

Gearóid Ó hAllmhuráin

Modern Music

Irish traditional music, at the beginning of the twentieth century, was generally played, sung, and danced in the domestic setting. Ireland still had a high proportion of Irish speakers, and singing was an important activity both to accompany work and as a form of entertainment. Musicians and dancers, apart from a few professional traveling musicians and dancing masters, were amateurs who played, sang, and danced for their own amusement at home or at house and crossroad dances in their locality. The better dancers gave solo dancing displays, but most took part in group dances, particularly set dances (dances that had developed in Ireland during the eighteenth century and which derived from the French dance, the quadrille). The transmission of music and song from one generation to the next was oral, and in rural Ireland regional repertoires and styles abounded. In many parts of the country Irish traditional music was the only music played and listened to.

The position of Irish traditional music by the end of the twentieth century, however, was very different. In common with Irish society, Irish music had undergone rapid changes and developments in the intervening years. The performance setting of the music had changed to the pub, concert hall, stadium, music festival, or radio/television studio. Instrumental music was most commonly played for listening to rather than for dancing. The prominence of singers and singing in the society waned, and Irish was no longer widely spoken. With increased prosperity, particularly in the latter part of the century, musical instruments were more easily purchased. Comhaltas Ceoltóirí Éireann, an organization for the promotion of Irish music, song, and dance, was formed in 1951. This and other organizations, such as Cáirde na Cruite (1960) and Na Píobairí Uilleann (1968), helped to rekindle interest in traditional music by providing lessons, and technical standards increased, particularly among young musicians.

The century also saw the rapid growth of céilí dancing and the céilí band as an instrumental grouping. Céilí dancing is a type of line or group dancing, which was introduced around the turn of the twentieth century and uses dances reconstructed or composed for the purpose. Music was provided by groups of musicians and these became known as céilí. U.S. céilí bands were influenced by the instrumental lineup of popular dance bands and adopted instruments such as drums and piano. This was copied at home in Ireland, and the céilí reached its pinnacle of popularity in the 1950s. In Ireland the Dance Hall Act of 1935 crushed the already dwindling house- and crossroad-dancing tradition by requiring a dance venue to be licensed, but a revival of set dancing spread countrywide in the 1980s and 1990s. Step dancing, incorporating both solo and group dancing, was widely taught by dancing masters particularly in the eighteenth and nineteenth centuries and differs from both set and céilí dancing. Irish step dancing was controlled by the Coimisiún le Rincí Gaelacha (Irish Dancing Commission), which organized dancing competitions known as feiseanna throughout Ireland and overseas.

Improved transport and communication, and the increased availability of radio, television, and recorded music, also helped to change the path of Irish music. Mass media often contributed to the popularization of Irish music as broadcasters such as Irish Radio, 2RN, which began in 1926, gave a high proportion of airtime to traditional music. The ready availability of traditional music meant that local styles faced competition from the music of other areas, even from the United States, and in many cases the local style ceased to exist. The 78 rpm recordings of Irish emigrant musicians in the United States in the 1920s and 1930s, such as Michael Coleman and James Morrison, had a wide-reaching effect on traditional playing in Ireland, with many Irish musicians copying the style and repertoire that they heard on the records.

In the 1960s the combination of voice and instruments was a new departure for the tradition. The vocal tradition in Irish music was heretofore unaccompanied and generally a solo art form. In New York the Clancy Brothers and Tommy Makem were influenced by the U.S. folk revival, and they combined instruments such as guitar and banjo with singing to form the first Irish ballad group. The Clancys and Makem became extremely popular in both the United States and Ireland and new ballad groups, including The Dubliners and The Wolfe Tones, sprang up at home. The ballad scene thrived during the 1960s with numerous groups throughout the country playing in lounge bars. The popularity of the ballad group diminished during the following decade.

The musical scene in Ireland increasingly encompassed different music genres. Irish traditional music was now a minority music rather than a majority one. Not only was there a diversity in the music available, but innovators of Irish traditional music began fusing Irish music with other genres, including classical, rock, folk, pop and various ethnic music. Seán Ó Riada, a classically trained musician and composer, was responsible for a new direction in Irish music in the 1950s and 1960s. He was the first person to introduce Irish music to the concert stage, and his compositions for orchestra, such as the music for the film Mise Éire, were hugely popular, bringing Irish music to a new, wider audience. Critical of the uniformity of the céilí-band sound, he developed a new type of traditional music group by forming the folk orchestra Ceoltóirí Cualann, which integrated solos, duets, trios, quartets, and an accompanied singer. Ó Riada helped to popularize the bodhrán and bones by using them to fill the percussive void left by the split between dancing and music. He used a harpsichord to recreate the sound of the Gaelic harp and also introduced countermelodies and harmonies in his arrangements. The Chieftains and Ceoltóirí Laighean developed from Ceoltóirí Cualann. In the 1970s another musician, Mícheál Ó Súilleabháin, combined Irish, classical, and jazz genres in his work for solo keyboard and in his compositions/arrangements for chamber orchestra, piano, and traditional instruments.

The era of the professional musician had arrived, with many bands and solo artists making a living from playing Irish music. Traditional music was popular not only in Ireland or with Irish emigrants abroad but also among non-Irish people. By the 1970s the trend of accompanied singing, together with the rise in instrumental playing and interest in Irish music produced groups such as Planxty, Horslips, De Danann, The Bothy Band, and Moving Hearts, who fused traditional music with rock, pop, or folk music. This involved the use of instruments such as keyboards, synthesizers, electric guitars, and ethnic instruments. Conflict between the purists and innovators caused controversy in the closing decades of the century. "Riverdance," "Lord of the Dance," and other stage shows belong to the 1990s, but their combination of dance and the portrayal of dance with modern costumes, theatrical effects, and staging effected a resurgence of interest in step dancing.

The twentieth century also marked a growth in the study of Irish music and in music literacy among practitioners. Early in the century, Captain Francis O'Neill published his volumes on Irish music in the United States. The Irish Folk Song Society operated in London from 1904 to the 1920s; its aim was the collection, publication, and study of Irish traditional music. In 1935 the Irish Folklore Commission was established to collect and preserve traditional culture. Beginning in the 1960s the study of Irish traditional music was a feature in third-level music courses. The Folk Music Society of Ireland was founded in 1971 and published some material and recordings during the final decades of the century. Breandán Breathnach published many collections of Irish music as well as a study of the music, *Folk Music and Dances of Ireland* (1971). Many and various publications ensued. Other projects included the establishment of the Irish Traditional Music Archive in 1987 as a reference archive and resource center for Irish traditional music.

SEE ALSO Arts: Early Modern Literature and the Arts from 1500 to 1800; Carolan, Turlough; Music: Early Modern Music; Music: Popular Music

Bibliography

Breathnach, Breandán. *Folk Music and Dances of Ireland.* 1971.

Carolan, Nicholas. "Acoustic and Electric: Traditional Music in the Twentieth Century." *The Journal of Music in Ireland* 1 (November/December 2000): 20–27.

O'Connor, Nuala. *Bringing It All Back Home: The Influence of Irish Music.* 1991.

Ó hAllmhuráin, Gearóid. *A Pocket History of Irish Traditional Music.* 1998.

Vallely, Fintan, ed. *The Companion to Irish Traditional Music.* 1999.

Colette Moloney

POPULAR MUSIC

Popular music in Ireland can most easily be assessed by acknowledging the impact of global trends on the Irish music scene. Since the 1960s Ireland has repeatedly produced musicians and groups essentially imitative of performers in Britain and the United States, though this imitation has been leavened by the intermarriage of imported styles with traditional Irish-music influences and by an occasional original idea. Through the 1950s and 1960s popular music was defined by the showbands, whose mix of rock-and-roll hits, country-and-western sentimentality, and novelty numbers and routines filled dance halls across the country. The showbands retained popularity into the 1970s—with some, such as Joe Dolan, prospering even into the new millennium—by continuously adding contemporary hits to old favorites. From the 1960s ballad singers and groups flourished because of the increased interest in traditional Irish music and the general proliferation of folk singers in western society. The Chieftains traveled widely with their instrument-based renditions of traditional music, and The Dubliners enjoyed similar success with a more ballad-based approach. Christy Moore, whose irreverent, socially aware narratives were very popular, was one of the foremost musicians who began playing traditional music before moving toward mainstream popular music. Others such as Enya successfully followed a similar path. In the 1990s a modernized packaging of Irish dancing that combined traditional Irish step dancing and tap dance into an extended stage show, "Riverdance," was an immensely profitable global phenomenon. The arrival of Van Morrison, Rory Gallagher, and Phil Lynnott in the late 1960s gave Ireland a credible position in the rock firmament. All three enjoyed acclaim as international artists, and Morrison's 1969 album "Astral Weeks" was accepted as a classic. His position in Irish popular music is second only to that of U2, whose multimillion-selling albums and groundbreaking world tours made them one of the most popular rock bands in the world in the mid-1980s. A Celtic subgenre of rock music from The Horslips in the 1970s to The Corrs in the 1990s brought national and international recognition, and an innovative fusing of punk rock, ballad, and traditional music in the 1980s brought great success to The Pogues, a London-Irish band whose singer Shane MacGowan has been acclaimed as the leading songwrit-

U2 concert at Slane Castle, Co. Meath, 25 August 2001. The success of Irish popular-music groups has helped to transform the image of Ireland. © REUTERS NEWMEDIA INC./CORBIS. REPRODUCED BY PERMISSION.

er of his generation. Beginning in the mid-1990s, most albums sold by Irish artists were by industry-created boybands such as Boyzone and Westlife, whose success at home and abroad lies in the marketing of formulaic music through suggestive dance routines that appeal to children and teenagers. Again, it was a trend imported from Britain.

SEE ALSO Fleadh Cheoil; Music: Modern Music

Bibliography

O'Connor, Nuala. *Bringing It All Back Home: The Influence of Irish Music.* 1991.

Power, Vincent. *Send 'em Home Sweatin': The Showband Story.* 2000.

Paul Rouse

~

Myth and Saga

A critically neutral term, the Irish saga denotes the large body of often heroic narrative composed over many centuries in medieval Ireland and surviving in the great monastic codices, such as *Lebor na hUidhre* (*Book of the Dun Cow*, late eleventh century) and *Lebor Laighneach* (*Book of Leinster*, twelfth century). The same narratives were once dubbed Early Irish literature, implying no antecedents in pre-Christian religion. An assertion that many elements from Celtic religion survived in Irish stories encouraged adoption of the term *Irish myths*, still widely used. The survival theory was challenged in the late twentieth century by Kim McCone, Donnchadh Ó Corráin and others, who argued that while some figures, for example Lug Lámfhota, Fionn mac Cumhaill, may indeed be based on lost divinities, the shape of the stories themselves drew more from the classically influenced ecclesiastics who committed them to writing. The death of Diarmait in a boar hunt, for example, is unmistakably modeled on the comparable death of Adonis. The term *saga* does not here carry its Icelandic denotation of a family story that is very likely based on historical incident.

Irish sagas should not be confused with Irish folklore. The huge volume of stories committed to writing in medieval Ireland enjoyed a prestige not accorded to those surviving in oral tradition among the oppressed and illiterate peasantry. Some figures from the sagas, such as Deirdre or the lovers Diarmait and Gráinne, were expanded and given variations in oral tradition. Yet much more in the whole corpus of Irish folklore has no correlative in the sagas.

On the basis of internal evidence, nineteenth-century scholars divided the corpus into four principal parts or cycles: the Mythological Cycle, the Ulster Cycle, the Fenian Cycle, and the Cycle of Kings or Historical Cycle. Beyond these are the stories of voyages to the otherworld and fanciful explanations of place-names. Medieval compilers of the sagas, however, may have been unaware of such cycles. Instead they denoted the tale type by the first word in the title. For example, the many titles that begin with the word *Táin* all concern cattle raids.

MYTHOLOGICAL CYCLE

The six-volume *Lebor Gabála Érenn* (Book of invasions) details the semihistorical invasions of prehistoric Ireland, leading to the triumph of the mortal Milesians (ancestors of the Gaels) over the immortal Tuatha Dé Danann. The climatic invasion story occurs in a separate text, *Cath Maige Tuired* (*The Second Battle of Mag Tuired/Moytura*), between the Tuatha Dé Danann and the Fomorians, demonic pirates. The principal hero of this cycle is Lug Lámfhota (Lug of the Long Arms), a figure whose roots can be traced to the Gaulish god Lugos, whom Julius Caesar (first century B.C.E.) called Mercury. The leader of the Tuatha Dé Danann is Nuadu Airgetlám (of the Silver Hand/Arm).

Important texts include *Tochmarc Étaíne* (The wooing of Étaín), about the supernatural love between King Midir and Étaín, a paragon of beauty, a myth whose form evolves over a millennium. Two of the "Three Sorrows of Storytelling" are in this cycle. *Oidheadh Chloinne Tuireann* (Tragic fate of the children of Tuireann) tells how three sons—Brian, Iuchar, and Iucharba—endure arduous tasks in exile for having murdered Cian, Lug's father. In a second "sorrow," *Oidheadh Chloinne Lir* (Tragic fate of the children of Lir), a king's children fostered to a distant royal household are transformed into swans by a wicked queen and suffer a three-hundred year exile at each of three places in Ire-

land. The last is on the Mayo coast, where the children are returned to human from and baptized in the Christian faith before they crumble into dust. The third "sorrow," the Deirdre story, appears in the Ulster Cycle.

THE ULSTER CYCLE

Earlier known as the Red Branch Cycle, the Ulster Cycle takes place near the hillfort "capital" of Ulster, Emain Macha, Co. Armagh, and the Hill of Tara, Co. Meath. Cúchulainn (the Hound of Culann), the greatest of all Irish heroes, is at the center of the action and is the key figure in *Táin Bó Cúailnge* (*Cattle Raid of Cooley*); he is a son of Lug Lámfhota. The bellicose and libidinous Queen Medb of Connacht initiates war with Ulster over Donn Cuailnge, the Brown Bull, which she covets in order to have status above her husband, Aillil. Her own white bull, Finnbennach, gives insufficient esteem, so Donn Cuailnge must be seized from Ulster. An epic with dozens of named characters and faceless armies, the Táin's most dramatic moments come in personal encounters, between Cúchulainn and Medb, especially Cúchulainn's duel at the ford with Ferdiad, his former friend and companion. At the end Medb takes home Donn Cuailnge, but Cúchulainn's story continues through several other texts. One tells of the wooing of his wife Emer, another of his unwitting slaying of his son Connla.

The tragic love story of Deirdre, the third "sorrow" of storytelling, exists in two medieval texts, one a foretale of the *Táin*, and in many oral tradition retellings. In all of them young Deirdre is unhappily betrothed to aging King Conchobar of Ulster (anglicized Conor) when she elopes with handsome Noíse, who is accompanied by his brothers Ardan and Ainnle. Conchobar pursues them and through the trickery of a surrogate captures the lovers, killing Noíse. Deirdre takes her own life rather than return to the embrace of Conchobar.

Prominent also in the Ulster Cycle are the heroes Cú Roí and Fergus mac Róich, the second a lover of Medb. The poison-tongued Briccriu sets heroes into violent conflict over the "hero's portion" of meat in the widely read *Fled Bricrenn* (Briccriu's feast).

THE FENIAN CYCLE

The Fenian Cycle, also known as the Finn or Ossianic Cycle, has produced by far the most extensive texts of any cycle and its stories have been the longest lived; yet it is called the "sow's ear of Irish literature" by Sean O'Faolain because the narratives often lack literary distinction. The central hero of the cycle, Fionn mac Cumhaill, unquestionably of divine origin, is portrayed as a poet-warrior-seer who heads the Fianna Éireann, a kind of freelance militia skilled in poetry. Many of the stories in the cycle are told in flashback by Fionn's son Oisín and the warrior Caílte, who are presumed to have survived until Christian times and engaged in dialogue with Saint Patrick. The Scottish charlatan James Macpherson borrowed Fenian themes in his bogus historical *Poems of Ossian* (1760–1763) in order to introduce the cycle's characters to a wider European audience as Fingal (Fionn), Ossian (Oisín), and Oscar (Fionn's grandson). Fionn sometimes appears to be an unattractive figure, as when he pursues the beautiful young Gráinne, who prefers the warrior Diarmait; this parallels the Deirdre story except that Gráinne returns to Fionn at the end.

THE CYCLE OF KINGS, OR HISTORICAL CYCLE

These stories may relate events thought to be historical, such as *Cath Maige Rath* (Battle of Moira), or may be rooted during the reigns of historical or semihistorical kings, *Fingal Rónáin* (How Rónán killed his son), the narrative of a seventh-century ruler whose name appears in the annals. A datable authenticity does not mean that stories within the cycle are always earthbound, as is seen in the highly regarded *Buile Shuibne* (Frenzy of Sweeney). In this sequel to *Cath Maige Rath*, Suibne, driven mad by the din of battle following a curse put upon him by a cleric, spends years living naked or nearly naked in the tops of trees, regretting his fate, but celebrating nature in haunting, lyrical verse.

Portrayals of themes and characters from Irish sagas in Irish writing in English in the nineteenth and twentieth centuries do not always draw on original texts or their translations, but often rely instead on modern popularizers.

SEE ALSO Celtic Migrations; Cruachain; Cú Chulainn; Emain Macha (Navan Fort); Literature: Early and Medieval Literature; Prehistoric and Celtic Ireland; *Táin Bó Cúailnge*

Bibliography

Cross, Tom Peete, and Harris Clark Slover. *Ancient Irish Tales.* 1936. Reprint, 1969.

McCone, Kim. *Pagan Past and Christian Present in Early Irish Literature.* 1990.

MacKillop, James. *Dictionary of Celtic Mythology.* 1998.

O'Rahilly, Thomas F. *Early Irish History and Mythology.* 1946. Reprint, 1971.

Rees, Alwyn and Brinley Rees. *Celtic Heritage: Ancient Tradition in Ireland and Wales.* 1961.

James MacKillop

N

Nagle, Honora (Nano)

Honora Nagle (1718–1784), founder of the Presentation Order of Catholic women religious and pioneering leader in the reestablishment of both Catholic education and women's religious institutions in Ireland during the eighteenth century, was born in Ballygriffin, Co. Cork, into a prominent, landowning Catholic family. Better known by her childhood nickname, Nano, Nagle was educated in a convent school in France and returned to Ireland in the 1740s with the intention of establishing a school for poor, illiterate Catholics in the city of Cork (an illegal act under the Catholic penal code in force at the time). She opened her first school in the early 1750s and by the end of the 1760s oversaw a total of seven establishments, each with several hundred students attending daily. Emboldened by the government's unwillingness to prosecute her, the support of some members of the Catholic clergy, and a large inheritance from her uncle Joseph Nagle, she expanded her enterprise by making a foundation of the French Ursuline Sisters in 1771, the first new establishment of religious women in Ireland for more than one hundred years. Although the Ursulines were able to staff Nagle's burgeoning schools, because they were an enclosed, or cloistered, order that had traditionally catered to the wealthy, they were not able to participate in her larger vision of having socially engaged religious women undertake active philanthropic work among the poor. Consequently, in 1775 Nagle founded a radically new congregation, the Sisters of the Presentation of the Blessed Virgin Mary (originally uncloistered and named the Sisters of the Charitable Instruction). At the age of fifty-seven, finally content that she had created the religious community she had earlier envisioned, Nagle took religious vows herself. Though the community experienced a slow and difficult start (and though it was deemed necessary to reorganize as an enclosed order after her death to gain greater support from wealthy Cork Catholics), by the end of the nineteenth century Nano Nagle's community was the second-largest women's order in Ireland, with foundations throughout the world.

SEE ALSO Religious Orders: Women; Roman Catholic Church: 1690 to 1829

Bibliography

Magray, Mary Peckham. *The Transforming Power of the Nuns: Women, Religion, and Cultural Change in Ireland, 1750–1900.* 1998.

Walsh, Thomas J. *Nano Nagle and the Presentation Sisters.* 1959.

Mary Peckham Magray

Neilson, Samuel

A prominent United Irishman from Ulster and the organization's most important publicist, Samuel Neilson (1761–1803) was born at Ballyroney, Co. Down, the son of a Presbyterian minister. He followed an older brother into the woolen trade in Belfast and had built up a prosperous business by the late 1780s. Sympathetic to the cause of Catholic relief, he joined the first Whig Club in Belfast in 1790, worked on Robert Stewart's election campaign in County Down later that year, and in 1791 was among the founders of the Belfast Society of United Irishmen and of the *Northern Star*, a radical newspaper which was forcibly closed by the government in September 1797. Neilson was a principal figure behind the Ulster United movement, which was more radical and more secretive than the corresponding society in Dublin. Neilson was in Dublin in the spring of 1798, and the arrests there left him as the only member of the Leinster Executive who was in a position to lead the rebellion when the moment to strike came. He himself was arrested as the rebel mobilization was in its early stages, however (his drinking problem may have contributed to this), and he spent the duration of the rising in Newgate prison. He was among the leaders who escaped execution thanks to British General Charles Cornwallis's clemency and their own promise to divulge the details of the conspiracy. He was sent to Fort George in Scotland in March 1799. Released in March 1802, he traveled secretly to Ireland, where he spent the next six months; he then sailed for the United States in December. He died suddenly of apoplexy on 29 August 1803 in Poughkeepsie, New York, where he was attempting to start a newspaper.

SEE ALSO Eighteenth-Century Politics: 1778 to 1795—Parliamentary and Popular Politics; Eighteenth-Century Politics: 1795 to 1800—Repression, Rebellion, and Union; United Irish Societies from 1791 to 1803; **Primary Documents:** United Irish Parliamentary Reform Plan (March 1794); Grievances of the United Irishmen of Ballynahinch, Co. Down (1795); Speech Delivered at a United Irish Meeting in Ballyclare, Co. Antrim (1795); The United Irish Organization (1797); Statement of Three Imprisoned United Irish Leaders (4 August 1798)

Bibliography

Curtin, Nancy. *The United Irishmen: Popular Politics in Ulster and Dublin, 1791–1798.* 1994.

Madden, R. R. *The United Irishmen, Their Lives and Times.* 1842–1846.

Daniel Gahan

~

Neutrality

Irish neutrality is one of the most misunderstood features of Irish foreign policy. It has been elevated into a sacred doctrine by its most avid domestic supporters and simultaneously criticized by pro-Western analysts in Europe and North America, especially as it was practiced during World War II and the Cold War. The reality is subtler than these diametrically opposed interpretations would suggest. Irish neutrality, for starters, is not legally based: It is enshrined neither in domestic law nor in international treaties and substantially departs, therefore, from the Swiss model. Instead, it has been a strategic and tactical tool that Irish political leaders have, depending on the circumstances, utilized in the pursuit of Irish national interests. The Irish electorate has consistently backed government officials and policymakers in how they have wielded neutrality. It has, accordingly, proved to be an essential component of Irish statecraft.

WORLD WAR I

Neutrality was actually mooted as a foreign-policy option even before Ireland gained independence. On the eve of World War I, Roger Casement envisioned Ireland being transformed into "a neutralised, independent European state under international guarantees." During the negotiations leading to the Anglo-Irish Treaty of 1921, Arthur Griffith asserted that "Ireland would want to be free to be neutral in the event of war declared by Britain." Future Irish leaders agreed. As storm clouds gathered on the European horizon during the 1930s, Eamon de Valera, taoiseach (Irish prime minister) and minister for foreign affairs, initially entrusted hopes for international peace to the League of Nations and collective security. But when the League failed to enforce sanctions against Japan for its invasion of Manchuria, and Italy for its aggression against Ethiopia, de Valera, wishing to sidestep a debilitating conflict that might do irreparable material and political harm to the new, nearly defenseless Irish state, made a crucial geostrategic decision: In any future war involving the great powers Ireland would, he insisted, "be neutral."

WORLD WAR II

De Valera transformed this diplomatic preference into a realistic alternative by signing the Anglo-Irish Agreement of 1938, which, inter alia, returned to Ireland the "treaty ports" of Cobh, Lough Swilly, and Berehaven, which had remained under British military control since

1922. On 2 September 1939, the day after World War II began, de Valera declared Ireland's neutrality, introduced the necessary legislation into Dáil Éireann and instructed the Department of External Affairs to notify all the belligerents in the conflict. The Irish government soon came under tremendous pressure to jettison neutrality from the United Kingdom, which feared, especially early in the war, that Nazi Germany might use Ireland as a staging ground for an invasion of the British mainland. The promise of a British commitment to a united Ireland in exchange for joining the Allies was even dangled before de Valera. He refused the offer. Across the Atlantic, neutrality strained relations between the Irish and American governments. In April 1941 President Franklin D. Roosevelt, who was doing all he could to support Great Britain's war effort, brusquely dismissed a request by Frank Aiken, minister for the coordination of defensive measures, to sway the British in favor of Irish unity. The American envoy in Dublin, David Gray, developed a particular disdain for Irish neutrality and tried to undermine it by utilizing his direct family connections to President Roosevelt.

Yet the American representative, like so many commentators since then, overlooked a critical dimension of Irish neutrality during the war: It was a powerful manifestation, only two decades since achieving independence, of Irish sovereignty. Ronan Fanning has noted that neutrality was conceived "not as an end in itself, but as a means to an end: the means whereby the end of sovereignty might be freely expressed in the form of an independent foreign policy—a policy independent, above all, of British policy." F. S. L. Lyons has defined neutrality as "the ultimate expression of Irish independence." Indeed, this aspect of it may partially account for de Valera's decision at the end of the war, for which he has rightly been excoriated, to pay his condolences at the German embassy in Dublin upon learning of the death of Adolf Hitler. It certainly accounts for de Valera's famous reply to a passage in Winston Churchill's May 1945 victory speech that was highly critical of Irish neutrality: "Even as a partitioned small nation, [Ireland] shall go on to play our part in the world, continuing unswervingly to work for the cause of true freedom and for peace and understanding between all nations."

The tendency of some Irish proponents of neutrality to transform de Valera's quasi-idealistic public interpretation into smug self-righteousness has been tempered by scholarship of the 1990s that has conclusively demonstrated how Irish neutrality in practice was heavily tilted in favor of the Allies during World War II. Irish officials shared intelligence and planning information with their Allied counterparts, granted overflight rights to Allied aircraft, and returned downed Allied pilots to their respective authorities. Indeed, when the United States entered the war, de Valera said "We can only be a friendly neutral." This high level of official cooperation, combined with the support of thousands of Irish men who joined the British army, outweighed the pro-Nazi sympathies of hard-core Irish republicans like Sean Russell and Frank Ryan, who collaborated with German agents in Ireland and across Europe during the conflict.

THE COLD WAR

Neutrality remained a feature of Irish foreign policy throughout the Cold War. It became entwined with Northern Ireland in 1949 when the first interparty government turned down an invitation to join NATO on the grounds that while Ireland remained partitioned, it could not be a member of a military alliance that included the United Kingdom. This policy was championed by Seán MacBride, Irish minister for external affairs and leader of the junior member of the coalition, the staunchly republican party Clann na Poblachta. A former Irish diplomat has argued; however, that a majority government led by Fine Gael (the senior partner in the interparty government) would have brought Ireland into NATO. Party politics thus became a component of the postwar debate over neutrality.

The Irish government differentiated between economic and military alliances, and, ironically, when the United Kingdom applied for membership in the European Economic Community in 1962, Ireland did likewise. During the application process, the taoiseach, Seán Lemass, repeatedly stressed Ireland's pro-Western credentials and the narrow limits of neutrality in the context of the Cold War: its absence from NATO did "not mean that we are indifferent to the great issues which divide mankind today, much less that we are neutral in regard to them." Indeed, "while Ireland did not accede to the North Atlantic Treaty, we have always agreed with the general aims of that Treaty." Neutrality, therefore, could be tactically downgraded in favor of economic or other interests as the government determined. Ireland did not join the European Economic Community until 1973, but in the interim its neutral status qualified it for numerous United Nations peacekeeping missions. Still, throughout the Cold War, Ireland, unlike many other neutral countries that participated in peacekeeping operations, was neither "neutralist" nor a member of the Third World-dominated nonaligned movement. It is best compared during this period to other European neutrals such as Sweden, Finland, and Austria.

In the post–Cold War era neutrality has remained a strategic and tactical option for the Irish government.

Ireland permitted Allied aircraft to refuel at Shannon airport during the Persian Gulf War in 1990 to 1991 since the war was sanctioned by the United Nations Security Council, but it did not send troops to the region. In 1999, Ireland became one of the last European nations to join NATO's Partnership for Peace. The government stipulated that it will participate only in Partnership for Peace humanitarian and peacekeeping operations authorized by the United Nations Security Council, and within this framework it has contributed troops to NATO-led, UN-approved missions in Bosnia and Kosovo. Some Irish politicians have recently called for full membership in NATO.

The Irish government is committed to the European Union's emerging Common Foreign and Security Policy (CFSP). It has concluded that humanitarian and rescue operations, peacekeeping missions, and crisis management efforts (the Petersberg Tasks), some of which will be conducted by the European Union's developing Rapid Reaction Force (RRF), pose no threat in principle to Ireland's military neutrality. Irish forces will participate only in European missions authorized by the UN and on a case-by-case basis. The Irish government has stressed that the CFSP and the RRF do not constitute a mutual-defense commitment. Yet growing popular apprehension that they do indeed pose a threat to neutrality, support for which has always been quite resilient among some sectors of the Irish electorate, contributed to the defeat of the Nice Treaty in a referendum in June 2001, even though the treaty is primarily concerned with the reform and enlargement of the European Union's political institutions and not with defense policy per se.

SEE ALSO de Valera, Eamon; European Union; Politics: Independent Ireland since 1922; United Nations; **Primary Documents:** "German Attack on Neutral States" (12 May 1940); "National Thanksgiving" (16 May 1945); Speech to Ministers of the Governments of the Member States of the European Economic Community (18 January 1962)

Bibliography

Dwyer, T. Ryle. *Strained Relations: Ireland at Peace and the USA at War, 1941–1945.* 1988.

Fanning, Ronan. "Irish Neutrality: An Historical Perspective." *Irish Studies in International Affairs* 1, no. 3 (1982): 27–38.

Fisk, Robert. *In Time of War: Ireland, Ulster, and the Price of Neutrality, 1939–1945.* 1983.

Keatinge, Patrick. *European Security: Ireland's Choices.* 1996.

Keogh, Dermot. *Twentieth-Century Ireland.* 1994.

Lee, Joseph. *Ireland, 1912–1985: Politics and Society.* 1989.

O'Halpin, Eunan. *Defending Ireland: The Irish State and Its Enemies since 1922.* 1999.

Salmon, Trevor. *Unneutral Ireland.* 1989.

Joseph M. Skelly

Newspapers

Newspapers have been published in Ireland since the late seventeenth century. In the mid-eighteenth century, newspapers became a regular part of the political, social, and commercial scene, and by the end of the century the press increasingly reflected the political debates on Catholic claims and the nature of the government of Ireland. At the beginning of the nineteenth century papers were being published in Dublin and in all the large towns of Ireland.

In 1774 taxes were imposed on newsprint, advertisements, and paper, and bonds had to be lodged with the revenue department. Dublin Castle regulated the press, partly through contracts to publish government proclamations and official advertisements, and partly through the distribution of secret service monies that were voted by Parliament to support newspapers acting in the government interest. Editors who published material thought to be seditious were prosecuted repeatedly, often by dubious means and before a prejudiced judiciary.

The press was used by the growing number of political movements to further their causes. Daniel O'Connell used newspapers both in Dublin and in the provinces as his allies in the repeal movement. From its founding in 1823, one of the aims of the Catholic Association was "a liberal and enlightened press" (Wyse 1829, appendix, p. xliii), and part of the Catholic "rent" was spent on press publicity. The provinces were always important to O'Connell, who supported the founding of the *Limerick Reporter* as a repeal newspaper in 1839. From the 1840s onwards, the Repeal Association founded reading rooms that subscribed to newspapers, which were often read aloud to groups of peasants.

The *Nation* (1842–1897) was founded in Dublin by Charles Gavan Duffy in collaboration with Thomas Davis and John Blake Dillon. Its aim was to further the campaign for repeal, and it became crucial to the rise of the Young Ireland movement, which eventually (in 1846) seceded from the movement for repeal. It claimed a readership of 250,000 and was distributed in the repeal reading rooms. The *Nation* had a program to disseminate the history and culture of Ireland, and it influenced the content of successive provincial papers. Dublin Castle thought that those whom it considered to be uneducated were susceptible to material that might lead them to commit violence and acts of sedition, so the *Nation* was suppressed during the 1848 rebellion; Duffy was twice prosecuted for sedition and twice discharged. Many other newspapers were also seized and the repeal reading rooms were closed down. The *Nation* was edited by A. M. and T. D. Sullivan from 1855 to 1874, and was used by them, too, as a major propaganda force for Irish nationalism.

In the 1850s the Tenant League was the first political movement to employ the press to its fullest extent. Charles Gavan Duffy of the *Nation* and John Gray of the *Freeman's Journal* (1763–1921) organized the conference that founded the League in 1850, and John Francis Maguire of the *Cork Examiner* (1841–) and James MacKnight of the *Banner of Ulster* (1842–1869) furthered its cause through articles and speeches.

Until the middle of the nineteenth century, newspapers in the provinces were published mostly by patent-medicine vendors and stationers. With the polarization of political parties at mid-century, newspapers were increasingly founded with political aims in mind. Elections proved profitable for the press, which charged for reporting meetings and printing leaflets. Between 1853 and 1861 stamps on newspapers and taxes on advertisements and paper were abolished, and this, together with the increase in literacy and a rise in consumer spending, brought about the rise of cheap newspapers, especially in the provinces. They were extensively read in the reading rooms established by mechanics' institutes, employers, and town governments throughout Ireland. Initially, new titles tended to be liberal, but a minority of editors and proprietors moved into nationalist politics. The move toward mass political movements was reflected in the press; there was a sharp rise in the number of nationalist papers, particularly in the provinces, where the numbers rose from none in 1861 to thirty-four in 1891. A number of provincial newspapermen went on to become nationalist members of Parliament. By 1879 there were 127 newspapers published outside Dublin, a rise of 85 percent over the previous thirty years.

Outside Ulster, Protestant unionist newspapers, which had flourished early in the nineteenth century all over Ireland, gradually decreased in number, and inside Ulster, the number of newspapers sympathetic to liberalism decreased. New newspapers reflected the sectarian divide: The *Belfast Telegraph* group was founded in 1870 in the interests of the Orange Order; the *Banner of Ulster* was the newspaper of the Presbyterian Church. Extreme Protestant views flourished around mid-century in William Johnston's *Downshire Protestant* (1855–1862).

The Fenians were slow to use newspapers for propaganda, although a number of provincial editors close to Fenianism, such as Denis Holland of the *Belfast Vindicator* and Martin O'Brennan of the *Connaught Patriot* in Tuam, Co. Galway, were advocating proto-Fenian ideas in the 1850s. James Stephens founded the *Irish People* (1863–1865) in Dublin as the voice of Fenianism, but it was suppressed and its journalists arrested. Its nationalist successor was the *Irishman* (1858–1881). It was owned by the journalist Richard Pigott who, during the Land War, changed his politics and aimed to destroy the Parnellite movement. To silence Pigott's propaganda, the Irish Nationalist Party bought out the *Irishman* and closed it down. In its stead Charles Stewart Parnell founded *United Ireland* (1881–1898), edited by William O'Brien, a paper in support of the Land League. With the split in the party following Parnell's involvement in the O'Shea divorce in 1890, *United Ireland* took an anti-Parnellite line until it was forcibly extended by Parnell and its editor, Matthew Bodkin, expelled. Parnell went on to found the *Irish Daily Independent* in 1891. Parnell's new paper was challenged by Martin Murphy's anti-Parnellite *National Press* (1891–1892), which amalgamated with the *Freeman's Journal*. Murphy later founded the *Daily Nation* (1897–1900), which merged with the *Irish Daily Independent* to become a mass-circulation paper, the *Irish Independent*. The *Irish Independent* supported Cumann na nGaedheal in 1923 and is now the largest-circulation morning newspaper in Ireland.

The Gaelic-speaking population declined rapidly during and after the Great Famine, owing in large part to emigration and the move to towns. Literacy in Gaelic was uncommon, but increasingly in the nineteenth century newspapers published columns in Gaelic. However, no Irish-language mass-circulation newspaper has yet been successful. In the twentieth century the Gaelic League founded *An Claidheamh Soluis* (1899–1938) as its official paper, but its circulation was small.

Eamon de Valera founded the daily *Irish Press* (1931–1995) to provide a platform for the Fianna Fáil Party, and he and his family kept tight editorial control. It was addressed to the lower middle class and to women especially, and had an Irish-language section and particularly good coverage of Gaelic sports. By the 1980s, however, the newspaper was in trouble, and after a legal judgment against it for damages as compensation that could not be paid and a dispute with its journalists, it closed in 1995.

By 2001 in the Republic there were two national morning daily papers, a regional daily, and four Sunday papers. Only Dublin and Cork have evening papers. There are about fifty local papers that are published weekly. Belfast has four morning papers and one evening paper. The *Belfast News-Letter*, first published in 1737, is the oldest newspaper in print in the British Isles. There are also three daily papers published in Northern Ireland outside Belfast. In addition, since the mid-1960s British papers have had a growing share of the Irish market, and several publish Irish editions.

SEE ALSO Balladry in English; de Valera, Eamon; Fenian Movement and the Irish Republican Brotherhood; Language and Literacy: Irish Language since 1922; Literacy and Popular Culture; O'Connell, Daniel; Parnell, Charles Stewart; Repeal Movement; Stephens, James; Sullivan Brothers (A. M. and T. D.); Murphy, William Martin; Young Ireland and the Irish Confederation

Bibliography

Aspinall, A. *Politics and the Press, c. 1780–1850*. 1946.

Inglis, Brian. *The Freedom of the Press in Ireland, 1784–1841*. 1954.

Legg, Marie-Louise. *Newspapers and Nationalism: The Irish Provincial Press, 1850–1892*. 1999.

Oxford Companion to Irish History. Edited by S. J. Connolly. 2002.

Wyse, Thomas. *Historical Sketch of the Late Catholic Association of Ireland*. 2 vols. 1829.

Marie-Louise Legg

~

Nine Years War

The Nine Years War, which lasted nearly ten years, from April 1593 to March 1603, is also known as Tyrone's rebellion after its main protagonist, Hugh O'Neill, earl of Tyrone. Fought throughout the island and at enormous financial and human cost, it was the climactic phase of the Elizabethan conquest of Ireland.

The war broke out as a result of centralizing pressure on the autonomous lordships of Ulster from the colonial government in Dublin headed by Lord Deputy Fitzwilliam. His execution of Hugh MacMahon in 1590 and reorganization of the MacMahon lordship into the county of Monaghan was a warning to other Ulster lords. Furthermore, the ambitions of Sir Henry Bagenal, a soldier and landowner based at Newry, to be lord president of a reorganized Ulster threatened the traditional regional overlordship of the O'Neills.

The commanding genius on the Irish side was Hugh O'Neill. After the creation of Monaghan he had sprung his son-in-law Red Hugh O'Donnell from jail in Dublin Castle and through him opened channels of communication with Spain. When the war began in the Maguire lordship of Fermanagh in 1593 over an attempt to establish an English sheriff there, the wily O'Neill initially fought on the side of the Crown. In fact, he was the head of a secret, oath-bound confederacy of Ulster lords connected to him by blood, marriage, and fosterage that transcended the long-standing provincial rivalry between the O'Neills and O'Donnells. O'Neill alleged an inability to control the military activities of his relatives while they were actually waging proxy wars on his behalf. The Crown, eventually exasperated by his stance, proclaimed him a traitor in 1595 after his half-brother Art McBaron O'Neill captured the Blackwater fort on the route into central Ulster. The interpretation of these early stages of the war has been confused by Sean O'Faolain's popular biographical study *The Great O'Neill* (1942), which portrays the Ulster leader as vacillating between loyalty and insurrection. It was guile, not vacillation.

O'Neill had taken advantage of the Crown's procrastination to build up an effective army which, by the time of his proclamation, had already won battles at the Ford of the Biscuits (1594) and Clontibret (1595). O'Neill had increased the number of men under arms in Ulster and had them trained by veterans from English and Spanish service. A third of the infantrymen now had firearms—an added incentive for the Irish to use a modified variant of their traditional guerrilla tactics. The battles of Clontibret and later the Yellow Ford were in fact large-scale ambushes of English armies that were attempting the relief of isolated garrisons at Monaghan and on the Blackwater. On both occasions the Crown's commander was Sir Henry Bagenal, and on the second he and 2,000 others were killed in the greatest victory ever won by the Irish against England. The Yellow Ford victory in August 1598 facilitated the spread of the revolt to Leinster and Munster. Within a fortnight the Munster plantation was overthrown after Onie O'More and Captain Richard Tyrell led a confederate force into the southern province. Those settlers (including the poet Edmund Spenser) who survived the sudden onslaught fled to the towns and subsequently to England. Queen Elizabeth's response was to send over her favorite and

Hugh O'Neill (1550–1616), second earl of Tyrone, was initially the Crown's great hope in late-sixteenth-century, heavily Gaelic Ulster. His cooperation gradually gave way to open rebellion, and at the Battle of the Yellow Ford (1598) his formidable forces were victorious. His subsequent negotiations with Queen Elizabeth I's earl of Essex (1567–1601) bought his resistance some time but led to Essex's recall to England and disgrace. Ultimately defeated at Kinsale in late 1601, O'Neill left Ireland a few years later and died in Rome in 1616. © HULTON ARCHIVE/ GETTY IMAGES. REPRODUCED BY PERMISSION.

England's leading soldier, the earl of Essex. He assembled the largest army yet seen in Ireland, but he dissipated his 19,000-strong force in fruitless marches and sieges in Leinster and Munster instead of confronting O'Neill in Ulster. Meanwhile, Red Hugh O'Donnell was achieving significant success in Connacht and Thomond. After the fall of Sligo in 1595 he ranged with impunity along the western seaboard and in 1599 scored a resounding victory of his own when Sir Conyers Clifford, the lord president of Connacht on another relief march, was defeated and killed at the battle of the Curlew Pass.

Essex manufactured his own downfall by foolishly negotiating alone with O'Neill at a river ford on the Ulster borders. Indeed, the confederates used negotiation as a tactic to confound the state and embarrass its officials, and the related ceasefires to delay or stymie its military operations. The contrasting personalities of the cautious O'Neill and the more belligerent O'Donnell were used to advantage in the frequent encounters with Crown commissioners that interspersed the bouts of fighting. In each negotiation O'Neill and O'Donnell

would increase their demands by incorporating those of new allies in their geographically expanding confederacy or by raising the stakes from the local to the national. The Irish were increasingly demanding religious liberty and an overturning of the colonial land settlement throughout Ireland. In the negotiations of early 1596 the Crown, militarily weak and fearful of foreign intervention, offered a compromise to the Ulster lords. However, Spanish agents arrived soon afterward, and O'Neill and O'Donnell agreed to abandon the peace in return for the offer of Spanish military aid. Having secretly become Spanish allies, the confederates embarked on a series of tactics to frustrate the English peace, including O'Neill's turning over of the "king of Spain's letter" to mislead the state. Further ceasefires and negotiations in the winter of 1597 to 1598 and the autumn and winter of 1599 were intended to delay English military activity.

By 1600 the Irish confederates controlled most of Ireland outside the towns, but lacking artillery and infrastructure generally, they required a Spanish expeditionary force to achieve military victory. In the meantime they tried to win over the English-speaking Catholic inhabitants of the towns and their hinterlands by political means. O'Neill launched an appeal on the basis of "faith and fatherland." In late 1599 he issued a proclamation to the Palesmen demanding their support as fellow Catholics and countrymen and threatening with destruction and damnation those who did not comply. Although a papal bull recognized him as Catholic commander in Ireland, O'Neill never managed to obtain permission from Rome to excommunicate those who refused to follow his banner. As an enticement to the hesitant, he put forward twenty-two articles which—if accepted—would have given Ireland political and religious independence under nominal English suzerainty. The Old English, who had spent three centuries fighting the Gaels, could not bring themselves to trust O'Neill, and the state glossed his demands as "Ewtopia" (i.e., utopian, or unrealistic). Far from winning over the Old English in Ireland, O'Neill's ideological démarche provoked the state in England into winning the war in Ireland conclusively.

Lord Deputy Mountjoy was dispatched to replace the disgraced Essex. The policy of parley and ceasefire, and of fruitless expeditions into the interior, was replaced by continuous warfare in which a network of small interconnected garrisons harried the Gaelic lords into submission by destroying their people through famine and slaughter. While Mountjoy cleared Leinster, he was ably seconded by Sir George Carew in Munster and Sir Henry Docwra in Ulster. The landing of an amphibious expedition under Docwra behind enemy lines at Derry was a critical development. The revolt in Ulster began to collapse as O'Neill and O'Donnell were deserted first by erstwhile allies and then by their own dependents. A Spanish force under Don Juan del Águila eventually landed at Kinsale in September 1601 but received no local support in Munster and soon found themselves besieged by Mountjoy. O'Neill and O'Donnell marched their forces the length of Ireland to rendezvous outside Kinsale and effectively turned the tables on Mountjoy, who now found himself trapped between their army and that of the Spaniards. But at the urging of the Spaniards, the Irish committed themselves to a pitched battle on Christmas Eve 1601 and were completely routed. The Spaniards promptly sought a truce and agreed to withdraw. O'Donnell took ship for Spain to lobby for further aid, fruitlessly, and he died there in September 1602. O'Neill fled back to Ulster and went into hiding. Eventually, he surrendered to Mountjoy at Mellifont in March 1603.

For the first time since the Norman invasion English sovereignty was effective throughout Ireland. The end of the sovereignty of the Gaelic lords was symbolized by Mountjoy's destruction of the O'Neill inaugural stone at Tullaghoge in late 1602. The war had cost the English exchequer nearly two million pounds sterling. Sustaining the costly garrison strategy in the final phases was achieved only by the expedient of debasement of the coinage, which reduced the silver content of the Irish pound. After the war O'Neill's position in Ulster was protected at Court by Mountjoy. When the latter lost the favor of King James, O'Neill came under increasing pressure, and in 1607 he and the other Gaelic lords of Ulster fled to the continent in an event which has been immortalized as "the Flight of the Earls." Their lands were subsequently confiscated to make way for the plantation of Ulster.

SEE ALSO Desmond Rebellions; English Political and Religious Policies, Responses to (1534–1690); O'Neill, Hugh, Second Earl of Tyrone; **Primary Documents:** Ferocity of the Irish Wars (1580s–1590s); Tyrone's Demands (1599); Accounts of the Siege and Battle of Kinsale (1601)

Bibliography

Morgan, Hiram. "Hugh O'Neill and the Nine Years War in Tudor Ireland." *Historical Journal* 36 (March 1993): 21–37.

Morgan, Hiram. *Tyrone's Rebellion: The Outbreak of the Nine Years War in Tudor Ireland.* 1993.

Ó Riain, Pádraig, ed. *Beatha Aodh Ruadh Uí Dhomnaill.* 2002. (Irish Texts Society, subsidiary series, no. 12, London, 2002.)

Silke, J. J. *Kinsale: Spanish Intervention in Ireland at the End of the Elizabethan Wars.* 1970.

Hiram Morgan

Norman Conquest and Colonization

The Anglo-Norman invasion of Ireland began with a trickle of mercenaries from South Wales landing in County Wexford in the summer of 1167, in aid of the exiled king of Leinster, Diarmait Mac Murchada; substantial reinforcements arrived two years later, who were intent on staying and winning Irish lands. The most famous of the invaders was Richard "Strongbow" de Clare, lord of Pembroke and Chepstow (Strigoil), who did not arrive until August 1170, when he married Mac Murchada's daughter, claimed the right to succeed him as king of Leinster, and conquered Dublin from its Hiberno-Norse rulers. These latter events caused the reigning king of England, Henry II, to reassess the benign but "hands-off" stance that had hitherto characterized his response to the invasion. Since his youth, he had been interested in conquering Ireland himself and adding it to the many territories that were his Angevin "empire." He had accepted Mac Murchada's declaration of fealty, made in Aquitaine in 1166 to 1167, carrying the reciprocal duty to protect Diarmait from his enemies, and had authorized him to seek support from among Henry's vassals.

The problem was that Strongbow was an errant vassal, out of royal favor after having taken the wrong side in the civil war that preceded Henry's accession. The latter had denied him the title of earl for his Welsh estates, and was hardly likely to allow him become king of Leinster, which Strongbow was intending to do following Mac Murchada's death in May 1171. Attempts having failed to forbid Strongbow's departure for Ireland, to call home his associates, and to blockade their supplies, Henry decided to come to Ireland, to regularize the position of Strongbow and the other adventurers who were making rapid strides there, and to oversee the conquest in person. And so, when he landed near Waterford on 17 October 1171, with five hundred knights and four thousand archers, Henry II became the first English king to enter Ireland.

It was no glittering prize, although its Viking-founded towns were certainly an asset, and Henry was quick to take possession of them from Strongbow and his followers. Without its wealthy ports, especially Dublin, Leinster was a far less attractive acquisition, and hence Henry allowed Strongbow to hold it in return for supplying the military service of 100 knights. The kings of Thomond and Desmond, Ó Briain and Mac Carthaig, voluntarily came to Henry at Waterford and submitted to him, and most other important kings and prelates did likewise, the kings hoping that Henry might restrain the more acquisitive of the invaders (he did so, to a degree, for several years), while the clergy believed that the Irish church could be more successfully modernized if subjected to English influence, an arrangement formalized at the Synod of Cashel during Henry's brief visit.

However, Henry did not meet the high king, Ruaidrí Ó Conchobair (Rory O'Connor), and the Anglo-Norman settlement did not proceed easily when faced with his opposition, although his armies proved ineffective against the sophistication of the Norman military machine and the invulnerability to Irish assault of the castles with which they were busy dotting the landscape. A compromise was required, and in 1175 the "treaty" of Windsor was negotiated whereby Ruaidrí accepted the Anglo-Norman colony, which was confined within its existing boundaries (Leinster, Munster from Waterford to Dungarvan, and Meath, which Henry had given to Hugh de Lacy in 1172), while Henry acknowledged Ruaidrí as the paramount power elsewhere. However, this had little appeal for the land-hungry colonists and was soon abandoned in favor of a policy of all-out conquest, with speculative grants of Desmond and Thomond being made to favorites of the king, while John de Courcy won east Ulster for himself in 1177. In that year, a royal council was held at Oxford at which the youngest of Henry's four sons, John, was made lord of Ireland. He was not expected to succeed to the throne, and so Henry envisaged a loose constitutional arrangement whereby Ireland would be ruled by a junior branch of the English royal family.

It was 1185 before John visited Ireland, but his youthful folly in his dealings with the Irish kings alienated them from their new lord, who was busy building castles on Leinster's frontier and granting lands in Munster to the ancestors of the Butlers and Burkes, while what is now County Louth was also taken from the Irish. In terms of fostering relations with the Irish, John's expedition proved disastrous, but it did advance the conquest and saw the establishment in Ireland of a form of government modeled on that of England, a pattern that has prevailed. John's later expedition in 1210 was hardly more productive since he was again inept in his treatment of the native rulers, although he reasserted his faltering authority over the colonists and further expanded the apparatus and reach of royal government. In the meantime, in 1199, John had ascended the throne, and hence the lordship of Ireland and kingship of England were, by an accident of history, reunited in the same person, as remained the case long thereafter.

By the time of John's second visit the country had been immeasurably transformed. The power of the Irish kings, except in the northwestern quadrant of the island, had been minimized, and their best ancestral lands taken from them by Anglo-Norman barons intent on expanding even further. They were able to do so by virtue of their advanced military equipment and tactics and their policy of encastellation. Beginning with rapidly erected timber structures atop earthen mounds (the motte-and-bailey), they were soon constructing massive stone fortresses like Trim and Carrickfergus, a sign for all to see that they were there to stay. But these would have meant nothing to the Irish if conquest were not followed by large-scale colonization. Only then, by the banishment of the native population from the fertile plains or their reduction to servile status, and the introduction of a new, loyal English population, could the colony feel secure and, just as important, provide a profit for those adventurers who had risked all on crossing the Irish Sea to start a new life.

In the aftermath of the invasion, therefore, Ireland witnessed nothing short of an economic and agricultural revolution. The great lords parceled up their conquests among members of the lesser gentry from their homelands who were prepared to join them on this new frontier. The latter in turn persuaded others to follow suit (probably not too difficult at a time of population growth), and as each took ownership of their new estates, they enticed over their English and Welsh tenants, offering more attractive terms of tenure. They built new towns and boroughs and persuaded burgesses to inhabit them by less rigorous taxes and regulation. Just as towns needed merchants, traders, and craftsmen, so too manors needed laborers and parishes needed priests. Everything required to turn this new colony into a facsimile of England was found and shipped over from the neighboring isle, and within a generation or two the transformation was immense. But it was never complete. In the north and west, and in the uplands and bogs, the native Irish remained intact. Denied access to the law and treated as enemies in their own land, they remained a potential threat, and although the colony continued to expand until about the year 1300, its unfinished nature meant that an Irish resurgence was inevitable.

SEE ALSO English Government in Medieval Ireland; MacMurrough, Dermot, and the Anglo-Norman Invasion; Norman Invasion and Gaelic Resurgence; **Primary Documents:** The Treaty of Windsor (1175); Grant of Prince John to Theobold Walter of Lands in Ireland (1185); Grant of Civic Liberties to Dublin by Prince John (1192)

Bibliography

Cosgrove, Art, ed. *A New History of Ireland.* Vol. 2, *Medieval Ireland, 1169–1534.* 1987. Reprint, 1993.

Duffy, Seán. *Ireland in the Middle Ages.* 1997.

Flanagan, Marie Therese. *Irish Society, Anglo-Norman Settlers, Angevin Kingship.* 1989.

Orpen, Goddard Henry, ed. *The Song of Dermot and the Earl.* 1892.

Orpen, Goddard Henry. *Ireland under the Normans.* 4 vols. 1911–1920.

Scott, Alexander Brian, and Francis Xavier Martin, eds. *Expugnatio Hibernica: The Conquest of Ireland by Giraldus Cambrensis.* 1978.

Seán Duffy

Norman French Literature

Although Welsh and Flemish may have been used by the Anglo-Norman force that landed on the Wexford coast in 1169, its leaders probably spoke Norman-French: The few generations that their ancestors spent on English soil had not altered that. As the language of the ruling Norman elite, French was used in acts of Parliament and in early town statutes. It was favored by the upper echelons of the church, especially those with strong French connections. Private letters written in French by Irish-born Normans demonstrate their acquaintance with French. Criticism of French love lyrics by the fourteenth-century bishop of Ossory indicates some familiarity with French among the common people.

French titles included in inventories of possessions suggest that French literature was read in medieval Ireland. The country also produced some French literature, such as the *Rithmus Facture Ville de Rosse*, a 200-line lighthearted poem describing the 1265 entrenchment of the Norman town of New Ross in County Wexford. The most extensive Norman-French text surviving from medieval Ireland is the *Song of Dermot and the Earl*. Its 3,459 lines recount the 1169 invasion from a Norman perspective. Straddling the *chanson de geste* and the rhymed chronicle so favored by the Normans, it tells of invasions, battles, danger, shifting allegiances, sieges, and slaughter. It is significant not as an accurate historical account but for providing insight into the besieged mentality of the early Norman community, for whom it was probably written. *Amour courtois* (courtly love) inspiration may have reached Ireland later via English literature.

Exactly how long French featured in the linguistic landscape of medieval Ireland is debatable. As early as 1285, French-linked religious orders were abandoning French for Irish. The famous Statutes of Kilkenny (1366), which promoted the English language, are couched in legal French—an unconsciously ironic indication that French was becoming fossilized. Gearóid Iarla (1338–1398), lord chief justice of Ireland, wrote poetry in Irish, whereas his grandfather, the first earl of

From Lucas de Heere, Theatre de tous les peuples et nations de la terre avec leurs habits et ornemens divers . . . , f° 80: Irlandois, Irlandoise, *or images of an Irish city woman from the Pale and a Gaelic man from the country,* sixteenth century. COURTESY OF GHENT UNIVERSITY, UNIVERSITY LIBRARY, MS 2466. REPRODUCED BY PERMISSION.

Desmond, wrote poetry in French. French may thus have yielded to Irish as speedily as the much later final shift from Irish to English in the nineteenth century. French still prospers in contemporary Ireland, from the renowned French writers who have made their homes there to the students who continue to study French in remarkably high numbers.

SEE ALSO Arts: Early and Medieval Arts and Architecture; Literature: Early and Medieval Literature; Middle English Literature

Bibliography

Cosgrove, Art, ed. *A New History of Ireland.* Vol. 2, *Medieval Ireland, 1169–1534.* Rev. edition, 1993.

Curtis, Edmund. "The Spoken Languages of Medieval Ireland." *Studies* 8 (1919): 234–254.

Orpen, Goddard Henry. *The Song of Dermot and the Earl: An Old French Poem Edited by Goddard Henry Orpen.* 1892.

Grace Neville

~

Norman Invasion and Gaelic Resurgence

The Norman invasion of 1169 at the request of Diarmaid Mac Murchadha (Dermot MacMurrough, 1110?–1171), king of Leinster, is traditionally identified as the start of non-Irish rule. But the first Norman invasion was almost a century earlier and was spiritual, not military.

RELIGIOUS BACKGROUND TO THE CONFLICT

William the Conqueror saw his ally Lanfranc installed as archbishop of Canterbury in 1070. Lanfranc claimed primacy over the entire archipelago (chiefly to assert his superiority to York), ordaining and winning the obedience of two bishops of Dublin, Patrick (in 1074) and Donngus (in 1085), both monks of Canterbury province, with Donngus directly under Lanfranc. In 1074 Lanfranc also sought to enlist Ireland's most powerful king, Terdelvacus (Turlough) Ó Briain (1009–1086) of Munster into the work of church reform, denouncing Irish polygamy and simony (notably in bishops taking money for ordaining priests). Lanfranc's successor, St. Anselm, ordained bishops of Dublin, Waterford, and Limerick, and his pressure on Turlough's son and successor Murtagh (d. 1119) brought about the reform Synod of Cashel in 1101.

The papacy was made aware of Irish church abuses, including lay control of ecclesiastical nominations, notably by St. Malachy (1094?–1148) and his friend and biographer St. Bernard of Clairvaux (1090–1153). Pope Adrian IV therefore granted crusader rights in 1155 to Henry II of England to control Ireland so as to effect church reform, a right confirmed by Pope Alexander III in 1172. (Both popes fought the issue of lay control against the Holy Roman Emperor Frederick Barbarossa with ultimate success.) Henry avoided personal intervention until it became desperately necessary to win back papal favor after the murder of Archbishop Saint Thomas Becket in 1170, allegedly on his orders.

The Military Invasion

Henry had permitted Diarmaid to seek aid from Norman Welsh vassals from 1166 to recover Leinster, from which the high king Rory O'Conor (1116?–1198) had ousted him. Diarmaid brought in a complex network of families headed by Richard de Clare (d. 1176), second earl of Pembroke ("Strongbow"), an opponent of Henry in the civil wars before his accession. Linked to him were many descendants and kinsfolk of Gerald of Windsor or at least of his wife, the Princess Nesta a Rhys ap Twedwr, whose paramours had included Henry I, grandfather of one of Diarmaid's allies, Meiler FitzHenry (who would serve as his cousin King John's Irish justiciar from 1200 to 1208). The arrival in Ireland of Henry II and his forces in 1171 was as much to control his old subjects as to convert his new ones.

After Diarmaid's death, Strongbow, now his son-in-law, claimed the kingship of Leinster, which accounted for Henry's enormous though unused army. Strongbow had foiled O'Conor's siege of Dublin, put its Norse jarl to death, recovered Waterford, and allied with Donal Mór Ó Briain (d. 1194) to attack Ossory, but he made no resistance to Henry, who reduced his Leinster title to an earldom and made Hugh de Lacy (d. 1186) his justiciar. De Lacy was made lord of Meath, but before his assassination he too would be accused of aspiring to independent Irish kinship. Before returning to Normandy in 1172, Henry received homage from Ó Briain and several other Gaelic kings. These proceedings were emblematic of the future relationships of English government, colonial magnates, and native leaders: constant maneuvering, short-term alliances, and a consistent belief down the centuries among the English that any of their number established in Ireland, however recently, were not to be trusted.

The Normans, unlike the Norse, could establish Irish bases far from the sea, and their kings depended on these to keep control. Norman castles, the open secret of their success, encouraged and proclaimed self-reliance, as did their modern armor, professional armies, and effective archers. The papacy supported Norman conquest in the perceived need of strong, centralized rule to facilitate reform, hierarchy, and control. However, the papacy found that excessive power in regal hands worked to its detriment, while regal weakness bred Norman as well as Gaelic autonomy and the emasculation of communications and tributes.

Early Chronicles and Commentary

There is no equivalent of the Bayeux Tapestry for the Norman invasion of Ireland, but two versions of the conquest of high literary value have survived. One is the *Song of Dermot and the Earl*, a heroic chanson so titled by its translator, the pro-Norman historian Goddard H. Orpen (*Ireland under the Normans*, 1911–1920). The chanson is tentatively ascribed to Morice Regan, an interpreter in Diarmaid's service who appears in its text in what seems an assertion of authorship. It may be no earlier in writing than 1225 but survived as a great dining-hall oral performance in Norman castles over the previous half-century. Although pro-Norman (its Irish natives are treacherous as well as primitive), it is a vivid narrative, with skillful deployment of character differentiation (possibly for reasons of sponsorship) and a companionable eagerness, which makes it as valuable for what it tells of its audience as for its events.

The other source is the various writings of Giraldus of Wales (Gerald de Barri, 1146?–1223), yet another grandson of the industrious Nesta, topographer, propagandist, historian, archdeacon, incessant autobiographer, and family partisan for the FitzGerald invaders of 1169 and 1170. His fullest portrait, more revealing than he realized, is of his assertive, gossipy, intriguing, persistent, iconoclastic, snobbish, affectionate, treacherous, comic, and tragic self. But he made fine stories and good descriptions of the invaders, producing *Topographia Hibernica* after one visit (1183) and *Expugnatio* (Conquest) *Hibernica*, which concludes with what he saw of the visit of Prince John in 1185, when the prince had been appointed lord of Ireland by his father, Henry II. Giraldus was ready to vilify the Irish partly to vindicate his Norman identity from the suspicion of undue Welshness that had cost him at least one bishopric, but his marginal status must have resembled that of many Irish in these years, including Morice Regan.

Meanwhile the Irish annalists continued their work at various periods, not always greatly concerned with the invasion. The contemporary Munster *Annals of Inisfallen* merely state of Henry's massive incursion ("arguably the single most important turning point in Irish history," wrote Sean Duffy in 1997), that he landed in Waterford, received submission from Ó Briain and from the southernmost major king Mac Carthaigh, and wintered in Dublin. Annalists had their own art, notably in invective: Diarmaid's death was recorded as of "a man who troubled and destroyed Ireland" by the Connacht contemporary chronicler in the *Annals of Tighearnach*, which noted for Strongbow's obituary that no greater brigand than he had existed since the Viking Turgesius. The same vigorous strain is audible in Gaelic poetry more than five centuries later.

Anglicization of the Irish Church

All of these writers (possibly excepting Regan) were clerics, and the ecclesiastical rationale for the invasion consolidated its advance. Henry II ensured a synod at Cashel during his visit and had its proposed reforms of marriage, liturgy, and so on reported to the pope. He had the new archbishop of Dublin, the Englishman John Cumin (d. 1212) elected under his auspices in 1181 and consecrated by the pope in 1182. Irish dioceses steadily fell into English or Norman hands in Leinster and east Munster over the next 150 years, but much of this seems to have been the result of local Norman influence, not royal demands or appointments. J. A. Watt (1972) estimates the anglicization of dioceses as having occurred in Meath (from 1192), Waterford (from c. 1200), Down, Ossory, and Leighlin (from c. 1202), Limerick (from 1215), Ferns and Kildare (from 1223), Lismore (1216–1246 and then from 1253), Emly (1212–1236 and then from 1286), Armagh (1217–1227 and then from 1306), Cork (1267–1276? and then from 1321), and Cloyne (1284–1321 and then from 1333). Leinster's dependence on Canterbury was preconquest, and east Munster reflected Norse as well as Norman and royal control of Waterford. (The former Mac Carthaigh capital and subsequent archbishopric of Cashel stayed under Gaelic influence.) But even before John Cumin, the diocese of Connor (County Antrim) was anglicized from c. 1178, which testified to a Norman breakthrough in eastern Ulster under John de Courcy (d. 1219?) in 1177, and the subsequent fates of Down and Armagh show consolidation and extension under successive magnates.

From the first, the invaders had intermarried with the natives: Hugh de Lacy married Rory O'Conor's daughter, which did not prevent O'Conor from leveling one of his castles a short time later. But ecclesiastical anglicization meant making the Irish church in all things akin to the church in England, and clerics of note had to be English-born or obviously English in culture. Cumin's successor was named Henry of London. It was essentially intellectuals, bards, annalists, and clerics who were supremely conscious of the Irish-English divide. That is not to say that they were always reliably on one side of it. De Courcy, carving out eastern Ulster for a quarter-century, became passionately attached to the cult of St. Patrick and saw to the transfer of what he was certain were the saint's remains to a grave in Downpatrick. De Courcy's native Cumbria is a popular candidate for Patrick's birthplace, so there may have been a personal identification, and de Courcy was a most generous ecclesiastical provider. Eventually de Courcy was ousted by Hugh de Lacy's eponymous son (d. 1242), who was first ennobled (earl of Ulster) and then in his turn ousted by King John. The effect was to gain security for the rise of the O'Neills of Tyrone.

The papacy's battles with John and with the infant Henry III's effective regent (and Anglo-Irish magnate)

William Marshal seriously impaired the initial papal principle of support for strong English rule as desirable for reform. The king's clerical friends might not be the pope's—Henry of London backed John under interdict and won the Dublin archbishopric when John gave way. And William Marshal's ukase that only Englishmen should be appointed to Irish dioceses was repudiated and condemned by Honorius III in 1220. Honorius also terminated at that point the papal legateship of Henry of London, who once again showed himself the king's man rather that the pope's in combining the office of justiciar with that of archbishop from 1221 to 1224, as he had done from 1213 to 1215. In practice the line dividing Irish and English clerical rule roughly approximated the pattern established in lay territorial control. Those Normans who penetrated beyond the line from Carrickfergus to Cork were even more conscious of the need to serve themselves, and sometimes such a reputation may have advanced them.

POST-CONQUEST ASSIMILATION

The first generations of Normans from Strongbow to de Courcy who established themselves and their successors or supplanters in eastern Ireland brought their followers with them, and the country took its pattern from this. In many ways the real division in Ireland remains between east and west rather than north and south. The Normans who arrived after King John's death in 1216 were much more on their own. Many of them might have made great conquests in the west, as the de Burghs did, but they then grew much more dependent on the native population, lost influence at court, found that lands they claimed were now awarded elsewhere, and became increasingly Gaelic in speech, manners, usages, and even law. As Victorian imperialists might put it, they "went native." This did not mean identification with Gaelic interests; it meant that they became further groups of Gaelic magnates playing off king's men against Norman barons and moving to a deeper level of mutual mistrust with royal officials and recent settlers.

The first fifty years of Norman Ireland had also established common law there, ultimately to form the basis of the present-day Irish legal system (cousin to the English and remote from the Scots). Local government on the shire principal was introduced then, where sheriffs could enforce their authority. Urban liberties were granted and regal councils were started, to evolve by the end of the thirteenth century into the Irish parliament. Irish intellectuals from 1169 to the present might curse the Normans, but Sean O'Faolain (1900–1991), evolving from his youthful nationalism, correctly spoke in his *The Irish* (1947) of "the Norman gift." Licensed brigandage begat democracy.

That history evolved thus was in part due to the crusading role in which Henry II had arrived: the native Irish were far from high in his priorities, but he and his successors had some sense of responsibility for them. The natives were expected to attend the early councils and first parliaments, and the language of apartheid or "Jim Crow" only came into legal use during periods when Normans had gone native and the English had lost confidence in their powers of assimilation. Giraldus, the classic exemplar of assimilation, wrote of Irish life and manners with the utmost contempt but with the assumption that under due royal or noble guidance, however rough the tutelage, civilization and salvation might ultimately extend to the Irish. Only after the lapse of two centuries did the tone change, when the Statutes of Kilkenny were passed in 1366 under Lionel (1338–1368), duke of Clarence and earl of Ulster, third son of Edward III. Lionel had married the de Burgh heiress Elizabeth (d. 1362), only to find her male kinsmen occupying her enormous inheritance of Connacht land and serving themselves by flaunting native status. In his rage and frustration Lionel had the statutes outlaw "alliance by marriage, . . . fostering of children, concubinage or amour or in any other manner . . . between the English and Irish." The English were also forbidden to adopt Irish names, customs, fashions, modes of riding, dress, shaving, and so on, or to sell horses or armor to the Irish on penalty of being adjudged traitors. It shows how deeply the Irish and English peoples had intermingled and would continue so to do, but it also asserted a government principle—however often ignored—separating natives from colonizers. Past regimes had exhibited metropolitan hostility to the periphery, but Lionel codified it—uselessly, as far as the next 150 years were concerned, since England had no military resources to overawe natives and bring the alienated to heel. It had to await the invention of gunpowder for any hope of realization.

NATIVE IRISH RESPONSE

The native Irish position from the start had been consistent in its divisions. High King Rory had suddenly replaced the previous strongman, Murtagh Mac Lochlainn of Tyrone (d. 1166), and driven out his ally Diarmaid from Leinster. Diarmaid's return with the Normans was welcomed by Ó Briain and other kings who disliked the thought of Rory becoming too powerful. The same considerations governed individual kings and chieftains in the formulation of policy over subsequent centuries: resist the foreigner by all means, but not so as to give too much strength to a native rival; assist the foreigner where appropriate, but not where it infringes unduly on your own power. King John in

1310 alienated two friendly native rulers, Cathal ("Red-Hand") O'Conor and Aedh Ó Néill, by demands for hostages. This was not simply a feeling that John was hardly a wise choice for guardian of a child: family feeling was not particularly delicate on either side of the Irish Sea (Rory, for instance, burned out the eyes of a son of his who guided a Norman raid on Connacht). They refused to turn alliance for the present into dependency for the future.

As the century progressed, disputed successions to Irish kingships were decided by Norman intervention, although sometimes later repudiated by the selected protégé. For instance, Hugh de Lacy the younger backed Brian Ó Néill in 1238. Brian cut his teeth as ruler in a 1241 massacre of his rivals for the rule of Tyrone, the Mac Lochlainns of Inishowen, but he subsequently allied with their remnant against Mael Seachlainn O'Donnell (d. 1247), who had supported him against them. He allied with the O'Conors of Connacht (now limited to Roscommon) against the English in 1249, and after de Lacy's death he withheld the tribute he had previously paid to the earldom of Ulster. In 1258 he met with Aedh O'Connor and Tadhg Ó Briain at Belleek and won Aedh's support (but probably not Tadhg's) as "king of the Irish in Ireland," only to be defeated and killed by the Normans at the battle of Down in 1260. It seems like a mark of Gaelic resurgence, and in effect it was, but not with the sense of unity implied by the readiness of the *Annals of Ulster* in 1248 to describe Brian as "high king of the north of Ireland" or of King Henry III to complain after Brian's death that he had "presumptuously borne himself as king of the kings of Ireland."

The high kingship had consistently bred fear and rivalry rather than any enduring unity and had thus given rise to the Norman invasion itself. Brian Ó Néill won no support from his O'Donnell neighbors for his high kingship ambitions, yet his career was paralleled by that of Godfrey O'Donnell (d. 1257), who repelled the attempts of Maurice FitzGerald (d. 1257) against O'Donnell territory by destroying his castle at Caol Uisce, wrecking his base at Sligo, and defeating his forces at Credran in 1257. FitzGerald had been a formidable member of his formidable family, threatening the northwest as well as supporting de Lacy's ill-advised intervention in the Ó Néill succession. This reminds us that Gaelic resurgence rose highest with the stimulation of an extended Norman threat. John fitz Thomas FitzGerald (d. 1261), menacing MacCarthaigh in south Munster, was comparably routed at the battle of Callan (1261) despite support both from the justiciar and from a cousin of Fineen MacCarthaigh who defeated him.

Re-Gaelicization

The Irish frontier remained a vortex of conflict but also of cultural exchange, and if its Normans became gaelicized, it no more limited their hostilities against their native Gaelic neighbors than it did against Norman rivals or against increasingly ineffectual royal attempts to assert authority. Kenneth Nicholls (1972), authoritative historian of medieval Gaelic Ireland, estimates that the re-gaelicization primarily turned on intermarriage, sometimes on Norman procreation of children with Gaelic tenants; the very looseness and secular character of marriage, still unreformed to clerical specifications, dramatically increased the intermingling of peoples. At the very time when Parliament was taking root under Edward I, Anglo-Norman control of the regions where initial Norman leaders had had few followers was now fraying away. But what succeeded it was broadly a synthesis, with clerics pulling toward anglicization. (Gaelic bishops even offered Edward I 8,000 marks to grant English law to all Ireland outside the impenetrably Gaelic Ulster, but Edward refused: it was too daunting for the conqueror of Wales and Scotland).

The Bruce invasion (1315–1318) proved something of a Pyrrhic victory for Crown forces, revealing how shaky royal government was (very much dependent on magnates such as the Red Earl of Ulster, whose lands were chiefly in gaelicized Norman possession within two generations). In Ulster itself Niall Mór Ó Néill was master of central and most of eastern Ulster by the end of the fourteenth century, partly by the use of Scottish troops, some of whom settled in Down and Antrim (MacDonnell, Magennis, possibly MacQuillin). English families were chiefly limited to the now-gaelicized "savages," surviving intermittently in the Ards peninsula. Meanwhile, in the extreme south of the once heavily anglicized Leinster, the Mac Murchadha (MacMurrough) family had maintained and extended its kingship of Leinster as though it had never been interrupted by Strongbow. Art Mór held the Barrow valley in Carlow and Wexford at the end of the century, and the O'Tooles and O'Byrnes threatened Dublin from the hills of Wicklow. In Munster the de Clares, to whom Edward I had granted all Thomond (i.e., north Munster) in 1276, were smashed by the O'Briens at the battle of Dysert O'Dea in 1318 and disappeared. Gaelicized FitzGeralds and Butlers continued to play a major part in English affairs, partly from lust for power, partly for self-protection: Butlers were Lancastrian and FitzGeralds Yorkist in the Wars of the Roses, and the successive English rulers worried more about them than about the Gaelic rulers of the late fifteenth century. Royal rule now extended little beyond Dublin, while church authorities bewailed the persistent raids on cathedrals and lands by incessantly predatory Gaels and Normans.

SEE ALSO Bruce Invasion; English Government in Medieval Ireland; Gaelic Recovery; Gaelic Society in the Late Middle Ages; MacMurrough, Dermot, and the Anglo-Norman Invasion; Magnates, Gaelic and Anglo-Irish; Norman Conquest and Colonization; Richard II in Ireland; **Primary Documents:** The Bull *Laudabiliter*, Pope Adrian IV's Grant of Ireland to Henry II (c. 1155); Three Letters of Pope Alexander III, Confirming Henry II's Conquest of Ireland (1172); The Treaty of Windsor (1175); The Statutes of Kilkenny (1366); King Richard II in Ireland (1395)

Bibliography

Cosgrove, Art, ed. *Medieval Ireland, 1169–1534*. Vol. 2 of *A New History of Ireland*. 1993.

Duffy, Sean. *Ireland in the Middle Ages*. 1997.

Edwards, R. Dudley. *A New History of Ireland*. 1972.

Frame, Robin. *Colonial Ireland, 1169–1369*. 1981.

Lyndon, James. *The Making of Ireland*. 1998.

Nicholls, Kenneth. *Gaelic and Gaelicised Ireland in the Middle Ages*. 1972.

Watt, John A. *The Church in Medieval Ireland*. 1972.

Owen Dudley Edwards

Norse Settlement

In 795 the first recorded raid on Ireland by the Vikings occurred when Reachrú (possibly Lambay Island off the coast of Dublin) was attacked. For the next forty-six years the Vikings continued to attack monasteries and other centers of wealth until in 841 they founded their first permanent settlements, called *longphorts*, at Dublin and Annagassan, Co. Louth. These were defended fortresses where the Vikings could protect their warships and, if necessary, overwinter in Ireland. (Longphorts were also established in other places, such as Cork, but they have yet to be located archaeologically.) To the immediate west of Viking-age Dublin, the largest Viking cemetery outside of Scandinavia was found in the nineteenth century and has been dated to the ninth century. Until recently, scholars have debated whether the original longphort was located here in 841, and then the urban settlement was established in 917 at the site where it is now, closer to the mouth of the River Liffey, but recent archaeological excavations have produced radiocarbon dates that indicate ninth-century settlement in the center of present-day Dublin at Temple Bar.

A characteristic Viking motif. This drawing incised on a ship's plank was found in a wood house excavated in Christchurch Place, Dublin. COPYRIGHT © NATIONAL MUSEUM OF IRELAND. REPRODUCED BY PERMISSION.

The Vikings established the major port towns on the east coast such as Dublin, Waterford, Wexford, Limerick, and Cork, which were all used as trading centers for their widespread economic empire that dominated much of western Europe. The excavations in the heart of Dublin, more than anywhere else in Ireland, have revealed the wealth and sophistication of the trade and industry concentrated in these ports in the eleventh and twelfth centuries. Dublin was famous for the production of fine metalwork, especially the ring pins that secured garments in the Viking period. Excavations have also produced much evidence of the layout of Viking Age Dublin. The remains of many structures, such as post-and-wattle sub-rectangular houses, and their associated artifacts reveal the intermixture of Gaelic-Irish and Scandinavian culture that made up the rich Hiberno-Norse artistic tradition that dominated Irish urban life, especially in the eleventh and early twelfth centuries. Archaeological evidence from the Wood Quay site in Dublin in the late 1970s also showed that a stone town wall was constructed around the core of the nucleated settlement in about 1100 C.E. This replaced a large earthen embankment with a wooden palisade on top, which had encircled the town from the tenth century. Along the southern edge of the river, docking facilities and buildings were also being constructed as the river silted up, with nine successive stages being identified archaeologically, dating from 900 to 1300.

Excavations within the walled city of Waterford have uncovered about 20 percent of the Viking and medieval occupation layers there, and have been especially valuable in putting the finds from Hiberno-Norse Dublin into a broader socioeconomic context. Although the range and quality of the Viking Age finds from Dublin are arguably more impressive than those of Waterford, the discovery of five sunken buildings in Waterford represents the greatest number yet found in any Irish urban center. To date, no archaeological evidence for the Vikings from a secure context has been found in Cork, but explorations in Limerick have provided traces of Hiberno-Norse constructions and occupation layers on the southwestern portion of King's Island, at the lowest fording point across the River Shannon.

This archaeological evidence from these Hiberno-Norse ports has provided a counterweight to the anti-Viking propaganda forcefully advanced by the contemporary annalistic sources, such as the *Annals of Ulster* and the *Annals of Inisfallen*, that have clouded historical judgment on the Norse until the last decade or so. As these written sources were largely compiled by the monks whose monasteries bore the brunt of the Viking raids, it is scarcely surprising that all of the ills of the church—such as pluralism and lay abbots—and indeed of Irish society generally, were laid at the feet of these invaders. Archaeology has emphasized the significant role that the Norse settlers played in the establishment of urban life in Ireland, and in bringing the island into the wider trading network established by the Vikings in Western Europe.

In popular mythology the Battle of Clontarf in 1014, which ended with the victory of the forces of the Irish high king Brian Boru over the Vikings of Dublin, marked the end of Norse dominance in Ireland. But the historical reality is more complex, because Vikings fought on both sides of the battle, and Dublin retained some political independence until 1052, when they had to accept Murchad, the son of King Diarmaid mac Maél na mBó of Leinster, as their ruler. Even after the Anglo-Normans captured these port towns at the end of the twelfth century, their Hiberno-Norse populations were segregated into areas called (for instance, in Dublin) the *villa Ostmanorrum*—"town of the Norsemen"—but they arguably ceased to have any distinctive identity by the fourteenth century. One of the major challenges facing future scholars will be to try to establish the true extent of Viking rural settlement. There is place-name evidence of such settlement outside the major urban settlements, including Dublin, where the term *Dyflinarskiri* was used to denote its rural hinterland, and Waterford, where the names Ballygunner and Ballytruckle probably refer to medieval inhabitants with the Scandinavian names Gunner and Thorkell.

Indeed, among the few reminders of this long period of Norse settlement in Ireland are some place-names that are Old Norse in origin, such as the fishing village Howth, which is located on a rocky promontory at the northern tip of Dublin Bay, whose named is derived from *höfuth* (headland). Waterford is probably the largest settlement in Ireland that has retained its Old Norse-derived place-name, originally *Vedrarfjordr*, which has been identified as meaning either "windy fjord" or "fjord of the ram" (i.e., where they were loaded for transport by sea). Recently it has been suggested that the first element of the place-name is derived from the Old Norse *Vedr* (wind or weather), referring to the fact that this inlet (or fjord, to the Scandinavians) of the River Suir was often exposed to the wind, and that this settlement offered a safe haven in any storm.

SEE ALSO Clontarf, Battle of; Dál Cais and Brian Boru; Early Medieval Ireland and Christianity; Uí Néill High Kings

Bibliography

Duffy, S., ed. *Medieval Dublin*. 3 vols. 2000, 2001, 2002.

Hurley, M. F., O. M. B. Scully, and S. W. J. McCutcheon, eds. *Late Viking Age and Medieval Waterford Excavations, 1986–1992*. 1997.

Roesdahl, E. *The Vikings*. 1991.

Wallace, P. F. *The Viking Age Buildings of Dublin*. 2 vols. 1992.

Terry Barry

~

Northern Ireland

CONSTITUTIONAL SETTLEMENT FROM SUNNINGDALE TO GOOD FRIDAY

There is a tendency to see a connection between the Sunningdale settlement of December 1973 and the Belfast Agreement of April 1998. Indeed, one of the clichés is that the latter was simply "Sunningdale for slow learners." This implies that there was not much more on offer in 1998 than could have been secured in 1974 and that the interim was a period of wasted years and lost lives. The sentiment has a certain superficial attraction but misses the vital point that both content and context need to be examined: peace agreements are only a part of a peace process. And it raises the question, Who were the slow learners?

The Sunningdale Agreement was innovative because it established a coalition government in Northern Ireland and recognized that the Irish government had a role to play in ending the conflict (the "Irish dimension"). The executive that took office on 1 January 1974 was composed of the Ulster Unionist Party (UUP) led by Brian Faulkner, the nationalist Social Democratic and Labour Party (SDLP) led by Gerry Fitt, and the biconfessional Alliance Party led by Oliver Napier. It was the first time in the history of Northern Ireland that a nationalist party had a share in power. That very fact contributed to its undoing. Ostensibly the executive collapsed because many objected to the Irish dimension: "Dublin is only a Sunningdale away" was the popular dissident slogan used in the British general election one month later. Northern Ireland returned eleven anti-Sunningdale candidates and only one in favor. The executive was redundant in less than five months, having been brought down by a loyalist uprising known as the Ulster Workers' Council (UWC) strike. Key workers (particularly those in the gas and electricity industries) withdrew their labor during May in protest over the Irish dimension. It was a masterful strategy because it crippled the Northern Ireland economy. The power-sharing executive ceased activities, and the first bold ex-

The Ulster Workers' Council Strike in May 1974 brought down the power-sharing executive established under the Sunningdale Agreement. Devolved government was not re-established in Northern Ireland until 1998. © Hulton-Deutsch Collection/Corbis. Reproduced by permission.

ample of constitutional innovation in Northern Ireland's history collapsed.

Over the next decade successive governments moved with more caution. The Labour governments of 1974 to 1979 placed greater emphasis on security and the economy than on constitutionalism. There was one attempt—in July 1974—to establish a constitutional convention "to consider what provisions for the government of Northern Ireland would be likely to command the most widespread acceptance throughout the community." Seventy-eight members were elected to the convention, which met during 1975 and 1976, but it split on the issue of partnership government versus simple majority rule. It was only when Prime Minister Margaret Thatcher's Conservatives came into office in May 1979 that constitutionalism and innovation were revived. They came in two forms—two further attempts at an internal settlement, and the creation of more formalized links between the British and Irish governments.

The attempts at settlement were associated with two secretaries of state, Humphrey Atkins and James Prior. Atkins established a conference of the constitutional parties which met in 1980 to examine the future governance of Northern Ireland. This initiative succeeded in narrowing the political options to a form of power-sharing, or a system of majority rule with a minority blocking mechanism. The conference had been boycotted from the outset by the largest party (the UUP) on the grounds that it was a dereliction of the government's policy of integrating Northern Ireland more fully into the British system. Atkins was succeeded by Prior, who introduced a more ambitious scheme of "rolling devolution" in April 1982, whereby an elected assembly was invested with inquiring and consultative powers to make direct rule more accountable. Powers were to be devolved to the assembly incrementally if it could win cross-community agreement by 70 percent. But the SDLP and Sinn Féin (SF) boycotted the assembly proceedings, and there was no cross-community consensus. The assembly struggled on

John Hume and David Trimble, joint winners of the 1998 Nobel Peace Prize, pictured with Bono from U2, at a rally to win support for the Belfast Agreement, 19 May 1998. © LEWIS ALAN/CORBIS SYGMA. REPRODUCED BY PERMISSION.

until 1986; by that stage the process had moved on to another (Anglo-Irish) dimension, especially after the signing of the 1985 Anglo-Irish Agreement.

In formalizing interstate cooperation, the 1985 agreement changed the nature of the debate from the endogenous to the exogenous. Henceforth dialogue would be conducted between the two governments of Britain and the Republic of Ireland rather than among the bickering parties in Northern Ireland. Unionism's failure to destroy the agreement led to a period of its internal exile which was only properly addressed in the 1990s, but within a British-Irish context. In essence, this meant that there were two strands to the peace process—one between Northern Ireland's constitutional parties and the second between the British and Irish governments. (Another strand—dialogue between North and South within Ireland—was added later.) Finally, the first strand was enhanced by the inclusion of SF and the small loyalist parties, the Ulster Democratic Unionist Party (UDP) and the Progressive Unionist Party (PUP)— parties close to the Irish Republican Army (IRA), the Ul-

ster Defence Association (UDA), and the Ulster Volunteer Force (UVF). Their entry became possible after the British and Irish prime ministers produced the "Downing Street Declaration" in December 1993, which led directly to republican and loyalist cease-fires by October 1994. The declaration offered the opportunity of negotiating the political future to "democratically mandated parties which establish a commitment to exclusively peaceful methods and which have shown that they abide by the democratic process" and referred (ambiguously) to the "right of self-determination" of the Irish people.

To advance the process, the governments sponsored the "Framework Documents" in February 1995, which outlined a blueprint for future discussions, but they had little immediate impact because the IRA abandoned its cease-fire in February 1996 in protest against British insistence that it decommission its weapons. On 30 May 1996 elections were held for a Northern Ireland forum to enable the politicians to engage in interparty negotiations. Eleven months later, the Labour Party defeated the Conservatives in the British general election, and a new opportunity for inclusive dialogue was created. SF was permitted to join interparty talks on 9 September 1997. (The IRA's cease-fire had been reinstated on 20 July.) Intensive negotiations under the chairmanship of former U.S. Senator George Mitchell (and with the blessing of the Clinton administration and the European Union) followed the now established three-strand formula: strand 1 dealt with internal Northern Ireland institutions, strand 2 with North-South relations, and strand 3 with East-West (British-Irish) relations. The negotiations culminated with the signing of the Belfast Agreement on 10 April 1998.

The Belfast Agreement was much more comprehensive than Sunningdale, and crucially it introduced the prospect of the total cessation of violence, a prospect not offered by Sunningdale. It was based on the doctrines of consent (Irish unity was conceivable only in a peaceful context) and sufficient consensus (cross-community cooperation). It created sophisticated institutions that linked the three strands together. It built on the earlier failed initiatives of 1974 by learning from their defects and had a full-fledged equality and human-rights agenda. The agreement had been achieved through an inclusive process without any form of coercion. It had the warm support of the international community and reflected changing conceptions of identity by moving away from the narrow designations of (simply) unionist or nationalist. Above all, in two referenda held throughout Ireland on 22 May 1998 it was endorsed by 71 percent of Northern Ireland's voters and by 94 percent of the Republic's. It offered a comprehensive peace that had eluded Ireland in the twentieth century and was hailed as a model for conflict transformation in other intractable struggles.

SEE ALSO Adams, Gerry; Anglo-Irish Agreement of 1985 (Hillsborough Agreement); Decommissioning; Economic Relations between North and South since 1922; Hume, John; Northern Ireland: History since 1920; Northern Ireland: The United States in Northern Ireland since 1970; Trimble, David; **Primary Documents:** Anglo-Irish Agreement (15 November 1985); Irish Republican Army (IRA) Cease-Fire Statement (31 August 1994); Text of the IRA Cease-Fire Statement (19 July 1997); The Belfast/Good Friday Agreement (10 April 1998)

Bibliography

Arthur, Paul. *Special Relationships: Britain, Ireland, and the Northern Ireland Problem.* 2001.

Cox, M., et al. *A Farewell to Arms? From "Long War" to Long Peace in Northern Ireland.* 2000.

Ruane, Joseph, and Jennifer Todd, eds. *The Good Friday Agreement: Analysing Political Change in Northern Ireland.* 1999.

Paul Arthur

DISCRIMINATION AND THE CAMPAIGN FOR CIVIL RIGHTS

Discrimination against Catholics predated the establishment of the Northern Ireland state. Catholics were disproportionately represented in lower economic and social categories and were rarely to be found in senior managerial positions. The political turmoil surrounding the consolidation of Ulster Unionist Party control further marked out the disadvantaged minority as disloyal. Thus local government constituencies were gerrymandered and Catholics were effectively barred from sensitive civil service positions. They were underrepresented in the new Royal Ulster Constabulary (RUC) and absent from the police auxiliaries known as the Specials.

BACKGROUND TO THE MOVEMENT

Unionists feared losing control of their devolved parliament and government (from 1932 known as Stormont, after new parliament buildings opened in that year) to an opportunistic alliance of nationalists, socialists, and unionist independents. Though the Government of Ireland Act of 1920 required proportional representation in Northern elections, it was repealed for the 1929 general election. This weakened minority parties, particularly Labour, and consolidated the unionist-nationalist rift. Representation for Labour, independent unionists, and other groups fell from eight seats in 1925 to four in 1929, although their share of the vote increased.

In common with the situation in Great Britain, the Northern Ireland local government electorate was based upon a ratepayers' franchise. But when it was abolished in Britain after World War II, Stormont politicians elected to remain as they were. Protestants made up the majority of the 250,000 thus deprived of the local government vote, but Catholics, being lower down on the socioeconomic scale and thus less likely to pay rates, were disproportionately outside the franchise. The importance to unionists of the ratepayers' franchise was that it locked in the principle that those who paid the highest rates were entitled to the biggest say in the conduct of local government. Richer areas were disproportionately unionist. The political results of this principle were starkly revealed in the 1923 redrawing of many

Members of the Royal Ulster Constabulary attack a civil-rights demonstration in Derry city, 5 October 1968. Television coverage of this demonstration brought the Northern Ireland civil-rights campaign to international attention. HULTON ARCHIVE/GETTY IMAGES. REPRODUCED BY PERMISSION.

local government constituency boundaries to reflect changing patterns of wealth. Nationalist councils fell in great numbers to unionist control. Similar, rejigging won or consolidated for Unionism Omagh Urban District in 1935, Derry County Borough in 1936, Armagh Urban District in 1946, and Fermanagh County Council in 1966. Perhaps one-fifth of Catholics lived under gerrymandered constituencies.

As a consequence, however, there was pressure to maintain the relative wealth disparities of Catholic and Protestant districts, or else the entire delicate framework would collapse. The government in practice could rely upon private employment discrimination to sustain Protestant economic influence. Local government also strove to maintain a robust proportion of Protestant employees. After the war, as local governments undertook slum clearance and built housing for rent, unionist-controlled local authorities made sure that Catholics and Protestants remained segregated. The inevitable housing bottlenecks caused much resentment. Even the large-scale infrastructural elements were carefully manipulated to minimize disruption of unionist electoral dominance.

ORGANIZATION AND STRUGGLE

In January 1964 the Campaign for Social Justice (CSJ) was founded in Dungannon, Co. Tyrone, "to collect data on all injustices done against all creeds and political opinions." Hitherto, civil rights propaganda had been simply one string in the antipartitionist bow. The CSJ's apolitical campaign was designed to appeal primarily to a British audience. In this they had some success, and a Campaign for Democracy in Ulster (CDU) pressure group won considerable support on the back benches of the British parliamentary Labour Party.

On 30 March 1966 a conference of more than eighty representatives, meeting at the International Hotel in Belfast, set up the Northern Ireland Civil Rights Association (NICRA), a "non-political pressure group modeled on the National Council for Civil Liberties." They organized the first civil rights march, in emulation of the movement in the United States, from Coalisland to Dungannon on 25 August 1968.

The city of Londonderry (Derry to nationalists) proved to be the powder keg, however. In a gerrymander in 1923, unionists wrested control from nationalists, an arrangement reinforced in the 1930s. A nationalist voting majority of 5,000 resulted in a unionist council of twelve unionists to eight nationalists. In the 1960s Derry was deprived of the New University, although there was general agreement that it was the most obvious location. Few were surprised when evidence emerged that there existed the "faceless men," a cabal of local unionists lobbying for investment to be directed away from Derry for fear of upsetting the delicate population balance behind the gerrymander.

On 27 August 1968 leftist activists in the Derry Housing Action Committee invited NICRA to organize a march there. This was rerouted to exclude it from the city center by the partisan minister of home affairs, Bill Craig. On 5 October 1968 the Derry march was stopped by police lines, and violence broke out after the Royal Ulster Constabulary moved in to disperse the crowd. This developed into two days of rioting and an immediate political crisis.

A thousand Queen's University students staged a sit-down in Linen Hall Street on 9 October after being barred from the Belfast City Hall area on the pretext of a Paisleyite counterdemonstration. They quickly went on to form People's Democracy, a radical and activist civil-rights group. In Derry, meanwhile, a broad-ranging Derry Citizens' Action Committee took over leadership of the city's civil-rights movement. An attempt to ban all demonstrations in Derry collapsed on 16 November when 16,000 marched and 2,000 staged a sit-down protest in the Diamond.

Police repression having failed, and under pressure from the British government, Stormont on 22 November announced a five-point reform package. This was a somewhat limited program, with the concessions of a points system for housing allocation and an ombudsman being the only U-turns.

Agitation continued, and on 30 November 8,000 civil rights demonstrators took to the streets of Armagh, only to be excluded from the city center by a belligerent and quite heavily armed crowd of 1,000 Paisleyites. On 9 December 1968, Prime Minister Terence O'Neill broadcast to the province, addressing directly the civil-rights marchers: "Your voice has been heard and clearly heard. Your duty now is to play your part in taking the heat out of the situation before blood is shed." Shortly afterward he sacked William Craig, his controversial minister of home affairs.

The immediate response was favorable, and most civil rights organizations called off demonstrations for at least a month. However, one group increasingly in thrall to socialist radicals, the People's Democracy, organized a "long march" from Belfast to Derry, starting on 1 January 1969. They were harassed on their way and seriously attacked by loyalists on 4 January at Burntollet Bridge and as they straggled into Derry. Subsequent disorder in Derry saw a breakdown in RUC discipline and the temporary removal of police from a nationalist district of the city. The civil-rights agitation reignited, but on the following weekend it was doused again when protestors attacked police and property in a poorly organized demonstration in the Catholic town of Newry.

When O'Neill called a general election on 3 February, primarily to still dissent in his own party, civil-rights activists redirected their energies into electoral politics. A slew of civil-rights campaigners, notably John Hume, Paddy Devlin, and Ivan Cooper, ousted traditionalist Nationalist Party MPs. Meanwhile O'Neill failed to effectively reshape his parliamentary party, and there was general agreement that the Unionist Party was sliding rightward. In this atmosphere civil rights demonstrations were reignited, now emphasizing the demand for "one person, one vote" in local government suffrage and the repeal of repressive legislation arising from recent disorders. Severe rioting in April 1969, however, not only precipitated the fall of O'Neill but also eclipsed civil-rights agitation as communal confrontation and preparation for conflict became the dominant concern.

SEE ALSO Faulkner, Brian; Northern Ireland: History since 1920; O'Neill, Terence; Ulster Unionist Party in Office; **Primary Documents:** On "A Protestant Parliament and a Protestant State" (24 April 1934)

Bibliography

Hennessy, Thomas. *A History of Northern Ireland, 1920–1996.* 1997.

Mulholland, Marc. *Northern Ireland at the Crossroads: Ulster Unionism in the O'Neill Years, 1960–9.* 2000.

Rose, Richard. *Governing without Consensus: An Irish Perspective.* 1971.

Whyte, John. "How Much Discrimination Was There under the Unionist Regime, 1921–1968." In *Contemporary Irish Studies*, edited by Tom Gallagher and James O'Connell. 1983.

Marc Mulholland

HISTORY SINCE 1920

The state of Northern Ireland was created in 1920 under the terms of the Government of Ireland Act, and comprised the northeastern counties of Antrim, Armagh, Down, Fermanagh, Londonderry, and Tyrone. This area was the heartland of Protestant unionist opposition to Irish nationalism, although it also contained a substantial number of Catholics—in 1926 there were 420,000 Catholics in a total Northern population of 1,257,000. This religious demography, allied to the bitter circumstances of the state's creation, would leave lasting political scars. Northern Ireland was launched in the context of the Anglo-Irish war, and the insurgents of the Irish Republican Army (IRA) were deeply opposed both to the partition of Ireland and to the creation of a unionist state in the northeast. They sustained operations against the new state from its inception, and in 1922 (after the Anglo-Irish Treaty with the British was signed) they launched an offensive designed to overturn its government. This campaign was not only unsuccessful but also counterproductive insofar as it helped to stimulate repressive official measures and attitudes that long outlasted the "Troubles" of the early 1920s.

NATIONALISTS IN NORTHERN IRELAND, 1920–1960

The Anglo-Irish Treaty of 1921 had made provision for the amendment of the border between Northern Ireland and the new Irish Free State, and nationalists throughout the island trusted that this promise of possible revision would truncate and destabilize the North. Ulster nationalists, believing in the transience of partition, generally boycotted the evolving institutions of the new state, including its parliament and its committees of inquiry into local government and educational reform. This, together with the unfriendly attitudes of the unionist elite, meant that the Northern minority was effectively denied a say at a crucial stage in the evolution of the North. A review of the North-South boundary was undertaken by a commission in 1924 and 1925, but it failed to deliver the radical revisions that had been expected. Northern nationalists were forced to accept that partition would survive and that they would have to coexist with the unionist regime. But the unionist governors of Northern Ireland, led by James Craig, the first prime minister of the new state, saw themselves as the political and military victors of the struggles of the early and mid-1920s; and they showed little magnanimity to the nationalist minority either at this time or later.

Nationalists emerged as a permanently alienated section of Northern society. They constituted a small minority in the devolved parliament and thus were never in government. They were underrepresented in most areas of the workplace, including the police force, and were dramatically underrepresented in the elite cad-

The Republic of Ireland and Northern Ireland

——— International border

• City

res of the public sector. The relationship between nationalists and the police was often antagonistic; the Royal Ulster Constabulary was unpopular but won some grudging acceptance, while the part-time policemen of the Ulster Special Constabulary were viewed as heavy-handed and oppressive. Local-government electoral boundaries favored the unionists, in some cases—Omagh, Derry city—so blatantly that they effectively disfranchised clear nationalist majorities. Proportional representation was abolished by unionist ministers for local-government elections in September 1922—a move that decisively weakened nationalist representation. The retention of a property qualification for the local-government (though not the parliamentary) franchise excluded many socially disadvantaged people from the vote, and though both the unionist and nationalist poor were affected, nationalists suffered disproportionately. Nationalists, who were concentrated in the west of Northern Ireland, believed that the unionist government actively favored the eastern counties in terms of industrial investment and social improvements.

Until the 1960s Northern nationalists expressed these resentments through a tacit disengagement from the state. There were occasional electoral mobilizations, as in the early and mid-1950s, when several republicans were elected to the Northern Ireland parliament (Stormont) and Westminster. The militant separatist tradition also provided an avenue for the disenchanted, although this survived only on a very small scale in West Belfast and other nationalist enclaves. The IRA launched campaigns against the Northern government in 1939 and again in 1956, but while some lives were lost and the unionist regime was unsettled, these were relatively unimportant affairs that were suppressed with comparative ease.

THE UNIONIST GOVERNMENT AND ITS DIFFICULTIES, 1920–1960

The unionist governors of Northern Ireland faced other profound challenges. The foundation charter of their state, the Government of Ireland Act of 1920, was a problem in that it defined political and economic relationships that were speedily outmoded. In particular, the act burdened the new regime in Belfast with financial constraints which, if they had been sustained, would have ensured its collapse, and the economic relationship between the Belfast and London governments had to be repeatedly overhauled in 1924 to 1925 and later. The act partitioned the island and created separate Home Rule administrations in Belfast and Dublin. The measure also envisaged the ultimate unity of the island, and much of its political engineering was designed to facilitate this end. But Irish revolutionaries wanted more than Home Rule by 1920 or 1921, and the unionists, while accepting a Home Rule administration in Belfast, emphatically did not want Irish unity. Only in 1925 were some of the legislative inducements for unity effectively dismantled. Still, the unionist government remained burdened with what was effectively a unitary constitution until the demise of Stormont in 1972.

But the core problem for the governors and people of Northern Ireland was the collapse of the regional economy in the interwar years. The staples of Northern industry were shipbuilding and linen, and both of these enterprises were in crisis. Unionist ministers sought to bolster shipbuilding and other existing businesses through loans guarantees and tried to tempt new enterprises into Northern Ireland with subventions and other inducements. Neither venture was successful, and the level of unemployment remained appallingly high throughout the interwar years. In 1938, 92,000 Northern citizens were on the dole, reflecting an unemployment rate of 29.5 percent (compared with 12.8 percent for the rest of the United Kingdom). High levels of un-

employment meant much personal misery, sustained pressure on welfare resources, and a high degree of political instability—the poor of both communities, Protestant and Catholic, rioted in October 1932. High levels of unemployment also threatened to disrupt the social alliance of Ulster Protestants upon which the Northern state rested, and in this context unemployment tended to reinforce the sectarian defensiveness of the unionist government.

The Second World War brought German air attacks and (in the raids of April and May 1941) some 1,100 civilian casualties. But in other senses the war brought a form of grim relief to many of the relentless problems confronting the unionist regime. The war created a heightened demand for the industrial goods of the region, and it therefore temporarily ameliorated (but by no means cured) the contagion of joblessness. The war also brought ultimately a greater degree of political security to the governing party: Northern Ireland was heavily involved in the support of the Allied war effort, and unionism was clearly bolstered by the victory of May 1945. The neutrality of the Dublin government, on the other hand, simultaneously focused and reinforced Irish patriotism and undermined the antipartitionist cause in the United States and Britain in the immediate postwar years. When the Irish government declared in 1948 that the twenty-six counties were to become a republic, the British government responded with its Ireland Act (1949), a measure that affirmed that Northern Ireland would cease to be a part of the United Kingdom only if the Stormont parliament so decided. This was the most solid legislative endorsement that the unionist regime had yet been or ever would be given.

Other, sometimes indirect results of the war had more ambiguous implications. The war was associated with an expansion of the British state, and in particular with the elaboration of social-welfare reform. This affected Northern Ireland, where the civil service grew rapidly in the postwar years, as did the provision of welfare relief (social services were now on a par with Britain and were largely subsidized by the British state). There were some short-term political benefits from this to the extent that the regime was able, through jobs and welfare, to bolster the Protestant social alliance upon which it was founded. But it was also the case that Catholic nationalist resentment was becoming more of a challenge, for the Catholic community now had greater educational opportunities than before and yet was still largely excluded from both political power and public employment.

Nor had the scourge of unemployment disappeared. Agriculture was a significant feature of the regional economy, but—with the onset of mechanization—was growing more efficient and employing fewer people. Shipbuilding and linen continued on their downward trajectory in the 1950s despite government subventions. By the early 1960s there were massive layoffs in the shipyards, and 10,000 jobs were lost in the linen industry between 1956 and 1961. This economic collapse recreated some of the political volatility that had been evident in the early 1930s, with massive protest demonstrations and the redirection of working-class Protestant votes away from unionism toward the Northern Ireland Labour Party.

O'NEILLISM AND THE PRELUDE TO VIOLENCE, 1960–1970

In 1963, against the backdrop of this crisis, Viscount Brookeborough, the prime minister of Northern Ireland and unionist leader, resigned. His replacement, Terence O'Neill, saw industrial modernization and the reform and consolidation of unionism as his key tasks, and he embarked upon a series of inclusivist gestures and economic improvements that were designed to attain these ends. O'Neill believed that the economic problems of Northern Ireland were susceptible to rational management, and he also argued that the "irrationality" of much of Northern politics would be undermined by enhanced prosperity. He maintained that it was possible to recast community relations within Northern Ireland and between the North and Dublin on the basis of well-publicized friendly political gestures, such as inviting the Southern taoiseach Seán Lemass to visit Belfast in January 1965.

But in fact the relationship between economic and political modernization was more complex than O'Neill understood, and the result of many of his actions was to inflame rather than ameliorate resentments, divisions, and expectations. The new industries that succumbed to O'Neill's blandishments tended to establish themselves in the east of the region. Nationalists, concentrated in the impoverished west, saw this as economic discrimination. Improvements in transport, particularly the closure of railways and the construction of motorways, also provoked criticisms concerning the neglect of the west. Any benefits accruing from other initiatives—a new university or a new town, for example—tended to be obscured by allegations concerning their location. The drive to build new homes also helped to inflame long-standing Catholic resentments concerning the unfair allocation of public housing.

Catholic anger on housing led to the creation of the Campaign for Social Justice in January 1964; this in turn fed into a wider protest organization, the Northern Ireland Civil Rights Association (NICRA), created in April 1967. Following the example of civil-rights protest in the United States, NICRA and its radical offshoot, the People's Democracy, organized a series of political marches in 1968 and 1969 that resulted in confrontations with the police and with ultraconservative Protestant counterdemonstrators. O'Neill, pressed by Harold Wilson's Labour government in London, hastily sought to enact a five-point reform program in November 1968, but this only alienated many unionists (who saw it as a surrender to militant pressure) without in any way defusing civil-rights anger. O'Neill sought an electoral mandate for his reformism in February 1969, but he only succeeded in entrenching the divisions within his own party. He had hoped to win the votes of substantial numbers of moderate Catholics but was disappointed. The election, combined with O'Neill's resignation in April 1969, signaled the extent to which the traditional governing elite was weakened and disoriented, and it helped to generate a radical realignment within Northern constitutional politics. In 1969 to 1971 the party structure of the North was completely reinvented with the establishment of a centrist Alliance Party in April 1970; a new constitutional nationalist grouping, the Social Democratic and Labour Party, in August 1970; and the hardline Democratic Unionists, led by Dr. Ian Paisley, in September 1971.

The apparent weakness of the governing elite also helped to stimulate civil unrest: Intercommunal rioting in Belfast and Derry marred the summer of 1969, and in August British troops were deployed on the streets in an effort to quell the disturbances. Some nationalists were for a brief time inclined to welcome these outside forces, believing that their traditional defenders, the IRA, had failed to offer adequate protection. But by January 1970, with the launch of a more aggressive republican force, the Provisional IRA (PIRA or "Provisionals"), many Northern Catholics believed that they had found a credible new focus for their loyalties.

THE PROVISIONAL IRA, 1970–1994

Born in the Catholic-Protestant interface areas of Belfast and armed by Southern sympathizers, the Provisionals were strong enough by 1972 to launch an offensive designed to overturn the Northern Irish state and remove the British presence from Ireland. Recruits were plentiful, particularly after August 1971 when in a last, desperate initiative on security the Stormont government presided over the heavy-handed and mismanaged application of internment without trial. The PIRA also received a grim boost on 30 January 1972 ("Bloody Sunday") when the British army opened fire on a demonstration in Derry, killing thirteen protestors. The Provisionals sustained their war, with only minor in-

On 21 July 1972 ("Bloody Friday") the IRA planted over twenty bombs in the Belfast city center, killing eleven people and injuring many more.
© LEIF SKOOGFORS/CORBIS. REPRODUCED BY PERMISSION.

terruptions, until the cease-fire of August 1994. Their strategies shifted somewhat over this period, with an initial emphasis on bombing economic targets—eleven people died in a series of PIRA bombs in central Belfast on "Bloody Friday," 21 July 1972—and the assassination of policemen and soldiers. In the later 1970s there was a shift toward the targeting of high-profile victims, such as Earl Mountbatten, an uncle of Prince Philip, who was killed on 27 August 1979. There was a plan to assassinate the Prince and Princess of Wales in July 1983, and Mrs. Thatcher and the Conservative cabinet narrowly missed death when a bomb exploded at the Grand Hotel in Brighton in October 1984. Bombing political and economic targets in England was a long-term strategy of the Provisionals.

In 1980 and 1981 the republican movement also returned to a highly emotive form of protest used in the Anglo-Irish War: hunger strikes. Between May and August 1981 eleven republican prisoners in the Maze Gaol near Belfast starved themselves to death in order to highlight a demand for "political" (as distinct from "criminal") status. Sinn Féin, the political wing of the Provisionals, was able to mobilize popular nationalist

anger and to achieve a degree of electoral momentum on this basis. The party contested elections for the Northern Ireland Assembly (October 1982), for Westminster (June 1983), and for local councils (May 1985). The degree of success that was sustained (the party won 13.4% of the vote at the 1983 Westminster general election) was sufficient to encourage further political action and to unsettle the Thatcher government.

BRITISH STRATEGIES, 1972–1990

The British response to the insurgency of the 1970s and 1980s was seemingly inconsistent. In March 1972 Edward Heath's Tory government suspended the devolved government at Stormont and thereby ended more than 50 years of uninterrupted unionist executive power. In July 1972 the British minister responsible for Northern Ireland, William Whitelaw, met leaders of PIRA in an apparent effort to explore the possibilities of agreement. Later British ministers (notably Merlyn Rees, secretary of state from 1974 to 1976) nurtured a similar hope that both loyalist and republican paramilitaries might be brought into the constitutional process, and also (briefly) pursued conciliationist strategies.

But the main pattern of British policy involved periodic efforts to reach an agreement between the main constitutional parties in Northern Ireland, followed by exasperation and military offensives. The Sunningdale Agreement of December 1973 was struck between the Northern constitutional parties (excluding the Democratic Unionist Party) along with the British and Irish governments, and involved an effort to create a power-sharing devolved administration in Belfast that would be linked by strong cross-border authorities with the administration in Dublin. But the plan was overthrown by popular Protestant protest action in May 1974. The balance of political influence on the whole shifted in the unionists' favor after this debacle, but no internal settlement was forthcoming. The failure of a conciliationist initiative by Rees in 1974 to 1975 was followed by a hardline stand on security taken by his successor, Roy Mason.

In the early 1980s, mindful of this political failure and of the rising support for Sinn Féin, the British government sought to re-engage the Irish government, and effectively excluded the unionists from a lengthy negotiation that concluded in November 1985 with the signing of the Anglo-Irish Agreement. The Irish saw this document as a stepping stone to a form of joint authority within Northern Ireland, whereas the British (who were more divided in their counsels) appear to have viewed it as a means of inculpating the Irish in the problems of governing the North without granting them any formal authority. The British also fervently hoped that the agreement would improve cross-border security arrangements. Both governments believed that the agreement would help to bolster constitutional nationalism and subvert the electoral progress of Sinn Féin.

The Peace Process, 1990–1998

Judged by its own apparent goals, the agreement might well be interpreted as a failure, for it undermined constitutional unionist politics while pushing the Social Democratic and Labour Party (SDLP) toward a form of rapprochement with Sinn Féin. Indeed, it is arguable that future political progress stemmed not so much from the agreement's achievements as from initiatives that ran contrary to its underlying principles. The starting points for the negotiations that culminated in the Belfast Agreement of April 1998 were the dialogue between SDLP leader John Hume and Sinn Féin leader Gerry Adams and overtures toward Irish republicanism that were made by Peter Brooke (British secretary of state for Northern Ireland from 1989 to 1992) and continued for

a time under his successor, Patrick Mayhew (secretary of state from 1992 to 1997). Gerry Adams had cautiously hinted in 1987 that he would be prepared to consider a constitutional means of securing the end of the British presence in Ireland, and this was seized upon by John Hume as a means of opening up dialogue with the republican movement. Brooke had an independent line of communication with Adams, and he also publicly declared in November 1990 in a message directed toward republicans that the British had "no selfish or strategic interest" in Northern Ireland. This mild overture was complemented by the launching of a talks process in March 1991 involving the constitutional parties and framed within three "strands": the proposed political structures of Northern Ireland, cross-border institutions and relationships, and the British-Irish connection. These talks collapsed in July 1991, but they were resurrected under Mayhew between April and November 1992.

Neither this diplomacy nor the resumed dialogue between Hume and Adams (1992–1993) was immediately successful. But the British and Irish governments led by John Major and Albert Reynolds were anxious to seize the initiative from Hume-Adams, and on 15 December 1993 they published the "Downing Street Declaration," a joint statement of shared principles for any future settlement in the North. The declaration emphasized again the lack of any "selfish strategic or economic [British] interest" in Northern Ireland, highlighted the need for "full respect" for all traditions, and affirmed the principle of political consent in the North. It fell far short of republican ideals, but on the other hand, it appeared to provide an opportunity for republicans, who were threatened at this time by a ferocious loyalist assault on the nationalist population, to explore the potentialities of constitutional action. After some hesitation, therefore, the Provisionals declared a cease-fire on 31 August 1994. This decision was apparently rewarded when in February 1995 the two governments published the "Frameworks Documents," a paper that raised the possibility of cross-border bodies with "executive" functions and that hinted at the possibility of joint British-Irish authority within Northern Ireland.

The key difficulty in the "Peace Process" (at this stage and later) arose from the issue of paramilitary weapons. The British envisaged that Sinn Féin would be admitted to negotiations on the constitutional future of the North once they had decommissioned their arms. But republicans saw this as tantamount to surrender, and with the peace process apparently stalled, in February 1996 the Provisionals detonated a bomb in London that killed two people. By the early summer of 1997 there were changes of administration in London and

Dublin, with the demise of John Major and John Bruton, the Fine Gael taoiseach, both of whom were disliked by republicans. The return of a Labour government under Tony Blair and a Fianna Fáil-led coalition with Bertie Ahern as taoiseach, together with the earlier re-election of Bill Clinton to the U.S. presidency, all appeared to augur well for republican political fortunes. In these contexts the Provisionals called a second cease-fire on 20 July 1997. The British government by now had substantially retreated from its earlier line on decommissioning, and the restoration of the cease-fire was sufficient for Sinn Féin to be admitted in September 1997 to constitutional talks. These negotiations, chaired by Senator George Mitchell and including the two governments, the Ulster Unionists, the SDLP, and a range of smaller parties, eventually produced the Belfast Agreement on Good Friday, 10 April 1998.

THE BELFAST AGREEMENT OF 1998

The Belfast Agreement restored a devolved executive and legislative assembly to Northern Ireland after an absence of twenty-four years. But the new institutions were very different from the Stormont government and Parliament. The new Assembly was twice the size of the old House of Commons, the better to represent the political diversity of Northern Ireland, and it was elected through a proportional-representation franchise and multimember constituencies. The executive was also larger, with ministers drawn from all the major parties represented in the Assembly. In addition, there was to be a North-South Ministerial Council, which (it was intended) would "take decisions by agreement on policies and action at an all-island and cross-border level." A complementary British-Irish Council was designed to bring together ministers from all the devolved and sovereign governments in the archipelago. As part of a constitutional swap, the Irish undertook to amend Articles Two and Three of the Republic's 1937 Constitution (which unionists found offensive), and the British agreed to repeal the Government of Ireland Act of 1920, for long a focus of republican hatred. Provision was also made for a review of policing and criminal justice. And the decommissioning of paramilitary weapons was mooted, albeit in highly aspirational and ambiguous language.

It is impossible to judge with certainty the intentions of the Belfast Agreement's signatories. It is still arguable that the agreement marks a radical new departure in the political history of modern Ireland. Militant republicans silenced their weapons, at least temporarily, and entered a "partition legislature." For their part, unionists shared power with historic adversaries and were involved in the operation of cross-border political institutions. It will be for long unclear whether the Belfast Agreement represents a secure settlement of the historic divisions within Northern Ireland. While a deal on institutions is a major advance and may conceivably reflect some fundamental changes within Northern Irish politics, the effects of twenty-five years of peculiarly intimate violence may well linger. Indeed, it can scarcely be hoped that the deeply rooted traditions of sectarian animosity within Ireland can be put to rest by any single document, however bold and imaginative.

SEE ALSO Bloody Sunday; Economic Relations between North and South since 1922; Economic Relations between Northern Ireland and Britain; Northern Ireland: Constitutional Settlement from Sunningdale to Good Friday; Northern Ireland: Discrimination and the Campaign for Civil Rights; Northern Ireland: Policy of the Dublin Government from 1922 to 1969; Northern Ireland: The United States in Northern Ireland since 1970; Proportional Representation; **Primary Documents:** On "A Protestant Parliament and a Protestant State" (24 April 1934); On Community Relations in Northern Ireland (28 April 1967); "Ulster at the Crossroads" (9 December 1968); Statement by the Taoiseach (13 August 1969); Irish Republican Army (IRA) Cease-Fire Statement (31 August 1994); Text of the IRA Cease-Fire Statement (19 July 1997); The Belfast/Good Friday Agreement (10 April 1998)

Bibliography

Bew, Paul, Peter Gibbon, and Henry Patterson. *Northern Ireland, 1921–1994: Political Forces and Social Classes.* 1995.

Cox, Michael, Adrian Guelke, and Fiona Stephen. *A Farewell to Arms? From "Long War" to Long Peace in Northern Ireland.* 2000.

De Bréadún, Deaglán. *The Far Side of Revenge: Making Peace in Northern Ireland.* 2001.

Elliott, Marianne. *The Catholics of Ulster: A History.* 2000.

Harkness, David. *Northern Ireland since 1920.* 1983.

Hennessey, Thomas. *A History of Northern Ireland, 1920–1996.* 1997.

Hennessey, Thomas. *The Northern Ireland Peace Process: Ending the Troubles?* 2000.

Jackson, Alvin. *Ireland, 1798–1998: Politics and War.* 1999.

Mulholland, Marc. *Northern Ireland at the Crossroads: Ulster Unionism in the O'Neill Years, 1960–69.* 2000.

Phoenix, Éamon. *Northern Nationalism: Nationalist Politics, Partition, and the Catholic Minority in Northern Ireland, 1890–1940.* 1994.

Alvin Jackson

POLICY OF THE DUBLIN GOVERNMENT FROM 1922 TO 1969

The Sinn Féin leaders who persuaded the British government to concede the 1921 Anglo-Irish Treaty were aware of the complexity of the Ulster question. They admitted that the northeast needed a custom-made solution and were willing to concede some form of local autonomy, provided that it was devolved from Dublin and not London. This was provided for in the Treaty but was undermined by another provision which granted the recently established Northern Ireland government the right to secede from the Irish Free State. This secession was inevitable, but it obliged northern leaders to accede to the findings of the Irish Boundary Commission which would revise the border between Northern Ireland and the Irish Free State.

Southern leaders remained publicly optimistic that the commission would so delimit Northern Ireland that it would prove unviable and that the logic of geography would deliver Irish unity. As it happened, the Irish Boundary Commission proposed only marginal changes to the border and—heresy to southern politicians—recommended the ceding of some territory to Northern Ireland. This threatened the very stability of the Free State, and a hastily convened Anglo-Irish summit resulted in the scrapping of the Irish Boundary Commission, the acceptance of the existing border, and the waiving by Britain of the Free State's contribution to the British national debt.

When W. T. Cosgrave described this as "a damned good bargain" it did not endear him to nationalists within Northern Ireland who felt betrayed by the Dublin government's acceptance of partition. This outcome encouraged those Irish nationalists most opposed to partition to vest their hopes in Eamon de Valera. He was a more pragmatic politician than his reputation had suggested, and in no way did he demonstrate his pragmatism more than in the manner in which he took ownership of the antipartition strategy during his decades of political ascendancy in the southern state. Having founded Fianna Fáil as the vehicle for his political rewriting of the Treaty settlement, de Valera repetitively lectured Irish republicans on how force would prove counterproductive in attempting to win Irish unity. He maintained that the issue was one for resolution between Dublin and London, and that it would only be resolved "in the larger general play of English interests."

While never missing a diplomatic or propagandistic opportunity to rail against the injustice of partition, de Valera remained vigilant in ensuring that the grievance did not destabilize the southern state. Vulnerable to the republican jibe that he had settled for leadership of a partitioned state—"three-quarters of a nation once again"—and under pressure to declare a united Ireland in his new constitution in 1937, his solution typified his genius for casuistry: Article 2 claimed for the nation jurisdiction over the entire island of Ireland; Article 3 accepted that de facto the laws of the state could only be exercised in the twenty-six counties "pending the reintegration of the national territory."

De Valera smuggled the partition issue into the Anglo-Irish talks of 1938 to the surprise of the British. Both he and Neville Chamberlain spoke at length about it, but these were not negotiations, merely the reiteration of what were by then the very well known views of both sides. When invited by the British to concede some trading preferences to Northern Ireland, de Valera declined, thereby underlining his disinclination to ever engage with the Ulster Unionists. During World War II, de Valera's Fianna Fáil government established and maintained Irish neutrality, eschewing a number of overtures by the British to join the Allies in return for some prospect of Irish unity. Although much has been made of these British kites, the small print invariably revealed that Churchill considered Ulster's acquiescence to be essential.

De Valera's policy of neutrality united all elements in the state; any other policy would probably have led to civil war, with the greatest threat to stability coming from the Irish Republican Army (IRA), which was actively encouraging Hitler to intervene in Ireland. Paradoxically, although it was often criticized by unionist and British sources, de Valera's policy was best suited to the interests of the Allies: thousands of volunteers joined the British forces; Irish emigrant labor and agricultural exports proved vital to Britain's war effort; and, strategically, de Valera's contribution to keeping the South as a demilitarized zone concided with the interests of the Allied war effort. Ironically, this in turn was facilitated by the presence in Northern Ireland of British and, later, U.S. troops. Partition facilitated Irish neutrality, itself the most solemn proof of sovereignty since the Treaty settlement.

The experience of the war consolidated partition, winning the Ulster Unionists new friends in London. Meanwhile, de Valera's lack of progress on Irish unity left his party electorally vulnerable to a new socialist and republican party, Clann naPoblachta, led by Seán MacBride. Winning only ten seats in the 1948 election, it joined an all-party government united on only one policy: to remove de Valera after sixteen years in power. MacBride, as foreign minister, developed what became known as "the sore thumb" approach to partition, instructing all Irish diplomats to engage in a propaganda onslaught on the issue. In a world recovering from the

Eamon de Valera (center) and Frank Aiken (far left) in Hawaii, April 1948. They were on a 'round-the-world tour to publicize the case against the partition of Ireland. PHOTOGRAPH FROM THE DE VALERA PAPERS, ARCHIVES DEPARTMENT, UNIVERSITY COLLEGE DUBLIN. REPRODUCED BY PERMISSION.

most catastrophic war in history, this proved futile. It did prompt de Valera to compete to be the best antipartitionist. This competition probably led to the controversial decision of the interparty government to break even those tenuous ties with the British Commonwealth that de Valera had maintained in the hope that they would prove a "bridge" to the Ulster Unionists.

Thus, what had been the Irish Free State from 1922 to 1937, and had been named Éire under de Valera's constitution, became from 1949 the Republic of Ireland. The British retaliated with the Ireland Act of 1949, which proved the most serious setback to the South's antipartition strategy. Whereas London had hitherto refused to consider Irish unity by citing Ulster's veto, under this act it granted custody of the veto to the Northern Ireland parliament. This precipitated an even shriller antipartition campaign, which arguably led to

a resurgence of the IRA and to the opening of a sporadic campaign of force against Northern Ireland in 1956. This proved futile and was opposed most successfully by Fianna Fáil, which had the self-confidence—as an avowed republican party itself—to end this campaign by introducing internment in the South.

De Valera retired from party politics to the largely ceremonial office of the president in 1959. His successor, Seán Lemass, had always shown a greater interest in pragmatic cooperation between North and South on issues of energy, transport, fisheries, and trade. Such cooperation had already yielded mutually beneficial outcomes since partition, but this had been delivered by civil servants who had left the cold war rhetoric to their political masters. Lemass saw partition not as an issue which London must undo, but rather as a matter which could be ameliorated only by better cooperation between North and South. To this end, in 1965 he made the historic journey to Stormont as a gesture of mutual friendship with the Northern Ireland prime minister, Captain Terence O'Neill.

Encouraged by an outstanding civil servant, T. K. Whitaker, secretary of finance, Lemass and his successor, Jack Lynch, pursued a constructive policy of North-South rapprochement whose potential can only be guessed at because it was overtaken by the rise of the civil rights movement and the failure—or inability—of the Ulster Unionists to accommodate its demands, which in turn led to the outbreak of the "Troubles" in the summer of 1969.

All governments in Dublin from the Treaty settlement and the North-South thaw of the 1960s had vehemently denounced partition, but they had also entrenched it. Their policies on the Irish language, on church-state relations, and on neutrality were all inimical to the very goal of Irish unity which they constantly espoused. Moreover, Dublin was expected to champion the complaints of northern nationalists, of which there was no shortage—many of them justified. But if Northern Ireland's first prime minister, Sir James Craig, could be mocked for calling Stormont "a Protestant parliament for a Protestant people," did not the southern state in its first half-century after independence come too close to fashioning "a Catholic state for a Catholic people"?

SEE ALSO Constitution; Declaration of a Republic and the 1949 Ireland Act; Northern Ireland: History since 1920; Politics: Nationalist Politics in Northern Ireland; **Primary Documents:** On Community Relations in Northern Ireland (28 April 1967); Statement by the Taoiseach (13 August 1969); "Towards Changes in the Republic" (1973)

Bibliography

Bowman, John. *De Valera and the Ulster Question, 1917–1973.* 1982.

Kennedy, Michael. *Division and Consensus: The Politics of Cross-Border Relations in Ireland, 1925–1969.* 2000.

O'Halloran, Clare. *Partition and the Limits of Irish Nationalism.* 1985.

John Bowman

THE UNITED STATES IN NORTHERN IRELAND SINCE 1970

Toward the end of the nineteenth century there was evidence of a "second front" in the United States in the British-Irish conflict—Fenian raids in Canada in 1866 and 1870 and a succession of "Irish race conventions." It was given greater credence during World War I when the "Irish Question" was transformed from an essentially domestic problem into one occupying the international stage; until December 1921 the Irish Question plagued Anglo-American relations. But there is little evidence that subsequently the conflict had any real impact on U.S. domestic or foreign policy. The reasons are simple: The United States and United Kingdom enjoyed a "special relationship" based on similar interests and ideologies, and secondly, Ireland's tradition of neutrality antagonized successive U.S. administrations, an attitude made clear by National Security Council (NSC) statements in 1950 and 1960. Indeed, a rare antipartition resolution that had made its way into the U.S. House of Representatives was decisively defeated in September 1951.

Following civil unrest in Northern Ireland in 1968, the situation began to change as Irish America became united in its sense of moral outrage. In June 1969 Representatives Tip O'Neill and Philip Burton obtained 100 signatures appealing to President Richard Nixon complaining about "discrimination against Catholics." By October 1971 Senator Edward Kennedy was calling for British withdrawal, and a month after Bloody Sunday there was a three-day public hearing of the House Foreign Affairs Subcommittee on Europe. None of this dented the administration's insistence that although what was happening in Northern Ireland was a tragedy, it was a matter internal to the United Kingdom.

After that, Irish America ceased to speak with one voice. As in Ireland, a split occurred between the physical-force and the constitutional wings. First came the Irish Northern Aid Committee (NORAID), founded in 1970 by a former member of the Irish Republican Army (IRA). Its stated aim was to raise funds for prisoners' families, but the authorities considered it to be an IRA front and forced it in 1984 to register with the attorney general as an agent of the IRA. Such was the concern about NORAID's activities that in a private meeting with President Ronald Reagan at a G7 summit in July 1981, Prime Minister Margaret Thatcher "thank[ed] him warmly for his tough stand against Irish terrorism and its NORAID supporters." The Irish National Caucus (INC) and the (Congressional) Ad Hoc Committee on Irish Affairs shared NORAID's declared goals but were concerned about its image. The INC, founded in 1974, was endorsed by thirty different Irish-American groups to lobby the U.S. government from a militant nationalist perspective. The Ad Hoc group, founded in 1977, sought to revise existing State Department policies. Both were opposed by the Irish government, Irish constitutional nationalists, and the "Four Horsemen"—Senators Kennedy and Daniel Patrick Moynihan, Speaker of the House Tip O'Neill, and New York Governor Hugh Carey. The Horsemen were influenced by the fundamental opposition of John Hume, leader of the Social Democratic and Labour Party (SDLP), to the IRA campaign, a fact reflected in their Saint Patrick's Day statement in 1977 and subsequently. In 1981 the Horsemen, anxious to counter the Ad Hoc group and conscious that the Republican Party controlled the White House, metamorphosed into the bipartisan Friends of Ireland.

The Irish-American split indicated weakness in Congress during the 1970s. In retrospect, the high point was President Jimmy Carter's statement in August 1977 in which he condemned violence, expressed support for a peaceful solution that would involve the Irish government, and promised U.S. investment in the event of such a settlement. Northern Ireland was now considered a legitimate concern of U.S. foreign policy. In addition, the president raised human rights and discrimination issues that were exploited by the lobbyists in the coming years. Finally, the sentiments were similar to those written into the preamble of the Anglo-Irish Agreement in November 1985. Intensive lobbying began to pay off during the Reagan presidency. Although Reagan and Mrs. Thatcher were committed to defeating the "international network of terrorism," the president needed the Speaker's support in Congress; in addition, he was influenced by his close friend William P. Clark, a member of his administration and a supporter of Irish unity. On the one hand, Reagan resisted Irish requests to intervene in the hunger strikes of 1980 and 1981 and in the deliberations of constitutional nationalism's New Ireland Forum (1984); on the other, he gave total support to the Anglo-Irish Agreement of November 1985.

The agreement created, inter alia, the International Fund for Ireland (IFI), a U.S.-sponsored investment program for Northern Ireland and the border counties of the Republic. But the IFI was not accepted by Congress until 17 July 1986, the same day that a Supplementary Extradition Treaty that enabled the United States to extradite certain IRA suspects back to the United Kingdom was signed. The linking of these measures illustrated the gap between Irish America and the administration. The Bush administration simply kept a watching brief. Nevertheless, Irish America had entered a convergence phase. In a bid to secure more visas for Irish emigrants, Irish America had entered into coalitions with other ethnic groups. Coalition-building, even among Irish Americans, became attractive, especially because the SDLP and Sinn Féin began discussions in 1988 and continued them during the Hume-Adams talks after 1990. When

Bill Clinton won the U.S. presidential election in 1992, Irish America was in a position to speak with one voice.

The appointment of Jean Kennedy Smith as Ireland's U.S. ambassador heralded a more interventionist period. By granting Gerry Adams a two-day visa in January 1994, Clinton enunciated a radical sea change in U.S. involvement in British-Irish relations. The British government, along with the U.S. State and Justice Departments, was furious—the president appeared to be "soft on terrorism." Granting the visa was a calculated and personal risk for Clinton, but he listened carefully to Irish Americans close to (Irish) republican thinking, to the Kennedys, to the Irish government and John Hume, and to trusted NSC staffers. All were satisfied that the IRA was serious about peace. The Adams visa unlocked the door: The president then tied the IRA more into the peace process through further visas, he sponsored a White House Conference on Trade and Investment in Northern Ireland, and he appointed former senator George Mitchell as his special adviser on economic initiatives in Ireland in February 1995. Mitchell's role changed dramatically when the British secretary of state introduced the decommissioning issue in Washington in March and the peace process went into crisis. To expedite matters the president visited Britain and Ireland in November 1995. This led to a hastily summoned British-Irish summit that attempted to make parallel progress on decommissioning and all (Northern Ireland) party negotiations. George Mitchell was empowered to chair an international decommisioning panel that reported on 22 January 1996. But it was not enough to save the peace—the Provisional IRA detonated a bomb in London's Canary Wharf on 9 February, killing two people.

Despite this setback, Clinton persisted. George Mitchell was reinvented as chair of multiparty talks in Northern Ireland in June 1996. Over the next two years Mitchell displayed tremendous patience and diplomacy. Sinn Féin entered the process in September 1997 only after the IRA announced a "complete cessation of military operations" in July. They recognized that with Prime Minister Tony Blair's decisive May 1997 general election victory, they could commit themselves wholeheartedly to the search for peace. Blair and Clinton set a one-year deadline for the multiparty talks. Mitchell was more specific when, on 25 March 1998, he set 9 April as the date for agreement between the parties. Agreement was reached on 10 April after Clinton worked the phones assiduously, persuading the parties to sign on. "The Agreement Reached in Multiparty Negotiations" was a triumph for Anglo-Irish, Anglo-American, and Irish-American diplomacy. It demonstrated the huge influence of the Clinton administration and the president's own tenacity and vision, and it also showed the huge leap that the Anglo-American special relationship had taken.

SEE ALSO Adams, Gerry; Anglo-Irish Agreement of 1985 (Hillsborough Agreement); Decommissioning; Hume, John; Northern Ireland: Constitutional Settlement from Sunningdale to Good Friday; Northern Ireland: History since 1920; Trimble, David; **Primary Documents:** Anglo-Irish Agreement (15 November 1985); The Belfast/Good Friday Agreement (10 April 1998)

Bibliography

Arthur, Paul. "Diasporan Intervention in International Affairs: Irish America as a Case Study." *Diaspora: A Journal of Transnational Studies* 1, no. 2 (fall 1991): 143–162.

Arthur, Paul. *Special Relationships: Britain, Ireland, and the Northern Ireland Problem.* 2001.

Mitchell, George J. *Making Peace.* 1999.

Wilson, Andrew J. *Irish America and the Ulster Conflict, 1968–1995.* 1995.

Paul Arthur

Oakboys and Steelboys

The agrarian violence committed by the Oakboys and the Steelboys was confined to Ulster and had sharply defined lifespans in the 1760s and early 1770s. The Hearts of Oak or Oakboys emerged in the summer of 1763, their insurrection lasting little over a month. Then in July 1769 the Hearts of Steel appeared, and this outbreak lasted, with ebbs and flows, until 1772. The causes for the two movements were different, as were the geographical areas in which they appeared and, on many occasions, the methods employed.

The spark for the Oakboys appears to have been the levels of cess, or county taxation, in Armagh and the efforts made by collectors to enforce their will on a barony in the north of the county. Violence was reported by 3 July 1763, with the news that large gatherings of people in the baronies of O'Neilland (the northern part of County Armagh) were forcing local landlords to swear that they would not collect or issue presentments to the county grand jury for more than one penny per acre in cess. These gatherings quickly spread in the following days to the surrounding county of Tyrone because of the surprising ease with which the local gentry capitulated to their demands. By that time the demands had broadened to incorporate the lowering of tithes and the abolition of "small dues" collected by the Church of Ireland clergy for funerals, weddings, and other ceremonies that they never performed. Emboldened by success, the Oakboy bands of Armagh and Tyrone sent what could be called agents to mobilize crowds throughout south Ulster and also to make a drive for Derry city, a move that was to cause the ultimate collapse of the movement.

The Steelboys, too, had specific beginnings that eventually grew into a wider agrarian rebellion, this time over a much longer period. Their origins lay in the reorganization of the huge Donegall and smaller Upton estates in County Antrim where leases were granted to middlemen. Many of these men, like Thomas Greg, were Belfast merchants and already tenants of Lord Donegall, who were pressed to find money for the large entry fines being charged. Upton's lands were released in July 1769, sparking the first outbreak, and the Donegall lands followed suit in June 1770. By that summer many of the undertenants on the Donegall estate were engaged in desperate resistance, fearing dispossession. This struggle peaked in December 1770, when a band of Steelboys entered Belfast, burned the house of Waddell Cunningham (a middleman and active magistrate), and freed one of their leaders, David Douglas, from the barracks. County Antrim was soon afterward overwhelmed with troops, and the trouble spread to the counties of Down, Armagh, and Derry in the winter and spring of 1771 to 1772. This was far from the original area of disturbance and the agrarian rioters in these areas may have used the Steelboy name to cover demands concerning cess, rents, and tithes. Another factor was the poor harvests of 1770 and 1771, which led to high prices and economic hardship. After substantial Steelboy mobilizations and a clash in Gilford, Co. Down, where a Presbyterian minister was killed, army reinforcements were sent north in March 1772 and brought a rapid end to the disturbances. The Oakboy and Steelboy organizations shared continuity in tactics and mobilization, but there were differences as well. The Oakboys organized daylight gatherings with large crowds (perhaps in the thousands), which only happened again in 1771 to 1772, when the Steelboy disturbances spread beyond County Antrim. In 1763 and 1771 to 1772, entire townlands and villages were sworn in at nominated times and places. Both movements saw violence against property and persons, but the second movement saw a greater concentration on nocturnal attacks (including burning of buildings, anonymous letters, shooting at houses, and maiming of farm animals) more reminiscent of the Munster agrarian troubles. The Oakboys also used a Munster tactic, portable gallows, to intimidate their targets. As to internal organization, there appears to have been some coordination of activity, such as the sending of agents, marches, and the raid on Belfast in December 1770, but no cell structures like later Ulster movements. Localized groups—some in west Down with their own distinctive names like Hearts of Gold or Flint—may have acted as a precursor for the later "fleets" of the Armagh troubles in the 1780s.

The Ulster agrarian movements were dominated by Protestants, possibly Presbyterians. The Protestant "tone" is most clearly seen in the propaganda, like Oakboy ballads and Steelboy newspaper statements. These purported to be the products of the Dissenters and, in many cases the indicted or tried leaders may have been Presbyterians. Indeed, in County Monaghan in 1763, leadership seems to have passed down to local Seceders, who espoused a rigid brand of Presbyterianism. However, there can be no doubt of Catholic involvement in both movements, particularly the Oakboys. Some of the areas involved and the evidence of a poem by Art McCooey, praising one of the O'Neills of the Fews (south Armagh) for leading an Oakboy band, suggest Catholic input. In both uprisings there seems little evidence in indictments or trials of "Gentlemen Oakboys," suggesting that the movements were led by tenant farmers and linen weavers. Tradesmen and craftsmen played minor roles, suggesting that rural towns, like Lurgan or Hillsborough, also gave support to the movements.

The effectiveness of the Oakboys and Steelboys is a difficult question. On the one hand, the response of the government was hardly an overreaction to the violence. There was just enough repression to curb the threat of the agrarian movements, and in the case of the Oakboys this was sharp enough in 1763 to prevent any recurrence in the following year. The problem after 1769 was that the Steelboys did not cease their activities, and few of their leaders were convicted at the assizes. By 1771 to 1772, the government was using a combination of methods, such as amnesty, alongside proclamations naming fifty-eight Steelboys, and a statute allowing trials of indicted rioters outside their county of residence. This extended and deeper repression hints at the greater effectiveness of the Steelboys. On the other hand, the collection of cess, rents, and fines recovered after both outbreaks had ceased. The apparently less successful Oakboys, however, managed to prevent cess collection in north Armagh between 1763 and 1770. Another mixed sign is that reforms were made to the way in which county grand juries raised the cess, though this did not automatically lead to lower levels or a fairer use of the tax.

The legacy of the Oakboys and Steelboys was probably much less prosaic than matters of rents or taxes. What these movements did was to damage the easy, complacent picture of Ulster held by those living in Dublin or London. The province had been seen, with some local exceptions, as generally peaceful and industrious, almost in spite of Presbyterian numbers there. After 1772, attitudes changed, and the expectation of quiescence was gradually replaced by one of suspicion of the motives of Ulster Protestants, first during the American War of Independence and later during the French Revolution. The Oakboys and Steelboys were not simple preradical movements, as some members were among the supporters of "Church and King" politics in Armagh and elsewhere in the 1780s and 1790s; they were early signs of independence and unrest in Ulster.

SEE ALSO Defenderism; Irish Tithe Act of 1838; Land Questions; Tenant Right, or Ulster Custom; Tithe War (1830–1838); Whiteboys and Whiteboyism

Bibliography

Bigger, Francis J. *The Ulster Land War of 1770.* 1910.

Donnelly, James S., Jr. "Hearts of Oak, Hearts of Steel." *Studia Hibernica* 21 (1981): 7–73.

Magennis, Eoin F. "A 'Presbyterian Insurrection': Reconsidering the Hearts of Oak disturbances of July 1763." *Irish Historical Studies* 31 (1998): 165–187.

Maguire, William A. "Lord Donegall and the Hearts of Steel." *Irish Historical Studies* 21 (1979): 351–376.

Eoin Magennis

O'Brien, William

Trade union leader William O'Brien (1881–1968) was born at Ballygurteen, Clonakilty, Co. Cork, youngest son of a Royal Irish Constabulary (RIC) officer. He grew up mainly in Dublin and was apprenticed to the tailoring trade at age fourteen. He developed an early interest in socialism under the influence of his older brothers, and in 1904 became chairman of the Amalgamated Society of Tailors and a leading advocate of "new unionism" in Ireland. An ally of James Larkin, he played an important role in the 1913 lockout when he was president of the Irish Trade Union Congress and secretary of the Dublin Trades Council. A clubfoot prevented O'Brien from becoming involved in the Easter Rising, but he was designated by James Connolly to establish a civilian committee to administer Dublin on behalf of the provisional government. On his release from internment after Rising, he threw himself into rebuilding the labor movement. He has been criticized by many historians and leftwing commentators for making trade union reorganization his priority within the movement and relegating political activity to a secondary role. He also supported the decision to give Sinn Féin a clear run against the Irish Parliamentary Party in the 1918 election rather than risk splitting the radical nationalist vote by running labor candidates.

O'Brien formally joined the Irish Transport and General Workers' Union (ITGWU) in 1917 and became its general treasurer in 1919. Despite his leftist rhetoric, O'Brien's main aim was not to wage revolution, but a strong organization to mediate on behalf of workers. When James Larkin returned from the United States in 1923, O'Brien successfully opposed Larkin's attempt to revive the revolutionary syndicalist policies of 1913. He succeeded Larkin as general secretary of the ITGWU in 1924 and held the post until his retirement in 1946. He served as a Labor TD (Member of Parliament) to the Dail in 1922-3, 1927 and 1937-8, but the ITGWU was his main power base. He used it to create the National Labour Party and the Congress of Irish Unions after Larkin was elected to the Dáil as a Labour deputy in 1943.

The decision to form a new party and trade union congress was not based on ideological disagreements within the labor movement but on fear of the growing influence of Larkin and his son James Larkin Jr., who was also elected to the Dail in 1943. To justify the split in the labor movement and generate support, the new Congress and National Labour Party played on the anti-communist mood of the early cold war period. Both constantly stressed their attachment to the values of the Catholic Church and emphasized their patriotism by attacking left-wing and British-based unions. It was an ironic end to the career of one of the pioneers of the modern Irish labor movement. O'Brien devoted his last years to writing and research. His papers, which were donated to the National Library of Ireland, are a major source of primary material for the history of the labor movement.

SEE ALSO Connolly, James; Labor Movement; Larkin, James; Lockout of 1913; Markievicz, Countess Constance; Murphy, William Martin

Bibliography

O'Brien, William. *Forth the Banners Go: Reminiscences of William O'Brien as Told to Edward MacLysaght D. Litt.* 1969.

O'Brien, William. Papers. National Library of Ireland, Dublin.

O'Connor Lysaght, D. R. "The Rake's Progress of a Syndicalist: The Political Career of William O'Brien, Irish Labour Leader." *Saothar* 9 (1983): 48–63.

Padraig Yeates

O'Carolan, Turlough

See Carolan, Turlough.

O'Connell, Daniel

A lawyer and politician who earned the moniker "the Great Liberator" for his efforts to secure full civil rights for Catholics, Daniel O'Connell (1775–1847) was born near Cahirciveen, Co. Kerry, on 6 August 1775. O'Connell belonged to a locally prominent Catholic landowning family and was adopted as heir by his wealthy uncle at an early age. Called to the Irish bar in 1798, he quickly established a very successful legal practice.

O'Connell became a national figure well before he founded the Catholic Association in 1823. Ably organized at the grassroots level by clergymen and others and led at the national level by the charismatic O'Connell, the Association is often regarded as the first European populist political movement. Assembling his supporters at huge meetings, O'Connell deployed thunderous oratory and militaristic language to intimidate the British government into granting Catholic Emancipation. After O'Connell was handily elected as MP for County Clare in June 1828, the government relented and the Emancipation Act was signed in April 1829.

Once in Parliament, O'Connell supported a number of radical causes, such as the secret ballot and separation

The most successful Catholic barrister of the early nineteenth century, Daniel O'Connell (1775–1847) led two mass political campaigns that transformed Irish politics and unsettled Anglo-Irish relations—the successful struggle for Catholic emancipation in the 1820s and the failed movement for repeal of the Act of Union in the 1840s. His challenge to the Protestant Ascendancy also included a term as mayor of Dublin in 1841–1842. Here he appears in his mayoral regalia, as painted by William Henry Holbrooke. NATIONAL GALLERY OF IRELAND, CAT. NO. 10 983. REPRODUCED BY PERMISSION.

empire. In October 1843 Peel called O'Connell's bluff by prohibiting a meeting announced for Clontarf outside Dublin. O'Connell backed down and cancelled the meeting rather than risk bloodshed, signaling the end of repeal as a credible political movement.

Heartbroken by his inability to secure more aid for famine-struck Ireland and in rapidly failing health, O'Connell set out several years later on a pilgrimage to Rome but died on the way at Genoa on 15 May 1847. Despite his failure to repeal the union, the Liberator is generally regarded as one of the most influential and certainly the most popular politician in modern Irish history.

SEE ALSO Catholic Emancipation Campaign; Davis, Thomas; Mitchel, John; Newspapers; Repeal Movement; Veto Controversy; Young Ireland and the Irish Confederation; **Primary Documents:** Origin of the "Catholic Rent" (18 February 1824); The Catholic Relief Act (1829); On Repeal of the Act of Union at the "Monster Meeting" at Mullingar (14 May 1843)

Bibliography

MacDonagh, Oliver. *The Hereditary Bondsman: Daniel O'Connell, 1775–1829.* 1988.

MacDonagh, Oliver. *The Emancipist: Daniel O'Connell, 1830–47.* 1989.

Nowlan, Kevin. B. *The Politics of Repeal: A Study in the Relations between Great Britain and Ireland, 1841–50.* 1965.

O'Connell, Maurice. *Daniel O'Connell: The Man and His Politics.* 1990.

Michael W. de Nie

of church and state. He also worked toward his second great political goal: repeal of the Act of Union of 1800. Finding Parliament firmly opposed to repeal, O'Connell pursued lesser concessions through an informal political alliance with the Whig party between 1835 and 1841. The fruits of this alliance included an overhaul of local government machinery in Ireland, which provided a large number of administrative and political posts for Catholics. Some of O'Connell's followers benefited greatly from this alliance, but others remained deeply dissatisfied. After the Conservative Party under Robert Peel regained control of Parliament in 1841, O'Connell decided to renew his campaign for repeal. Once again O'Connell combined a widespread popular organization, the Repeal Association, with numerous large public meetings at which he used fiery language and thinly veiled threats to pressure the government. This time the government was not willing to yield for fear that repeal of the union would lead to the dissolution of the British

O'Connors of Connacht

The O'Connors were one of the royal families of medieval Ireland that ruled Síl Muiredaig, roughly the modern county of Roscommon, in the province of Connacht in the northwest of Ireland. The family produced several high kings (most powerful kings) of Ireland in the twelfth century, and was originally descended from Conchobair, king of Connacht, who died in 973. Conchobair was of the line of the Uí Bruín Aí who originally controlled central Roscommon. By the eleventh century the O'Connors had successfully subdued the other major families of Connacht, notably the O'Flahertys, the O'Rourkes, and the Uí Bruín Bréifni. Contemporaneously, successive O'Connor kings also tried to rid themselves of the overlordship of the O'Brien high kings. This conflict was temporarily resolved when Turloch Mór O'Connor, with the active support of his maternal uncle, the high king Muirchertach O'Brien, was inaugurated as king over the Síl Muiredaig in 1106. Because of his powerful position he soon became provincial king of the whole of Connacht, and in about 1120 he replaced the O'Briens as high king with opposition.

Later in his reign, around 1150, he had to defer to the northern high king, Muirchertach Mac Lochlainn. But on Muirchertach's death in 1166, Turloch's son, Rory, who had succeeded him on his death in 1156, took control of the whole of Ireland. As high king, he presided over two national assemblies in 1167 and 1168, and on the advice of Ua Ruairc of Bréifne he also banished Dermot MacMurrough, king of Leinster, who fled to England to gain the support of King Henry II in his attempt to recover Leinster. This caused the Anglo-Norman invasion of Ireland after Dermot brought foreign troops back with him in 1167 and again in 1169. For more than two years Rory, with the support of his Norse allies, fought the army of Strongbow, who had landed in Ireland with at least two hundred knights in 1170. However, in 1171, Henry, worried by the success of his nobles in Ireland, came over to Ireland to stamp his authority on the island. At the Treaty of Windsor (1175) Rory submitted to Henry, who in return agreed to maintain Rory as king of Connacht and high king of Ireland over those parts of northern and western Ireland that had not yet been taken over by the Anglo-Normans. On Rory's death in 1198 his brother Cathal Crobderg O'Connor was able to hold all of Connacht by a royal charter, and he also maintained good relations with the Dublin government of the English Crown.

SEE ALSO Dál Cais and Brian Boru; Uí Néill High Kings

Bibliography

Byrne, F. J. *Irish Kings and High-Kings.* 2d edition, 2001.

Orpen, G. H. *Ireland under the Normans.* 4 vols. 1911–1920.

Simms, K. *From Kings to Warlords.* 2000.

Terry Barry

~

O'Conor, Charles, of Balenagare

Historian, pamphleteer, and cofounder of the Catholic Committee, Charles O'Conor's (1710–1791) lifelong commitment to the Irish language, Irish history, and the Catholic religion derived from his belief that, in the absence of an independent nation, this was the means to sustain Irish culture and identity. Imbued with this conviction by the Gaelic-speaking priests who were responsible for his early education, and by the members of the famous Ó Neachtain circle with whom he came into contact while attending Father Walter Skelton's academy in Dublin in 1727 to 1728, he commenced a lifelong practice of copying manuscripts. Following his return to Belanagare, Co. Roscommon, where he spent most of his life, O'Conor devoted his energies largely to scholarship.

He entered the realm of public controversy in 1749 with the first of a sequence of pamphlets promoting greater toleration of Irish Catholics, notably his *Seasonable Thoughts Relating to Our Civil and Ecclesiastical Constitution* (1751, 1754), which proffered an oath of allegiance that Catholics might take. His historical works included *Dissertations on the History of Ireland* (1753, 1766), which argued that preconquest Ireland was a land of industry, piety, and learning. He encouraged other writers, such as Ferdinando Warner, Thomas Leland, and especially John Curry, who, together with O'Conor and Thomas Wyse, founded the Catholic Committee in 1756 in order to elicit the repeal of the penal laws. O'Conor's literary efforts, and his belief in the efficacy of affirming that Catholics no longer posed a threat to the security of the Protestant succession, assisted the committee in gaining the repeal of most of the penal laws appertaining to land and religion during the 1770s and early 1780s. O'Conor was elected to the Select Committee for Antiquities of the Dublin Society and to membership of the Royal Irish Academy. His scholarship and the moderation with which he pursued the cause of Catholic rights brought him a measure of respect from all ranks of Irish society.

SEE ALSO Catholic Committee from 1756 to 1809; Eighteenth-Century Politics: 1714 to 1778—Interest Politics; Penal Laws

Bibliography

Coogan, Catherine, and Robert E. Ward. *The Letters of Charles O'Conor of Belanagare.* 2 vols. 1980.

Leighton, Cador D. A. *Catholicism in a Protestant Kingdom: A Study of the Irish Ancien Régime.* 1994.

Love, Walter D. "Charles O'Conor of Belanagare and Thomas Leland's 'Philosophical' *History of Ireland.*" *Irish Historical Studies* 13 (1962): 1–25.

James Kelly

∽

O'Donovan, John

John O'Donovan (1806–1861), historian and topographer, was born at Atateemore in the Irish-speaking Slieverue district of south Kilkenny in July 1806. By the time that he reached late middle age, he had become one of the most prominent interpreters of ancient Irish language, literature, and history.

After moving to Dublin in 1823, he attended until 1827 a Latin school on Arran Quay—Saint Patrick's Seminary. In 1828, James Hardiman employed him to transcribe Irish and Anglo-Norman manuscripts; in that year he gave some lessons in Irish to Thomas Larcom of the Ordnance Survey, which had been established in 1824 to map the country. From the autumn of 1830 he was employed by the Ordnance Survey to determine the most appropriate English spellings of the names to be engraved on the Ordnance Survey maps; for this purpose he made extracts from topographical ancient manuscripts in the Royal Irish Academy and Trinity College and other early sources. In 1831 he met George Petrie, later head of the place-names and antiquities section of the Ordnance Survey, where Eugene O'Curry and his brother Anthony, James Clarence Mangan, Thomas O'Conor, and Patrick O'Keeffe later worked. Through Petrie's influence O'Donovan was able to publish his first articles in 1832 and 1833 in the *Dublin Penny Journal*, beginning with a translation of an eleventh-century poem ascribed to Alfred, king of Northumbria, who had been a student in Ireland in the seventh century. In these articles he demonstrated his ability to read and translate early medieval Irish and Latin texts. In March 1834, O'Donovan began field-work in County Down, meeting informants face-to-face to hear the local pronunciation of the names and ascertain their derivation form the Irish language, and writing regular reports to Larcom in Dublin. These reports later became known as the *Ordnance Survey Letters*. They exist for twenty-nine of the thirty-two counties of Ireland, the exceptions being Antrim, Tyrone, and Cork. He collected the place-names from Anglo-

Norman and other late medieval sources, and from maps such as William Petty's seventeenth-century Down Survey. On the basis of these and the pronunciations he heard in the field, he chose or adapted anglicised spellings for the names that would appear on the maps.

When in 1842 the place-names and antiquities department of the Survey was closed, O'Donovan began to publish editions of early Irish texts for the Irish Archaeological Society and the Celtic Society with translations (see the list in Boyne 1987, pp. 136–139). His *Grammar of the Irish Language* appeared in 1845, and the first part of his magisterial edition of the *Annals of the Four Masters (Annála Ríoghachta Éireann)* was published in 1848. He was elected a member of the Royal Irish Academy in 1847, he was awarded their prestigious Cunningham Medal in 1848. In August 1849 he was appointed professor of the Irish language at Queen's University, Belfast. Trinity College conferred on him an honorary Ll.D. in 1850, and in 1856 Jakob Grimm initiated his election to membership of the Royal Prussian Academy of Sciences. O'Donovan died in Dublin on 9 December 1861 and was buried in Glasnevin cemetery, leaving his widow and five boys in poor circumstances.

SEE ALSO *Annals of the Four Masters*; Antiquarianism; Literature: Gaelic Literature in the Nineteenth Century; Ordnance Survey

Bibliography

Andrews, John H. *A Paper Landscape.* 1975.

Boyne, Patricia. *John O'Donovan (1806–61): A Biography.* 1987.

De Valera, Ruaidhrí. "Seán Ó Donnabháin agus a Lucht Cúnta." *Journal of the Royal Society of Antiquaries of Ireland* 79 (1949): 146–159.

Herity, Michael. "John O'Donovan's Early Life and Education." In *Ordnance Survey Letters*, *Down*, edited by Michael Herity. 2001.

Michael Herity

∽

Old English

The Old English comprised those whose ancestors had settled in Ireland since the twelfth century. They preserved an English lifestyle, incorporating the common law, the English language, and English political and civil institutions. Members of the community served as officials in the colonial administration and also acted as officers in local governments.

The quandary for the Old English community of Ireland originated in the late middle ages: Although very conscious of their English roots, the members were tightly enmeshed in social, political, and economic networks throughout the country. Yet their sense of themselves as separate from the rest of the island's population is symbolized by the evolution of the English Pale, a defended area with defined boundaries, consisting of the English parts of the counties around Dublin (viz. Dublin, Kildare, Meath, and Houth), in the eastern counties of Ireland. For members of the community, the ascendancy of the Fitzgeralds of Kildare up until the 1530s represented the nub of their dilemma: the emphasis on self-governance was welcome, but not the compromising of English mores and identity in which the earls indulged.

The closer engagement of the English monarchy with its Irish domain after 1534 had far-reaching implications for the community of Old English. An English-born governor was not unwelcome as an impartial arbiter among the political factions, but the appointment by Thomas Cromwell of New English officials to the principal offices of state was ominous. Also unsettling were the ecclesiastical changes: while reform of religious life might be acceptable to most, the implications of the change in management from pope to king were problematic because the usual role of Old English clergy as upholders of the papal bull *Laudabiliter* (which gave Anglo-Norman involvement in the Irish polity and church its charter) was threatened. Royal supremacy stressed the Anglicanism (English centeredness) of the Irish church, whereas the Old English clergy saw themselves as successors of generations of reform-minded personnel who had established a characteristically Irish church. While grants of dissolved monastic lands may have assuaged lay leaders, ecclesiastics were perturbed about the future.

On the face of it, the constitutional and political initiatives of the mid-Tudor period were consonant with Old English aspirations. The declaration by Henry VIII of the kingship of Ireland in 1541 created an all-island entity in which the two long-standing communities, Gaelic and English, were to be equal partners. An acknowledgment of the de facto political position, it represented a cessation of the conquest initiated in the twelfth century. The arrangements under the "surrender and regrant" scheme—a policy whereby the principal Gaelic and gaelicized lords surrendered their lands and titles to the Crown and received new grants of those lands and titles to be held directly from the Crown—were meant to assimilate the Gaelic lordships into the institutions of the Englishry. Within this new framework the Old English would apparently have a part to play as agents of reform among the Gaelic population. It appeared that the English viceroy who presided over the program, Sir Anthony Saint Leger, was complaisant in this agenda. He also managed the ecclesiastical changes of the 1540s in an adroit manner, using persuasive—rather than coercive—methods to push ahead with monastic closures and the imposition of royal supremacy.

The removal of Saint Leger and his replacement with governors whose methods were more rigorous presaged a change in the relationship of the Old English with the state government. The alienation of Archbishop George Dowdall of Armagh, an Old English representative, by the enforcement of Protestant dogma in the early 1550s was also significant. Although Dowdall returned under the Catholic reign of Queen Mary, he and a number of local politicians were at odds with the governor, the earl of Sussex, in the later 1550s over his failure to consult with them regarding Old English interests. As the weight of administration became greater, the expenditure involved in maintaining the political and military establishment mounted. Sussex and successive governors resorted to innovative and unpopular forms of taxation, involving levying of goods, services, and money, which collectively became known among the Old English by the pejorative term *cess*.

The fusing of the cess campaign with the intensification of recusancy (religious dissent) created a cause to which the Old English would rally in the 1570s and 1580s. Essentially, their aim was the conservation of their old constitution whereby they were consulted in parliament, particularly in the matter of taxation, and also the preservation of the older church institutions in which they had a vested interest. The growing burden of cess and the sporadic imposition of religious penalties galvanized the community into a campaign of passive resistance and constitutional lobbying at court. This campaign was headed by leading gentlemen such as the barons of Delvin and Howth.

Not all of the Old English activists were prepared to restrict their methods to constitutional agitation in support of ancient liberties. Throughout the provinces, members of old Norman families such as the Butlers, the Fitzgeralds of Desmond, and the Burkes of Clanricard rose up in arms against the curtailment of autonomy and the threat of new English colonization of lands. In the cases of James Fitzmaurice and James Eustace, Viscount Baltinglass, secular grievances merged with religious ones, and Fitzmaurice's own death and those of both his and Baltinglass's followers forged a sharper Old English consciousness of collective identity. Then, when in the 1590s Hugh O'Neill emerged as a champion of Catholic restoration as well as a defender of the political status quo, the Old English community faced an acute dilemma: Should their deep-seated loyalty to the English monarchy override the imperative to engage in militancy in order to bring about the restoration of their faith? They resolved it by sometimes siding with the forces of the state against the rebellious confederates, and by sometimes maintaining a precarious neutrality.

With the Stuart accession in 1603, a number of demonstrations in favor of a Catholic restoration took place in the Old English boroughs (excluding, notably, Dublin). The new regime made it clear that freedom of worship was not contemplated, and furthermore there were bouts of repression of recusancy, especially in 1604 to 1605 and 1611 to 1612. Thereafter, the Old English attempted to maintain the delicate balance of dual loyalty—to London in politics and to Rome in religion. The fragility of the position was demonstrated by the perceived subversion by the state of the Old English majority in parliament in 1613 to 1615, but the possibility of a Stuart marriage into the Spanish royal house revived hopes of official toleration for Catholics. Then Charles I was moved to negotiate a series of concessions to the Old English, including religious and landed rights, in return for military and monetary assistance; these concessions wre known as the "Graces." The governorship of Thomas Wentworth in the 1630s, however, succeeded in antagonizing the Old English (among others). When rebellion broke out in 1641, the Old English leadership committed itself to arms in support of its religious and political aims while claiming loyalty to the monarchy. The confederation of Kilkenny in the 1640s was the constitutional expression of its campaign for religious toleration and political recognition.

With the Cromwellian conquest in 1649 to 1650, the campaign of the Old English was irreparably damaged. After the Restoration in 1660, there was little recognition by the monarchy of the community's loyalty, and the gains of New English were consolidated. The position of the Old English in town and county was irrevocably undermined as they were replaced by a new Protestant elite. The fragile tolerance extended to Catholic activity could not now be guaranteed by Old English patronage. With the accession of James II in 1685 the expectation of Catholic restoration buoyed the hopes of the Old English as Tyrconnell, one of their number, became chief governor. But the defeat of the Jacobite campaign in Ireland marked the end of the aspiration of the Old English for recognition of their ambiguous position. Although the next ascendant elite in Ireland, the New English, soon began to feel a similar political alienation, their Protestant identity inhibited their isolation.

SEE ALSO Church of Ireland: Elizabethan Era; Graces, The; Monarchy; Rebellion of 1641; Sidney, Henry

Bibliography

Brady, Ciaran. "Conservative Subversives: The Community of the Pale and the Dublin Administration, 1556–86." In *Radicals, Rebels and Establishments*, edited by Patrick J. Corish. *Historical Studies* 15 (1985): 11–32.

Canny, Nicholas. *The Formation of an Old English Elite in Ireland.* 1975.

Clarke, Aidan. *The Old English in Ireland, 1625–1642.* 1966.

Clarke, Aidan. *The Graces, 1625–1641.* 1968.

Corish, Patrick J. "Ormond, Rinuccini, and the Confederates, 1645–9." In *Early Modern Ireland, 1534–1691.* Vol. 3 of *A New History of Ireland*, edited by T. W. Moody, F. X. Martin, and F. J. Byrne. 1976. Reprint, 1991.

Corish, Patrick J. "The Rising of 1641 and the Catholic Confederacy, 1641–5." In *Early Modern Ireland 1534–1691.* Vol. 3 of *A New History of Ireland*, edited by T. W. Moody, F. X. Martin, and F. J. Byrne. 1976. Reprint, 1991.

Lennon, Colm. "Richard Stanihurst (1547–1618) and Old English Identity." *Irish Historical Studies* 21 (1978–1979): 121–143.

Ó Siochrú, Micheál. *Confederate Ireland, 1642–9: A Constitutional and Political Analysis.* 1999.

Colm Lennon

O'Mahony, Conor, S. J.

Jesuit academic and author Conor O'Mahony was probably of Munster origin but spent much of his life in the Iberian Peninsula, where he became a professor at the University of Evora in Portugal. The experience of living in Portugal during the Braganza revolt against the Spanish Habsburgs, and, almost certainly, personal acquaintance with several of the Jesuit scholars who provided intellectual justification for the Braganza position, were of critical importance in conditioning his own reaction to rebellion in Ireland and the formation of the Confederate Catholic Association in 1642. In 1645 he published in Lisbon the text on which his historical reputation rests, the *Disputatio apologetica de iure regni Hiberniae pro Catholicis Hibernis adversus haereticos Anglos* (Explanatory argument concerning the authority of the kingdom of Ireland on behalf of Irish Catholics against English heretics), a two-part work consisting of a *disputatio* and an *exhortatio*.

O'Mahony's purpose was to demonstrate that the *Hiberni*, a generic term that he used to denote all the Catholics of the island, had the right to reject the authority of the monarchs of England over Ireland. In the *disputatio* he first rehearsed a series of arguments that might be advanced to legitimize English authority and then proceeded to attack them. His arguments were intensely legalistic, and the historical underpinning was somewhat weak. The second part of the *disputatio* was relatively stronger. It adapted the work of Bellarmine, Suarez, and Molina to build a case that even if English monarchs had once legitimately ruled over Ireland, the Irish retained the right to eliminate their authority because of the lapse into heresy of Charles I and his two predecessors. The *exhortatio* that followed, drawing heavily on biblical example, urged the Irish people to choose a new Catholic and native monarch and to eliminate all the remaining heretics in the island.

Although emotional resonances with O'Mahony's book can be detected in some manuscript material produced after the rebellion of 1641, it received almost no public support among the audience for which it was avowedly written, the Confederate Catholics of Ireland. The book ran counter to the dominant current in Irish Catholic political ideology, which stressed the legitimacy of Stuart rule. In 1645, the year of its publication, even the clerical convocation, the most militant group within the association, dismissed out of hand the idea that Charles was not the Confederates' legitimate king. Radical Catholics within the association opted to refer to the Confederate oath of association to justify their objectives rather than to O'Mahony's dangerously divisive argumentation. Moreover, the frank approbation in the *exhortatio* for the killing of tens of thousands of Protestants in the rebellion of 1641 was particularly unwelcome to the great mass of the Confederate Catholic leadership, which wished to avoid any link to these alleged atrocities.

SEE ALSO Confederation of Kilkenny; Rinuccini, Giovanni Battista; Wild Geese—The Irish Abroad from 1600 to the French Revolution

Bibliography

Canny, Nicholas. "Religion, Politics, and the Irish Rising of 1641," In *Religion and Rebellion*, edited by Judith Devlin and Ronan Fanning. 1997.

Ó Buachalla, Breandán. "James Our True King: The Ideology of Irish Royalism in the Seventeenth Century." In *Political Thought in Ireland since the Seventeenth Century*, edited by George Boyce, Robert Eccleshall, and Vincent Geoghegan. 1993.

Ó hAnnracháin, Tadhg. "'Though Hereticks and Politicians Should Misinterpret Their Goode Zeal': Political Ideology and Catholicism in Early Modern Ireland." In *Political Thought in Seventeenth-Century Ireland: Kingdom or Colony*, edited by Jane Ohlmeyer. 2000.

O'Mahony, Conor. *Disputatio apologetica de iure regni Hiberniae pro Catholicis Hibernis adversus haereticos Anglos: Accessit eiusdem authoris ad eosdem Catholicos exhortation* [Explanatory argument concerning the authority of the Kingdom of Ireland on behalf of Irish Catholics against English heretics: To which is joined the exhortation of the same author to the said Catholics]. 1645.

Silke, John J. "Primate Lombard and James I." *Irish Theological Quarterly* 22 (1955): 124–150.

Tadhg Ó hAnnracháin

O'Neill, Hugh, Second Earl of Tyrone

Hugh O'Neill (1550–1616), the second earl of Tyrone and last inaugurated chief of the O'Neills, was the major Irish leader of the Counter-Reformation period. An able soldier and wily negotiator with a charismatic personality, he was summed up by the English historian William Camden as a man "born either to the very great good or the great hurt of Ireland." After the assassination of his father Matthew by Shane O'Neill in 1558, he was fostered in the Pale by the Hovendens, a New English settler family, and *not* brought up at court in England as mistakenly asserted by his mid-twentieth-century biographer Sean O'Faolain.

In 1568 Hugh O'Neill was reestablished in Ulster by Lord Deputy Sidney, and for the next twenty years he was the English Crown's agent there against the pretensions of Shane's sons and his eventual successor Turlough Luineach O'Neill. By 1585 he controlled half of Tyrone and in 1587 was acknowledged by the Crown as earl of Tyrone. He had achieved this power not only by English connections and support but also through an extensive network of marriage alliances and fosterage arrangements. The Crown set out to contain this power by kidnapping and jailing Red Hugh O'Donnell, his son-in-law and the heir apparent of Tirconnell. Then followed Lord Deputy Fitzwilliam's attempt to reform Ulster by dismantling the power of the great lords generally, which was inaugurated by the execution of Hugh

MacMahon and the partition of the lordship of Monaghan in 1589 and 1590. The major beneficiary of this process was O'Neill's opponent, the prospective governor of Ulster, Sir Henry Bagenal.

O'Neill's countermeasures included murdering rival O'Neills, bribing Crown officials, liberating Red Hugh from prison in Dublin, and opening up channels of communication with Spain. Less successfully, he eloped with Mabel Bagenal, which embittered relations with her ambitious family. When the Crown attempted to replicate the Monaghan settlement in County Fermanagh, O'Neill organized his relatives and adherents in a proxy war, but to allay suspicion, he fought on the government side, even getting himself wounded at the battle of the Erne (1593). Eventually, he was proclaimed a traitor by the Crown in 1595, and in the same year he succeeded Turlough Luineach as holder of the banned Gaelic title of "The O'Neill."

In the so-called Nine Years War O'Neill gained a Europe-wide reputation as a soldier. He won great victories over English armies at Clontibret (1595) and the Yellow Ford (1598), and he exploited these victories to extend his oath-bound confederacy throughout Ireland in an Irish Catholic revolt against English Protestant colonial domination. O'Neill also proved an astute diplomat in negotiations with the state. By 1596 he had secured a compromise peace with England but decided instead to take up an offer of support from Spain. His most famous such negotiation was his encounter with the earl of Essex at the Ford of Bellaclinthe on the borders of Ulster (1599). His departure left O'Neill in charge of most of Ireland outside the towns. Yet O'Neill's increasingly overt Catholic stance and propaganda in Ireland failed to win over the Old English Catholics of the towns, who did not trust his threats and blandishments.

In 1600 Spain made a decisive commitment to the Irish struggle, and O'Neill sent over his second son Henry as a hostage. But O'Neill and his allies were already on the defensive in Ulster when in the following year a relatively small Spanish expeditionary force landed at Kinsale in the extreme south of the country. He and O'Donnell marched their armies south to relieve the Spaniards besieged in Kinsale but were decisively defeated. O'Neill's hitherto victorious army was smashed in an English cavalry charge that resulted in the death of one Englishman and 1,200 Irish. Deserted by his allies and with Ulster reduced to starvation, O'Neill surrendered to Lord Deputy Mountjoy at Mellifont in March 1603.

Although he was restored to his earldom, interference from English officials, soldiers, and churchmen soon began in earnest. In 1607 O'Neill and a large entourage fled to the Continent. This departure, romanticized as the Flight of the Earls, opened the way for land confiscation and plantation in Ulster. Spain, at peace with England, did not want O'Neill and pensioned him off to Rome.

SEE ALSO English Political and Religious Policies, Responses to (1534–1690); Nine Years War; **Primary Documents:** Ferocity of the Irish Wars (1580s–1590s); Accounts of the Siege and Battle of Kinsale (1601); Tyrone's Demands (1599); English Account of the Flight of the Earls (1607); Irish Account of the Flight of the Earls (1608)

Bibliography

Morgan, Hiram. "Hugh O'Neill and the Nine Years War in Tudor Ireland." *Historical Journal* 36 (March 1993): 21–37.

Morgan, Hiram. *Tyrone's Rebellion: The Outbreak of the Nine Years War in Tudor Ireland.* 1993.

O'Faolain, Sean. *The Great O'Neill.* 1942.

Walsh, Micheline Kerney. *"Destruction by Peace": Hugh O'Neill after Kinsale.* 1986.

Hiram Morgan

O'Neill, Owen Roe

Owen Roe O'Neill (c. 1583–1649), a native Irish leader and general of the northern army of the Kilkenny Confederation, was born in Ulster, educated by continental-trained Franciscans, and during the last Elizabethan Irish war was "bred in a nursery of arms" ("Aphorismical Discovery," in Gilbert 1879, p. 172). At the conflict's end, he joined an Irish regiment in the Spanish Netherlands and became its tacit commander. His goals were the recovery of confiscated estates and the restoration of the Catholic faith. Years later, he proposed the liberation of Ireland and its oppressed religion through a unifying Catholic "republic and kingdom."

Despite decades of exile, O'Neill kept in touch with his homeland by recruiting and giving military advice to native dissidents. When the crisis of the Stuart monarchy spilled over into Ireland, O'Neill stepped up his activities in hopes of concessions from the troubled Charles I. Ensuing setbacks led to a rebellion in late 1641 and Owen Roe's return to Ireland, where he supported a Catholic confederation meeting in Kilkenny. In May 1642 this embryonic commonwealth brought together the king's Irish Catholic subjects under the motto "United for God, King, and the Irish fatherland." Their task was to lay the foundation for a Catholic *patria (fatherland)* in a provincial-minded and religiously fractious society.

Appointed general of the northern forces, O'Neill assembled an army against Protestant English planters and Scottish settlers. His efforts were forestalled by a September 1643 cessation of arms with the king's lord deputy, the marquis of Ormond, a devout Old English royalist and Protestant convert. Ormond's negotiations failed to satisfy the clerical confederates and the new papal nuncio, Archbishop Rinuccini, who resisted royalist terms and succored O'Neill's army for an aggressive northern campaign. On 5 June 1646 O'Neill routed a Protestant-settler army at the battle of Benburb. His victory raised hopes for a more advantageous accord with Ormond.

These expectations splintered the Catholic confederacy. In August, O'Neill's army came to Kilkenny to support the clerical party. The Supreme Council, the executive branch of the Kilkenny Federation, was purged and a new executive led by Rinuccini took control. New fissures developed over the negotiations with Ormond and the appointment of O'Neill as the sole commander for an attack on Dublin. The campaign failed and the clerical coup lost its momentum.

Over the next year O'Neill remained in the Confederate heartland, as the nuncio and Ormondist factions jockeyed for power. The final breach came on 20 May 1648 when the Supreme Council, believing that Protestant royalists were likely to rekindle negotiations with Ormond, joined them in another cessation of arms. O'Neill supported Rinuccini's condemnation and censure of the Council, which rescinded O'Neill's military command. On 30 September the new General Assembly declared O'Neill a traitor—a rebel against the king and the fundamental laws of the Confederation.

Over the next four months O'Neill's position deteriorated. Ormond and the Confederation concluded a treaty, Charles I was executed, and an embittered Rinuccini returned to Rome. Ostracized and without allies, Owen Roe signed truces with parliamentary commanders, but their benefits were short-lived. Ormond's defeat at Rathmines, followed by Cromwell's arrival in August 1649, compelled the weakened confederate-royalist cause to turn to O'Neill once more. On 12 October 1649 articles of peace were finally concluded. Severely ill, O'Neill dispatched forces to Ormond's service and re-

tired to County Cavan, where he died of natural causes on 6 November.

SEE ALSO Confederation of Kilkenny; Rebellion of 1641; **Primary Documents:** Confederation of Kilkenny (1642)

Bibliography

"An Aphorismical Discovery of Treasonable Faction." In *A Contemporary History of Affairs in Ireland from 1641 to 1652*, edited by John T. Gilbert. 6 vols. 1879–1880.

Casway, Jerrold I. *Owen Roe O'Neill and the Struggle for Catholic Ireland.* 1984.

Casway, Jerrold I. "Gaelic Maccabeanism: The Politics of Reconciliation." In *Political Thought in Seventeenth-Century Ireland: Kingdom or Colony*, edited by Jane H. Ohlmeyer. 2000.

Gillespie, Raymond. "Owen Roe O'Neill: Soldier and Politician." In *Nine Ulster Lives*, edited by G. O'Brien and Peter Roebuck. 1992.

Ohlmeyer, Jane H. *Civil War and Restoration in the Three Kingdoms: The Career of Randall MacDonnell, Marquis of Antrim, 1609–1683.* 1993.

Ó Siochrú, Micheál. *Confederate Ireland, 1642–1649: A Constitutional and Political Analysis.* 1999.

Jerrold I. Casway

O'Neill, Terence

Prime minister of Northern Ireland Terence Marne O'Neill (1914–1990) was born on 10 September 1914 in London. Having served in the Irish Guards, he came to live in Northern Ireland in 1945. He was returned unopposed for the Stormont seat of Bannside in November 1946 for the Ulster Unionist Party and ten years later reached cabinet rank. When Lord Brookeborough retired as prime minister in March 1963, O'Neill succeeded as the apostle of technocratic modernization who could see off the Northern Ireland Labour Party. In community relations O'Neill was unprecedentedly liberal, visiting Catholic schools and, more dramatically, meeting with the taoiseach of the Irish Republic, Sean Lemass, at Stormont on 14 January 1964. O'Neill hoped to encourage Catholic acceptance of the state, but he more quickly aggravated suspicious unionist and loyalist opinion.

The eruption of the civil-rights movement of 1968 multiplied pressures for substantive reform from the

Irish prime minister Seán Lemass and Northern Ireland prime minister Terence O'Neill at Stormont, 14 January 1965, the first meeting between the leaders of the two Irish states since 1922. Courtesy of The Deputy Keeper of the Records, Public Record Office of Northern Ireland, ref. no. INF/7A/5/110.

British government. O'Neill impressed on his cabinet colleagues the necessity of concessions. On 22 November he unveiled a program of reforms, notably the closing down of the gerrymandered Londonderry Corporation. However, the local government's rate-based franchise was for the time untouched. In a television broadcast on 9 December 1968, O'Neill warned that Northern Ireland stood at the crossroads. He called for an end to street demonstrations but also promised meaningful reforms. There was a massive response from the public, but attitudes polarized again when a radical civil-rights march from Belfast to Derry was attacked by loyalists at Burntollet Bridge on 4 January 1969.

O'Neill's failure to preserve governmental authority by repression or concession led to discontent in his party. In an attempt to regain the initiative and remake the Unionist Party, he called for an election for 24 February 1969. He refused to campaign for official unionist candidates opposed to his leadership and lent his support to Independent candidates who vowed to support him personally. Breaking with unionist convention, O'Neill openly canvassed for Catholic votes. Such strategic innovations failed to produce a clear victory, however, and a phalanx of anti-O'Neill unionists returned. There was little evidence that O'Neill's re-branded unionism had succeeded in attracting Catholic votes. Amid a renewal of rioting and a campaign of bombing by loyalists, he announced his resignation as prime minister on 28 April 1969. Before leaving, he secured "one person, one vote" in place of the ratepayers' franchise in local elections as well as the succession of the relatively loyal James Chichester-Clarke.

SEE ALSO Economic Relations between North and South since 1922; Lemass, Seán; Northern Ireland: Discrimination and the Campaign for Civil Rights; Trimble, David; Ulster Unionist Party in Office; **Primary Documents:** On Community Relations in Northern Ireland (28 April 1967); "Ulster at the Crossroads" (9 December 1968)

Bibliography

Cochrane, Feargal. "'Meddling at the Crossroads': The Decline and Fall of Terence O'Neill within the Unionist Community." In *Unionism in Modern Ireland: New Perspectives on Politics and Culture,* edited by Richard English and Graham Walker. 1966.

Mulholland, Marc. *Northern Ireland at the Crossroads: Ulster Unionism in the O'Neill Years, 1960–9.* 2000.

O'Neill, Terence. *The Autobiography of Terence O'Neill.* 1972.

Marc Mulholland

Orange Order

ORIGINS, 1784 TO 1800	SEAN FARRELL
SINCE 1800	BRIAN WALKER

ORIGINS, 1784 TO 1800

The process that led to the September 1795 formation of the Orange Order originated in the Armagh Troubles, a complex and long-running sectarian conflict that started in the early 1780s. Like so many of modern Ulster's sectarian clashes, the Armagh Troubles were rooted in Protestant insecurity over the loss of privileges deemed necessary to protect them from their Catholic rivals. In Armagh the major destabilizing force proved to be the formation of the Irish Volunteers, a home-defense force that became the muscle behind efforts to gain parliamentary reform in Ireland. Individual Volunteer companies called for Catholics to join their ranks. While few did so in Ulster, the prospect of Catholics carrying arms was worrisome for many lower-class Ulster Protestants, particularly in County Armagh, which was precariously divided between Anglicans, Catholics and Presbyterians. For many Protestants these changes were particularly problematic because they occurred in an era when the government was removing many of the economic and political restrictions that had been placed on Irish Catholics in the early eighteenth century. The tide seemed to be flowing in a Catholic direction.

In 1784 bands of plebeian Protestants known as the Peep o' Day Boys ransacked Catholic homes throughout mid-Ulster, ostensibly in search of arms. Almost inevitably, these assaults brought a reaction from Catholics, who increasingly joined the Defenders, a secret society originally designed to protect Catholics from such attacks. Recognizing the Peep o' Day Boys as the primary aggressors, members of the Armagh gentry attempted to bring them under control. They were largely successful by the late 1780s; the arms raids had stopped and sectarian conflict was now limited to sporadic and highly ritualized "battles" between Catholic and Protestant combatants.

The famous Battle of the Diamond started as just such an affair. On 17 September 1795 Catholic and Protestant crowds squared off at a crossroads near Loughgall, Co. Armagh. For three days the "battle" proceeded in typical fashion, with threatening shots fired in the air amid negotiations to disperse the combatants. On 21 September, however, a real fight broke out in which dozens of Catholics were killed by the better-armed Protestants. In the wake of the clash many of the Protestant participants met at an inn near Loughgall, where they founded the Loyal Orange Order.

The men who founded the Orange Order were not members of the elite—farmers and weavers from Armagh and Tyrone dominated the first meeting. The plebeian origins of the Order can be seen in its early rules and regulations, which refer to the Twelfth of July festivities, where Protestant loyalists marched in procession to commemorate late seventeenth-century Protestant victories at the Battle of the Boyne and Aughrim. Although such marches long predated the creation of the Orange Order, they quickly became associated with the organization. The Twelfth celebration would prove to be one of the most controversial aspects of Orangeism, as marchers often clashed with Catholics offended by the partisan display of power and ascendancy. Wanting to avoid controversy, gentry members tended to downplay the marching tradition. Of course, Orangeism was about much more than marching. Like many of its predecessors, the Orange Order was above all a Protestant association, dedicated to preserving the Protestant constitution and advancing the Protestant cause in Ireland.

What made the Orange Order different from its predecessors was that it soon gained the support of the Protestant elite and the acquiescence of the British state. This was largely a consequence of the tumult of the 1790s, for with the rising threat of organized rebellion,

House of Dan Winter near Loughgall, Co. Armagh, in which the Orange Order is said to have been organized after the Battle of the Diamond in 1795. Repaired and rethatched in 2000. COURTESY OF DAN WINTER'S HOUSE, ANCESTRAL HOME, 9 DERRYLOUGHAN ROAD, THE DIAMOND, LOUGHGALL. REPRODUCED BY PERMISSION.

both the British government and its elite supporters searched for loyal groups that could be depended upon. If the Orange Order's anti-Catholic excesses caused discomfort in some government circles, most members of the establishment argued that this was a small price to pay for such a loyal body. The growing acceptance of the Orange Order was marked by two public events in 1797: the formation of an Orange lodge in Dublin that soon attracted a number of influential leaders of the Irish Protestant establishment, and General Gerard Lake's public review of an Orange procession in Lurgan, Co. Armagh. By early 1798 the Loyal Orange Order had become a national institution.

The 1798 Rebellion greatly strengthened Orangeism's position in Ireland. The story of the rebellion is inextricably tied with the Society of United Irishmen, an organization formed in Belfast in 1791 to push for radical reform. Frustrated by the absence of meaningful reform and forced underground by increasing state pressure, the Society abandoned reform for revolution as the 1790s progressed. Although United Irish leaders had called for a union of Irishmen of all creeds, the rebellion

that broke out in 1798 took on a nakedly sectarian appearance in Wexford and other locations. Orangemen participated actively in putting down the revolt, committing a host of sectarian atrocities in Wexford in particular. But Orange excesses were largely overlooked in the aftermath of the rebellion. By seemingly confirming the Orangemen's view of Irish Catholics as untrustworthy rebels, the 1798 Rebellion accelerated the Orange Order's move to respectability and influence. While members of the Order initially had opposed the Act of Union of 1800, Orangemen quickly became its most fervent supporters, seeing a more formalized union with Britain as their best protection against Irish Catholics. The weavers and tenant farmers who had founded the Loyal Orange Order could now rest easy: Their exclusivist vision of Irish society had won and would dominate Irish politics for the next two decades.

SEE ALSO Act of Union; Church of Ireland: Since 1690; Defenderism; Eighteenth-Century Politics: 1778 to 1795—Parliamentary and Popular Politics; Eigh-

Chair of French origin believed to have been brought with the Winter family when they immigrated in 1665 and, according to tradition, used in the 1795 meeting at which the Orange Order was organized. COURTESY OF DAN WINTER'S HOUSE, ANCESTRAL HOME, 9 DERRYLOUGHAN ROAD, THE DIAMOND, LOUGHGALL. REPRODUCED BY PERMISSION.

teenth-Century Politics: 1795 to 1800—Repression, Rebellion, and Union; Orange Order: Since 1800

Bibliography

Farrell, Sean. *Rituals and Riots: Sectarian Violence and Political Culture in Ulster, 1784–1886.* 2000.

Gibbon, Peter. *The Origins of Ulster Unionism: The Formation of Popular Protestant Politics and Ideology.* 1975.

Miller, David W. "The Armagh Troubles, 1784–1795." In *Irish Peasants: Violence and Political Unrest, 1780–1914,* edited by J. S. Donnelly, Jr., and Samuel Clark. 1983.

Senior, Hereward. *Orangeism in Britain and Ireland, 1795–1836.* 1966.

Sean Farrell

SINCE 1800

The Orange Order, an organization of loyalist Protestants, was founded in County Armagh during the political agitation that led to the 1798 rebellion. Although some individual Orange lodges opposed the Act of Union as undermining local and Protestant power, the Orange Order quickly moved to support the union. Orange parades on 12 July, the anniversary of the Battle of the Boyne in 1690, continued to be a prominent feature of the movement, which was to be found especially but not exclusively in Ulster. The government had initially welcomed Orange support for the state, but in the early decades of the nineteenth century the authorities sought to adopt a more neutral stance toward Orangeism because the parades often led to disturbances.

Between 1825 and 1828 the Order was suppressed under the Unlawful Societies Act. The Anti-Processions Act of 1832 curbed parades, and following a critical parliamentary report into the organization, the Orange Order was dissolved in 1835. Popular support for the movement survived, however, and when the Anti-Processions Act was lifted in 1845, the organization was re-formed and Twelfth of July processions resumed. Confrontations between Orangemen and Catholics still occurred, and after a large-scale fight at Dolly's Brae near Castlewellan, Co. Down, on 12 July 1849, which left a number of Catholics dead, the government introduced a new Party Processions Act forbidding public demonstrations.

Over the next two decades the authorities took firm action in support of this ban on parades, although some infringements did occur. In protest against the ban, William Johnston of Ballykilbeg, Co. Down, led an illegal Orange parade in 1867 from Newtownards to Bangor, Co. Down, which resulted in his imprisonment. He emerged from jail to become an Orange hero and was elected MP for Belfast in 1868. His protest led to the repeal of the act in 1872 and the resumption of legal Orange parades.

At this point the Orange Order's support was fairly limited, and it drew its membership mainly from small farmers and laborers in Ulster, most of whom belonged to the Church of Ireland. By the early 1880s, however, in response to the growing conflict between supporters of Home Rule and supporters of the union, the Order's membership increased and its social basis expanded to include large farmers and members of the middle and professional classes, many of them Presbyterians. The Order was seen by most unionists as a bulwark in support of the union that transcended social and denominational divisions. At the general elections of 1885 and 1886 the Order achieved an extra level of influence when local lodges secured representation on many of the new

Early nineteenth-century banner of the Fountainville Loyal Orange Lodge, depicting William III. Banners of this type are carried each year on the 12th of July to celebrate William's victory at the Battle of the Boyne in 1690. PHOTOGRAPH REPRODUCED WITH THE KIND PERMISSION OF THE TRUSTEES OF THE NATIONAL MUSEUMS AND GALLERIES OF NORTHERN IRELAND, X–38-1976.

local unionist constituency associations. A majority of the Ulster Unionist MPs in 1886 were Orangemen.

Although Orange influence was strongest in Ulster, support for the movement was also found outside Ireland in other parts of the world such as Scotland, Australia, and New Zealand. Lodges were often started in these countries by emigrants from Ulster. The Order was especially prevalent in Canada. To link these different national Orange organizations, an Imperial Orange Council was established in 1867 to meet triennially.

At the 1892 Ulster Unionist Convention, delegates from the Orange Order assumed an important role. When the Ulster Unionist Council was formed in 1904, numerous places were allocated to nominees of the Orange Order. Early in the twentieth century, as a result of social and religious conflict, divisions arose in Orange ranks that led to the founding in 1903 of the Independent Orange Order by R. L. Crawford. This movement produced some radical political ideas, but in 1908, Crawford was expelled and the Independent Orange Order returned to a mainstream unionist stance, although it remained an autonomous body.

During the fierce Ulster resistance to Home Rule in 1912 to 1914, members of the Orange Order played a significant part. Orange demonstrations continued during most of the war years, although attendance was greatly reduced owing to the large number of Orangemen who had joined the armed forces. Because of the many casualties from Ulster at the Battle of the Somme, which commenced on 1 July 1916, Orange parades were cancelled on the Twelfth of July that year and church services were held instead. Following partition in 1920 and 1921, the headquarters of the Orange Order moved from Dublin to Belfast. The vast majority of Orangemen on the island were then to be found within the new Northern Ireland, although there was still a significant membership in the Ulster counties of Donegal, Monaghan, and Cavan that were part of the Irish Free State.

Membership in the Orange Order has generally been regarded as obligatory for unionist politicians since the founding of Northern Ireland in 1921. Especially since the outbreak of the "Troubles" in the late 1960s, the annual summer "marching season," of which the Twelfth of July is the climax, has been a continual source of tension and often violence. Catholics take offense at Orange parades as triumphalist rituals intended to humiliate them, while Orangemen regard the right to parade as a fundamental civil liberty. During the 1990s public attention came to focus on one particular parade—the annual march by a Portadown, Co. Armagh, lodge following their attendance at a special Sunday service at Drumcree parish church. The traditional route for this parade passes through a modern residential area occupied by Catholics. Intransigence on both sides has created a recurring confrontation and posed special dilemmas, especially for unionist elected representatives seeking to make the larger peace process successful.

SEE ALSO Ancient Order of Hibernians; Church of Ireland: Since 1690; Orange Order: Origins, 1784 to 1800; Sodalities and Confraternities

Bibliography

Bryan, Dominic. *Orange Parades: The Politics of Ritual, Tradition, and Control.* 2000.

Edwards, Ruth Dudley. *The Faithful Tribe: An Intimate Portrait of the Loyal Institutions.* 1999.

Brian Walker

Ordnance Survey

The Ordnance Surveys of Ireland (OSI) and Northern Ireland (OSNI) are the official state mapping agencies in Ireland. The Ordnance Survey developed in the late 1820s out of an earlier wartime British mapping initiative by the Board of Ordnance in England. The need to reform Ireland's local taxation system called for a comprehensive valuation of land and buildings, and the Royal Engineers Artillery formed the core of the new Ordnance Survey, which was based in the Phoenix Park in Dublin. Its greatest pioneering achievement was the mapping of Ireland at a scale of six inches to the mile between 1833 and 1846. This project recorded all townland units, field boundaries, and acreages, buildings in urban and rural areas, place-names, and data on heights above sea level; it has become an invaluable topographic record of the Irish landscape on the eve of the Great Famine. The *Ordnance Survey Memoirs* were intended by the director Thomas Colby as a comprehensive textual profile of each civil parish to accompany the maps, but officials succeeded in publishing only one parish memoir. The material on the remaining parishes for much of Ulster was published in the 1990s. The Ordnance Survey Letters of John O'Donovan, an Irish language scholar who was almost single-handedly responsible for standardizing the thousands of place-names on the maps, will be published in the early twenty-first century.

The 6-inch maps were published in county volumes, which were revised at various times throughout nineteenth century. Maps at 1:2500 ("twenty-five inches to the mile") were undertaken from 1864 until the early twentieth century. These maps provided detail on acreages of fields, which was of great use for the implementation of the Irish Land Acts and the transfer of farms from landlords to tenants, as well as for the reform of *rundale* (field system) plots and settlements in the west of the country by the Congested Districts Board and the Land Commission. The Ordnance Survey also produced large-scale town plans from the 1840s, some at 1:1056, or 5 feet to 1 mile; others at 10 feet to 1 mile; and still others at more economical scales. The 1-inch maps were designed as a popular scale from the 1850s, and the half-inch map was produced in the early twentieth century.

The OSI today produces urban, rural, and leisure mapping for a range of different scales, in digital and paper format. The 1:50,000 Discovery series is the most popular product in the early twenty-first century. The Ordnance Survey's digital data are used under license for many computer-based applications, such as Computer-Aided Design (CAD) and Geographic Information Systems (GIS).

SEE ALSO Landscape and Settlement; O'Donovan, John

Bibliography

Andrews, John H. *A Paper Landscape: The Ordnance Survey in Nineteenth-Century Ireland.* 1975.

Day, Angelique, and Patrick McWilliams, eds. *Ordnance Survey Memoirs of Ireland.* 40 vols. 1992.

Patrick J. Duffy

Overseas Investment

The unprecedented expansion of the Irish economy during the 1990s was due in large measure to the country's success in attracting inward investment. The thirteen hundred overseas companies located in Ireland and assisted by the Investment and Development Agency of Ireland (IDA Ireland), the state investment and development agency, are the main contributors to economic growth. They employ 150,000 people, equivalent to more than half the workforce in manufacturing; they export 90 percent of their output and account for over 80 percent of Ireland's manufactured exports; they contribute one-third of the gross domestic product (GDP); and they spend E15 billion annually in Ireland on salaries, components, materials, and services.

Overseas companies have been the dominant factor in the opening up of new export markets. Ireland is no longer over dependent on the United Kingdom, which in 1970 took 75 percent of Irish exports. In the year 2000 the proportion was down to 22 percent, with the rest of the European Union taking 40 percent and the United States, 17 percent. Free access to the 370 million people of the European market has been critical to this transformation. Foreign direct investment (FDI), especially from the United States, has helped to develop the Irish economy in other, less quantifiable ways. Major corporations, leaders in their industry sectors, have brought world-class standards of manufacturing, marketing, management, and research and development. They have created a market within Ireland for subsuppliers and have stimulated native enterprise.

The United States is by far the most important source of new investment from abroad; it provided 60

Northern Ireland % FDI market share in comparison to rest of British Isles (including Republic of Ireland)

	FDI into NI		FDI into British Isles		
	No.	%	No.	%	Total
1999	7	7.3	141	95.3	**148**
2000	15	4.5	134	89.9	**149**
Total	**22**	**5.8**	**275**	**92.6**	**297**

(1) Figures are for those projects that IDB can offer support (i.e., manufacturing and internationally traded service sector projects)
(2) Does not include any intra-U.K. investment

SOURCE: IDB Northern Ireland.

percent to 70 percent of the new investment projects and 80 percent of the foreign capital investment in the ten years between 1990 and 2000. The 524 U.S. affiliates in Ireland employ 86,000 workers, and account for three-quarters of the E43 billion in export sales of overseas-owned companies. Substantial investment has also come from the United Kingdom (179 subsidiaries), Germany (166), the Asia/Pacific region (54), and from other European countries (291). These foreign-owned companies dominate the high-tech sectors: information and communications technologies (ICT); pharmaceuticals and healthcare; internationally traded services, including software, teleservices, e-business, and financial services. Dublin's new International Financial Services Centre (IFSC), a public/private partnership venture on the north bank of the Liffey, dwarfs Gandon's superb neoclassical Custom House building. The IFSC has four hundred of the world's leading banks and finance houses, providing specialist services to international clients.

MARKET SHARE

Consistent comparative statistics on FDI are notoriously difficult to obtain. FDI includes new investment in all sectors as well as mergers and acquisitions. IDA Ireland's remit covers only manufacturing and international services; it does not include tourism, retail sales, property, or oil and gas, for example, and it counts mergers and acquisitions only when there is associated incremental investment or employment in Ireland. However, it is clear from independent reviews that Ireland wins a disproportionately large share of all available new investment in Europe. It attracts close to a quarter of all new U.S. manufacturing projects (excluding mergers and acquisitions, and expansions of existing facilities) that locate in Europe, although it accounts for a mere 1 percent of European Union population and GDP. In 1997 it was the fifth largest recipient of all U.S. investment abroad; typically, Ireland's share of U.S. FDI

is about 8 percent, up from less than 3 percent in the 1980s. The *World Investment Report 2001*, published by the United Nations Conference on Trade and Development (UNCTAD), shows FDI flows into Ireland rising from $2.7 billion in 1997 to $16.3 billion in 2000; the figures for the United Kingdom were $33.2 billion and $130.4 billion respectively; and the United States had inward FDI of $281 billion in 2000. Per capita, therefore, Ireland wins twice as much investment as the United Kingdom and more than four times the U.S. level. The value of total FDI stock in Ireland rose tenfold during the 1990s to $60 billion, while U.K. FDI stock barely doubled over the same period.

Ireland's emergence as a highly successful location for inward investment, and as one of the world's most open economies, really began in the 1960s, although many of the sagacious policy decisions that prepared the way for the "tiger economy" date from the 1950s. The 1950s were a period of transition, from the protectionist self-sufficiency of the Irish Free State (1922–1949), to an economy actively promoting free trade and foreign direct investment. The Control of Manufactures Act (1932) mandated that Irish-based companies must be majority Irish owned, reflecting the economic zeitgeist of the period between the world wars. By the time that the last controls on foreign ownership of Irish businesses were removed in 1958, the Industrial Development Authority (IDA), established in 1949 as a relatively minor investment-promotion agency, had been given new powers to seek inward investors by offering capital grants and tax breaks as incentives. The most compelling incentive was export sales relief (ESR), introduced in 1956: It gave full tax relief on profits from exports of manufactured products. ESR was terminated for new investors in 1981 and replaced by a 10 percent rate of corporation tax for all manufacturers, and for services companies trading internationally.

Since 1970, when it became responsible for all aspects of planning, promoting, and negotiating industrial investment, IDA has concentrated on sectors appropriate to Ireland's attributes and in which Ireland could offer investors a competitive advantage. The agency has been successful in identifying emerging new sectors, often ahead of its competitors—call centers, shared services, and specialist financial services are examples from the 1990s. Most of the current inward investment is targeted at high-growth, high-productivity sectors.

IDA negotiates more than one hundred new investments each year; about half come from existing investors. The agency works with foreign subsidiaries in Ireland helping them to upgrade the value and quality of their activities (by adding marketing and research and development to a basic production unit, for example) in order to make them more secure in times of economic crisis. Inevitably, given the volatility of the high-technology sector, Ireland has had its share of plant closures; the attrition rate is in line with international trends. While the policy of encouraging inward investment has the support of all sections of the community, the critical impact of U.S. investment leaves Ireland vulnerable to downturns in the American economy.

With Ireland in effect enjoying full employment, IDA will shift its emphasis away from single projects, mainly in manufacturing, to establishing "strategic business areas," clusters of technology companies, venture capitalists, corporate and academic research centers, and consultants, on the Silicon Valley model. Over time, more of the incoming investment will be based on innovation and research, involving knowledge-intensive projects needing the high skills and expertise that Ireland is determined to have available.

NORTHERN IRELAND

At the time of Ireland's independence in 1922 the six counties of Northern Ireland, which remained part of the United Kingdom, were more industrialized than the agricultural South. Shipbuilding and linen manufacturing were strong sectors (the *Titanic* was built in Belfast), and through the 1940s and 1950s heavy industry flourished. Exposure to foreign competition brought a decline in manufacturing in the 1960s and 1970s. Between 1973 (when Northern Ireland became part of the European Union) and 1990, employment in manufacturing fell by 36 percent.

As in the republic, measures to encourage industrial investment were first introduced in the 1950s; capital grants date back to 1954. The range of supports for industrial development has grown steadily since 1970. The Industrial Development Board was established in 1982 as an amalgamation of two existing agencies; it had responsibility for encouraging inward and indigenous industrial investment, for promoting exports, and for expanding small industry. At the beginning of 2002 the inward-investment arm of IDB was hived off as a new agency called Invest Northern Ireland (INI).

Northern Ireland has a long tradition of inward investment, but continuing civil unrest since 1970 has significantly curtailed the flow of new projects. In 1990 there were 207 externally owned plants in the province, including 129 from mainland Britain. By 2001 the total had risen to 388 establishments—100 from the rest of the United Kingdom, 95 from the United States, and 59 from the Irish Republic. They employ 55,000 workers, and their export sales are equivalent to almost one-fifth of N.I. GDP. IDB secured thirteen new FDI projects in

2000; the key targets are the knowledge-based sectors of software, telecommunications, network services, and e-business, which account for 69 percent of projects and 79 percent of FDI capital.

SEE ALSO Celtic Tiger; Economies of Ireland, North and South, since 1920; European Union; Industry since 1920; Investment and Development Agency (IDA Ireland); Lemass, Seán; **Primary Documents:** From the 1937 Constitution; Speech to Ministers of the Governments of the Member States of the European Economic Community (18 January 1962)

Bibliography

Forfás. *Shaping Our Future.* 1996.

Goerg, Holger. "Foreign Investment in the EU: The Case of Ireland in a European Context." M. Litt. thesis, Trinity College, Dublin. 1996.

IDB. *Annual Report 1999/2000.* 2000.

OECD. *Economic Survey: Ireland.* 1999.

UNCTAD. *World Investment Report 2001.* 2001.

Finn Gallen

Overseas Missions

In the modern period Ireland's first overseas missionaries came from the Protestant churches. The Irish auxiliary to the Society for the Propagation of the Gospel was founded as early as 1714. Members of the auxiliary worked in the American colonies, South Africa, India, Japan, and West Africa. No less active was the Hibernian Church Missionary Society, founded in 1814. Many Irish men and women were also involved in English or international missionary agencies such as the South American Missionary Society, the Church of England Missionary Society, the Bible Churchmen's Missionary Society, the Moravian missions, the Baptist missions, the Methodist Missionary Society, the Sudan Interior Mission, and the Sudan United Mission. Among the homegrown agencies were the Irish Presbyterian missions and the Mission to Lepers.

With the flood of emigration from Ireland during the nineteenth century the Irish Roman Catholic Church increasingly focused on the pastoral care of Irish emigrants to Great Britain, the United States, Canada, Australia, New Zealand, South Africa, Argentina, and the West Indies. There were also considerable numbers of Irish soldiers and civil servants in British territories such as India who required pastoral care. The first institution to train missionaries specifically for this diaspora was All Hallows College, established in Dublin in 1842 by Father John Hand with the support of the church hierarchy. Before then the emigrants had been served by priests from Irish diocesan seminaries, principally Saint Kieran's College, Kilkenny (1782); Saint Patrick's College, Carlow (1793); Saint John's College, Waterford (1807); and Saint Peter's College, Wexford (1819). Saint Patrick's College, Maynooth (1795), Ireland's national seminary, also contributed priests, mainly for India and Australia. Irish convents were just as active: Loreto Sisters, Irish Sisters of Mercy, Presentation Sisters, Irish Sisters of Charity, Dominicans, and Ursulines all established foundations in the Irish diaspora countries. Irish Christian Brothers, De La Salle Brothers, and Patrician Brothers participated equally in serving the emigrant Irish.

Within the worldwide Roman Catholic communion there was a strong revival of missionary services to non-Christian peoples during the late seventeenth century, spearheaded by the French church and led by new agencies established exclusively for missionary work. This revival came in the wake of the decline and virtual disappearance of the great missionary movement which had followed the era of exploration and had endured down to the time of the French Revolution. During the third quarter of the nineteenth century this movement came to include Italy, Belgium, Germany, Holland, and England. Its arrival in Ireland dates from the establishment of the movement's main promotion and fundraising agency—the Association for the Propagation for the Faith (1838)—and the arrival of a number of continental agencies in search of candidates for their missions in British colonies, principally the Congregation of the Holy Ghost (1858) and the Society of African Missions (1877). These agencies set down roots in Ireland and promoted the missionary message. Several continental orders of women religious recruited successfully in Ireland, but they were less influential because, with few exceptions (Sisters of the Good Shepherd [1852], Sisters of the Holy Family [1875] and Sisters of Our Lady of Apostles [1887]), they rarely established convents in the nineteenth century. The Irish Church, too, growing more confident and outward looking since revocation of the penal laws, experienced a steady increase in young people offering themselves as priests, sisters or brothers to serve not only in Ireland, but overseas among the emigrant Irish and among non-Christian peoples.

In the opening decades of the twentieth century interest in missionary activity intensified within the Irish Church. The formation of the Maynooth mission to China (Saint Columban's Foreign Mission Society) in 1916 was the great watershed in the history of the missionary movement. Influenced by Ireland's growing interest in missions and by the new spirit of cultural and political identity, the stream of missionary vocations became a flood. Existing religious orders such as the Vincentians, Dominicans, Augustinians, Jesuits, and Franciscans increasingly took on commitments to non-Christian missions. Presentation and Loreto Sisters were in the forefront of work among non-Christians in India. Christian Brothers went to Africa. Most significant of all, within the space of two decades four additional indigenous missionary bodies were established: The Missionary Sisters of Saint Columban (1922); the Sisters of the Holy Rosary (1924); Saint Patrick's Missionary Society (1932); and the Medical Missionaries of Mary (1937). Missionaries from these agencies worked principally in the Far East and Asia, in Africa, and in South and Central America.

During the nineteenth century and much of the twentieth century Irish laity supported overseas missions with money that was channeled through the Association for the Propagation of the Faith and other mission-aid societies. There were some laypersons who took a more active part, assisting in the promotion of missionary magazines, and forming groups of apostolic workers who supplied sacred vessels and liturgical materials. Laity also served overseas mainly as teachers, nurses, doctors, and catechists. Lay participation increased significantly with the establishment of lay missionary organizations such as the Viatores Christi (1962) and an Irish branch of the Volunteer Missionary Movement (1972).

By the late 1960s Ireland had more than 7,000 Protestant and Catholic missionaries overseas. Since then the number has been gradually diminishing. In 1982, reflecting a decline in recruitment, there were 5,613 missionaries working in 86 developing countries, including 142 missionaries from Protestant denominations working in ten countries. Today the figure is significantly smaller, and the average age of the missionary is rapidly rising. But Irish missionaries, both to emigrants and to non-Christians, have made a signal contribution in establishing many young churches that are now growing to maturity. They continue to help in the development of countries through their work for education, health care, and other social needs, and they play an important role in alerting the global community to injustice and poverty.

SEE ALSO Evangelicalism and Revivals; Church of Ireland: Since 1690; Presbyterianism; Religious Orders:

Men; Religious Orders: Women; Roman Catholic Church: 1829 to 1891; Roman Catholic Church: Since 1891

Bibliography

Condon, Kevin. *The Missionary College of All Hallows, 1842–1891.* 1986.

Hickey, Raymond, ed. *Modern Missionary Documents and Africa.* 1982.

Hogan, Edmund M. *The Irish Missionary Movement: A Historical Survey, 1830–1980.* 1990.

McGlade, Joseph. *The Missions: Africa and the Orient.* 1967.

Edmund M. Hogan